Lecture Notes in Computer Science 12973

More information about this subseries at http://www.springer.com/series/7410

Elisa Bertino · Haya Shulman ·
Michael Waidner (Eds.)

Computer Security – ESORICS 2021

26th European Symposium
on Research in Computer Security
Darmstadt, Germany, October 4–8, 2021
Proceedings, Part II

 Springer

Editors
Elisa Bertino 🆔
Purdue University
West Lafayette, IN, USA

Michael Waidner 🆔
National Research Center for Applied
Cybersecurity ATHENE
Technische Universität Darmstadt,
Fraunhofer Institute for Secure Information
Technology SIT
Darmstadt, Germany

Haya Shulman 🆔
National Research Center for Applied
Cybersecurity ATHENE
Fraunhofer Institute for Secure Information
Technology SIT
Darmstadt, Germany

ISSN 0302-9743   ISSN 1611-3349   (electronic)
Lecture Notes in Computer Science
ISBN 978-3-030-88427-7   ISBN 978-3-030-88428-4   (eBook)
https://doi.org/10.1007/978-3-030-88428-4

LNCS Sublibrary: SL4 – Security and Cryptology

This Springer imprint is published by the registered company Springer Nature Switzerland AG
The registered company address is: Gewerbestrasse 11, 6330 Cham, Switzerland

Preface

The 26th European Symposium on Research in Computer Security (ESORICS 2021) was held together with the affiliated workshops during the week of October 4–8, 2021. Due to the COVID-19 pandemic the conference and the workshops took place digitally, hosted by the Fraunhofer Institute for Secure Information Technology (Fraunhofer SIT), within the National Research Center for Applied Cybersecurity ATHENE, Germany.

This year's ESORICS introduced for the first time in the ESORICS conference series two review cycles: a winter cycle and a spring cycle. This follows the general trends for conferences of providing multiple submission deadlines and is not only more convenient for the authors but also allows revision and resubmission for papers. In the case of ESORICS, papers submitted in the winter cycle could be recommended for revision and resubmission to the spring cycle.

In response to the call for papers 351 papers were submitted to the conference. These papers were peer reviewed and subsequently discussed based on their novelty, quality, and contribution by the members of the Program Committee. The submissions were single blind, and all the members of the Program Committee had access to all the submissions and their reviews at all times to facilitate discussions among the members. The submission of the papers and the review process were carried out using the Easychair platform. Based on the reviews and the discussion 71 papers were selected for presentation at the conference. As a result ESORICS had an interesting program covering timely and interesting security and privacy topics in theory, systems, networks, and applications.

The papers that were selected for presentation at ESORICS 2021 were published in a two volume set of proceedings: LNCS 12972 and LNCS 12973.

ESORICS is a flagship European security conference. The aim of ESORICS is to advance the research in computer security and privacy by establishing a European forum, bringing together researchers in these areas, and promoting the exchange of ideas with the developers, standardization bodies, and policy makers and by encouraging links with researchers in related fields.

We were honoured to have four keynote speakers: Shafi Goldwasser, Christof Paar, Nicolas Papernot, and Yuval Yarom. Their talks provided interesting insights and research directions in important research areas. The program was complemented by six tutorials given by Anna Cinzia Squicciarini, Yossi Oren, Michael Schwarz, Avishai Wool, and Daphne Yao. For tutorials, ESORICS introduced a novel organization, in that tutorials were given in advance with respect to the conference dates, with the first tutorial given on June 30, 2021, and the last one on September 8, 2021. Tutorial presentations were recorded and are available online. This arrangement takes advantage of today's availability of content dissemination platforms and allows researchers to access the tutorial contents at their own pace.

The Program Committee consisted of 185 members across 31 countries. There were submissions from a total of 1150 authors across 41 countries, with 25 countries represented among the accepted papers. We would like to thank the members of the Program Committee and the external referees for their hard work in supporting the review process as well as everyone who supported the organization of ESORICS. We are grateful to the workshops chairs, Adrian Perrig and David Hay, and all of the workshop co-chairs, the poster chair, Simone Fischer-Hübner, and the ESORICS Steering Committee. We are also grateful to Huawei and IBM Research – Haifa, Israel, for supporting the organization of ESORICS 2021. Finally, we would like to thank the authors for submitting their papers to ESORICS 2021. We hope that the proceedings will promote the research and facilitate future work in the field of security.

September 2021   Elisa Bertino
                                                                       Haya Shulman
                                                                  Michael Waidner

Organization

General Chair

Michael Waidner National Research Center for Applied Cybersecurity
ATHENE/Technische Universität
Darmstadt/Fraunhofer SIT, Germany

Program Committee Chairs

Elisa Bertino Purdue University, USA
Haya Shulman National Research Center for Applied Cybersecurity
ATHENE/Fraunhofer SIT, Germany

Steering Committee

Joachim Biskup
Véronique Cortier
Frédéric Cuppens
Sabrina De Capitani di Vimercati
Joaquin Garcia-Alfaro
Dieter Gollmann
Sokratis Katsikas
Mirosław Kutyłowski
Javier Lopez
Jean-Jacques Quisquater
Peter RYAN
Pierangela Samarati
Einar Arthur Snekkenes
Michael Waidner

Program Committee

Ruba Abu-Salma International Computer Science Institute / University
of California, Berkeley, USA
Yehuda Afek Tel Aviv University, Israel
Mitsuaki Akiyama NTT, Japan
Cristina Alcaraz UMA, Spain
Mark Allman International Computer Science Institute, USA
Vijay Atluri Rutgers University, USA
Erman Ayday Case Western Reserve University, USA
Guangdong Bai University of Queensland, Australia
Lejla Batina Radboud University, The Netherlands

Neil Gong   Duke University, USA
Stefanos Gritzalis   University of Piraeus, Greece
Daniel Gruss   Graz University of Technology, Austria
Zhongshu Gu   IBM T.J. Watson Research Center, USA
Thomas Haines   Norwegian University of Science and Technology,
                               Norway
Feng Hao   University of Warwick, UK
Juan Hernández-Serrano   Universitat Politècnica de Catalunya, Spain
Xinyi Huang   Fujian Normal University, China
Syed Hussain   Pennsylvania State University, USA
Sotiris Ioannidis   Technical University of Crete, Greece
Tibor Jager   Bergische Universität Wuppertal, Germany
Philipp Jeitner   Fraunhofer SIT, Germany
Yuseok Jeon   Ulsan National Institute of Science and Technology,
                               South Korea
Shouling Ji   Zhejiang University, China
Ghassan Karame   NEC Laboratories Europe, Germany
Sokratis Katsikas   Norwegian University of Science and Technology,
                               Norway
Aggelos Kiayias   University of Edinburgh, UK
Hyoungshick Kim   Sungkyunkwan University, South Korea
Ryan Ko   University of Queensland, Australia
Juliane Krämer   TU Darmstadt, Germany
Steve Kremer   Inria France
Marina Krotofil   Honeywell Industrial Cyber Security Lab, USA
Christopher Kruegel   University of California, Santa Barbara, USA
Yonghwi Kwon   University of Virginia, USA
Costas Lambrinoudakis   University of Piraeus, Greece
Shir Landau-Feibish   The Open University of Israel, Israel
Kyu Hyung Lee   University of Georgia, USA
Corrado Leita   VMware, UK
Shujun Li   University of Kent, UK
Zitao Li   Purdue University, USA
Kaitai Liang   Delft University of Technology, The Netherlands
Xiaojing Liao   Indiana University Bloomington, USA
Hoon Wei Lim   Trustwave, Singapore
Zhiqiang Lin   Ohio State University, USA
Xiangyu Liu   Alibaba Group, China
Joseph Liu   Monash University, Australia
Rongxing Lu   University of New Brunswick, Canada
Xiapu Luo   Hong Kong Polytechnic University, Hong Kong
Shiqing Ma   Rutgers University, USA
Leandros Maglaras   De Montfort University, UK
Fabio Martinelli   IIT-CNR, Italy
Sjouke Mauw   Université du Luxembourg, Luxembourg
Weizhi Meng   Technical University of Denmark, Denmark

Yang Zhang	CISPA Helmholtz Center for Information Security, Germany
Yinqian Zhang	Southern University of Science and Technology, China
Yuan Zhang	Fudan University, China
Zhenfeng Zhang	Chinese Academy of Sciences, China
Yunlei Zhao	Fudan University, China
Jianying Zhou	Singapore University of Technology and Design, Singapore
Sencun Zhu	Pennsylvania State University, USA

Workshop Chairs

| David Hay | Hebrew University of Jerusalem, Israel |
| Adrian Perrig | ETH Zurich, Switzerland |

Posters Chair

| Simone Fischer-Hübner | Karlstad University, Sweden |

Publication Chairs

| Philipp Jeitner | Fraunhofer SIT, Germany |
| Hervais Simo | Fraunhofer SIT, Germany |

Publicity Chairs

| Oliver Küch | Fraunhofer SIT, Germany |
| Anna Spiegel | Fraunhofer SIT, Germany |

Sponsorship Chair

| Ute Richter | Fraunhofer SIT, Germany |

Local Arrangements Chair

| Linda Schreiber | National Research Center for Applied Cybersecurity ATHENE, Germany |

Web Chair

| Ingo Siedermann | Fraunhofer SIT, Germany |

Posters Program Committee

Patricia Arias	KIT, Germany
Xinlei He	CISPA Helmholtz Center for Information Security, Germany
Juliane Krämer	TU Darmstadt, Germany
Erwin Quiring	TU Braunschweig, Germany
Neta Shiff Rozen	Hebrew University of Jerusalem, Israel
Tobias Urban	Westphalian University of Applied Sciences, Germany
Di Wang	King Abdullah University of Science and Technology, Saudi Arabia
Zhikun Zhang	CISPA Helmholtz Center for Information Security, Germany

Additional Reviewers

Alexopoulos, Nikolaos
Amiri Eliasi, Parisa
Andreina, Sebastien
Angelogianni, Anna
Avizheh, Sepideh
Bag, Samiran
Bagheri, Sima
Bamiloshin, Michael
Bampatsikos, Michail
Baumer, Thomas
Baumgärtner, Lars
Binun, Alexander
Bolgouras, Vaios
Bonte, Charlotte
Brighente, Alessandro
Böhm, Fabian
Cao, Yanmei
Caprolu, Maurantonio
Catuogno, Luigi
Cecconello, Stefano
Chen, Jinrong
Chen, Long
Chen, Min
Chen, Xihui
Ciampi, Michele
Cicala, Fabrizio
Dang, Hai-Van
Daudén, Cristòfol
Davies, Gareth

Diemert, Denis
Ding, Hailun
Divakaran, Dinil Mon
Dolev, Shlomi
Dong, Naipeng
Du, Jianqi
Du, Minxin
Duman, Onur
Dutta, Sabyasachi
Eckhart, Matthias
Ehsanpour, Maryam
El Kassem, Nada
Empl, Philip
Esgin, Muhammed F.
Feng, Qi
Ferrag, Mohamed Amine
Freisleben, Bernd
Gaballah, Sarah
Gangwal, Ankit
Gellert, Kai
Ghaedi Bardeh, Navid
Gong, Boru
Han, Donggyun
Handirk, Tobias
Hao, Shuai
Hassan, Fadi
Hatzivasilis, George
Hou, Huiying
Huang, Mengdie

Huang, Zonghao
Ismail, Maliha
Jiang, Hetong
Jiang, Shaoquan
Judmayer, Aljosha
Junming, Ke
Kantarcioglu, Murat
Karim, Imtiaz
Kasinathan, Prabhakaran
Kasra Kermanshahi, Shabnam
Kelarev, Andrei
Kern, Andreas
Kern, Sascha
Kim, Hyungsub
Klement, Felix
Komissarov, Rony
Koutroumpouchos, Nikolaos
Kuchta, Veronika
Kumar, Manish
Kwon, Yonghwi
Köstler, Johannes
Lai, Jianchang
Lakka, Eftychia
Lal, Chhagan
Lampropoulos, Konstantinos
Lee, Jehyun
Li, Rui
Li, Yanan
Li, Yannan
Liber, Matan
Lima Pereira, Hilder Vitor
Lin, Chengyu
Lin, Yan
Liu, Guannan
Liu, Lin
Livsey, Lee
Lopez, Christian
Loss, Julian
Lyu, Lin
Ma, Haoyu
Ma, Jack P. K.
Ma, Mimi
Makriyannis, Nikolaos
Mariot, Luca
Marson, Giorgia Azzurra
Martínez, Sergio

Mateu, Victor
Merzouk, Mohamed-Amine
Mestel, David
Mitropoulos, Charalambos
Mohammadi, Farnaz
Niehues, David
Noorman, Job
O'Connell, Sioli
Oppermann, Alexander
Palamidessi, Catuscia
Pan, Jing
Pang, Bo
Panwar, Nisha
Park, Jeongeun
Petroulakis, Nikolaos
Poeplau, Sebastian
Pradel, Gaëtan
Qiu, Tian
Qiu, Zhi
Rabbani, Md Masoom
Ramírez-Cruz, Yunior
Ringerud, Magnus
Rivera, Esteban
Rizomiliotis, Panagiotis
Román-García, Fernando
Saha, Sayandeep
Sanchez-Rola, Iskander
Schindler, Philipp
Schlette, Daniel
Sentanoe, Stewart
Setayeshfar, Omid
Sharifian, Setareh
Shen, Jun
Shen, Xinyue
Silde, Tjerand
Singla, Ankush
Skrobot, Marjan
Song, Zirui
Spolaor, Riccardo
Stifter, Nicholas
Striecks, Christoph
Struck, Patrick
Tabatabaei, Masoud
Tan, Teik Guan
Teague, Vanessa
Tengana, Lizzy

Tian, Guangwei
Trujillo, Rolando
Tschorsch, Florian
Tu, Binbin
Turrin, Federico
Van Strydonck, Thomas
Vielberth, Manfred
Wang, Coby
Wang, Jiafan
Wang, Kailong
Wang, Qian
Wang, Xiaofeng
Wang, Xiaolei
Wang, Yi
Watanabe, Yohei
Wen, Rui
Wisiol, Nils
Wong, Harry W. H.
Wu, Chen
Wu, Huangting

Xu, Fenghao
Xu, Jia
Yang, Rupeng
Yang, S. J.
Yang, Shishuai
Yang, Xu
Yang, Xuechao
Yang, Zheng
Ying, Jason
Yung, Moti
Zhang, Cong
Zhang, Min
Zhang, Wenlu
Zhang, Yanjun
Zhang, Yubao
Zhang, Yuexin
Zhang, Zhiyi
Zhao, Yongjun
Zou, Yang
Zuo, Cong

Additional Reviewers for Posters

Alexopoulos, Nikolaos
Ma, Yihan
Wang, Cheng-Long

Wen, Rui
Xiang, Zihang
Zhang, Minxing

Contents – Part II

Cryptography

Privacy

Differential Privacy

Zero Knowledge

Key Exchange

Multi-party Computation

Posters

Contents – Part I

Malware

User Behaviour and Underground Economy

Blockchain

Automotive

Anomaly Detection

Encryption

Bestie: Very Practical Searchable Encryption with Forward and Backward Security

Tianyang Chen[1], Peng Xu[1](✉), Wei Wang[2], Yubo Zheng[1], Willy Susilo[3], and Hai Jin[1]

[1] National Engineering Research Center for Big Data Technology and System, Services Computing Technology and System Lab, Hubei Engineering Research Center on Big Data Security, School of Cyber Science and Engineering, Huazhong University of Science and Technology, Wuhan 430074, China
{chentianyang,xupeng,zhengyubo,hjin}@mail.hust.edu.cn
[2] Cyber-Physical-Social Systems Lab, School of Computer Science and Technology, Huazhong University of Science and Technology, Wuhan 430074, China
viviawangwei@hust.edu.cn
[3] Institute of Cybersecurity and Cryptology, School of Computing and Information Technology, University of Wollongong, Wollongong, Australia
wsusilo@uow.edu.au

Abstract. *Dynamic searchable symmetric-key encryption* (DSSE) is a promising crypto-tool that enables secure keyword searching over dynamically added or deleted ciphertexts. Currently, many works on DSSE devote their efforts to obtaining *forward and backward security* and practical performance. However, it is still challenging to design a single DSSE scheme that simultaneously achieves this security, high performance, and real deletion. Note that real deletion is a critical feature to guarantee *the right of the user to be forgotten* stipulated by GDPR. Due to this fact, we propose a new *forward-and-backward secure* DSSE scheme named Bestie. To achieve high search performance, Bestie takes the traditional hash and pseudorandom functions and symmetric-key encryption as building blocks and supports parallel keyword search. Bestie also achieves non-interactive real deletion for avoiding the client to do a *clean-up* process. This feature not only guarantees the above GDPR rule but also makes Bestie more suitable for managing large-scale data. Bestie also saves the client's computation and communication costs. Finally, we experimentally compare Bestie with five previous well-known works and show that Bestie is much better in most respects. For example, Bestie requires approximately 3.66 microseconds to find a matching ciphertext. In contrast, Bestie has search performance at least 2 times faster than both Mitra* (CCS'18) and Diana$_{del}$ (CCS'17), 1,032× faster than Fides (CCS'17), and 38,332× faster than Janus++ (CCS'18), respectively. Compared with Mitra (CCS'18), Bestie saves at least 80% client time cost during a search.

© Springer Nature Switzerland AG 2021
E. Bertino et al. (Eds.): ESORICS 2021, LNCS 12973, pp. 3–23, 2021.
https://doi.org/10.1007/978-3-030-88428-4_1

Keywords: Dynamic searchable symmetric-key encryption · Forward and backward security · High performance · Real deletion

1 Introduction

Dynamic searchable symmetric-key encryption (DSSE) [18] originates from searchable symmetric-key encryption [25] (SSE). DSSE allows a client to delegate keyword searches over ciphertexts to an honest-but-curious server while preserving the keyword privacy as SSE does. Additionally, DSSE uniquely enables the client to dynamically update his ciphertexts on the server, such as adding a new ciphertext or deleting an existing ciphertext.

A DSSE scheme usually consists of two parties, namely, a client and an honest-but-curious server, and three protocols between these two parties, such as Setup, Update, and Search. In the beginning, the client runs the Setup protocol to generate his/her symmetric keys, and the server initializes an empty database. The Update protocol allows the client to add a new ciphertext to or delete an existing ciphertext from the server. Each ciphertext contains a keyword-and-file-identifier entry. The Search protocol enables the client to delegate a secure keyword search to the server. The server then returns all found ciphertexts (namely, the ciphertexts containing the expected keyword) to the client.

In terms of the DSSE security, the research community continues to attempt to reduce the information leakage caused by Update and Search protocols as much as possible. The possible information leakage includes keyword privacy and access and search patterns. Recently, researchers have devoted their efforts to developing DSSE schemes with *forward and backward security* [1,2]. Forward security can resist file-injection attack [31] by hiding the relationship between a newly issued Update query and any previously issued Search queries. Backward security can hide the historically deleted ciphertexts from the server when running a Search operation. Hence, *forward and backward security* is widely accepted and strong security in practice.

In terms of the DSSE performance, we say that a DSSE scheme is practical if it achieves high search performance, low client overhead, and non-interactive real deletion. The importance of the first two features is very evident. High search performance means that a DSSE scheme can search over large-scale encrypted data. Low client overhead alleviates the minimum limits on the capability of the client's device. The client, even with a mobile device, can also apply a DSSE scheme. Non-interactive real deletion allows a DSSE scheme to erase the deleted or invalid ciphertexts from the server without the client's help. This not only saves the storage cost of the server but also benefits a DSSE scheme to manage large-scale ciphertexts. Moreover, (non-interactive) real deletion satisfies the GDPR stipulation that *a data subject should have the right to have his or her personal data erased and no longer processed where the personal data are no longer necessary in relation to the purposes for which they are collected or otherwise processed* [23].

However, it is still challenging to design a single DSSE scheme with *forward and backward security* and practical performance. We extensively investigate

Table 1. SSE Scheme Comparison. Note that column "Search Cost" presents the average time cost to find one matching ciphertext if no Delete query was issued before. Symbol n_w denotes the number of ciphertexts matching a keyword search. Column "Encryption Cost" is the average time cost for the client to generate one ciphertext. Column "Real Deletion" describes the deletion type a DSSE scheme can achieve.

Scheme	BP	Search cost (μs)			Round trips	Encryption cost (μs)	Real deletion
		Client	Server	Total			
Fides [2]	II	4,142.63	24.18	4,166.81	2	4,145.22	Interactive
Mitra [4]	II	5.91	0.53	6.44	2	5.81	Failed
Mitra* [4]	II	12.06	3.92	15.98	2	7.38	Interactive
Diana$_{del}$ [2]	III	82.73/n_w	11.83	>11.83	2	13.21	Failed
Janus++ [29]	III	480.58/n_w	154,569	>154,569	1	154,692	Non-interactive
Bestie (ours)	III	0.89	2.77	3.66	2	7.83	Non-interactive

previous well-known DSSE schemes with *forward and backward security*. Table 1 lists some of these schemes and shows that they are still not effective in terms of performance. Concretely, both Fides [2] and Janus++ [29] suffer from low search performance and high client overhead during encryption. Fides also introduces high client time cost into a search process. Fides and Diana$_{del}$ both from [2] and Mitra*[1] [4] consume more bandwidth to transfer re-encrypted ciphertexts or to determine which ciphertexts should be deleted. Both Diana$_{del}$ and Mitra [4] fail to achieve real deletion. Both Fides and Mitra* achieve interactive real deletion. It means that both Fides and Mitra* require the client to re-encrypt and re-upload all matching and still-valid ciphertexts to the server. Clearly, achieving interactive real deletion is not practical for handling large-scale data. The above observations motivate us to develop a practical *forward-and-backward-secure* DSSE scheme that achieves high search performance, low client overhead, and non-interactive real deletion, simultaneously.

In this paper, we present Bestie, a very practical and *forward-and-Type-III-backward-secure* DSSE scheme. As shown in Table 1, Bestie achieves a Search protocol with the highest search performance and the non-interactive real deletion. Hence, Bestie is very suitable for managing large-scale data. In the Search protocol, Bestie only offers a slightly higher client time cost during a search than both Diana$_{del}$ and Janus++, since the Bestie client requires some time cost to decrypt the returned file identifiers from the server. However, the decryption cost of Bestie does not influence the practicality because modern CPUs are equipped with hardware instructions to accelerate the decryption process, such as AES-NI of Intel CPUs. In addition, although Bestie slightly increases the client's time cost, the total time cost of Bestie during a search is still the best one compared with all the above-mentioned schemes.

Some may worry that *forward and Type-III-backward security* is not strong enough. However, it is a fact that *forward and Type-III-backward security* is enough to mitigate the widely-concerned file-injection attack. Meanwhile, it

---

[1] Mitra* is a variant of Mitra that achieves interactive real deletion by the client to re-encrypt and re-upload the still-valid searchable ciphertexts.

seems impossible to achieve Type-I or Type-II backward security and practical performance, simultaneously. To achieve Type-I or Type-II backward security, we have to adopt the costly cryptographic primitive oblivious random access machine (ORAM) (or similar techniques, e.g., Horus [4] and FB-DSSE [32]), occupy client storage resources to stash deletion queries (e.g., Aura [28]), or simply omit (non-interactive) real deletion (e.g., Mitra and Mitra* both from [4], SD_a and SD_d both from [8], and CLOSE-FB [13]). Adopting ORAM (or similar techniques) means that a DSSE scheme must transfer largely redundant data or consume a considerable computation cost.

In summary, we outline our main contributions as below:

- We propose a new DSSE scheme, named Bestie, and prove that it is *forward-and-Type-III-backward secure*;
- We comprehensively compare Bestie with previous DSSE schemes and show that Bestie offers much better performance;
- We introduce the parallelization method to implement the Search protocol of Bestie and experimentally evaluate its efficiency.

We organize the remaining sections of this paper as follows. Section 2 reviews the background knowledge of DSSE. Section 3 presents our Bestie. Section 4 experimentally compares Bestie with previous works. We introduce the related works in Sect. 5. Section 6 finally concludes this paper.

2   Background

Notations. In the remaining sections, we use $\lambda \in \mathbb{N}$ to denote the security parameter. We use symbol $e \xleftarrow{\$} \mathcal{X}$ to denote randomly choosing an element e from space or set $\mathcal{X}$. Symbol $\{0, 1\}^k$ indicates all strings that are of binary length $k \in \mathbb{N}$, and symbol $\{0, 1\}^*$ represents all strings of arbitrary binary length. Let 0^λ be the string of binary length λ whose bits are all zero. We assume that no file has the identifier 0^λ. Let symbol poly(λ) denote a polynomial with input parameter λ. Let symbol $\perp$ denote the abort operation.

Definition 1 (DSSE). *A DSSE scheme Σ consists of three protocols between the client and the server, such as $\Sigma.Setup$, $\Sigma.Update$, and $\Sigma.Search$. Their definitions are given below:*

- *Protocol $\Sigma.Setup(\lambda)$: In this protocol, the client initializes his secret key K_Σ and an empty state-set σ for the given security parameter λ and sends an empty encrypted database **EDB** to the server. The client keeps both his key K_Σ and state-set σ private.*
- *Protocol $\Sigma.Update(K_\Sigma, \sigma, op, (w, id); \mathbf{EDB})$: In this protocol, the client either adds a new keyword-and-file-identifier entry (w, id) to or deletes an existing entry from the server according to parameter $op \in \{add, del\}$. Given key K_Σ and state-set σ, the client sends a new ciphertext of entry (w, id) to the server if $op = add$; otherwise (namely, $op = del$), he sends a delete token of entry (w, id) to the server. When receiving the above message, the server updates its database **EDB** correspondingly.*

– *Protocol Σ.Search($K_\Sigma, \sigma, w; \boldsymbol{EDB}$): In this protocol, given key K_Σ and state-set σ, the client sends a search trapdoor of the expected keyword w to the server. Then, the server searches the keyword over the database $\boldsymbol{EDB}$ and returns all valid file identifiers to the client.*

A DSSE scheme must be correct in the sense that all valid file identifiers can always be found. The formal definition can be found in [18].

A popular method to define the adaptive security of DSSE is to define the indistinguishability between a real game and an ideal game of DSSE. In both games, the adversary can adaptively issue Update and Search queries. In the real game, all keyword-and-file-identifier entries and secret keys are real, and both protocols Σ.Update and Σ.Search are correctly implemented. In contrast, in the ideal game, a simulator only uses leakage functions to simulate the responses to all queries of the adversary. We say that DSSE is adaptively secure if a simulator can simulate an ideal game that is indistinguishable from the real game. The fewer leakage functions the simulator uses, the more secure DSSE is.

Definition 2 (Adaptive Security of DSSE). *Given leakage functions $\mathcal{L} = (\mathcal{L}^{Stp}, \mathcal{L}^{Updt}, \mathcal{L}^{Srch})$, a DSSE scheme Σ is said to be $\mathcal{L}$-adaptively secure if for any sufficiently large security parameter $\lambda \in \mathbb{N}$ and adversary $\mathcal{A}$, there exists an efficient simulator $\mathcal{S} = (\mathcal{S}.Setup, \mathcal{S}.Update, \mathcal{S}.Search)$ for which $|Pr[Real_\mathcal{A}^\Sigma(\lambda) = 1] - Pr[Ideal_{\mathcal{A},\mathcal{S},\mathcal{L}}^\Sigma(\lambda) = 1]|$ is negligible in λ, where games $Real_\mathcal{A}^\Sigma(\lambda)$ and $Ideal_{\mathcal{A},\mathcal{S},\mathcal{L}}^\Sigma(\lambda)$ are defined as below:*

– *$Real_\mathcal{A}^\Sigma(\lambda)$: The real game exactly implements all DSSE protocols. Adversary $\mathcal{A}$ can adaptively issue Update and Search queries with input $(op, (w, id))$ and w, respectively, and observe the real transcripts generated by the DSSE protocols. At the end, adversary $\mathcal{A}$ outputs a bit.*
– *$Ideal_{\mathcal{A},\mathcal{S},\mathcal{L}}^\Sigma(\lambda)$: All transcripts are simulated by the simulator $\mathcal{S}$. Adversary $\mathcal{A}$ can issue the same queries as in the real game. The simulator $\mathcal{S}$ simulates the corresponding transcripts by taking leakage functions $\mathcal{L}$ as input. At the end, adversary $\mathcal{A}$ outputs a bit.*

Let list Q be a set of all Update and Search queries, where each entry in list Q has the form of either $(u, op, (w, id))$ or (u, w) for Update and Search queries, respectively, where parameter u denotes the timestamp of issuing a query. Given a keyword w, let function $sp(w)$ return all timestamps of the Search queries about keyword w, function $TimeDB(w)$ return all undeleted file identifiers of keyword w and the history timestamps for adding these files, and function $DelHist(w)$ return the history timestamps of all paired Add and Delete operations about keyword w. The formal definitions of the above three functions are given below.

$$sp(w) = \{u | (u, , w) \in Q\}$$

$$TimeDB(w) = \{(u, id) | (u, add, (w, id)) \in Q \text{ and } \forall u', (u', del, (w, id)) \notin Q\}$$

$$DelHist(w) = \{(u^{add}, u^{del}) | \exists id, (u^{add}, add, (w, id)) \in Q$$
$$\text{and } (u^{del}, del, (w, id)) \in Q\}$$

With the above functions, *forward and Type-III-backward security* is defined as follows.

Definition 3 (Forward and Type-III-Backward Security [1,2]). *An $\mathcal{L}$-adaptively secure DSSE scheme Σ is forward-and-Type-III-backward secure iff the Update and Search leakage functions $\mathcal{L}^{Updt}$ and $\mathcal{L}^{Srch}$ can be written as*

$$\mathcal{L}^{Updt}(op, w, id) = \mathcal{L}'(op) \text{ and } \mathcal{L}^{Srch}(w) = \mathcal{L}''(sp(w), TimeDB(w), DelHist(w))$$

where $\mathcal{L}'$ and $\mathcal{L}''$ are two stateless functions.

Besides the Type-III backward security, there exist two other levels of backward security, namely Type-I backward security and Type-II backward security. Type-I backward security requires that a Search query leaks only $TimeDB(w)$ and the total number of updating w. In contrast, Type-II backward security additionally allows a Search query to leak the timestamps of updating w. This paper focuses on the Type-III backward security. The formal definitions of Type-I and Type-II backward securities can be found in [2].

3   Construction of Bestie

As shown in Table 1, our proposed Bestie is practical in almost all aspects. To achieve this, the construction of Bestie adopts the following three core ideas:

- To achieve high search performance, Bestie generates searchable ciphertexts in a counter-based design and collects all found ciphertexts into a group for each Search query. This method avoids redundant computation in the next-time search on these ciphertexts. The counter-based design enables the server to find all matching ciphertexts by traversing all valid counter values, and the resulting search complexity is sub-linear with respect to the total number of ciphertexts. Additionally, Bestie avoids any expensive cryptographic operation and adopts some hash computations. Hence, Bestie achieves faster search performance than the previous works, such as Fides and Janus++.
- To realize non-interactive real deletion while ensuring minimal information leakage, we apply the idea of combining logical deletion and real deletion introduced by Xu et al. [30]. Bestie additionally achieves higher security (less information leakage) than the scheme in [30]. In short, when issuing an Update query to delete a historical ciphertext, Bestie uploads a new ciphertext to the server. This ciphertext contains the index of a historical ciphertext that the client expects to delete. When a Search query finds this new ciphertext, the server can decrypt the contained index, and this index can guide the server to really delete the corresponding historical ciphertext.
- To achieve forward security, Bestie chooses a new key for a keyword to generate the keyword ciphertexts after each search for the keyword. In other words, after each search for a keyword, Bestie chooses a new key to generate the following ciphertexts of the keyword. To avoid storing many keys for a keyword on the client-side, Bestie allows the client to maintain a Search

counter for each keyword and dynamically generate any historical key of a keyword. Moreover, the use of a group on the server-side enables `Bestie` to send a constant-size search trapdoor for each `Search` query, instead of delegating many search trapdoors generated by the different historical keys of a keyword to the server. To achieve backward security, `Bestie` encrypts all file identifiers such that the server learns nothing about the deleted file identifier.

3.1 Our Construction

Let λ be the security parameter. `Bestie` utilizes a PRF function $\mathbf{F} : \mathcal{K}_{\mathbf{F}} \times \mathcal{X}_{\mathbf{F}} \to \mathcal{Y}_{\mathbf{F}}$, where $\mathcal{K}_{\mathbf{F}} = \{0,1\}^{\lambda}$ is the secret key space, $\mathcal{X}_{\mathbf{F}} = \{0,1\}^{*}$ is the domain and $\mathcal{Y}_{\mathbf{F}} = \{0,1\}^{\lambda}$ is the range. The security of PRF ensures that the output of $\mathbf{F}$ is indistinguishable from a randomly sampled value from $\mathcal{Y}_{\mathbf{F}}$, except for a negligible probability in the parameter λ. `Bestie` also uses a semantically secure and probabilistic symmetric encryption scheme ξ. ξ comprises of a probabilistic encryption algorithm $\mathcal{E} : \mathcal{K}_{\xi} \times \mathcal{M}_{\xi} \to \mathcal{C}_{\xi}$ and the corresponding decryption algorithm $\mathcal{D} : \mathcal{K}_{\xi} \times \mathcal{C}_{\xi} \to \mathcal{M}_{\xi} \cup \{\bot\}$, where $\mathcal{K}_{\xi} = \{0,1\}^{\lambda}$ is the symmetric key space, $\mathcal{M}_{\xi} = \{0,1\}^{*}$ is the plaintext space, and $\mathcal{C}_{\xi} = \{0,1\}^{*}$ is the ciphertext space. Algorithm 1 presents the pseudocode of protocols `Bestie.Setup`, `Bestie.Update`, and `Bestie.Search`. The following content explains the details of `Bestie`.

`Bestie.Setup` **Protocol.** Upon inputting a security parameter λ, this protocol mainly initializes two keys K_{ξ} and S and some empty storage structures **Count** and **EDB** = (**CDB, GRP**). Key K_{ξ} will be used as a symmetric key to encrypt (or decrypt, resp.) file identifiers when updating an entry (or receiving the search results from the server, resp.). Key S is a master key. When issuing an `Update` query or a `Search` query of a keyword, the client will dynamically generate two sub-keys from the master key for the keyword to complete the query. Such a method avoids storing many keys on the client-side. Structure **Count** stores the update times of a keyword after the last search of the keyword and the keyword search times. The client must locally store structure **Count** and ensure its privacy. The server uses structure **CDB** to store all newly updated ciphertexts that are never searched and uses group **GRP** to group the still-valid ciphertexts of the same keyword when receiving a `Search` query.

`Bestie.Update` **Protocol.** This protocol enables the client to issue an `Update` query for adding or deleting a keyword-and-file-identifier entry, such as (w, id). For a given entry (w, id), the client locally queries structure **Count** to obtain the existing update times c_w^{updt} after the last search of keyword w and the existing search times c_w^{srch} of keyword w (refer to Steps 1 to 3). Then, the client computes two special keys K_w and K_w' with the master key S and the search times c_w^{srch} of keyword w (refer to Step 4). As a result, the client will use a new key K_w to generate the subsequent ciphertexts of keyword w after each search of this keyword. Each ciphertext consists of three parts, namely, (L, D, C). Part L is taken as a unique address to store the ciphertext in structure **CDB**. Part D encrypts the inputted operation type op and a hash value $\mathbf{G}(K_w', id)$. When searching

---

Algorithm 1. Protocols `Bestie.Setup`, `Bestie.Update` and `Bestie.Search`.

Setup(λ)

1: Choose two hash functions $\mathbf{H}$: $\{0,1\}^*$ → $\{0,1\}^{\lambda'+\lambda+1}$, where λ' = poly(λ) and $\mathbf{G}$: $\{0,1\}^*$ → $\{0,1\}^\lambda$
2: Initialize three empty maps **Count**, **CDB**, and **GRP**, and let **EDB** = (**CDB**, **GRP**)
3: Let $op \in \{add, del\}$ with the binary codes $add = 1$ and $del = 0$
4: Pick a symmetric key $K_\xi \xleftarrow{\$} \mathcal{K}_\xi$ and a secret key $S \xleftarrow{\$} \mathcal{K}_{\mathbf{F}}$, and set $K_\Sigma = (S, K_\xi)$
5: Store **EDB** on the server

Update(K_Σ, **Count**, op, (w, id); **EDB**)

Client:

1: Retrieve the current count values (c_w^{updt}, c_w^{srch}) ← **Count**[w] with the inputted keyword w
2: Initialize (c_w^{updt}, c_w^{srch}) ← $(0, 0)$ if **Count**[w] is NULL
3: Accumulate the update times of keyword w by setting c_w^{updt} ← $c_w^{updt}+1$ and update such modification to **Count**[w]
4: Compute two special keys K_w ← $\mathbf{F}(S, w||c_w^{srch})$ and K'_w ← $\mathbf{F}(S, w|| - 1)$ for encrypting keyword w
5: Encrypt keyword w as $(L||D)$ ← $\mathbf{H}(K_w, c_w^{updt}) \oplus (0^{\lambda'}||op||\mathbf{G}(K'_w, id))$, where L represents the most significant λ' bits of the result and D denotes the remaining $\lambda + 1$ bits (Note that we have assumed that id cannot be 0^λ in Section 2)
6: Encrypt the inputted file identifier as C ← $\mathcal{E}(K_\xi, id)$
7: Send ciphertext (L, D, C) to the server

Server:

1: Store the received ciphertext by setting **CDB**[L] ← (D, C)

Search(K_Σ, **Count**, w; **EDB**)

Client:

1: Retrieve the current count values (c_w^{updt}, c_w^{srch}) ← **Count**[w]
2: Abort if **Count**[w] is NULL

3: Compute two special keys K_w ← $\mathbf{F}(S, w||c_w^{srch})$ and K'_w ← $\mathbf{F}(S, w|| - 1)$ for generating the search trapdoor of keyword w
4: Compute index I_w^{grp} ← $\mathbf{G}(K'_w, 0^\lambda)$ for the server to group the search results of this time with the results of the previous searches of the same keyword
5: Send search trapdoor $(c_w^{updt}, K_w, I_w^{grp})$ to the server

Server:

1: Initialize an empty set $\mathcal{D}$, and set i ← c_w^{updt}
2: **repeat**
3:   Break if $i = 0$
4:   Compute $(L||D')$ ← $\mathbf{H}(K_w, i)$, where L represents the most significant λ' bits of the hash value and D' denotes the remaining $\lambda + 1$ bits
5:   Retrieve ciphertext (D, C) ← **CDB**[L] according to index L
6:   Decrypt $(op||X)$ ← $D \oplus D'$
7:   **if** $op = del$ **then**
8:     Record X into $\mathcal{D}$ ← $\mathcal{D} \cup \{X\}$
9:     Remove all old ciphertexts $(X', C') \in \mathbf{GRP}[I_w^{grp}]$ with $X' = X$ that already exist in $\mathbf{GRP}[I_w^{grp}]$ before this search
10:   **else if** $op = add$ **then**
11:     Record (X, C) into group $\mathbf{GRP}[I_w^{grp}]$ if $X \notin \mathcal{D}$
12:   **end if**
13:   Set $i = i - 1$
14: **until** $(i = 0)$
15: Remove all above ciphertexts found from structure **CDB**
16: Return all remaining file identifier ciphertexts in group $\mathbf{GRP}[I_w^{grp}]$ to the client

Client:

1: Use the symmetric key K_ξ to decrypt all received ciphertexts and return the obtained file identifiers
2: Accumulate the search times of keyword w by setting c_w^{srch} ← $c_w^{srch} + 1$ and updating **Count**[w]
3: Update **Count**[w] by setting $c_w^{updt} = 0$

---

keyword w in the future, this hash value will inform the server which ciphertext must be deleted if $op = del$. Part C encrypts the inputted file identifier.

Bestie.Search Protocol. This protocol allows the client and the server to complete a search task together. The protocol contains three steps: the client generates and uploads a search trapdoor to the server, the server then finds and returns the matching ciphertexts, and finally, the client receives and decrypts the returned file identifiers. For searching a keyword w, the generated search trapdoor consists of three parts: the current counter value c_w^{updt}, the sub-key K_w, and a group index I_w^{grp}. The value c_w^{updt} denotes the number of newly updated ciphertexts of keyword w after the last search of keyword w. Upon receiving both c_w^{updt} and K_w, the server can find the matching ciphertexts from these newly updated ones. The group index I_w^{grp} allows the server to retrieve the historical matching ciphertexts from group **GRP**. The final search results include these two parts.

When searching a keyword w, first, the server finds all new matching ciphertexts from structure **CDB** (refer to Steps 2 to 14). The server handles these matching ciphertexts as two cases according to their contained operation types (refer to Steps 7 to 12). In the case of $op = del$, the decrypted value X means that the server will remove a ciphertext from either structure **CDB** or group **GRP**$[I_w^{grp}]$ if the ciphertext contains the same value X. Note that when using the value X to delete ciphertexts from group **GRP**$[I_w^{grp}]$, the server only removes the old ciphertexts found in previous search queries. This guarantees that a Delete query only removes the early corresponding Add queries, not the subsequent Add queries. In the case of $op = add$, the server will add the corresponding ciphertext into group **GRP**$[I_w^{grp}]$ if the ciphertext is still valid (not deleted). Second, the server retrieves all matching and still-valid ciphertexts from group **GRP**$[I_w^{grp}]$ and returns them to the client. Finally, the client decrypts the matching file identifiers, accumulates the search times c_w^{srch}, and clears the counter value c_w^{updt}.

Correctness of Bestie. The correctness of Bestie comes straightforwardly from the collision-resistant property of hash functions **H** and **G**. Concretely, when searching a keyword w, the server repeats computing hash value $\mathbf{H}(K_w, i)$ for i decreasing successively from c_w^{updt} to 1 and obtains the number of c_w^{updt} distinct addresses. These addresses guarantee the search correctness of finding all matching ciphertexts from structure **CDB**. The uniqueness of hash value $I_w^{grp} = \mathbf{G}(K_w', 0^\lambda)$ guarantees that group **GRP**$[I_w^{grp}]$ contains all historical matching ciphertexts. In addition, the uniqueness of hash value $\mathbf{G}(K_w', id)$ guarantees that the server can correctly delete the expected ciphertext.

Security of Bestie. In terms of security, Bestie is *forward-and-Type-III-backward secure*. Formally, we have the following theorem, which is proven in Appendix A.

Theorem 1. *Suppose that the hash function **H** is a random oracle, **G** is a cryptographic hash function, function **F** is a secure PRF function, and ξ is a CPA-secure symmetric encryption scheme; then, Bestie is an adaptively secure DSSE scheme with leakage functions $\mathcal{L}^{Stp}(\lambda) = \lambda$, $\mathcal{L}^{Updt}(op, w, id) = \emptyset$, and $\mathcal{L}^{Srch}(w) = \{sp(w), TimeDB(w), DelHist(w)\}$.*

Remarks on Improving the Performance. To reduce the hash function iterations as much as possible, Bestie computes the partial ciphertexts L and D by only one hash computation (refer to Step 5 in protocol Update), instead of independently generating them by running a hash function twice. This approach is very effective in reducing the time cost. For example, our experiment shows that the time cost to run hash function SHA-256 twice by the OpenSSL library is approximately 20% more than running hash function SHA-512 once.

When searching for a keyword, the server can find the matching ciphertexts by a parallel method to improve the performance. Refer to Steps 2 to 14 in protocol Search. The repeated computations to find all matching ciphertexts from structure **CDB** can be transformed into a parallel algorithm since each computation relies on the sub-key K_w and the parameter $i \in [1, c_w^{updt}]$. The server can traverse all possible values of parameter i in parallel to improve the search performance. We will show a parallel execution of protocol Search to demonstrate its significant advantage in Sect. 4.

3.2 An Example of Bestie

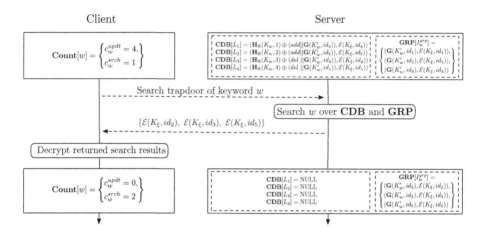

Fig. 1. Example of Bestie. Note that $\mathbf{H}_R$ denotes the least significant $\lambda + 1$ bits of the output of hash function $\mathbf{H}$. The ciphertexts with $op = del$ colored with red or blue mean to delete the corresponding ciphertexts with $op = add$ of the same color, respectively.

We introduce an example to clearly present the search procedures of Bestie. For keyword w, suppose that in the first time search of this keyword, the server finds three matching ciphertexts from structure **CDB** and transfers them to group $\mathbf{GRP}[I_w^{grp}]$. Then, the client issues four Update queries for adding entries (w, id_4) and (w, id_5) and deleting entries (w, id_4) and (w, id_1). The two upperside rectangles of Fig. 1 shows the states of both the client and the server after completing the above operations, respectively. The client records the current counter values. The server stores the four newly uploaded ciphertexts in structure **CDB**.

Now, suppose the client to issue the search query of keyword w again. Upon receiving the corresponding search trapdoor, the server first finds the four matching ciphertexts $\mathbf{CDB}[L_4]$, $\mathbf{CDB}[L_3]$, $\mathbf{CDB}[L_2]$, and $\mathbf{CDB}[L_1]$ and decrypts $del||\mathbf{G}(K_w', id_1)$, $del||\mathbf{G}(K_w', id_4)$, $add||\mathbf{G}(K_w', id_5)$, and $add||\mathbf{G}(K_w', id_4)$, sequentially. Secondly, the server performs the following steps: (1) use $del||\mathbf{G}(K_w', id_1)$ to delete entry $(\mathbf{G}(K_w', id_1), \mathcal{E}(K_\xi, id_1))$ from group $\mathbf{GRP}[I_w^{grp}]$ and temporarily store $\mathbf{G}(K_w', id_1)$ for future (possible) deletions, (2) temporarily store $\mathbf{G}(K_w', id_4)$ for future (possible) deletions, (3) store entry $(\mathbf{G}(K_w', id_5), \mathcal{E}(K_\xi, id_5))$ in group $\mathbf{GRP}[I_w^{grp}]$, and (4) ignore ciphertext $\mathbf{CDB}[L_1]$ since it contains $\mathbf{G}(K_w', id_4)$.

Thirdly, the server empties structures $\mathbf{CDB}[L_4/L_3/L_2/L_1]$ and returns the three matching and still-valid ciphertexts in group $\mathbf{GRP}[I_w^{grp}]$ to the client. Finally, the client decrypts the returned search results and updates his counter values. The lower-side rectangles of Fig. 1 shows the new states of both the client and the server after the search, respectively.

4   Evaluation

We code `Bestie` and comprehensively evaluate its performance. To show the significant advantages of `Bestie`, we compare `Bestie` with five existing *forward-and-backward-secure* DSSE schemes, such as `Fides` and `Diana`$_{del}$ both from [2], `Mitra` and `Mitra`* both from [4], and `Janus++` [29].

4.1   Implementation

We code `Bestie` and recode the above five existing DSSE schemes for unifying their security parameters and testing environments.

Table 2. Hardware and software configuration

Hardware platform			
CPU	Intel E5-2630 v3	Memory	64 GB
Software environment			
Operation system	CentOS 7.3.1611 x64	Compiler	GCC 4.8.5
Cryptographic library	OpenSSL 1.1.1c [10]	Mathematical library	GMP Library 6.1.2 [9]

Programming Environment. Table 2 lists the hardware and software configurations. We code the above mentioned six DSSE schemes with C++ language and choose suitable security parameters to guarantee that they satisfy the 128-bit security level. To mitigate the influence of hard disk I/O, we store all generated ciphertexts in memory with the C++ STL library's data structures, such as *unordered_map*. Some graphs of our experiment are produced with Matplotlib [15].

Cryptographic Primitives. We apply the OpenSSL library and choose the SHA-2 hash family, the SHA-256-based HMAC, and AES-128 encryption to realize the hash function, the PRF function, and the symmetric encryption that appear in above mentioned six DSSE schemes, respectively. `Janus++` is the most complex one to be coded compared with others. In `Janus++`, each ciphertext includes a unique tag. When the client wants to delete a ciphertext, he generates a punctured key according to the ciphertext tag. This key can revoke the capability of the server to decrypt the ciphertext. The chosen binary length of the tag (namely, 16 bits) in [29] is too short to support a large volume of data. Hence, we apply the SHA-256-based HMAC algorithm to securely generate 256-bit tag. In addition, we set the maximum deletion number of `Janus++` to be 2,000 and apply `Diana`$_{del}$ as a building block to realize `Janus++`. We apply the GMP library to realize the 2048-bit RSA-based trapdoor permutation employed by `Fides`.

4.2   Data Description

Table 3. The 18 representative keywords and their frequencies

Keyword	Freq.	Keyword	Freq.	Keyword	Freq.	Keyword	Freq.	Keyword	Freq.
2001	246,613	pst	218,860	2000	208,551	call	102,807	thu	93,835
question	83,882	follow	75,409	regard	68,923	contact	60,270	energi	54,090
current	47,707	legal	39,923	problem	31,282	industri	21,472	transport	12,879
target	7,311	exactli	4,644	enterpris	3,130				

We run the *Porter Stemming* algorithm [24] on the Enron dataset [20] to extract keywords as [16] does. We extract a total of 42,014,587 keyword-and-file-identifier entries after excluding stop words, such as "a", "an", and "the". The total number of distinct keywords is 856,131. To succinctly present experimental results, we choose the 18 representative keywords listed in Table 3. These keywords have distinct frequencies. In particular, we choose the keyword "2001", which has the highest frequency, as a representative one. Ultimately, our test dataset includes 1,381,588 keyword-and-file-identifier entries. In addition, for each email, we set its file identifier to be the hexadecimal representation of the SHA-256 hash digest of its full path. Each file identifier consists of 64 bytes.

4.3   Experimental Results

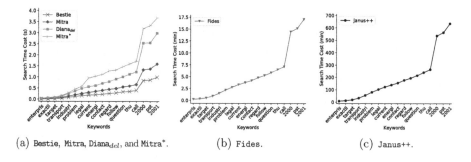

(a) Bestie, Mitra, Diana$_{del}$, and Mitra*.   (b) Fides.   (c) Janus++.

Fig. 2. Total Search time cost without deletion.

Search Performance without Any Deletion. The search performance consists of three respects, such as total Search time cost, bandwidth cost, and client time cost. Note that the search performance here does not contain any deletion operation. Figure 2 compares the above-mentioned six schemes in terms of total Search time cost, namely the sum of both the server and the client time costs. The numerical results demonstrate that Bestie is the best one. It achieves a

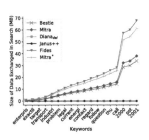

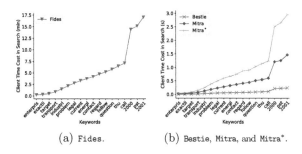

(a) Fides.

(b) Bestie, Mitra, and Mitra*.

Fig. 3. Bandwidth cost without deletion.

Fig. 4. Client time cost without deletion.

Search time cost that is at least 2, 1,032, and 38,332 times faster than both Mitra* and Diana$_{del}$, Fides, and Janus++, respectively. Bestie is also faster than Mitra. Bestie takes approximately 3.66 microseconds to find one matching ciphertext in average.

Figure 3 gives comparisons in terms of bandwidth cost. The bandwidth cost means the transferred data during a search. Figure 3 shows that Bestie achieves the lowest bandwidth cost compared with those schemes that need the client to return file identifiers to the server, like Mitra, Mitra*, and Fides. Both Janus++ and Diana$_{del}$ achieve the cheapest bandwidth cost, since they allow the server to learn the file identifiers without the help of the client.

Figure 4 compares Bestie, Mitra, Mitra*, and Fides in terms of client time cost. We omit the comparisons with both Janus++ and Diana$_{del}$, since both of them require quite small client time cost during a search. The numerical results show that the client time cost of Bestie to find one matching ciphertext is approximately 0.89 microsecond, which is the minimum one in Fig. 4.

Search Performance with Deletions. In this part, we consider deletion operations and test the search performance again. This experiment selects keyword "2001" as a representation and its corresponding file identifiers as the test dataset for testing Bestie, Mitra, Mitra*, Fides, and Diana$_{del}$. In contrast, we select keyword "enterpris" for testing Janus++. The difference is caused by the reasons that the maximum deletion number of Janus++ is set to be 2,000, and this number is much smaller than the total number of file identifiers of keyword "2001". If we set the maximum deletion number to be a much bigger one, the Search time cost of Janus++ is too high. To test the search performance, we add 246,613 (3,130, resp.) ciphertexts for keyword "2001" ("enterpris", resp.) at first. Secondly, we issue different number of Delete queries and then search keyword "2001" ("enterpris", resp.) over these ciphertexts. Each Delete query is to delete a randomly chosen file identifier.

Figure 5 shows how the different number of Delete queries affect the total Search time cost of a scheme. The numerical results show that Bestie achieves the lowest total Search time cost compared with others. Moreover, the increasing number of Delete queries has very little influence on the total Search time cost of

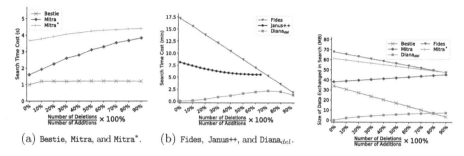

(a) Bestie, Mitra, and Mitra*.   (b) Fides, Janus++, and Diana$_{del}$.

Fig. 5. Total Search time cost with deletions.   **Fig. 6.** Bandwidth cost with deletions.

Bestie. This is because that the total number of memory-writing operations in protocol Bestie.Search is decreasing along with the increasing number of Delete queries. The saved time cost caused by the decreasing number of memory-writing operations nearly counteracts the time cost caused by the increasing number of Delete queries.

Figure 6 show that Bestie achieves the lowest bandwidth cost compared with Mitra, Mitra*, and Fides. Moreover, the bandwidth cost of Bestie is decreasing along with the increasing number of Delete queries. We omit the comparison with Janus++ in terms of bandwidth cost, since Janus++ does not need the client to help the server get the matching file identifiers.

Figure 7 shows that Bestie saves at least 80% client time cost compared with others except Janus++ if $\frac{\text{Number of Deletions}}{\text{Number of Additions}} \times 100\% \geq 10\%$. We also omit to test the client time cost of Janus++ due to the same reason as the last experiment.

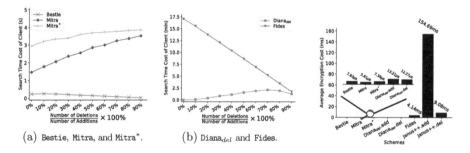

(a) Bestie, Mitra, and Mitra*.   (b) Diana$_{del}$ and Fides.

Fig. 7. Client time cost with deletions.   **Fig. 8.** Update time cost.

Update Time Cost. This experiment tests the time cost to generate one Update query, including Add and Delete queries. The above-mentioned six schemes has an identical time cost in generating that two kinds of queries, except Diana$_{del}$ and Janus++. Figure 8 shows that Bestie has a little more Update time cost only than both Mitra and Mitra*. But Bestie is more useful since both Mitra and Mitra* cannot achieve non-interactive real deletion.

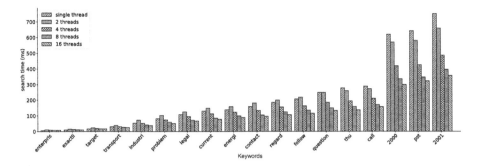

Fig. 9. Time costs of `Bestie.Search` with different threads.

Parallel Keyword Search. Section 3 explains that `Bestie` can achieve parallel keyword search. This means that compared with other schemes, `Bestie` can also retain its performance advantage when searching a keyword in the multi-threading setting. To highlight this feature, we implement the search procedures of the `Bestie.Search` protocol with different numbers of threads, such as two, four, eight, and sixteen threads. According to the numerical results shown in Fig. 9, generally, the more threads the server uses, the more efficient the search performance `Bestie` can obtain. The opposite results are observed only in the case of two threads when the number of matching ciphertexts is too small. The main reason for such an exception is the competition among threads for writing memory.

5   Other Related Works

Traditional SSE Schemes. The seminal work of Song *et al.* in 2000 [25] started the research on SSE. The proposed SSE scheme needs to scan the whole database during the search therefore is not efficient. In 2006, Curtmola *et al.* firstly improved the search efficiency of SSE to the sub-linear setting [7]. However, their construction with sub-linear search efficiency is not secure against adaptive chosen-keyword attacks (CKA2). Chase *et al.* exhibited the first CKA2-secure SSE scheme that has sub-linear search complexity [6] in 2010. Their work adopts padding in the encryption algorithm, which results in waste of storage and bandwidth resources. In 2012, Islam *et al.* introduced the first attack against SSE, which relies on the access pattern leakage of SSE and some background knowledge [16], such as the distribution of the keyword space.

Early DSSE Schemes. In 2010, Liesdonk *et al.* proposed the first CKA2-secure DSSE scheme, for which the search efficiency is logarithmic with the number of unique keywords [22]. However, the underlying cryptographical primitives produce redundant data, which results in a non-optimal search bandwidth. Additionally, the scheme is not scalable enough to support a large number of file identifiers. In 2012, Kamara *et al.* formally defined the security notion of DSSE over information leakage [7] and presented a CKA2-secure DSSE construction with sub-linear search efficiency [18]. In 2013, Kamara *et al.* presented a CKA2-secure DSSE scheme that is built upon a keyword red-black tree, and the scheme supports parallel search [17]. However, the generated encrypted index of their construction is very large. Cash *et al.* later proposed a counter-based DSSE scheme that supports very large datasets [3]. In the same year, Stefanov *et al.* proposed a DSSE scheme that is forward secure [27]. However, the Update protocol of their scheme is costly because it requires the client to interact with the server to perform re-encryption operations. In 2014, Hahn *et al.* constructed an efficient DSSE scheme [12]. However, when adding searchable ciphertexts, the scheme directly classifies the ever-searched keywords and stores the corresponding ciphertexts in specific places, which reveals the semantic information of the ciphertexts. In 2017, Xu *et al.* proposed a DSSE scheme with sub-linear search efficiency and small leakage [30]. The scheme constructs a hidden chain in those generated ciphertexts that contain the same keyword and combines the physical and logical deletion. In 2016, Zhang *et al.* presented the file-injection attack against DSSE [31]. The file-injection attack is a proactive attack wherein the adversary injects files into the target scheme.

Forward-and-Backward-Secure DSSE Schemes. As illustrated by Zhang *et al.*, forward security is an important property that can defend against file-injection attacks [31]. The first forward-secure DSSE scheme was proposed by Chang *et al.* in 2005 [5]. In 2014, Stefanov *et al.* first formally defined forward security with leakage functions [27]. Later, Bost improved the performance of the proposed scheme in the aspects of both computation and bandwidth by using the trapdoor permutation [1]. In 2016, Garg *et al.* constructed a forward-secure DSSE scheme based on their TWORAM [11], but it suffers from low Update and Search efficiency. In 2017, Kim *et al.* utilized the dual dictionary to construct a forward-secure DSSE scheme that supports real deletion [19]. In 2018, Song *et al.* proposed a counter-based forward-secure DSSE scheme with real deletion support [26]. Their proposed scheme achieves I/O efficiency by caching historical search results.

In 2014, Stefanov *et al.* proposed backward security, which requires that search queries cannot be executed over deleted ciphertexts [27]. In 2016, Hoang *et al.* presented *forward-and-backward-secure* DOD-DSSE [14]. The core idea of DOD-DSSE is to let the client fetch all related data from the server and to perform Search or Update operations locally. In 2017, Bost *et al.* formulated backward security with leakage functions [2]. In their work, they defined three types of backward security for ensuring different levels of security strength. In work [2], Bost *et al.* constructed four *forward-and-backward-secure* DSSE schemes: Fides, $Diana_{Del}$, Moneta and Janus. Moneta is based on TWORAM, which is not practical. In 2019, Li *et al.* constructed a *forward-and-backward-secure* DSSE with the hidden pointer ciphertext structure and partition search technique [21]. In 2020, He *et al.* [13] presented a *forward-and-backward-secure* DSSE scheme with constant client storage. He *et al.*'s approach is to combine the counter and chain structure and use the global counter to find all chain structures of ciphertexts.

In the same year, Demertzis *et al.* [8] proposed three *forward-and-backward-secure* DSSE scheme with constant client storage. The first two schemes in [8] achieve interactive real deletion, and the third scheme uses *oblivious map* and a tree-based encrypted index as building blocks. Recently in 2021, Sun *et al.* [28] proposed a *forward-and-backward-secure* DSSE scheme Aura, which achieves non-interactive real deletion in the cost of extra client-side storage resources to stash Delete queries.

6   Conclusion

In this paper, we analyse the requirements for a DSSE scheme to be practical and note that most existing *forward-and-backward-secure* DSSE schemes are not practical enough in terms of performance or real deletion. This fact motivates us to propose Bestie, a very practical and *forward-and-backward-secure* DSSE scheme. Bestie also supports non-interactive real deletion and parallel keyword search. The experimental results show that Bestie achieves the best Search time cost compared with Fides, Mitra, Mitra*, Diana$_{del}$, and Janus++. During a search, Bestie achieves the lowest client time cost and the lowest bandwidth cost compared with Fides, Mitra, and Mitra*. Although Bestie introduces a little more client time cost and bandwidth cost during a search than Janus++ and Diana$_{del}$, it is much faster than Janus++ during a search and achieves non-interactive real deletion that Diana$_{del}$ fails to achieve. In summary, Bestie is very practical, especially for managing large-scale data.

Acknowledgements. We would like to thank our shepherd Prof. Xun Yi and the anonymous reviewers for their insightful comments and valuable suggestions. This work was partly supported by the National Natural Science Foundation of China under Grant No. 61872412, the Wuhan Applied Foundational Frontier Project under Grant No. 2020010601012188, and the Guangdong Provincial Key R&D Plan Project under Grant No. 2019B010139001.

A   Proof of Theorem 1

Proof. To prove the *forward and Type-III-backward security* of the proposed Bestie, we construct a $\mathcal{S}$ simulator, which takes as inputs leakage functions $\mathcal{L}^{Stp}(\lambda) = \lambda$, $\mathcal{L}^{Updt}(op, w, id) = \emptyset$, and $\mathcal{L}^{Srch}(w) = \{sp(w), TimeDB(w), DelHist(w)\}$ to simulate protocols Bestie.Setup, Bestie.Update, and Bestie.Search, respectively. We will demonstrate that the simulated Bestie is indistinguishable from the real Bestie under the adaptive attacks. Algorithm 2 describes the simulator $\mathcal{S}$. Specifically, the simulator $\mathcal{S}$ consists of the following three phases.

Protocol $\mathcal{S}$.Setup. This protocol simulates protocol Bestie.Setup. In this protocol, simulator $\mathcal{S}$ takes leakage function $\mathcal{L}^{Stp}(\lambda) = \lambda$ as input and initializes five empty maps **CDB**, **GRP**, **CipherList**, **GIndlist**, and **Xlist**, where

---

Algorithm 2. Construction of Simulator $\mathcal{S}$ in the Ideal Game of `Bestie`

Setup($\mathcal{L}^{Stp}(\lambda)$)
1: Initialize five empty maps **CDB**, **GRP**, **CipherList**, **GIndlist** and **Xlist** and a timestamp parameter $u \leftarrow 0$
2: Send **EDB** $\leftarrow$ (**CDB**, **GRP**) to the server

Update($\mathcal{L}^{Updt}(op, (w, id))$)
1: Accumulate the timestamp parameter by setting $u \leftarrow u + 1$
2: Randomly pick a triplet $(L, D, C) \xleftarrow{\$} \{0,1\}^{\lambda'} \times \{0,1\}^{\lambda+1} \times \mathcal{C}_\xi$ as the generated ciphertext
3: Record the triplet (L, D, C) in **CipherList**$[u]$
4: Send the triplet (L, D, C) to the server

Search($\mathcal{L}^{Srch}(w) = (\text{sp}(w), \text{TimeDB}(w), \text{DelHist}(w))$
1: Accumulate the timestamp parameter by setting $u \leftarrow u + 1$
2: Extract the timestamp u_0 of the last Search query from $\text{sp}(w)$, where $u_0 = 0$ if $\text{sp}(w) = \emptyset$
3: Extract all timestamps $\{u_1, ..., u_n\}$ between u_0 and u from both $\text{TimeDB}(w)$ and $\text{DellHist}(w)$, where $u_i < u_j$ if $i < j$
4: Abort if $n = 0$ and $u_0 = 0$ (namely, keyword w never appears in any historical Update query)
5: Extract the timestamp u_s of the first Search query from $\text{sp}(w)$, where $u_s = u$ if no earlier Search query of keyword w occurs
6: If the index $I^{grp}_{u_s}$ stored in **GIndlist**$[u_s]$ is NULL, then randomly choose $I^{grp}_{u_s} \xleftarrow{\$} \{0,1\}^\lambda$ and update **GIndlist**$[u_s] \leftarrow I^{grp}_{u_s}$
7: Randomly choose a key $K \xleftarrow{\$} \{0,1\}^\lambda$ for searching keyword w, and retrieve $I^{grp}_{u_s} \leftarrow$ **GIndlist**$[u_s]$
8: **for** $i = 1$ to n **do**
9:     Retrieve the simulated ciphertext $(L_{u_i}, D_{u_i}, C_{u_i}) \leftarrow$ **CipherList**$[u_i]$
10:    If the timestamp u_i was extracted from $\text{TimeDB}(w)$ in the above Step 3, then set parameter $u_{min} = u_i$
11:    Otherwise (namely, the timestamp u_i was extracted from $\text{DelHist}(w)$), set parameter u_{min} to be the smaller of the timestamp u_i and the timestamp paired with u_i in $\text{DelHist}(w)$
12:    If **Xlist**$[u_{min}]$ is NULL, then randomly set **Xlist**$[u_{min}] \xleftarrow{\$} \{0,1\}^\lambda$
13:    If the Update query at timestamp u_i has operation type add, then program oracle **H** such that $\mathbf{H}(K, i) = (L_{u_i} || D_{u_i}) \oplus (0^{\lambda'} || add || \textbf{Xlist}[u_{min}])$
14:    Otherwise, program oracle **H** such that $\mathbf{H}(K, i) = (L_{u_i} || D_{u_i}) \oplus (0^{\lambda'} || del || \textbf{Xlist}[u_{min}])$
15: **end for**
16: Send search trapdoor (n, K, I^{grp}_w) to the server
17: **return** all file identifiers in $\text{TimeDB}(w)$ after receiving the response from the server

---

(**CDB**, **GRP**) will be sent to the server and the remaining maps are kept as internal states of simulator $\mathcal{S}$. The map **CipherList** records the ciphertexts generated by simulator $\mathcal{S}$. The map **GIndList** records the group indexes for the following Search queries. Map **XList** records the simulated values of hash function **G**. Clearly, the simulated protocol is indistinguishable from the real one in the view of adversary $\mathcal{A}$.

Protocol $\mathcal{S}$.Update. This protocol simulates protocol `Bestie.Update`. In this protocol, simulator $\mathcal{S}$ takes nothing as input. It randomly chooses a random triplet (L, D, C) as the generated ciphertext and uploads it to the server. In the real world, **H** is a collision-free hash function, and ξ is a semantically secure symmetric encryption scheme. Hence, the random triplet is indistinguishable from a real ciphertext if adversary $\mathcal{A}$ does not know the corresponding search trapdoor. The following content will prove that the random triplet is still indistinguishable from a real ciphertext, even in the opposite case.

Protocol $\mathcal{S}$.Search. This protocol simulates protocol Bestie.Search. In this protocol, simulator $\mathcal{S}$ takes the leaked information sp(w), TimeDB(w), and DelHist(w) as inputs. Simulator $\mathcal{S}$ first checks whether there exists any historical Update query about keyword w. If not, simulator $\mathcal{S}$ aborts, as the real protocol does (refer to Steps 2 to 4). Otherwise, simulator $\mathcal{S}$ sets or retrieves the group index $I_{u_s}^{grp}$ of keyword w (refer to Steps 5 and 6). In the following content, simulator $\mathcal{S}$ must program oracle **H** such that the randomly generated search trapdoor is still valid in the view of adversary $\mathcal{A}$ (refer to Steps 8 and 15).

In this part, simulator $\mathcal{S}$ mainly achieves two aims: (1) simulate hash values of function **G** for all Update queries of keyword w as well as guarantee that the Update queries of the same keyword-and-file-identifier entry have the same hash value (refer to Steps 10 to 12) and (2) program oracle **H** such that all simulated ciphertexts of keyword w can be correctly found by the server with the randomly generated search trapdoor (refer to Steps 13 and 14). Finally, simulator $\mathcal{S}$ sends the randomly generated search trapdoor to the server. The transcripts generated by the simulated Search protocol are indistinguishable from those of the real protocol since all operations are consistent with the real protocol in the view of adversary $\mathcal{A}$.

To summarize, there exists a $\mathcal{S}$ simulator to simulate Bestie with the given leakage functions, and the simulation is indistinguishable from the real Bestie. Thus, Theorem 1 is true. □

References

1. Bost, R.: $\sum o\varphi o\varsigma$: forward secure searchable encryption. In: Proceedings of the 2016 ACM SIGSAC Conference on Computer and Communications Security, Vienna, Austria, pp. 1143–1154 (2016)
2. Bost, R., Minaud, B., Ohrimenko, O.: Forward and backward private searchable encryption from constrained cryptographic primitives. In: Proceedings of the 2017 ACM SIGSAC Conference on Computer and Communications Security, CCS 2017, Dallas, TX, USA, pp. 1465–1482 (2017)
3. Cash, D., et al.: Dynamic searchable encryption in very-large databases: data structures and implementation. In: 21st Annual Network and Distributed System Security Symposium, NDSS 2014, San Diego, California, USA (2014)
4. Chamani, J.G., Papadopoulos, D., Papamanthou, C., Jalili, R.: New constructions for forward and backward private symmetric searchable encryption. In: Proceedings of the 2018 ACM SIGSAC Conference on Computer and Communications Security, CCS 2018, Toronto, ON, Canada, pp. 1038–1055 (2018)
5. Chang, Y.-C., Mitzenmacher, M.: Privacy preserving keyword searches on remote encrypted data. In: Ioannidis, J., Keromytis, A., Yung, M. (eds.) ACNS 2005. LNCS, vol. 3531, pp. 442–455. Springer, Heidelberg (2005). https://doi.org/10.1007/11496137_30
6. Chase, M., Kamara, S.: Structured encryption and controlled disclosure. In: Abe, M. (ed.) ASIACRYPT 2010. LNCS, vol. 6477, pp. 577–594. Springer, Heidelberg (2010). https://doi.org/10.1007/978-3-642-17373-8_33
7. Curtmola, R., Garay, J.A., Kamara, S., Ostrovsky, R.: Searchable symmetric encryption: improved definitions and efficient constructions. In: Proceedings of

the 13th ACM Conference on Computer and Communications Security, CCS 2006, Alexandria, VA, USA, pp. 79–88 (2006)

8. Demertzis, I., Chamani, J.G., Papadopoulos, D., Papamanthou, C.: Dynamic searchable encryption with small client storage. In: 27th Annual Network and Distributed System Security Symposium, NDSS 2020, San Diego, California, USA. The Internet Society (2020)

9. Foundation, F.S.: The GNU MP bignum library. https://gmplib.org/. Accessed 8 Oct 2019

10. Foundation, O.S.: OpenSSL. https://www.openssl.org/. Accessed 8 Oct 2019

11. Garg, S., Mohassel, P., Papamanthou, C.: TWORAM: efficient oblivious RAM in two rounds with applications to searchable encryption. In: Robshaw, M., Katz, J. (eds.) CRYPTO 2016, Part III. LNCS, vol. 9816, pp. 563–592. Springer, Heidelberg (2016). https://doi.org/10.1007/978-3-662-53015-3_20

12. Hahn, F., Kerschbaum, F.: Searchable encryption with secure and efficient updates. In: Ahn, G., Yung, M., Li, N. (eds.) Proceedings of the 2014 ACM SIGSAC Conference on Computer and Communications Security, Scottsdale, AZ, USA, pp. 310–320. ACM (2014)

13. He, K., Chen, J., Zhou, Q., Du, R., Xiang, Y.: Secure dynamic searchable symmetric encryption with constant client storage cost. IEEE Trans. Inf. Forensics Secur. **16**, 1538–1549 (2021)

14. Hoang, T., Yavuz, A.A., Guajardo, J.: Practical and secure dynamic searchable encryption via oblivious access on distributed data structure. In: Schwab, S., Robertson, W.K., Balzarotti, D. (eds.) Proceedings of the 32nd Annual Conference on Computer Security Applications, ACSAC 2016, Los Angeles, CA, USA, pp. 302–313. ACM (2016)

15. Hunter, J.D.: Matplotlib: a 2D graphics environment. Comput. Sci. Eng. **9**(3), 90–95 (2007)

16. Islam, M.S., Kuzu, M., Kantarcioglu, M.: Access pattern disclosure on searchable encryption: ramification, attack and mitigation. In: 19th Annual Network and Distributed System Security Symposium, NDSS 2012, San Diego, California, USA (2012)

17. Kamara, S., Papamanthou, C.: Parallel and dynamic searchable symmetric encryption. In: Sadeghi, A.-R. (ed.) FC 2013. LNCS, vol. 7859, pp. 258–274. Springer, Heidelberg (2013). https://doi.org/10.1007/978-3-642-39884-1_22

18. Kamara, S., Papamanthou, C., Roeder, T.: Dynamic searchable symmetric encryption. In: the ACM Conference on Computer and Communications Security, CCS 2012, Raleigh, NC, USA, pp. 965–976 (2012)

19. Kim, K.S., Kim, M., Lee, D., Park, J.H., Kim, W.: Forward secure dynamic searchable symmetric encryption with efficient updates. In: Thuraisingham, B.M., Evans, D., Malkin, T., Xu, D. (eds.) Proceedings of the 2017 ACM SIGSAC Conference on Computer and Communications Security, CCS 2017, Dallas, TX, USA, pp. 1449–1463. ACM (2017)

20. Klimt, B., Yang, Y.: Introducing the Enron corpus. In: CEAS 2004 - First Conference on Email and Anti-Spam, Mountain View, California, USA (2004)

21. Li, J., et al.: Searchable symmetric encryption with forward search privacy. IEEE Trans. Dependable Secur. Comput. **18**(1), 460–474 (2021)

22. van Liesdonk, P., Sedghi, S., Doumen, J., Hartel, P., Jonker, W.: Computationally efficient searchable symmetric encryption. In: Jonker, W., Petković, M. (eds.) SDM 2010. LNCS, vol. 6358, pp. 87–100. Springer, Heidelberg (2010). https://doi.org/10.1007/978-3-642-15546-8_7

23. Parliament, E., Council: on the protection of natural persons with regard to the processing of personal data and on the free movement of such data, and repealing directive 95/46/ec (general data protection regulation) (2016). https://eur-lex.europa.eu/eli/reg/2016/679/oj. Accessed 16 Jan 2020
24. Porter, M.F.: An algorithm for suffix stripping. Program **14**(3), 130–137 (1980)
25. Song, D.X., Wagner, D.A., Perrig, A.: Practical techniques for searches on encrypted data. In: 2000 IEEE Symposium on Security and Privacy, Berkeley, California, USA, pp. 44–55 (2000)
26. Song, X., Dong, C., Yuan, D., Xu, Q., Zhao, M.: Forward private searchable symmetric encryption with optimized I/O efficiency. IEEE Trans. Dependable Secur. Comput. **17**(5), 912–927 (2020)
27. Stefanov, E., Papamanthou, C., Shi, E.: Practical dynamic searchable encryption with small leakage. In: 21st Annual Network and Distributed System Security Symposium, NDSS 2014, San Diego, California, USA (2014)
28. Sun, S., et al.: Practical non-interactive searchable encryption with forward and backward privacy. In: 28th Annual Network and Distributed System Security Symposium, NDSS 2021, virtually, 21–25 February 2021. The Internet Society (2021). https://www.ndss-symposium.org/ndss-paper/practical-non-interactive-searchable-encryption-with-forward-and-backward-privacy/
29. Sun, S., et al.: Practical backward-secure searchable encryption from symmetric puncturable encryption. In: Proceedings of the 2018 ACM SIGSAC Conference on Computer and Communications Security, CCS 2018, Toronto, ON, Canada, pp. 763–780 (2018)
30. Xu, P., Liang, S., Wang, W., Susilo, W., Wu, Q., Jin, H.: Dynamic searchable symmetric encryption with physical deletion and small leakage. In: Pieprzyk, J., Suriadi, S. (eds.) ACISP 2017, Part I. LNCS, vol. 10342, pp. 207–226. Springer, Cham (2017). https://doi.org/10.1007/978-3-319-60055-0_11
31. Zhang, Y., Katz, J., Papamanthou, C.: All your queries are belong to us: the power of file-injection attacks on searchable encryption. In: 25th USENIX Security Symposium, USENIX Security 16, Austin, TX, USA, pp. 707–720 (2016)
32. Zuo, C., Sun, S.-F., Liu, J.K., Shao, J., Pieprzyk, J.: Dynamic searchable symmetric encryption with forward and stronger backward privacy. In: Sako, K., Schneider, S., Ryan, P.Y.A. (eds.) ESORICS 2019, Part II. LNCS, vol. 11736, pp. 283–303. Springer, Cham (2019). https://doi.org/10.1007/978-3-030-29962-0_14

Geo-DRS: Geometric Dynamic Range Search on Spatial Data with Backward and Content Privacy

Shabnam Kasra Kermanshahi[1]([✉]), Rafael Dowsley[2], Ron Steinfeld[2], Amin Sakzad[2], Joseph K. Liu[2], Surya Nepal[3], and Xun Yi[1]

[1] RMIT University, Melbourne, VIC 3000, Australia
{shabnam.kasra.kermanshahi,xun.yi}@rmit.edu.au
[2] Monash University, Melbourne, VIC 3800, Australia
{rafael.dowsley,ron.steinfeld,amin.sakzad,joseph.liu}@monash.edu
[3] CSIRO Data 61, Epping, NSW 1710, Australia
surya.nepal@data61.csiro.au

Abstract. Driven by the cloud-first initiative taken by various governments and companies, it has become a common practice to outsource spatial data to cloud servers for a wide range of applications such as location-based services and geographic information systems. Searchable encryption is a common practice for outsourcing spatial data which enables search over encrypted data by sacrificing the full security via leaking some information about the queries to the server. However, these inherent leakages could equip the server to learn beyond what is considered in the scheme, in the worst-case allowing it to reconstruct of the database. Recently, a novel form of database reconstruction attack against such kind of outsourced spatial data was introduced (Markatou and Tamassia, IACR ePrint 2020/284), which is performed using common leakages of searchable encryption schemes, i.e., access and search pattern leakages. An access pattern leakage is utilized to achieve an *order reconstruction attack*, whereas both access and search pattern leakages are exploited for the *full database reconstruction attack*. In this paper, we propose two novel schemes for outsourcing encrypted spatial data supporting dynamic range search. Our proposed schemes leverage R^+tree to partition the dataset and binary secret sharing to support secure range search. They further provide backward and content privacy and do not leak the access pattern, therefore being resilient against the above mentioned database reconstruction attacks. Our evaluation shows the practicality of our schemes, due to (a) the minimal round-trip between the client and the server, and (b) low overhead in the client side in terms of computation and storage.

1 Introduction

The information retrieval community has been studying geometric range search (GRS) for decades [1,21] and it has a wide range of applications in geosciences,

E. Bertino et al. (Eds.): ESORICS 2021, LNCS 12973, pp. 24–43, 2021.
https://doi.org/10.1007/978-3-030-88428-4_2

location-based services, geographical information system, geo-medical engineering, and so on. Besides its use in applications assisting in our daily life activities such as taking an Uber, finding nearby locations on Google Maps or friends on Facebook, GRS can be used in some significant emerging public health and safety applications. For instance, with the current COVID-19 outbreak, governments and researchers need to collect information (e.g. number of the test taken, confirmed cases, death toll, etc.) in a specific geometric area. The need is the same in other emergency situations, e.g., a bushfire emergency situation.

Driven by the cloud-first policy of many companies and governments, outsourcing the spatial data to a cloud server is a common practice around the world. The cloud provides the scalable infrastructure to handle large datasets and supports on-demand access through its highly available services. Data privacy is a necessity in such scenarios. Although public cloud providers are trusted in providing their services, they cannot be fully trusted for data privacy. One obvious solution is to only store encrypted data in the cloud. However, downloading and decrypting large datasets every time a search or update operation needs to be performed is completely impractical. Hence, searchable encryption (SE) is considered as a solution to correctly perform queries (search/update) over outsourced encrypted data.

Searchable Symmetric Encryption (SSE) efficiently enables search over encrypted data at the cost of revealing some well-defined information to the server, known as the leakage. The most common SSE leakage functions are access pattern and search pattern. Access pattern leaks all file identifiers that are matching a search query. In contrast, search pattern leaks the repetition of search queries (i.e., it is possible to determine if two search tokens correspond to the same query). Exploiting SSE leakages might enable an adversary (often an honest-but-curious cloud server) to infer information about the database beyond what is considered in an SSE scheme (e.g. leakage abuse attacks [8,23]).

Most of the existing SSE schemes that support geometric range search are designed in the static setting (i.e., updates of the database records after the setup are not possible or come at the cost of re-encryption and re-upload of the database). Although the dynamic setting provides more flexibility to the schemes and supports more real-world applications, it introduces more leakages. To capture new leakages in a dynamic setting, Bost et al. [5] introduced security notions for dynamic SSE, so called forward and backward privacy. Recently, Kasra-Kermanshahi et al. [15] showed that there might be additional leakages when dealing with geometric data that are not captured by Bost's forward and backward privacy models, and introduced a new security notion for dynamic SSE over spatial data (called content privacy) that hides the access pattern both in search and update operations.

Different cryptographic primitives have been used to support secure range search over geometric data such as order-preserving encryption (OPE), somewhat/fully homomorphic encryption, Geohash, and so on [15,19,27–29,31–33]. However, due to the inherent leakages associated with geometric range search, the majority of them fail to resist the newly developed leakage abuse attacks that target SSE schemes designed for GRS [20,24].

1.1 Our Contributions

In this paper, we propose two dynamic searchable symmetric encryption schemes to support geometric range search, Geo-DRS and Geo-DRS$^+$. The first scheme illustrates a novel approach to support geometric range search using R$^+$tree where more round trips between the client and the server are required to achieve content privacy (alternatively homomorphic encryption can be used at higher computational cost). Our Geo-DRS$^+$ scheme provides an efficient dynamic range search by leveraging R$^+$tree and secret sharing in $\mathbb{Z}_2$. Moreover, it uses two non-colluding servers to avoid multiple rounds of client-to-server interactions. Thus, it has only one round trip between the client and the servers during searches and updates, with a logarithmic number of communication rounds between the two servers. Geo-DRS$^+$ is efficient and scalable while resilient against *Full Database Reconstruction* (FDR) and *Approximate Database Reconstruction* (ADR) attacks. Our security analysis shows that Geo-DRS$^+$ is backward and content private.

1.2 Motivation and Related Works

Order Preserving Encryption (OPE) [2] is one of the most popular approaches to perform range search over encrypted data due to its efficiency. However, several studies have shown that it is possible to perform inference attacks on one-dimensional datasets using OPE leakages [10,14,16,17]. The search and access pattern leakages are the most common leakages used in performing inference attacks. For example, Naveed et al. [23] used frequency analysis to perform sorting and cumulative attack. Later, Durak et al. [8] discovered two more types of attacks (*Inter-column correlation-based attacks* and *Inter+Intra-column correlation-based attack*) using OPE leakages that have not been considered by Naveed's work. Grubbs et al. [10] designed a leakage abuse attack which takes advantages of both frequency and order leakage of OPE. Grubbs's attack is faster, with a higher recovery rate in comparison with Naveed's cumulative attack. Furthermore, a passive adversary is also able to perform FDR without requiring auxiliary information, as discussed by Kellaris et al. [14].

   The above discussed attacks mainly focused on one-dimensional data. Recently, Pan et al. [24] investigated data inference attacks against multi-dimensional OPE-encrypted databases. They designed a greedy and polynomial-time algorithm with approximation guarantees. The FDR attacks for geometric datasets were introduced recently by Markatou and Tamassia [20]. They utilized access pattern leakage to reconstruct the horizontal and vertical order of the points, and both access and search pattern leakages to recover the coordinates of the points.

   Several studies have begun to support range search over encrypted spatial data [15,19,27–29,31–33]. For example, Wang et al. [27–29] proposed several constructions for geometric range search using SSW[1] encryption [26], which is a pairing-based public-key encryption (PBKE). The main idea of these works is to enumerate all possible points and then check whether they are in the queried range. Due to the use of SSW, it is necessary to perform a pairing computation for each database point. Similarly, bilinear pairing operations are used by Zhu et al. [33] to support range search for location-based services. Both Xu et al. [31] and Zheng et al. [32] proposed an OPE-based scheme which utilizes R-tree for range search over spatial data. Luo et al. [19] used asymmetric scalar-product-preserving encryption (ASPE) [30] and a geometric transformation to achieve efficient range search. However, Li et al. [18] showed that Luo's scheme has some security flaws and cannot achieve the stated security notion. They proposed an enhanced version of Luo's scheme to overcome the security issues. However, both schemes are designed in a static setting; hence the update (insertion/deletion) of the points in the datasets is either not possible or requires re-encryption of the entire dataset. Guo et al. [11] proposed a dynamic searchable encryption scheme for geometric range search called GeoMix. They utilized Geohash and predicate symmetric searchable encryption to achieve efficient linear search and update. Although, the scheme supports update of the dataset points, there is no discussion about forward and backward privacy of the scheme as well as resilience against leakage abuse attacks.

Unlike other existing works in the area of geometric range search, Kasra-Kermanshahi et al. [15] proposed two constructions which consider forward and backward privacy. Moreover, they have defined a new security notion for spatial data named content privacy. Their constructions utilize binary tree and a special type of additive symmetric homomorphic encryption (ASHE). To the best of our knowledge, only three of the state-of-the-art symmetric searchable encryption schemes that support geometric range search are presented in a dynamic setting. Only one of them, Kasra-Kermanshahi et al. [15], considered forward, backward, and content privacy. However, the constructions are not scalable as the size of the utilized binary tree grows linearly with the number of grid points in each dimension of the environment.

2 Building Blocks

2.1 Notation

Some of the notations that are used more frequently in the work are given in Table 1.

2.2 R-Tree and R+tree

R-tree was first introduced by Antonin Guttman in 1984 [12], to handle spatial data efficiently. This data structure is a height-balanced tree-structure with index records in its leaf nodes containing pointers to data objects. In this paper, we

---

[1] *Shen-Shi-Waters.*

Table 1. Table of notations.

Notation	Description
$\mathcal{D}$	Spatial dataset
N	Number of objects in $\mathcal{D}$
ℓ	Bit length of database objects (64 bits)
$[\![x]\!]$	A secret share of x over $\mathbb{Z}_2$
$\mathrm{ID}_i \in \{0,1\}^{\ell}$	ℓ-bit object identifier
m	Maximum number of objects per leaf node
$\mathcal{E}$	Encrypted dataset
$\mathcal{ST}$	Search token
$\mathcal{R}$	Search results

use R$^+$tree [25], a variation of R-tree in which overlapping rectangles in intermediate nodes are avoided. Moreover, R$^+$trees have better searching performance
compared to R-trees [25].

We briefly review the example from [25] as shown in Figs. 1, 2 and 3 to see
how a R$^+$tree is formed (for the sake of simplicity, the values of the bounding
boxes (Rect) are not mentioned in this example).

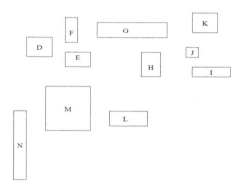

Fig. 1. The sample dataset.

In R$^+$trees leaf nodes consist of (ID, Rect), where ID is the object identifier and Rect represents the bounding box where the object is located. That is,
Rect $= (x_{min}, x_{max}, y_{min}, y_{max})$ which are the coordinates of the lower left corner and the coordinate of the upper right corner. Non-leaf nodes contain entries
of the form (p, Rect), where p is the pointer to the address of the lower nodes
(children nodes) and Rect covers the rectangles in the lower node's entries. A
R$^+$tree has the following properties:

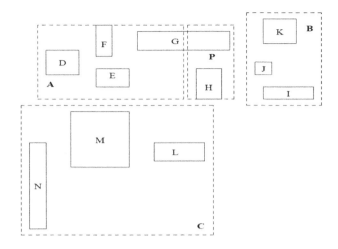

Fig. 2. The rectangles of Fig. 1 grouped to form an R+tree.

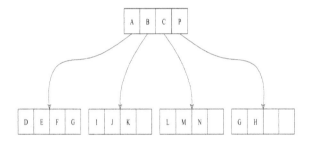

Fig. 3. The R+tree built for Fig. 2.

- For each entry (p, Rect) in an intermediate node, the corresponding subtree contains a rectangle R if and only if R is covered by Rect unless R is a rectangle at a leaf node; in which case R must just overlap with Rect.
- There is no overlap in any two entries in an intermediate node.
- The root has at least two children unless it is a leaf.
- All leaves are at the same level/height.

2.3 Secure Bitwise Comparison

This work uses secure two-party computation based on bitwise secret sharings. An additively secret sharing of $x \in \mathbb{Z}_2$ consists of two shares x_1 and x_2 chosen uniformly at random subject to the constraint that $x = x_1 + x_2 \mod 2$. The two shares are distributed to two servers, respectively. We will denote this secret sharing by $[\![x]\!]$. All secret sharing operations are modulo 2 and the modular notation is omitted for conciseness. Note that modulo 2, addition and subtraction are equivalent. Given secret sharings $[\![x]\!]$ and $[\![y]\!]$, the two servers can locally compute in a trivial way secret sharings corresponding to $z = x + y$. This operation will be denoted by $[\![z]\!] \leftarrow [\![x]\!] + [\![y]\!]$. It is also trivial to add the constant 1 to a secret sharing, one of the servers simply adds it locally.

In this work, secure multiplications of secret shared values are performed in a standard way using pre-distributed multiplications triples [3,7], which consist of ($[\![a]\!]$, $[\![b]\!]$, $[\![c]\!]$) for uniformly random a and b, and $c = ab$. These triples are pre-distributed by the data owner to the two computing servers. In order to improve the communication costs, a pseudorandom function (PRF) is used to generate the triples: (1) the data owner sends a key $K1$ of the PRF to $S1$ and a key $K2$ to $S2$; (2) the data owner and $S1$ use the PRF to obtain pseudorandom values $a_1, b_1, c_1 \in \mathbb{Z}_2$, while the data owner and $S2$ use the PRF to obtain pseudorandom values $a_2, b_2 \in \mathbb{Z}_2$; (3) the data owner fixes c_2 such that $c = ab$ and transmits the share c_2 to $S2$. With this optimization the communication cost for pre-distributing each multiplication triple is reduced to a single bit.

For performing secure bitwise comparison, we use the same protocol as De Cock et al. [6], which is a variant of the protocol of Garay et al. [9] using bitwise secret sharings in the field $\mathbb{Z}_2$ (a detailed description of the underlying protocol can be found in Sect. 4.3.3 of De Hoogh's PhD thesis [13]). For ℓ-bits values x and y, the two servers have as inputs secret shares $[\![x_i]\!]$ and $[\![y_i]\!]$ for $i \in \{0, \ldots, \ell - 1\}$, where $x = \Sigma_{i=0}^{\ell-1} x_i 2^i$ and $y = \Sigma_{i=0}^{\ell-1} y_i 2^i$. The protocol **GEQ** outputs a secret shared value $[\![z]\!]$, where z is equal to 1 if $x \geq y$; and equal to 0 otherwise. The protocol, which uses the divide and conquer paradigm, is presented in Algorithm 1. It outputs the inverse of the output of the protocol **LT** that outputs a secret shared value $[\![z]\!]$, where z is equal to 1 if $x < y$; and equal to 0 otherwise. **LT** uses as a subprotocol **LTEQ**, which outputs ($[\![z]\!]$, $[\![w]\!]$) such that z is equal to 1 if and only if $x < y$ and w is equal to 1 if and only if $x = y$. The protocol **GEQ** has $\log \ell + 1$ rounds and needs to perform $3\ell - \log \ell - 2$ secure multiplications of values that are secret shared in $\mathbb{Z}_2$.

3 Definitions, Security Notions and Model

3.1 Syntax of Our Geometric Dynamic Range Search (Geo-DRS$^+$)

Our geometric dynamic range search (Geo-DRS$^+$) scheme consists of the following algorithms:

1. **Setup**(DB): The first step is to generate the shares of the database records to be outsourced to the servers. This phase is run by the data owner as follows:
   - **Build.R$^+$tree**(DB, m) $\rightarrow$ (RT): Given a database DB and the tree parameter m (which determines the maximum number of the points in each node), this algorithm outputs a height-balanced R$^+$tree.
   - **SecretShare**(RT) $\rightarrow$ ($\mathbb{S}1, \mathbb{S}2$): This algorithm gets the R$^+$tree as input and outputs its bitwise secret shares.

   The Setup phase also generates the multiplications triples (that will be needed for the executions of Protocol **GEQ**) and the database state δ. $\mathbb{S}1$ is given to the first server and $\mathbb{S}2$ to the second server.

Algorithm 1. Comparison Protocols

GEQ$(\ell, [\![x_\ell]\!], \ldots, [\![x_1]\!], [\![y_\ell]\!], \ldots, [\![y_1]\!])$
Input: $\ell, [\![x_\ell]\!], \ldots, [\![x_1]\!], [\![y_\ell]\!], \ldots, [\![y_1]\!]$
Output: $[\![z]\!]$

1: return $[\![z]\!] \leftarrow 1 + \mathbf{LT}(\ell, [\![x_\ell]\!], \ldots, [\![x_1]\!], [\![y_\ell]\!], \ldots, [\![y_1]\!])$

LT$(k, [\![x_k]\!], \ldots, [\![x_1]\!], [\![y_k]\!], \ldots, [\![y_1]\!])$
Input: $k, [\![x_k]\!], \ldots, [\![x_1]\!], [\![y_k]\!], \ldots, [\![y_1]\!]$
Output: $[\![z]\!]$

1: if $k = 1$ then
2:    return $[\![z]\!] \leftarrow [\![y_1]\!] + [\![y_1]\!][\![x_1]\!]$
3: else
4:    $k' \leftarrow \lfloor k/2 \rfloor$
5:    $([\![a]\!], [\![b]\!]) \leftarrow \mathbf{LTEQ}(k - k', [\![x_k]\!], \ldots, [\![x_{k'+1}]\!], [\![y_k]\!], \ldots, [\![y_{k'+1}]\!])$
6:    $[\![c]\!] \leftarrow \mathbf{LT}(k', [\![x_{k'}]\!], \ldots, [\![x_1]\!], [\![y_{k'}]\!], \ldots, [\![y_1]\!])$
7:    return $[\![z]\!] \leftarrow [\![a]\!] + [\![b]\!][\![c]\!]$
8: end if

LTEQ$(k, [\![x_k]\!], \ldots, [\![x_1]\!], [\![y_k]\!], \ldots, [\![y_1]\!])$
Input: $k, [\![x_k]\!], \ldots, [\![x_1]\!], [\![y_k]\!], \ldots, [\![y_1]\!]$
Output: $[\![z]\!], [\![w]\!]$

1: if $k = 1$ then
2:    $[\![z]\!] \leftarrow [\![y_1]\!] + [\![y_1]\!][\![x_1]\!]$
3:    $[\![w]\!] \leftarrow 1 + [\![x_1]\!] + [\![y_1]\!]$
4:    return $([\![z]\!], [\![w]\!])$
5: else
6:    $k' \leftarrow \lfloor k/2 \rfloor$
7:    $([\![a]\!], [\![b]\!]) \leftarrow \mathbf{LTEQ}(k - k', [\![x_k]\!], \ldots, [\![x_{k'+1}]\!], [\![y_k]\!], \ldots, [\![y_{k'+1}]\!])$
8:    $([\![c]\!], [\![d]\!]) \leftarrow \mathbf{LTEQ}(k', [\![x_{k'}]\!], \ldots, [\![x_1]\!], [\![y_{k'}]\!], \ldots, [\![y_1]\!])$
9:    $[\![z]\!] \leftarrow [\![a]\!] + [\![b]\!][\![c]\!]$
10:    $[\![w]\!] \leftarrow [\![b]\!][\![d]\!]$
11:    return $([\![z]\!], [\![w]\!])$
12: end if

2. **Search**$(\mathrm{Rect}_q/\mathbb{S}1/\mathbb{S}2)$ is a protocol between a client and the servers. To find the desirable range query Rect_q, the client secret shares the query coordinates with the servers whom run the **GEQ** protocol over their stored shares $\mathbb{S}1/\mathbb{S}2$ traversing the R$^+$tree jointly to find the minimum bounding boxes (leaf nodes) that cover the query. The servers output the shares of the result set, $\mathcal{R}1$ and $\mathcal{R}2$.

3. **Update**$(n_i, \delta, \mathbb{S}1/\mathbb{S}2)$ is a protocol between the data owner and the servers. To insert or delete an object, the data owner should generate the new shares of the corresponding leaf node. Upon receiving the shares, the servers update their stored shares $\mathbb{S}1/\mathbb{S}2$ by replacing them with the new shares. At the end, the servers update the dataset state to $\delta + 1$.

Remark. Note that, in our model we assume that the data owner sets m large enough according to the size of the environment such that the insertion of new objects would not require node splitting (see [25] for more details). Thus, to add/delete an object only the corresponding leaf nodes would be updated. Moreover, even if the number of objects in a leaf node become larger than m, the data owner can proceed with splitting the corresponding leaf node and updating the encrypted records accordingly.

3.2   Generic Dynamic SSE Leakage Functions

The leakage function $\mathcal{L}$ keeps as state the query list $\mathcal{Q}$, i.e., the list of all queries issued so far. The entries are (t, w) for a search query on keyword w, or $(\mathsf{t}, op, (w, ind))$ for an update query, where t is the timestamp, w is the search keyword, $op \in \{Add, Del\}$ denoting the operation, and ind is a list of file identifiers to be updated. According to Bost [5] the general leakage functions associated with dynamic SSE schemes are the following:

- $sp(w) = \{\mathsf{t} : (\mathsf{t}, w) \in \mathcal{Q}\}$ is the search pattern which leaks if two search queries correspond to the same keyword w.
- UpHist(w) is a history which outputs the list of all updates on keyword w. Each element of this list is an update query tuple $q_u = (\mathsf{t}, op, (w, ind))$.
- TimeDB(w) is the list of all documents matching w, excluding the deleted ones, together with the timestamp of when they were inserted in the database.
- Updates(w) is the list of timestamps of updates on w.
- DelHist(w) is the deletion history of w, which is the list of timestamps for all deletion operations together with the timestamp of the inserted entry it removed.

3.3   Range Search Leakage Functions

We denote the leakage function of our Geo-DRS$^+$ scheme by $\mathcal{L}$. That is, the information which each server is allowed to learn about the dataset and the queries. This leakage function corresponds to the Setup, Search and Update of Geo-DRS$^+$; $\mathcal{L} = (\mathcal{L}^{Stp}, \mathcal{L}^{Srch}, \mathcal{L}^{Updt})$.

- *Search pattern* (s): Similar to most of the existing searchable encryption schemes, our scheme leaks some information about whether any two queries are generated from the same range search or not. In our design, the servers learn if the minimum bounding boxes match the minimum bounding boxes of previous searches. That is, every time a search happens, the client will generate new random secret shares of the coordinates. So, even if the same search query happens twice or more, the random secret shares of the coordinates will be different from the point of view of any single server, and he cannot link the search queries using this part of the protocol. But the servers learns the resulting minimum bounding boxes and can compare with the respective boxes of previous search queries.
- *Number of updates* (Nu): The server learns how many updates are performed on the dataset but he cannot recognize the type of the update (insertion, deletion, modification) and also on which point the update is performed. Therefore, the update does not leak any information about the dataset and the search queries.

- *Range search size* (rs): the server learns which minimum bounding boxes cover the range for each search query.
- *Range update size* (ru): the server learns which minimum bounding boxes cover the range for each update query.
- R^+*tree structure* (R^+): The structure of R^+tree is leaked to the servers.

Therefore, Geo-DRS$^+$ leakage consists of $\mathcal{L}^{Stp}(\mathcal{D}) = R^+$, $\mathcal{L}^{Srch}(r) = (\mathsf{s}, \mathsf{rs})$, and $\mathcal{L}^{Updt}(op, \mathrm{ID}_i) = (\mathsf{ru}, \mathsf{Nu})$.

3.4 Security Notions and Definitions

Kasra-Kermanshahi et al. [15] introduced a new security notion for spatial data called content privacy. They formulated a leakage that was not captured in previous definitions such as forward/backward privacy [4,5]. In short, there should be no leakage on updated points neither in the search phase nor during the update. Content privacy and backward privacy (Type-II) have some common properties: both protect the content and do not leak anything about the documents' identifiers in the update queries. However, backward privacy (Type-II) leaks information about the content in the search queries via the access pattern.

Backward privacy (Type-II) reveals all of the information contained in Backward privacy (Type-I)[2] and also reveals when all updates over the search keyword happened without their content.

Definition 1 (Backward Security with Update Pattern). *A $\mathcal{L}$-adaptively-secure SSE scheme is update pattern revealing backward-secure if, and only if, the search and update leakage functions $\mathcal{L}^{Srch}$, $\mathcal{L}^{Updt}$ can be written as: $\mathcal{L}^{Updt}$ $(op, w, ind) = \mathcal{L}'(op, w)$ and $\mathcal{L}^{Srch}(w) = \mathcal{L}''(TimeDB(w), Updates(w), sp(w))$, where $\mathcal{L}'$ and $\mathcal{L}''$ are stateless.*

Definition 2 (Content Privacy for Spatial Dataset). *A $\mathcal{L}$-adaptively-secure SSE scheme is content-private if, and only if, the search and update leakage functions $\mathcal{L}^{Srch}$, $\mathcal{L}^{Updt}$ can be written as: $\mathcal{L}^{Updt}(op, r, P) = \mathcal{L}'(op, r)$ and $\mathcal{L}^{Srch}(r) = \mathcal{L}''(r)$ where $\mathcal{L}'$ and $\mathcal{L}''$ are stateless. Here, r represents a range of coordinates and a point identifier is denoted by P.*

3.5 Security Model

The security model of the proposed constructions is formulated using two games; $\mathrm{REAL}_{\mathcal{A}}^{\Sigma}(\lambda)$ and $\mathrm{IDEAL}_{\mathcal{A},\mathcal{S}}^{\Sigma}(\lambda)$, for a security parameter λ. The former is executed using our Geo-DRS$^+$ scheme (denoted by Σ), whereas the latter is simulated using the leakage of our scheme as defined in Sect. 3.3. The leakage is parameterised by a function $\mathcal{L} = (\mathcal{L}^{Stp}, \mathcal{L}^{Srch}, \mathcal{L}^{Updt})$, which describes what information is leaked to the adversary $\mathcal{A}$. If the adversary $\mathcal{A}$ cannot distinguish these two games, then we can say that there is no leakage beyond what is defined in the leakage function. These games can be formally defined as followed;

---

[2] The document identifiers matching the issued search keyword when they were inserted, and the total number a_w of updates over the search keyword.

- $\text{REAL}_{\mathcal{A}}^{\Sigma}(\lambda)$: On input a dataset chosen by the adversary $\mathcal{A}$, it outputs the shares of the R^+tree nodes by using **Setup**(DB) to $\mathcal{A}$. The adversary can repeatedly perform search and update queries. The game outputs the results generated by running **Search**($\text{Rect}_q/\mathbb{S}1/\mathbb{S}2$) and **Update**($n_i, \delta, \mathbb{S}1/\mathbb{S}2$) to $\mathcal{A}$. Eventually, $\mathcal{A}$ outputs a bit.

- $\text{IDEAL}_{\mathcal{A},\mathcal{S}}^{\Sigma}(\lambda)$: On input a database chosen by $\mathcal{A}$, it outputs the shares of R^+tree nodes to the adversary $\mathcal{A}$ by using a simulator $\mathcal{S}(\mathcal{L}^{Stp})$. Then, it simulates the results for search queries using the leakage function $\mathcal{S}(\mathcal{L}^{Srch})$ and uses $\mathcal{S}(\mathcal{L}^{Updt})$ to simulate the results for update queries. Eventually, $\mathcal{A}$ outputs a bit.

Definition 3. *The scheme Σ is $\mathcal{L}$-adaptively-secure if for every PPT adversary $\mathcal{A}$, there exists an efficient simulator $\mathcal{S}$ such that $|\Pr[\text{REAL}_{\mathcal{A}}^{\Sigma}(\lambda) = 1] - \Pr[\text{IDEAL}_{\mathcal{A},\mathcal{S}}^{\Sigma}(\lambda) = 1]| \leq negl(\lambda)$.*

4 Dynamic Secure Range Search on Encrypted Spatial Data

This section first presents the Geo-DRS scheme to address the challenge of secure range search on spatial data in a dynamic manner. Figure 4 demonstrates the overview of Geo-DRS scheme. This base scheme imposes a logarithmic number of communication rounds between the client and the server to perform the search. One possible solution to avoid this communication overhead is to store the R^+tree structure from root to the leaf nodes on the client side and put the rest on the server. However, this is not desirable as it contradicts the main goal of outsourcing the data and also is not appropriate for resource constrained devices. Therefore, we design Geo-DRS$^+$, an enhanced version of the Geo-DRS scheme in which the single-server model of Geo-DRS is replaced with a two non-colluding server model, see Fig. 5. This enables us to shift the communication between the client and a server to the communication between the two non-colluding servers. To enable the servers to perform secure computation over the outsourced data and achieve backward and content privacy, we utilize binary secret sharing in Geo-DRS$^+$.

4.1 Geo-DRS Scheme

To explain the ideas underlying our main construction (Geo-DRS+), we first describe the details of the Geo-DRS scheme in Algorithm 2. This scheme consists of three main algorithms: SETUP, SEARCH, UPDATE.

- SETUP: The data owner proceeds as follows:
  - On input the dataset $\mathcal{D}$, security parameter λ and the tree parameter m, she partitions the environment and builds a height-balanced R^+tree.
  - Encrypt each of the tree nodes and outsource it to the server.
- SEARCH: The protocol is executed between the client and the server as follows:

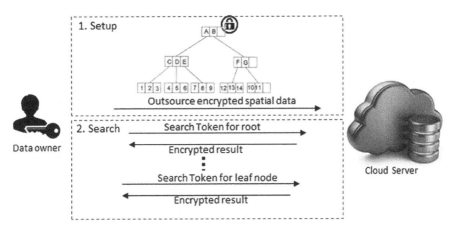

Fig. 4. The system model of Geo-DRS scheme

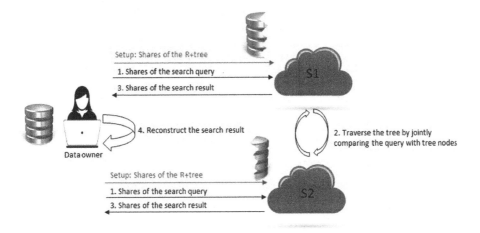

Fig. 5. The system model of Geo-DRS$^+$ scheme

- Client: Given the desired range query $\text{Rect}_q = ([x_{LL}(q), x_{UR}(q)], [y_{LL}(q), y_{UR}(q)])$, the client generates the search token $\mathcal{ST}$ for the tree root and sends it to the server. Upon receiving the corresponding result $\mathcal{R}$ from the server, he decrypts it to find the next node in the R$^+$tree and continues this procedure to reach the desirable object.
- Server: Given the encrypted dataset $\mathcal{E}$ and the search token $\mathcal{ST}$, it outputs $\mathcal{R}$ which contains the ciphertext of the nodes corresponding to the issued search token.
- UPDATE[3]: The data owner and the server perform the following protocol:

---

[3] It is also possible to use additive homomorphic encryption to perform the update at the server side (e.g. update in [15]), here we want to show only a basic scenario.

- Data Owner: Given the update query $\mathcal{Q}_u = \mathrm{ID}_i$, whether it is an insertion or a deletion, they first perform the SEARCH protocol so that the data owner finds the corresponding leaf node, n_i. Then, the data owner re-encrypts n_i and sends the re-encryption to the server.
- Server: The server replaces the corresponding entry for n_i with the given value from the data owner and updates the encrypted dataset $\mathcal{E}$ state.

4.2   Geo-DRS$^+$: Optimised Geometric Dynamic Range Search

In our model, we use a R$^+$tree to categorise the data before creating the inverted index. We applied the technique of De Cock et al. [6] with the secret sharing of [9] in the field $\mathbb{Z}_2$ to perform the secure search. The protocols for the setup, search and update work as follows (Fig. 6 illustrates the details of Geo-DRS$^+$ scheme):

- **Setup($\mathcal{D}$):** This algorithm is performed by the data owner that inputs the the spatial dataset $\mathcal{D}$. He first partitions the environment to build the R$^+$tree. Then he creates bitwise secret sharings of the inverted index based on each node in the tree, and sends the sets of shares $\mathbb{S}1$ and $\mathbb{S}2$ to S1 and S2, respectively. He also pre-distributes to the servers the multiplications triples that will be needed for the executions of the **GEQ** protocol.[4]
- **Search(Rect$_q$/$\mathbb{S}1$/$\mathbb{S}2$):** This protocol is executed by the client and the servers. On an input query Rect$_q$ = $([x_{LL}(q),\ x_{UR}(q)], [y_{LL}(q), y_{UR}(q)])$, the client generates bitwise secret sharings of those coordinates and send the set of shares $\mathcal{ST}1$ and $\mathcal{ST}2$ to the corresponding servers. Given the shares of the search token and of the inverted index, the servers S1 and S2 jointly perform the search and return shares of the results, $(\mathcal{R}1, \mathcal{R}2)$, to the client. Finally, the client reconstructs the results, $\mathcal{R}$.
- **Update($n_i, \delta, \mathbb{S}1$/$\mathbb{S}2$):** This protocol is executed between the data owner and the servers. To update (i.e., insertion/deletion) an object in the outsourced dataset, the data owner should update the corresponding leaf node. That is, it first updates the object and then generates the new shares of that leaf node. As the entire entry for the leaf node is getting updated the servers would not learn which particular object is being updated. To update the leaf node n_i, the data owner generates the corresponding shares $\mathcal{U}1$ and $\mathcal{U}2$ for the servers. Given such shares, the servers update their shares by replacing them with the new shares. Finally, the servers update the dataset state to $\delta + 1$.

Remark. The security analysis of our scheme is presented in Appendix A.

---

[4] The data owner can initially distribute some reasonable number of multiplication triples, and once the servers are about to run out of triples, they can request more triples to the data owner.

Algorithm 2. Geo-DRS Construction

Setup($\lambda, \mathcal{D}, m$)

Input: $\lambda, \mathcal{D}, m$
Output: $\mathcal{E}, K$
1: The data owner partitions $\mathcal{D}$
2: $RT \leftarrow R^+tree(\mathcal{D}, m)$ // generates a R^+tree where each node has m entries, filling up the empty spaces with dummy values
3: Append each partition of size m of $ID_i \in \mathcal{D}$ to the corresponding leaf node
4: Initialize $UT \leftarrow \emptyset$ indexed by nodes' Tag
5: $K_s, K_t \xleftarrow{\$} \{0, 1\}^\lambda$, $\mathcal{E} \leftarrow \{\}$, $\delta \leftarrow 1$ // state of $\mathcal{E}$
6: **for** all $n_i \in RT$ **do**
7:     $K_i \leftarrow F(K_s, n_i)$ // F is a pseudo-random function (PRF)
8:     $Tag_i \leftarrow F(K_t, n_i)$
9:     **for** $j = 1, ..., m$ **do**
10:        **for** $\mathsf{R}_j(n_i) \in RT$ **do** // $\mathsf{R}_j(n_i)$ is the records associated with a node
11:            $e_i \leftarrow Enc_{K_i}(\mathsf{R}_j(n_i))$
12:            $UT(Tag_i) \leftarrow e_i$
13:        **end for**
14:    **end for**
15: **end for**
16: Append UT to $\mathcal{E}$
17: **return** $\mathcal{E}, K_s, K_t$ // The data owner stores $K = (K_s, K_t)$ and the identifier of the root of RT which is n_0, and sends $\mathcal{E}$ to the server

Search($\text{Rect}_q, \mathcal{E}$)

Input: $\text{Rect}_q = ([x_{LL}(q), x_{UR}(q)], [y_{LL}(q), y_{UR}(q)]), n_0, \mathcal{E}$
Output: $\mathcal{R}$
1: The client starts from the root n_0 and performs **Sch(n_0)**
2: Returns $\mathcal{R}$ as the list of objects which overlap with the queried rectangle

Sch(n_i)

1: The client computes $Tag_i \leftarrow F(K_t, n_i)$
2: $K_i \leftarrow F(K_s, n_i)$
3: Send Tag_i to the server
4: The server computes $e_i \leftarrow UT(Tag_i)$ and send e_i to the client
5: **if** n_i is a leaf node **then**
6:     $\mathcal{R} = \{R_j(n_i) = (ID_o, rect_o)\}_{j=1,...,m}^{o \in \{1,...,N\}} \leftarrow Dec_{K_i}(e_i)$
7:     **return** $\mathcal{R}$
8: **else**
9:     $\mathcal{R} = \{R_j(n_i) = (n_c, rect_c)\}_{j=1,...,m}^{c \in \{1,...,n\}} \leftarrow Dec_{K_i}(e_i)$
10:    **for** $j = 1, ..., m$ **do**
11:        // Check if Rect_q collides with $rect_{n_c}$
12:        **if** $((y_{LL}(n_i) \leq y_{UR}(q) \leq y_{UR}(n_i))$ OR $(y_{LL}(n_i) \leq y_{LL}(q) \leq y_{UR}(n_i)))$
           AND
           $((x_{LL}(n_i) \leq x_{LL}(q) \leq x_{UR}(n_i))$ OR $(x_{LL}(n_i) \leq x_{UR}(q) \leq x_{UR}(n_i)))$ **then**
13:            **Sch(n_c)**
14:        **end if**
15:    **end for**
16:    **return** $\mathcal{R}$
17: **end if**

Update($ID_i; \mathcal{E}, \delta$)

Input: $ID_i; \mathcal{E}, \delta$
Output: $\mathcal{E}, \delta$
1: **if** $op = Add$ **then**
2:     The data owner append ID_i to $R_j(n_i)$
3: **else**
4:     The data owner replaces ID_i with dummy value in $R_j(n_i)$
5: **end if**
6: $Tag_i \leftarrow F(K_t, n_i)$
7: $e'_i \leftarrow Enc_{K_i}(\mathsf{R}_j(n_i))$ and send (Tag_i, e'_i) to the server
8: The server finds $e_i \leftarrow UT(Tag_i)$ and replace e_i with e'_i in $\mathcal{E}$
9: $\delta \leftarrow \delta + 1$
10: **return** $\mathcal{E}, \delta$

Setup($\mathcal{D}$)

1. The data owner generates the R$^+$tree, $RT \leftarrow R^+tree(\mathcal{D}, m)$
2. For each $n_i \in RT$ and for $j \in \{0, ..., \ell - 1\}$ (where ℓ is the bit-length used to represent the coordinates), the data owner secret shares between S1 and S2 the values ($[\![x^j_{LL}(n_i)]\!]$, $[\![y^j_{LL}(n_i)]\!]$, $[\![x^j_{UR}(n_i)]\!]$, $[\![y^j_{UR}(n_i)]\!]$). Let $\mathbb{S}1$ denote the shares of S1, and $\mathbb{S}2$ those of S2.
3. The data owner sets the state $\delta = 0$
4. The data owner generates the multiplication triples that are necessary to execute the **GEQ** protocol and sends the respective shares of the triples, as well as δ, to S1 and S2.

Search($\mathbf{Rect}_q$; /$\mathbb{S}1$/$\mathbb{S}2$)

1. The client $\mathcal{C}$ secret shares the query coordinates ($[\![x^j_{LL}(q)]\!]$, $[\![y^j_{LL}(q)]\!]$, $[\![x^j_{UR}(q)]\!]$, $[\![y^j_{UR}(q)]\!]$) between the servers S1 and S2.
2. S1 and S2 run the protocol **GEQ** over the shared query coordinates and R$^+$tree nodes starting from the root to determine which children need to be searched. If the following condition hold (the output of comparison is "1") then S1 and S2 traverse the R$^+$tree via that node until they reach the leaf node
$((y_{LL}(n_i) \leq y_{UR}(q) \leq y_{UR}(n_i))$ OR $(y_{LL}(n_i) \leq y_{LL}(q) \leq y_{UR}(n_i)))$ AND $((x_{LL}(n_i) \leq x_{LL}(q) \leq x_{UR}(n_i))$ OR $(x_{LL}(n_i) \leq x_{UR}(q) \leq x_{UR}(n_i)))$.
3. Once S1 and S2 reach the leaf nodes they output their shares of the result set, $\mathcal{R}1$ and $\mathcal{R}2$.
4. The client $\mathcal{C}$ reconstructs the results $\mathcal{R}$ using the given shares $\mathcal{R}1$ and $\mathcal{R}2$.

Update($n_i, \delta, \mathbb{S}1$/$\mathbb{S}2$)
1. The data owner sends the new shares of the entries to be updated, $\mathcal{U}1$ and $\mathcal{U}2$, to the servers S1 and S2, respectively.
2. S1 and S2 replace their old shares with the new ones and update the state $\delta \leftarrow \delta+1$.

Fig. 6. Geo-DRS$^+$ scheme

5   Evaluation

We consider that the dataset objects are represented in a metre scale where coordinate values are 64 bits ($\ell = 64$). To compare the queried coordinate value with the bounding box coordinates in each level of the R$^+$tree, we require a Boolean circuit of depth $\log \ell + 1$ for ℓ-bit integers. Note that, this logarithmic-round protocol for secure integer comparison is performed between the two non-colluding servers during the search, hence no overhead to the client. For each comparison $3\ell - \log \ell - 2$ bit multiplications are required. Therefore, the size of the circuit is 184 secure multiplication with the depth of 7.

Our scheme requires the pre-distribution of random binary multiplication triples by the data owner to the servers in the setup phase which are needed for the secure comparisons during the search. This enables the servers to perform the search without further online interaction with the data owner. With the optimization explained in Sect. 2.3, the communication cost for pre-distributing

Table 2a. Comparison

Scheme	Guo2019	Li 2019	Zheng 2020	Kasra-I 2020	Kasra-II 2020	Geo-DRS$^+$
Search complexity (server)	$O(N)$	$O(n\eta \log N)$	$O(m \log mN)$	$O(\log(2R)N)$	$O(\log(2R)N)$	$O(\ell m \log m)$
Search complexity (client)	$O(\theta)$	$O((n+d)\eta^2)$	$O(1)$	$O((\log R)N)$	$O((\log R)N)$	$O(1)$
Update complexity (server)	$O(N)$	NA	NA	$O(1)$	$O(2^t N)$	$O(1)$
Update complexity (client)	$O(1)$	NA	NA	$O(ktN)$	$O(1)$	$O(1)$
#client-server roundtrips (search)	2	1	1	1	1	1
#client-server roundtrips (update)	2	NA	NA	$O(\log R)$	1	1
Dynamic	✓	✗	✗	✓	✓	✓
Avoid Search pattern leakage	✗	✗	✗	✗	✗	✗
Avoid access pattern leakage	✗	✗	✗	✓	✓	✓
Content privacy	✗	NA	NA	✓	✓	✓
Cryptographic primitive	Geohash and PBKE	ASPE	OPE	SE	ASHE	SS

SE: Symmetric Encryption; ASHE: Additive Symmetric Homomorphic Encryption; PBPKE: Pairing-based Public Key Encryption; OPE: Order Preserving Encryption; Geohash: public domain geocoding system [22]; ASPE: Asymmetric Scalar-product-Preserving Encryption; SS: Secret Sharing R: Radius of the circle query; t: Bit length of coordinates (x and y); N: Number of the data points in the dataset; N_{deg}: highest degree of a term in the used fitted polynomial θ: size of Bloom filter; n: number of the matching result; k: number of update point; T_{exp} exponentiation time in token generation of SSW; η: Plain-text vector size; d: number of dimensions; ℓ: Bit length of database objects (64 bits)

Table 2b. Comparison

Scheme	Zhu 2015	Wang 2015	Wang 2016	Luo 2017	Wang 2017	Xu 2019
Search complexity (server)	$O(RNT_pT_{mul})$	$O(R^2 N)$	$O(\theta N)$	$O(N\delta d')$	$O(2^t)$	$O(Nt^2 N_{deg}^3)$
Search Complexity (Client)	$O(1)$	$O(RT_{exp})$	$O(2^{2t}T_{exp})$	$O(\delta d')$	$O(R^2 2^t T_{exp})$	$O(N_{deg}^4 t^2)$
Update complexity (server)	NA	NA	NA	NA	$O(2^t N)$	$O(1)$
Update complexity (client)	NA	NA	NA	NA	$O(1)$	$O(kt)$
# client-server roundtrips (Search)	3	1	2	δ	δ	1
# client-server roundtrips (Update)	NA	NA	NA	NA	NA	1
Dynamic	✗	✗	✗	✗	✗	✓
Avoid search pattern leakage	✗	✗	✗	✗	✗	✗
Avoid access pattern leakage	✗	✗	✗	✗	✗	✗
Content privacy	NA	NA	NA	NA	NA	✗
Cryptographic primitive	PBKE	PBKE	PBKE	ASPE	PBKE	OPE

each multiplication triple is a single bit. To compare the search query with each bonding box, four comparisons are required. As mentioned earlier each comparison costs less than 3ℓ secure multiplications in $\mathbb{Z}_2$. Therefore, the overall search complexity in the worst-case scenario is $4m \log m \times 3\ell = 12\ell m \log m$ multiplications in $\mathbb{Z}_2$. Here, m is the maximum number of entries that can fit in each node in the tree. The number of roundtrips between the two servers is $\log m(\log \ell + 1)$ as the four comparisons of the search query with each bonding box can be performed in parallel. Finally, to perform the update the client should generate new shares for the leaf node to be updated. There is only one round of communication to send these values to the servers. Moreover, the server only require to replace the current value of a leaf node with the updated values.

Table 2a and Table 2b illustrate the comparison between our Geo-DRS$^+$ scheme with the state-of-the-art schemes supporting spatial range queries of encrypted data from different aspects. Except our scheme and Wang-2017, the search complexity on the server side in all of the existing related works is linearly dependent to the number of data points/records in the database. The token generation (search on client side) complexity is constant only in Geo-DRS$^+$, Zhu-2015, and Zheng-2020, whereas in the rest of the related works it varies from scheme to scheme and depends on different factors such as radius of the circle query, bit length of coordinates, and number of data points/records in the database.

Beside of our Geo-DRS$^+$ scheme, about half of the proposed schemes for geometric range search are presented in the dynamic setting, the rest have limited application as the update of the database cost the re-encryption and re-uploading the entire database. Among the dynamic schemes in this domain only our construction, Xu-2019, and Kasra-II-2020 have only one round of communication between the client and the server for search and update queries.

In terms of the leakages, the search pattern is inherent and unavoidable in all of the discussed schemes. Both constructions of Kasra-2020 and Geo-DRS$^+$ support content privacy as they are not leaking the access pattern. More importantly the access pattern leakage is required to perform the order reconstruction attack, whereas both access and search pattern leakages are exploited for the full database reconstruction attack [20].

6 Conclusion

We first proposed a dynamic scheme for secure range search over spatial data and then extend it to a more efficient (in terms of client storage and round trips between client and server) version which we named Geo-DRS$^+$. In terms of security and data privacy, Geo-DRS$^+$ scheme has backward and content privacy. As Geo-DRS$^+$ does not leak access pattern and does not rely on OPE, it is resilient against recently developed ADR and FDR attacks targeting the searchable encryption schemes supporting geometric range search. The comparisons between Geo-DRS$^+$ and state-of-the-art schemes indicates that it is more appealing in practice due to lower computation and communication overhead.

A Security analysis

In our construction, each search result is a share of a list associated with a leaf node and client is the one who reconstructs the final result using these shares. To insert or delete an object within a list, the client generates the new shares of the list and the servers will replace the old shares with the new ones. Thus, 1) there is no leakage regarding the content of the dataset (object's identifier), 2) it is impossible to distinguish which object was being updated, 3) the search queries do not leak matching objects after they have been deleted. As a result, our construction is content and backward private as proved below.

Theorem 1. *Let $\mathcal{L}$ denote the leakage function of our Geo-DRS$^+$ scheme as defined in Sect. 3.3. Our constructed Geo-DRS$^+$ is $\mathcal{L}$-adaptively-secure, if the protocol of De Cock et al.(we call it π_s) [6] is secure. Let Σ represents Geo-DRS$^+$, and $\mathcal{A}$ be the adversary (the honest-but-curious server)[5], who breaks the security of Σ. Suppose $\mathcal{A}$ make at most $q_u > 0$ update queries. One can construct an algorithm $\mathcal{B}$ that can break the UC-security of De Cock et al. [6] protocol by running $\mathcal{A}$ as a subroutine with non-negligible probability if $\log_2 q_s + \ell \geq \lambda$, for security parameter λ.*

Proof
The proof proceeds using a hybrid argument, by game hopping, starting from the real-world game $\text{REAL}_{\mathcal{A}}^{\Sigma}(\lambda)$.

- **Game G_0:** This game is exactly the same as the real world security game $\text{REAL}_{\mathcal{A}}^{\Sigma}(\lambda)$. Hence, we have

$$\mathbb{P}\left[\text{REAL}_{\mathcal{A}}^{\Sigma}(\lambda) = 1\right] = \mathbb{P}\left[G_0 = 1\right].$$

- **Game G_1:** In this game, we pick random values instead of the output of π_s as a share of a search query and store it in a table to be reused if same query is issued. The advantage of the adversary in distinguishing between G_0 and G_1 is exactly the same as advantage for π_s. Thus, we can build a reduction $\mathcal{B}$ which is able to distinguish between π_s and a truly random function.

$$\left|\mathbb{P}\left[G_0 = 1\right] - \mathbb{P}\left[G_1 = 1\right]\right| \leq \text{Adv}_{\mathcal{S}_{\pi_s},\mathcal{B}}^{\pi_s}(\lambda).$$

- **Game G_2:** To update (delete/insert) an object from the list associated to a leaf node on the R$^+$tree, this game replaces the shares of the leaf node with random shares. For update token, it uses the leakage to learn which node should be updated. The adversary $\mathcal{A}$ cannot distinguish the real shares from the truly random shares. Suppose $\mathcal{A}$ makes at most $q_u > 0$ update queries, then we have

$$\left|\mathbb{P}\left[G_2 = 1\right] - \mathbb{P}\left[G_1 = 1\right]\right| \leq \frac{1}{q_u \cdot 2^{\ell}}.$$

- **Simulator.** We can simulate the IDEAL game like Game G_2. Let $\mathcal{S}_{\pi_s}$ be the simulator for De Cock et al. [6] protocol; then we construct a simulator $\mathcal{S}$ for our construction to perform the search. The algorithm $\mathcal{B}$ uses $\mathcal{S}_{\pi_s}$ to construct the simulator $\mathcal{S}$ in order to answer the queries issued by $\mathcal{A}$. We just need to use $\mathcal{S}_{\pi_s}$ for $\mathcal{A}_{\pi_s}$, to construct $\mathcal{S}$ for $\mathcal{A}$. We have that

$$\left|\mathbb{P}\left[\text{REAL}_{\mathcal{A}}^{\Sigma}(\lambda) = 1\right] - \mathbb{P}\left[\text{IDEAL}_{\mathcal{A},\mathcal{S}}^{\Sigma}(\lambda) = 1\right]\right| \leq \text{Adv}_{\mathcal{S}_{\pi_s},\mathcal{B}}^{\pi_s}(\lambda) + \frac{1}{q_u \cdot 2^{\ell}}.$$

For the update, simulator $\mathcal{S}$ works the same as G_1 without knowing the content (objects' identifiers). The simulator only uses ru to identify the bounding box of the update query and not the object's identifier. Therefore, it can simulate the attacker's view using only $\mathcal{L}^{Updt}$.

---

[5] Who follows the protocol instructions correctly, but try to learn additional information.

As a result, our construction satisfies content and backward privacy as the search leakage does not include TimeDB(w) or Updates(w).   □

References

1. Agarwal, P.K., Erickson, J., et al.: Geometric range searching and its relatives. Contemp. Math. **223**, 1–56 (1999)
2. Agrawal, R., Kiernan, J., Srikant, R., Xu, Y.: Order preserving encryption for numeric data. In: Proceedings of the 2004 ACM SIGMOD, pp. 563–574. ACM (2004)
3. Beaver, D.: Commodity-based cryptography (extended abstract). In: Proceedings of the Twenty-Ninth Annual ACM Symposium on the Theory of Computing, El Paso, Texas, USA, 4–6 May 1997, pp. 446–455 (1997)
4. Bost, R.: σoφoς: forward secure searchable encryption. In: Proceedings of the 2016 ACM SIGSAC Conference on Computer and Communications Security, pp. 1143–1154. ACM (2016)
5. Bost, R., Minaud, B., Ohrimenko, O.: Forward and backward private searchable encryption from constrained cryptographic primitives. In: Proceedings of the 2017 ACM SIGSAC Conference on Computer and Communications Security, pp. 1465–1482. ACM (2017)
6. Cock, M.D., et al.: Efficient and private scoring of decision trees, support vector machines and logistic regression models based on pre-computation. IEEE TDSC **16**(2), 217–230 (2019)
7. Dowsley, R.: Cryptography based on correlated data: foundations and practice. Ph.D. thesis, Karlsruhe Institute of Technology, Germany (2016)
8. Durak, F.B., DuBuisson, T.M., Cash, D.: What else is revealed by order-revealing encryption? In: Proceedings of the 2016 ACM SIGSAC Conference on Computer and Communications Security, pp. 1155–1166. ACM (2016)
9. Garay, J., Schoenmakers, B., Villegas, J.: Practical and secure solutions for integer comparison. In: Okamoto, T., Wang, X. (eds.) PKC 2007. LNCS, vol. 4450, pp. 330–342. Springer, Heidelberg (2007). https://doi.org/10.1007/978-3-540-71677-8_22
10. Grubbs, P., Lacharité, M., Minaud, B., Paterson, K.G.: Learning to reconstruct: statistical learning theory and encrypted database attacks. In: 2019 IEEE Symposium on Security and Privacy, pp. 1067–1083 (2019)
11. Guo, R., Qin, B., Wu, Y., Liu, R., Chen, H., Li, C.: MixGeo: efficient secure range queries on encrypted dense spatial data in the cloud. In: Proceedings of the International Symposium on Quality of Service, pp. 1–10 (2019)
12. Guttman, A.: R-trees: a dynamic index structure for spatial searching. In: Proceedings of the 1984 ACM SIGMOD International Conference on Management of Data, SIGMOD 1984, pp. 47–57. ACM, New York (1984)
13. de Hoogh, S.: Design of large scale applications of secure multiparty computation: secure linear programming. Ph.D. thesis, Department of Mathematics and Computer Science (2012)
14. Kellaris, G., Kollios, G., Nissim, K., O'neill, A.: Generic attacks on secure outsourced databases. In: Proceedings of the 2016 ACM SIGSAC, pp. 1329–1340. ACM (2016)
15. Kermanshahi, S.K., et al.: Geometric range search on encrypted data with forward/backward security. IEEE Trans. Dependable Secure Comput. 1–20 (2020)

16. Kornaropoulos, E.M., Papamanthou, C., Tamassia, R.: Data recovery on encrypted databases with k-nearest neighbor query leakage. In: 2019 IEEE Symposium on Security and Privacy, San Francisco, CA, USA, 19–23 May 2019, pp. 1033–1050 (2019)
17. Lacharité, M.-S., Minaud, B., Paterson, K.G.: Improved reconstruction attacks on encrypted data using range query leakage. In: 2018 IEEE Symposium on Security and Privacy (SP), pp. 297–314. IEEE (2018)
18. Li, X., Zhu, Y., Wang, J., Zhang, J.: Efficient and secure multi-dimensional geometric range query over encrypted data in cloud. J. Parallel Distrib. Comput. **131**, 44–54 (2019)
19. Luo, Y., Fu, S., Wang, D., Xu, M., Jia, X.: Efficient and generalized geometric range search on encrypted spatial data in the cloud. In: 2017 IEEE/ACM 25th International Symposium on Quality of Service (IWQoS), pp. 1–10. IEEE (2017)
20. Markatou, E.A., Tamassia, R.: Database reconstruction attacks in two dimensions. Cryptology ePrint Archive, Report 2020/284 (2020). https://eprint.iacr.org/2020/284
21. Matoušek, J.: Geometric range searching. ACM Comput. Surv. (CSUR) **26**(4), 422–461 (1994)
22. Morton, G.M.: A computer oriented geodetic data base and a new technique in file sequencing. Technical report, IBM (1966)
23. Naveed, M., Kamara, S., Wright, C.V.: Inference attacks on property-preserving encrypted databases. In: Proceedings of the 22nd ACM SIGSAC Conference on Computer and Communications Security, pp. 644–655. ACM (2015)
24. Pan, Y., et al.: Data inference from encrypted databases: a multi-dimensional order-preserving matching approach. arXiv:2001.08773 (2020)
25. Sellis, T., Roussopoulos, N., Faloutsos, C.: The R+-tree: a dynamic index for multi-dimensional objects. Technical report, University of Maryland (1987)
26. Shen, E., Shi, E., Waters, B.: Predicate privacy in encryption systems. In: Reingold, O. (ed.) TCC 2009. LNCS, vol. 5444, pp. 457–473. Springer, Heidelberg (2009). https://doi.org/10.1007/978-3-642-00457-5_27
27. Wang, B., Li, M., Wang, H.: Geometric range search on encrypted spatial data. IEEE Trans. Inf. Forensics Secur. **11**(4), 704–719 (2016)
28. Wang, B., Li, M., Wang, H., Li, H.: Circular range search on encrypted spatial data. In: 2015 IEEE CNS, pp. 182–190. IEEE (2015)
29. Wang, B., Li, M., Xiong, L.: FastGeo: efficient geometric range queries on encrypted spatial data. IEEE TDSC **16**(2), 245–258 (2019)
30. Wong, W.K., Cheung, D.W.-L., Kao, B., Mamoulis, N.: Secure kNN computation on encrypted databases. In: Proceedings of the 2009 ACM SIGMOD International Conference on Management of data, pp. 139–152 (2009)
31. Xu, G., Li, H., Dai, Y., Yang, K., Lin, X.: Enabling efficient and geometric range query with access control over encrypted spatial data. IEEE Trans. Inf. Forensics Secur. **14**(4), 870–885 (2019)
32. Zheng, Z., Shen, J., Cao, Z.: Practical and secure circular range search on private spatial data. Cryptology ePrint Archive, Report 2020/242 (2020). https://eprint.iacr.org/2020/242
33. Zhu, H., Lu, R., Huang, C., Chen, L., Li, H.: An efficient privacy-preserving location-based services query scheme in outsourced cloud. IEEE Trans. Veh. Technol. **65**(9), 7729–7739 (2015)

Efficient Multi-client Order-Revealing Encryption and Its Applications

Chunyang Lv[1,2], Jianfeng Wang[1,2](✉), Shi-Feng Sun[3], Yunling Wang[4], Saiyu Qi[5], and Xiaofeng Chen[1,2](✉)

[1] State Key Laboratory of Integrated Service Networks (ISN), Xidian University, Xi'an 710071, China
cylv_1@stu.xidian.edu.cn, {jfwang,xfchen}@xidian.edu.cn
[2] State Key Laboratory of Cryptology, P. O. Box 5159, Beijing 100878, China
[3] Shanghai Jiao Tong University, Shanghai 200240, China
shifeng.sun@sjtu.edu.cn
[4] School of Cyberspace Security, Xi'an University of Posts and Telecommunications, Xi'an 710121, China
ylwang@xupt.edu.cn
[5] School of Computer Science and Technology, Xi'an Jiaotong University, Xi'an 710049, China
syqi@connect.ust.hk

Abstract. Order-revealing encryption (ORE) is a cryptographic primitive that enables ciphertext comparison while leaking nothing about the underlying plaintext beyond their lexicographic ordering. However, how to achieve efficient and secure ciphertext comparison for multi-user settings is still a challenging problem. In this work, we propose an efficient multi-client order-revealing encryption scheme (named m-ORE) by introducing a new token-based comparison method. Specifically, data owner is enabled to delegate token generation ability to some authorized users without revealing his secret key, and then each authorized user can perform comparison on ciphertexts from multiple data owners by generating the associated comparison tokens. Benefiting from our new method, m-ORE can not only reduce ciphertext size but also improve comparison efficiency, compared with the state-of-the-art (Cash et al. Asiacrypt 2018). Further, we present a non-interactive multi-client range query scheme by extending m-ORE. Finally, we show a formal security analysis and implement our scheme. The evaluation result demonstrates that m-ORE outperforms the scheme by Cash et al. in terms of both query and storage cost while achieving the same level of security.

Keywords: Order-revealing encryption · Property-presering hash · Range query · Multi-client searchable encryption

1 Introduction

Order-revealing encryption (ORE) [5], as a generation of order-preserving encryption (OPE) [2], enables client to perform efficient range queries on encrypted data while ensuring strong security guarantee. Different from OPE,

© Springer Nature Switzerland AG 2021
E. Bertino et al. (Eds.): ESORICS 2021, LNCS 12973, pp. 44–63, 2021.
https://doi.org/10.1007/978-3-030-88428-4_3

the ciphertexts of ORE can be represented as arbitrary form rather than only numeric-valued in OPE. Furthermore, an additional *publicly comparison* algorithm is introduced to perform ciphertext comparison.

Boneh et al. [5] first formalized the notion of ORE and presented an ORE scheme based on multilinear maps that satisfies the "best-possible" security, i.e., IND-OCPA security. It means that the ciphertext should reveal nothing about the underlying plaintexts other than the ordering. However, the proposed scheme is too impractical to deploy in real-world scenarios. To overcome the efficiency limit of ORE, Chenette et al. [8] proposed an efficient ORE scheme from symmetric cryptographic primitives at the cost of certain security loss, which leaks the most significant different bit. Subsequently, Lewi and Wu [16] designed a new ORE scheme that leaks the position of the most significant differing blocks. Recently, a line of works [6,9,19] investigated vulnerability of ORE schemes. Surprisingly, an *ideal* ORE scheme may be insecure even only the order of the plaintexts is leaked. That is, a significant amount of useful information can be inferred by the order of plaintexts. The underlying reason is that the adversary can compromise the privacy of plaintext when enough knowledge on prior distribution is obtained. To address this drawback, Cash et al. [7] introduced the notion of parameter-hiding ORE that leaks less than all existing (practical) ORE schemes. The main idea is to use a new primitive named property-preserving hash (PPH), where it only allows the server to reveal whether two messages (c_1, c_2) satisfy the following equation $c_1 \overset{?}{=} c_2 + 1$. Due to the property of PPH, the adversary cannot count how many elements two ciphertexts have in common. As a consequence, the location of the first differing bit will not be leaked. Nevertheless, the proposed scheme can only support comparisons on ciphertexts from a single user. Li et al. [17] presented the notion of delegatable ORE, which enables ciphertext comparisons among different users by delegating the ciphertext comparison privilege. However, their proposed scheme leaks the most significant different bit. Therefore, a natural question following the above discussion is that:

Is there an efficient multi-client ORE scheme without leaking the location of the first differing bit?

In this paper, we first introduce the notion of multi-client order-revealing encryption (m-ORE). Then we put forward a concrete construction by employing PPH, which achieves better comparison efficiency than the state-of-the-art [7] while supporting cross-users ciphertext comparison. The main contributions are summarized as follows:

- We first formalize the notion of multi-client order-revealing encryption (m-ORE), where the server can perform ciphertext comparison among different clients by receiving the comparison token. We propose, to the best of our knowledge, the first m-ORE scheme without leaking the location of the differing bit. For ciphertext comparison, our scheme m-ORE requires $O(n)$ pairings in contrast to $O(n^2)$ in [7].
- We present an efficient multi-client range query scheme from m-ORE and multi-client searchable encryption. The proposed construction only requires

Table 1. Comparison with existing ORE schemes

Scheme	Ciphertext size	Encrypt cost	Compare cost	Leakage	Multi client	Token size
Chenette et al. [8]	$\lceil n \log M \rceil$	nPrf	nM	MSDB	✗	–
Lewi et al. [16]	$b(2d+\lceil \log d \rceil)$	$b(d+1)$Prf	bdM	MSDB	✗	–
Cash et al. [7]	$2n(\tau_{G_1}+\tau_{G_2})$	$2n(\text{Exp}_1+\text{Exp}_2)$	$4n^2$P	EQ	✗	–
Li et al. [17]	$4n\tau_{G_1}$	$6n\text{Exp}_1$	$8n$P	MSDB	✓	$2\tau_{G_2}$
Our m-ORE	$(n+1)\tau_{G_1}$	$n\text{Exp}_1$	$3n$P	EQ	✓	$(2n+1)\tau_{G_2}$
Our s-ORE	$n(\tau_{G_1}+2\tau_{G_2})$	$n(\text{Exp}_1 + 2\text{Exp}_2)$	$3n$P	EQ	–	–

n is the bit-length of the plaintext; M denotes the modulo as in [8]; b and d are the amount of block in a plaintext and the bit-length of one block respectively as in [16]; τ_{G_1} and τ_{G_2} is the size of elements of groups G_1 and G_2; Prf, M, Exp_1, Exp_2, P are pseudorandom function, modular comparison, group exponentiation in G_1 and G_2 and bilinear pairing, respectively; MSDB refers to leak most-significant differing bit/block, EQ refers to the Equality pattern of most-significant differing bit; Our s-ORE denotes a variant of our m-ORE scheme in single-user setting.

the data owner to generate an authorized query key to the client. Then each authorized client can generate a comparison token from the query key in a non-interactive manner.

- We implement our proposed m-ORE in both multi-user and single-user settings and perform a comprehensive comparison with existing constructions (as shown in Table 1). The results demonstrate that m-ORE in single-user settings brings a saving of 23% in server storage cost and achieves a speedup of 50× in comparison latency compared to [7].

1.1 Related Work

Agrawal et al. [2] first introduced the notion of order-preserving encryption (OPE), where the ciphertext preserves the numerical ordering of the plaintext. Subsequently, Boldyreva et al. [3] formalized the security model of OPE, namely indistinguishability under ordered chosen-plaintext attack (IND-OCPA). Informally, it means that given two ciphertexts, nothing is leaked other than the order-relations among the plaintexts, which is known as the best possible security under the order-preserving constraint. However, Boldyreva et al. also pointed out that this security cannot be achieved unless the size of its ciphertext-space is exponential in the size of its plaintext-space.

The first OPE scheme that achieves IND-OCPA security was presented by Popa et al. [20]. Their scheme mOPE (mutable order-preserving encoding) adopting a stateful structure and interactive protocol is inefficient since it requires a large communication complexity of $O(\log n)$ rounds for answering range queries. For other existing OPE schemes [4,10,14,15,21] with different levels of security, they are either interactive or less secure.

To achieve better security guarantees with a non-interactive and stateless approach, Boneh et al. [5] introduced the notion of order-revealing encryption (ORE), where the ciphertexts have no particular order and look more like semantically secure encryption. The first ORE scheme was achieved by the primitive of multilinear map. To improve the efficiency, Chenette et al. [8] presented a practical ORE scheme by employing pseudorandom function. However, their scheme leaks the location of the first differing bit. Subsequently, Lewi et al. [16] presented an improved ORE scheme that leaks only the location of the first differing block. Note that a block can be a byte or can be flexibly adjusted to balance efficiency and security. Nonetheless, Cash et al. [7] pointed out that these leakage profiles are still unacceptable and introduced the notion of parameter-hiding ORE, which only leaks the equality pattern of most-significant differing bit.

Recently, another line of work is to design ORE scheme supports ciphertexts comparison among multiple clients, which can strengthen the applicability of ORE. Eom et al. [11] initially introduced multi-client ORE by depending on a trusted third party. Subsequently, Li et al. [17] presented a delegatable ORE scheme that allows clients to search other client's data after being authorized. However, it also leaks the index of the first differing bit.

2 Preliminaries

2.1 Notation

We use $[n]$ to denote a set of integers $\{1, 2, \cdots, n\}$. For a decimal integer $m = (b_1 b_2 b_3 \cdots b_n)_2$, the string $b_1 b_2 b_3 \cdots b_n$ is the binary form of m where b_1 is the highest digit bit and b_n is the lowest digit bit. Let λ be the security parameter. For a string α and a string β, we use $\alpha \| \beta$ to denote the concatenation of the two strings. PPT is stands for probabilistic polynomial time and $x \leftarrow A^{\mathcal{O}_1, \mathcal{O}_2, \cdots}(m_1, m_2, \cdots)$ means that x is the output of the algorithm A which runs with the inputs $m_1, m_2, \cdots$ and access to the random oracles $\mathcal{O}_1, \mathcal{O}_2, \cdots$. When $\mathbb{Z}_p$ is a group, we use $r \leftarrow \mathbb{Z}_p$ to denote r is chosen from group $\mathbb{Z}_p$ uniformly and randomly. If $\mathcal{P}$ is a predicate on x, we write $\mathbf{1}(\mathcal{P}(x))$ to denote the indicator function for $\mathcal{P}$: that is $\mathbf{1}(\mathcal{P}(x))=1$ if and only if $\mathcal{P}(x) = 1$.

2.2 Bilinear Maps

Let $\mathbb{G}_1$, $\mathbb{G}_2$ and $\mathbb{G}_T$ be three cyclic multiplicative groups of prime order p, and g_1, g_2 be the generators of $\mathbb{G}_1$, $\mathbb{G}_2$ respectively. A bilinear pairing is a mapping $e : \mathbb{G}_1 \times \mathbb{G}_2 \to \mathbb{G}_T$ with the following properties:

1. Bilinearity: $e(u^a, v^b) = e(u, v)^{ab}$ for all $u \in \mathbb{G}_1$, $v \in \mathbb{G}_2$, and $a, b \in \mathbb{Z}_p$.
2. Non-degeneracy: $e(g_1, g_2) \neq 1$, where 1 represents the identity of group $\mathbb{G}_T$.
3. Computability: there exists an algorithm to efficiently compute $e(u, v)$ for any $u \in \mathbb{G}_1$ and $v \in \mathbb{G}_2$.

A pairing is Type-3 if there is no efficient computable isomorphism between $\mathbb{G}_1$ and $\mathbb{G}_2$, we use Type-3 bilinear map in this work. Then we recall the following assumption.

2.3   Complexity Assumption

Definition 1. Symmetric eXternal Diffie-Hellman (SXDH) Assumption: We say the symmetric external Diffie-Hellman (SXDH) assumption holds with respect to these groups and pairing if for all probabilistic polynomial-time adversary $\mathcal{A}$, the advantage $\epsilon_{sxdh} = max\{\epsilon_1, \epsilon_2\}$ is negligible for $a, b, c, d, r_1, r_2 \in \mathbb{Z}_p$. Where

$$\epsilon_1 = | \Pr[\mathcal{A}(g_1, g_1^a, g_1^b, g_1^{ab}) = 1] - \Pr[\mathcal{A}(g_1, g_1^a, g_1^b, g_1^{r_1}) = 1] |$$

and

$$\epsilon_2 = | \Pr[\mathcal{A}(g_2, g_2^c, g_2^d, g_2^{cd}) = 1] - \Pr[\mathcal{A}(g_2, g_2^c, g_2^d, g_2^{r_2}) = 1] |$$

This essentially says that the Decisional Diffie-Hellman (DDH) assumption holds for both $\mathbb{G}_1$ and $\mathbb{G}_2$.

3   Property-Preserving Hash

In this section, we first recall the definitions of Property-Preserving Hash (PPH) [7]. Then we present a concrete PPH from Bilinear Maps.

Definition 2. A property-preserving hash (PPH) scheme consists of three algorithms $\Gamma = (PPH.KeyGen, PPH.Hash, PPH.Test)$ as follows:

- PPH.KeyGen(1^λ): The key generation algorithm takes as input the security parameter and outputs (pp, hk, tk) that denotes as the public parameter, hash key and test key. These implicitly define a domain D and range R for the hash.
- PPH.Hash(hk, x): The hash evaluation algorithm takes as input the hash key hk, an input $x \in D$, and emits a single output $h \in R$ that we refer to as the hash of x.
- PPH.Test(tk, h_1, h_2): The test algorithm takes as input the test key tk and two hashes h_1, h_2, and outputs a bit $b \in \{0, 1\}$.

Correctness: Let P be some predicate. We say that Γ is computationally correct with respect to P if the probability

$$\Pr\left[PPH.Test(tk, h, h') \neq P(x, y) : \begin{array}{l} (pp, hk, tk) \leftarrow PPH.KeyGen(1^\lambda) \\ h \leftarrow PPH.Hash(hk, x) \\ h' \leftarrow PPH.Hash(hk, y) \end{array} \right]$$

is a negligible function of λ.

Security: Let P be some predicate and $\Gamma = (PPH.KeyGen, PPH.Hash, PPH.Test)$ be a PPH scheme with respect to P. For a PPT adversary $\mathcal{A}$, we define its advantage as $\text{Adv}_{P,\mathcal{A}}^{\text{w-pph}}(\lambda) = 2\Pr[\text{IND}_P^{\text{w-pph}}(\mathcal{A}) = 1] - 1$. Here $\text{IND}_P^{\text{w-pph}}(\mathcal{A})$ is a furter restricted version of the PPH security game in [7] and the adversary is not allowed to query $x = x^*$. If for all PPT adversaries, the advantage $\text{Adv}_{P,\mathcal{A}}^{\text{w-pph}}(\lambda)$ is negligible, we say that Γ is restricted-chosen-input secure.

Game $\mathrm{IND}_P^{\mathsf{w\text{-}pph}}(\mathcal{A})$:

$(\mathsf{pp}, \mathsf{hk}, \mathsf{tk}) \leftarrow \mathsf{PPH.KeyGen}(1^\lambda); x^* \leftarrow \mathcal{A}(\mathsf{tk})$

$h_0 \leftarrow \mathsf{PPH.Hash}(\mathsf{hk}, x^*); h_1 \overset{\$}{\leftarrow} R; b \overset{\$}{\leftarrow} \{0,1\}; b' \leftarrow \mathcal{A}^{\mathsf{Hash}}(\mathsf{tk}, x^*, h_b)$

$\mathrm{Return}(b \overset{?}{=} b')$

$\underline{\mathsf{Hash}(x)}$:

If $P(x, x^*) = 1$ or $x = x^*$, then $h \leftarrow \perp$, Else $h \leftarrow \mathsf{PPH.Hash}(\mathsf{hk}, x)$

$\mathrm{Return}(h)$

3.1 PPH from Bilinear Maps

We present a concrete PPH scheme for the predicate P where $P(x, y) = 1$ if and only if $x = y \pm 1$. The PPH consists of a tuple of algorithms $\Gamma = (\mathsf{PPH.KeyGen}, \mathsf{PPH.Hash}, \mathsf{PPH.Test})$ as follows:

- $\mathsf{PPH.KeyGen}(1^\lambda)$: It takes as input a security parameter λ, then picks $k_1, k_{2,1}, k_{2,2} \leftarrow \mathbb{Z}_p$ and sets the hash key $\mathsf{hk} = (k_1, (k_{2,1}, k_{2,2}))$. Let $H : \{0,1\}^\lambda \times \{0,1\}^\lambda \to \mathbb{Z}_p$ be a secure PRF. It samples groups $\mathbb{G}_1$, $\mathbb{G}_2$ and $\mathbb{G}_T$ with prime order p and an associated bilinear map $e : \mathbb{G}_1 \times \mathbb{G}_2 \to \mathbb{G}_T$. Then it randomly chooses generators $g_1 \in \mathbb{G}_1$, $g_2 \in \mathbb{G}_2$ and sets the test key as $\mathsf{tk} = (g_1^{k_{2,1}}, g_2^{k_{2,2}})$. Let $(\mathbb{G}_1, \mathbb{G}_2, \mathbb{G}_T, e)$ be the public parameter pp. Finally it outputs $(\mathsf{pp}, \mathsf{hk}, \mathsf{tk})$.

- $\mathsf{PPH.Hash}(\mathsf{hk}, x)$: It takes as input the prime hash key hk and a message x, then outputs the hash value:

$$\overrightarrow{h} = (h_1 = g_1^{H(k_1, x) \cdot k_{2,1}}, h_2 = g_2^{H(k_1, x+1) \cdot k_{2,2}}, h_3 = g_2^{H(k_1, x-1) \cdot k_{2,2}})$$

- $\mathsf{PPH.Test}(\mathsf{tk}, \overrightarrow{h}, \overrightarrow{h}')$: It takes as input two hash values $\overrightarrow{h}, \overrightarrow{h}'$ and the test key $\mathsf{tk} = (g_1^{k_{2,1}}, g_2^{k_{2,2}})$, and computes $e(h_1, g_2^{k_{2,2}})$, $e(g_1^{k_{2,1}}, h_2')$ and $e(g_1, h_3')$. Then it returns 1 if $e(h_1, g_2^{k_{2,2}}) = e(g_1^{k_{2,1}}, h_2')$ or $e(h_1, g_2^{k_{2,2}}) = e(g_1^{k_{2,1}}, h_3')$, otherwise returns 0.

Correctness: The correctness of PPH depends on whether $H(k_1, x) = H(k_1, y \pm 1)$. If so, the correctness holds. Otherwise, we can show that finding such a pair (x, y) that satisfies this property with non-negligible probability will deduce an adversary that can break the security of PRF.

Remark 1. Informally, the proposed PPH is similar to that in [7]. The main difference is that the hash value of our PPH is deterministic while random in [7]. In additon, tk and hk here are reorganized for our application.

3.2   Security Analysis

Theorem 1. *Assuming that H is a secure PRF and the SXDH assumption holds, the proposed restrictive PPH scheme Γ is restricted-chosen-input secure.*

Proof. The proof is very similar to that in [7]. For completeness, we show the details below. The theorem is proved via a sequence of games. Particularly, we start from the real game and end with a game that perfectly hides the random bit b. Then we need to show any two adjacent games are indistinguishable. Here, we denote by $\Pr[G_i = 1]$ the probability of Game G_i outputting 1.

- Game G_0: This is exactly the real game. The challenger generates the test key tk and the challenge hash value $(h_1, h_2, h_3) \in \mathbb{G}_1 \times \mathbb{G}_2^2$.
- Game G_1: G_1 is exactly the same as G_0 except that we repalce the pseudorandom function $H(k_1, \cdot)$ with a real random function $H^*(\cdot)$.
- Game G_2: G_2 is exactly the same as G_1 except the challenge hash values are replace by (r, h_2, h_3), where $r \xleftarrow{\$} \mathbb{G}_1$.
- Game G_3: G_3 can be obtained by slightly modifying the challenge hash values of G_2 to $(r, \overline{r}, h_3)$, where $\overline{r} \xleftarrow{\$} \mathbb{G}_2$.
- Game G_4: G_4 is exactly the same as G_3 except the challenge hash values are replaced by $(r, \overline{r}, \overline{\overline{r}})$, where $\overline{\overline{r}} \xleftarrow{\$} \mathbb{G}_2$.

Then by the definition of PPH security, we have

$$\mathrm{Adv}_{\Gamma,P,\mathcal{A}}^{\mathsf{w\text{-}pph}}(\lambda) = |\Pr[G_0 = 1] - \Pr[G_4 = 1]|$$

It is easy to obtain that G_0 and G_1 are computationally indistinguishable based on the security of PRF. Next, we argue G_1 and G_2 are computationally indistinguishable by the following lemma.

Lemma 1. $G_1 \approx G_2$ *assuming that SXDH assumption holds.*

Proof. Assume that there is an adversary $\mathcal{A}$ that can distinguish between G_1 and G_2, we define its advantage as $\epsilon = |\Pr[G_1 = 1] - \Pr[G_2 = 1]|$. Then we can deduce an adversary $\mathcal{B}$ that can solve SXDH problem with the same advantage ϵ. On input of (g_1, g_2, B, C) and the challenge term T, the adversary $\mathcal{B}$ executes the following steps:

1. First, $\mathcal{B}$ randomly chooses $k_{2,2} \xleftarrow{\$} \mathbb{Z}_p$, sets tk $= (C, g_2^{k_{2,2}})$ and sends it to $\mathcal{A}$. Then, $\mathcal{A}$ sends x^* to $\mathcal{B}$. $\mathcal{B}$ simulates the random function H^* and it implicitly sets $H^*(x^*) = b$, the discrete logarithm of B. It then computes

$$\left(h_1 = T, h_2 = g_2^{H^*(x^*+1)\cdot k_{2,2}}, h_3 = g_2^{H^*(x^*-1)\cdot k_{2,2}}\right)$$

and sends (h_1, h_2, h_3) to $\mathcal{A}$. Note that $c = k_{2,1}$ and $C = g_1^c$.
2. Second, to answer a new hash query satisfying $x \neq x^*$ and $x \pm 1 \neq x^*$ from $\mathcal{A}$, $\mathcal{B}$ computes:

$$\left(h_1 = C^{H^*(x)}, h_2 = g_2^{H^*(x+1)\cdot k_{2,2}}, h_3 = g_2^{H^*(x-1)\cdot k_{2,2}}\right)$$

3. Finally, the output of $\mathcal{B}$ is equal to that of $\mathcal{A}$.

We say that $\mathcal{B}$ correctly simulates the game (without querying $\mathcal{A}(x^* \pm 1)$ and $\mathcal{A}(x^*)$). If the challenge term $T = g_1^{bc}$, it means that $\mathcal{B}$ simulates G_1, and if T is a random group element of $\mathbb{G}_1$, then $\mathcal{B}$ simulates G_2. As a result, $\mathcal{B}$ can break the SXDH assumption with advantage ϵ. We complete the proof.

Similarly, we have the following lemmas:

Lemma 2. $G_2 \approx G_3$ *assuming that SXDH assumption holds.*

Lemma 3. $G_3 \approx G_4$ *assuming that SXDH assumption holds.*

The proofs of both Lemma 2 and 3 are similar to the proof of Lemma 1, so we omit the details here. By combining the above lemmas, we complete the proof of Theorem 1.

4   Multi-client Order-Revealing Encryption (m-ORE)

In this section, we first formalize the definition of m-ORE. We then present a concrete m-ORE scheme from the PPH scheme Γ.

4.1   Definition of m-ORE

Definition 3. *A m-ORE scheme consists of four algorithms Π_m =(m-ORE.KGen, m-ORE.Enc, m-ORE.TGen, m-ORE.Cmp) as follows:*

- *m-ORE.KGen(1^λ): On input the security parameter λ, the key generation algorithm m-ORE.KGen outputs master key msk and query key qk.*
- *m-ORE.Enc(msk, m): On input the master key msk and a message m, the encryption algorithm m-ORE.Enc outputs a ciphertext c.*
- *m-ORE.TGen(qk, m): On input the query key qk and a queried message m, the token generation algorithm m-ORE.TGen outputs a token t.*
- *m-ORE.Cmp(c, t): On input a ciphertext c and a token t, the compariton algorithm m-ORE.Cmp outputs a bit $b \in \{0, 1\}$.*

Correctness: We say that Π_m is computationally correct if the probability

$$\Pr\left[\text{m-ORE.Cmp}(c,t) \neq \mathbf{1}(m_1 > m_2) : \begin{array}{c} \text{msk}, \text{qk} \leftarrow \text{m-ORE.KGen}(1^\lambda) \\ c \leftarrow \text{m-ORE.Enc}(\text{msk}, m_1) \\ t \leftarrow \text{m-ORE.TGen}(\text{qk}, m_2) \end{array} \right]$$

is negligible of λ.

Security: Similar to Cash et al. [7], Our m-ORE scheme can achieve non-adaptive simulation-based security. We provide the formal definition as follows:

Definition 4. *Let Π_m = (m-ORE.KGen, m-ORE.Enc, m-ORE.TGen, m-ORE.Cmp) be an m-ORE scheme. For a PPT adversary $\mathcal{A}$, a simulator $\mathcal{S}$ and leakage function $\mathcal{L}(\cdot)$, we define the non-adaptive experiments $\text{Real}_{\mathcal{A}}^{m\text{-}ore}(\lambda)$ and $\text{Sim}_{\mathcal{A},\mathcal{L},\mathcal{S}}^{m\text{-}ore}(\lambda)$ as follows.*

$$\underline{\text{Real}_{\mathcal{A}}^{\text{m-ore}}(\lambda)}:$$

$\text{msk}, \text{qk} \leftarrow \text{m-ORE.KGen}(1^\lambda)$

$(m_1, \ldots, m_q) \leftarrow \mathcal{A}(\lambda)$

for $1 \le i \le q$:

$\quad c_i \leftarrow \text{m-ORE.Enc}(\text{msk}, m_i)$

$\quad t_i \leftarrow \text{m-ORE.TGen}(\text{qk}, m_i)$

output $(c_1, \ldots, c_q)$ and $(t_1, \ldots, t_q)$

$$\underline{\text{Sim}_{\mathcal{A}, \mathcal{L}, \mathcal{S}}^{\text{m-ore}}(\lambda)}:$$

$\text{st}_{\mathcal{S}} \leftarrow \mathcal{S}(\lambda)$

$(m_1, \ldots, m_q) \leftarrow \mathcal{A}(\lambda)$

$((c_1, \ldots, c_q), (t_1, \ldots, t_q)) \leftarrow \mathcal{S}(\text{st}_{\mathcal{S}},$

$\mathcal{L}(m_1, \ldots, m_q))$

output $(c_1, \ldots, c_q)$ and $(t_1, \ldots, t_q)$

Then Π_{m} is a secure m-ORE scheme with leakage function $\mathcal{L}(\cdot)$, if for any PPT adversary $\mathcal{A}$, there exists a polynomial-size simulator $\mathcal{S}$ such that the outputs of the two distributions $\text{Real}_{\mathcal{A}}^{\text{m-ore}}(\lambda)$ and $\text{Sim}_{\mathcal{A}, \mathcal{L}, \mathcal{S}}^{\text{m-ore}}(\lambda)$ are computationally indistinguishable.

We remark that the notion of m-ORE is compatible with that of single-user ORE. In particular, we will obtain a single-user ORE s-ORE by appending token t to the corresponding ciphertext c.

4.2   m-ORE Scheme from PPH

Let λ be the security parameter and $F : [n] \times \{0, 1\}^n \to \{0, 1\}^\lambda$ be a secure PRF. Let $\Gamma = (\text{PPH.KeyGen}, \text{PPH.Hash}, \text{PPH.Test})$ be a PPH scheme w.r.t. a predicate P that $P(x, y) = 1$ iff $x = y \pm 1$. Then our m-ORE scheme $\Pi_{\mathsf{m}} = (\text{m-ORE.KGen}, \text{m-ORE.Enc}, \text{m-ORE.TGen}, \text{m-ORE.Cmp})$ is as follows:.

– m-ORE.KGen(1^λ): It takes as input a security parameter λ, and obtains $\text{pp} = (\mathbb{G}_1, \mathbb{G}_2, \mathbb{G}_T, e), \text{hk} = (k_1, (k_{2,1}, k_{2,2}))$ and $\text{tk} = (g_1^{k_{2,1}}, g_2^{k_{2,2}})$ by running PPH.KeyGen(1^λ). And then it sets $\text{msk} = \text{hk}$ and $\text{qk} = (k_1, g_2^{k_{2,2}})$ and outputs (msk, qk).

– m-ORE.Enc(msk, m): With input msk and message m, it picks $r \leftarrow \mathbb{Z}_p$ and computes the binary representation of $m = (b_1, \cdots, b_n)$ and $c_0 = g_1^{k_{2,1} \cdot r}$. Then it sets $\overline{k_{2,1}} \leftarrow k_{2,1} \cdot r$, $\text{hk} = (k_1, (\overline{k_{2,1}}, k_{2,2}))$ and for $i = 1, \cdots, n$ computes:

$$u_i = F(i, b_1 b_2 \cdots b_{i-1} \| 0^{n-i+1}) + b_i \bmod 2^\lambda, v_i = h_1 \leftarrow \text{PPH.Hash}(\text{hk}, u_i).$$

Finally it chooses a random permutation $\pi : [n] \to [n]$, sets $c_i = v_{\pi(i)}$, and outputs the ciphertext $c = (c_0, c_1, \cdots, c_n)$.

– m-ORE.TGen($\text{qk}, \overline{m}$): It takes as input the query key $\text{qk} = (k_1, g_2^{k_{2,2}})$ and message $\overline{m}$ and computes the binary representation of $\overline{m} = (b_1, \cdots, b_n)$ and $t_0 = g_2^{k_{2,2} \cdot r'}$, where $r' \leftarrow \mathbb{Z}_p$. Then for $i = 1, \cdots, n$, it computes

$$u_i = F(i, b_1 b_2 \cdots b_{i-1} \| 0^{n-i+1}) + b_i \bmod 2^\lambda,$$

$$t_{i,1} = g_2^{k_{2,2} \cdot r' H(k_1, u_i + 1)}, \quad t_{i,2} = g_2^{k_{2,2} \cdot r' H(k_1, u_i - 1)}$$

Finally it chooses a random permutation $\pi : [n] \to [n]$, sets $t_i = (t_{\pi(i),1}, t_{\pi(i),2})$, and outputs the token $t = (t_0, (t_{1,1}, t_{1,2}), \cdots, (t_{n,1}, t_{n,2}))$. Note that this algorithm generates the hash value using the query key rather than hk, and the self-generated hash value is applicable to the PPH.Test function.

- m-ORE.Cmp(c, t): Taking as input a ciphertext $c = (c_0, c_1, \cdots, c_n)$ and a token $t = (t_0, (t_{1,1}, t_{1,2}), \cdots, (t_{n,1}, t_{n,2}))$, it extracts tk $= (c_0, t_0) = (g_1^{k_{2,1} \cdot r}, g_2^{k_{2,2} \cdot r'})$ and runs PPH.Test(tk, $c_i, t_{j,1}$) and PPH.Test(tk, $c_i, t_{j,2}$) for every $i, j \in [n]$. If there exists a pair (i^*, j^*) such that PPH.Test(tk, $c_{i^*}, t_{j^*,1}) = 1$, it returns 1 and stops, meaning $m > \overline{m}$; else if there exists a pair (i^*, j^*) such that PPH.Test(tk, $c_{i^*}, t_{j^*,2}$), it returns 0 and stops, meaning $m < \overline{m}$; otherwise it returns $\perp$, meaning $m = \overline{m}$, where m is the underlied plaintext of ciphertext c and $\overline{m}$ is the underlied plaintext of token t.

Correctness: Let $(b_1 \cdots b_n)$ and $(b'_1 \cdots b'_n)$ be the binary form of m and $\overline{m}$ respectively. If $m > \overline{m}$, there must exist an index $i^* \in [n]$ such that $b_{i^*} = b'_{i^*} + 1$. Therefore the correctness of Π_m is followed by correctness of PPH. For $m < \overline{m}$ or $m = \overline{m}$, we use the same argument.

Remark 2. Note that our m-ORE scheme can perform ciphertext comparison only by receiving the associated token. Given a ciphertext $c = (c_0, c_1, \cdots, c_n)$ and a search token $t = (t_0, (t_{1,1}, t_{1,2}), \cdots, (t_{n,1}, t_{n,2}))$, it needs to compare all $(c_i, t_{j,1})$ and $(c_i, t_{j,2})$ pair in sequence. That is, the server tests if $e(c_i, g_2^{k_{2,2} \cdot r'}) = e(g_1^{k_{2,1} \cdot r}, t_{j,1})$ or $e(c_i, g_2^{k_{2,2} \cdot r'}) = e(g_1^{k_{2,1} \cdot r}, t_{j,2})$ for every $i, j \in [n]$. It seems that m-ORE requires $O(n^2)$ pairings for ciphertext comparison. However, we argue that it only requires to compute $e(c_i, g_2^{k_{2,2} \cdot r'})$ once for some c_i due to that all $(t_{j,1}, t_{j,2})$ shares a unique random value $g_2^{k_{2,2} \cdot r'}$. Similarly, $e(g_1^{k_{2,1} \cdot r}, t_{j,1})$ and $e(g_1^{k_{2,1} \cdot r}, t_{j,2})$ are reusable. As a result, the required computation of each ciphertext reduced to $3n$ pairings.

4.3   Security Analysis

Note that the leakage of m-ORE scheme is identical to that of [7]. That is,

$$\mathcal{L}_f(m_1, \cdots, m_q) = (\forall 1 \leq i, j, k \leq q | \mathbf{1}(m_i < m_j),$$
$$\mathbf{1}(\mathsf{msdb}(m_i, m_j) = \mathsf{msdb}(m_i, m_k)))$$

It basically means that apart from the order of underlying plaintexts, the leakage is only whether $\mathsf{msdb}(m_i, m_j)$ equals to $\mathsf{msdb}(m_i, m_k)$ for any three messages i, j, k. Then following the analysis of parameter-hiding ORE [7], we have the following theorem.

Theorem 2. *Assuming that the underlying PPH scheme Γ is restricted-chosen-input secure, our m-ORE Π_m scheme is $\mathcal{L}_f$-non-adaptively-simulation secure.*

Proof. We prove the security of our m-ORE scheme through a series of games that are defined as following.

- Game G_{-1}: This is exactly the real game $\mathsf{Real}_{\mathcal{A}}^{\mathsf{m\text{-}ore}}(\lambda)$.
- Game G_0: This game is same as G_{-1} except the the pseudorandom function F in the m-ORE.Enc algorithm is replaced by a truely random function F^*.
- Game $G_{i \cdot q + j}$: These games are the same as G_0 except during the m-ORE.Enc algorithm, for every two adjacent games, u_i^j may be replaced by a random string depending on a predicate Switch.
- Game G_{qn+1}: This game is exactly the simulation $\mathsf{Sim}_{\mathcal{A},\mathcal{L}_f,\mathcal{S}}^{\mathsf{m\text{-}ore}}(\lambda)$.

We prove that any two consecutive games are indistinguishable, and then we construct an efficient simulator $\mathcal{S}$ such that the output of G_{qn} and $\mathsf{Sim}_{\mathcal{A},\mathcal{L}_f,\mathcal{S}}^{\mathsf{m\text{-}ore}}(\lambda)$ are indistinguishable. To define the predicate Switch, following the idea of [7], we say that $\mathsf{Switch}_{i,j} = 1$ if $\forall l \in [q], \mathsf{msdb}(m_j, m_l) \neq i$, it implies that the i-th bit of m_j can be replaced by a random string. When $\mathsf{Switch}_{i,j} = 0$, there must exists u_i^l such that $u_i^j = u_i^l \pm 1$, this property can be revealed by the PPH.Test algorithm hence we can not switch the i-th bit of m_j to a random string. Therefore, we say this bit (i.e. m_i^j) is leaked.

First, we have $G_{-1} \approx G_0$ due to the security of pseudorandom function F. Then we have the following lemma:

Lemma 4. *Assuming that our PPH scheme Γ is restricted-chosen-input secure, we have $G_{k-1} \approx G_k$ for any $k \in [1, qn]$.*

Proof. To prove $G_{k-1} \approx G_k$ for any $k \in [1, qn]$, we argue that it is sufficient to prove $G_{i^* \cdot q + j^* - 1} \approx G_{i^* \cdot q + j^*}$ where $i^* \in [0, n-1], j^* \in [1, q]$ under the condition $\mathsf{Switch}_{i^*, j^*} = 1$. Note that for $\mathsf{Switch}_{i^*, j^*} = 0$, we have $G_{i^* \cdot q + j^* - 1} = G_{i^* \cdot q + j^*}$ because there is no alteration between these two games. We show that if there exists an adversary $\mathcal{A}$ that can distinguish G_k from G_{k-1} with non-negligible advantage ϵ, then we obtain a simulator $\mathcal{B}$ that can win the restricted-chosen-input game with the same advantage ϵ. $\mathcal{B}$ executes the following steps:

1. It first runs $\mathsf{IND}_P^{\mathsf{w\text{-}pph}}$ and sends tk to $\mathcal{A}$. After receiving a vector of plaintext $m_1, \cdots, m_q$, it uses the truely random function F^* to sets the challenge ciphertext bit as $u_{i^*}^{j^*} = F^*(i^*, b_1^{j^*} b_2^{j^*} \cdots b_{i^*-1}^{j^*} || 0^{n-i^*+1}) + b_{i^*}^{j^*} \bmod 2^\lambda$ where $b_{i^*}^{j^*}$ is the i^*-th bit of m_{j^*} in binary form.
2. Then $\mathcal{B}$ sends the challenge bit $u_{i^*}^{j^*}$ to the challenger in the $\mathsf{IND}_P^{\mathsf{w\text{-}pph}}$ game. After receiving the challenge term T, it sets $c_{i^*}^{j^*} = T$.
3. To simulate the other bit in the ciphertext vector, $\mathcal{B}$ executes the followings.
4. If for all the ciphertext bit $u_{i'}^{j'}$ after $u_{i^*}^{j^*}$ (i.e. $i'q + j' > i^*q + j^*$), $\mathcal{B}$ first selects q elements $r_1, \cdots, r_q \leftarrow \mathbb{Z}_p$ for every $j \in [1, q]$ and computes:

$$u_{i'}^{j'} = F^*(i', b_1^{j'} b_2^{j'} \cdots b_{i'-1}^{j'} || 0^{n-i'+1}) + b_{i'}^{j'} \bmod 2^\lambda;$$

$$c_{i'}^{j'} = h_1 \leftarrow \mathsf{PPH.Hash}(\mathsf{hk}, u_{i'}^{j'}).$$

Else if for all the ciphertext bit $u_{i'}^{j'}$ before $u_{i*}^{j^*}$ (i.e. $i'q + j' < i^*q + j^*$) and Switch$_{i',j'} = 0$, then the same as above, else for Switch$_{i',j'} = 1$, it computes $u_{i'}^{j'} \xleftarrow{\$} \{0,1\}^{\lambda}; c_{i'}^{j'} = h_1 \leftarrow$ PPH.Hash(hk, $u_{i'}^{j'}$).

5. Finally, after $\mathcal{B}$ simulates all the ciphertext bits, for all $j^* \in [q]$, it picks a random permutation π_{j^*} and outputs $c_{j^*} = (c_{\pi_{j^*}(1)}^{j^*}, \cdots, c_{\pi_{j^*}(n)}^{j^*}; g_1^{r_{j^*}})$ to $\mathcal{A}$. Then $\mathcal{B}$ outputs to its challenger a bit based on the output of $\mathcal{A}$.

Then we say that $\mathcal{B}$ correctly simulates the encryption oracle since F^* is a truly random function and the probability of $u_{i*}^{j^*} = u_{i'}^{j'} \pm 1$ is negligible for all $i'q + j' \neq i^*q + j^*$, which means $\mathcal{B}$ fails to simulate the encryption oracle with only negligible probability. Also, $\mathcal{B}$ correctly simulates G_{k-1} when $T = h_1 \leftarrow$ PPH.Hash(hk, $u_{i'}^{j'}$), and if T is random, due to the security of pseudorandom function F, $\mathcal{B}$ simulates G_k correctly. Hence, if $\mathcal{A}$'s advantage in distinguishing G_k from G_{k-1} is noticeable, then $\mathcal{B}$'s advantage in wining the IND$_P^{\text{w-pph}}$ game is also noticeable. Since we already proved that an adversary's advantage in wining IND$_P^{\text{w-pph}}$ game is negligible, we have $G_{k-1} \approx G_k$ for any $k \in [1, qn]$. Note that we skip the prove of $G_{k-1} \approx G_k$ with respect to token due to the fact that it is very similar from the proof of ciphertexts. This will complete the proof of Lemma 4.

We then have the following lemma:

Lemma 5. *There exists an efficient simulator $\mathcal{S}$ that the output of G_{qn} and G_{qn+1} are indistinguishable.*

Proof. To simulate the encryption function correctly, for any i-th of m_j that Switch$_{i,j} = 1$, we first set u_i^j as a random string since it would not affect the leakage profile. Thus it is sufficient to only simulate the bit that Switch$_{i,j} = 0$. Before we give the description of the simulator $\mathcal{S}$, we first introduce an recursive algorithm FillMatrix(i, j, k, m, M) as presented in Algorithm 1. This algorithm takes a set of messages $(m_1, \cdots, m_q)$, which we assume $m_1 > \cdots > m_q$ without

---

Algorithm 1. FillMatrix(i, j, k, m, M)

Input: (i, j, k) where $i \in [n], j \leq k \in [q]$, a set of messages $m = (m_1, \cdots, m_q)$, an matrix $M_{q \times n}$.
Output: a filled matrix M

1: **if** $j = k$ **then**
2:     for all $i' \in [i, n]$, set $M[j][i'] = r$ where $r \xleftarrow{\$} \{0,1\}^{\lambda}$;
3:     return 0;
4: **else**
5:     search for the smallest $j^* \in [j, k]$ such that msdb$(m_j, m_{j^*}) = $ msdb(m_j, m_k);
6:     for all $j' \in [j, j^* - 1]$, set $M[j'][i] = r'$ where $r' \xleftarrow{\$} \{0,1\}^{\lambda}$;
7:     for all $j' \in [j^*, k]$, set $M[j'][i] = r' - 1$;
8:     runs FillMatrix$(i + 1, j, j^* - 1, m, M)$ and FillMatrix$(i + 1, j^*, k, m, M)$;
9: **end if**

loss of generality, and (i, j, k) that $i \in [n], j \leq k \in [q]$, where n is the bit-length of every message and q is the total number of messages, it outputs a matrix M.

To simulate the encryption oracle for a set of messages $m = (m_1, \cdots, m_q)$, the simulator $\mathcal{S}$ first calls the FillMatrix$(1, 1, q, m, M)$ to get a matrix $M_{q \times n}$, then it calls the PPH.KeyGen(1^λ) to get hk $= (k_1, (k_{2,1}, k_{2,2}))$ and tk. After that, $\mathcal{S}$ chooses q elements $r_1, \cdots, r_q \leftarrow \mathbb{Z}_p$ and q random permutations $\pi_1, \cdots, \pi_q$ for every $j \in [1, q]$ and sets $c_0 = g_1^{k_{2,1} \cdot r_j}$, $\overline{k_{2,1}} \leftarrow k_{2,1} \cdot r_j$ and hk $= (k_1, (\overline{k_{2,1}}, k_{2,2}))$, then it computes $c_i^j = h_1 \leftarrow$ PPH.Hash(hk, $M[j][i]$) for every $i \in [n], j \in [q]$. Finally, it outputs a set of ciphertexts $(c_1, \cdots, c_q)$ such that $c_j = (c_0, c_{\pi_j(1)}^j, \cdots, c_{\pi_j(n)}^j)$ for every $j \in [q]$.

Additionally, in order to simulate m-ORE.TGen function, $\mathcal{S}$ constructs the tokens as follows. After simulating the ciphertexts, $\mathcal{S}$ chooses q new elements $r_1, \cdots, r_q \leftarrow \mathbb{Z}_p$ and q new random permutations $\pi_1, \cdots, \pi_q$ for every $j \in [1, q]$ and sets $t_0 = g_2^{k_{2,2} \cdot r_j}$, $t_{i,1}^j = g_2^{k_{2,2} \cdot r_j H(k_1, M[j][i]+1)}$ and $t_{i,2}^j = g_2^{k_{2,2} \cdot r_j H(k_1, M[j][i]-1)}$ for every $i \in [n], j \in [q]$. Then, it outputs a set of token $(t_1, \cdots, t_q)$ such that $t_j = (t_0, (t_{\pi_j(1),1}^j, t_{\pi_j(1),2}^j), \cdots, (t_{\pi_j(n),1}^j, t_{\pi_j(n),2}^j))$ for every $j \in [q]$.

Note that during the simulation, the probability of $\exists i, i^* \in [n]$ that satisfies $M[j][i] = M[j][i^*]$ for any $j \in [q]$ is negligible, hence the restriction of the security definition of our PPH (i.e. the adversary is not allowed to query $x = x^*$) is reasonable and it does not affect the security of our m-ORE.

We argue that the simulator $\mathcal{S}$ is correct for the following reasons. First, the simulator identifies how many leaked bits for a set of messages $(m_1, \cdots, m_q)$ just like the game G_{qn}. The FillMatrix algorithm first identifies that if $(m_1, \cdots, m_q)$ share the same 1st prefix. If there exists the first m_{j^*} such that msdb$(m_1, m_{j^*}) =$ msdb(m_1, m_q), we can infer that messages $(m_1, \cdots, m_{j^*-1})$ have 1 on their first bit, and messages $(m_{j^*}, \cdots, m_k)$ have 0 on their first bit. It means that the 1st bit of total q messages is leaked. Then this algorithm runs recursively to identify other leaked bit and get a total number of leaked bit. This information also can be identified in the game G_{qn} by counting the number of Switch$_{i,j} = 0$ for all $i \in [n], j \in [q]$. Note that the simulator $\mathcal{S}$ and game G_{qn} do not only identify the total number of leaked bit but also the exact position of this leaked bit due to the ordered messages set. Hence the output of ciphertext set also leaks the msdb of any two ciphertexts. But the random permutation π will hide these indexes of the leaked bit except the total number both for this game and G_{qn}. Accordingly, the simulation Sim$_{\mathcal{A}, \mathcal{L}_f, \mathcal{S}}^{\text{m-ore}}(\lambda)$ is identical to G_{qn}, hence we establish the proof of Lemma 5.

By combining proofs of Lemma 4 and Lemma 5, we complete the proof of Theorem 2.

5   Multi-client Range Query from m-ORE

Refer to the construction of multi-party searchable encryption (MPSE) scheme [22]. We now describe how to build a multi-client range query scheme using our m-ORE construction $\Pi_m = $ (m-ORE.KGen, m-ORE.Enc, m-ORE.TGen, m-ORE.Cmp) from Sect. 4. At a high level, the server's encrypted database **DB** consists of different data owners' ciphertexts generated by m-ORE.Enc algorithm, each query q consists of tokens generated by m-ORE.TGen. To answer a range query, the server performs m-ORE.Cmp algorithm to find the lower and upper boundaries in the encrypted database corresponding to its query and returns all ciphertexts lying within those bounds. The client then decrypts the ciphertexts to learn the response.

Our multi-client range query scheme involves a server and a group of users. Users are divided into data owners and followers. The data owners are responsible for outsourcing ciphertext to the server. The followers are authorized to generate query tokens using query keys. The server can perform range query over ciphertext by receiving the query token. Note that every user can be data owner and follower concurrently or individually.

5.1 The Proposed Construction

We present a concrete multi-client range query scheme from our m-ORE construction $\Pi_\mathsf{m} = (\mathsf{m\text{-}ORE.KGen}, \mathsf{m\text{-}ORE.Enc}, \mathsf{m\text{-}ORE.TGen}, \mathsf{m\text{-}ORE.Cmp})$. Let $H_1 : \{0,1\}^\lambda \to \mathbb{Z}_p$ and $H_2 : \{0,1\}^\lambda \to \mathbb{G}_2$ be two secure PRFs. Formally, we define our multi-client range query scheme $\Sigma = (\mathsf{Setup}, \mathsf{Update}, \mathsf{Search})$ as follows. Without loss of generality, we assume that a client j is authorized by client i.

- $\mathsf{Setup}(1^\lambda)$: The setup algorithm between the clients proceeds as follows:
  - All $\mathsf{Clients}(1^\lambda)$: The clients take as input the security parameter λ, generate the master key and query key $\mathsf{msk}, \mathsf{qk} \leftarrow \mathsf{m\text{-}ORE.KGen}(1^\lambda)$, and generate a secret key and a public key $sk = x \leftarrow \mathbb{Z}_p$, $pk = g_2^x$.
  - Client $i(\mathsf{qk}_i, sk_i, pk_j)$: The client i takes as input his own query key qk_i, parses qk_i as $(k_1, g_2^{k_{2,2}})$, secret key $sk_i = x_i$, and client j's public key pk_j, encrypts his query key as $QK_{i \to j} = (pk_i, H_1(pk_j^{x_i}||j||i) \cdot k_1, H_2(pk_j^{x_i}||j||i) \cdot g_2^{k_{2,2}})$. Then client i sends $QK_{i \to j}$ to client j.
  - Client $j(QK_{i \to j}, sk_j)$: The client j takes as input the encrypted query key $QK_{i \to j} = (pk_i, H_1(pk_j^{x_i}||j||i) \cdot k_1, H_2(pk_j^{x_i}||j||i) \cdot g_2^{k_{2,2}})$ and his own secret key $sk_j = x_j$, first computes a $H_1(pk_i^{x_j}||j||i)^{-1}, H_2(pk_i^{x_j}||j||i)^{-1}$ and then decrypts $QK_{i \to j}$ to get the $\mathsf{qk}_i = (k_1, g_2^{k_{2,2}})$. The qk_i will be used for token generation.
- $\mathsf{Update}(\mathsf{msk}_i, \mathcal{M})$: The update algorithm between the client and server proceeds as follows:
  - Client $i(\mathsf{msk}_i, \mathcal{M})$: The client i takes as input his own master key msk_i and a set of messages $\mathcal{M}$, for each $m \in \mathcal{M}$, client i computes $c = \mathsf{m\text{-}ORE.Enc}(\mathsf{msk}_i, m)$, and sends $\mathcal{C}_i = \{c\}$ to the server.
  - Server$(\mathcal{C}_i)$: The server simply sets $\mathbf{DB}_i \leftarrow \mathcal{C}_i$.
- $\mathsf{Search}(\mathsf{qk}_i, \mathbf{DB}_i)$: The search algorithm between the client and server proceeds as follows:

- Client $j(\mathsf{qk}_i)$: The client j takes as input the query key qk_i and range query for the range $[x, y]$, produces the query token $\mathsf{q} = (t_1, t_2) = (\text{m-ORE.TGen}(\mathsf{qk}_i, x), \text{m-ORE.TGen}(\mathsf{qk}_i, y))$ which is sent to the server.
- Server($\mathbf{DB}_i, \mathsf{q}$): The server takes as input the current database $\mathbf{DB}_i = \{c\}$ of client i and the query token $\mathsf{q} = (t_1, t_2)$. It performs m-ORE.Cmp(c, t_1) and m-ORE.Cmp(c, t_2) for every $c \in \mathbf{DB}_i$ to find the ciphertext c in $\mathbf{DB}_i$ that the underlied plaintexts are at least x and at most y. Let res be the set of ciphertexts lying in this interval. The server sends the response res to client j.
- Client $j(\mathsf{res})$: The client j takes as input the response res, decrypt to get the plaintext set $S \leftarrow \text{m-ORE.Dec}(\mathsf{key}, c)$ for every $c \in \mathsf{res}$. (Our m-ORE scheme can be attached with a decryption algorithm. That is, each m-ORE.Enc is accompanied by a CPA-secure symmetric encryption scheme).

Remark 3. Note that our range query scheme is insusceptible to the sorting attack presented by Naveed et al. [19]. Sorting attack basically means that an adversary is able to find a one-to-one correspondence between the plaintext and the sorted ciphertext thus recovering all ciphertexts trivially. We circumvent this problem by outsourcing only the m-ORE ciphertext to the server. That is, our ciphertext alone cannot be compared without a token. Note that even after the ciphertext being queried with tokens, the server cannot obtain the order of all ciphertexts but only the relative order between the tokens and ciphertexts. Therefore our range query scheme is insusceptible to sorting attacks.

Due to space constraints, the detailed security analysis is presented in Appendix A.

6   Experimental Evaluation

In this section, we provide a thorough experimental evaluation of our proposed m-ORE scheme. We first depict the configuration of the experiment environment and the selection of parameters. Then we evaluate our scheme by comparing it with Chenette et al.'s scheme [8], Lewi et al.'s scheme [16], Cash et al.'s scheme [7] and Li et al.'s delegatable ORE scheme [17].

6.1   Setup

We implement the compared schemes in C and use OpenSSL [1] library to implement cryptographic primitives, i.e., SHA-256 and HMAC-SHA-256. We use SHA-256 as pseudorandom function for our m-ORE scheme, Lewi et al.'s scheme [16] and Li et al.'s scheme [17], while HMAC-SHA-256 as keyed PRF for our m-ORE scheme, schemes [8] and [7]. Besides, we use GMP library [12] to implement big integer arithmetic, and PBC library [18] to implement bilinear pairing.

Regarding experiments, we deploy the compared schemes on a virtual machine with 4-cores Intel(R) Core(TM) i5-9500 CPU @ 3.00 GHz, 4 GB of

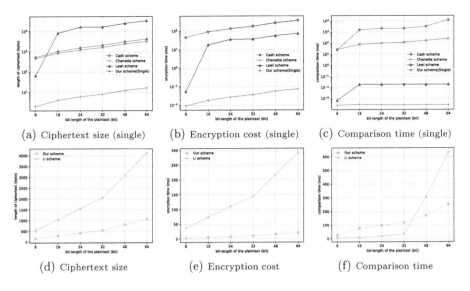

(a) Ciphertext size (single)   (b) Encryption cost (single)   (c) Comparison time (single)

(d) Ciphertext size   (e) Encryption cost   (f) Comparison time

Fig. 1. Performance comparison

RAM and 21GB SSD disk, running on Ubuntu 18.04 LTS. For comparison, we use the opensource code of FastORE[1] for the implementation of [8] and [16]. The code of m-ORE and scheme of [7] and [17] are published at GitHub[2].

6.2   Evaluation

We implement the compared schemes in the aspect of the ciphertext size, the time cost for encryption and comparison. Note that m-ORE and the schemes of [7,8] and [17] encrypt a message bit-by-bit, while the scheme [16] encrypts a message block-by-block. Specifically, the block size is 8-bit for 8-bit plaintext, and the block size is 16-bit for larger plaintext. We implement m-ORE both in single-user setting and multi-user setting, the magenta line denotes the single-user setting and the yellow line denotes the multi-user setting. In Fig. 1, the first row (Fig. 1(a), 1(b), 1(c)) compares all the single-user ORE scheme, and the second row (Fig. 1(d), 1(e), 1(f)) compares the ORE scheme in multi-client settings.

Ciphertext Size Comparison. In Fig. 1(a) and 1(d), we evaluate the cipher-text size of the schemes. The experimental results show that Lewi et al.'s scheme [16] has a good performance when the size of the plaintext is small. However, the ciphertext size expands immensely when the plaintext size is larger than 8 bits. Specifically, the ciphertext expansion of their scheme is about 10× to the single-user mode of our scheme regarding a 64-bit plaintext. We also achieve less ciphertext expansion than Cash et al.'s scheme [7] in single-user settings. As for

---

[1] https://github.com/kevinlewi/fastore.
[2] https://github.com/collisionl/m-ORE.

multi-client settings of our scheme, the ciphertext size is about one-third compare to the single-user settings and it outperforms the delegatable ORE scheme [17] immensely as shown in Fig. 1(d).

Encryption Cost Comparison. As depicted in Figure 1(b) and 1(e), regarding the encryption efficiency, despite our scheme is only slightly efficient than Cash et al.'s scheme [7] in single-user mode, for encrypting a 64-bit plaintext, we achieve a speedup of 17× in the multi-client settings compared to our single-user mode. As for the comparison to Li et al.'s scheme [17] which is depicted in Fig. 1(e), our scheme takes 20.12ms to encrypt a 64-bit plaintext in multi-client settings, which achieves a speedup of 14× compared to their scheme. Note that Chenette et al.'s scheme [8] has a good performance on encryption efficiency at the cost of degrading the security.

Comparison Time Comparison. In Fig. 1(c) and 1(f), we evaluate the comparative efficiency of the five schemes. Note the comparison time of our m-ORE scheme in single-user settings performs identically to multi-user settings. As seen, our scheme outperforms Cash et al.'s scheme [7] because of less pairing computation. Specifically, for 64-bit plaintext, our scheme achieves a speedup of 50× compared to theirs. Despite Li et al.'s scheme [17] outperforms ours when the plaintext size is less than 48-bit, it soon increases and exceeds ours. In particular, for a 64-bit plaintext, we achieve less than half of the comparison time compared to their scheme. Moreover, we note that our m-ORE achieved a fine-grained access control on ciphertext comparison, that is the server can only compare the ciphertext with the uploaded token. While their scheme only achieved coarse-grained access control on ciphertext comparison, that is the server is able to compare all the ciphertexts of a user once it received the token of the corresponding user. In addition, although schemes [16] and [8] have a speedup in comparison efficiency, they cannot achieve the same security level as ours.

In conclusion, our scheme achieves multi-client comparison with the same security level as scheme [7] while achieving less ciphertext expansion and comparable efficiency of encryption and comparison.

7 Conclusion

In this paper, we presented a multi-client ORE (m-ORE) scheme that allows the data owner to securely delegate the token generation ability to authorized users, which enables the server to perform ciphertext comparison for multi-user settings. Compared with the state-of-the-art [7], our m-ORE is superior to it in comparison complexity and storage overhead. Furthermore, we extend m-ORE to an non-interactive multi-client range query scheme. Note that our proposed scheme requires that the number of tokens is linear with the number of data owners. Thus, how to design a multi-client ORE scheme with only a single comparison token remains a challenging problem.

Acknowledgments. This work was supported by the National Natural Science Foundation of China (Nos. 62072357 and 61960206014), the Preferential Funding for Scientific and Technological Activities of Overseas Students in Shaanxi Province (No. 2019-25), the Fundamental Research Funds for the Central Universities (No. JB211503), and Innovation Fund of Xidian University (No. YJS2114).

Appendix

A   Security Analysis of Range Query Scheme

To define the security of multi-client range query scheme in Sect. 5.1, we first introduce a slight modification to the security notions that by our m-ORE scheme from Sect. 4. Recall that an m-ORE scheme is secure with respect to a leakage profile $\mathcal{L}_f(\cdot)$ if for any adversarially-chosen sequence of messages $(m_1, \cdots, m_q)$, there is an efficient simulator $\mathcal{S}$ that can simulate the real m-ORE ciphertext and token given the leakage $\mathcal{L}_f(m_1, \cdots, m_q)$.

Similar to [16], we define a leakage function $\mathcal{L}_f(\cdot, \cdot)$ that if there exists an efficient simulator such that for any two adversarially-chosen collections of plaintexts $(m_1, \cdots, m_q)$ and $(m_1, \cdots, m_k)$, the simulator can simulate the outputs of m-ORE.Enc$(\cdot, m_i)$ and m-ORE.TGen$(\cdot, m_j)$ for all $i \in [q], j \in [k]$ given only the leakage $\mathcal{L}_f((m_1, \cdots, m_q), (m_1, \cdots, m_k))$. That is:

$$\mathcal{L}_f((m_1, \cdots, m_q), (m_1, \cdots, m_k)) = (\forall 1 \le i, l \le q, 1 \le j \le k | \mathbf{1}(m_i < m_j),$$
$$\mathbf{1}(\mathsf{msdb}(m_j, m_i) = \mathsf{msdb}(m_j, m_l)))$$

in which $q = k$. We argue that this leakage profile is essentially the same as $\mathcal{L}_f(m_1, \cdots, m_q)$.

We then define the security of our range query scheme Σ in two different aspects, online and offline security. Online security models the information revealed to a malicious server during **Update** and **Search**, while offline security considers the situation of an adversary obtains a one-time snapshot of the encrypted database from the server which was studied by Naveed et al. [19] and Grubbs et al. [13]. First, we formalize the online security as follows:

Theorem 3. *For a database $\boldsymbol{DB}_i$ containing user i's data which is essentially a set of m-ORE ciphertext $(c_1, \cdots, c_q)$ on the server and a sequence of queries $\boldsymbol{q}_i$ from user i which is a set of m-ORE token $(t_1, \cdots, t_k)$. Let $\mathcal{L}_{RQ}$ be the leakage function.*

$$\mathcal{L}_{RQ}(\boldsymbol{DB}_i, \boldsymbol{q}_i) = \mathcal{L}_f((m_1, \cdots, m_q), (m_1, \cdots, m_k))$$

We say that the range query scheme Σ achieves online security with respect to the leakage function $\mathcal{L}_{RQ}$.

Proof. The proof follows the proof of Theorem 2 except the leakage profile were substituted by $\mathcal{L}_f((m_1, \cdots, m_q), (m_1, \cdots, m_k))$ which is very similar. And the simulator $\mathcal{S}$ only needs to output the ciphertexts for m_i where $\forall i \in [q]$ and token for m_j where $\forall j \in [k]$.

Note that we define the leakage function $\mathcal{L}_{RQ}$ under a condition that **DB** and **q** are from the same user. It is clear that the leakage will be none if these are from different users. The reason is that m-ORE.Cmp will not work in this case and $\mathsf{msdb}(m_j, m_i) = \mathsf{msdb}(m_j, m_l)$ will always hold for all i and j.

The offline security of our range query scheme follows directly from the fact that the encrypted database stored on the server only contains a collection group elements from $\mathbb{G}_1$ and were generated with random factor, which is simulatable given just the size of the collection.

Theorem 4. *The range query scheme Σ is offline secure.*

Proof. The proof follows the proof of Theorem 2 except the simulator $\mathcal{S}$ only needs to simulate the ciphertext for all the messages.

References

1. OpenSSL: Cryptography and SSL/TLS toolkit. https://www.openssl.org/
2. Agrawal, R., Kiernan, J., Srikant, R., Xu, Y.: Order preserving encryption for numeric data. In: Proceedings of the 2004 ACM SIGMOD International Conference on Management of Data, SIGMOD 2004, pp. 563–574 (2004)
3. Boldyreva, A., Chenette, N., Lee, Y., O'Neill, A.: Order-preserving symmetric encryption. In: Joux, A. (ed.) EUROCRYPT 2009. LNCS, vol. 5479, pp. 224–241. Springer, Heidelberg (2009). https://doi.org/10.1007/978-3-642-01001-9_13
4. Boldyreva, A., Chenette, N., O'Neill, A.: Order-preserving encryption revisited: improved security analysis and alternative solutions. In: Rogaway, P. (ed.) CRYPTO 2011. LNCS, vol. 6841, pp. 578–595. Springer, Heidelberg (2011). https://doi.org/10.1007/978-3-642-22792-9_33
5. Boneh, D., Lewi, K., Raykova, M., Sahai, A., Zhandry, M., Zimmerman, J.: Semantically secure order-revealing encryption: multi-input functional encryption without obfuscation. In: Oswald, E., Fischlin, M. (eds.) EUROCRYPT 2015. LNCS, vol. 9057, pp. 563–594. Springer, Heidelberg (2015). https://doi.org/10.1007/978-3-662-46803-6_19
6. Cash, D., Grubbs, P., Perry, J., Ristenpart, T.: Leakage-abuse attacks against searchable encryption. In: Ray, I., Li, N., Kruegel, C. (eds.) Proceedings of the 22nd ACM SIGSAC Conference on Computer and Communications Security, CCS 2015, pp. 668–679. ACM (2015)
7. Cash, D., Liu, F.-H., O'Neill, A., Zhandry, M., Zhang, C.: Parameter-hiding order revealing encryption. In: Peyrin, T., Galbraith, S. (eds.) ASIACRYPT 2018. LNCS, vol. 11272, pp. 181–210. Springer, Cham (2018). https://doi.org/10.1007/978-3-030-03326-2_7
8. Chenette, N., Lewi, K., Weis, S.A., Wu, D.J.: Practical order-revealing encryption with limited leakage. In: Peyrin, T. (ed.) FSE 2016. LNCS, vol. 9783, pp. 474–493. Springer, Heidelberg (2016). https://doi.org/10.1007/978-3-662-52993-5_24
9. Durak, F.B., DuBuisson, T.M., Cash, D.: What else is revealed by order-revealing encryption? In: Proceedings of the 2016 ACM SIGSAC Conference on Computer and Communications Security, CCS 2016, pp. 1155–1166 (2016)
10. Dyer, J., Dyer, M., Djemame, K.: Order-preserving encryption using approximate common divisors. J. Inform. Secur. Appl. **49**, 102391 (2019)

11. Eom, J., Lee, D.H., Lee, K.: Multi-client order-revealing encryption. IEEE Access **6**, 45458–45472 (2018)
12. Granlund, T., the GMP development team: GNU MP: the GNU multiple precision arithmetic library. https://gmplib.org/
13. Grubbs, P., Sekniqi, K., Bindschaedler, V., Naveed, M., Ristenpart, T.: Leakage-abuse attacks against order-revealing encryption. In: Proceedings of the 2017 IEEE Symposium on Security and Privacy, S&P 2017, pp. 655–672. IEEE (2017)
14. Kerschbaum, F.: Frequency-hiding order-preserving encryption. In: Proceedings of the 22nd ACM SIGSAC Conference on Computer and Communications Security, CCS 2015, pp. 656–667 (2015)
15. Kerschbaum, F., Schröpfer, A.: Optimal average-complexity ideal-security order-preserving encryption. In: Proceedings of the 2014 ACM SIGSAC Conference on Computer and Communications Security, CCS 2014, pp. 275–286 (2014)
16. Lewi, K., Wu, D.J.: Order-revealing encryption: new constructions, applications, and lower bounds. In: Proceedings of the 2016 ACM SIGSAC Conference on Computer and Communications Security, CCS 2016, pp. 1167–1178 (2016)
17. Li, Y., Wang, H., Zhao, Y.: Delegatable order-revealing encryption. In: Proceedings of the 2019 ACM Asia Conference on Computer and Communications Security, AsiaCCS 2019, pp. 134–147 (2019)
18. Lynn, B., other contributors: The pairing-based cryptography library. https://crypto.stanford.edu/pbc/
19. Naveed, M., Kamara, S., Wright, C.V.: Inference attacks on property-preserving encrypted databases. In: Proceedings of the 22nd ACM SIGSAC Conference on Computer and Communications Security, CCS 2015, pp. 644–655 (2015)
20. Popa, R.A., Li, F.H., Zeldovich, N.: An ideal-security protocol for order-preserving encoding. In: Proceedings of the 2013 IEEE Symposium on Security and Privacy, S&P 2013, pp. 463–477. IEEE (2013)
21. Roche, D.S., Apon, D., Choi, S.G., Yerukhimovich, A.: POPE: partial order preserving encoding. In: Proceedings of the 2016 ACM SIGSAC Conference on Computer and Communications Security, CCS 2016, pp. 1131–1142 (2016)
22. Tang, Q.: Nothing is for free: security in searching shared and encrypted data. IEEE Trans. Inf. Forensics Secur. **9**(11), 1943–1952 (2014)

Versatile and Sustainable Timed-Release Encryption and Sequential Time-Lock Puzzles (Extended Abstract)

Peter Chvojka[1]($\boxtimes$), Tibor Jager[1], Daniel Slamanig[2], and Christoph Striecks[2]

[1] University of Wuppertal, Wuppertal, Germany
{chvojka,tibor.jager}@uni-wuppertal.de
[2] AIT Austrian Institute of Technology, Vienna, Austria
{daniel.slamanig,christoph.striecks}@ait.ac.at

Abstract. Timed-release encryption (TRE) makes it possible to send messages "into the future" such that a pre-determined amount of time needs to pass before a message can be accessed. Malavolta and Thyagarajan (CRYPTO'19) recently introduced an interesting variant of TRE called homomorphic time-lock puzzles (HTLPs), making TRE more versatile and greatly extending its applications. Here one considers multiple independently generated puzzles and the homomorphic evaluation of a circuit over these puzzles. Solving the so obtained puzzle yields the output of a circuit evaluated on the messages locked by the original puzzles.

We observe that viewing HTLPs more abstractly gives rise to a simple generic construction of homomorphic TRE (HTRE) that is not necessarily based on sequential squaring, but can be instantiated based on any TLP, e.g., from the LWE assumption (via randomized encodings). This construction has slightly different properties, but provides essentially the same functionality for applications. It makes TRE versatile and can be used beyond HTRE, for instance to construct timed-release functional encryption. Interestingly, it achieves a new *"solve one, get many for free"* property, which supports that an arbitrary number of independently time-locked (homomorphically evaluated) messages can all be obtained simultaneously after solving only a single puzzle. This puzzle is independent of the number of time-locked messages and thus achieves optimal amortized cost.

Moreover, we define and construct *sequential* TLPs as a particularly useful generalization of TLPs and TRE. Such puzzles can be solved sequentially in a way that solving a puzzle additionally considers the previous solution and the time required to solve the puzzle is determined

This work was supported by the German Federal Ministry of Education and Research (BMBF) project REZEIVER, the European Research Council (ERC) under the European Union's Horizon 2020 research and innovation programme, grant agreement n°802823, the EU's Horizon 2020 ECSEL Joint Undertaking under grant agreement n°783119 (SECREDAS) and by the Austrian Science Fund (FWF) and netidee SCIENCE under grant agreement P31621-N38 (PROFET). This is an extended abstract, the full version of this paper is available at [11].

© Springer Nature Switzerland AG 2021
E. Bertino et al. (Eds.): ESORICS 2021, LNCS 12973, pp. 64–85, 2021.
https://doi.org/10.1007/978-3-030-88428-4_4

by the difference in the time parameters. When instantiated from sequential squaring, this allows to realize public "sequential squaring services", where everyone can time-lock messages, but only one entity needs to perform the computations required to solve puzzles. Thus, this removes the burden of wasting computational resources by every receiver and makes TRE economically and ecologically more sustainable.

1 Introduction

Timed-release encryption (TRE) has the goal of sending information into the future in a way that the sender can be sure that a pre-determined amount of time needs to pass before the information can be decrypted. This idea was firstly discussed by May [25], who introduced this notion and proposed a solution based on trusted agents, which after the pre-determined time has passed releases some secret which allows to obtain the information (see also [10,12]). In this work we will focus on an alternative idea proposed by Rivest *et al.* in [29] and called time-lock puzzles (TLPs), which does not require trusted agents. TLPs allow to seal messages in such a way that one is able to obtain the sealed message only by executing an expensive *sequential* computation. The amount of time required to perform this sequential computation is determined by a hardness parameter T of the TLP, which can be freely chosen. Here, a sender can just publish a puzzle whose solution hides the message until enough time has elapsed for the puzzle to be solved. TLPs have found numerous applications such as sealed-bid auctions [29], fair contract signing [6], zero-knowledge arguments [13], or non-malleable commitments [20].

TLP Constructions. The TLP proposed by Rivest *et al.* in [29] uses sequential squaring in an RSA group $\mathbb{Z}_N^*$, i.e., for hardness T compute $s = x^{2^T}$. An interesting feature of this TLP construction is that creating a puzzle, i.e., knowing the factorization of N, is much faster than the expensive sequential computation to solve the puzzle. This is an important property of TLPs when the required amount of time until the puzzle should be solved is very large. Interestingly, TLPs with this property seem hard to find. In [23] Mahmoody *et al.* show that in the random-oracle model it is impossible to construct TLPs from one-way permutations and collision-resistant hash-functions that require more parallel time to solve than the total work required to generate a puzzle and thus ruling out black-box constructions of such TLPs. On the positive side, Bitansky *et al.* [4] show how to construct TLPs with the aforementioned property from randomized encodings [2,18] relying on indistinguishability obfuscation. Interestingly, when slightly relaxing the requirements and allowing efficient parallel computation in the generation of the puzzles or a solution independent preprocessing (so-called *weak* TLPs), then such TLPs can be constructed generically from one-way functions and directly from the learning with errors (LWE) assumption, respectively, via randomized encodings.

Homomorphic TLPs. Recently, Malavolta and Thyagarajan [24] (MT19 henceforth) proposed an interesting variant called *homomorphic* TLPs (HTLPs).

Here one considers multiple puzzles $(Z_1, \ldots, Z_n)$ with hardness parameter T, which can be independently generated by different entities. Without knowing the corresponding solutions $(s_1, \ldots, s_n)$ one can homomorphically evaluate a circuit C over these puzzles to obtain as result a puzzle $\widehat{Z}$ with solution $C(s_1, \ldots, s_n)$, where the hardness of this resulting puzzle does not depend on the size of the circuit C that was evaluated (which is called compactness). Consequently, this allows to aggregate a potentially large number of puzzles in a way that only a single puzzle needs to be solved. While this concept is interesting on its own, MT19 also shows that it extends the applications of TLPs and in particular present applications to e-voting, multi-party coin flipping as well as multi-party contract signing, or more recently verifiable timed signatures [31], again yielding a number of interesting further applications.

MT19 conjecture that any application that involves a large number of users and thus the constraint of requiring to solve multiple puzzles (in parallel) constitute one of the main obstacles that so far prevented the large scale adoption of TLPs. As already, mentioned, this can be partly mitigated via HTLPs by MT19 and in particular if one is only interested in homomorphic evaluations over multiple messages. We additionally stress that applications requiring to solve multiple puzzles will also represent a huge waste of resources and are thus problematic from an economic and ecological perspective. Moreover, even the requirement for a receiver to only solve a single puzzle on its own may already prevent the application of TRE, e.g., for resource constrained receivers of messages as omnipresent within the Internet of Things (IoT).

Motivation for Our Work. The motivation of our work is twofold. Firstly, our goal is to make TRE more versatile in order to improve on existing applications and to broaden the scope of applications even further. For instance, when we look at the HTLPs in MT19, they construct a linearly homomorphic TLP (LHTLP) from the sequential squaring TLP and Paillier encryption [28] which is linearly homomorphic and the evaluation is independent of the hardness T (and one can also turn this into a multiplicatively homomorphic TLP). In order to extend this to fully HTLPs (FHTLPs), MT19 requires sub-exponentially hard indistinguishability obfuscation, whereas in follow-up work Brakerski et al. in [8] proposed FHTLPs from standard assumption which itself requires an LHTLP (where to the best of our knowledge the aforementioned is the only known construction). In particular, the idea in [8] is to use a multi-key fully-homomorphic encryption (MK-FHE) scheme [22] to encrypt every message with a fresh key and an LHTP to lock the respective MK-FHE secret keys. To be compatible with the LHTLP, Brakerski et al. in particular require a MK-FHE scheme with a linear decryption algorithm.

Unfortunately, all these constructions are not generic as they rely on a single particular construction of an HTLP from sequential squaring (and additionally a very specific MK-FHE scheme in [8]). Moreover, for every such puzzle including the one obtained from homomorphically evaluating on many such puzzles, one can only start to solve it after having produced it. Consequently, although the homomorphic property makes it scalable in a setting where one is only interested in the homomorphic evaluation over all encrypted messages, it would be convenient to have an approach that also supports a *"solve one, get many for free"* property. And this even if one wants to obtain *all* encrypted messages in full, instead of only the result of a homomorphic evaluation. Note that, if in contrast to the homomorphically evaluated function over all the messages, one wants to unlock n of the input messages with the approaches in [8,24], it requires to solve n puzzles. Consequently, we ask whether it is possible to come up with an approach that provides the *"solve one, get many for free"* property on an arbitrary number of independently time-locked messages such that it is possible to decrypt all single messages and at the same time. So essentially having a solution that *can be* homomorphic but does not need to be if one is only interested in the single messages and all with only solving a single puzzle. Ideally this approach is generic in nature and thus would allow to construct (homomorphic) timed-release encryption (TRE) generically from *any* TLP.

Secondly, a central drawback of TRE is that it puts considerable computational overhead on the message receiver, i.e., the receiver has to invest lots of computational resources to solve the puzzle to obtain the time-locked message. This makes it undesirable for real-life scenarios from an economic as well as ecological perspective. While HTLPs of MT19 address this problem from a different angle, i.e., homomorphically combine many TLPs such that only one puzzle needs to be solved, this will not reveal the individual messages without solving all puzzles. And while this functionality is a helpful feature in certain applications, it can not be considered a general purpose solution, because the amount of recoverable data is bounded by the amount of data that can be encapsulated in a single ciphertext. Moreover, it still requires the receiver to waste potentially significant resources for solving a new puzzle. Consequently, we ask whether this can be avoided.

Due to the lack of space we defer a discussion on recent concurrent and independent work on TLPs to Appendix A.

2 Technical Overview and Contributions

Before we discuss our contributions we stress, that the terms time-lock puzzle (TLP) [29], timed-release encryption (TRE) [25], and time-lock encryption (TLE) [21] are often used interchangeably in the literature. For our constructions we need to distinguish between them. In particular, TRE will denote an encryption scheme which allows us send messages "into the future". A TLP provides the core functionality of a puzzle that needs a certain amount of time to be solved, without considering any messages. TLPs will be used as a building block for TRE. Now, we are ready to discuss our contributions.

Versatile Timed-Release Encryption. We introduce a generic approach to construct TRE. The basic and indeed very simple idea is that given *any* TLP we can use it to generate a puzzle Z and its solution s, and we can use s as the random coins for the key generation algorithm $\mathsf{Gen}(1^\lambda; s)$ of a public key encryption (PKE) scheme. Then, we provide the respective public key pk as parameters of the TRE and solving the puzzle Z reveals s and thus sk allowing to decrypt *all* of the ciphertexts computed with respect to pk. Note that when using s as the random coins for a partially homomorphic encryption scheme, e.g., ElGamal [14], or a fully homomorphic encryption scheme, e.g., BGV [9], this immediately yields (fully) homomorphic TRE. Interestingly, this approach then allows us to obtain the *"solve one, get many for free"* property for both, the result of a homomorphic evaluation of many ciphertexts, but also if we want to decrypt all ciphertexts individually. Consequently, solving one puzzle allows to decrypt all ciphertexts associated to a hardness parameter (generated by many potentially independent entities). We note that our approach to HTRE satisfies the basic definition of HTLPs from MT19, where the time required to solve the puzzles starts with the generation of the parameters. In contrast, MT19 also provides the notion of a reusable setup for their LHTLP, where one can use the same parameters to generate many puzzles in a way that for every single puzzle the time only starts to run from the point where the puzzle is generated (this characteristic is also inherited by [8]). However, we observe that for all the applications discussed in [24] it seems sufficient, and in some applications even more desirable, when the runtime of the puzzle is counted from the point of running the puzzle setup algorithm. For instance, MT19 discuss an application to e-voting, where it rather seems to complicate issues when one can only start solving the puzzle after the last voter cast its vote. It seems more practical to set-up the puzzle such that the solution can be made available at a certain pre-defined point in time. And even if this is not required, it might be easy to adjust the setup in a way that it outputs a set of public parameters, and a user can choose which public parameters to use when computing a puzzle. We defer a detailed discussion of the applications to Appendix B.

Moreover, we demonstrate that our TRE framework can be used to obtain other variants of TRE in a generic way. We showcase this using the regime of functional encryption. In particular, we introduce timed-release functional encryption (TRFE) which allows to time-lock a function f. After a certain time has passed everyone can learn the function $f(x)$ of any ever encrypted message x. As an application we discuss identity-based encryption (IBE) [5] with locked keys, where the key generator at registration gives locked IBE secret keys for various validity periods (e.g., each for a month) to the user and the respective secret keys then unlock over time.

Sustainable Timed-Release Encryption. We introduce the notion of sequential TLPs as a particularly useful generalization of TLPs, which yields practical and particularly sustainable TRE schemes (from the perspective of consumption of computational resources). The basic idea is that the puzzle generation takes a sequence of hardness parameters $T_1, \ldots, T_n$ (where we assume that $T_i < T_{i+1}$ for all $i \in [n-1]$) and outputs a sequence of puzzles and solutions $(Z_i, s_i)_{i \in [n]}$. Now the distinguishing feature is that puzzles can be solved sequentially in a way that solving Z_i additionally considers solution s_{i-1} and the time required to solve puzzle Z_i is determined by the hardness $T_i - T_{i-1}$ (note that having $n = 1$ this yields a conventional TLP). From this, we then build a sequential TRE scheme, where security is based on the security of a sequential TLP. Unfortunately, it turns out that such a construction is non-trivial. For a TRE scheme to be secure, we require that any adversary that runs in time $T < T_i$ is not able to break the security of an encryption with respect to time slot T_i. For such an adversary, we need to simulate all values up to T_{i-1}, in particular all TLP solutions $s_1, \ldots, s_{i-1}$ up to T_{i-1}, properly, as otherwise the reduction would not simulate the security experiment properly for an adversary running in time $T = T_{i-1} < T_i$, for instance. However, it is not possible to build a reduction which receives as input $s_1, \ldots, s_{i-1}$ as part of the TLP instance, because then the reduction would only be able to break the assumption that the puzzle is hard if it runs in time less than $T_i - T_{i-1}$. Our solution to overcome this difficulty is to construct a TRE scheme which does not directly use the real solutions s_i, but instead $\mathsf{F}(T_i, s_i)$, where one can think of F as a hard-to-invert function. This way we are able to formulate a hardness assumption for TLPs where the reduction in the security proof of the TRE scheme receives $\mathsf{F}(T_1, s_1), \ldots, \mathsf{F}(T_{i-1}, s_{i-1}), \mathsf{F}(T_{i+1}, s_{i+1}), \ldots, \mathsf{F}(T_n, s_n)$ as additional "advice", and thus is able to provide a proper simulation. At the same time it is reasonable to assume that no adversary is able to distinguish $\mathsf{F}(T_i, s_i)$ from random, even if it runs in time up to $T < T_i$, which is exactly the upper bound that we have on the TRE adversary. We note that MT19 [24, Section 5.2] also proposed a construction that allows to use multiple time slots, by describing a specific construction which is similar to our notion of sequential TRE. The technical difficulty that we encounter should arise in their construction as well. Unfortunately, they do not provide a formal security analysis, so that this is not clarified. We, however, believe that a similar assumption involving an "advice" for the reduction is also necessary for a security proof of the construction suggested in their work.

In order to construct sequential TLPs, we introduce the so called *gap sequential squaring assumption*, which extends the sequential squaring assumption by an oracle which takes as input the hardness parameter T' and a value y' and outputs 1 if and only if $y' = x^{2^{T'}} \bmod N$. This is akin to other gap problems [26] such as the well known gap Diffie-Hellman problem. As evidence for the hardness of this assumption, we provide an analysis in the strong algebraic group model (SAGM) and in particular show that our assumption holds as long as factoring is hard. The SAGM was introduced by Katz *et al.* [19] as a variant of the algebraic group model (AGM) [16] and enables to work with time-sensitive assumption. Finally, when modeling the above mentioned function F as a random oracle, we obtain a provably secure construction of a sequential TLP and finally a sequential TRE.

Summary and Discussion of Properties of Our Approach. There exist different approaches to construct TRE in the literature, which all aim at achieving a similar goal from a high-level perspective, but which provide very different properties from a low-level perspective, with sometimes subtle but crucial differences. We briefly summarize the properties achieved by our (sequential) TRE approach again and discuss how it enables novel applications.

Homomorphic TRE. We recall that the *homomorphic* timed-release encryption from MT19 (called HTLPs in [24]) supports homomorphic evaluation of functions on encrypted messages and avoids expensive parallel computations to solve one puzzle per ciphertext, while it still achieves the desired security against time-bounded adversaries. In some applications it may be desirable to enable the homomorphic evaluation of ciphertexts before decryption. This might be useful to save space, since it does not require storage of n encryptions of $m_1, \ldots, m_n$, but only of their homomorphic evaluation. Also a sufficiently expressive homomorphic encryption scheme that supports the homomorphic evaluation of function f is required in order to take advantage of the *"solve one, get many"* property. Practically efficient instantiations of additively and multiplicatively homomorphic schemes are readily available, but fully-homomorphic schemes [17] are currently still much less practical. So for applications that require a complex function f, the homomorphic approach from [24] is conceptually interesting, but not yet practical.

Our modular TRE costruction follows a different approach, which supports this in a black-box manner by simply replacing the PKE scheme with a *homomorphic* PKE scheme that supports homomorphic evaluation of ciphertexts. Since the existence of an additional homomorphic evaluation algorithm is merely an additional *functional* feature of the encryption scheme, the security analysis carries over without any modifications. In particular, note that our construction readily supports any (additively/multiplicatively/fully) homomorphic encryption scheme in a modular way. It thus can be based on arbitrary hardness assumptions and without introducing further requirements, such as the need for indistinguishability obfuscation for the fully-homomorphic TLP construction in [24], or the need for a specific *multi-key* fully-homomorphic encryption scheme [22] as in [8]. We note also that our construction of sequential TRE equally provides homomorphic computations *within* a single time period. Homomorphic computations *across* different time slots can easily be realized using any *multi-key* homomorphic encryption scheme [22].

Optimal Amortized Costs. Note that while MT19 [24] achieve the "solve one, get many" property only for homomorphic evaluations over many time-locked messages and thus only for functions evaluated over the time-locked messages, our TRE construction achieves this even without requiring an underlying homomorphic encryption scheme, but for all the original ciphertexts. This is because solving a puzzle yields the randomness to generate the secret key sk of the PKE scheme, which makes it possible to decrypt all ciphertexts efficiently without requiring to solve many puzzles in parallel. Note that the approach of MT19 is thus limited with respect to applicability. The homomorphic evaluation of ciphertexts is only useful when an application needs to decrypt only a function $f(m_1, \ldots, m_n)$ of all encrypted messages $m_1, \ldots, m_n$. However, if it needs to learn all n messages $m_1, \ldots, m_n$ explicitly, then MT19 still requires to solve n puzzles in parallel.

With our TRE approach it is possible to achieve the "solve one, get many" property even for applications that require the full decryption of all independently encrypted messages. Note that for a number n of independently time-locked messages $m_1, \ldots, m_n$ our scheme is thus the first one to achieve an optimal amortized cost of decryption per ciphertext of $(n \cdot T_{\mathsf{PKE.Dec}} + T_{\mathsf{TLP}})/n$ where $T_{\mathsf{PKE.Dec}}$ is the time required to run the decryption algorithm $\mathsf{PKE.Dec}$ and T_{TLP} is the time required to solve the puzzle. Note that this approaches $T_{\mathsf{PKE.Dec}}$ with increasing n. We note that this equally applies to our sequential TRE approach.

Public Verifiability. In [15], Ephraim *et al.* recently introduced the notion of *public verifiability* for TLPs, meaning that after a party solves the puzzle, they can publish the underlying solution together with a proof which can be later used by anyone to quickly verify the correctness of the solution. Ephraim et al. require this property to hold even if the puzzle is maliciously generated and might have no valid solution. We briefly discuss how our TRE construction provides a public verifiability property, but since in our TRE the puzzles are honestly generated and part of the public parameters, we do not consider malicious puzzle generation. Note that in our TRE construction from the generated puzzle $(Z, s) \leftarrow \mathsf{TLP.Gen}(T)$ the solution s is used as the random coins to obtain $(\mathsf{pk}, \mathsf{sk}) \leftarrow \mathsf{PKE.Gen}(1^\lambda; s)$. Now, our public TRE parameters include $\mathsf{pp}_e := \mathsf{pk}$ and $\mathsf{pp}_d = Z$ and given a potential solution s' one wants to guarantee that $(\mathsf{pk}, \mathsf{sk}) \leftarrow \mathsf{PKE.Gen}(1^\lambda; s')$ generates the same public key and an equivalent secret key. Therefore, if the used PKE scheme $\mathsf{PKE} = (\mathsf{PKE.Gen}, \mathsf{PKE.Enc}, \mathsf{PKE.Dec})$ provides perfect correctness, this public verifiability property is perfectly satisfied, i.e.,. for one pk there cannot be different secret keys output by $\mathsf{PKE.Gen}$ that behave differently in their decryption behavior. In particular, the publicly verifiable proof is then simply the solution s' and the verification is to check whether $s' \in \mathcal{R}$, to run $(\mathsf{pk}', \mathsf{sk}') \leftarrow \mathsf{PKE.Gen}(1^\lambda; s')$ and to check whether $\mathsf{pk}' = \mathsf{pp}_e$, which represents an efficient check.

Sequential TRE with Public Servers. One particularly interesting feature of our notion of sequential TRE is that one can use a *single* centralized server that continuously computes and publishes solutions $s_i = \mathsf{Solve}(s_{i-1})$ to decrypt an arbitrary number of ciphertexts. Most importantly, the server would be *independent* of these ciphertexts, which is not achieved by prior constructions. This yields TRE where the decrypting parties would not have to solve any puzzle, but merely would have to wait until the server publishes a solution. Note that here the fact that the amortized complexity of decrypting n ciphertexts approaches the complexity of running $\mathsf{PKE.Dec}$ with increasing n is particularly useful.

We stress that this must not be confused with TRE schemes in a trusted-agent based setting. Loosely speaking, in such schemes a so called time server publishes a single time-dependent trapdoor that then allows decryption of ciphertexts. As shown in [10], this concept is essentially equivalent to identity-based encryption (IBE) [5]. Most importantly, in any such agent-based TRE scheme there is a trusted party which is not only involved in running the setup, but this party then also needs to be online and, in particular, needs to be trusted to keep the secret keys that are supposed to be released at a later point in time confidential until the time has passed. In our approach of sequential TRE with public servers, however, only the setup needs to be trusted. Even for the service that actually performs the squaring there are no shortcuts to revealing the decryption keys before the respective time has passed.

If one is worried about a trusted setup performed by a third-party server, or about the fact that one server might run out of service, then one could use $N > 1$ servers. The public parameters of each server would be used to encrypt a share of the message, using an (K, N)-threshold secret sharing scheme (e.g., [30]). Even with $K - 1$ colluding servers, the message would remain hidden. Even if up to $N - K$ servers go out of service, messages would still be recoverable using the K shares obtained from the remaining servers.

3 Definitions and Constructions of Time Lock-Puzzles

Simple Time-Lock Puzzles. In this section we give a new definition for time-lock puzzles (TLPs) and explain how it relates to the old definition.

Definition 1. *A time-lock puzzle is pair of algorithms* TLP = (Gen, Solve) *with the following syntax.*

- $(Z, s) \leftarrow$ Gen(T) *is a probabilistic algorithm which takes as input a hardness parameter* $T \in \mathbb{N}$ *and outputs a puzzle* Z *together with the unique solution* s *of the puzzle. We require that* Gen *runs in time at most* poly$(\log T, \lambda)$ *for some polynomial* poly.
- $s \leftarrow$ Solve(Z) *is a deterministic algorithm which takes as input a puzzle* Z *and outputs a solution* $s \in S$, *where* S *is a finite set. We require that* Solve *runs in time at most* $T \cdot$ poly(λ). *There will also be a lower bound on the running time, which is part of the security definition.*

We say TLP *is correct if for all* $\lambda \in \mathbb{N}$ *and for all polynomials* T *in* λ *it holds:*

$$\Pr[s = s' : (Z, s) \leftarrow \text{Gen}(T), s' \leftarrow \text{Solve}(Z)] = 1.$$

Relation to Prior Definitions. In the definitions of TLPs from Bitansky *et al.* [4] and Malavolta and Thyagarajan [24] algorithm Gen receives s as an additional input and output a puzzle Z. This immediately yields a timed-release encryption (TRE) scheme by viewing s as a message that is encrypted. Our definition enables a slightly simpler generic construction of (homomorphic) TRE. Intuitively, our new definitions relates to the prior one in a similar way like a key encapsulation mechanism relates to an encryption scheme. Concretely, let TLP = (Gen, Solve) be a puzzle according to our new definition. Then we obtain a puzzle TLP$'$ = (Gen$'$, Solve$'$) of the old form as follows:

- Gen$'(T, m)$ computes $Z \leftarrow$ Gen(T) outputs $Z' = (Z, m \oplus s)$.
- Solve$'(Z' = (Z, c))$ computes $s \leftarrow$ Solve(Z) and outputs $c \oplus s$.

$$\begin{aligned}
&\underline{\mathsf{ExpTLP}^b_{\mathcal{A}}(\lambda):} \\
&(Z, s) \leftarrow \mathsf{Gen}(T(\lambda)) \\
&\text{if } b = 0 : c := s \\
&\text{if } b = 1 : c \xleftarrow{\$} S \\
&\text{return } b' \leftarrow \mathcal{A}_\lambda(Z, c)
\end{aligned}$$

Fig. 1. Security experiment for time-lock puzzles.

Security. For security we require that the solution of a TLP is indistinguishable from random, unless the adversary has sufficient running time to solve the puzzle. The following definition is inspired by those from Bitansky *et al.* [4] and Malavolta and Thyagarajan [24], but adopted to our slightly modified definition of the Gen algorithm.

Definition 2. *Consider the security experiment* $\mathsf{ExpTLP}^b_{\mathcal{A}}(\lambda)$ *in Fig. 1. We say that a time-lock puzzle* TLP *is secure with gap* $\epsilon < 1$, *if there exists a polynomial* $\tilde{T}(\cdot)$ *such that for all polynomials* $T(\cdot) \geq \tilde{T}(\cdot)$ *and every polynomial-size adversary* $\mathcal{A} = \{\mathcal{A}_\lambda\}_{\lambda \in \mathbb{N}}$ *of depth* $\leq T^\epsilon(\lambda)$ *there exists a negligible function* $\mathsf{negl}(\cdot)$ *such that for all* $\lambda \in \mathbb{N}$ *it holds*

$$\mathbf{Adv}^{\mathrm{TLP}}_{\mathcal{A}} = \left| \Pr\left[\mathsf{ExpTLP}^0_{\mathcal{A}}(\lambda) = 1\right] - \Pr\left[\mathsf{ExpTLP}^1_{\mathcal{A}}(\lambda) = 1\right] \right| \leq \mathsf{negl}(\lambda).$$

Other Variants of TLPs. In the full version we also discuss weaker forms of TLPs as introduced by Bitansky *et al.* [4]. Moreover, we present instantiations of TLPs based on different variants of randomized encodings [2,18] and in particular the approach of constructing TLPs from them by Bitansky et al. [4]. Furthermore, we discuss how they can be cast into our TLP framework.

Instantiating TLPs from Sequential Squaring. Subsequently, we discuss instantiations of TLPs based on the sequential squaring. Therefore, we recall a definition of the sequential squaring assumption which was implicitly introduced by Rivest et al. [29]. Let p be an odd prime number. We say that p is a strong prime, if $p = 2p' + 1$ for some prime number p'. Let GenMod be a probabilistic polynomial-time algorithm which, on input 1^λ, outputs two λ-bit strong primes p and q and modulus N that is the product of p and q. Let $\varphi(\cdot)$ denotes Euler's totient function. We denote by $\mathbb{QR}_N$ the cyclic group of quadratic residues which has order $|\mathbb{QR}_N| = \frac{\varphi(N)}{4} = \frac{(p-1)(q-1)}{4}$.

Definition 3 (The Sequential Squaring Assumption). *The* sequential squaring assumption *with gap* $0 < \epsilon < 1$ *holds relative to* GenMod *if there exists a polynomial* $\tilde{T}(\cdot)$ *such that for all polynomials* $T(\cdot) \geq \tilde{T}(\cdot)$ *and for every* *non-uniform polynomial-size adversary* $\mathcal{A} = \{\mathcal{A}_\lambda\}_{\lambda \in \mathbb{N}}$, *where the depth of* $\mathcal{A}_\lambda$ *is at most* $T^\epsilon(\lambda)$, *there exists a negligible function* $\mathsf{negl}(\cdot)$ *such that for all* $\lambda \in \mathbb{N}$

$$\left| \Pr \left[b = b' : \begin{array}{c} (p, q, N) \leftarrow \mathsf{GenMod}(1^\lambda) \\ x \xleftarrow{\$} \mathbb{QR}_N, b \xleftarrow{\$} \{0, 1\} \\ \text{if } b = 0 : y := x^{2^{T(\lambda)}} \bmod N \\ \text{if } b = 1 : y \xleftarrow{\$} \mathbb{QR}_N \\ b' \leftarrow \mathcal{A}_\lambda(N, T(\lambda), x, y) \end{array} \right] - \frac{1}{2} \right| \leq \mathsf{negl}(\lambda).$$

The instantiation of TLP from the sequential squaring assumption is straightforward:

- $\mathsf{Gen}(T)$: Run $(p, q, N) \leftarrow \mathsf{GenMod}(1^\lambda)$. Randomly sample $x \xleftarrow{\$} \mathbb{QR}_N$ and compute the value $s := x^{2^T} \bmod N$. Notice that value s can be efficiently computed knowing the values p and q. Set $Z := (N, T, x)$ and output (Z, s).
- $\mathsf{Solve}(Z)$: compute $s := x^{2^T} \bmod N$ by repeated squaring.

The security of this construction is directly implied by the security of the sequential squaring assumption.

4   Sequential Time-Lock Puzzles

In this section we introduce *sequential* time-lock puzzles along with their security and propose an instantiation which we prove secure under a new assumption called the *gap sequential squaring* assumption. We also show this assumption to hold, assuming factoring is hard, in the strong algebraic group model (SAGM) of Katz et al. [19].

Defining Sequential Time-Lock Puzzles. *Sequential time-lock puzzles* are a particularly useful generalization of basic TLPs, which yields particularly practical time-lock encryption schemes. To this end, we generalize Definition 1 by allowing the Gen algorithm to take multiple different time parameters as input, which then produces a corresponding set of puzzles.

Definition 4. *A sequential time-lock puzzle is tuple of algorithms* $\mathsf{sTLP} = (\mathsf{Gen}, \mathsf{Solve})$ *with the following syntax.*

- $(Z_i, s_i)_{i \in [n]} \leftarrow \mathsf{Gen}((T_i)_{i \in [n]})$ *is a probabilistic algorithm which takes as input n integers* $(T_i)_{i \in [n]}$ *and outputs n puzzles together with their solutions* $(Z_i, s_i)_{i \in [n]}$ *in time at most* $\mathsf{poly}((\log T_i)_{i \in [n]}, \lambda)$. *Without loss of generality we assume in the sequel that set* $(T_i)_{i \in [n]}$ *is ordered and hence* $T_i < T_{i+1}$ *for all* $i \in [n-1]$.
- $s_i \leftarrow \mathsf{Solve}(Z_i, s_{i-1})$ *is a deterministic algorithm which takes as input a puzzle* Z_i *and a solution for puzzle* Z_{i-1} *and outputs a solution* s_i, *where we define* $s_0 := \perp$. *We require that* Solve *runs in time at most* $(T_i - T_{i-1}) \cdot \mathsf{poly}(\lambda)$, *where we define* $T_0 := 0$.

We say a sequential time-lock puzzle is correct *if for all* $\lambda, n \in \mathbb{N}$, *for all* $i \in [n]$ *and for polynomials* T_i *in* λ *such that* $T_i < T_{i+1}$ *it holds:*

$$\Pr\left[s_i = s'_i : (Z_i, s_i)_{i \in [n]} \leftarrow \mathsf{Gen}((T_i)_{i \in [n]}), s'_i \leftarrow \mathsf{Solve}(Z_i, s_{i-1})\right] = 1.$$

Security. In order to define a security notion for sequential time-lock puzzles that is useful for our application of constructing particularly efficient timed-release encryption schemes, we need to introduce an additional function F : $\mathbb{N} \times S \rightarrow Y$, which takes as input a pair a hardness parameter $T \in \mathbb{N}$ together with solution $s \in S$ and outputs elements of some set Y. Instead of requiring that elements s_i are indistinguishable from random, we require that $y_i = \mathsf{F}(T_i, s_i)$ is indistinguishable from random.

$\mathsf{ExpsTLP}^b_{\mathcal{A}_i}(\lambda)$:

$(Z_j, s_j)_{j \in [n]} \leftarrow \mathsf{Gen}(1^\lambda, (T_j(\lambda))_{j \in [n]})$

$(y_j := \mathsf{F}(T_j(\lambda), s_j))_{j \in \{[n] \setminus \{i\}\}}$

if $b = 0 : y_i := \mathsf{F}(T_i(\lambda), s_i)$

if $b = 1 : y_i \xleftarrow{\$} Y$

return $b' \leftarrow \mathcal{A}_{i,\lambda}((Z_j, y_j)_{j \in [n]})$

Fig. 2. Security experiment for sequential time-lock puzzles.

Definition 5. *Consider the security experiment* $\mathsf{ExpsTLP}^b_{\mathcal{A}_i}(\lambda)$ *in Fig. 2. We say that a sequential time-lock puzzle* sTLP *is secure with gap* $0 < \epsilon < 1$ *and with respect to the function* F, *if for all polynomials* n *in* λ *there exists a polynomial* $\tilde{T}(\cdot)$ *such that for all sets of polynomials* $(T_j(\cdot))_{j \in [n]}$ *fulfilling that* $\forall j \in [n]$: $T_j(\cdot) \geq \tilde{T}(\cdot)$, *for all* $i \in [n]$ *and every polynomial-size adversary* $\mathcal{A}_i = \{\mathcal{A}_{i,\lambda}\}_{\lambda \in \mathbb{N}}$, *where the depth of* $\mathcal{A}_{i,\lambda}$ *is bounded from above by* $T_i^\epsilon(\lambda)$, *there exists a negligible function* $\mathsf{negl}(\cdot)$ *such that for all* $\lambda \in \mathbb{N}$ *it holds*

$$\mathbf{Adv}^{\mathsf{sTLP}}_{\mathcal{A}_i} = \left| \Pr\left[\mathsf{ExpsTLP}^0_{\mathcal{A}_i}(\lambda) = 1\right] - \Pr\left[\mathsf{ExpsTLP}^1_{\mathcal{A}_i}(\lambda) = 1\right]\right| \leq \mathsf{negl}(\lambda).$$

Instantiating Sequential TLPs from Sequential Squaring. In order to obtain a sequential TLP, we define a variant of the sequential squaring assumption in which an adversary is given oracle access to a *decisional sequential squaring verification function* DSSvf. DSSvf takes as input hardness parameter T' and value $y' \in \mathbb{QR}_N$ and outputs 1 if $y' = x^{2^{T'}} \bmod N$, otherwise it outputs 0. The values x and N are defined in security experiment. The assumption essentially states that computational sequential squaring assumption remains hard, even if the adversary is given access to DSSvf, akin to other gap assumptions [26]. We discuss the necessity of this assumption in Appendix C.

Definition 6 (The Gap Sequential Squaring (GGS) Assumption). *The gap sequential squaring assumption with gap $0 < \epsilon < 1$ holds relative to* GenMod *if there exists a polynomial $\tilde{T}(\cdot)$ such that for all polynomials $T(\cdot) \geq \tilde{T}(\cdot)$ and for every polynomial-size adversary $\mathcal{A} = \{\mathcal{A}_\lambda\}_{\lambda \in \mathbb{N}}$, where the depth of $\mathcal{A}_\lambda$ is bounded from above by $T^\epsilon(\lambda)$, there exists a negligible function* negl$(\cdot)$ *such that for all $\lambda \in \mathbb{N}$ it holds*

$$\mathbf{Adv}_{\mathcal{A}}^{\mathsf{GSS}} = \Pr\left[y = x^{2^T} \bmod N : \begin{array}{c} (p,q,N) \leftarrow \mathsf{GenMod}(1^\lambda), x \xleftarrow{\$} \mathbb{QR}_N \\ y \leftarrow \mathcal{A}_\lambda^{\mathsf{DSSvf}(\cdot,\cdot)}(N, T(\lambda), x) \end{array} \right] \leq \mathsf{negl}(\lambda),$$

where DSSvf$(\cdot, \cdot)$ *is an oracle which takes as input a hardness parameter T' and a value y' and outputs 1 if and only if $y' = x^{2^{T'}} \bmod N$.*

Now we are ready to construct our sequential TLP:

- Gen$((T_i)_{i \in [n]})$: Run $(p,q,N) \leftarrow$ GenMod(1^λ). Randomly sample $x \xleftarrow{\$} \mathbb{QR}_N$ and compute values $s_i := x^{2^{T_i}} \bmod N$ for all $i \in [n]$. Value s_i can be efficiently computed knowing the values p and q. Output $((N, x, T_i, T_{i-1}), s_i))_{i \in [n]}$.
- Solve$((N, x, T_i, T_{i-1}), s_{i-1})$: Compute value $s_{i-1}^{T_i - T_{i-1}} \bmod N$ by repeated squaring.

Theorem 1. *If the gap sequential squaring assumption with gap ϵ holds relative to* GenMod *and* F *is modelled as a random oracle, then for any $\underline{\epsilon} < \epsilon$, the* sTLP $=$ (Gen, Solve) *defined above is a secure sequential time-lock puzzle with gap $\underline{\epsilon}$ and with respect to the function* F.

In the full version we prove that the gap sequential squaring problem is at least as hard as factoring N in the Strong Algebraic Group Model (SAGM), which was introduced by Katz *et al.* [19] to consider time-sensitive assumptions.

Theorem 2. *If the factoring assumption holds relative to* GenMod, *then the gap sequential squaring assumption with gap ϵ holds relative to* GenMod *in the SAGM for any $0 < \epsilon < 1$.*

5 (Sequential) Timed-Release Encryption

In this section we give generic constructions of (sequential) timed-release encryption (TRE) schemes based on (sequential) TLPs. There exist several definitions for TRE and we base ours on that of Unruh [32]. However, we introduce two additional algorithms Setup and Solve which leads to better modularity and applicability of TRE, as we will illustrate in Supplementary Material B.

Definition 7. *A sequential timed-release encryption scheme with message space $\mathcal{M}$ is tuple of algorithms* TRE $=$ (Setup, Enc, Solve, Dec) *with the following syntax.*

- $(\mathsf{pp}_{e,i}, \mathsf{pp}_{d,i})_{i \in [n]} \leftarrow \mathsf{Setup}(1^\lambda, (T_i)_{i \in [n]})$ *is a probabilistic algorithm which takes as input a security parameter* 1^λ *and a set of time hardness parameters* $(T_i)_{i \in [n]}$ *with* $T_i < T_{i+1}$ *for all* $i \in [n-1]$, *and outputs set of public encryption parameters and public decryption parameters* $\mathsf{PP} := (\mathsf{pp}_{e,i}, \mathsf{pp}_{d,i})_{i \in [n]}$. *We require that* Setup *runs in time* $\mathsf{poly}((\log T_i)_{i \in [n]}, \lambda)$.

- $s_i \leftarrow \mathsf{Solve}(\mathsf{pp}_{d,i}, s_{i-1})$ *is a deterministic algorithm which takes as input public decryption parameters* $\mathsf{pp}_{d,i}$ *and a solution from a previous iteration* s_{i-1}, *where* $s_0 := \bot$, *and outputs a solution* s_i. *We require that* Solve *runs in time at most* $(T_i - T_{i-1}) \cdot \mathsf{poly}(\lambda)$.

- $c \leftarrow \mathsf{Enc}(\mathsf{pp}_{e,i}, m)$ *is a probabilistic algorithm that takes as input public encryption parameters* $\mathsf{pp}_{e,i}$ *and message* $m \in \mathcal{M}$, *and outputs a ciphertext* c.

- $m/\bot \leftarrow \mathsf{Dec}(T_i, s_i, c)$ *is a deterministic algorithm which takes as input a hardness parameter* T_i, *a solution* s_i *and a ciphertext* c, *and outputs* $m \in \mathcal{M}$ *or* $\bot$.

We say a sequential timed-release encryption scheme is correct *if for all* $\lambda, n \in \mathbb{N}$, *for all sets of hardness parameters* $(T_j)_{j \in [n]}$ *such that* $\forall j \in [n-1]$: $T_j < T_{j+1}$, *for all* $i \in [n]$ *and for all messages* $m \in \mathcal{M}$ *it holds:*

$$\Pr\left[m = m' : \begin{array}{l} \mathsf{PP} \leftarrow \mathsf{Setup}(1^\lambda, (T_j)_{j \in [n]}), s_i \leftarrow \mathsf{Solve}(\mathsf{pp}_{d,i}, s_{i-1}) \\ m' \leftarrow \mathsf{Dec}(T_i, s_i, \mathsf{Enc}(\mathsf{pp}_{e,i}, m_i)) \end{array} \right] = 1.$$

Note that the above definition also defines "non-sequential" TRE, by setting $n = 1$. In that case the value T_i is not needed as an input for Dec algorithm, however, for sequential TRE, this value is necessary. For ease of the notation, it is unified.

Definition 8. *A sequential timed-release encryption scheme is* secure with gap $0 < \epsilon < 1$ *if for all polynomials* n *in* λ *there exists a polynomial* $\tilde{T}(\cdot)$ *such that for all sets of polynomials* $(T_j)_{j \in [n]}$ *fulfilling that* $\forall j \in [n] : T_j(\cdot) \geq \tilde{T}(\cdot)$, *for all* $i \in [n]$ *and every polynomial-size adversary* $\mathcal{A} = \{(\mathcal{A}_{1,\lambda}, \mathcal{A}_{2,\lambda})\}_{\lambda \in \mathbb{N}}$ *there exists a negligible function* $\mathsf{negl}(\cdot)$ *such that for all* $\lambda \in \mathbb{N}$ *it holds*

$$\mathbf{Adv}_{\mathcal{A}}^{\mathrm{TRE}} = \left| \Pr\left[b = b' : \begin{array}{l} \mathsf{PP} \leftarrow \mathsf{Setup}(1^\lambda, (T_j)_{j \in [n]}) \\ (i, m_0, m_1,) \leftarrow \mathcal{A}_{1,\lambda}(\mathsf{PP}) \\ b \xleftarrow{\$} \{0,1\}; c \leftarrow \mathsf{Enc}(\mathsf{pp}_{e,i}, m_b) \\ b' \leftarrow \mathcal{A}_{2,\lambda}(c,) \end{array} \right] - \frac{1}{2} \right| \leq \mathsf{negl}(\lambda).$$

We require that $|m_0| = |m_1|$ and an adversary $\mathcal{A}_\lambda = (\mathcal{A}_{1,\lambda}, \mathcal{A}_{2,\lambda})$ where $\mathcal{A}_{1,\lambda}$ outputs i in the second step of the above security experiment consists of two circuits with total depth at most $T_i^\epsilon(\lambda)$ (i.e., the total depth is the sum of the depth of $\mathcal{A}_{1,\lambda}$ and $\mathcal{A}_{2,,\lambda}$).

$$
\begin{array}{|ll|}
\hline
\mathsf{Setup}(1^\lambda, T) & \mathsf{Solve}(\mathsf{pp}_d) \\
(Z, s) \leftarrow \mathsf{TLP.Gen}(T) & s \leftarrow \mathsf{TLP.Solve}(\mathsf{pp}_d) \\
(\mathsf{pk}, \mathsf{sk}) \leftarrow \mathsf{PKE.Gen}(1^\lambda; s) & \text{return } s \\
\text{return } \mathsf{pp}_e := \mathsf{pk}, \mathsf{pp}_d := Z & \\
 & \\
\mathsf{Enc}(\mathsf{pp}_e, m) & \mathsf{Dec}(s, c) \\
\text{return } c \leftarrow \mathsf{PKE.Enc}(\mathsf{pp}_e, m) & (\mathsf{pk}, \mathsf{sk}) \leftarrow \mathsf{PKE.Gen}(1^\lambda; s) \\
 & \text{return } m \leftarrow \mathsf{PKE.Dec}(\mathsf{sk}, c) \\
\hline
\end{array}
$$

Fig. 3. Construction of TRE

5.1   Basic TRE Construction

Building Blocks. Our construction combines a time-lock puzzle (TLP) with a CPA secure public-key encryption (PKE) scheme. We refer to [11] for standard formal syntactical and security definitions of PKE. We require standard CPA security of the PKE scheme, since this is sufficient to construct a TRE scheme achieving Definition 8[1].

Construction. Let TLP = (TLP.Gen, TLP.Solve) be a TLP with solution space S and let PKE = (PKE.Gen, PKE.Enc, PKE.Dec) be a PKE scheme. Figure 3 describes our construction of a TRE scheme. As we have already mentioned, the hardness parameter T is not necessary as input for Dec, hence we leave it out in the construction. Observe that correctness is directly implied by correctness of the PKE scheme and the TLP.

Theorem 3. *If* TLP = (TLP.Gen, TLP.Solve) *is secure time-lock puzzle with gap* ϵ *in the sense of Definition 2 and* PKE = (PKE.Gen, PKE.Enc, PKE.Dec) *is a CPA secure encryption scheme, then* TRE = (Setup, Solve, Enc, Dec) *defined in Fig. 3 is a secure timed-release encryption scheme with gap* $\underline{\epsilon} < \epsilon$ *in the sense of Definition 8.*

5.2   Sequential TRE

In the sequel let sTLP = (sTLP.Gen, sTLP.Solve) be a sequential TLP in the sense of Definition 4 and let PKE = (PKE.Gen, PKE.Enc, PKE.Dec) be a PKE scheme. Let $F : \mathbb{N} \times S \to Y$ be a function that maps the hardness parameter space $\mathbb{N}$ and the solution space S of sTLP to the randomness space of algorithm PKE.Gen. Our constructions of a sequential TRE scheme TRE = (Setup, Enc, Solve, Dec) is given in Fig. 4. Note that correctness of the scheme is directly implied by correctness of the PKE scheme and the sequential TLP.

---

[1] We note that by replacing the PKE with a CCA secure one, we can straightforwardly obtain a CCA secure TRE. This is easily achieved as our puzzles are included in the public parameters and thus do not need to be non-malleable and we only require non-malleability on the ciphertexts.

$\text{Setup}(1^\lambda, (T_i)_{i \in [n]})$

$(Z_i, s_i)_{i \in [n]} \leftarrow \text{sTLP.Gen}((T_i)_{i \in [n]})$

$((\text{pk}_i, \text{sk}_i) \leftarrow \text{PKE.Gen}(1^\lambda; F(T_i, s_i)))_{i \in [n]}$

$\text{return } (\text{pp}_{e,i} := \text{pk}_i, \text{pp}_{d,i} := Z_i)_{i \in [n]}$

$\text{Solve}(\text{pp}_{d,i}, s_{i-1})$

$s_i \leftarrow \text{sTLP.Solve}(\text{pp}_{d,i}, s_{i-1})$

$\text{return } s_i$

$\text{Enc}(\text{pp}_{e,i}, m)$

$\text{return } c \leftarrow \text{PKE.Enc}(\text{pp}_{e,i}, m)$

$\text{Dec}(T_i, s_i, c)$

$(\text{pk}_i, \text{sk}_i) \leftarrow \text{PKE.Gen}(1^\lambda; F(T_i, s_i))$

$\text{return } m \leftarrow \text{PKE.Dec}(\text{sk}_i, c)$

Fig. 4. Construction of sequential TRE

$\text{Gen}(1^\lambda, \mathcal{F}, (T_j)_{j \in [n]})$

$(\text{pk}, \text{msk}) \leftarrow \text{FE.Gen}(1^\lambda, \mathcal{F})$

$(\text{pp}_{e,j}, \text{pp}_{d,j})_{j \in [n]} \leftarrow \text{TRE.Setup}(1^\lambda, (T_j)_{j \in [n]})$

$\text{return } (\text{pk}, \text{msk}, (\text{pp}_{e,j}, \text{pp}_{d,j})_{j \in [n]})$

$\text{Enc}(\text{pk}, x)$

$\text{return } c \leftarrow \text{FE.Enc}(\text{pk}, x)$

$\text{KeyGen}(\text{msk}, (\text{pp}_{e,j})_{j \in [n]}, f, i)$

$\text{sk}_f \leftarrow \text{FE.KeyGen}(\text{msk}, f)$

$c_i \leftarrow \text{TRE.Enc}(\text{pp}_{e,i}, \text{sk}_f)$

$\text{return } \text{dk}_i := c_i$

$\text{Dec}(\text{dk}_i, T_i, s_i, c)$

$c_i := \text{dk}_i$

$\text{sk}_f := \text{TRE.Dec}(T_i, s_i, c_i)$

$\text{return } f(x) := \text{FE.Dec}(\text{sk}_f, c)$

$\text{Solve}(\text{pp}_{d,i}, s_{i-1})$

$\text{return } s_i := \text{TRE.Solve}(\text{pp}_{d,i}, s_{i-1})$

Fig. 5. Construction of TRFE.

Theorem 4. *If* $\text{sTLP} = (\text{sTLP.Gen}, \text{sTLP.Solve})$ *is a secure sequential time-lock puzzle with gap* ϵ *w.r.t. function* F *and* $\text{PKE} = (\text{PKE.Gen}, \text{PKE.Enc}, \text{PKE.Dec})$ *is a CPA secure encryption scheme, then* $\text{TRE} = (\text{Setup}, \text{Enc}, \text{Solve}, \text{Dec})$ *defined in Fig. 4 is a secure sequential timed-release encryption with gap* $\underline{\epsilon} < \epsilon$.

5.3 Integrating Timed-Release Features into Functional Encryption

In this section, we connect sequential timed-release features with functional encryption (FE) [7,27] and introduce the notion of a (sequential) timed-release functional encryption (TRFE) scheme. The basic idea is that in such a scheme, similarly to an FE scheme, there is a public key pk used for encryption of any message x and a main secret key msk which is associated to a class of functions $\mathcal{F} : \mathcal{X} \to \mathcal{Y}$. In contrast to an FE scheme, however, in a TRFE scheme, msk can be used to generate decryption keys for a function $f \in \mathcal{F}$ which is associated to a time hardness parameter T_i (and, hence, to its solution s_i). Decryption takes the associated decryption key dk_i, the solution s_i, a function $f \in \mathcal{F}$, and a ciphertext to message x and outputs $f(x)$. Security-wise, an adversary is allowed to query *any* secret function key for any public encryption parameter associated to T_i as long as its solution s_i is not retrievable. Due to limited space, we present the formal definitions of FE, the formal framework of timed-release functional encryption (TRFE) as well as the proof that the construction in Fig. 5 is a secure TRFE in the full version.

Construction of TRFE. Let TRE = (TRE.Setup, TRE.Solve, TRE.Enc, TRE.Dec) be a (sequential) TRE scheme and FE = (FE.Gen, FE.KeyGen, FE.Enc, FE.Dec) be an FE scheme. We construct a TRFE scheme TRFE = (Setup, KeyGen, Enc, Solve, Dec) as given in Fig. 5. Let the message space of TRE be the functional-secret-key space of FE which is the output of FE.KeyGen and all functional secret keys for function $f \in \mathcal{F}$ and any main secret key of FE are of equal length.

Application to Locked-Key IBE. With TRFE, we are able to lock secret keys of an IBE scheme with a sequential timed-release feature. When the central authority in an IBE scheme generates the identity-based secret keys, it can attach hardness parameters to it such that those keys only become usable sequentially. This, for example, enables an IBE central authority to produce all secret keys in the beginning and afterwards go off-line.

A   Concurrent and Independent Work

Recently, there have been some independent and concurrent works investigating different aspects of TLPs, which we want to briefly discuss. Most closely related to our work is the one of Katz *et al.* [19] who show that sequential squaring is as hard as factoring in the strong algebraic group model (SAGM) and construct non-malleable timed commitments based upon a novel building block called timed public-key encryption (TPKE). The similarities are that we will also rely on the SAGM to prove the generic hardness of our new gap sequential squaring assumption. However, their TRPKE approach is different to our TRE approach. Firstly, they support a fast and a slow decryption, where former uses the secret key and latter requires solving a TLP. Secondly, while in our setting encryption is efficient, in their TPKE which is constructed from sequential squaring and the Naor-Yung double encryption paradigm one has to compute twice a T-times sequential squaring. This construction achieves CCA security, but they also discuss a CPA secure version where encryption is equivalently expensive. Note that in contrast to our TRE, in their TPKE time starts running with encryption and not with parameter generation.

In [15] Ephraim *et al.* investigate efficient constructions of concurrent non-malleable TLPs in the auxiliary-input random oracle model (whereas previous constructions in the plain model [3] are not practically efficient). The idea, which is similar to our idea, is essentially to evaluate random oracle on hardness parameter T and solution s of a puzzle Z and use the output of the oracle as a randomness for Gen algorithm of any TLP. An interesting property introduced and investigated in [15] is public verifiability of TLPs. As we have already discussed we can achieve public verifiability for our generic TRE when basing them on perfectly correct PKE schemes. We note however that while Ephraim et al. consider this notion in a setting with malicious puzzle generation, we consider a weaker notion with honest puzzle generation which is sufficient for our TRE.

Abadi and Kiayias [1] construct so-called Multi-Instance Time-Lock Puzzles (MITLPs) which are similar to our notion of sequential TRE. The crucial difference is that MILTPs allow to encrypt messages with respect to consecutive multiples of one hardness parameter by chaining TLPs which requires that all messages of interest must be known at the time when MITLP is generated.

B   Applications: Simpler and More Efficient Instantiations

Subsequently, we discuss the applications in [24] when we use our (homomorphic) TRE approach in contrast to HTLPs of MT19. All the following application have in common that they require decrypting a set of encrypted messages at some required time. Our approach to TRE allows to decrypt arbitrary number of messages at the specified time by solving one puzzle. In [24] this is achieved by homomorphic evaluation of puzzles and then solving one or more resulting puzzles. The drawback of this solution is that one needs to wait until all puzzles of interest have been collected, then execute homomorphic evaluation and only after that the resulting puzzles can be solved. Our scheme allows to start to solve the puzzle immediately after Setup is run. In all of this applications we are able to use our TRE approach *without* any homomorphic property.

E-voting. We focus on designing an e-voting protocol in absence of trusted party, where voters are able to cast their preference without any bias. Similarly to [24], we do not consider privacy nor authenticity of the votes. The crucial property of our TRE is that setup can be reused for producing an arbitrary number of ciphertexts and for that reason it is enough to run Solve only once. The output s of Solve allows to obtain the secret key which is then used to decrypt all ciphertexts that have been produced using corresponding pp_e. Therefore, if we encrypt all votes using the same pp_e, we are able to decrypt all ciphertexts at the same time. Then it is easy to obtain final result by combining decrypted plaintexts. Notice that the security of the TRE scheme guarantees that all votes remain hidden during the whole voting phase. In the e-voting protocol proposed in [24], we have to wait until the voting phase is finished and then we can combine puzzles from voting phase to m resulting puzzles (one per candidate where votes are encoded as 0 and 1 respectively). Then, these m puzzles can be solved, which requires at least time T and solving m puzzles in parallel. Hence, it requires time T after the voting phase is over to be able to announce the results. This is in contrast to what we can do with our TRE, in which we can encrypt the respective encoding of the candidate, e.g., $i \in [m]$ directly, and can start to solve a *single* puzzle immediately after Setup is run and hence the results are available at the beginning of the counting phase.

Multi-party Coin Flipping. In multi-party coin flipping we assume n parties which want to flip a coin in the following way: 1) The value of the coin is unbiased even if $n - 1$ parties collude and 2) all parties agree on the same value for the coin. The approach proposed in [24] relies on HTLPs and their protocol consist of three phases: Setup, Coin Flipping and Announcement of the result. Similarly to the e-voting protocol, one is only able to start solving the puzzle in the last phase and hence obtains the results after time T. We are able to avoid this problem, by using our TRE approach, where we can start to solve the puzzle already after the Setup phase.

Sealed Bid Auctions. Here we consider an auction with n bidders. The protocol consist of two phases - the bidding phase and the opening phase. Bids should be kept secret during the bidding phase and later revealed in opening phase. Time-lock puzzles are used in this scenario to mitigate the issue that some bidders can go offline after the bidding phase. If we use only standard time-lock puzzles, then the number of puzzles which has to be solved in the opening phase is equal to number of bidders who went offline. In [24] this problem was resolved by using HLTPs. Again, this solution has the same issues as the ones discussed above and can be avoided using our TRE approach.

Multi-party Contract Signing. In multi-party contract signing we assume n parties which want to jointly sign a contract. The parties are mutually distrusting and the contract is valid only if it is signed by all parties. The protocol in [24] consists of four phases - Setup, Key Generation, Signing and Aggregation, and combines aggregate signatures from RSA with multiplicatively homomorphic time-lock puzzles with a setup that allows producing puzzles for multiple hardness parameters. We remark that this type of time-lock puzzles are in some sense equivalent to our sequential timed-release encryption.[2] The protocol runs in ℓ-rounds and in the i-th round every party should create a puzzle with hardness $T_{\ell-i+1}$ which contains a signature of the required message. Hence, the hardness of the puzzles decrease in every round. If some parties have not broadcasted their puzzles in any round, the parties will homomorphically evaluate puzzles from the previous round and solve the resulting puzzle.

Consider a scenario, where in the i-th round some party does not broadcast its puzzle. Then if we do not take into account time for homomorphic evaluation, we need time $T_{\ell-i+1}$ to solve the resulting puzzle after this event happened. On the other hand, if we use sequential TRE, we are able to obtain result in time $T_{\ell-i+1}$ after the setup was executed. Moreover, we can combine sequential TRE with an arbitrary aggregate signature scheme, because we do not need to perform any homomorphic evaluation.

C   On the Necessity of the Gap Sequential Squaring Assumption

One might ask why the following seemingly simple solution does not yield a secure sequential TLP:

---

[2] Though they only discuss them informally in [24] and as mentioned in Sect. 1 it seems that it is not possible to prove it secure as it is proposed.

- Generate a set of (non-sequential) puzzles $(Z_1, s_1), ..., (Z_n, s_n)$, such that the delay parameter for puzzle i is $T_i - T_{i-1}$.
- Let $(\mathsf{Enc}, \mathsf{Dec})$ be some CPA-secure symmetric encryption scheme.
- Publish $(Z_1, (\mathsf{Enc}_{s_{i-1}}(Z_i))_{i=2}^n)$.

Unfortunately, this approach does not work (see also page 16 of the full version [11]). Concretely, suppose we have an adversary which has sufficient running time to solve $n-1$ puzzles, and then successfully attacks the n-th puzzle (say, with success probability 1, for instance). Now note that we cannot use the CPA security of any of the first $n-1$ encryptions to "hide" any intermediate puzzle, because the adversary has enough time to notice this (as it has enough running time to solve all the first $n-1$ puzzles). However, then, since we cannot use the CPA security as an argument in the proof, we can equivalently consider the first $n-1$ encryption as completely insecure.

But if we have no security guarantees for the first $n-1$ encryptions, this means that we also cannot argue that the adversary cannot obtain the n-th puzzle instance Z_n quickly, without solving $n-1$ prior instances, because it could simply "break" the $(n-1)$-th encryption to obtain Z_n (which might be very quick, e.g., in just a few computational steps, because we cannot argue that the scheme is secure in the sense of CPA or some other notion). And then an adversary with sufficient running time to solve $n-1$ puzzles can simply solve only the last puzzle using the standard Solve algorithm.

So in conclusion, we do not claim that the construction is insecure, but only that CPA security or a similar notion seems not sufficient, as we cannot perform a reduction to the CPA security in the usual way. It might be possible to prove security under a non-standard assumption (e.g., by essentially assuming that the proposed construction is secure), however, this would also be an additional assumption, which we want to avoid.

References

1. Abadi, A., Kiayias, A.: Multi-instance publicly verifiable time-lock puzzle and its applications. In: Financial Cryptography and Data Security (2021)
2. Applebaum, B., Ishai, Y., Kushilevitz, E.: Computationally private randomizing polynomials and their applications. Comput. Complex **15**, 115–162 (2006)
3. Ball, M., Dachman-Soled, D., Kulkarni, M., Lin, H., Malkin, T.: Non-malleable codes against bounded polynomial time tampering. Cryptology ePrint Archive, Report 2018/1015. https://eprint.iacr.org/2018/1015
4. Bitansky, N., Goldwasser, S., Jain, A., Paneth, O., Vaikuntanathan, V., Waters, B.: Time-lock puzzles from randomized encodings. In: 7th Conference on Innovations in Theoretical Computer Science, ITCS 2016 (2016)
5. Boneh, D., Franklin, M.: Identity-based encryption from the Weil pairing. In: Kilian, J. (ed.) CRYPTO 2001. LNCS, vol. 2139, pp. 213–229. Springer, Heidelberg (2001). https://doi.org/10.1007/3-540-44647-8_13
6. Boneh, D., Naor, M.: Timed commitments. In: Bellare, M. (ed.) CRYPTO 2000. LNCS, vol. 1880, pp. 236–254. Springer, Heidelberg (2000). https://doi.org/10.1007/3-540-44598-6_15

7. Boneh, D., Sahai, A., Waters, B.: Functional encryption: definitions and challenges. In: Ishai, Y. (ed.) TCC 2011. LNCS, vol. 6597, pp. 253–273. Springer, Heidelberg (2011). https://doi.org/10.1007/978-3-642-19571-6_16

8. Brakerski, Z., Döttling, N., Garg, S., Malavolta, G.: Leveraging linear decryption: rate-1 fully-homomorphic encryption and time-lock puzzles. In: Hofheinz, D., Rosen, A. (eds.) TCC 2019, Part II. LNCS, vol. 11892, pp. 407–437. Springer, Cham (2019). https://doi.org/10.1007/978-3-030-36033-7_16

9. Brakerski, Z., Gentry, C., Vaikuntanathan, V.: (Leveled) fully homomorphic encryption without bootstrapping. In: 3rd Innovations in Theoretical Computer Science, ITCS 2012 (2012)

10. Cheon, J.H., Hopper, N., Kim, Y., Osipkov, I.: Provably secure timed-release public key encryption. ACM Trans. Inf. Syst. Secur. 11, 1–44 (2008)

11. Chvojka, P., Jager, T., Slamanig, D., Striecks, C.: Versatile and sustainable timed-release encryption and sequential time-lock puzzles. Cryptology ePrint Archive, Report 2020/739. https://eprint.iacr.org/2020/739

12. Di Crescenzo, G., Ostrovsky, R., Rajagopalan, S.: Conditional oblivious transfer and timed-release encryption. In: Stern, J. (ed.) EUROCRYPT 1999. LNCS, vol. 1592, pp. 74–89. Springer, Heidelberg (1999). https://doi.org/10.1007/3-540-48910-X_6

13. Dwork, C., Naor, M.: Zaps and their applications. In: 41st Annual Symposium on Foundations of Computer Science (2000)

14. ElGamal, T.: A public key cryptosystem and a signature scheme based on discrete logarithms. In: Blakley, G.R., Chaum, D. (eds.) CRYPTO 1984. LNCS, vol. 196, pp. 10–18. Springer, Heidelberg (1985). https://doi.org/10.1007/3-540-39568-7_2

15. Ephraim, N., Freitag, C., Komargodski, I., Pass, R.: Non-malleable time-lock puzzles and applications. Cryptology ePrint Archive, Report 2020/779. https://eprint.iacr.org/2020/779

16. Fuchsbauer, G., Kiltz, E., Loss, J.: The algebraic group model and its applications. In: Shacham, H., Boldyreva, A. (eds.) CRYPTO 2018, Part II. LNCS, vol. 10992, pp. 33–62. Springer, Cham (2018). https://doi.org/10.1007/978-3-319-96881-0_2

17. Gentry, C.: Fully homomorphic encryption using ideal lattices. In: 41st Annual ACM Symposium on Theory of Computing (2009)

18. Ishai, Y., Kushilevitz, E.: Randomizing polynomials: a new representation with applications to round-efficient secure computation. In: 41st Annual Symposium on Foundations of Computer Science (2000)

19. Katz, J., Loss, J., Xu, J.: On the security of time-lock puzzles and timed commitments. In: Pass, R., Pietrzak, K. (eds.) TCC 2020, Part III. LNCS, vol. 12552, pp. 390–413. Springer, Cham (2020). https://doi.org/10.1007/978-3-030-64381-2_14

20. Lin, H., Pass, R., Soni, P.: Two-round and non-interactive concurrent non-malleable commitments from time-lock puzzles. In: 58th Annual Symposium on Foundations of Computer Science (2017)

21. Liu, J., Jager, T., Kakvi, S.A., Warinschi, B.: How to build time-lock encryption. Des. Codes Cryptogr. 86(11), 2549–2586 (2018). https://doi.org/10.1007/s10623-018-0461-x

22. López-Alt, A., Tromer, E., Vaikuntanathan, V.: On-the-fly multiparty computation on the cloud via multikey fully homomorphic encryption. In: 44th Annual ACM Symposium on Theory of Computing (2012)

23. Mahmoody, M., Moran, T., Vadhan, S.: Time-lock puzzles in the random oracle model. In: Rogaway, P. (ed.) CRYPTO 2011. LNCS, vol. 6841, pp. 39–50. Springer, Heidelberg (2011). https://doi.org/10.1007/978-3-642-22792-9_3

24. Malavolta, G., Thyagarajan, S.A.K.: Homomorphic time-lock puzzles and applications. In: Boldyreva, A., Micciancio, D. (eds.) CRYPTO 2019, Part I. LNCS, vol. 11692, pp. 620–649. Springer, Cham (2019). https://doi.org/10.1007/978-3-030-26948-7_22

25. May, T.C.: Timed-release crypto. Technical report (1993)

26. Okamoto, T., Pointcheval, D.: The gap-problems: a new class of problems for the security of cryptographic schemes. In: Kim, K. (ed.) PKC 2001. LNCS, vol. 1992, pp. 104–118. Springer, Heidelberg (2001). https://doi.org/10.1007/3-540-44586-2_8

27. O'Neill, A.: Definitional issues in functional encryption. Cryptology ePrint Archive, Report 2010/556. https://eprint.iacr.org/2010/556

28. Paillier, P.: Public-key cryptosystems based on composite degree residuosity classes. In: Stern, J. (ed.) EUROCRYPT 1999. LNCS, vol. 1592, pp. 223–238. Springer, Heidelberg (1999). https://doi.org/10.1007/3-540-48910-X_16

29. Rivest, R.L., Shamir, A., Wagner, D.A.: Time-lock puzzles and timed-release crypto. Technical report (1996)

30. Shamir, A.: How to share a secret. Commun. ACM (1979)

31. Thyagarajan, S.A.K., Bhat, A., Malavolta, G., Döttling, N., Kate, A., Schröder, D.: Verifiable timed signatures made practical. In: ACM CCS 2020 (2020, to appear). https://verifiable-timed-signatures.github.io/web/assets/paper.pdf

32. Unruh, D.: Revocable quantum timed-release encryption. In: Nguyen, P.Q., Oswald, E. (eds.) EUROCRYPT 2014. LNCS, vol. 8441, pp. 129–146. Springer, Heidelberg (2014). https://doi.org/10.1007/978-3-642-55220-5_8

Multipath TLS 1.3

Marc Fischlin[(⊠)], Sven-André Müller, Jean-Pierre Münch, and Lars Porth

Technische Universität Darmstadt, Darmstadt, Germany
marc.fischlin@cryptoplexity.de

Abstract. In a multipath key exchange protocol (Costea et al., CCS'18) the parties communicate over multiple connection lines, implemented for example with the multipath extension of TCP. Costea et al. show that, if one assumes that an adversary cannot attack all communication paths in an active and synchronized way, then one can securely establish a shared key under mild cryptographic assumptions. This holds even if classical authentication methods like certificate-based signatures fail. They show how to slightly modify TLS to achieve this security level.

Here we discuss that the multipath security can also be achieved for TLS 1.3 without having to modify the crypto part of protocol at all. To this end one runs a regular handshake over one communication path and then a key update (or resumption) over the other path. We show that this already provides the desired security guarantees. At the same time, if only a single communication path is available, then one obtains the basic security properties of TLS 1.3 as a fall back guarantee.

1 Introduction

Secure connection establishment ultimately relies on the ability to authenticate the intended communication partner. Otherwise sensitive data may be transmitted to the wrong party, rendering any attempt to protect data-in-transit useless. Modern key establishment methods such as TLS therefore use various forms of authenticating the partner (unilaterally or mutually), ranging from shared secrets to the common certificate-based signatures.

However, the reliable binding of certified keys to identities is often hard to realize. These may be due to rogue certificates, issued to the wrong party such as in the Comodo and DigiNotar cases [20]. Another source of problems are misconfigured libraries which skip (parts of) the verification [14] or implementation errors as in Apple's goto fail [18]. Sometimes, connection proxies may also break up end-to-end connections and thereby weaken security, e.g., by insufficient certificate checks [4].

1.1 Multipath Key Exchange

Some solutions towards hedging against certificate misbinding have been proposed, including certificate pinning [10] to temporarily store known links, and certificate transparency [19] to log valid certificates. Recently, Costea et al. [5]

© Springer Nature Switzerland AG 2021
E. Bertino et al. (Eds.): ESORICS 2021, LNCS 12973, pp. 86–105, 2021.
https://doi.org/10.1007/978-3-030-88428-4_5

discussed another possibility to enhance security by using the multipath extension of the TCP connection protocol (MPTCP) in [13]. Roughly, the multipath extension allows to establish further sub flows in a TCP connection to ensure reliable and possibly parallel data transmission over different communication channels (such as WiFi and mobile networks). While being primarily a tool for network efficiency, Costea et al. [5] point out that it can also be used to build *multipath key exchange* protocols.

In a multipath key exchange protocol the two parties send partial information of the key exchange protocol over different connections to create a shared key. One usually assumes that there are two connections available. The optimistic assumption is that an adversary can either be active on both connections but then cannot synchronize during the execution, called A/A adversary in [5]. This happens if the latency of the sub connections is small. Or, the adversary may be able to synchronize during the key establishment but then does not have means to actively attack both connections and thus only passively eavesdrop on one of the connections. This is called an $A-P$ attacker in [5].

Costea et al. [5] continue by designing a multipath key exchange scheme *SMKEX* based on the Diffie-Hellman problem. The protocol only requires a Diffie-Hellman exchange over one flow, and the exchange of nonces over the other flow, together with a hash confirmation value. No further authentication is required. They prove their protocol to be secure in a multipath variant of the Canetti-Krawcyzk (CK) model [3] in the random oracle model, against A/A and $A-P$ adversaries. In addition, they also comprehensively discuss the practical feasibility of the multipath approach, and how to modify the crypto part of TLS slightly to incorporate the enhanced security guarantees. The resulting protocol is called *MTLS*.

1.2   Our Contribution

We adopt the idea to relax the assumption about authentication guarantees by using multiple communication paths. We present here a TLS 1.3 compliant protocol [21] to enhance the security of the key establishment. The idea is to run a regular handshake execution over the MPTCP main flow, followed by the key update sub protocol of TLS 1.3 over the MPTCP sub flow. See Fig. 1. The key update step renews the traffic secrets. Alternatively, one may run the resumption sub protocol of TLS 1.3 over the sub flow. The advantage of running the more expensive resumption step is that it updates all keys which TLS 1.3 established, including for example the resumption and exporter master secrets.

In comparison to the *SMKEX* and *MTLS* proposals in [5], our approach has some advantages:

- Our protocol works on top of existing TLS 1.3 implementation, without requiring any modifications of the cryptography. This is contrast to *SMKEX* which is built from scratch, and *MTLS* which modifies TLS slightly.
- Our protocol provides security against A/A and $A-P$ adversaries simultaneously, even if the TLS certificates are completely broken, relying on network

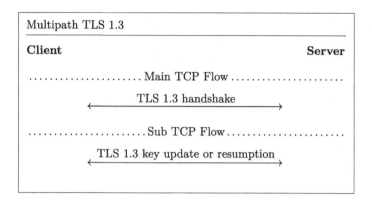

Fig. 1. MPTCP-TLS 1.3 overview

assumptions instead. However, since it runs the basic TLS 1.3 mechanisms, even if the network assumptions turn out to be false, e.g., the parties exchange the information only over a single connection, then one still has the original TLS 1.3 security guarantees as fallback. *MTLS* in [5] is also considered to have this property.

– We discuss our approach concretely for TLS 1.3, but the idea of running the key exchange step over one flow, and then some form of key update or confirmation message over the other flow, should be applicable in general.

In terms of the security model, we introduce a multipath extension of the Bellare-Rogaway (BR) model [1,2]. The difference to the CK model [3] essentially is the latter allows for session-state reveals. But TLS 1.3 has not been designed to withstand such attacks and so far has been analyzed only in (multi-stage extensions [11] of) the BR model [8,9]. We note that we only consider security of the traffic secrets such that we restrict ourselves to a single-stage security model here. We also introduce some minor strengthenings compared to the model in [5].

We finally prove the TLS 1.3 (EC)DHE key exchange followed by a key update to be secure against A/A and $A-P$ adversaries in our security model. We do not rely on the random oracle assumption but need some standard assumptions about the Diffie-Hellman problem, the pseudorandomness of HKDF, and the integrity of the record protocol (which follows from the security of the AEAD schemes stipulated in TLS 1.3). In the $A-P$ case we also need a slightly stronger integrity assumption for the record protocol and discuss its plausibility.

2 Preliminaries

2.1 Multipath TCP

The MPTCP protocol [13] allows to establish multiple TCP subflows underneath an (MPTCP) connection. This allows for an improved and more reliable throughput. For establishing an MPTCP connection the initiator and responder start a regular TCP connection but use a special flag MP_CAPABLE, i.e., both sides agree on an MPTCP connection by setting the MP_CAPABLE flag in the TCP flow of SYN,SYN/ACK, and ACK messages. In the course of this the parties also pick random cryptographic keys and a locally unique 32-bit token, which are all transmitted (in clear) to the other side. The token is in fact a truncated hash value of the responder's key.

To open up a new subflow between addresses either party can start a new TCP connection, but this time include the MP_JOIN flag in the SYN,SYN/ACK,ACK flow. The link to the initial connection is via the token which is included in the MP_JOIN part. During the new establishment both parties exchange nonces, and authenticate both nonces via a (truncated) HMAC computation for the keys from the initial MPTCP connection. The nonces should prevent replay attacks.

While the deployment of MPTCP should be transparent for TCP-only connections, the sender of data over an MPTCP connection in principle has full control over the distribution of data through different sub flows. The routing can be set arbitrarily through the scheduler, albeit not all operating system may support arbitrary choices by default. The receiver may request to prioritize a sub flow via the MP_PRIO flag, and the sender should obey to this request. For our advanced security guarantees, however, we require that the second part of our key agreement protocol indeed runs over a fresh sub flow. If not then one falls back to the ordinary security of TLS 1.3 against active network attackers.

2.2   Transport Layer Security

We give a high-level overview of the Transport Layer Security (TLS) protocol, in particular version 1.3 [21]. Given that our focus in this work is on multipath connection security without authentication we omit the mechanisms for server and client authentication in the description here; our model and security proof still takes this part into account. Instead in the description here we focus on the main anonymous handshake, the record protocol, as well as the protocol to update the record layer keys for an existing connection. More details, which are especially relevant for the proof, appear in Appendix A.

The (EC)DHE handshake of TLS 1.3 runs a Diffie–Hellman-based key derivation. The client initiates the communication with its client hello message CH, including a nonce, and a client key share CKS carrying a Diffie-Hellman value. The server responds with its server hello SH message with its nonce, and its SKS part with a Diffie-Hellman value. The server computes the finished message SF, including a MAC under the derived key, and the client responds with its finished message CF.

For us, the most relevant part is key derivation. With a convoluted key derivation schedule based on the HKDF functions HKDF.Extract and HKDF.Expand, the parties compute (among others) a resumption master secret RMS, a client application traffic secret client_application_traffic_secret, and a server application traffic secret server_application_traffic_secret. The former key is used for the session resumption step only, and the latter keys are used to protect the communication

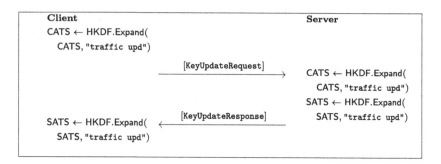

Fig. 2. The TLS 1.3 key update protocol. All messages are protected by the TLS record protocol using the current CATS and SATS, this is indicated by the square brackets.

via the record layer protocol (with an individual key for each sending party). We usually abbreviate the latter keys as CATS and SATS.

We omit the details about session resumption here and instead focus on the key update step. Figure 2 depicts the sub protocol to update the application traffic secrets, as well as the associated computations [21, Section 7.2]. In essence the initiator sends a fixed message requesting a key update and updates their sender secret which the responder is required to respond to with a fixed message, repeating the key updates as well as updating their keys.

Finally, the record layer protocol for TLS 1.3 enforces the use of an authenticated encryption with associated data (AEAD) scheme. It uses a secret IV as the initial nonce, derived from CATS or SATS, depending on whether the sender is the client or the server. The IV is derived as HKDF.Expand(CATS, "iv") for the client, and analogously for the server and its traffic secret. The keys are derived similarly as HKDF.Expand(CATS, "key") using a different label. The nonce is incremented with each sent message.

3 Security Model

3.1 Overview

We follow the description in [5] to motivate the different attacker models, especially $A-P$ and A/A. We always assume there are two communication paths between parties on which messages can be exchanged. The parties can choose the path for each message. On each path we assume there is one adversarial instance present, either active or passive. An *active* attacker may intercept and change messages. A *passive* attacker can monitor the communication between the two parties, but cannot modify it. Both types of adversaries can delay delivery of network messages at will.

We next distinguish between the communication between the different path attackers while a certain attacked execution is running. We let $X_1 - X_2$ denote two path instances which can communicate arbitrarily during the execution, and X_1/X_2 to be two instances with restrictions. That is, let X_1-X_2 (resp. X_1/X_2) denote a pair of *synchronized* (resp. *unsynchronized*) attackers, which can (resp. cannot) exchange information during the protocol execution. In both cases the attackers may exchange information before or after the protocol execution. The variable X_i can be either A for an *active* attacker (capable of altering messages) or P for a *passive* attacker.

Observe that we can disregard the scenario of $A-A$ where we have two synchronized active attackers. This scenario degenerates to a single attacker on a single path since the attackers can act as a single entity then. Also, according to our model $A-P$ and $P-A$ describe the same set of admissible adversaries. As pointed out by [5] it then suffices to consider types $A-P$ and A/A, synchronized adversaries with one passive party, and active but unsynchronized adversaries.

3.2 Security of Multi-path Key Exchange

We next define security of multi-path key exchange by adopting the common game-based security models, similar to [5]. We assume that we have n parties $P_1, \ldots, P_n$ all running the key exchange protocol. Each party may receive a pair of public and secret keys. When executing the protocol both parties obtain a session key which can be used to secure subsequent data flow. In TLS 1.3 these session keys are actually pairs, consisting of the client_application_traffic_secret key (for the communication from client to server) and server_application_traffic_secret key (for the communication from server to client). It is usually assumed that in a genuine execution both parties derive identical session keys.

Attack Model. Neglecting the restrictions due to synchronization, the adversary against the key exchange protocol has full control over the network and can inject, modify, or drop network messages. It can interact with each party by initiating a session between parties P_i (as client) and P_j (as server) for administrative identifier id, and then send protocol messages to either of the two parties, receiving immediately the party's response. In addition the adversary can ask to reveal session keys, modeling leakage of session keys, e.g., if used in weak applications. The adversary can also corrupt parties in which case it receives the long-term secrets like the secret key or the PSK in TLS 1.3.

The goal of the adversary is to distinguish a genuine session key from a random string, significantly better than with the guessing probability of $1/2$. For this the adversary can call a Test oracle which, initialized with a random bit $b \xleftarrow{\$} \{0,1\}$, returns either the session key (if $b = 0$) or an independently chosen random key (if $b = 1$), but answering queries consistently. There are usually some restrictions on testing a session, namely, that neither the session key of the tested session nor of its partner have been revealed. Here, partnering is usually defined by session identifiers sid.

To capture the different communication paths we distinguish between main and sub connection of a session id. That is, id.main denotes the identity of the initial connection and id.sub of the joined sub flow. We restrict ourselves to a single sub flow here but the model can be easily extended to handle more sub flows. To deal with the different attack models we assume that we have two adversarial instances, $\mathcal{A}_{main}$ and $\mathcal{A}_{sub}$, both initialized with independent randomness. The main adversary $\mathcal{A}_{main}$ can initialize new sessions, test or reveal session keys, and corrupt users, and can communicate (only) with the main part of a session. In contrast, $\mathcal{A}_{sub}$ can only interact with sessions with identifier sub via Send queries. The two algorithms can interact via special Sync oracle, which allows to pass arbitrary information between the two algorithms, and Relinquish to go idle and hand over control to the other adversarial instance (but passing no further information).

Formally, we assume that the adversary $\mathcal{A}_{main}$ can make the following queries during the attack:

- NewSession($P_i, P_j, role$) creates a new session for party P_i with role $role \in \{client, server\}$, supposedly communicating with P_j, picks a fresh administrative identifier id with two sub identifiers id.main and id.sub, and returns id. One also creates entries id.user $\leftarrow P_i$, id.partner $\leftarrow P_j$, id.role $\leftarrow role$, and id.key $\leftarrow \bot$ for the session key. It notes its status as id.status $\leftarrow$ *running* and holds two other entries id.main.sid and id.sub.sid for the session identifiers of the two flows (where id.sid = (id.main.sid, id.sub.sid)).
- Send(m, id.main) sends the next protocol message to the session with identity id.main (resp. drops the request and returns $\bot$ if no session with identifier id has been initialized). The message m may be of the special form init if the party is supposed to start the communication. The session is invoked for this protocol message and may return a protocol message (which is forwarded to the adversary). In addition, the session may change its status id.status to *accepted* or *rejected*. In the former case it also sets the session key id.key to some bit string and the session identifier id.sid to be (parts of) the ordered sequence of incoming and outgoing messages for each flow; details are provided as part of the protocol description.
  Analogously, adversary $\mathcal{A}_{sub}$ may call Send(m, id.sub), which is processed as above.
- Reveal(id) ignores the request if id.status $\neq$ *accepted*, else returns id.key and sets the status to id.status $\leftarrow$ *revealed*.
- Corrupt(P) returns the long-term signing key of the party P. We keep this oracle here for sake of compatibility with ordinary models, but since we are interested in trading authentication for multiple paths we will later assume that the adversary immediately corrupts all parties anyway.
- Test$_b$(id) ignores the request if id.status $\neq$ *accepted*, else returns id.key for $b = 0$ resp. a random string from $\{0,1\}^{|id.key|}$ if $b = 1$, and sets the status to id.status $\leftarrow$ *tested*. We assume that Test is only called once during the attack (by $\mathcal{A}_{main}$) and denote the corresponding identity by id$_{Test}$.

Both adversaries $\mathcal{A}_{main}$ and $\mathcal{A}_{sub}$ have access to two additional oracles:

- Sync(x) can be called by either adversary and forwards x to the other adversary. This is immediately followed by a Relinquish execution.

– Relinquish() lets the other adversary become active (and the calling adversary inactive). We assume that initially $\mathcal{A}_{\text{main}}$ is active and $\mathcal{A}_{\text{sub}}$ inactive, and that only the active adversary can make oracle calls.

At the end of the execution algorithm $\mathcal{A}_{\text{main}}$ outputs a guess $a \in \{0,1\}$ for the hidden bit b. We declare the adversary to lose if it tests the session id_{Test} (with $\text{id}_{\text{Test}}.\text{status} = \text{tested}$) and reveals the session key of an honest partner, that is, if there is a session $\text{id}' \neq \text{id}_{\text{Test}}$ such that $\text{id}'.\text{sid} = \text{id}_{\text{Test}}.\text{sid}$ and $\text{id}'.\text{status} = \text{revealed}$. If this happens we automatically set a Boolean variable $\text{lose} \leftarrow \texttt{true}$ (which initially is $\texttt{false}$).

In addition, we also declare the adversary to lose if it violates the A/A or $A{-}P$ properties for the test session. For the former we let the *lifetime* of the test session id_{Test} cover all the actions of the adversaries between the NewSession call which returned id_{Test} and the call which changes the status to $\text{id}_{\text{Test}}.\text{status} \neq \text{running}$. Let $\mathcal{I}$ be the set of session identities $\text{id}' \neq \text{id}_{\text{Test}}$ which $\mathcal{A}_{\text{main}}$ either calls an oracle about or has received from a NewSession call during the lifetime of id_{Test}. Then we set $\text{lose} \leftarrow \texttt{true}$ unless

– there is another session $\text{id}' \neq \text{id}_{\text{Test}}$ to the tested session id_{Test} which is partnered in one of the flows, i.e., such that $\text{id}'.\text{main}.\text{sid} = \text{id}_{\text{Test}}.\text{main}.\text{sid}$ or $\text{id}'.\text{sub}.\text{sid} = \text{id}_{\text{Test}}.\text{sub}.\text{sid}$ ($A{-}P$ property satisfied), or
– there is no Sync call and at most one Relinquish call during the lifetime of id_{Test}, and no Send call of $\mathcal{A}_{\text{sub}}$ to some identity $\text{id}' \in \mathcal{I}$ (A/A property satisfied).

In the A/A case we forbid the adversary $\mathcal{A}_{\text{sub}}$ to make any call to some "alive" session $\text{id}' \in \mathcal{I}$. This prevents the adversary from communicating by, say, observing the behavior of other sessions. An example could be $\mathcal{A}_{\text{main}}$ putting session id' into a certain state which triggers a certain response when $\mathcal{A}_{\text{sub}}$ calls id' after the handover. This could allow $\mathcal{A}_{\text{main}}$ to pass arbitrary bit strings to $\mathcal{A}_{\text{sub}}$ while the test session is still active, thus violating the A/A property.

Note also that we do not make any stipulations about corruptions of party. The idea of the multipath extension of TLS is exactly to withstand attacks where no authentication happens, or where the adversary controls the long-term signing key used for authentications.

We have defined security with respect to a single-test setting, i.e., where the adversary can only test a single session during the attack. This simplifies the definition compared to a multi-test scenario where the same secret bit b is used in multiple Test calls of the adversary. In the latter case one would need to make the above stipulation for each test session, preventing the adversary from communicating for any of the tested sessions. Depending on the scheme it may then be possible to show via a hybrid argument that the multi-test case can be reduced to the single-test case.

Security Definitions. We always assume that two accepting sessions with the same session identifier also derive the same session key. This is always the case in TLS 1.3 and in the following we do not discuss this further. We also note that, because of the freshly chosen nonces, the probability of three honest parties deriving the same (sub) session identifiers is negligible. This is called Match-security:

Definition 1 (Match-Security). *For a multi-path key exchange protocol* KE *and adversary pair* $\mathcal{A} = (\mathcal{A}_{main}, \mathcal{A}_{sub})$ *in the experiment above let* $\mathbf{Adv}_{KE,\mathcal{A}}^{Match}$ *be the probability that* $\mathcal{A}$ *manages to make three sessions have the same session identifier,* id, id', id'' *with* id.sid = id'.sid = id''.sid, *or that two sessions have the same session identifier but different keys,* id.sid = id'.sid *but* id.key $\neq$ id'.key. *The protocol is* Match-*secure if for any efficient adversary pair* $\mathcal{A} = (\mathcal{A}_{main}, \mathcal{A}_{sub})$ *the advantage is negligible.*

Next we define key secrecy for simultaneous A/A and $A-P$ attacks:

Definition 2 (Key Secrecy). *A multi-path key exchange protocol* KE *is simultaneously key-secret against* A/A *and* $A-P$ *adversaries if for any efficient adversary pair* $\mathcal{A} = (\mathcal{A}_{main}, \mathcal{A}_{sub})$ *in the experiment above*

$$\mathbf{Adv}_{KE,\mathcal{A}}^{A-P\&A/A\text{-}secrecy} := \mathrm{Prob}\left[a = b \wedge \neg\mathsf{lose} \right] - \tfrac{1}{2} \leq negl.$$

In comparison to previous models we make the following changes:

- The work by Costea et al. [5] models A/A adversaries by splitting the adversary when communicating with the test session. We split the adversary from the beginning but allow for an explicit information transfer through Sync queries (and disallow such queries when attacking the test session).
- Unlike [5] we do not enable session state reveals where the adversary receives the ephemeral randomness of the protocol participant. The reason is that TLS 1.3 does not account for such attacks.
- We account for security against $A-P$ and A/A simultaneously. That is, the adversary can decide during the attack on the type of attempt.
- Costea et al. [5] in the $A-P$ case explicitly consider adversaries which are passive on one of the two flows for the attacked session. Here we only demand that there exists a sub flow with some honest session, not necessarily in the same attacked session, where the adversary remains passive. Our model hence also captures cross-over attacks for different sessions.
- We do not consider multi-stage security of the TLS 1.3 session keys [11]. This notion is useful when one argues security of the intermediate keys derived during the handshake protocol, but we aim to protect the actual session keys client_application_traffic_secret and server_application_traffic_secret which are only derived at the very end.

4   Multipath Extension for TLS 1.3

4.1   Protocol

We present the MPTCP extension of the TLS 1.3 protocol in Fig. 3. The client and server first execute a regular (EC)DHE handshake to derive application traffic secrets CATS, SATS. Then they run a key update on the added sub flow to derive the new keys $\mathsf{CATS}^{\mathrm{ku}}, \mathsf{SATS}^{\mathrm{ku}}$. Note that the protocol messages in the update step on the sub flow are still secured under the current keys, namely client_write_iv ← HKDF.Expand(CATS, "iv") for the initialization vector and client_write_key ← HKDF.Expand(CATS, "key") for the key for the client, and analogously for the server.

We view the multipath protocol execution as consisting of both flows. The protocol session accepts only after a successful key update, and only then status changes from *running* to *accepted*. The session key pair, which is subsequently used to protect communication, is the updated pair $\mathsf{CATS}^{\mathrm{ku}}, \mathsf{SATS}^{\mathrm{ku}}$. In particular, this means that Reveal queries of the adversary in the attack only make sense after completion of the sub flow. The adversary then receives the key pair $\mathsf{CATS}^{\mathrm{ku}}, \mathsf{SATS}^{\mathrm{ku}}$ but still does not have access to the intermediate key pair CATS, SATS.

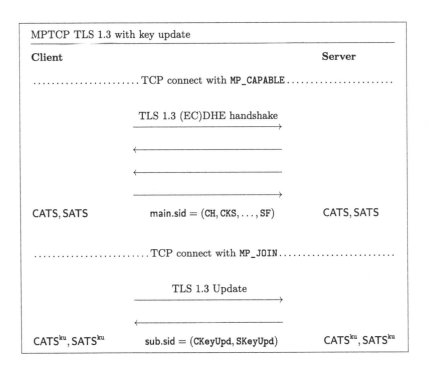

Fig. 3. Protocol Overview over MPTCP-TLS 1.3 with key update. The final session key(s) are the application-traffic-secrets $\mathsf{CATS}^{\mathrm{ku}}, \mathsf{SATS}^{\mathrm{ku}}$ after the key update. CKeyUpd and SKeyUpd denote the (secured) record-layer messages for the key update.

We note that the cryptographic part of TLS 1.3 remains unaltered. Only the socket interface to MPTCP would need to be changed, possibly enabling TLS 1.3 to demand a path change for the key update or resumption. Still, if for some reason MPTCP only runs plain TCP in backward compatibility mode, the network communication of our protocol looks like a common TLS 1.3 execution. Furthermore, even if the TLS application was not aware that the connection runs plain TCP, we would still have the basic security guarantees of TLS 1.3.

4.2 Security Assumptions

To show security we need several assumptions about the cryptographic primitives. We define them briefly below. Some assumptions like collision resistance of the hash function H are standard and can be found also in text books like [15]. For assumptions about the authenticated encryption with associated data (AEAD) in the record layer see [22]. We also need some slightly non-standard assumptions which nonetheless appear to be highly reasonable.

We let $\mathbf{Adv}_{\mathbb{G},\mathcal{D}}^{\mathrm{DDH}}(\lambda)$ be the advantage of an algorithm $\mathcal{D}$ deciding Diffie-Hellman values in the group $\mathbb{G}$. That is, $\mathbf{Adv}_{\mathbb{G},\mathcal{D}}^{\mathrm{DDH}}(\lambda)$ denotes the absolute difference between the probabilities that $\mathcal{D}$, on input a description of the group $\mathbb{G}$ with generator g and three values g^x, g^y, g^{xy} resp. g^x, g^y, g^z for random x, y, z, outputs 1. In our case we assume that $\mathbb{G}$ is the weakest of the elliptic curve groups of TLS 1.3.

We assume that the hash function H for computing the transcript hash is collision resistant. In other words, letting $\mathbf{Adv}_{\mathsf{H},\mathcal{C}}^{\mathrm{coll}}$ be the probability that an algorithm $\mathcal{C}$ outputs a collision $x \neq x'$ with $\mathsf{H}(x) = \mathsf{H}(x')$ is small.

We also assume that HKDF.Extract and HKDF.Expand are pseudorandom functions (for random inputs in the second input for Extract and in the first input for Expand, distributed according to some distribution D). That is, let $\mathbf{Adv}_{\mathsf{HKDF.Extract},D,\mathcal{D}}^{\mathrm{prf}}$ for an algorithm $\mathcal{D}$ be the absolute difference in outputting 1 when having oracle access to HKDF.Extract(key, ·) for key $\xleftarrow{\$} D$ resp. to a random function with the same input-output size. Define $\mathbf{Adv}_{\mathsf{HKDF.Expand},D,\mathcal{D}}^{\mathrm{prf}}$ analogously for function HKDF.Expand(·, key).

For A/A attacks we sometimes even consider pseudorandomness of HKDF for partially adversarial chosen distributions key $\leftarrow D(x; r)$ where an adversary can choose the input x after learning the distribution's randomness r. The distinguisher $\mathcal{D}$, however, does not get to learn x, r (such that the key still has high entropy) but only gets oracle access to HKDF.Expand(·, key) or a random function. In other words, we assume that HKDF.Expand is a good extractor for the adaptively biased source D. This seems to be very plausible given that HKDF was designed to have this property [16,17].

Finally, for the record layer protocol we assume that the probability of sending a protocol message through the record layer which is not rejected is infeasible. That is, let $\mathbf{Adv}_{\mathsf{AEAD},\mathcal{B}}^{\mathrm{int}}$ be the probability that an algorithm $\mathcal{B}$ first outputs a message m, then a key key is generated for the AEAD scheme, and an initial random nonce N_0 according to the record layer is picked. Then the adversary receives $C \leftarrow \mathsf{AEAD.Enc}(\mathsf{key}, N_0, m)$ and is supposed to output $C^* \neq C$ such that $\mathsf{AEAD.Dec}(\mathsf{key}, N_0, C^*) \neq \bot$. The fact that the adversary's success probability is small is implied by the common authentication or integrity assumption for AEAD schemes [22].

We also need a stronger but still reasonable assumption about the ability to use a different key key' and nonce N' to generate a valid record which can be successfully decrypted under the original key key and nonce N. We define this "correlation" property in combination with HKDF because the alternative key key' cannot be chosen directly but needs to be generated by calling HKDF, making attacks less likely. That is, for any adversary $\mathcal{E}$ define $\mathbf{Adv}^{\mathsf{corr}}_{\mathsf{AEAD},\mathsf{HKDF},\mathcal{E}}$ to be the probability that $\mathcal{E}$ outputs $(MS,x) \neq (MS',x')$, and m such that the following holds: Let $\mathsf{CATS} \leftarrow \mathsf{HKDF.Expand}(MS,x)$, $\mathsf{key} \leftarrow \mathsf{HKDF.Expand}(\mathsf{CATS},\texttt{"key"})$, $N \leftarrow \mathsf{HKDF.Expand}(\mathsf{CATS},\texttt{"iv"})$, as well as $\mathsf{CATS}' \leftarrow \mathsf{HKDF.Expand}(MS',x')$, $\mathsf{key}' \leftarrow \mathsf{HKDF.Expand}(\mathsf{CATS}',\texttt{"key"})$, $N' \leftarrow \mathsf{HKDF.Expand}(\mathsf{CATS}',\texttt{"iv"})$, $C' \leftarrow \mathsf{AEAD.Enc}(\mathsf{key}',N',m)$, and check that $\mathsf{AEAD.Dec}(\mathsf{key},N,C') \neq \perp$.

The assumption appears to hold for common AEAD schemes. If we assume that HKDF behaves like a random oracle then the different inputs $(MS,x) \neq (MS',x')$ yield independently distributed outputs. But then the probability that two random key-nonce combinations can be used to encrypt and successfully decrypt is unlikely. Otherwise one could attack the AEAD scheme by trying to decrypt with a fresh random key-nonce pair and succeed with high probability.

4.3   Security

We first show Match-security. Note that we count the number s of sessions via the $\mathsf{NewSession}$ calls of the (main) adversary, and the (full) session identifiers consist of both sub identifiers.

Proposition 1. *The MPTCP TLS 1.3 extension, (EC)DHE handshake with key update, is Match-secure. More precisely, for any adversary $\mathcal{A}$ initiating a maximum number s of sessions and for nonce length $|nonce| = 256$ we have* $\mathbf{Adv}^{\mathsf{Match}}_{\mathsf{KE},\mathcal{A}} \leq s^2 \cdot 2^{-|nonce|}$.

Proof. The property follows as for regular TLS 1.3 in [8,9]. The probability that there are three sessions among the s sessions with the same sid is bounded from above by $s^2 \cdot 2^{-|nonce|}$, since the probability that an honest party picks the same nonce as the (potentially partnered) other two sessions is given by the birthday bound. The fact that the same sid yields the same key follows straightforwardly, because the session identifier contains all information which enters the key derivation for CATS and SATS and if this key is identical, then the same update messages $\mathsf{CKeyUpd},\mathsf{SKeyUpd}$ also cause the same update step to $\mathsf{CATS}^{\mathsf{ku}}$ and $\mathsf{SATS}^{\mathsf{ku}}$. $\qquad\square$

Theorem 1. *The MPTCP TLS 1.3 extension, (EC)DHE handshake with key update, is simultaneously key-secret against $A-P$ and A/A adversaries. More precisely, for any adversary $\mathcal{A} = (\mathcal{A}_{main}, \mathcal{A}_{sub})$ initiating at most s sessions we have that there are algorithms $\mathcal{D}, \mathcal{D}_1, \ldots, \mathcal{D}_{16}, \mathcal{D}', \mathcal{B}, \mathcal{B}', \mathcal{C}, \mathcal{E}$ and distributions $D_1, \ldots, D_{16}, D'$ with*

$$\mathbf{Adv}_{\mathsf{KE},\mathcal{A}}^{A-P\mathcal{E}\mathcal{A}/A\text{-}secrecy}$$

$$\leq s^2 \cdot \Big(\mathbf{Adv}_{\mathbb{G},\mathcal{D}}^{DDH} + \sum_{i=1}^{16} \mathbf{Adv}_{\mathsf{HKDF.Extract/Expand},D_i,\mathcal{D}_i}^{prf} + 2 \cdot \mathbf{Adv}_{\mathsf{AEAD},\mathcal{B}}^{int}$$

$$+ \mathbf{Adv}_{\mathsf{H},\mathcal{C}}^{coll} + \mathbf{Adv}_{\mathsf{AEAD},\mathsf{HKDF},\mathcal{E}}^{corr}$$

$$+ \mathbf{Adv}_{\mathsf{HKDF.Expand},D',\mathcal{D}'}^{prf} + \mathbf{Adv}_{\mathsf{AEAD},\mathsf{HKDF},\mathcal{E}}^{corr} \Big).$$

Here the other algorithms have roughly the same run time as $\mathcal{A}$ plus the time to execute the attack on the key exchange protocol.

Proof. Consider an adversary $\mathcal{A} = (\mathcal{A}_{\mathsf{main}}, \mathcal{A}_{\mathsf{sub}})$ against the key secrecy of the key exchange protocol. We discuss first the $A-P$ case. That is, the adversary may be active in one flow and passive in the other one. More formally, assume that for the test session $\mathsf{id}_{\mathsf{Test}}$ there exists another session id' with the same session identifier in either the main or sub flow. We assume that we know the right sessions $\mathsf{id}_{\mathsf{Test}}$ and id' in advance; this can be accomplished by guessing the sessions with probability at least $1/s^2$ among all s sessions.

Further note that we can make all Corrupt queries at the outset, such that the adversary immediately knows the signing keys. This is valid since key secrecy does not depend on authentication. Note that this in particular means that $\mathcal{A}$ could simulate all other sessions different from $\mathsf{id}_{\mathsf{Test}}$ and id' itself.

An important observation for the proof steps below is to note, once more, that Reveal queries of the adversary only make sense after the successful update step. Then the status changes to *accepted* and the Reveal queries returns the updated key pair $\mathsf{CATS}^{\mathsf{ku}}, \mathsf{SATS}^{\mathsf{ku}}$ (but not the keys $\mathsf{CATS}, \mathsf{SATS}$). We will take advantage of this observation multiple times below.

We next make a case distinction, depending on whether the main or sub flow of $\mathsf{id}_{\mathsf{Test}}$ and id' match:

Case A: Passive in Main Flow, $\mathsf{id}'.\mathsf{main}.\mathsf{sid} = \mathsf{id}_{\mathsf{Test}}.\mathsf{main}.\mathsf{sid}$. In this case we argue that the session key $\mathsf{CATS}, \mathsf{SATS}$ in the two sessions is secure. To see this we can perform a sequence of game hops, where we let $G_{A.i}$ denote the event that $\mathcal{A}$ wins in the corresponding game.

Game $G_{A.0}$. Is the original attack, with the simplifications about knowing $\mathsf{id}_{\mathsf{Test}}$ and id' at the beginning and corrupting all long-term keys at the outset.

Game $G_{A.1}$. Modify the game and replace the internally used Diffie-Hellman value g^{xy} in the two main executions of $\mathsf{id}_{\mathsf{Test}}$ and id' by a random value g^z. A simple reduction to the DDH problem shows that this cannot decrease the adversary's success probability in the key secrecy game $G_{A.1}$ by more than the advantage against the DDH problem:

$$\mathrm{Prob}[\,G_{A.0}\,] \leq \mathrm{Prob}[\,G_{A.1}\,] + \mathbf{Adv}_{\mathbb{G},\mathcal{D}}^{DDH}.$$

The reduction $\mathcal{D}$ receives (g^x, g^y, g^z) as input, runs the entire key exchange attack with $\mathcal{A}$, also picking the test bit b, and inserts g^x and g^y into the test session $\mathsf{id_{Test}}$ as well as the partner session id' on the honest parties side. But when both parties are supposed to compute g^{xy} reduction $\mathcal{D}$ uses g^z instead. Eventually, $\mathcal{D}$ checks if $\mathcal{A}$ succeeds in predicting b and does not lose. Algorithm $\mathcal{D}$ outputs 1 if this is the case. Note that if $g^z = g^{xy}$ we perfectly simulate $G_{A.0}$ whereas for a random g^z we perfectly simulate $G_{A.1}$. It follows that the difference in probabilities is bounded by the advantage against the DDH problem (for the admissible group $\mathbb{G}$ used in the execution).

Game $G_{A.2}$. Replace all output values in the HKDF evaluations (after, and including the computation of $HS \leftarrow \mathsf{HKDF.Extract}(xES, g^z)$) in the two main executions of sessions $\mathsf{id_{Test}}$ and id' by random values. This includes the Expand calls to derive SS, server_finished_key, CS, client_finished_key, xHS, RMS and SATS as well as CATS, but also the Extract step to compute MS. Finally, we also replace the derived data client_write_key, client_write_iv, and $\mathsf{CATS^{ku}}$ from CATS, and server_write_key, server_write_iv, and $\mathsf{SATS^{ku}}$ from SATS by random values. Note that we can already replace the keys $\mathsf{CATS^{ku}}$ and $\mathsf{SATS^{ku}}$ as if they were computed, although we have not yet shown that they are actually derived; this will be shown below.

The proof replaces all the key values step wise, starting with computation of HS from the input source g^z, such that we can argue that the derivation of SS from the now random HS via Expand can be substituted by picking SS randomly etc. In each of the in total 16 steps we have an input distribution D_i and a distinguisher $\mathcal{D}_i$ such that we can show that the winning difference in each step is bounded by $\mathbf{Adv}^{\mathrm{prf}}_{\mathsf{HKDF.Extract/Expand},\mathcal{D}_i}$. Altogether we thus have

$$\mathrm{Prob}\left[G_{A.1}\right] \leq \mathrm{Prob}\left[G_{A.2}\right] + \sum_{i=1}^{16} \mathbf{Adv}^{\mathrm{prf}}_{\mathsf{HKDF.Extract/Expand},D_i,\mathcal{D}_i}.$$

In particular, we now have that CATS and SATS and the channel key-iv values derived from them, as well as $\mathsf{CATS^{ku}}$ and $\mathsf{SATS^{ku}}$, are random keys which are independent of the protocol messages between $\mathsf{id_{Test}}$ and id'.

Game $G_{A.3}$. Declare the adversary to lose if it successfully executes the key update in the sub flow of session $\mathsf{id_{Test}}$ or id' with $\mathsf{id_{Test}.sub.sid} \neq \mathsf{id}'.\mathsf{sub.sid}$. Note that the adversary can only make any of the two sessions accept if it sends a valid record layer message to the corresponding party, either under the now random channel key-nonce pair client_write_key, client_write_iv or server_write_key, server_write_iv. The adversary may first receive a message under the other key from the honest client or server before producing a successful forgery against the other party's key. We can simulate this by a single query before creating the forgery which is admissible in the integrity game. But then we give a reduction $\mathcal{B}$ to the security of either of the two keys, such that

$$\mathrm{Prob}\left[G_{A.2}\right] \leq \mathrm{Prob}\left[G_{A.3}\right] + 2 \cdot \mathbf{Adv}^{\mathrm{int}}_{\mathsf{AEAD},\mathcal{B}}.$$

Here we use that Reveal queries do not reveal the intermediate keys and only give reasonable answers after completion of the entire execution.

We finally note that, in this game, sessions $\mathsf{id}_{\mathsf{Test}}$ and id' can only complete the sub flow execution if the adversary relays the communication between the two sessions which update the keys to $\mathsf{CATS}^{\mathsf{ku}}$ and $\mathsf{SATS}^{\mathsf{ku}}$. In particular, the adversary cannot Reveal the session key in session id' since it is partnered with the test session in both flows.

In the final game the adversary has no advantage to predict the secret bit b because this game does not depend on b anymore; the final session keys are independent random values in both cases. It follows that $\mathrm{Prob}[G_{A.3}] \leq \frac{1}{2}$.

Case B: Passive in Sub Flow, $\mathsf{id}'.\mathsf{sub}.\mathsf{sid} = \mathsf{id}_{\mathsf{Test}}.\mathsf{sub}.\mathsf{sid}$. Note that this stipulates that $\mathsf{id}'.\mathsf{main}.\mathsf{sid} \neq \mathsf{id}_{\mathsf{Test}}.\mathsf{sub}.\mathsf{sid}$ or else we are again in case A. But then, since the session identifier in the main flow contains exactly the data entering the transcript hash, we can conclude that key derivation uses different inputs, at least if we assume collision resistance of the hash function:

$G_{B.0}$. Is the simplified starting attack as above.

$G_{B.1}$. As game $G_{B.0}$ but declare the adversary to lose if $\mathsf{H}(\mathsf{id}_{\mathsf{Test}}.\mathsf{main}.\mathsf{sid}) = \mathsf{H}(\mathsf{id}'.\mathsf{main}.\mathsf{sid})$. This would immediately contradict the collision-resistance, i.e., we can give a reduction $\mathcal{C}$ such that

$$\mathrm{Prob}[G_{B.0}] \leq \mathrm{Prob}[G_{B.1}] + \mathbf{Adv}_{\mathsf{H},\mathcal{C}}^{\mathrm{coll}}.$$

$G_{B.2}$. As game $G_{B.1}$ but declare the adversary to lose if $\mathsf{id}_{\mathsf{Test}}$ or id' accept. We can again give a reduction $\mathcal{E}$ against the correlation intractability of the AEAD scheme (in combination with HKDF). Adversary $\mathcal{E}$ can impersonate the client resp. server in the sessions $\mathsf{id}_{\mathsf{Test}}$ and id' such that it knows the keys MS_{Test} and MS' on both sides. These keys may or may not match. But for sure the transcript hashes do not match by the previous game hop, such that we obtain key derivation inputs $(MS_{\mathsf{Test}}, x) \neq (MS', x')$ which the (relayed) sub flow would make both sides accept. This, however, would contradict the correlation integrity of the AEAD scheme:

$$\mathrm{Prob}[G_{B.1}] \leq \mathrm{Prob}[G_{B.2}] + \mathbf{Adv}_{\mathsf{AEAD},\mathsf{HKDF},\mathcal{E}}^{\mathrm{corr}}.$$

In the final game it follows that neither party $\mathsf{id}_{\mathsf{Test}}$ nor id' has accepted, such that the adversary cannot do any better than guessing the bit b:

$$\mathrm{Prob}[G_{B.2}] \leq \frac{1}{2}.$$

Case C: Active in Both Flows But Acting Independently. Finally, we need to argue that A/A attacker cannot predict the bit b significantly beyond guessing it. For this consider the test session $\mathsf{id}_{\mathsf{Test}}$ as before. We assume that there is no other flow with identical session identifier, neither in the main step nor in the sub flow. Else we would be already in cases A or B.

First note that, once the test session $\mathsf{id}_{\mathsf{Test}}$ has been started by $\mathcal{A}_{\mathrm{main}}$, the sub adversaries cannot exchange information through Sync calls, nor via any other oracle calls during the lifetime of session $\mathsf{id}_{\mathsf{Test}}$. It follows that the main flow uses random inputs such as the party's nonce to compute the transcript hash $\mathsf{H}(\mathsf{CH}\|\mathsf{SH}\|\dots)$. We can therefore cast this input to HKDF.Expand via some distribution $D'(x;r)$ where the r part describes the honest party's contribution to the transcript, and x the contribution of $\mathcal{A}_{\mathsf{main}}$, possibly chosen adaptively. Note that, while the transcript hash has no entropy from $\mathcal{A}_{\mathsf{main}}$'s point of view, for $\mathcal{A}_{\mathsf{sub}}$ it is still unknown, because no information flows from $\mathcal{A}_{\mathsf{main}}$ to $\mathcal{A}_{\mathsf{sub}}$.

We next define the following game hops:

$G_{C.0}$. Is the attack as above.

$G_{C.1}$. As game $G_{C.0}$ but declare $\mathcal{A}$ to lose if the sub flow in $\mathsf{id}_{\mathsf{Test}}$ accepts.

It follows from the pseudorandomness of HKDF.Expand for the transcript-hash input distribution D' above that we can replace CATS and SATS computed over the transcript in the moment when $\mathcal{A}_{\mathsf{sub}}$ is active in $\mathsf{id}_{\mathsf{Test}}$ by random values. We argue that the probability that $\mathcal{A}_{\mathsf{sub}}$ makes the sub flow accept cannot change significantly, else we derive a contradiction to the pseudorandomness of HKDF.Expand via some reduction $\mathcal{D}'$. Note that for this we merely need to wait for $\mathcal{A}_{\mathsf{sub}}$ to make the sub flow accept or to hand over to $\mathcal{A}_{\mathsf{main}}$ again (or abort the execution).

Once we have replaced the traffic application secrets by random values we immediately get a reduction $\mathcal{B}'$ to the integrity of AEAD, as in Case A. Hence,

$$\mathrm{Prob}\,[G_{C.0}] \leq \mathrm{Prob}\,[G_{C.1}] + \mathbf{Adv}^{\mathrm{prf}}_{\mathsf{HKDF.Expand},D',\mathcal{D}'} + \mathbf{Adv}^{\mathrm{corr}}_{\mathsf{AEAD},\mathsf{HKDF},\mathcal{B}'}.$$

In the final game the adversary $\mathcal{A}_{\mathsf{sub}}$ does not make the sub flow accept. It follows that $\mathcal{A}$ does not learn any information about b from the Test query (since the session key is not set). It follows that the probability of predicting b is bounded by $\frac{1}{2}$.

Summing over all possibilities yields the claimed bound. $\square$

4.4   Sub Flow Resumption

Instead of using the simple key update procedure we may alternatively use resumption to update the keys over the sub flow. The advantage is that all TLS 1.3 keys are updated by this, not only the application traffic secrets. The security argument would be very similar to the one above, only that we need to take the key RMS into account.

A noteworthy point is that we can actually relax the correlation integrity condition on the AEAD scheme if we run resumption in the mode with the (EC)DHE step. In this case the sub flow would create a fresh Diffie-Hellman share in the sub flow as well, and we can argue that in Case B with relayed sub flow the adversary thus cannot distinguish the derived keys from random, just as we argue along the DDH assumption for passive adversaries in the main flow.

4.5   Practical Considerations

We discuss here some aspects when running the above multipath TLS 1.3 version. The first thing to note is that, in order to take advantage of the stronger security guarantees, the parties need to ensure that the communication of the update step is routed through the second communication channel. Luckily, even if the parties are not aware of this, or cannot ensure this, they can still rely on the basic security of TLS 1.3. Hence, from a security viewpoint the failure of using multiple communication lines does not make our protocol insecure.

Concerning efficiency observe that MPTCP in principle allows for parallel communication through the different channels. Our protocol, on the other hand, needs to complete the regular handshake execution before being able to run the update via the other communication line.

Next suppose that the key update step fails—if the handshake already fails then the protocol execution cannot be continued. At this point the two parties have already established a joint key via the handshake part. It may thus be tempting to still use that key. For security reasons and for compatibility it is nevertheless recommend to cautiously follow the TLS 1.3 specification [21] that the connection must be closed.

5 Conclusions

We have shown that update steps in key exchange protocols can be used to provide multipath security. We have discussed this specifically for the case of TLS 1.3, assuming that one can reliably assign protocol messages to communication paths. An interesting question is to analyze what kind of security can still be achieved if some of the messages may be unexpectedly transmitted over the other path. Also, we have not investigated the possibility of 0RTT modes and the security of the intermediate session keys. Note that any cryptographic analysis of 0RTT modes must take into account the possibility of replay attacks [12].

Our security analysis provides a non-tight security bound with respect to the underlying cryptographic primitives, in the sense that the key secrecy bound depends quadratically on the number s of sessions. Furthermore, we work in the single-test setting, and a potential hybrid argument to extend this to the multi-test setting would incur another factor s. Recent efforts for TLS 1.3 [6,7], however, have shown that it is possible to derive tight security bounds. It would be interesting to see if this is applicable here in the split adversary model as well.

Another interesting question is how smoothly one can use multipath connections. The work by Costea et al. [5] already provides a comprehensive set of experiments, indicating that it is doable in practice. It remains to investigate if this is also true for applications which rely on fast connection times of TLS 1.3, inciting the development of 0RTT modes.

Acknowledgments. We thank the anonymous reviewers for valuable comments. Marc Fischlin has been [co-]funded by the Deutsche Forschungsgemeinschaft (DFG) – SFB 1119 – 236615297.

A Transport Layer Security

Figure 4 depicts the basic TLS 1.3 anonymous (EC)DHE handshakes including the essential steps of the Diffie–Hellman-based key derivation. The key update step has already been explained in Sect. 2.2. A session resumption is similar to the handshake but adds some additional steps. It requires the server to have

Client | **Server**

$r_c \xleftarrow{\$} \{0,1\}^{256}$

$X \xleftarrow{\$} g^x$

ClientHello : r_c

ClientKeyShare : X →

$r_s \xleftarrow{\$} \{0,1\}^{256}$

$Y \xleftarrow{\$} g^y$

$ES \leftarrow$ HKDF.Extract("", "")

$xES \leftarrow$ HKDF.Expand(ES, "derived")

$HS \leftarrow$ HKDF.Extract(xES, X^y)

$SS \leftarrow$ HKDF.Expand(HS, "s hs traffic"||H(CH|| ... ||SKS))

server_finished_key ← HKDF.Expand(SS, "finished")

SF ← HMAC(server_finished_key, H(CH|| ... ||EE))

← ServerHello : r_s

ServerKeyShare : Y

{EncryptedExtensions*}

{ServerFinished}

$ES \leftarrow$ HKDF.Extract("", "")

$xES \leftarrow$ HKDF.Expand(ES, "derived")

$HS \leftarrow$ HKDF.Extract(xES, Y^x)

compute SS, server_finished_key

check SF

$CS \leftarrow$ HKDF.Expand(HS, "c hs traffic"||H(CH|| ... ||SKS))

client_finished_key ← HKDF.Expand(CS, "finished")

CF ← HMAC(client_finished_key, H(CH|| ... ||SF))

{ClientFinished} →

check CF

$xHS \leftarrow$ HKDF.Expand(HS, "derived")

$MS \leftarrow$ HKDF.Extract("", xHS)

$RMS \leftarrow$ HKDF.Expand(MS, "res master"||H(CH|| ... ||CF))

client_application_traffic_secret ← HKDF.Expand(MS, "c ap traffic"||H(CH|| ... ||SF))

server_application_traffic_secret ← HKDF.Expand(MS, "s ap traffic"||H(CH|| ... ||SF))

Fig. 4. The TLS 1.3 anonymous (EC)DHE handshake protocol. Starred messages are situation-dependent and not always sent. Messages enclosed in curly brackets are protected by the handshake traffic secrets CS resp. SS.

issued a ticket to the client containing a nonce and identifying information which are used for the resumption handshake. The client uses an additional extension `ClientPreSharedKey` in the first message to indicate potential identifiers. The server acknowledges one in its `ServerPreSharedKey` extension with the second message. The parties then use the resumption secret RMS from before to compute a pre-shared key PSK, which this time enters the computation $ES \leftarrow$ HKDF.Extract($""$, PSK). They also derive a binder key BK which is used to verify the key. From there on the steps are identical to the one of a handshake execution. We note that resumption can be executed with and without the Diffie-Hellman step.

References

1. Bellare, M., Pointcheval, D., Rogaway, P.: Authenticated key exchange secure against dictionary attacks. In: Preneel, B. (ed.) EUROCRYPT 2000. LNCS, vol. 1807, pp. 139–155. Springer, Heidelberg (2000). https://doi.org/10.1007/3-540-45539-6_11
2. Bellare, M., Rogaway, P.: Entity authentication and key distribution. In: Stinson, D.R. (ed.) CRYPTO 1993. LNCS, vol. 773, pp. 232–249. Springer, Heidelberg (1994). https://doi.org/10.1007/3-540-48329-2_21
3. Canetti, R., Krawczyk, H.: Analysis of key-exchange protocols and their use for building secure channels. In: Pfitzmann, B. (ed.) EUROCRYPT 2001. LNCS, vol. 2045, pp. 453–474. Springer, Heidelberg (2001). https://doi.org/10.1007/3-540-44987-6_28
4. de Carnavalet, X.C., Mannan, M.: Killed by proxy: analyzing client-end TLS interception software. In: 23rd Annual Network and Distributed System Security Symposium, NDSS 2016, San Diego, California, USA, 21–24 February 2016. The Internet Society (2016)
5. Costea, S., Choudary, M.O., Gucea, D., Tackmann, B., Raiciu, C.: Secure opportunistic multipath key exchange. In: Lie, D., Mannan, M., Backes, M., Wang, X. (eds.) Proceedings of the 2018 ACM SIGSAC Conference on Computer and Communications Security, CCS 2018, Toronto, ON, Canada, 15–19 October 2018, pp. 2077–2094. ACM (2018)
6. Davis, H., Günther, F.: Tighter proofs for the SIGMA and TLS 1.3 key exchange protocols. IACR Cryptol. ePrint Arch. 2020, 1029 (2020). https://eprint.iacr.org/2020/1029
7. Diemert, D., Jager, T.: On the tight security of TLS 1.3: theoretically-sound cryptographic parameters for real-world deployments. IACR Cryptol. ePrint Arch. 2020, 726 (2020). https://eprint.iacr.org/2020/726
8. Dowling, B., Fischlin, M., GÄnther, F., Stebila, D.: A cryptographic analysis of the TLS 1.3 handshake protocol. Cryptology ePrint Archive, Report 2020/1044 (2020). https://eprint.iacr.org/2020/1044
9. Dowling, B., Fischlin, M., Günther, F., Stebila, D.: A cryptographic analysis of the TLS 1.3 handshake protocol candidates. In: Ray, I., Li, N., Kruegel, C. (eds.) Proceedings of the 22nd ACM SIGSAC Conference on Computer and Communications Security, Denver, CO, USA, 12–16 October 2015, pp. 1197–1210. ACM (2015)
10. Evans, C., Palmer, C., Sleevi, R.: Public key pinning extension for HTTP. RFC 7469, April 2015. https://rfc-editor.org/rfc/rfc7469.txt

11. Fischlin, M., Günther, F.: Multi-stage key exchange and the case of Google's QUIC protocol. In: Ahn, G., Yung, M., Li, N. (eds.) Proceedings of the 2014 ACM SIGSAC Conference on Computer and Communications Security, Scottsdale, AZ, USA, 3–7 November 2014, pp. 1193–1204. ACM (2014)

12. Fischlin, M., Günther, F.: Replay attacks on zero round-trip time: the case of the TLS 1.3 handshake candidates. In: 2017 IEEE European Symposium on Security and Privacy, EuroS&P 2017, Paris, France, 26–28 April 2017, pp. 60–75. IEEE (2017). https://doi.org/10.1109/EuroSP.2017.18

13. Ford, A., Raiciu, C., Handley, M.J., Bonaventure, O., Paasch, C.: TCP extensions for multipath operation with multiple addresses. RFC 8684, March 2020. https://rfc-editor.org/rfc/rfc8684.txt

14. Georgiev, M., Iyengar, S., Jana, S., Anubhai, R., Boneh, D., Shmatikov, V.: The most dangerous code in the world: validating SSL certificates in non-browser software. In: Yu, T., Danezis, G., Gligor, V.D. (eds.) The ACM Conference on Computer and Communications Security, CCS 2012, Raleigh, NC, USA, 16–18 October 2012, pp. 38–49. ACM (2012)

15. Katz, J., Lindell, Y.: Introduction to Modern Cryptography, 2nd edn. CRC Press, Boca Raton (2014)

16. Krawczyk, D.H., Eronen, P.: HMAC-based extract-and-expand key derivation function (HKDF). RFC 5869, May 2010. https://rfc-editor.org/rfc/rfc5869.txt

17. Krawczyk, H.: Cryptographic extraction and key derivation: the HKDF scheme. In: Rabin, T. (ed.) CRYPTO 2010. LNCS, vol. 6223, pp. 631–648. Springer, Heidelberg (2010). https://doi.org/10.1007/978-3-642-14623-7_34

18. Langley, A.: Apple's SSL/TLS bug. ImperialViolet (2014). https://www.imperialviolet.org/2014/02/22/applebug.html

19. Laurie, B., Langley, A., Kasper, E.: Certificate transparency. RFC 6962, June 2013. https://rfc-editor.org/rfc/rfc6962.txt

20. Menn, J.: E-mail breach in Iran raises surveillance fears. Financial Times, 31 August 2011 (2011)

21. Rescorla, E.: The Transport Layer Security (TLS) Protocol Version 1.3. RFC 8446, August 2018. https://rfc-editor.org/rfc/rfc8446.txt

22. Rogaway, P.: Authenticated-encryption with associated-data. In: Atluri, V. (ed.) Proceedings of the 9th ACM Conference on Computer and Communications Security, CCS 2002, Washington, DC, USA, 18–22 November 2002, pp. 98–107. ACM (2002)

SyLPEnIoT: Symmetric Lightweight Predicate Encryption for Data Privacy Applications in IoT Environments

Tran Viet Xuan Phuong[1(✉)], Willy Susilo[1], Guomin Yang[1], Jongkil Kim[1], Yang-Wai Chow[1], and Dongxi Liu[2]

[1] Institute of Cybersecurity and Cryptology, School of Computing and Information Technology, University of Wollongong, Wollongong, Australia
{wsusilo,gyang,jongkil,caseyc}@uow.edu.au
[2] Data61, CSIRO, Syndey, Australia
Dongxi.Liu@data61.csiro.au

Abstract. Privacy preserving mechanisms are essential for protecting data in IoT environments. This is particularly challenging as IoT environments often contain heterogeneous resource-constrained devices. One method for protecting privacy is to encrypt data with a pattern or metadata. To prevent information leakage, an evaluation using the pattern must be performed before the data can be retrieved. However, the computational costs associated with typical privacy preserving mechanisms can be costly. This makes such methods ill-suited for resource-constrained devices, as the high energy consumption will quickly drain the battery. This work solves this challenging problem by proposing SyLPEnIoT – Symmetric Lightweight Predicate Encryption for IoT, which is lightweight and efficient compared with existing encryption schemes. Based on the bitwise-XOR operation, we use this basic gate to construct a scheme that transfers encrypted data onto more powerful machines. Furthermore, for resource-constrained IoT devices, the requester can authenticate devices at different levels based on the type of communication. SyLPEnIoT was meticulously designed to run on a gamut of IoT devices, including ultra low-power sensors that are constrained in terms of CPU processing, memory and energy consumption, which are widely deployed in real IoT ecosystems.

1 Introduction

The Internet of Things (IoT) was recognized as one of the Gartner Hype Cycle's emerging technologies in 2018. IoT devices are getting increasingly popular, and are hence becoming a core element in the next generation of information and communication architectures, e.g., smart cities, smart factories, smart homes, smart healthcare systems and many others. Current statistics show that there are 30 billion objects connected to the Internet due to IoT technology [13].

IoT systems comprise of heterogeneous embedded devices with limited computing capacity and battery power, such as sensors and actuators. They can

E. Bertino et al. (Eds.): ESORICS 2021, LNCS 12973, pp. 106–126, 2021.
https://doi.org/10.1007/978-3-030-88428-4_6

only afford lightweight computation to conserve their energy. The search for advanced cryptographic solutions for IoT devices remains an intriguing problem due to these restrictions, i.e. heterogeneity and limited resources.

◇ **Motivating Scenarios.** To improve the body's health, many people wear smart watches to track things like walking time, heart rate, blood pressure, and so on. Data collected from a user's smart watch is sent to the cloud for storage. This data can be retrieved and analyzed at a later stage based on a selection criteria, such as data type or time window, through a specific application program on a user's mobile device. However, user health data is sensitive, and requires a data privacy mechanism in place to protect the data. In practice, there is a lot of information that can be collected by a smart watch on a daily basis. This requires large storage space and results in increased latency when retrieving data for IoT devices. When using a mobile device to query the collected data stored in the cloud, the user may only want specific information, such as heart rate, blood pressure, or GPS location. As the amount of data can be very large, a secure mechanism is required to evaluate the specific data before downloading and decrypting it.

Some representative topics include secure search over encrypted data [14,17, 37] and enhanced data privacy in range queries [33–35], which enable interesting applications in IoT infrastructure. Existing research has demonstrated that the heterogeneity of IoT devices, as well as the data they produce, are further aggravated by the lack of metadata associated with these devices [5]. Therefore, the use of privacy computational methods is often very challenging due to the type of device, the nature of the data being produced, and their compatibility for secure data integration tasks.

◇ **Security and Resource Constraints.** IoT technology enables connections among various things, including sensors, actuators, and their compositions, for applications ranging from connected vehicles to online services and social networks. Hence, in typical IoT environments, many different types of processors with various resource constraints are embedded in IoT devices. For example, based on the wearable devices and low-cost environmental sensors categorized on the official NXP website [28], the ARM Cortex-53 processor and the ARM-Cortex M3/M4 are the main processors embedded in smartphones and wearable devices, respectively. In addition, there are recent low-power and ultra low-power micro-controllers, such as the 32-bit ARM Cortex-M0+ processor, which is very heavily resource-constrained. As such, security issues are increasingly challenging when it comes to these low resource devices. There will definitely be trade-offs in the design of new cryptographic algorithms in theory and when deploying them on these devices in practice. In general, although solutions to the aforementioned problems have been developed by the cryptographic research community in recent years, existing solutions require resource intensive computations, which make them impractical for IoT environments. These two requirements seem contradictory, as advanced cryptographic algorithms usually require expensive computation (such as pairing), while IoT devices can only cope with simple algorithms to reduce energy consumption. Driven by practical requirements, in this paper we aim to bridge the gap between the need for constructing such advanced cryptographic algorithms and the capabilities of lightweight IoT devices. To achieve this, we aimed to produce a predicate encryption scheme to support lightweight computation. The reason why we targeted predicate encryption, is because it can support complex and expressive inner product queries.

◇ **Predicate Encryption.** Predicate Encryption (PE) [9,22] is a promising candidate to address the problems of search and pattern matching on encrypted data. A PE scheme allows the owner to create a master secret key and to issue secret key tokens to other users. Tokens are associated with predicates that can be evaluated over encrypted data. Specifically, encrypted data x can be evaluated using a token TK_f associated with a predicate f to determine whether $f(x) = 1$. In the IoT scenario that was previously shown in Fig. 1, a smart watch encrypts the data, while a mobile device has the token to decrypt it. The devices can share the master key, since they are owned by the same user. The use of symmetric PE on the client's side is sufficient for users to preserve the privacy of their private data. While the underlying strategy of our method is based on the PE in [22], the purpose of our method is for lightweight symmetric PE.

The implementation of this type of encryption gives rise to a practical problem, which prevents clients from efficiently accessing and using their data. Specifically, Katz et al.'s [22] proposed PE is based on composite bilinear pairing order groups introduced by [15], which is inefficient when it comes to computation on lightweight devices. As shown in [15], the pairing operation in composite order groups requires extensive computational power. To evaluate the computational cost of [22], we conducted an experiment to test the encryption and decryption times of an arbitrary binary vector on a Raspberry Pi 3 Model B V1.2 with an ARM Cortex-A53 processor. As depicted in Fig. 1, the encryption and decryption times increase linearly with vector length. It is impractical in real applications for the decryption process to take over 15 s for a 100-bit vector. Hence, the existing method is ill-suited for practical deployment in IoT environments. IoT devices with limited computational resources do not have sufficient capacity to realize current search or evaluation operations on encrypted data. Moreover, this method also increases the encrypted data storage requirements, which does not suit resource-constrained devices. The PE schemes in [9,22] are based on composite order bilinear pairing groups introduced by [15], which is too expensive for computation on resource-constrained devices.

To reduce the cost, Bishop et al. [7,23] proposed a function private secret-key PE scheme for the inner product functionality that supports any arbitrary polynomial number of key and message queries. The construction makes use of asymmetric bilinear maps for greater efficiency in reducing ciphertext and key sizes. Recently, due to the threat of quantum computers, the security of PE schemes is in jeopardy. Shor's efficient quantum algorithm [36] for discrete logarithms for elliptic curve groups can solve problems beyond integer factorization. It was shown that a 160-bit elliptic curve cryptographic key can be broken on a hypothetical quantum computer.

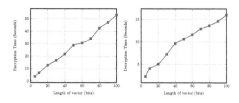

Fig. 1. Encryption and decryption times of [22] on a Raspberry Pi 3 with an ARM Cortex-A53 processor.

Whilst quantum computers pose a great threat to public key cryptography, the security of symmetric key cryptography remains unchanged. According to the evaluation criteria of the NIST Post Quantum Cryptography standardization project [27], hard lattice problems (e.g., Learning With Errors (LWE) [29,31]), and symmetric primitives (e.g., AES and PRF) are resistant to quantum attacks. In [2,7,18], LWE was used to construct PE schemes. Abdalla et al. [2] proposed Multi Input Functional Encryption for inner products under LWE assumptions, which is an instantiation of a single input PE construction. However, most PE schemes [2–4] constructed from the LWE problem are complex when it comes to generating the ciphertext and secret key, and are too computationally expensive for deployment on practical applications. In addition, in the new direction of lightweight constructions, PRF is considered to be a useful tool for dealing with many efficient protocols in [12,30]. Hence, an ideal PE scheme is conjectured to achieve both efficiency and quantum resistance, which uses PRF to construct PE schemes supporting inner products. This gives rise to the question:

"Can we utilize the fundamentals of symmetric primitives to construct a new efficient Predicate Encryption scheme for practical deployment on IoT environments?"

Therefore, our goal in this work is to construct a lightweight symmetric-key PE scheme that supports inner product queries.

1.1 Overview of SyLPEnIoT

This paper proposes SyLPEnIoT, a symmetric lightweight predicate encryption that accommodates resource constraints. SyLPEnIoT encrypts the message using a application-specific predicate, and generates the token using the query-specific predicate. When these two predicates match, the encrypted message is decrypted. In this work, we only investigate the symmetric scenario, where the key for encryption and the key for generation are agreed via a common key exchange protocol. Similar to [22], SyLPEnIoT uses the same master secret key to create the ciphertext and tokens. Let $\vec{v}$ be a non-zero vector, indicating the application-specific predicate, and $\vec{x}$ be a vector of the same length, indicating the query-specific predicate. SyLPEnIoT uses the exclusive-or operation as a critical component for reducing the high computational cost that current PE schemes suffer from. For this, we employ pseudo-random function and symmetric-key encryption primitives to realize our proposed scheme. In conjunction with the pseudo-random function, we exploit the exclusive-or ($\oplus$) operation to compute the inner product of two vectors ($\vec{v}, \vec{x}$) in a lightweight setting. However, using the $\oplus$ operation to determine the value of the inner product of two vectors is a challenging problem, since the inner product requires the sum of multiplications of each pairwise number between two vectors. Moreover, the predicates $\vec{v}$ and $\vec{x}$ must be kept secret in the cloud, making it more challenging to compute their inner product using the XOR gate.

Our Strategy. We will illustrate our strategy with the following two examples; the first case is when the inner product of two vectors is NON-ZERO, while the second case is when the inner product of two vectors is ZERO.

The Inner Product of Two Vectors Equals to NON-ZERO.

$$\vec{v} = (1_1, 0_2, 1_3, 0_4), \vec{x} = (1_1, 1_2, 0_3, 0_4).$$

We consider two binary vectors $\vec{v}$, and $\vec{x}$. Obviously, the inner product of the two vectors does not equal to zero, since $v_1 = x_1 = 1$ at position *one*. Rather than relying on the usual inner product computation between two vectors, i.e. $\sum_{i=1}^{4} v_i \cdot x_i = 1$, we only require computation using the $\oplus$ gate. We propose a way to detect whether there exists at least one position i, where $v_i = x_i = 1$, as the existence of $v_i = 1, x_i = 1$ leads to a non-zero inner product between two vectors.

Suppose that there is a Pseudo-Random Function $\mathsf{PRF} : \{0,1\} \times \{0,1\}^{\lambda} \rightarrow \{0,1\}^{\lambda}$ and a master secret key $\mathsf{SK} = \{0,1\}^{\lambda}$. We also need a typical symmetric-key encryption system SKE including the three main algorithms, namely, KeyGen, Encrypt, and Decrypt. Briefly, the KeyGen algorithm takes the security parameter λ as input and outputs a secret-key SK; the Encrypt algorithm takes a key SK and a plaintext x as input to perform encryption; the Decrypt algorithm takes a key SK and a ciphertext c as input and outputs the decrypted plaintext x.

We consider that $\vec{v}$ is generated in the ciphertext, and $\vec{x}$ is generated in the user's token. We then present our strategy for detecting whether the position i exists between the vector $\vec{v}$ and $\vec{x}$, where $v_i = x_i = 1$ for $i \in [1,4]$ in a secure manner using the PRF. The encoding function is computed as:

$$\delta_{ui} = \mathsf{PRF}(\mathsf{SK}, u||i) \tag{1}$$

where u is the arbitrary input, and i is the number.

With the input vector $\vec{v} = (1_1, 0_2, 1_3, 0_4)$, we generate the encoding as:

$$c = \delta_{11} \oplus \delta_{02} \oplus \delta_{13} \oplus \delta_{04}. \tag{2}$$

With the input vector $\vec{x}$ is $(1_1, 1_2, 0_3, 0_4)$, we similarly generate the encoding as:

$$t = \delta_{11} \oplus \delta_{12} \oplus \delta_{03} \oplus \delta_{04}. \tag{3}$$

However, when $c \oplus t = \delta_{02} \oplus \delta_{12} \oplus \delta_{13} \oplus \delta_{03}$ returns, the value at position *one* that we want to detect is unavailable. Therefore, our strategy is to transform the original $\vec{v} = (1_1, 0_2, 1_3, 0_4)$ to the complementary vector $\vec{v}' = (1_1 - 1_1, 1_2 - 0_2, 1_3 - 1_3, 1_4 - 0_4) = (0_1, 1_2, 0_3, 1_4)$, which leads to the new encoding for c:

$$c = \delta_{01} \oplus \delta_{12} \oplus \delta_{03} \oplus \delta_{14}. \tag{4}$$

In addition, we employ the wildcard symbol '*' to generate δ_{*i} to attach to the position where the original v_i equals to 1. This will conveniently enable to detect the positions i, where $v_i = x_i = 1$. Hence, c is regenerated as:

$$c = \delta_{*1} \oplus \delta_{01} \oplus \delta_{12} \oplus \delta_{*3} \oplus \delta_{03} \oplus \delta_{14}. \tag{5}$$

Then, we XOR c from (5) with t:

$$c \oplus t = \delta_{*1} \oplus \delta_{11} \oplus \delta_{01} \oplus \underbrace{\delta_{*3} \oplus \delta_{14} \oplus \delta_{04}}_{\text{redundant components}}. \tag{6}$$

Redundant Cancellation. From (6), we can extract the full-fledged values at position *one*. We also observe that at positions *three* and *four*, the value of $\vec{x}$ equals to *zero*. In the next step, we present the strategy on how to cancel out the values at positions *three* and *four*.

Based on the returned value of redundant components, we generate the adding component c_i' from $i = 1 \to 4$ based on the input value of the original $\vec{v} = (1_1, 0_2, 1_3, 0_4)$. If $v_i = 1$, it will set δ_{*i}. Otherwise, it sets $\delta_{1i} \oplus \delta_{0i}$. Then c_i' is as follows:

$$(c_1', c_2', c_3', c_4') = (\delta_{*1}, \delta_{12} \oplus \delta_{02}, \delta_{*3}, \delta_{14} \oplus \delta_{04}). \tag{7}$$

Furthermore, $\vec{x}$ is $(1_1, 1_2, 0_3, 0_4)$, we only select the positions i, where $x_i = 0$. As the observation from (5), we only extract c_3', c_4' at positions *three*, *four*, which is derived from the positions $x_3 = x_4 = 0$ of vector $\vec{x}$. Then, we compute:

$$c \oplus t \oplus c_3' \oplus c_4' = \delta_{*1} \oplus \delta_{11} \oplus \delta_{01}. \tag{8}$$

The aggregate $\oplus$ value at (8) equals non-zero, meaning that the inner product of two vectors, $\vec{v}$ and $\vec{x}$, is non-zero.

Collusion Resistance. Suppose that Alice queries $\vec{x}_1 = (1, 1, 0, 0)$ to get $t_A = \delta_{11} \oplus \delta_{12} \oplus \delta_{03} \oplus \delta_{04}$, with regards to the Eq. (3). In addition, when querying $\vec{x}_2 = (0, 0, 1, 1)$, Bob can obtain $t_B = \delta_{01} \oplus \delta_{02} \oplus \delta_{13} \oplus \delta_{14}$. Subsequently, even if the inner products of $<\vec{v}, \vec{x}_1>$, $<\vec{v}, \vec{x}_1>$ equal to non-zero, Alice and Bob together can produce t together through

$$t = t_A \oplus t_B = \delta_{11} \oplus \delta_{12} \oplus \delta_{03} \oplus \delta_{04} \oplus \delta_{01} \oplus \delta_{02} \oplus \delta_{13} \oplus \delta_{14}$$

Eventually, they can use the colluded value t to compute:

$$c_{(5)} \oplus t \oplus c_1' \oplus c_2' \oplus c_3' \oplus c_4' = 0.$$

To prevent such collusion attacks, we present a solution to achieve collusion resistance.

Based on the original equation of (4): $c = \delta_{01} \oplus \delta_{12} \oplus \delta_{03} \oplus \delta_{14}$, we reproduce $\hat{c}_i$ by separating each components in c:

$$\hat{c}_i = (\delta_{01}, \delta_{12}, \delta_{03}, \delta_{14}) \tag{9}$$

To prevent the collusion attack, in the generation of $\vec{x} = (1_1, 1_2, 0_3, 0_4)$ side, we uniformly sample $U_0, U_1, U_2 \xleftarrow{R}$ SKE.KeyGen(1^λ). Then, we add the component as

$$(\hat{t}_1, \hat{t}_2) = (\delta_{11} \oplus U_1, \delta_{12} \oplus U_2), \tag{10}$$

where we only consider the positions $i = \{1, 2\}$ in $\vec{x}$, which $x_1 = x_2 = 1$.

Then we set $t_0 = $ SKE.Encrypt($U_1 \oplus U_2, U_0$). We also XOR U_0 to t in (3)

$$t = \delta_{11} \oplus \delta_{12} \oplus \delta_{03} \oplus \delta_{04} \oplus U_0. \tag{11}$$

In the first step, we compute: $U_0' = \oplus_{i=1, x_i=1}^{\ell} \hat{t}_i \oplus \hat{c}_i = \hat{t}_1 \oplus \hat{c}_1 \oplus \hat{t}_2 \oplus \hat{c}_2$. Then use U_0' to decrypt t_0 to recover U_0 as $U_0'' = $ SKE.Decrypt(U_0', t_0).

We note that the SKE.Decrypt algorithm is deterministic, then we can use U_0'' to compute this later even though we do not know the exact value U_0.

Then, we achieve the computation similar to (8) as

$$c_{(5)} \oplus t_{(10)} \oplus c_3' \oplus c_4' \oplus U_0'' = \delta_{*1} \oplus \delta_{11} \oplus \delta_{01}. \tag{12}$$

Consequently, by adding the components $\hat{c}_i, \hat{t}_i$, even when the adversaries collude to attack the ciphertext corresponding to $\vec{v} = (1, 0, 1, 0)$, he/she attempts to make many queries as $\vec{x}_1 = (1, 1, 0, 0), \vec{x}_2 = (0, 0, 1, 1)$, ... Eventually, the aggregate values as in (12) cannot be canceled out.

Based on the strategy in case 1, with $\vec{v} = (1_1, 0_2, 1_3, 0_4)$, $\vec{x} = (1_1, 1_2, 0_3, 0_4)$ associated with the ciphertext generation and token generation, respectively, we also demonstrate the case where the inner product of two vectors, such as $\vec{v} = (1_1, 0_2, 1_3, 0_4)$ and $\vec{x} = (0_1, 1_2, 0_3, 0_4)$, equals to ZERO, in a more condensed manner.

The Inner Product of Two Vectors Equals to ZERO.

$$\vec{v} = (1_1, 0_2, 1_3, 0_4), \vec{x} = (0_1, 1_2, 0_3, 0_4).$$

Obviously, when the inner product of two vectors $\vec{v}, \vec{x}$ equals zero, there does not exist any pair of $v_i = x_i = 1$, where $i \in [1, 4]$. Having presented the strategy in case 1, we show the solution in case 2 compactly as.

Ciphertext Generation. From the original $\vec{v} = (1_1, 0_2, 1_3, 0_4)$, we generate the complementary vector $\vec{v}'$ as $(1_1 - 1_1, 1_2 - 0_2, 1_3 - 1_3, 1_4 - 0_4) = (0_1, 1_2, 0_3, 1_4)$. Then we apply $c_{(5)}, (c_i')_{(7)}, \hat{c}_{i(9)}$ to generate $c, c_i', \hat{c}_i$ for $i \in [1, 4]$ as follows:

$$\hat{c}_i = (\delta_{01}, \delta_{12}, \delta_{03}, \delta_{04}), c = \delta_{*1} \oplus \delta_{01} \oplus \delta_{12} \oplus \delta_{*3} \oplus \delta_{03} \oplus \delta_{14},$$

$$c_i' = (\delta_{*1}, \delta_{12} \oplus \delta_{02}, \delta_{*3}, \delta_{14} \oplus \delta_{04})$$

Token Generation. From $\vec{x} = (0_1, 1_2, 0_3, 0_4)$, we uniformly sample $U_0, U_2 \xleftarrow{R}$ SKE.KeyGen(1^λ). Then, we add the component on the side of $\vec{x}$ as $\hat{t}_i = \delta_{12} \oplus U_2$. Then, we apply (11) to generate t as follows: $t = \delta_{01} \oplus \delta_{12} \oplus \delta_{03} \oplus \delta_{04} \oplus U_0$, In addition, we create $t_0 = $ SKE.Encrypt(U_2, U_0).

Decryption. In the first step, we compute $U_0' = t_2 \oplus c_2$, where we only extract $\hat{c}_2$ in terms of $\hat{c}_i$. Then, we use U_0' to decrypt t_0 to recover U_0 as $U_0'' = $ SKE.Decrypt(U_0', t_0). In terms of c_i', we extract c_1', c_3', c_4', where we only consider positions $x_1 = x_3 = x_4 = 0$ in the token.

$$K = c \oplus t \oplus \underbrace{c_1' \oplus c_3' \oplus c_4'}_{x_1 = x_3 = x_4 = 0}$$
$$= \delta_{*1} \oplus \delta_{01} \oplus \delta_{12} \oplus \delta_{*3} \oplus \delta_{03} \oplus \delta_{14} \oplus \delta_{01} \oplus \delta_{12} \oplus \delta_{03} \oplus \delta_{04} \oplus U_0$$
$$\oplus \delta_{*1} \oplus \delta_{*3} \oplus \delta_{14} \oplus \delta_{04} \oplus U_0'' = 0$$

Since $U_0 = U_0''$, K equals to zero, meanwhile we can conclude that $<\vec{v}, \vec{x}> = 0$, which means that pairs of $(v_i = 1, x_i = 1)$ *do not exist* as $<\vec{v}, \vec{x}> = 0$.

1.2 Our Contributions

Main Contributions: We summarize our contributions as follows:

- Our SyLPEnioT scheme is based on the fundamental primitives of PRF and symmetric cryptography, which uses the exclusive-or operation to determine the inner product of two vectors, which will either evaluate to zero or non-zero. However, using an exclusive-or operation to determine the value of the inner product of two vectors is tricky, since the under-workings of an inner product requires summing the multiplications of each pairwise component between two vectors. In this work, we propose an encoding solution to evaluate the inner product between two binary vectors to determine whether it equals to zero. Therefore, SyLPEnioT provides a new lightweight construction from the original definition of PE [22] in the symmetric setting. We prove that SyLPEnioT is secure under the selective simulation-secure standard model against probabilistic polynomial-time adversaries that can make an unrestricted number of ciphertext generation and secret key generation queries.
- With the low-priced data storage and computation services offered by cloud providers, people outsource their large-scale data to the cloud to reduce their cost in spending on local devices.

Evaluations: We use SyLPEnioT to encrypt the pattern, generate the token, and in the decryption phase. We then integrated it on a spectrum of IoT devices. First, we ran it on a typical machine, i.e. a laptop. Second, we deployed it on a high-end IoT device, i.e. a Raspberry Pi 3 Model B V1.2 with an ARM Cortex-A53 processor. To prove our expressive SyLPEnioT model, we demonstrate its feasibility on an ultra low-power micro-controller of a typical device in the form of an Arduino Nano 33 IoT Board, which uses a 32-bit ARM Cortex-M0 CPU with 256 KB Flash and 16 KB RAM. In terms of the physical configuration, the Raspberry Pi 3's performance is an order of magnitude slower than the Laptop's performance, and its performance on the Arduino Nano 33 board is an additional two-to-three order of magnitude slower.

2 Related Work

Low-Powered Devices via Garbled Circuits. Kamara et al. [20] investigated garbled-circuit-based protocols, a set of mutually distrustful parties to evaluate a function of their joint inputs without revealing their inputs to each other. Later, Cater et al. [10] created a protocol that allows mobile devices to securely outsource the majority of computation required to evaluate a garbled circuit, which builds on the most efficient garbled circuit evaluation techniques.

Research on privacy-preserving wildcard pattern matching has become a hot topic in recent years. Hazay and Toft [19] showed that wildcard pattern matching can be converted to exact pattern matching using additive homomorphic encryption. However, their solution is impractical to deploy on resource-constrained IoT devices.

Predicate Encryption. A predicate encryption system [8, 9, 22, 23, 26, 34, 35] makes use of the bilinear/composite group order for the construction. In order to protect the predicate, Shi et al. [33] proposed predicate-only encryption. Moving a step forward, Abdalla et al. [1] propose a simple inner-product encryption scheme, meaning that decrypting an encrypted vector $\vec{v}$ with a key for a vector $\vec{y}$ will reveal only $<x, y>$ and nothing else. However, privacy of the predicate is not achieved. As a type of predicate encryption, a Hidden Vector Encryption (HVE) scheme [25, 32] supports equality test, which can include wildcard symbols. However, in HVE schemes, wildcard symbols will appear in the attribute string associated with the user secret key rather than that of the ciphertext. In another cryptographic primitive, Sergey et al. [18] constructed a leveled predicate encryption scheme for all circuits, assuming the hardness of the sub-exponential Learning With Errors (LWE) problem. In addition, Agrawal et al. [3] proposed a lattice-based functional encryption scheme for inner product predicates whose security follows from the difficulty of the LWE problem. This construction enables applications such as range and subset queries, polynomial evaluation, and CNF/DNF formulas on encrypted data. Gay et al. [16] produced a lattice-based predicate encryption scheme for multi-dimensional range and multi-dimensional subset queries. Lai et al. [24] proposed lightweight HVE to hide the pattern when boolean querying is issued [11]. Abdalla et al. [2] proposed a Multi Input Functional Encryption for inner products under the Decisional Diffie-Hellman (DDH), LWE, and Decisional Composite Residuosity (DCR) assumptions. Very recently, Agrawal et al. [4] constructed the inner product encryption, which achieves adaptive simulation-security for an unbounded number of key queries and a single challenge ciphertext under DDH, DCR, and LWE assumptions. Also, Katsumata et al. [21] proposed the lattice-based adaptively secure inner product encryption over integers $\mathbb{Z}$.

3   Background and Assumptions

3.1   SyLPEnIoT's Model and Threat Model

We consider the environment of an IoT system typically assumed in the literature, as depicted in Fig. 2. The system consists of three main entities: a lightweight device $\mathcal{A}$ such as the smart watch, a mobile device $\mathcal{B}$, and cloud storage provider $\mathcal{C}$. $\mathcal{A}$ encrypts message M, and $\mathsf{pattern}_{\vec{v}}$ using the key $\mathcal{K}$, then stores it in cloud $\mathcal{C}$. $\mathcal{B}$ will use $\mathsf{pattern}_{\vec{x}}$ and the key $\mathcal{K}$ for evaluation. We also note that key $\mathcal{K}$ is set up and managed by owners of mobile devices in any preferred way.

Fig. 2. Applying SyLPEnIoT to an IoT system.

On commencement, the smartwatch $\mathcal{A}$ uses $\mathsf{pattern}_{\vec{v}}$ and key $\mathcal{K}$ to generate the predicate ciphertext ($\mathsf{Enc}_{\mathcal{K}}(\vec{v})$), and generates a data ciphertext ($\mathsf{Enc}_{\mathcal{K}}(M)$) by encrypting the collected data M. The smartwatch uploads both predicate and data ciphertexts to a cloud server. Later, a mobile device $\mathcal{B}$ first downloads predicate ciphertext $\mathsf{Enc}_{\mathcal{K}}(\vec{v})$, and uses its predicate pattern $\mathsf{pattern}_{\vec{x}}$ and key $\mathcal{K}$ for evaluation. If the evaluation is true, which means $\mathsf{pattern}_{\vec{v}}$ matches $\mathsf{pattern}_{\vec{x}}$, $\mathcal{B}$ will download and decrypt the corresponding $\mathsf{Enc}_{\mathcal{K}}(M)$ and obtain the data M. Note that we aim to hide both the $\mathsf{pattern}_{\vec{v}}$ and data M from the cloud server, thus providing both predicate and data (or payload) privacy.

3.2   Definitions

Lightweight Symmetric-Key Predicate Encryption. Let Σ denote a set $\{0,1\}^{\ell}$, and $\mathcal{F}$ a finite set of predicates $f : \Sigma \rightarrow \{0,1\}$. We say that $v \in \Sigma$ satisfies a predicate f if $f_{\vec{x}}(\vec{v}) = 1$. Suppose that the input is described as a vector $\vec{v}$, and a predicate is defined as a vector $\vec{x}$, and the evaluation returns $f_{\vec{x}}(\vec{v}) = 1$ iff the inner product $<\vec{v}, \vec{x}> = 0$. A symmetric-key predicate encryption scheme for the class of predicates $\mathcal{F}$ over the set of binaries Σ consists of the following probabilistic polynomial time (PPT) algorithms.

- $\mathsf{Setup}(1^{\lambda}, \ell)$: The algorithm inputs the security parameter 1^{λ} and ℓ, and outputs a secret key SK.
- $\mathsf{Encryption}(\mathsf{SK}, \vec{v}, M)$: The algorithm inputs a secret key SK, a vector $\vec{v} \in \Sigma$, a message M, and outputs a ciphertext CT.
- $\mathsf{GenToken}(\mathsf{SK}, \vec{x})$: The algorithm inputs a secret key SK, a vector $\vec{x}$, and outputs a token TK.

– Decrypt(TK, CT): The algorithm inputs a token TK, and a ciphertext CT. It outputs M iff $<\vec{v}, \vec{x}> = 0$, and $\perp$ otherwise.

Correctness:
For all SK $\leftarrow$ Setup($1^\lambda, \ell$), all CT $\leftarrow$ Encryption(SK, $\vec{v}, M$), all TK $\leftarrow$ GenToken(SK, $\vec{x}$):

– If $<\vec{v}, \vec{x}> = 0$, Decrypt(TK, CT) $= M$;
– If $<\vec{v}, \vec{x}> \neq 0$, $Pr[\text{EvalThenDecrypt(TK,CT)} = \perp] \geq 1 - \text{negl}(\lambda)$;

where $\text{negl}(\lambda)$ is a negligible function in λ.

Security Definition. This section formally defines the security of our SyLPE-nIoT scheme. We define the notion Q_{Tkn} as the total number of token queries, and the notion Q_{Enc} as the total number of ciphertext queries.

Definition 1 *(Token Query Pattern). Given a query history* $(f_1, \ldots, f_{Q_{Tkn}})$ *of the SyLPEnIoT scheme, we set* $f_j = (x_{j,1}, \ldots, x_{j,\ell})$ *for each* $j \in [1, Q_{Tkn}]$, *where* ℓ *is the length of f in SyLPEnIoT. The token query pattern* $\alpha(f_1, \ldots, f_{Q_{Tkn}})$ *is a set of values*

$$\{\alpha_{i,j,k}\}_{i,j \in [1,Q_{Tkn}], k \in [1,\ell]} \ \textit{such that:} \ \alpha_{i,j,k} = \begin{cases} 1, & x_{i,k} = x_{j,k} \\ 0, & \textit{otherwise} \end{cases}, \ \textit{where} \ i, j \in$$

$[1, Q_{Tkn}], k \in [1, \ell]$.

Definition 2 *(Decryption Pattern). Let* CT *denote a ciphertext obtained upon encryption of plaintext* $(\mathcal{I}, M)$. *From the SyLPEnIoT scheme, it provides a query history* $(\mathcal{I}, M, f_1, \ldots, f_{Q_{Tkn}})$, *and a secret key* TK_{f_j} *corresponding to the predicate* f_j, *where* $j \in [1, Q_{Tkn}]$. *The output of decrypting* CT *using* TK_{f_j} *is a decryption pattern as a set of values* $\{\beta_j\}_{j \in [1, Q_{Tkn}]}$, *which is also defined as:*

$$\beta_j = \begin{cases} M, & f_j(\mathcal{I}) = 1 \\ \perp, & \textit{otherwise} \end{cases}, \ \textit{where} \ j \in [1, Q_{Tkn}].$$

We define the security notions of SyLPEnIoT scheme in the simulation setting, which analyze the security of SyLPEnIoT in a real experiment and a simulation experiment. In the real experiment, a probabilistic polynomial time algorithm $\mathcal{A}$ interacts with a challenger who knows the master key SK. Firstly, $\mathcal{A}$ invokes the ciphertext and token queries corresponding to the plaintext and predicate chosen by $\mathcal{A}$ to the challenger. In the experiment, a probabilistic polynomial time simulator algorithm $\mathcal{S}$ plays the challenger role, which only has access to the decryption pattern corresponding to the chosen query by $\mathcal{A}$, and has no permission to obtain the master secret key SK.

Selective Simulation-Secure SyLPEnIoT. We define the selective simulation security for SyLPEnIoT where the adversary must specify the entire query history non-adaptively at the beginning of both real and simulation experiments. For a security parameter $\lambda \in \mathbb{N}$, a SyLPEnIoT scheme with four algorithms (Setup, Encryption, GenToken, Decrypt), and a uniform probabilistic polynomial-time algorithm $\mathcal{A}$, we define the real and simulation experiments $\mathsf{Expt}^{sel,real}_{\mathsf{SyLPEnIoT},\mathcal{A}}(\lambda, n)$ as follows:

1. $\mathsf{SK} \xleftarrow{R} \mathsf{Setup}(1^\lambda)$
2. $((\mathcal{I}_1, M_1), \ldots, (\mathcal{I}_{Q_{\mathsf{Enc}}}, M_{Q_{\mathsf{Enc}}}), f_1, \ldots, f_{Q_{\mathsf{Tkn}}}) \xleftarrow{R} \mathcal{A}(1^\lambda)$
3. For $i \in [1, Q_{\mathsf{Enc}}]$, $\mathsf{CT}_i \xleftarrow{R} \mathsf{Encryption}(\mathsf{SK}, \mathcal{I}_i, M_i)$
4. For $j \in [1, Q_{\mathsf{Tkn}}]$, $\mathsf{TK}_{f_j} \xleftarrow{R} \mathsf{GenToken}(\mathsf{SK}, f_j)$
5. Output $(\{\mathsf{CT}_i\}_{i \in [1, Q_{\mathsf{Enc}}]}, \{\mathsf{TK}_{f_j}\}_{j \in [1, Q_{\mathsf{Tkn}}]})$,

where $Q_{\mathsf{Enc}}, Q_{\mathsf{Tkn}} \leq \mathsf{poly}(\lambda)$.

Let $\mathcal{S}$ be a uniform probabilistic polynomial-time simulator. We then define a second experiment $\mathsf{Expt}^{sel,sim}_{\mathsf{SyLPEnIoT},\mathcal{A}}(\lambda)$ as follows:

1. $((\mathcal{I}_1, M_1), \ldots, (\mathcal{I}_{Q_{\mathsf{Enc}}}, M_{Q_{\mathsf{Enc}}}), f_1, \ldots, f_{Q_{\mathsf{Tkn}}}) \xleftarrow{R} \mathcal{A}(1^\lambda)$
2. $\{\mathsf{CT}_i\}_{i \in [1, Q_{\mathsf{Enc}}]}, \{\mathsf{TK}_{f_j}\}_{j \in [1, Q_{\mathsf{Tkn}}]} \xleftarrow{R} \mathcal{S}(1^\lambda,$
   $\alpha(f_1, \ldots, f_{Q_{\mathsf{Tkn}}}), \beta(f_1, \ldots, f_{Q_{\mathsf{Tkn}}}))$
3. Output $(\{\mathsf{CT}_i\}_{i \in [1, Q_{\mathsf{Enc}}]}, \{\mathsf{TK}_{f_j}\}_{j \in [1, Q_{\mathsf{Tkn}}]})$.

Definition 3. *A SyLPEnIoT is selectively simulation-secure if for any uniform probabilistic polynomial-time algorithm $\mathcal{A}$, there exists a uniform probabilistic polynomial time simulator $\mathcal{S}$, such that the following ensemble distributions:*

$$(\{CT_i\}_{i \in [1, Q_{Enc}]}, \{TK_{f_j}\}_{j \in [1, Q_{Tkn}]}) \xleftarrow{R} \mathsf{Expt}^{sel,real}_{\mathsf{SyLPEnIoT},\mathcal{A}}(\lambda)$$

and $(\{CT_i\}_{i \in [1, Q_{Enc}]}, \{TK_{f_j}\}_{j \in [1, Q_{Tkn}]}) \xleftarrow{R} \mathsf{Expt}^{sel,sim}_{\mathsf{SyLPEnIoT},\mathcal{A},\mathcal{S}}(\lambda)$ are computationally indistinguishable.

4 Main Constructions in SyLPEnIoT

In this section, we first present our SyLPEnIoT construction in the standard model. Unlike existing PE constructions in the literature, our construction does not use bilinear pairings. Instead we use the following cryptographic primitives:

4.1 Pseudo-Random Function

A Pseudo-Random Function (PRF) is a polynomial time computable function $PRF : \{0,1\} \times \{0,1\}^\lambda \to \{0,1\}^\lambda$ such that for all polynomial-size algorithms $\mathcal{A}$:

$$|Pr[\mathcal{A}^{\mathsf{PRF}(K, \cdot)} = 1 : K \xleftarrow{R} \{0,1\}^\lambda] - Pr[\mathcal{A}^{g(\cdot)} = 1 : g \xleftarrow{R} \mathsf{Func}(\ell, m)]| \leq \mathsf{negl}(\lambda),$$

where the probabilities are taken over all possible choices of K and g.

4.2   Symmetric-Key Encryption

A symmetric-key encryption system SKE may be described as an ensemble of the following polynomial-time algorithms:

- SKE.KeyGen(1^λ): A probabilistic algorithm that takes the security parameter λ as input and outputs a secret-key SK.
- SKE.Encrypt(SK, s): A deterministic algorithm that takes as input a key SK and a plaintext x. It outputs a ciphertext c.
- SKE.Decrypt(SK, c): A deterministic algorithm that takes as input a key SK and a ciphertext c. It outputs the decrypted plaintext x.

4.3   Construction

In the construction, we use the definition of [22]; we take the class of attributes to be $\Sigma = \{0,1\}^\lambda \cup *$, and $\mathcal{F}$ a finite set of predicates $f : \Sigma \to \{0,1\}$. We say that $\mathcal{I} \in \Sigma$ satisfies a predicate f if $f(\mathcal{I}) = 1$. Suppose that the input $\mathcal{I}$ is described as a vector $\vec{v}$, and a predicate is defined as a vector $\vec{x}$. Then the evaluation returns the inner product $<\vec{v}, \vec{x}> = 0$, which means that $f(\mathcal{I}) = 1$. In addition, we assume a message space $\mathcal{M}$ is a small subset of $\{0,1\}^\lambda$, $|\mathcal{M}| < 2^\lambda/\mathrm{poly}(\lambda)$.

Our SyLPEnIoT scheme for the class of predicates $\mathcal{F}$ over the set of binaries Σ consists of the following probabilistic polynomial time (PPT) algorithms. Our construction utilizes a pseudo-random function: PRF : $\{0,1\} \times \{0,1\}^\lambda \to \{0,1\}^\lambda$, and a secure symmetric-key encryption SKE with the key-space $\{0,1\}^\lambda$, where $\lambda \in \mathbb{N}$ is the security parameter. This makes our construction more lightweight and efficiently implementable.

- Setup($1^\lambda, \ell$): On taking the security parameter λ and the fixed length ℓ of vectors as input, the setup algorithm samples SK $\leftarrow \{0,1\}^\lambda$, and outputs SK.
- Encryption(SK, $\vec{v}, M$): The encryption algorithm takes as input the secret key SK, a vector $\vec{v} = (v_1, \ldots, v_\ell) \in \{0,1\}$, and message M. First, with i from 0 to ℓ, the algorithm uniformly samples $K \xleftarrow{R} $ SKE.KeyGen(1^λ). Second, it generates the ciphertext as:

  1: **for** each $i \in [1, \ell]$ **do**

  2:   $\hat{c}_i = \begin{cases} \mathsf{PRF}(\mathsf{SK}, 1 - v_i || i), & \text{if } v_i = 1 \\ \mathsf{PRF}(\mathsf{SK}, 1 - v_i || i), & \text{otherwise} \end{cases}$

  3:   $c_i = \begin{cases} \mathsf{PRF}(\mathsf{SK}, * || i) \oplus \mathsf{PRF}(\mathsf{SK}, 1 - v_i || i), & \text{if } v_i = 1 \\ \mathsf{PRF}(\mathsf{SK}, 1 - v_i || i), & \text{otherwise} \end{cases}$

  4:   $c'_i = \begin{cases} \mathsf{PRF}(\mathsf{SK}, * || i), & \text{if } v_i = 1 \\ \mathsf{PRF}(\mathsf{SK}, 1 - v_i || i) \oplus \mathsf{PRF}(\mathsf{SK}, v_i || i), & \text{otherwise} \end{cases}$

  5: $c = \oplus_{i=1}^\ell c_i \oplus K$

  It then computes $c_0 = $ SKE.Encrypt(K, M). Finally, it produces the ciphertext as CT $= (c_0, c, \{\hat{c}_i, c'_i\}_{i \in [1, \ell]})$.

- GenToken(SK, $\vec{x}$): The algorithm takes as input the secret key SK, and a vector $\vec{x} = (x_1, \ldots, x_\ell) \in \{0,1\}$. With i from 1 to ℓ and $x_i = 1$, the algorithm uniformly samples $U_0, U_i \xleftarrow{R}$ SKE.KeyGen(1^λ). In addition, for i from 1 to ℓ and $x_i = 0$, it uniformly samples $R_i \xleftarrow{R} \{0,1\}^\lambda$. Next, the algorithm generates the token as:

  1: **for** each $i \in [1, \ell]$ **do**

  2: $\quad \hat{t}_i = \begin{cases} \mathsf{PRF}(\mathsf{SK}, x_i || i) \oplus U_i, & \text{if } x_i = 1 \\ R_i, & \text{otherwise} \end{cases}$

  3: $\quad t_i = \mathsf{PRF}(\mathsf{SK}, x_i || i)$

  4: $t = \oplus_{i=1}^{\ell} t_i \oplus U_0$

  It then sets $U_0' = \oplus_{i=1, x_i=1}^{\ell} U_i$, and computes $t_0 = \mathsf{SKE.Encrypt}(U_0', U_0)$. Then, the token is generated as: $\mathsf{TK} = (t_0, t, \{\hat{t}_i\}_{i \in [1,\ell]})$.

- Decrypt(TK, CT): the algorithm takes as input a ciphertext $\mathsf{CT} = (c_0, c, \{\hat{c}_i, c_i'\}_{i \in [1,\ell]})$ and a token $\mathsf{TK} = (t_0, t, \{\hat{t}_i\}_{i \in [1,\ell]})$. The decryption algorithm computes the following: $U_0' = \oplus_{i=1, x_i=1}^{\ell} \hat{t}_i \oplus \hat{c}_i$. Then uses U_0' to decrypt t_0 to recover U_0 as $U_0 = \mathsf{SKE.Decrypt}(U_0', U_0)$. Finally, it computes: $K = t \oplus c \oplus_{i=1, x_i=0}^{\ell} c_i' \oplus U_0$. $M = \mathsf{SKE.Decrypt}(K, c_0)$, which means that $<\vec{v}, \vec{x}> \; == 0$. Otherwise, the decryption outputs $\perp$.

Correctness. Consider a ciphertext $\mathsf{CT} = (c_0, c_1, c_2, \{c_i'\}_{i \in [1,\ell]})$ corresponding to $\vec{v}$, and a token $\mathsf{TK} = (t_1, t'')$ corresponding to $\vec{x}$. Hence, the correctness of the SyLPEnIoT scheme is established as follows:

1. If $<\vec{v}, \vec{x}> \; = 0$, then there does not exist any pair $(v_i = 1, x_i = 1)$. Firstly, we can recover the key U_0 correctly by computing $U_0' = \oplus_{i=1, x_i=0}^{\ell} \hat{t}_i \oplus \hat{c}_i$, and decrypting $U_0 = \mathsf{SKE.Decrypt}(U_0', U_0)$. Then $T = t \oplus c \oplus_{i=1, x_i=0}^{\ell} c_i' \oplus U_0 = K$, which in turn implies that $M = \mathsf{SKE.Decrypt}(T, c)$, Therefore $<\vec{v}, \vec{x}> \; = 0$, the payload message is recovered correctly.

2. If $<\vec{v}, \vec{x}> \; \neq 0$, then there exists at least a pair $(v_k = 1, x_k = 1)$. Subsequently, there is $x_k = 1$ with $t_k = \mathsf{PRF}(\mathsf{SK}, 1 || k)$, and $c_{x_k k} = \mathsf{PRF}(\mathsf{SK}, 0 || k) \oplus K_k$. Firstly, U_0 cannot be recovered successfully. If we keep using the uncorrected form U_0, the key K cannot be recovered successfully, and returns the message $M' = \mathsf{SKE.Decrypt}(K, c)$, which is a uniformly random string in $\{0,1\}^\lambda$. Since the payload message space $\mathcal{M}$ is assumed to be small, the probability of a uniformly random message M' lies in message space $\mathcal{M}$. Meanwhile, if $<\vec{v}, \vec{x}> \; \neq 0$, the decryption algorithm returns $\perp$ with overwhelming large probability.

Theorem 1. *The SyLPEnIoT scheme is selectively simulation-secure in the standard model under the assumption that PRF is a pseudo-random function.*

5   Evaluation

5.1   Microbenchmarks

The first benchmark was produced on a DELL laptop with an Intel Core I7-7820HQ CPU @ 2.90 GHz. The second benchmark was on a Raspberry Pi 3 Model B V1.2 with an ARM Corter-A53 @ 1.4 Ghz. Finally, we conducted a feasibility test of SyLPEnIoT on an ultra low-power device, an Arduino Nano 33 micro-controller using 32-bit ARM Cortex-M0 CPU with 256 KB Flash and 16 KB RAM.

5.2   SyLPEnIoT Construction

In this implementation, we generated the zero inner product pair of two binary vectors $\vec{v}, \vec{x}$, and the non-zero inner product pair of two binary vectors $\vec{v}, \vec{x}$. We ran this experiment by varying the lengths of two vectors. Figure 3 illustrate the encryption and decryption times of the original PE schemes and the proposed SyLPEnIoT schemes. Because the bilinear pairing operations in PE [22] require heavy computation, we only ran samples from five to one hundred order to compare the computational cost with our SyLPEnIoT. As can be seen, the encryption and decryption times of SyLPEnIoT are significantly reduced in comparison with the original PE scheme. The computation time marginally increases with the size of the data. Even with a large set (e.g., $\ell = 100$), both encryption and decryption operations can be completed in the order of milliseconds.

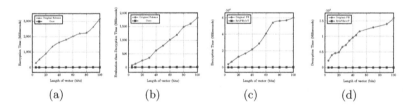

(a)   (b)   (c)   (d)

Fig. 3. (a)(b) Comparison of encryption and decryption times between the original PE and SyLPEnIoT on a Windows 10 Core i7 processor with 16 GB RAM. (c)(d) Comparison of encryption and decryption times between the original PE and SyLPEnIoT on a Linux Raspberry Pi 3 ARM Corter-A53 processor.

In addition, we demonstrate the practicality of SyLPEnIoT on IoT devices through experiments on the ARM Cortex-53 processor and the ARM Cortex-M0+ processor, which are embedded in Raspberry Pi 3. In (c)(d) of Fig. 3, we show its performance in terms of encryption time (seconds), total storage cost (KB), token generation time (seconds), and evaluation to decryption time (seconds). The experiments were conducted in real-time without optimization, and the evaluation to decryption algorithm requires $O(log_n)$ search time. This can be improved by executing search time synchronously to reduce the overall decryption time.

5.3   SyLPEnIoT on Ultra Low-Power Devices

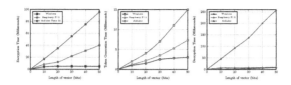

Fig. 4. Comparisons of the total encryption time, token generation time, and evaluation to decryption time (miliseconds) of SyLPEnIoT on a Windows 10 Core i7 processor with 16 GB RAM, a Linux Raspberry Pi 3 ARM Corter-A53 processor, and an Arduino Nano 33 IoT 32-bit ARM Cortex-M0 CPU with 256 KB Flash and 16 KB RAM.

We first reprogrammed the SALSA20 [6] encryption to be compatible with Raspberry Pi 3, as well as to enable it to function on the Arduino Nano 33, which is an ultra low-power device. The Arduino Nano 33 device is heavily resource-constrained, as it only has a 32-bit ARM Cortex-M0 CPU with 256 KB Flash and 16 KB RAM. WiFi and Bluetooth connectivity is performed with a module from u-blox, NINA-W10, a low power chipset operating in the 2.4 GHz range. Our target was to validate that SyLPEnIoT is practical for an ultra low sensor platform like Arduino Nano 33, which uses one of the common ultra low processors. We show the feasibility our SyLPEnIoT on the Arduino Nano 33 by conducting experiments for encryption, token generation, decryption, then provide a comparison in Fig. 4. From the results, the performance of SyLPEnIoT on Arduino 33 is reasonably good, which demonstrates that it can be extended to the other ultra low-power embedded devices. To the best of our knowledge, SyLPEnIoT is the first lightweight predicate encryption scheme that can run on such ultra low-end devices with a maximum vector length of 50-bits.

A   Security Proof

Theorem 2. *The SyLPEnIoT scheme is selectively simulation-secure in the standard model under the assumption that PRF is a pseudo-random function.*

Again, we use the notion Q_{Tkn} as the total number of token queries, and the notion Q_{Enc} as the total number of ciphertext queries.

Proof. We show that for any uniform probabilistic polynomial-time algorithm $\mathcal{A}$, there exists a uniform probabilistic polynomial-time simulator $\mathcal{S}$, such that the ensemble distribution: $(\{\mathsf{CT}_i\}_{i\in[1,Q_{\mathsf{Enc}}]}, \{\mathsf{TK}_{f_j}\}_{j\in[1,Q_{\mathsf{Tkn}}]}) \xleftarrow{R} \mathsf{Expt}^{sel,real}_{\mathsf{SyLPEnIoT},\mathcal{A}}$ (λ, ℓ) and the ensemble distribution: $(\{\mathsf{CT}_i\}_{i\in[1,Q_{\mathsf{Enc}}]}, \{\mathsf{TK}_{f_j}\}_{j\in[1,Q_{\mathsf{Tkn}}]}) \xleftarrow{R}$ $\mathsf{Expt}^{sel,sim}_{\mathsf{SyLPEnIoT},\mathcal{A}}(\lambda, \ell)$ are computationally indistinguishable. We then construct the simulator $\mathcal{S}$ in the experiment sim. First, we consider the simplest scenario where $\mathcal{A}$ makes $Q_{\mathsf{Enc}} = 1$ ciphertext query and $Q_{\mathsf{Tkn}} \le \mathsf{poly}(\lambda)$ gen-token queries.

Since in our main SyLPEnIoT scheme, the input $\mathcal{I}$ is described as a vector $\vec{v}$, and a predicate is defined as a vector $\vec{x}$, and the evaluation returns $f_{\vec{x}}(\vec{v}) = 1$ iff the inner product $<\vec{v}, \vec{x}> = 0$. In this proof, we describe directly the simulation of $\vec{v}, \vec{x}$ instead of attribute $\mathcal{I}$, predicate f.

- **Inputs to Simulator** $\mathcal{S}$. Let $Q_{\mathsf{Enc}} = 1$, we assume that $\mathcal{A}$ queries the simulator with a query history of the form $\mathcal{H} = (\vec{v}, M, \vec{x}_1, \ldots, \vec{x}_Q)$. $\mathcal{S}$ receives the security parameter 1^λ along with the query history $\mathcal{H}$. We recall the definition of query pattern $\alpha(\mathcal{H})$, and decryption pattern $\beta(\mathcal{H})$ as:
  - Given a query history $\mathcal{H} = (\vec{v}, M, \vec{x}_1, \ldots, \vec{x}_{Q_{\mathsf{Tkn}}})$ for SyLPEnIoT scheme, we set $\vec{x}_j = (x_{j,1}, \ldots, x_{j,\ell})$ for each $j \in [1, Q_{\mathsf{Tkn}}]$, where ℓ is the length of f in SyLPEnIoT scheme. The token query pattern $\alpha(\mathcal{H})$ is a set of of values

    $\{\alpha_{i,j,k}\}_{i,j \in [1,Q_{\mathsf{Tkn}}], k \in [1,\ell]}$ such that: $\alpha_{i,j,k} = \begin{cases} 1, & x_{i,k} = x_{j,k} \\ 0, & otherwise \end{cases}$, where $i, j \in$

    $[1, Q_{\mathsf{Tkn}}]$, $k \in [1, \ell]$.
  - Then let TK_{f_j} be the gen-token corresponding to $\vec{x}_j$ in $\mathcal{H} = (\vec{v}, M, \vec{x}_1, \ldots, \vec{x}_{Q_{\mathsf{Tkn}}})$, where $j \in [1, Q_{\mathsf{Tkn}}]$. Also, let CT denotes a ciphertext upon the encryption of the plaintext $\vec{v}, M$. The decryption pattern $\beta(\mathcal{H})$ received by $\mathcal{S}$ is defined as a set of values $\{\beta_j\}_{j \in [1,Q_{\mathsf{Tkn}}]}$:

    $\beta_j = \begin{cases} M, & <\vec{v}, \vec{x}_j> = 0 \\ \bot, & otherwise \end{cases}$,

    We choose the values $W_1, \ldots, W_\ell \xleftarrow{R} \{0,1\}^\lambda$ to simulate the $\mathsf{PRF}(\mathsf{SK}, *\|k)$ for $k \in [1, \ell]$.
- **Simulating GenToken.** The simulator $\mathcal{S}$ now generates GenToken $\{\mathsf{TK}_{f_j}\}_{j \in [1,Q_{\mathsf{Tkn}}]}$ using the algorithm below. Note that since the GenToken algorithm is deterministic, $\mathcal{S}$ ensures the GenToken generate are consistent with the predicate vectors.

  1: Initialize a $Q \times \ell$ matrix d to empty, $T = 0$
  2: **for** each $j \in [1, Q]$ **do do**
  3:     **for** each $k \in [1, \ell]$ **do do**
  4:         Uniformly samples $U_0, U_k \xleftarrow{R} \mathsf{SKE.KeyGen}(1^\lambda)$.
  5:         **if** there exists $i \in [1, j-1]; \alpha_{i,j,k} = 1$ **then**
  6:             $\hat{t}_{j,k} = \hat{t}_{i,k} \oplus U_k; T = \oplus U_k; t_{j,k} = t_{i,k}$
  7:         **else**
  8:             $t_{j,k} \xleftarrow{R} \{0,1\}^\lambda; \hat{t}_{j,k} \xleftarrow{R} \{0,1\}^\lambda$
  9:     **if** $T = 0$ **then**
  10:         $t_{j0}, \xleftarrow{R} \{0,1\}^\lambda$
  11:     **else**
  12:         $t_{j0} \leftarrow \mathsf{SKE.Encrypt}(T, U_0)$
  13:     $t_j = \oplus_{k=1}^{\ell} t_{j,k}$
  14:     $\mathsf{TK}_{f_j} = (t_{j0}, t_j, \hat{t}_{j,k}, \ldots, \hat{t}_{j,\ell})$

- **Simulating the Ciphertext.** The plaintext $(\vec{v}, M)$ is not known to $\mathcal{S}$. The only things that the simulator can learn are the various leakages of encrypted data and the secret keys. To simulate the components including the wild-card '$*$', the values $W_1, W_2, \ldots, W_\ell \xleftarrow{R} \{0,1\}^\lambda$ are used by $\mathcal{S}$ to simulate $\mathsf{PRF}(\mathsf{SK}, *\|k)$ for $k \in [1, \ell]$.

- If some $j \in [1, Q_{\mathsf{Tkn}}]$, $<\vec{v}, \vec{x}_j> = 0$, then at the positions k where $\vec{x}_{j_k} = 1$, it can deduce $\vec{v}_k = 0$, and from $\vec{x}_{j_k} = 0$; it can infer $\vec{v}_k = 1$ or $\vec{v}_k = 0$. This information allows $\mathcal{S}$ to simulate the ciphertext components as:

  1: **if** there exists $j \in [1, Q_{\mathsf{Tkn}}] \wedge \beta_j \neq\perp$ **then**
  2: $\quad M \leftarrow \beta_j$
  3: **else**
  4: $\quad M \xleftarrow{R} \{0,1\}^\lambda$
  5: Uniformly samples $K \xleftarrow{R} \mathsf{SKE.KeyGen}(1^\lambda)$.
  6: **for** each $k \in [1, \ell]$ do **do**
  7: $\quad$ **if** $j \in [1, Q_{\mathsf{Tkn}}] : \beta_j \neq\perp \wedge \alpha(j,k) = 0 \wedge x_{j,k} = 1$ **then**
  8: $\quad\quad \hat{c_1}_k = \hat{t_j}_k; c_{1_k} = t_{j_k} \oplus W_k; c'_{1_k} = W_k$
  9: $\quad$ **else**
  10: $\quad\quad$ **if** $j \in [1, Q_{\mathsf{Tkn}}] : \beta_j \neq\perp \wedge \alpha(j,k) = 0 \wedge x_{j,k} = 0$ **then**
  11: $\quad\quad\quad \hat{c_1}_k = \hat{t_j}_k; c_{1_k} = t_{j_k}; r_k \xleftarrow{R} \{0,1\}^\lambda; c'_{1_k} = t_{j_k} \oplus r_k$
  12: $\quad\quad$ **else**
  13: $\quad\quad\quad \hat{c_1}_k =\xleftarrow{R} \{0,1\}^\lambda; c_{1_k} =\xleftarrow{R} \{0,1\}^\lambda; c'_{1_k} =\xleftarrow{R} \{0,1\}^\lambda$
  14: $c_k = \oplus_{k=1}^\ell c_{1_k} \oplus K$
  15: $c = \mathsf{SKE.Encrypt}(K, M)$.

- The final step is to simulate the c component. Recall that the decryption pattern is the set of value $\beta_1, \ldots, \beta_Q$. For $j \in [1, Q_{\mathsf{Tkn}}]$, β_j output of 1 if $<\vec{v}, \vec{x}> = 0$, then M is a message. Otherwise, then M is set as the string $\{\perp\}^\lambda$. Later, M is used to generate the $c = \mathsf{SKE.Encrypt}(K, M)$ as in the real world. This ensures that *decrypting* C using TK_{f_j}, the message M is recovered correctly. On the other hand, $<\vec{v}, \vec{x}_j> = 1$ for $j \in [1, Q_{\mathsf{Tkn}}]$, *decrypting* with any the token TK_{f_j} always returns the string $\{\perp\}^\lambda$.

- **The Indistinguishability Argument.** This argues that a probabilistic polynomial-time distinguisher $\mathcal{D}$ cannot computationally distinguish $(\mathsf{CT}, \{\mathsf{TK}_{f_j}\}_{j\in[1, Q_{\mathsf{Tkn}}]}) \xleftarrow{R} \mathsf{Expt}^{sel,real}_{\mathsf{SyLPEnIoT}, \mathcal{A}}(\lambda, \ell)$ from $(\mathsf{CT}, \{\mathsf{TK}_{f_j}\}_{j\in[1, Q_{\mathsf{Tkn}}]}) \xleftarrow{R} \mathsf{Expt}^{sel,sim}_{\mathsf{SyLPEnIoT}, \mathcal{A}}(\lambda, \ell)$. The indistinguishability is presented as:

  - At the first simulation of $\mathsf{Expt}^{sel,sim}_{\mathsf{SyLPEnIoT}, \mathcal{A}}$ as $((\mathcal{I}_1, M_1), \ldots, (\mathcal{I}_{Q_{\mathsf{Enc}}}, M_{Q_{\mathsf{Enc}}}),$ $f_1, \ldots, f_{Q_{\mathsf{Tkn}}}) \xleftarrow{R} \mathcal{A}(1^\lambda)$, it does not include the secret key SK with all but negligible probability, and the secret keys generated in the real mode of experiment using the pseudo-random function PRF are indistinguishable from the uniformly random secret keys generated by the simulator $\mathcal{S}$. Then, this can distinguish between the output of PRF and a uniformly random string of size λ without knowing the corresponding secret key SK. In the same way, the components of the ciphertext CT in the real experiment must also be indistinguishable from those generated by the simulator $\mathcal{S}$.

- Finally, if there exists at least one $j \in [1, Q_{\mathsf{Tkn}}]$ such that $<\vec{v}, \vec{x}_j> = 0$, $\mathcal{S}$ gains knowledge of the message M, which is used to generate $c = \mathsf{SKE.Encrypt}(K, M)$ as in the real world. In this case, the indistinguishability is trivial. On the other hand, $<\vec{v}, \vec{x}_j> = 1$ for $j \in [1, Q_{\mathsf{Tkn}}]$, *decrypting* CT using any TK_{f_j} does not reveal the secret key K, which is used to encrypt M.

- **Polynomial Ciphertext Queries.** The simulator $\mathcal{S}$ can address polynomially many ciphertext queries of the form $\{(\mathcal{I}_i, M_i)\}_{i \in [1, Q_{\mathsf{Enc}}]]}$. The simulator $\mathcal{S}$ essentially repeats the same ciphertext simulation phase for each such query. As our security definition, the simulator $\mathcal{S}$ receives as input the decryption pattern corresponding to each ciphertext query $(\mathcal{I}_i, M_i)$. Hence, it can either infer the corresponding payload message M_i or a string $\{\bot\}^\lambda$. Additionally, the components for CT_i are chosen consistently with the tokengen $\{\mathsf{TK}_{f_j}\}_{j \in [1, Q_{\mathsf{Tkn}}]}$. This ensures that, if $f_j(\mathcal{I}_i) = 1$ for some $j \in [1, Q_{\mathsf{Tkn}}]$, then decrypting CT_i using TK_{f_j} correctly recovers the string $\{0,1\}^\lambda$. Finally, the simulation of two ciphertexts CT_i and CT'_i can proceed independent of whether the corresponding attributes $\mathcal{I}_i$ and $\mathcal{I}'_i$ match in one or more components. This completes the proof of Theorem 1.

References

1. Abdalla, M., Bourse, F., De Caro, A., Pointcheval, D.: Simple functional encryption schemes for inner products. In: Katz, J. (ed.) PKC 2015. LNCS, vol. 9020, pp. 733–751. Springer, Heidelberg (2015). https://doi.org/10.1007/978-3-662-46447-2_33
2. Abdalla, M., Catalano, D., Fiore, D., Gay, R., Ursu, B.: Multi-input functional encryption for inner products: function-hiding realizations and constructions without pairings. In: Shacham, H., Boldyreva, A. (eds.) CRYPTO 2018. LNCS, vol. 10991, pp. 597–627. Springer, Cham (2018). https://doi.org/10.1007/978-3-319-96884-1_20
3. Agrawal, S., Freeman, D.M., Vaikuntanathan, V.: Functional encryption for inner product predicates from learning with errors. In: Lee, D.H., Wang, X. (eds.) ASIACRYPT 2011. LNCS, vol. 7073, pp. 21–40. Springer, Heidelberg (2011). https://doi.org/10.1007/978-3-642-25385-0_2
4. Agrawal, S., Libert, B., Maitra, M., Titiu, R.: Adaptive simulation security for inner product functional encryption. In: Kiayias, A., Kohlweiss, M., Wallden, P., Zikas, V. (eds.) PKC 2020. LNCS, vol. 12110, pp. 34–64. Springer, Cham (2020). https://doi.org/10.1007/978-3-030-45374-9_2
5. Atzori, L., Iera, A., Morabito, G.: The internet of things: a survey. Comput. Netw. **54**(15), 2787–2805 (2010)
6. Bernstein, D.J.: The Salsa20 family of stream ciphers. In: Robshaw, M., Billet, O. (eds.) New Stream Cipher Designs. LNCS, vol. 4986, pp. 84–97. Springer, Heidelberg (2008). https://doi.org/10.1007/978-3-540-68351-3_8
7. Bishop, A., Jain, A., Kowalczyk, L.: Function-hiding inner product encryption. In: Iwata, T., Cheon, J.H. (eds.) ASIACRYPT 2015. LNCS, vol. 9452, pp. 470–491. Springer, Heidelberg (2015). https://doi.org/10.1007/978-3-662-48797-6_20
8. Boneh, D., Di Crescenzo, G., Ostrovsky, R., Persiano, G.: Public key encryption with keyword search. In: Cachin, C., Camenisch, J.L. (eds.) EUROCRYPT 2004.

LNCS, vol. 3027, pp. 506–522. Springer, Heidelberg (2004). https://doi.org/10. 1007/978-3-540-24676-3_30

9. Boneh, D., Waters, B.: Conjunctive, subset, and range queries on encrypted data. In: Vadhan, S.P. (ed.) TCC 2007. LNCS, vol. 4392, pp. 535–554. Springer, Heidelberg (2007). https://doi.org/10.1007/978-3-540-70936-7_29

10. Carter, H., Mood, B., Traynor, P., Butler, K.: Secure outsourced garbled circuit evaluation for mobile devices. In: Proceedings of the 22nd USENIX, pp. 289–304 (2013)

11. Cash, D., Jarecki, S., Jutla, C., Krawczyk, H., Roşu, M.-C., Steiner, M.: Highly-scalable searchable symmetric encryption with support for Boolean queries. In: Canetti, R., Garay, J.A. (eds.) CRYPTO 2013. LNCS, vol. 8042, pp. 353–373. Springer, Heidelberg (2013). https://doi.org/10.1007/978-3-642-40041-4_20

12. Chase, M., Miao, P.: Private set intersection in the internet setting from lightweight oblivious PRF. In: Micciancio, D., Ristenpart, T. (eds.) CRYPTO 2020. LNCS, vol. 12172, pp. 34–63. Springer, Cham (2020). https://doi.org/10.1007/978-3-030-56877-1_2

13. CISCO: Cisco IoT System Security: Mitigate Risk, Simplify Compliance, and Build Trust (2015)

14. Curtmola, R., Garay, J., Kamara, S., Ostrovsky, R.: Searchable symmetric encryption: improved definitions and efficient constructions. In: Proceedings of the 13th ACM CCS 2006, pp. 79–88 (2006)

15. Freeman, D.M.: Converting pairing-based cryptosystems from composite-order groups to prime-order groups. In: Gilbert, H. (ed.) EUROCRYPT 2010. LNCS, vol. 6110, pp. 44–61. Springer, Heidelberg (2010). https://doi.org/10.1007/978-3-642-13190-5_3

16. Gay, R., Méaux, P., Wee, H.: Predicate encryption for multi-dimensional range queries from lattices. In: Katz, J. (ed.) PKC 2015. LNCS, vol. 9020, pp. 752–776. Springer, Heidelberg (2015). https://doi.org/10.1007/978-3-662-46447-2_34

17. Golle, P., Staddon, J., Waters, B.: Secure conjunctive keyword search over encrypted data. In: Jakobsson, M., Yung, M., Zhou, J. (eds.) ACNS 2004. LNCS, vol. 3089, pp. 31–45. Springer, Heidelberg (2004). https://doi.org/10.1007/978-3-540-24852-1_3

18. Gorbunov, S., Vaikuntanathan, V., Wee, H.: Predicate encryption for circuits from LWE. In: Gennaro, R., Robshaw, M. (eds.) CRYPTO 2015. LNCS, vol. 9216, pp. 503–523. Springer, Heidelberg (2015). https://doi.org/10.1007/978-3-662-48000-7_25

19. Hazay, C., Toft, T.: Computationally secure pattern matching in the presence of malicious adversaries. In: Abe, M. (ed.) ASIACRYPT 2010. LNCS, vol. 6477, pp. 195–212. Springer, Heidelberg (2010). https://doi.org/10.1007/978-3-642-17373-8_12

20. Kamara, S., Mohassel, P., Riva, B.: Salus: a system for server-aided secure function evaluation. In: Proceedings of the 2012 ACM CCS, pp. 797–808 (2012)

21. Katsumata, S., Nishimaki, R., Yamada, S., Yamakawa, T.: Adaptively secure inner product encryption from LWE. Cryptology ePrint Archive, Report 2020/1135 (2020). https://eprint.iacr.org/2020/1135

22. Katz, J., Sahai, A., Waters, B.: Predicate encryption supporting disjunctions, polynomial equations, and inner products. In: Smart, N. (ed.) EUROCRYPT 2008. LNCS, vol. 4965, pp. 146–162. Springer, Heidelberg (2008). https://doi.org/10. 1007/978-3-540-78967-3_9

23. Kim, S., Lewi, K., Mandal, A., Montgomery, H., Roy, A., Wu, D.J.: Function-hiding inner product encryption is practical. In: Catalano, D., De Prisco, R. (eds.) SCN 2018. LNCS, vol. 11035, pp. 544–562. Springer, Cham (2018). https://doi.org/10.1007/978-3-319-98113-0_29

24. Lai, S., et al.: Result pattern hiding searchable encryption for conjunctive queries. In: Proceedings of the 2018 ACM CCS 2018, pp. 745–762 (2018)

25. Lee, K., Lee, D.H.: Improved hidden vector encryption with short ciphertexts and tokens. Des. Codes Cryptogr. **58**(3), 297–319 (2011). https://doi.org/10.1007/s10623-010-9412-x

26. Lewko, A., Okamoto, T., Sahai, A., Takashima, K., Waters, B.: Fully secure functional encryption: attribute-based encryption and (hierarchical) inner product encryption. In: Gilbert, H. (ed.) EUROCRYPT 2010. LNCS, vol. 6110, pp. 62–91. Springer, Heidelberg (2010). https://doi.org/10.1007/978-3-642-13190-5_4

27. NIST: Post-Quantum Cryptography PQC, Security (Evaluation Criteria) (2020). https://csrc.nist.gov/projects/post-quantum-cryptography/post-quantum-cryptography-standardization/evaluation-criteria/security-(evaluation-criteria)

28. NXP: https://www.nxp.com/applications/solutions/mobile/wearables/smart-watches:wrist-worn-wearable-smart-watch

29. Peikert, C.: Public-key cryptosystems from the worst-case shortest vector problem: extended abstract. In: Proceedings of the Forty-First Annual ACM Symposium on Theory of Computing, pp. 333–342 (2009)

30. Pinkas, B., Rosulek, M., Trieu, N., Yanai, A.: SpOT-light: lightweight private set intersection from sparse OT extension. In: Boldyreva, A., Micciancio, D. (eds.) CRYPTO 2019. LNCS, vol. 11694, pp. 401–431. Springer, Cham (2019). https://doi.org/10.1007/978-3-030-26954-8_13

31. Regev, O.: On lattices, learning with errors, random linear codes, and cryptography (2009)

32. Sedghi, S., van Liesdonk, P., Nikova, S., Hartel, P., Jonker, W.: Searching keywords with wildcards on encrypted data. In: Garay, J.A., De Prisco, R. (eds.) SCN 2010. LNCS, vol. 6280, pp. 138–153. Springer, Heidelberg (2010). https://doi.org/10.1007/978-3-642-15317-4_10

33. Shen, E., Shi, E., Waters, B.: Predicate privacy in encryption systems. In: Reingold, O. (ed.) TCC 2009. LNCS, vol. 5444, pp. 457–473. Springer, Heidelberg (2009). https://doi.org/10.1007/978-3-642-00457-5_27

34. Shi, E., Bethencourt, J., Chan, T.H., Song, D., Perrig, A.: Multi-dimensional range query over encrypted data. In: 2007 IEEE Symposium on Security and Privacy. SP 2007, pp. 350–364 (2007)

35. Shi, E., Waters, B.: Delegating capabilities in predicate encryption systems. In: Aceto, L., Damgård, I., Goldberg, L.A., Halldórsson, M.M., Ingólfsdóttir, A., Walukiewicz, I. (eds.) ICALP 2008. LNCS, vol. 5126, pp. 560–578. Springer, Heidelberg (2008). https://doi.org/10.1007/978-3-540-70583-3_46

36. Shor, P.W.: Algorithms for quantum computation: discrete logarithms and factoring. In: Proceedings 35th FOCS, pp. 124–134 (1994)

37. Song, D.X., Wagner, D., Perrig, A.: Practical techniques for searches on encrypted data. In: Proceedings of the SP 2000, p. 44 (2000)

Security Analysis of SFrame

Takanori Isobe[1,2,3], Ryoma Ito[2(⊠)], and Kazuhiko Minematsu[4]

[1] University of Hyogo, Kobe, Japan
`takanori.isobe@ai.u-hyogo.ac.jp`
[2] National Institute of Information and Communications Technology, Koganei, Japan
`itorym@nict.go.jp`
[3] PRESTO, Japan Science and Technology Agency, Kawaguchi, Japan
[4] NEC Corporation, Kawasaki, Japan
`k-minematsu@nec.com`

Abstract. As people become more and more privacy conscious, the need for end-to-end encryption (E2EE) has become widely recognized. We study the security of SFrame, an E2EE mechanism recently proposed to IETF for video/audio group communications over the Internet. Although a quite recent project, SFrame is going to be adopted by a number of real-world applications. We inspected the original specification of SFrame. We found a critical issue that will lead to an impersonation (forgery) attack by a malicious group member with a practical complexity. We also investigated the several publicly-available SFrame implementations, and confirmed that this issue is present in these implementations.

Keywords: End-to-End Encryption · SFrame · Authenticated encryption · Signature · Impersonation

1 Introduction

End-to-end encryption (E2EE) is a technology that ensures the secrecy and authenticity of communications from the intermediaries between the communicating parties. When E2EE is deployed in a communication application over the Internet, even the servers that facilitate communications cannot read or tamper the messages between the users of this application.

Due to the numerous evidences of massive surveillance, most notably by the case of Snowden, E2EE has received significant attentions and deemed as a key feature to protect users' privacy and integrity for a wide range of communication applications. This also holds for the video calling/meeting applications, such as Zoom[1] or Webex[2]. The end-to-end security of video group meeting applications has been actively studied, and various approaches to E2EE have been proposed. Studying the security of E2EE systems in practice is also a hot topic, as shown by [6, 12–14, 31].

---

[1] https://zoom.us/.
[2] https://www.webex.com.

© Springer Nature Switzerland AG 2021
E. Bertino et al. (Eds.): ESORICS 2021, LNCS 12973, pp. 127–146, 2021.
https://doi.org/10.1007/978-3-030-88428-4_7

In this article, we study SFrame, which is one such approach aiming to providing E2EE over the Internet. Technically, it is a mechanism to encrypt RTC (Real-Time Communication) traffic in an end-to-end manner. RTC (or WebRTC, an RTC protocol between web browsers) is a popular protocol used by video/audio communication, and SFrame is carefully designed to suppress communication overheads that would be introduced when E2EE is deployed. It was proposed to IETF by a team of Google and CoSMo Software (Omara, Uberti, Gouaillard and Murillo) at 2020 as a form of Internet draft [26]. Although a quite recent proposal, it quickly gains lots of attentions. One can find a large variety of ongoing plans to adopt SFrame as a crucial component for E2EE including major proprietary software to open-source applications, such as Google Duo [25], Cisco Webex [4,5], and Jitsi Meet [15,32].

1.1 Our Contributions

We looked into the original specification of SFrame [26], and made several observations. Most notably, we found an issue regarding the use of authenticated encryption with associated data (AEAD) and signature algorithm. The specification [26] defines two AEAD algorithms, namely a generic composition of AES-CTR and HMAC-SHA256, dubbed AES-CM-HMAC, and AES-GCM for encryption of video/audio packets. We show an *impersonation (forgery)* attack by a malicious group member who owns a shared group key for the specified AEAD algorithm. The attack complexity depends on the AEAD algorithm. More specifically for AES-CM-HMAC the complexity depends on the tag length, and for AES-GCM the complexity is negligible for any tag length. We observe that AES-CM-HMAC is specified with particularly short tags, such as 4 or 8 bytes, making the attack complexity practical. The following shows the overview of our security analysis.

AEAD Security. In Sect. 4.1, we study the classical AEAD security (namely, confidentiality and integrity) of SFrame encryption scheme. While SFrame adopts existing, well-analyzed AEAD schemes, they are used in a way different from what standard security analysis assumes, hence the existing AEAD security proofs do not necessarily carry over to the entire protocol. Despite this discrepancy, we show that encryption schemes defined by SFrame are provably secure in the context of standard AEAD.

Impersonation Against AES-CM-HMAC with Short Tags. In Sect. 4.2, we show an impersonation attack on AES-CM-HMAC with short tags by a malicious group member. This attack exploits a vulnerability of very short tag length. Since the malicious group member owns a shared group key, she can precompute multiple ciphertext/tag pairs from any input set, and store them into a precomputation table. After that, she can forge by intercepting a target message frame and replacing the ciphertext in that frame with a properly selected ciphertext from the precomputation table. For example, when the tag length is 4 bytes, she can practically perform an impersonation attack with a success probability of almost one by preparing 2^{32} precomputation tables in advance.

Security of AES-CM-HMAC with Long Tags. In Sect. 4.3, we discuss the security of AES-CM-HMAC with long tags. We show that AES-CM-HMAC with long tags is secure against the impersonation attack proposed in Sect. 4.2. In more detail, we prove that AES-CM-HMAC is second-ciphertext unforgeability (SCU) security, which was defined by Dodis *et al.* [7], and SCU security covers the class of impersonation attacks described above, i.e., forging a ciphertext using the knowledge of the secret key so that the forged ciphertext has the same tag value as a previously observed ciphertext. Concretely, we show that the SCU security of AES-CM-HMAC depends on the security of SHA256, which is the underlying hash function of SFrame. Since SHA256 has an everywhere second-preimage resistance, which was defined by Rogaway and Shrimpton [30], AES-CM-HMAC with long tags can be considered as the SCU-secure AEAD.

Impersonation Against AES-GCM with Any Long Tags. In Sect. 4.4, we show an impersonation attack on AES-GCM with any long tags by a malicious group member. This attack exploits a vulnerability of the linearity of GHASH function in the known key setting. The malicious group member who owns the GCM key and observes a legitimate GCM input/output set including a tag is able to create another distinct set with the same tag. The remaining value in this set, excluding the tag, can be chosen almost freely from the linearity of GHASH function and the knowledge of the GCM key; thus, this attack works with negligible complexity irrespective of the tag length unlike the case of AES-CM-HMAC.

Authentication Key Recovery against AES-GCM with Short Tags. In Sect. 4.5, we consider an authentication key recovery attack on AES-GCM with short tags. This attack exploits the fact that there is no restriction regarding the NIST requirements on the usage of GCM with short tags. Actually, available implementations of the original [33], Cisco Webex [4], and Jitsi Meet [15] have no restriction regarding such requirements. When these available implementations employ the 4-byte tag, the authentication key is recovered with the data complexity of 2^{32}, which is practically available in by the adversary.

Our results are based solely on the Internet draft [26] and publicly available source code [4,15,33], and we have not implemented the proposed attacks to verify their feasibility. It is difficult to implement the proposed attacks because the SFrame specification is still a draft version and no product that implements the current version of SFrame [26] has actually been deployed. Accordingly, instead of implementing the proposed attacks, we discussed with the designers to confirm the feasibility of the proposed attacks.

Since the specification remains abstract at some points and may be subject to change, besides the real-world implementation often do not strictly follow what was specified in [26], this issue does not immediately mean the practical attacks against the existing E2EE video communication applications that adopt SFrame. Nevertheless, considering the practicality of our attacks, we think there is a need to improvement of the current SFrame specification.

Responsible Disclosure. In March 2021, we reported our results in this article to the SFrame designers via email and video conference. They acknowledged that our attacks are feasible under the existence of a malicious group member, quickly decided to remove the signature mechanism [10] and extend tag calculation to cover nonces [9], and updated the specification in the Internet draft on March 29, 2021 [27]. They have a plan to review the SFrame specification and support signature mechanism again in the future.

Organization of the Paper. The paper is organized as follows. Section 2 provides the specification of SFrame including the underlying AEAD, and also a brief survey on the publicly available implementations of SFrame. Section 3 describes the security goals of E2EE recently proposed. We present our analysis in Sect. 4 which shows impersonation attacks against SFrame. Several other observations are also made, followed by our recommendations. Section 5 concludes the article.

2   SFrame

2.1   Specification

Overview. SFrame is a group communication protocol for end-to-end encryption (E2EE) used by video/audio meeting systems. It involves multiple users and a (media) server which mediates communication between users. They are connected via the server, and communication between a user and the server is protected by a standard Internet client-server encryption protocol, specifically Datagram Transport Layer Security-Secure Real-time Transport Protocol (DTLS-SRTP).

SFrame is specified in the Internet draft [26]. However, it does not specify the key exchange protocol between the parties and the choice is left to the implementors. In practice Signal protocol [28], Olm protocol [20], or Message Layer Security (MLS) protocol [2] could be used. With SFrame, users encrypt/decrypt video and audio frames prior to RTP packetization. A generic RTP packetizer splits the encrypted frame into one or more RTP packets and adds an original SFrame header to the beginning of the first packet and an authentication tag to the end of the last packet. The SFrame header contains a signature flag S, a key ID number KID, and a counter value CTR for a nonce used for encryption/decryption.

Cryptographic Protocol. Suppose there is a group of users, G. All users in G first perform a predetermined key exchange protocol as suggested above, and share multiple group keys K_{base}^{KID} associated with the key ID number KID, which is called *base key* in the original specification [26]. In addition, each user establishes a digital signature key pair, (K_{sig}, K_{verf}).

An E2EE session for SFrame uses a single ciphersuite that consists of the following primitives:

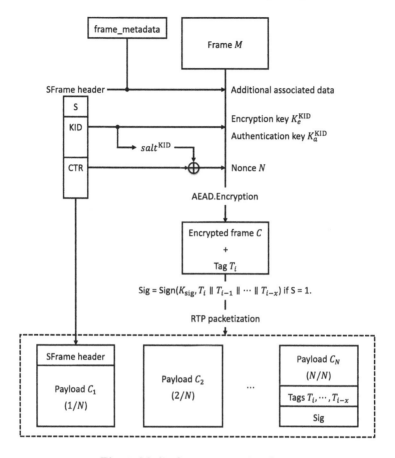

Fig. 1. Media frame encryption flow.

- A hash function used for key derivation, tag generation, and hashing signature inputs, e.g., SHA256 and SHA512.
- An authenticated encryption with associated data (AEAD) [22,29] used for frame encryption, e.g., AES-GCM and AES-CM-HMAC. The authentication tag may be truncated.
- An optional signature algorithm, e.g., EdDSA over Ed25519 and ECDSA over P-521.

Specifically, the original specification [26] defines the following symmetric-key primitives for the ciphersuite:

- AES-GCM with a 128- or 256-bit key and no specified tag length.
- AES-CM-HMAC, which is a combination of AES-CTR with a 128-bit key and HMAC-SHA256 with a 4- or 8-byte truncated authentication tag.

Algorithm 1. Media frame encryption scheme

Input: S: signature flag, KID: key ID, CTR: counter value,frame_metadata: frame metadata, M: frame
Output: C: encrypted frame, T: authentication tag
1: **procedure** ENCRYPTION(S, KID, CTR, frame_metadata, M)
2:    **if** An AEAD encryption algorithm is AES-GCM **then**
3:        $K_e^{KID}, salt^{KID} = $ KeyStore[KID]
4:    **else**
5:        $K_e^{KID}, K_a^{KID}, salt^{KID} = $ KeyStore[KID]
6:    **end if**
7:    $ctr = $ encode(CTR, NonceLen)   ▷ encode CTR as a big-endian of NonceLen.
8:    $N = salt^{KID} \oplus ctr$ ▷ N is a Nonce.
9:    header = encode(S, KID, CTR)
10:    aad = header + frame_metadata   ▷ aad is an additional associated data.
11:    **if** an AEAD encryption algorithm is AES-GCM **then**
12:        $C, T = $ AEAD.ENCRYPTION($K_e^{KID}, N,$ aad, M)
13:    **else**
14:        $C, T = $ AEAD.ENCRYPTION($K_e^{KID}, K_a^{KID}, N,$ aad, M)
15:    **end if**
16: **end procedure**

Figure 1 and Algorithm 1 show the media frame encryption flow in an E2EE session for SFrame using the above ciphersuites. When AES-GCM is adopted as the ciphersuite, AEAD.ENCRYPTION in Algorithm 1 is executed according to NIST SP 800-38D [8]. Before performing by the AEAD encryption procedure by AES-GCM, HKDF [19] is used to generate the encryption key K_e^{KID} and the salt $salt^{KID}$ for encrypting/decrypting media frames as follows:

$$\text{SFrameSecret} = \text{HKDF}(K_{base}^{KID}, '\text{SFrame10}'),$$
$$K_e^{KID} = \text{HKDF}(\text{SFrameSecret}, '\text{key}', \text{KeyLen}),$$
$$salt^{KID} = \text{HKDF}(\text{SFrameSecret}, '\text{salt}', \text{NonceLen}),$$

where KeyLen and NonceLen are the length (byte) of an encryption key and a nonce for the encryption algorithm, respectively. Then, each user stores K_e^{KID} and $salt^{KID}$, such as KeyStore[KID] $= (K_e^{KID}, salt^{KID})$. When AES-CM-HMAC is adopted as the ciphersuite, AEAD.ENCRYPTION in Algorithm 1 is executed according to Algorithm 2. Before performing AES-CM-HMAC, HKDF [19] is used as well as the case of AES-GCM, however in a slightly different manner:

$$\text{AEADSecret} = \text{HKDF}(K_{base}^{KID}, '\text{SFrame10 AES CM AEAD}'),$$
$$K_e^{KID} = \text{HKDF}(\text{AEADSecret}, '\text{key}', \text{KeyLen}),$$
$$K_a^{KID} = \text{HKDF}(\text{AEADSecret}, '\text{auth}', \text{HashLen}),$$
$$salt^{KID} = \text{HKDF}(\text{AEADSecret}, '\text{salt}', \text{NonceLen}),$$

where HashLen is the output length (byte) of the hash function. Also, each user stores the encryption key K_e^{KID}, the authentication key K_a^{KID}, and the salt $salt^{KID}$, such as KeyStore[KID] $= (K_e^{KID}, K_a^{KID}, salt^{KID})$.

Algorithm 2. AEAD encryption by AES-CM-HMAC

Input: K_a^{KID}: authentication key, aad: additional associated data, C: encrypted frame
Output: T: truncated authentication tag
 1: **procedure** TAG.GENERATION(K_a^{KID}, aad, C)
 2:     $\mathsf{aad}Len = \mathsf{encode}(len(\mathsf{aad}), 8)$ ▷ encode aad length as a big-endian of 8 bytes
 3:     $D = \mathsf{aad}Len + \mathsf{aad} + C$
 4:     $tag = \mathsf{HMAC}(K_a^{\mathsf{KID}}, D)$
 5:     $T = \mathsf{trancate}(tag, \mathsf{TagLen})$
 6: **end procedure**
Input: K_e^{KID}, K_a^{KID}, N: Nonce, aad, M: frame
Output: C, T
 1: **procedure** AEAD.ENCRYPTION(K_e^{KID}, K_a^{KID}, N, aad, M)
 2:     $C = \mathsf{AES\text{-}CTR.ENCRYPTION}(K_e^{\mathsf{KID}}, N, M)$
 3:     $T = \mathsf{TAG.GENERATION}(K_a^{\mathsf{KID}}, \mathsf{aad}, C)$
 4: **end procedure**

While an AEAD enables to detect forgeries by an entity who does not own $K_{\mathsf{base}}^{\mathsf{KID}}$, it does not prevent from an impersonation by a malicious group member who owns a shared group key. To detect such an impersonation, a common countermeasure is to attach a signature for each encrypted packet. This can incur a significant overhead both in time and bandwidth. SFrame addresses this problem by reducing the frequency and input length of signature computations. Namely a signature Sig is computed over a list of authentication tags with a fixed size, $(T_i, T_{i-1}, \ldots, T_{i-x})$, as follows:

$$\mathsf{Sig} = \mathsf{Sign}(K_{\mathsf{sig}}, T_i \parallel T_{i-1}, \parallel \cdots \parallel T_{i-x}),$$

where Sign denotes the signature function. This signature is appended to the end of the data which consists of SFrame header, the current encrypted payload, its corresponding authentication tag T_i, and the list of authentication tags $(T_{i-1}, \ldots, T_{i-x})$ which correspond to the previously encrypted payload so that any group user can verify the authenticity of the entire payload.

2.2 Available Implementations

We list some implementations of SFrame that are publicly available. Some of them do not strictly follow the original specification [26] and exhibit some varieties. In this article, we particularly focus on the specified AEAD schemes and the allowed tag length in each of the implementation since this determines the complexity of our attack.

The Original. There is a Javascript implementation by one of the designers of SFrame (Sergio Garcia Murillo) [33]. It is based on webcrypt. In his implementation, it supports

– AES-CM-HMAC with 4 or 10-byte tag, where 4 (10) byte tag is used for audio (video) packets.

Google Duo. Duo[3] is a video calling application developed by Google. For group calling, it adopts Signal protocol as a key exchange mechanism and SFrame as a E2EE mechanism. There is a technical paper [25] written by one of the coauthors (Emad Omera) of the original specification [26]. The source code is not available, however, according to the technical paper, it supports

- AES-CM-HMAC.

The technical paper does not describe the tag length. Note that we confirmed that Google Duo does not currently use the signature feature.

Cisco Webex. Webex is a major video meeting application developed by Cisco. There is a recent whitepaper entitled "Zero-Trust Security for Webex White Paper" [5]. The whitepaper describes the path to their goal called Zero-Trust Security, and suggests to use MLS protocol as a key exchange mechanism and SFrame as a media encryption to enhance the end-to-end security of Webex. The corresponding SFrame implementation is available at Github [4]. The repository maintainer warns that the specification is in progress. As of March 2021, it supports

- AES-GCM with 128 or 256-bit key, with 16-byte tag,
- AES-CM-HMAC with 4 or 8-byte tag.

Jitsi Meet. An open-source video communication application called Jitsi Meet[4] was presented at FOSDEM 2021, a major conference for open source projects[5]. Although a quite recent project, it is getting popularity as an open-source alternative to other major systems. It adopts SFrame with Olm protocol as the underlying key exchange protocol. The source code is available [15]. It supports

- AES-CM-HMAC with 4 or 10-byte tag, where 4 (10) byte tag is used for audio (video) packets.

3   Adversary Models and Security Goals

3.1   Adversary Models

The designers did not define adversary models in the original specification [26]. Then, we define the adversary models for our security analysis with reference to them defined by Isobe and Minematsu [14].

Definition 1 (Malicious User). *A malicious user, who is a legitimate user but does not possess a shared group key, tries to break one of the subsequently defined security goals of the other E2EE session by maliciously manipulating the protocol.*

---

[3] https://duo.google.com/about/.

[4] https://meet.jit.si/.

[5] https://fosdem.org/2021/schedule/.

Definition 2 (Malicious Group Member). *A malicious group member, who is a legitimate group member and possesses a shared group key, tries to break the subsequently defined security goals by deviating from the protocol.*

In addition, *E2E adversary* is defined in [14], however, we do not explain this definition because this adversary is out of scope for our security analysis.

3.2 Security Goals of E2EE

In February 2021, the Internet draft entitled "Definition of End-to-end Encryption" was released [17]. According to this draft, the fundamental features for E2EE require *authenticity, confidentiality*, and *integrity*, which are defined as follows:

Definition 3 (Authenticity). *A system provides message authenticity if the recipient is certain who sent the message and the sender is certain who received it.*

Definition 4 (Confidentiality). *A system provides message confidentiality if only the sender and intended recipient(s) can read the message plaintext, i.e., messages are encrypted by the sender such that only the intended recipient(s) can decrypt them.*

Definition 5 (Integrity). *A system provides message integrity when it guarantees that messages has not been modified in transit, i.e. a recipient is assured that the message they have received is exactly what the sender intented to sent.*

In addition, *availability, deniability, forward secrecy*, and *post-compromise security* are defined in this draft as the optional/desirable features to enhance the E2EE systems, however, we do not explain these definitions because these features are out of scope for our security analysis.

3.3 Security Goals of AEAD for E2EE

Dodis *et al.* [7] proposed a new primitive called *encryptment* for the message franking scheme, which enables cryptographically verifiable reporting of malicious content in end-to-end encrypted messaging. In addition, they defined *confidentiality* and *second-ciphertext unforgeability* (SCU) as security goals to ensure the securily level of the encryptment scheme.

Definition 6 (Second-Ciphertext Unforgeability (SCU)). *An adversary $\mathcal{A}$ is given $K \xleftarrow{\$} \mathcal{K}$, which means a randomly chosen key K form the key space $\mathcal{K}$, and is allowed to perform AEAD encryption/decryption in the local environment. Then, we define the second-ciphertext unforgeability (SCU) advantage of $\mathcal{A}$ against AEAD for E2EE as*

$$\begin{aligned}\mathbf{Adv}_{\mathsf{AEAD}}^{\mathsf{SCU}}(\mathcal{A}) = \Pr\big[&K \xleftarrow{\$} \mathcal{K} : \mathcal{A}(K) \to (N, A, C, N^*, A^*, C^*, T),\\ &\mathsf{Dec}(K, N, A, C, T) = M,\\ &\mathsf{Dec}(K, N^*, A^*, C^*, T) = M^* \text{ for some } M, M^* \neq \bot\big],\end{aligned}$$

where **Dec** *denotes the decryption algorithm of AEAD, N and N* denote nonces, A and A* denote associated data, C and C* denote ciphertexts, M and M* denote plaintexts, T denotes a tag, and* $\perp$ *denotes a symbol that represents a decryption failure.*

The adversary in SCU game is given with key, hence this is not captured by the standard AEAD security notions of confidentiality and integrity [3,29]. When there exists a malicious group member in an E2EE application, she can actually work as a SCU adversary $\mathcal{A}$ by intercepting the target frame (N, A, C, T) since she knows the shared group key K.

3.4   Security Goals of Hash Functions

A secure hash function H typically has three fundamental properties: *preimage resistance, second-preimage resistance,* and *collision resistance.* Here, we focus on two types of second-preimage resistance, and define them with references to [23,30] as follows:

Definition 7 (Second-Preimage Resistance). *Let $\mathcal{A}$ be an adversary attempting to find any second input which has the same output as any specified input, i.e., for any given message $M \xleftarrow{\$} \mathcal{M}$, which means a randomly chosen message M form the message space $\mathcal{M}$, to find a second-preimage $M^* \neq M$ such that $H(M) = H(M^*)$. Then, we define the second-preimage (Sec) resistance advantage of $\mathcal{A}$ against H as*

$$\mathbf{Adv}_H^{\mathsf{Sec}}(\mathcal{A}) = \Pr\left[M \xleftarrow{\$} \mathcal{M}; M^* \leftarrow \mathcal{A} : (M \neq M^*) \wedge \left(H(M) = H(M^*)\right)\right].$$

Definition 8 (Everywhere Second-Preimage Resistance). *For a positive integer n, let $\{0,1\}^{\leq n}$ be a set of bit strings not longer than n. Let $\mathcal{M} = \{0,1\}^*$ and $\mathcal{Y} = \{0,1\}^n$. Suppose $H : \mathcal{K} \times \mathcal{M} \to \mathcal{Y}$ be a keyed hash function. Let $\mathcal{A}$ be an adversary against H to find a second preimage for the target input $M \in \mathcal{M}$ that is fixed with $|M| \leq \ell$. Then, we define the everywhere second-preimage (eSec) resistance advantage of $\mathcal{A}$ against H as*

$$\mathbf{Adv}_H^{\mathsf{eSec}[\leq \ell]}(\mathcal{A})$$

$$= \max_{M \in \{0,1\}^{\leq \ell}} \left\{ \Pr\left[K \xleftarrow{\$} \mathcal{K}; M^* \leftarrow \mathcal{A}(K) : (M \neq M^*) \wedge \left(H_K(M) = H_K(M^*)\right)\right] \right\}.$$

The everywhere second-preimage or eSec resistance, introduced by Rogaway and Shrimpton [30], is called (a slight extension of) a strong form of second-preimage resistance. In this article, we assume the standard hash function (SHA2) as an instantiation of keyed function, say by using IV as a key, since otherwise standard security reduction is not possible (see [30]). For simplicity, we assume this key is implicit and do not describe it in the proofs.

4   Security Analysis

4.1   Security of AEAD Under SFrame

We first discuss on the security of AEAD used by SFrame. Here we view Algorithm 1 as an encryption of AEAD for the reason that viewing Algorithm 2 as a full-fledged AEAD does not make sense (see below). Then, effectively, the keys are contained by KeyStore[KID] and the nonce is CTR, the associated data is a tuple (S, KID, frame_metadata), and the plaintext is M.

In Algorithm 1, the variable N is a sum of $salt^{KID}$ and ctr (Line 8), where the former is essentially a part of key (via HKDF), the latter is an encoded form of CTR. This N serves as nonce for the internal AEAD algorithm at Line 12/14. The data aad serves as AD for the internal AEAD and consists of header and frame_metadata, where the former contains an encoded form of (S, KID,CTR). Since aad contains CTR as well as N, if the internal AEAD is AES-CM-HMAC of Algorithm 2, HMAC takes the nonce (CTR) in addition to AD (frame_metadata) and the ciphertext C. Hence the lack of $N = salt^{KID} \oplus ctr$ is not a problem. Moreover, adding a pseudorandom value to the nonce of AES-CTR does not degrade security as long as that value is computationally independent of the key of AES-CTR.

A slightly more formal analysis is given below. Algorithm 1 combined with AES-CM-HMAC can be interpreted as an encryption routine the encryption-then-MAC AEAD construction. More specifically, it takes nonce $\widetilde{N} =$ CTR, associated data $\widetilde{A} = $ (S, KID, frame_metadata), and plaintext M to produce the ciphertext C and the tag T:

$$C = \widetilde{\mathsf{Enc}}_K(\widetilde{N}, M)$$
$$T = \widetilde{\mathsf{MAC}}_{K'}(\widetilde{N}, \widetilde{A}, C),$$

where K and K' are derived via a master key with a key derivation function (HKDF), and $\widetilde{\mathsf{Enc}}_K$ denotes the plain counter mode encryption with a pseudorandom offset to nonce (i.e., $salt^{KID}$, which is derived via HKDF), and $\widetilde{\mathsf{MAC}}_{K'}$ denotes the HMAC with a certain bijective input encoding. This means that Algorithm 1 is exactly reduced to the encryption-then-MAC generic composition (assuming HKDF as a PRF) whose security is proved when $\widetilde{\mathsf{Enc}}$ is IND-CPA secure and $\widetilde{\mathsf{MAC}}$ is a PRF [18,24]. Proving the latter claim is trivial. Hence Algorithm 1 is secure under the standard assumptions that AES is a pseudorandom permutation and HMAC is a PRF. We remark that Algorithm 2 itself is not a generically secure (i.e., when nonce N and AD aad are independently chosen) AEAD as it ignores N in the computation of tag. This issue was raised at the discussion in CFRG[6] and our analysis provides an answer.

---

[6] https://mailarchive.ietf.org/arch/browse/cfrg/?q=SFrame.

4.2 Impersonation Against AES-CM-HMAC with Short Tags

While the AEAD security of Algorithm 1 is sound, it does not necessarily mean the full E2EE security. In this section we point out that there is a risk of *impersonation* by a malicious group member who owns the group key. The impersonation attack implies that the scheme does not achieve the security goal of integrity in E2EE.

Hereafter, we simplify the model and stick to the standard AEAD notation, namely the input is (N, A, M) for nonce N, associated data A, plaintext M and the output is (C, T) for ciphertext C and tag T. Also we consider the case that the signature is computed for each tag for simplicity. The notational discrepancies from Algorithm 1 and Algorithm 2 do not change the essential procedure of our attacks. With this simplified model, each group member sends an encrypted frame to all other members, and this frame consists of an AEAD output (N, A, C, T) and a signature $\mathsf{Sig} = \mathsf{Sign}(K_{\mathsf{sig}}, T)$ signed by the user's signing key K_{sig}. The encryption input is (N, A, M) and the frame encryption by AES-CM-HMAC is abstracted as follows:

$$C \leftarrow \text{AES-CTR}(K_e^{\mathsf{KID}}, N, M)$$

$$T \leftarrow \mathsf{truncate}(\text{HMAC-SHA256}(K_a^{\mathsf{KID}}, (N, A, C)), \tau), \qquad (8)$$

where τ denotes the tag length in bits. Note that N is included as a part of HMAC's input, for the reason described at Sect. 4.1.

Suppose there is a communication group G containing a malicious group member U_M and another member U_T which we call a target user. This U_M is able to mount a forgery attack (impersonation) by manipulating a frame sent by U_T. The forgery attack by U_M consists of offline and online phases.

In the offline phase, U_M determines (N, A, M), and precomputes a set of (ciphertext,tag) tuples (C, T) by using K_e^{KID} and K_a^{KID}, which are known to all group members, and stores these into a table tb. Here, N and A are determined so that it is likely to be used by U_T (these information are public and N is a counter so this is practical).

In the online phase, the malicious group member observes the frames sent by U_T. If she finds the frame $(N, A, C', T', \mathsf{Sig})$ such that (C^*, T^*) is included in tb and $T^* = T'$, $C^* \neq C'$, then she replaces C' in that frame with C^*. Since the signature Sig is computed over the tag T' which is not changed after the replacement, this manipulated frame will pass the verification. Figure 2 shows the overview of the attack. The details of attack procedures are given as follows.

Offline Phase

1. U_M chooses the encryption input tuple (N, A, M).
2. U_M computes a ciphertext C and a τ-bit tag T for (N, A, M) following Eq. (8), where KID is set to point the target user.
3. U_M stores a set of (M, C, T) into the table tb.
4. U_M repeats Step 1–3 2^t times with different messages.

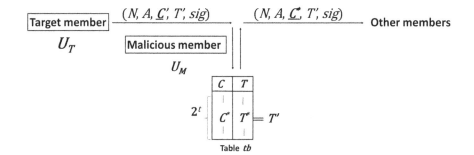

Fig. 2. Impersonation against AES-CM-HMAC with short tags. In the offline phase, a malicious group member U_M stores a set of (M, C, T) into the table tb. In the online phase, U_M intercepts a target frame $(N', A', C', T', \mathsf{Sig})$ sent by the target user U_T, searches a tuple (M^*, C^*, T^*) in tb such that $T^* = T'$ and $C^* \neq C'$, replaces C' with C^* in the target frame, and sends $(N', A', C^*, T', \mathsf{Sig})$ to other group members.

Online Phase

1. U_M intercepts a target frame $(N', A', C', T', \mathsf{Sig})$ sent by the target user, where $N' = N$ and $A' = A$.
2. U_M searches a tuple (M^*, C^*, T^*) in tb such that $T^* = T'$ and $C^* \neq C'$.
3. If U_M finds such a tuple, replaces C' with C^* in the target frame, and sends $(N', A', C^*, T', \mathsf{Sig})$ to other group members.

The manipulated frame including (C^*, T') successfully pass the signature verification by other group members due to a tag collision, *i.e.*, no one can detect that the frame is manipulated by U_M, and the group members will accept M^* as a valid message from U_T. The above is for the case where $x = 1$, *i.e.*, each tag is independently signed by the signature key. It is naturally extend to the case where x is more than one, namely the case where a list of tags is signed altogether for efficiency.

To mount the attack described above, the adversary needs to intercept a legitimate message. It implies the adversary may collude with an intermediate server, or E2EE adversary, which is the central operating server. The practicality of this is beyond the scope of this article, however we remark that preventing colluding attack with E2EE adversary is one of the fundamental goals of E2EE.

We note that the attack without intercept is also possible by creating a forged tuple $(N', A', C', T', \mathsf{Sig})$ such that $T' = T$ and $(N', A', C') \neq (N, A, C)$ by observing some legitimate tuple $(N, A, C, T, \mathsf{Sig})$ that was previously sent without corruption; here (N', A') is chosen so that it is likely to be used by U_T in the next frame which is yet sent. This is essentially a reply of signature and we guess whether it is detected as replay depends on the actual system, so we keep it open. The cost of detecting a reply of randomized algorithm is generally high since the receiver must keep the all random IVs used.

Complexity Evaluation. The computational cost to make the precomputation table tb in the offline phase is estimated as 2^t, and the success probability of Step 2 in the online phase is estimated as $2^{-\tau+t}$.

Practical effects on SFrame. In case $\tau = 32$ (i.e. 4-byte tags) if U_M prepares 2^{32} precomutation tables in the offline, the success probability is almost one. Thus, this forgery attack is practically feasible with a high success probability for the 4-byte tag. Besides, in this attack, the adversary fully controls the decryption result (M^*) of the manipulated frame except 32 bits which are used for generating 2^{32} different tags in the offline phase.

To perform an actual attack on SFrame, since each SFrame header includes the frame counter to avoid replay attacks, the adversary has to decide the target frame and set the target frame counter to the SFrame header file in M when generating tags in the offline phase.

Even in the case of 8- and 10-byte tag, if U_M prepares 2^{56} tables, which is feasible by the nation-level adversary, the success probability is non-negligible, 2^{-8} and 2^{-24}, respectively.

4.3   Security of AES-CM-HMAC with Long Tags

We first discuss the security of AES-CM-HMAC with long tags, e.g., 16-byte tags, against impersonation attack as described in Sect. 4.2. Even if a malicious group member prepares 2^{56} precomputation tables, it is infeasible because the success probability of the attack is 2^{-72}; therefore, AES-CM-HMAC with long tags can be secure against the impersonation attack proposed in Sect. 4.2.

We justify the above observation by showing SCU security of AES-CM-HMAC with long tags. According to Algorithm 2, let D and D^* be (N, A, C) and (N^*, A^*, C^*), respectively (see Line 3 in TAG.GENERATION procedure). Note that N is included in A (aad) as partial information (see Lines 7–10 in Algorithm 1). For simplicity, the tag generation by HMAC is abstracted as follows:

$$\text{HMAC}(K_a^{\text{KID}}, D) = H\big((K \oplus opad) \,\|\, H\big((K \oplus ipad) \,\|\, D\big)\big),$$

where H denotes a hash function, e.g., SHA256 used in SFrame, *ipad* and *opad* denote fixed padding values, and K is generated from K_a^{KID} according to the padding rule in HMAC algorithm (see [34] for details). The following theorem is simple to prove.

Theorem 1. *Let $\mathcal{A}$ be a SCU adversary against AES-CM-HMAC with the target encryption output being at most ℓ bits. Then, SCU advantage of $\mathcal{A}$ against AES-CM-HMAC is bounded as*

$$\mathbf{Adv}_{\text{AES-CM-HMAC}}^{\text{SCU}}(\mathcal{A}) < 2\mathbf{Adv}_H^{\text{eSec}[\le(\ell')]}(\mathcal{A}')$$

for some eSec adversary $\mathcal{A}'$ against H, which denotes the underlying SHA256 hash function, where $\ell' = \ell + 512$ (i.e., one block larger).

Proof. Let K be the key of HMAC. Thanks to the generic composition, we can assume that the adversary is given the key for the counter mode. The resulting game is that, given a transcript of encryption query (N, A, M, C, T) derived on

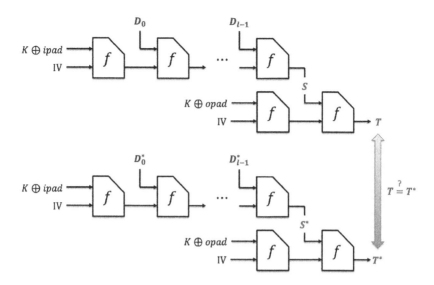

Fig. 3. SCU scenario against AES-CM-HMAC with long tags for E2EE. In this scenario, given a transcript of encryption query (N, A, M, C, T) derived on K, the adversary $\mathcal{A}$ is required to find a successful forgery (N^*, A^*, C^*, T^*) on K such that $T^* = T$ and $D^* \neq D$, i.e., $(N^*, A^*, C^*) \neq (N, A, C)$.

K, the adversary is required to find a successful forgery (N^*, A^*, C^*, T) on K such that $D^* \neq D$, i.e., $(N^*, A^*, C^*) \neq (N, A, C)$. Note that the tag T is the output of HMAC taking K and $D = (N, A, C)$ and thus the plaintext M is not needed in the attack. Figure 3 illustrates this scenario, where IV denotes the initial hash value, $D = D_0 \| \ldots \| D_{l-1}$, $D^* = D_0^* \| \ldots \| D_{l-1}^*$, $S = H((K \oplus ipad) \| D)$, and $S^* = H((K \oplus ipad) \| D^*)$. Each D_i and D_i^* denotes an input block to HMAC. The last block may need padding but we simply ignore this (the analysis is pretty much the same). In this scenario, we consider the following two cases: $\mathcal{A}$ finds $S^* = S$ (Case 1) which implies $T = T^*$ or $S^* \neq S$ and $T = T^*$ (Case 2).

For Case 1, observe that $S = S^*$ means $H(K \oplus ipad \| D) = H(K \oplus ipad \| D^*)$, hence a second preimage against the target input $K \oplus ipad \| D$ is obtained. For Case 2, when $S \neq S^*$ and $T = T^*$, it means the adversary finds a second preimage against the target (2-block, thus 1024-bit) input $K \oplus opad \| S$. Both cases are covered by the eSec security of H, hence we have

$$\mathbf{Adv}_{AES\text{-}CM\text{-}HMAC}^{\mathsf{SCU}}(\mathcal{A}) \leq \mathbf{Adv}_H^{\mathsf{eSec}[\leq(\ell')]}(\mathcal{A}') + \mathbf{Adv}_H^{\mathsf{eSec}[\leq 1024]}(\mathcal{A}')$$
$$< 2\mathbf{Adv}_H^{\mathsf{eSec}[\leq(\ell')]}(\mathcal{A}'),$$

which concludes the proof.   □

Theorem 1 tells that the SCU security of AES-CM-HMAC with long tags depends on the security of underlying hash function. According to the Internet draft [26], SFrame adopts SHA256 as the hash function used in AES-CM-HMAC.

Second-Preimage Security of SHA256. Ideally, a n-bit hash function provides a n-bit security level against second-preimage attacks. That is, we can find a second-preimage on SHA256 with a time complexity of 2^{256}. Khovratovich *et al.* [16] proposed a new concept of biclique as a technique for preimage attacks, and applied it to the reduced-round SHA2 family. Their second-preimage attack on the reduced-round SHA256 performs up to 45 rounds (out of 64) with a time complexity of $2^{255.5}$ and a memory complexity of 2^6 words. After that, Andreeva *et al.* [1] presented new generic second-preimage attacks on the basic Merkle-Damgård hash functions. Their best attack allow us to find a second-preimage on the full SHA256 with a time complexity of 2^{173} and a memory complexity of 2^{83}, but this attack is required too long message blocks, e.g., a 2^{118}-block message.

To the best of our knowledge, no study has been reported on a second-preimage attack that is more efficient than the above described attacks; therefore, AES-CM-HMAC with long tags can be considered as the SCU-secure AEAD.

4.4   Impersonation Against AES-GCM with Any Long Tags

The impersonation attacks described above is a generic attack and the offline attack complexity depends on the tag length. In contrast, if we use AES-GCM, it is easy to mount a similar attack without the offline phase. This is because, the adversary who owns the GCM key and observes a legitimate GCM output of (N, A, C, T) is able to create another distinct tuple of (N', A', C', T') with $T' = T$. The remaining $(N', A', C') \neq (N, A, C)$ can be chosen almost freely from the linearity of GHASH and the knowledge of the key. In particular, the attack works with negligible complexity irrespective of the tag length unlike the case of AES-CM-HMAC.

Once the adversary intercepts a legitimate tuple (N, A, C, T) created by GCM, it is trivial to compute (N', A', C', T') such that $T' = T$ and $(N', A', C') \neq (N, A, C)$, for almost any choice of (N', A', C').

For example, suppose GCM with 96-bit nonce and 128-bit tag, which is one of the most typical settings. Given any GCM encryption output tuple (N, A, C, T) with 2-block $C = (C_1, C_2)$ and 1-block $A = A_1$, we have

$$T = \mathsf{GHASH}(L, A \parallel C \parallel \mathsf{len}(A, C)) \oplus E_K(N \parallel 1_{32})$$
$$= A \cdot L^4 \oplus C_1 \cdot L^3 \oplus C_2 \cdot L^2 \oplus \mathsf{len}(A, C) \cdot L \oplus E_K(N \parallel 1_{32}),$$
$$C_1 = E_K(N \parallel 2_{32}) \oplus M_1,$$
$$C_2 = E_K(N \parallel 3_{32}) \oplus M_2,$$

where $M = (M_1, M_2)$ is the plaintext. Here, $\mathsf{len}(A, C)$ is a 128-bit encoding of lengths of A and C, and multiplications are over $\mathrm{GF}(2^{128})$. $E_K(*)$ denotes the encryption by AES with key K and $L = E_K(0^{128})$, and i_{32} for a non-negative integer i denotes the 32-bit encoding of i. It is straightforward to create a valid tuple (N', A', C', T') such that $T' = T$ and $(N', A', C') \neq (N, A, C)$ as we know

Table 1. NIST requirements on the usage of GCM with short tags.

t	32						64					
L	2^1	2^2	2^3	2^4	2^5	2^6	2^{11}	2^{13}	2^{15}	2^{17}	2^{19}	2^{21}
q	2^{22}	2^{20}	2^{18}	2^{15}	2^{13}	2^{11}	2^{32}	2^{29}	2^{26}	2^{23}	2^{20}	2^{17}
c	2^{62}	2^{62}	2^{61}	2^{65}	2^{66}	2^{67}	2^{75}	2^{74}	2^{73}	2^{72}	2^{71}	2^{70}

K. Say, we first arbitrary choose N' and A', and the fake plaintext block M_1' to compute C_1', and finally set C_2' so that

$$C_2' \cdot L^2 = T' \oplus A' \cdot L^4 \oplus C_1' \cdot L^3 \oplus \mathsf{len}(A', C') \cdot L \oplus E_K(N' \parallel 1_{32})$$

holds. This will make the last decrypted plaintext block M_2' random. It works even if the tag is truncated. That is, the malicious group member can impersonate other member and the forged plaintext is almost arbitrary except the last block. We note that the plaintext is video or audio hence a tiny random block will not be recognized. This attack severely harms the integrity of group communication.

This difference from the case of AES-CM-HMAC is rooted in the authentication mechanism – while HMAC maintains a collision resistance once the key is known, GHASH with a known key is a simple function without any sort of known-key security.

4.5   Considerations on Authentication Key Recovery

The specification [26] appears to implicitly allow 4 and 8-byte tags with AES-GCM. In addition to the attacks described above, it is known that the use of short tags in GCM will lead to a complete recovery of the authentication key (*i.e.*, the key of GHASH) by a class of attacks called reforging. This leads to a universal forgery.

Ferguson [11] first pointed out this attack, and Mattsson and Westerlund [21] further refined the attack and provided a concrete complexity estimation. According to [21], they point out that the security levels are only 62–67 bits and 70–75 bits for 32-bit and 64-bit tags, respectively, even if we follow NIST requirements on the usage of GCM with short tags, which is shown in Table 1. In Table 1, L is the maximum combined length of A and C, and q is the maximum number of invocations of the authenticated decryption function. Table 1 also shows the required data complexity c for the authentication key recovery under each restriction of L and q. For example, for $L = 2^3$ and $q = 2^{18}$, the required data to recover the key of GHASH is 2^{61}.

If there is no restriction regarding L and q, the authenticated key is recovered with data complexity of 2^t as the complexity of the first forgery is dominated. Thus, for 4-byte ($= 32$-bit) tag length, the authenticated key recovery is feasible with 2^{32} data complexity. It seems that the specification [26] does not explicitly mention the restrictions of q and L.

Practical effects on SFrame. As far as we checked available implementations of the original [33], Cisco Webex [4], and Jitsi Meet [15], there is no restriction regarding L and q. In this case, for the 4-byte tag, the authenticated key is recovered with data complexity of 2^{32}, which is practically available by a malicious user.

4.6 Recommendations

From the vulnerabilities shown in Sects. 4.2 to 4.5, we recommend the followings.

- For AES-CM-HMAC, short tags, especially 4-byte tag, should not be used.
- For AES-GCM, a signature should be computed over a whole frame, not only tags.
- For AES-GCM, the specification should clearly forbid short tags, or refer to NIST requirements on the usage of GCM with short tags.
- As discussed at Sect. 3, switch to other ciphersuite that works as a secure encryptment scheme, such as HFC [7], with a sufficiently long tag is another option.

5   Conclusions

We have shown our security analysis on SFrame, a recently proposed end-to-end encryption mechanism built on RTC, developed by Google and CoSMo Software and proposed to IETF. SFrame is a young project but going to be adopted by a number of real-world products. Our results show that there is a practical risk of impersonation by a malicious group member. This problem is caused by the digital signature computed only on (a list of) AEAD tags, and the attack becomes practical when tags are short or the used AEAD algorithm allows to create a collision on tags with the knowledge of the key. The former applies to the case of AES-CM-HMAC, and the latter applies to the case of AES-GCM. We also showed that AES-CM-HMAC with a long tag avoids this problem as it fulfills a "committing" property introduced by Dodis *et al.* [7]. Moreover, AES-CM-HMAC is, if it is correctly used by the upper layer, a provably secure AEAD because it can be interpreted as a standard encryption-then-MAC generic composition. We notify our findings to the designers, and they acknowledged them and revised the specification including the removal of the signature feature and a patch for the AEAD algorithm. Considering its quick deployment, we think SFrame should be studied more actively and hope our work help its improvement.

Acknowledgments. We are grateful to the SFrame designers (Emad Omara, Justin Uberti, Alex Gouaillard, and Sergio Garcia Murillo) for the fruitful discussion and feedback about our findings. We would like to thank the anonymous reviewers for their insightful comments, and Shiguredo Inc. for helpful discussion about real-world applications of the end-to-end encryption. Takanori Isobe is supported by JST, PRESTO Grant Number JPMJPR2031, Grant-in-Aid for Scientific Research (B)(KAKENHI 19H02141) and SECOM science and technology foundation.

References

1. Andreeva, E., et al.: New second-preimage attacks on hash functions. J. Cryptol. **29**(4), 657–696 (2016). https://doi.org/10.1007/s00145-015-9206-4

2. Barnes, R., Beurdouche, B., Millican, J., Omara, E., Cohn-Gordon, K., Robert, R.: The Messaging Layer Security (MLS) Protocol, October 2020. https://tools. ietf.org/html/draft-ietf-mls-protocol-10

3. Bellare, M., Namprempre, C.: Authenticated encryption: relations among notions and analysis of the generic composition paradigm. In: Okamoto, T. (ed.) ASI-ACRYPT 2000. LNCS, vol. 1976, pp. 531–545. Springer, Heidelberg (2000). https://doi.org/10.1007/3-540-44448-3_41

4. Cisco Systems: SFrame (2020). https://github.com/cisco/sframe

5. Cisco Systems: Zero-Trust Security for Webex White Paper (2021). https://www. cisco.com/c/en/us/solutions/collateral/collaboration/white-paper-c11-744553. pdf

6. Cohn-Gordon, K., Cremers, C., Dowling, B., Garratt, L., Stebila, D.: A formal security analysis of the signal messaging protocol. J. Cryptol. **33**(4), 1914–1983 (2020)

7. Dodis, Y., Grubbs, P., Ristenpart, T., Woodage, J.: Fast message franking: from invisible salamanders to encryptment. In: Shacham, H., Boldyreva, A. (eds.) CRYPTO 2018. LNCS, vol. 10991, pp. 155–186. Springer, Cham (2018). https:// doi.org/10.1007/978-3-319-96884-1_6

8. Dworkin, M.: NIST SP 800–38D, Recommendation for Block Cipher Modes of Operation: Galois/Counter Mode (GCM) and GMAC (2007). U.S. Department of Commerce/National Institute of Standards and Technology

9. Omara, E.: Extend Tag Calculation to Cover Nonce #59 (2021). https://github. com/eomara/sframe/pull/59

10. Omara, E.: Remove Signature #58 (2021). https://github.com/eomara/sframe/ pull/58

11. Ferguson, N.: Authentication Weaknesses in GCM. Comments submitted to NIST Modes of Operation Process (2005). http://csrc.nist.gov/groups/ST/toolkit/ BCM/documents/comments/CWC-GCM/Ferguson2.pdf

12. Garman, C., Green, M., Kaptchuk, G., Miers, I., Rushanan, M.: Dancing on the lip of the volcano: chosen ciphertext attacks on apple iMessage. In: Holz, T., Savage, S. (eds.) USENIX Security 2016, pp. 655–672. USENIX Association, August 2016

13. Isobe, T., Ito, R.: Security analysis of end-to-end encryption for zoom meetings. IEEE Access **9**, 90677–90689 (2021)

14. Isobe, T., Minematsu, K.: Breaking message integrity of an end-to-end encryption scheme of LINE. In: Lopez, J., Zhou, J., Soriano, M. (eds.) ESORICS 2018. LNCS, vol. 11099, pp. 249–268. Springer, Cham (2018). https://doi.org/10.1007/978-3-319-98989-1_13

15. Jitsi: Jitsi Meet API library (2020). https://github.com/jitsi/lib-jitsi-meet/

16. Khovratovich, D., Rechberger, C., Savelieva, A.: Bicliques for preimages: attacks on Skein-512 and the SHA-2 family. In: Canteaut, A. (ed.) FSE 2012. LNCS, vol. 7549, pp. 244–263. Springer, Heidelberg (2012). https://doi.org/10.1007/978-3-642-34047-5_15

17. Knodel, M., Baker, F., Kolkman, O., Celi, S., Grover, G.: Definition of End-to-end Encryption, February 2021. https://datatracker.ietf.org/doc/draft-knodel-e2ee-definition/

18. Krawczyk, H.: The order of encryption and authentication for protecting communications (or: how secure is SSL?). In: Kilian, J. (ed.) CRYPTO 2001. LNCS, vol. 2139, pp. 310–331. Springer, Heidelberg (2001). https://doi.org/10.1007/3-540-44647-8_19

19. Krawczyk, H., Eronen, P.: HMAC-based Extract-and-Expand Key Derivation Function (HKDF). Internet Engineering Task Force - IETF, Request for Comments 5869, May 2010

20. Matrix.org Foundation: Olm: a Cryptographic Ratchet (2016). https://gitlab.matrix.org/matrix-org/olm/-/blob/master/docs/olm.md

21. Mattsson, J., Westerlund, M.: Authentication key recovery on Galois/Counter Mode (GCM). In: Pointcheval, D., Nitaj, A., Rachidi, T. (eds.) AFRICACRYPT 2016. LNCS, vol. 9646, pp. 127–143. Springer, Cham (2016). https://doi.org/10.1007/978-3-319-31517-1_7

22. McGrew, D.A.: An Interface and Algorithms for Authenticated Encryption. Internet Engineering Task Force - IETF, Request for Comments 5116, January 2008

23. Menezes, A.J., Oorschot, P.C.V., Vanstone, S.A.: Handbook of Applied Cryptography. CRC Press, Boca Raton (1996)

24. Namprempre, C., Rogaway, P., Shrimpton, T.: Reconsidering generic composition. In: Nguyen, P.Q., Oswald, E. (eds.) EUROCRYPT 2014. LNCS, vol. 8441, pp. 257–274. Springer, Heidelberg (2014). https://doi.org/10.1007/978-3-642-55220-5_15

25. Omara, E.: Google Duo End-to-End Encryption Overview - Technical Paper (2020). https://www.gstatic.com/duo/papers/duo_e2ee.pdf

26. Omara, E., Uberti, J., Gouaillard, A., Murillo, S.G.: Secure Frame (SFrame), November 2020. https://tools.ietf.org/html/draft-omara-sframe-01

27. Omara, E., Uberti, J., Gouaillard, A., Murillo, S.G.: Secure Frame (SFrame), March 2021. https://tools.ietf.org/html/draft-omara-sframe-02

28. Open Whisper Systems.: Signal Github Repository (2017). https://github.com/WhisperSystems/

29. Rogaway, P.: Authenticated-encryption with associated-data. In: Atluri, V. (ed.) ACM CCS 2002, pp. 98–107. ACM Press, November 2002. https://doi.org/10.1145/586110.586125

30. Rogaway, P., Shrimpton, T.: Cryptographic hash-function basics: definitions, implications, and separations for preimage resistance, second-preimage resistance, and collision resistance. In: Roy, B., Meier, W. (eds.) FSE 2004. LNCS, vol. 3017, pp. 371–388. Springer, Heidelberg (2004). https://doi.org/10.1007/978-3-540-25937-4_24

31. Rösler, P., Mainka, C., Schwenk, J.: More is less: on the end-to-end security of group chats in signal, WhatsApp, and Threema. In: 2018 IEEE European Symposium on Security and Privacy (EuroS&P), pp. 415–429. IEEE (2018)

32. Corretgé, S.I.: The road to End-to-End Encryption in Jitsi Meet (2021). https://fosdem.org/2021/schedule/event/e2ee/attachments/slides/4435/export/events/attachments/e2ee/slides/4435/E2EE.pdf

33. Murillo, S.G.: SFrame.js (2020). https://github.com/medooze/sframe

34. Turner, J.M.: The keyed-hash message authentication code (HMAC). Federal Inf. Process. Stand. Publ. **198**(1) (2008)

Attribute-Based Conditional Proxy Re-encryption in the Standard Model Under LWE

Xiaojian Liang, Jian Weng$^{(\boxtimes)}$, Anjia Yang, Lisha Yao, Zike Jiang, and Zhenghao Wu

College of Cyber Security, Jinan University, Guangzhou, China

Abstract. Attribute-based conditional proxy re-encryption (AB-CPRE) allows delegators to carry out attribute-based control on the delegation of decryption by setting policies and attribute vectors. The fine-grained control of AB-CPRE makes it suitable for a variety of applications, such as cloud storage and distributed file systems. However, all existing AB-CPRE schemes are constructed under classical number-theoretic assumptions, which are vulnerable to quantum cryptoanalysis. Therefore, we propose the first AB-CPRE scheme based on the learning with errors (LWE) assumption. Constructed from fully key-homomorphic encryption (FKHE) and key-switching techniques, our scheme is unidirectional, single-hop, and enables a polynomial-depth boolean circuit as its policy. Furthermore, we split the ciphertext into two independent parts to avoid two-level or multi-level encryption/decryption mechanisms. Taking advantage of it, we then extend our single-hop AB-CPRE into an efficient and concise multi-hop one. No matter how many transformations are performed, the re-encrypted ciphertext is in constant size, and only one encryption/decryption algorithm is needed. Both of our schemes are proved to be selective secure against chosen-plaintext attacks (CPA) in the standard model.

Keywords: Conditional proxy re-encryption · Learning with errors · Fine-grained control

1 Introduction

Proxy re-encryption (PRE) allows a semi-trusted proxy with a re-encryption key to transform a ciphertext intended for Alice (i.e. delegator) to another ciphertext intended for Bob (i.e.delegatee) without revealing the underlying plaintext [5]. PRE schemes can be classified into two types: one is single-hop, whose ciphertext can be transformed at most once, e.g., a ciphertext can be converted from Alice to Bob and cannot be further converted; the other is multi-hop, which means a ciphertext can be transformed multiple times, e.g., a ciphertext can be converted from Alice to Bob and to Carol, and so on. Based on the direction of transformation, PRE can be further categorized into bidirectional and unidirectional. In a

© Springer Nature Switzerland AG 2021
E. Bertino et al. (Eds.): ESORICS 2021, LNCS 12973, pp. 147–168, 2021.
https://doi.org/10.1007/978-3-030-88428-4_8

bidirectional scheme, a re-encryption key enables the transformation from Alice to Bob and vise versa. Whereas, in the unidirectional setting, a re-encryption key only supports the transformation from Alice to Bob. Notice that a bidirectional scheme can be built by running a unidirectional one in both directions.

PRE has found lots of applications that require delegation, but it may not be sufficient to facilitate flexible delegation. More specifically, once the proxy obtains a re-encryption key, it can re-encrypt all ciphertexts for delegator into the ciphertexts for delegate without any discrimination. Suppose that some of Alice's ciphertexts are highly confidential, and they should remain secret from Bob. To implement the delegation control, a trusted proxy is needed. Such a trusted model makes PRE unrealistic in complex applications.

To address the above problem, conditional proxy re-encryption (CPRE) was introduced by Weng et al. [32]. A CPRE is a variant of PRE supporting control on re-encryption. The ciphertext is associated with a condition, and the proxy can perform a transformation correctly only if the re-encryption key is associated with the same condition. The delegation control of CPRE makes it applicable to complex applications, such as encrypted email systems [30], online medical systems [13], distributed files systems [33] and cloud storage systems [18,19].

An open problem left by Weng et al. is how to construct a CPRE scheme supporting expressive predicates over the condition [32]. To address this problem, two types of CPRE are proposed: one is fuzzy conditional proxy re-encryption (F-CPRE), which does not require the condition in the re-encryption key and ciphertext to exactly match [12]; the other is attribute-based conditional proxy re-encryption (AB-CPRE), which supports attribute-based control on delegation [24,33,34]. Accurately, AB-CPRE is a kind of CPRE with fine-grained control, in which the ciphertext is associated with an attribute vector $\mathbf{x}$ and the re-encryption key is related to a policy f. The proxy is able to perform a transformation if $f(\mathbf{x}) = 0$ only. However, as far as our knowledge, there only exist CPRE [23] and F-CPRE [17] based on learning with errors (LWE). In other words, there is no quantum-resistant AB-CPRE construction to date.

On the other hand, several multi-hop PRE schemes are available in the literature [3,9,15,16,22,29,31]. However, the majority of them do not capture conditional re-encryption property. To achieve delegation control, Mo et al. proposed a unidirectional multi-hop conditional proxy re-encryption [26]. Liang et al. suggested a bidirectional multi-hop identity-based conditional proxy re-encryption (IBCPRE) with constant-size ciphertexts [18]. But, how to construct a multi-hop CPRE with fine-grained control remains open.

The existing lattice-based CPRE and multi-hop IBCPRE leave us two interesting problems: AB-CPRE over lattices and multi-hop AB-CPRE with constant-size ciphertexts. Therefore, the new scheme should be secure under lattice-based assumptions, e.g., LWE, but it should also enjoy constant-size ciphertexts no matter how many transformations are performed.

1.1   Contribution

We first formalize the definition and security notation for unidirectional multi-hop AB-CPRE. Specially, to achieve multi-hop, we require that a ciphertext with an attribute vector $\mathbf{x}$ for user α could be transformed into another ciphertext with a different attribute vector $\mathbf{y}$ for user β. Regarding security notation of AB-CPRE, we define a selective security and key privacy against chosen-plaintext attacks.

We also present two LWE-based unidirectional AB-CPRE schemes: the first one is single-hop; the second one is multi-hop. Our designs are obtained from fully key-homomorphic encryption (FKHE) and key-switching techniques. Table 1 makes a comparison between existing lattice-based CPRE, multi-hop CPRE, and ours. Our LWE-based constructions have the following features:

- The majority of PRE schemes are built with 2-level encryption/decryption mechanisms, where the second-level ciphertext allows to be transformed into the first-level one. To make CPRE more concise, we split ciphertext CT into two parts: one is ct, the ciphertext for message; the other is cc, the ciphertext for attributes. As a result, only one encryption/decryption is needed. Moreover, by reconstructing cc, our single-hop AB-CPRE can be extended into a multi-hop one with constant-size ciphertexts.
- Combining with FKHE, the delegation policy enables any polynomial-depth boolean circuit. As a consequence, our schemes support fine-grained delegation control.
- Our schemes enjoy selective indistinguishability of re-encryption keys and encryptions against chosen-plaintext attacks (sKP-CPA, sIND-CPA) in the standard model.

Table 1. Comparison between ours and existing schemes

Schemes	Types	Policy	Assumption	Security	Key Privacy	Standard model	Direction	Multi-hop
[23]	IBCPRE	\	LWE	CPA	✓	✗	→	✗
[17]	F-CPRE	Threshold	LWE	sCPA	✗	✓	→	✗
[34]	AB-CPRE	Access Tree	3-QDBDH	sCCA	✗	✓	→	✗
[33]	AB-CPRE	Access Tree	BDH	CPA	✗	✗	→	✗
[24]	AAB-CPRE	LSSS	3-wDBDHI	RCCA	✗	✓	→	✗
Scheme I	AB-CPRE	Boolean Circuit	LWE	sCPA	✓	✓	→	✗
[26]	CPRE	\	DDH	CCA	✗	✗	→	✓
[18]	IBCPRE	\	3-wBDHI	CCA	✗	✓	↔	✓
Scheme II	AB-CPRE	Boolean Circuit	LWE	sCPA	✓	✓	→	✓

1.2   Related Work

In 2010, Zhao et al. [34] supposed the first AB-CPRE scheme to improve the expressiveness and flexibility of the condition construction. Later, Yang et al. [33] presented a ciphertext-policy AB-CPRE, whose re-encryption key is related to a set of attributes whereas the ciphertext is associated with a policy. In 2018, Mao et al. [24] constructed the first anonymous AB-CPRE (AAB-CPRE) by linear secret sharing schemes (LSSS), which achieved replayable CCA (RCCA) security [10] in the standard model. But all stated AB-CPRE schemes were constructed under classical number-theoretic assumptions and none of them considers multi-hop case. We are thus motivated to propose AB-CPRE schemes over lattices that is secure against quantum attacks.

1.3   Organization

The rest of paper is organized as follows. The introductions of lattices, such as LWE, lattice trapdoor, and Gaussian sampling are presented in Sect. 2. The definition and security notation of universal AB-CPRE are formalized in Sect. 3. In Sect. 4, we propose our single-hop AB-CPRE scheme in the standard model and give the corresponding security proof. In Sect. 5, we give a multi-hop AB-CPRE scheme as an extension from our single-hop one. Finally, Sect. 6 concludes this paper.

2   Preliminaries

In this paper, we use a lower-case bold letter to denote a column vector $\mathbf{a}$, while an upper-case bold letter to denote a matrix $\mathbf{A}$. The (centered) discrete Gaussian distribution over $\mathcal{L}$ with parameter σ is denoted $\mathcal{D}_\sigma(\mathcal{L})$. For vector $\mathbf{u}$, we let $\|\mathbf{u}\|$ denote its ℓ_2 norm. For matrix $\mathbf{R} \in \mathbb{Z}^{k \times m}$, we denote by $\|\mathbf{R}\|$ the maximum length of column vector of $\mathbf{R}$. $\|\mathbf{R}\|_{GS} := \|\tilde{\mathbf{R}}\|$ where $\tilde{\mathbf{R}}$ is the Gram-Schmidt(GS) orthogonalization of $\mathbf{R}$, and $\|\mathbf{R}\|_2 := \sup_{\|\mathbf{e}\|=1} \|\mathbf{Re}\|$. Then, we have $\|\mathbf{R}\|_{GS} \leq \|\mathbf{R}\| \leq \|\mathbf{R}\|_2 \leq \sqrt{k}\|\mathbf{R}\|$ and $\|\mathbf{RS}\|_2 \leq \|\mathbf{R}\|_2 \cdot \|\mathbf{S}\|_2$. Moreover, we denote horizontal concatenation of vectors and/or matrices using a vertical bar, e.g., $[\mathbf{A}|\mathbf{B}]$, and vertical concatenation of vectors and/or matrices using a semicolon, e.g., $[\mathbf{A}; \mathbf{B}]$.

2.1   Lattice Background

We use m-dimensional full-rank integers lattices Λ, which are discrete additive subgroups of $\mathbb{Z}^m$. A q-ary integer lattice and a "shift" integer lattice are defined as follows.

Definition 1. *(q-ary Lattices) Given a matrix* $\mathbf{A} \in \mathbb{Z}_q^{n \times m}$ *for some positive integers* n, m, q *and a vector* $\mathbf{u} \in \mathbb{Z}_q^n$, *we define:*

$$\Lambda_q^\perp(\mathbf{A}) = \{\mathbf{x} \in \mathbb{Z}^m : \mathbf{Ax} = \mathbf{0} \mod q\}.$$
$$\Lambda_q^{\mathbf{u}}(\mathbf{A}) = \{\mathbf{x} \in \mathbb{Z}^m : \mathbf{Ax} = \mathbf{u} \mod q\}.$$

Definition 2. *A noise distribution χ over $\mathbb{Z}$ is B-bounded, if $\Pr\limits_{x \leftarrow \chi} \left[\|x\| \geq B \right] \leq 2^{-\tilde{\Omega}(n)}$.*

Definition 3. *(Decisional learning with errors) Given integers n, $q \geq 1$, $m \geq O(n \log q)$, and a B-bounded noise distribution χ over integers, the $LWE_{n,q,\chi}$ problem is to distinguish the following two distributions:*

$$(\mathbf{A}, \mathbf{A}^T \mathbf{s} + \mathbf{e}) \ and \ (\mathbf{A}, \mathbf{u})$$

where $\mathbf{A} \leftarrow \mathbb{Z}_q^{n \times m}, \mathbf{s} \leftarrow \mathbb{Z}_q^n, \mathbf{e} \leftarrow \chi^m, \mathbf{u} \leftarrow \mathbb{Z}_q^m$ are sampled independently.

Theorem 1. *([8,27,28]) If there exists an efficient algorithm for deciding the $LWE_{n,q,\chi}$ problem for some $B = B(n), q/B \geq 2^{n^\varepsilon}, m = poly(n)$, then there is an efficient quantum algorithm for $SIVP_\gamma$ and a classical algorithm for $GapSVP_\gamma$ for $\gamma = 2^{\Omega(n^\varepsilon)}$ in the worst case.*

Corollary 1. *(Hermite normal form [4]) There exists a useful transformation that reduces $LWE_{n,q,\chi}$ problem into one where the secret is chosen from its noise distributions χ, which illustrates that distinguish the following two distributions is no easier than solving $LWE_{n,q,\chi}$ problem.*

$$(\mathbf{A}, \mathbf{A}^T \mathbf{s} + \mathbf{e}) \ and \ (\mathbf{A}, \mathbf{u})$$

where $\mathbf{A} \leftarrow \mathbb{Z}_q^{n \times m}, \mathbf{s} \leftarrow \chi^n, \mathbf{e} \leftarrow \chi^m, \mathbf{u} \leftarrow \mathbb{Z}_q^m$ are sampled independently.

Corollary 2. *([21]) Applying standard hybrid argument, these distributions below are computational indistinguishable. Otherwise, there exists an efficient algorithm to solve $LWE_{n,q,\chi}$ problem.*

- $(\mathbf{A}, \mathbf{A}^T \mathbf{X} + \mathbf{E})$ and $(\mathbf{A}, \mathbf{U})$, where $\mathbf{A} \leftarrow \mathbb{Z}_q^{n \times m}, \mathbf{X} \leftarrow \chi^{n \times \ell}, \mathbf{E} \leftarrow \chi^{m \times \ell}, \mathbf{U} \leftarrow \mathbb{Z}_q^{m \times \ell}$.
- $(\mathbf{A}, \mathbf{D}, \mathbf{A}^T \mathbf{X} + \mathbf{E}, \mathbf{D}^T \mathbf{X} + \mathbf{E}')$ and $(\mathbf{A}, \mathbf{D}, \mathbf{A}^T \mathbf{X} + \mathbf{E}, \mathbf{D}^T \mathbf{X}' + \mathbf{E}')$ where $\mathbf{A}, \mathbf{D} \leftarrow \mathbb{Z}_q^{n \times m}, \mathbf{X}, \mathbf{X}' \leftarrow \chi^{n \times \ell}, \mathbf{E}, \mathbf{E}' \leftarrow \chi^{m \times \ell}$.
- $(\mathbf{A}, \{\mathbf{A}^T \mathbf{X}_i + \mathbf{E}_i\}_{i \in [t]})$ and $(\mathbf{A}, \{\mathbf{U}_i\}_{i \in [t]})$, where $\mathbf{A} \leftarrow \mathbb{Z}_q^{n \times m}, \mathbf{X}_i \leftarrow \chi^{n \times \ell}, \mathbf{E}_i \leftarrow \chi^{m \times \ell}, \mathbf{U}_i \leftarrow \mathbb{Z}_q^{n \times \ell}$ for all $i \in [t], t = poly(n)$.

Lemma 1. *([1]) Given $q > 2$ and $m > (n+1) \log q + \omega(\log n)$, for some polynomial $k = k(n)$, choose three uniformly random matrices $\mathbf{U} \in \{-1,1\}^{m \times k}, \mathbf{A} \in \mathbb{Z}_q^{n \times m}$, and $\mathbf{B} \in \mathbb{Z}_q^{n \times k}$. For all vectors $\mathbf{r} \in \mathbb{Z}_q^m$, the distributions $(\mathbf{A}, \mathbf{AU}, \mathbf{U}^T \mathbf{r})$ and $(\mathbf{A}, \mathbf{B}, \mathbf{U}^T \mathbf{r})$ are statistically indistinguishable.*

2.2 Trapdoor and Sampling

The following lemmas show the properties of lattice trapdoor and efficient Gaussian preimage sampling respectively.

Definition 4. *(Gadget matrix [6,25]) For integers $q \geq 2$ and $n \geq 1$, there is a special, structured matrix $\mathbf{G} = \mathbf{I}_n \otimes \mathbf{g}^T \in \mathbb{Z}_q^{n \times kn}$ where $k = \lceil \log(q) \rceil, \mathbf{g} = (1, 2, ..., 2^{k-1}) \in \mathbb{Z}_q^k$.*

- The lattice $\Lambda_q^\perp(\mathbf{G})$ has a public known basis $\mathbf{T_G} \in \mathbb{Z}^{kn \times kn}$ with $\|\mathbf{T_G}\|_{GS} \leq \sqrt{5}$.
- For any $m \geq kn$, $\mathbf{G} \in \mathbb{Z}_q^{n \times kn}$ can be extended to a matrix $\mathbf{G'} \in \mathbb{Z}_q^{n \times m}$ by adding zero columns on the right of $\mathbf{G}$.

Lemma 2. ([1,6,11]) Given $n \geq 1$, $q \geq 2$ and $m \geq \lceil 6n \log q \rceil$, we have the following polynomial-time algorithms:

- There is a randomized algorithm **TrapGen**$(1^n, 1^m, q)$ that outputs a full-rank matrix $\mathbf{A} \in \mathbb{Z}_q^{n \times m}$ and a short basis $\mathbf{T_A} \in \mathbb{Z}^{m \times m}$ for $\Lambda_q^\perp(\mathbf{A})$ such that $\mathbf{A}$ is statistically close to uniform and $\|\mathbf{T_A}\|_{GS} = O(\sqrt{n \log q})$, with all but negligible probability in n.
- There is a deterministic algorithm **ExtendRight**$(\mathbf{A}, \mathbf{T}_A, \mathbf{B})$ that given matrices $\mathbf{A}, \mathbf{B} \in \mathbb{Z}_q^{n \times m}$ and a basis $\mathbf{T_A}$ of $\Lambda_q^\perp(\mathbf{A})$ outputs a basis $\mathbf{T_{A|B}}$ of $\Lambda_q^\perp(\mathbf{A}|\mathbf{B})$ such that $\|\mathbf{T_{A|B}}\|_{GS} = \|\mathbf{T_A}\|_{GS}$.
- There is a deterministic algorithm **ExtendLeft**$(\mathbf{A}, \mathbf{G}, \mathbf{T_G}, \mathbf{S})$ that given full-rank matrices $\mathbf{A}, \mathbf{G} \in \mathbb{Z}_q^{n \times m}$ and a basis $\mathbf{T_G}$ of $\Lambda_q^\perp(\mathbf{G})$ outputs a basis $\mathbf{T_{A|AS+G}}$ of $\Lambda_q^\perp(\mathbf{A}|\mathbf{AS+G})$ such that $\|\mathbf{T_{A|AS+G}}\|_{GS} \leq \|\mathbf{T_G}\|_{GS} \cdot (1 + \|\mathbf{S}\|_2)$.

Lemma 3. ([2,11,14]) Given integers $n, q > 2$ and $m > n$. Let $\mathbf{A} \in \mathbb{Z}_q^{n \times m}$ and $\mathbf{T_A}$ be a basis for $\Lambda_q^\perp(\mathbf{A})$, for any $\sigma \geq \|\mathbf{T_A}\|_{GS} \cdot \omega(\sqrt{\log m})$. We have

- A random vector $\mathbf{x}$ sampled from $D_\sigma(\Lambda_q^\mathbf{u}(\mathbf{A}))$ has ℓ_2 norm less than $\sigma\sqrt{m}$ all but with negligible probability in m.
- There is a randomized algorithm **SamplePre**$(\mathbf{A}, \mathbf{T_A}, \mathbf{D}, \sigma)$, which outputs a random matrix $\mathbf{X} \in \Lambda_q^\perp(\mathbf{A})$ such that $\mathbf{AX} = \mathbf{D}$ from a distribution that is statistically close to $\mathcal{D}_\sigma(\Lambda_q^\mathbf{D}(\mathbf{A}))$.
- There is a randomized algorithm **RandBasis**$(\mathbf{A}, \mathbf{T_A}, \sigma)$, which outputs a random basis $\mathbf{T'_A}$ of $\Lambda_q^\perp(\mathbf{A})$ sampled from a distribution that is statistically close to $\mathcal{D}_\sigma(\Lambda_q^\mathbf{D}(\mathbf{A}))$.

2.3   Key Homomorphism and Vector Decomposition

Let us recall some notions, used in fully homomorphic encryption.

Definition 5. For any positive integers ℓ, d, we define the family of functions $\mathcal{F}_{\ell,d} = \{f : \{0,1\}^\ell \to \{0,1\}\}$, where f is a boolean circuit of depth $\leq d$.

Lemma 4. ([6,22]) Given positive integers n, q, ℓ, d, m where $m \geq \lceil n \log(q) \rceil$ and a B-bounded noise distribution χ, for any matrices $\mathbf{B}_1, ..., \mathbf{B}_\ell \in \mathbb{Z}_q^{n \times m}$, any boolean circuit $f \in \mathcal{F}_{\ell,d}$ and any $\mathbf{x} \in \{0,1\}^\ell$, if

$$\forall i \in [\ell] : \mathbf{c}_i = (x_i \mathbf{G} + \mathbf{B}_i)^T \mathbf{s} + \mathbf{e}_i$$

where $\mathbf{s} \leftarrow \mathbb{Z}_q^n, \mathbf{e}_i \leftarrow \chi^m$ for $i \in [\ell]$, then we have,

- A deterministic algorithm **Eval**$_{pk}(f, \{\mathbf{B}_i\}_{i \in [\ell]})$ that given a circuit f and ℓ matrices $\{\mathbf{B}_i\}_{i \in [\ell]}$, outputs a matrix $\mathbf{B}_f$.

- A deterministic algorithm $\mathbf{Eval}_{ct}(f, \{(x_i, \mathbf{B}_i, \mathbf{c}_i)\}_{i\in[\ell]})$ that given a circuit f, a vector $\mathbf{x} \in \{0,1\}^\ell$, ℓ matrices $\{\mathbf{B}_i\}_{i\in[\ell]}$ and ℓ vectors $\{\mathbf{c}_i\}_{i\in[\ell]}$, outputs a vector $\mathbf{c}_f$, satisfying

$$\mathbf{c}_f = (f(\mathbf{x})\mathbf{G} + \mathbf{B}_f)^T \mathbf{s} + \mathbf{e}_f$$

where $\mathbf{B}_f = \mathbf{Eval}_{pk}(f, \{\mathbf{B}_i\}_{i\in[\ell]})$ and $\|\mathbf{e}_f\| \leq B\sqrt{m}(m+1)^d$ with all but negligible probability.

- For all $i \in [\ell]$, it holds that $\mathbf{B}_i = \mathbf{AS}_i - x_i^*\mathbf{G}$ where $\mathbf{x}^* = \{x_i^*\}_{i\in[\ell]} \in \{0,1\}^\ell$ and $\mathbf{S}_i \in \{-1,1\}^{m\times m}$. A deterministic algorithm $\mathbf{Eval}_{sim}(f, \{x_i^*, \mathbf{S}_i\}_{i\in[\ell]}, \mathbf{A})$ that given a circuit f, a vector $\mathbf{x}^* \in \{0,1\}^\ell$, ℓ matrices $\{\mathbf{S}_i\}_{i\in[\ell]}$ and a matrix $\mathbf{A}$, outputs a matrix $\mathbf{S}_f$ satisfying

$$\mathbf{AS}_f - f(\mathbf{x}^*)\mathbf{G} = \mathbf{B}_f$$

where $\mathbf{B}_f = \mathbf{Eval}_{pk}(f, \{\mathbf{B}_i\}_{i\in[\ell]})$ and $\|\mathbf{S}_f\|_2 \leq 20\sqrt{m}(m+1)^d$ with all but negligible probability.

Definition 6. *(Vector Decomposition [3,7]) We define the function mapping vectors to their bit representations as below:*

- A deterministic function $\mathbf{Bits}_q(\mathbf{v})$ that given a vector $\mathbf{v} \in \mathbb{Z}_q^n$, let $\mathbf{v}_i \in \{0,1\}^n$ be such that $\mathbf{v} = \sum_{i=1}^{\lceil \log q\rceil-1} 2^i \mathbf{v}_i$, outputs a vector $\tilde{\mathbf{v}} \in \{0,1\}^{n\cdot\lceil \log q\rceil}$, where $\tilde{\mathbf{v}} = (\mathbf{v}_0; \ldots; \mathbf{v}_{\lceil \log q\rceil-1})$.
- A deterministic function $\mathbf{Power2}_q(\mathbf{X})$ that given a matrix $\mathbf{X} \in \mathbb{Z}_q^{n\times m}$, outputs a matrix $\overline{\mathbf{X}} \in \mathbb{Z}_q^{n\lceil\log q\rceil\times m}$, where $\overline{\mathbf{X}} = [\mathbf{X}; 2\mathbf{X}; \ldots; 2^{\lceil\log q\rceil-1}\mathbf{X}]$.
- For all positive integers $q, n, m \in \mathbb{Z}$, a vector $\mathbf{v} \in \mathbb{Z}_q^n$ and a matrix $\mathbf{X} \in \mathbb{Z}^{n\times m}$, it holds that $\mathbf{v}^T\mathbf{X} = \mathbf{Bits}_q(\mathbf{v})^T \cdot \mathbf{Power2}_q(\mathbf{X}) = \tilde{\mathbf{v}}^T\overline{\mathbf{X}} \in \mathbb{Z}_q^{1\times m}$.

3   Model of Attribute-Based CPRE

In this section, we present the formalization of unidirectional AB-CPRE and its corresponding security notation. We start with multi-hop AB-CPRE, which implies single-hop AB-CPRE.

3.1   Multi-hop AB-CPRE

Definition 7. *(Multi-hop AB-CPRE) A unidirectional multi-hop attribute-based conditional proxy re-encryption scheme comprises the following six algorithms:*

- **Setup**(n): *the setup algorithm is run by a semi-trusted agent. Given a security parameter n as input, it outputs the public parameters pp.*
- **KeyGen**(pp, α): *the key generation algorithm is run by a user in the system. Given the public parameters pp, it generates the public/private key pair (pk_α, sk_α) for user α.*

- **Enc**$(pp, pk_\alpha, \boldsymbol{\mu}, \mathbf{x})$: *the encryption algorithm, takes as input the public parameters pp, a public key pk_α, a plaintext $\boldsymbol{\mu}$, and an attribute vector $\mathbf{x}$. It outputs a ciphertext CT_α associated with $\mathbf{x}$ under public key pk_α.*
- **Dec**$(pp, sk_\alpha, CT_\alpha)$: *the decryption algorithm, takes as input the public parameters pp, a private key sk_α and a ciphertext CT_α under public key pk_α. It outputs a message $\boldsymbol{\mu}$.*
- **ReKeyGen**$(pp, sk_\alpha, pk_\beta, f, \mathbf{y})$: *the re-encryption key generation algorithm is run by user α, takes as input the public parameters pp, the private key sk_α for user α, the public key pk_β for another user β, a control policy/function f and an attribute vector $\mathbf{y}$. It outputs a re-encryption key $rk_{\alpha,f\to\beta,\mathbf{y}}$ associated with f.*
- **ReEnc**$(pp, CT_\alpha, rk_{\alpha,f\to\beta,\mathbf{y}})$: *the re-encryption algorithm run by the proxy, takes as input a ciphertext CT_α associated with $\mathbf{x}$ under a public key pk_α for user α, a public key pk_β for user β and a re-encryption key $rk_{\alpha,f\to\beta,\mathbf{y}}$. It outputs a ciphertext CT_β associated with $\mathbf{y}$ under the public key pk_β when $f(\mathbf{x}) = 0$ holds, otherwise outputs $\bot$.*

Remark 1. In AB-CPRE scheme, a ciphertext can be associated with null attribute, which means vector $\mathbf{x}$ in **Enc** algorithm or vector $\mathbf{y}$ in **ReKeyGen** and **ReEnc** algorithms may be a null vector. Specially, a ciphertext with null attribute cannot be re-encrypted. For simplification, if the attribute vector is a null vector, we will omit it, e.g., $rk_{\alpha,f\to\beta} \leftarrow$ **ReKeyGen**$(pp, sk_\alpha, pk_\beta, f)$.

Correctness. In a unidirectional multi-hop attribute-based proxy re-encryption scheme. We require the correctness for encryption and re-encryption as follows,

- For any key pair $(pk_\alpha, sk_\alpha) \leftarrow$ **KeyGen**(pp, α), any attribute vector $\mathbf{x}$ and any message $\boldsymbol{\mu}$, it holds that

$$\Pr[\mathbf{Dec}(pp, sk_\alpha, \mathbf{Enc}(pp, pk_\alpha, \boldsymbol{\mu}, \mathbf{x})) = \boldsymbol{\mu}] = 1 - negl(n).$$

- For any attribute vectors $\mathbf{y}_1, ..., \mathbf{y}_t$, any key pairs $(pk_{\beta_1}, sk_{\beta_1})...(pk_{\beta_t}, sk_{\beta_t})$, and any message $\boldsymbol{\mu}$, for all $i \in \{2, ..., t\}$, $f_{i-1}(\mathbf{y}_{i-1}) = 0$, it holds that

$$rk_{\beta_{i-1}, f_{i-1}\to\beta_i, \mathbf{y}_i} \leftarrow \mathbf{ReKeyGen}(pp, sk_{\beta_{i-1}}, pk_{\beta_i}, f_{i-1}, \mathbf{y}_i),$$
$$CT_{\beta_i}^{(i-1)} = \mathbf{ReEnc}(pp, CT_{\beta_{i-1}}^{(i-2)}, rk_{\beta_{i-1}, f_{i-1}\to\beta_i, \mathbf{y}_i}),$$
$$\Pr[\mathbf{Dec}(pp, sk_{\beta_i}, CT_{\beta_i}^{(i-1)}) = \boldsymbol{\mu}] = 1 - negl(n)$$

where $t = poly(n)$, $CT_{\beta_1}^{(0)} = \mathbf{Enc}(pp, pk_{\beta_1}, \boldsymbol{\mu}, \mathbf{y}_1)$.

3.2 Single-Hop AB-CPRE

Unidirectional single-hop AB-CPRE, whose ciphertext can be transformed at most once, can be viewed as a weak concept of unidirectional multi-hop AB-CPRE. CPRE scheme does not require the attribute vector (or conditional vector) as an input to decrypt the transformed ciphertext. Thus, different from multi-hop one, single-hop AB-CPRE does not require delegator to set an attribute vector **y** in **ReKeyGen** and **ReEnc** algorithms. Particularly, in single-hop scheme, we would call the ciphertext with attributes as original ciphertext, and the ciphertext with null attribute as transformed ciphertext.

3.3   Security Notation

In this section, we concentrate on formulating the universal security notation for unidirectional AB-CPRE. Before proceeding, we define the notations used in security definitions.

– **Delegation chain.** Suppose in an unidirectional AB-CPRE scheme there is a re-encryption key set $RK = \{rk_{\beta_1, f_1 \to \beta_2, \mathbf{y}_2}, ..., rk_{\beta_{t-1}, f_{t-1} \to \beta_t, \mathbf{y}_t}\}$, or $RK' = \{rk_{\beta_1, f_1 \to \beta_2, \mathbf{y}_2}, ..., rk_{\beta_{t-2}, f_{t-2} \to \beta_{t-1}, \mathbf{y}_{t-1}}, rk_{\beta_{t-1}, f_{t-1} \to \beta_t}\}$, where $t \geq 2$ and $f_i(\mathbf{y}_i) = 0$ for all $i \in \{1, ..., t-1\}$. Specially, we can learn that users $\beta_1, \beta_2, ..., \beta_t$ are able to decrypt all ciphertexts with $\mathbf{y}_1$ for user β_1. Thus, we say that there exists a delegation chain under $(\beta_1, \mathbf{y}_1)$ from user β_1 to user β_t. For convenience, we denote this delegation chain as $(\mathbf{y}_1, \beta_1, ..., \beta_t)$.
– **Uncorrupted/corrupted user.** If the private key of a user is compromised by an adversary, then we consider this user as a corrupted user. Otherwise, this user is an uncorrputed user.
– **Uncorrupted/corrupted delegation chain.** Suppose there exists a delegation chain $(\mathbf{y}_1, \beta_1, ..., \beta_t)$. If all users on the chain are uncorrputed users, then it is an uncorrputed chain. Otherwise, it is a corrupted chain, which implies at least one corrupted user could decrypt all ciphertexts with $\mathbf{y}_1$ for user β_1.

Remark 2. In single-hop AB-CPRE, the delegation chain at most contains two users, e.g., $(\mathbf{x}, \alpha, \beta)$. Whereas, in multi-hop one, the delegation chain could contain $O(n)$ users.

sIND-CPA Game. The selective security of AB-CPRE on ciphertext is defined through the following security game between a challenger $\mathcal{C}$ and an adversary $\mathcal{A}$.

Init Adversary $\mathcal{A}$ announces an attributes vector $\mathbf{x}^*$ before seeing public parameters pp.
Setup Challenger $\mathcal{C}$ runs the **Setup** algorithm to generate public parameters pp, and then executes **KeyGen** algorithm with a random user identity θ to get a key pair (pk_θ, sk_θ). Finally, the challenger passes pp and pk_θ to the adversary $\mathcal{A}$.
Phase 1 $\mathcal{C}$ initializes three empty collections Ψ_u, Ψ_c, and Ψ_{rk}. Then, $\mathcal{C}$ inserts (pk_θ, sk_θ) into Ψ_u. $\mathcal{A}$ sends queries $q_1, ..., q_t$ to $\mathcal{C}$. Each query is one of the following:

    1) Uncorrupted key generation query $\mathcal{O}_u(\beta)$: $\mathcal{C}$ first runs algorithm **KeyGen**(pp, β) to get a key pair (pk_β, sk_β), and then inserts it into collection Ψ_u. Finally, $\mathcal{C}$ outputs a public key pk_β.

2) Corrupted key generation query $\mathcal{O}_c(\beta)$: $\mathcal{C}$ first executes algorithm **KeyGen**(pp, β) to get a key pair (pk_β, sk_β), and then inserts it into collection Ψ_c. Finally, $\mathcal{C}$ outputs a key pair (pk_β, sk_β).

3) Re-encryption key query $\mathcal{O}_{rk}(pk_\alpha, pk_\beta, f, \mathbf{y})$: If $\alpha = \beta$ or $pk_\alpha \notin \Psi_u \cup \Psi_c$ or $pk_\beta \notin \Psi_u \cup \Psi_c$, then $\mathcal{C}$ outputs $\bot$. $\mathcal{C}$ generates a re-encryption key $rk_{\alpha, f \to \beta, \mathbf{y}}$ by executing **ReKeyGen**$(pp, sk_\alpha, pk_\beta, f, \mathbf{y})$. If there exists a corrupted delegation chain $(\mathbf{x}^*, \theta, ...)$ in $\Psi_{rk} \cup \{rk_{\alpha, f \to \beta, \mathbf{y}}\}$, then $\mathcal{C}$ outputs $\bot$. Otherwise, $\mathcal{C}$ inserts $rk_{\alpha, f \to \beta, \mathbf{y}}$ into Ψ_{rk} and then outputs $rk_{\alpha, f \to \beta, \mathbf{y}}$.

4) Re-encryption query $\mathcal{O}_{re}(CT_\alpha, rk_{\alpha, f \to, \beta, \mathbf{y}})$: If $rk_{\alpha, f \to, \beta, \mathbf{y}} \in \Psi_{rk}$, then $\mathcal{C}$ outputs **ReEnc**$(pp, CT_\alpha, rk_{\alpha, f \to, \beta, \mathbf{y}})$. Otherwise, $\mathcal{C}$ outputs $\bot$.

Challenge $\mathcal{A}$ submits two equal-length messages $\boldsymbol{\mu}_0^*$ and $\boldsymbol{\mu}_1^*$. $\mathcal{C}$ flips a random coin $b \in \{0, 1\}$, executes $CT^* \leftarrow$ **Enc**$(pp, pk_\theta, \mathbf{x}^*, \boldsymbol{\mu}_b^*)$, and returns the original ciphertext CT^* to $\mathcal{A}$.

Phase 2 The same as **Phase 1**.

Guess $\mathcal{A}$ outputs a bit b', which is a guess on b.

sKP-CPA Game. The selective security of AB-CPRE on re-encryption key is the same as sIND-CPA game, except the Challenge phase.

Challenge $\mathcal{A}$ submits an uncorrupted user's public key pk_β and a policy f. If there exists a re-encryption key $rk_{\beta, f \to \theta} \in \Psi_{rk}$ or $rk_{\beta, f \to \theta, \mathbf{y}} \in \Psi_{rk}$ where $\mathbf{y}$ is an attribute vector, then $\mathcal{C}$ outputs $\bot$. Otherwise, $\mathcal{C}$ tosses a random coin $b \in \{0, 1\}$, outputs a re-encryption key $rk_{\beta, f \to \theta}$ by executing **ReKeyGen**$(pp, sk_\beta, pk_\theta, f)$ if $b = 1$, or returns random re-encryption key rk^* in re-encryption key space if $b = 0$.

Definition 8. *(sIND-CPA Security) An attribute-based CPRE scheme is selective secure against chosen-plaintext attacks if for any probabilistic polynomial time (PPT) adversary $\mathcal{A}$, it holds that $Pr[b' = b] = 1/2 + negl(n)$ in sIND-CPA game, where negl is a negligible function.*

Definition 9. *(sKP-CPA security) An attribute-based CPRE scheme is selective key privacy under chosen-plaintext attacks if for any PPT adversary $\mathcal{A}$, it holds that $Pr[b' = b] = 1/2 + negl(n)$ in sKP-CPA game, where negl is a negligible function.*

4   Single-Hop AB-CPRE Scheme

In this section, we propose the single-hop AB-CPRE scheme. Firstly, we introduce the core techniques and the main idea behind our scheme. Then, we present our concrete scheme, its correctness as well as security proof.

4.1   Technique Review

We start with a brief overview of fully key-homomorphic public-key encryption (FKHE) [6] and key switching [3], which are the core techniques of our scheme.

In [6], Boneh et al. put forward a kind of FKHE. For any boolean circuit $f : \{0,1\}^\ell \to \{0,1\}$ and its ℓ bits input $\mathbf{x} \in \{0,1\}^\ell$, there exist three efficient algorithms $\mathbf{Eval}_{pk}$, $\mathbf{Eval}_{ct}$ and $\mathbf{Eval}_{sim}$ (See Lemma 4 for more details).

Applying FKHE, a KP-ABE system can be constructed. The master public key contains ℓ attribute matrices $\{\mathbf{B}_i\}_{i \in [\ell]}$ and two matrices $\mathbf{A}, \mathbf{D}$. The master secret key is a short basis $\mathbf{T}$ for lattice $\Lambda^\perp(\mathbf{A})$.

- For a user with policy f, use $\mathbf{T}$ to extract a secret key $\mathbf{R}_f$ such that $[\mathbf{A}|\mathbf{B}_f]\mathbf{R}_f = -\mathbf{D}$, where $\mathbf{B}_f = \mathbf{Eval}_{pk}(f, \{\mathbf{B}_i\}_{i \in [\ell]})$.
- For a ciphertext $(\mathbf{A}^T\mathbf{s} + \mathbf{e}_{in}, \mathbf{D}^T\mathbf{s} + \mathbf{e}_{out} + \lfloor q/2 \rfloor \boldsymbol{\mu}, \{(x_i\mathbf{G} + \mathbf{B}_i)^T\mathbf{s} + \mathbf{e}_i\}_{i \in [\ell]})$ of a message $\boldsymbol{\mu}$ with an attribute vector $\mathbf{x}$, the user can execute the $\mathbf{Eval}_{ct}$ to assemble a ciphertext $\mathbf{c}_f = (\mathbf{B}_f + f(\mathbf{x})\mathbf{G})^T\mathbf{s} + \mathbf{e}_f$. The user can recover the message $\boldsymbol{\mu}$ correctly by secret key $\mathbf{R}_f$ if his policy f satisfies $f(\mathbf{x}) = 0$.

First Attempt. Easily, we can construct a naive AB-CPRE scheme by FKHE. Firstly, a random matrix $\mathbf{D}$ and ℓ attribute matrices $\{\mathbf{B}_i\}_{i \in [\ell]}$ are chosen and shared among users. Then, each user chooses his public key $\mathbf{A}$ and the corresponding private key $\mathbf{T}$, the short basis of lattice $\Lambda^\perp(\mathbf{A})$. At last, if user α wants to delegate the decryption right with policy f to user β, user α could use $\mathbf{T}_\alpha$ to extract the re-encryption key $\mathbf{R}_{\alpha, f \to \beta}$ such that $[\mathbf{A}_\alpha|\mathbf{B}_f]\mathbf{R}_{\alpha, f \to \beta} = \mathbf{A}_\beta$.

Although this naive scheme seems to work, there is no formal proof to show the indistinguishability under chosen-plaintext attack. The FKHE system of [6] only achieves selective IND-CPA secure. In other words, in FKHE system, $\mathcal{A}$ would announce an attribute vector $\mathbf{x}^*$ in the beginning, and $\mathcal{C}$ does not need to answer the query on function f such that $f(\mathbf{x}^*) = 0$. But the security notation of AB-CPRE needs $\mathcal{C}$ to answer the query on $\mathcal{O}_{rk}(pk_\theta, pk_\beta, f)$. In the case that $f(\mathbf{x}^*) = 0$ and $pk_\beta \in \Psi_u$, $\mathcal{C}$ cannot generate the corresponding re-encryption key by **ExtendLeft**, and then abort.

To address the constrain in the naive scheme, we have to apply the key-switching technique, which was originally used in fully homomorphic encryption [7]. Aono et al. [3] constructed an interactive PRE with key privacy using key-switching. Intuitively, we can convert it into a non-interactive one as follows,

- For user α, the public key is a pair of LWE instance $(\mathbf{A}_\alpha, \mathbf{D}_\alpha)$ while the private key is $\mathbf{S}_\alpha$, where $\mathbf{D}_\alpha = \mathbf{R}_\alpha - \mathbf{A}_\alpha\mathbf{S}_\alpha$ and $\mathbf{R}_\alpha, \mathbf{S}_\alpha$ are sampled from error distribution.
- The re-encryption key is a matrix $\mathbf{Q}_{\alpha \to \beta}$ as below,

$$\mathbf{Q}_{\alpha \to \beta} = \begin{bmatrix} \mathbf{E}_1\mathbf{A}_\beta + \mathbf{E}_2 & \mathbf{E}_1\mathbf{D}_\beta + \mathbf{E}_3 + \mathbf{Power2}_q(\mathbf{S}_\alpha) \\ \mathbf{0} & \mathbf{I} \end{bmatrix}.$$

where $\mathbf{E}_1, \mathbf{E}_2, \mathbf{E}_3$ are chosen from error distribution.
- In the transformation process, the proxy converts user α's ciphertext $(\mathbf{c}_{in}, \mathbf{c}_{out})$ into $(\mathbf{Bits}_q(\mathbf{c}_{in}), \mathbf{c}_{out})$ and then returns $[\mathbf{Bits}(\mathbf{c}_{in})^T | \mathbf{c}_{out}^T]\mathbf{Q}_{\alpha \to \beta}$ as transformed ciphertext ($\mathbf{Power2}_q$ and $\mathbf{Bits}_q$ are defined as Definition 6).

Combining key-switching technique with our naive scheme, we propose a provably-secure single-hop AB-CPRE scheme. The main idea is showed as follows,

- ℓ attribute matrices $\{\mathbf{B}_i\}_{i\in[\ell]}$ are chosen uniformly at random and shared among users.
- Each user chooses two matrices $\mathbf{A}, \mathbf{D}$ as their public key, and the short basis $\mathbf{T}$ for lattice $\Lambda^\perp(\mathbf{A})$ as their private key.
- Ciphertext of message $\boldsymbol{\mu}$ with attribute vector $\mathbf{x}$ under pk_α is $CT_\alpha = (ct, cc)$,

$$ct = (\mathbf{A}_\alpha^T \mathbf{s} + \mathbf{e}_{in}, \mathbf{D}_\alpha^T \mathbf{s} + \mathbf{e}_{out} + \lfloor q/2 \rfloor \boldsymbol{\mu}) \ , \ cc = \{(x_i\mathbf{G} + \mathbf{B}_i)^T \mathbf{s} + \mathbf{e}_i\}_{i\in[\ell]}$$

where $\mathbf{A}_\alpha, \mathbf{D}_\alpha$ is the public key of user α and $\mathbf{s}$ is selected uniformly at random.
- Since user α has the short basis $\mathbf{T}_\alpha$, only ct is needed in decryption process. Whereas cc only works for delegation of decryption.
- If user α wants to delegate the decryption right with policy f to user β, then user α extracts a matrix $\mathbf{R}_{\alpha,f}$ with small norm such that $(\mathbf{A}_\alpha|\mathbf{B}_f)\mathbf{R}_{\alpha,f} = -\mathbf{D}_\alpha$ and returns a matrix $\mathbf{Q}_{\alpha,f\to\beta}$ as re-encryption key.

4.2   Construction

Before giving our AB-CPRE scheme, we list the parameters that will be used.

- (n, q, m, χ) - lattice parameters, where $m \geq \lceil 6n\log q \rceil$, $q/4 \geq B \cdot (m+1)^{O(d)}$ and χ is a B-bounded ($B \geq \sqrt{n} \cdot \omega(\log n)$) distribution.
- ℓ - number of attributes.
- d - the maximum depth of the boolean circuit.
- σ - Gaussian parameter, where $\sigma = \omega((m+1)^{d+1}) \cdot \omega(\sqrt{\log m})$.

Our scheme works for $\ell, d, q = poly(n), k = \lceil \log q \rceil$.

- **Setup**(n): Choose ℓ random uniform matrices $\mathbf{B}_1, ..., \mathbf{B}_\ell \leftarrow \mathbb{Z}_q^{n\times m}$ and an error sampling algorithm χ, which is a B-bounded distribution. Output public parameters $pp := (\{\mathbf{B}_i\}_{i\in[\ell]}, \chi)$.
- **KeyGen**(pp, α): Select a matrix $\mathbf{D}_\alpha \leftarrow \mathbb{Z}_q^{n\times m}$ uniformly at random and generate a pair $(\mathbf{A}_\alpha, \mathbf{T}_\alpha) \leftarrow \mathbf{TrapGen}(1^n, 1^m, q)$. Then run

$$\mathbf{R}_\alpha \leftarrow \mathbf{SamplePre}(\mathbf{A}_\alpha, \mathbf{T}_\alpha, -\mathbf{D}_\alpha, \sigma) \text{ s.t. } \mathbf{A}_\alpha\mathbf{R}_\alpha = -\mathbf{D}_\alpha.$$

Output public key $pk_\alpha = (\mathbf{A}_\alpha, \mathbf{D}_\alpha)$ and private key $sk_\alpha = (\mathbf{T}_\alpha, \mathbf{R}_\alpha)$.
- **Enc**$(pp, pk_\alpha, \boldsymbol{\mu}, \mathbf{x})$: Given $pp = (\{\mathbf{B}_i\}_{i\in[\ell]}, \chi)$, $pk_\alpha = (\mathbf{A}_\alpha, \mathbf{D}_\alpha)$, a plaintext $\boldsymbol{\mu} \in \{0,1\}^m$ and an attribute vector $\mathbf{x} = \{x_i\}_{i\in[\ell]}$. Choose a random vector $\mathbf{s} \leftarrow \mathbb{Z}_q^n$ and error vectors $\mathbf{e}_{in}, \mathbf{e}_{out} \leftarrow \chi^m$. Compute $ct = (\mathbf{c}_{in}, \mathbf{c}_{out})$ as

$$\mathbf{c}_{in} = \mathbf{A}_\alpha^T \mathbf{s} + \mathbf{e}_{in}, \mathbf{c}_{out} = \mathbf{D}_\alpha^T \mathbf{s} + \mathbf{e}_{out} + \lfloor q/2 \rfloor \boldsymbol{\mu}.$$

If $\mathbf{x}$ is none or null, then set $cc = \emptyset$. Otherwise, choose ℓ uniformly random matrices $\mathbf{S}_i \leftarrow \{-1, 1\}^{m\times m}$ and compute

$$cc = (\{\mathbf{c}_i = (x_i\mathbf{G} + \mathbf{B}_i)^T \mathbf{s} + \mathbf{S}_i^T \mathbf{e}_{in}\}_{i\in[\ell]}) \in \mathbb{Z}_q^{\ell m}.$$

Output ciphertext $CT_\alpha := (ct, cc)$.

- **Dec**$(pp, sk_\alpha, CT_\alpha)$: Parse $sk_\alpha = (\mathbf{T}_\alpha, \mathbf{R}_\alpha)$ and $CT_\alpha = (ct, cc)$. Let $ct = (\mathbf{c}_{in}, \mathbf{c}_{out})$, then compute

$$\widehat{\mu} = \begin{bmatrix} \mathbf{c}_{in}^T & \mathbf{c}_{out}^T \end{bmatrix} \cdot \begin{bmatrix} \mathbf{R}_\alpha \\ \mathbf{I}_{m \times m} \end{bmatrix}.$$

  For $j \in [m]$, set $\boldsymbol{\mu}_j = 1$ if $|\widehat{\mu}_j - \lfloor q/2 \rfloor| < q/4$, otherwise set $\boldsymbol{\mu}_j = 0$. Finally, output $\boldsymbol{\mu} \in \{0, 1\}^m$.

- **ReKeyGen**$(pp, sk_\alpha, pk_\beta, f)$: Given $pp = (\{\mathbf{B}_i\}_{i \in [\ell]}, \chi)$, $sk_\alpha = (\mathbf{T}_\alpha, \mathbf{R}_\alpha)$, $pk_\beta = (\mathbf{A}_\beta, \mathbf{D}_\beta)$ and a policy $f \in \mathcal{F}_{\ell,d}$. Let $\mathbf{B}_f = \mathbf{Eval}_{pk}(f, \{\mathbf{B}_i\}_{i \in [\ell]})$ and $\mathbf{F} = (\mathbf{A}_\alpha | \mathbf{B}_f) \in \mathbb{Z}^{n \times 2m}$. To construct $\mathbf{R}_{\alpha, f}$, build the basis $\mathbf{T}_{\alpha, f}$ for $\mathbf{F}$ as $\mathbf{T}_{\alpha, f} \leftarrow \mathbf{ExtendRight}(\mathbf{A}_\alpha, \mathbf{T}_\alpha, \mathbf{B}_f)$. Then run **SamplePre**$(\mathbf{F}, \mathbf{T}_{\alpha, f}, -\mathbf{D}_\alpha, \sigma)$ to generate $\mathbf{R}_{\alpha, f}$ such that $\mathbf{F} \mathbf{R}_{\alpha, f} = -\mathbf{D}_\alpha$ where $\mathbf{R}_{\alpha, f} \in \mathbb{Z}^{2m \times m}$. Set $\overline{\mathbf{R}}_{\alpha, f} = \mathbf{Power2}_q(\mathbf{R}_{\alpha, f})$, sample matrices $\mathbf{E}_1 \leftarrow \chi^{2km \times n}, \mathbf{E}_2, \mathbf{E}_3 \leftarrow \chi^{2km \times m}$ and build matrix

$$\mathbf{Q} = \begin{bmatrix} \mathbf{E}_1 \mathbf{A}_\beta + \mathbf{E}_2 & \mathbf{E}_1 \mathbf{D}_\beta + \mathbf{E}_3 + \overline{\mathbf{R}}_{\alpha, f} \\ \mathbf{0}_{m \times m} & \mathbf{I}_{m \times m} \end{bmatrix} \in \mathbb{Z}_q^{(2km+m) \times 2m}.$$

  Output $rk_{\alpha, f \to \beta} = \mathbf{Q}$ as re-encryption key.

- **ReEnc**$(pp, rk_{\alpha, f \to \beta}, CT_\alpha)$: Parse $pp = (\{\mathbf{B}_i\}_{i \in [\ell]}, \chi)$, $rk_{\alpha, f \to \beta} = \mathbf{Q}$, and $CT_\alpha = (ct, cc)$. If $f(\mathbf{x}) \neq 0$ or $cc = \emptyset$ then output $\perp$, otherwise let $ct = (\mathbf{c}_{in}, \mathbf{c}_{out}), cc = \{\mathbf{c}_i\}_{i \in [\ell]}$, set $\mathbf{c}_f = \mathbf{Eval}_{ct}(f, \{(x_i, \mathbf{B}_i, \mathbf{c}_i)\}_{i \in [\ell]})$ and $\widetilde{\mathbf{c}}_{in, f} = \mathbf{Bits}_q([\mathbf{c}_{in}; \mathbf{c}_f])$,

$$(\mathbf{c}_{in}'^T | \mathbf{c}_{out}'^T) = [\widetilde{\mathbf{c}}_{in, f}^T | \mathbf{c}_{out}^T] \cdot \mathbf{Q}.$$

  Output $CT_\beta = (ct' = (\mathbf{c}_{in}', \mathbf{c}_{out}'), cc' = \emptyset)$ as transformed ciphertext.

4.3   Correctness

According to the parameters given at the beginning, the correctness is as follows.

Original Ciphertext. $(\mathbf{c}_{in}, \mathbf{c}_{out})$ is the ct of ciphertext under pk_α as follows,

$$\mathbf{c}_{in} = \mathbf{A}_\alpha^T \mathbf{s} + \mathbf{e}_{in}, \mathbf{c}_{out} = \mathbf{D}_\alpha^T \mathbf{s} + \mathbf{e}_{out} + \lfloor q/2 \rfloor \boldsymbol{\mu}.$$

Since, $\mathbf{A}_\alpha \cdot \mathbf{R}_\alpha = -\mathbf{D}_\alpha$ where $\|\mathbf{R}_\alpha\|_2 \leq m\sigma$ with overwhelming probability. Therefore, we have

$$\begin{bmatrix} \mathbf{c}_{in}^T & \mathbf{c}_{out}^T \end{bmatrix} \cdot \begin{bmatrix} \mathbf{R}_\alpha \\ \mathbf{I}_{m \times m} \end{bmatrix} = \mathbf{e}_{in}^T \mathbf{R}_\alpha + \mathbf{e}_{out}^T + \lfloor q/2 \rfloor \boldsymbol{\mu}^T$$

where $\|\mathbf{e}_{in}^T \mathbf{R}_\alpha + \mathbf{e}_{out}^T\| \leq m\sqrt{m}\sigma B + \sqrt{m}B \leq B \cdot (m+1)^{O(d)} \leq q/4$ with overwhelming probability, which ensures correct decryption of $\boldsymbol{\mu}$.

Transformed Ciphertext. $(ct = (\mathbf{c}_{in}, \mathbf{c}_{out}), cc = (\{\mathbf{c}_i\}_{i \in [\ell]}))$ is the original ciphertext associated with attribute vector $\mathbf{x}$ under pk_α. $rk_{\alpha, f \to \beta}$ is a re-encryption key, where $f(\mathbf{x}) = 0$. By Lemma 6 and Lemma 4, we have

$$\widetilde{\mathbf{c}}_{in, f}^T \cdot \overline{\mathbf{R}}_{\alpha, f} = (\mathbf{s}^T [\mathbf{A}_\alpha | \mathbf{B}_f] + [\mathbf{e}_{in}^T | \mathbf{e}_f^T]) \mathbf{R}_{\alpha, f} = -\mathbf{s}^T \mathbf{D}_\alpha + [\mathbf{e}_{in}^T | \mathbf{e}_f^T] \mathbf{R}_{\alpha, f}$$

where $\mathbf{R}_{\alpha,f} \leq \sqrt{2}m\sigma$ and $\|\mathbf{e}_f\| \leq B\sqrt{m}(m+1)^d$ with overwhelming probability. Then, the transformed ciphertext is computed as follows,

$$[\mathbf{c}_{in}'^T | \mathbf{c}_{out}'^T]$$

$$= [\tilde{\mathbf{c}}_{in,f}^T | \mathbf{c}_{out}^T] \begin{bmatrix} \mathbf{E}_1\mathbf{A}_\beta + \mathbf{E}_2 & \mathbf{E}_1\mathbf{D}_\beta + \mathbf{E}_3 + \overline{\mathbf{R}}_{\alpha,f} \\ \mathbf{0}_{m\times m} & \mathbf{I}_{m\times m} \end{bmatrix}$$

$$= [\tilde{\mathbf{c}}_{in,f}^T(\mathbf{E}_1\mathbf{A}_\beta + \mathbf{E}_2) \,|\, \tilde{\mathbf{c}}_{in,f}^T(\mathbf{E}_1\mathbf{D}_\beta + \mathbf{E}_3) + [\mathbf{e}_{in}^T | \mathbf{e}_f^T]\mathbf{R}_{\alpha,f} + \mathbf{e}_{out}^T + \lfloor q/2 \rfloor \boldsymbol{\mu}]$$

where $\mathbf{A}_\beta$ and $\mathbf{D}_\beta$ is public key of user β, $\|\mathbf{E}_1\| \leq \sqrt{2k}mB$, $\|\mathbf{E}_2\| \leq \sqrt{2k}mB$ and $\|\mathbf{E}_3\| \leq \sqrt{2k}mB$ with overwhelming probability. Therefore, we have

$$[\mathbf{c}_{in}'^T | \mathbf{c}_{out}'^T] \cdot \begin{bmatrix} \mathbf{R}_\beta \\ \mathbf{I}_{m\times m} \end{bmatrix} = \tilde{\mathbf{c}}_{in,f}^T\mathbf{E}_2\mathbf{R}_\beta + \tilde{\mathbf{c}}_{in,f}^T\mathbf{E}_3 + [\mathbf{e}_{in}^T | \mathbf{e}_f^T]\mathbf{R}_{\alpha,f} + \mathbf{e}_{out}^T + \lfloor q/2 \rfloor \boldsymbol{\mu}$$

where $\|\tilde{\mathbf{c}}_{in,f}^T\mathbf{E}_2\mathbf{R}_\beta + \tilde{\mathbf{c}}_{in,f}^T\mathbf{E}_3 + [\mathbf{e}_{in}^T | \mathbf{e}_f^T]\mathbf{R}_{\alpha,f} + \mathbf{e}_{out}^T\| \leq 2km^2\sqrt{m}\sigma B + 2km\sqrt{m}B + 2m\sqrt{m}(m+1)^d\sigma B + \sqrt{m}B \leq B(m+1)^{O(d)} \leq q/4$ with overwhelming probability, which means that decryption of $\boldsymbol{\mu}$ is correct.

4.4   Security Proof

In this subsection, we show that our AB-CPRE scheme is sIND-CPA secure and sKP-CPA secure in the standard model.

Theorem 2. *Our single-hop AB-CPRE scheme is sIND-CPA secure and sKP-CPA secure in the standard model under $LWE_{n,q,\chi}$ assumption.*

The full proof can be found in Appendix A. Here, we outline our proof sketch only. Our security proof employs proof idea from [1,6]. We build a challenger $\mathcal{C}$, who solves $LWE_{n,q,\chi}$ problem by invocating a PPT adversary $\mathcal{A}$.

Given a random matrix $[\mathbf{A}_\theta | \mathbf{D}_\theta]$, $\mathcal{C}$ will be given a uniform vector $\mathbf{u}$ or an LWE instance $[\mathbf{A}_\theta | \mathbf{D}_\theta]^T\mathbf{s} + \mathbf{e}$, where $\mathbf{e}$ is sampled from error distribution χ. Then $\mathcal{A}$ announces a challenge attribute vector $\mathbf{x}^* \in \{0,1\}^\ell$ before $\mathcal{C}$ selects the public parameters and the specific public key. After receiving $\mathbf{x}^*$, $\mathcal{C}$ generates ℓ matrices $\{\mathbf{S}_i^*\}_{i\in[\ell]}$ with small norm uniformly at random, computes $\{\mathbf{B}_i = \mathbf{A}_\theta\mathbf{S}_i^* - x_i^*\mathbf{G}\}_{i\in[\ell]}$, sets $(\{\mathbf{B}_i\}_{i\in[\ell]}, \chi)$ as the public parameters pp and sets $(\mathbf{A}_\theta, \mathbf{D}_\theta)$ as the specific public key pk_θ. When adversary $\mathcal{A}$ makes a query on $\mathcal{O}_{rk}(pk_\theta, pk_\beta, f)$ such that $f(\mathbf{x}^*) \neq 0$, challenger $\mathcal{C}$ would check whether there exists a corrupted delegation chain $(\mathbf{x}^*, \theta, ...)$. If not, $\mathcal{C}$ executes $\mathbf{Eval}_{\mathrm{sim}}$, defined as Lemma 4, produces a short basis $\mathbf{T}_{\theta,f}$ for lattice $\Lambda^\perp(\mathbf{A}_\theta | \mathbf{B}_f)$ by $\mathbf{ExtendLeft}$ and then compute a re-encryption key $rk_{\theta,f\to\beta} = \mathbf{Q}$. In Challenge phase, challenger $\mathcal{C}$ assembles a challenge ciphertext by LWE instance $[\mathbf{A}_\theta | \mathbf{D}_\theta]^T\mathbf{s} + \mathbf{e}$ or a uniform vector $\mathbf{u}$. Finally, challenger $\mathcal{C}$ outputs adversary $\mathcal{A}$'s answer as result.

However, adversary $\mathcal{A}$ may make a query on $\mathcal{O}_{rk}(pk_\theta, pk_\beta, f)$ where $f(\mathbf{x}^*) = 0$ and $pk_\beta \in \Psi_u$. In this case, $\mathbf{B}_f = \mathbf{A}_\theta\mathbf{S}_f$, challenger $\mathcal{C}$ cannot generate the corresponding short basis $\mathbf{T}_{\theta,f}$ by $\mathbf{ExtendLeft}$, which will make $\mathcal{C}$ abort.

To fix such a problem, we have to use key-switching technique to avoid to generate $\mathbf{T}_{\theta,f}$, where $f(\mathbf{x}^*) = 0$. By LWE assumption, $\mathbf{E}_1\mathbf{D}_\beta + \mathbf{E}_3 + \mathbf{Power2}_q(\mathbf{R}_{\alpha,f})$ is computational indistinguishable from uniform matrix $\mathbf{M}$. As a result, we will sample a random $\mathbf{M}$ instead of computing $\mathbf{E}_1\mathbf{D}_\beta + \mathbf{E}_3 + \mathbf{Power2}_q(\mathbf{R}_{\alpha,f})$ when asking for $rk_{\theta,f\to\beta}$, $f(\mathbf{x}^*) = 0$ and $pk_\beta \in \Psi_u$.

5 Extension: Multi-hop AB-CPRE Scheme

In this section, we construct a multi-hop AB-CPRE scheme from the single-hop scheme in Sect. 4.

Let us show transformed ciphertext $CT_\beta = (ct, cc = \emptyset)$ in single-hop AB-CPRE, detailedly,

$$ct^T = [\widetilde{\mathbf{c}}_{in,f}^T | \mathbf{c}_{out}^T] \begin{bmatrix} \mathbf{E}_1\mathbf{A}_\beta + \mathbf{E}_2 & \mathbf{E}_1\mathbf{D}_\beta + \mathbf{E}_3 + \overline{\mathbf{R}}_{\alpha,f} \\ \mathbf{0}_{m\times m} & \mathbf{I}_{m\times m} \end{bmatrix}$$
$$\approx (\widetilde{\mathbf{c}}_{in,f}^T\mathbf{E}_1) \cdot [\mathbf{A}_\beta + error \,|\, \mathbf{D}_\beta + error'] + [\,\mathbf{0}\,|\,\lfloor q/2\rfloor\boldsymbol{\mu}] \in \mathbb{Z}_q^{1\times 2m}.$$

Method 1. Obviously, ct is in the form of dual Regev's ciphertext [14]. Thus, we can apply key-switching to generate a re-encryption key $rk_{\beta\to\pi}$ from user β to user π (mentioned in Subsect. 4.1). However, in such way, once the proxy obtains a re-encryption key $rk_{\beta\to\pi}$, the proxy could transform all ciphertext of user β to user π without any discrimination.

Method 2. Compared to original ciphertext, transformed ciphertext does not contain any $cc = \{(x_i\mathbf{G} + \mathbf{B}_i)^T\mathbf{s} + \mathbf{e}_i\}_{i\in[\ell]}$, which plays an important role in delegation. Thus, we can make subtle change in **ReKeyGen** algorithm to achieve multi-hop capacity. **ReKeyGen** would return a re-encryption key in single-hop AB-CPRE together with an extra matrix,

$$\mathbf{P} = [\mathbf{E}_1(y_1\mathbf{G} + \mathbf{B}_1) + \mathbf{E}_{B_1}|...|\mathbf{E}_1(y_\ell\mathbf{G} + \mathbf{B}_\ell) + \mathbf{E}_{B_\ell}]$$

where $\mathbf{y}$ is the attribute vector set by delegator, $\mathbf{E}_1$ is the same as in **ReKeyGen**, and the elements of $\mathbf{E}_{B_i}$ are chosen from error distribution χ. With matrix $\mathbf{P}$, the proxy could compute the new cc for the transformed ciphertext

$$cc^T = [\mathbf{c}_1; ...; \mathbf{c}_\ell]^T = \widetilde{\mathbf{c}}_{in,f}^T\mathbf{P}$$
$$= \widetilde{\mathbf{c}}_{in,f}^T \cdot [\mathbf{E}_1(y_1\mathbf{G} + \mathbf{B}_1) + \mathbf{E}_{B_1}|...|\mathbf{E}_1(y_\ell\mathbf{G} + \mathbf{B}_\ell) + \mathbf{E}_{B_\ell}].$$

Therefore, the transformed ciphertext (ct, cc) would be associated with a new attribute vector $\mathbf{y}$ set by delegator.

5.1 Construction

The parameters are the same as in Sect. 4, and our scheme works for $\ell, d, q = poly(n)$, $m \geq \lceil 6n\log q\rceil$, $q/4 \geq B \cdot (m+1)^{O(d)}$, $\sigma = \omega((m+1)^{d+1}) \cdot \omega\sqrt{\log m}$, $k = \lceil\log q\rceil$.

- **Setup**(n): the same as **Setup**(n) in Sect. 4.
- **Enc**($pp, pk_\alpha, \boldsymbol{\mu}, \mathbf{x}$): the same as **Enc**($pp, pk_\alpha, \boldsymbol{\mu}, \mathbf{x}$) in Sect. 4.
- **Dec**(pp, sk_α, CT_α): the same as **Dec**(pp, sk_α, CT_α) in Sect. 4.
- **ReKeyGen**($pp, sk_\alpha, pk_\beta, f, \mathbf{y}$): Parse $pp = (\{\mathbf{B}_i\}_{i\in[\ell]}, \chi)$, $sk_\alpha = (\mathbf{T}_\alpha, \mathbf{R}_\alpha)$, $pk_\beta = (\mathbf{A}_\beta, \mathbf{D}_\beta)$, a policy $f \in \mathcal{F}_{\ell,d}$ and an attribute vector $\mathbf{y} = \{y_i\}_{i\in[\ell]}$. Let $\mathbf{B}_f = \mathbf{Eval}_{pk}(f, \{\mathbf{B}_i\}_{i\in[\ell]})$ and $\mathbf{F} = (\mathbf{A}_\alpha | \mathbf{B}_f) \in \mathbb{Z}^{n\times 2m}$. To construct $\mathbf{R}_{\alpha,f}$, build the basis $\mathbf{T}_{\alpha,f}$ for $\mathbf{F}$ as $\mathbf{T}_{\alpha,f} \leftarrow \mathbf{ExtendRight}(\mathbf{A}_\alpha, \mathbf{T}_\alpha, \mathbf{B}_f)$. Then run $\mathbf{R}_{\alpha,f} \leftarrow \mathbf{SamplePre}(\mathbf{F}, \mathbf{T}_{\alpha,f}, -\mathbf{D}_\alpha, \sigma)$ s.t. $\mathbf{FR}_{\alpha,f} = -\mathbf{D}_\alpha$ where $\mathbf{R}_{\alpha,f} \in \mathbb{Z}^{2m\times m}$. Set $\overline{\mathbf{R}}_{\alpha,f} = \mathbf{Power2}_q(\mathbf{R}_{\alpha,f})$, sample matrices $\mathbf{E}_1 \leftarrow \chi^{2km\times n}, \mathbf{E}_2, \mathbf{E}_3 \leftarrow \chi^{2km\times m}$ and build matrix

$$\mathbf{Q} = \begin{bmatrix} \mathbf{E}_1\mathbf{A}_\beta + \mathbf{E}_2 & \mathbf{E}_1\mathbf{D}_\beta + \mathbf{E}_3 + \overline{\mathbf{R}}_{\alpha,f} \\ \mathbf{0}_{m\times m} & \mathbf{I}_{m\times m} \end{bmatrix} \in \mathbb{Z}_q^{(2km+m)\times 2m}.$$

If $\mathbf{y}$ is none or null, then set $\mathbf{P}$ as a null matrix. Otherwise, samples ℓ matrices $\mathbf{E}_{B_i}$ from error distribution $\chi^{2km\times m}$ and compute,

$$\mathbf{P} = [(\mathbf{E}_1(y_i\mathbf{G} + \mathbf{B}_1) + \mathbf{E}_{B_1}) | ... | (\mathbf{E}_1(y_i\mathbf{G} + \mathbf{B}_\ell) + \mathbf{E}_{B_\ell})] \in \mathbb{Z}_q^{2km\times \ell m}.$$

Output $rk_{\alpha,f\to\beta,\mathbf{y}} = (\mathbf{Q}, \mathbf{P})$ as re-encryption key.
- **ReEnc**($pp, rk_{\alpha,f\to\beta,\mathbf{y}}, CT_\alpha$): Parse $pp = (\{\mathbf{B}_i\}_{i\in[\ell]}, \chi)$, $rk_{\alpha,f\to\beta} = (\mathbf{Q}, \mathbf{P})$, and $CT_\alpha = (ct, cc)$. If $f(\mathbf{x}) \neq 0$ or $cc = \emptyset$ then $\perp$, otherwise let $ct = (\mathbf{c}_{in}, \mathbf{c}_{out})$, $cc = \{\mathbf{c}_i\}_{i\in[\ell]}$, set $\mathbf{c}_f = \mathbf{Eval}_{ct}(f, \{(x_i, \mathbf{B}_i, \mathbf{c}_i)\}_{i\in[\ell]})$ and $\tilde{\mathbf{c}}_{in,f} = \mathbf{Bits}_q([\mathbf{c}_{in}; \mathbf{c}_f])$, then compute

$$(\mathbf{c}_{in}'^T | \mathbf{c}_{out}'^T) = [\tilde{\mathbf{c}}_{in,f}^T | \mathbf{c}_{out}^T] \cdot \mathbf{Q}.$$

If $\mathbf{P}$ is a null matrix, then set $cc' = \emptyset$. Otherwise, compute

$$[\mathbf{c}_1'; ...; \mathbf{c}_\ell']^T = \tilde{\mathbf{c}}_{in,f}^T \cdot \mathbf{P}.$$

and then set $cc' = \{\mathbf{c}_i'\}_{i\in[\ell]}$. Output $CT_\beta = (ct' = (\mathbf{c}_{in}', \mathbf{c}_{out}'), cc')$ as transformed ciphertext.

5.2　Correctness and Security Proof

Theorem 3. *Our multi-hop scheme supports $O(n)$ times transformations.*

Suppose $t = O(n)$ and $(ct^{(t)} = (\mathbf{c}_{in}^{(t)}, \mathbf{c}_{out}^{(t)}), cc^{(t)} = \{\mathbf{c}_i^{(t)}\}_{i\in[\ell]})$ is the ciphertext that has been transformed t times, then we have $\|\mathbf{e}_{out}^{(t)}\| \leq \sqrt{m}B + 2km\sqrt{m}Bt + 2\sqrt{2}km^2(m+1)^d\sigma Bt$ and $\|\mathbf{e}_{in}^{(t)}\| \leq 2km\sqrt{m}B$ (See Appendix B for more details).

Therefore, $\|\mathbf{e}_{in}^{(t)^T}\mathbf{R}_\alpha + \mathbf{e}_{out}^{(t)^T}\| \leq 2km^2\sqrt{m}\sigma B + \sqrt{m}B + 2km\sqrt{m}B \cdot O(n) + 2\sqrt{2}km^2(m+1)^d\sigma B \cdot O(n) \leq B \cdot (m+1)^{O(d)} \leq q/4$ holds with overwhelming probability, which ensures the correctness.

Theorem 4. *Our multi-hop AB-CPRE scheme is sIND-CPA secure and sKP-CPA secure in standard model under $LWE_{n,q,\chi}$ assumption.*

Due to the space limitations, we just outline our proof sketch here. Our proof idea is similar to single-hop one. The difference between multi-hop scheme and single-hop scheme is the form of re-encryption key. In single-hop scheme, the re-encryption key $rk_{\theta, f \to \beta}$ contains a matrix $\mathbf{Q} \in \mathbb{Z}_q^{(2km+m) \times 2m}$. Whereas, in the multi-hop scheme, the re-encryption key $rk_{\theta, f \to \beta, \mathbf{y}}$ would contain an extra $\mathbf{P} \in \mathbb{Z}_q^{2km \times \ell m}$. Thus, in the sequence of sIND-CPA game or sKP-CPA game, $\mathcal{C}$ would generate an extra matrix $\mathbf{P}$ honestly, when asking for a re-encryption key (see Appendix C for more details).

6 Conclusion

In this paper, we propose two LWE-based AB-CPRE schemes against quantum-attack. Single-hop one is unidirectional, and supports fine-grained delegation of control as polynomial-depth circuit. Multi-hop one, an extension of single-hop scheme, is the first multi-hop AB-CPRE scheme. No matter how many trans-formations are performed, the ciphertext of multi-hop AB-CPRE is in constant size. Besides, we prove that both of our schemes are sIND-CPA and sKP-CPA without relying on random oracle.

At last, we leave two open problems. One is to construct an IND-CCA secure AB-CPRE scheme from lattices. Another is to construct a multi-hop lattice-based IND-CPA secure AB-CPRE scheme in adaptive model.

Acknowledgements. We all thank the anonymous reviewers for their valuable comments and suggestions which improve the content and presentation of this work a lot. Jian Weng was supported by Major Program of Guangdong Basic and Applied Research Project under Grant No. 2019B030302008, National Key Research and Development Plan of China under Grant Nos. 2020YFB1005600, National Natural Science Foundation of China under Grant Nos. 61825203, U1736203 and 61732021, and Guangdong Provincial Science and Technology Project under Grant No. 2017B010111005. Anjia Yang was partially supported by Key-Area Research and Development Program of Guangdong Province (Grant No. 2020B0101360001), National Natural Science Foundation of China (Grant No. 62072215, 61702222). Xiaojian Liang, Zhenghao Wu, and Zike Jiang were supported by Special Funds for the Cultivation of Guangdong College Students' Scientific and Technological Innovation. ("Climbing Program" Special Funds.) (No. pdjh2021a0050).

A   Proof for Single-hop AB-CPRE

All details of proof can be found in full version [20]. Due to space limitations, we only present the simulator algorithms used in our proof.

- **Setup**$_{SIM}(n, \mathbf{x}^*)$: Let $\mathbf{x}^* = \{x_i^*\}_{i \in [\ell]}$ to be the attribute vector selected by adversary $\mathcal{A}$. Sample a uniform matrix $\mathbf{D}_\theta \leftarrow \mathbb{Z}_q^{n \times m}$ and generate a random identity's public key $\mathbf{A}_\theta \leftarrow \mathbb{Z}_q^{n \times m}$, then choose ℓ random matrices $\mathbf{S}_1^*, ..., \mathbf{S}_\ell^* \leftarrow \{-1, 1\}^{m \times m}$. Set $\mathbf{B}_i = \mathbf{A}_\theta \mathbf{S}_i^* - x_i^* \mathbf{G}$ for all $i \in [\ell]$. Select an error sampling algorithm χ, which is a $B-$bounded distribution. Keep matrices $\{\mathbf{S}_i^*\}_{i\in[\ell]}$ as secret and output public parameters $pp := (\{\mathbf{B}_i\}_{i\in[\ell]}, \chi)$ and specific public key $pk_\theta := (\mathbf{A}_\theta, \mathbf{D}_\theta)$.

– $\mathbf{Enc}_{SIM}(pp, pk_\theta, \boldsymbol{\mu}_b, \mathbf{x}^*)$: Let $pp = (\{\mathbf{B}_i\}_{i\in[\ell]}, \chi)$, $pk_\theta = (\mathbf{A}_\theta, \mathbf{D}_\theta)$, a challenge message $\boldsymbol{\mu}_b \in \{0,1\}^m$, and a selected attribute vector $\mathbf{x}^* = (\{x_i^*\}_{i\in[\ell]})$. Choose a random vector $\mathbf{s} \leftarrow \mathbb{Z}_q^n$ and two error vectors $\mathbf{e}_{in}, \mathbf{e}_{out} \leftarrow \chi^m$. Compute $ct = (\mathbf{c}_{in}, \mathbf{c}_{out})$ as

$$\mathbf{c}_{in} = (\mathbf{A}_\theta)^T\mathbf{s} + \mathbf{e}_{in}, \mathbf{c}_{out} = (\mathbf{D}_\theta)^T\mathbf{s} + \mathbf{e}_{out} + \lfloor q/2 \rfloor \boldsymbol{\mu}_b.$$

Use $\{\mathbf{S}_i^*\}_{i\in[\ell]}$ chosen in $Setup_{SIM}$ instead of uniform matrices in $\{-1,1\}^{m\times m}$ and then assemble $cc^* = (\{\mathbf{c}_i = (x_i^*\mathbf{G} + \mathbf{B}_i)^T\mathbf{s} + (\mathbf{S}_i^*)^T\mathbf{e}_{in}\}_{i\in[\ell]}) \in \mathbb{Z}_q^{\ell m}$. Output a challenge ciphertext $CT^* = (ct^*, cc^*)$.

– $\mathbf{ReKeyGen}_{SIM}(pp, pk_\beta, f)$: Parse $pp = (\{\mathbf{B}_i\}_{i\in[\ell]}, \chi)$, $pk_\beta = (\mathbf{A}_\beta, \mathbf{D}_\beta)$, and a policy $f \in \mathcal{F}_{\ell,d}$. Let $\mathbf{S}_f^* = \mathbf{Eval}_{sim}(f, (x_i^*, \mathbf{S}_i^*)_{i\in[\ell]}, \mathbf{A}_\theta)$.

1) In the case that $f(\mathbf{x}^*) \neq 0$, let $\mathbf{B}_f = \mathbf{A}_\theta\mathbf{S}_f^* - f(\mathbf{x}^*)\mathbf{G}$ and set $\mathbf{F} = [\mathbf{A}_\theta|\mathbf{B}_f - f(\mathbf{x}^*)\mathbf{G}] \in \mathbb{Z}^{n\times 2m}$. Compute the basis $\mathbf{T}_{\theta,f}$ for $\mathbf{F}$ as $\mathbf{T}_{\theta,f} \leftarrow \mathbf{ExtendLeft}(\mathbf{A}_\theta, \mathbf{G}, \mathbf{T}_\mathbf{G}, \mathbf{S}_f)$. Then generate a matrix $\mathbf{R}_{\theta,f} \in \mathbb{Z}^{2m\times m}$ such that $\mathbf{FR}_{\theta,f} = -\mathbf{D}_\theta$ by executing $\mathbf{SamplePre}(\mathbf{F}, \mathbf{T}_{\theta,f}, -\mathbf{D}_\theta, \sigma)$, set $\overline{\mathbf{R}}_{\alpha,f} = \mathbf{Power2}_q(\mathbf{R}_{\alpha,f})$, sample $\mathbf{E}_1 \leftarrow \chi^{2km\times n}, \mathbf{E}_2, \mathbf{E}_3 \leftarrow \chi^{2km\times m}$ and compute

$$\mathbf{Q} = \begin{bmatrix} \mathbf{E}_1\mathbf{A}_\beta + \mathbf{E}_2 & \mathbf{E}_1\mathbf{D}_\beta + \mathbf{E}_3 + \overline{\mathbf{R}}_{\theta,f} \\ \mathbf{0}_{m\times m} & \mathbf{I}_{m\times m} \end{bmatrix} \in \mathbb{Z}_q^{(2km+m)\times 2m}.$$

2) In the case that $f(\mathbf{x}^*) = 0$, sample two matrices $\mathbf{E}_1 \leftarrow \chi^{2km\times n}, \mathbf{E}_2 \leftarrow \chi^{2km\times m}$, choose a matrices $\mathbf{M}' \leftarrow \mathbb{Z}^{2km\times m}$ uniformly at random, and compute

$$\mathbf{Q} = \begin{bmatrix} \mathbf{E}_1\mathbf{A}_\beta + \mathbf{E}_2 & \mathbf{M}' \\ \mathbf{0}_{m\times m} & \mathbf{I}_{m\times m} \end{bmatrix} \in \mathbb{Z}_q^{(2km+m)\times 2m}.$$

Output $rk_{\theta,f\to\beta} = \mathbf{Q}$ as re-encryption key.

B   Correctness for Multi-hop AB-CPRE

The correctness of original ciphertext is the same as the correctness in Sect. 4. Then the correctness of transformed ciphertext is presented as follows.

Transformed Ciphertext. $(ct^{(t-1)} = (\mathbf{c}_{in}^{(t-1)}, \mathbf{c}_{out}^{(t-1)}), cc^{(t-1)} = \{\mathbf{c}_i^{(t-1)}\}_{i\in[\ell]})$ is the ciphertext which has been transformed $t-1$ times and associated with attribute vector $\mathbf{x}$ under pk_α. For convenience, $rk_{\alpha,f\to\beta,\mathbf{y}} = (\mathbf{Q}, \mathbf{P})$ is the re-encryption key, where $f(\mathbf{x}) = 0$. Set $\widetilde{\mathbf{c}}_{in,f}^{(t-1)} = \mathbf{Bits}_q([\mathbf{c}_{in}^{(t-1)}; \mathbf{c}_f^{(t-1)}])$ and $\overline{\mathbf{R}}_{\alpha,f} = \mathbf{Power2}_q(\mathbf{R}_{\alpha,f})$. Then the t times transformed ciphertext $(ct^{(t)}, cc^{(t)})$ is showed as following;

$$\mathbf{c}_{in}^{(t)} = (\mathbf{s}^{(t)})^T\mathbf{A}_\beta + \mathbf{e}_{in}^{(t)} = (\widetilde{\mathbf{c}}_{in,f}^{(t-1)})^T\mathbf{E}_1\mathbf{A}_\beta + (\widetilde{\mathbf{c}}_{in,f}^{(t-1)})^T\mathbf{E}_2,$$

$$\mathbf{c}_{out}^{(t)} = (\widetilde{\mathbf{c}}_{in,f}^{(t-1)})^T\mathbf{E}_1\mathbf{D}_\beta + (\widetilde{\mathbf{c}}_{in,f}^{(t-1)})^T\mathbf{E}_3 + [\mathbf{e}_{in}^{(t-1)}; \mathbf{e}_f^{(t-1)}]^T\mathbf{R}_{\alpha,f} + (\mathbf{e}_{out}^{(t-1)})^T + \lfloor q/2 \rfloor \boldsymbol{\mu},$$

$$\{\mathbf{c}_i^{(t)} = (\mathbf{s}^{(t)})^T(y_i\mathbf{G} + \mathbf{B}_i) + (\mathbf{e}_i^{(t)})^T = (\widetilde{\mathbf{c}}_{in,f}^{(t-1)})^T\mathbf{E}_1(y_i\mathbf{G} + \mathbf{B}_i) + (\widetilde{\mathbf{c}}_{in,f}^{(t-1)})^T\mathbf{E}_{B_i}\}_{i\in[\ell]}.$$

For any $t > 0$, we can learn that, $\|\mathbf{e}_{in}^{(t)}\| \leq 2km\sqrt{m}B$ and $\|\mathbf{e}_i^{(t)}\| \leq 2km\sqrt{m}B$. Because $\|\mathbf{e}_{out}^{(0)}\| \leq \sqrt{m}B$ and $\|\mathbf{e}_f^{(t)}\| \leq \sqrt{2}mkB(m+1)^d$, we have,

$$\|\mathbf{e}_{out}^{(t)}\| \leq \sqrt{m}B + 2km\sqrt{m}Bt + 2\sqrt{2}km^2(m+1)^d\sigma Bt.$$

Therefore, for the t times transformed ciphertext $(ct^{(t)}, cc^{(t)})$,

$$\begin{bmatrix} (\mathbf{c}_{in}^{(t)})^T & (\mathbf{c}_{out}^{(t)})^T \end{bmatrix} \cdot \begin{bmatrix} \mathbf{R}_\alpha \\ \mathbf{I}_{m\times m} \end{bmatrix} = (\mathbf{e}_{in}^{(t)})^T\mathbf{R}_\alpha + (\mathbf{e}_{out}^{(t)})^T + \lfloor q/2 \rfloor \boldsymbol{\mu}^T.$$

where $\|(\mathbf{e}_{in}^{(t)})^T\mathbf{R}_\alpha + (\mathbf{e}_{out}^{(t)})^T\| \leq \|(\mathbf{e}_{in}^{(t)})^T\| \cdot \|\mathbf{R}_\alpha\| + \|(\mathbf{e}_{out}^{(t)})^T\| \leq 2km^2\sqrt{m}\sigma B + \sqrt{m}B + 2km\sqrt{m}Bt + 2\sqrt{2}km^2(m+1)^d\sigma Bt \leq B \cdot (m+1)^{O(d)} \leq q/4$ with overwhelming probability, which ensures the correctness.

C   Simulator Algorithms for Multi-hop AB-CPRE

We only present $\mathbf{ReKeyGen}_{SIM}$ for multi-hop scheme and the other simulator algorithms can be found in the full version [20].

- $\mathbf{ReKeyGen}_{SIM}(pp, pk_\beta, f, \mathbf{y})$: Parse $pp = (\{\mathbf{B}_i\}_{i\in[\ell]}, \chi)$, $pk_\beta = (\mathbf{A}_\beta, \mathbf{D}_\beta)$, a policy $f \in \mathcal{F}_{\ell,d}$ and an attribute vector $\mathbf{y} = \{y_i\}_{i\in[\ell]}$. Compute $\mathbf{S}_f^*$ by executing $\mathbf{Eval}_{sim}(f, (x_i^*, \mathbf{S}_i^*)_{i\in[\ell]}, \mathbf{A}_\theta)$, sample matrices $\mathbf{E}_1 \leftarrow \chi^{2km\times n}$, $\mathbf{E}_2, \mathbf{E}_3 \leftarrow \chi^{2km\times m}$.
  1) In the case that $f(\mathbf{x}^*) \neq 0$, let $\mathbf{B}_f = \mathbf{A}_\theta\mathbf{S}_f^* - f(\mathbf{x}^*)\mathbf{G}$ and set $\mathbf{F} = [\mathbf{A}_\theta|\mathbf{B}_f - f(\mathbf{x}^*)\mathbf{G}] \in \mathbb{Z}^{n\times 2m}$. Compute the basis $\mathbf{T}_{\theta,f}$ for $\mathbf{F}$ as $\mathbf{T}_{\theta,f} \leftarrow \mathbf{ExtendLeft}(\mathbf{A}_\theta, \mathbf{G}, \mathbf{T}_\mathbf{G}, \mathbf{S}_f)$. Then generate a matrix $\mathbf{R}_{\theta,f} \in \mathbb{Z}^{2m\times m}$ such that $\mathbf{FR}_{\theta,f} = -\mathbf{D}_\theta$ by executing $\mathbf{SamplePre}(\mathbf{F}, \mathbf{T}_{\theta,f}, -\mathbf{D}_\theta, \sigma)$, set $\overline{\mathbf{R}}_{\alpha,f} = \mathbf{Power2}_q(\mathbf{R}_{\alpha,f})$, and compute

$$\mathbf{Q} = \begin{bmatrix} \mathbf{E}_1\mathbf{A}_\beta + \mathbf{E}_2 & \mathbf{E}_1\mathbf{D}_\beta + \mathbf{E}_3 + \overline{\mathbf{R}}_{\theta,f} \\ \mathbf{0}_{m\times m} & \mathbf{I}_{m\times m} \end{bmatrix} \in \mathbb{Z}_q^{(2km+m)\times 2m}.$$

  2) In the case that $f(\mathbf{x}^*) = 0$, choose a matrices $\mathbf{M} \leftarrow \mathbb{Z}^{2km\times m}$ uniformly at random, and compute

$$\mathbf{Q} = \begin{bmatrix} \mathbf{E}_1\mathbf{A}_\beta + \mathbf{E}_2 & \mathbf{M} \\ \mathbf{0}_{m\times m} & \mathbf{I}_{m\times m} \end{bmatrix} \in \mathbb{Z}_q^{(2km+m)\times 2m}.$$

If $\mathbf{y}$ is none or null, then set $\mathbf{P}$ as a null matrix. Otherwise, samples ℓ matrices $\mathbf{E}_{B_i}$ from error distribution $\chi^{2km\times m}$ and compute,

$$\mathbf{P} = [(\mathbf{E}_1(y_i\mathbf{G} + \mathbf{B}_1) + \mathbf{E}_{B_1}) \mid ... \mid (\mathbf{E}_1(y_i\mathbf{G} + \mathbf{B}_\ell) + \mathbf{E}_{B_\ell})] \in \mathbb{Z}_q^{2km\times \ell m}.$$

Output $rk_{\theta,f\to\beta,\mathbf{y}} = (\mathbf{Q}, \mathbf{P})$ as re-encryption key.

References

1. Agrawal, S., Boneh, D., Boyen, X.: Efficient lattice (h)ibe in the standard model. In: Gilbert, H. (ed.) EUROCRYPT 2010. LNCS, vol. 6110, pp. 553–572. Springer, Heidelberg (2010). https://doi.org/10.1007/978-3-642-13190-5_28
2. Alwen, J., Peikert, C.: Generating shorter bases for hard random lattices. In: 26th International Symposium on Theoretical Aspects of Computer Science STACS 2009, pp. 75–86. IBFI Schloss Dagstuhl (2009)
3. Aono, Y., Boyen, X., Phong, L.T., Wang, L.: Key-private proxy re-encryption under LWE. In: Paul, G., Vaudenay, S. (eds.) INDOCRYPT 2013. LNCS, vol. 8250, pp. 1–18. Springer, Cham (2013). https://doi.org/10.1007/978-3-319-03515-4_1
4. Applebaum, B., Cash, D., Peikert, C., Sahai, A.: Fast cryptographic primitives and circular-secure encryption based on hard learning problems. In: Halevi, S. (ed.) CRYPTO 2009. LNCS, vol. 5677, pp. 595–618. Springer, Heidelberg (2009). https://doi.org/10.1007/978-3-642-03356-8_35
5. Blaze, M., Bleumer, G., Strauss, M.: Divertible protocols and atomic proxy cryptography. In: Nyberg, K. (ed.) EUROCRYPT 1998. LNCS, vol. 1403, pp. 127–144. Springer, Heidelberg (1998). https://doi.org/10.1007/BFb0054122
6. Boneh, D., et al.: Fully key-homomorphic encryption, arithmetic circuit ABE and compact garbled circuits. In: Nguyen, P.Q., Oswald, E. (eds.) EUROCRYPT 2014. LNCS, vol. 8441, pp. 533–556. Springer, Heidelberg (2014). https://doi.org/10. 1007/978-3-642-55220-5_30
7. Brakerski, Z.: Fully homomorphic encryption without modulus switching from classical GapSVP. In: Safavi-Naini, R., Canetti, R. (eds.) CRYPTO 2012. LNCS, vol. 7417, pp. 868–886. Springer, Heidelberg (2012). https://doi.org/10.1007/978-3-642-32009-5_50
8. Brakerski, Z., Langlois, A., Peikert, C., Regev, O., Stehlé, D.: Classical hardness of learning with errors. In: Proceedings of the Forty-Fifth Annual ACM Symposium on Theory of Computing, STOC '13, pp. 575–584. Association for Computing Machinery, New York (2013)
9. Canetti, R., Hohenberger, S.: Chosen-ciphertext secure proxy re-encryption. In: Proceedings of the 14th ACM Conference on Computer and Communications Security, pp. 185–194 (2007)
10. Canetti, R., Krawczyk, H., Nielsen, J.B.: Relaxing chosen-ciphertext security. In: Boneh, D. (ed.) CRYPTO 2003. LNCS, vol. 2729, pp. 565–582. Springer, Heidelberg (2003). https://doi.org/10.1007/978-3-540-45146-4_33
11. Cash, D., Hofheinz, D., Kiltz, E., Peikert, C.: Bonsai trees, or how to delegate a lattice basis. In: Gilbert, H. (ed.) EUROCRYPT 2010. LNCS, vol. 6110, pp. 523–552. Springer, Heidelberg (2010). https://doi.org/10.1007/978-3-642-13190-5_27
12. Fang, L., Wang, J., Ge, C., Ren, Y.: Fuzzy conditional proxy re-encryption. Sci. China Inf. Sci. 56(5), 1–13 (2013). https://doi.org/10.1007/s11432-012-4623-6
13. Ge, C., Susilo, W., Wang, J., Fang, L.: Identity-based conditional proxy re-encryption with fine grain policy. Comput. Stand. Interfaces 52, 1–9 (2017)
14. Gentry, C., Peikert, C., Vaikuntanathan, V.: Trapdoors for hard lattices and new cryptographic constructions. In: Proceedings of the Fortieth Annual ACM Symposium on Theory of Computing, pp. 197–206 (2008)
15. Green, M., Ateniese, G.: Identity-based proxy re-encryption. In: Katz, J., Yung, M. (eds.) ACNS 2007. LNCS, vol. 4521, pp. 288–306. Springer, Heidelberg (2007). https://doi.org/10.1007/978-3-540-72738-5_19

16. Lai, J., Huang, Z., Au, M.H., Mao, X.: Constant-size CCA-secure multi-hop unidirectional proxy re-encryption from indistinguishability obfuscation. Theoret. Comput. Sci. **847**, 1–16 (2020)
17. Li, B., Xu, J., Liu, Y.: Lattice-based fuzzy conditional proxy re-encryption. J. Internet Technol. **20**(5), 1379–1385 (2019)
18. Liang, K., Chu, C.K., Tan, X., Wong, D.S., Tang, C., Zhou, J.: Chosen-ciphertext secure multi-hop identity-based conditional proxy re-encryption with constant-size ciphertexts. Theoret. Comput. Sci. **539**, 87–105 (2014)
19. Liang, K., Susilo, W., Liu, J.K., Wong, D.S.: Efficient and fully CCA secure conditional proxy re-encryption from hierarchical identity-based encryption. Comput. J. **58**(10), 2778–2792 (2015)
20. Liang, X., Weng, J., Yang, A., Yao, L., Jiang, Z., Wu, Z.: Attribute-based conditional proxy re-encryption in the standard model under LWE. Cryptology ePrint Archive, Report 2021/613 (2021). https://ia.cr/2021/613
21. Lindner, R., Peikert, C.: Better key sizes (and attacks) for LWE-based encryption. In: Kiayias, A. (ed.) CT-RSA 2011. LNCS, vol. 6558, pp. 319–339. Springer, Heidelberg (2011). https://doi.org/10.1007/978-3-642-19074-2_21
22. Luo, F., Al-Kuwari, S., Wang, F., Chen, K.: Attribute-based proxy re-encryption from standard lattices. Theoret. Comput. Sci. **865**, 52–62 (2021)
23. Ma, C., Li, J., Ouyang, W.: Lattice-based identity-based homomorphic conditional proxy re-encryption for secure big data computing in cloud environment. Int. J. Found. Comput. Sci. **28**(06), 645–660 (2017)
24. Mao, X., Li, X., Wu, X., Wang, C., Lai, J.: Anonymous attribute-based conditional proxy re-encryption. In: Au, M.H., et al. (eds.) NSS 2018. LNCS, vol. 11058, pp. 95–110. Springer, Cham (2018). https://doi.org/10.1007/978-3-030-02744-5_7
25. Micciancio, D., Peikert, C.: Trapdoors for lattices: simpler, tighter, faster, smaller. In: Pointcheval, D., Johansson, T. (eds.) EUROCRYPT 2012. LNCS, vol. 7237, pp. 700–718. Springer, Heidelberg (2012). https://doi.org/10.1007/978-3-642-29011-4_41
26. Mo, L., Yao, G.: Multi-use conditional proxy re-encryption. In: 2013 International Conference on Information Science and Cloud Computing Companion, pp. 246–251. IEEE (2013)
27. Peikert, C.: Public-key cryptosystems from the worst-case shortest vector problem: extended abstract. In: Proceedings of the Forty-First Annual ACM Symposium on Theory of Computing, STOC 2009, pp. 333–342. Association for Computing Machinery, New York (2009)
28. Regev, O.: On lattices, learning with errors, random linear codes, and cryptography. J. ACM **56**(6), 1–40 (2009)
29. Shao, J., Cao, Z.: Multi-use unidirectional identity-based proxy re-encryption from hierarchical identity-based encryption. Inf. Sci. **206**, 83–95 (2012)
30. Shao, J., Wei, G., Ling, Y., Xie, M.: Identity-based conditional proxy re-encryption. In: 2011 IEEE International Conference on Communications (ICC), pp. 1–5. IEEE (2011)
31. Wang, H., Cao, Z., Wang, L.: Multi-use and unidirectional identity-based proxy re-encryption schemes. Inf. Sci. **180**(20), 4042–4059 (2010)
32. Weng, J., Deng, R.H., Ding, X., Chu, C.K., Lai, J.: Conditional proxy re-encryption secure against chosen-ciphertext attack. In: Proceedings of the 4th International Symposium on Information, Computer, and Communications Security, pp. 322–332 (2009)

33. Yang, Y., Lu, H., Weng, J., Zhang, Y., Sakurai, K.: Fine-grained conditional proxy re-encryption and application. In: Chow, S.S.M., Liu, J.K., Hui, L.C.K., Yiu, S.M. (eds.) ProvSec 2014. LNCS, vol. 8782, pp. 206–222. Springer, Cham (2014). https://doi.org/10.1007/978-3-319-12475-9_15
34. Zhao, J., Feng, D., Zhang, Z.: Attribute-based conditional proxy re-encryption with chosen-ciphertext security. In: 2010 IEEE Global Telecommunications Conference GLOBECOM 2010, pp. 1–6. IEEE (2010)

Lattice-Based HRA-secure Attribute-Based Proxy Re-Encryption in Standard Model

Willy Susilo, Priyanka Dutta$^{(\boxtimes)}$, Dung Hoang Duong, and Partha Sarathi Roy

Institute of Cybersecurity and Cryptology, School of Computing and Information Technology, University of Wollongong, Northfields Avenue, Wollongong, NSW 2522, Australia
{wsusilo,pdutta,hduong,partha}@uow.edu.au

Abstract. Proxy re-encryption (PRE), introduced by Blaze, Bleumer, and Strauss at EUROCRYPT 98, offers delegation of decryption rights, i.e., it securely enables the re-encryption of ciphertexts from one key to another, without relying on trusted parties. PRE allows a semi-trusted third party termed as a "proxy" to securely divert ciphertexts of a user (delegator) to another user (delegatee) without revealing any information about the underlying messages to the proxy. Attribute-based proxy re-encryption (ABPRE) generalizes PRE by allowing such transformation of ciphertext under an access-policy into another ciphertext under a new access policy. Such a primitive facilitates fine-grained secure sharing of encrypted data in the cloud.

In order to capture the application goals of PRE, the security model of (Attribute-based) PRE evolves over the decades. There are two well-established notions of security for (Attribute-based) proxy re-encryption schemes: security under chosen-plaintext attacks (CPA) and security under chosen-ciphertext attacks (CCA). Both definitions aim to address the security that the delegator enjoys against both proxy and delegatee. Recently, at PKC 19, Cohen points out that CPA security guarantees much less security against delegatee than was previously understood. In particular, CPA security does not prevent delegatee from learning delegator's secret key after receiving a single honestly re-encrypted ciphertext. To circumvent this issue, Cohen proposes security against honest re-encryption attacks (HRA) to strengthen CPA security that better captures the goals of PRE, and shows that two existing proxy re-encryption schemes are HRA-secure, one of them is quantum-safe, which is constructed from fully homomorphic encryption scheme (FHE).

In this work, we advance the studies on HRA-secure PRE for the ABE setting. We first formalize the definition of HRA-secure Key-Policy ABPRE (KP-ABPRE) and propose a construction, which is quantum-safe and secure in the standard model based on the hardness of the LWE. As an important consequence, we have the first quantum-safe HRA-secure Identity-based PRE. Moreover, the underlying PRE of the proposed KP-ABPRE is the first quantum-safe HRA-secure PRE without FHE.

© Springer Nature Switzerland AG 2021
E. Bertino et al. (Eds.): ESORICS 2021, LNCS 12973, pp. 169–191, 2021.
https://doi.org/10.1007/978-3-030-88428-4_9

Keywords: Proxy Re-Encryption · (Key-Policy) Attribute-based
Encryption · Learning with errors · HRA security

1   Introduction

Consider a scenario when Alice wants to allow Bob to decrypt a message
encrypted under her public key without giving her secret key to Bob. A naive way
for Alice to have a proxy implementing such a mechanism is to simply store her
private key at the proxy: when a ciphertext arrives for Alice, the proxy decrypts
it using the stored secret key and re-encrypts the plaintext using Bob's public
key and sends to Bob. The obvious problem with this strategy is that the proxy
learns the plaintext and Alice's secret key. Blaze, Bleumer, and Strauss [5] introduced the concept of PRE to achieve an elegant solution that offers delegation
of decryption rights without compromising privacy of underlying message and
Alice's secret key. Here, Alice provides a piece of secret information to a semi-
trusted proxy called re-encryption key (but not her secret key) that allows it
to re-encrypt a ciphertext computed under Alice's public key into one that can
be opened using Bob's secret key. Since Alice delegates her decryption rights
to Bob, Alice is termed as a 'delegator' and Bob as a 'delegatee'. Based on
the direction of the delegation, PRE schemes are classified into bidirectional and
unidirectional schemes. In unidirectional schemes, a proxy can re-encrypt ciphertexts from Alice to Bob but not from Bob to Alice, while in the bidirectional
schemes, the proxy is allowed to re-encrypt ciphertexts in both directions. It is
worth mentioning that unidirectional constructions are much desirable because
bidirectional construction can be easily implemented using a unidirectional one.
PRE schemes are also classified into single-hop and multi-hop schemes. In a
single-hop scheme, a proxy cannot re-encrypt ciphertexts that have been re-
encrypted once. In a multi-hop scheme, the proxy can further re-encrypt the
re-encrypted ciphertexts. PRE has various interesting applications ranging from
encrypted email forwarding [4,5,23], securing distributed file systems [4], single-
writer many-reader encrypted storage [28], to digital rights management systems
[30]. We notice a real-world file system employing a PRE scheme by Toshiba Corporation [26]. On the other hand, various emerging ideas and techniques have
shown connections between re-encryption with other cryptographic primitives,
such as program obfuscation [12,22], and fully-homomorphic encryption [10].
Hence, further studies along this line are both important and interesting for
theory and practice.

In a PRE scheme, the communication model is one-to-one, in the sense that a
ciphertext can be re-encrypted only towards a particular public key. In practice,
however many scenarios require the re-encryption functionality without exact
knowledge of the set of intended recipients. One such major application is data
sharing in untrusted cloud storage. In the cloud, a data owner may wish to share
her encrypted data with users satisfying a specified access policy. Attribute-based
proxy re-encryption (ABPRE) [18,24] enables such fine-grained data sharing.
ABPRE designates a semi-trusted proxy to transform ciphertexts of delegators

satisfying an access policy into ciphertexts of delegatees satisfying a new access policy. ABPRE integrates the notion of PRE with attribute-based encryption (ABE) to effectively enhance the flexibility of delegation of decryption capability.

1.1 Motivation and Related Works

Recently, Cohen [13] demonstrates the insufficiency of CPA-secure PRE for various applications, viz., encrypted email forwarding, key escrow, single-writer many-reader encrypted storage. In particular, CPA security does not prevent delegatee from learning delegator's secret key after receiving a single honestly re-encrypted ciphertext. Such an attack can be withstood by a CCA-secure PRE. However, CCA-secure PRE is much more expensive than CPA-secure PRE. To this end, Cohen proposes security under honest re-encryption attacks (HRA) to strengthen CPA security that better captures the goals of proxy re-encryption. Informally, both notions of CPA and HRA security are typically defined using a security game between an adversary and a challenger in which the adversary's task is to distinguish between encryptions of two messages. Both notions allow the adversary to corrupt either delegatee (learning secret key of delegatee) or proxy (learning the re-encryption key). However, in a CPA security game, the adversary is not allowed to have access to re-encryption oracle of honestly generated ciphertexts. In contrast, HRA security provides the adversary with a restricted re-encryption oracle which re-encrypt honestly generated ciphertexts.

In [13], Cohen shows that two existing proxy re-encryption schemes are HRA-secure – one of them is quantum-safe, which is constructed from FHE using the procedure based on double encryption of plaintext and evaluation of the decryption circuit [19]. However, this approach relies on heavyweight tools generally used for bootstrapping for FHE, which is very inefficient. Two subsequent recent works [14,17] forward the studies on HRA-secure proxy re-encryption. Fuchsbauer et al. [17] study HRA-secure proxy re-encryption in an adaptive corruption model. Very recently, Döttling and Nishimaki [14] extend HRA security to the universal setting, where ciphertexts can be converted between different public-key encryption schemes – a problem that is coined as universal PRE. However, to address efficiently the wider horizon of application by removing certificate respiratory or to embed fine-grained access control, it is required to extend HRA security for the identity-based and attribute-based PRE schemes.

1.2 Our Contributions and Future Direction

To date, HRA security has not been introduced for identity-based and attribute-based PRE schemes, which leaves a research gap. In this work, we fill this gap in the literature by formalizing the definition of HRA-secure Key-Policy Attribute-based PRE (KP-ABPRE) and proposing a construction. The proposed construction is quantum-safe and secure in the standard model based on the hardness of the learning with errors problem. We show that HRA-secure KP-ABPRE is also CPA-secure KP-ABPRE. While HRA is a stronger security notion than CPA, we show that if a CPA-secure KP-ABPRE scheme has an additional property, viz., *re-encryption simulatability* (see Sect. 3.1), then it must also be HRA-secure. It is worth mentioning that KP-ABPRE was first formalized in [18] and proposed a CCA-secure construction. Unfortunately, in [18], re-encrypted ciphertext follows the phenomena of Ciphertext-Policy Attribute-based PRE instead of KP-ABPRE. Hence, this work first presents the precise definition of CPA-secure KP-ABPRE as well. In nutshell, contributions of this paper are as follows:

– Formalization of HRA-secure KP-ABPRE and CPA-secure KP-ABPRE.
– Construction of single-hop unidirectional HRA-secure KP-ABPRE scheme. The proposed scheme enjoys the properties of proxy transparency, non-interactivity, key optimality, non-transitivity. The proposed construction is quantum-safe and secure in the standard model based on the hardness of the learning with errors problem (LWE).
– Considering attribute set as an identity, we will have the first HRA-secure Identity-based PRE in the selective identity model[1].
– Underlying PRE of the proposed KP-ABPRE is the first HRA-secure quantum-safe PRE without FHE.

This work left open interesting problems to construct variants of proposed constructions in multi-hop setting and initiate the study of HRA-secure Ciphertext-Policy Attribute-based PRE.

1.3   Technical Overview

A possible way to construct KP-ABPRE is to use Attribute-based FHE [21] following the procedure based on double encryption of plaintext and evaluation of the decryption circuit [19]. However, this approach relies on heavyweight tools generally used for bootstrapping. Instead, we convert KP-ABE by Boneh et al. [6] to KP-ABPRE by using the idea of "key switching" technique from [7].

KP-ABPRE consists of six algorithms, namely, SetUp, KeyGen, ReKeyGen, Enc, ReEnc, Dec. To construct KP-ABPRE, we design re-encryption key generation algorithm (ReKeyGen) and re-encryption algorithm (ReEnc) maintaining compatibility with SetUp, KeyGen, Enc, Dec algorithms of [6]. Let us assume attribute vectors for KP-ABPRE are ℓ-tuples over $\mathbb{Z}_q$ and the supported key-policies are functions in $\mathcal{F} := \{f : \mathbb{Z}_q^\ell \longrightarrow \mathbb{Z}_q\}$. Let $f : \mathbb{Z}_q^\ell \longrightarrow \mathbb{Z}_q$ be a function represented as a polynomial-size arithmetic circuit. It is required to use evaluation algorithms [6], namely $\mathsf{Eval}_{pk}, \mathsf{Eval}_{ct}, \mathsf{Eval}_{sim}$, for the underlying *key-homomorphic* features of KP-ABE - hence to construct KP-ABPRE. Informally, Eval_{pk} helps to compute public parameters under some functions, such as f; Eval_{ct} translates the ciphertext encrypted under the attribute vectors $\mathbf{x}$ to a ciphertext under the function f, and Eval_{sim} is only useful in the simulation for the security reduction. For SetUp, we generate $(\mathbf{A}_0, \mathbf{T}_{\mathbf{A}_0})$ using TrapGen algorithm [2,3,25], where $\mathbf{A}_0$ is a random $n \times m$ matrix over $\mathbb{Z}_q$, and $\mathbf{T}_{\mathbf{A}_0} \in \mathbb{Z}_q^{m \times m}$ is a basis of $\Lambda_q^\perp(\mathbf{A}_0)$. We call $\mathbf{T}_{\mathbf{A}_0}$ the associated trapdoor for $\mathbf{A}_0$. Also, choose ℓ random $n \times m$ matrices over

---

[1] It may possible to prove HRA security for the Identity-based constructions by Dutta et al. [15,16] with appropriate modifications.

$\mathbb{Z}_q$, denoted by $\mathbf{A}_1, \cdots, \mathbf{A}_\ell$ and $\mathbf{U}$. Let $\mathbf{G}$ be the gadget matrix, whose associated trapdoor $\mathbf{T_G}$ (i.e., a short basis for the q-ary lattice $\Lambda_q^\perp(\mathbf{G})$) is publicly known (see [25] for details). We set $\{\mathbf{A}_0, \mathbf{A}_1, \cdots, \mathbf{A}_d, \mathbf{U}, \mathbf{G}\}$ as the public parameters and $\mathbf{T_{A_0}}$ as the master secret key. One of the main challenging tasks to design the proposed KP-ABPRE is the design of re-encryption key, which we describe briefly in next paragraph:

In KP-ABPRE, every secret key sk_f is associated with some function f and an encryption of a message $\boldsymbol{\mu}$ is labeled with a public attribute vector $\mathbf{x} \in \mathbb{Z}_q^\ell$. The encryption of $\boldsymbol{\mu}$ can be decrypted using sk_f only if $f(\mathbf{x}) = 0 \in \mathbb{Z}_q$. To compute a re-encryption key from the policy f to g $(rk_{f \to g})$, we need to ensure that the re-encrypted ciphertext (suppose labeled with the attribute vector $\mathbf{y}$) should be decrypted only by sk_g while $g(\mathbf{y}) = 0$. We first choose an attribute vectors $\mathbf{y}$, which satisfies the policy g i.e. $g(\mathbf{y}) = 0$. Treating $\mathbf{H_y} = \left[\mathbf{A}_0 | y_1 \mathbf{G} + \mathbf{A}_1 | \cdots | y_\ell \mathbf{G} + \mathbf{A}_\ell \right]$ as the public key for $\mathbf{y}$ and the secret key sk_f for the policy f, we construct the unidirectional re-encryption key

$$rk_{f \to g} = \begin{bmatrix} \mathbf{R}_1 \mathbf{H_y} + \mathbf{R}_2 & \mathbf{R}_1 \mathbf{U} + \mathbf{R}_3 - P2(sk_f) \\ \mathbf{0} & \mathbf{I} \end{bmatrix},$$

where $P2$ represents *power of* 2 (Suppose $\mathbf{x} \in \mathbb{Z}_q^n$, we denote $(\mathbf{x}, 2 \cdot \mathbf{x}, \cdots, 2^{\lceil \log q \rceil} \cdot \mathbf{x}) \in \mathbb{Z}_2^{n \cdot \lceil \log q \rceil}$ by $P2(\mathbf{x})$), $\mathbf{R}_1$ is chosen uniformly random from $\mathbb{Z}_q$ of order $2mk \times n$, and $\mathbf{R}_2, \mathbf{R}_3$ are chosen from χ-distribution (see Definition 1) of order $2mk \times (\ell + 1)m$ and $2mk \times m$ respectively. Note that, we embed $\mathbf{y}$ at $\mathbf{H_y}$, which ensure that the re-encrypted ciphertexts can not be decrypted by sk_g while $g(\mathbf{y}) \neq 0$. Since, the order and structure of the original ciphertext and the re-encrypted ciphertext are same in our scheme, we can use same decryption algorithm for both original and re-encrypted ciphertext to decrypt.

We prove the security of Selective-KP-ABPRE under the hardness of decisional LWE (dLWE). Here, adversary announces the target set of attributes $\mathbf{x}^* = (x_1^*, \cdots, x_\ell^*)$ before seeing the public parameters. During security reduction, $\mathbf{A}_1, \cdots, \mathbf{A}_\ell$ from the public parameter change as follows: $\mathbf{A}_i = \mathbf{A}_0 \mathbf{S}_i^* - x_i^* \mathbf{G}$ for $i \in \{1, \cdots, \ell\}$, where $\mathbf{S}_1^*, \cdots, \mathbf{S}_\ell^* \longleftarrow \{+1, -1\}^{m \times m}$ are random matrices. We show that $\mathbf{A}_0 \mathbf{S}_i^*$ are uniform in $\mathbb{Z}_q^{n \times m}$, so that $\mathbf{A}_i$'s are distributed as required. Also, the challenger chooses a low-norm matrix $\mathbf{R}_{\mathbf{x}^*}$ from the discrete Gaussian distribution and construct $\mathbf{U}$ as $\left[\mathbf{A}_0 | x_1^* \mathbf{G} + \mathbf{A}_1 | \cdots | x_\ell^* \mathbf{G} + \mathbf{A}_\ell \right] \cdot \mathbf{R}_{\mathbf{x}^*} = \mathbf{U}$. $\mathbf{R}_{\mathbf{x}^*}$ will play a vital role during the simulation of re-encryption query. Now, to respond to secret key query for policy f, where $f(\mathbf{x}^*) \neq 0$, the challenger must produce a low-norm matrix $\mathbf{R}_f$ satisfying $\left[\mathbf{A}_0 | \mathbf{A}_f \right] \cdot \mathbf{R}_f = \mathbf{U}$, where $\mathbf{A}_f = \mathbf{A}_0 \mathbf{S}_f^* - f(\mathbf{x}^*) \mathbf{G}$ and low-norm matrix $\mathbf{S}_f^*$ is the output of Eval_{sim} taking $\mathbf{S}_1^*, \cdots, \mathbf{S}_\ell^*$ as input. It is worth mentioning that the challenger cannot construct a secret key that decrypts ciphertexts under the target set of attributes $\mathbf{x}^*$ – hence, secret key sk_f can not be constructed for the functions f, where $f(\mathbf{x}^*) = 0$. Otherwise, the challenger can generate secret keys for the functions f for which $f(\mathbf{x}^*) \neq 0$.

To respond to re-encryption key query from the policy f to g, the challenger will construct the secret key for f whenever $f(\mathbf{x}^*) \neq 0$, then following ReKeyGen algorithm, the challenger will create the re-encryption key. For functions f where $f(\mathbf{x}^*) = 0$, the challenger does not have secret key. So, it is not possible for the challenger to construct re-encryption key following ReKeyGen algorithm. In such case, the challenger simulates re-encryption key in the following way: for $f(\mathbf{x}^*) = 0$ and $g(\mathbf{x}^*) = 0$, the challenger simulates the re-encryption key $rk_{f \to g}$ as $\begin{bmatrix} \mathbf{X}_1 & \mathbf{X}_2 \\ \mathbf{0}_{m \times (\ell+1)m} & \mathbf{I}_{m \times m} \end{bmatrix}$, where $\mathbf{X}_1, \mathbf{X}_2$ are randomly chosen matrices over $\mathbb{Z}_q$ of order $(2mk \times n)$ and $(2mk \times m)$ respectively; otherwise, challenger outputs $\bot$.

One of the main challenges to achieve the HRA security is to provide access of re-encryption of honestly generated ciphertexts to the adversary. That is, the challenger needs to re-encrypt the ciphertext under the set of attributes $\mathbf{x}$ (except the challenge ciphertext) from the policy f to g when $f(\mathbf{x}) = 0$ and also $f(\mathbf{x}^*) = 0$. Since, $f(\mathbf{x}^*) = 0$, challenger does not have corresponding secret key – hence, challenger does not have actual re-encryption key, which rises a nontrivial challenge to simulate re-encryption oracle. To construct honestly generated re-encrypted ciphertext, challenger first choose $\mathbf{y}$ satisfies $g(\mathbf{y}) = 0$ and then construct a dummy re-encryption key $rk_{sim}^{\mathbf{x} \to \mathbf{y}}$. For $\mathbf{x} = \mathbf{x}^*$, challenger uses $\mathbf{R}_{\mathbf{x}^*}$ from SetUp; Otherwise, chooses a low-norm matrix $\mathbf{R}_{\mathbf{x}}$ satisfying $\mathbf{H}_{\mathbf{x}} \cdot \mathbf{R}_{\mathbf{x}} = \mathbf{U}$ to create the dummy re-encryption key

$$\begin{bmatrix} \mathbf{R}_1 \mathbf{H}_{\mathbf{y}} + \mathbf{R}_2 & \mathbf{R}_1 \mathbf{U} + \mathbf{R}_3 - P2(\mathbf{R}_{\mathbf{x}^*}) \text{or}(P2(\mathbf{R}_{\mathbf{x}})) \\ \mathbf{0}_{m \times (\ell+1)m} & \mathbf{I}_{m \times m} \end{bmatrix}.$$

Here, $\mathbf{R}_1$ is chosen uniformly random from $\mathbb{Z}_q$ of order $(\ell+1)mk \times n$, and $\mathbf{R}_2, \mathbf{R}_3$ are chosen from χ-distribution of order $(\ell+1)mk \times (\ell+1)m$ and $(\ell+1)mk \times m$ respectively. Note that, to compute $\mathbf{R}_{\mathbf{x}}$ for $\mathbf{x} \neq \mathbf{x}^*$, challenger needs to have a trapdoor for $\mathbf{H}_{\mathbf{x}}$. Thanks to publicly known trapdoor $\mathbf{T}_{\mathbf{G}}$ of $\mathbf{G}$ to compute trapdoor for $\mathbf{H}_{\mathbf{x}}$. Since, $\mathbf{x} \neq \mathbf{x}^*$, there exist at least one $i \in \{1, \cdots, \ell\}$ for which $(x_i - x_i^*) \neq 0$. Without loss of generality, we assume that $(x_\ell - x_\ell^*) \neq 0$. Challenger constructs $\mathbf{H}_{\mathbf{x}} = \begin{bmatrix} \mathbf{A}_0 | (x_1 - x_1^*)\mathbf{G} + \mathbf{A}_0 \mathbf{S}_1^* | \cdots | (x_\ell - x_\ell^*)\mathbf{G} + \mathbf{A}_0 \mathbf{S}_\ell^* \end{bmatrix}$. Since, $\mathbf{T}_{\mathbf{G}}$ is a trapdoor for $\mathbf{G}$ and $(x_\ell - x_\ell^*) \neq 0$, $\mathbf{T}_{\mathbf{G}}$ is also a trapdoor for $(x_\ell - x_\ell^*)\mathbf{G}$. By using this trapdoor, challenger can compute a trapdoor for $\mathbf{H}_{\mathbf{x}}$. Multiplying the binary decomposition of ciphertext with this dummy re-encryption key, challenger constructs the re-encrypted ciphertext. Finally, for the target set of attributes $\mathbf{x}^*$ the challenger can produce a challenge ciphertext and solves the given dLWE challenge using the decision of the adversary.

Efficiency. Table 1 summarizes the asymptotic bit-size of public parameter, master secret key, secret key, re-encryption key, ciphertext and re-encrypted ciphertext. We can see that the public parameter size is a linear function in the size of attribute vectors ℓ. The master secret key size and secret key size are independent of ℓ. The re-encryption key size is a linear function in ℓ. Lastly, the ciphertext size and the re-encrypted ciphertext size are same, and linear function of ℓ. Note that, after converting KP-ABE of [6] to KP-ABPRE, sizes of public parameter, master secret key, secret Key and ciphertext are remain same.

Table 1. Data sizes of proposed KP-ABPRE

Public parameter size	$O((\ell + 3) \cdot n^2 \log^2 q)$
Master Secret key size	$O(n^2 \log^3 q)$
Secret Key size	$O(2n^2 \log^3 q)$
Re-encryption key size	$O((\ell + 2) \cdot (n^2 \log^4 q))$
Ciphertext size	$O((\ell + 2) \cdot n \log^2 q))$
Re-encrypted Ciphertext size	$O((\ell + 2) \cdot n \log^2 q))$

**ℓ is the size of attribute vectors; n is an integer; $q = poly(n)$.

2 Preliminaries

We denote the real numbers and the integers by $\mathbb{R}, \mathbb{Z}$, respectively. We denote column-vectors by lower-case bold letters (e.g. $\mathbf{b}$), so row-vectors are represented via transposition (e.g. $\mathbf{b}^t$). Matrices are denoted by upper-case bold letters and treat a matrix $\mathbf{X}$ interchangeably with its ordered set $\{\mathbf{x}_1, \mathbf{x}_2, \ldots\}$ of column vectors. We use $\mathbf{I}$ for the identity matrix and $\mathbf{0}$ for the zero matrix, where the dimension will be clear from context. We use $[*|*]$ to denote the concatenation of vectors or matrices. For $\mathbf{x} \in \mathbb{Z}_q^n$, we denote $(\mathbf{u}_0, \cdots, \mathbf{u}_{\lceil \log q \rceil}) \in \mathbb{Z}_2^{n \cdot \lceil \log q \rceil}$ by $BD(\mathbf{x})$, where $x = \sum_{j=0}^{\lceil \log q \rceil} 2^j \cdot \mathbf{u}_j$ and $\mathbf{u}_j \in \mathbb{Z}_2^n$. For $\mathbf{x} \in \mathbb{Z}_q^n$, we denote $(\mathbf{x}, 2 \cdot \mathbf{x}, \cdots, 2^{\lceil \log q \rceil} \cdot \mathbf{x}) \in \mathbb{Z}_2^{n \cdot \lceil \log q \rceil}$ by $P2(\mathbf{x})$. By Lemma 2 of [7], we have $BD(\mathbf{x})^t \cdot P2(\mathbf{y}) = \mathbf{x}^t \mathbf{y}$. A negligible function, denoted by $\mathsf{negl}(\lambda)$. We say that a probability is overwhelming if it is $1 - \mathsf{negl}(\lambda)$. The *statistical distance* between two distributions $\mathbf{X}$ and $\mathbf{Y}$ over a countable domain Ω defined as $\frac{1}{2} \sum_{w \in \Omega} |\mathsf{Pr}[\mathbf{X} = w] - \mathsf{Pr}[\mathbf{Y} = w]|$. We say that a distribution over Ω is ϵ-far if its statistical distance from the uniform distribution is at most ϵ.

Lattices: A *lattice* Λ is a discrete additive subgroup of $\mathbb{R}^m$. Specially, a lattice Λ in $\mathbb{R}^m$ with basis $\mathbf{B} = [\mathbf{b}_1 | \cdots | \mathbf{b}_n] \in \mathbb{R}^{m \times n}$ is defined as $\Lambda := \{\sum_{i=1}^n \mathbf{b}_i x_i | x_i \in \mathbb{Z} \; \forall i = 1, \ldots, n\} \subseteq \mathbb{R}^m$. We call n the rank of Λ and if $n = m$ we say that Λ is a full rank lattice. The dual lattice Λ^* is the set of all vectors $\mathbf{y} \in \mathbb{R}^m$ satisfying $\langle \mathbf{x}, \mathbf{y} \rangle \in \mathbb{Z}$ for all vectors $\mathbf{x} \in \Lambda$. If $\mathbf{B}$ is a basis of an arbitrary lattice Λ, then $\mathbf{B}^* = \mathbf{B}(\mathbf{B}^t \mathbf{B})^{-1}$ is a basis for Λ^*. For a full-rank lattice, $\mathbf{B}^* = \mathbf{B}^{-t}$. We refer to $\widetilde{\mathbf{B}}$ as a Gram-Schmidt orthogonalization of $\mathbf{B}$.

In this paper, we mainly consider full rank lattices containing $q\mathbb{Z}^m$, called q-ary lattices, defined as the following, for a given matrix $\mathbf{A} \in \mathbb{Z}_q^{n \times m}$ and $\mathbf{u} \in \mathbb{Z}_q^n$: $\Lambda_q^\perp(\mathbf{A}) := \{\mathbf{z} \in \mathbb{Z}^m : \mathbf{A}\mathbf{z} = 0 \bmod q\}$; $\Lambda_q(\mathbf{A}) := \{\mathbf{z} \in \mathbb{Z}^m : \exists \, \mathbf{s} \in \mathbb{Z}_q^n \; s.t. \; \mathbf{z} = \mathbf{A}^\top \mathbf{s} \bmod q\}$; $\Lambda_q^\mathbf{u}(\mathbf{A}) := \{\mathbf{z} \in \mathbb{Z}^m : \mathbf{A}\mathbf{z} = \mathbf{u} \bmod q\} = \Lambda_q^\perp(\mathbf{A}) + \mathbf{x} \; for \; \mathbf{x} \in \Lambda_q^\mathbf{u}(\mathbf{A})\}$.

Matrix Norms: For a vector $\mathbf{u}$, we let $\|\mathbf{u}\|$ denotes its ℓ_2 norm. For a matrix $\mathbf{R} \in \mathbb{Z}^{k \times m}$, let $\widetilde{\mathbf{R}}$ is the result of applying Gram-Schmidt (GS) orthogonalization to the columns of $\mathbf{R}$. We denote three matrix norms as follows:

$\|\mathbf{R}\|$ denotes the ℓ_2 length of the longest column of $\mathbf{R}$.

$\|\mathbf{R}\|_{GS} = \left\|\widetilde{\mathbf{R}}\right\|$, where $\widetilde{\mathbf{R}}$ is the GS orthogonalization of $\mathbf{R}$.

$\|\mathbf{R}\|_2$ is the operator norm of $\mathbf{R}$ defined as $\|\mathbf{R}\|_2 = \sup_{\|\mathbf{x}\|=1} \|\mathbf{Rx}\|$.

Gaussian on Lattices: Let $\Lambda \subseteq \mathbb{Z}^m$ be a lattice. For a vector $\mathbf{c} \in \mathbb{R}^m$ and a positive parameter $\sigma \in \mathbb{R}$, define: $\rho_{\mathbf{c},\sigma}(\mathbf{x}) = \exp\left(\pi \frac{\|\mathbf{x}-\mathbf{c}\|^2}{\sigma^2}\right)$ and $\rho_{\mathbf{c},\sigma}(\Lambda) = \sum_{\mathbf{x} \in \Lambda} \rho_{\mathbf{c},\sigma}(\mathbf{x})$. The discrete Gaussian distribution over Λ with center $\mathbf{c}$ and parameter σ is $\mathcal{D}_{\mathbf{c},\sigma}(\Lambda)(\mathbf{y}) = \frac{\rho_{\mathbf{c},\sigma}(\mathbf{y})}{\rho_{\mathbf{c},\sigma}(\Lambda)}, \forall \mathbf{y} \in \Lambda$.

Lemma 1. (Lemma 2.5. [6]). *Let $n, m, k, q, \sigma > 0$ and $\mathbf{A} \in \mathbb{Z}_q^{n \times m}, \mathbf{U} \in \mathbb{Z}_q^{n \times k}$. For $\mathbf{R} \in \mathbb{Z}^{m \times k}$ sampled from $\mathcal{D}_\sigma(\Lambda_q^{\mathbf{u}}(\mathbf{A}))$ and $\mathbf{S}$ sampled uniformly from $\{+1, -1\}^{m \times m}$, the followings hold with overwhelming probability in m:*

$$\left\|\mathbf{R}^\top\right\|_2 \leq \sigma\sqrt{mk}, \quad \|\mathbf{R}\|_2 \leq \sigma\sqrt{mk} \quad and \quad \|\mathbf{S}\|_2 \leq 20\sqrt{m}.$$

Learning With Errors (LWE) [29]: The Learning with Errors (LWE) problem was introduced by Regev [29]. Here we define the decisional version of LWE. The security of our schemes are based on this hardness assumption.

Definition 1 (Decisional LWE (dLWE)). *Consider a prime integer q, positive integers n, m, and a noise distribution χ over $\mathbb{Z}_q$. The $\mathsf{dLWE}_{n,m,q,\chi}$ problem is to distinguish the following two distributions:*

$$(\mathbf{A}, \mathbf{A}^\top \mathbf{s} + \mathbf{e}) \quad and \quad (\mathbf{A}, \mathbf{u})$$

Where $\mathbf{A} \xleftarrow{\$} \mathbb{Z}_q^{n \times m}$, $\mathbf{s} \xleftarrow{\$} \mathbb{Z}_q^n$, $\mathbf{u} \xleftarrow{\$} \mathbb{Z}_q^m$ and $\mathbf{e} \xleftarrow{\$} \chi^m$ are sampled.

Let the noise distribution χ is B- bounded if its support is in $[-B, B]$. For any constant $d > 0$ and sufficiently large q, Regev [29] through a quantum reduction showed that taking χ as a q/n^d-bounded discretized Gaussian distribution, the $\mathsf{dLWE}_{n,m,q,\chi}$ problem is as hard as approximating the worst-case $GapSVP$ to $n^{O(d)}$ factors, which is believed to be hard. In subsequent works, (partial) dequantization of the Regev's reduction were achieved [8,27]. More generally, let $\chi_{max} < q$ be the bound on the noise distribution. The difficulty of the problem is measured by the ratio q/χ_{max}. The problem appears to remain hard even when $q/\chi_{max} < 2n^\epsilon$ for some fixed ϵ that is $0 < \epsilon < 1/2$. We refer the reader to [6,9,27,29] for more information.

Trapdoor Generators and Related Algorithms: Here, we briefly describe the properties of algorithms for generating short basis of lattices and algorithms for finding a low-norm matrix $\mathbf{X} \in \mathbb{Z}^{m \times k}$ such that $\mathbf{AX} = \mathbf{U}$.

Lemma 2. *Let $n, m, q > 0$ be integers with q prime. There are polynomial time algorithms as follows:*

1. $(\mathbf{A}, \mathbf{T_A}) \longleftarrow \mathsf{TrapGen}(1^n, 1^m, q)$ *[2, 3, 25]: A randomized algorithm that, when $m = \Theta(n \log q)$, outputs a full-rank matrix $\mathbf{A} \in \mathbb{Z}_q^{n \times m}$, and a basis $\mathbf{T_A} \in \mathbb{Z}^{m \times m}$ for $\Lambda_q^\perp(\mathbf{A})$ such that $\mathbf{A}$ is $\mathsf{negl}(\lambda)$-close to uniform and $\|\mathbf{T}\|_{GS} = O(\sqrt{n \log q})$ with all but negligible probability in n.*

2. $\mathbf{T}_{(\mathbf{A}|\mathbf{B})} \longleftarrow$ ExtendRight$(\mathbf{A}, \mathbf{T_A}, \mathbf{B})$ [11]: A deterministic algorithm that given full-rank matrices $\mathbf{A}, \mathbf{B} \in \mathbb{Z}_q^{n \times m}$, and a basis $\mathbf{T_A}$ of $\Lambda_q^\perp(\mathbf{A})$ outputs a basis $\mathbf{T}_{(\mathbf{A}|\mathbf{B})}$ of $\Lambda_q^\perp(\mathbf{A}|\mathbf{B})$ such that $\|\mathbf{T_A}\|_{GS} = \|\mathbf{T}_{(\mathbf{A}|\mathbf{B})}\|_{GS}$.

3. $\mathbf{T_M} \longleftarrow$ ExtendLeft$(\mathbf{A}, \mathbf{G}, \mathbf{T_G}, \mathbf{R})$, where $\mathbf{M} = \begin{bmatrix} \mathbf{A} | \mathbf{G} + \mathbf{AR} \end{bmatrix}$ [1]: A deterministic algorithm that given full-rank matrices $\mathbf{A}, \mathbf{G} \in \mathbb{Z}_q^{n \times m}$, and a basis $\mathbf{T_G}$ of $\Lambda_q^\perp(\mathbf{G})$ outputs a basis $\mathbf{T_M}$ of $\Lambda_q^\perp(\mathbf{M})$ such that $\|\mathbf{T_M}\|_{GS} \leq \|\mathbf{T_G}\|_{GS} \cdot (1 + \|\mathbf{R}\|_2)$.

Lemma 3. *Let $\mathbf{A} \in \mathbb{Z}_q^{n \times m}$, $\mathbf{T_A} \in \mathbb{Z}^{m \times m}$ be a basis for $\Lambda_q^\perp(\mathbf{A})$ and $\mathbf{U} \in \mathbb{Z}_q^{n \times k}$. There are polynomial time algorithms that output $\mathbf{X} \in \mathbb{Z}^{m \times k}$ satisfying $\mathbf{AX} = \mathbf{U}$ with the properties below:*

1. $\mathbf{X} \longleftarrow$ SampleD$(\mathbf{A}, \mathbf{T_A}, \mathbf{U}, \sigma)$ [20]: A randomized algorithm that, when $\sigma = \|\mathbf{T_A}\|_{GS} \cdot \omega(\sqrt{\log m})$, outputs a random sample $\mathbf{X}$ from a distribution that is statistically close to $\mathcal{D}_\sigma(\Lambda_q^\mathbf{u}(\mathbf{A}))$.

2. $\mathbf{T}_\mathbf{A}' \longleftarrow$ RandBasis$(\mathbf{A}, \mathbf{T_A}, \sigma)$ [11]: A randomized algorithm that, when $\sigma = \|\mathbf{T_A}\|_{GS} \cdot \omega(\sqrt{\log m})$, outputs a basis $\mathbf{T}_\mathbf{A}'$ of $\Lambda_q^\perp(\mathbf{A})$ sampled from a distribution that is statistically close to $(\mathcal{D}_\sigma(\Lambda_q^\perp(\mathbf{A})))^m$. Here $\|\mathbf{T}_\mathbf{A}'\|_{GS} < \sigma\sqrt{m}$ with all but negligible probability.

Lemma 4. *1.* $\mathbf{X} \longleftarrow$ SampleRight$(\mathbf{A}, \mathbf{T_A}, \mathbf{B}, \mathbf{U}, \sigma)$: A randomized algorithm that given full-rank matrices $\mathbf{A}, \mathbf{B} \in \mathbb{Z}_q^{n \times m}$, and a matrix $\mathbf{U} \subset \mathbb{Z}_q^{n \times m}$, a basis $\mathbf{T_A}$ of $\Lambda_q^\perp(\mathbf{A})$ and $\sigma = \|\mathbf{T_A}\|_{GS} \cdot \omega(\sqrt{\log m})$, outputs a random sample $\mathbf{X} \in \mathbb{Z}^{2m \times m}$ from a distribution that is statistically close to $\mathcal{D}_\sigma(\Lambda_q^\mathbf{u}((\mathbf{A}|\mathbf{B})))$. This algorithm is the composition of two algorithms: $\mathbf{T}_{(\mathbf{A}|\mathbf{B})} \longleftarrow$ ExtendRight$(\mathbf{A}, \mathbf{T_A}, \mathbf{B})$ and $\mathbf{X} \longleftarrow$ SampleD$((\mathbf{A}|\mathbf{B}), \mathbf{T}_{(\mathbf{A}|\mathbf{B})}, \mathbf{U}, \sigma)$.

2. $\mathbf{X} \longleftarrow$ SampleLeft$(\mathbf{A}, \mathbf{S}, y, \mathbf{U}, \sigma)$: A randomized algorithm that given full-rank matrix $\mathbf{A} \in \mathbb{Z}_q^{n \times m}$, and matrices $\mathbf{S}, \mathbf{U} \in \mathbb{Z}_q^{n \times m}$, $y \neq 0 \in \mathbb{Z}_q$ and $\sigma = \sqrt{5} \cdot (1 + \|\mathbf{S}\|_2) \cdot \omega(\sqrt{\log m})$, outputs a random sample $\mathbf{X} \in \mathbb{Z}^{2m \times m}$ from a distribution that is statistically close to $\mathcal{D}_\sigma(\Lambda_q^\mathbf{u}((\mathbf{A}|y\mathbf{G} + \mathbf{AS})))$. This algorithm is the composition of two algorithms: $\mathbf{T}_{(\mathbf{A}|y\mathbf{G}+\mathbf{AS})} \longleftarrow$ ExtendLeft$(\mathbf{A}, y\mathbf{G}, \mathbf{T_G}, \mathbf{S})$ and $\mathbf{X} \longleftarrow$ SampleD$((\mathbf{A}|y\mathbf{G} + \mathbf{AS}), \mathbf{T}_{(\mathbf{A}|y\mathbf{G}+\mathbf{AS})}, \mathbf{U}, \sigma)$.

Next, we define three types of evaluation algorithms from [6]. Let n and $q = q(n)$, and $m = \Theta(n \log q)$ be positive integers. Let $\mathbf{G} \in \mathbb{Z}_q^{n \times m}$ be the fixed matrix. For $x \in \mathbb{Z}_q, \mathbf{B} \in \mathbb{Z}_q^{n \times m}, \mathbf{s} \in \mathbb{Z}_q^n$, and $\delta > 0$ define the set

$$E_{\mathbf{s}, \delta}(x, \mathbf{B}) = \{(x\mathbf{G} + \mathbf{B})^\top \mathbf{s} + \mathbf{e} \in \mathbb{Z}_q^m, \text{where} \|\mathbf{e}\| < \delta\}.$$

Lemma 5 (Evaluation Algorithms (Sect. 4. [6])). *The three efficient deterministic evaluation algorithms* Eval$_{pk}$, Eval$_{ct}$, Eval$_{sim}$ *satisfy the following properties with respect to the family of functions $\mathcal{F} = \{f : (\mathbb{Z}_q)^\ell \longrightarrow \mathbb{Z}_q\}$, in which each function can be computed by some circuit of a family of depth d, polynomial-size arithmetic circuits $(\mathcal{C}_\lambda)_{\lambda \in \mathbb{N}}$ and a positive integer-valued function $\alpha_\mathcal{F} : \mathbb{Z} \longrightarrow \mathbb{Z}$:*

1. $\mathbf{B}_f \longleftarrow$ Eval$_{pk}(f \in \mathcal{F}, \{\mathbf{B}_i\}_{i=1}^\ell)$, where $\mathbf{B}_f$ and each $\mathbf{B}_i \in \mathbb{Z}_q^{n \times m}$.

2. $\mathbf{c}_f \longleftarrow \mathsf{Eval}_{ct}(f \in \mathcal{F}, \{x_i, \mathbf{B}_i, \mathbf{c}_i\}_{i=1}^{\ell})$, where $\mathbf{c}_f \in \mathbb{Z}_q^m$, and each $x_i \in \mathbb{Z}_q, \mathbf{B}_i \in \mathbb{Z}_q^{n \times m}$, and $\mathbf{c}_i \in E_{\mathbf{s},\delta}(x_i, \mathbf{B}_i)$ for some $\mathbf{s} \in \mathbb{Z}_q^n$ and $\delta > 0$. The output $\mathbf{c}_f$ must satisfy $\mathbf{c}_f \in E_{\mathbf{s},\Delta}(f(\mathbf{x}), \mathbf{B}_f)$, where $\mathbf{B}_f \longleftarrow \mathsf{Eval}_{pk}(f \in \mathcal{F}, \{\mathbf{B}_i\}_{i=1}^{\ell})$, $\mathbf{x} = (x_1, \cdots, x_{\ell})$, and $\Delta < \delta \cdot \alpha_{\mathcal{F}}(n)$, where $\alpha_{\mathcal{F}}(n)$ measures the increase in the noise magnitude in $\mathbf{c}_f$ compared to the input ciphertext.

3. $\mathbf{R}_f \longleftarrow \mathsf{Eval}_{sim}(f \in \mathcal{F}, \{x_i^*, \mathbf{R}_i\}_{i=1}^{\ell}, \mathbf{A})$, where $\mathbf{R}_f$ and each $\mathbf{R}_i \in \mathbb{Z}_q^{m \times m}$, and each $x_i^* \in \mathbb{Z}_q$. For $\mathbf{x}^* = (x_1^*, \cdots, x_{\ell}^*)$, the output $\mathbf{R}_f$ satisfies the relation $\mathbf{A}\mathbf{R}_f - f(\mathbf{x}^*)\mathbf{G} = \mathbf{B}_f$, where $\mathbf{B}_f \longleftarrow \mathsf{Eval}_{pk}(f \in \mathcal{F}, \{\mathbf{A}\mathbf{R}_i - x_i^*\mathbf{G}\}_{i=1}^{\ell})$. For all $f \in \mathcal{F}$, and for $\mathbf{R}_1, \cdots, \mathbf{R}_{\ell} \xleftarrow{\$} \{+1, -1\}^{m \times m}$, $\|\mathbf{R}_f\|_2 < \alpha_{\mathcal{F}}(n)$ with all but negligible probability.

Next, we state a variant of the Left-over Hash Lemma from [1].

Lemma 6 (Left-over Hash Lemma (Lemma 13. [1])). *Suppose that $m > (n+1)\log_2 q + \omega(\log n)$ and that $q > 2$ is prime. Let $\mathbf{R}$ be an $m \times k$ matrix chosen uniformly in $\{1, -1\}^{m \times k}$ mod q, where $k = k(n)$ is polynomial in n. Let $\mathbf{A}$ and $\mathbf{B}$ be matrices chosen uniformly in $\mathbb{Z}^{n \times m}$ and $\mathbb{Z}^{n \times k}$ respectively. Then, for all vectors $\mathbf{e} \in \mathbb{Z}_q^m$, the distribution $(\mathbf{A}, \mathbf{A}\mathbf{R}, \mathbf{R}^{\top}\mathbf{e})$ is statistically close to the distribution $(\mathbf{A}, \mathbf{B}, \mathbf{R}^{\top}\mathbf{e})$.*

3   Key-Policy Attribute-Based Proxy Re-Encryption

In this section, we define the HRA-secure KP-ABPRE and it's relation with CPA-secure KP-ABPRE.

Definition 2 (KP-ABPRE). *Let $\mathcal{F} = \{f : \mathcal{X}^{\ell} \longrightarrow \mathcal{Y}\}$ be the family of functions. Attribute vectors for the ABPRE are ℓ-tuples over $\mathcal{X}$ and the supported Key-Policies are functions in $\mathcal{F}$. A single-hop unidirectional KP-ABPRE scheme is a tuple of algorithms (SetUp, KeyGen, ReKeyGen, Enc, ReEnc, Dec) :*

- $(PP, msk) \longleftarrow \mathsf{SetUp}(1^{\lambda}, \ell)$: *On input a security parameter 1^{λ}, and the number of attributes ℓ, output the public parameter PP and a master secret key msk.*
- $sk_f \longleftarrow \mathsf{KeyGen}(PP, msk, f)$: *On input the public parameter PP, the master secret key msk, and a policy $f \in \mathcal{F}$, output a secret key sk_f for the policy f.*
- $rk_{f \to g} \longleftarrow \mathsf{ReKeyGen}(PP, sk_f, f, g)$: *On input the public parameter PP, two policy f, g, and a secret key sk_f for the policy f, output the unidirectional re-encryption key $rk_{f \to g}$. This key can be used to re-encrypt a ciphertext under attribute vector $\mathbf{x}$ to a ciphertext under attribute vector $\mathbf{y}$, where $f(\mathbf{x}) = 0$ and $g(\mathbf{y}) = 0$.*
- $ct \longleftarrow \mathsf{Enc}(PP, \mathbf{x} \in \mathcal{X}^{\ell}, \mu)$: *On input the public parameter PP, an attribute vector $\mathbf{x}$, and a plaintext $\mu \in \mathcal{M}$, output a ciphertext ct along with the attribute vector $\mathbf{x}$.*
- $\bar{ct} \longleftarrow \mathsf{ReEnc}(PP, rk_{f \to g}, ct)$: *On input the public parameter PP, an original ciphertext ct under the attribute vector $\mathbf{x}$ and a re-encryption key $rk_{f \to g}$, output a re-encrypted ciphertext $\bar{ct}$ along with attribute vector $\mathbf{y}$ if $f(\mathbf{x}) = 0$ or the error symbol $\perp$ indicating ct is invalid.*

- $\mu \longleftarrow \mathsf{Dec}(PP, sk_f, ct)$: *On input the ciphertext ct under the attribute vector* **x** *and a secret key sk_f of a policy f, output a plaintext μ if $f(\mathbf{x}) = 0$, otherwise output the error symbol $\perp$.*

Definition 3 (KP-ABPRE Correctness). *A single-hop unidirectional Key-Policy Attribute-Based Proxy Re-Encryption scheme* (SetUp, KeyGen, ReKeyGen, Enc, ReEnc, Dec) *decrypts correctly for the message $\mu \in \mathcal{M}$ if:*

- *For all sk_f output by* KeyGen *under policy f and for the message $\mu \in \mathcal{M}$, it holds that*
$\mathsf{Dec}(PP, sk_f, \mathsf{Enc}(PP, \mathbf{x}, \mu)) = \mu$ *if $f(\mathbf{x}) = 0$.*
- *For any re-encryption key $rk_{f \to g}$ output by* ReKeyGen(PP, sk_f, f, g) *and any $ct = \mathsf{Enc}(PP, \mathbf{x}, \mu)$, it holds that* $\mathsf{Dec}(PP, sk_g, \bar{ct}) = \mu$ *if $g(\mathbf{y}) = 0$, Where $\bar{ct} \longleftarrow \mathsf{ReEnc}(PP, rk_{f \to g}, ct)$ and $f(\mathbf{x}) = 0$.*

Security Game of Selectively Secure Single-hop Unidirectional KP-ABPRE against Honest Re-Encryption Attacks (IND-HRA-ABPRE): Let $\mathcal{A}$ be the PPT adversary and $\Pi = $ (SetUp, KeyGen, ReKeyGen, Enc, ReEnc, Dec) be an KP-ABPRE scheme with a plaintext space $\mathcal{M}$ and a ciphertext space $\mathcal{C}$. Let $\mathcal{F} = \{f : \mathcal{X}^\ell \longrightarrow \mathcal{Y}\}$ be the family of functions. Attribute vectors for the KP-ABPRE are ℓ-tuples over $\mathcal{X}$ and the supported Key-Policies are functions in $\mathcal{F}$. Security game is defined according to the following game $\mathsf{Exp}_{\mathcal{A}}^{\mathsf{IND\text{-}HRA\text{-}ABPRE}}(\lambda)$ between $\mathcal{A}$ and the challenger:

1. **Initial:** $\mathcal{A}$ sends the target set of attributes $\mathbf{x}^*$.
2. **SetUp:** The challenger runs SetUp$(1^\lambda, \ell)$ to get (PP, msk) and give the public parameter PP to $\mathcal{A}$. Also, the challenger introduces a counter $numCt$ to 0, a key-value store $\mathcal{H}$ to be empty, and a set $Derive$ to be empty.
3. **Query Phase 1:** The adversary $\mathcal{A}$ may make queries polynomially many times in any order to the following oracles:
   - $\mathcal{O}^{\mathsf{KeyGen}}$: an oracle that on input a policy $f \in \mathcal{F}$, outputs $\perp$ whenever $f(\mathbf{x}^*) = 0$; Otherwise, outputs the secret key $sk_f \longleftarrow$ KeyGen(PP, msk, f) for the policy f.
   - $\mathcal{O}^{\mathsf{ReKeyGen}}$: an oracle that on input two policy f, g, outputs $\perp$ whenever $f(\mathbf{x}^*) = 0$ and $g(\mathbf{x}^*) \neq 0$; Otherwise, outputs the re-encryption key $rk_{f \to g} \longleftarrow$ ReKeyGen(PP, sk_f, f, g).
   - $\mathcal{O}^{\mathsf{Enc}}$: an oracle that on input the set of attributes $\mathbf{x}$, and message μ, outputs ciphertext $ct \longleftarrow$ Enc$(PP, \mathbf{x} \in \mathcal{X}^\ell, \mu)$ under $\mathbf{x}$. Increment $numCt$ and add ct to the set $\mathcal{H}$ with key $(\mathbf{x}, numCt)$.
   - $\mathcal{O}^{\mathsf{ReEnc}}$: an oracle that on input the policy f, g, and $(\mathbf{x}, k)$ where $k \leq numCt$, outputs $\perp$ if there is no value in $\mathcal{H}$ with key $(\mathbf{x}, k)$. Otherwise, let ct be that value in $\mathcal{H}$. If $f(\mathbf{x}) \neq 0$, output $\perp$ indicating ct is invalid. Otherwise, outputs re-encrypted ciphertext $ct' \longleftarrow$ ReEnc$(PP, rk_{f \to g}, ct)$.
4. **Challenge:** $\mathcal{A}$ submits two messages $\mu_0, \mu_1 \in \mathcal{M}$ under the set of attributes $\mathbf{x}^*$ to the challenger. The challenger outputs a challenge ciphertext $ct_\beta^* \longleftarrow$ Enc$(PP, \mathbf{x}^* \in \mathcal{X}^\ell, \mu)$ for either $\beta = 0$ or $\beta = 1$, by choosing a random bit $\beta \in \{0, 1\}$. Increment $numCt$ and add $numCt$ to the set $Derive$. Store the value ct_β^* to the set $\mathcal{H}$ with key $(\mathbf{x}^*, numCt)$.

5. **Query Phase 2:** After receiving the challenge ciphertext, $\mathcal{A}$ continues to have access to the $\mathcal{O}^{\mathsf{KeyGen}}$, $\mathcal{O}^{\mathsf{ReKeyGen}}$, $\mathcal{O}^{\mathsf{Enc}}$, and $\mathcal{O}^{\mathsf{ReEnc}}$ as in **Query Phase 1** except the following constraints for $\mathcal{O}^{\mathsf{ReEnc}}$ oracle: Outputs $\perp$ if $g(\mathbf{x}^*) \neq 0 \wedge k \in Derive$.
6. **Guess:** On input β' from $\mathcal{A}$, this oracle outputs 1 if $\beta = \beta'$ and 0 otherwise.

The advantage of an adversary in the above experiment $\mathsf{Exp}_{\mathcal{A}}^{\mathsf{IND\text{-}HRA\text{-}ABPRE}}(\lambda)$ is defined as $|\Pr[\beta' = \beta] - \frac{1}{2}|$.

Definition 4. *An* KP-ABPRE *scheme is* IND-HRA-ABPRE *secure if all PPT adversaries* $\mathcal{A}$ *have at most a negligible advantage in experiment* $\mathsf{Exp}_{\mathcal{A}}^{\mathsf{IND\text{-}HRA\text{-}ABPRE}}(\lambda)$.

We can get the Chosen Plaintext Attacks (CPA) game from the Honest Reencryption Attacks (HRA) game by the following modifications:

1. In SetUp, the challenger does not need to add $numCt$, $\mathcal{H}$ and $Derive$.
2. There will be no $\mathcal{O}^{\mathsf{Enc}}$ in both the Query phases.
3. In $\mathcal{O}^{\mathsf{ReEnc}}$, outputs $\perp$ whenever $f(\mathbf{x}^*) = 0$ and $g(\mathbf{x}^*) \neq 0$ in the both phases. Otherwise, outputs the re-encrypted ciphertext.

The resulting notion is selectively secure single-hop unidirectional KP-ABPRE Scheme against chosen plaintext attack and is denoted by IND-CPA-ABPRE.

Remark 1. Ge et al. [18] introduced KP-ABPRE. Unfortunately, according to [18] and its follow-up works, only the secret key sk_g can decrypt the re-encrypted ciphertext $ct' \longleftarrow$ ReEnc$(PP, rk_{f \to g}, ct)$, which is the property CP-ABE. However, for KP-ABPRE, re-encrypted ciphertext should follow the property of KP-ABE instead of CP-ABE. In this paper, we remove this inconsistency.

Theorem 1. *Let* KP-ABPRE *be an* IND-HRA-ABPRE *secure scheme, then* KP-ABPRE *is* IND-CPA-ABPRE *secure.*

Proof. Follows from the similar argument of [13, Theorem 3].   □

3.1   Re-Encryption Simulatability

We show that IND-HRA-ABPRE follows from IND-CPA-ABPRE if the KP-ABPRE scheme has an additional property, namely, *re-encryption simulatability*. Informally, re-encryption simulatability means that the resulting ciphertexts from ReEnc$(rk_{f \to g}, ct_{\mathbf{x}})$ can be simulated without knowledge of the delegator's secret key sk_f, but with knowledge of the plaintext message μ and the delegatee's secret key sk_g. Note that, Re-encryption Simulatability is not a necessary condition to prove HRA security.

Definition 5 (Re-encryption Simulatability). KP-ABPRE *is Re-encryption Simulatable if there exists a probabilistic polynomial-time algorithm* ReEncSim *such that with high probability over* aux, *for all* $\mu \in \mathcal{M}$: (ReEncSim(aux), aux) $\approx_s$

$(\mathsf{ReEnc}(rk_{f \to g}, ct_\mathbf{x}), \mathsf{aux})$, *where $\approx_s$ denotes statistical indistinguishability, and $ct_\mathbf{x}$, aux are sampled according to*

$$(PP, msk) \longleftarrow \mathsf{SetUp}(1^\lambda, \ell);$$
$$sk_f \longleftarrow \mathsf{KeyGen}(PP, msk, f);$$
$$sk_g \longleftarrow \mathsf{KeyGen}(PP, msk, g);$$
$$rk_{f \to g} \longleftarrow \mathsf{ReKeyGen}(PP, sk_f, f, g);$$
$$ct_\mathbf{x} \longleftarrow \mathsf{Enc}(PP, \mathbf{x} \in \mathcal{X}^\ell, \mu);$$

where $\mathsf{aux} = (PP, f, g, sk_g, ct_\mathbf{x}, \mu)$ and $f(\mathbf{x}) = 0$. Re-encrypted ciphertext generated under some attribute vector, say, $\mathbf{y}$. g is some policy that satisfies by $\mathbf{y}$. Here, sk_g can be a secret key of any policy g that is satisfies by the corresponding vector $\mathbf{y}$.

Theorem 2. *Let KP-ABPRE be an IND-CPA-ABPRE secure and Re-encryption Simulatable scheme, then KP-ABPRE is IND-HRA-ABPRE secure.*

Proof. We construct an algorithm $\mathcal{A}_{CPA}$ (the CPA adversary) from any probabilistic polynomial-time algorithm $\mathcal{A}_{HRA}$ (the HRA adversary), such that $Adv_{\mathcal{A}_{CPA}}(\lambda) \geq Adv_{\mathcal{A}_{HRA}}(\lambda) - \mathsf{negl}(\lambda)$. Since, KP-ABPRE is an IND-CPA-ABPRE secure, $Adv_{\mathcal{A}_{CPA}}(\lambda)$ is $\mathsf{negl}(\lambda)$ – hence, $Adv_{\mathcal{A}_{HRA}}(\lambda)$ is $\mathsf{negl}(\lambda)$, completing the proof.

$\mathcal{A}_{CPA}$ runs $\mathcal{A}_{HRA}$ and simulates the HRA security game. If $\mathcal{A}_{HRA}$ does not follow the specification of the HRA security game, $\mathcal{A}_{CPA}$ simply aborts. To answer oracle calls by $\mathcal{A}_{HRA}$ to any oracle other than $\mathcal{O}^{\mathsf{ReEnc}}$, $\mathcal{A}_{CPA}$ simply forwards the calls and answers unaltered to the corresponding CPA oracles.

To answer oracle calls to $\mathcal{O}^{\mathsf{ReEnc}}$, $\mathcal{A}_{CPA}$ considers following cases to re-encrypt from a policy f to g. For $f(\mathbf{x}^*) \neq 0$, adversary has the secret key for that policy f, otherwise not. Lets consider the following cases:

$$case\ 1 : f(\mathbf{x}^*) \neq 0 \text{ and } g(\mathbf{x}^*) \neq 0;$$
$$case\ 2 : f(\mathbf{x}^*) = 0 \text{ and } g(\mathbf{x}^*) = 0;$$
$$case\ 3 : f(\mathbf{x}^*) \neq 0 \text{ and } g(\mathbf{x}^*) = 0;$$
$$case\ 4 : f(\mathbf{x}^*) = 0 \text{ and } g(\mathbf{x}^*) \neq 0.$$

For case 1, 2, and 3, $\mathcal{A}_{CPA}$ simply forwards the calls and answers unaltered to the corresponding CPA oracles. On the other hand, for case 4, $\mathcal{A}_{CPA}$ simulates the re-encryption using ReEncSim, which is possible because $\mathcal{A}_{CPA}$ knows the underlying message μ along with the other information in aux. Re-encryption simulatability implies that the views of $\mathcal{A}_{HRA}$ in the real security game using the original $\mathcal{O}^{\mathsf{ReEnc}}$ and the simulated security game using ReEncSim are statistically close. Hence, $\mathcal{A}_{CPA}$ wins the CPA security game if and only if $\mathcal{A}_{HRA}$ wins in the simulated HRA game. $\qquad\square$

4   Construction of HRA-secure **KP-ABPRE**

In this section, we present our construction of KP-ABPRE. We set the *parameters* as the following:

- $\mathbf{G} \in \mathbb{Z}_q^{n \times m}$ is a gadget matrix for integer n, large enough prime power $q = poly(n)$, and $m = \Theta(n \log q)$. Let $k = \lceil \log q \rceil$.
- consider the message space is $\mathcal{M} = \{0, 1\}^m$.
- Let χ be a χ_{max}-bounded distribution for which dLWE$_{n,2m,q,\chi}$ is hard.
- For the trapdoor algorithms to work correctly and the security to work, set the Gaussian parameters $\sigma = \omega(\alpha_{\mathcal{F}} \cdot \sqrt{\log m})$, where $\alpha_{\mathcal{F}} > \sqrt{n \log m}$.
- Let $\mathcal{F} = \{f : \mathbb{Z}_q^\ell \longrightarrow \mathbb{Z}_q\}$ be the family of functions. Attribute vectors are ℓ-tuples over $\mathbb{Z}_q$ and the supported Key-Policies are functions in $\mathcal{F}$.

The proposed KP-ABPRE consists of the following algorithms:

SetUp$(1^\lambda, \ell)$: On input a security parameter λ, and ℓ, do as follows:

1. Generate $(\mathbf{A}_0, \mathbf{T}_{\mathbf{A}_0}) \longleftarrow$ TrapGen$(1^n, 1^m, q)$, where $\mathbf{A}_0 \leftarrow \mathbb{Z}_q^{n \times m}$, and $\mathbf{T}_{\mathbf{A}_0} \in \mathbb{Z}_q^{m \times m}$, a basis of $\Lambda_q^\perp(\mathbf{A}_0)$.
2. Choose $\ell + 1$ uniformly random matrices $\mathbf{A}_1, \cdots, \mathbf{A}_\ell, \mathbf{U} \in \mathbb{Z}_q^{n \times m}$.
3. Output the public parameter $PP = \{\mathbf{A}_0, \mathbf{A}_1, \cdots, \mathbf{A}_\ell, \mathbf{U}, \mathbf{G}\}$ and the master secret key $msk = \{\mathbf{T}_{\mathbf{A}_0}\}$.

KeyGen$(PP, msk, f \in \mathcal{F})$: On input the public parameter PP, master secret key msk, and a policy $f \in \mathcal{F}$, do as follows:

1. Evaluate $\mathbf{A}_f \longleftarrow$ Eval$_{pk}(\{\mathbf{A}_i\}_{i=1}^\ell, f)$.
2. Compute $\mathbf{T}_{(\mathbf{A}_0|\mathbf{A}_f)}^{\mathrm{ER}} \longleftarrow$ ExtendRight$(\mathbf{A}_0, \mathbf{A}_f, \mathbf{T}_{\mathbf{A}_0})$.
3. sample $\mathbf{R}_f \longleftarrow$ SampleD$\left([\mathbf{A}_0|\mathbf{A}_f], \mathbf{T}_{(\mathbf{A}_0|\mathbf{A}_f)}^{\mathrm{ER}}, \mathbf{U}, \sigma\right)$.
4. Output the secret key $sk_f = \mathbf{R}_f \in \mathbb{Z}_q^{2m \times m}$ for the policy f.

Enc$(PP, \mathbf{x} \in \mathbb{Z}_q^\ell, \boldsymbol{\mu} \in \{0, 1\}^m)$: On input the public parameter PP, the set of attributes $\mathbf{x} = (x_1, \cdots, x_\ell) \in \mathbb{Z}_q^\ell$, and message $\boldsymbol{\mu} \in \{0, 1\}^m$, do as follows:

1. Choose a uniformly random vector $\mathbf{s} \leftarrow \mathbb{Z}_q^n$.
2. Choose ℓ uniformly random matrices $\mathbf{S}_i \longleftarrow \{+1, -1\}^{m \times m}$ for $i \in 1, \cdots, \ell$.
3. Choose error vectors $\mathbf{e}_0, \mathbf{e}_{out} \in \chi^m$.
4. Set $\mathbf{H}_{\mathbf{x}} = [\mathbf{A}_0 | x_1\mathbf{G} + \mathbf{A}_1 | \cdots | x_\ell\mathbf{G} + \mathbf{A}_\ell] \in \mathbb{Z}_q^{n \times (\ell+1)m}$.
5. Set $\mathbf{e} = [\mathbf{I}_m | \mathbf{S}_1 | \cdots | \mathbf{S}_\ell]^\top \cdot \mathbf{e}_0 = (\mathbf{e}_{in}^\top, \mathbf{e}_1^\top, \cdots, \mathbf{e}_\ell^\top)^\top \in \mathbb{Z}_q^{(\ell+1)m}$.
6. Compute $\mathbf{c} = \mathbf{H}_{\mathbf{x}}^\top \mathbf{s} + \mathbf{e} \in \mathbb{Z}_q^{(\ell+1)m}$ and $\mathbf{c}_{out} = \mathbf{U}^\top \mathbf{s} + \mathbf{e}_{out} + \lfloor q/2 \rfloor \cdot \boldsymbol{\mu} \in \mathbb{Z}_q^m$.
   Here, $\mathbf{c} = [\mathbf{c}_{in} | \mathbf{c}_1 | \cdots | \mathbf{c}_\ell] \in \mathbb{Z}_q^{(\ell+1)m}$, where $\mathbf{c}_{in} = \mathbf{A}_0^\top \mathbf{s} + \mathbf{e}_{in}$, and $\mathbf{c}_i = (x_i\mathbf{G} + \mathbf{A}_i)^\top \mathbf{s} + \mathbf{e}_i$ for all $i \in \{1, \cdots, \ell\}$.
7. Output the ciphertext $ct = (\mathbf{c}_{in}, \mathbf{c}_1, \cdots, \mathbf{c}_\ell, \mathbf{c}_{out}) \in \mathbb{Z}_q^{(\ell+2)m}$ along with the set of attributes $\mathbf{x}$.

$\mathsf{Dec}(PP, sk_f, (ct, \mathbf{x}))$: On input the public parameter PP, the secret key $sk_f = \mathbf{R}_f$, and a ciphertext ct under the set of attributes $\mathbf{x}$, do as follows:

1. If $f(\mathbf{x}) \neq 0$, output $\perp$.
2. Otherwise, do as follows:
   - Parse ct as $(\mathbf{c}_{in}, \mathbf{c}_1, \cdots, \mathbf{c}_\ell, \mathbf{c}_{out})$, and evaluate $\mathbf{c}_f \longleftarrow \mathsf{Eval}_{ct}(\{x_i, \mathbf{A}_i, \mathbf{c}_i\}_{i=1}^\ell, f)$. Let $\mathbf{c}'_f = [\mathbf{c}_{in}|\mathbf{c}_f] \in \mathbb{Z}_q^{2m}$.
   - Compute $\boldsymbol{\mu} = (\mu_1, \cdots, \mu_m) = \mathbf{c}_{out} - \mathbf{R}_f^\top \mathbf{c}'_f$. For each i, if $|\mu_i| < q/4$, take $\mu_i = 0$, otherwise take $\mu_i = 1$.
   - Output $\boldsymbol{\mu} = (\mu_1, \cdots, \mu_m)$.

$\mathsf{ReKeyGen}(PP, sk_f, f, g)$ On input the public parameter PP, two policy f, g and the secret key $sk_f = \mathbf{R}_f$ for the policy f, do as follows:

1. Select an attribute set $\mathbf{y} = (y_1, \cdots, y_\ell)$ such that $g(\mathbf{y}) = 0$.
2. Construct $\mathbf{H_y} = \begin{bmatrix} \mathbf{A}_0 | y_1 \mathbf{G} + \mathbf{A}_1 | \cdots | y_\ell \mathbf{G} + \mathbf{A}_\ell \end{bmatrix} \in \mathbb{Z}_q^{n \times (\ell+1)m}$.
3. Choose a uniformly random matrix $\mathbf{R}_1 \leftarrow \mathbb{Z}_q^{2mk \times n}$.
4. Choose $\mathbf{R}_2 \leftarrow \chi^{2mk \times (\ell+1)m}$ and $\mathbf{R}_3 \leftarrow \chi^{2mk \times m}$.
5. Construct the unidirectional re-encryption key
$$rk_{f \to g} = \begin{bmatrix} \mathbf{R}_1 \mathbf{H_y} + \mathbf{R}_2 & \mathbf{R}_1 \mathbf{U} + \mathbf{R}_3 - P2(\mathbf{R}_f) \\ \mathbf{0}_{m \times (\ell+1)m} & \mathbf{I}_{m \times m} \end{bmatrix} \in \mathbb{Z}_q^{(2mk+m) \times (\ell+2)m}.$$
6. Output $rk_{f \to g}$ along with the attribute vector $\mathbf{y}$.

$\mathsf{ReEnc}(PP, rk_{f \to g}, (ct, \mathbf{x}))$ On input the public parameter, the re-encryption key $rk_{f \to g}$, and ciphertext ct under the set of attributes $\mathbf{x}$, do as follows:

1. If $f(\mathbf{x}) \neq 0$, output $\perp$.
2. Otherwise, do as follows:
   - parse ct as $(\mathbf{c}_{in}, \mathbf{c}_1, \cdots, \mathbf{c}_\ell, \mathbf{c}_{out})$, and evaluate $\mathbf{c}_f \longleftarrow \mathsf{Eval}_{ct}(\{x_i, \mathbf{A}_i, \mathbf{c}_i\}_{i=1}^\ell, f)$. Let $\mathbf{c}'_f = [\mathbf{c}_{in}|\mathbf{c}_f] \in \mathbb{Z}_q^{2m}$.
   - Compute the re-encrypted ciphertext $\bar{ct} = (\bar{\mathbf{c}}_{in}, \bar{\mathbf{c}}_1, \cdots, \bar{\mathbf{c}}_\ell, \bar{\mathbf{c}}_{out})$ as follows:
$$\bar{ct}^\top = \begin{bmatrix} BD((\mathbf{c}'_f)^\top) | \mathbf{c}_{out}^\top \end{bmatrix} \cdot rk_{f \to g} \in \mathbb{Z}_q^{1 \times (\ell+2)m}.$$
   - Output the re-encrypted ciphertext $\bar{ct}$ along with the attribute vector $\mathbf{y}$.

4.1 Correctness and Security

In this section, we analyze the correctness and security of the proposed scheme.

Theorem 3 (Correctness). *The* KP-ABPRE *scheme is correct with respect to* $\mathcal{F}$ *if* $3\alpha_\mathcal{F}^2 \cdot \chi_{max} \cdot m < q/4$.

Proof. To show that the decryption algorithm outputs a correct message, it is required for Eval_{ct} that for $f(\mathbf{x}) = 0$, the resulting ciphertext $\mathbf{c}_f \in \mathbf{E}_{\mathbf{s},\Delta}(0, \mathbf{B}_f)$ so that $\mathbf{c}_f = \mathbf{A}_f^\top \mathbf{s} + \mathbf{e}_f$ with $\|\mathbf{e}_f\| < \Delta < \alpha_\mathcal{F} \cdot \chi_{max}$. Using Lemma 4.6, 4.7 and 5.3 of [6], we have the bound function $\alpha_\mathcal{F}(n) = O((p^\ell m)^D \sqrt{m})$, where the upper bound on the intermediate values in the circuit is $p < q$ and $\mathcal{F}$ is computable by depth D circuits.

We consider correct decryption of both original and re-encrypted ciphertext. Let $sk_f = \mathbf{R}_f$ and $sk_g = \mathbf{R}_g$ be the secret key for the policy f and g respectively. From ReKeyGen(PP, sk_f, f, g) algorithm, we get

$$rk_{f \to g} = \begin{bmatrix} \mathbf{R}_1 \mathbf{H_y} + \mathbf{R}_2 & \mathbf{R}_1 \mathbf{U} + \mathbf{R}_3 - P2(\mathbf{R}_f) \\ \mathbf{0}_{m \times (\ell+1)m} & \mathbf{I}_{m \times m} \end{bmatrix}.$$

Let $ct = (\mathbf{c}_{in}, \mathbf{c}_1, \cdots, \mathbf{c}_\ell, \mathbf{c}_{out})$ be the original ciphertext of a message $\boldsymbol{\mu} \in \{0, 1\}^m$ under the set of attributes $\mathbf{x}$ and $\bar{ct} = (\bar{\mathbf{c}}_{in}, \bar{\mathbf{c}}_1, \cdots, \bar{\mathbf{c}}_\ell, \bar{\mathbf{c}}_{out}) = $ (ReEnc($PP, rk_{f \to g}, ct$)) be the re-encrypted ciphertext under the set of attributes $\mathbf{y}$. Thus, we need to prove that Dec(PP, sk_f, ct) = Dec($PP, sk_g, \bar{ct}$) = $\boldsymbol{\mu}$.

For correctness of the original ciphertext, when $f(\mathbf{x}) = 0$, we know by the requirement on Eval$_{ct}$ that the resulting ciphertext $\mathbf{c}_f \in \mathbf{E}_{\mathbf{s}, \Delta}(0, \mathbf{B}_f)$. After evaluating $\mathbf{c}_g \longleftarrow$ Eval$_{ct}(\{y_i, \mathbf{A}_i, \bar{\mathbf{c}}_i\}_{i=1}^\ell, g)$, we have the magnitude of the noise in $\mathbf{c}_g$, i.e., $\|\mathbf{e}_g\| < \Delta$. Consequently, $\mathbf{c}'_f = [\mathbf{c}_{in} | \mathbf{c}_f] = (\mathbf{A}_0 | \mathbf{A}_f)^\top \mathbf{s} + (\mathbf{e}_{in} | \mathbf{e}_f)$, where $\|(\mathbf{e}_{in} | \mathbf{e}_f)\| < \Delta + \chi_{max} < (\alpha_{\mathcal{F}} + 1)\chi_{max}$. Since, $\mathbf{R}_f \in \mathbb{Z}^{2m \times m}$ is sampled from the distribution $\mathcal{D}_\sigma(\Lambda_q^{\mathbf{u}}((\mathbf{A}_0 | \mathbf{A}_f)))$, we have $(\mathbf{A}_0 | \mathbf{A}_f) \cdot \mathbf{R}_f = \mathbf{U}$, and $\left\| \mathbf{R}_f^\top \right\|_2 < 2m\sigma$ with overwhelming probability by Lemma 1. Now, $\boldsymbol{\mu} = \mathbf{c}_{out} - \mathbf{R}_f^\top \mathbf{c}'_f = (\mathbf{U}^\top \mathbf{s} + \mathbf{e}_{out} + \lfloor q/2 \rfloor \cdot \boldsymbol{\mu}) - (\mathbf{U}^\top \mathbf{s} + \mathbf{R}_f^\top (\mathbf{e}_{in} | \mathbf{e}_f)) = \lfloor q/2 \rfloor \cdot \boldsymbol{\mu} + (\mathbf{e}_{out} - \mathbf{R}_f^\top (\mathbf{e}_{in} | \mathbf{e}_f))$. To get a correct decryption, the norm of the error term should be less than $q/4$, i.e., $\left\| \mathbf{e}_{out} - \mathbf{R}_f^\top (\mathbf{e}_{in} | \mathbf{e}_f) \right\| < q/4$.

Now, $\left\| \mathbf{e}_{out} - \mathbf{R}_f^\top (\mathbf{e}_{in} | \mathbf{e}_f) \right\| \leq \chi_{max} + 2m\sigma \cdot (\alpha_{\mathcal{F}} + 1)\chi_{max} \leq 3\alpha_{\mathcal{F}}^2 \cdot \chi_{max} \cdot m$ with overwhelming probability. By choosing the parameters such that, $3\alpha_{\mathcal{F}}^2 \cdot \chi_{max} \cdot m < q/4$, the decryption of the original ciphertext is correct.

Now, for the re-encrypted ciphertext $\bar{ct}$, we have

$$\bar{ct}^\top = \left[BD((\mathbf{c}'_f)^\top) \big| \mathbf{c}_{out}^\top \right] \cdot rk_{f \to g}$$

$$= \left[BD((\mathbf{c}'_f)^\top)(\mathbf{R}_1 \mathbf{H_y} + \mathbf{R}_2) \big| BD((\mathbf{c}'_f)^\top)(\mathbf{R}_1 \mathbf{U} + \mathbf{R}_3 - P2(\mathbf{R}_f)) + \mathbf{c}_{out}^\top \right].$$

Hence, $\bar{ct} = \left[\mathbf{H_y^\top} \bar{\mathbf{s}} + \bar{\mathbf{e}} \big| \mathbf{U}^\top \bar{\mathbf{s}} + \bar{\mathbf{e}}_{out} + \lfloor q/2 \rfloor \cdot \boldsymbol{\mu} \right] = \left[\bar{\mathbf{c}} \big| \bar{\mathbf{c}}_{out} \right] = $ $(\bar{\mathbf{c}}_{in}, \bar{\mathbf{c}}_1, \cdots, \bar{\mathbf{c}}_\ell, \bar{\mathbf{c}}_{out}) \in \mathbb{Z}_q^{(\ell+2)m}$, where $\bar{\mathbf{s}} = (BD((\mathbf{c}'_f)^\top)\mathbf{R}_1)^\top$, $\bar{\mathbf{e}} = (BD((\mathbf{c}'_f)^\top)\mathbf{R}_2)^\top$, and $\bar{\mathbf{e}}_{out} = (BD((\mathbf{c}'_f)^\top)\mathbf{R}_3)^\top + \mathbf{e}_{out} - \mathbf{R}_f^\top (\mathbf{e}_{in} | \mathbf{e}_f)$.

After evaluating $\mathbf{c}_g \longleftarrow$ Eval$_{ct}(\{y_i, \mathbf{A}_i, \bar{\mathbf{c}}_i\}_{i=1}^\ell, g)$, we have the magnitude of the noise in $\mathbf{c}_g$, i.e., $\|\mathbf{e}_g\| < \Delta$. For correctness of the re-encrypted ciphertext, when $g(\mathbf{y}) = 0$, we know by the requirement on Eval$_{ct}$ that the resulting ciphertext $\mathbf{c}_g \in \mathbf{E}_{\mathbf{s}, \Delta}(0, \mathbf{A}_g)$. Consequently, $\mathbf{c}'_g = [\mathbf{c}_{in} | \mathbf{c}_g] = (\mathbf{A}_0 | \mathbf{A}_g)^\top \mathbf{s} + (\mathbf{e}_{in} | \mathbf{e}_g)$, where $\|(\mathbf{e}_{in} | \mathbf{e}_g)\| < \Delta + \chi_{max} < (\alpha_{\mathcal{F}} + 1)\chi_{max}$. Since, $\mathbf{R}_g \in \mathbb{Z}^{2m \times m}$ is sampled from the distribution $\mathcal{D}_\sigma(\Lambda_q^{\mathbf{u}}((\mathbf{A}_0 | \mathbf{A}_g)))$, we have $(\mathbf{A}_0 | \mathbf{A}_g) \cdot \mathbf{R}_g = \mathbf{U}$, and $\left\| \mathbf{R}_g^\top \right\|_2 < 2m\sigma$ with overwhelming probability by Lemma 1. Now, $\boldsymbol{\mu} = $

$c_{out} - \mathbf{R}_g^{\top} c_g' = (\mathbf{U}^{\top} \mathbf{s} + \mathbf{e}_{out} + \lfloor q/2 \rfloor \cdot \boldsymbol{\mu}) - (\mathbf{U}^{\top} \mathbf{s} + \mathbf{R}_g^{\top} (\mathbf{e}_{in} | \mathbf{e}_g)) = \lfloor q/2 \rfloor \cdot \boldsymbol{\mu} +$
$(\mathbf{e}_{out} - \mathbf{R}_g^{\top} (\mathbf{e}_{in} | \mathbf{e}_g))$. To get a correct decryption, the norm of the error term
should be less than $q/4$, i.e., $\left\| \mathbf{e}_{out} - \mathbf{R}_g^{\top} (\mathbf{e}_{in} | \mathbf{e}_g) \right\| < q/4$.
Now, $\left\| \mathbf{e}_{out} - \mathbf{R}_g^{\top} (\mathbf{e}_{in} | \mathbf{e}_g) \right\| \leq \chi_{max} + 2m\sigma \cdot (\alpha_{\mathcal{F}} + 1)\chi_{max} \leq 3\alpha_{\mathcal{F}}^2 \cdot \chi_{max} \cdot m$ with
overwhelming probability. By choosing the parameters such that, $3\alpha_{\mathcal{F}}^2 \cdot \chi_{max} \cdot m < q/4$, the decryption of the re-encrypted ciphertext is correct. □

Theorem 4 (Security). *The above scheme is* IND-HRA-ABPRE *secure assuming the hardness of* dLWE$_{n,2m,q,\chi}$.

Proof. Let $\mathbf{x}^* = (x_1^*, x_2^*, \cdots, x_\ell^*) \in \mathbb{Z}_q^\ell$ be the target set of attributes. The challenger introduces a counter $numCt$ to 0, a key-value store $\mathcal{H}$ to be empty, and a set $Derive$ to be empty. First, we define the following simulation algorithms Sim.SetUp, Sim.KeyGen, Sim.ReKeyGen and Sim.ReEn$_1$, Sim.ReEn$_2$.

Sim.SetUp$((1^\lambda, \ell))$: The algorithm does the following:

1. Choose a random $\mathbf{A}_0$ from $\mathbb{Z}_q^{n \times m}$.
2. Choose ℓ uniformly random matrices $\mathbf{S}_i^* \longleftarrow \{+1, -1\}^{m \times m}$ for $i \in \{1, \cdots, \ell\}$ and set $\mathbf{A}_i = \mathbf{A}_0 \mathbf{S}_i^* - x_i^* \mathbf{G}$ for $i \in \{1, \cdots, \ell\}$.
3. choose $\mathbf{R}_{\mathbf{x}^*}$ from $\mathcal{D}$ distribution of order $(\ell + 1)m \times m$ and construct $\mathbf{U}$ as $\left[\mathbf{A}_0 | x_1^* \mathbf{G} + \mathbf{A}_1 | \cdots | x_\ell^* \mathbf{G} + \mathbf{A}_\ell \right] \cdot \mathbf{R}_{\mathbf{x}^*} = \mathbf{U}$; i.e., $\left[\mathbf{A}_0 | \mathbf{A}_0 \mathbf{S}_1^* | \cdots | \mathbf{A}_0 \mathbf{S}_\ell^* \right] \cdot \mathbf{R}_{\mathbf{x}^*} = \mathbf{U}$.
4. Output the public parameter $PP = \{\mathbf{A}_0, \mathbf{A}_1, \cdots, \mathbf{A}_\ell, \mathbf{U}, \mathbf{G}\}$.

Sim.KeyGen$(PP, f \in \mathcal{F}, where f(\mathbf{x}^*) \neq 0)$: The algorithm does the following:

1. Evaluate $\mathbf{A}_f \longleftarrow \mathsf{Eval}_{pk}(\{\mathbf{A}_i\}_{i=1}^\ell, f)$.
2. Run $\mathbf{S}_f^* \longleftarrow \mathsf{Eval}_{sim}(f, \{x_i^*, \mathbf{S}_i^*\}_{i=1}^\ell, \mathbf{A}_0)$ and let $\mathbf{A}_f = \mathbf{A}_0 \mathbf{S}_f^* - f(\mathbf{x}^*)\mathbf{G}$, where $\left\| \mathbf{S}_f^* \right\|_2 \leq \alpha_{\mathcal{F}}$. Since, $T_{\mathbf{G}}$ is a trapdoor for $\mathbf{G}$ and $f(\mathbf{x}^*) \neq 0$, it is also a trapdoor for $f(\mathbf{x}^*)\mathbf{G}$.
3. Obtain a trapdoor $\mathbf{T}_{(\mathbf{A}_0 | \mathbf{A}_f)}^{EL} \longleftarrow \mathsf{ExtendLeft}(\mathbf{A}_0, f(\mathbf{x}^*)\mathbf{G}, T_{\mathbf{G}}, \mathbf{S}_f^*)$.
4. Sample $\mathbf{R}_f \longleftarrow \mathsf{SampleD}\left(\left[\mathbf{A}_0 | \mathbf{A}_f \right], \mathbf{T}_{(\mathbf{A}_0 | \mathbf{A}_f)}^{EL}, \mathbf{U}, \sigma \right)$.
5. Output the secret key $sk_f = \mathbf{R}_f$.

Sim.ReKeyGen$(PP, f, g \in \mathcal{F}, where f(\mathbf{x}^*) = 0)$: The algorithm does as follows:

1. For $f(\mathbf{x}^*) = 0$, outputs $\perp$ if $g(\mathbf{x}^*) \neq 0$.
2. For $f(\mathbf{x}^*) = 0$ and $g(\mathbf{x}^*) = 0$, simulate the re-encryption key $rk_{f \to g}$ as follows: $\begin{bmatrix} \mathbf{X}_1 & \mathbf{X}_2 \\ \mathbf{0}_{m \times (\ell+1)m} & \mathbf{I}_{m \times m} \end{bmatrix}$, where $\mathbf{X}_1, \mathbf{X}_2$ are randomly chosen matrices over $\mathbb{Z}_q$ of order $(2mk \times n)$ and $(2mk \times m)$ respectively.
3. Output the re-encryption key $rk_{f \to g}$.

Sim.ReEn$_1(PP, (ct, \mathbf{x}^*), f, g \in \mathcal{F})$: The algorithm does the following:

1. If $f(\mathbf{x}^*) \neq 0$, output $\perp$.
2. Otherwise for $f(\mathbf{x}^*) = 0$, do as follows:
   - Select an attribute set $\mathbf{y} = (y_1, \cdots, y_\ell)$ such that $g(\mathbf{y}) = 0$.
   - Construct $\mathbf{H_y} = \begin{bmatrix} \mathbf{A}_0 | y_1 \mathbf{G} + \mathbf{A}_1 | \cdots | y_\ell \mathbf{G} + \mathbf{A}_\ell \end{bmatrix}$.
   - Choose a uniformly random matrix $\mathbf{R}_1 \leftarrow \mathbb{Z}_q^{(\ell+1)mk \times n}$.
   - Choose $\mathbf{R}_2 \leftarrow \chi^{(\ell+1)mk \times (\ell+1)m}$ and $\mathbf{R}_3 \leftarrow \chi^{(\ell+1)mk \times m}$.
   - Construct a dummy key for re-encryption from $\mathbf{x}^*$ to $\mathbf{y}$ as follows:
     $$rk_{sim}^{\mathbf{x}^* \to \mathbf{y}} = \begin{bmatrix} \mathbf{R}_1 \mathbf{H_y} + \mathbf{R}_2 & \mathbf{R}_1 \mathbf{U} + \mathbf{R}_3 - P2(\mathbf{R}_{\mathbf{x}^*}) \\ \mathbf{0}_{m \times (\ell+1)m} & \mathbf{I}_{m \times m} \end{bmatrix} \in \mathbb{Z}_q^{((\ell+1)mk+m) \times (\ell+2)m}.$$
   - Compute the re-encrypted ciphertext $\bar{ct} = (\bar{\mathbf{c}}_{in}, \bar{\mathbf{c}}_1, \cdots, \bar{\mathbf{c}}_\ell, \bar{\mathbf{c}}_{out})$ as
     $$\bar{ct}^\top = \begin{bmatrix} BD(([\mathbf{c}_{in}|\mathbf{c}_1|\cdots|\mathbf{c}_\ell])^\top)|\mathbf{c}_{out}^\top \end{bmatrix} \cdot rk_{sim}^{\mathbf{x}^* \to \mathbf{y}} \in \mathbb{Z}_q^{1 \times (\ell+2)m}.$$
   - Output the re-encrypted ciphertext $\bar{ct}$ with the attribute vector $\mathbf{y}$.

$\mathsf{Sim.ReEn}_2(PP, (ct, \mathbf{x}(\neq \mathbf{x}^*)), f, g \in \mathcal{F}, where\ f(\mathbf{x}^*) = 0)$: The algorithm does the following:

1. If $f(\mathbf{x}) \neq 0$, output $\perp$.
2. Otherwise for $f(\mathbf{x}) = 0$, do as follows:
   - Since, $\mathbf{x} \neq \mathbf{x}^*$, there exist atleast one $i \in \{1, \cdots, \ell\}$ for which $(x_i - x_i^*) \neq 0$. Without loss of generality, assume that $(x_\ell - \mathbf{x}_\ell^*) \neq 0$. Construct

     $$\mathbf{H_x} = \begin{bmatrix} \mathbf{A}_0 | x_1 \mathbf{G} + \mathbf{A}_1 | \cdots | x_\ell \mathbf{G} + \mathbf{A}_\ell \end{bmatrix}$$
     $$= \begin{bmatrix} \mathbf{A}_0 | (x_1 - x_1^*)\mathbf{G} + \mathbf{A}_0 \mathbf{S}_1^* | \cdots | (x_\ell - x_\ell^*)\mathbf{G} + \mathbf{A}_0 \mathbf{S}_\ell^* \end{bmatrix}.$$

   - Since, $T_{\mathbf{G}}$ is a trapdoor for $\mathbf{G}$ and $(x_\ell - x_\ell^*) \neq 0$, it is also a trapdoor for $(x_\ell - x_\ell^*)\mathbf{G}$. To obtain a trapdoor for $\mathbf{H_x}$, first compute $\mathbf{T}_{(\mathbf{A}_0|(x_\ell - x_\ell^*)\mathbf{G} + \mathbf{A}_0 \mathbf{S}_\ell^*)}^{EL} \longleftarrow \mathsf{ExtendLeft}\,(\mathbf{A}_0, (x_\ell - x_\ell^*)\mathbf{G}, \mathbf{T_G}, \mathbf{S}_\ell^*)$. Then compute a trapdoor $\mathbf{T}_{(\mathbf{A}_0|x_\ell \mathbf{G} + \mathbf{A}_\ell|x_1 \mathbf{G} + \mathbf{A}_1|\cdots|x_{\ell-1}\mathbf{G} + \mathbf{A}_{\ell-1})}^{ER}$ by running $\mathsf{ExtendRight}\left((\mathbf{A}_0|x_\ell \mathbf{G} + \mathbf{A}_\ell), \mathbf{T}_{(\mathbf{A}_0|x_\ell \mathbf{G} + \mathbf{A}_\ell)}^{EL}, (x_1 \mathbf{G} + \mathbf{A}_1|\cdots|x_{\ell-1}\mathbf{G} + \mathbf{A}_{\ell-1})\right)$. By switching the rows of the matrix $\mathbf{T}_{(\mathbf{A}_0|x_\ell \mathbf{G} + \mathbf{A}_\ell|x_1 \mathbf{G} + \mathbf{A}_1|\cdots|x_{\ell-1}\mathbf{G} + \mathbf{A}_{\ell-1})}^{ER}$, get $\mathbf{T}_{(\mathbf{A}_0|x_1 \mathbf{G} + \mathbf{A}_1|\cdots|x_{\ell-1}\mathbf{G} + \mathbf{A}_{\ell-1}|x_\ell \mathbf{G} + \mathbf{A}_\ell)}^{ER}$, which is a trapdoor for $\mathbf{H_x}$. Let us assume $\mathbf{T}_{\mathbf{H_x}}^{ER} = \mathbf{T}_{(\mathbf{A}_0|x_1 \mathbf{G} + \mathbf{A}_1|\cdots|x_{\ell-1}\mathbf{G} + \mathbf{A}_{\ell-1}|x_\ell \mathbf{G} + \mathbf{A}_\ell)}^{ER}$.
     Here, $\|\mathbf{T}_{\mathbf{H_x}}^{ER}\|_{GS} \leq \|\mathbf{T_G}\|_{GS} \cdot \|\mathbf{S}_\ell^*\|_2 \leq \sqrt{5}\alpha_{\mathcal{F}}$ by Lemma 2.
   - Sample $\mathbf{R_x} \longleftarrow \mathsf{SampleD}\,(\mathbf{H_x}, \mathbf{T}_{\mathbf{H_x}}^{ER}, \mathbf{U}, \sigma)$.
   - Select an attribute set $\mathbf{y} = (y_1, \cdots, y_\ell)$ such that $g(\mathbf{y}) = 0$.
3. Construct $\mathbf{H_y} = \begin{bmatrix} \mathbf{A}_0 | y_1 \mathbf{G} + \mathbf{A}_1 | \cdots | y_\ell \mathbf{G} + \mathbf{A}_\ell \end{bmatrix}$.
   - Choose a uniformly random matrix $\mathbf{R}_1 \leftarrow \mathbb{Z}_q^{(\ell+1)mk \times n}$.
   - Choose $\mathbf{R}_2 \leftarrow \chi^{(\ell+1)mk \times (\ell+1)m}$ and $\mathbf{R}_3 \leftarrow \chi^{(\ell+1)mk \times m}$.
   - Construct a dummy key for re-encryption from $\mathbf{x}$ to $\mathbf{y}$ as follows:
     $$rk_{sim}^{\mathbf{x} \to \mathbf{y}} = \begin{bmatrix} \mathbf{R}_1 \mathbf{H_y} + \mathbf{R}_2 & \mathbf{R}_1 \mathbf{U} + \mathbf{R}_3 - P2(\mathbf{R_x}) \\ \mathbf{0}_{m \times (\ell+1)m} & \mathbf{I}_{m \times m} \end{bmatrix} \in \mathbb{Z}_q^{((\ell+1)mk+m) \times (\ell+2)m}.$$
   - Compute the re-encrypted ciphertext $\bar{ct} = (\bar{\mathbf{c}}_{in}, \bar{\mathbf{c}}_1, \cdots, \bar{\mathbf{c}}_\ell, \bar{\mathbf{c}}_{out})$ as
     $$\bar{ct}^\top = \begin{bmatrix} BD(([\mathbf{c}_{in}|\mathbf{c}_1|\cdots|\mathbf{c}_\ell])^\top)|\mathbf{c}_{out}^\top \end{bmatrix} \cdot rk_{sim}^{\mathbf{x} \to \mathbf{y}} \in \mathbb{Z}_q^{1 \times (\ell+2)m}.$$
   - Output the re-encrypted ciphertext $\bar{ct}$ with the attribute vector $\mathbf{y}$.

The simulated re-encrypted ciphertexts generated by $\mathsf{Sim.ReEn_1}$ or $\mathsf{Sim.ReEn_2}$ need to be decrypted correctly. For the correctness of the simulated re-encrypted ciphertext, when $g(\mathbf{y}) = 0$, we know by the requirement on Eval_{ct} that the resulting ciphertext $\mathbf{c}_g \in \mathbf{E}_{\mathbf{s},\Delta}(0, \mathbf{A}_g)$. After evaluating $\mathbf{c}_g \longleftarrow \mathsf{Eval}_{ct}(\{y_i, \mathbf{A}_i, \bar{\mathbf{c}}_i\}_{i=1}^{\ell}, g)$, we have the magnitude of the noise in $\mathbf{c}_g$, i.e., $\|\mathbf{e}_g\| < \Delta$. Consequently, $\mathbf{c}'_g = [\mathbf{c}_{in} | \mathbf{c}_g] = (\mathbf{A}_0 | \mathbf{A}_g)^{\top}\mathbf{s} + (\mathbf{e}_{in} | \mathbf{e}_g)$, where $\|(\mathbf{e}_{in} | \mathbf{e}_g)\| < \Delta + \chi_{max} < (\alpha_{\mathcal{F}} + 1)\chi_{max}$. Since, $\mathbf{R}_g \in \mathbb{Z}^{2m \times m}$ is sampled from the distribution $\mathcal{D}_{\sigma}(\Lambda_q^{\mathbf{u}}((\mathbf{A}_0 | \mathbf{A}_g)))$, we have $(\mathbf{A}_0 | \mathbf{A}_g) \cdot \mathbf{R}_g = \mathbf{U}$, and $\|\mathbf{R}_g^{\top}\|_2 < 2m\sigma$ with overwhelming probability by Lemma 1. Now, $\boldsymbol{\mu} = \mathbf{c}_{out} - \mathbf{R}_g^{\top}\mathbf{c}'_g = (\mathbf{U}^{\top}\mathbf{s} + \mathbf{e}_{out} + \lfloor q/2 \rfloor \cdot \boldsymbol{\mu}) - (\mathbf{U}^{\top}\mathbf{s} + \mathbf{R}_g^{\top}(\mathbf{e}_{in} | \mathbf{e}_g)) = \lfloor q/2 \rfloor \cdot \boldsymbol{\mu} + (\mathbf{e}_{out} - \mathbf{R}_g^{\top}(\mathbf{e}_{in} | \mathbf{e}_g))$. To get a correct decryption, the norm of the error term should be less than $q/4$, i.e., $\|\mathbf{e}_{out} - \mathbf{R}_g^{\top}(\mathbf{e}_{in} | \mathbf{e}_g)\| < q/4$. Now, $\|\mathbf{e}_{out} - \mathbf{R}_g^{\top}(\mathbf{e}_{in} | \mathbf{e}_g)\| \leq \chi_{max} + 2m\sigma \cdot (\alpha_{\mathcal{F}} + 1)\chi_{max} \leq 3\alpha_{\mathcal{F}}^2 \cdot \chi_{max} \cdot m$ with overwhelming probability. By choosing the parameters such that, $3\alpha_{\mathcal{F}}^2 \cdot \chi_{max} \cdot m < q/4$, the decryption of the simulated re-encrypted ciphertext is correct.

The rest of the proof proceeds in a sequence of games. The first game is identical to the original IND-HRA-ABPRE game from the Definition 4. The last two games are indistinguishable due to the hardness of the dLWE problem.

Game 0: This is the original IND-HRA-ABPRE game from definition between an adversary $\mathcal{A}$ against scheme and an IND-HRA-ABPRE challenger.

Game 1: Here, the challenger generates the public parameter PP as in $\mathsf{Sim.SetUp}$. Due to Lemma 6, $\mathbf{A}_0\mathbf{S}_1^*, \cdots, \mathbf{A}_0\mathbf{S}_\ell^*$ are statistically indistinguishable with uniform distribution. So, $\mathbf{A}_1, \cdots, \mathbf{A}_\ell$, as defined in $\mathsf{Sim.SetUp}$, are close to uniform. Also, due to Lemma 6, $[\mathbf{A}_0 | \mathbf{A}_0\mathbf{S}_1^* | \cdots | \mathbf{A}_0\mathbf{S}_\ell^*] \cdot \mathbf{R}_{\mathbf{x}^*}$ is statistically indistinguishable with uniform distribution. Hence, $\mathbf{U}$ is statistically indistinguishable with uniform distribution. In Query Phase 1, adversary issues following queries adaptively and the challenger does as follows:

$\mathcal{O}^{\mathsf{KeyGen}}$: Given a policy f, challenger does as follows:

1. Output $\perp$ whenever $f(\mathbf{x}^*) = 0$.
2. Otherwise, runs $\mathsf{Sim.KeyGen}$ to get the secret key sk_f for the policy f.

$\mathcal{O}^{\mathsf{ReKeyGen}}$: On input two policy f, g, challenger does as follows:

– For $f(\mathbf{x}^*) = 0$, runs $\mathsf{Sim.ReKeyGen}$.
– For $f(\mathbf{x}^*) \neq 0$, first computes $sk_f = \mathbf{R}_f$ by running $\mathsf{Sim.KeyGen}$, then use $\mathsf{ReKeyGen}$ algorithm to compute the re-encryption key $rk_{f \to g}$. Outputs the re-encryption key $rk_{f \to g}$.

$\mathcal{O}^{\mathsf{Enc}}$: On input the set of attributes $\mathbf{x}$, and message μ, outputs ciphertext $ct \longleftarrow \mathsf{Enc}(PP, \mathbf{x} \in \mathcal{X}^{\ell}, \mu)$ under $\mathbf{x}$. Increment $numCt$ and add ct to the set $\mathcal{H}$ with key $(\mathbf{x}, numCt)$.

$\mathcal{O}^{\mathsf{ReEnc}}$: On input the policy f, g and $(\mathbf{x}, k)$ where $k \le numCt$, challenger does as follows:

If $\mathbf{x} = \mathbf{x}^*$, outputs $\perp$ if there is no value in $\mathcal{H}$ with key $(\mathbf{x}^*, k)$. Otherwise, let $ct = (\mathbf{c}_{in}, \mathbf{c}_1, \cdots, \mathbf{c}_\ell, \mathbf{c}_{out})$ be that value in $\mathcal{H}$ and compute re-encrypted ciphertext by running Sim.ReEnc$_1$.

If $\mathbf{x} \ne \mathbf{x}^*$, outputs $\perp$ if there is no value in $\mathcal{H}$ with key $(\mathbf{x}, k)$. Otherwise, let $ct = (\mathbf{c}_{in}, \mathbf{c}_1, \cdots, \mathbf{c}_\ell, \mathbf{c}_{out})$ be that value in $\mathcal{H}$ and consider the following cases:

- If $f(\mathbf{x}^*) = 0$, compute the re-encrypted ciphertext by running Sim.ReEnc$_2$.
- If $f(\mathbf{x}^*) \ne 0$, compute $rk_{f \to g} \longleftarrow \mathcal{O}^{\mathsf{ReKeyGen}}$. Using this re-encryption key, compute the re-encrypted ciphertext according to the ReEnc algorithm.

Game 1 is otherwise same as Game 0. Since the public parameters and responses to the queries are statistically close to those in Game 0, the adversary $\mathcal{A}$'s advantage in Game 1 is at most negligibly different from its advantage in Game 0.

Game 2: Game 2 is identical to Game 1 except that the challenge ciphertext $ct^* = (\mathbf{c}_{in}, \mathbf{c}_1, \cdots, \mathbf{c}_\ell, \mathbf{c}_{out})$ chosen randomly from $\mathbb{Z}_q^{(\ell+2)m}$. Therefore, the adversary $\mathcal{A}$'s advantage in Game 2 is zero.

We show that Game 1 and Game 2 are computationally indistinguishable for a PPT adversary, by giving a reduction from the dLWE problem.

Reduction from dLWE: Suppose $\mathcal{A}$ has non-negligible advantage in distinguishing Game 1 and Game 2. Using $\mathcal{A}$, we construct a dLWE solver $\mathcal{B}$.

- **dLWE instance:** $\mathcal{B}$ begins by obtaining an dLWE challenge consisting of two random matrices $\mathbf{A}_0, \mathbf{U} \in \mathbb{Z}_q^{n \times m}$ and two $\mathbf{c}_{in}, \mathbf{c}_{out} \in \mathbb{Z}_q^m$. Here, $\mathbf{c}_{in}, \mathbf{c}_{out}$ are either random in $\mathbb{Z}_q^m$ or $\mathbf{c}_{in} = \mathbf{A}_0^\top \mathbf{s} + \mathbf{e}_0$ and $\mathbf{c}_{out} = \mathbf{U}^\top \mathbf{s} + \mathbf{e}_{out}$ for some random vector $\mathbf{s} \in \mathbb{Z}_q^n$ and $\mathbf{e}_0, \mathbf{e}_{out} \in \chi^m$. The goal of $\mathcal{B}$ is to distinguish these two cases with non-negligible advantage by using $\mathcal{A}$.
- **Initial:** $\mathcal{A}$ announces the target set of attributes $\mathbf{x}^* = (x_1^*, x_2^*, \cdots, x_\ell^*) \in \mathbb{Z}_q^\ell$ that it intends to attack.
- **SetUp:** $\mathcal{B}$ constructs the public parameter as Game 1: choose ℓ random matrices $\mathbf{S}_i^*$ from $\{+1, -1\}^{m \times m}$ for $i \in \{1, \cdots, \ell\}$ and set $\mathbf{A}_1, \cdots, \mathbf{A}_\ell$ as $\mathbf{A}_i = \mathbf{A}_0 \mathbf{S}_i^* - x_i^* \mathbf{G}$ for $i \in \{1, \cdots, \ell\}$. Sends $PP = \{\mathbf{A}_0, \mathbf{A}_1, \cdots, \mathbf{A}_\ell, \mathbf{U}, \mathbf{G}\}$ to $\mathcal{A}$.
- **Query Phase 1:** $\mathcal{B}$ answers $\mathcal{A}$'s all key queries as in Game 1.
- **Challenge:** $\mathcal{A}$ sends two messages $\boldsymbol{\mu}_0, \boldsymbol{\mu}_1 \in \{0, 1\}^m$ to $\mathcal{B}$. $\mathcal{B}$ chooses a random bit $\beta \in \{0, 1\}$ and compute $\mathbf{c}^* = [\mathbf{I}_m | \mathbf{S}_1^* | \cdots | \mathbf{S}_\ell^*]^\top \cdot \mathbf{c}_{in} \in \mathbb{Z}_q^{(\ell+1)m}$ and $\mathbf{c}_{out}^* = \mathbf{c}_{out} + \lfloor q/2 \rfloor \cdot \boldsymbol{\mu}_\beta \in \mathbb{Z}_q^m$. $\mathcal{B}$ sends $ct^* = (\mathbf{c}^*, \mathbf{c}_{out}^*) \in \mathbb{Z}_q^{(\ell+2)m}$ to $\mathcal{A}$ as the challenge ciphertext. Increment $numCt$ and add $numCt$ to the set $Derive$. Store the value ct^* to the set $\mathcal{H}$ with key $(\mathbf{x}^*, numCt)$.

- Suppose $\mathbf{c}_{in}, \mathbf{c}_{out}$ are generated by dLWE, i.e., $\mathbf{c}_{in} = \mathbf{A}_0{}^\top \mathbf{s} + \mathbf{e}_0$ and $\mathbf{c}_{out} = \mathbf{U}^\top \mathbf{s} + \mathbf{e}_{out}$. Then from the Enc algorithm, we have,
$$\mathbf{H}_{\mathbf{x}^*} = \begin{bmatrix} \mathbf{A}_0 | x_1^* \mathbf{G} + \mathbf{A}_1 | \cdots | x_\ell^* \mathbf{G} + \mathbf{A}_\ell \end{bmatrix} = \begin{bmatrix} \mathbf{A}_0 | \mathbf{A}_0 \mathbf{S}_1^* | \cdots | \mathbf{A}_0 \mathbf{S}_\ell^* \end{bmatrix} \in \mathbb{Z}_q^{n \times (\ell+1)m}$$
(Substituting the value of $\mathbf{A}_0$ and $\mathbf{A}_i$'s). Then, $\mathbf{c}^* = \begin{bmatrix} \mathbf{I}_m | \mathbf{S}_1^* | \cdots | \mathbf{S}_\ell^* \end{bmatrix}^\top \cdot (\mathbf{A}_0{}^\top \mathbf{s} + \mathbf{e}_0) = \mathbf{H}_{\mathbf{x}^*}^\top \mathbf{s} + \mathbf{e}$, where $\mathbf{e} = \begin{bmatrix} \mathbf{I}_m | \mathbf{S}_1^* | \cdots | \mathbf{S}_\ell^* \end{bmatrix}^\top \cdot \mathbf{e}_0$. It is easy to see that $\mathbf{c}^*$ is computed as in Game 1. Also, $\mathbf{c}_{out}^* = \mathbf{U}^\top \mathbf{s} + \mathbf{e}_{out} + \lfloor q/2 \rfloor \cdot \boldsymbol{\mu}_\beta$. Then $ct^* = (\mathbf{c}^*, \mathbf{c}_{out}^*)$ is a valid ciphertext of $\boldsymbol{\mu}_\beta$ under $\mathbf{x}^*$.
- When $\mathbf{c}_{in}, \mathbf{c}_{out}$ are random in $\mathbb{Z}_q^m$, we have $\mathbf{c}^*$ is random in $\mathbb{Z}_q^{(\ell+1)m}$ by standard left over hash lemma. Also, $\mathbf{c}_{out}$ is uniform. So, ct^* is uniform in $\mathbb{Z}_q^{(\ell+2)m}$, as in Game 2.

- **Query Phase 2:** As in Query Phase 1 with the following constrain: ReEnc oracle output $\perp$ if $g(\mathbf{x}^*) \neq 0 \wedge k \in Derive$.
- **Guess:** $\mathcal{A}$ guesses if it is interacting with a Game 1 or Game 2 challenger. $\mathcal{B}$ outputs $\mathcal{A}$'s guess as the answer to the corresponding dLWE challenge.

Hence, $\mathcal{B}$'s advantage in solving dLWE is the same as $\mathcal{A}$'s advantage in distinguishing Game 1 and Game 2, as required. This completes the description of algorithm $\mathcal{B}$. This completes the proof. $\qquad \square$

Remark 2. We have proved the HRA security of the proposed scheme by following the HRA security game of Sect. 3. Theorem 2 may be easier to prove HRA security for pairing-based scheme.

Acknowledgement. This work is partially supported by the Australian Research Council Linkage Project LP190100984

References

1. Agrawal, S., Boneh, D., Boyen, X.: Efficient lattice (H)IBE in the standard model. In: Gilbert, H. (ed.) EUROCRYPT 2010. LNCS, vol. 6110, pp. 553–572. Springer, Heidelberg (2010). https://doi.org/10.1007/978-3-642-13190-5_28
2. Ajtai, M.: Generating hard instances of the short basis problem. In: Wiedermann, J., van Emde Boas, P., Nielsen, M. (eds.) ICALP 1999. LNCS, vol. 1644, pp. 1–9. Springer, Heidelberg (1999). https://doi.org/10.1007/3-540-48523-6_1
3. Alwen, J., Peikert, C.: Generating shorter bases for hard random lattices. In: STACS 2009, pp. 75–86 (2009)
4. Ateniese, G., Fu, K., Green, M., Hohenberger, S.: Improved proxy re-encryption schemes with applications to secure distributed storage. ACM Trans. Inf. Syst. Secur. **9**(1), 1–30 (2006)
5. Blaze, M., Bleumer, G., Strauss, M.: Divertible protocols and atomic proxy cryptography. In: Nyberg, K. (ed.) EUROCRYPT 1998. LNCS, vol. 1403, pp. 127–144. Springer, Heidelberg (1998). https://doi.org/10.1007/BFb0054122
6. Boneh, D., et al.: Fully key-homomorphic encryption, arithmetic circuit ABE and compact garbled circuits. In: Nguyen, P.Q., Oswald, E. (eds.) EUROCRYPT 2014. LNCS, vol. 8441, pp. 533–556. Springer, Heidelberg (2014). https://doi.org/10.1007/978-3-642-55220-5_30

7. Brakerski, Z., Gentry, C., Vaikuntanathan, V.: (Leveled) fully homomorphic encryption without bootstrapping. In: ITCS 2012, pp. 309–325. ACM (2012)
8. Brakerski, Z., Langlois, A., Peikert, C., Regev, O., Stehlé, D.: Classical hardness of learning with errors. In: STOC 2013, pp. 575–584 (2013)
9. Brakerski, Z., Vaikuntanathan, V.: Circuit-ABE from LWE: unbounded attributes and semi-adaptive security. In: Robshaw, M., Katz, J. (eds.) CRYPTO 2016. LNCS, vol. 9816, pp. 363–384. Springer, Heidelberg (2016). https://doi.org/10.1007/978-3-662-53015-3_13
10. Canetti, R., Lin, H., Tessaro, S., Vaikuntanathan, V.: Obfuscation of probabilistic circuits and applications. In: Dodis, Y., Nielsen, J.B. (eds.) TCC 2015. LNCS, vol. 9015, pp. 468–497. Springer, Heidelberg (2015). https://doi.org/10.1007/978-3-662-46497-7_19
11. Cash, D., Hofheinz, D., Kiltz, E., Peikert, C.: Bonsai trees, or how to delegate a lattice basis. In: EUROCRYPT 2010, pp. 523–552 (2010)
12. Chandran, N., Chase, M., Vaikuntanathan, V.: Functional re-encryption and collusion-resistant obfuscation. In: Cramer, R. (ed.) TCC 2012. LNCS, vol. 7194, pp. 404–421. Springer, Heidelberg (2012). https://doi.org/10.1007/978-3-642-28914-9_23
13. Cohen, A.: What about bob? The inadequacy of CPA security for proxy reencryption. In: Lin, D., Sako, K. (eds.) PKC 2019. LNCS, vol. 11443, pp. 287–316. Springer, Cham (2019). https://doi.org/10.1007/978-3-030-17259-6_10
14. Döttling, N., Nishimaki, R.: Universal proxy re-encryption. In: Garay, J.A. (ed.) PKC 2021. LNCS, vol. 12710, pp. 512–542. Springer, Cham (2021). https://doi.org/10.1007/978-3-030-75245-3_19
15. Dutta, P., Susilo, W., Duong, D.H., Baek, J., Roy, P.S.: Identity-based unidirectional proxy re-encryption in standard model: a lattice-based construction. In: You, I. (ed.) WISA 2020. LNCS, vol. 12583, pp. 245–257. Springer, Cham (2020). https://doi.org/10.1007/978-3-030-65299-9_19
16. Dutta, P., Susilo, W., Duong, D.H., Roy, P.S.: Collusion resistant identity-based proxy re-encryption: lattice-based constructions in standard model. Theor. Comput. Sci. **871**, 16–29 (2021)
17. Fuchsbauer, G., Kamath, C., Klein, K., Pietrzak, K.: Adaptively secure proxy reencryption. In: Lin, D., Sako, K. (eds.) PKC 2019. LNCS, vol. 11443, pp. 317–346. Springer, Cham (2019). https://doi.org/10.1007/978-3-030-17259-6_11
18. Ge, C., Susilo, W., Fang, L., Wang, J., Shi, Y.: A CCA-secure key-policy attribute-based proxy re-encryption in the adaptive corruption model for dropbox data sharing system. Des. Codes Crypt. **86**(11), 2587–2603 (2018)
19. Gentry, C.: A Fully Homomorphic Encryption Scheme, vol. 20. Stanford university Stanford, Stanford (2009)
20. Gentry, C., Peikert, C., Vaikuntanathan, V.: Trapdoors for hard lattices and new cryptographic constructions. In: STOC 2008, pp. 197–206 (2008)
21. Gentry, C., Sahai, A., Waters, B.: Homomorphic encryption from learning with errors: conceptually-simpler, asymptotically-faster, attribute-based. In: Canetti, R., Garay, J.A. (eds.) CRYPTO 2013. LNCS, vol. 8042, pp. 75–92. Springer, Heidelberg (2013). https://doi.org/10.1007/978-3-642-40041-4_5
22. Hohenberger, S., Rothblum, G.N., Vaikuntanathan, V.: Securely obfuscating re-encryption. In: Vadhan, S.P. (ed.) TCC 2007. LNCS, vol. 4392, pp. 233–252. Springer, Heidelberg (2007). https://doi.org/10.1007/978-3-540-70936-7_13
23. Jakobsson, M.: On quorum controlled asymmetric proxy re-encryption. In: Imai, H., Zheng, Y. (eds.) PKC 1999. LNCS, vol. 1560, pp. 112–121. Springer, Heidelberg (1999). https://doi.org/10.1007/3-540-49162-7_9

24. Liang, X., Cao, Z., Lin, H., Shao, J.: Attribute based proxy re-encryption with delegating capabilities. In: AsiaCCS 2009, pp. 276–286 (2009)

25. Micciancio, D., Peikert, C.: Trapdoors for lattices: simpler, tighter, faster, smaller. In: Pointcheval, D., Johansson, T. (eds.) EUROCRYPT 2012. LNCS, vol. 7237, pp. 700–718. Springer, Heidelberg (2012). https://doi.org/10.1007/978-3-642-29011-4_41

26. Miki, M., Hayashi, E., Shingai, H.: Highly reliable and highly secure online storage platform supporting "timeon" regza cloud service. Toshiba Rev. **68**(5), 25–27 (2013)

27. Peikert, C.: Public-key cryptosystems from the worst-case shortest vector problem. In: STOC 2009, pp. 333–342 (2009)

28. Polyakov, Y., Rohloff, K., Sahu, G., Vaikuntanathan, V.: Fast proxy re-encryption for publish/subscribe systems. ACM Trans. Priv. Secur. **20**(4), 1–31 (2017)

29. Regev, O.: On lattices, learning with errors, random linear codes, and cryptography. In: STOC 2005, pp. 84–93 (2005)

30. Smith, T.: Dvd jon: buy drm-less tracks from apple itunes (2005). https://www.theregister.co.uk/2005/03/18/itunes_pymusique/

Server-Aided Revocable Attribute-Based Encryption Revised: Multi-User Setting and Fully Secure

Leixiao Cheng[1] and Fei Meng[2,3]($\boxtimes$)

[1] School of Mathematics, Shandong University, Jinan 250100, China
lxcheng@sdu.edu.cn
[2] Ding Lab, Beijing Institute of Mathematical Sciences and Applications, Beijing, China
[3] Yau Mathematical Center, Tsinghua University, Beijing, China

Abstract. Attribute-based encryption (ABE) is a promising cryptographic primitive achieving fine-grained access control on encrypted data. However, efficient user revocation is always essential to keep the system dynamic and protect data privacy. Cui et al. (ESORICS 2016) proposed the first server-aided revocable attribute-based encryption (SR-ABE) scheme, in which an untrusted server manages all the long-term transform keys and update keys generated by key generation center (KGC) in order to achieve efficient user revocation. So, there's no need for any user to communicate with KGC to update his/her decryption key regularly. In addition, the most part of computational overhead of decryption is outsourced to the server and user keeps a small size of private key to decrypt the final ciphertext. Then, Qin et al.'s (CANS 2017) extended Cui et al.s' work to be decryption key exposure resistant (DKER).

Unfortunately, current SR-ABE schemes could only be provably secure in one-user setting, which means there's only one "target user" id^* with an attribute set S_{id^*} satisfying the access structure $(\mathbb{M}^*, \rho)$ in the challenge ciphertext, i.e., $S_{id^*} \vDash (\mathbb{M}^*, \rho)$. However, a more reasonable security model, i.e., multi-user setting, requires that any user id in the system can be with an attribute set $S_{id} \vDash (\mathbb{M}^*, \rho)$, and the adversary is allowed to query on any user's private key SK_{id} and his/her long-term transform key $PK_{id, S_{id}}$ as long as his/her identity id is revoked at or before the challenge time t^*. How to construct a SR-ABE secure in multi-user setting is still an open problem.

In this paper, we propose the first SR-ABE scheme provably secure in multi-user setting. In addition, our SR-ABE is fully secure and decryption key exposure resistant. Our scheme is constructed based on dual system encryption methodology and novelly combines a variant of Lewko et al.'s work in EUROCRYPT 2010 and Lewko et al.'s work in TCC 2010. As a result, we solve the remaining open problem.

Keywords: Attribute-based encryption · Revocation · Server-aided · Multi-user setting · Fully secure

© Springer Nature Switzerland AG 2021
E. Bertino et al. (Eds.): ESORICS 2021, LNCS 12973, pp. 192–212, 2021.
https://doi.org/10.1007/978-3-030-88428-4_10

1   Introduction

Attribute-based Encryption (ABE)[22], as an extension of identity-based encryption (IBE), is a powerful cryptographic primitive achieving fine-grained access control on encrypted data. ABE schemes are usually divided into two types: Key-Policy ABE (KP-ABE) [9] and Ciphertext-Policy ABE (CP-ABE) [3]. In this paper, we only focus on CP-ABE. In CP-ABE scheme, the data owner is allowed to define a specific access policy in the ciphertext which can only be decrypted by users with attributes satisfying the policy. CP-ABE is very suitable for encrypted data sharing in public cloud storage scenarios.

In the IBE or ABE system, when users lose their secret keys or exit the system, efficient user revocation is very crucial for preserving data privacy and keeping the system dynamic. In 2001, Boneh et al. [6] proposed a simple identity revocation mechanism, in which the Key Generation Center (KGC) has to generate $O(N - r)$ new secret keys for all unrevoked users at time period t, where N is the total number of users and r is the number of revoked users. To reduce the workload of KGC, Boldyreva et al. [4] proposed a more efficient identity revocation mechanism based on the binary-tree structure of [15]. In [4], each user keeps $O(\log N)$ long-term secret keys and the KGC broadcasts $O(r \log(N/r))$ update keys at time period t. Only non-revoked users can obtain their corresponding update keys. However, there are two drawbacks in [4]: every user needs to keep at least $O(\log N)$ long-term secret keys; all non-revoked users are required to communicate with the KGC regularly. As a result, [4] is not suitable for users with limited resources or who cannot communicate with KGC in real-time.

To solve this problem, Qin et al. [17] proposed a novel system model i.e., server-aided revocation in IBE scenario (SR-IBE). In [17], user's original long-term secret keys and update keys are all managed by an untrusted server, which honestly follows the protocol but is curious about data encrypted in the ciphertext, and each user keeps only one short private key. Since the original long-term secret keys are stored in the server, those keys are renamed as long-term transform keys. In this case, user no longer needs to communication with KGC for key updating regularly. To extend server-aided revocation mechanism from IBE to ABE scenario, in 2016, Cui et al. [8] proposed the first server-aided revocable ABE (SR-ABE). [8] not only inherits the advantages of server-aided revocation mechanism, but also achieves the decryption outsourcing, i.e., user could decrypt the ciphertext with little computational overhead. However, the scheme fails to satisfy (local) decryption key exposure resistance (DKER). Specifically, in [8], user's decryption key is his/her private key, which does not change with time, so exposing the user's decryption key will make the scheme completely insecure. Seo and Emura [23] has shown that the exposure of decryption keys is a very realistic threat to many revocable cryptosystems. Then, Qin et al. [18,19] revisited the security model of [8] and enhanced it by capturing the decryption key exposure attacks on user's local decryption keys while allowing the adversary to fully corrupt the server. In [18,19], the user keeps just a short private key, and can delegate his/her decryption capacity to a decryption key with any specified time period. Even if the local decryption key of a certain time period is leaked, the security of the decryption key of other time periods will not be affected. Similarly, [18,19] maintain the properties of server-aided revocation and outsourced decryption.

In general, the system framework of SR-ABE is shown in Fig. 1. The ABE ciphertext generated by data owner is transformed by an untrusted server using a short-term transformation key which is generated by combining the long-term transformation key and the key update message. However, once a user is revoked, the server cannot assist him/her to accomplish the transformation. In [8], user's private key is the decryption key, so once the decryption key is exposed, user's privacy is totally leaked. However, in [18,19], user's decryption key is derived from the private key, so even a decryption key of time period t is exposed, it will not affect decryption keys in other time periods.

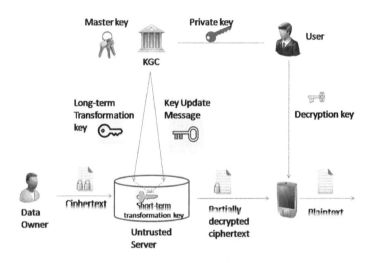

Fig. 1. System framework of SR-ABE

1.1 Motivation

The existing SR-ABE schemes [8,18,19] can only prove secure under "one-user setting", in which only one user id^* (called "target user") has the capacity to access the challenge ciphertext and the adversary can corrupt his private key. In [8,18,19], the adversary is divided into two distinct types: (1) the adversary is allowed to corrupt id^*'s private key, but id^* has to be revoked at or before the challenge time period t^*; (2) the adversary is not allowed to corrupt id^*'s private key, then id^* is not revoked but the adversary can obtain decryption keys for any time period except t^*. Note that [8,18,19] can only simulate the security game for these two types of adversaries separately, which do not cross with each other. However, this is too restrictive in a real world scenario, since the two different adversaries may exist simultaneously even for two target users.

But unfortunately, the restriction seems necessary for the proof technique used in [8,18,19].

Let us analyze why this is the case. In this paper, we focus on SR-ABE scheme with DKER. Note that [8] is improved by [18,19] which achieves DKER, so we take [18,19] as example. The analysis works similarly for [8] as well. First, we briefly recall some algorithms in the construction of [18,19]:

Setup(1^λ): This algorithm outputs master secret key $msk = \alpha$, the public parameter $par = (g, w, v, u, h, u_0, h_0, e(g, g)^\alpha)$, along with a revocation list RL and a state st, where g is the generator of a group G, w, v, u, h, u_0, h_0 are randomly chosen from G, α is randomly chosen from $\mathbb{Z}_p$, st is set to be the binary tree BT (BT is introduced in Sect. 2.3).

UserKG(par, msk, id, S, st): This algorithm randomly chooses $\beta_{id} \in \mathbb{Z}_p$ and set $sk_{id} = g^{\beta_{id}}$. Then, it chooses an undefined leaf node θ_{id} from BT, stores id in this node. For each $x \in \mathsf{Path}(\mathsf{BT}, \theta_{id})$, it runs as follows.

1. It fetches g_x from the node x. If x has not been defined, it randomly chooses $g_x \in G$, computes $g'_x = g^{\alpha - \beta_{id}}/g_x$ and stores g_x in the node x.
2. It randomly chooses $r_x, r_{x,1}, \ldots, r_{x,k} \in \mathbb{Z}_p$, computes

$$P_{x,0} = g'_x \cdot w^{r_x}, \quad P_{x,1} = g^{r_x}, \quad P_{x,2}^{(i)} = g^{r_{x,i}}, \quad P_{x,3}^{(i)} = (u^{s_i}h)^{r_{x,i}} \cdot v^{-r_x}.$$

3. it outputs $pk_{id,S} = \{x, P_{x,0}, P_{x,1}, P_{x,2}^{(i)}, P_{x,3}^{(i)}\}_{x \in \mathsf{Path}(\mathsf{BT},\theta_{id}), i \in [1,k]}$ as the long-term transformation key and $sk_{id} = g^{\beta_{id}}$ as the secret key.

TKeyUp$(par, msk, \mathsf{RL}, t, st)$: This algorithm inputs par, msk, a revocation list RL, a time period t and a state st. For each $x \in \mathsf{KUNodes}(\mathsf{BT}, \mathsf{RL}, t)$, it randomly chooses $s_x \in \mathbb{Z}_p$, fetches g_x from the node x, outputs a key update message $tku_t = \{x, Q_{x,1}, Q_{x,2}\}_{x \in \mathsf{KUNodes}(\mathsf{BT},\mathsf{RL},t)}$, where

$$Q_{x,0} = g_x \cdot (u^t h)^{s_x}, \quad Q_{x,1} = g^{s_x}.$$

Encrypt$(par, (\mathbb{M}, \rho), t, M)$: This algorithm inputs par, an LSSS access structure $(\mathbb{M}, \rho)$, a time period t and a message M, randomly chooses $\mathbf{v} = (s, y_2, \ldots, y_n)^\perp \in \mathbb{Z}_p^n$ and $\mu_1, \ldots, \mu_l \in \mathbb{Z}_p$, computes $\lambda_i = \mathbb{M}_i \cdot \mathbf{v}$, outputs the ciphertext $CT = \{C, C_0, \{C_{i,1}, C_{i,2}, C_{i,3}\}, C_4\}$, where

$$C = e(g, g)^{\alpha s} \cdot M, \quad C_0 = g^s, \quad C_{i,1} = w^{v_i} \cdot v^{\mu_i},$$
$$C_{i,2} = (u^{s_{\rho(i)}}h)^{-\mu_i}, \quad C_{i,3} = g^{\mu_i}, \quad C_4 = (u^t h)^s.$$

As we can see, Qin et al. [18,19] used the "random splitting technique" to divide a master secret key "α" into two parts. Specifically, "α" is split into "$\alpha - \beta_{id}$" and "β_{id}" for identity id, where β_{id} is randomly chosen and $g^{\beta_{id}}$ serves as the user's private key in **UserKG**. In order to achieve user revocation, $g^{\alpha - \beta_{id}}$ will be further divided into random g_x and $g'_{x,id}$ to generate key update message in **TKeyUp** and long-term transformation key in **UserKG** respectively (g_x is stored in the node x of BT, and does not change once stored; $g'_{x,id}$ changes with different identities), such that

$$g_x \cdot g'_{x,id} = g^{\alpha - \beta_{id}}, \quad x \in \mathsf{Path}(\mathsf{BT}, \theta_{id}). \tag{1}$$

The security of the SR-ABE scheme [18,19] is reduced to the Rouselakis-Waters CP-ABE scheme [20]. It seems that [18,19] cannot prove secure in multi-user setting. This is because if the adversary $\mathcal{A}$, who attacks the SR-ABE scheme [18,19], is allowed to simultaneously corrupt two separate users in two different types, as we mentioned at the beginning of this section, then the simulator $\mathcal{B}$, who was built using $\mathcal{A}$ to attack [20], can break [20] itself, which leads to the failure of the security reduction. The detail is as follows.

The simulator $\mathcal{B}$ is given the public parameters of Rouselakis-Waters, and the master key α is hidden from $\mathcal{B}$. Assume that there are two identities id_0^* and id_1^* with attribute sets S_0 and S_1 satisfying the challenge access structure $(\mathbb{M}^*, \rho)$ such that:

(1) $\mathcal{A}$ corrupts id_0^*'s private key and id_0^* is revoked before the time period t^*;
(2) $\mathcal{A}$ doesn't corrupts id_1^*'s private key and id_1^* is not revoked.

According to Eq. (1), we have

$$g_x \cdot g'_{x,id_0} = g^{\alpha - \beta_{id_0}}, \quad x \in \mathsf{Path}(\mathsf{BT}, \theta_{id_0}) \tag{2}$$

$$g_x \cdot g'_{x,id_1} = g^{\alpha - \beta_{id_1}}, \quad x \in \mathsf{Path}(\mathsf{BT}, \theta_{id_1}) \tag{3}$$

Since $S_0 \models (\mathbb{M}^*, \rho)$, g'_{x,id_0} for $x \in \mathsf{Path}(\mathsf{BT}, \theta_{id_0})$, are known to $\mathcal{B}$ in order to generate the long-term transformation key pk_{id_0,S_0} for $\mathcal{A}$; Since $\mathcal{A}$ corrupts id_0^*'s private key, β_{id_0} is a known value to $\mathcal{B}$; Since id_1 is non-revoked, $\mathcal{B}$ has to know g_x for $x \in \mathsf{Path}(\mathsf{BT}, \theta_{id_1})$ to generate the key update message at time period t^* for $\mathcal{A}$, especially the value g_{x^*} for $x^* \in \mathsf{Path}(\mathsf{BT}, \theta_{id_0}) \cap \mathsf{Path}(\mathsf{BT}, \theta_{id_1})$. According to Equation (2), $\mathcal{B}$ knows the value

$$g^\alpha = (g_{x^*} \cdot g'_{x^*,id_0}) \cdot g^{\beta_{id_0}},$$

which enables $\mathcal{B}$ to break the underlying Rouselakis-Waters CP-ABE scheme [20], and thus the security reduction fails. For the similar reason, [8] also cannot prove secure in multi-user setting and it is still a practical open problem to construct an SR-ABE scheme probably secure under such setting.

1.2 Our Approach

As we analyzed above, in previous SR-ABE schemes [8,18,19], if the adversary $\mathcal{A}$ is allowed to simultaneously corrupt two separate users in two different types, then the simulator $\mathcal{B}$ is able to compute g^α (α is the master secret key) and solve the underlying complexity assumption itself, thus the security reduction breaks down. This hints that we need to find a new construction and proof system so that the exposure of g^α will not lead to the failure of the security reduction. Fortunately, Waters et al. [11,13,24] introduced dual system methodology, which opens up a new way to prove security of IBE, ABE and other related encryption systems.

Briefly speaking, in the dual encryption system [11, 13], both ciphertext and private key can be in one of two indistinguishable forms: normal and semi-functional. Unless both the key and ciphertext are semi-functional, the key will decrypt the ciphertext correctly. However, when a semi-functional key is used to decrypt a semi-functional ciphertext, the semi-functional components of the key and ciphertext will interact to generate an additional random term, and decryption will fail. In the real system, the normal keys and ciphertexts are used, while semi-functional objects are gradually presented in hybrid security proof: firstly in Game_0, the normal challenge ciphertext is switched to a semi-functional one; then, from Game_1 to Game_q, the secret keys given the adversary are changed from normal to semi-functional one by one and Game_q is a security game where the simulator only generates semi-functional objects; finally, we end up in $\mathsf{Game}_{\mathsf{Final}}$ where the challenge ciphertext is a semi-function encryption on a *random* group element and *all* of the private key queries result in semi-functional key, hence security can be proved straightforward.

When arguing that Game_{k-1} and Game_k are indistinguishable for $k \in [1, q]$, the simulator $\mathcal{B}$ who attacks the underlying assumptions (Assumption 1 and 2 in Sect. 2.1) always chooses the master secret key α by himself so that he is ready to make *any* key and *any* challenge ciphertext for adversary $\mathcal{A}$ who attacks the scheme. When claiming that Game_q and $\mathsf{Game}_{\mathsf{Final}}$ are indistinguishable, the simulator $\mathcal{B}$ who attacks Assumption 3 (Sect. 2.1) takes as input parameters $g, g^{\alpha}X_2, X_3, g^s Y_2, Z_2, T$ (T is either $e(g, g)^{\alpha}$ or a random element in G_T), then it makes use of the Assumption 3 parameter $g^{\alpha}X_2$ to generate semi-functional objections to answer *any* key query from $\mathcal{A}$.

Based on this observation, the dilemma encountered in proving multi-user security in the previous SR-ABE schemes could be overcome, because we no longer need to worry about the exposure of g^{α} or $g^{\alpha}X_2$. In other words, leveraging dual system methodology into SR-ABE may lead us down the right path to prove the security under multi-user setting. Therefore, we novelly combine the ABE scheme [11] and the IBE scheme [13] in the dual system to construct our SR-ABE scheme. Thanks to the powerful dual system encryption methodology, in our security proof, even the adversary $\mathcal{A}$ corrupts two separate users in two different types simultaneously, the simulator $\mathcal{B}$, who knows α or $g^{\alpha}X_2$, is able to answer *any* key query on these two users from $\mathcal{A}$, and thus the security reduction works. As a result, our SR-ABE is provably secure in multi-user setting. The only remaining question is how to combine those two schemes in the dual system organically to obtain a concrete SR-ABE scheme. We put this detail at the beginning of Sect. 4.

1.3   Our Contributions

In this paper, we construct the first (fully secure) server-aided revocable attribute-based encryption scheme with decryption key exposure resistance, achieving the security requirement in the multi-user setting. We solve the open problem of how to construct a SR-ABE scheme that is provably secure in the

Table 1. Comparison between our scheme and other indirect revocable ABE schemes.

	[4]	[1]	[21]	[8]	[18]	Ours
Revocation Mode	Indirect	Indirect	Indirect & Direct	Indirect	Indirect	Indirect
Type of ABE	KP-ABE	KP-ABE	KP-ABE & CP-ABE	CP-ABE	CP-ABE	CP-ABE
Server	-	-	-	Untrusted	Untrusted	Untrusted
Decryption Outsource	No	No	No	Yes	Yes	Yes
DKER	No	No	No	No	Yes	Yes
Fully Secure	No	No	No	No	No	Yes
Secure Channel	Yes	Yes	Yes	No	Yes/No	Yes/No
Multi-User Setting	Yes	Yes	Yes	No	No	Yes
Size of Key Updates	$O(r \log \frac{N}{r})$	$O(r \log \frac{N}{r})$ & -	$O(r \log \frac{N}{r})$	$O(r \log \frac{N}{r})$	$O(r \log \frac{N}{r})$	$O(r \log \frac{N}{r})$
Size of Key Stored by User	$O(l \log N)$	$O(l \log N)$	$O(l \log N)$ & $O(k \log N)$	$O(1)$	$O(1)$	$O(1)$

multi-user setting. Specifically, our scheme novelly combines a variant of a fully secure (H)IBE [13] and a fully secure ABE [11] in the dual encryption system.

In Table 1, we compare our SR-ABE scheme with several related indirect revocable ABE schemes [1,4,8,18,21]. Let N be the number of user in the system, r be the number of revoked users, l be the number of attributes presented in an access structure, and k be the size of the attribute set associated with an attribute-key. Also, let "-" denote not-applicable. As shown in Table 1, compared with [1,4,21], our scheme has inherited the wonderful merits of SR-ABE schemes [8] and [18], i.e., decryption outsourced and small size of key storage in the user side. There's no need for any user to communicate with KGC to update his/her decryption key regularly as well. In addition, compared with [8] and [18], our scheme is fully secure and provably secure in multi-user setting. Furthermore, different from [8], our SR-ABE satisfies DKER.

2   Preliminaries

In this section, we briefly introduce some basic cryptographic definitions.

2.1   Composite Order Bilinear Groups

We recall the definition of composite order bilinear groups in [13]. A group generator $\mathcal{G}$ is defined as an algorithm that takes a security parameter λ as input and outputs $(p_1, p_2, p_3, G, G_T, e)$, where p_1, p_2, p_3 are distinct primes, G and G_T are two cyclic groups of order $N = p_1 p_2 p_3$, and $e : G \times G \to G_T$ is a bilinear map with the following properties:

Bilinear: $\forall u, v \in G$ and $a, b \in \mathbb{Z}_p$, we have $e(u^a, v^b) = e(u, v)^{ab}$.
Non-degenerate: $\exists g \in G$ such that $e(g, g) \in G_T$ is the generator of G_T.

The group operations in G and G_T as well as the bilinear map e are computable in polynomial time. Let $G_{p_1}, G_{p_2}, G_{p_3}$ denote the subgroups of order p_1, p_2, p_3 in G respectively, then when $h_i \in G_{p_i}$ and $h_j \in G_{p_j}$ for $i \neq j$, $e(h_i, h_j)$ is the identity element in G_T. This orthogonality property of $G_{p_1}, G_{p_2}, G_{p_3}$ will be used to implement semi-functionality in our SR-ABE.

We now introduce the complexity assumptions [11,12]. Let $G_{p_1 p_2}$ and $G_{p_1 p_3}$ denote the subgroup of order $p_1 p_2$ and $p_1 p_3$ in G, respectively.

Assumption 1. (Subgroup decision problem for 3 primes). Given a group generator $\mathcal{G}$, we define the following distribution:

$$\mathbb{G} = (N = p_1 p_2 p_3, G, G_T, e) \xleftarrow{R} \mathcal{G}, g \xleftarrow{R} G_{p_1}, X_3 \xleftarrow{R} G_{p_3}, D = (\mathbb{G}, g, X_3)$$

$$T_1 \xleftarrow{R} G_{p_1 p_2}, T_2 \xleftarrow{R} G_{p_1}.$$

The advantage of an algorithm $\mathcal{A}$ in breaking Assumption 1 is defined as:

$$Adv1_{\mathcal{G},\mathcal{A}}(\lambda) := \mid \Pr[\mathcal{A}(D, T_1)] - \Pr[\mathcal{A}(D, T_2)] \mid.$$

Definition 1. *We say that $\mathcal{G}$ satisfies Assumption 1 if $Adv1_{\mathcal{G},\mathcal{A}}(\lambda)$ is a negligible function of λ for any polynomial time algorithm $\mathcal{A}$.*

Note that T_1 can be written uniquely as the product of an element of G_{p_1} and an element of G_{p_2}. We refer to these elements as the G_{p_i} part of T_1 for $i = 1, 2$.

Assumption 2. Given a group generator $\mathcal{G}$, we define the following distribution:

$$\mathbb{G} = (N = p_1 p_2 p_3, G, G_T, e) \xleftarrow{R} \mathcal{G}, g, X_1 \xleftarrow{R} G_{p_1}, X_2, Y_2 \xleftarrow{R} G_{p_2},$$

$$X_3, Y_3 \xleftarrow{R} G_{p_3}, D = (\mathbb{G}, g, X_1 X_2, X_3, Y_2 Y_3), T_1 \xleftarrow{R} G, T_2 \xleftarrow{R} G_{p_1 p_3}.$$

The advantage of an algorithm $\mathcal{A}$ in breaking Assumption 2 is defined as:

$$Adv2_{\mathcal{G},\mathcal{A}}(\lambda) := \mid \Pr[\mathcal{A}(D, T_1)] - \Pr[\mathcal{A}(D, T_2)] \mid.$$

Definition 2. *We say that $\mathcal{G}$ satisfies Assumption 2 if $Adv2_{\mathcal{G},\mathcal{A}}(\lambda)$ is a negligible function of λ for any polynomial time algorithm $\mathcal{A}$.*

Note that T_1 can be written uniquely as the product of an element of G_{p_1}, an element of G_{p_2} and an element of G_{p_3}. We refer to these elements as the G_{p_i} part of T_1 for $i = 1, 2, 3$. T_2 can be written as the product of an element of G_{p_1} and an element of G_{p_3} similarly.

Assumption 3. Given a group generator $\mathcal{G}$, we define the following distribution:

$$\mathbb{G} = (N = p_1 p_2 p_3, G, G_T, e) \xleftarrow{R} \mathcal{G}, \alpha, s \xleftarrow{R} \mathbb{Z}_N, g \xleftarrow{R} G_{p_1}, X_2, Y_2, Z_2 \xleftarrow{R} G_{p_2},$$

$$X_3 \xleftarrow{R} G_{p_3}, D = (\mathbb{G}, g, g^\alpha X_2, X_3, g^s Y_2, Z_2), T_1 = e(g, g)^{\alpha s}, T_2 \xleftarrow{R} G_T.$$

The advantage of an algorithm $\mathcal{A}$ in breaking Assumption 3 is defined as:

$$Adv3_{\mathcal{G},\mathcal{A}}(\lambda) := \mid \Pr[\mathcal{A}(D, T_1)] - \Pr[\mathcal{A}(D, T_2)] \mid.$$

Definition 3. *We say that $\mathcal{G}$ satisfies Assumption 3 if $Adv3_{\mathcal{G},\mathcal{A}}(\lambda)$ is a negligible function of λ for any polynomial time algorithm $\mathcal{A}$.*

2.2   Access Structures and Linear Secret Sharing

Definition 4 (Access structure[3]). *Let $\{P_1, P_2, \ldots, P_n\}$ be a set of parties. A collection $\mathbb{A} \subseteq 2^{\{P_1, P_2, \ldots, P_n\}}$ is monotone if $\forall B, C$: if $B \in \mathbb{A}$ and $B \subseteq C$ then $C \in \mathbb{A}$. An access structure (respectively, monotone access structure) is a collection (respectively, monotone collection) $\mathbb{A}$ of non-empty subsets of $\{P_1, P_2, \ldots, P_n\}$, i.e., $\mathbb{A} \subseteq 2^{\{P_1, P_2, \ldots, P_n\}} \setminus \{\emptyset\}$. The sets in $\mathbb{A}$ are called the authorized sets, and the sets not in $\mathbb{A}$ are called the unauthorized sets.*

Definition 5 (Linear Secret Sharing Schemes (LSSS)[3]). *A secret sharing scheme Π over a set of parties P is a linear secret-sharing scheme over Z_p if:*

- *The shares for each party form a vector over Z_p.*
- *There exists a matrix $\mathbb{M}$ with l rows and n columns, called the share generating matrix, for Π. For $i = 1, \ldots, l$, the ith row of matrix $\mathbb{M}$, i.e., $\mathbb{M}_i$, is labelled by a party $\rho(i)$, where $\rho : \{1, \ldots, l\} \to P$ is a function that maps a row to a party for labelling. Considering that the column vector $\vec{v} = (s, r_2, \ldots, r_n)$, where $s \in Z_p$ is the secret to be shared and $r_2, \ldots, r_n \in Z_p$ are randomly chosen, then $\mathbb{M}\vec{v}$ is the vector of l shares of the secret s according to Π. The share $\mathbb{M}_i\vec{v}$ belongs to party $\rho(i)$.*

The linear reconstruction property states that there exist constants $\{\omega_i \in \mathbb{Z}_p\}_{i \in I}$ such that, for any valid shares $\{\lambda_i\}_i$ of a secret s according to Π, we have: $\Sigma_{i \in I}\omega_i\lambda_i = s$, where $I = \{i \mid \rho(i) \in S\}$ for an authorized set S [2]. We note that for unauthorized sets, no such constants $\{\omega_i\}$ exist.

2.3   Binary Tree

We recall the definition of binary-tree data structure, as with [5,7,10,16,23]. This structure uses a node selection algorithm called KUNodes. In the algorithm, we use the following notations: BT denotes a binary-tree. root denotes the root node of BT. x denotes a node in the binary tree and θ emphasizes that the node x is a leaf node. The set Path(BT, θ) stands for the collection of nodes on the path from the leaf θ to the root (including θ and the root). If x is a non-leaf node, then x_ℓ, x_r denote the left and right child of x, respectively. The KUNodes algorithm takes as input a binary tree BT, a revocation list RL and a time t, and outputs the minimal set Y of nodes, such that the corresponding key update information can only be used by the non-revoked users to generate a valid short-term transformation key. Specifically, the KUNodes algorithm first marks all ancestor of users that were revoked by t as revoked nodes, then outputs all the non-revoked children of revoked nodes. The description of the KUNodes algorithm is as follows:

KUNodes(BT, RL, t):
    $X, Y \leftarrow \emptyset$; $\forall(\theta_i, t_i) \in$ RL, and $t_i \leq t$, add Path(BT, θ_i) to X;
    $\forall x \in X$: if $x_\ell \notin X$ then add x_ℓ to Y, if $x_r \notin X$ then add x_r to Y;
    If $Y = \emptyset$ then add root to Y;   Return Y.

3   Framework and Security Model

Our SR-ABE scheme involves four types of entities: a key generation center (KGC), data owners, data users and an untrusted server.

Setup$(1^\lambda, U) \rightarrow (PK, MSK, \mathsf{RL}, st)$: Taking as input a security parameter λ and an attribute set U containing all possible attributes, KGC runs this algorithm to generate the public key PK, the master secret key MSK, an initially empty revocation list RL and a state st.

UserKG$(PK, MSK, id, S, st) \rightarrow (PK_{id,S}, SK_{id}, st)$: KGC runs the user key generation algorithm and outputs user's long-term transformation key $PK_{id,S}$ for the untrusted server and a private key SK_{id} for the user, then updates the state st.

TKeyUp$(PK, MSK, \mathsf{RL}, t, st) \rightarrow (tku_t, st)$: KGC runs the transformation key update algorithm and outputs a key update message tku_t for server and an updated state st.

TranKG$(PK, id, PK_{id,S}, tku_t) \rightarrow tk_{id,t}/ \perp$: The server runs the transformation key generation algorithm and outputs a short-term transformation key $tk_{id,t}$ for id if id is not revoked at t. Otherwise, it outputs $\perp$.

DecKG$(PK, id, SK_{id}, t) \rightarrow dk_{id,t}$: The user runs the decryption key generation algorithm and outputs a decryption key $dk_{id,t}$ for id in time period t.

Enc$(PK, (\mathbb{M}, \rho), t, M) \rightarrow CT$: Taking the public key PK, an access structure $(\mathbb{M}, \rho)$, a time period t and a message M as the input, the data owner runs the encryption algorithm to generate a ciphertext CT and then submits CT to server.

Transform$(PK, id, S, tk_{id,t}, CT) \rightarrow CT'/ \perp$: The server runs the ciphertext transformation algorithm to generate a partially decrypted ciphertext CT' for id if the attribute set S associated with the transformation key $tk_{id,t}$ satisfies the access structure of the ciphertext CT. Otherwise, it outputs $\perp$.

Decrypt$(PK, id, dk_{id,t}, CT') \rightarrow M/ \perp$: The user runs the decryption algorithm and outputs the message M or a failure symbol $\perp$.

Revoke$(id, t, \mathsf{RL}, st) \rightarrow \mathsf{RL}$: KGC runs the revocation algorithm and outputs an updated revocation list RL.

3.1   Security Model

Now, we introduce the security definition of indistinguishability under chosen plaintext attacks (IND-CPA security) for SR-ABE between an adversary $\mathcal{A}$ and the challenger $\mathcal{B}$.

Setup: $\mathcal{B}$ runs the **Setup** algorithm, and returns the public key to $\mathcal{A}$, then keeps the master secret key MSK, an initially empty revocation list RL, a state st, and two empty sets T, T' by itself.

Phase 1: $\mathcal{A}$ adaptively issues a sequence of following queries to $\mathcal{B}$:

– Create(id, S). $\mathcal{B}$ runs **UserKG**(PK, MSK, id, S, st) to obtain the pair $(PK_{id,S}, SK_{id})$, stores in table T the entry $(id, S, PK_{id,S}, SK_{id})$ and returns $PK_{id,S}$ to $\mathcal{A}$.

- Corrupt(id). If there exists an entry indexed by id in table T, then $\mathcal{B}$ retrieves the entry $(id, S, PK_{id,S}, SK_{id})$, sets $T' = T' \cup \{(id, S)\}$, returns SK_{id}. If no such entry exists, then it returns $\perp$.
- TKeyUp(t). $\mathcal{B}$ runs **TKeyUp**($PK, MSK, \mathsf{RL}, t, st$) and returns tku_t.
- DecKG(id,t). If there exists an entry indexed by id in table T, then $\mathcal{B}$ retrieves the entry $(id, S, PK_{id,S}, SK_{id})$, runs DecKG($PK, id, SK_{id}, t$) and returns $dk_{id,t}$. If no such entry exists, then it returns $\perp$.
- Revocation(id,t). $\mathcal{B}$ runs **Revoke**(id, t, RL, st) and outputs an updated revocation list RL.

Challenge: $\mathcal{A}$ submits two messages (M_0, M_1) of the same size, an access structure $(\mathbb{M}^*, \rho)$ and a time period t^* with the following restrictions:
- If $(id, S) \in T'$ and $S \vDash (\mathbb{M}^*, \rho)$, then $\mathcal{A}$ must query the revocation oracle on (id, t) at or before t^*.
- If there exists a tuple $(id, S, PK_{id,S}, SK_{id}) \in T$, $S \vDash (\mathbb{M}^*, \rho)$ and id is not revoked at or before t^*, then $\mathcal{A}$ cannot query Corrupt(id) and DecKG(id,t^*).

$\mathcal{B}$ picks a random bit $\beta \in \{0, 1\}$, and returns the challenge ciphertext $CT^* \leftarrow$ **Enc**($PK, (\mathbb{M}^*, \rho), t^*, M_\beta$) to $\mathcal{A}$.

Phase 2: $\mathcal{A}$ continues submits queries to $\mathcal{B}$ as in Phase 1, with the restrictions defined in the Challenge phase.

Guess: $\mathcal{A}$ outputs a guess β' of β, and it wins the game if $\beta' = \beta$. The advantage of $\mathcal{A}$ in this game is defined as $\mathsf{Adv}_{\mathcal{A}}(l) = \mid \Pr[\beta' = \beta] - 1/2 \mid$.

Definition 6. *An SR-ABE scheme is adaptively IND-CPA secure if the advantage* $\mathsf{Adv}_{\mathcal{A}}(l)$ *is negligible in l for all polynomial time adversary $\mathcal{A}$.*

4 Construction

In this section, we propose the construction of our SR-ABE with DKER, which is fully secure in multi-user setting. As we have discussed in Sect. 1.2, we try to construct an SR-ABE by the dual system encryption technique. However, we find that if we trivially follow the construction of SR-ABE with DKER [18,19] by just replacing their underlying ABE block [20] with dual ABE [11], then it will cause "authority abuse": (1) anyone can generate a valid private key, since it is computed without the system master secret key; (2) user id with his private key SK_{id} can easily change the identity embedded in his long-term transform key $PK_{id,S}$ from id to id'. Adding up these two points, user id can maliciously generate a new $SK_{id'}$ and $PK_{id',S'}$, where $S' \subseteq S$, for an unauthorized user id' by the key re-randomization technique, resulting in the authority abuse.

In our scheme, we novelly combine dual ABE [11] and dual IBE [13]. Firstly, we embed the system master key into user's private key to ensure that only the KGC can distribute users' private keys. Specifically, we view the system master key α as the master key of a variant of the 2-level HIBE [13] to generate 1-level user private key SK_{id} (id as identity), which is then used to delegate a 2-level decryption key $dk_{id,t}$ (($id \parallel t$) as identity). It should be noted that the exposure of decryption key $dk_{id,t}$ on time t will not affect the decryption key $dk_{id,t'}$ on time $t' \neq t$, so that our SR-ABE is decryption key exposure resistant (DKER). Secondly, we generate user's long-term transformation key $PK_{id,S}$ by combining the key generation algorithms of both [11] and the variant of [13]. The unique random r embedded in both SK_{id} and $PK_{id,S}$ guarantees that, without knowing r, anyone cannot change the identity embedded in SK_{id} and $PK_{id,S}$, so that the authority abuse is prevented. The detail of our scheme is shown as follows.

- **Setup**$(1^\lambda, U) \to (PK, MSK)$: The setup algorithm chooses a bilinear group G of order $N = p_1 p_2 p_3$, where p_1, p_2, p_3 are three distinct primes. We let G_{p_i} denote the subgroup of order p_i in G. It then chooses random exponents $\alpha, a \in \mathbb{Z}_N$, and random group elements $g, u, h, u_0, h_0 \in G_{p_1}$. For each attribute $i \in U$, it chooses a random value $s_i \in \mathbb{Z}_N$. Then, the algorithm outputs the public parameters PK and master secret key MSK as follows:

$$PK = \{N, g, g^a, u, h, u_0, h_0, e(g,g)^\alpha, \{T_i = g^{s_i}\}_{i \in U}\}, MSK = \{\alpha, X_3\} \quad (4)$$

where X_3 is a generator of G_{p_3}.
- **UserKG**$(PK, MSK, id, S, st) \to (PK_{id,S}, SK_{id}, st)$: The algorithm chooses an undefined leaf node θ from the binary tree BT, and stores id in this node. Then, it randomly chooses $r \in \mathbb{Z}_N$. For each node $x \in \mathsf{Path}(\mathsf{BT}, \theta)$, it runs as follows.
  - It fetches g_x from the node x. If x has not been defined, it randomly picks $g_x \in G_{p_1}$, then stores g_x in node x.
  - It randomly chooses $t_x \in \mathbb{Z}_N, R_{x,0}, \bar{R}_{x,0}, R_{x,i} \in G_{p_1}$, and computes

$$PK_{id,S,x} = \left\{ \begin{array}{l} K_x = g^{\alpha + at_x r}((u^{id}h)^r/g_x) \cdot R_{x,0}, \ L_x = g^{t_x r} \cdot \bar{R}_{x,0} \\ \{K_{x,i} = T_i^{t_x r} \cdot R_{x,i}\}_{i \in S} \end{array} \right\}. \quad (5)$$

Then, the algorithm picks a random element $R_3 \in G_{p_3}$ and computes

$$SK_{id} = g^\alpha (u^{id}h)^r \cdot R_3. \quad (6)$$

Finally, the algorithm outputs the long-term transformation key $PK_{id,S} = \{x, PK_{id,S,x}\}_{x \in \mathsf{Path}(\mathsf{BT}, \theta)}$, the private key SK_{id} and updates the state st.
- **TKeyUp**$(PK, MSK, \mathsf{RL}, t, st) \qquad\qquad \to \qquad\qquad (tku_t, st)$: For each $x \in \mathsf{KUNodes}(\mathsf{BT}, \mathsf{RL}, t)$, the algorithm fetches g_x from x (g_x should always be predefined in the above UserKG algorithm), randomly chooses $\hat{R}_{x,3}, \bar{R}_{x,3} \in G_{p_3}, s_x \in \mathbb{Z}_N$, and computes

$$Q_{x,0,t} = g^\alpha g_x \cdot (u_0^t h_0)^{s_x} \hat{R}_{x,3}, \qquad Q_{x,1,t} = g^{s_x} \bar{R}_{x,3}. \quad (7)$$

Finally, the algorithm generates the transformation key update information $tku_t = \{x, Q_{x,0,t}, Q_{x,1,t}\}_{x \in \mathbf{KUNodes}(\mathsf{BT}, \mathsf{RL}, t)}$ and updates the state st.
- **TranKG**$(PK, id, PK_{id,S}, tku_t) \to tku_{id,t}/ \perp$: Suppose θ is the leaf node corresponding with id. If $\mathsf{Path}(\mathsf{BT}, \theta) \bigcap \mathsf{KUNodes}(\mathsf{BT}, \mathsf{RL}, t) = \emptyset$, the algorithm returns $\perp$. Otherwise, there must exist one node x such that $x \in$

$\mathsf{Path}(\mathsf{BT}, \theta) \bigcap \mathsf{KUNodes}(\mathsf{BT}, \mathsf{RL}, t)$. Then, it computes

$$
\left\{
\begin{array}{ll}
tk_0 = K_x \cdot Q_{x,0,t} = g^{2\alpha + at_x r}(u^{id}h)^r(u_0^t h_0)^{s_x} \cdot R_{x,0}\hat{R}_{x,3} \\
tk_1 = L_x = g^{t_x r} \cdot \bar{R}_{x,0} \\
tk_{2,i} = K_{x,i} = T_i^{t_x r} R_{x,i} \qquad \forall i \in S \\
tk_3 = Q_{x,1,t} = g^{s_x} \bar{R}_{x,3}
\end{array}
\right\}. \tag{8}
$$

Finally, it returns the transformation key $tk_{id,t} = \{tk_0, tk_1, \{tk_{2,i}\}_{i \in S}, tk_3\}$.

- **DecKG**$(PK, id, SK_{id}, t) \rightarrow dk_{id,t}$: It randomly chooses $r_t \in \mathbb{Z}_N$ and outputs a decryption key $dk_{id,t} = \{SK_{id}(u_0^t h_0)^{r_t}, g^{r_t}\} = \{g^\alpha(u^{id}h)^r(u_0^t h_0)^{r_t} R_3, g^{r_t}\}$.
- **Enc**$(PK, (\mathbb{M}, \rho), t, M) \rightarrow CT$: Given an LSSS access structure $(\mathbb{M}, \rho)$, $\mathbb{M}$ is an $l \times n$ matrix and ρ is a map from each row $\mathbb{M}_i$ of $\mathbb{M}$ to an attribute $\rho(i)$. The algorithm randomly chooses a random vector $\vec{v} \in \mathbb{Z}_N^n$ and denotes $\vec{v} = (s, y_2, \ldots, y_n)^\perp$. Then it computes the shares $\lambda = (\lambda_1, \ldots, \lambda_l)^\perp = \mathbb{M} \cdot \vec{v}$, where $\lambda_i = \mathbb{M}_i \cdot \vec{v}$. Finally, it randomly chooses $r_1, \ldots, r_l \in \mathbb{Z}_N$ and outputs the ciphertext CT as

$$
CT = \left\{
\begin{array}{l}
C = M \cdot e(g,g)^{\alpha s}, C_0 = g^s, C_t = (u_0^t h_0)^s \\
\{C_i = g^{a\lambda_i} T_{\rho(i)}^{-r_i}, D_i = g^{r_i}\}_{i \in [1,l]}
\end{array}
\right\}. \tag{9}
$$

- **Transform**$(PK, id, S, tk_{id,t}, CT) \rightarrow CT'/ \perp$: If the user has been revoked at time period t or the attribute set $S \not\models (\mathbb{M}, \rho)$, the algorithm returns $\perp$. Otherwise, the algorithm computes a set of constants $\{\omega_i \in \mathbb{Z}_N\}$ such that $\sum_{\rho(i) \in S} \omega_i \mathbb{M}_i = (1, 0, \ldots, 0)$. Next, it computes

$$
\begin{aligned}
B_0 &= \prod_{\rho(i) \in S} (e(tk_{2,i}, D_i) \cdot e(C_i, tk_1))^{\omega_i} \\
&= \prod_{\rho(i) \in S} (e(T_i^{t_x r}, g^{r_i}) \cdot e(g^{a\lambda_i} T_{\rho(i)}^{-r_i}, g^{t_x r} \bar{R}_{x,0}))^{\omega_i} \tag{10} \\
&= e(g,g)^{at_x r \sum_{\rho(i) \in S} \lambda_i \omega_i} = e(g,g)^{at_x rs},
\end{aligned}
$$

and $B_1 = e(tk_0, C_0) = e(g,g)^{2\alpha s} \cdot e(g,g)^{at_x rs} \cdot e((u^{id}h)^r, g^s) \cdot e((u_0^t h_0)^{s_x}, g^s)$ and $B_2 = e(tk_3, C_t) = e(g^{s_x} \bar{R}_{x,3}, (u_0^t h_0)^s) = e(g^{s_x}, (u_0^t h_0)^s)$. Finally, the algorithm computes

$$
D = \frac{B_1}{B_0 \cdot B_2} = e(g,g)^{2\alpha s} \cdot e((u^{id}h)^r, g^s). \tag{11}
$$

and returns the transformed ciphertext $CT' = (C, C_0, C_t, D)$

- **Decrypt**$(PK, id, dk_{id,t}, CT') \rightarrow M$: Set $dk_{id,t} = (dk_0, dk_1)$, it computes

$$
\begin{aligned}
D_0 &= e(dk_0, C_0) = e(g,g)^{\alpha s} \cdot e((u^{id}h)^r, g^s) \cdot e((u_0^t h_0)^{r_t}, g^s) \\
D_1 &= e(dk_1, C_t) = e(g^{r_t}, (u_0^t h_0)^s) \tag{12}
\end{aligned}
$$

and then computes

$$
M = \frac{C \cdot D_0}{D \cdot D_1} = \frac{M \cdot e(g,g)^{2\alpha s} \cdot e((u^{id}h)^r, g^s) \cdot e((u_0^t h_0)^{r_t}, g^s)}{e(g,g)^{2\alpha s} \cdot e((u^{id}h)^r, g^s) \cdot e(g^{r_t}, (u_0^t h_0)^s)}. \tag{13}
$$

– **Revoke**$(id, t, \mathsf{RL}, st) \to \mathsf{RL}$: If a user's identity id is revoked at time period t, the algorithm adds (x, t) into the revocation list RL for all nodes x associated with identity id.

5   Security Analysis

In this section, we provide a security analysis of our SR-ABE scheme in the multi-user setting. Following the basic technique of dual system encryption [11,13], we define two additional structures: semi-functional ciphertexts and semi-functional keys. These will not be used in the real system, but will be essential in the security proof.

Semi-functional Ciphertext: Let g_2 be a generator of G_{p_2}. Randomly pick $c, z_{t^*}, z_1, \ldots, z_l, \gamma_1, \ldots, \gamma_l \in \mathbb{Z}_N$ and $\vec{u} \in \mathbb{Z}_N^n$. Then:

$$C_0 = g^s g_2^c, \qquad C_t = (u_0^t h_0)^s g_2^{cz_{t^*}},$$
$$C_i = g^{a\lambda_i} T_{\rho(i)}^{-r_i} g_2^{\mathbb{M}_i \vec{u} + \gamma_i z_{\rho(i)}}, \qquad D_i = g^{r_i} g_2^{-\gamma_i} \quad \forall i \in [1, l]. \tag{14}$$

Semi-functional Key: There are two types of semi-functional key. A semi-functional key of type 1 is formed as follows. Chose random elements $z_{id}, b, d, z_t \in \mathbb{Z}_N$, set

$$SK_{id} = g^\alpha (u^{id} h)^r \cdot R_3 \cdot g_2^{bz_{id}}; \tag{15}$$

for each node $x \in \mathsf{Path}(\mathsf{BT}, \theta)$, set

$$K_x = g^{\alpha + at_x r}((u^{id}h)^r / g_x) \cdot R_{x,0} \cdot g_2^{dt_x} \cdot g_2^{bz_{id}}, \quad L_x = g^{t_x r} \cdot \bar{R}_{x,0} \cdot g_2^{bt_x},$$
$$K_{x,i} = T_i^{t_x r} R_{x,i} \cdot g_2^{bt_x z_{\rho(i)}} \quad \forall i \in S; \tag{16}$$

for each node $x \in \mathsf{KUNodes}(\mathsf{BT}, \mathsf{RL}, t)$, pick random element $\gamma_x \in \mathbb{Z}_N$, set:

$$Q_{x,0,t} = g^\alpha g_x \cdot (u_0^t h_0)^{s_x} \hat{R}_{x,3} \cdot g_2^{\gamma_x z_t}, \quad Q_{x,1,t} = g^{s_x} \bar{R}_{x,3} \cdot g_2^{\gamma_x}. \tag{17}$$

A semi-functional key of type 2 is formed as:

$$SK_{id} = g^\alpha (u^{id} h)^r \cdot R_3 \cdot g_2^{bz_{id}}; \tag{18}$$

for $\forall x \in \mathsf{Path}(\mathsf{BT}, \theta)$,

$$K_x = g^{\alpha + at_x r}((u^{id}h)^r / g_x) \cdot R_{x,0} \cdot g_2^{dt_x} \cdot g_2^{bz_{id}}, \qquad L_x = g^{t_x r} \cdot \bar{R}_{x,0},$$
$$K_{x,i} = T_i^{t_x r} R_{x,i} \quad \forall i \in S; \tag{19}$$

for $\forall x \in \mathsf{KUNodes}(\mathsf{BT}, \mathsf{RL}, t)$,

$$Q_{x,0,t} = g^\alpha g_x \cdot (u_0^t h_0)^{s_x} \hat{R}_{x,3} \cdot g_2^{\gamma_x z_t}, \quad Q_{x,1,t} = g^{s_x} \bar{R}_{x,3} \cdot g_2^{\gamma_x}. \tag{20}$$

It should be noted that if we use a semi-functional key to decrypt a semi-functional ciphertext, we get the following additional term:

$$e(g_2, g_2)^{(cd - bu_1)t_x + c\gamma_x(z_t - z_{t^*})}, \tag{21}$$

where u_1 denotes the first coordinate of $\vec{u}$ (i.e. $(1, 0, \ldots, 0) \cdot \vec{u}$). Note that the values z_i, which are used to hide u_1 from an attacker, are common to semi-functional ciphertexts and semi-functional keys of type 1. Similar to [11], our security proof will depend on the restriction that each attribute can only be used once in the row labeling of an access matrix. Based on this restriction, the attacker gains very limited information-theoretic knowledge of z_i.

We call a semi-functional key of type 1 "nominally" semi-functional if $(cd - bu_1)t_x + c\gamma_x(z_t - z_{t^*}) = 0$. If we use such a key to decrypt a corresponding semi-functional ciphertext, the decryption still succeeds.

We will prove the security of our system from Assumptions 1, 2, and 3 using a hybrid argument over a sequence of games. The first game, $\mathbf{Game}_{Real}$, is the real security game (the ciphertext and all the keys are normal). The next game $\mathbf{Game}_{Restricted}$ will be like the real security game except that the attacker cannot ask for the transformation key update information and decryption keys for times which are equal to the challenge time t^* modulo p_2. Also, the attacker cannot ask for long-term transformation keys, private keys and decryption keys for identities $id_i \neq id_j$ modulo N such that $id_i = id_j$ modulo p_2. In the next game, $\mathbf{Game}_0$, all of the keys will be normal, but the challenge ciphertext will be semi-functional. We let q denote the number of key queries made by the attacker. For k from 1 to q, we define:

$\mathbf{Game}_{k,1}$ In this game, the challenge ciphertext is semi-functional, the first $k - 1$ keys are semi-functional of type 2, the kth key is semi-functional of type 1, and the remaining keys are normal.

$\mathbf{Game}_{k,2}$ In this game, the challenge ciphertext is semi-functional, the first k keys are semi-functional of type 2, and the remaining keys are normal.

In $\mathbf{Game}_{q,2}$, all of the keys are semi-functional of type 2. In the final game, $\mathbf{Game}_{Final}$, all keys are semi-functional of type 2 and the ciphertext is a semi-functional encryption of a random message, independent of the two messages provided by the attacker. Thus, the adversary's advantage in winning the final game is 0. Now, we will prove that these games are indistinguishable. The proof of Lemmas 2, 4, 5 is given in Appendix.

Lemma 1. *Supposed that a PPT adversary $\mathcal{A}$ can distinguish the $\mathbf{Game}_{Real}$ and $\mathbf{Game}_{Restricted}$ with a non-negligible advantage $\epsilon > 0$, then there exists a PPT simulator $\mathcal{B}$ that can break either Assumption 1 or Assumption 2 with advantage $\geq \frac{\epsilon}{2}$.*

Proof. This proof is similar with Lemma 1 of [13], so we omit it here.

Lemma 2. *Supposed that a PPT adversary $\mathcal{A}$ can distinguish $\mathbf{Game}_{Restricted}$ and $\mathbf{Game}_0$ with a non-negligible advantage $\epsilon > 0$, then there exists a PPT simulator $\mathcal{B}$ that can break Assumption 1 with advantage ϵ.*

Lemma 3. *Supposed that a PPT adversary $\mathcal{A}$ can distinguish the $\mathbf{Game}_{k-1,2}$ and $\mathbf{Game}_{k,1}$ with a non-negligible advantage $\epsilon > 0$, then there exists a PPT simulator $\mathcal{B}$ that can break Assumption 2 with advantage ϵ.*

Proof. $\mathcal{B}$ is given $(g, X_1X_2, X_3, Y_2Y_3, T)$ and simulates $\mathbf{Game}_{k-1,2}$ or $\mathbf{Game}_{k,1}$ with $\mathcal{A}$. It randomly picks $a, \alpha, a_0, a_1, b_0, b_1 \in \mathbb{Z}_N$ and $s_i \in \mathbb{Z}_N$ for each attribute i in the system, then sets $u = g^{a_1}, h = g^{b_1}, u_0 = g^{a_0}, h_0 = g^{b_0}$ and returns the public parameters $PK = \{N, g, g^a, u, h, u_0, h_0, e(g,g)^{\alpha}, \{T_i = g^{s_i}, \forall i\}\}$ to $\mathcal{A}$.

To make the first $k-1$ keys semi-functional of type 2, $\mathcal{B}$ responds to each key request as follows. Choose an undefined leaf node θ from BT and store id in this node. Randomly choose $f, r, z_{id}, d', z_t \in \mathbb{Z}_N$, $R'_3 \in G_{p_3}$, set

- $SK_{id} = g^{\alpha}(u^{id}h)^r \cdot R'_3 \cdot (Y_2Y_3)^{fz_{id}}$;
- For each $x \in \mathsf{Path}(\mathsf{BT}, \theta)$, fetch g_x from the node x (if g_x has not been defined, randomly pick $g_x \in G_{p_1}$ and store in node x), randomly choose $t_x \in \mathbb{Z}_N$, $R'_{x,0}, \bar{R}_{x,0}, \{R_{x,i}\}_{i \in S} \in G_{p_3}$, set

$$K_x = g^{\alpha + at_x r}((u^{id}h)^r/g_x) \cdot R'_{x,0} \cdot (Y_2Y_3)^{d't_x + fz_{id}}, \quad L_x = g^{t_x r} \cdot \bar{R}_{x,0},$$
$$K_{x,i} = T_i^{t_x r} R_{x,i} \quad \forall i \in S; \tag{22}$$

- For each $x \in \mathsf{KUNodes}(\mathsf{BT}, \mathsf{RL}, t)$, fetch g_x from the node x, randomly choose $s_x, \gamma'_x \in \mathbb{Z}_N$ and $\hat{R}'_{x,3}, \bar{R}'_{x,3} \in G_{p_3}$, set

$$Q_{x,0,t} = g^{\alpha}g_x(u_0^t h_0)^{s_x} \cdot \hat{R}'_{x,3}(Y_2Y_3)^{\gamma'_x z_t}, Q_{x,1,t} = g^{s_x} \cdot \bar{R}'_{x,3}(Y_2Y_3)^{\gamma'_x}. \tag{23}$$

The above keys are properly distributed. To make normal keys for requests $> k$, $\mathcal{B}$ can simply run the key generation algorithm by using the MSK.

To answer the kth key request, $\mathcal{B}$ will implicity set g^r be the G_{p_1} part of T. Choose an undefined leaf node θ from BT and store id in this node. Randomly choose $R'_3 \in G_{p_3}$, set

- $SK_{id} = g^{\alpha}T^{a_1id+b_1} \cdot R'_3$;
- For each $x \in \mathsf{Path}(\mathsf{BT}, \theta)$, fetch g_x from the node x, choose random elements $t_x \in \mathbb{Z}_N$, $R'_{x,0}, \bar{R}'_{x,0}, \{R'_{x,i}\}_{i \in S} \in G_{p_3}$, set

$$K_x = g^{\alpha}T^{at_x}(T^{a_1id+b_1}/g_x) \cdot R'_{x,0}, \quad L_x = T^{t_x} \cdot \bar{R}'_{x,0},$$
$$K_{x,i} = T^{s_it_x}R'_{x,i} \quad \forall i \in S; \tag{24}$$

- For each $x \in \mathsf{KUNodes}(\mathsf{BT}, \mathsf{RL}, t)$, fetch g_x from the node x, choose random elements $\hat{R}'_{x,3}, \bar{R}'_{x,3} \in G_{p_3}$ and $s'_x \in \mathbb{Z}_N$, set

$$Q_{x,0,t} = g^{\alpha}g_x \cdot (T^{a_0t+b_0})^{s'_x}\hat{R}'_{x,3}, \qquad Q_{x,1,t} = T^{s'_x}\bar{R}'_{x,3}. \tag{25}$$

If $T \in G_{p_1p_3}$, we set $s_x = rs'_x$ and this is a properly distributed normal key. Otherwise $T \in G$, this is a semi-functional key of type 1. In this case, we implicitly set $z_i = s_i$. If we set g_2^b as the G_{p_2} part of T, then we have that $d = ba$, $z_{id} = a_1id + b_1$, $z_t = a_0t + b_0$, $\gamma_x = bs'_x$, $s_x = rs'_x$. Note that the value of s'_x, s_i modulo p_2 are uncorrelated from these values modulo p_1. Since $\phi(id) = a_1 id + b_1$ ($\varphi(t) = a_0 t + b_0$) is pairwise independent function modulo p_2, as long as $id_i \neq id_j (\mathrm{mod}\, p_2)$ ($t \neq t^* (\mathrm{mod}\, p_2)$), z_{id_i} and z_{id_j} (z_t and z_{t^*}) will seem randomly distributed to $\mathcal{A}$. If $id_i = id_j (\mathrm{mod}\, p_2)$ or $t = t^* (\mathrm{mod}\, p_2)$, then $\mathcal{A}$ has made invalid key requests, this is why we use additional restrictions.

$\mathcal{A}$ sends $\mathcal{B}$ two messages (M_0, M_1), a challenge access matrix $(\mathbb{M}^*, \rho)$ and a challenge time t^*. To generate the semi-functional challenge ciphertext CT^*, $\mathcal{B}$ will implicitly set $g^s = X_1$ and $g_2^c = X_2$. It randomly chooses $u_2, \ldots, u_n \in \mathbb{Z}_N$, $r'_i \in \mathbb{Z}_N$ for $i \in [1, l]$ and a random bit $\beta \in \{0, 1\}$ and sets $\vec{u}' = (a, u_2, \ldots, u_n)$. Finally, $\mathcal{B}$ generates the challenge ciphertext CT^* as:

$$CT^* = \left\{ \begin{array}{l} C = M_\beta \cdot e(g^\alpha, X_1 X_2), C_0 = X_1 X_2, C_t = (X_1 X_2)^{a_0 t^* + b_0} \\ C_i = (X_1 X_2)^{\mathbb{M}_i^* \vec{u}'} T^{-r'_i s_{\rho(i)}}, D_i = (X_1 X_2)^{r'_i} \quad \forall i \end{array} \right\}. \qquad (26)$$

We set $\vec{v} = sa^{-1} \vec{u}'$ and $\vec{u} = c\vec{u}'$ (i.e., $u_1 = ca$). Then, s is shared in the G_{p_1} while ca is shared in the G_{p_2}. We also implicitly set $r_i = sr'_i$ and $\gamma_i = -cr'_i$. The values $z_{\rho(i)} = s_{\rho(i)}$ match those in the kth key if it is semi-functional key of type 1, as required.

The kth key and challenge ciphertext are almost properly distributed. However, the first coordinate of $\vec{u}$ (i.e., u_1) is correlated with the value of a modulo p_2, since a also appears in the kth key if it is semi-functional. We argue that this is information theoretically hidden from the adversary $\mathcal{A}$, who cannot request any keys that can decrypt the challenge ciphertext. This argument has been carefully proved in Lemma 8 of [11], so we omit it here.

In addition, with the setting of $z_{id} = a_1 id + b_1$ and $z_t = a_0 t + b_0$, if $\mathcal{B}$ use the kth key to decrypt a semi-functional ciphertext, which is embedded with the same time period with k^{th} key query, we would have $(cd - bu_1)t_x + c\gamma_x(z_t - z_t) = (cba - bca)t_x + c\gamma_x(z_t - z_t) = 0 \mod p_2$, so the kth key is either normal key or nominally semi-functional key.

Thus, if $T \in G_{p_1 p_3}$, then $\mathcal{B}$ has properly simulated $\mathbf{Game}_{k-1,2}$. Otherwise, $T \in G$ and $\mathcal{B}$ has properly simulated $\mathbf{Game}_{k,1}$. Therefore, $\mathcal{B}$ can use the output of $\mathcal{A}$ to gain advantage negligibly close to ϵ in breaking Assumption 2. $\qquad \square$

Lemma 4. *Supposed that a PPT adversary $\mathcal{A}$ can distinguish the $\mathbf{Game}_{k,1}$ and $\mathbf{Game}_{k,2}$ with a non-negligible advantage $\epsilon > 0$, then there exists a PPT simulator $\mathcal{B}$ that can break Assumption 2 with advantage ϵ.*

Lemma 5. *Supposed that a PPT adversary $\mathcal{A}$ can distinguish the $\mathbf{Game}_{q,2}$ and $\mathbf{Game}_{Final}$ with a non-negligible advantage $\epsilon > 0$, then there exists a PPT simulator $\mathcal{B}$ that can break Assumption 3 with advantage ϵ.*

6   Conclusion

In this paper, we propose the first (fully secure) SR-ABE scheme with DKER, which is provably secure in multi-user setting. The construction of our scheme relies on the basic technique of dual encryption system in composite order bilinear groups. In our security proof, we inherited the shortcomings of the one-use restriction in the fully secure ABE scheme [11], meaning that a single attribute could only be used once in a policy. Later, [14] relaxed the restriction and allowed unrestricted use of attributes while still proving full security in the standard model. However, these frameworks only work in composite-order bilinear groups, where the computations (especially pairing operation) are very slow. In practice, prime-order bilinear groups are preferable because they provide more efficient and compact instantiations. Our SR-ABE can be further improved by using the techniques of above works. Due to the limited space, we leave it as future work.

Acknowledgments. We thank anonymous reviewers for helpful feedback.

A   Proof of Lemma 2

Proof. $\mathcal{B}$ is given (g, X_3, T) and simulates $\mathbf{Game}_{Restricted}$ or $\mathbf{Game}_0$ with $\mathcal{A}$. It sets the public parameters as follows. It randomly picks $a, \alpha, a_0, a_1, b_0, b_1 \in \mathbb{Z}_N$ and $s_i \in \mathbb{Z}_N$ for each attribute i in the system, then sets $u = g^{a_1}, h = g^{b_1}, u_0 = g^{a_0}, h_0 = g^{b_0}$, returns the public parameters to $\mathcal{A}$ as:

$$PK = \{N, g, g^a, u, h, u_0, h_0, e(g,g)^\alpha, \{T_i = g^{s_i}, \forall i\}\}, \tag{27}$$

and keeps $MSK = \{\alpha, X_3\}$ as secret. In this case, $\mathcal{B}$ can answer any normal key query (including Create(id,S), Corrupt(id), TKeyUp(t), DecKG(id,t)) from $\mathcal{A}$ by running the corresponding key generation algorithm with MSK.

$\mathcal{A}$ sends $\mathcal{B}$ two messages (M_0, M_1), a challenge access matrix $(\mathbb{M}^*, \rho)$ and a challenge time t^*. To generate the challenge ciphertext CT^*, $\mathcal{B}$ will implicitly set g^s to be the G_{p_1} part of T (T is the product of g^s and possible an element of G_{p_2}). It randomly chooses $v'_2, \ldots, v'_n \in \mathbb{Z}_N, r'_i \in \mathbb{Z}_N$ for $i \in [1, l], \beta \in \{0, 1\}$ and sets $\vec{v}' = (1, v'_2, \ldots, v'_n)^\perp$. Finally, $\mathcal{B}$ generates the challenge ciphertext CT^* as:

$$CT^* = \begin{cases} C = M_\beta \cdot e(g^\alpha, T), & C_0 = T, & C_t = T^{a_0 t^* + b_0} \\ C_i = T^{a \mathbb{M}_i^* \vec{v}'} T^{-r'_i s_{\rho(i)}}, & D_i = g^{r'_i} & \forall i \end{cases}. \tag{28}$$

We note that this implicitly sets $\vec{v} = (s, sv'_2, \ldots, sv'_n)$ and $r_i = sr'_i$. Modulo p_1, v is a random vector with first coordinate s and r_i is a random value. Thus, if $T \in G_{p_1}$, CT^* is a properly distributed normal ciphertext. Otherwise, $T \in G_{p_1 p_2}$, we let g_2^c as the G_{p_2} part of T (i.e. $T = g^s g_2^c$). We then have a semi-functional ciphertext with $z_{t^*} = a_0 t^* + b_0$, $u = ca\vec{v}'$, $\gamma_i = -cr'_i$, and $z_{\rho(i)} = s_{\rho(i)}$. By the Chinese Remainder Theorem, $a_0, b_0, a, v'_2, \ldots, v'_n, r'_i, s_{\rho(i)}$ modulo p_2 are uncorrelated from these values modulo p_1, so CT^* is a properly distributed semi-functional ciphertext. Therefore, $\mathcal{B}$ can break Assumption 1 with advantage ϵ by the output of $\mathcal{A}$. $\square$

B   Proof of Lemma 4

Proof. $\mathcal{B}$ is given $(g, X_1X_2, X_3, Y_2Y_3, T)$ and simulates $\mathbf{Game}_{k,1}$ or $\mathbf{Game}_{k,2}$ with $\mathcal{A}$. It randomly picks $a, \alpha, a_0, a_1, b_0, b_1 \in \mathbb{Z}_N$ and $s_i \in \mathbb{Z}_N$ for each attribute i in the system, then sets $u = g^{a_1}, h = g^{b_1}, u_0 = g^{a_0}, h_0 = g^{b_0}$ and returns the public parameters $PK = \{N, g, g^a, u, h, u_0, h_0, e(g,g)^\alpha, \{T_i = g^{s_i}, \forall i\}\}$ to $\mathcal{A}$.

The first $k-1$ semi-functional keys of type 2, the normal keys $> k$, and the challenge ciphertext are all constructed the same as the above lemma. Hence, the ciphertext is sharing the value ac in the G_{p_2} subgroup. However, this will not be correlated with the kth key any way, so the value is random modulo p_2. To answer the kth key request, $\mathcal{B}$ choose a random element $R_3' \in G_{p_3}$ and set

- $SK_{id} = g^\alpha T^{a_1 id + b_1} \cdot R_3'$;
- For each $x \in \mathsf{Path}(BT, \theta)$, fetch g_x from the node x, choose random elements $t_x \in \mathbb{Z}_N, R_{x,0}', \bar{R}_{x,0}', \{R_{x,i}'\}_{i \in S} \in G_{p_3}$, and an additional $h_x \in \mathbb{Z}_N$, set

$$K_x = g^\alpha T^{a t_x} (T^{a_1 id + b_1}/g_x) \cdot R_{x,0}' \cdot (Y_2Y_3)^{h_x}, \qquad L_x = T^{t_x} \cdot \bar{R}_{x,0}',$$
$$K_{x,i} = T^{s_i t_x} R_{x,i}' \quad \forall i \in S; \tag{29}$$

- For each $x \in \mathsf{KUNodes}(BT, RL, t)$, fetch g_x from the node x, choose random elements $\hat{R}_{x,3}, \bar{R}_{x,3} \in G_{p_3}$ and $s_x' \in \mathbb{Z}_N$, set

$$Q_{x,0,t} = g^\alpha g_x \cdot (T^{a_0 t + b_0})^{s_x'} \hat{R}_{x,3}, \quad Q_{x,1,t} = T^{s_x'} \bar{R}_{x,3}. \tag{30}$$

Note that we add the $(Y_2Y_3)^{h_x}$ term. This randomizes the G_{p_2} part of K_x, so the key is no longer nominally semi-functional. If we use the kth key to decrypt the semi-functional ciphertext, the decryption would fail.

Thus, if $T \in G_{p_1 p_3}$, then $\mathcal{B}$ has properly simulated $\mathbf{Game}_{k,2}$. Otherwise, $T \in G$, then $\mathcal{B}$ has properly simulated $\mathbf{Game}_{k,1}$. Therefore, $\mathcal{B}$ can use the output of $\mathcal{A}$ to gain advantage to ϵ in breaking Assumption 2.   □

C   Proof of Lemma 5

Proof. $\mathcal{B}$ is given $(g, g^\alpha X_2, X_3, g^s Y_2, Z_2, T)$ and simulates $\mathbf{Game}_{q,2}$ or $\mathbf{Game}_{Final}$ with $\mathcal{A}$. It randomly picks $a, , a_0, a_1, b_0, b_1 \in \mathbb{Z}_N$ and $s_i \in \mathbb{Z}_N$ for each attribute i in the system, then sets $u = g^{a_1}, h = g^{b_1}, u_0 = g^{a_0}, h_0 = g^{b_0}$ and returns $PK = \{N, g, g^a, u, h, u_0, h_0, e(g, g^\alpha X_2) = e(g,g)^\alpha, \{T_i = g^{s_i}, \forall i\}\}$ to $\mathcal{A}$.

To make semi-functional keys of type 2, randomly choose $f, r, z_{id}, d', z_t \in \mathbb{Z}_N$, $R_3' \in G_{p_3}$ and set

- $SK_{id} = g^\alpha (u^{id} h)^r \cdot R_3' \cdot Z_2^{f z_{id}}$;
- For each $x \in \mathsf{Path}(BT, \theta)$, fetch g_x from the node x, randomly choose $t_x \in \mathbb{Z}_N$, $R_{x,0}', \bar{R}_{x,0}', \{R_{x,i}\}_{i \in S} \in G_{p_3}$, set

$$K_x = g^{\alpha + a t_x r} ((u^{id} h)^r / g_x) \cdot R_{x,0}' \cdot Z_2^{d' t_x + f z_{id}}, \quad L_x = g^{t_x r} \cdot \bar{R}_{x,0}',$$
$$K_{x,i} = T_i^{t_x r} R_{x,i}' \quad \forall i \in S; \tag{31}$$

– For each $x \in \mathsf{KUNodes}(\mathsf{BT}, \mathsf{RL}, t)$, fetch g_x from the node x, randomly choose $s_x, \gamma'_x \in \mathbb{Z}_N$ and $\hat{R}'_{x,3}, \bar{R}'_{x,3} \in G_{p_3}$, set

$$Q_{x,0,t} = g^\alpha g_x \cdot (u_0^t h_0)^{s_x} \hat{R}'_{x,3} \cdot Z_2^{\gamma'_x z_t}, \quad Q_{x,1,t} = g^{s_x} \bar{R}'_{x,3} \cdot Z_2^{\gamma'_x}. \tag{32}$$

$\mathcal{A}$ sends $\mathcal{B}$ two messages (M_0, M_1), a challenge access matrix $(\mathbb{M}^*, \rho)$ and a challenge time t^*. $\mathcal{B}$ chooses $u_2, \ldots, u_n, r'_i \in \mathbb{Z}_N$, a random bit $\beta \in \{0, 1\}$ and sets $\vec{u}' = (a, u_2, \ldots, u_n)$. Finally, $\mathcal{B}$ generates the challenge ciphertext CT^* as:

$$CT^* = \left\{ \begin{array}{l} C = M_\beta \cdot T, C_0 = g^s Y_2, C_t = (g^s Y_2)^{a_0 t^* + b_0} \\ C_i = (g^s Y_2)^{\mathbb{M}_i^* \vec{u}'} (g^s Y_2)^{-r'_i s_{\rho(i)}}, D_i = (g^s Y_2)^{r'_i} \quad \forall i \end{array} \right\}. \tag{33}$$

We set $Y_2 = g_2^c$, $\vec{v} = sa^{-1}\vec{u}'$ and $\vec{u} = c\vec{u}'$ (i.e., $u_1 = ac$), so s is shared in the G_{p_1} and ca is shared in the G_{p_2}. This implicitly sets $u_1 = ca$, $r_i = sr'_i$ and $\gamma_i = -cr'_i$.

Thus, if $T = e(g, g)^{\alpha s}$, then $\mathcal{B}$ has properly simulated $\mathbf{Game}_{q,2}$ and CT^* is a semi-functional ciphertext with encryption of M_β. Otherwise, $T \in G_T$, then $\mathcal{B}$ has properly simulated $\mathbf{Game}_{Final}$ and CT^* is a semi-functional ciphertext with encryption of a random message in G_T. Therefore, $\mathcal{B}$ can use the output of $\mathcal{A}$ to gain advantage to ϵ in breaking Assumption 3. $\qquad\square$

References

1. Attrapadung, N., Imai, H.: Attribute-based encryption supporting direct/indirect revocation modes. In: Parker, M.G. (ed.) IMACC 2009. LNCS, vol. 5921, pp. 278–300. Springer, Heidelberg (2009). https://doi.org/10.1007/978-3-642-10868-6_17
2. Beimel, A.: Secure schemes for secret sharing and key distribution. PhD thesis Israel institute of technology Technion (1996)
3. Bethencourt, J., Sahai, A., Waters, B.: Ciphertext-policy attribute-based encryption. In: IEEE Symposium on Security and Privacy 2007, pp. 321–334 (2007)
4. Boldyreva, A., Goyal, V., Kumar, V.: Identity-based encryption with efficient revocation. In: CCS 2008, pp. 417–426 (2008)
5. Boldyreva, A., Goyal, V., Kumar, V.: Identity-based encryption with efficient revocation. IACR Cryptology ePrint Archive **2012**, 52 (2012)
6. Boneh, D., Franklin, M.: Identity-based encryption from the weil pairing. In: Kilian, J. (ed.) CRYPTO 2001. LNCS, vol. 2139, pp. 213–229. Springer, Heidelberg (2001). https://doi.org/10.1007/3-540-44647-8_13
7. Chen, J., Lim, H.W., Ling, S., Wang, H., Nguyen, K.: Revocable identity-based encryption from lattices. In: Susilo, W., Mu, Y., Seberry, J. (eds.) ACISP 2012. LNCS, vol. 7372, pp. 390–403. Springer, Heidelberg (2012). https://doi.org/10.1007/978-3-642-31448-3_29
8. Cui, H., Deng, R.H., Li, Y., Qin, B.: Server-aided revocable attribute-based encryption. In: Askoxylakis, I., Ioannidis, S., Katsikas, S., Meadows, C. (eds.) ESORICS 2016. LNCS, vol. 9879, pp. 570–587. Springer, Cham (2016). https://doi.org/10.1007/978-3-319-45741-3_29
9. Goyal, V., Pandey, O., Sahai, A., Waters, B.: Attribute-based encryption for fine-grained access control of encrypted data. In: CCS 2006, pp. 89–98 (2006)

10. Katsumata, S., Matsuda, T., Takayasu, A.: Lattice-based revocable (hierarchical) IBE with decryption key exposure resistance. In: PKC 2019, pp. 441–471 (2019)
11. Lewko, A., Okamoto, T., Sahai, A., Takashima, K., Waters, B.: Fully secure functional encryption: attribute-based encryption and (hierarchical) inner product encryption. In: Gilbert, H. (ed.) EUROCRYPT 2010. LNCS, vol. 6110, pp. 62–91. Springer, Heidelberg (2010). https://doi.org/10.1007/978-3-642-13190-5_4
12. Lewko, A.B., Sahai, A., Waters, B.: Revocation systems with very small private keys. In: IEEE Symposium on Security and Privacy, S&P 2010, pp. 273–285. IEEE Computer Society (2010)
13. Lewko, A., Waters, B.: New techniques for dual system encryption and fully secure HIBE with short ciphertexts. In: Micciancio, D. (ed.) TCC 2010. LNCS, vol. 5978, pp. 455–479. Springer, Heidelberg (2010). https://doi.org/10.1007/978-3-642-11799-2_27
14. Lewko, A., Waters, B.: New proof methods for attribute-based encryption: achieving full security through selective techniques. In: Safavi-Naini, R., Canetti, R. (eds.) CRYPTO 2012. LNCS, vol. 7417, pp. 180–198. Springer, Heidelberg (2012). https://doi.org/10.1007/978-3-642-32009-5_12
15. Naor, D., Naor, M., Lotspiech, J.: Revocation and tracing schemes for stateless receivers. In: CRYPTO, pp. 41–62 (2001)
16. González-Nieto, J.M., Manulis, M., Sun, D.: Fully private revocable predicate encryption. In: Susilo, W., Mu, Y., Seberry, J. (eds.) ACISP 2012. LNCS, vol. 7372, pp. 350–363. Springer, Heidelberg (2012). https://doi.org/10.1007/978-3-642-31448-3_26
17. Qin, B., Deng, R.H., Li, Y., Liu, S.: Server-aided revocable identity-based encryption. In: Pernul, G., Ryan, P.Y.A., Weippl, E. (eds.) ESORICS 2015. LNCS, vol. 9326, pp. 286–304. Springer, Cham (2015). https://doi.org/10.1007/978-3-319-24174-6_15
18. Qin, B., Zhao, Q., Zheng, D., Cui, H.: Server-aided revocable attribute-based encryption resilient to decryption key exposure. In: Capkun, S., Chow, S.S.M. (eds.) CANS 2017. LNCS, vol. 11261, pp. 504–514. Springer, Cham (2018). https://doi.org/10.1007/978-3-030-02641-7_25
19. Qin, B., Zhao, Q., Zheng, D., Cui, H.: (Dual) server-aided revocable attribute-based encryption with decryption key exposure resistance. Inf. Sci. **490**, 74–92 (2019)
20. Rouselakis, Y., Waters, B.: Practical constructions and new proof methods for large universe attribute-based encryption. In: Sadeghi, A., Gligor, V.D., Yung, M. (eds.) CCS 2013, pp. 463–474. ACM (2013)
21. Sahai, A., Seyalioglu, H., Waters, B.: Dynamic credentials and ciphertext delegation for attribute-based encryption. In: Safavi-Naini, R., Canetti, R. (eds.) CRYPTO 2012. LNCS, vol. 7417, pp. 199–217. Springer, Heidelberg (2012). https://doi.org/10.1007/978-3-642-32009-5_13
22. Sahai, A., Waters, B.: Fuzzy identity-based encryption. In: Cramer, R. (ed.) EUROCRYPT 2005. LNCS, vol. 3494, pp. 457–473. Springer, Heidelberg (2005). https://doi.org/10.1007/11426639_27
23. Seo, J.H., Emura, K.: Revocable identity-based encryption revisited: security model and construction. In: Kurosawa, K., Hanaoka, G. (eds.) PKC 2013. LNCS, vol. 7778, pp. 216–234. Springer, Heidelberg (2013). https://doi.org/10.1007/978-3-642-36362-7_14
24. Waters, B.: Dual system encryption: realizing fully secure IBE and HIBE under simple assumptions. In: Halevi, S. (ed.) CRYPTO 2009. LNCS, vol. 5677, pp. 619–636. Springer, Heidelberg (2009). https://doi.org/10.1007/978-3-642-03356-8_36

Cryptography

Precomputation for Rainbow Tables has Never Been so Fast

Gildas Avoine[1], Xavier Carpent[2], and Diane Leblanc-Albarel[1(✉)]

[1] CNRS, INSA Rennes, IRISA, Rennes, France
{gildas.avoine,diane.leblanc-albarel}@irisa.fr
[2] KU Leuven, COSIC, Leuven, Belgium
xavier.carpent@kuleuven.be

Abstract. Cryptanalytic time-memory trade-offs (TMTOs) are techniques commonly used in computer security e.g., to crack passwords. However, TMTOs usually encounter in practice a bottleneck that is the time needed to perform the precomputation phase (preceding to the attack). We introduce in this paper a technique, called *distributed filtration-computation*, that significantly reduces the precomputation time without any negative impact the online phase. Experiments performed on large problems with a 128-core computer perfectly match the theoretical expectations. We construct a rainbow table for a space $N = 2^{42}$ in approximately 8 h instead of 50 h for the usual way to generate a table. We also show that the efficiency of our technique is very close from the theoretical time lower bound.

Keywords: Cryptography · Time-Memory Trade-Offs (TMTO) · Rainbow table · Distributed precomputation

1 Introduction

Inverting a hash function (or equivalent cryptographic problem) can be addressed using an exhaustive search when the problem is reasonably sized. An illustrative case is password cracking, which consists in recovering a password from its hash stored by the targeted system. The computation cost may be prohibitive, though, when the attack is repeated. A time-memory trade-off (TMTO) is then an efficient alternative to an exhaustive search. It consists of a precomputation phase – or offline phase – performed once then stored, and an online phase performed each time the hash function should be inverted. The precomputation phase is therefore exploited to accelerate the online phase.

A TMTO, introduced by Martin Hellman [1], offers a significant speedup in practice. Given a problem of size N (i.e., $N = |A|$ where A is the considered set of possible solutions) and a memory M, the time complexity of the online phase is $O(N^2/M^2)$ instead of N for the exhaustive search. It is worth noting that the time complexity of the precomputation phase remains $O(N)$. This means that using a TMTO makes sense in specific scenarios: the attack has to be performed

© Springer Nature Switzerland AG 2021
E. Bertino et al. (Eds.): ESORICS 2021, LNCS 12973, pp. 215–234, 2021.
https://doi.org/10.1007/978-3-030-88428-4_11

several times, the attack itself has to last for a short period of time ("lunch time" attack), or the attacker is not powerful enough to perform an exhaustive search but he can download the result of a precomputed phase, stored in what is called *tables*.

Hellman's work has been improved over time, particularly with the rainbow tables [2] and the distinguished points [3]. These variants are faster [2,4,5] than the original time-memory trade-off. A few improvements [6,7] have been suggested on the distinguished points, and the rainbow tables also benefited from various optimizations concerning the online phase, notably the way of storing and using tables [8–11], checkpoints [12] and the use of data [13]. In 2016, Lee and Hong [4] demonstrated that, in the absence of excessive constraints such as a very limited memory, rainbow tables are the most efficient TMTOs for both online and precomputation phases. We consequently focus on rainbow tables in this paper.

The precomputation phase is very costly, though, typically of the order of $160\,N$ when considering practical scenarios, even for rainbow tables. The precomputation phase must consequently be distributed on many computers.

This paper introduces *distributed filtration-computation*, a technique that drastically decreases the cost of the precomputation phase and that is compliant with a distribution of that phase. The filtration process identifies computations that will eventually be useless, avoiding so to carry out computations that would be thrown out at the end precomputation phase. The distribution trivially consists in sharing the computing load among several computing units. In common scenarios, the technique we introduce divides by 6 the precomputation time, but the speedup can be much higher in extreme cases, namely when considering what are called *maximum* tables. As far as we know, this is the first time a technique is introduced to improve the precomputation phase of TMTOs.

After providing background on rainbow tables in Sect. 2, we introduce the filters and a lower bound on the precomputation in Sect. 3. We provide a distributed version of the filters in Sect. 4, with an optimization algorithm for their positions, and we finally illustrate the theory with practical results in Sect. 5. Note that Table 4. in Appendix D recaps the notations used through this paper.

2   Background

2.1   Rainbow Tables

Given a hash function $h : A \to B$, and given $h(x) \in B$, the purpose of a TMTO is to retrieve $x \in A$. To do so, the precomputation phase of the TMTO precomputes rainbow *matrices*, which consist of *chains* of elements $x_i \in A$ ($0 \leqslant i \leqslant t$) such that $x_{i+1} = f_i(x_i)$, where x_0 is an arbitrary value, introduced below, and f_is are *hash-reduction* functions defined as follows:

$$f_i : A \to \quad A$$
$$x \mapsto R_i(h(x))$$

where each $R_i : B \to A$ is a *reduction* function, that is a function that aims to map each value in B to a value in A. The choice of the reduction functions is out of the scope of this article, and interested readers can refer to [2]. Note however that using a different reduction function in every iteration is a key feature of rainbow-based TMTOs that reduces the number of merging chains. It is also important to note that the execution time of a reduction function is negligible compared to that of a hash function.

Once the precomputation phase is completed, the matrix (see Fig. 1) consists of $m \times (t + 1)$ values denoted $X_{j,i}$ with $0 < j \leqslant m$ and $0 \leqslant i \leqslant t$, and $X_{j,i}$ the element in row j and column i.

The *length t*, of a chain is the number of application of the Hash-Reduction functions f_i performed to construct the chain.

$$
\begin{array}{ccccc}
 & f_1 & & f_2 & \\
\mathbf{X_{1,0}} & \longrightarrow & X_{1,1} & \longrightarrow & X_{1,2} \ldots \mathbf{X_{1,t}} \\
 & f_1 & & f_2 & \\
\mathbf{X_{2,0}} & \longrightarrow & X_{2,1} & \longrightarrow & X_{2,2} \ldots \mathbf{X_{2,t}} \\
\vdots & & \vdots & & \vdots \qquad \vdots \\
 & f_1 & & f_2 & \\
\mathbf{X_{m,0}} & \longrightarrow & X_{m,1} & \longrightarrow & X_{m,2} \ldots \mathbf{X_{m,t}}
\end{array}
$$

Fig. 1. Rainbow matrix

Once the rainbow matrix is computed, only the first column that contains the so-called *Start Points* (SP) and the last column that contains the *End Points* (EP) are saved in what is called a *table*[1]. All intermediary columns are discarded to save memory.

Using a different reduction function in each column reduces the number of merging chains. Indeed, with rainbow tables, two chains merge if they collide in the same column.

From here on we consider a single matrix for the sake of clarity, but a rainbow-based TMTO usually consists of a few independently-computed matrices in order to reach a high success rate, typically 4 tables guarantee the success of the online phase with a probability greater than 99.96%.

2.2   Clean Rainbow Tables

Using a different reduction function per column reduces the number of merging chains, but two chains colliding in the same column can still happen. Detecting such a merge is however trivial, as it necessarily leads to equal EPs.

---

[1] This paper will not discuss how to use the rainbow tables during the online phase, as the approach is developed in other papers.

Given that colliding chains make the TMTO less memory-efficient due to the overlapping values, Philippe Oechslin introduced [2] tables without merges, which are called *clean* tables[2] [14].

Merging chains are deleted to obtain clean tables, so if a matrix contains m_0 chains, the corresponding clean table only contains $m_t < m_0$ chains, with m_t the number of chains with distinct EPs in a matrix of length t.

2.3 Maximum Rainbow Tables

Given a set A with $N = |A|$, there is a limit to the number of EPs that can be obtained without duplicates. This number, denoted $m_t^{\max}$, depends on N and the number of columns t in the table[3]. $m_t^{\max}$ is obtained from Eq. (1) [12] where m_i is the theoretical number of different elements in column i:

$$m_i \approx \frac{2N}{i + \gamma}, \quad \text{with} \quad \gamma = \frac{2N}{m_0}. \tag{1}$$

Given a number of columns $t + 1$ and a sufficiently large number of elements N, the expected maximum number of chains $m_t^{\max}$ per clean rainbow table is hence given by Theorem 1 [12].

Theorem 1. *Given t and a sufficiently large N, the expected maximum number of chains per clean rainbow table is:*

$$m_t^{\max} \approx \frac{2N}{t + 2}.$$

Proof. The proof is presented in [12].

In practice, computing $m_0 = N$ chains is prohibitively expensive, so the chosen m_0 is generally markedly smaller than N. This produces tables of size $\alpha\, m_t^{\max}$ with $0 < \alpha < 1$. Usually, chains are generated until a satisfactory α is reached and m_0 is then determined retrospectively. A satisfactory α allow to have an online success rate close to the rate of a maximal table[4]. When α is close to one (e.g., $\alpha = 0.95$), the table is said to be *quasi-maximum*.

3 Filtering Chains

3.1 Preliminary Result on Quantifying Precomputation

In order to generate clean tables containing $m_t = \alpha\, m_t^{\max}$ chains, the common approach consists in computing chains until obtaining the desired number of

---

[2] Initially called *perfect* tables by Philippe Oechslin.

[3] The number of elements in a clean table is constant which implies that t is inversely proportional to m. The larger m is, the faster the online phase will be, but the more memory is needed for storage and inversely.

[4] The probability of success for a single maximal table is 86% when t is large. For the same t and a table of size $0.95 m_t^{max}$, the probability of success for a single table is 85%.

unique end points. We provide in Lemma 1 and Proposition 1 formulas to predict the value m_0 required to reach on average $\alpha\, m_t^{\max}$ unique end points. α is called the *maximality factor*.

Lemma 1. *Let $r = m_0/m_t^{\max}$. The expected number of unique EPs is given by:*

$$m_t \approx \frac{1}{(1 + \frac{1}{r})} m_t^{\max}.$$

Proof. From Eq. (1), we have $m_0 = \frac{2N}{\gamma}$. Given that $m_0 = r\, m_t^{\max}$, we can write $\gamma = \frac{2N}{r\, m_t^{\max}}$. Using Theorem 1, we then obtain $\gamma \approx \frac{t+2}{r} \approx \frac{t}{r}$. Replacing γ in Eq. (1) for $i = t$, we finally have:

$$m_t \approx \frac{2N}{t(1 + \frac{1}{r})} = \frac{1}{(1 + \frac{1}{r})} m_t^{\max}.$$

$\square$

Proposition 1. *With a target of $m_t = \alpha\, m_t^{\max}$ unique endpoints, $m_0 = rm_t^{\max}$ chains need to be generated, with:*

$$r \approx \frac{\alpha}{1 - \alpha}.$$

Proof

From Lemma 1:	$m_t \approx \frac{1}{(1+\frac{1}{r})} m_t^{\max}.$
Since $m_t = \alpha\, m_t^{\max}$:	$\alpha \approx \frac{1}{(1+\frac{1}{r})}$
Which conduct to:	$\frac{1}{r} \approx \frac{1}{\alpha} - 1 \Leftrightarrow r \approx \frac{\alpha}{1-\alpha}$

$\square$

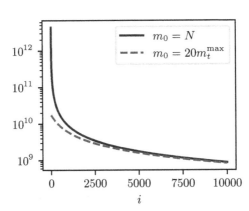

Fig. 2. Number of unique elements m_i remaining in column i (log scale) according to the value of m_0 for $N = 2^{42}$ and $t = 10\,000$.

To illustrate Proposition 1, let us consider the case $r = 20$, which results in $m_t \approx 0.95\,m_t^{\max}$. This is a reasonable number that provides a high quality table (m_t relatively close to $m_t^{\max}$), while significantly reducing the precomputation cost (compared to the $m_0 = N$ case). With $N = 2^{42}$ and $t = 10\,000$ for instance, generating $20\,m_t^{\max}$ chains instead of N brings the number of chains to be generated from 440×10^{10} to 1.7×10^{10} – a 258-fold reduction – while keeping the number of endpoints very close to the maximum, and thus preserving the density of the trade-off.

Figure 2 illustrates the difference between the scenarios $m_0 = r m_t^{\max}$ and $m_0 = N$ in terms of maximum number of elements in each column.

3.2   Intermediary Filtration

Classically, computing a rainbow table requires $m_0 \times (t+1)$ elements to compute, although only $m_t \times (t+1)$ elements are represented in the final (clean) matrix. Discarding merged chains at the end of the precomputation is a wasted effort, because a single chain is kept among multiple chains with the same EP (i.e., hash operations performed after a merge occurs are useless). An option to mitigate this waste is to remove duplicated values progressively.

So, instead of computing the full chains in a row, from the SPs to the EPs, chains are divided into sub-chains, and merging chains are detected and discarded at the end of each sub-chain. A *sub-chain* is delimited by Intermediary Points (IPs). Computation of chains is thus performed "column by column" (or group of columns after group of columns), as opposed to the typical "chain-by-chain" method. A *filter* is placed in selected columns (IPs): when all sub-chains have been computed up to the filter, a *filtration* is performed: only one of the merged chains is saved. Figure 7 in Appendix C, presents the mechanism of filtration with an example zooming on 2 filters.

3.3   Filtration in Each Column

The minimum number of elements to be computed to generate a table is obtained when duplicates are removed in each column, i.e., if each chain of length t is divided in t sub-chains of length 1.

Proposition 2. *Let m_i denote the number of unique elements in column i of a rainbow matrix. The number P of hash operations to precompute a $m_t \times (t+1)$ clean rainbow matrix is lower bounded by:*

$$P \geq \sum_{i=0}^{t-1} m_i.$$

Proof. Given that the minimum hash operations to compute in order to obtained a table is when duplicates are removed in each column and that m_i denote the number of unique elements in column i, then the expression of the lower bound is trivial.

□

Theorem 2 quantifies this with results from Sect. 3.1.

Theorem 2. *Given* $m_0 = r m_t^{\max}$ *the number of SPs,* $t + 1$ *the number of columns, and* $r \ll t$, *we have that the naïve precomputation cost is:*

$$P_{naive} = m_0 t \approx 2rN, \qquad (2)$$

and the minimum precomputation cost is:

$$P_{min} = \sum_{i=0}^{t-1} m_i \approx 2N \ln(1 + r). \qquad (3)$$

Proof. The proof of Eq. (2) follows directly from $m_0 = \frac{2N}{\gamma} \approx \frac{2rN}{t}$. For Eq. (3), we have:

$$\sum_{i=0}^{t-1} m_i = 2N \sum_{i=0}^{t-1} \frac{1}{i + \gamma} = 2N \sum_{i=\gamma}^{t+\gamma-1} \frac{1}{i} = 2N \left[\sum_{i=1}^{t+\gamma-1} \frac{1}{i} - \sum_{i=1}^{\gamma-1} \frac{1}{i} \right]$$

$$= 2N \left[H_{t+\gamma-1} - H_{\gamma-1} \right] \approx 2N \left[\ln(t + \gamma - 1) - \ln(\gamma - 1) \right]$$

$$= 2N \ln \left(\frac{t + \gamma - 1}{\gamma - 1} \right)$$

with $H_n = \sum_{k=1}^{n} \frac{1}{k}$ the n-th harmonic number. Using $\gamma \approx \frac{t}{r}$ and given that $r \ll t$, the expected result is obtained. □

For values of r such that $m_0 \ll N$ (i.e., "reasonable" values), we can make the approximation that γ is large (leading itself to the asymptotic approximation of H_n). This allows an expression of P_{min} that only depends on N and r and is in particular virtually independent of t. For $m_0 = N$ however these approximations do not hold, and the resulting expression of P_{min} does depend on t (Corollary 1). We remark that the precomputation cost in all cases is linear in N.

Corollary 1. *For the case* $m_0 = N$, *precomputation costs are respectively* $P_{naive} = Nt$ *and* $P_{min} \approx 2N(H_{t+1} - 1)$, *with* H_n *the* n-th *harmonic number.*

Proof. The expression for P_{min} results from instantiating $2N \left[H_{t+\gamma-1} - H_{\gamma-1} \right]$ (similarly to the proof of 2) to $\gamma = 2$ (from Eq. (1)).

From Theorem 2, we observe, for instance, that using a filter in each column with a typical $r = 20$ reduces the number of performed hash operations by about 85% (regardless of N or t). Tables 1 and 2 display the maximum speedup $P_{\text{naive}}/P_{\text{min}}$ that can be obtained when filtering in each column with respect to no intermediary filtering. Results in Table 1 are valid for any (sensible) N and t.

Table 1. Speedup for quasi-maximum tables for different values of r.

r	10	15	**20**	30	50
$\frac{r}{\ln(1+r)}$	4.17	5.41	**6.57**	8.74	12.72

Table 2. Speedup for maximum tables of various lengths.

t	1 000	10 000	100 000
$\frac{t}{2(H_{t+1}-1)}$	77.03	568.98	4508.50

3.4   Filtration in Chosen Columns

In practice, it may not always be beneficial to filter in every column, because this may involve an excessive overhead due to the filtering cost (results provided in Sect. 3.3 consider the number of hash operations, but they do not consider the additional time due to filtration and communication). Before considering this cost, an intermediary step consists in evaluating the number P of hash operations to be performed if the filtering technique is applied to $a < t + 1$ columns only:

$$P = \sum_{i=0}^{a} m_{c_i}(c_{i+1} - c_i),\qquad(4)$$

where c_i the column of the i-th filter, and $c_0 = 0$ and $c_a = t+1$. Given a number of filters a and t very large compared to this number[5], the optimal average number of hash operations is given in Theorem 3.

Theorem 3. *The optimal average number of hash operations for precomputation with a filters and $a \ll t$ is:*

$$P = 2Na\left[\left(\frac{t+\gamma-1}{\gamma}\right)^{\frac{1}{a}} - 1\right].$$

The optimal placement of the filters is given by:

$$c_i = \gamma\left(\frac{t+\gamma-1}{\gamma}\right)^{\frac{i}{a}} - \gamma + 1.$$

Proof. See Appendix A.   □

Figure 3 illustrates Theorem 3 for $N = 2^{42}$, $t = 10\,000$, and $r = 20$. It shows the number of hash operations needed for precomputation with varying number of filters a, placed according to Theorem 3. It also displays the lower bound ($P_{\min}$) in terms of hash operations, which is reached when a filter is applied in each column. The case $a = 1$ corresponds to P_{naive} (filtration only in the last column).

It indicates diminishing returns in increasing a. For instance in that scenario, P with a single filter is 2.88 times faster than using no filter. On the other

---

[5] If a is too close to t, several filters could be affected to the same column. Choosing $a \ll t$ is not a problem, as presented in Fig. 3.

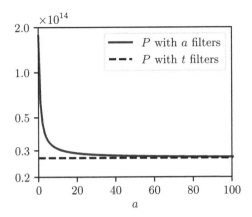

Fig. 3. Number of hash operations P (log scale) according to the number of filters used a, with $N = 2^{42}$, $t = 10\,000$, and $r = 20$. P with a filters according to Theorem 3 and P with t filters according to Theorem 2.

hand, using a filter in each column is only about 1% faster than using 50 filters. Note that the optimal distribution of filters is actually not uniform. Indeed, detecting merges as soon as they occur avoids to waste time computing the useless remaining parts of the chains. As a consequence filters are mostly located on the left-hand parts of the chains.

This, together with the fact that the cost of non-hashing operations is not necessarily negligible in a practical implementation, implies that a limited number of filters is preferable. The next sections discuss an implementation and quantify this effect.

4   Distributing Precomputation

4.1   Distribution and Filtration

Even with filters, generating rainbow tables on a single computing node takes too much time when considering practical cases. To compute m_0 chains of length t, $m_0 t = 2rN$ hash operations are needed. For example, for $N = 2^{42}$ and $r = 20$, building a clean table of about $0.95\,m_t^{\max}$ chains with optimal filters requires 2.7×10^{13} hash operations, which would take about 40.5 days on a single processor core.

To generate tables of such size, precomputation should be distributed. Without filters, the precomputation phase is easily parallelizable. If n_h hashing nodes are available, the total precomputation time is simply divided by n_h, with each hashing node performing $\frac{2rN}{n_h}$ hash operations (assuming only the hashing time is taken into account and all hashing nodes have the same performances).

However, as seen in Sect. 3.2, precomputing a (quasi-maximum) clean rainbow table without intermediary filtering wastes significant effort due to merging chains. Therefore considering both distributing and filtering is essential[6].

4.2 Distributed Architecture

Distribution of the precomputation phase with intermediate filtering requires the nodes to communicate. We consider in what follows that n_h nodes are dedicated to perform hash operations and n_f nodes to filter chains, with $n_h + n_f = n$. Filtration and computation of chains are carried out in parallel[7], in an effort to minimize the number of non-hashing operations. Sub-chains computed by the n_h *hashing nodes* are sent eagerly to the n_f *filtration nodes*.

In the environments and problem sizes we considered, the filtration effort was not significant enough compared to the hashing effort to warrant using more than a single filtration node. It is possible that for other environments (e.g., low bandwidth) or larger spaces, dedicating more nodes to filtering could be beneficial.

4.3 Estimation of the Precomputation Time

Precomputation Process. In an environment with a single filtration node, this node is also in charge of the different tasks sequencing. A *job* is defined as a number of sub-chains to be computed between two filters. A job of size s contains s SP-IP pairs. Precomputations are hence divided in two main parts: jobs to be performed between filters and the filtration of these jobs. Precomputations consists of managing, for each filter, the sending of jobs to the hashing nodes and the filtration of the completed jobs.

The rationale behind choosing to bundle sub-chains into jobs is to mitigate the communication overhead. Using $s = 1$ is, for instance, a bad idea, because the overhead due to the communication, would significantly hinder performance. On the other hand, using a very large s may result in additional idle time by the computing nodes, for instance if there is no available chains left to compute for an idling computing node but some other computing nodes are still busy[8]. In what follows, we consider that the value of s is reasonable.

Once receiving a job, a hashing node starts from each IP to compute the new IPs corresponding to the column of the next filter. Once these computations are done, it returns the SPs and the new IPs to the filtration node, which sends a new job back to it. The filtration node purpose is to receive jobs from hashing nodes

---

[6] Distributed filtration-computation has negligible impact on the online phase, including its many improvements. See Appendix B for more details.

[7] Technically, filtration starts and stops slightly after computation of chains.

[8] Experiments show that, for the typical problem sizes and architecture considered, choosing s to be anywhere from 1 000 to 100 000 mitigates both of these issues. The particular choice of s therefore has negligible impact on the performance, provided it lies in that range.

and send new ones as soon as it receive it. At the meantime the filtration node filters already received jobs. This procedure is repeated between each filter until the end of the computation phase. As described in Sect. 3.4, it is not possible in a distributed architecture to filter in every column since the filtration adds an overhead. The problem of choosing the positions of the filters is discussed in Sect. 4.4.

Impacting Functionalities. Several functionalities are required to perform the precomputation phase: hashing (i.e., computing sub-chains), filtration, and communication. In this section the way to evaluate the time needed for each of these functionalities is described.

Hashing Time (H). Jobs computations are carried out by hashing nodes. Given a filters with $a < t + 1$, the total number of hash operations to be performed is $\sum_{i=1}^{a} m_{c_{i-1}}(c_i - c_{i-1})$ (Eq. (4)) with c_i the column of the i-th filter, $c_0 = 0$ and $c_a = t + 1$. A hashing node can perform v_h applications of $f_i = R_i \circ h$ per second. v_h is determined before the beginning of precomputations and depends of the hashing nodes performance. Computations of chains are considered to be done in parallel, by n_h hashing nodes with equal performances. The total hashing time can therefore be estimated as:

$$H = \frac{1}{n_h v_h} \sum_{i=1}^{a+1} m_{c_{i-1}}(c_i - c_{i-1}). \tag{5}$$

Filtration Time (F). For a filter in column i, the number of points that have to be filtered is $m_{c_{i-1}}$. The total number of points that have to be filtered in the entire precomputation is hence $\sum_{i=1}^{a+1} m_{c_{i-1}}$. We consider that a filtration node can perform v_f filtrations per second. The total time due to filtration is thus:

$$F = \frac{1}{v_f n_f} \sum_{i=1}^{a+1} m_{c_{i-1}}. \tag{6}$$

We also model for a potential overhead due to the filtration. This can for instance result from processing the output of the filtration into jobs to be sent to hashing nodes. This overhead depends on the number of elements generated and depends on the implementation (filtration algorithm, memory allocation, etc.). Given d_o the average overhead time per point, the total overhead O can be expressed as:

$$O = d_o \sum_{i=1}^{a+1} m_{c_{i-1}}. \tag{7}$$

Communication Time (C). Communication time is the time needed for the communication of jobs between filtration nodes and computing nodes. Let d_c be the average time for a job to be sent from a filtration node to a hashing node and back. We assume that when a communication is in progress with one hashing node all the other hashing nodes are computing. The impacting communication time can then be estimated by:

$$C = \frac{d_c}{n_h} \sum_{i=1}^{a+1} m_{c_{i-1}} \tag{8}$$

Total Time. Given that computation of sub-chains and filtration are performed in parallel, the most impacting component in the total time spend to generate a rainbow table is the maximum time between the hashing time H and the filtration time F i.e., $\text{Max}(H, F)$[9]. To obtain the total time, the communication time has to be added as well as the overhead time due to filtration. The total time T needed to generate a clean rainbow table is hence:

$$T = \text{Max}(H, F) + C + O. \tag{9}$$

4.4   Optimal Configuration

The number of filters and their positions have a considerable impact on the precomputation time. Let a *configuration* be a set $C = \{c_1, \ldots, c_a\}$, where a is the number of filters, and c_i the position (column number) of the i-th filter. Let C_a^* be the configuration of a filters that minimizes Eq. (9), and $C^* = \min_a C_a^*$.

Due to the various operations outside of hashing, in particular the filtering process (which, to some extent, can be done in parallel to hashing) and other communication/data processing overheads, the configuration given by Theorem 3 typically gives sub-optimal results. For this reason we rely instead of numerical minimization of Eq. (9), which models the precomputation time given by our implementation.

We settled on a truncated-Newton method [15], an optimization algorithm suitable to solving bounded optimization problems with many variables (see e.g., [16] for a thorough description). The minimization is used to find C_a^*, coupled with an exhaustive search on a[10]. The optimality of the configuration found by the numerical minimization is predicated on the two following conjectures: (1) C_a^* is a convex function of a and (2) Eq. (9) is smooth enough (w.r.t. C) to guarantee or approach the conditions of optimality of the truncated-Newton search[11] [15]. We offer no proof of these conjectures, but note that they seem to hold true both intuitively and after extensive testing.

---

[9] In general, for an architecture with a single filtration node, hashing time is much bigger than the filtering time. If the parameters of the problem and the architecture are such that it is not the case, then an other architecture with several filtration nodes should be considered.

[10] To keep things efficient, the search is from 0 up to a reasonable upper bound $a_{\max}$. A more sophisticated approach could be used here (e.g., Newton descent on a), but we found it to be unnecessary.

[11] Namely strong convexity and Lipschitz-continuous Hessian.

Regardless of the validity of these conjectures however, the configuration obtained through numerical minimization presents a significant improvement over the analytical minimization that assumes no overhead or filtration cost (Theorem 3). In addition, the estimated precomputation time comes very close to the theoretical minimum, as detailed in Sect. 5.

5 Experiments

5.1 Computing Environments

We conducted our experiments on two different environments that are described below. We benchmarked these two environments before starting the precomputation phase in order to measure the hashing speed v_h, the filtration speed v_f, the overhead d_o related to the implementation of the filtration, and the communication cost d_c. The benchmark has been done by generating tables on a small-sized problem ($N = 2^{32}$) with filters placed according to Theorem 3.

Environment 1 consists of a computer hosting two AMD EPYC 7742 3.2 GHz processors composed of 64 cores each, for a total of 128 cores[12]. The benchmark measured $v_h = 7\,747\,002$ hashs per seconds, $v_f = 15\,949\,709$ filtrations per second, and $v_0 = 1.37 \times 10^{-10}$. The communication overhead is negligible compared to v_h and v_f, it can hence be considered that $d_c = 0$ which implies that $d_o + \frac{d_c}{n_h} = d_o = 1.37 \times 10^{-10}$ s to treat one point.

Environment 2 is a cluster of 8 computers with 2 CPUs per machine and 14 cores for each CPU, i.e., a total of 224 cores. Each CPU is an Intel Xeon E5-2680 v4 (Broadwell, 2.40 GHz, 14 cores). The computers are directly connected through switches, meaning that they communicate using the ethernet protocol. The benchmark provided $v_h = 6\,403\,611$ hashs per seconds, $v_f = 7\,918\,745$ filtrations per second, and $d_o + \frac{d_c}{sn_h} = 7.5 \times 10^{-10}$ s to treat one point.

5.2 Filtration Implementation

For the filtration, we used an open addressing hash table with the following parameters:

- A load factor $\lambda = 2/3$, which is a good compromise between size overhead and low probability of collision.
- The number of slots of the table is $k = m_{c_i}/\lambda = 1.5m_{c_i}$ with m_{c_i} the theoretical number of different points after filtration (given by Eq. (1)).
- The hash function used is $IP \bmod k$.

We used linear probing for collision resolution (with interval of 1). This is appropriate because inputs to the hash table are uniformly distributed in A (by construction). At each filtration the following steps are carried out:

---

[12] We used 127 of them to be sure that all cores are fully exploited for the precomputation, and the last core was left available for the basic operations performed by the system.

- A hash table of size $k = 1.5m_{c_i}$ is created.
- As soon as a job is received by the filtration node this job is filtered as follow:
  1. For each couple $(SP;IP)$ of the job, $IP \bmod k$ is computed.
  2. The index $IP \bmod k$ of the table is checked.
  3. If at the index computed no value is present then IP and its corresponding SP are inserted at this index.
  4. If at the index computed the same value equals to IP is present then a merge has occurred between two chain and IP and its corresponding SP are deleted.
  5. If at the index computed, a different value of IP is present then a new value of index is computed and is equals to $IP + 1 \bmod k$, the index $IP + 1 \bmod k$ is checked and the steps 3. to 5. are repeated.
- When all jobs have been filtered, the hash table is scanned and all the IPs and their corresponding SPs are transferred by copying them to an array in a form facilitating the sending of the jobs.
- The hash table is deleted.

5.3   Positions of the Filters

We conducted experiments where filters were optimally placed using the Truncated Newton Constrained (TNC) algorithm (Sect. 4.4) applied to Eq. (9).

For environment 1, the optimal configuration was 31 filters, with positions as provided in Fig. 4. The latter figure also displays the positions of the 31 filters in the theoretical case where filtering and communicating are free (Theorem 3).

Figure 5 displays the number of hash operations needed to generate a clean rainbow table in our scenario, when: (left case) there are no filters, which is the current state of the art; (middle case) there are filters optimally placed, which is our approach; and (right case) filtration and communication are free, with so a filter in each column, which is the theoretical lower bound. It is worth noting that our approach is tightly close to the theoretical lower bound (about 10% of the theoretical lower bound).

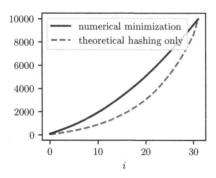

Fig. 4. Positions of the 31 filters

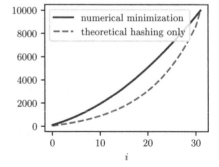

Fig. 5. Number of hash operations

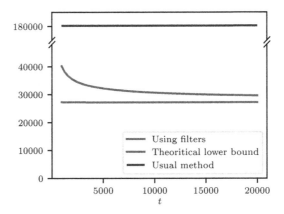

Fig. 6. Time (sec) to generate a clean rainbow table according to t ($N = 2^{42}$, $r = 20$)

5.4   Considered Parameters

Experiments were performed with the following parameters that represents a realistic scenario: $N = 2^{42}$, $t = 10\,000$, and $r = 20$.

Corollary 1 provides the number of starting points in the experiment: $m_0 = 2rN/t \approx 1.76 \times 10^{10}$. According to Proposition 1, the expected number of chains in a single such table is: $0.9524\,m_t^{\max} \approx 8.38 \times 10^8$.

The chain length ($t = 10\,000$) has an impact on the online phase: when t decreases, the time required for the online phase decreases as well, but the required memory increases. The chain length also has an impact on the precomputation phase when filters are used, but this effect is *much* smaller. As shown in Fig. 6, the smaller t is, the greater the precomputation time.

We chose $t = 10\,000$ because this value leads to a very fast online phase in the order of a few seconds with a reasonably-sized memory (for $N = 2^{42}$). Choosing $t = 20\,000$ for instance would provide a 20% faster precomputation but would increase the time of the online phase four-fold.

Figure 6, also shows that our experimental results (green curve) is close to the theoretical lower bound (red curve) and that our method is much more efficient that the usual way to generate table (blue curve) as detailed in Sect. 5.5.

5.5   Results

Environment 1. Precomputing a single rainbow table without any filter requires $m_0\,t$ hash operations in our scenario, which is 100×2^{42}. Given that $v_h = 7\,747\,002$ and the environment consists of 127 cores (each core corresponding to one node) with 1 filtration node and 126 hashing nodes, the precomputation time is estimated to be $180\,225$ s (50 h and 3 min), which is very close from our experimental result of $179\,850$ s (49 h and 57 min).

Now, using 31 filters optimally placed significantly reduces the precomputation time. Using Eq. (9), we obtain that the predicted precomputation time is as low as 30 657 s (about 8 h). Filters thus divide by 5.9 the precomputation time in this scenario. The experimental result is 31 029 s.

Environment 2. According to the TNC algorithm, without any filter, the precomputation time of a single rainbow table should be around 123 194 s (about 34 h and 13 min).

If 11 filters optimally placed are used, our experimental results show that a table can be generated in 26 499 s (about 7 h and 20 min). According to TNC algorithm with the parameters for this second environment, given in Sect. 5.1, this precomputation time is estimated to 26 139 s (about 7 h and 12 min). Our experimental results are therefore very close from the predicted one.

Utilization of filters on this environment hence allows to generate a table in about 5 times less time than the naive method. Table 3 provides a summary of the results obtained for environments 1 and 2.

Table 3. Summary of the results ($N = 2^{42}$, $t = 10\,000$, $r = 20$)

Scenario	#Filters	#Hashes ($\times 10^{12}$)	#Cores	Time	
				Experimental	Predicted
Environment 1 (state of the art)	0	176	127	179 850	180 225
Environment 1 (our approach)	31	28	127	31 029	30 657
Environment 1 (theoretical bound)	10 000	26.8	127	–	27 452
Environment 2 (state of the art)	0	176	224	123 717	123 194
Environment 2 (our approach)	11	31	224	26 499	26 139
Environment 2 (theoretical bound)	10 000	26.8	224	–	18 765

6   Conclusion

This paper introduces the concept of distributed filters to precompute rainbow tables. Such tables are widely used by the community of security experts, especially, but not only, to tests passwords. Given that the precomputation phase is highly resource-consuming, the technique we introduce in this paper has a strong practical impact. It also comes with formulas to compute the optimal positions of the filters, and to evaluate the precomputation time.

We illustrate our technique on a typical scenario, namely a problem of size $N = 2^{42}$ ($t = 10\,000$ and $r = 20$). In such a scenario, the precomputation phase requires 1.76×10^{14} hash operations, which takes about 50 h on a 128-core computer, while our technique requires 2.8×10^{13} hash operations, which were performed (including filtering) in about 8 h and 36 min on the same 128-core computer. Distributed filtration-computation thus divides by about 6 the expected precomputation time. It is also close to the theoretical lower bound of 27 452 s i.e., 7 h and 33 min (for $r = 20$), with the difference due to the filtering and communication overheads.

We considered a typical scenario in the sense that we used quasi-maximum tables ($r = 20$) instead of maximum tables. Such maximum tables (corresponding to $r = 5\,001$ in our case) are usually considered in the literature, but they are never used in practice because precomputing maximum tables is prohibitive. However, considering maximum tables would make distributed filtration-computation much more valuable still (e.g., increasing the speedup from 6 to $4\,500$ with the same parameters).

It is worth noting that our technique to speed up the precomputation phase has been applied to classical rainbow tables but we state in this article that it is fully compliant with the improvements published during the last years to make the online phase more efficient.

Appendix

A   Proof of Theorem 3

We have $P = \sum_{i=0}^{a} m_{c_i}(c_{i+1} - c_i)$. Deriving for each filter column position, we obtain:

$$\frac{\partial P}{\partial c_i} = \frac{\partial}{\partial c_i} \left[m_{c_i}(c_{i+1} - c_i) + m_{c_{i-1}} c_i \right].$$

Inserting $m_i = \frac{2N}{i+\gamma-1}$ we have:

$$\frac{\partial P}{\partial c_i} = 2N \frac{\partial}{\partial c_i} \left[\frac{c_{i+1} - c_i}{c_i + \gamma - 1} + \frac{c_i}{c_{i-1} + \gamma - 1} \right]$$

$$= 2N \left[\frac{1}{c_{i-1} + \gamma - 1} - \frac{c_{i+1} + \gamma - 1}{(c_i + \gamma - 1)^2} \right].$$

To minimize P, we must have $\frac{\partial P}{\partial c_i} = 0$, and thus:

$$c_i = \sqrt{(c_{i-1} + \gamma - 1)(c_{i+1} + \gamma - 1)} - \gamma + 1.$$

It is easy to verify that a solution to this recurrence relation with terminal conditions $c_0 = 1$ and $c_a = t$ is:

$$c_i = \gamma \left(\frac{t + \gamma - 1}{\gamma} \right)^{\frac{i}{a}} - \gamma + 1.$$

Replacing in the expression for P gives the expected result.

B   Online Phase Improvements and Their Impact on Precomputation

There exists many significant algorithmic improvements on the online phase and optimizations of the storage of tables. Their impact on the distribution and intermediate filtering of precomputation is briefly discussed below.

- Chain storage optimizations (prefix/suffix decomposition or compressed delta encoding [9]): lossless compression can be applied at the end of the table generation, with no impact on the precomputation process.
- Truncated endpoints [8]: Endpoints can be truncated at the end of the table generation, again with no impact.
- Checkpoints [8,12]: Saving checkpoints can be done during the filtered and distributed precomputation with ease, although specific care must be taken. Hashing nodes must be made aware of which columns are checkpoint columns, and the filtration node needs to keep track of this. This adds no significant burden on either.
- Heterogeneous tables [10]: Precomputation of tables of different shapes is done independently, regardless of whether they operate on the same input set. Consequently The use of heterogeneous tables has no impact on precomputation improvements.
- Interleaving [11]: Just like with heterogeneous tables, the different tables are independently computed, again having no impact on precomputation improvements

C   Intermediary Filtration

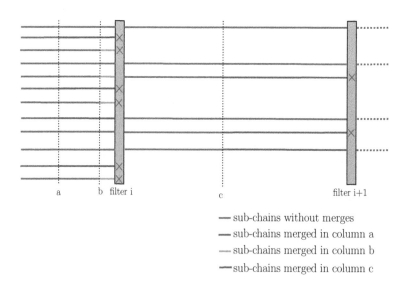

— sub-chains without merges
— sub-chains merged in column a
— sub-chains merged in column b
— sub-chains merged in column c

Fig. 7. Intermediary filtration with 2 filters.

D   Notation Through this Paper

Table 4. Notation

N	Cardinality of A
t	Number of columns in a table
m	Number of rows in a table
m_i	Number of different elements in column i
a	Number of filters
n_h	Number of computing nodes
n_f	Number of filtration nodes
n	Number of nodes $n = n_h + n_f$
α	maximality factor
r	$\frac{\alpha}{1-\alpha}$
c_i	Column of the ith filter
s	Job size
v_h	hashing speed
v_f	Filtration speed
d_c	Communication cost
d_o	Filtration overhead

References

1. Hellman, M.E.: A cryptanalytic time-memory trade-off. IEEE Trans. Inf. Theory **26**(4), 401–406 (1980)
2. Oechslin, P.: Making a faster cryptanalytic time-memory trade-off. In: Boneh, D. (ed.) CRYPTO 2003. LNCS, vol. 2729, pp. 617–630. Springer, Heidelberg (2003). https://doi.org/10.1007/978-3-540-45146-4_36
3. Denning, D.E.R.: Cryptography and Data Security, p. 100. Addison-Wesley Longman Publishing Co., Inc. (1982)
4. Lee, G.W., Hong, J.: Comparison of Perfect Table Cryptanalytic Tradeoff Algorithms, vol. 80, pp. 473–523. Kluwer Academic Publishers (2016)
5. Hong, J., Moon, S.: A comparison of cryptanalytic tradeoff algorithms. J. Cryptol. **26**, 559–637 (2013)
6. Hong, J., Jeong, K.C., Kwon, E.Y., Lee, I.-S., Ma, D.: Variants of the distinguished point method for cryptanalytic time memory trade-offs. In: Chen, L., Mu, Y., Susilo, W. (eds.) ISPEC 2008. LNCS, vol. 4991, pp. 131–145. Springer, Heidelberg (2008). https://doi.org/10.1007/978-3-540-79104-1_10
7. Standaert, F.-X., Rouvroy, G., Quisquater, J.-J., Legat, J.-D.: A time-memory tradeo. Using distinguished points: new analysis & FPGA results. In: Kaliski, B.S., Koç, K., Paar, C. (eds.) CHES 2002. LNCS, vol. 2523, pp. 593–609. Springer, Heidelberg (2003). https://doi.org/10.1007/3-540-36400-5_43

8. Avoine, G., Bourgeois, A., Carpent, X.: Analysis of rainbow tables with finger-prints. In: Foo, E., Stebila, D. (eds.) ACISP 2015. LNCS, vol. 9144, pp. 356–374. Springer, Cham (2015). https://doi.org/10.1007/978-3-319-19962-7_21
9. Avoine, G., Carpent, X.: Optimal storage for rainbow tables. In: Lee, H.-S., Han, D.-G. (eds.) ICISC 2013. LNCS, vol. 8565, pp. 144–157. Springer, Cham (2014). https://doi.org/10.1007/978-3-319-12160-4_9
10. Avoine, G., Carpent, X.: Heterogeneous rainbow table widths provide faster crypt-analyses. In: Proceedings of the 2017 ACM on Asia Conference on Computer and Communications Security, ASIA CCS 2017, pp. 815–822. Association for Computing Machinery, New York (2017)
11. Avoine, G., Carpent, X., Lauradoux, C.: Interleaving cryptanalytic time-memory trade-offs on non-uniform distributions. In: Pernul, G., Ryan, P.Y.A., Weippl, E. (eds.) ESORICS 2015. LNCS, vol. 9326, pp. 165–184. Springer, Cham (2015). https://doi.org/10.1007/978-3-319-24174-6_9
12. Avoine, G., Junod, P., Oechslin, P.: Characterization and Improvement of Time-Memory Trade-Off Based on Perfect Tables, vol. 11. Association for Computing Machinery, New York (2008)
13. Biryukov, A., Mukhopadhyay, S., Sarkar, P.: Improved time-memory trade-offs with multiple data. In: Preneel, B., Tavares, S. (eds.) SAC 2005. LNCS, vol. 3897, pp. 110–127. Springer, Heidelberg (2006). https://doi.org/10.1007/11693383_8
14. Avoine, G., Carpent, X., Kordy, B., Tardif, F.: How to handle rainbow tables with external memory. In: Pieprzyk, J., Suriadi, S. (eds.) ACISP 2017. LNCS, vol. 10342, pp. 306–323. Springer, Cham (2017). https://doi.org/10.1007/978-3-319-60055-0_16
15. Nash, S.G.: A survey of truncated-newton methods. Numerical Analysis 2000. Vol. IV: Optimization and Nonlinear Equations, vol. 124, pp. 45–59 (2000)
16. Nash, S.G.: A survey of truncated-newton methods. J. Comput. Appl. Math. 124(1–2), 45–59 (2000)

Cache-Side-Channel Quantification and Mitigation for Quantum Cryptography

Alexandra Weber[1]($\boxtimes$) iD, Oleg Nikiforov[2] iD, Alexander Sauer[2] iD,
Johannes Schickel[1], Gernot Alber[2] iD, Heiko Mantel[1] iD,
and Thomas Walther[2] iD

[1] Department of Computer Science, Technical University of Darmstadt,
Darmstadt, Germany
{weber,schickel,mantel}@mais.informatik.tu-darmstadt.de
[2] Department of Physics, Technical University of Darmstadt,
Darmstadt, Germany
{oleg.nikiforov,alexander.sauer,gernot.alber,
thomas.walther}@physik.tu-darmstadt.de

Abstract. Quantum cryptography allows one to transmit secret information securely, based on the laws of quantum physics. It consists of (1) the transmission of physical particles like photons and (2) the software-based processing of measurements during the transmission. Quantum key distribution (QKD), e.g., transmits material for establishing a shared crypto key in this way. The key material is encoded into the particles in a way that leakage can be detected and mitigated via so-called privacy amplification.

In this article, we investigate the role of the software implementation for the security of quantum cryptography. More concretely, we quantify the security of QKD software against cache side channels and show how to integrate cache-side-channel mitigation with the privacy amplification in QKD. We evaluate our approach at one variant of a QKD software that is in practical use. During our evaluation, we detect a cache-side-channel vulnerability, for which we develop a parametric mitigation that combines privacy amplification and program rewriting. We propose a cost model for the combined mitigation, which allows one to optimize the interaction between privacy amplification and program rewriting for the mitigation.

1 Introduction

Quantum cryptography [31,56] is a promising approach to protect secret communication. It is based on the laws of quantum physics, which ensure that an attacker will be detected if he intercepts the communication. Quantum crypto is fundamentally different from post-quantum crypto, which is based on mathematical problems that are hard to solve even with quantum computers.

© Springer Nature Switzerland AG 2021
E. Bertino et al. (Eds.): ESORICS 2021, LNCS 12973, pp. 235–256, 2021.
https://doi.org/10.1007/978-3-030-88428-4_12

A prominent example of quantum crypto is Quantum Key Distribution (QKD). QKD is a promising candidate for post-quantum key exchange [30]. The German government, e.g., is investing 165M€ in a QKD network among governmental agencies [25] and Quapital [36] aims at a QKD network across Europe. In China, a QKD network between Beijing, Shanghai and other cities was established in 2018 and is in a trial period for applications like banking [78].

QKD consists of a physical part and a software part. In the physical part, the key material on Alice's side is encoded into quantum properties of particles, usually photons. The particles are transmitted to Bob via a so-called quantum channel, and Bob measures their properties to recover the key material. In the software part, the key material on both sides is converted into a shared key.

Information leakage during the physical part can be quantified based on traces that an attacker inevitably leaves in intercepted particles. It is mitigated by privacy amplification, which increases the number of particles and compresses the resulting key in the software part. Information leakage during the software part can be quantified using Quantitative Information Flow (QIF) [3,70] and mitigated by privacy amplification or, more traditionally, by program rewriting.

When the physical and software parts are combined, new threats arise. For instance, an attacker might combine attacks on the physical part with cache-side-channel attacks, which exploit that a software unintentionally uses a shared cache in a secret-dependent way [1,7,33,43,59,69,77]. In QKD setups like [67] (for secure video conferencing at Mitsubishi) or [68], it is common to use regular PCs for postprocessing. PCs, especially those that process measurements, are often multi-purpose. That is, when setups like [67,68] go into production, communication, e.g., of corporate secrets, might be at risk because the postprocessing software for the encryption key might share a cache with other software. Given efforts to move QKD to the cloud [11,53] and to end-user devices like smartphones [72], cache side channels will be even more dangerous for future QKD.

In this article, we focus on two research questions: (1) How can cache-side-channel mitigation by program rewriting be integrated with privacy amplification? (2) What is a good split between program rewriting and privacy amplification from a performance perspective? Being able to integrate both mitigation techniques in a reliable and cost-efficient fashion is crucial for achieving end-to-end security for QKD across quantum physics and software in practice.

Our first step is to quantify the cache side channels in QKD software. To this end, we develop a program analysis that computes upper leakage bounds. The main novelty of our analysis is that it supports x86 binaries with floating-point instructions. Prior analyses that compute reliable cache-side-channel leakage bounds for x86 binaries (including [8,19,20,51]) did not support floating-point instructions. As QKD software inherently deals with probabilities, e.g., to process imperfect measurements, floating-point support is crucial in this domain.

We evaluate our analysis at the example of the BB84 protocol for QKD [6]. More concretely, we analyze the BB84 implementation from [42,57], which is one of the few publicly available QKD implementations. It uses the low-density parity check (LDPC) technique, which is very popular in QKD [29,34,38,52].

In our evaluation, we discovered a vulnerability in a part of the implementation that optimizes the LDPC. An attacker might recover the entire secret key from one cache trace. We show how to harden the implementation by program rewriting and use our analysis to confirm that the hardening is, indeed, effective.

Naturally, the program rewriting induces performance overhead. To increase flexibility in trading performance against security, we develop a mitigation technique that combines selective program rewriting with privacy amplification. Given a set of key bits that might be leaked by the software, we cannot simply identify the corresponding particles and drop them from the transmission. The reasons are (1) that the postprocessing relies on relations across multiple bits, e.g., that a certain percentages of bits survives the first postprocessing phase (key-sifting phase) and (2) that privacy amplification relies on hash-functions, i.e., there is no one-to-one mapping between the original bits and the final key bits. Therefore, we use our program analysis to show how much privacy amplification is needed to mitigate potential leakage that remains after selective rewriting. Finally, we develop a cost model for the combined mitigation technique and evaluate it for realistic QKD-setup parameters.

In summary, our main technical contributions are (1) a static program analysis that computes reliable upper bounds on the cache-side-channel leakage of programs that use floating-point operations,[1] (2) an evaluation on real-world QKD software, (3) the detection and mitigation of a vulnerability in the QKD software that might leak the entire key, (4) a mitigation technique that integrates program rewriting with privacy amplification, and (5) an evaluation how to optimize performance across program rewriting and privacy amplification.

2 Basic Notions and Notation

2.1 Cache-Side-Channel Quantification

To quantify the leakage of an implementation, we model the secret as a random variable X with prior $\vec{\pi}$, the potential attacker observations as a random variable Obs, and the implementation as a deterministic discrete memoryless channel $C : X \to Obs$. Let $p(x_i)$ and $p(obs_j)$ be the probabilities for $x_i \in X$ and $obs_j \in Obs$. Let $p(obs_j|x_i)$ be the conditional probability for obs_j given x_i. Min-entropy $H_\infty(X) = -\log_2 \max_i p(x_i)$ and conditional min-entropy $H_\infty(X|Obs) = -\log_2 \Sigma_{j=1}^{|Obs|} p(obs_j) \cdot \max_i \frac{p(obs_j|x_i) \cdot p(x_i)}{p(obs_j)}$ [70] capture the uncertainty of a one-try attacker about the secret before, resp., after his observation. The leakage $L(\vec{\pi}, C) = H_\infty(X) - H_\infty(X|Obs)$ is maximized for a uniform $\vec{\pi}$ [41] and then amounts to $L(\vec{\pi}, C) = \log_2 |Obs|$ [70].

We capture Obs for a given implementation using an execution model of the target platform. We call a model that captures the exact values on which the implementation computes (e.g., values of registers) a concrete execution model. It consists of a concrete domain $\mathcal{D}$, which is the set of all possible execution states, and a concrete semantics $upd_\mathcal{D} : \mathcal{D} \times \mathcal{I} \to \mathcal{D}$, which models how executing an instruction from the set $\mathcal{I}$ changes the execution state. Since computing Obs on

---

[1] Available at https://www.mais.informatik.tu-darmstadt.de/qkd-esorics21.html.

such a concrete execution model is usually not computationally feasible, we use abstract interpretation [15] to make the computation tractable. We represent concrete execution states by abstract execution states from an abstract domain $\overline{\mathcal{D}}$ and overapproximate the concrete semantics by an abstract semantics $\mathrm{upd}_{\overline{\mathcal{D}}}$: $\overline{\mathcal{D}} \times \mathcal{I} \to \overline{\mathcal{D}}$. We perform a reachability analysis on $\mathrm{upd}_{\overline{\mathcal{D}}}$ to obtain the set $Obs^{\overline{\mathcal{D}}}$ of observations an attacker might make in any concrete execution modeled by the possible abstract executions. This set overapproximates the actual set Obs, i.e., $\log_2 |Obs^{\overline{\mathcal{D}}}| \geq \log_2 |Obs| \geq L(\vec{\pi}, C)$. Overall, we compute upper bounds on the cache-side-channel leakage of an implementation as $\log_2 |Obs^{\overline{\mathcal{D}}}|$.

This combination of abstract interpretation and information theory was pioneered in [40] and then broadened (e.g., [8,19,20,51]), but the particular analysis that we present is a novel contribution of this article.

2.2   Quantum Key Distribution

Quantum Key Distribution (QKD) [56] aims at establishing a shared secret key between two parties, Alice and Bob, in the presence of an attacker, Eve, who has access to a quantum computer. A QKD implementation consists of a physical part and a software part. Overall, there are five stages in a QKD implementation: one stage in the physical part and four stages in the software part.

In the first stage, the *raw-key exchange*, Alice generates a random bitstring, her so-called raw key b_r^A. She transmits b_r^A to Bob using qbits (quantum bits). BB84 [6] implements qbits using the polarization of photons. A polarization is a linear combination of two orthogonal base vectors. In BB84, two bases are used: $\oplus$ ($\uparrow$ and $\rightarrow$) and $\otimes$ ($\nearrow$ and $\nwarrow$). For each bit in b_r^A, Alice randomly chooses base $\oplus$ or $\otimes$ and polarizes a photon along the base vectors to encode the bit.

Alice sends the photons to Bob, who measures their polarization and obtains his raw key, b_r^B. Bob picks the bases for his measurements independently. This is introducing errors, but crucial for security. If Eve intercepts photons without knowing the bases, she will use the wrong base with a 50% chance. Based on the laws of quantum physics, a wrong measurement will disturb the actual polarization. When resending photons to Bob, Eve can only guess the original polarization of the photons that she measured wrongly. Overall, she will, hence, introduce errors in 25% of the intercepted photons, which can be detected later.

Overall, b_r^A and b_r^B might differ due to (i) mismatching bases, (ii) attacks, or (iii) measurement errors. We refer to the error rate from (ii) and (iii) by err_{true}.

Starting from the second stage, the remaining QKD stages happen in software. The second stage of QKD is the *key sifting*. Bob sends his polarization bases to Alice, who checks which of these bases are wrong. Alice and Bob discard all bits from b_r^A and b_r^B for which Bob used a wrong base, and they obtain the shorter bitstrings b_{si}^A and b_{si}^B. Note that, Bob sends the polarization bases via a conventional electromagnetic channel. Eve might intercept and modify messages on this channel but cannot impersonate other parties and cannot use information she obtains to hide an attack, because the raw-key exchange is over.

The third stage of QKD, *parameter estimation*, has two purposes: (1) to detect attacks and (2) to determine an estimated error rate err_{est} to be used in the fourth step of QKD. Alice and Bob compare randomly selected bits of b_{si}^A and b_{si}^B to obtain err_{est}. All bits used to compute err_{est} are discarded, resulting in the shorter bitstrings b_s^A and b_s^B, called sifted keys. Alice and Bob restart the QKD if err_{est} exceeds a predefined threshold, which indicates an attack.

The fourth stage, called *error correction* eliminates any remaining differences between b_s^A and b_s^B so that Alice and Bob obtain the bitstrings x_{ec}^A and x_{ec}^B, respectively, the so-called error-corrected keys. There are multiple coding techniques that can be used for error correction, including Cascade [9] and LDPC [28]. We focus on LDPC, which optimizes the required amount of communication [18]. Alice and Bob first agree on a length $n = k + m$ (for k message bits and m parity bits) and on a public $k \times n$ parity matrix H. The error correction then consists of an *encoding* by Alice and a *decoding* by Bob. Alice splits b_s^A into blocks of length k. For each block, she computes m parity bits using H and sends them to Bob. For herself, Alice sets $x_{ec}^A = b_s^A$. Bob computes the most likely guess for each sifted-key block based on b_s^B and the parity bits. He concatenates the resulting blocks to obtain x_{ec}^B. If m is sufficiently large based on err_{est} (see [61]), then $x_{ec}^B = x_{ec}^A$.

The final step, *privacy amplification*, compresses x_{ec}^B and x_{ec}^A using hash functions to compensate for leakage to Eve. One example of suitable hash functions are Toeplitz matrices (matrices in which each descending diagonal consists of equal values). Alice and Bob agree on a length l and on a public $l \times k$ Toeplitz matrix T. They multiply T with each k-bit block of the error-corrected key and concatenate the results to obtain the final key $x_{pa}^A = x_{pa}^B$. Naturally, the more the key is compressed in the end, the more qbits need to be transmitted during the first stage of the QKD in order to achieve the same key length.

3   Analysis for Cache-Side-Channel Quantification

In the error-correction step of QKD, Bob computes the most likely values of the sifted-key bits based on his measurements and on additional information received from Alice. That is, software implementations for QKD need to handle probabilities, which are most naturally represented using floating-point values.

To enable cache-side-channel quantification for x86 binaries with floating-point instructions, we define an execution model that captures both, the regular x86 architecture and the components specific to floating-point instructions. Based on this model, we define an abstract reachability analysis that handles floating-point values reliably. We provide tool support to automate the analysis.

Attacker Model. We consider an attacker who observes a victim's interaction with a cache. More concretely, we consider an attacker who has access to a trace of the cache hits and misses encountered, e.g., based on CPU performance counters. Such trace-based attacks have been mounted, e.g., on OpenSSL AES [1], and on reference implementations of the CAMELLIA and CLEFIA ciphers [62,64].

We capture such an attacker by the attacker model *csc-att*. An attacker under *csc-att* observes a trace of the victim binary's execution that we call *cache trace*.

This trace contains the entry "Hit" for each cache hit, the entry "Miss" for each cache miss, and the entry "None" for each instruction without memory access.

3.1   Execution Model

In our execution model, we model a 32-bit architecture, which is supported by older lab machines, as well as newer machines in compatibility mode. That is, we focus on the execution of 32-bit x86 instructions in combination with x87 floating-point instructions. While regular x86 instructions are executed by the CPU, x87 instructions are executed by the floating-point unit (FPU).

CPU (x86). The CPU operates on 32-bit memory entries and CPU registers. It maintains six 1-bit status flags that store information on the results of comparisons and arithmetic operations [37]: Carry Flag (CF), Parity Flag (PF), Auxiliary Carry Flag (AF), Zero Flag (ZF), Sign Flag (SF), and Overflow Flag (OF).

In our model, $\mathcal{X}_{32}$ is the set of all CPU registers and memory locations. By $\mathcal{F}_{CPU} = \{CF, PF, AF, ZF, SF, OF\}$ we model the set of all CPU flags and by $\mathcal{V}_{32}$ we model the set of all 32-bit values. We capture a CPU state by two functions of types $\mathcal{F}_{CPU} \rightarrow \mathbb{B}$ and $\mathcal{X}_{32} \rightarrow \mathcal{V}_{32}$ that map each CPU flag to a boolean value and each CPU register and memory entry to a 32-bit value, respectively.

FPU (x87). The FPU operates on the same memory entries as the CPU. In addition, it operates on a stack that consists of 8 dedicated 80-bit FPU registers (consisting of 1 bit sign, 15 bits exponent and 64 bit mantissa) [37]. For each stack entry, the FPU stores a tag: "valid" for a valid number, "zero" for entry 0, "special" for entries with a special value (e.g., not-a-number) or "empty" if the entry is empty. Like the CPU, the FPU maintains status flags, the so-called condition-code flags, to realize conditional control flow: C0, C1, C2, C3.

We model the set of all FPU registers by $\mathcal{S}_{64}$ and the set of all possible floating-point values by $\mathcal{V}_{64}$. Let $\mathcal{F}_{FPU} = \{C0, C1, C2, C3\}$ be the set of all FPU condition-code flags and $\mathcal{T} = \{valid, empty\}$ be the set of FPU-stack tags, where *empty* models the tag "empty" and *valid* models all other tags. We capture an FPU state by two functions of types $\mathcal{F}_{FPU} \rightarrow \mathbb{B}$ and $\mathcal{S}_{64} \rightarrow \mathcal{T} \times \mathcal{V}_{64}$, which map FPU flags to booleans and FPU registers to tagged floating-point values.

Cache. Frequently-used memory entries are stored in caches for quick access. Most contemporary architectures incorporate a multi-level hierarchy of caches.

We model the memory hierarchy by distinguishing between the main memory and one level of cache. We focus on a 32KB 8-way set-associative data cache with line size 64B (like the L1 cache of the Skylake architecture [37]) and LRU replacement. By $\mathcal{C}_{pos}$, we model the set of all possible positions in the cache, including the position "uncached". We capture a cache state by a function of type $\mathcal{X}_{32} \rightarrow \mathcal{C}_{pos}$, which maps each memory entry to its position in the cache.

Combined State and Executions. We model the possible execution states by

$$\mathcal{D} = (\mathcal{F}_{CPU} \to \mathbb{B}) \times (\mathcal{F}_{FPU} \to \mathbb{B}) \times$$
$$(\mathcal{X}_{32} \to \mathcal{V}_{32}) \times (\mathcal{S}_{64} \to \mathcal{T} \times \mathcal{V}_{64}) \times (\mathcal{X}_{32} \to \mathcal{C}_{pos}).$$

That is, a state in the concrete domain $\mathcal{D}$ is a combination of a CPU state, FPU state, and cache state. Let $\mathcal{I}$ be the set of x86 and x87 instructions. We model their concrete semantics by a function $\mathrm{upd}_{\mathcal{D}} : \mathcal{D} \times \mathcal{I} \to \mathcal{D}$.

Note that, overall we made two key simplifications in our model of execution: We focus on 32-bit binaries and on a single level of cache. Both simplifications are sensible ones and also common in existing analyses [8,19,20,51].

3.2   Abstract Reachability Analysis

We define the abstract domain for our abstract reachability analysis by

$$\overline{\mathcal{D}} = ((\mathcal{F}_{CPU} \to \mathbb{B}) \times (\mathcal{F}_{FPU} \to \mathbb{B})) \to$$
$$((\mathcal{X}_{32} \to 2^{\mathcal{V}_{32}}) \times (\mathcal{S}_{64} \to 2^{\mathcal{T}} \times 2^{\mathcal{V}_{64}}) \times (\mathcal{X}_{32} \to 2^{\mathcal{C}_{pos}})).$$

The values of CPU flags and FPU flags are captured by functions of types $\mathcal{F}_{CPU} \to \mathbb{B}$ and $\mathcal{F}_{FPU} \to \mathbb{B}$ like in the concrete domain. The values of CPU registers and memory entries with concrete type $\mathcal{X}_{32} \to \mathcal{V}_{32}$ are abstracted from by a function of type $\mathcal{X}_{32} \to 2^{\mathcal{V}_{32}}$, i.e., by a set abstraction. Analogously, the tags and values of FPU registers with concrete type $\mathcal{S}_{64} \to \mathcal{T} \times \mathcal{V}_{64}$ are abstracted from by a function of type $\mathcal{S}_{64} \to 2^{\mathcal{T}} \times 2^{\mathcal{V}_{64}}$, and the cache positions with the concrete type $\mathcal{X}_{32} \to \mathcal{C}_{pos}$ are abstracted from by a function of type $\mathcal{X}_{32} \to 2^{\mathcal{C}_{pos}}$.

Unlike in the concrete domain, the state of the flags and the state of memory, registers and cache are not combined using the Cartesian product $\times$ in the abstract domain. Instead, the abstract domain is defined as a mapping $\to$ from the state of the flags to the state of memory, registers and cache. That is, the domain allows to distinguish between the states of memory, registers and cache that are possible across different states of the flags. Since the flags determine the control flow of binaries, this means that the abstract domain allows to distinguish between the execution states across different control-flow branches.

Abstract Semantics. We define the abstract semantics of x86 and x87 instructions by $\mathrm{upd}_{\overline{\mathcal{D}}} : \overline{\mathcal{D}} \times \mathcal{I} \to \overline{\mathcal{D}}$, which overapproximates the effect of instructions on operands that are sets. In the definition, we faced two main challenges.

Firstly, the pointer for the FPU stack is stored in a register and, hence, has an abstract value of type $2^{\mathcal{V}_{32}}$. That is, instructions operate on a set of candidate stack pointers. To treat such situations sufficiently precisely, our abstract semantics takes into account the tag of the stack entries pointed to by the candidate pointers. For instance, on a stack entry tagged {valid}, a pop instruction will yield the tag {valid, empty} and an unmodified stack value, while a push instruction will yield the tag {valid} and a stack value that is the union of the previous value and the singleton set containing the loaded value.

Secondly, values in memory are Byte-aligned but not necessarily aligned to the borders of memory blocks (chunks of memory that are cached together in one cache line) [37]. Large values like floating-point values might cross the border between two memory blocks. Instructions that retrieve such values from the memory might affect multiple cache lines. To reliably overapproximate the effect of such accesses, our abstract semantics splits such values into individual Bytes and updates all cache lines in which at least one of the Bytes is cached.

Computation of Leakage Bounds. Based on an abstract initial configuration $\bar{d}$, we compute all possible abstract executions using $\text{upd}_{\overline{\mathcal{D}}}$. These executions overapproximate the possible concrete executions and corresponding attacker observations. Based on the abstract executions, we determine the set $Obs^{\overline{\mathcal{D}}}$ of attacker observations that an attacker under *csc-att* might make in any concrete execution modeled by the possible abstract executions and compute $\log_2 |Obs^{\overline{\mathcal{D}}}|$ as the leakage bound (see Sect. 2.1) with respect to an attacker under *csc-att*.

3.3   Automation Through Tool Support

To create tool support for our analysis, we implemented the model and semantics for the FPU from scratch, because no such implementation for the FPU was available. Our implementation covers a large set of x87 instructions, including load, store, arithmetic and compare instructions. For the models of the CPU and cache, as well as the semantics of CPU instructions, we aimed at maximum code reuse from existing tools. While no previously existing tool provides support for all required CPU features and instructions, CacheAudit [20] provides a model of the cache and a model of the CPU for selected status flags and instructions. We reused the code from CacheAudit and augmented it with support for 34 additional CPU instructions and the parity flag, which occurs in jumps that are conditional on whether a floating-point value is NaN (not-a-number).

When building on CacheAudit, we noticed that CacheAudit's abstract semantics cannot handle memory entries that map to multiple cache lines. We implemented a solution based on our semantics, splitting values into Bytes.

Overall, the resulting analysis tool takes an x86/x87 binary as input and returns the upper bound $\log_2 |Obs^{\overline{\mathcal{D}}}|$ on the leakage to attackers under *csc-att*.

4   Practical Evaluation

For the evaluation of our program analysis, we consider an implementation of the BB84 protocol. More concretely, we consider the implementation from [42,57], which is both, in practical use and publicly available.

The implementation covers all stages of QKD that happen in software: key sifting, parameter estimation, error correction and privacy amplification. For our evaluation, we selected the two last stages: error correction and privacy amplification, because they involve non-trivial computations on secret bitstrings. More concretely, we selected functions for the encoding part of error correction, for the decoding part of error correction, and for privacy amplification from [42].

Before we apply our program analysis, we perform well-defined simplifications to the functions. We then lift the analysis results to the original functions in a separate step. That is, our results are independent of the simplifications.

For the explanation of our simplified functions, we focus on their high-level C code. For the evaluation of our program analysis, we considered binaries obtained with gcc 7.4.0 with the flags -m32 -fno-stack-protector.

Encoding. We created the simplified version of the function dense_encode shown in Fig. 1. The parameter sblk with size $k = 4$ is the sifted-key block to be encoded. It is copied into the vector u (Line 9) and passed to function mod2dense_multiply (Line 10), which multiplies the sifted-key block with a generator matrix G that is derived from the parity matrix H. The resulting code block (the sifted-key block and $m = 3$ parity bits) is stored in cblk.

Figure 1 simplifies the original code in two aspects: (1) it stores matrices and vectors in fixed-size arrays instead of dynamically allocated pointer structures and (2) it stores the variables G and cols locally instead of globally. We tested with a Hamming(7,4) code that the simplifications do not alter the functionality.

```
1  #define M 3  #define K 4  #define N M+K [...]
2  void mod2dense_multiply(char m1[M][K], char m2[K][1], char r[M][1]){
3    for (int i=0;i<M;i++){ r[i][0]=0; }
4    for(int k=0;k<K;k++){ if (m2[k][0]==1){
5      for(int m=0;m<M;m++){ r[m][0]^=m1[m][k]; }}}}
6  void dense_encode(char sblk[K],char cblk[N],char u[K][1],char v[M][1]){
7    int cols[N]={4,5,6,0,1,2,3}; char G[M][K]; int j;
8    for(j=M;j<N;j++){ cblk[cols[j]] = sblk[j-M]; }
9    for(j=M;j<N;j++){ mod2dense_set(u,j-M,0,sblk[j-M]);}
10   mod2dense_multiply(G,u,v);
11   for(j=0;j<M;j++){cblk[cols[j]]=mod2dense_get(v,j,0);}}
12 void main(){ char sblk[K]; char cblk[N]; char u[N][1]; char v[M][1];
13   dense_encode(sblk,cblk,u,v);}
```

Fig. 1. Target encoding implementation

Decoding. We created simplified versions of the functions initprp and iterprp (Fig. 2). They perform LDPC decoding with a parity matrix stored in an array H_val. They compute the correct values of the bits in the sifted-key block based on probabilities stored in the auxiliary arrays H_lr and H_pr. Function initprp initializes the probabilities using a vector lratio of likelihood ratios based on Bob's measurements. Function iterprp then iteratively updates the probabilities. The resulting error-corrected-key block is stored in dblk.

Our simplified implementation (1) uses fixed-size arrays instead of pointer structures, (2) performs only one iteration of iterprp, (3) uses a fixed instead of a variable parity matrix, and (4) performs overflow handling on dummy variables if no overflow occurred instead of skipping the step. Again, we tested the functionality of the simplified implementation on a Hamming(7,4) code.

Note that the variables H_lr, H_pr and lratio are of type double, i.e., floating-point values. Our simplification preserves these datatypes, because the corresponding values represent probabilities and likelihood ratios. Representing them as integers would loose precision and cause a great deviation from

```
1  #include "math.h"  #define M 3  #define K 4  #define N M+K
2  void initprp (char H_val[M][N], double H_lr[M][N], double H_pr[M][N], double
      lratio[N], char dblk[N], double bprb[N]){ int e; int j;
3    for (j = 0; j<N; j++){ for (e = 0; e < M; e++){
4      if (H_val[e][j] == 1){ H_pr[e][j] = lratio[j]; H_lr[e][j] = 1.0;}}
5      if (bprb) bprb[j] = 1 - 1/(1+lratio[j]); dblk[j] = lratio[j]>=1;}}
6  void iterprp(char H_val[M][N], double H_lr[M][N], double H_pr[M][N], double
      lratio[N], char dblk[N], double bprb[N]){
7    double pr, dl, t; int e, i, j; double temp; double temp2; double dummy;
8    for (i = 0; i<M; i++){ dl = 1; for (e = 0; e < N; e++){
9      if (H_val[i][e] == 1){ H_lr[i][e] = dl; dl *= 2/(1+H_pr[i][e])-1;}}
10     dl = 1; for (e = N-1; e >= 0; e--){
11       if (H_val[i][e] == 1){ t = H_lr[i][e]*dl;
12         H_lr[i][e] = (1-t)/(1+t); dl *= 2/(1+H_pr[i][e]) - 1;}}}
13   for (j = 0; j<N; j++){ pr = lratio[j]; for (e = 0; e < M; e++){
14     if (H_val[e][j] == 1){ H_pr[e][j] = pr; pr *= H_lr[e][j];}}
15     if (isnan(pr)){ pr = 1;} else{dummy=1;__asm__("nop":::);}
16     if (bprb) bprb[j] = 1 - 1/(1+pr); dblk[j] = pr>=1; pr = 1;
17     for (e = M-1; e >= 0; e--){
18       if (H_val[e][j] == 1){ H_pr[e][j] *= pr; temp = H_pr[e][j];
19         if (isnan(temp)){temp = 1;} else{temp2=1;__asm__("nop":::);}
20         H_pr[e][j] = temp; pr *= H_lr[e][j];}}}}
21   void main(){char H_val[M][N]={{1,1,0,1,1,0,0},{1,0,1,1,0,1,0},{0,1,1,1,0,0,1}};
22     double H_lr[M][N]; double H_pr[M][N]; double lratio[N]; char dblk[N];
23     double bprb[N]; initprp(H_val, H_lr, H_pr, lratio, dblk, bprb);
24     iterprp(H_val, H_lr, H_pr, lratio, dblk, bprb);}
```

Fig. 2. Target decoding implementation

the original code due to the additional encoding needed to represent probabilities as integers. Therefore, the binary of our simplified implementation contains floating-point instructions that need to be handled by our program analysis.

Privacy Amplification. We created the simplified version of the function calcPA shown in Fig. 3. It takes an error-corrected key block key and the target length paLen for the privacy-amplified key block as inputs. It hashes the error-corrected key block by multiplying it with the Toeplitz matrix in Line 8.

The simplified calcPA differs from the original calcPA by (1) using fixed-size instead of variable-size arrays, (2) using local variables and parameters instead of class members and (3) initializing each entry of the Toeplitz matrix to the least-significant bit (lsb) of the value stored at the uninitialized address 0x4 (to make explicit that the Toeplitz matrix is binary). Again, we tested the functionality of the simplified implementation on a Hamming(7,4) code.

5   Vulnerability in the QKD Implementation

With our analysis tool, we detected a vulnerability in the QKD implementation from [42], which might leak the entire secret key. In this section, we describe the detection, assessment, and mitigation of this vulnerability.

Note that, the vulnerability is located in the encoding part of the error-correction step. We also analyzed the decoding part of the error-correction step and the privacy-amplification step, but we did not detect vulnerabilities in these implementations. We will describe the security analysis for the hardened QKD software, including decoding and privacy amplification, in Sect. 6.

Detection and Assessment. For dense_encode from Fig. 1, our analysis computes the leakage bound 4 bit with respect to *csc-att*. Recall that the sifted-key-block here has 4 bit, i.e., leaking 4 bit might reveal the entire sifted key.

Recall from Sect. 4 that the differences between the original and the simplified implementation of dense_encode are only the datatypes and scope of the variables that store matrices and vectors. These differences do not impact the control flow and the locations of memory accesses in the encoding implementation. Thus, they do not impact the leakage with respect to *csc-att*. That is, our leakage bound indicates a potential leakage also in the original encoding implementation from [42]. We investigate this potential leakage in the following.

Figure 4 shows excerpts of two functions from the original encoding implementation. The function dense_encode encodes the sifted-key block sblk using the generator matrix G. To this end, the sifted-key block is passed to the function mod2dense_multiply in Line 10 via vector u. The function mod2dense_multiply multiplies the sifted-key block (m2) by the generator matrix (m1).

```
1  #include "string.h"  #include "stdbool.h"
2  #define KEYLENGTH 4  #define PAKEYLENGTH 2
3  void calcPAKey(bool* key, int paLen){
4    int toepMatLen=KEYLENGTH+paLen-1; char paKey[paLen]; char toepMat[toepMatLen];
5    for(int i=0;i<toepMatLen;++i){ toepMat[i]= *((int*)0x4)&1;}
6    for(int i=0;i<paLen;i++){ paKey[i]=0;
7     for(int j=0;j<KEYLENGTH;j++){ int id=i-j+KEYLENGTH-1;
8      paKey[i]+=toepMat[id]*key[j]; paKey[i]=paKey[i]%2;}}}
9  void main(){bool key[KEYLENGTH];calcPAKey(key,PAKEYLENGTH);}
```

Fig. 3. Target privacy-amplification implementation

For each column of the generator matrix and result matrix (Line 2), the function mod2dense_multiply iterates over the sifted-key block (Line 3). If a bit in the sifted-key block is set (Line 4), the function adds the corresponding row of the generator matrix m1 to the intermediate result r of the multiplication in Line 5 and Line 6. That is, the function mod2dense_multiply only accesses those rows of m1 that correspond to set bits of the sifted-key block.

Consider an attacker under *csc-att*. He observes the cache trace while Alice executes the encoding. He recognizes which parts of the trace correspond to iterations of the loop in Line 3 in which the branch in Line 4 is taken because in these iterations cache accesses occur between the non-memory-access steps corresponding to the loop guard. As the branch in Line 4 is taken exactly for each set bit in the sifted-key block m2, the attacker learns which bits in the sifted-key block are 1 and which are 0. That is, he learns the entire sifted-key block.

The attacker can obtain all blocks of Alice's sifted key by observing all executions of the encoding function. By concatenating the blocks, he obtains Alice's entire sifted key. Recall that Alice's sifted key is identical to the error-corrected key (Sect. 2.2). That is, once the attacker knows Alice's sifted key, he can emulate the privacy-amplification step by applying the public hash function to the error-corrected key. As a result, he obtains the privacy-amplified key and can use it to decrypt the subsequent communication between Alice and Bob.

This vulnerability is not only a concern for the QKD software from [42]. It is caused by the optimization to skip multiplications with zero, which is a very natural optimization in a matrix multiplication. Furthermore, the encoding implementation in [42] reuses the original implementation of LDPC encoding by Radford Neal [55], who rediscovered LDPC codes together with MacKay in the 1990s [46]. The vulnerability we detected is also contained in Neal's implementation [55], which has been forked by many others [32]. Overall, a solution for hardening implementations against the vulnerability is highly desirable.

Hardening of the QKD Software. We provide a hardened implementation of mod2dense_multiply in Fig. 5. The implementation iterates through all rows of the generator matrix, independently of the value of the respective sifted-key bit. That is, control flow and memory accesses are independent of the sifted key.

To preserve the functionality of the multiplication, the term to be added to the intermediate result is masked by the value of the sifted-key bit in Line 3. This technique is inspired by conditional assignment [54]. We tested the functionality of the hardened implementation with a Hamming(7,4) code.

```
1   void mod2dense_multiply(mod2dense *m1,mod2dense *m2, mod2dense *r){ [...]
2    for(j=0;j<mod2dense_cols(r);j++){
3     for(i=0;i<mod2dense_rows(m2);i++){
4      if(mod2dense_get(m2,i,j)){
5       for(k=0;k<r->n_words;k++){
6        r->col[j][k]^=m1->col[i][k];}}}}}
7   void dense_encode(char *sblk,char *cblk, mod2dense *u,mod2dense *v){ int j;
8    for(j=M;j<N;j++){cblk[cols[j]]=sblk[j-M];}
9    for(j=M;j<N;j++){ mod2dense_set(u,j-M,0,sblk[j-M]);}
10   mod2dense_multiply(G,u,v);
11   for(j=0;j<M;j++){ cblk[cols[j]]=mod2dense_get(v,j,0);}}
```

Fig. 4. Excerpt from [42]: encoding

As the modified function mod2dense_multiply preserves the functionality of the multiplication function from Fig. 1, it can be plugged into the simplified encoding implementation from Fig. 1. To apply the hardening to [42] and [55], the data types of m1, m2 and r in the function mod2dense_multiply need to be changed back to pointer structures before integrating the function.

6   Security of the Hardened Implementation

By applying our program analysis to the hardened QKD software, consisting of the mitigated encoding implementation, the decoding implementation, and the privacy-amplification implementation, we obtain security guarantees with respect to attackers under *csc-att*. In the following, we describe the security guarantees for each of the analyzed QKD steps.

Hardened Encoding. For the hardened encoding implementation from Sect. 5, our analysis computes the leakage bound 0 bit. That is, the implementation does not leak any information to attackers under *csc-att*. If the hardening is deployed in the encoding implementation from [42] as described in Sect. 5, the resulting implementation will also be secure with respect to *csc-att*, because the data type and scope of the variables do not influence the possible traces.

Decoding. For the implementation from Fig. 2, our analysis also returns the leakage bound 0 bit, i.e., there is no leakage to attackers under *csc-att*.

The implementation simplifies [42] in four aspects (see Sect. 4). We lift the leakage bound to the original implementation by discussing each simplification:

1. While [42] iterates through a pointer structure storing only the set bits of the parity matrix, the simplified version iterates over the complete matrix. This eliminates a dependence of the cache trace on the parity matrix. Since the parity matrix is public, this simplification does not influence the leakage.
2. The parity matrix is fixed to a random matrix in the simplified implementation. This eliminates another dependence of the cache trace on the parity matrix. Again, the leakage is not affected because the parity matrix is public.
3. The simplified implementation calls `iterprp`, which would usually be iterated, only once. Since the leakage bound for decoding is 0 bit, no leakage might accumulate, i.e., the simplification does not influence the leakage.
4. Overflows of probabilities are handled in [42] by resetting the probabilities to 50%. The cache trace reveals the number of overflows encountered. This is hidden by the simplified version. This simplification does not influence the leakage since overflowing probabilities are reset to 50%. Nothing about the final probabilities is revealed by the occurrence of an overflow.

```
1   void mod2dense_multiply(char m1[M][K], char m2[K][1], char r[M][1]){
2     for (int m=0; m<M; m++){r[m][0] = '0';
3       for (int k=0; k<K; k++){r[m][0]^= m1[m][k] & m2[k][0];}
4     r[m][0] = r[m][0] % 2;}}
```

Fig. 5. Hardening of the encoding function

Overall, the zero leakage bounds can be translated to the original decoding implementation, which is, hence, also secure against attackers under *csc-att*.

Privacy Amplification. For Fig. 3, our analysis yields the leakage bound 0 bit. That is, the implementation does not leak to attackers under *csc-att*.

Recall from Sect. 4 that the only differences between Fig. 3 and the original implementation are the fixed size of variables, the scope of variables and the explicit marking of the Toeplitz matrix as uninitialized binary matrix. None of these has an influence on the control flow or memory accesses during the privacy amplification. That is, the zero leakage bound also applies to the original implementation. No need for additional hardening arises.

Together with the bounds for the encoding and decoding implementations, we now have a set of security guarantees for the hardened QKD software.

7 Combining Rewriting and Privacy Amplification

While our hardening by program rewriting in Sect. 5 is effective, it also removes an optimization and thereby increases the running time of the encoding step (by about 50% on average for a uniformly distributed sifted key). In this section, we present a more flexible mitigation strategy, which allows to optimize performance cost across the physical and software-based part of QKD.

```
5   void mod2dense_multiply(char m1[M][K], char m2[K][1], char r[M][1]){
6     for (int i=0; i<M; i++){r[i][0] = 0;}
7     for (int k=0; k<K; k++){
8       if (k < SEC_PARAM || m2[k][0] == 1){
9         for (int m = 0; m < M; m++){r[m][0] ^= m1[m][k] & m2[k][0];}}}}
```

Fig. 6. Parametric mitigation in the encoding function

Parametric Mitigation of the Vulnerability. Figure 6 shows a parametric program rewriting of the encoding implementation. Instead of iterating through all of the block m2 as in the hardening from Fig. 5, the function iterates through the first SEC_PARAM bits of m2 and only iterates through the remaining bits if they are set. That is, the optimization is disabled selectively. While Fig. 6 still leaks a consecutive key portion, additionally randomizing the indices where the optimization is disabled would even hide where the leaked bits belong.

We use our program analysis to verify whether the security guarantees are, indeed, improved incrementally by incrementally disabling the optimization. We obtain the following leakage bounds: 3 bit for SEC_PARAM $= 1$, 2 bit for SEC_PARAM $= 2$, and 1 bit for SEC_PARAM $= 3$. That is, our mitigation allows us to trade performance against security locally within the encoding function.

Integration with Privacy Amplification. Traditional security analyses of QKD solutions [65] aim at guarantees for the secret key resulting after privacy amplification. They take into account leakage to Eve during the raw-key exchange and through the electromagnetic channel.

Privacy amplification requires the transmission of more particles during the raw-key exchange, which lead to more remaining key material after error correction. This key material of length l_{block} is then compressed with a hash function to a key of target length l_{target}. To compensate for potential leaks across the different stages of QKD, privacy amplification relies on upper leakage bounds b_{raw} for the raw-key exchange and b_{parity} for the electromagnetic channel. The length l_{target} of the privacy-amplified key should be $l_{target} < l_{block} - b_{raw} - b_{parity}$ bit. The smaller l_{target} is compared to $l_{block} - b_{raw} - b_{parity}$, the more secure is the final key.

We integrate our leakage bounds as follows. Let b_{cache} be the leakage bound derived with our analysis. To compensate the potential cache-side-channel leakage in addition to the leakage from the raw-key exchange and the electromagnetic channel, the target length should be $l_{target} < l_{block} - b_{raw} - b_{parity} - b_{cache}$ bit. The reason is that the information leaked during a traditional attack on QKD and the information leaked through the side channel might be distinct.

Consider the parametric cache-side-channel mitigation from Fig. 6 for SEC_PARAM = 3. In this case, only one bit of cache-side-channel leakage remains to be mitigated, i.e., $l_{target} < 4 - b_{raw} - b_{parity} - 1 = 3 - b_{raw} - b_{parity}$ bit. That is, only a slightly stronger privacy amplification than usual will be required.

But how should one choose how much leakage to mitigate by program rewriting and how much to mitigate by privacy amplification?

Optimizing the Combined Mitigation. The combination of program rewriting and privacy amplification allows one to split the mitigation overhead across the physical and software parts of QKD. In the following, we present a cost model that allows one to choose an optimal split based on a given QKD setup.

Let c_{raw} be the cost for the raw-key exchange, sifting and parameter estimation for one sifted-key block. Let c_{ec} and c_{pa} be the costs of the encoding and privacy amplification, respectively, for one sifted-key block without any software-based cache-side-channel mitigation. Given a bound b_{cache} on cache-side-channel leakage, the cost for obtaining a key of the length l_{target} is $\frac{(c_{raw} + c_{ec} + c_{pa}) \cdot l_{target}}{l_{block} - b_{raw} - b_{parity} - b_{cache}}$
That is, the cost for the same level of security in the privacy-amplified key increases linearly with b_{cache}. If b_{cache} is too high compared to l_{block}, the key exchange becomes impossible, as the cost would become infinite.

With our mitigation that decreases b_{cache} to b'_{cache}, the cost becomes

$$\frac{\left(c_{raw} + c_{ec} \cdot \frac{l_{block} - 0.5 b'_{cache}}{0.5 \cdot l_{block}} + c_{pa}\right) \cdot l_{target}}{l_{block} - b_{raw} - b_{parity} - b'_{cache}}$$

The encoding becomes more expensive because instead of performing actions for 50% of the bits in the block (on average given a uniform distribution of the sifted key), it needs to perform actions for 50% of the b'_{cache} bits which are not protected and for all of the $l_{block} - b'_{cache}$ bits, which are protected.

If we know the cost of the individual phases, we can find the leakage bound b'_{cache} which minimizes the cost. Given the desired b'_{cache}, we can then set the mitigation strength SEC_PARAM to $l_{block} - b'_{cache}$ in the code.

We evaluate this technique for a set of realistic parameters for cost and leakage bounds. Consider a QKD setup that implements LDPC following IEEE standard 802.11n-2009 [35] like, e.g., the implementation in [73]. Let the block length be $l_{block} = 1458$ bit with corresponding parity-bit length $b_{parity} = 486$ bit.

The leakage per bit during the raw-key exchange is $-err_{true} \cdot \log_2(err_{true}) - (1 - err_{true}) \cdot \log_2(1 - err_{true})$ [22]. Assuming an error rate $err_{true} = 5\%$, we arrive at a leakage of about 0.2864, i.e., $b_{raw} \approx 0.2864 \cdot l_{block} \approx 418$ bit.

The bit-rates that can be achieved for the raw-key exchange vary across different experimental setups between 10^{-3} and 13 Mbit/s [76]. Consider a setup with a bit-rate of $10 Mbit$ of sifted key per second, i.e., where the transmission of one block takes $c_{raw} = 145.8 \cdot 10^{-6}$ s. Let the cost of encoding and privacy amplification be $c_{ec} = 0.001$ and $c_{pa} = 0.01$ s per sifted-key block. The latter two numbers are rounded based on performance measurements we performed on the code from Fig. 1 and 3 across random inputs on a Lenovo ThinkPad X250 M93p with an i7-5600U CPU at 2.60 GHz.

If we now aim to minimize the cost for the exchange of, e.g., $l_{target} = 5,000$ bit of symmetric key, we arrive at $(60.729 - 0.003429355 \cdot b'_{cache})/(554 - b'_{cache})$.

Hence, in this scenario, $b'_{cache} = 0$ bit minimizes the overhead. That is, the complete hardening from Sect. 5 would be the most beneficial here, because the cost of privacy amplification outweighs the software overhead.

For different QKD setups or implementations, the result might differ. In particular, as research in physics is pushing the limits of photon detectors to achieve higher bit-rates [17], the effect of software performance might become more relevant. We hope that our program analysis and flexible mitigation technique will also be beneficial for future QKD setups and implementations.

8   Related Work

We are not aware of any prior work in the intersection of cache side channels and the security of QKD software. The closest are works on cache-side-channel assessment in general, on cache-side-channel attacks on other software, on the security of the quantum-channel transmission in QKD, and on the combination of QIF with concepts from quantum theory. We discuss these areas briefly below.

Assessment of Cache-Side-Channel Security. Side channels are traditionally detected manually as in [24,43]. Recently, complementary approaches have become popular, ranging from systematic testing [75] to empirical methods [14] like distinguishing experiments [49,50] to program analysis [16,20,48]. In the following, we describe the most related tools for cache-side-channel analysis.

The tool CacheAudit [20] quantifies the cache-side-channel leakage of x86 binaries through upper bounds on Shannon-entropy leakage and min-entropy leakage. To this end, CacheAudit performs an abstract reachability analysis for x86. Different versions of CacheAudit have been used in multiple side-channel analyses, e.g., of AES implementations [51], lattice-based cryptography [8] and modular exponentiation [19]. While CacheAudit provides reliable upper bounds on cache-side-channel leakage, it covers only parts of the x86 instruction set architecture. None of the existing versions supports floating-point instructions.

CaSym [10] uses symbolic execution and SMT solving to explore the possible program executions and deduce the existence of a leaking pair of executions. CaSym does not provide upper bounds on cache-side-channel leakage. It only provides security guarantees for software that is free from cache side channels.

The tools LeakiEst [12] and LeakWatch [13] quantify side-channel leakage using statistical methods based on samples of side-channel observations. Both tools provide an estimation of leakage within a confidence interval. That is, they do not provide sound upper bounds on the leakage.

The tools DATA [75] and CacheD [74] detect potential cache-side-channel leakage in software based on execution traces. DATA is based on statistical methods and CacheD is based on symbolic execution and constraint solving. Both, DATA and CacheD are intended to support developers in debugging against cache side channels. They do not provide any security guarantees.

Cache-Side-Channel Attacks. Cache-side-channel attacks were first discussed by Page [60] in 2002. Since then, multiple variants have been developed, including access-based attacks like PRIME+PROBE, EVICT+TIME [59] or FLUSH+RELOAD [77], trace-based attacks [1] and time-based attacks [7]. Cache-side-channel attacks have also been mounted in the cloud [66] and on mobile devices [43,71]. Recently, cache-side-channel attacks became an even more serious concern based on their role in the Spectre [39] and Meltdown [44] attacks.

Security of Quantum-Channel Transmissions. The key idea of QKD is to create a setup where eavesdropping can be detected. To this end, information is encoded into photons [6,21], e.g., using equipment like beam splitters and photodiodes as in [23]. Atoms have been considered as an alternative to photons, e.g., in [26]. An eavesdropper will likely destroy the correlation (measured, e.g., using quantum discord, classical correlation or quantum entanglement [2,58]) between the particles on the sender and receiver side. Thus, there will be a higher error rate in the transmission, by which the eavesdropper can be detected.

Existing research about attacks on QKD focuses primarily on attacking the quantum channel. Existing attacks include, e.g., the injection of bright light [45], the manipulation of the data received by Bob through adversarially constructed light pulses [47], tricking Alice's hardware into producing an erroneous encoding in the photons [27], or time-shifting the transmitted qbits [63].

Quantum Quantitative Information Theory. While we apply classical information theory in the context of quantum cryptography, Américo and Malacaria [4] apply concepts from the context of quantum systems to information theory. The applications presented in [4] are based on classical systems. They use a notion of quantum quantitative information flow (QQIF) to model the choice between different attacks and to model probabilistic program behavior. But the aim of QQIF is to also quantify the security of quantum systems. In the future, a combination of QQIF and our analysis might be an interesting direction for generalizing the integration between security guarantees in quantum cryptography.

9 Conclusion

We presented a solution for quantitative security of QKD, which takes Physics and Computer Science into consideration, at the example of cache side channels.

Our program analysis is the first for automatically computing reliable upper bounds on the cache-side-channel leakage of x86 binaries that use floating-point instructions. We evaluated the analysis on a simplified implementation of the QKD protocol BB84 and subsequently lifted the results to the original code.

During the evaluation, we discovered a vulnerability in the original code that might leak the entire secret key. The vulnerability is caused by an optimization in the application of an LDPC matrix to the secret key. Note that QKD is not the only place where LDPC is applied to secret information. Applications of LDPC to secrets can also be found, for instance, in post-quantum cryptography [5] and, hence, our findings should be of interest beyond QKD.

We showed how to mitigate the vulnerability by program rewriting and presented a parametric mitigation that combines the physical and software parts of QKD. Since currently the exchange of polarized photons is the performance bottleneck, a purely rewriting-based mitigation provides the best results to date. As improving the performance of the photon exchange is subject to intensive research, we expect progress in the future that might affect the trade-off, and our finding about the best trade-off should then be revisited.

Acknowledgements. Funded by the Deutsche Forschungsgemeinschaft (DFG, German Research Foundation) - SFB 1119 - 236615297. We also gratefully acknowledge support by the German Federal Ministry of Education and Research and the Hessian Ministry of Higher Education, Research, Science and the Arts within their joint support of the National Research Center for Applied Cybersecurity ATHENE. We thank the reviewers and Boris Köpf for their helpful comments, Tim Weißmantel for his implementation contributions, and the authors of CacheAudit for making the tool publicly available.

References

1. Acıiçmez, O., Koç, Ç.K.: Trace-driven cache attacks on AES (short paper). In: Ning, P., Qing, S., Li, N. (eds.) ICICS 2006. LNCS, vol. 4307, pp. 112–121. Springer, Heidelberg (2006). https://doi.org/10.1007/11935308_9

2. Ali, M., Rau, A.R.P., Alber, G.: Quantum discord for two-qubit X states. Phys. Rev. A **81**(4), 042105-1–042105-7 (2010)

3. Alvim, M.S., Chatzikokolakis, K., Palamidessi, C., Smith, G.: Measuring information leakage using generalized gain functions. In: CSF, pp. 265–279 (2012)

4. Américo, A., Malacaria, P.: QQIF: quantum quantitative information flow (invited paper). In: HotSpot, pp. 1–10 (2020)

5. Baldi, M., Bianchi, M., Maturo, N., Chiaraluce, F.: Improving the efficiency of the LDPC code-based McEliece cryptosystem through irregular codes. In: ISCC, pp. 000197–000202 (2013)

6. Bennett, C.H., Brassard, G.: Quantum cryptography: public key distribution and coin tossing. In: CSSP, pp. 175–179 (1984)

7. Bernstein, D.J.: Cache-timing attacks on AES. Technical report, University of Illinois (2005)

8. Bindel, N., Buchmann, J., Krämer, J., Mantel, H., Schickel, J., Weber, A.: Bounding the cache-side-channel leakage of lattice-based signature schemes using program semantics. In: Imine, A., Fernandez, J.M., Marion, J.-Y., Logrippo, L., Garcia-Alfaro, J. (eds.) FPS 2017. LNCS, vol. 10723, pp. 225–241. Springer, Cham (2018). https://doi.org/10.1007/978-3-319-75650-9_15

9. Brassard, G., Salvail, L.: Secret-key reconciliation by public discussion. In: Helleseth, T. (ed.) EUROCRYPT 1993. LNCS, vol. 765, pp. 410–423. Springer, Heidelberg (1994). https://doi.org/10.1007/3-540-48285-7_35

10. Brotzman, R.L., Liu, S.L., Zhang, D., Tan, G., Kandemir, M.T.: CaSym: cache aware symbolic execution for side channel detection and mitigation. In: S&P, pp. 505–521 (2018)

11. Cho, J.Y., Szyrkowiec, T., Griesser, H.: Quantum key distribution as a service. In: QCrypt, pp. 1–3 (2017)

12. Chothia, T., Kawamoto, Y., Novakovic, C.: A tool for estimating information leakage. In: Sharygina, N., Veith, H. (eds.) CAV 2013. LNCS, vol. 8044, pp. 690–695. Springer, Heidelberg (2013). https://doi.org/10.1007/978-3-642-39799-8_47

13. Chothia, T., Kawamoto, Y., Novakovic, C.: LeakWatch: estimating information leakage from Java programs. In: Kutyłowski, M., Vaidya, J. (eds.) ESORICS 2014. LNCS, vol. 8713, pp. 219–236. Springer, Cham (2014). https://doi.org/10.1007/978-3-319-11212-1_13

14. Cock, D., Ge, Q., Murray, T., Heiser, G.: The last mile: an empirical study of timing channels on seL4. In: CCS, pp. 570–581 (2014)

15. Cousot, P., Cousot, R.: Abstract interpretation: a unified lattice model for static analysis of programs by construction or approximation of fixpoints. In: POPL, pp. 238–252 (1977)

16. Dewald, F., Mantel, H., Weber, A.: AVR processors as a platform for language-based security. In: Foley, S.N., Gollmann, D., Snekkenes, E. (eds.) ESORICS 2017. LNCS, vol. 10492, pp. 427–445. Springer, Cham (2017). https://doi.org/10.1007/978-3-319-66402-6_25

17. Diamanti, E., Lo, H.K., Qi, B., Yuan, Z.: Practical challenges in quantum key distribution. NPJ Quantum Inf. **2**(1), 1–12 (2016)

18. Dixon, A.R., Sato, H.: High speed and adaptable error correction for megabit/s rate quantum key distribution. Sci. Rep. **4**(7275), 1–6 (2014)

19. Doychev, G., Köpf, B.: Rigorous analysis of software countermeasures against cache attacks. In: PLDI, pp. 406–421 (2017)

20. Doychev, G., Köpf, B., Mauborgne, L., Reineke, J.: CacheAudit: a tool for the static analysis of cache side channels. ACM Trans. Inf. Syst. Secur. **18**(1), 4:1–4:32 (2015)

21. Ekert, A.K.: Quantum cryptography based on Bell's theorem. Phys. Rev. Lett. **67**(6), 661–663 (1991)

22. Elkouss, D., Leverrier, A., Alléaume, R., Boutros, J.H.: Efficient reconciliation protocol for discrete-variable quantum key distribution. In: ISIT, pp. 1879–1883 (2009)

23. Euler, S., Beier, M., Sinther, M., Walther, T.: Spontaneous parametric down-conversion in waveguide chips for quantum information. In: AIP Conference Proceedings, vol. 1363, no. 1, pp. 323–326 (2011)

24. Fardan, N.J.A., Paterson, K.G.: Lucky thirteen: breaking the TLS and DTLS record protocols. In: S&P, pp. 526–540 (2013)

25. Fraunhofer HHI: Fraunhofer HHI participates in major initiative for Quantum Communication supported by German Federal Ministry of Education and Research (2019). https://www.hhi.fraunhofer.de/en/press-media/news/2019/fraunhofer-hhi-participates-in-major-initiative-for-quantum-communication-supported-by-german-federal-ministry-of-education-and-research.html. Accessed 30 Sept 2020

26. Fry, E.S., Walther, T., Li, S.: Proposal for a loophole-free test of the Bell inequalities. Phys. Rev. A **52**(6), 4381–4395 (1995)

27. Fung, C.H.F., Qi, B., Tamaki, K., Lo, H.K.: Phase-remapping attack in practical quantum-key-distribution systems. Phys. Rev. A **75**(3), 032314-1–032314-12 (2007)
28. Gallager, R.: Low-density parity-check codes. IRE Trans. Inf. Theory **8**(1), 21–28 (1962)
29. Gehring, T., et al.: Implementation of continuous-variable quantum key distribution with composable and one-sided-device-independent security against coherent attacks. Nat. Commun. **6**(8795), 1–7 (2015)
30. Geihs, M., et al.: The status of quantum-key-distribution-based long-term secure Internet communication. IEEE T-SUSC **6**(1), 19–29 (2021)
31. Gisin, N., Ribordy, G., Tittel, W., Zbinden, H.: Quantum cryptography. Rev. Mod. Phys. **74**(1), 145–195 (2002)
32. GitHub Inc: Forks of radfordneal/LDPC-codes (2019). https://github.com/radfordneal/LDPC-codes/network/members. Accessed 30 Sept 2020
33. Gullasch, D., Bangerter, E., Krenn, S.: Cache games - bringing access-based cache attacks on AES to practice. In: S&P, pp. 490–505 (2011)
34. Hui, C., Wang, Y., Lu, X.: Implementation of a high throughput LDPC codec in FPGA for QKD system. In: ICSICT, pp. 1494–1496 (2016)
35. IEEE Computer Society: IEEE Standard for Information technology - Telecommunications and information exchange between systems - Local and metropolitan area networks - Specific requirements - Part 11: Wireless LAN Medium Access Control (MAC) and Physical Layer (PHY) Specifications - Amendment 5: Enhancements for Higher Throughput. Technical report. IEEE Std 802.11n-2009, IEEE (2009)
36. Institute for Quantum Optics and Quantum Information, Austrian Academy of Sciences: QUAPITAL: Building the first reliable Quantum Internet on top of Europe's glass fiber network (2020). https://quapital.eu/. Accessed 30 Sept 2020
37. Intel Corporation: Intel® 64 and IA-32 Software Developer's Manual. Order Number: 325462–069US (2019)
38. Jouguet, P., Kunz-Jacques, S., Leverrier, A., Grangier, P., Diamanti, E.: Experimental demonstration of long-distance continuous-variable quantum key distribution. Nat. Photonics **7**(5), 378–381 (2013)
39. Kocher, P., et al.: Spectre attacks: exploiting speculative execution. In: S&P, pp. 1–19 (2019)
40. Köpf, B., Mauborgne, L., Ochoa, M.: Automatic quantification of cache side-channels. In: Madhusudan, P., Seshia, S.A. (eds.) CAV 2012. LNCS, vol. 7358, pp. 564–580. Springer, Heidelberg (2012). https://doi.org/10.1007/978-3-642-31424-7_40
41. Köpf, B., Smith, G.: Vulnerability bounds and leakage resilience of blinded cryptography under timing attacks. In: CSF, pp. 44–56 (2010)
42. Laser and Quantum Optics group (LQO) at TU Darmstadt: Open source software for control of the quantum key distribution and its postprocessing (2020). https://git.rwth-aachen.de/oleg.nikiforov/qkd-tools. Accessed 07 Sept 2020
43. Lipp, M., Gruss, D., Spreitzer, R., Maurice, C., Mangard, S.: ARMageddon: cache attacks on mobile devices. In: USENIX Security, pp. 549–564 (2016)
44. Lipp, M., et al.: Meltdown: reading kernel memory from user space. In: USENIX Security, pp. 973–990 (2018)
45. Lydersen, L., Wiechers, C., Wittmann, C., Elser, D., Skaar, J., Makarov, V.: Hacking commercial quantum cryptography systems by tailored bright illumination. Nat. Photonics **4**(10), 686–689 (2010)
46. MacKay, D.J.C., Neal, R.M.: Near Shannon limit performance of low density parity check codes. Electron. Lett. **32**(18), 1645–1646 (1996)

47. Makarov, V., Hjelme, D.R.: Faked states attack on quantum cryptosystems. J. Mod. Opt. **52**(5), 691–705 (2005)

48. Malacaria, P., Khouzani, M., Pasareanu, C.S., Phan, Q., Luckow, K.S.: Symbolic side-channel analysis for probabilistic programs. In: CSF, pp. 313–327 (2018)

49. Mantel, H., Schickel, J., Weber, A., Weber, F.: How secure is green IT? The case of software-based energy side channels. In: Lopez, J., Zhou, J., Soriano, M. (eds.) ESORICS 2018. LNCS, vol. 11098, pp. 218–239. Springer, Cham (2018). https://doi.org/10.1007/978-3-319-99073-6_11

50. Mantel, H., Starostin, A.: Transforming out timing leaks, more or less. In: Pernul, G., Ryan, P.Y.A., Weippl, E. (eds.) ESORICS 2015. LNCS, vol. 9326, pp. 447–467. Springer, Cham (2015). https://doi.org/10.1007/978-3-319-24174-6_23

51. Mantel, H., Weber, A., Köpf, B.: A systematic study of cache side channels across AES implementations. In: Bodden, E., Payer, M., Athanasopoulos, E. (eds.) ESSoS 2017. LNCS, vol. 10379, pp. 213–230. Springer, Cham (2017). https://doi.org/10.1007/978-3-319-62105-0_14

52. Milicevic, M., Feng, C., Zhang, L.M., Gulak, P.G.: Quasi-cyclic multi-edge LDPC codes for long-distance quantum cryptography. NPJ Quantum Inf. **4**(21), 1–9 (2018)

53. Mohammad, O.K.J., Abbas, S.: Detailed quantum cryptographic service and data security in cloud computing. In: Alfaries, A., Mengash, H., Yasar, A., Shakshuki, E. (eds.) ICC 2019. CCIS, vol. 1097, pp. 43–56. Springer, Cham (2019). https://doi.org/10.1007/978-3-030-36365-9_4

54. Molnar, D., Piotrowski, M., Schultz, D., Wagner, D.: The program counter security model: automatic detection and removal of control-flow side channel attacks. In: Won, D.H., Kim, S. (eds.) ICISC 2005. LNCS, vol. 3935, pp. 156–168. Springer, Heidelberg (2006). https://doi.org/10.1007/11734727_14

55. Neal, R.M.: Software for Low Density Parity Check Codes, Version 2012–02-11 (2012). http://www.cs.utoronto.ca/~radford/ftp/LDPC-2012-02-11/. Accessed 20 Sept 2020

56. Nielsen, M.A., Chuang, I.L.: Quantum Computation and Quantum Information: 10th Anniversary Edition. Cambridge University Press, New York (2011)

57. Notz, P., Nikiforov, O., Walther, T.: Software bundle for data post-processing in a quantum key distribution experiment. Technical report, TU Darmstadt (2020)

58. Ollivier, H., Zurek, W.H.: Quantum discord: a measure of the quantumness of correlations. Phys. Rev. Lett. **88**(1), 017901-1–017901-4 (2002)

59. Osvik, D.A., Shamir, A., Tromer, E.: Cache attacks and countermeasures: the case of AES. In: Pointcheval, D. (ed.) CT-RSA 2006. LNCS, vol. 3860, pp. 1–20. Springer, Heidelberg (2006). https://doi.org/10.1007/11605805_1

60. Page, D.: Theoretical use of cache memory as a cryptanalytic side-channel. IACR Cryptology ePrint Archive **2002**(169), 1–23 (2002)

61. Pearson, D.: High-speed QKD reconciliation using forward error correction. In: AIP Conference Proceedings, vol. 734, no. 1, pp. 299–302 (2004)

62. Poddar, R., Datta, A., Rebeiro, C.: A cache trace attack on CAMELLIA. In: Joye, M., Mukhopadhyay, D., Tunstall, M. (eds.) InfoSecHiComNet 2011. LNCS, vol. 7011, pp. 144–156. Springer, Heidelberg (2011). https://doi.org/10.1007/978-3-642-24586-2_13

63. Qi, B., Fung, C.H.F., Lo, H.K., Ma, X.: Time-shift attack in practical quantum cryptosystems. Quantum Inf. Comput. **7**(1), 73–82 (2006)

64. Rebeiro, C., Mukhopadhyay, D.: Differential cache trace attack against clefia. IACR Cryptology ePrint Archive **2010**(012), 1–11 (2010)

65. Renner, R.: Security of quantum key distribution. Ph.D. thesis, Swiss Federal Institute of Technology Zurich (2005)
66. Ristenpart, T., Tromer, E., Shacham, H., Savage, S.: Hey, you, get off of my cloud: exploring information leakage in third-party compute clouds. In: CCS, pp. 199–212 (2009)
67. Sasaki, M., et al.: Field test of quantum key distribution in the Tokyo QKD network. Opt. Express **19**(11), 10387–10409 (2011)
68. Schmitt-Manderbach, T., et al.: Experimental demonstration of free-space decoy-state quantum key distribution over 144 km. Phys. Rev. Lett. **98**(1), 010504-1–010504-4 (2007)
69. Schwarz, M., et al.: KeyDrown: eliminating software-based keystroke timing side-channel attacks. In: NDSS, pp. 1–15 (2018)
70. Smith, G.: On the foundations of quantitative information flow. In: de Alfaro, L. (ed.) FoSSaCS 2009. LNCS, vol. 5504, pp. 288–302. Springer, Heidelberg (2009). https://doi.org/10.1007/978-3-642-00596-1_21
71. Spreitzer, R., Moonsamy, V., Korak, T., Mangard, S.: Systematic classification of side-channel attacks: a case study for mobile devices. IEEE Commun. Surv. Tutor. **20**(1), 465–488 (2018)
72. Vest, G., et al.: Design and evaluation of a handheld quantum key distribution sender module. IEEE J. Sel. Top. Quantum Electron. **21**(3), 131–137 (2015)
73. Walenta, N., et al.: A fast and versatile quantum key distribution system with hardware key distillation and wavelength multiplexing. New J. Phys. **16**(013047), 1–20 (2014)
74. Wang, S., Wang, P., Liu, X., Zhang, D., Wu, D.: CacheD: identifying cache-based timing channels in production software. In: USENIX Security, pp. 235–252 (2017)
75. Weiser, S., Zankl, A., Spreitzer, R., Miller, K., Mangard, S., Sigl, G.: DATA – differential address trace analysis: finding address-based side-channels in binaries. In: USENIX Security, pp. 603–620 (2018)
76. Xu, F., Ma, X., Zhang, Q., Lo, H.K., Pan, J.W.: Secure quantum key distribution with realistic devices. Rev. Mod. Phys. **92**(2), 025002-1–025002-60 (2020)
77. Yarom, Y., Falkner, K.: FLUSH+RELOAD: a high resolution, low noise, L3 cache side-channel attack. In: USENIX Security, pp. 719–732 (2014)
78. Zhang, Q., Xu, F., Li, L., Liu, N.L., Pan, J.W.: Quantum information research in China. Quantum Sci. Technol. **4**(040503), 1–7 (2019)

Genetic Algorithm Assisted State-Recovery Attack on Round-Reduced Xoodyak

Zimin Zhang, Wenying Zhang[✉], and Hongfang Shi

School of Information Science and Engineering, Shandong Normal University, Jinan 250358, China
zhangwenying@sdnu.edu.cn

Abstract. Genetic algorithm (GA) has led to significant improvements in many challenging tasks, including combinatorial optimization, signal processing, and artificial life. It shows enormous potential for cryptanalysis. This paper designed a heuristic algorithm based on GA for the known-plaintext attack on round-reduced Xoodyak, a finalist of the NIST lightweight cryptography project, under the nonce-respecting setting. To accomplish this, we firstly remodel Xoodoo, the underlying permutation of Xoodyak, portraying it as a function whose input and output are continuous variables defined in $[0, 1]$, representing the likelihood that each bit is equal to 1 and describing the goal of cryptanalysis as an objective function optimized with GA secondly. Consequently, we can abstract the potential information of the unknown state of Xoodyak from the results given by GA. Compared with traditional methods, ours requires less knowledge about complex cryptanalysis as GA can work well with lower complexity, both in time complexity and data complexity, and can be carried out under more restricted conditions.

Keywords: Xoodyak · Xoodoo · Genetic algorithm · AEAD · Known-plaintext attack

1 Introduction

As the foundation of information security, cryptography plays a vital role in modern society. The three prime goals of cryptography are confidentiality, integrity, and authenticity. Therefore, designing a cryptographic primitive that can protect the data from eavesdropping or tampering and enable the receiver to authenticate the data source has become an inevitable demand for cryptography to develop.

Authenticated encryption (AE) and its variant authenticated encryption with associated data (AEAD) are cryptographic primitives that can encrypt data and generate message authentication code (MAC) simultaneously, providing confidentiality, integrity, and authenticity for data. The study of AE started late last century when combining an encryption algorithm and a hash function was

© Springer Nature Switzerland AG 2021
E. Bertino et al. (Eds.): ESORICS 2021, LNCS 12973, pp. 257–274, 2021.
https://doi.org/10.1007/978-3-030-88428-4_13

the primary way for designing an AE algorithm. The cryptographers developed three authenticated encryption modes: Encrypt-then-MAC (EtM), Encrypt-and-MAC (E&M), and MAC-then-Encrypt (MtE) [2]. These modes have the virtue of versatility and the vice of unconvincing security, so they are not satisfactory results.

Another approach is to design brand-new cryptographic algorithms that interweave the encryption and authentication process by sharing computation and strives for better security, applicability, and robustness for algorithms designed in this fashion. Under the leadership of Bernstein, an AE algorithm competition, CAESAR, was launched in January 2013. The competition received extensive attention worldwide, collected 57 algorithms till March 2014, and attracted numerous scholars to conduct a series of cryptanalysis on these algorithms, which significantly promoted the progress of AE. In July 2015, the competition selected 29 algorithms to enter the next round of evaluation. Several algorithms (like Ascon, ICEPOLE, Ketje, Keyak, NORX, and PAEQ) [1,4,8,9,16,19] adopt sponge structure, and four algorithms were designed based on Keccak [3]-like permutation among them. Besides, NIST has initiated a process to solicit, evaluate, and standardize AEAD and hashing for restricted environments. Several algorithms with such structure have been selected for finalists, such as ASCON [8] and Xoodyak [6]. As can be seen, the idea of coupling sponge structure and Keccak-like permutation greatly influences AE algorithms' design. How to effectively evaluate the performance of the algorithms as mentioned above and propose new analysis methods based on the unique design of AE algorithms has also become a concern.

Xoodyak, one of the finalists for the NIST's Lightweight Cryptography project, is the official AEAD scheme based on Xoodoo (a Keccak-like permutation proposed by Daemen et al. on ToSC 2018 [5]). Xoodyak accord with the characteristics we mentioned above, and the analysis of the Xoodyak will help us understand such structure more deeply. Most current analysis methods against Xoodyak share a common feature: the attack needs to be carried out under the nonce-reuse settings. That is, the sender encrypts data with the same nonce, which brings more significant security risks by Xoodyak's definition. The method of analyzing Xoodyak under nonce-respecting conditions needs to be further explored.

Various artificial intelligence (AI) technologies have caused dramatic changes in many fields, including cryptanalysis [10,12]. Among them, Genetic Algorithm (GA) [11] has led to significant improvements on many challenging tasks. GA is commonly used to generate high-quality solutions to optimization and search problems by relying on biologically inspired operators such as mutation, crossover, and selection. In cryptography, practical work using GA has mainly focused on side-channel analysis. How to solve the specific problems in cryptanalysis using GA effectively is worth exploring.

Our Contribution. This paper presents a new cryptoanalysis method for Xoodyak using GA, which can be carried out under more restricted conditions: the sender uses a different nonce for each message. We can think of Xoodyak as a black box with input for plaintext and output for ciphertext. The attacker's goal is to recover the black box's internal state by abstracting the potential and valuable information from plaintext-ciphertext pairs. However, according to the characteristics of Xoodyak, as the nonce changes, the black box's internal state will be entirely different, which means that the attacker can only get one pair of plaintext-ciphertext for internal state analysis. Under this condition, the means of attack are extremely limited. Traditional methods like differential attack, linear attack, and algebraic attack, which need numerous plaintext-ciphertext pairs, are unlikely to work.

Therefore, we designed a new attack method for this condition. Firstly, we set each bit of Xoodoo's internal state as a continuous variable defined in $[0, 1]$, representing the likelihood that this bit is equal to 1, in place of a discrete variable that is either 0 or 1. Secondly, we remodeled Xoodoo so that its input and output are continuous variables that conform to our definition. Finally, combined with our model, we portray the target of the attack as an objective function and find its optimal solutions with the assistant of GA, which are close to the true value of the unknown state. Based on this, we designed an algorithm for the state-recovery attack against round-reduced Xoodyak under the nonce-respecting setting. Furthermore, our method can analyze other AE/AEAD algorithms similar to Xoodyak with a slight modification.

Outline. The rest of the paper is organized as follows. In Sect. 2, we briefly introduce Xoodoo, Xoodyak, and some notations used in this paper. Then, we introduce some related works in Sect. 3. In Sect. 4, we introduce our method of remodeling Xoodoo, followed by an introduction of a new cryptoanalysis method for Xoodyak based on our model in Sect. 5. We conclude the paper with some open problems in Sect. 6.

2 Preliminaries

2.1 Notations

- l, h, w are the number of columns, of rows, and of bits on a lane, respectively.
- (i, j, k) is the index of bit.
- $(*, j, k)$, $(i, *, k)$, $(i, j, *)$ are the indexes of column, row, and lane.
- One-dimensional index for $(i, j, k) = (i + l * j) * w + k$
- $S[i]$ the i-th bit of state S in one-dimensional representation.
- $S[i : j]$ the i-th to j-th bits of state S in one-dimensional representation.
- $S[\{i, j, k\}]$ the i-th, j-th, and the k-th bit of state S in one-dimensional representation.
- $S[i][j]$ the lane indexed by $(i, j, *)$ of state S.
- $S[i][j][k]$ the bit indexed by (i, j, k) of state S.
- S_0 represents the initial state, and S_r represents the state S_0 after r rounds of Xoodoo permutation.
- $|x|$ represents the absolute value of x.
- $||S||_1 = \sum_{a_i \in S} |a_i|$
- Σ denote all kinds of summation operations $(+, \oplus, \bar{\oplus}, \hat{\oplus})$, the actual meaning of a specific use instance should be clear from the context.

2.2   Xoodoo

Xoodoo, proposed by Daemen et al., is a permutation operate on the 384 state bits whose design is similar to Keccak. As depicted in Fig. 1, the state is arranged in a three-dimensional matrix of bits $S[l][h][w]$, where $l = 4, h = 3, w = 32$ (indexed by x, y, z respectively), or in a two-dimensional matrix of 32-bit words $S[l][h]$. Xoodoo iteratively applies a round function to a state.

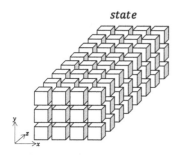

state $S[i,j]$

0,2	1,2	2,2	3,2
0,1	1,1	2,1	3,1
0,0	1,0	2,0	3,0

Fig. 1. (a) The Xoodoo state with w reduced to 8 bits, (b) State in 2-dimension with $0 \leq i \leq 3$ for the index of column and $0 \leq j \leq 2$ for the index of row.

The round function of Xoodoo has five operations: a mixing layer θ, a plane shifting ρ_{west}, the addition of round constants ι (see Table 1), a non-linear layer χ, and another plane shifting ρ_{east}. Round function $R = \rho_{east} \circ \chi \circ \iota \circ \rho_{west} \circ \theta$, and the details are as follows:

$$\theta : S[x][y][z] = S[x][y][z] \oplus \sum_{j=0}^{2} (S[x-1][j][z-5] \oplus S[x-1][j][z-14]).$$

$$\rho_{west} : S[x][1][z] = S[x-1][1][z], S[x][2][z] = S[x][2][z-11].$$

$$\iota : S[0][0] = S[0][0] \oplus RC_i. \tag{1}$$

$$\chi : S[x][y][z] = S[x][y][z] \oplus ((S[x][y+1][z] \oplus 1) \wedge S[x][y+2][z]).$$

$$\rho_{east} : S[x][1][z] = S[x][1][z-1], S[x][2][z] = S[x-2][2][z-8].$$

χ is the only non-linear operation in the Xoodoo, which can be treated as a 3-bit S-box (Table 2) acting on each column of Xoodoo's state. Xoodoo can be parameterized by its number of rounds r and denoted $Xoodoo^r$.

2.3   Xoodyak

As a finalist of the NIST lightweight cryptography project, Xoodyak has an AEAD scheme combined with Xoodoo permutation and sponge structure, which uses a new operation mode called Cyclist. As shown in Fig. 2, f is the 12-round

Table 1. The round constants RC_i with $0 \leq i \leq 11$, in hexadecimal notation (the least significant bit is at $z = 0$)

i	RC_i	i	RC_i	i	RC_i	i	RC_i
0	0x00000058	3	0x000000D0	6	0x00000060	9	0x000000F0
1	0x00000038	4	0x00000120	7	0x0000002C	10	0x000001A0
2	0x000003C0	5	0x00000014	8	0x00000380	11	0x00000012

Table 2. The S-box of Xoodoo

x	0	1	2	3	4	5	6	7
S(x)	0	5	3	2	6	1	4	7

permutation $Xoodoo^{12}$. Xoodyak first absorbs the 128-bit key into the 384 bits internal state and refreshes the state through $Xoodoo^{12}$. Then, absorb a 128-bit nonce and refresh by $Xoodoo^{12}$, absorb 192-bit associated data and refresh; then absorb the 192-bit plaintext and output the ciphertext; then enter the finalization stage. Please refer to [6] for more details.

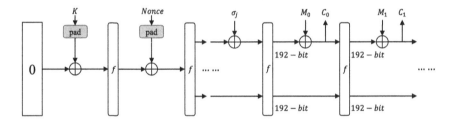

Fig. 2. Framework of Xoodyak-AEAD, where the finalization is omitted.

According to the settings, the attacker can obtain half the state information before and after permutation through $M_0 \oplus C_0$ and $M_1 \oplus C_1$ respectively. The attacker's goal is to recover the other 192 unknown bits. Once the whole 384-bit state is known, the attacker can compute the key inversely.

3   Related Works

Related Cryptographic Work: Song and Guo [17] gave the first Key-recovery attack on 6-round Xoodoo-AE, an artificial AE algorithm using Xoodoo in Ketje style. Li et al. [13] proposed a new conditional cube attack on Keccak, which reduces the time complexity of the key-recovery attack against 7-round Keccak-MAC-512. Then, Zhou et al. [21] found a new property on Li et al.'s method, modified the new conditional cube attack, and applied it to 6-round Xoodyak.

Liu et al. constructed a practical zero-sum distinguisher for 12-round Xoodoo in [14]. Liu et al. [15] developed a new technology called rotational differential-linear cryptanalysis and applied it to Xoodoo. These works directly or indirectly examined the security of Xoodyak.

Prior Work on GA in Cryptanalysis mainly concentrated on the side channel. In 2015, Zhang et al. [20] presented a GA-based correlation power analysis (CPA), which took full use of information in the power consumption traces generated by multiple S-boxes. Ding et al. [7] also proposed a method using GA to conduct attack on bitwise linear leakages in 2020. Wang et al. [18] put forward a GA-CPA framework that improves the convergence rate of GA and reduces the number of traces required in the power analysis on cryptographic algorithms implemented with parallel S-boxes and large noise.

4   Remodel Xoodoo

As shown in Fig. 3, the output of Xoodoo are functions of the input variables, and these variables are discrete variables defined in $\{0, 1\}$. When the function's input changes slightly, the function's output will change dramatically. This change is almost random, and it is challenging to reveal its laws. To reveal the pattern that output changes with input, we need to remodel the Xoodoo permutation. Firstly, set each bit of Xoodoo's internal state as a continuous variable defined in $[0, 1]$, representing the likelihood that this bit is equal to 1. The larger the value, the higher the likelihood that the bit is equal to 1. Conversely, the smaller the value, the greater the likelihood that the bit is equal to 0. Secondly, Remodel the components of the round function into continuous functions, whose input and output variables conform to our definition. Finally, we assemble the remodeled components into a continuous version of Xoodoo. In this manner, the output of Xoodoo convert to continuous functions of the input variables. When an input variable changes in a continuous field of definition, the output variables will also change in a continuous domain, revealing more information about input and output relations.

Since Xoodoo's ρ_{west} and ρ_{east} are shift operations, we just need to shift the variables according to the setting. The critical part of modeling is the re-characterization of the linear and the nonlinear layer of Xoodoo.

4.1   Remodel Linear Layer

The key to remodeling the linear layer is to re-portrait the operator $\oplus$. Set two independent bits a and b, $p(a \oplus b = 1) = p(a \neq b)$, and $p(a \neq b) = p(a = 1; b = 0) + p(a = 0; b = 1) = p(a = 1)(1 - p(b = 1)) + p(b = 1)(1 - p(a = 1))$. Namely,

$$p(a \oplus b = 1) = p(a = 1) + p(b = 1) - 2p(a = 1)p(b = 1). \tag{2}$$

Therefore, we can define the operator $\bar{\oplus}$, for two continuous variables x, y defined in $[0, 1]$, $x \bar{\oplus} y = x + y - 2xy$. In particular $x \bar{\oplus} 1 = 1 - x$ and $x \bar{\oplus} 0 = x$.

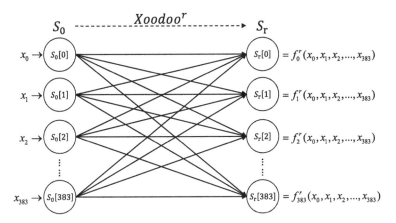

Fig. 3. Each output bit of Xoodoo is a function of all input bits. We can denote these functions as f_i^r, where $0 \leq i \leq 383$ represent the ith output of S_r.

For Xoodoo's component ι, since the round constants have been determined, we can replace $\oplus$ in ι with $\bar{\oplus}$ so that ι' can handle continuous variables.

$$\iota' : S[0][0] = S[0][0]\bar{\oplus}RC_i. \tag{3}$$

Unfortunately, we cannot use $\bar{\oplus}$ instead of $\oplus$ in θ directly. We can observe from the function image shown in Fig. 4(a) that the function's change rate is very low in the central area, which will cause the corresponding relationship between input and output to become insignificant in this area. Besides, according to the optimization theory, this function will easily make the optimizer fall into the local optimum, and it is not easy to get the desired results. Therefore, we need to reduce the area in which the rate of function change is low.

The Sigmoid function is a monotonic increasing function that is often used as the activation function of neural networks to map variables between 0 and 1. The function is smooth, easy to derive, and the rate of function change increases as x approaches 0. $Sigmoid(x) = 1/1 + e^{-x}$. According to these characteristics of the Sigmoid function, we can define the operator $\hat{\oplus}$, for two continuous variables x, y defined in $[0,1]$, $x\hat{\oplus}y = Sigmoid[w((x\bar{\oplus}y) - 0.5)]$ where w is the enhancement coefficient, the larger the value, the more drastic the function changes. This paper defaults the w to 10. If we bring in $x = p(a = 1)$, $y = p(b = 1)$, the value of $x\hat{\oplus}y$ can be treated as a measure of likelihood that $a \oplus b = 1$. It can be seen from Fig. 4(b) that the slow-changing area is reduced. Consequently, we can use $\hat{\oplus}$ instead of $\oplus$ in θ to complete the operation θ remodeling.

$$\theta' : S[x][y][z] = S[x][y][z]\hat{\oplus}\sum_{j=0}^{2} (S[x-1][j][z-5]\hat{\oplus}S[x-1][j][z-14]). \tag{4}$$

Finally, we can replace θ and ι in Xoodoo with θ' and ι'. Similarly, we can remodel the inverse functions θ^{-1} and ι^{-1} to get $\theta^{-1'}$, $\iota^{-1'}$.

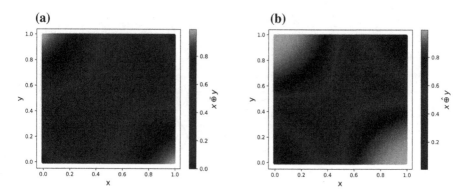

Fig. 4. (a) The function image of $\bar{\oplus}$. (b) The function image of $\hat{\oplus}$ with $w = 10$.

4.2 Remodel Non-linear Layer

χ can be treated as a 3-bit S-box (Table 2) acting on each column of Xoodoo's state. This S-box maps a point containing three discrete variables to another, namely $Sbox(x, y, z) = (a, b, c)$. In addition, since $Sbox(Sbox(x, y, z)) = (x, y, z)$, $\chi = \chi^{-1}$. According to these characteristics, the re-characterize χ' should be a self-reciprocal function of continuous point in three-dimensional space. We first turn our attention to S-box, according to our remodeled linear layer, the point entering the S-box consist of three continuous variables defined in $[0, 1]$, which respectively represent the likelihood that x, y, and z are equal to 1.

We assume that x, y, and z are independent bits. When we know the value of $p(x = 1)$, $p(y = 1)$, and $p(z = 1)$, we can calculate the probability of each value of the point (a, b, c) as shown in Table 3. Based on this, we can get $p(a = 1) = p_1+p_4+p_6+p_7$, $p(b = 1) = p_2+p_3+p_4+p_7$, $p(c = 1) = p_1+p_2+p_5+p_7$, then define function $Sbox'((p(x = 1), p(y = 1), p(z = 1))) = (p(a = 1), p(b = 1), p(c = 1))$.

We may get a deeper understanding of $Sbox'$ by Fig. 5. S-box determines the relationships between coordinate systems $O(x, y, z)$ and $O'(a, b, c)$. The input and output of $Sbox'$ are continuous points defined in a cube of length 1 whose eight vertices are the mapping relationship between (x, y, z) and (a, b, c). If we consider the probability of each vertex as the mass of that vertex, input point $(p(x = 1), p(y = 1), p(z = 1))$ is actually the coordinate of the centroid of the eight vertices in $O(x, y, z)$. The closer the centroid is to a certain vertex, the more likely this mapping will occur, so the output of point $(p(a = 1), p(b = 1), p(c = 1))$ is actually the coordinate of the centroid of the eight vertices in $O'(a, b, c)$. $Sbox'$ reveals the pattern that dependent variables change with the variation of independent variables, which facilitates the optimizer to search the optimization path. For example, if we fix $p(y = 1)$, $p(z = 1)$ at point O, and let $p(x = 1)$ gradually increases, $p(a = 1)$, $p(b = 1)$ will increase at the same rate, and $p(c = 1)$ will remain constant.

Table 3. Probability of vector (a, b, c) taking each value

i	(x, y, z)	$(a, b, c) = Sbox(x, y, z)$	Probability p_i
0	$(0,0,0)$	$(0,0,0)$	$(1 - p(x = 1))(1 - p(y = 1))(1 - p(z = 1))$
1	$(0,0,1)$	$(1,0,1)$	$(1 - p(x = 1))(1 - p(y = 1))p(z = 1)$
2	$(0,1,0)$	$(0,1,1)$	$(1 - p(x = 1))p(y = 1)(1 - p(z = 1))$
3	$(0,1,1)$	$(0,1,0)$	$(1 - p(x = 1))p(y = 1)p(z = 1)$
4	$(1,0,0)$	$(1,1,0)$	$p(x = 1)(1 - p(y = 1))(1 - p(z = 1))$
5	$(1,0,1)$	$(0,0,1)$	$p(x = 1)(1 - p(y = 1))p(z = 1)$
6	$(1,1,0)$	$(1,0,0)$	$p(x = 1)p(y = 1)(1 - p(z = 1))$
7	$(1,1,1)$	$(1,1,1)$	$p(x = 1)p(y = 1)p(z = 1)$

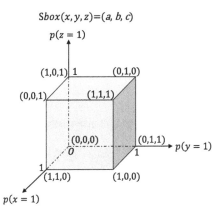

Fig. 5. Image understanding of $Sbox'$

We define the χ' operation as letting $Sbox'$ act on each column of the state so that Xoodoo's nonlinear layer can handle continuous variables. It is easy to verify, $\chi'^{-1} = \chi'$.

4.3   Assemble into $Xoodoo'$

In summary, we can get $Xoodoo' = \rho_{east} \circ \chi' \circ \iota' \circ \rho_{west} \circ \theta'$ and its inverse function $Xoodoo'^{-1} = \theta'^{-1} \circ \rho_{west}^{-1} \circ \iota'^{-1} \circ \chi'^{-1} \circ \rho_{east}^{-1}$, whose input and output are both 384-dimensional vectors and each dimension of the vector is a continuous variable defined in $[0, 1]$. It is worth noting that we assume that each bit in the state is mutually independent when modeling. However, there are various linear and nonlinear relationships between the bits, so this assumption does not square with the fact. Nevertheless, from the experimental results, the impact of these relationships is negligible. Considering these relationships will not significantly improve model precision but will only make the model more complex. Besides, we omit the addition of round constants in the following sections because it does not affect the accuracy of the model and the optimization results in GA.

We can design an example to verify the effectiveness of our model. To facilitate the observation, we reduce the w in Xoodoo to 8 and adjust our model accordingly. We can treat the state as a 96-dimensional vector. The following p, $c = Xoodoo(p)$ are the vector before and after one round mini version of Xoodoo permutation.

$$p = \begin{bmatrix} 1\,1\,1\,0\,1\,1\,0\,1\,1\,0\,0\,1\,1\,0\,1\,1 \\ 0\,1\,1\,0\,1\,0\,0\,1\,1\,1\,1\,0\,0\,1\,0\,0 \\ 1\,1\,1\,1\,1\,1\,1\,0\,1\,1\,1\,0\,1\,1\,0\,1 \\ 1\,1\,1\,0\,0\,1\,0\,1\,0\,0\,0\,0\,0\,1\,0\,1 \\ 0\,0\,0\,0\,0\,1\,1\,1\,0\,1\,0\,1\,1\,1\,0\,0 \\ 0\,0\,0\,1\,1\,0\,1\,1\,1\,0\,1\,1\,1\,0\,0\,0 \end{bmatrix} \quad c = \begin{bmatrix} 0\,1\,0\,1\,0\,0\,1\,0\,1\,1\,1\,0\,1\,1\,1\,1 \\ 1\,1\,0\,1\,0\,0\,0\,0\,0\,1\,0\,0\,0\,1\,0\,1 \\ 1\,1\,0\,1\,0\,0\,1\,0\,1\,0\,0\,1\,1\,1\,0\,1 \\ 1\,1\,0\,0\,1\,1\,1\,0\,0\,0\,0\,0\,1\,1\,0\,0 \\ 0\,1\,0\,1\,0\,0\,0\,1\,0\,1\,0\,1\,0\,0\,1\,1 \\ 1\,0\,1\,1\,0\,0\,0\,0\,1\,0\,0\,0\,0\,1\,0\,1 \end{bmatrix}$$

Then we can design a test vector p', which is close to p, and we can get $c' = Xoodoo'(p')$ though our model.

$$p' = \begin{bmatrix} 0.61 & 0.62 & 0.61 & 0.13 & 0.9 & 0.83 & 0.09 & 0.73 & 0.79 & 0.06 & 0.04 & 0.73 & 0.86 & 0.31 & 0.67 & 0.76 \\ 0.05 & 0.79 & 0.93 & 0.37 & 0.93 & 0.21 & 0.31 & 0.79 & 0.65 & 0.71 & 0.8 & 0.23 & 0.26 & 0.96 & 0.01 & 0.25 \\ 0.7 & 0.84 & 0.98 & 0.87 & 0.76 & 0.74 & 0.72 & 0.09 & 0.78 & 0.98 & 0.75 & 0.39 & 0.85 & 0.65 & 0.37 & 0.85 \\ 0.78 & 0.94 & 0.61 & 0.15 & 0.18 & 0.95 & 0.07 & 0.84 & 0.14 & 0.13 & 0.27 & 0.13 & 0.27 & 0.79 & 0.17 & 0.75 \\ 0.27 & 0.08 & 0.25 & 0.28 & 0.29 & 0.6 & 0.93 & 0.94 & 0.07 & 0.81 & 0.33 & 0.71 & 0.93 & 0.98 & 0.25 & 0.08 \\ 0.31 & 0.3 & 0.18 & 0.8 & 0.76 & 0.22 & 0.63 & 0.88 & 0.74 & 0.34 & 0.87 & 0.65 & 0.77 & 0.25 & 0.09 & 0.03 \end{bmatrix}$$

$$c' = \begin{bmatrix} 0.18 & 0.73 & 0.16 & 0.69 & 0.18 & 0.09 & 0.79 & 0.29 & 0.74 & 0.8 & 0.68 & 0.31 & 0.83 & 0.61 & 0.61 & 0.76 \\ 0.7 & 0.7 & 0.09 & 0.58 & 0.15 & 0.17 & 0.18 & 0.12 & 0.22 & 0.63 & 0.22 & 0.19 & 0.29 & 0.93 & 0.32 & 0.63 \\ 0.84 & 0.75 & 0.42 & 0.81 & 0.17 & 0.23 & 0.93 & 0.36 & 0.8 & 0.14 & 0.43 & 0.62 & 0.89 & 0.81 & 0.08 & 0.5 \\ 0.86 & 0.64 & 0.17 & 0.32 & 0.62 & 0.96 & 0.84 & 0.36 & 0.14 & 0.37 & 0.19 & 0.11 & 0.69 & 0.84 & 0.17 & 0.16 \\ 0.05 & 0.85 & 0.35 & 0.59 & 0.28 & 0.19 & 0.42 & 0.74 & 0.28 & 0.7 & 0.18 & 0.6 & 0.37 & 0.15 & 0.82 & 0.73 \\ 0.67 & 0.34 & 0.67 & 0.76 & 0.34 & 0.2 & 0.22 & 0.33 & 0.85 & 0.32 & 0.08 & 0.38 & 0.16 & 0.67 & 0.31 & 0.92 \end{bmatrix}$$

We define the $error = ||c - c'||_1$. In this case, $error = 23.59$. Let a small variation $\Delta x = 0.1$. Since the value of $p[0]$ is 1, the closer the value of $p'[0]$ is to 1, the smaller the value of $error$ will be. As the experiment proves, the $error$ decrease to 22.84 when $p'[0] + \Delta x$, and the $error$ increase to 26.63 when $p'[0] - \Delta x$.

5   State-Recovery Attack on Round-Reduced Xoodyak

For the convenience of illustration, we continued to use the mini version of Xoodoo defined above whose states is reduced to 96 bits. As mentioned before, we can obtain half the state information before and after permutation through

$S_0[i] = M_0[i] \oplus C_0[i]$ and $S_r[i] = M_1[i] \oplus C_1[i], 0 \le i \le 47$ respectively. Our goal is to recover the remaining 48-bit unknown state $S_0[48:95]$ or $S_r[48:95]$ through $S_0[0:47]$ and $S_r[0:47]$. In this section, we introduce the method of obtaining information about $S_0[48:95]$.

5.1   4/5-Round Attack Against Xoodyak

Since Xoodoo is a bijective mapping in $\{0,1\}^{96}$ space: $S_0 \overset{f^r}{\underset{f^{-r}}{\rightleftharpoons}} S_r$, and half of the state $S_0[0:47]$ has been fixed by message($M_0 \oplus C_0$), the possible values of $S_r = f^r(S_0)$ are restricted in $\{0,1\}^{48}$ space. Similarly, since half of the state $S_r[0:47]$ has been fixed by message($M_1 \oplus C_1$), the possible values of $S_0 = f^{-r}(S_r)$ are also restricted in $\{0,1\}^{48}$ space. Therefore, the feasible states of Xoodoo are restricted in the intersection of these two spaces. If we can find all the elements in the intersection and get all feasible solutions of $S_0[48:95]$, we can count the frequency of each bit in $S_0[48:95]$ that is equal to 0 or 1. Due to the limited number of elements and inadequate permutation caused by shortened rounds, we can assume that these frequencies are not uniform, and the bits are constrained to each other. However, the computation complexity of finding the intersection of these two spaces is too high (2^{48}). We can set the unknown bits of S_0 as variable x, $S_0[48:95] = x[0:47]$. The value of $x[i]$ can be understood as a guess about the likelihood that the value of the corresponding bit is equal to 1. Then let $error = \sum_{i=0}^{47} |Xoodoo'^r(S_0)[i] - S_r[i]|$, which is a function of x. The closer the value of x is to the feasible value of $S_0[48:95]$, the lower the $error$.

We can use GA to search for several optimal feasible solutions of $S_0[48 : 95]$ for minimum $error$: $x_1, x_2, ..., x_n$ and the corresponding $error_1, error_2, ..., error_n$. These optimal feasible solutions are not necessarily an approximation of the actual value of $S_0[48:95]$, but approximations of certain elements in the intersection of two $\{0,1\}^{48}$ spaces we mentioned earlier and the smaller the $error_i$ corresponding to x_i, the closer x_i is to these elements. We can choose a weight w_i representing the degree of proximity to calculate the weighted average of $x_i[j]$, where $1 \le i \le n, 0 \le j \le 47$, which is equivalent to sampling the feasible solutions for $S_0[48 : 95]$. Eventually, we can use this information to guess the true value of $S_0[48:95]$ like Algorithm 1.

Under the setting of $r = 4$, $n = 4$, the search process of GA at the first iteration is shown in Fig. 6. Judging results, GA can reduce the $error$ roughly to 9.6 in total and 0.2 on average.

Here, we elaborate on one of the experimental results shown in Fig. 6 to illustrate the effectiveness of GA. We set p and $c = Xoodoo^4(p)$ as follows, the true value of the state we need to recover is $true$, and one of the results given by GA is $guess$. We can classify $guess$'s value into two categories: let the value greater than 0.5 equal to 1, the value less than 0.5 equal to 0. According to this classification method, the correct rate is 62.5%. $MostConfident(guess) = 6$, and $true[6] == guess[6]$. Based on these characteristics, the algorithm we designed will combine the results given by GA in one iteration to determine the value of

---

Algorithm 1. State-recovery Attack on Round-reduced Xoodyak.

Input: Plaintext M_0, M_1; Ciphertext C_0, C_1;

Output: Unknown states $S_0[48:95]$;

1: n is an artificially set parameter representing the number of optimal feasible solutions that need to be searched by GA, r is the number of attack rounds, $UnknownIndex$ is the set of unknown state indexes of S_0. The function $MostConfident(x)$ returns the index of the maximum value in the array $|x - 0.5|$.

2: $S_0[0:47] \leftarrow M_0 \oplus C_0$, $S_r[0:47] \leftarrow M_1 \oplus C_1$, $UnknownIndex \leftarrow \{48, 49, ..., 95\}$;

3: **while** $UnknownIndex \neq \emptyset$ **do**

4:     Define $error$ as $\sum_{i=0}^{47} |Xoodoo'^r(S_0)[i] - S_r[i]|$;

5:     Search optimal solutions $x_1, ..., x_n$ of $S_0[UnknownInedx]$ for min $error$ by GA;

6:     $w_1 \leftarrow \frac{(1/error_1)}{\sum_{i=1}^{n}(1/error_i)}, w_2 \leftarrow \frac{(1/error_2)}{\sum_{i=1}^{n}(1/error_i)}, ..., w_n \leftarrow \frac{(1/error_n)}{\sum_{i=1}^{n}(1/error_i)}$;

7:     $Avg\_x \leftarrow \sum_{i=1}^{n} w_i x_i$;

8:     $i \leftarrow MostConfident(Avg\_x)$, $j \leftarrow UnknownInedx[i]$;

9:     **if** $Avg\_x[i] > 0.5$ **then**

10:        $S_0[j] \leftarrow 1$;

11:    **else if** $Avg\_x[i] < 0.5$ **then**

12:        $S_0[j] \leftarrow 0$;

13:    **else**

14:        continue;

15:    **end if**

16:    $UnknownIndex \leftarrow UnknownIndex - \{j\}$;

17: **end while**

18: **return** $S_0[48:95]$;

---

the state with the highest degree of confidence, which will decrease the number of variables in the next iteration, thereby reducing the GA search space.

$$p = \begin{bmatrix} 1\,1\,1\,0\,1\,1\,0\,1\,1\,0\,0\,1\,1\,0\,1\,1 \\ 0\,1\,1\,0\,1\,0\,0\,1\,1\,1\,1\,0\,0\,1\,0\,0 \\ 1\,1\,1\,1\,1\,1\,1\,0\,1\,1\,1\,0\,1\,1\,0\,1 \\ 1\,1\,1\,0\,0\,1\,0\,1\,0\,0\,0\,0\,0\,1\,0\,1 \\ 0\,0\,0\,0\,0\,1\,1\,1\,0\,1\,0\,1\,1\,1\,0\,0 \\ 0\,0\,0\,1\,1\,0\,1\,1\,1\,0\,1\,1\,1\,0\,0\,0 \end{bmatrix} \quad c = \begin{bmatrix} 0\,0\,0\,0\,1\,1\,1\,1\,0\,0\,0\,1\,1\,1\,0\,1 \\ 1\,0\,0\,0\,0\,0\,0\,0\,0\,1\,1\,0\,0\,1\,0\,1 \\ 1\,0\,0\,0\,0\,0\,1\,1\,0\,0\,1\,1\,0\,1\,0\,0 \\ 1\,1\,1\,0\,0\,0\,0\,1\,1\,0\,0\,0\,0\,1\,0\,0 \\ 1\,0\,0\,0\,0\,0\,0\,1\,1\,0\,0\,1\,0\,0\,0\,1 \\ 1\,1\,1\,0\,0\,0\,0\,0\,0\,0\,0\,0\,0\,0\,0\,1 \end{bmatrix}$$

$$true = \begin{bmatrix} 1\,1\,1\,0\,0\,1\,0\,1 \\ 0\,0\,0\,0\,0\,1\,0\,1 \\ 0\,0\,0\,0\,0\,1\,1\,1, \\ 0\,1\,0\,1\,1\,1\,0\,0 \\ 0\,0\,0\,1\,1\,0\,1\,1 \\ 1\,0\,1\,1\,1\,0\,0\,0 \end{bmatrix} \quad guess = \begin{bmatrix} 0.95\,0.17\,0.16\,0.93\,0.26\,0.82\ \ 0.\ \ 0.75 \\ 0.22\,0.88\,0.94\,0.14\,0.74\,0.34\,0.36\,0.75 \\ 0.28\,0.18\,0.12\,0.14\,0.01\,0.75\ \ 0.9\ \ 0.8 \\ 0.9\ \ 0.13\,0.94\ \ 0.8\ \ 0.85\,0.06\ \ 0.2\ \ 0.07 \\ 0.2\ \ 0.34\,0.12\,0.07\,0.27\,0.82\,0.87\,0.94 \\ 0.1\ \ 0.95\,0.82\ \ 0.2\ \ 0.01\,0.18\,0.09\,0.06 \end{bmatrix}$$

We experiment with the 5-round state-recovery attack for Xoodyak in the same method, and the results are shown in Fig. 7. Judging from the barely satisfactory results, several populations quickly fall into the local optimum, and sometimes GA cannot find a non-trivial solution. More importantly, under the current parameter settings, GA cannot find a non-trivial solution in most 6-round

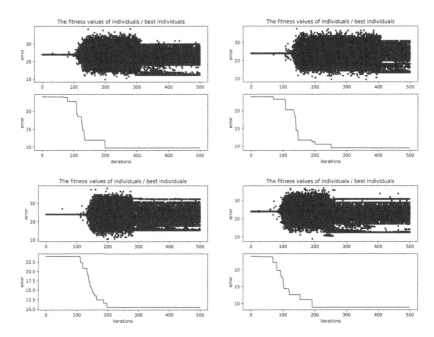

Fig. 6. Parallel search for four optimal feasible solutions of $S_0[48 : 95]$ by GA, whose population size = 500; iterations = 500; mutation rate = 0.0015, took about 40 min on a personal computer equipped with i7-9700K CPU.

experiments, which means that we need to increase the w in $\hat{\oplus}$ further to avoid GA trapping in the local optimum and increase population size to obtain better global search capabilities. However, the increase of w means that the change rate of $\hat{\oplus}$ will be more drastic, which is not conducive to the optimization search of GA, and a larger population size means a larger amount of calculation. Another approach is to extend one round based on the 4-round or 5-round method to achieve the 5-round or 6-round attack without adjusting parameters.

5.2 Extended to 5/6-Round

This section introduces an attack method that expands the number of attack rounds without adjusting parameters. Our goal is to recover the state information of S_1 through the state information of $S_0[0 : 47]$ and $S_r[0 : 47]$. We can set the unknown bits of S_1 as variable x, $S_1[0 : 95] = x[0 : 95]$. Then let $error = \sum_{i=0}^{47} |Xoodoo'^{-1}(S_1)[i] - S_0[i]| + \sum_{i=0}^{47} |Xoodoo'^{(r-1)}(S_1)[i] - S_r[i]|$, which is a function of x. The closer the value of x is to the feasible value of $S_1[0 : 95]$, the lower the $error$. Then, we can design an algorithm similar to Algorithm 1 to guess the true value of S_1, which will not be described in detail here. For $r = 5$, the search process of GA at the first iteration is shown in Fig. 8. Judging results, GA can reduce the $error$ roughly to 26.5 in total and 0.27 on average.

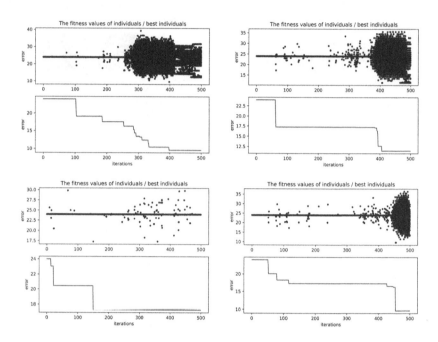

Fig. 7. Experiment results where $r = 5$.

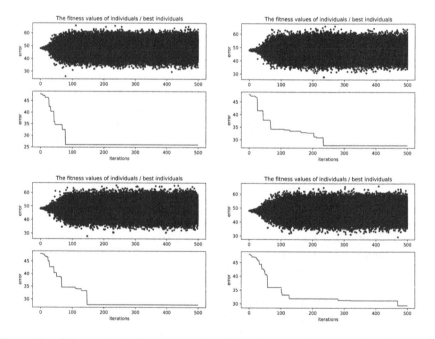

Fig. 8. Parallel search for four optimal feasible solutions of $S_1[0 : 95]$ by GA, whose population size $= 500$; iterations $= 500$; mutation rate $= 0.0015$, took about one hour on a personal computer equipped with i7-9700K CPU.

We experiment with the 6-round state-recovery attack for Xoodyak in the same method, and the results are shown in Fig. 9. GA can reduce the *error* roughly to 28 in total and 0.29 on average.

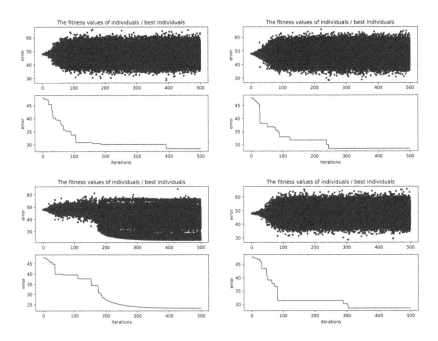

Fig. 9. Experiment results where $r = 6$.

5.3   Attack Against Xoodyak Under the Nonce-Reuse Setting

This section appropriately relaxes the attack conditions, assuming that the attacker can intercept several plaintext-ciphertext pairs generated with the same nonce. With the relaxation of the conditions, the attacker can obtain more information for recovering the unknown state. Specifically, since the same nonce, the Xoodoo state S_0 before absorbing the message is identical. We denote the messages intercepted by the attacker as $(M_0^{(i)}, C_0^{(i)}; M_1^{(i)}, C_1^{(i)})$, $1 \le i \le n$. After absorbing the message, $S_0^{(i)}[48:95]$ remained constant while

$$\begin{cases} S_0^{(1)}[0:47] = M_0^{(1)} \oplus C_0^{(1)} \\ S_0^{(2)}[0:47] = M_0^{(2)} \oplus C_0^{(2)} \\ \quad\vdots \\ S_0^{(n)}[0:47] = M_0^{(n)} \oplus C_0^{(n)} \end{cases} ; \quad \begin{cases} S_r^{(1)}[0:47] = M_1^{(1)} \oplus C_1^{(1)} \\ S_r^{(2)}[0:47] = M_1^{(2)} \oplus C_1^{(2)} \\ \quad\vdots \\ S_r^{(n)}[0:47] = M_1^{(n)} \oplus C_1^{(n)} \end{cases}$$

and attacker's goal is to recover $S_0[48:95]$ based on this information. According to the previous introduction, each plaintext-ciphertext pairs has a feasible solution set of $S_0^{(i)}[48:95]$. The intersection of these sets is the feasible solutions of $S_0[48:95]$ that can satisfy all pairs. We can set the unknown bits of S_0 as variable x, $S_0[48:95] = x[0:47]$. Define $error^{(i)}$ as $\sum_{j=0}^{47} |Xoodoo'^r(S_0^{(i)})[j] - S_r^{(i)}[j]|$, $1 \leq i \leq n$, and $Sum\_error = \sum_{i=1}^{n} error^{(i)}$, which is a function of x. With the assistance of GA, we can find the optimal solutions x that minimizes Sum_error. Then, we can guess the true value of $S_0[48:95]$ based on the information of these solutions.

6   Conclusion

In this paper, we design a heuristic algorithm based on GA for the known-plaintext attack on round-reduced Xoodyak under the nonce-respecting setting and give the experimental results of 4, 5, and 6 rounds. Although our results are far from threatening the security of Xoodyak, they provide new insights into the security analysis of Xoodyak. More importantly, the performance of GA is encouraging, proving that GA can be an approach to analyze cryptographic algorithms in general. However, GA-based cryptanalysis is still in the early stages, needs further research, and more sophisticated attack methods are yet to be developed. Future work amounts to evaluate our model to improve the accuracy; characterize the cryptanalysis problem into a more suitable objective function or a multi-objective optimization task, allowing GA to reach the globally optimized solution; find more suitable parameters to attack higher rounds. In addition, we can apply our method to other AE/AEAD algorithms with a similar structure to Xoodyak and examine whether it can produce better results.

Acknowledgements. The authors thank the anonymous reviewers for their helpful comments and suggestions, the editors for shepherding this final version of the paper. This paper is supported by the National Natural Science Foundation of China (Grants No. 61672330, 62071280, 61802235) and the Natural Science Foundation of Shandong Province (Grants No. ZR2020KF011, ZR2020MF056).

References

1. Aumasson, J.-P., Jovanovic, P., Neves, S.: NORX: parallel and scalable AEAD. In: Kutyłowski, M., Vaidya, J. (eds.) ESORICS 2014. LNCS, vol. 8713, pp. 19–36. Springer, Cham (2014). https://doi.org/10.1007/978-3-319-11212-1_2

2. Bellare, M., Namprempre, C.: Authenticated encryption: relations among notions and analysis of the generic composition paradigm. In: Okamoto, T. (ed.) ASIACRYPT 2000. LNCS, vol. 1976, pp. 531–545. Springer, Heidelberg (2000). https://doi.org/10.1007/3-540-44448-3_41

3. Bertoni, G., Daemen, J., Peeters, M., Van Assche, G.: Keccak. In: Johansson, T., Nguyen, P.Q. (eds.) EUROCRYPT 2013. LNCS, vol. 7881, pp. 313–314. Springer, Heidelberg (2013). https://doi.org/10.1007/978-3-642-38348-9_19

4. Biryukov, A., Khovratovich, D.: PAEQ: parallelizable permutation-based authenticated encryption. In: Chow, S.S.M., Camenisch, J., Hui, L.C.K., Yiu, S.M. (eds.) ISC 2014. LNCS, vol. 8783, pp. 72–89. Springer, Cham (2014). https://doi.org/10.1007/978-3-319-13257-0_5

5. Daemen, J., Hoffert, S., Assche, G.V., Keer, R.V.: The design of Xoodoo and Xoofff. IACR Transactions on Symmetric Cryptology **2018**, 1–38 (2018). https://doi.org/10.13154/tosc.v2018.i4.1-38

6. Daemen, J., Hoffert, S., Peeters, M., Van Assche, G., Van Keer, R.: Xoodyak, a lightweight cryptographic scheme. IACR Transactions on Symmetric Cryptology, pp. 60–87 (2020). https://doi.org/10.13154/tosc.v2020.iS1.60-87

7. Ding, Y., Shi, Y., Wang, A., Wang, Y., Zhang, G.: Block-oriented correlation power analysis with bitwise linear leakage: an artificial intelligence approach based on genetic algorithms. Futur. Gener. Comput. Syst. **106**, 34–42 (2020). https://doi.org/10.1016/j.future.2019.12.046

8. Dobraunig, C., Eichlseder, M., Mendel, F., Schläffer, M.: ASCON v1.2: lightweight Authenticated Encryption and Hashing. J. Cryptol. **34**(3), 1–42 (2021). https://doi.org/10.1007/s00145-021-09398-9

9. Geltink, G.: Concealing KETJE: a lightweight PUF-based privacy preserving authentication protocol. In: Bogdanov, A. (ed.) LightSec 2016. LNCS, vol. 10098, pp. 128–148. Springer, Cham (2017). https://doi.org/10.1007/978-3-319-55714-4_9

10. Gohr, A.: Improving attacks on round-reduced speck32/64 using deep learning. In: Boldyreva, A., Micciancio, D. (eds.) CRYPTO 2019. LNCS, vol. 11693, pp. 150–179. Springer, Cham (2019). https://doi.org/10.1007/978-3-030-26951-7_6

11. Holland, J.H., et al.: Adaptation in Natural and Artificial Systems: An Introductory Analysis with Applications to Biology, Control, and Artificial Intelligence. MIT Press, Cambridge (1992). https://doi.org/10.7551/mitpress/1090.001.0001

12. Hou, B., Li, Y., Zhao, H., Wu, B.: Linear attack on round-reduced DES using deep learning. In: Chen, L., Li, N., Liang, K., Schneider, S. (eds.) ESORICS 2020. LNCS, vol. 12309, pp. 131–145. Springer, Cham (2020). https://doi.org/10.1007/978-3-030-59013-0_7

13. Li, Z., Dong, X., Bi, W., Jia, K., Wang, X., Meier, W.: New conditional cube attack on Keccak keyed modes. IACR Transactions on Symmetric Cryptology, pp. 94–124 (2019). https://doi.org/10.13154/tosc.v2019.i2.94-124

14. Liu, F., Isobe, T., Meier, W., Yang, Z.: Algebraic attacks on round-reduced Keccak/Xoodoo. Cryptology ePrint Archive, Report 2020/346 (2020). https://eprint.iacr.org/2020/346

15. Liu, Y., Sun, S., Li, C.: Rotational cryptanalysis from a differential-linear perspective. In: Canteaut, A., Standaert, F.-X. (eds.) EUROCRYPT 2021. LNCS, vol. 12696, pp. 741–770. Springer, Cham (2021). https://doi.org/10.1007/978-3-030-77870-5_26

16. Morawiecki, P., et al.: ICEPOLE: high-speed, hardware-oriented authenticated encryption. In: Batina, L., Robshaw, M. (eds.) CHES 2014. LNCS, vol. 8731, pp. 392–413. Springer, Heidelberg (2014). https://doi.org/10.1007/978-3-662-44709-3_22

17. Song, L., Guo, J.: Cube-attack-like cryptanalysis of round-reduced Keccak using MILP. IACR Transactions on Symmetric Cryptology, pp. 182–214 (2018). https://doi.org/10.13154/tosc.v2018.i3.182-214

18. Wang, A., Li, Y., Ding, Y., Zhu, L., Wang, Y.: Efficient framework for genetic-algorithm-based correlation power analysis. Cryptology ePrint Archive, Report 2021/179 (2021). https://eprint.iacr.org/2021/179

19. Wetzels, J., Bokslag, W.: Sponges and engines: an introduction to Keccak and Keyak. Cryptology ePrint Archive, Report 2016/028 (2016). https://eprint.iacr.org/2016/028

20. Zhang, Z., Wu, L., Wang, A., Mu, Z., Zhang, X.: A novel bit scalable leakage model based on genetic algorithm. Secur. Commun. Netw. **8**(18), 3896–3905 (2015). https://doi.org/10.1002/sec.1308

21. Zhou, H., Li, Z., Dong, X., Jia, K., Meier, W.: Practical key-recovery attacks on round-reduced Ketje Jr, Xoodoo-AE and Xoodyak. Comput. J. **63**(8), 1231–1246 (2020). https://doi.org/10.1093/comjnl/bxz152

Moving the Bar on Computationally Sound Exclusive-Or

Catherine Meadows[(✉)]

Naval Research Laboratory, Washington DC, USA
`catherine.meadows@nrl.navy.mil`

Abstract. Soundness of symbolic security with respect to computational security was originally investigated from the point of cryptographic protocol design. However, there has been an emerging interest in applying it to the automatic generation and verification of cryptographic algorithms. This creates a challenge, since it requires reasoning about low-level primitives like exclusive-or whose actual behavior may be inconsistent with any possible symbolic behavior.

In this paper we consider symbolic and computational soundness of cryptographic algorithms defined in terms of block ciphers and exclusive-or. We present a class of algorithms in which security is defined in terms of IND\$-CPA-security, that is, security against an adaptive chosen plaintext adversary's distinguishing the output of the cryptosystem from a random string. We develop conditions for symbolic security and show that they imply computational security. As a result of this, we are able to identify a class of cryptosystems to which results such as Unruh's [25] on the impossibility of computationally sound exclusive-or do not apply, in the sense that symbolic security implies computational security against an adaptive adversary. We also show how our results apply to a practical class of cryptosystems: cryptographic modes of operation.

1 Introduction

Symbolic methods have been in use in cryptography for a long time, starting with Dolev and Yao's seminal paper [12], progressing on to powerful crypto protocol analysis tools, and most recently, to methods for the automated generation and analysis of cryptographic algorithms. Ideally, one would like these methods to be sound with respect to some computational model, so that symbolic security implies computational security. Although results in this area exist, it has been found difficult to extend them to certain low-level primitives such as group operations. To the best of my knowledge, it was Unruh [25] who first pointed out the difficulty, using low-level behavior of exclusive-or that can't be captured in a symbolic model.

Such behavior can have a direct effect on security proofs of cryptosystems. For example, many proofs of indistinguishability depend upon proving that the probability of a collision between random functions is negligible. But consider the counter-example below, which is similar, but not identical, to Unruh's.[1]

---

[1] I am grateful to an anonymous reviewer for this example.

© Springer Nature Switzerland AG 2021
E. Bertino et al. (Eds.): ESORICS 2021, LNCS 12973, pp. 275–295, 2021.
https://doi.org/10.1007/978-3-030-88428-4_14

Example 1. Let f be a random function from λ-length bitstrings to λ-length bit-strings (blocks, for short) computed by a challenger, and let $r_0, \ldots, r_m$ be randomly chosen bitstrings. Suppose that the challenger sends $f(r_0), r_1, \ldots, r_{\lambda+1}$ to the adversary, and the adversary returns a subset S of $\{r_1, \ldots r_{\lambda+1}\}$ to the challenger, who returns $f(r_0 \oplus \bigoplus_{r_i \in S} r_i)$, where $\bigoplus_{r_i \in S} r_i$ stands for the exclusive-or of all r_i such that $r_i \in S$. The adversary can never succeed in distinguishing the challenger's output from random in the symbolic model, since each term sent by the challenger is a different term standing for a different randomly generated bitstring. However, in the computational model the set of λ-bit strings is the vector space $\mathbb{Z}_2^\lambda$, and so no set of $m > \lambda$ bitstrings can be linearly independent modulo $\oplus$. Thus there is a subset S of $r_1, \ldots, r_m$ such that $\bigoplus_{r_i \in S} r_i = 0^\lambda$, which the adversary can find via Gaussian elimination. It can then send S to the challenger, which computes $f(r_0 \oplus \bigoplus_{r_i \in S} r_i) = f(r_0)$ and returns it to the adversary. In this way the adversary can force the first and last bitstrings sent by the challenger to be equal, and so its output is distinguishable from random.

One important feature of this counterexample is that the adversary is given all the information it needs in order to make its choice. If it was not shown any of the bitstrings before the final response from the encryptor, it would not know which subset would result in a collision with $f(r_0)$. Thus, for any subset it chose, the probability of a collision would be $2^{-\lambda}$. In some cases it may not be practical to deprive the adversary of adaptive choice altogether, but it may be possible to limit it so that its contribution to the adversary's advantage is negligible. For example, we can limit the adversary's choice of functions that it can compute. Consider the case in which the adversary is limited to choosing, instead of any subset of $r_1, \ldots, r_m$, one of a polynomial number $q(\lambda)$ of subsets of $r_1, \ldots, r_m$. In this case, the probability of a collision between $f(r_0)$ and $f(r_0 \oplus \bigoplus_{r_i \in S} r_i)$, for some S chosen by the adversary, would be bounded by $q(\lambda) \cdot 2^{-\lambda}$, a negligible function of λ. In this paper we will consider cryptosystems that impose a stronger condition on the adversary, in which not only adaptive choice, but any choice, is limited. For the purposes of this paper, it has the advantage that, not only it is simpler to reason about, but, as we shall see, there are non-trivial classes of cryptosystems that have this property. To the best of my knowledge this feature of a cryptosystem does not have a specific name; we shall call it *polynomially bounded execution choice* (PBEC). We will define this more formally later on.

Consider the following example: the cryptographic mode of operation Cipher Block Chaining.

Example 2 (Cipher Block Chaining (CBC)). Let E be a block cipher, and let $f = E_K$ denote encryption with E using a key K. The input to the algorithms is a sequence x_1 through x_n of plaintext blocks, and the output is a list of ciphertext blocks $C_0, \ldots, C_n$ returned only after all plaintext blocks are received:

1. $C_0 = r$, where r is a randomly generated block known as an *initialization vector* (IV), and;
2. $C_i = f(x_i \oplus C_{i-1})$ for $i > 0$.

Suppose that f is indistinguishable from a random function. Suppose also that the number of different terms $f(s)$ and r_i that the adversary can request the encryptor to compute is bounded by a polynomial in λ. Thus the maximum number of messages and the maximum length of a message must also be polynomially bounded, say by $p_1(\lambda)$ and $p_2(\lambda)$ respectively. It follows that the set of all terms that the adversary could possibly request the encryptor to compute is contained in the set $D_0 = \{r_i \mid 1 \leq i \leq p_1(\lambda)\} \cup D_1 = \{f(C_{i,j-1} \oplus x_{i,j}) \mid (1 \leq i \leq p_1) \wedge (1 \leq j \leq p_2(\lambda) - 1)\}$, where $C_{i,j}$ (respectively $x_{i,j}$) denotes the i'th ciphertext (respectively, plaintext) block in the j'th message. The cardinality of this set is $p_1(\lambda) \cdot p_2(\lambda)$, so the probability of a collision is bounded by $p_1(\lambda)^2 \cdot p_2(\lambda)^2 \cdot 2^{-\lambda}$, thus giving us polynomially bounded execution choice.

In the remainder of this paper we describe a class of cryptosystems using the symbols $\mathbf{f}$ for E_K as in Example 2, $\oplus$ for bitwise exclusive-or, a set $\mathbf{R}$ of bound variables r standing for random bitstrings, and a set of free variables $\mathbf{X}$ standing for blocks of adversarial input. A *symbolic history* of such a cryptosystem describes a sequence in which an adversary sends plaintext blocks to an encryptor and gets encrypted blocks in return. However, in a symbolic history the plaintext blocks are replaced by free variables, and the ciphertext blocks are replaced by symbolic terms that serve as recipes for computing the ciphertext blocks, with the free variables standing as placeholders for the plaintext. We show that such a cryptosystem satisfies IND\$-CPA-security (essentially, indistinguishability from random against an adaptive chosen plaintext adversary) if the following hold:

1. Nondegeneracy: There is no subset of terms sent in any symbolic history $\mathbf{H}$ whose elements $\oplus$-sum to zero.
2. Safety: There are no two subterms $\mathbf{f(s)}$ and $\mathbf{f(t)}$ of terms sent in any symbolic history $\mathbf{H}$ such that the normal form of $\mathbf{s} \oplus \mathbf{t}$ is $\mathbf{x} \oplus \mathbf{u}$ and $\mathbf{u}$ can be derived by $\oplus$-summing terms received by the adversary before it sends $\mathbf{x}$.
3. Polynomially bounded execution choice.

The rest of this paper is organized as follows. In Sect. 2 we give background and related work. We give symbolic preliminaries necessary for understanding the paper in Sect. 3. We describe our symbolic and computational models in Sect. 4 and give a precise statement of our main theorem sketched above. In Sect. 5 we prove the theorem. In Section 6 we describe some applications to cryptographic modes of operation. In Sect. 7 we conclude and discuss future work.

2   Background and Related Work

Probably the earliest work on proving computational soundness and completeness of symbolic methods for cryptographic proofs of security for protocols is that of Abadi and Rogaway in [2], against passive attackers. Shortly afterword, Backes et al. [4] and Micciancio and Warinschi [24] separately proved soundness and completeness of a symbolic model including a full Dolev-Yao adversary that interacts with principals over a network it completely controls. This work and the work that followed tended to avoid equational theories (e.g. $\mathbf{d}(\mathbf{e}(\mathbf{k}, \mathbf{m})) = \mathbf{m}$) as much as possible, relying instead on derivation rules (e.g. $\mathbf{k}, \mathbf{e}(\mathbf{d}, \mathbf{m}) \vdash \mathbf{m}$). These are equally expressive, as long as you can rely on the cryptographic mechanisms to rule out ill-formed terms such as $\mathbf{d}(\mathbf{k}, \mathbf{m})$. Moreover, since well-designed protocols generally outlaw such ill-formed terms, this is a reasonable restriction. Appropriate abstractions have even been found for more equationally rich algorithms such as Diffie-Hellman [9]. But it is harder to distinguish ill-formed terms for exclusive-or, since $\oplus$ is self-cancelling. Unruh's and others' examples give evidence that including the $\oplus$ theory in such systems may be problematic.

In spite of these issues, some progress has been made on computational soundness of symbolic models with equational theories. In [7] Baudet et al. develop computational implementations of equational theories for which soundness can be proved assuming a passive adversary, thus avoiding Unruh's counter-example. In [20] Kremer and Mazaré extend this to a computationally sound implementation of static equivalence (a symbolic analogue of indistinguishability) against an adversary that can adaptively request the encryptor to send members of a set of pre-defined message. We note, however, that Example 1 is secure according to their computational definition of static equivalence. This is not because of any fault in their computational realization. Rather, it is because static equivalence itself, which is expressed in terms of conditions on possible histories of message exchanges, does not fully capture the abilities of an adaptive adversary.

In the meantime, work has been ongoing on developing symbolic methods for reasoning about cryptoalgorithms that use exclusive-or and other Abelian group theories, much of it motivated by recent interest in the automatic generation and verification of cryptoalgorithms. In this approach, multiple instances of a particular class of algorithms (e.g. cryptographic modes of operation [17,22], garbled circuit schemes [11], collision-resistant hash functions [23], padding-based public key encryption algorithms [6]) are generated, usually automatically, and then checked for security and other desirable properties. Because a large number of candidate cryptosystems are generated, the verification techniques must be efficient. Symbolic verification of cryptosystems can often be easily automated, so symbolic verification techniques that can be proved sound and/or complete with respect to a computational model of security have become of more interest. Interestingly, many of the cryptosystems to which this automatic generation and verification approach have been applied involve exclusive-or or other types of group operations. However, these techniques tend to be applied to specific classes of algorithms, so general soundness and completeness results have not been as important. Indeed, we note that many of the cryptosystems have similar restrictions on the adversary; for example the modes of operation in [17,22] are PBEC, and the adversary in [11] is honest-but-curious.

We also discuss some related work on the symbolic design and analysis of cryptographic modes of operation. Gagné et al. [14] have developed a Hoare logic for proving semantic security of block cipher modes of encryption, and a program implementing the logic that can be used to automatically prove their security. However, their work concentrates on heuristically driven theorem proving techniques rather than on evaluating symbolic security conditions. We also note the work of Bard [5], who considers circumstances under which security for modes of encryption can be reduced to a collision-freeness property. Although [5] does not address symbolic security directly, our approach to deriving criteria for collision-freeness owes much to it. The work of Malezomoff et al. [22] and Hoang et al. [17] is probably the closest to that in this paper. They prove adaptive chosen plaintext security for cryptographic modes of operation based on deterministic block ciphers [22] and authenticated modes of encryption using block ciphers with tweaks [17] by defining a set of symbolic conditions checked on automatically generated modes using a messagewise schedule, in which the encryptor delays returning ciphertext until it has received all plaintext blocks, and they prove these conditions sufficient for security. The results in this paper extend the results of [22] to sufficient symbolic conditions for arbitrary schedules.

3   Symbolic Preliminaries

In this section we give definitions and results term in term algebras and unification used in this paper. Readers interested in a more in-depth discussion may find it in Baader and Nipkow's book *Term Rewriting and All That* [3].

A *signature* is a finite set of function symbols Σ of different arities. We write $\mathcal{T}_\Sigma(\mathcal{X})$ for the set of all terms constructed using function symbols from Σ and variables from a countable infinite set $\mathcal{X}$. $\mathcal{T}_\Sigma(\mathcal{X})$ is referred to as a *term algebra*. If $\mathbf{T} \subseteq \mathcal{T}_\Sigma(\mathcal{X})$, we write $Sub(\mathbf{T})$ for the set of subterms of elements of $\mathbf{T}$. [2] Thus, if $\mathbf{T} = \{\mathbf{f(g(x), a), h(f(a, b))}\}$, $Sub(\mathbf{T}) = \{\mathbf{f(g(x), a), g(x), a, x, h(f(a, b)), f(a, b), b}\}$. The set $\mathcal{X}$ is divided into a countable set of *names* bound by a quantifier ν and a countable set of free variables. We write $Var(\mathbf{t})$ (respectively $bv(\mathbf{t})$, $fv(\mathbf{t})$) for the set of variables (respectively, bound variables, free variables) present in a term $\mathbf{t}$. We say that a term is *ground* if it contains only function symbols and bound variables.

A Σ-*equation* is a pair $\mathbf{t} = \mathbf{t}'$. where $\mathbf{t}, \mathbf{t}' \in \mathcal{T}_\Sigma(\mathcal{X})$. A set E of Σ-equations induces a congruence relation $=_E$ on terms $\mathbf{t}, \mathbf{t}' \in \mathcal{T}_\Sigma(\mathcal{X})$, so that $\mathbf{t} =_E \mathbf{t}'$ if and only if $\mathbf{t}$ can be made equal to $\mathbf{t}'$ via applications of equations from E. An *equational theory* is a pair (Σ, E), where Σ is a signature and E a set of Σ-equations. We will refer to a term algebra $\mathcal{T}_\Sigma(\mathcal{X})$ together with an equational theory (Σ, E) as $(\mathcal{T}_\Sigma(\mathcal{X}), E)$. For example, suppose $\Sigma = \{\mathbf{d}/2, \mathbf{e}/2, \mathbf{k}/0, \mathbf{a}/0\}$, and $E = \{\mathbf{d(x, e(x, y))} = \mathbf{y}\}$. Then $\mathbf{e(k, d(k, e(k, a)))} =_\mathbf{E} \mathbf{e(k, a)}$, by setting $\mathbf{x} = \mathbf{k}$ and $\mathbf{y} = \mathbf{a}$ in the equation $\mathbf{d(x, e(x, y))} = \mathbf{y}$.

A *substitution* σ is a mapping from free variables to $\mathcal{T}_\Sigma(\mathcal{X})$ that is the identity on all but a finite subset of the free variables known as the *domain* of σ. Substitutions are homomorphically extended to $\mathcal{T}_\Sigma(\mathcal{X})$. Application of σ to a term $\mathbf{t}$ is denoted by $\sigma \mathbf{t}$. The composition of two substitutions is $\sigma\theta \mathbf{t} = \sigma(\theta \mathbf{t})$. A substitution σ is an E-*unifier* of a system of equations $\mathbf{S} = \{\ldots, \mathbf{s_i} =^? \mathbf{t_i}. \ldots\}$ if

---

[2] We write symbolic terms in **bold** and computational terms in *italic* to make it easier to distinguish between the two.

$\sigma s_i =_E \sigma t_i$ for every $s_i =^? t_j \in S$. For example, consider $S = \{w =^? e^{-1}(k, z)\}$ over the algebra $(\mathcal{T}_\Sigma(\mathcal{X}), \{e^{-1}(x, e(x, y)) = y\})$ described in the previous paragraph. Then the substitutions $\sigma_1 : w \mapsto e^{-1}(k, z)$ and $\sigma_2 : z \mapsto e(k, w)$ are both unifiers of S modulo E. We will be interested in the algebra whose signature is the free unary symbol f plus an exclusive-or operator $\oplus$ and a null operator 0. We say that a term is f-*rooted* if it is of the form $f(s)$ for some term s. The $\oplus$ operator is associative and commutative and satisfies $X \oplus 0 = 0$ and $X \oplus X = 0$. Equality of two terms modulo this theory is equivalent to equality under the theory $(R_\oplus \uplus AC)$ where AC is the associative and commutative rules for $\oplus$, and $R_\oplus$ is a set of *rewrite rules*, $\{X \oplus 0 \to X,\ X \oplus X \to\ 0,\ X \oplus (X \oplus Y) \to Y\}$ oriented from left to right. A rewrite rule $\ell \to r$ is applied to a term t by first finding a subterm s of t such that $s = \sigma\ell$ modulo AC for some substitution σ, and then replacing s in t with $\sigma\ell$. Thus $0 \oplus a \oplus b$ can be reduced to $a \oplus b$ by noting that $0 \oplus a \oplus b = (0 \oplus a) \oplus b = \sigma\ell \oplus b$ modulo AC, where ℓ is the left-hand side of $X \oplus 0 \to X$, and $\sigma X = a$. In addition, every term t reduces after a finite number of steps to a *normal form* $\downarrow_\oplus t$ to which no further rewrite rules can be applied, and this normal form is unique up to AC-equivalence. We refer to $(R_\oplus \uplus AC)$ as the $\oplus$ theory for brevity, and use $\mathcal{T}_{(\Sigma_f, \oplus)}(\mathcal{X})$ to refer to the term algebra with signature $\{f/1, \oplus/2, 0/0\}$ and equational theory $\oplus$.

4   Symbolic and Computational Models

In this section we give a brief description of how we model the relationship between symbolic terms and computational functions. This is based on the abstract and concrete models of cryptosystems introduced by Baudet et al. in [7], with the main difference being that we allow free variables in the symbolic model to be replaced in the computational model by the output of Turing machines, instead of restricting ourselves to concrete computational representations of symbolic terms.

4.1   The Computational Model

We begin by giving a definition of IND\$-CPA security below. It uses the assumption that a block cipher is a member of a family of pseudorandom permutations index by a key K.

Definition 1. *Let $\mathcal{E}$ be a cryptosystem built using a keyed pseudorandom permutation from λ-length blocks to λ-length blocks. Let K be a key chosen uniformly at random. Suppose that a challenger, by flipping a coin, chooses either an encryption oracle that computes $\mathcal{E}_K$ on input from an adversary or a \$-oracle that returns a uniformly randomly chosen bitstring of the same length as the encryption oracle's response. The adversary is then allowed multiple queries to the oracle, and at the end of the game it outputs a bit. We say that $\mathcal{A}^{\mathcal{E}_K}(1^\lambda) = 1$ if the adversary outputs 1 after interacting with the encryption oracle, and $\mathcal{A}^\$(1^\lambda) = 1$*

if the adversary outputs 1 after interacting with the \$-oracle. We define the adversary's advantage to be

$$|Pr(K \xrightarrow{\$} Key; \mathcal{A}^{\mathcal{E}_K}(1^\lambda) = 1) - Pr(\mathcal{A}^\$(1^\lambda) = 1)|$$

We say that $\mathcal{E}$ is IND\$-CPA *secure if there is a negligible function τ of λ such that the advantage of any PPT adversary is bounded by $\tau(\lambda)$.*

4.2   Relationship Between Computational and Symbolic Models

We use the construction of Baudet et al. [7] as the basis for ours. Let λ be a security parameter. Each sequence of n ground terms $\mathbf{T} \subset \mathcal{T}_{(\mathbf{\Sigma}, \oplus)}(\mathcal{X})$ determines a probability distribution T_λ over $\{0, 1\}^{\lambda \cdot n}$ called the *computational realization T_λ of* $\mathbf{T}$. This is defined as follows: To compute the output of a bound variable $\mathbf{r}$, we choose a λ-length bitstring uniformly at random. If $\mathbf{r}$ occurs more than once in $\mathbf{T}$, it is replaced with the same random λ-length bitstring wherever it occurs. We also replace 0 by a bitstring of λ zeroes, $\oplus$ by bitwise exclusive-or on λ-length bitstrings, and f by a keyed pseudorandom permutation. Each time the recipe defined above is followed, it will produce an $n \cdot \lambda$-length bitstring sampled from the distribution T_λ, called an *output* of T and denoted by $[\![T]\!]_\lambda$. This is an abuse of notation, since T may have many possible outputs, but in general we will use $[\![T]\!]_\lambda$ to mean "the output just produced by T", so which output is meant should be clear. In addition, when we can do so without confusion, we will drop the λ.

We expand on [7] to consider the case where $\mathbf{T}$ contains free variables. Free variables play a special role: they are place holders for inputs to a term. In our case they will always stand for inputs from the adversary. In particular, the free variables $\mathbf{x}_1, \ldots \mathbf{x}_\ell$ appearing in $\mathbf{T}$ stand for inputs supplied to the computational realization T of $\mathbf{T}$ by $\theta_1, \ldots, \theta_\ell$ where each θ_i is a suite of $\theta_{i,\lambda}$ programs run by the adversary, whose input is the adversary's state, that supply λ-bit blocks used as input to T_λ. Note that we do not require that the θ_i themselves be computational realizations of elements of $\mathcal{T}_{(\Sigma, \oplus)}(\mathcal{X})$; they can be arbitrary probabilistic polynomial-time Turing machines. We call a map θ that maps a finite set of variables of $\mathcal{T}_{(\Sigma, \oplus)}(\mathcal{X})$ to such programs and is the identity on all other variables a *computational substitution*. If θ is a computational substitution, and $\mathbf{T}$ is a finite subset of $\mathcal{T}_{(\Sigma, \oplus)}(\mathcal{X})$, we define $\theta\mathbf{T}$ to be the substitution obtained by replacing each variable x used by the computational functions in T with θx. The composition of two computational substitutions is defined in the natural way.

If a θ is a computational substitution to t we define $[\![\theta t]\!]$ to be the output obtained from t by using $[\![\theta x]\!]$ wherever a free variable $\mathbf{x}$ appears in $\mathbf{t}$.

4.3 $MOO_\oplus$ Cryptosystems and Symbolic Histories

A *symbolic $MOO_\oplus$ history*[3] (symbolic history for short) gives a recipe for constructing a sequence of messages exchanged between an adversary and an encryp-

---

[3] The term comes from"mode of operation".

tor. The adversary's input to the encryptor is represented by free variables, where each free variable sent by the adversary is unique. The encryptor's output to an adversary is a sequence of $\mathcal{T}_{(\Sigma_f, \oplus)}(\mathcal{X})$ terms representing computations on input from the adversary, whose free variables are limited to variables previously received from the adversary in the history. $MOO_\oplus$ histories are analogous to the *frames* defined by Abadi and Fournet [1]; that is, they represent records of protocol executions.[4]

To give an example of a symbolic history, we consider the case, using cipher block chaining, in which an adversary interacts with an encryptor that allows it to encrypt two messages in parallel, timing its response so that the adversary receives the two IVs first, and the two first blocks of ciphertext right after sending the two first blocks of plaintext:

$$\nu r_1.\nu r_2[r_1, r_2.x_1.x_2.f(r_1 \oplus x_1).f(r_2 \oplus x_2)]$$

A $MOO_\oplus$ *program* specifies the possible interactions between the adversary and the encryptor. A $MOO_\oplus$ program is a program of bounded size that specifies 1) the encryptor's schedule for receiving input and sending output and 2) what terms the adversary can request the encryptor to evaluate and when.

Since the adversary in the IND\$-CPA game is polynomially bounded, there is a polynomial function p of the security parameter λ such that the number of blocks it can send and receive is bounded by $p(\lambda)$. This means that, for any symbolic history $\mathbf{H}$, a concrete adversary using security parameter λ can execute $\mathbf{H}$ as long as $length(\mathbf{H}) \leq p(\lambda)$. Thus, for every history $\mathbf{H}$, there is an infinite set $V_\mathbf{H}$ of values λ of the security parameter (namely, all (λ such that $length(\mathbf{H}) \leq p(\lambda)$)) such that the adversary can interact with H_λ. Moreover, if $\mathbf{H}'$ extends $\mathbf{H}$, then $V_{\mathbf{H}'} \subseteq V_\mathbf{H}$. This makes it possible to allow arbitrarily long histories in the symbolic model.

5 $MOO_\oplus$ Games and Security Proofs

In this section we define a sequence of games and use them to prove our main result: that if a $MOO_\oplus$ -cryptosystem satisfies PBEC, then there are symbolic conditions that imply IND\$-CPA security.

There are four such games, described in Section Sect. 5.1: G_{crypt}, in which f is a pseudorandom permutation, G_{rperm}, where f is a random permutation of strings, G_{rstr}, where f is a random function from λ-length strings to λ-length strings, and G_{rsymb} in which f is a random function from symbolic terms to λ-length blocks. We also show that the output of G_{rsymb} is random as long as the cryptosystem is nondegenerate, and then show via game transformations that G_{rstr} and G_{rsymb} are identical up to *bad*, where the *bad* event is a collision between the input of any two f-rooted terms computed by the encryptor.

---

[4] We could indeed define histories as frames, but since in this work we have no need of the main feature of frames (that they are substitutions) we choose a simpler option.

In Sect. 5.2 we formally define the symbolic conditions, and show that, as long as the cryptosystem satisfies PBEC, then the probability of *bad* is negligible. We then use these results to derive security criteria for cryptographic modes of operation.

5.1 $MOO_\oplus$ Games G_{rstr} and G_{rsymb}

We begin by defining the games. We note that all four games are identical except for the method used to compute f. We will thus begin by describing a generic game G_{gen} which can be instantiated to any of the four games by choosing the appropriate method for computing f. Moreover, since the adversary's the advantage in distinguishing between G_{crypt}, G_{rperm}, and G_{rstr} can be estimated by assumption or known results from the literature, we will only describe in detail how f is computed in G_{rstr} and G_{rsymb}

G_{gen} proceeds in a series of steps. In each step the adversary sends the encryptor a sequence of symbolic terms **I.O** and a set of λ-length bitstrings B, such that **I** is a (possibly empty) sequence of free variables $\mathbf{x_1}.\ \ldots\ .\mathbf{x_n}$, **O** is a sequence of terms, and **B** is a sequence of bitstrings $b_1 \ldots b_n$ such that $b_i = [\![\sigma x_i]\!]$, where σ is the substitution computed by the adversary. The encryptor checks whether the adversary is able to submit a request at this point, and if so, if this is a legal request to submit. If it is not, the game is aborted. If the request is valid, the encryptor returns the encrypted blocks specified by **O**.

We now describe how the encryptors in G_{rstr} and G_{rsymb} work. In the following, we say "the encryptor" when both encryptors behave the same way. Otherwise we identify the encryptor as a G_{rstr} or a G_{rsymb} encryptor.

The encryptor maintains a symbolic history **H** describing its interaction with the adversary so far, as well as two databases that describe the output $[\![\sigma H]\!]$. The first database, DBI, stores the plaintext blocks sent by the adversary and the second, DBO, stores results of the random functions computed by the encryptor.

DBI consists of tuples of the form $[\mathbf{x}, [\![\sigma x]\!]]$, where $\mathbf{x}$ is a free variable, and $[\![\sigma x]\!]$ is the output of σx, where σ is the substitution computed by the adversary. DBO contains two types of tuples. The first are of the form $[\mathbf{r}, outstr]$, where $\mathbf{r}$ is a bound variable and $outstr$ is $[\![r]\!]$. The second are of the form $[instr, \mathbf{F}, outstr]$, where $\mathbf{F}$ is a set of **f**-rooted terms, and $instr$ and $outstr$ are λ-length bitstrings. The entries in this form of tuple are computed differently in G_{rstr} and G_{rsymb}. At the beginning, **H**, DBO and DBI are all empty. They are extended by the encryptor as the protocol evolves.

We now describe the computations made by the encryptors. Suppose that an encryptor, whether in G_{rstr} or G_{rsymb}, receives an input $[\![\sigma I]\!]$ from the adversary and is required to return $[\![\sigma O]\!]$. It performs the following steps for each variable or **f**-rooted term $\mathbf{t} = \mathbf{f}(\mathbf{s}) \in Sub(\mathbf{O})$ that has not been computed already, computing each bitstring $[\![\sigma s]\!]$ such that $\mathbf{s}$ is a proper subterm of $\mathbf{t}$ before computing $[\![\sigma t]\!]$.

1. If $\mathbf{I} = \mathbf{x_1}, \ldots, \mathbf{x_k}$, where the $\mathbf{x_i}$ are free variables, it stores $[\mathbf{x_i}, [\![\sigma x_i]\!]]$ in DBI.
2. For any bound variable $\mathbf{r} \in Sub(\mathbf{O})$ such that there is no tuple $[\mathbf{r}, str]$ in DBO, it chooses a λ-length bitstring str' uniformly at random and stores $[\mathbf{r}, str']$ in DBO.
3. For each $\mathbf{f(t)} \in Sub(\mathbf{O})$ such that there is not already a tuple $[a, \mathbf{W}, b]$ in DBO with $\mathbf{f(t)} \in \mathbf{W}$, the encryptor computes $instr$ using the outputs stored in DBI and DBO. That is, if

$$\mathbf{t} = \left(\bigoplus_{i=0}^{m} \oplus \alpha_i \mathbf{x_i}\right) \oplus \left(\bigoplus_{i=1}^{n} \oplus \beta_i \mathbf{r_i}\right) \oplus \left(\bigoplus_{i=1}^{q} \oplus \gamma_i \mathbf{f(s_i)}\right)$$

where the α_i, β_i, and γ_i are booleans, then for each $\alpha_i \neq \mathbf{0}$ (respectively, $\beta_i \neq \mathbf{0}$, $\gamma_i \neq \mathbf{0}$) the encryptor finds the tuple $[\mathbf{x_i}, [\![\sigma x_i]\!]] \in DBI$ (respectively, $[\mathbf{r_i}, [\![r_i]\!]] \in DBO$, $[instr, \mathbf{W}, outstr] \in DBO$ such that $\mathbf{f(s_i)} \in \mathbf{W}$), and computes the $\oplus$-sum of the final bitstrings of the tuples found. The result is bitstring $instr_0$ that will be used as the input to f.
4. If there is already a tuple $[instr, \mathbf{F}, outstr] \in DBO$ such that $\mathbf{f(t)} \in \mathbf{F}$ then the encryptor takes no action. If not, G_{rstr} and G_{rsymb} differ as follows:
   (a) If there is already a tuple $[instr_1, \mathbf{F}, outstr_1] \in DBO$ such that $instr_0 - instr_1$, the G_{rstr} encryptor replaces it with $[instr_1, \mathbf{F} \cup \{\mathbf{f(t)}\}, outstr_1]$. Otherwise, it picks a random λ-length bitstring $outstr_0$ and stores the tuple $[instr_0, \{\mathbf{f(t)}\}, outstr_0]$ in DBO. $\sigma f(t)$ is defined to be $outstr_0$.
   (b) The G_{rsymb} encryptor picks a random λ-length bitstring $outstr_0$ and stores $[instr_0, \{\mathbf{f(t)}\}, outstr_0]$ in DBO. $\sigma f(t)$ is defined to be $outstr_0$.
5. The encryptor uses the output values stored in DBI and DBO to construct $[\![\sigma O]\!]$, and returns it to the adversary.

A pseudocode description of the top-level algorithm is given in Algorithm 1. Descriptions of the two implementations of f are given in Algorithms 2 and 3. Both of these make use of the subroutine given in Algorithm 4.

We note that the entire tuple $[instr, \mathbf{F}, outstr]$ is not necessary to compute f in either G_{rstr} or G_{rsymb}. G_{rstr} does not need the second entry in the tuple, and G_{rsymb} does not need the first. Their only purpose is to reduce the number of steps needed to transform the two games in a pair of identical-until-bad games. We make the real dependencies of these functions explicit in the following lemma.

Lemma 1. *Let f_{rstr} denote the function defined by $f_{rstr}(instr) = outstr$ if $[instr, \mathbf{F}, outstr] \in DBO$ in G_{rstr}, and let f_{rsymb} denote the function defined by $f_{rsymb}(\mathbf{f(t)}) = outstr$ if $[instr, \{\mathbf{f(t)}\}, outstr] \in DBO$ in G_{rsymb}. Then f_{rstr} is a random function from λ-bit strings to λ-bit strings, and f_{rsymb} is a random function from $\mathbf{f}$-rooted terms in $\mathbf{H}$ to λ-bit strings.*

Proof. This follows directly from the fact that, in the case of G_{rstr}, $outstr$ is chosen at uniformly at random when and only when a tuple $[instr, \mathbf{f(t)}, \_]$ needs to be added to DBO for a new string $instr$, and in the case of G_{rsymb}, $outstr$ is chosen uniformly at random when and only when a tuple $[instr, \{\mathbf{f(t)}\}, \_]$ is added to DBO for a new $\mathbf{f}$-rooted term $\mathbf{f(t)}$. □

Algorithm 1. G_{gen}

1: ... Begin Setup ... $K \xleftarrow{\$} \{0,1\}^{\lambda}$ ... End Setup ...
2: Freevar, Bdvar $\subset$ Term
3: Integer: i, n, λ ; String: $instr, outstr$; Term: $\mathbf{x}, \mathbf{t}, \mathbf{s}, \mathbf{u}, \mathbf{v}$; Set_of_Records: DBI, DBO, a, a_0; Boolean: $b, b', STOP$; Freevar: $\mathbf{x}, \mathbf{x_i}$, Bdvar: $, \mathbf{r}, \mathbf{r_i}$; Seq_of_Terms: $\mathbf{U_1}, \mathbf{U_2}, \mathbf{O}, \mathbf{O'}, \mathbf{H}, \mathbf{W}$; Seq_of_Freevars: $\mathbf{I}$
4: $DBI, DBO \leftarrow \emptyset$; $\mathbf{H} \leftarrow []$; $i \leftarrow 0$; $b \leftarrow 0$; $STOP \leftarrow 0$
5: $a \leftarrow \emptyset$ {a is the information the encryptor has sent to the adversary}
6: **while** $STOP \neq 1$ **do**
7:    $i \leftarrow i + 1$; $[\mathbf{I.O}] \leftarrow \mathcal{A}(1^{\lambda}, a)$ {Adversary picks next tuple to execute}
       {Below, encryptor checks that adversary's request is valid}
8:    **if** $valid(\mathbf{H}, \mathbf{I.O})$ **then**
9:       $\mathbf{H} \leftarrow \mathbf{H.I.O}$
10:      **while** $\mathbf{I} = \mathbf{x.I'}$ **do**
11:         $outstr \leftarrow \mathcal{A}(1^{\lambda}, a)$ {Adversary sends plaintext block to encryptor}
12:         $DBI \leftarrow DBI \cup \{[\mathbf{x}, outstr]\}$ {Encryptor stores plaintext block in DBI}
13:         $\mathbf{I} \leftarrow \mathbf{I'}$
14:      **end while**
15:      $\mathbf{U_1} \leftarrow$ set of all bound variables in $sub(\mathbf{O})$ not yet computed
16:      $\mathbf{U_2} \leftarrow$ set of all f-rooted terms in $sub(\mathbf{O})$ not yet computed
17:      **while** $\mathbf{U_1} \neq \emptyset$ **do**
18:         Choose $\mathbf{r} \in \mathbf{U_1}$; $outstr \xleftarrow{\$} \{0,1\}^{\lambda}$
19:         $DBO \leftarrow DBO \cup \{[0, \{\mathbf{r}\}, outstr]\}$
20:         $\mathbf{U_1} \leftarrow \mathbf{U_1} \setminus \{\mathbf{r}\}$
21:      **end while**
22:      **while** $\mathbf{U_2} \neq \emptyset$ **do**
23:         Choose a minimal element $\mathbf{f(s)}$ of $\mathbf{U_2}$ in the subterm partial order {We say $\mathbf{u} < \mathbf{v}$ in the subterm partial order if $\mathbf{u}$ is a proper subterm of $\mathbf{v}$.}
24:         $DBO \leftarrow$ Compute-f$(\mathbf{f(s)}, \mathbf{DBO})$
25:         $\mathbf{U_2} \leftarrow \mathbf{U_2} \setminus \{\mathbf{f(s)}\}$
26:      **end while**
27:      **while** $\mathbf{O} = \mathbf{t.O'}$ **do**
28:         $a_0 \leftarrow Construct(\mathbf{t}, DBI \cup DBO)$
29:         $a \leftarrow a.a_0$; $\mathbf{O} \leftarrow \mathbf{O'}$
30:      **end while**
31:   **end if**
32:   $STOP \leftarrow \mathcal{A}(1^{\lambda}, a)$
33: **end while**
34: $b \leftarrow \mathcal{A}(1^{\lambda}, a)$
35: **return** b

Example 3. We can now use the G_{rstr} encryptor to model an attack on CBC when the blockwise schedule is used. In the blockwise schedule, each ciphertext block is sent by the encryptor as soon as it is able to compute it.

1. The adversary sends the encryptor a request for the initialization vector $\mathbf{r_0}$. The encryptor sets $\mathbf{H}$ equal to $\mathbf{r_0}$. The encryptor computes a random bitstring $outstr_0$, stores $[\{\mathbf{r_0}\}, outstr_0]$ in DBO, and sends $outstr_0$ to the adversary.

Algorithm 2. Subroutine Compute-f(f(s), DBI, DBO) (for G_{rstr})

```
1: if ∃[instr, F ∪ {f(s)}, outstr] ∈ DBO then
2:     DBO ← DBO
3: else
4:     instr ← construct(s, DBI, DBO)
5:     if ∃F, outstr₀ s.t. [instr, F, outstr₀] ∈ DBO then
6:         DBO ← (DBO \ {[instr, F, outstr₀]}) ∪ {[instr, {f(s)} ∪ F, outstr₀]}
7:     else
8:         outstr₁ ←$ {0,1}^λ ; DBO ← DBO ∪ {[instr, }{f(s)}, outstr₁]}
9:     end if
10: end if
11: return (DBO)
```

Algorithm 3. Subroutine Compute-f($\mathbf{f(s)}$, DBI, DBO) (for G_{rsymb})

```
1: if ∃[instr, {f(s)}, outstr] ∈ DBO then
2:     DBO ← DBO
3: else
4:     instr ← construct(s, DBI, DBO)
5:     outstr ←$ {0,1}^λ
6:     DBO ← DBO ∪ {[instr, {f(s)}, outstr]}
7: end if
8: return (DBO)
```

Algorithm 4. Subroutine Construct($\mathbf{s}$, $DBI \cup DBO$)

```
1: if s is a free variable x then
2:     Find [x, outstr] ∈ DBI ; c ← outstr
3: else if s is a bound variable r then
4:     Find [0, r, outstr] ∈ DBO ; c ← outstr
5: else if s is an f-rooted term then
6:     Find [instr, F, outstr] ∈ DBO such that s ∈ F; c ← outstr
7: else if s = ⊕ᵏᵢ₌₁ ⊕sᵢ, where each sᵢ is an f-rooted term or a free variable then
8:     outstr ← construct(s₁, DBO) ; c ← outstr ⊕ construct(⊕ᵏᵢ₌₂ ⊕sᵢ, DBO)
9: end if
10: return c
```

2. The adversary computes $\llbracket \sigma x_1 \rrbracket = 0^\lambda$ and sends it to the encryptor, along with $\{x_1\}.\{f(x_1 \oplus r_0)\}$. The encryptor sets $\mathbf{H} = r_0.x_1.f(x_1 \oplus r_0)$. It then stores $[x_1, 0^\lambda]$ in DBI. Next it chooses a random bitstring $outstr_1$ and sets

$$\llbracket \sigma_1 f(x_1 \oplus r_0) \rrbracket = \llbracket f(0 \oplus r_0) \rrbracket = f(outstr_0) = outstr_1$$

and stores $[outstr_0, \{f(x_1 \oplus r_0)\}, outstr_1]$ in DBO. It returns $\llbracket f(r_0) \rrbracket = outstr_1$ to the adversary.

3. The adversary computes $\llbracket \sigma x_2 \rrbracket = \llbracket r_0 \rrbracket \oplus \llbracket f(r_0) \rrbracket = outstr_0 \oplus outstr_1$ and sends it to the encryptor, along with the sequence $x_2.f(x_2 \oplus f(x_1 \oplus r_0))$. $\mathbf{H}$ is updated by the encryptor as before. The encryptor computes the string

---

Algorithm 5. G_{rstr} and G_{rsymb} Algorithm (($\mathbf{f(s)}$, DBI, DBO)

1: **if** $\exists[instr, \mathbf{U} \cup \{\mathbf{f(s)}\}, outstr] \in DBO$ **then**
2:   $DBO \leftarrow DBO$
3: **else**
4:   $\mathbf{W} \leftarrow \emptyset$
5:   $instr \leftarrow construct(\mathbf{s}, DBI, DBO)$
6:   $outstr \xleftarrow{\$} \{0,1\}^{\lambda}$
7:   $outstr_0 \leftarrow outstr$
8:   **if** $\exists \mathbf{F}, outstr_1$ s.t. $[instr, \mathbf{F}, outstr_1] \in DBO$ **then**
9:     $bad \leftarrow 1$
10:     $\underline{outstr_0 \leftarrow outstr_1}$
11:     $\underline{\mathbf{W} \leftarrow \mathbf{F}}$
12:     $\underline{DBO \leftarrow (DBO \setminus \{[instr, \mathbf{F}, outstr_0]\})}$
13:   **end if**
14:   $DBO \leftarrow DBO \cup \{[instr, \mathbf{W} \cup \{\mathbf{f(s)}\}, outstr_0]\}$
15: **end if**
16: **return** (DBO)

$[\![\sigma(x_2 \oplus f(x_1 \oplus r_0))]\!] = [\![r_0]\!] \oplus [\![\ f(r_0)\ ]\!] \oplus [\![\ f(r_0)]\!] = outstr_0 \oplus outstr_1 \oplus outstr_1 = outstr_0$. It finds the tuple $[outstr_0, \{\mathbf{f(x_1 \oplus r_0)}\}, outstr_1]$ in DBO, which it replaces with $[outstr_0, \{\mathbf{f(x_1 \oplus r_0)}, \mathbf{f(x_2 \oplus f(x_1 \oplus r_0))}\}, outstr_1]$, forcing a collision between the inputs to the two $\mathbf{f}$-rooted terms. It then sends $outstr_1$ to the adversary.

We note that such an attack is *not* possible when the G_{rsymb} encryptor is used. In that case the strings returned by the encryptor will be independently randomly generated, since the symbolic terms $\mathbf{r_0}, \mathbf{f(x_1 \oplus r_0)}$ and $\mathbf{f(x_2 \oplus f(x_1 \oplus r_0))}$ are all different. We now give the result that will be needed to prove our main theorem.

Lemma 2. *Algorithms 2 and 3 are equivalent to the identical-until-bad algorithms given in Algorithm 5.*

Proof. We first prove the result for Algorithm 3. Since lines 7 through 11 in Algorithm 5 result in no change once the underlined code is removed, we remove them. Once that is done, $\mathbf{W}$ is always empty, so we can remove line 4 and remove $\mathbf{W}$ from line 12. This gives us Algorithm 3.

For Algorithm 2, we open up a new "else" clause in Algorithm 5 and move statement 6 inside it. This is equivalent to Algorithm 5 because the statement is not used in the first clause. We then note that we can move line 14 inside both clauses of the "if" statement without changing the results. The rest is eliminating unnecessary assignments and variables, giving us Algorithm 2. □

By the fundamental lemma of game-playing [8], the adversary's advantage in distinguishing between the use of the f_{rstr} and f_{rsymb} functions in constructing $\mathbf{H}$ is bounded by the probability that bad is set to 1 in either of them. This only happens when $[\![\sigma u]\!] = [\![\sigma v]\!]$, where $\mathbf{f(u)}$ and $\mathbf{f(v)}$ are subterms of terms returned by the encryptor, so we will concentrate on estimating the probability of this occurring when the f_{rsymb} function is used.

5.2   Conditions Implying IND\$-CPA Security

In this section we define PBEC $MOO_\oplus$ cryptosystems. We also define two symbolic conditions that, together with PBEC, imply IND\$-CPA and use the games described in Sect. 5.1 to show that is the case. We first give some notation:

Definition 2. *Let* $\mathbf{H}$ *be a symbolic history,* $\mathbf{t}$ *a term, and* $\mathbf{x}$ *a free variable.*

1. *We say that* $\mathbf{H} \vdash_\oplus \mathbf{t}$ *if* $\mathbf{t}$ *can be derived by* $\oplus$-*summing a subset of* $\mathbf{H}$.
2. *We define* $\mathbf{H}[\mathbf{x}]$ *to be the sequence of terms exchanged between the adversary and the encryptor before the adversary sends* $\mathbf{x}$, *i.e.* $\mathbf{H} = \mathbf{H}[\mathbf{x}].\mathbf{x}.\mathbf{H}'$, *where* $\mathbf{x} \notin sub(\mathbf{H}[\mathbf{x}])$.
3. *We say that* $\mathbf{x} >_\mathbf{H} \mathbf{u}$ *if* $\mathbf{H}[\mathbf{x}] \vdash_\oplus \mathbf{u}$

Next, we define the two conditions.

Definition 3. *Let* $\mathbf{H}$ *be a symbolic history.*

1. *If* $\mathbf{f}(\mathbf{s})$ *and* $\mathbf{f}(\mathbf{t})$ *are terms in* $sub(\mathbf{H})$, *we say that* $\{\mathbf{f}(\mathbf{s}), \mathbf{f}(\mathbf{t})\}$ *is an* unsafe pair *if there is a free variable* $\mathbf{x}$ *such that* $\downarrow_\oplus (\mathbf{s} \oplus \mathbf{t}) =_{AC} \mathbf{x} \oplus \mathbf{u}$ *for some term* $\mathbf{u}$ *such that* $\mathbf{x} >_\mathbf{H} \mathbf{u}$, *and that* $\{\mathbf{f}(\mathbf{s}), \mathbf{f}(\mathbf{t})\}$ *is a* safe pair *otherwise. We say that a symbolic history is safe if it contains no unsafe pairs, and that it is safe otherwise. Finally, we say that a* $MOO_\oplus$ *program is* safe *if it admits only safe histories, and that it is* unsafe *otherwise.*
2. *We say that a symbolic history* $\mathbf{H}$ *is* degenerate *if there is a subset of* $\mathbf{H}$ *that* $\oplus$-*sums to* 0. *If a* $MOO_\oplus$ *program* $\mathcal{C}$ *admits a degenerate history, we say it is a degenerate program. If not, we say it is non-degenerate.*

Proposition 1. *1. Let* $\{\mathbf{f}(\mathbf{s}), \mathbf{f}(\mathbf{t})\}$ *be an unsafe pair in a symbolic history* $\mathbf{H}$. *Then there is an adversary that can compute a substitution* σ *such that* $[\![\sigma f(s)]\!] = [\![\sigma f(t)]\!]$ *with probability 1.*
2. *No degenerate* $MOO_\oplus$ *program is* IND\$-CPA-*secure.*

Proof. 1. By hypothesis, $\downarrow_\oplus (\mathbf{s} \oplus \mathbf{t}) = \mathbf{x} \oplus \mathbf{u}$, where $\mathbf{x} >_\mathbf{H} \mathbf{u}$. Since $[\![\sigma u]\!]$ has thus already been computed by the time $[\![\sigma x]\!]$ is computed, the adversary can thus choose σx such that $[\![\sigma x]\!] = [\![\sigma u]\!]$.
2. If there is a subset $\mathbf{T}$ of the terms returned by the encryptor in a symbolic history, such that $\sum_{t \in \mathbf{T}} \oplus t =_\oplus 0$, then for any substitution σ computed by the adversary, $\sum_{t \in \mathbf{T}} \oplus [\![\sigma t]\!] = 0$ as well. $\square$

Definition 4. *Let* $\mathcal{C}$ *be a* $MOO_\oplus$ *program. Let* $\mathbb{H}_\mathcal{C}(n)$ *denote the set of all* $\mathcal{C}$ *symbolic histories of length* $\leq n$. *We say that* $\mathcal{C}$ *satisfies* polynomially bounded execution choice *(PBEC) if there is a polynomial* $p(n)$ *such that the number of different* f-*rooted subterms of* $\mathbb{H}_\mathcal{C}(n)$ *is* $\leq p(n)$ *for all* n.

Theorem 1. *Nondegenerate, safe, PBEC, MOO$_\oplus$ programs are* IND\$-CPA *secure.*

Proof. Let $\mathcal{C}$ be a $MOO_\oplus$ cryptosystem. The proof is by game transformation, starting with G_{crypt} (f is a block cipher), followed by G_{perm} (f is a random permutation), G_{rstr}, and then by G_{rsymb}. WLOG we assume that the adversary's computational bounds are the same for all games.

Advantage in Distinguishing G_{crypt} from G_{perm} and G_{perm} from G_{rstr}: By assumption, the adversary's advantage in distinguishing the block cipher from a random permutation is bounded by some negligible quantity ϵ_λ. In addition, it is known [8] that the adversary's advantage in distinguishing G_{perm} from G_{rstr} bounded by $q(\lambda) \cdot (q(\lambda) - 1) \cdot 2^{-\lambda-1}$, where $q(\lambda)$ is the maximum number of times the function f may be computed when the security parameter is λ. The maximum number of blocks exchanged between the adversary and the encryptor is bounded by a polynomial function ℓ of λ, and, $\mathcal{C}$ is PBEC, we have $q(\lambda)$ is bounded by $w(\ell(\lambda))$ where w is a polynomial. Thus $q(\lambda)$ is polynomially bounded, and hence so is $q(\lambda) \cdot (q(\lambda) - 1) \cdot 2^{-\lambda-1}$.

*Probability of a Collision Between Two **f**-rooted terms in G_{rsymb}:* Safety implies that for any pair of terms $\mathbf{f(s)}$ and $\mathbf{f(t)}$, the G_{rsymb} adversary knows nothing about the potential value $[\![\sigma(s \oplus t)]\!]$ at the time it is computing σ on the free variables of $\mathbf{s}$ and $\mathbf{t}$, so $P([\![\sigma(s \oplus t)]\!] = 0)$ for any given $\mathbf{f(s)}$ and $\mathbf{f(t)}$ is $2^{-\lambda}$.

Advantage in distinguishing between G_{rstr} and G_{rsymb} : Suppose that the encryptor has already computed a set $\mathbf{A}$ of $\mathbf{f}$-rooted terms. Let $\mathbf{B}$ be the set of $\mathbf{f}$-rooted terms the adversary can potentially request to be evaluated. By hypothesis $|\mathbf{A}| \leq q(\lambda)$ and $|\mathbf{B}| \leq \ell(\lambda)$, where both are polynomially bounded. The number of possible new collisions offered by $\mathbf{B}$ is $|\mathbf{A}| \cdot |\mathbf{B}| + 1/2 |\mathbf{B}| \cdot (|\mathbf{B}| - 1)$, which is bounded by $q(\lambda) \cdot w(\ell(\lambda)) + \frac{1}{2} \cdot w(\ell(\lambda)) \cdot (w(\ell(\lambda)) - 1)$. Since the adversary has at most $\ell(\lambda)$ opportunities to request evaluated terms from the encryptor, the probability of two input strings being equal is bounded by

$$(\ell(\lambda) \cdot w(\ell(\lambda)) \cdot (q(\lambda) + \frac{1}{2} \cdot (w(\ell(\lambda)) - 1))) \cdot 2^{-\lambda}$$

Summing up the Results: Finally, we recall from Proposition 1 that in the non-degenerate case the output of the G_{rsymb} encryptor is random, so the adversary's advantage in distinguishing the G_{rsymb} encryptor from random is zero. Summing the remaining advantages in the sequences of games, we obtain an advantage of

$$\epsilon(\lambda) + q(\lambda) \cdot (q(\lambda) - 1) \cdot 2^{-\lambda-1} + (\ell(\lambda) \cdot w(\ell(\lambda)) \cdot (q(\lambda) + \frac{1}{2} \cdot (w(\ell(\lambda)) - 1))) \cdot 2^{-\lambda}$$

$\square$

We now finish up with a result on cryptographic modes of operation. Although to the best of my knowledge there is no definition that precisely sets out the properties that modes must have, some conditions that are satisfied by most modes in the literature are given below.

Definition 5. *A MOO$_\oplus$ program is* well-behaved *if it satisfies the following properties:*

1. *The i'th term returned by the encryptor in any message is the i'th iteration of a deterministic recursive function;*
2. *for any single message, ciphertext blocks are returned according to a fixed schedule;*
3. *symbolic histories of different encrypted messages may be interleaved in an arbitrary fashion, and;*
4. *the number of new* **f**-*rooted terms in any term returned by the encryptor is bounded by a constant D.*

Corollary 1. *Any safe, non-degenerate well-behaved MOO$_\oplus$ program is is* IND\$-CPA *secure.*

Proof. By Theorem 1 it is enough to show the program is PBEC, i.e. that for any n the set of f-rooted terms in $\mathbb{H}_\mathcal{C}(n)$ is bounded by a polynomial function of λ.

We call a symbolic history *unary* if it is a history the encryption of a single message, or an initial subsequence of such histories. Consider any length n interleaving of unary symbolic histories. We note that the symbolic terms sent in any such interleaving are the same no matter how the interleaving is done. We also note that at most n unary histories may be interleaved (the bound being achieved when the resulting symbolic history consists of n initial terms), and the length of any symbolic history may be at most n (the bound being achieved when a unary history of length n is used). Thus the number of different f-rooted terms in $\mathbb{H}_\mathcal{C}(n)$ is bounded by $D \cdot n^2$. Since the adversary is PPT, n is bounded by a polynomial function of λ. □

We illustrate these results with an example.

Example 4. Consider Cipher Feedback (CFB) mode, in which $C_0 = r$, and $C_i = f(C_{i-1}) \oplus x_i$ for $i > 0$, where r is a random block. Clearly, CFB is well-behaved. We show that CFB encryption is secure under the *blockwise schedule*, in which ciphertext is sent to the adversary as soon as it is computed. We note that no set of ciphertext terms $\oplus$ sums to 0, so CFB is nondegenerate. We now let $\mathbf{f}(\mathbf{C_{i,j}})$ and $\mathbf{f}(\mathbf{C_{\ell,k}})$ be two different f-rooted terms appearing in a symbolic history **H**, where $\mathbf{C_{i,j}}$ denotes the i'th ciphertext block in the encryption of message j. Without loss of generality we may assume that $\mathbf{f}(\mathbf{C_{i,j}})$ appears after $\mathbf{f}(\mathbf{C_{\ell,k}})$ in **H**. We note that $\mathbf{C_{i,j}} = \mathbf{f}(\mathbf{C_{i-1,j}}) \oplus \mathbf{x_{i,j}}$, and $\mathbf{f}(\mathbf{C_{i-1,j}}) \notin sub(\mathbf{H_{x_{i,j}}})$. Thus, $(\mathbf{f}(\mathbf{C_{i,j}}), f(C_{\ell,k})$ is a safe pair. It follows that CFB is SBN-secure, and hence by from Corollary 1 it is IND\$-CPA secure.

6   Using Our Results to Analyze Modes

In this section we show how the results of this paper can be applied to the analysis of cryptorgraphic modes of operation. We begin by stating and proving some lemmas that allow us decide security by examining properties of single $\mathbf{f}$ rooted terms appearing in a symbolic history instead of properties of pairs of such terms.

Lemma 3. *Suppose that a mode $\mathcal{C}$ admits a history $\mathbf{H}$ containing a term $\mathbf{f}(\mathbf{x} \oplus \mathbf{t})$ where $\mathbf{x} >_\mathbf{H} \mathbf{t}$. Then $\mathcal{C}$ is unsafe. Moreover, if $\mathbf{H} \vdash_\oplus \mathbf{f}(\mathbf{x} \oplus \mathbf{t})$, $\mathcal{C}$ is not* IND\$-CPA.

Proof. Suppose that the first condition of the lemma holds. Then consider an adversary that runs $\mathbf{H}$ followed by $\mathbf{H}'$, where $\mathbf{H}'$ is identical to $\mathbf{H}$ except for different (both bound and unbound) variable names. Let $\mathbf{f}(\mathbf{x}' \oplus \mathbf{t}')$ be the copy of $\mathbf{f}(\mathbf{x} \oplus \mathbf{t})$ computed in $\mathbf{H}'$. Then $\mathbf{x}' >_\mathbf{H} \mathbf{x} \oplus \mathbf{t} \oplus \mathbf{t}'$. If $\mathbf{H} \vdash_\oplus \mathbf{f}(\mathbf{x} \oplus \mathbf{t})$, then the adversary is able to derive $\mathbf{f}(\mathbf{x} \oplus \mathbf{t})$ and $\mathbf{f}(\mathbf{x}' \oplus \mathbf{t}')$ from $\mathbf{H}.\mathbf{H}'$ and is able to both compute the substitution $\sigma x = x' \oplus t \oplus t'$ and observe that $\sigma f(x \oplus t) = \sigma f(x' \oplus t')$, thus distinguishing the two blocks from random. $\square$

Lemma 4. *Let $\mathcal{C}$ be a well-behaved $MOO_\oplus$ program, such that for any $\mathbf{f}(\mathbf{s})$ appearing as a subterm of a term in some symbolic history $\mathbf{H}$, $\mathbf{s}$ has at least one $\mathbf{f}$-rooted or bound variable summand that does not appear in any term sent by the encryptor prior to computing $\mathbf{s}$. Then $\mathcal{C}$ is safe. If it is also non-degenerate, then it is* IND\$-CPA *secure.*

Proof. Suppose $\mathcal{C}$ is not safe. Let $\mathbf{H}$ be an unsafe history, and let $\mathbf{f}(\mathbf{s}), \mathbf{f}(\mathbf{x} \oplus \mathbf{t})$ be the first unsafe pair in $\mathbf{H}$, where $\mathbf{x} >_\mathbf{H} \downarrow_\oplus (\mathbf{s} \oplus \mathbf{t})$. The proofs in the case in which $\mathbf{f}(\mathbf{x} \oplus \mathbf{t})$ is computed after $\mathbf{f}(\mathbf{s})$ and $\mathbf{f}(\mathbf{s})$ is computed after $\mathbf{f}(\mathbf{x} \oplus \mathbf{t})$ are similar, so we prove only the first case. If $\mathbf{f}(\mathbf{x} \oplus \mathbf{t})$ is computed after $\mathbf{f}(\mathbf{s})$, then $\mathbf{t}$ must contain a summand $\mathbf{f}(\mathbf{w})$ that does not appear in any term sent by the encryptor prior to computing $\mathbf{t}$. But $\mathbf{f}(\mathbf{w})$ is not a summand of $\mathbf{s}$, it must be a summand of $\mathbf{s} \oplus \mathbf{t}$, contradicting our hypothesis. Thus, since $\mathbf{x} \not>_\mathbf{H} \mathbf{f}(\mathbf{w})$, we have $\mathbf{x} \not>_\mathbf{H} \mathbf{s} \oplus \mathbf{t}$.

The conclusion that, if $\mathcal{C}$ is also non-degenerate, then it is IND\$-CPA secure, follows directly from Theorem 1. $\square$

For modes, security often depends on the schedule in which ciphertext is returned to the adversary. The most conservative is the messagewise schedule, in which ciphertext blocks are not returned until all plaintext blocks have been received. The most eager is the blockwise schedule, in which the ciphertext blocks are returned as soon as they are computed. The delay-by-one schedule lies between the two: the ciphertext block encrypting the i'th plaintext block is returned after the $i + 1$'st block is received.

We now apply Lemmas 3 and 4 to some modes discussed by Bard [5]. They are listed in Table 1. The first column give the name of the mode. The references give where the mode was first described (if known), and where an attack was first described, if relevant. The second column describes the mode. The third column describes the most conservative schedule (if any) under which the mode is insecure, and the fifth the most eager schedule under which it is secure.

Table 1. Different modes and their security properties

Mode	Description	Insecure	Why	Secure	Why
CBC [13, 18]	$C_0 = r$ $C_i = f(x_i \oplus C_{i-1})$	C_0 sent before x_1	Lemma 3 $x_1 >_H r$	1-delay	Lemma 4 C_{i-1} sent after x_i
PCBC	$C_0 = r$ $C_i = f(x_i \oplus x_{i-1} \oplus C_{i-1})$	C_0 sent before x_1	Lemma 3 $x_1 >_H r$	1-delay	Lemma 4 C_{i-1} sent after x_i
CFB	$C_0 = r$ $C_i = f(C_{i-1}) \oplus x_i$	none		bw	Lemma 4 $f(C_{i-1})$ new in C_i
OFB	$E_0 = f(r), E_i = f(E_{i-1})$ $C_i = E_i \oplus x_i$	none		bw	Lemma 4 $f(C_{i-1})$ new in C_i
IGE [10, 15]	$C_0 = r, P_0 = r'$ $P_i = x_i$ $C_i = f(P_i \oplus C_{i-1}) \oplus P_{i-1}$	bw P_0 secret	Lemma 3 $x_i >_H C_{i-1}$	1-delay	Lemma 4 x_i sent after C_{i-1}
S-ABC [19]	$C_0 = r, E_0 = r'$ $E_i = x_i \oplus f(E_{i-1})$ $C_i = f(E_i \oplus C_{i-1}) \oplus E_{i-1}$	none		bw	Lemma 4 $f(E_i \oplus C_{i-1})$ new in C_i
H-IACBC [16, 18]	$C_0 = E_0 = f(r)$, $E_i = f(x_i \oplus (E_{i-1}))$ $C_i = E_i \oplus S_i$ $S_i \oplus S_j =_\oplus S_i' \oplus S_j'$ any 2 mess. streams	C_0 sent before x_1	Lemma 3 plus identities on S_i	1-delay	Lemma 4 C_{i-1} sent after x_i

7   Conclusion and Open Problems

We have identified symbolic conditions sufficient to guarantee IND$-CPA security
for a class of cryptosystems that use exclusive-or. We used these results to generate conditions applicable to cryptographic modes of operation. Our approach
relies on the use of identical-until-*bad* games that allow us to pinpoint a property implying a cryptosystem's security. Even though this property (in this case,
negligible probability of collisions) is not always preserved in the computational
model, it is possible to determine further conditions that guarantee that it will
be, avoiding known problems with the computational soundness of exclusive-or.

This work opens up several directions for future research.

Verification of Symbolic Criteria: The first is to develop algorithms for checking
the symbolic criteria developed in this paper, and for generating cryptosystems
that meet them. We have already begun work on developing verification algorithms and a tool for generating and checking cryptosystems (https://symcollab.

github.io/CryptoSolve/). In addition, we have begun to study the complexity of the problem. In particular, in [21]it is shown that degeneracy is undecidable by reducing it to the Post correspondence problem.

Enriching the Set of Cryptographic Primitives and Properties: Block ciphers and exclusive-or are not the only cryptographic primitives that can be reasoned about symbolically. Some others include hash functions, modular exponentiation, finite field and Abelian group operations, and bilinear pairings. Computational interpretations of the symbolic versions of many of these have already been covered by Baudet et al. in [7] for the case of a passive adversary, but may still need to be adapted for the case of an adaptive one. For properties, we would be interested not only in secrecy properties but properties such as authentication, collision-freeness and so forth.

Weaker Properties: Several of the properties we use in this paper are stronger than strictly necessary. In particular, polynomially bounded execution choice-limits the adversarial choices, but although $MOO_\oplus$ programs satisfy it, all that is really required is that the adversary's *adaptive* choice be polynomially limited. Indeed, this is the case for the cryptosystem used as an example by Kremer and Mazaré in [20]. The adversary first non-adaptively compromises a proper subset of the principals in a network, and then interacts with the remaining principals in a polynomially bounded execution choice fashion. Counting opportunities for adaptive execution choice is more complex than counting opportunities for execution choice, but identifying design choices such that make such counting easier may make the analysis more tractable.

In addition, the safety property defined in this paper is stronger than is strictly necessary: it is possible for a cryptosystem to have internal collisions that are not visible to the adversary. For example, consider the symbolic history $\nu \mathbf{r}.\mathbf{r}.\mathbf{x_1}.\mathbf{x_2}.\mathbf{f}(\mathbf{r} \oplus \mathbf{f}(\mathbf{x_1}) \oplus \mathbf{f}(\mathbf{x_2}))$.[5] The pair $(\mathbf{f}(\mathbf{x_1}), \mathbf{f}(\mathbf{x_2}))$, and the adversary can force a collision by setting $\mathbf{x_1} = \mathbf{x_2}$. However, in that case the ciphertext $\mathbf{r}.\mathbf{f}(\mathbf{r})$ is still indistinguishable from random. But the technique used to prove IND\$-CPA for safe cryptosystems does not extend easily to cryptosystems whose only unsafe pairs are invisible, because safeness or unsafeness of a pair may now depend on where it is located with respect to other $\mathbf{f}$-rooted terms in a symbolic history.

Design and Analysis of Protocols: Although the work we describe is applied to cryptosystems, they are cryptosystems that are themselves simple protocols, whose security depends on communication rules governing the schedule used by the encryptor to return ciphertext. Thus the question of whether or not these results can be extended to more complex protocols is more a question of to what degree than of whether it is possible at all. Thus it may be possible to augment previous work on computationally sound symbolic cryptographic protocol analysis, which has employed more of a top-down approach in which algorithms are modeled as equation-free abstractions, with a more bottom-up approach in which one starts with equational theories that are more tightly connected to the computational model. However, the question of scale is not a

---

[5] I am grateful to Christopher Lynch for this example.

trivial one, in particular, since, as Unruh has shown, providing too much adaptive choice to an adversary can break the link between symbolic and computational security. This question will need to be studied in more depth.

Acknowledgements. I am grateful to Jonathan Katz for helpful comments on earlier versions of this paper, as well as for the comments of many anonymous reviewers. I am also grateful the fruitful discussions I have had with fellow members of the Crypto-Solve group, including Wei Du, Serdar Erbatur, Hai Lin, Christopher Lynch, Andrew Marshall, Paliath Narendran, Danielle Radosta, Veena Ravishankar, Brandon Rozek, and Luis Rovera. Any problems that remain with this paper are of course my own responsibility. This work was funded by ONR Code 311.

References

1. Abadi, M., Fournet, C.: Mobile values, new names, and secure communication. In: Proceedings of POPL 2001, pp. 104–115. ACM (2001)
2. Abadi, M., Rogaway, P.: Reconciling two views of cryptography. In: van Leeuwen, J., Watanabe, O., Hagiya, M., Mosses, P.D., Ito, T. (eds.) TCS 2000. LNCS, vol. 1872, pp. 3–22. Springer, Heidelberg (2000). https://doi.org/10.1007/3-540-44929-9_1
3. Baader, F., Nipkow, T.: Term Rewriting and All That. Cambridge University Press, Cambridge (1998)
4. Backes, M., Pfitzmann, B.: A cryptographically sound security proof of the Needham-Schroeder-Lowe public-key protocol. In: Pandya, P.K., Radhakrishnan, J. (eds.) FSTTCS 2003. LNCS, vol. 2914, pp. 1–12. Springer, Heidelberg (2003). https://doi.org/10.1007/978-3-540-24597-1_1
5. Bard, G.V.: Blockwise-adaptive chosen-plaintext attack and online modes of encryption. In: Galbraith, S.D. (ed.) Cryptography and Coding 2007. LNCS, vol. 4887, pp. 129–151. Springer, Heidelberg (2007). https://doi.org/10.1007/978-3-540-77272-9_9
6. Barthe, G., et al.: Fully automated analysis of padding-based encryption in the computational model. In: ACM Conference on Computer and Communications Security (2013)
7. Baudet, M., Cortier, V., Kremer, S.: Computationally sound implementations of equational theories against passive adversaries. In: Caires, L., Italiano, G.F., Monteiro, L., Palamidessi, C., Yung, M. (eds.) ICALP 2005. LNCS, vol. 3580, pp. 652–663. Springer, Heidelberg (2005). https://doi.org/10.1007/11523468_53
8. Bellare, M., Rogaway, P.: The security of triple encryption and a framework for code-based game-playing proofs. In: Vaudenay, S. (ed.) EUROCRYPT 2006. LNCS, vol. 4004, pp. 409–426. Springer, Heidelberg (2006). https://doi.org/10.1007/11761679_25
9. Bresson, E., Lakhnech, Y., Mazaré, L., Warinschi, B.: A generalization of DDH with applications to protocol analysis and computational soundness. In: Menezes, A. (ed.) CRYPTO 2007. LNCS, vol. 4622, pp. 482–499. Springer, Heidelberg (2007). https://doi.org/10.1007/978-3-540-74143-5_27
10. Campbell, C.: Design and specification of cryptographic capabilities. IEEE Commun. Soc. Mag. **16**(6), 15–19 (1978)
11. Carmer, B., Rosulek, M.: Linicrypt: a model for practical cryptography. In: Robshaw, M., Katz, J. (eds.) CRYPTO 2016. LNCS, vol. 9816, pp. 416–445. Springer, Heidelberg (2016). https://doi.org/10.1007/978-3-662-53015-3_15

12. Dolev, D., Yao, A.C.-C.: On the security of public key protocols. IEEE Trans. Inf. Theory **29**(2), 198–207 (1983)
13. Ehrsam, W.F., Meyer, C.H., Smith, J.L., Tuchman, W.L.: Message verification and transmission error detection by block chaining, US Patent 4,074,066, 14 February 1978
14. Gagné, M., Lafourcade, P., Lakhnech, Y., Safavi-Naini, R.: Automated proofs of block cipher modes of operation. J. Autom. Reason. **56**(1), 49–94 (2016). https://doi.org/10.1007/s10817-015-9341-5
15. Gligor, V.D., Donescu, P., Katz, J.: On message integrity in symmetric encryption. In: 1st NIST Workshop on AES Modes of Operation (2000)
16. Halevi, S.: An observation regarding Jutla's modes of operation. IACR Cryptol. ePrint Arch. 2001:15 (2001)
17. Hoang, V.T., Katz, J., Malozemoff, A.J.: Automated analysis and synthesis of authenticated encryption schemes. In: Proceedings of 22nd ACM CCS, pp. 84–95 (2015)
18. Joux, A., Martinet, G., Valette, F.: Blockwise-adaptive attackers revisiting the (in)security of some provably secure encryption modes: CBC, GEM, IACBC. In: Yung, M. (ed.) CRYPTO 2002. LNCS, vol. 2442, pp. 17–30. Springer, Heidelberg (2002). https://doi.org/10.1007/3-540-45708-9_2
19. Knudsen, L.R.: Block chaining modes of operation. In: Proceedings of Symmetric Key Block Cipher Modes of Operation Workshop (2000)
20. Kremer, S., Mazaré, L.: Adaptive soundness of static equivalence. In: Biskup, J., López, J. (eds.) ESORICS 2007. LNCS, vol. 4734, pp. 610–625. Springer, Heidelberg (2007). https://doi.org/10.1007/978-3-540-74835-9_40
21. Lin, H., et al.: Algorithmic problems in the symbolic approach to the verification of automatically synthesized cryptosystems. In: Konev, B., Reger, G. (eds.) FroCoS 2021. LNCS, vol. 12941, pp. 253–270. Springer, Heidelberg (2021). https://doi.org/10.1007/978-3-030-86205-3_14
22. Malozemoff, A.J., Katz, J., Green, M.D.: Automated analysis and synthesis of block-cipher modes of operation. In: 2014 IEEE 27th Computer Security Foundations Symposium (CSF), pp. 140–152. IEEE (2014)
23. McQuoid, I., Swope, T., Rosulek, M.: Characterizing collision and second-preimage resistance in Linicrypt. In: Hofheinz, D., Rosen, A. (eds.) TCC 2019. LNCS, vol. 11891, pp. 451–470. Springer, Cham (2019). https://doi.org/10.1007/978-3-030-36030-6_18
24. Micciancio, D., Warinschi, B.: Soundness of formal encryption in the presence of active adversaries. In: Naor, M. (ed.) TCC 2004. LNCS, vol. 2951, pp. 133–151. Springer, Heidelberg (2004). https://doi.org/10.1007/978-3-540-24638-1_8
25. Unruh, D.: The impossibility of computationally sound XOR. IACR Cryptology ePrint Archive, 2010:389 (2010)

Optimal Verifiable Data Streaming Protocol with Data Auditing

Jianghong Wei[1,2,3], Guohua Tian[1], Jun Shen[1], Xiaofeng Chen[1,2(✉)],
and Willy Susilo[4]

[1] State Key Laboratory of Integrated Service Networks, Xidian University,
Xi'an, China
xfchen@xidian.edu.cn
[2] State Key Laboratory of Cryptology, P. O. Box 5159, Beijing 100878, China
[3] State Key Laboratory of Mathematical Engineering and Advanced Computing,
PLA Strategic Support Force Information Engineering University, Zhengzhou, China
[4] School of Computing and IT, University of Wollongong,
Wollongong 2522, NSW, Australia
wsusilo@uow.edu.au

Abstract. As smart devices connected to networks like Internet of
Things and 5G become popular, the volume of data generated over time
(i.e., stream data) by them is growing rapidly. As a consequence, for
these resources-limited client-side devices, it becomes very challenging
to store the continuously generated stream data locally. Although the
cloud storage provides a perfect solution to this problem, the data owner
still needs to ensure the integrity of the outsourced stream data, since
various applications built upon stream data are sensitive of both its
context and order. To this end, the notion of verifiable data streaming (VDS) was proposed to effectively append and update stream data
outsourced to an untrusted cloud server, and has received significant
attention. However, previous VDS constructions adopt Merkle hash tree
to capture the integrity of outsourced data, and thus inevitably have
logarithmic costs. In this paper, we further optimize the construction of
VDS in terms of communication and computation costs. Specifically, we
use the digital signature scheme to ensure the integrity of outsourced
stream data, and employ a recently proposed RSA accumulator (v.s.
Merkle hash tree) to invalidate the corresponding signature after each
data update operation. Benefited from this approach, the resulted VDS
construction achieves optimal, i.e., having constant costs. Furthermore,
by specifying the underly signature scheme with the BLS short signature and carefully combining it with the RSA accumulator, we finally
obtain an optimal verifiable data streaming protocol with data auditing.
We prove the security of the proposed VDS construction in the random
oracle model.

Keywords: Verifiable data streaming · Outsourced storage · Data
auditing · Cryptographic accumulator

© Springer Nature Switzerland AG 2021
E. Bertino et al. (Eds.): ESORICS 2021, LNCS 12973, pp. 296–312, 2021.
https://doi.org/10.1007/978-3-030-88428-4_15

1   Introduction

With the extensive use of smart devices connected to networks like Internet of Things and 5G, both individuals and enterprises have been generating huge amounts of data. In particular, as a kind of important and common data type, stream data appears in various application scenarios, such as network intrusion detection, DNA sequence analysis, stock trading, and so on [2]. Although there has been a lot of research focusing on how to effectively store and manage stream data [1,12], the explosive and unpredicted growth of stream data scale still brings serious storage issues, especially for those resource-restricted client-side devices.

Fortunately, the emergence of cloud computing provides an economical and convenient storage mode for big stream data. That is, users can continuously stream the local data to cloud storage servers (e.g., Dropbox, Google Driver and Microsoft Azure), and then access the outsourced data via lightweight devices connected networks at anytime and anywhere. However, after the data is outsourced to cloud storage servers, the data owner completely loses its control right. This means that, to ensure the security of the outsourced data, the data owner has to trust these cloud storage servers. On the other hand, a large number of cloud data leakage incidents have shown that cloud storage servers are not completely trusted in fact [16]. To this end, a lot of active studies have been proposed to conquer the security issues of outsourced data in the context of cloud computing, e.g., proof of retrievability [26], secure duplication [3], verifiable update [10] and cryptographically enforced access control [28].

Among these security issues, the integrity of the outsourced data is especially important, since it is directly related to the data availability. In other words, a data user should be convinced that the data returned back by the cloud storage server is consistent with the data that was originally outsourced by the data owner. Otherwise, the analysis results based on the retrieved data may be biased or even maliciously misled. When focusing on stream data, due to its own features of unpredictable size and location-sensitive, this problem becomes more challenging.

As the first step towards solving the above problem, Schröder and Schröder [24] introduced the notion of verifiable data streaming (VDS) protocol. They put forward an efficient instantiation built upon a novel authenticated data structure named as chameleon authentication tree (CAT), which is essentially a generalized Merkle hash tree. Specifically, in their construction, the data owner assigns data items to leaf nodes of the CAT in a natural order, and thus binds the data content and the corresponding position. At the same time, the one-way nature of the underlying hash functions ensures that the outsourced data cannot be tampered with. In addition, by using a chameleon hash function and maintaining a dynamic verification key[1], the data owner can update previously outsourced data items in an efficient manner, and also invalidate them. On the other hand, any data user can independently verify the integrity of a requested data item by reconstructing the hash value at the root node of the CAT and further comparing it with that

---

[1] The verification key is updated after each data update operation.

contained in the verification key. On the whole, this VDS construction almost satisfies all of the above listed properties, except that it requires to fix the size of the CAT at the beginning. In other words, the number of data items that can be authenticated is bounded, which violates the first property. Moreover, both the computation cost and communication overhead of this construction are logarithmic in the bounded number of data items.

Towards optimizing the above VDS protocol, Schröder and Simkin [25] used the CAT in a black-box way, and proposed a more efficient VDS protocol. Particularly, in this construction, the number of data items is unbounded, and both the computation and communication costs are only logarithmic in the number of all authenticated data items so far. However, their construction was just proved secure in the random oracle model, at the cost of achieving these optimization goals. Furthermore, Krupp et al. [18] formally defined the notion of chameleon vector commitment (CVC), based on which they put forward the first unbounded VDS protocol in the standard model. Since they also followed the idea of Merkle hash tree used in previous constructions, the complexity of their VDS protocol built upon CVC is the same as Schröder and Simkin's [25] protocol. In addition, they also proposed another VDS construction by combining the digital signature scheme and the cryptographic accumulator. Notably, such a VDS construction is nearly optimal, that is, to achieve constant communication overhead and computation cost. But the computation cost of the cloud server responding to a query is linear in the number of update operations conducted so far.

Although a lot of valuable research efforts have been made, the state-of-the-art VDS construction is still not optimal, i.e., achieving constant computation and communication costs. In addition, the complexity of previous VDS protocols is evaluated under a single query. That is, for concurrent queries that retrieve multiple data items at once, the cost of these protocols is linear in the size of concurrent queries. In view of this state of affairs, a nature and important problem is how to design an optimal VDS protocol.

1.1   Our Contribution

In this paper, we focus on the problem of constructing more efficient VDS protocols, and improve upon the state-of-the-art. Roughly, to achieve this goal, we employ the approach of digital signature plus cryptographic accumulator to instantiate VDS, rather than the traditional method of Merkle hash tree. That is, the digital signature scheme is used to bind the content of each data item and its position, and also to ensure their integrity. Moreover, to invalidate the old signature after each data update operation, we add it to the cryptographic accumulator, and let the cloud server generate a non-membership witness for the current signature of each queried data item, so as to resist replay attacks.

In more detail, we adopt BLS signature [6] as the underlying digital signature scheme. It not only guarantees the integrity of the retrieved data, but also allows the data owner or other third party to audit the integrity of those previously outsourced data items without retrieving them. With respect to the cryptographic accumulator, we employ Boneh et al.'s [5] RSA accumulator that can batch non-membership witnesses. By carefully combining these two primitives, we finally obtain a verifiable and auditable data streaming (VADS for short) protocol that has constant costs.

Specifically, we conduct the following contributions:

- We formalize the syntax and security notion of VADS protocol, and propose a concrete VADS construction built upon the Boneh-Lynn-Shacham (BLS) signature [6] and the RSA accumulator due to Boneh et al. [5].
- We prove the security of our proposal in the random oracle model, and reduce its security to the computational Diffie-Hellman assumption over bilinear groups as well as the security of the underlying RSA accumulator, which in turn depends on the adaptive root assumption over hidden order groups.
- We theoretically analyze the performance of the proposed VADS construction. Specifically, when considering our VADS construction as a VDS protocol, it outperforms the state-of-the-art, and achieves optimal. In addition, it also features the functionality of data auditing.

1.2   Related Work

A naive solution to verify the integrity of outsourced stream data is to use a simple Merkle hash tree [21]. Specifically, all data items are stored at the leaves of the tree, and each internal node is associated with the hash value of the concatenation of its children's values. Then, the hash value of the root node is used as the public verification key, and the integrity proof of each data item consists of all node values that are required for reconstructing root node's value from the corresponding leaf node. The shortcoming of this solution is that the verification key needs to be immediately updated after either updating an old data item or appending a new data item, which brings an infeasible burden of managing the verification key, especially for stream data with large scale and high transmission rate.

Towards overcoming the above shortcoming, Schröder and Schröder [24] introduced the notion of verifiable data streaming protocols, and proposed the first VDS construction supporting a bounded number of authenticated data items. In their protocol, appending a new data item no longer needs to update the verification key, but the total number of data items is initially fixed. Subsequently, Schröder and Simkin [25] removed such a limitation, and constructed the first unbounded VDS protocol in the random oracle model. Krupp et al. [18] further presented nearly optimal VDS constructions in terms of communication and computation costs.

In addition, there are several other related works that extend the original VDS protocol. For instance, Chen et al. [9] and Xu et al. [32] combined VDS with homomorphic encryption to realize verifiable computation on stream data. Zhang et al. [36] proposed a VDS construction with accountability. Xu et al. [31] presented a lightweight VDS construction supporting range queries. Recently,

Sun et al. [27] employed Schröder and Simkin's [25] approach[2] to propose a VDS protocol with public data auditing. However, Li et al. [20] demonstrated that their construction can be invalidated by any adversarial cloud server, and thus failed to achieve the goal of data auditing.

Another cryptographic primitive similar to VDS is verifiable databases (VDB) proposed by Benabbas et al. [4]. The main difference between the two is that the database size needs to be fixed in the setup phase of VDB schemes, while it is allowed to be unbounded in the setting of VDS. Therefore, VDS can be regarded as a generalization of VDB. Since its introduction, a lot of research around VDB has been conducted, such as new primitives for constructing VDB [8,19], VDB with efficient updates and deletions [11,22], VDB supporting various SQL queries [33,35] as well as public auditing [29]. In addition, Papamanthou et al. [23] also introduced a similar notion named as streaming authenticated data structures, which enable the data owner to efficiently compute a verification key, and then use it to verify the computation results of the stream data from the server. However, the verification key in their construction dynamically changes after streaming or uploading each data item.

Juels and Kaliski [17] put forward the notion of proof of retrievability (PoR, a.k.a data auditing), which is also closely related to VDS. This cryptographic primitive allows the data owner to verify the integrity of those outsourced data without retrieving them again, and has been extensively studied. Those early PoR constructions [17,26] are static, and cannot be used in the dynamic setting due to replay attacks. As discussed in [13], in order to resist replay attacks, authenticated data structures (e.g., Merkle hash trees and authenticated dictionaries) must be employed to invalidate those previously authenticated data items in the case of dynamic. However, dynamic PoR or data auditing schemes [14,15,30,34] following this manner usually incur logarithmic costs. Also note that in the setting of VDS, the data user first retrieves the data, and further checks its integrity for downstream processing. Thus, adding the functionality of data auditing to VDS makes it more flexible, and can also ensure the integrity of the outsourced stream data when we do not need to retrieve and use them.

1.3   Organization

The reset of this paper is organized as follows: In Sect. 2, we introduce necessary preliminaries. Section 3 formalizes the syntax and security notion of verifiable and auditiable data streaming protocol. We put forward a concrete VADS construction in Sect. 4, and prove its security in the random oracle model. The performance analysis of the proposed VADS construction is presented in Sect. 5. We conclude this paper in Sect. 6.

---

[2] In Sun et al.'s construction, they used the notion of adaptive trapdoor hash authentication tree. But we note that it is essentially the fully dynamic CATs constructed by Schröder and Simkin.

2   Preliminaries

2.1   Notations

Throughout this paper, we use the following notations:

- $\mathsf{Primes}(\lambda)$: The set of primes belonging to $[0, 2^\lambda)$.
- $\mathsf{EEA}(\cdot, \cdot)$: The extended euclidean algorithm.
- $\mathsf{H}_\mathbb{G}$, $\mathsf{H}_{\mathbb{G}'}$: Hash functions with domains $\mathbb{G}$, $\mathbb{G}'$.
- H_λ, $\mathsf{H}_{\mathsf{Prime}}$: Hash functions with domains $[0, 2^\lambda)$, $\mathsf{Primes}(\lambda)$.
- S: Unbounded stream data.
- $s[i]$: The i-th data item of the stream data S.
- $S[J]$: The data item set $\{s[j] | j \in J\}$.
- $[n]$: The integer set $\{1, 2, \ldots, n\}$.
- $x \xleftarrow{\$} R$: Randomly sampling x from the set R.
- $I \xleftarrow{\$} R$: Randomly sampling a subset I of the set R.

2.2   Bilinear Groups and CDH Assumption

Let $\mathbb{G}$ and $\mathbb{G}_T$ be two cyclic groups with the prime order p in the size λ, and g be a random generator of the group $\mathbb{G}$. A map $e : \mathbb{G} \times \mathbb{G} \to \mathbb{G}_T$ is said to be bilinear if the following properties hold:

- *Bilinearity*: For any group elements $u, v \in \mathbb{G}$ and integers $\alpha, \beta \in \mathbb{Z}_p$, it holds that $e(u^\alpha, v^\beta) = e(u, v)^{\alpha\beta}$.
- *Non-degeneracy*: $e(g, g) \neq 1_{\mathbb{G}_T}$, where $1_{\mathbb{G}_T}$ is the unit element of $\mathbb{G}_T$.
- *Computability*: For any group elements $u, v \in \mathbb{G}$, there exists a probabilistic polynomial-time (PPT) algorithm that can efficiently compute $e(u, v)$.

To simplify subsequent descriptions, we assume that there exists a PPT algorithm BilGen that takes the security parameter λ as input, and then generates bilinear groups, i.e., $(\mathbb{G}, \mathbb{G}_T, e, p, g) \leftarrow \mathsf{BilGen}(\lambda)$.

The security of our protocol is partially built upon the computational Diffie-Hellman (CDH) assumption over bilinear groups, which is formalized as follows:

Definition 1 (CDH Assumption [6]). *Let $(\mathbb{G}, \mathbb{G}_T, e, p, g) \leftarrow \mathsf{BilGen}(\lambda)$ be bilinear groups, α and β be two random integers sampled from $\mathbb{Z}_p$. We say the CDH assumption holds if for any PPT adversary given (g, g^α, g^β), its probability of outputting $g^{\alpha\beta}$ is negligible in the security parameter λ.*

2.3   Groups of Unknown Order and RSA Accumulator

Our protocol employs a cryptographic accumulator based on a group $\mathbb{G}'$ of unknown order. Given a security parameter λ, we assume there exists a PPT algorithm $\mathsf{UGen}(\lambda) \to \mathbb{G}'$ that can generate such a group with order in a range $[a, b]$ such that $\frac{1}{a}$, $\frac{1}{b}$ and $\frac{1}{b-a}$ are all negligible in λ. As discussed by Boneh et al. [5], available two concrete instantiations of $\mathbb{G}'$ include class groups and the quotient group $\mathbb{Z}_N^*/\{-1,1\}$ of an RSA group, where N is an RSA modulus.

Specifically, we use Boneh et al.'s [5] RSA accumulator that supports batching non-membership witnesses. Since our protocol only involves adding elements to the accumulator and producing non-membership witnesses, here we just present a simplified version. In more detail, it consists of the following algorithms:

- Setup(1^λ): The setup algorithm takes as input a security parameter λ. It first generates a hidden order group $\mathbb{G}' \leftarrow \mathsf{UGen}(\lambda)$, and randomly chooses an element $h \in \mathbb{G}'$. Furthermore, it initializes the element set as $R \leftarrow \emptyset$ and the corresponding accumulator as $\mathsf{Acc}(\emptyset) \leftarrow h$.
- Add($\mathsf{Acc}(R), R, z$): The addition algorithm takes as input the current accumulator $\mathsf{Acc}(R)$ and element set R as well as a prime $z \in \mathsf{Primes}(\lambda)$. If $z \in R$, then it directly outputs $\mathsf{Acc}(R)$. Otherwise, it updates the element set as $R' \leftarrow R \cup \{z\}$ and the accumulator as $\mathsf{Acc}(R') \leftarrow (\mathsf{Acc}(R))^z$.
- WitCreate($\mathsf{Acc}(R), R, z$): This non-membership witness creation algorithm takes as input the current accumulator $\mathsf{Acc}(R)$ and element set R as well as an element $z \notin R$. It first computes $z^* = \prod_{z' \in R} z'$, and employs the extended euclidean algorithm to compute coefficients $x, y \in \mathbb{Z}$ such that $x \cdot z^* + y \cdot z = 1$. Then, it assigns $Y = h^y$, and outputs $\pi = (x, Y)$ as the witnesses of $z \notin R$.
- Verify($\mathsf{Acc}(R), \pi, z$): This verification algorithm takes as input the accumulator $\mathsf{Acc}(R)$, the non-membership witness π and the corresponding element z. It first parses the witness π as (x, Y). Then, it outputs 1 if $(\mathsf{Acc}(R))^x \cdot Y^z = h$ and 0 otherwise.

2.4 Hashing to Primes

In our VADS construction, we need a hash function $\mathsf{H}_{\mathsf{Prime}}$ that maps arbitrary strings to primes belonging to $[0, 2^\lambda)$ for the given security parameter λ. We make use of such a hash function introduced in [7].

Specifically, let $\mathsf{H}_\lambda : \{0,1\}^* \to [0, 2^\lambda)$ be a collision resistant hash function and $i \leftarrow 0$. Given an input $x \in \{0,1\}^*$, if $y \leftarrow \mathsf{H}_\lambda(x, i)$ is a prime then directly assign $y \leftarrow \mathsf{H}_{\mathsf{Prime}}(x)$, otherwise let $i \leftarrow i + 1$ and continue to evaluate $\mathsf{H}_\lambda(x, i)$, until a prime is found. If H_λ was a random function, then the running time of $\mathsf{H}_{\mathsf{Prime}}$ is $\mathcal{O}(\lambda)$, since the number of primes less than 2^λ is $\mathcal{O}(\frac{2^\lambda}{\lambda})$.

3   Verifiable and Auditable Data Streaming Protocol

In this section, we formalize the syntax of VADS protocol and its security requirement.

In the context of a VADS protocol, a client $\mathcal{C}$ can outsource some unbounded data $S = s[1], s[2] \ldots$ to an untrusted server $\mathcal{S}$ in a streaming manner. That is, $\mathcal{C}$ reads a data item $s[i] \in \{0,1\}^\lambda$ at a time and sends it to $\mathcal{S}$, who then stores it in a database DB. The outsourced stream data must be publicly verifiable and auditable in the sense that the server $\mathcal{S}$ can neither modify the position and content of any data item nor append additional data items to the database. In addition, given some proof[3] generated and returned by the server, the client $\mathcal{C}$ (or a third party) can publicly verify that the requested data item $s[i]$ was indeed located at the position i of the outsourced stream data, and can also publicly judge that the server $\mathcal{S}$ has not deleted the data without retrieving it. Moreover, the client $\mathcal{C}$ is allowed to update any data item $s[i]$ with a new one $s'[i]$.

Formally, a verifiable and auditable data streaming protocol $\mathcal{VADS}$ = (Setup, Append, Query, Audit, Verify, Judge, Update) is seven-tuple of algorithms and protocols, and is interactively executed between a client $\mathcal{C}$ and a server $\mathcal{S}$, which are both modeled as PPT algorithms. The details of these algorithms are specified as follows:

- Setup(1^λ): The setup algorithm is performed by the client $\mathcal{C}$, and takes a security parameter λ as input. It outputs a verification key vk and a secret key sk. The former is sent to the server $\mathcal{S}$, and the later is held by the client $\mathcal{C}$. To simplify descriptions, we assume that vk is part of sk.

- Append(sk, s): The append protocol is initiated by the client $\mathcal{C}$, and takes the secret key sk and a data item s as input. It appends s to the database DB maintained by the server $\mathcal{S}$, and may output a new secret key sk'.

- Query(vk, i, DB): The query protocol takes as input the verification key vk and the database DB provided by the server $\mathcal{S}$ as well as an index $i \in \mathbb{N}^*$ from the client $\mathcal{C}$. At the end of this protocol, the server $\mathcal{S}$ outputs the i-th entry $s[i]$ of the database DB along with a proof π_q, or an error symbol $\perp$.

- Verify(vk, $s[i]$, i, π_q): The verification algorithm is run by the client $\mathcal{C}$, and takes as input the verification key vk, an index i and a data item $s[i]$ as well as a proof π_q. It outputs the data item $s[i]$ if $s[i]$ is actually the i-th entry of the database DB. Otherwise, it outputs an symbol $\perp$.

- Audit(I): The audit protocol is initiated by the client $\mathcal{C}$, and takes as input an index set $I \subset \mathbb{N}^*$. At the end of this protocol, it outputs a proof π_a returned by the server $\mathcal{S}$.

- Judge(vk, π_a): The judge algorithm is performed by the client $\mathcal{C}$, and takes the verification key vk and a proof π_a as input. It outputs 1 if the server passes the judge and 0 otherwise.

- Update(sk, i, s', vk, DB): The update protocol is conducted between the server $\mathcal{S}$ that provides the verification key vk as well as the database DB and the client $\mathcal{C}$ that provides the secret key sk, an index i as well as a data item s'. At the end of this protocol, the server $\mathcal{S}$ will replace the original i-th data item $s[i]$ of the database DB with s', and both $\mathcal{S}$ and $\mathcal{C}$ update the original verification key to vk'.

A VADS protocol must fulfill the usual requirement of correctness. That is, when all algorithms/protocols of a VDS protocol are honestly executed, it should work as expected. This is formally defined as follows.

---

[3] For different tasks (i.e. query and auditing), the corresponding proofs are also different.

Definition 2 (Correctness). *A VADS protocol $\mathcal{VADS}$ is said to be correct provided that for correctly generated verification and secret key* $(\text{vk}, \text{sk}) \leftarrow$ *Setup(λ) and any stream data* $S = s[1], s[2], \ldots$, *if* $\text{sk}' \leftarrow$ *Append$(\text{sk}, s[i])$ and* $(s[i], \pi_q) \leftarrow$ *Query(vk, DB, i) as well as* $\pi_a \leftarrow$ *Audit(I), then* *Verify$(\text{vk}, i, s[i], \pi_q) \rightarrow s[i]$ and Judge$(\text{vk}, \pi_a) \rightarrow 1$ must hold with an overwhelming probability. Furthermore, the correctness must hold even after performing an arbitrary number of updates.*

The intuition behind the security of the VADS protocol is that an adversary $\mathcal{A}$ should not be able to modify those data items stored in the database, including their contents and positions, and nor should it be able to append new elements to the database. Moreover, for an updated data item $s'[i]$, its old value $s[i]$ should no longer pass verification. This can be modeled in a security game played between a challenger $\mathcal{B}$ that plays the role of the client and an adversary $\mathcal{A}$ that plays the role of the server. The security game comprises of the following three phases:

Setup Phase. In this phase, $\mathcal{B}$ runs the setup algorithm Setup$(\lambda) \rightarrow (\text{vk}, \text{sk})$, and sends the verification key vk to the adversary $\mathcal{A}$. In addition, $\mathcal{B}$ creates a database DB and a set Q both initialized as empty.

Query Phase. The adversary $\mathcal{A}$ is allowed to adaptively add a new data item s to the database DB by streaming it to the challenger $\mathcal{B}$. As a response, $\mathcal{B}$ performs the algorithm Append(sk, s), and returns the index i of s and corresponding proof π_q to the adversary $\mathcal{A}$. Furthermore, the adversary $\mathcal{A}$ can also update a data item $s[i] \in DB$ with a new one $s'[i]$ by providing a tuple $(i, s'[i])$ to the challenger $\mathcal{B}$, who then executes the algorithm Update$(\text{vk}, DB, i, s'[i])$ and returns a new proof $\hat{\pi}_q$ to $\mathcal{A}$. Throughout this phase, the challenger $\mathcal{B}$ always immediately updates the verification/secret keys after each query, and adds new data items and corresponding indexes to the set Q, i.e., $Q = \{(1, s[1]), \ldots, (q(\lambda), s[q(\lambda)])\}$.

Challenge Phase. Finally, when the adversary $\mathcal{A}$ decides to end the game, it outputs a tuple $(i^*, I^*, s[i^*], \pi_q^*, \pi_a^*)$. Then, let $s^* \leftarrow$ Verify$(\text{vk}, i^*, s[i^*], \pi_q^*)$ and $b^* \leftarrow$ Judge(vk, π_a^*). We say the adversary $\mathcal{A}$ wins this security game if it holds that:

$$\left(s^* \neq \perp \wedge (i^*, s^*) \notin Q\right) \vee \left(b^* = 1 \wedge \exists i' \in I^* \ s.t. \ (i', s[i']) \notin Q\right)$$

We denote by $\text{Adv}_{\mathcal{A}}^{\text{VADS}}(\lambda)$ the probability of $\mathcal{A}$ winning in the game.

Definition 3 (Security). *A VADS protocol is secure if for any PPT adversary $\mathcal{A}$, the probability $\text{Adv}_{\mathcal{A}}^{\text{VADS}}(\lambda)$ is negligible in the security parameter λ.*

4   The Construction of VADS

In this section, we propose a concrete construction of verifiable and auditable data streaming protocol. To this end, we first outline our techniques, and provide an overview for ease of understanding. Then, we specify our VADS protocol that supports a single query, just like previous VDS constructions.

4.1   Overview

Our solution to the problem of verifying the integrity of the outsourced stream data starts from a trivial idea, i.e., signing each data item and its position in the stream data with a digital signature scheme. Obviously, the unforgeability of signatures makes the outsourced data items can neither be tampered with nor re-ordered. Here, the problem is how to update data items. Note that for a position i, simply signing i and the new data item $s'[i]$ is not sufficient, since the old signature σ_i for i and the original data item $s[i]$ would still remain valid. In other words, upon a query about retrieving the data item at position i, the cloud server can legitimately return $s[i]$ and σ_i, rather than $s'[i]$, although the data owner has conducted the update operation at the position i.

Observe that the key to making the above solution effective is to invalidate the old signature after each update operation. But here the verification key is the public key of the underlying signature scheme, and does not relate to the updated data item. Thus, to realize data update, the data owner has to generate a new pair of public key and secret key, and signs all data items again, which is clearly infeasible. This is also why previous VDS constructions [18,24,25] use the approach of Merkle hash tree to invalidate those old data items. But at the same time, this manner inevitably brings logarithmic costs.

Towards constructing optimal VDS protocol, we still follow the above trivial idea, but adopt the cryptographic accumulator to revoke those old signatures. More precisely, we use the state-of-the-art RSA accumulator proposed by Boneh et al. [5] to invalidate the old signature after each update operation. That is, we add the old signature into the current accumulator after the corresponding data item was updated. Then, upon a query for position i, the cloud server needs to create a non-membership proof π, so as to prove that the returned signature σ_i and the corresponding data item $s[i]$ are the newest ones. The data user employs the proof π to verify the membership of σ_i against the current accumulator, which is a short digest of all revoked signatures and assigned as part of the verification key. On the whole, by dynamically freshing the accumulator with each update operation, those old signatures can be effectively invalidated. In addition, since the underlying accumulator features of batching non-membership witnesses, the resulted VDS construction achieves constant computation and communication costs, and therefore is optimal.

Furthermore, since we use the digital signature scheme to ensure the integrity of the outsourced stream data, then it may be possible to enable the above VDS construction to capture the functionality of public data auditing as done in PoR schemes [26,30]. To this end, we instantiate the underlying signature scheme of the above VDS construction with the BLS signature [6], and achieve the goal of data auditing with the approach of Shacham and Waters [26]. Here we emphasize that we focus on dynamic stream data, but Shacham and Waters dealt with the case of static. Therefore, to resist replay attacks during the auditing procedure, we additionally require the cloud server to return a non-membership proof for those challenged data items along with a tag set that identifies them. This also makes the communication cost of data auditing in our VDS construction is linear in the set of challenge set.

Finally, by carefully combing the BLS signature with Boneh et al.'s [5] RSA accumulator, we obtain a optimal VDS protocol with data auditing.

4.2 The Construction

The concrete construction consists of the following algorithms.

- Setup(1^λ): Given a security parameter λ, the client $\mathcal{C}$ first generates bilinear groups $(\mathbb{G}, \mathbb{G}_T, e, p, g) \leftarrow \mathsf{BilGen}(\lambda)$ and a hidden order group $\mathbb{G}' \leftarrow \mathsf{UGen}(\lambda)$. Then, $\mathcal{C}$ randomly picks an integer $\alpha \in \mathbb{Z}_p$ and two elements $u \in \mathbb{G}, h \in \mathbb{G}'$. The client $\mathcal{C}$ also selects four collision-resistant hash functions defined in the following way: $\mathsf{H}_\mathbb{G} : \{0,1\}^* \to \mathbb{G}$, $\mathsf{H}_{\mathbb{G}'} : \{0,1\}^* \to \mathbb{G}'$, $\mathsf{H}_{\mathsf{Prime}} : \{0,1\}^* \to$ $\mathsf{Primes}(\lambda)$ and $\mathsf{H}_\lambda : \{0,1\}^* \to [0, 2^\lambda)$. In addition, the client $\mathcal{C}$ initializes a counter $\mathsf{cnt} \leftarrow 1$ and an accumulator $\mathsf{Acc}(\emptyset) \leftarrow h$. Finally, The client outputs the verification key $\mathsf{vk} = \{(\mathbb{G}, \mathbb{G}_T, e, p, g), \mathbb{G}', \mathsf{H}_\mathbb{G}, \mathsf{H}_{\mathbb{G}'}, \mathsf{H}_{\mathsf{Prime}}, \mathsf{H}_\lambda, \mathsf{Acc}(\emptyset), A = g^\alpha, u, h\}$ and the secret key $\mathsf{sk} = \{\alpha, \mathsf{cnt}, \mathsf{vk}\}$. After that, sk is kept privately by $\mathcal{C}$, and vk is sent publicly to the server $\mathcal{S}$, which further creates a database DB and a revocation list R that are both initialized as empty.
- Append(sk, s, DB): To append a data item $s \in \mathbb{Z}_p$ to the database DB, the client $\mathcal{C}$ first retrieves the current counter cnt from the secret key sk, and assigns an index $i \leftarrow \mathsf{cnt}$ for s. Then, $\mathcal{C}$ generates a signature $\sigma_i \leftarrow \big(\mathsf{H}_\mathbb{G}(i\|\mathsf{tag}_i) \cdot u^s\big)^\alpha$, and forwards the tuple $(i, s, \sigma_i, \mathsf{tag}_i)$ to $\mathcal{S}$, where $\mathsf{tag}_i{}^4$ is a random string sampled from $\{0,1\}^\lambda$. Meanwhile, $\mathcal{C}$ updates the counter $\mathsf{cnt} \leftarrow \mathsf{cnt} + 1$. Upon receiving the tuple, the server $\mathcal{S}$ first verifies the validity of the signature as follows:

$$e(\sigma_i, g) \stackrel{?}{=} e\big(A, \mathsf{H}_\mathbb{G}(i\|\mathsf{tag}_i) \cdot u^s\big) \qquad (1)$$

  If it passes the verification, then $\mathcal{S}$ stores s at the position i of the database DB. Otherwise, $\mathcal{S}$ rejects $\mathcal{C}$'s append request.
- Query(vk, i, DB): When the client $\mathcal{C}$ intends to query some data item that was stored in the database DB, it sends the corresponding index i to the server $\mathcal{S}$. To answer such a query, $\mathcal{S}$ first retrieves the tuple $(i, s[i], \sigma_i, \mathsf{tag}_i)$ from the database DB. Then, it needs to produce a non-membership proof with respect to the current accumulator $\mathsf{Acc}(R)$, so as to demonstrate that the signature σ_i has not been revoked by the client $\mathcal{C}$. To this end, $\mathcal{S}$ computes $z_i \leftarrow \mathsf{H}_{\mathsf{Prime}}(\mathsf{tag}_i)$ and directly retrieves[5] $z^* \leftarrow \prod_{\mathsf{tag} \in R} \mathsf{H}_{\mathsf{Prime}}(\mathsf{tag})$. It then lets $(x, y) \leftarrow \mathsf{EEA}(z^*, z_i)$, and assigns $\pi = (x, Y = h^y)$. Finally, the server $\mathcal{S}$ returns the requested data item $s[i]$ and the proof $\pi_{\mathsf{q}} = \{\sigma_i, \mathsf{tag}_i, \pi\}$ to the client $\mathcal{C}$.

---

[4] We assume that each signature has a unique tag. So we can use it to identify the corresponding signature as we do in the Query protocol.

[5] Note that the value z^* is computed with the revocation list R and is independent of i, and thus can be refreshed after each update operation.

- Verify(vk, $s[i], i, \pi_q$): After getting the response from the server $\mathcal{S}$, the client $\mathcal{C}$ first parses the proof π_q as $\{\sigma_i, \mathsf{tag}_i, \pi\}$, where $\pi = (x, Y)$. After that, it recomputes $z_i \leftarrow \mathsf{H}_{\mathsf{Prime}}(\mathsf{tag}_i)$, and verifies if the following condition holds:

$$\left(\mathsf{Acc}(R)\right)^x \cdot Y^{z_i} \stackrel{?}{=} h \tag{2}$$

If not, it outputs $\perp$ and terminates. Otherwise, it further checks if the following condition holds:

$$e(\sigma_i, g) \stackrel{?}{=} e\left(A, \mathsf{H}_{\mathbb{G}}(i\|\mathsf{tag}_i) \cdot u^{s[i]}\right) \tag{3}$$

If yes, it outputs $s[i]$. Otherwise, it outputs $\perp$.
- Audit(I): To check the retrievability of the outsourced stream data, the client $\mathcal{C}$ (or a third party) first retrieves the current counter cnt, and selects a random c-element subset $I \subseteq [\mathsf{cnt}]$. Then, for each $i \in I$, it chooses a random integer $\nu_i \in \mathbb{Z}_p$, and sends the set $\{(i, \nu_i)|i \in I\}$ to the server $\mathcal{S}$. After receiving this set, $\mathcal{S}$ retrieves $\{(i, s[i], \sigma_i, \mathsf{tag}_i)|i \in I\}$ from the database DB, and lets $\nu = \sum_{i \in I} \nu_i s[i] \mod p$ and $\sigma_I = \prod_{i \in I} \sigma_i^{\nu_i}$. In addition, it needs to produce an aggregated non-membership proof with respect to the current accumulator $\mathsf{Acc}(R)$ for the set $\{\sigma_i|i \in I\}$, i.e., proving each σ_i has not been revoked by $\mathcal{C}$. To this end, it assigns $Q_I = \{\mathsf{H}_{\mathsf{Prime}}(\mathsf{tag}_i)|i \in I\}$, and generates the aggregated non-membership proof as $\pi_I \leftarrow \mathsf{WitCreate}^*(\mathsf{Acc}(R), R, Q_I)$ (see Algorithm 1). Finally, the server $\mathcal{S}$ returns the proof $\pi_a = \{\nu, \sigma_I, \pi_I, \{\mathsf{tag}_i|i \in I\}\}$ to $\mathcal{C}$.
- Judge(vk, π_a): Given the challenge set $\{(i, \nu_i)|i \in I\}$ and the returned proof $\pi_a = \{\nu, \sigma_I, \pi_I, \{\mathsf{tag}_i|i \in I\}\}$, the client $\mathcal{C}$ reconstructs $Q_I = \{\mathsf{H}_{\mathsf{Prime}}(\mathsf{tag}_i)|i \in I\}$, and judges the validity of the received proof with the following condition:

$$\mathsf{WitVerify}^*(\mathsf{Acc}(R), R, Q_I, \pi_I) \stackrel{?}{=} 1 \tag{4}$$

If the proof fails to pass the above verification, then $\mathcal{C}$ outputs 0. Otherwise, $\mathcal{C}$ further checks the following condition:

$$e(\sigma_I, g) \stackrel{?}{=} e\left(A, \prod_{i \in I} \mathsf{H}_{\mathbb{G}}(i\|\mathsf{tag}_i)^{\nu_i} \cdot u^\nu\right) \tag{5}$$

The client $\mathcal{C}$ outputs 1 if it holds, and 0 otherwise.
- Update(sk, i, s', vk, DB): To replace a previously outsourced data item $s[i]$ with a new one s', the client $\mathcal{C}$ first retrieves the current tuple $(i, s[i], \sigma_i, \mathsf{tag}_i)$ from the server $\mathcal{S}$, and then checks its validity via the equation (1). If it passes the verification, $\mathcal{C}$ creates $\sigma_i' \leftarrow \left(\mathsf{H}_{\mathbb{G}}(i\|\mathsf{tag}_i') \cdot u^{s'}\right)^\alpha$, where tag_i' is a new random string uniformly sampled from $\{0, 1\}^\lambda$, and updates the current accumulator $\mathsf{Acc}(R) \leftarrow (\mathsf{Acc}(R))^{\mathsf{H}_{\mathsf{Prime}}(\mathsf{tag}_i)}$. Furthermore, $\mathcal{C}$ sends $(s', \sigma_i', \mathsf{tag}_i')$ and $\mathsf{Acc}(R)$ to $\mathcal{S}$. After that, $\mathcal{S}$ checks the validity of s' according to the equation (1) again, and replaces $(i, s[i], \sigma_i, \mathsf{tag}_i)$ with $(i, s', \sigma_i', \mathsf{tag}_i')$ if it passes the verification. Finally, the client $\mathcal{C}$ updates $R \leftarrow R \cup \{\mathsf{tag}_i\}$. In addition, both $\mathcal{C}$ and $\mathcal{S}$ use the updated accumulator $\mathsf{Acc}(R)$ to update the verification key vk.

Algorithm 1. Batching Non-membership Witnesses of the RSA Accumulator

---

Require: WitCreate*$(\mathrm{Acc}(R), R, Q)$:

1: $z^* \leftarrow \prod_{z' \in R} z'$
2: $w' \leftarrow \prod_{w \in Q} w$
3: $(x, y) \leftarrow \mathrm{EEA}(z^*, w')$
4: $V \leftarrow (\mathrm{Acc}(R))^x$
5: $Y \leftarrow h^y$
6: $\ell_1 \leftarrow \mathsf{H}_{\mathrm{Prime}}(w', Y, h \cdot V^{-1})$
7: $t_1 \leftarrow \lfloor \frac{w'}{\ell_1} \rfloor$, $T_1 = Y^{t_1}$
8: $h' \leftarrow \mathsf{H}_{\mathbb{G}'}(\mathrm{Acc}(R), V)$
9: $X' = (h')^x$
10: $\ell_2 \leftarrow \mathsf{H}_{\mathrm{Primes}}(\mathrm{Acc}(R), V, X')$,
11: $\gamma \leftarrow \mathsf{H}_\lambda(\mathrm{Acc}(R), V, X', \ell_2)$
12: $t_2 \leftarrow \lfloor \frac{x}{\ell_2} \rfloor$, $r \leftarrow x \bmod \ell_2$
13: $T_2 \leftarrow (\mathrm{Acc}(R) \cdot (h')^\gamma)^{t_2}$
14: **return** $\pi = \{V, Y, T_1, T_2, X', r\}$

Require: WitVerify*$(\mathrm{Acc}(R), R, Q, \pi)$:

1: $\{V, Y, T_1, T_2, X', r\} \leftarrow \pi$
2: $w' \leftarrow \prod_{w \in Q} w$
3: $\ell_1 \leftarrow \mathsf{H}_{\mathrm{Prime}}(w', Y, h \cdot Y^{-1})$
4: $r' \leftarrow w' \bmod \ell_1$
5: **if** $T_1^{\ell_1} \cdot Y^{r'} \neq h \cdot V^{-1}$ **then**
6:     **return** 0
7: **end if**
8: $h' \leftarrow \mathsf{H}_{\mathbb{G}'}(\mathrm{Acc}(R), V)$
9: $\ell_2 \leftarrow \mathsf{H}_{\mathrm{Prime}}(\mathrm{Acc}(R), V, X')$
10: $\gamma \leftarrow \mathsf{H}_\lambda(\mathrm{Acc}(R), V, X', \ell_2)$
11: **if** $T_2^{\ell_2} \cdot (\mathrm{Acc}(R) \cdot (h')^\gamma)^r \neq V \cdot (X')^\gamma$ **then**
12:     **return** 0
13: **end if**
14: **return** 1

CORRECTNESS. The correctness of the above VADS protocol is guaranteed by the Eqs. (1–5), which in turn depend on the correctness of the underlying BLS signature and RSA accumulator. Specifically, for a correctly generated signature σ_i for the i-th data item $s[i]$, if it has not been revoked by the client, then it can naturally pass through the verification of the Eqs. (1–4) due to the correctness of the BLS signature and RSA accumulator. Furthermore, for correctly generated and non-revoked signature set $\{\sigma_i | i \in I\}$, as shown below, the Eq. (5) also holds:

$$
\begin{aligned}
e(\sigma_I, g) &= e\left(\prod_{i \in I} \sigma_i^{\nu_i}, g \right) = e\left(\prod_{i \in I} \mathsf{H}_{\mathbb{G}}(i || \mathrm{tag}_i)^{\nu_i} \cdot u^{s[i] \cdot \nu_i}, g^\alpha \right) \\
&= e\left(\prod_{i \in I} \mathsf{H}_{\mathbb{G}}(i || \mathrm{tag}_i)^{\nu_i} \cdot u^{\sum_{i \in I} s[i] \cdot \nu_i}, A \right) \\
&= e\left(A, \prod_{i \in I} \mathsf{H}_{\mathbb{G}}(i || \mathrm{tag}_i)^{\nu_i} \cdot u^\nu \right).
\end{aligned}
$$

SECURITY. The security of the above VADS construction is guaranteed by the following theorem.

Theorem 1. *If the hash function* $\mathsf{H}_{\mathrm{prime}}$ *is collision-resistant, the adaptive root assumption holds in the RSA group, the CDH assumption holds in the bilinear group, then the proposed VADS protocol is secure in the random oracle model.*

Due to the limit of space, we provide the proof in the full version of this paper.

5   Performance Analysis

In this section, we theoretically discuss the performance of our proposal by comparing it with previous VDS constructions in terms of computation and communication costs as well as security properties.

Table 1. Comparisons with previous works in terms of costs

VDS Protocols	Communication Cost		Computation Cost					
	$|\pi_a|$	$|\pi_q|$	Append	Query	Verify	Update	Audit	Judge
Schröder and Schröder [24]	N/A	$\mathcal{O}(\log M)$	$\mathcal{O}(\log M)$	$\mathcal{O}(\log M)$	$\mathcal{O}(\log M)$	$\mathcal{O}(\log M)$	N/A	N/A
Schröder and Simkin [25]	N/A	$\mathcal{O}(\log N)$	$\mathcal{O}(\log N)$	$\mathcal{O}(\log N)$	$\mathcal{O}(\log N)$	$\mathcal{O}(\log N)$	N/A	N/A
Krupp et al. CVC [18]	N/A	$\mathcal{O}(\log N)$	$\mathcal{O}(1)$	$\mathcal{O}(\log N)$	$\mathcal{O}(\log N)$	$\mathcal{O}(\log N)$	N/A	N/A
Krupp et al. ACC [18]	N/A	$\mathcal{O}(1)$	$\mathcal{O}(1)$	$\mathcal{O}(1)$	$\mathcal{O}(1)$	$\mathcal{O}(U)$	N/A	N/A
Sun et al. [27]	N/A	$\mathcal{O}(\log N)$	$\mathcal{O}(\log N)$	$\mathcal{O}(\log N)$	$\mathcal{O}(\log N)$	$\mathcal{O}(\log N)$	N/A	N/A
Ours	$\mathcal{O}(|I|)$	$\mathcal{O}(1)$	$\mathcal{O}(1)$	$\mathcal{O}(1)$	$\mathcal{O}(1)$	$\mathcal{O}(1)$	$\mathcal{O}(|I|)$	$\mathcal{O}(|I|)$

* $|I|$ is the size of challenge index set I used in the auditing protocol. $|\pi_a|$ is the proof size in the audit protocol. $|\pi_q|$ is the proof size in the query protocol. M is the maximum number of data entries allowed to store into the database. N is the number of data entries currently stored in the database. U denotes the number of previous update operations. N/A means this item is not applicable to the corresponding scheme. We only consider those dominant operations like pairing and exponentiation.

As demonstrated in Table 1, for a single query, the communication and computation costs of our construction achieve constant, and is independent of either the size of outsourced stream data or the number of update operations. From this perspective, the proposed VDS protocol outperforms the state-of-the-art, and is optimal. What is more, for concurrent queries, our proposal also has constant costs, but that of other VDS constructions are linear in the size of concurrent queries[6]. On the other hand, for each data auditing, the computation and communication costs of our VADS construction grows linearly with the size of the challenge set. This is mainly because that the cloud server has to return those tags assigned to challenged data items, so as to enable the data owner to verify the returned non-membership proof against the current accumulator. In fact, for the pure data auditing scheme, only those schemes in the case of statics have constant cost, while the cost of those schemes in the case of dynamics is usually logarithmic in the size of authenticated data items. Therefore, the auditing cost of our VADS construction, which deals with dynamic data, is acceptable.

Table 2. Comparisons with previous works in terms of properties

VDS Protocols	Unbounded	Auditability	Security Model	Complexity Assumption
Schröder and Schröder [24]	✗	✗	Standard Model	Discrete Logarithm
Schröder and Simkin [25]	✓	✗	Random Oracle	Discrete Logairthm
Krupp et al. CVC [18]	✓	✗	Standard Model	CDH
Krupp et al. ACC [18]	✓	✗	Standard Model	q-strong DH
Sun et al. [27]	✓	✗	Random Oracle	Discrete Logairthm
Ours	✓	✓	Random Oracle	CDH and Adaptive Root

---

[6] Due to limited space, here we omit how to extend our VADS protocol to support concurrent queries. In fact, it is straightforward, and just needs to create an aggregated non-membership proof for those requested data items by invoking the Algorithm 1.

In Table 2, we compare the security properties of the proposed VADS construction with previous VDS protocols. Observe that, except for Schröder and Schröder's [24] VDS protocol, the other protocols are all unbounded, and meet the unbounded feature of stream data. Although Krupp et al.'s [18] CVC construction is proved secure in the standard model and also is more efficient than other VDS constructions [18,24], its security is built upon a non-standard assumption, i.e., q-strong Diffie-Hellman assumption. At the same time, other listed VDS schemes are proved secure under standard assumptions. In particular, our VADS construction uniquely enjoys the functionality of data auditing, and thus allows the data owner to check the integrity of outsourced stream data without retrieving them.

6   Conclusion

In this paper, we revisit the problem of verifiable data streaming, and focus on further optimizing the efficiency of previous constructions. Specifically, by carefully combing the BLS signature with a recently proposed RSA accumulator, we put forward an optimal verifiable data streaming protocol with data auditing. That is, it achieves constant communication and computation costs, and outperforms the state-of-the-art. Additionally, compared with the original VDS, it features of public data auditing, and thus enables the data owner to verify the integrity of outsourced stream data in the case of not having to retrieve them. We prove its security under standard assumptions in the random oracle model.

Acknowledgment. This work was supported by the National Nature Science Foundation of China under Grants 61960206014 and 62172434, and in part by the Project funded by China Postdoctoral Science Foundation No. 2020M673348 and No. 2021T140531.

References

1. Arasu, A., et al.: STREAM: the Stanford stream data manager. In: Proceedings of the 2003 ACM SIGMOD International Conference on Management of Data, p. 665. ACM (2003)
2. Babcock, B., Babu, S., Datar, M., Motwani, R., Widom, J.: Models and issues in data stream systems. In: Proceedings of the Twenty-first ACM SIGACT-SIGMOD-SIGART Symposium on Principles of Database Systems, pp. 1–16. ACM (2002)
3. Bellare, M., Keelveedhi, S., Ristenpart, T.: Message-locked encryption and secure deduplication. In: Johansson, T., Nguyen, P.Q. (eds.) EUROCRYPT 2013. LNCS, vol. 7881, pp. 296–312. Springer, Heidelberg (2013). https://doi.org/10.1007/978-3-642-38348-9_18
4. Benabbas, S., Gennaro, R., Vahlis, Y.: Verifiable delegation of computation over large datasets. In: Rogaway, P. (ed.) CRYPTO 2011. LNCS, vol. 6841, pp. 111–131. Springer, Heidelberg (2011). https://doi.org/10.1007/978-3-642-22792-9_7
5. Boneh, D., Bünz, B., Fisch, B.: Batching techniques for accumulators with applications to IOPs and stateless blockchains. In: Boldyreva, A., Micciancio, D. (eds.) CRYPTO 2019. LNCS, vol. 11692, pp. 561–586. Springer, Cham (2019). https://doi.org/10.1007/978-3-030-26948-7_20

6. Boneh, D., Lynn, B., Shacham, H.: Short signatures from the weil pairing. In: Boyd, C. (ed.) ASIACRYPT 2001. LNCS, vol. 2248, pp. 514–532. Springer, Heidelberg (2001). https://doi.org/10.1007/3-540-45682-1_30

7. Campanelli, M., Fiore, D., Greco, N., Kolonelos, D., Nizzardo, L.: Incrementally aggregatable vector commitments and applications to verifiable decentralized storage. In: Moriai, S., Wang, H. (eds.) ASIACRYPT 2020. LNCS, vol. 12492, pp. 3–35. Springer, Cham (2020). https://doi.org/10.1007/978-3-030-64834-3_1

8. Catalano, D., Fiore, D.: Vector commitments and their applications. In: Kurosawa, K., Hanaoka, G. (eds.) PKC 2013. LNCS, vol. 7778, pp. 55–72. Springer, Heidelberg (2013). https://doi.org/10.1007/978-3-642-36362-7_5

9. Chen, C., Wu, H., Wang, L., Yu, C.: Practical integrity preservation for data streaming in cloud-assisted healthcare sensor systems. Comput. Netw. **129**, 472–480 (2017)

10. Chen, X., et al.: Publicly verifiable databases with all efficient updating operations. IEEE Trans. Knowl. Data Eng. (2020). https://doi.org/10.1109/TKDE.2020.2975777

11. Chen, X., Li, J., Huang, X., Ma, J., Lou, W.: New publicly verifiable databases with efficient updates. IEEE Trans. Dependable Secure Comput. **12**(5), 546–556 (2015)

12. Cugola, G., Margara, A.: Processing flows of information: from data stream to complex event processing. ACM Comput. Surv. **44**(3), 15:1–15:62 (2012)

13. Erway, C.C., Küpçü, A., Papamanthou, C., Tamassia, R.: Dynamic provable data possession. ACM Trans. Inf. Syst. Secur. **17**(4), 15:1–15:29 (2015)

14. Esiner, E., Kachkeev, A., Braunfeld, S., Küpçü, A., Özkasap, Ö.: FlexDPDP: flexlist-based optimized dynamic provable data possession. ACM Trans. Storage **12**(4), 23:1–23:44 (2016)

15. Etemad, M., Küpçü, A.: Generic dynamic data outsourcing framework for integrity verification. ACM Comput. Surv. **53**(1), 8:1–8:32 (2020)

16. Grobauer, B., Walloschek, T., Stöcker, E.: Understanding cloud computing vulnerabilities. IEEE Secur. Priv. **9**(2), 50–57 (2011)

17. Juels, A., Kaliski Jr, B.S.: PORs: proofs of retrievability for large files. In: Proceedings of the 2007 ACM Conference on Computer and Communications Security, pp. 584–597. ACM (2007)

18. Krupp, J., Schröder, D., Simkin, M., Fiore, D., Ateniese, G., Nuernberger, S.: Nearly optimal verifiable data streaming. In: Cheng, C.-M., Chung, K.-M., Persiano, G., Yang, B.-Y. (eds.) PKC 2016. LNCS, vol. 9614, pp. 417–445. Springer, Heidelberg (2016). https://doi.org/10.1007/978-3-662-49384-7_16

19. Lai, R.W.F., Malavolta, G.: Subvector commitments with application to succinct arguments. In: Boldyreva, A., Micciancio, D. (eds.) CRYPTO 2019. LNCS, vol. 11692, pp. 530–560. Springer, Cham (2019). https://doi.org/10.1007/978-3-030-26948-7_19

20. Li, S., Zhang, Y., Xu, C., Chen, K.: Cryptoanalysis of an authenticated data structure scheme with public privacy-preserving auditing. IEEE Trans. Inf. Forensics Secur. **16**, 2564–2565 (2021)

21. Merkle, R.C.: Protocols for public key cryptosystems. In: Proceedings of the 1980 IEEE Symposium on Security and Privacy, pp. 122–134. IEEE Computer Society (1980)

22. Miao, M., Ma, J., Huang, X., Wang, Q.: Efficient verifiable databases with insertion/deletion operations from delegating polynomial functions. IEEE Trans. Inf. Forensics Secur. **13**(2), 511–520 (2018)

23. Papamanthou, C., Shi, E., Tamassia, R., Yi, K.: Streaming authenticated data structures. In: Johansson, T., Nguyen, P.Q. (eds.) EUROCRYPT 2013. LNCS, vol. 7881, pp. 353–370. Springer, Heidelberg (2013). https://doi.org/10.1007/978-3-642-38348-9_22

24. Schröder, D., Schröder, H.: Verifiable data streaming. In: 19th ACM Conference on Computer and Communications Security (CCS'12), pp. 953–964. ACM (2012)

25. Schöder, D., Simkin, M.: VeriStream – a framework for verifiable data streaming. In: Böhme, R., Okamoto, T. (eds.) FC 2015. LNCS, vol. 8975, pp. 548–566. Springer, Heidelberg (2015). https://doi.org/10.1007/978-3-662-47854-7_34

26. Shacham, H., Waters, B.: Compact proofs of retrievability. J. Cryptol. **26**(3), 442–483 (2013). https://doi.org/10.1007/s00145-012-9129-2

27. Sun, Y., Liu, Q., Chen, X., Du, X.: An adaptive authenticated data structure with privacy-preserving for big data stream in cloud. IEEE Trans. Inf. Forensics Secur. **15**, 3295–3310 (2020)

28. Wang, F., Mickens, J., Zeldovich, N., Vaikuntanathan, V.: Sieve: cryptographically enforced access control for user data in untrusted clouds. In: 13th USENIX Symposium on Networked Systems Design and Implementation, pp. 611–626. USENIX Association (2016)

29. Wang, J., Chen, X., Huang, X., You, I., Xiang, Y.: Verifiable auditing for outsourced database in cloud computing. IEEE Trans. Comput. **64**(11), 3293–3303 (2015)

30. Wang, Q., Wang, C., Ren, K., Lou, W., Li, J.: Enabling public auditability and data dynamics for storage security in cloud computing. IEEE Trans. Parallel Distrib. Syst. **22**(5), 847–859 (2011)

31. Xu, J., Meng, Q., Wu, J., Zheng, J.X., Zhang, X., Sharma, S.: Efficient and lightweight data streaming authentication in industrial control and automation systems. IEEE Trans. Ind. Inf. **17**(6), 4279–4287 (2021)

32. Xu, J., Wei, L., Zhang, Y., Wang, A., Zhou, F., Gao, C.: Dynamic fully homomorphic encryption-based Merkle tree for lightweight streaming authenticated data structures. J. Netw. Comput. Appl. **107**, 113–124 (2018)

33. Xue, K., Li, S., Hong, J., Xue, Y., Yu, N., Hong, P.: Two-cloud secure database for numeric-related SQL range queries with privacy preserving. IEEE Trans. Inf. Forensics Secur. **12**(7), 1596–1608 (2017)

34. Zhang, Y., Blanton, M.: Efficient dynamic provable possession of remote data via update trees. ACM Trans. Storage **12**(2), 9:1–9:45 (2016)

35. Zhang, Y., Genkin, D., Katz, J., Papadopoulos, D., Papamanthou, C.: VSQL: verifying arbitrary SQL queries over dynamic outsourced databases. In: 2017 IEEE Symposium on Security and Privacy, pp. 863–880. IEEE Computer Society (2017)

36. Zhang, Z., Chen, X., Ma, J., Tao, X.: New efficient constructions of verifiable data streaming with accountability. Ann. Telecommun. **74**(7–8), 483–499 (2019). https://doi.org/10.1007/s12243-018-0687-7

One-More Unforgeability of Blind ECDSA

Xianrui Qin$^{(\boxtimes)}$ ⓘ, Cailing Cai, and Tsz Hon Yuen

The University of Hong Kong, Hong Kong, China
{xrqin,clingcai,thyuen}@cs.hku.hk

Abstract. In this paper, we give the *first* formal security analysis on the one-more unforgeability of blind ECDSA. We start with giving a general attack on blind ECDSA, which is similar to the ROS attack on the blind Schnorr signature. We formulate the ECDSA-ROS problem to capture this attack.

Next, we give a generic construction of blind ECDSA based on an additive homomorphic encryption and a corresponding zero-knowledge proof. Our concrete instantiation is about 40 times more bandwidth efficient than the blind ECDSA in AsiaCCS 2019.

After that, we give the *first* formal proof of one-more unforgeability for blind ECDSA, under a new model called *algebraic bijective random oracle*. The security of our generic blind ECDSA relies on the hardness of a discrete logarithm-based interactive assumption and an assumption of the underlying elliptic curve.

Finally, we analyze the hardness of the ECDSA-ROS problem in the algebraic bijective random oracle model.

Keywords: Blind signature · ECDSA · One-more unforgeability

1 Introduction

A blind signature scheme [8] consists of an interactive protocol between a user and a signer. The signer holds a secret key sk and the user holds a message m of its choice. After the interaction, the user learns a valid signature σ on the message m. The signer can neither learn the message that it signs, nor link the transcripts of protocol that it creates.

The blind signature can be applied to various privacy sensitive scenarios, such as anonymous credentials, eCash, and e-voting. In particular, for blind ECDSA, Bitcoin developers are exploring its usage to blind coin swaps, trustless tumbler services, and more [17,22].

The security model of blind signature is called the *one-more unforgeability* against chosen message attack. It means that the adversary cannot generate $\ell + 1$ blind signatures from ℓ interactions with the signer. Blind Schnorr signature was shown to be one-more unforgeable if the *one-more discrete logarithm* (OMDL) assumption and the *ROS* assumption hold [20]. Unfortunately, the ROS

© Springer Nature Switzerland AG 2021
E. Bertino et al. (Eds.): ESORICS 2021, LNCS 12973, pp. 313–331, 2021.
https://doi.org/10.1007/978-3-030-88428-4_16

assumption is recently broken in [5]. The clause blind Schnorr signature [12] is secure based on the OMDL assumption and the modified ROS assumption in the algebraic group model.

Blind ECDSA. For decades of study, many constructions of blind signatures are proposed [1,2,6,8,10,12–15,19], including those based on ECDSA [16,22]. ECDSA is one of the most widely deployed signature schemes in practice. For a signing key x, the signature on a message m is a pair $\sigma = (r, s)$ satisfying

$$s = k^{-1}(H(m) + xr) \mod p, \quad r = f(kG),$$

where G is a generator of an ECC group of prime order p, k is randomly chosen from $\mathbb{Z}_p$, H is a hash function, and f is a *conversion function* which returns the x-part of the input ECC point modulus p.

Although blind ECDSA has already been explored in 2004 [16], to the best of our knowledge, no formal security proof of one-more unforgeability has been provided for it yet. In [22], the authors only give a heuristic argument for the security of scheme. On the contrary, the security of blind Schnorr signature has been studied for decades [12,20]. It is mainly because an elegant linearity exists in the Schnorr signature, while it disappears in the ECDSA with the usage of division k^{-1} and the conversion function f during the signature generation.

Our Contributions. In this paper, we solve the open problem of constructing a blind ECDSA signature with a *formal* security proof of one-more unforgeability. We have the following contributions.

1. General Attack on One-more Unforgeability. We first demonstrate an attack on the one-more unforgeability of *any* blind ECDSA signature. We propose an *ECDSA-ROS problem* to capture this attack. The hardness of the ECDSA-ROS problem will be further analyzed in Sect. 5.
2. Generic Construction with Efficient Instantiation. We propose a generic construction of blind ECDSA from an additive homomorphic encryption and a corresponding non-interactive zero-knowledge (NIZK) proof.
   Our blind ECDSA can be instantiated with the additive homomorphic Castagnos-Laguillaumie (CL) encryption [7] with the corresponding NIZK proof in [23]. Our scheme is about 40 times more bandwidth efficient than [22].
3. Formal Security Proof. We give the *first* formal security proof of one-more unforgeability of blind ECDSA. The proof uses a new model called Algebraic Bijective Random Oracle (ABRO), which is a non-trivial combination of the bijective random oracle (BRO) [9] and the algebraic group model (AGM) [11]. The new ABRO model is of independent interest.
   We show that the one-more unforgeability of our generic blind ECDSA relies on some assumptions related to the discrete logarithm and the underlying elliptic curve.

A high level summary will be given in the rest of this section.

1.1   ECDSA-ROS Attack on Blind ECDSA

Now we consider the following attack on the one-more unforgeability of blind ECDSA. No matter how the blind ECDSA protocol is implemented, the user eventually obtains ℓ signatures (r_j, s_j) on messages m_j for $j \in [\ell]$ such that:

$$R_j = s_j^{-1}(h_j G + r_j X), \quad r_j = f(R_j), \quad h_j = H(m_j).$$

The adversary can break the one-more unforgeability if he can find (m^*, R^*, s^*) and a vector $\boldsymbol{\rho} = (\rho_1, \ldots, \rho_\ell)$ that satisfies:

$$\frac{H(m^*)}{s^*} = \sum_{j=1}^{\ell} \frac{\rho_j h_j}{s_j}, \tag{1}$$

$$\frac{f(R^*)}{s^*} = \frac{r^*}{s^*} = \sum_{j=1}^{\ell} \frac{\rho_j r_j}{s_j}, \tag{2}$$

$$R^* = \sum_{j=1}^{\ell} \rho_j R_j. \tag{3}$$

The one-more forgery includes the extra signature $(r^* = f(R^*), s^*)$ on the message m^*. We call this attack as the *ECDSA-ROS attack*, because Eq. 1 is similar to the ROS attack on the blind Schnorr signature. The *ECDSA-ROS attack* does not rely on solving the discrete logarithm of the public key X.

Hardness of the ECDSA-ROS Problem. We conjecture that the ECDSA-ROS problem is hard to solve even under the recent attack on the ROS problem [5], since the attacker needs to solve three equations simultaneously, with two non-linear functions f and H involved. The hardness of the ECDSA-ROS problem will be further analyzed in Sect. 5.

1.2   Generic Construction

Our generic blind ECDSA can be constructed with any additive homomorphic encryption HE and a corresponding NIZK proof. Suppose that the signer knows a secret key x and the user knows the message m. They jointly compute $R = k_a k_b G$, where k_a (resp. k_b) is chosen by the signer (resp. the user). The user encrypts $H(m)$ and $r = f(R)$ with HE and sends the ciphertext to the signer, with a NIZK proof of the well-formedness of the ciphertext. The signer returns the ciphertext of $k_a^{-1}(H(m) + rx)$ using the additive homomorphic property. The user decrypts it and then divides the plaintext with k_b to obtain s. The blind signature is (r, s).

Efficiency Analysis. The blind ECDSA in [22] used a modified Paillier encryption with a modulus $N = pqt$, where q and t are two random large prime numbers. Hence, it is even more inefficient than the standard Paillier encryption. Furthermore, [22] proposed a NIZK proof for the modified Paillier ciphertext with a binary challenge. In order to achieve a soundness error of $2^{-\ell_s}$, the NIZK proof has to be repeated for ℓ_s times. The resulting blind ECDSA in [22] is inefficient.

Our blind ECDSA can be instantiated with the additive homomorphic CL encryption [7] with the corresponding NIZK proof in [23]. Consider 128 bit security level, the ciphertext size of the CL encryption is 3654 bits, about 55% of the ciphertext size of the modified Paillier encryption (6656 bits). The NIZK proof for CL encryption in [23] is 1488 bytes, but the NIZK proof for modified Paillier encryption in [22] is 69120 bytes for a soundness error of 2^{-80}. Our scheme is about 40 times more bandwidth efficient than [22].

1.3 Algebraic Bijective Random Oracle Model

We propose a new Algebraic Bijective Random Oracle (ABRO) model for the security analysis of blind ECDSA. The idea comes from the bijective random oracle (BRO) [9] and the algebraic group model (AGM) [11]. The BRO was used to prove the unforgeability of ECDSA in [9]. The AGM was used to prove the one-more unforgeability of the clause blind Schnorr signature [12]. Hence, the ABRO model is a reasonable security model to analyze the security of blind ECDSA.

The BRO models the algebraically disruptive behaviour of f similar to the random oracles, which model the disordered behavior of cryptographic hash functions. The BRO decomposes the conversion function f into three independent functions as:

$$f = \varphi \circ \Pi \circ \psi,$$

where φ is a function which maps a group element G into $\{0,1\}^L$ (which is the x-part of G for ECDSA). Π is a bijective mapping from $\{0,1\}^L$ to $[0..2^L - 1]$, and ψ is a mapping from $[0..2^L - 1]$ to $\mathbb{Z}_p$. The BRO requires that the adversary must query the oracles for the computation of Π and Π^{-1}.

The AGM lies between the standard model and the generic group model. With every group element Z that the adversary outputs, he also gives a representation z of Z in terms of the group elements it has received so far. The AGM can be instantiated in an *algebraic wrapper*, as introduced in [3].

New ABRO Model. Our new ABRO model is not a trivial combination of BRO and AGM. Our goal is to minimize the use of AGM in the security model. The ABRO model only requires the adversary to output a representation for the group element R asked in the query $\Pi(\varphi(R))$. The representations are in terms of group elements that has received so far, including the output of the signing oracle and the Π^{-1} oracle.

In contrast with the AGM, the ABRO model does not require the adversary to output representations for group elements used in other oracle queries. Since the mapping Π does not appear in the real scheme, our model does not need to be instantiated with the algebraic wrapper [3].

1.4 Security Proof of Blind ECDSA

ECDSA. As a stepping stone for understanding the security proof for blind ECDSA, we briefly describe the security proof of ECDSA in the ABRO model.

The public key X comes from the discrete logarithm (DL) problem instance (G, X). For a valid forgery signature (r^*, s^*) on a message m^*, we have $s^* R^* = H(m^*)G + r^* X$ and $r^* = f(R^*)$. In the BRO, either Π or Π^{-1} must be queried for R^* or r^*. By the setting of the ABRO, either the representation of R^* is known when $\Pi(\varphi(R^*))$ is asked, or the representation of R^* is set by the simulator when $\Pi^{-1}(\psi^{-1}(r^*))$ is asked. In either case, the representation of R^* can be expressed as a pair (a, b), where $R^* = aG + bX$. Hence, the answer to the DL problem $\log_G X$ can be computed from $s^*(aG + bX) = H(m^*)G + r^* X$.

Blind ECDSA. The main contribution of the paper is the reduction of the one-more unforgeability of blind ECDSA to the Multi-Base Discrete Logarithm (MBDL) assumption in the ABRO model. The (n, q)-MBDL is the generalization of the $(n, 1)$-MBDL problem in [4]: Given group elements $(G, X, R_1, \ldots, R_n)$ and q DL oracle queries (which takes (i, P) as input and outputs $\log_{R_i} P$), output $\log_G X$, with the restriction that i must be distinct in all DL oracle queries. This restriction is essential because $\log_G X$ can be easily computed from $\log_{R_i} G$ and $\log_{R_i} X$.

In the security proof of one-more unforgeability, the blind signing oracle is simulated by the DL oracle of the (n, q)-MBDL problem. Roughly speaking, the simulator sets $kG = R_i$ first. If the adversary asks the blind signature s with respect to kG for some r and a message m, the simulator asks the DL oracle with input $(i, H(m)G + rX)$. The DL oracle returns s such that $sR_i = H(m)G + rX$. Hence s can be used to build a valid answer for the blind signing oracle query. Similar to the security proof of ECDSA, we eventually get $aG + bX = 0$ from the forgery signature for some $a, b \in \mathbb{Z}_p$. The value $\log_G X$ can be extracted to answer the MBDL problem. For the case of $a = 0$, we prove that it happens in negligible probability. During the security proof, we also need an assumption on the underlying elliptic curve that for all points on the elliptic curve, there is only one subgroup whose order is p. This assumption is needed to ensure the correctness of the simulation of the BRO oracle. This assumption holds for most common elliptic curves defined in various standards.

1.5 Related Work

In the security analysis of the blind ECDSA in [22], the authors claimed that 'the proposed blind signature scheme has unforgeability if the ECDSA is unforgeable.' However, this claim is not formally proven. In particular, they did not discuss one-more type assumption (like other blind signature schemes) or ROS type assumption (like the blind Schnorr signature).

2   Preliminaries

Notations. We denote the (closed) integer interval from a to b by $[a, b]$. We use $[b]$ as shorthand for $[1, b]$.

2.1   ECDSA

We define a group generation algorithm for elliptic curve.

- GpGen. On input a security parameter λ, it picks a prime q, an elliptic curve E defined over $\mathbb{F}_p$, and a cyclic group $\mathbb{G}$ in $E(\mathbb{F}_p)$ with a generator G of prime order p. Finally, it outputs $(p, \mathbb{G}, G)$.

ECDSA requires two independent functions (denoted as H and f) to map the messages and group elements into a field $\mathbb{Z}_p$ respectively. The function H is a cryptographic hash function. The function f is known as the *conversion function*, mapping a point A to $A.x \bmod p$, which is an encoding of the x-coordinate of A as an integer.

If x is a signing key and $X = xG$ is the corresponding verification key, a signature on a message m is a pair $\sigma = (r, s)$ satisfying $r = f(kG)$ and $s = k^{-1}(H(m) + xr) \bmod p$. Signatures are verified by recovering $R = \frac{H(m)}{s}G + \frac{r}{s}X$ and checking that $f(R) = r$.

2.2   Blind Signature

Syntax. We follow the definition of [12]. A blind signature scheme BS consists of the following algorithms:

- par $\leftarrow$ BS.Setup(1^λ): the setup algorithm takes the security parameter λ in unary and returns public parameters par;
- (sk, pk) $\leftarrow$ BS.KeyGen(par): the key generation algorithm takes the public parameters par and returns a secret/public key pair (sk, pk);
- $(b, \sigma) \leftarrow \langle$BS.Sign(sk), BS.User(pk, m)$\rangle$: an interactive protocol is run between the signer with private input a secret key sk and the user with private input a public key pk and a message m; the signer outputs $b = 1$ if the interaction completes successfully and $b = 0$ otherwise, while the user outputs a signature σ if it terminates correctly, and $\bot$ otherwise. For a 2-round protocol the interaction can be realized by the following algorithms:

$$(msg_{U,0}, \text{state}_{U,0}) \leftarrow \text{BS.User}_0(\text{pk}, m)$$
$$(msg_{S,1}, \text{state}_S) \leftarrow \text{BS.Sign}_1(\text{sk}, msg_{U,0})$$
$$(msg_{U,1}, \text{state}_{U,1}) \leftarrow \text{BS.User}_1(\text{state}_{U,0}, msg_{S,1})$$
$$(msg_{S,2}, b) \leftarrow \text{BS.Sign}_2(\text{state}_S, msg_{U,1})$$
$$\sigma \leftarrow \text{BS.User}_2(\text{state}_{U,1}, msg_{S,2})$$

(Typically, BS.User$_0$ just initiates the session, thus $msg_{U,0} = ()$ and state$_{U,0} = $ (pk, m).)

- $b' \leftarrow$ BS.Ver(pk, m, σ): the (deterministic) verification algorithm takes a public key pk, a message m and a signature σ as input, and returns 1 if σ is valid on m under pk and 0 otherwise.

Game $\mathsf{UNF}^{\mathcal{A}}_{\mathsf{BS}}(\lambda)$	$\mathsf{Sign}_1(msg)$	$\mathsf{Sign}_2(j, msg)$
1: $par \leftarrow \mathsf{BS.Setup}(1^\lambda)$	1: $k_1 := k_1 + 1$	1: **if** $j \notin S$ **then return** $\bot$
2: $(sk, pk) \leftarrow \mathsf{BS.KeyGen}(par)$	2: $(msg', state_{k_1}) \leftarrow \mathsf{BS.Sign}_1(sk, msg)$	2: $(msg', b) \leftarrow \mathsf{BS.Sign}_2(state_j, msg)$
3: $k_1 := 0; k_2 := 0; S := \emptyset$	3: $S := S \cup \{k_1\}$	3: **if** $b = 1$
4: $(m_i^*, \sigma_i^*)_{i \in [n]} \leftarrow \mathcal{A}^{\mathsf{Sign}_1, \mathsf{Sign}_2}(par, pk)$	4: **return** (k_1, msg')	4: $\quad S := S \backslash \{j\}, \quad k_2 := k_2 + 1$
5: $a_1 = (k_2 < n)$		5: **return** msg'
6: $a_2 = (\forall i \neq j \in [n] : (m_i^*, \sigma_i^*) \neq (m_j^*, \sigma_j^*))$		
7: $a_3 = (\forall i \in [n] : \mathsf{BS.Ver}(pk, m_i^*, \sigma_i^*) = 1)$		
8: **return** $(a_1 \wedge a_2 \wedge a_3)$		

Fig. 1. The one-more unforgeability game for a blind signature scheme BS.

Correctness requires that for any λ and any message m, when running $par \leftarrow \mathsf{BS.Setup}(1^\lambda)$, $(sk, pk) \leftarrow \mathsf{BS.KeyGen}(par)$, $(b, \sigma) \leftarrow \langle \mathsf{BS.Sign}(sk), \mathsf{BS.User}(pk, m) \rangle$, and $b' \leftarrow \mathsf{BS.Ver}(pk, m, \sigma)$, we have $b = 1 = b'$ with probability 1.

One-More Unforgeability. The standard security notion of blind signatures demands that no user, after arbitrary interactions with a signer and ℓ of these interactions were considered successful by the signer, can produce more than ℓ signatures. Moreover, the adversary can schedule and interleave its sessions with the signer in any arbitrary way.

In Game $\mathsf{UNF}^{\mathcal{A}}_{\mathsf{BS}}(\lambda)$ defined in Fig. 1 the adversary has access to two oracles Sign_1 and Sign_2 corresponding to the two phases of the interactive protocol. The game maintains two counters k_1 and k_2 (initially set to 0), where k_1 is used as session identifier, and a set S of "open" sessions. Oracle Sign_1 takes the user's first message, increments k_1, adds k_1 to S and runs the first round on the signer's side, storing its state as state k_1. Oracle Sign_2 takes as input a session identifier j and a user message; if $j \in S$, it runs the second round on the signer's side; if successful, it removes j from S and increments k_2, representing the number of successful interactions.

Blindness. Blindness requires that a signer cannot link a message/signature pair to a particular execution of the signing protocol. The formal security model of blindness is given in Appendix B.

3   Algebraic Bijective Random Oracle Model

In this paper, we propose a new model called *algebraic bijective random oracle model* (ABRO) for proving the security of blind ECDSA. It is developed from the Bijective Random Oracle (BRO) model and the Algebraic Group Model (AGM).

3.1   AGM and BRO

Algebraic Group Model. The *algebraic group model* (AGM) [11] lies between the standard model and the generic group model. On the one hand, the adversary has direct access to group elements; on the other hand, it is assumed to only produce new group elements by applying the group operation to receive group elements. In particular, with every group element Z that it outputs, the adversary also gives a representation z of Z in terms of the group elements it has received so far. Security results in the AGM are proved via reductions to computationally hard problems, like in the standard model.

Bijective Random Oracle Model. As introduced in Sect. 1, the BRO does not allow the adversary to compute the conversion function f completely by itself (which is similar to the restriction on computing the hash function in the random oracle model). The BRO decomposes the function f as $f = \varphi \circ \Pi \circ \psi$ for some bijective mapping Π. The adversary has to query an oracle BRO to compute Π, and an oracle BRO^{-1} to compute Π^{-1}.

3.2 Algebraic Bijective Random Oracle Model

We define a new model by demanding the algebraic representation in the BRO. All queries to the BRO oracle with a group element input must come with the corresponding algebraic representation. We call this new model as Algebraic Bijective Random Oracle (ABRO) Model.

Two changes are made from the definition of the BRO model with oracles BRO and BRO^{-1}.

1. The BRO^{-1} oracle takes as input an integer $x \in [0..2^L - 1]$ (L is the bit length of x) and returns $y = \Pi^{-1}(x)$. In addition, the outputs of $\varphi^{-1}(y)$ are added to the list of received group elements.[1]
2. The BRO oracle takes as input a group element R and its algebraic representation r. The representation is in terms of group elements that it has received so far, including the public key, signatures obtained from the signing oracle, and the group elements defined above by BRO^{-1}. The oracle outputs $x = \Pi(\psi(R))$.

We can see that the algebraic representation requirement in the ABRO is only needed for the query of the BRO oracle. This is the advantage of the ABRO as compared to the trivial combination of the BRO and the AGM.

4   Blind ECDSA

We first give the blind ECDSA protocol. It uses an additive homomorphic encryption and a corresponding non-interactive zero-knowledge (NIZK) proof.

4.1 Building Blocks

Additive Homomorphic Encryption. Denote $\mathsf{HE} = (\mathsf{Setup}, \mathsf{KeyGen}, \mathsf{Enc}, \mathsf{Dec})$ as an additive homomorphic encryption scheme, such that $\mathsf{Enc}_{\mathsf{pk}}(m_1) \cdot$

---

[1] Since φ is a semi-injective function for ECDSA, two group elements are added for each BRO^{-1} query for the case of ECDSA.

$\mathsf{Enc_{pk}}(m_2) = \mathsf{Enc_{pk}}(m_1 + m_2)$. Paillier encryption [18], modified Paillier encryption [22] and CL encryption [7] are some examples of additive homomorphic encryption.

Denote the message space of HE as $\mathcal{M}$. For HE that has a message space $\mathcal{M}$ different from $\mathbb{Z}_p$ (e.g., Paillier encryption), we further require that $\mathcal{M}$ is larger than $p^3 + p^2$.

NIZK Proof. Denote $\mathsf{NIZK} = (\mathsf{Setup}, \mathsf{Pf}, \mathsf{Vf})$ as a non-interactive zero-knowledge proof for the relation $\mathcal{R}$ for the ciphertext of HE:

$$\mathcal{R} = \{(m_1, m_2, r_1, r_2) : c_1 = \mathsf{Enc_{pk}}(m_1; r_1) \wedge c_2 = \mathsf{Enc_{pk}}(m_2; r_2) \wedge m_1, m_2 \in \mathbb{Z}_p\},$$

where r_1 (resp. r_2) is the randomness used to encrypt the message m_1 (resp. m_2). If the HE has a message space of $\mathbb{Z}_p$ (e.g., modified Paillier encryption [22], or CL encryption [7]), the range proof of $m_1, m_2 \in \mathbb{Z}_p$ is not needed.

4.2 Construction

The blind ECDSA protocol BS is as follows.

- Setup. On input a security parameter λ, it runs $(p, \mathbb{G}, G) \leftarrow \mathsf{GpGen}(1^\lambda)$ and picks a cryptographic hash function $H : \{0,1\}^* \rightarrow \mathbb{Z}_p$. It runs $\mathsf{par}' \leftarrow \mathsf{HE.Setup}(1^\lambda)$ and $\mathsf{crs} \leftarrow \mathsf{NIZK.Setup}(1^\lambda)$. It returns $\mathsf{par} = (p, \mathbb{G}, G, H, \mathsf{par}', \mathsf{crs})$.
- KeyGen. On input par, it picks $\mathsf{sk} := x \leftarrow_\$ \mathbb{Z}_p$ and computes $\mathsf{pk} := X = xG$.
- Sign, User. The user runs $(\mathsf{upk}, \mathsf{usk}) \leftarrow \mathsf{HE.KeyGen}(\mathsf{par})$ and sends upk to the signer. Then they run the interactive blind signing protocols in Fig. 2.
- Verify. To verify a signature $\sigma = (r, s)$ for a message m and a public key X, it computes $R = \frac{H(m)}{s}G + \frac{r}{s}X$. It returns 1 if $r = f(R)$, or returns 0 otherwise.

4.3 Assumptions

Before proving the security of ECDSA in the ABRO model, we first introduce the assumptions needed for the security proof.

Firstly, we propose an assumption on the underlying elliptic curves chosen by GpGen in the Setup phase above.

Assumption 1. Let $(p, \mathbb{G}, G) \leftarrow \mathsf{GpGen}(\lambda)$ and $E(\mathbb{F}_q)$ is a group of points on the elliptic curve E. There is only one subgroup in $E(\mathbb{F}_q)$ whose order is p.

Assumption 1 is not always true for all elliptic curves. In general, $E(\mathbb{F}_q)$ can contain more than one subgroup whose order is a prime $p > 2$. For example, let E be the elliptic curve $y^2 = x^3 + 2$ over $\mathbb{F}_7$. Then $E(\mathbb{F}_7) = \{\infty, (0,3), (0,4), (3,1), (3,6), (5,1), (5,6), (6,1), (6,6)\}$, and there are four different subgroups whose order is 3:

$$\{(0,3), (0,4), \infty\}, \{(3,1), (3,6), \infty\}, \{(5,1), (5,6), \infty\}, \{(6,1), (6,6), \infty\}.$$

BS.Sign$((par, upk, X), x)$		BS.User$((par, upk, X), m, usk)$
$k_a \xleftarrow{\$} \mathbb{Z}_p$		
$R = k_a G$. Abort if $R = \mathcal{O}$	$\xrightarrow{\quad R \quad}$	$k_b \xleftarrow{\$} \mathbb{Z}_p, \quad h = H(m)$
		$(r, \cdot) = \tilde{R} = k_b R = k_a k_b G$
		Abort if $\tilde{R} = \mathcal{O} \vee r = 0$
		$c_1 = \mathsf{HE.Enc_{upk}}(r; r_1)$
		$c_2 = \mathsf{HE.Enc_{upk}}(h; r_2)$
if $\mathsf{NIZK.Vf}((c_1, c_2, upk), \pi) = 1$,	$\xleftarrow{c_1, c_2, \pi}$	$\pi = \mathsf{NIZK.Pf}((r, h, r_1, r_2), (c_1, c_2, upk))$
$t \xleftarrow{\$} [0, |\mathcal{M}|/p - p^2 - p]^3$		
$\bar{k} := k_a^{-1} \mod p$		
$c = c_1^{x\bar{k}} \cdot c_2^{\bar{k}} \cdot \mathsf{HE.Enc_{upk}}(tp)$	$\xrightarrow{\quad c \quad}$	$s = \mathsf{HE.Dec_{usk}}(c)/k_b \mod p$
		Abort if $s = 0 \wedge \mathsf{Verify}((r, s), m, X) = 0$
		return (r, s)

Fig. 2. The signing protocol of the blind ECDSA signature scheme. If the message space of HE is equal to $\mathbb{Z}_p$, then t can be fixed to 0. Here, r_1, r_2 are Encrandomness. For the range of t, firstly, here t is used for rerandomizing the message($xr\bar{k} + h\bar{k}$) encrypted in the ciphertext c. Secondly, the range in which t is chosen is set to prevent $|xr\bar{k} + h\bar{k} + tp| \geq |\mathcal{M}|$, Otherwise it will result in decryption error of c, i.e., $|xr\bar{k} + h\bar{k}| \neq \mathsf{HE.Dec_{usk}}(c) \mod p$.

However in practice, the common elliptic curves defined in various standards have the order of the subgroup $\mathbb{G}$ that is closed to the order of the curves themselves. In other words, Assumption 1 holds in practice. For example, for NIST P-256,

$q = $ 0xffffffff 00000001 00000000 00000000 00000000 ffffffff ffffffff ffffffff,

$p = $ 0xffffffff 00000000 ffffffff ffffffff bce6faad a7179e84 f3b9cac2 fc632551.

For secp256k1 used in Bitcoin,

$q = $ 0xffffffff ffffffff ffffffff ffffffff ffffffff fffffffe fffffc2f,

$p = $ 0xffffffff ffffffff ffffffff fffffffe baaedce6 af48a03b bfd25e8c d0364141.

Remark 1. Assumption 1 is crucial for our proof, since the argument that we use in the proof "$pU = \mathcal{O}$ implies $U \in E(\mathbb{F}_q)$ falls in the subgroup $\mathbb{G}$ whose order is p" is not always correct without using Assumption 1.

(n, q)**-MBDL Problem.** We give the (n, q)-MBDL problem in Fig. 3, which is the generalization of the Multi-base Discrete Logarithm (MBDL) problem in [4]. The $(n, 1)$-MBDL problem is introduced by Bellare and Dai [4], and they give a tight security reduction of the Schnorr signature to the $(1, 1)$-MBDL problem.

Game $\mathrm{MBDL}^{\mathcal{A}}_{\mathsf{GpGen},n,q}(\lambda)$	Oracle $\mathrm{DLo}(i, W)$
$(p, \mathbb{G}, G) \leftarrow \mathsf{GpGen}(1^{\lambda}); S := \emptyset; y \leftarrow_\$ \mathbb{Z}_p; Y := yG$	**if** $i \in S$ or $i \notin [n]$, **return** $\perp$
for $i = 1, \ldots, n,$	$S := S \cup \{i\}$
$\quad x_i \leftarrow_\$ \mathbb{Z}_p; X_i := x_i G$	**return** $\log_{X_i}(W)$
$y' \leftarrow \mathcal{A}^{\mathrm{DLO}}(p, \mathbb{G}, G, Y, X_1, \ldots, X_n)$	
return $(y' = y \wedge |S| \leq q)$	

Fig. 3. The (n, q)-MBDL problem.

4.4   Security Proof

Theorem 1. *Assume that Assumption 1 holds for* GpGen. *Let* $\mathcal{A}_{\mathsf{alg}}$ *be an algebraic adversary against the one-more unforgeability security of the blind EDCSA signature running in time at most* τ *and making at most* ℓ *queries to* Sign_1, q_r *queries to the random oracle* H *and* q_b *queries to the bijective random oracles. If* NIZK *has soundness, then there exists an algorithm* $\mathcal{B}_1$ *solving the* (ℓ, ℓ)-MBDL *problem, and an algorithm* $\mathcal{B}_2$ *breaking the collision resistant of* H, *both running in time at most* $\tau + O(\ell + q_r + q_b)$, *such that:*

$$\mathsf{Adv}^{\mathsf{om\text{-}unf}}_{\mathcal{A}_{\mathsf{alg}}}(\lambda) \leq \mathsf{Adv}^{(\ell,\ell)-\mathsf{MBDL}}_{\mathcal{B}_1}(\lambda) + \mathsf{Adv}^{\mathsf{cr}}_{\mathcal{B}_2}(\lambda) + \frac{q_b^2}{(p-1)/2 - q_b} + \left(\frac{q_r \cdot q_b}{p}\right)^{\ell+1}.$$

Proof. The one-more unforgeability of our blind ECDSA is proved by a sequence of games.

$\underline{\mathsf{Game}_0}$. As shown in Fig. 4, the first game is the one-more unforgeability game for scheme BS played with $\mathcal{A}_{\mathsf{alg}}$ in the ABRO model. Hence we have $\mathsf{Adv}^{\mathsf{om\text{-}unf}}_{\mathcal{A}_{\mathsf{alg}}}(\lambda) = \mathsf{Adv}^{\mathsf{Game}_0}_{\mathcal{A}_{\mathsf{alg}}}(\lambda)$.

$\underline{\mathsf{Game}_1}$. By Fig. 4, Game_1 is the same as Game_0 except that in the Fin procedure, it rejects the collision of the challenge message m^* with any message queried in the signing oracle. Hence $\mathsf{Adv}^{\mathsf{Game}_0}_{\mathcal{A}_{\mathsf{alg}}}(\lambda) \leq \mathsf{Adv}^{\mathsf{Game}_1}_{\mathcal{A}_{\mathsf{alg}}}(\lambda) + \mathsf{Adv}^{\mathsf{cr}}_{\mathcal{B}_2}(\lambda)$, where $\mathsf{Adv}^{\mathsf{cr}}_{\mathcal{B}_2}(\lambda)$ is the probability of breaking the collision resistance of H by some algorithm $\mathcal{B}_2$.

Fig. 4. Game_0 and Game_1 used in the proof of Blind ECDSA

BRO(R, ρ) Game$_2$	BRO$^{-1}(\beta)$
1: **if** $R \neq \rho \cdot U$, **return** $\bot$	1: **if** $(\cdot, \beta) \in \Pi$, **return** $\Pi^{-1}(\beta)$
2: $\alpha = \varphi(R)$	2: $\alpha' \leftarrow_\$ \mathbb{A} \setminus Dom(\Pi)$
3: **if** $(\alpha, \cdot) \in \Pi$, **return** $\Pi(\alpha)$	3: $(U, -U) := \varphi^{-1}(\alpha')$
4: $\beta \leftarrow_\$ \mathbb{B} \setminus Rng(\Pi)$	4: **if** $pU = \mathcal{O}$
5: $\Pi \leftarrow \Pi \cup \{(\alpha, \beta)\}$	5: $v \leftarrow_\$ \mathbb{Z}_p; V := vG$
6: **return** β	6: **else**
	7: $V := U$
	8: $\alpha = \varphi(V)$
	9: **if** $(\alpha, \cdot) \in \Pi$: *Abort*
	10: $\Pi \leftarrow \Pi \cup \{(\alpha, \beta)\}$
	11: $U = U \| V$
	12: **return** α

Fig. 5. Game$_2$ used in the proof of Blind ECDSA.

<u>Game$_2$.</u> By Fig. 5, Game$_2$ is the same as Game$_1$, except that the bijection Π is now implemented by:

- BRO: lazy sampling in $\mathbb{B}$.
- BRO^{-1}: lazy sampling α' in $\mathbb{A}$ and then try to convert it to an ECC point U. If $pU = \mathcal{O}$, it means that $U \in \mathbb{G}$ by Assumption 1. We picks a random $v \in \mathbb{Z}_p$ and sets $\alpha = \varphi(vG)$. Otherwise, we just set $\alpha = \alpha'$.

The input-output pairs (α, β) to these two oracles are stored in Π. By assumption of the BRO model, $\mathcal{A}$ does not output a forgery without having posed the corresponding bijective random oracle query first. Procedure Fin is not affected by the switch to sampling and remains unmodified.

We assess the probability that Game$_2$ aborts in BRO^{-1} as follows: a uniformly distributed value of a set of cardinality at least $2^L - q_b$ is sampled and checked for containedness in a set of at most q_b elements. That is, the probability of Game$_2$ aborts in BRO^{-1} is at most $q_b/(2^L - q_b)$. As these lines are executed at most q_b times in total, the overall probability of abort is bounded by $q_b^2/(2^L - q_b)$. Since φ is semi-injective, we have $(p-1)/2 \leq 2^L$. Since Game$_1$ and Game$_2$ are identical, if no abort happens, we obtain $\mathsf{Adv}_{\mathcal{A}_{\mathsf{alg}}}^{\mathsf{Game}_1}(\lambda) \leq \mathsf{Adv}_{\mathcal{A}_{\mathsf{alg}}}^{\mathsf{Game}_2}(\lambda) + q_b^2/((p-1)/2 - q_b)$.

<u>Final Reduction.</u> In our last step, we construct an algorithm $\mathcal{B}_1$ solving the (ℓ, ℓ)-MBDL problem whenever $\mathcal{A}_{\mathsf{alg}}$ wins Game$_2$. Algorithm $\mathcal{B}_1$, which has access to the oracle DLO takes as input a group description $(p, \mathbb{G}, G)$ and $(Y, X_1, \ldots, X_\ell)$. It sets the public key $X := Y$, and runs $\mathcal{A}_{\mathsf{alg}}$ on input $(p, \mathbb{G}, G, X)$. Each time $\mathcal{A}_{\mathsf{alg}}$ makes a Sign$_1$() query, $\mathcal{B}_1$ sets $R_j = X_j$. It simulates Sign$_2(j, c_1, c_2, \pi)$ in the following way: firstly it uses the extractor of the NIZK to extract $r_j, h_j \in \mathbb{Z}_p$ from the proof π_j. Then it queries the oracle

upon $(j, h_j G + r_j X)$ and get $s_j = \log_{R_j}(h_j G + r_j X)$. Finally, $\mathcal{B}_1$ returns c as $\mathsf{HE.Enc_{upk}}(s_j + tp)$, where $t \leftarrow_\$ |\mathcal{M}|/p - 1^2$.

Finally, $\mathcal{A}_{\mathsf{alg}}$ returns (m_i^*, r_i^*, s_i^*) for all $i \in \{\ell + 1\}$. Since the i-th forgery is valid, we have $r_i^* = f(R_i^*)$ and:

$$s_i^* R_i^* = H(m_i^*)G + r_i^* X. \tag{4}$$

There are two possible cases:

1. For all $i \in [\ell + 1]$, $r_i^* = f(R_i^*)$ is queried via BRO.
2. For some $i \in [\ell + 1]$, $\pm R_i^* = f^{-1}(r_i^*)$ is queried in BRO^{-1}.

Case 1. $(\gamma_i^*, \xi_i^*, \zeta_i^*,, \boldsymbol{\mu}_i^*)$ is a representation of R_i^* asked in BRO, i.e.,

$$R_i^* = \gamma_i^* G + \xi_i^* X + \sum_{j=1}^{\ell} \zeta_{i,j}^* R_j + \sum_{j=1}^{q_b} \mu_{i,j}^* V_j. \tag{5}$$

Denote $\bar{V}_j$ (resp. $V_j' := v_j G$) as the ECC points generated from line 6 (resp. line 4) of BRO^{-1} and $\bar{\mu}_{i,j}$ (resp. $\mu_{i,j}'$) as the corresponding coefficients in Eq. (5). If $\sum_{\forall j} \bar{\mu}_{i,j} \bar{V}_j \neq 0$, $\mathcal{B}_1$ aborts since R_i^* is not in $\mathbb{G}$. Otherwise, combining Eqs. (4) and (5), we get

$$s_i^*((\gamma_i^* + \sum_{\forall j} \mu_{i,j}' v_j)G + \xi_i^* X + \sum_{j=1}^{\ell} \zeta_{i,j}^* R_j) = H(m_i^*)G + r_i^* X. \tag{6}$$

By the Sign$_2$ oracle query, we have $s_j R_j = h_j G + r_j X$. Then we have:

$$\underbrace{[s_i^*(\xi_i^* + \sum_{j=1}^{\ell} \frac{\zeta_{i,j}^* r_j}{s_j}) - r_i^*]}_{=:\chi_i} X + \underbrace{[s_i^*(\gamma_i^* + \sum_{\forall j} \mu_{i,j}' v_j + \sum_{j=1}^{\ell} \frac{\zeta_{i,j}^* h_j}{s_j}) - H(m_i^*)]}_{=:\theta_i} G = 0.$$

If $\chi_i = 0$ for all $i \in [\ell + 1]$, it means

$$s_i^* = (\xi_i^* + \sum_{j=1}^{\ell} \frac{\zeta_{i,j}^* r_j}{s_j})^{-1} r_i^*. \tag{7}$$

for all $i \in [\ell + 1]^3$. Plugging (7) in (4), we have

$$r_i^* C_i^* = H(m_i^*)G \tag{8}$$

---

[2] This range is set to ensure that the distribution of simulated message $s_j + tp$ is the same as the distribution of the real message $xr\bar{k} + h\bar{k} + tp$.

[3] Note that $r_i^* \neq 0$ and $s_i^* \neq 0$ for a valid ECDSA signature. If $\chi_i = 0$, it means that $\xi_i^* + \sum_{j=1}^{\ell} \frac{\zeta_{i,j}^* r_j}{s_j}$ would not be 0.

where $C_i^* = (\xi_i^* + \sum_{j=1}^{\ell} \frac{\zeta_{i,j}^* r_j}{s_j})^{-1} R_i^* - X$. Observe that C_i^* is fixed when $f(R_i^*)$ is queried via BRO[4]. Since r_i^* is randomly chosen after fixing C_i^*, and $h_i^* = H(m_i^*)$ is also randomly chosen from $\mathbb{Z}_p$ in the random oracle $H(\cdot)$, the probability that Eq. (8) holds is $\frac{q_r \cdot q_b}{p}$ at maximum for each i.

Case 2. By the simulation of BRO^{-1}, if it is computed by line 6 of BRO^{-1}, $\mathcal{B}_1$ aborts since $R_i^* \notin \mathbb{G}$[5]. Otherwise, $R_i^* = \pm v_i G$. Combining it with Eq. (4), we have $\pm v_i s_i^* G = H(m_i^*)G + r_i^* X$. Then $\mathcal{B}_1$ can return $(\pm v_i s_i^* - H(m_i^*))/r_i^*$ as the solution to the MBDL problem since $r_i^* \neq 0$.

Hence, we have $\mathrm{Adv}_{\mathcal{A}_{\mathrm{alg}}}^{\mathsf{Game}_3}(\lambda) \leq \mathrm{Adv}_{\mathcal{B}_1}^{(\ell,\ell)-\mathsf{MBDL}}(\lambda) + (\frac{q_r \cdot q_b}{p})^{\ell+1}$ □

Theorem 2. *The blind ECDSA has blindness if* HE *is IND-CPA secure and* NIZK *has zero-knowledge property.*

The security proof of blindness is given in Appendix B.

4.5   EUF-CMA Security of ECDSA in the ABRO Model

Similar to the proof of one-more unforgeability for blind ECDSA, we can prove the EUF-CMA security of ECDSA directly in the ABRO model. As compared to the ECDSA security proof in [9], the advantage of our proof is that our reduction does not involve rewinding, and hence the reduction is tight.

The high level idea of the EUF-CMA security of ECDSA is described in Sect. 1.4. We omit the details due to the space limit for the paper submission.

5   Hardness of the ECDSA-ROS Problem

In the previous section, we prove the security of our blind ECDSA without directly using any assumption related to the ECDSA-ROS attack mentioned in Sect. 1. In this section, we want to show that the ECDSA-ROS problem is hard to solve if the DL assumption holds in the ABRO and the random oracle model. Hence, we do not need to have an extra ECDSA-ROS assumption in the security proof.

Recall that the ECDSA-ROS problem is that, given (r_j, s_j) on messages m_j for $j \in [\ell]$, output (m^*, R^*, s^*) and a vector ρ such that:

$$\frac{H(m^*)}{s^*} = \sum_{j=1}^{\ell} \frac{\rho_j h_j}{s_j},$$

$$\frac{f(R^*)}{s^*} = \frac{r^*}{s^*} = \sum_{j=1}^{\ell} \frac{\rho_j r_j}{s_j},$$

$$R^* = \sum_{j=1}^{\ell} \rho_j R_j.$$

---

[4] Also, $f(-R_i^*)$ refers to the same C_i^*.
[5] If R_i^* satisfies $s_i^* R_i^* = H(m_i^*)G + r_i^* X$, there must be $R_i^* \in \mathbb{G}$.

Theorem 3. *Assume that $\mathcal{A}_{\mathsf{alg}}$ is the adversary solving the ECDSA-ROS problem, with q_r queries to the random oracle H and q_b queries to the bijective random oracle. Then there exists an algorithm $\mathcal{B}$ solving the DL problem such that:*

$$\mathsf{Adv}_{\mathcal{A}_{\mathsf{alg}}}(\lambda) \leq \mathsf{Adv}_{\mathcal{B}}^{\mathsf{DL}}(\lambda) + \frac{q_r \cdot q_b}{p}.$$

Proof. The algorithm $\mathcal{B}$ is given a DL problem (G, Y) and wants to solve $\log_G Y$. Assume that there is an adversary $\mathcal{A}_{\mathsf{alg}}$ that can break the ECDSA-ROS problem. Then $\mathcal{B}$ picks $x \leftarrow\!\!{\scriptstyle\$}\, \mathbb{Z}_p$ and computes $X = xG$, which is forwarded to $\mathcal{A}_{\mathsf{alg}}$. $\mathcal{B}$ samples random messages m_j for $j \in [\ell]$ and computes ECDSA signatures (r_j, s_j). These are given to the adversary $\mathcal{A}_{\mathsf{alg}}$.

When $\mathcal{A}_{\mathsf{alg}}$ queries the BRO with a new input $(R, \boldsymbol{\rho})$, $\mathcal{B}$ returns a random $\beta \leftarrow\!\!{\scriptstyle\$}\, \mathbb{B} \setminus Rng(\Pi)$ as reply. When $\mathcal{A}_{\mathsf{alg}}$ queries the BRO^{-1} with input β, $\mathcal{B}$ picks a random $\delta \leftarrow\!\!{\scriptstyle\$}\, \mathbb{Z}_p$ and returns $\varphi(\delta Y)$ as reply. The function H is simulated as a normal random oracle.

Finally, $\mathcal{A}_{\mathsf{alg}}$ outputs (m^*, R^*, s^*) and a vector ρ. There are two cases:

1. $r^* = f(R^*)$ is queried via BRO.
2. $\pm R^* = f^{-1}(r^*)$ is queried in BRO^{-1}.

Case 1: Observe that

$$s^* = H(m^*)/\sum_{j=1}^{\ell} \frac{\rho_j h_j}{s_j} = r^*/\sum_{j=1}^{\ell} \frac{\rho_j r_j}{s_j}.$$

Let $z^* = \sum_{j=1}^{\ell} \frac{\rho_j r_j}{s_j} / \sum_{j=1}^{\ell} \frac{\rho_j h_j}{s_j}$, the above means the adversary can find $m^*, \boldsymbol{\rho}$ such that

$$H(m^*) = z^* r^*. \tag{9}$$

But r^* is calculated from the output of BRO is randomly distributed in $\mathbb{Z}_p$ and independent from z^* (which is fixed by $\boldsymbol{\rho}$ when $f(R^*)$ is queried), and $H(m^*)$ output is also randomly chosen from $\mathbb{Z}_p$, which means (9) happens with the probability of $\frac{q_r \cdot q_b}{p}$ in maximum.

Case 2: By the simulation of BRO^{-1}, if it is computed by line 6 of BRO^{-1}, $\mathcal{B}_1$ aborts since $R^* \notin \mathbb{G}$. Otherwise, $\mathcal{B}$ returns $\varphi(\delta^* Y)$ as a reply for some $\delta^* \neq 0$. If the adversary can find a valid pair of (m^*, r^*, s^*) and a vector $\boldsymbol{\rho} = (\rho_1, \ldots, \rho_\ell)$, we have that satisfies:

$$R^* = f^{-1}(r^*) = \delta^* Y = \sum_{j=1}^{\ell} \frac{\rho_j h_j}{s_j} G + \sum_{j=1}^{\ell} \frac{\rho_j r_j}{s_j} X. \tag{10}$$

then $\mathcal{B}$ forwards $(\sum_{j=1}^{\ell} \frac{\rho_j h_j}{s_j} + \sum_{j=1}^{\ell} \frac{\rho_j r_j}{s_j} x)/\delta^*$ to the challenger as the solution to the DL problem. $\qquad\square$

The Best Attack Against the ECDSA-ROS Problem. We only reduce the ECDSA-ROS problem to the DL problem in the ABRO model and random oracle model above. Their relation in the standard model is not clear.

We conjecture that the best attack against the ECDSA-ROS problem is to use Wagner's generalized birthday algorithm [21]. We left the analysis on the complexity of attack against the ECDSA-ROS problem as an interesting open problem.

6 Conclusion

ECDSA is a significant signature scheme in applications, especially in cryptocurrency like Bitcoin and Ethereum. Blind signature is also popular in constructing privacy-preserving applications. In this paper, we give the first formal security proof for blind ECDSA. One of the assumptions that we use is the MBDL assumption, which is relatively new. An interesting question is whether we can prove the security of blind ECDSA under some well-studied assumptions, like one-more discrete logarithm assumption. We leave this as future work.

Game BLIND$_{BS}^{B}(\lambda)$	INIT(pk, m_0, m_1)	Oracle U$_1(i, R_i)$	Oracle U$_2(i, s_i)$
1: $b \leftarrow \{0,1\}$	1: $sess_0 :=$ init	1: **if** $i \notin \{0,1\} \vee sess_i \neq$ init **then return** $\perp$	1: **if** $sess_i \neq$ open **then return** $\perp$
2: $b_0 := b$; $b_1 := 1 - b$	2: $sess_1 :=$ init	2: $sess_i :=$ open	2: $sess_i :=$ closed
3: par $\leftarrow$ BS.Setup(1^λ)		3: (state, c_i) $\leftarrow$ BS.User$_1$(pk, R_i, m_{b_i})	3: $\sigma_{b_i} \leftarrow$ BS.User$_2$(state$_i, s_i$)
4: $b' \leftarrow B^{\text{INIT}, U_1, U_2}$(par)		4: **return** c_i	4: **if** $sess_0 = sess_1 =$ closed **then**
5: **return** ($b' = b$)			5: **if** $\sigma_0 = \perp \vee \sigma_1 = \perp$ **then** $(\sigma_0, \sigma_1) := (\perp, \perp)$
			6: **return** (σ_0, σ_1)
			7: **else return** ϵ

Fig. 6. The blindness game for a blind ECDSA scheme BS.

A   Comparison with Existing Blind ECDSA Protocols

We compare our blind ECDSA with the blind ECDSA proposed in [22].

Efficiency Analysis. We first analyze the blind ECDSA protocol in [22]. For the security level of 3072-bit RSA, the modified Paillier ciphertext uses N, which is a product of two large primes times p (3328 bits). The modified Paillier ciphertext is an integer modulus N^2, which is 6656 bits. The NIZK proof for each modified Paillier ciphertext is two integers modulus N^2 and an integer modulus p, which is 864 bytes for each NIZK proof. To achieve a soundness error of 2^{-80}, the NIZK proof is run 80 times. The total bandwidth is 69120 bytes.

We can instantiate our blind ECDSA with the CL encryption using class groups of imaginary quadratic order. Consider 128-bit security level, the size of a class group element is 1827 bits [7]. A CL ciphertext has two class group elements, which is 3654 bits. The NIZK proof for CL encryption is 1488 bytes ([23], Table 2) for a soundness error of 2^{-80}.

B   Blindness

B.1   Security Model of Blindness

A formal definition of blindness can be found in Fig. 6. The adversary chooses two messages m_0 and m_1, and the experiment runs the signing protocol acting as the user with the adversary, first obtaining a signature (σ_b) on m_b, and then (σ_{1-b}) on m_{1-b} for a random bit b. If both signatures are valid, the adversary is given (σ_0, σ_1) and must determine the value of b.

B.2   Security Proof of Blindness

Proof. Let $\mathcal{A}$ be an adversary playing in Game $\mathsf{BLIND}_{\mathsf{BS}}^{\mathcal{B}}(\lambda)$. After its execution, $\mathcal{A}$ holds $(m_0, \sigma_0), (m_1, \sigma_1)$ where σ_0 is a signature on m_0 and σ_1 is a signature on m_1. The adversary $\mathcal{A}$ furthermore learns two transcripts $T_1 = (R_1, c'_{1,1}, c'_{1,2}, \pi_1, c_1)$ and $T_2 = (R_2, c'_{2,1}, c'_{2,2}, \pi_2, c_2)$ from its interaction with the first and the second signer session, respectively. The goal of $\mathcal{A}$ is to match the message/signature pairs with the two transcripts.

We show that no adversary is able to distinguish whether the message m_0 was used by the experiment to create the transcript T_1 or T_2. We define Game_1 that is the same as $\mathsf{Game\ BLIND}$, except that the proof π returned from the Oracle U_1 is replaced by the simulator of the NIZK proof. If NIZK has the zero-knowledge property, then no PPT adversary can distinguish these two games.

We define Game_2 that is the same as Game_1, except that the ciphertext (c_1, c_2) returned from the Oracle U_1 is changed from the encryption of m_{b_i} to m_{1-b_i}. If HE is IND-CPA secure, then no PPT adversary can distinguish these two games.

We define Game_3 that is the same as Game_2, except that the proof π returned from the Oracle U_1 is changed back to the real NIZK proof on message m_{1-b_i}.

Finally, we can see that in Game_3 is the same as the original $\mathsf{Game\ BLIND}$, except that the bit b is flipped in these two games.   □

References

1. Abe, M.: A secure three-move blind signature scheme for polynomially many signatures. In: Pfitzmann, B. (ed.) EUROCRYPT 2001. LNCS, vol. 2045, pp. 136–151. Springer, Heidelberg (2001). https://doi.org/10.1007/3-540-44987-6_9
2. Abe, M., Okamoto, T.: Provably secure partially blind signatures. In: Bellare, M. (ed.) CRYPTO 2000. LNCS, vol. 1880, pp. 271–286. Springer, Heidelberg (2000). https://doi.org/10.1007/3-540-44598-6_17
3. Agrikola, T., Hofheinz, D., Kastner, J.: On instantiating the algebraic group model from falsifiable assumptions. In: Canteaut, A., Ishai, Y. (eds.) EUROCRYPT 2020. LNCS, vol. 12106, pp. 96–126. Springer, Cham (2020). https://doi.org/10.1007/978-3-030-45724-2_4
4. Bellare, M., Dai, W.: The multi-base discrete logarithm problem: tight reductions and non-rewinding proofs for Schnorr identification and signatures. In: Bhargavan, K., Oswald, E., Prabhakaran, M. (eds.) INDOCRYPT 2020. LNCS, vol. 12578, pp. 529–552. Springer, Cham (2020). https://doi.org/10.1007/978-3-030-65277-7_24

5. Benhamouda, F., Lepoint, T., Loss, J., Orrù, M., Raykova, M.: On the (in)security of ROS. In: Canteaut, A., Standaert, F.-X. (eds.) EUROCRYPT 2021. LNCS, vol. 12696, pp. 33–53. Springer, Cham (2021). https://doi.org/10.1007/978-3-030-77870-5_2

6. Camenisch, J.L., Piveteau, J.-M., Stadler, M.A.: Blind signatures based on the discrete logarithm problem. In: De Santis, A. (ed.) EUROCRYPT 1994. LNCS, vol. 950, pp. 428–432. Springer, Heidelberg (1995). https://doi.org/10.1007/BFb0053458

7. Castagnos, G., Laguillaumie, F.: Linearly homomorphic encryption from DDH. In: Nyberg, K. (ed.) CT-RSA 2015. LNCS, vol. 9048, pp. 487–505. Springer, Cham (2015). https://doi.org/10.1007/978-3-319-16715-2_26

8. Chaum, D.: Blind signatures for untraceable payments. In: Chaum, D., Rivest, R.L., Sherman, A.T. (eds.) Advances in Cryptology, pp. 199–203. Springer, Boston, MA (1983). https://doi.org/10.1007/978-1-4757-0602-4_18

9. Fersch, M., Kiltz, E., Poettering, B.: On the provable security of (EC)DSA signatures. In: Weippl, E.R., Katzenbeisser, S., Kruegel, C., Myers, A.C., Halevi, S. (eds.) CCS 2016, pp. 1651–1662. ACM (2016)

10. Fischlin, M.: Round-optimal composable blind signatures in the common reference string model. In: Dwork, C. (ed.) CRYPTO 2006. LNCS, vol. 4117, pp. 60–77. Springer, Heidelberg (2006). https://doi.org/10.1007/11818175_4

11. Fuchsbauer, G., Kiltz, E., Loss, J.: The algebraic group model and its applications. In: Shacham, H., Boldyreva, A. (eds.) CRYPTO 2018. LNCS, vol. 10992, pp. 33–62. Springer, Cham (2018). https://doi.org/10.1007/978-3-319-96881-0_2

12. Fuchsbauer, G., Plouviez, A., Seurin, Y.: Blind Schnorr signatures and signed ElGamal encryption in the algebraic group model. In: Canteaut, A., Ishai, Y. (eds.) EUROCRYPT 2020. LNCS, vol. 12106, pp. 63–95. Springer, Cham (2020). https://doi.org/10.1007/978-3-030-45724-2_3

13. Garg, S., Rao, V., Sahai, A., Schröder, D., Unruh, D.: Round optimal blind signatures. In: Rogaway, P. (ed.) CRYPTO 2011. LNCS, vol. 6841, pp. 630–648. Springer, Heidelberg (2011). https://doi.org/10.1007/978-3-642-22792-9_36

14. Hauck, E., Kiltz, E., Loss, J.: A modular treatment of blind signatures from identification schemes. In: Ishai, Y., Rijmen, V. (eds.) EUROCRYPT 2019. LNCS, vol. 11478, pp. 345–375. Springer, Cham (2019). https://doi.org/10.1007/978-3-030-17659-4_12

15. Kiayias, A., Zhou, H.-S.: Equivocal blind signatures and adaptive UC-security. In: Canetti, R. (ed.) TCC 2008. LNCS, vol. 4948, pp. 340–355. Springer, Heidelberg (2008). https://doi.org/10.1007/978-3-540-78524-8_19

16. Metet, A.: Blind signatures with DSA/ECDSA? https://www.metzdowd.com/pipermail/cryptography/2004-April/006790.html

17. Nick, J.: Blind signatures in scriptless scripts. https://building-on-bitcoin.com/docs/slides/Jonas_Nick_BoB_2018.pdf

18. Paillier, P.: Public-key cryptosystems based on composite degree residuosity classes. In: Stern, J. (ed.) EUROCRYPT 1999. LNCS, vol. 1592, pp. 223–238. Springer, Heidelberg (1999). https://doi.org/10.1007/3-540-48910-X_16

19. Rückert, M.: Lattice-based blind signatures. In: Abe, M. (ed.) ASIACRYPT 2010. LNCS, vol. 6477, pp. 413–430. Springer, Heidelberg (2010). https://doi.org/10.1007/978-3-642-17373-8_24

20. Schnorr, C.P.: Security of blind discrete log signatures against interactive attacks. In: Qing, S., Okamoto, T., Zhou, J. (eds.) ICICS 2001. LNCS, vol. 2229, pp. 1–12. Springer, Heidelberg (2001). https://doi.org/10.1007/3-540-45600-7_1

21. Wagner, D.: A generalized birthday problem. In: Yung, M. (ed.) CRYPTO 2002. LNCS, vol. 2442, pp. 288–304. Springer, Heidelberg (2002). https://doi.org/10. 1007/3-540-45708-9_19
22. Yi, X., Lam, K.Y.: A new blind ECDSA scheme for bitcoin transaction anonymity. In: Galbraith, S.D., Russello, G., Susilo, W., Gollmann, D., Kirda, E., Liang, Z. (eds.) AsiaCCS 2019, pp. 613–620. ACM (2019)
23. Yuen, T.H., Cui, H., Xie, X.: Compact zero-knowledge proofs for threshold ECDSA with trustless setup. In: Garay, J.A. (ed.) PKC 2021. LNCS, vol. 12710, pp. 481–511. Springer, Cham (2021). https://doi.org/10.1007/978-3-030-75245-3_18

MPC-in-Multi-Heads: A Multi-Prover Zero-Knowledge Proof System
(or: How to Jointly Prove Any NP Statements in ZK)

Hongrui Cui[1], Kaiyi Zhang[1], Yu Chen[2,3,4], Zhen Liu[1],
and Yu Yu[1,5(✉)]

[1] Department of Computer Science, Shanghai Jiao Tong University,
Shanghai 200240, China
{rickfreeman,kzoacn,liuzhen,yyuu}@sjtu.edu.cn
[2] School of Cyber Science and Technology, Shandong University,
Qingdao 266237, China
[3] State Key Laboratory of Cryptology, P.O. Box 5159, Beijing 100878, China
[4] Key Laboratory of Cryptologic Technology and Information Security,
Ministry of Education, Shandong University, Qingdao 266237, China
yuchen@sdu.edu.cn
[5] Shanghai Qizhi Institute, Shanghai 200232, China

Abstract. With the rapid development of distributed computing, the traditional zero-knowledge proofs (ZKP) are becoming less adequate for privacy-preserving applications in the distributed setting. Take "double financing" as an example: multiple financial providers jointly prove that the sum of their committed values is no more than a given threshold, which generalizes the "range proof" to the multiple-prover setting. Therefore, traditional zero-knowledge proof does not seemingly lend itself to this problem on its own.

We identify and fill this gap by formalizing the ZKP system in the multi-prover setting (MPZK) that proves arbitrary NP statements with distributed witnesses. Our MPZK system offers zero-knowledge as long as one prover is honest (while others can collude arbitrarily), and thus is applicable to "double financing", "credit checking", and various other multi-prover applications. We then propose a generic black-box construction from multiparty computation, referred to as "MPC-in-Multi-Heads", and prove its security under the simulation-based paradigm. We also offer a proof-of-concept implementation and present its experimental results.

1 Introduction

Zero-knowledge proof (ZKP) is a powerful cryptographic primitive that enables a *prover* to convince a *verifier* of the membership of a problem instance in an $\mathcal{NP}$ language *without* revealing anything substantial beyond its validity. Since the proposal of ZKP by Goldwasser, Micali, and Rackoff in [GMR85] and non-interactive zero-knowledge (NIZK) by Blum, Feldman, and Micali [BFM88], numerous efforts have been devoted to improving the efficiency of those primitives, namely the computational complexity of proving and verification and the

© Springer Nature Switzerland AG 2021
E. Bertino et al. (Eds.): ESORICS 2021, LNCS 12973, pp. 332–351, 2021.
https://doi.org/10.1007/978-3-030-88428-4_17

proof size (or communication complexity in general). Specifically, by settling with computational soundness (commonly referred to as argument systems), a rich body of research [Kil92, Mic94, Gro10, GGPR13, GKR08, BCC16, XZZ19, ZXZS20] (and many others) has focused on building *succinct* argument systems with proof size and verification complexity sub-linear in the size of the statement.

Generalizing to Multiple Provers. Before exhibiting our main contributions, it is helpful to consider the following motivating problem of *Double Financing.*

> A corporate seeks financial support from several banks by a single document (e.g., a \$10 million invoice). Due to the need for risk control, each bank needs to *verify* that the sum of their loans does not exceed a certain percentage of the invoice (e.g., \$9 million), since otherwise the corporate may abuse its power by applying for more than it legally deserves. The verification process should be 1) preserving the privacy of each bank's loan amount; and 2) verifiable by any third party (e.g., the regulator of jurisdiction).

If we consider the whole bank loan amounts as the *witness* then the above process is essentially the verification of the $\mathcal{NP}$ relation (banks as provers and regulator as the verifier) that sums up the amounts against a threshold value.

Solutions Implied by Completeness Results. Intuitively, the completeness theorems of multiparty computation (MPC) [GMW86, BGW88, CCD88] and the existence of efficient NIZK suggest that the above problem can be solved by computing the zero-knowledge functionality using existing MPC protocols. Such an adaptation, nevertheless, could be tremendously inefficient in practice due to the difference of computational models commonly considered in both worlds. Within general MPC frameworks, computation are mostly represented as arithmetic or Boolean circuits. However, expressing aforementioned prover's algorithm of NIZK in such circuits may incur a significant overhead that renders the result impractical. This indicates that the combination of two efficient constructions may be inefficient in practice.

Therefore, the result implied by combining NIZK and MPC should be more viewed as a feasibility result. We are thus motivated to seeking a more practical solution. We take the MPC-in-the-Head framework as our starting point. The reason for this choice is due to its distributed nature and good efficiency. To best illustrate our idea, we first briefly recall this paradigm as below.

Revisiting the Classics. Recall that ZKP in the MPC-in-the-Head paradigm of Ishai et al. [IKOS07] works as follows. Prover first simulates the multiparty verification process some $\mathcal{NP}$ relation locally and then commits to the generated views, a random subset of which will be challenged for consistency checking.

As the main observation of this work, we discover that such a paradigm generalizes naturally in the multi-prover setting where the proof must be generated in a distributed manner. Particularly, the proving program itself defines a multiparty computation process. Multiple provers can simply follow the original proving program by each simulating some virtual parties (similar ideas appeared in designing maliciously-secure MPC, e.g., [IPS08]).

There are nevertheless a number of technical hurdles: 1) since virtual parties are simulated by multiple real provers, inter-prover communication corresponds to the actual communication among the multiple provers—a fact absent in the original single-prover MPC-in-the-Head construction, which is however crucial for the performance in our multi-prover setting; 2) towards proving security of the new scheme, we need to handle the possible inconsistency between inter-prover interaction and that implicit in the proof string.

Our Contributions. We conclude this section by listing out our contributions.

Extending ZK in the Distributed Setting. We motivate the study of *efficient* ZK in the multi-prover setting by formalizing the syntax and security requirements of such proof systems. Moreover, we present the multi-prover counterpart of the classical Fiat-Shamir transform [FS87] that compiles a constant-round public-coin protocol into a non-interactive one in the random oracle model.

"MPC-in-Multi-Heads". As the second contribution of this paper, we discover that the "MPC-in-the-Head" approach is well suited for the multi-prover setting. Our adaptation of the MPC-in-the-Head paradigm to the multi-prover setting, which we call "MPC-in-Multi-Heads", is shown to be an MPZK as previously defined via careful analysis.

Implementation and Experiments. We implement our protocol and report its performance in Sect. 5. Our implementation is the *first* practical realization of the MPZK functionality to our best knowledge. While further optimizations are desirable, our work constitutes a basis against which subsequent works can be compared.

1.1 Related Works

Here we survey works in the field of multiparty computation and zero-knowledge that are related to our goal. We mainly focus on those similar or relevant to the our MPZK functionality. Nevertheless, none of them is comparable to our functionality despite the superficial similarities.

Multiparty Computation with Public Verifiability. This concept was introduced and studied in the work of Asharov and Orlandi [AO12] whose result was later improved in a line of subsequent works [SV15,KM15,HKK19,BOSS20]. The notion "MPC with public verifiability" (PV-MPC) is an extension of the "identifiable abort" concept of multiparty computation (ID-MPC), which allows honest parties to identify any cheating ones once a deviation is detected. In PV-MPC, the error-detection property of ID-MPC is enhanced such that honest participants can locally generate a certificate, by which any third party can detect whether anyone cheated during protocol execution. A weaker notion of "auditability" is introduced by Baum, Damgård, and Orlandi in [BDO14] where the certificate only shows cheating occurs but does not pinpoint the cheater.

Although similar in functionality, we note that there are some technical differences between our work and theirs. The construction of Schoenmakers and

Veeningen [SV15] only guarantees privacy with an honest majority, while our construction could preserve zero-knowledge even if all-but-one prover is corrupted. Moreover, the works of Baum et al. [BDO14,BOSS20] inherently relies on an ideal "bulletin board" functionality, which is usually instantiated using a blockchain protocol. Our construction, on the other hand, can be based on a variety of assumptions depending on the requirement of the underlying MPC.

Zero-Knowledge Proof on Secret Shared Data. Boneh et al. introduced ZKP on distributed data in [BBC19] where the proof *instance* is shared among multiple verifiers by a linear secret sharing scheme. With this new primitive, this and some subsequent works [BGIN19,BGIN20] improved the communication complexity of some honest-majority MPC protocols.

The syntax of our proof system differs fundamentally from theirs. The constructions of Boneh et al. relies on a single prover that holds all of the proof instance and witness, whereas in our setting this party does not exist. The witness in our case is shared across multiple provers, and the proof system offers protection of the privacy of witness shares.

We note that Boneh et al. demonstrated a means to circumvent the aforementioned limitation by letting multiple parties jointly emulate the proof generation process [BBC19, Sect. 7.4], which is conceptually similar to the construction in this paper. Nevertheless, we stress a couple of crucial differences. First of all, in our setting the witness can be shared arbitrarily conditioned on the existence of *efficient* reconstruction, whereas in their construction the statement must be *linearly* shared. Secondly, the construction in their paper inherently relies on threshold CNF sharing, which renders it inefficient when the number of parties becomes large, whereas our construction offers efficient communication with a large number of provers. Finally, the technique in this paper is orthogonal to that in Boneh et al.'s construction, where a key component is a *fully-linear PCP* generalizing the linear PCP of Gennaro et al. [GGPR13] (causing the reliance on central prover). Therefore, our work is mostly incomparable to theirs.

Multi-prover ZKPoK. Baum et al. introduced *multi-prover ZKPoK* in the context of improving the efficiency of actively-secure MPC protocols in [BCS19]. While the syntax and functionality of their construction is similar to ours, the two notions differs in several ways. First of all, a knowledge extractor in [BCS19] can only extract witnesses for a larger language, in contrast to the standard knowledge extraction property in this work. What's more, the provers in [BCS19] do not communicate with each other while ours does not pose such a restriction. Last but not least, the authors of [BCS19] only offer a construction for proving the plaintext knowledge of BGV encryption scheme but our constructions can be applied to any $\mathcal{NP}$ languages.

Multi-prover Interactive Proofs. MIP was first introduced by Ben-Or et al. [BGKW88] as a generalization of interactive proofs. Perhaps the most widely-known result related to this notion is the groundbreaking work of Babai and

Fortnow [BF90] showing $\mathcal{MIP} = \mathcal{NEXP}$. Nevertheless, MIP qualitatively differs from our notion in several aspects. MIP is more of a theoretical notion, in which the provers do *not* communicate with each other during the protocol and the relation is not necessarily an $\mathcal{NP}$ relation. In sharp contrast, our notion aims to extend the usage of zero-knowledge proof with the efficient prover. Thereby, our notion focuses on $\mathcal{NP}$ relations, and multiple provers do communicate with each other since individual prover is presumed unable to convince the verifier.

2   Preliminaries

In this section, we define the symbols and notions of this work. Additionally, we also introduce the fundamental concepts and definitions upon which we will build our proof system in Sect. 4. Readers familiar with the basic notions of multiparty computation and zero-knowledge proof may safely skip this section.

2.1   Basic Notations

A negligible function, denoted as $\mathsf{negl}(n)$, represents a function $f : \mathbb{N} \to \mathbb{R}$ that for any constant c, there exists an integer N such that for all $n > N$, $f(n) \leq n^{-c}$. We also use $\mathsf{poly}(n)$ to denote *some* polynomial. For integer $m, n \in \mathbb{N}$ and $m < n$, we use $[m, n]$ to denote the set $\{m, m+1, \ldots, n\}$ and $[n]$ to denote $[1, n]$. We use the common definitions of computational and statistical indistinguishable distribution ensembles. Throughout this work, we use κ (resp. λ) to denote computational (resp. statistical) security parameters. We use PPT to indicate probabilistic polynomial-time and sometimes use the term "efficient" and PPT interchangeably

2.2   Secure Computation

For an interactive process among m Turing machines $M_1, \ldots, M_m$ with a public input x and private inputs $w_1, \ldots, w_m$ respectively, we denote the interaction generating the concatenated output z as $z \leftarrow \langle M_1(w_1), \ldots, M_m(w_m) \rangle(x)$. We use a subscript to denote the output of a particular party.

When considering multiparty computation between n parties, we assume secure point-to-point channels between all pairs of parties. Moreover, we consider MPC with synchronized communication, i.e., the participating parties communicate in synchronized rounds. And therefore the program M_i of a party P_i can be divided into several "next-message functions", i.e., the function that maps local input, local state, and incoming messages into updated local states and outgoing messages. We use $\mathcal{A}$ to denote a PPT adversary that may corrupt a subset $\mathcal{I} \subseteq [n]$ of parties and use $\bar{\mathcal{I}}$ to denote the honest ones.

We use the definition of secure computation in the work of Lindell [Lin16]. An interactive protocol is said to *securely* compute a multi-input functionality, as shown in Definition 1, if the interaction process is essentially indistinguishable from that in an idealized model where a trusted party receives inputs from all participants, computes the functionality, and delivers the output faithfully.

Definition 1 (Secure Computation). *An n-party protocol defined by n interactive Turing machines $M_1, \ldots, M_n$ is said to* securely compute *an n-party functionality $\mathcal{F}$ if there exists a* PPT *simulator S, such that for all* PPT *adversaries $\mathcal{A}$ that may corrupt a subset $\mathcal{I}$ of parties, the joint outputs of the adversary and honest parties in the real world are indistinguishable from that of the simulated outputs of $\mathcal{A}$ and honest parties in the ideal world.*

If the only limitation of the corrupted set $\mathcal{I}$ is its size smaller than t, we use the shorthand notation t-secure computation.

Additionally, we define notions related to the "MPC-in-the-Head" paradigm. In particular, we need to specify the notion of consistent views. Intuitively, views of two parties are *consistent* if messages reported in the transcript agree with those defined by input and protocol definition. This is captured by Definition 2.

Definition 2 (Consistent Views). *For an m-party protocol defined by m interactive Turing machines $M_1, \ldots, M_m$ and any two indices $i, j \in [m]$, the two views V_i, V_j are called* consistent *if all the messages that M_i sends to M_j induced from V_i are consistent with the respective incoming messages in V_j and the same condition holds vice versa.*

For a set $S \subseteq [n]$ of players, the set of views $\{V_i : i \in S\}$ is consistent *if for all $i, j \in S$, V_i, V_j are consistent.*

2.3 Helper Functionalities

We define three helper functionalities necessary for our construction in Sect. 4.

Commitment. The ideal commitment as defined in Fig. 1 allows each party to register a message which can be later revealed to all parties.

Functionality $\mathcal{F}^{\mathsf{com}}$

The functionality $\mathcal{F}^{\mathsf{com}}$ interacts with n parties $M_1, \ldots, M_n$ in the following way:

- On input (sid, com, x) from party M_i, the functionality sends (sid, com, i) to every other parties and stores (sid, i, x) internally.
- On input (sid, decom) from party M_i, the functionality checks if (sid, i, x) is stored for some x. If not, it ignores this message; Otherwise, it sends (sid, decom, i, x) to all other parties.

Fig. 1. The ideal n-party commitment functionality $\mathcal{F}^{\mathsf{com}}$ between $M_1, M_2, \ldots, M_n$.

Broadcast. The ideal *detectable* broadcast functionality $\mathcal{F}^{\mathsf{bcast}}$ allows a party to deliver a message to a group of parties who either receive the message or jointly abort [FGMv02]. In this paper, we assume broadcast messages are always sent to all parties. This functionality is shown in Fig. 2.

Functionality $\mathcal{F}^{\mathsf{bcast}}$

The ideal functionality $\mathcal{F}^{\mathsf{bcast}}$ receives messages (sid, i, m) from M_i. The adversary $\mathcal{A}$ gets the message (sid, i, m) and decides whether to continue or abort by sending one bit to the ideal functionality.

- If $\mathcal{A}$ continues, then $\mathcal{F}^{\mathsf{bcast}}$ sends (sid, i, m) to all parties;
- Otherwise, $\mathcal{F}^{\mathsf{bcast}}$ sends (sid, $\perp$) instead.

Fig. 2. The ideal n-party broadcast functionality $\mathcal{F}^{\mathsf{bcast}}$ between $M_1, \ldots, M_n$. Here m is the broadcast message, whose syntax remains to be specified by upper-level protocols. The adversary $\mathcal{A}$ may corrupt a subset $\mathcal{I}$ of players.

Random Oracle. We use $\mathcal{F}^{\mathsf{ro}}$ to denote an ideal functionality that implements a truly random function. In practice, such functionality is usually implemented by a cryptographically-secure hash function.

3   Multi-Prover Zero-Knowledge

In this section, we introduce the formal definition of *multi-prover* zero-knowledge proof system (MPZK hereafter). We start by extending the common definition of $\mathcal{NP}$ relation and language for the multi-prover setting, and then define the syntax of this proof system, and finally formalize its simulation-based definition.

3.1   Relation and Language

We extend the common definition of an $\mathcal{NP}$ relation $R(x, y)$ by allowing multiple witnesses to fit the multi-prover setting. In particular, for an integer $m \in \mathbb{N}$ we consider such a relation R^m defined by a polynomial-sized uniform circuit family $\{C_n\}$ where C_n has $m+1$ inputs, and $(x, y_1, \ldots, y_m) \in R^m$ iff $C(x, y_1, \ldots, y_m) = 1$. We then define the corresponding language $L(R)$ induced by this relation as $L(R) = \{x : \exists y_1, \ldots, y_m \text{ s.t. } C(x, y_1, \ldots, y_m) = 1\}$.

3.2   Proof System Syntax

A multi-prover zero-knowledge proof system Π with m provers for an extended $\mathcal{NP}$ relation R^m is defined by $m+1$ interactive Turing machines: m provers P_1, $\ldots$, P_m and a verifier V. Each prover P_i holds a public input x and a private witness w_i while the verifier V only holds the public input. The provers try to convince the verifier that $x \in L(R)$.

3.3   Formal Definition

We define our multi-prover generalization of the zero-knowledge proof system in the simulation-based paradigm. In particular, an ideal zero-knowledge functionality with regard to m provers for an extended $\mathcal{NP}$ relation R^m, denoted as

$\mathcal{F}_{R^m}^{\mathsf{zk}}$, receives the instance x from all parties, and witness w_i from prover P_i for $i \in [m]$, checks whether $R(x, w_1, \ldots, w_m) = 1$, and finally sends the result to all parties. This process is shown in Fig. 3.

Functionality $\mathcal{F}_{R^m}^{\mathsf{zk}}$

On input (sid, x, w_i) from P_1, ..., P_m and (sid, x) from V, the functionality checks whether all parties have sent consistent x values.

- If the check fails, it sends a message (sid, $\bot$) indicating failure to all parties.
- Otherwise, it sets $y = C(x, w_1, \ldots, w_m)$ and then sends (sid, y) to $\mathcal{A}$
  - If $\mathcal{A}$ sends back (sid, continue), then it forwards (sid, y) to honest parties;
  - Otherwise, it sends (sid, $\bot$) instead.

Fig. 3. The m-prover zero-knowledge functionality $\mathcal{F}_{R^m}^{\mathsf{zk}}$ for extended $\mathcal{NP}$ relation R^m.

We call an $(m + 1)$-party protocol following the syntax of Sect. 3.2 as an *m-prover* zero-knowledge proof system if it securely computes the ideal zero-knowledge functionality $\mathcal{F}_{R^m}^{\mathsf{zk}}$ in Fig. 3 against efficient adversaries with abilities that correspond to classical definitions of soundness and zero-knowledge. In cases that mutual trust does not necessarily exist amongst provers, we require that inputs of honest provers remain secret even if a *fraction* of provers actively or passively collude to disrupt the protocol execution. Formally, we have Definition 3.

Definition 3 (MPZK). *With regard to an extended $\mathcal{NP}$ relation R^m, an $(m + 1)$-party protocol Π following the syntax of Sect. 3.2 is an m-prover zero-knowledge proof system if it securely compute the ideal zero-knowledge functionality $\mathcal{F}_{R^m}^{\mathsf{zk}}$ defined in Fig. 3 against a* PPT *adversary $\mathcal{A}$ that may corrupt a subset $\mathcal{I}$ of parties with different controlling capabilities.*

Let $\mathcal{S}_P = \{P_1, \ldots, P_m\}$ denote the set of all provers. The corrupted parties $\mathcal{I}$ can be the following cases:

- **Soundness.** *$\mathcal{I}$ contains all provers that are* actively *controlled;*
- **Standard ZK.** *$\mathcal{I}$ contains the verifier that is* actively *controlled.*
- **Honest-Verifier ZK.** *$\mathcal{I}$ contains the verifier that is* passively *controlled.*

Additionally, this proof system has passive/active $\mathcal{S}$-partial witness privacy ($\mathcal{S}$ contains subsets of $\mathcal{S}_P$) if the adversary has the power to passively/actively control a subset $Q \in \mathcal{S}$ of provers with the possible additional ability to passively control the verifier (i.e. $V \in \mathcal{I} \wedge \mathcal{I} \setminus \{V\} \in \mathcal{S}$).

If the definition of $\mathcal{S}$ is based on a threshold $t \in \mathbb{N}$ (namely, $\mathcal{S} = \{S \subseteq \mathcal{S}_P : |S| \leq t\}$), then we call it t-partial witness privacy.

Remark 1 (Comparison with the Classics). We argue the above definition has subsumed the classical definitions (e.g., [GMW91, FLS90]) of zero-knowledge and further extended the security guarantees to the more general case. Consider the following facts.

- When $m = 1$ the syntax "collapses" to that of the classical proof system.
- When we eliminate the verifier, the syntax "collapses" to the multiparty computation process of the NP relation.
- Completeness is guaranteed by the correctness of multiparty computation.
- Soundness and Standard/Honest-Verifier ZK correspond to the three corruption cases, respectively.
- Additionally in the multi-prover setting, partial witness privacy protects the security of the protocol even when some provers collude with the verifier.

Remark 2 (One Bit of Leakage). Recall that the ideal functionality in Fig. 3 allows all parties to get the one-bit value $y = C(x, w_1, \ldots, w_m)$ regardless of whether $x \in L(R)$ or not. This means that when the adversary controls some of the provers, then even if it does not hold the valid partial witnesses, it will get the output bit correlated to the inputs of other honest provers. In such a situation, the adversary will effective acquire an oracle $O(C(x, w_{\bar{I}}, \cdot))$ from the proving process. Notice that such a problem is unique to the multi-prover setting, since if a single prover holds the witness then such information is efficiently implied. Nevertheless, we note that this problem seems inherent in the multi-prover setting since a naïve construction based on computing the NIZK program by MPC among all provers also has this leakage from the generated proof.

3.4   Public-Coin and Non-interactive Proof

We call such proof system *public coin* if the verifier's messages are public randomness as captured in Definition 4.

Definition 4. *We call an MPZK proof system public-coin if it satisfies Definition 3 and additionally the verifier messages satisfy the following constraints.*

1. *They are randomly sampled according to some distribution, independent of any other randomness (i.e. fresh random coins);*
2. *All such coins are broadcasted to all provers (i.e. public).*

Such extension is meaningful to our work because we can mimic the template of constructing (single-prover) non-interactive argument system: first designing an honest-verifier zero-knowledge protocol and then compiling it into a non-interactive one in the random oracle model using general constructions (namely Fiat-Shamir [FS84] or BCS [BCS16]).

In more detail, our characterization of the multi-prover proof system (Definition 3) requires the interaction between parties being indistinguishable to an ideal process, and if a protocol satisfies the public coin property above, one can replace the verifier messages with random oracle responses. The two interaction processes are indistinguishable except when additional RO queries collide with those defining random challenges, which happens with negligible probability for proper parameter choices.

And thus interaction between provers and verifier can be compressed into one single message. To rigorously capture this intuition, we first define the multi-party equivalence of non-interactive proof. Since in the multi-prover setting no prover has the ability to convince the verifier of the validity of the statement, we argue that limiting prover-verifier communication is the best one can hope for. Formally we have the following definition.

Definition 5. *We call a multi-prover honest-verifier zero-knowledge proof system* non-interactive *if it satisfies Definition 3 and additionally throughout the proof process the provers only send one message to the verifier.*

The public coin property allows us to transform the proving process into a non-interactive one in the random oracle model, in the same spirit as existing general transformations. Formally, we have the following lemma.

Lemma 1 (Multi-Prover Fiat-Shamir). *Suppose Π is a multi-prover honest-verifier zero-knowledge proof system as in Definition 3 with the additional public coin property as in Definition 4, the verifier's message count is a constant n, and challenge space in each n steps are super-polynomial in the statistical parameter λ, then by replacing for $i \in [n]$ the verifier's message c_i with random oracle response $\tilde{c}_i := \mathcal{F}^{ro}(\tau_i)$ where τ_i is the verifier's partial transcript before sending c_i in Π, one can acquire a protocol $\tilde{\Pi}$ that is a non-interactive proof as in Definition 5 in the $\mathcal{F}^{ro}$-hybrid model.*

Proof. Dividing the random oracle queries in the execution of $\tilde{\Pi}$ into two classes: the ones that define verifier's challenges, denoted as q_c and all others, denoted as $q_{\bar{c}}$. When these two classes return distinct outputs, the protocols $\tilde{\Pi}$ and Π are equivalent in the sense that adversarial strategy in $\tilde{\Pi}$ can be efficiently translated to one in Π by simulating additional random oracle responses. And thus it suffices to prove this event Collide happens with overwhelming probability.

Since the size of q_c is a constant and the challenge space is super-polynomial, the probability of the ith query in $q_{\bar{c}}$ collides with response of q_c is $\Pr[\mathsf{Collide}_i] = \lambda^{-\omega(1)}$. This probability is still negligible after applying a union bound on all queries in $q_{\bar{c}}$. Namely,

$$\Pr[\mathsf{Collide}] \leq \sum_i \Pr[\mathsf{Collide}_i] = \mathsf{poly}(\lambda) \cdot \lambda^{-\omega(1)} = \lambda^{-\omega(1)} \ .$$

As we shall see, our construction in Sect. 4 is public coin and can be made non-interactive using this transformation.

4   MPC-in-Multi-Heads: A Black-Box Construction from MPC

In this section, we present a protocol that realizes a multi-prover zero-knowledge proof system defined in Definition 3. Our protocol can be viewed as a natural extension to the original "MPC-in-the-Head" paradigm of Ishai et al. [IKOS07]. We first introduce the intuition behind our method, then elaborate our protocol in detail, and finally prove its security.

4.1 Intuitions

Recall that in the original "MPC-in-the-Head" paradigm, the prover first shares the witness w among n virtual parties, and then simulates the secure execution of the verification circuit locally. The prover then broadcasts the commitment of these n views, and on request of the verifier, opens some views to show that 1) the output is unanimously accepting and 2) the execution process is consistent with the protocol specification.

In our setting, the witness is distributed among m provers, and therefore no single prover can complete the view generation process. Instead, we let each party split their witness into n/m pieces and simulate respective parties (hence "MPC-in-Multi-Heads"). All provers would therefore jointly simulate n parties and commit to generated views, a subset of which will be checked by the verifier.

In more detail, the next-message function of any secure computation protocol of that verification circuit relies on the input, random tape, and incoming messages. It is thus sufficient to let each party deliver outgoing messages to the respective parties, in order to jointly simulate the protocol execution. Once this step is completed, the rest of the protocol follows the original scheme.

Remark 3 (Choosing Inner Protocol). In our setting, multiple provers hold inputs to be protected against the verifier (traditional zero-knowledge) and in some cases against each other (partial witness privacy). And thus the inner protocol, in this case, should satisfy the following two constraints: 1) when instantiated in the original framework, soundness, and zero-knowledge should hold; 2) when considering the adversary's ability to control a subset of provers and the verifier, simulation of the inner protocol should not break the security of the overall protocol. This corresponds to the partial-prover corruption cases in Definition 3.

4.2 Protocol Description

We describe our protocol in the $\mathcal{F}^{\mathsf{com}}$, $\mathcal{F}^{\mathsf{bcast}}$-hybrid model, as illustrated in Fig. 5. We denote the m-prover protocol for relation R^m that makes an oracle use of another (inner) protocol π as $\Pi^\pi_{R^m}$.

Let R^m be a generalized $\mathcal{NP}$ relation and C its verification circuit. Let t, ℓ be constant integers and $n = (t+1) \cdot m$. Let $\mathcal{D}$ be a distribution over all subsets of $[n]$ and π an n-party (denoted as $M_1, \ldots, M_n$) protocol that computes C. Each prover, denoted as $P_1, \ldots, P_m$ holds partial witness $w_1, \ldots, w_m$ respectively.

The provers first additively split their witness into $t+1$ random shares and then they collectively simulate the n parties in π via the point-to-point channel and corresponding two-party protocols for any two-party functionalities in π (e.g. OT channels).

Functionality $\mathcal{F}_{R^m, t}^{\text{ext}}$

On input (sid, x, w_i) from M_i for $i \in [m \cdot (t+1)]$ the functionality first checks all x values are consistent. If not it sends (sid, $\perp$) to all parties. Otherwise, it computes $y = C\left(\sum_{i=1}^{t+1} w_i, \ldots, \sum_{i=m(t+1)-t}^{m(t+1)} w_i\right)$ and sends (sid, y) to $\mathcal{A}$.

- If $\mathcal{A}$ returns (sid, $\perp$) then the functionality forwards it to honest parties;
- If $\mathcal{A}$ returns (sid, continue) then it sends the output (sid, y) instead.

Fig. 4. The extended $m \cdot (t+1)$ party verification functionality for extended $\mathcal{NP}$ relation R^m. t is a parameter to be specified by upper-level protocols.

Protocol $\Pi_{R^m}^{\pi}$

The protocol proceeds in three stages like classical "sigma protocols". We denote the set of players $M_{i \cdot (t+1)-t}, \ldots, M_{i \cdot (t+1)}$ of protocol π as G_i.

Preparation. Each prover P_i perform the following steps:

- Uniformly samples $w_i^1, \ldots, w_i^{t+1}$ s.t. $w_i^1 \oplus \ldots \oplus w_i^{t+1} = w_i$;
- Simulate the parties of G_i in π by sending simulated messages bound for G_j to P_j;
- Runs corresponding two-party protocol with P_j if two parties in group G_i and G_j calls a two-party functionality.

After the emulation of protocol π, each prover will generate $t+1$ views denoted as V_i^j for $i \in [m]$ and $j \in [t+1]$. They are then sent to ideal commitment functionality $\mathcal{F}^{\text{com}}$ by their respective owners.

Challenge. The verifier randomly samples a set S from the distribution $\mathcal{D}$ and broadcasts this set to all provers though the ideal broadcast functionality $\mathcal{F}^{\text{bcast}}$.

Response. On receiving S, each prover P_i opens respective views in $S \cap [i \cdot (t+1) - t, i \cdot (t+1)]$ by calling the ideal commitment functionality $\mathcal{F}^{\text{com}}$. On receiving the views in S, the each party checks that

- Outputs of all views are accepting, i.e., $y = 1$,
- All views in S are consistent, i.e., for all V_i and V_j, the incoming messages of V_i are consistent with the implicit outgoing ones in V_j, and vice versa.

Repeat the above process for ℓ times. If all checks pass and outputs are consistent, the verifier outputs y. Otherwise, it outputs $\perp$.

Fig. 5. The m-prover zero knowledge proof system $\Pi_{R^m}^{\pi}$ for an extended $\mathcal{NP}$ relation R^m. The verification circuit for R^m is $C(x, w_1, \ldots, w_m)$. Here t, ℓ are constant integers that defines the simulated parties of each prover and repetition count. $\mathcal{D}$ is a distribution defined over all subsets of $[n]$. π is an $(t+1) \cdot m$ party protocol that computes the extended verification functionality $\mathcal{F}_{R^m, t}^{\text{ext}}$ as in Fig. 4.

After the simulation of π, each prover collectively holds n views. Then the protocol could proceed as the original MPC-in-the-Head scheme. This process is repeated ℓ times in sequential order.

4.3   Instantiation with Different Inner Protocols

In this section, we introduce two instantiations of the protocol in Fig. 5. These two implementations differ in whether the adversary can actively or passively control *a subset of* provers and correspond to the two constructions in [IKOS07, Sect. 3, 4]. Formally, we have the following theorems.

Theorem 1 (Active Partial Control). *Let t be a constant multiple of statistical security parameter λ, $\ell = 1$, π be a $(m - 1) \cdot (t + 1)$-secure protocol, and $\mathcal{D}$ be the uniform distribution over all size-t subsets of $[n]$, protocol $\Pi_{R^m}^\pi$ as defined in Fig. 5 is an m-prover honest-verifier zero-knowledge proof system for the extended relation R^m with additional active $(m - 1)$-partial witness privacy as defined in Definition 3.*

Theorem 2 (Passive Partial Control). *Let $t = 2$, $\ell = \lceil \lambda / \log (3/2) \rceil$, π be a $(n-1)$-secure protocol, and $\mathcal{D}$ be the uniform distribution over the set $\mathcal{S}_1 \times \ldots \times \mathcal{S}_m$ where $\mathcal{S}_i$ is the set of all size-2 subsets of $[(t+1) \cdot (i-1) + 1, (t+1) \cdot i]$, protocol $\Pi_{R^m}^\pi$ as defined in Fig. 5 is an m-prover honest-verifier zero-knowledge proof system for the extended relation R^m with additional passive $(m - 1)$-partial witness privacy as defined in Definition 3.*

We defer the complete proofs to the appendix, and only state the high-level ideas here. The two theorems share the same structure and proof strategy.

Proof (Sketch). In both theorems, the parameter settings of π and $\mathcal{D}$ leaves the adversary negligible probability to bypass the consistency check, and therefore for $x \notin L$ the probability of verifier outputting $y = 1$ is negligible in the real execution. Except for this unlikely event, a simulator in the ideal world could simulate the preparation phase from the security guarantees of π and then observe all inputs to $\mathcal{F}^{\mathsf{com}}$. With all this information, it can simulate challenges of the verifier and thus effectively simulate the real protocol execution. A malicious adversary may not commit to views faithfully, but a careful analysis shows that the effect of such malicious behavior can be efficiently simulated in the ideal world and thus does not affect security.

5   Implementation and Experimental Results

We have implemented the protocol in Sect. 4 by instantiating the inner MPC with the passive secure protocol of Goldreich, Micali, and Wigderson [GMW86] (hence secure against adversary with passive partial control) and the

Table 1. Parameter setting of our experiments. The two numbers in "Circuit Size" denote the number of linear and non-linear gates, respectively. In "Simulated Party", "$m \times n$" denotes that each of the m provers simulates n virtual parties, resulting in a total of mn virtual parties. "Repetition Count" is the number of linear repetition needed to achieve required soundness error.

Relation	$\mathcal{R}^{\text{hash}}$	$\mathcal{R}^{\text{comp}}$	$\mathcal{R}^{\text{sum}}$
Circuit Size	94,302/22,528	189,450/45,312	1,821/288
Simulated Party	2×3	2×3	8×3
Soundness Error	2^{-40}	2^{-40}	2^{-40}
Repetition Count	70	70	70
Proving Time	109 min	223 min	26 min 31 s
Verification Time	23.7 s	50.0 s	1.44 s
Proof Size	4.0 MB	8.0 MB	1.3 MB

Multi-Prover Fiat-Shamir transform with the SHA256 hash function. Based on this implementation, we conducted experiments on the following relations:

- $\mathcal{R}^{\text{hash}}(y; (x_1, x_2)) : y = \texttt{SHA256}(x_1 \oplus x_2)$, where $x_1, x_2 \in \{0,1\}^{512}$, and $y \in \{0,1\}^{256}$;
- $\mathcal{R}^{\text{comp}}((y, h_1, h_2) : ((x_1, r_1), (x_2, r_2))) : y < (x_1 + x_2) \wedge h_1 = \texttt{SHA256}(x_1 \| r_1) \wedge h_2 = \texttt{SHA256}(x_2 \| r_2)$, where $x_1, x_2, y \in \{0,1\}^{32}$, $r_1, r_2 \in \{0,1\}^{480}$, $h_1, h_2 \in \{0,1\}^{256}$, "$\|$" denotes concatenation of bit strings, and x_1, x_2, y are interpreted as unsigned 32-bit integers for addition and comparison operations.
- $\mathcal{R}^{\text{sum}}(y; (x_1, ..., x_8)) : y = \sum_{i=1}^{8} x_i$ for $x_1, ..., x_8, y \in \{0,1\}^{32}$ interpreted as 32-bit unsigned integers for addition and comparison operations.

Throughout the experiment, we use the SHA256 circuit in the works of Campanelli et al. [CGGN17] which has optimized the AND gate count. We run the experiments on a Ubuntu 20.04 LTS machine with AMD®Ryzen 5 3600 CPU and 16 GB of RAM in LAN setting. The simulated communication channel has 10 Gbps bandwidth and 1 ms delay. Parameters and results for the experiments are reported in Table 1.

When compared with the state-of-the-art in ZKP, results from our experiments seem very rudimentary. We provide justifications for this phenomenon. First of all, our construction implements a generalized functionality 1) that "collapses" to regular ZKP in the single prover case; 2) that, in absence of the verifier, "collapses" to a multiparty computation of the NP relation verification circuit, where the communication size of the challenge and response phases relates to the proof size, and running time corresponds to proving time. Moreover, the functionality we realized has never been implemented before and our result should be interpreted as a proof-of-concept result. Finally, the protocol in Sect. 4 is built upon the vanilla approach of "MPC-in-the-Head" which has proof size linear in the verification circuit size. Despite the initial performance is far from desirable, subsequent works has substantially improved the asymptotic/concrete efficiency to the extent of being competitive in the ZKP literature. Thus, we expect subsequent improvement over our work following these optimizations.

6   Conclusion and Future Directions

In this paper, we formalize the syntax and security requirements for *multi-prover zero-knowledge*, the multi-prover extension of ZKP for proving arbitrary $\mathcal{NP}$ statements with distributed witnesses. Inspired by the MPC-in-the-Head paradigm, we then design a protocol named "MPC-in-Multi-Heads" that efficiently realizes the multi-prover zero-knowledge functionality. Finally, we instantiate and implement the proof system with the classical GMW protocol and report experimental results.

We expect further optimizations considering the numerous improvements (e.g., [GMO16, CDG17, KKW18, AHIV17, BFH20]) following the proposal of the MPC-in-the-Head paradigm. As a byproduct of this work, we advocate a new metric of ZK, referred to as "MPC-friendliness"[1], to capture the property of being efficiently computable in the multiparty setting and thus more suitable for multi-prover applications.

Acknowledgements. We would like to thank the reviewers for their helpful suggestions. Yu Chen is supported by National Natural Science Foundation of China (Grant No. 61772522, No. 61932019). Zhen Liu is supported by the National Natural Science Foundation of China (Grant No. 62072305) and the National Cryptography Development Fund (Grant No. MMJJ20170111). Yu Yu was supported by the National Key Research and Development Program of China (Grant Nos. 2020YFA0309705 and 2018YFA0704701) and the National Natural Science Foundation of China (Grant Nos. 62125204, 61872236, and 61971192).

A   Missing Proofs

In this section, we present the missing proofs in the body.

Proof (of Thm. 1). The $(m-1) \cdot (t+1)$-threshold security of π implies the existence of a simulator $S_{\mathcal{A}'}^{\pi}$ such that for any PPT adversary $\mathcal{A}'$ corrupting at most $(m-1) \cdot (t+1)$ parties, the concatenated outputs of all parties in the real world is indistinguishable with that in the ideal world where the simulator $S_{\mathcal{A}'}^{\pi}$ interacts with the ideal functionality $\mathcal{F}_{R^m,t}^{\text{ext}}$ and $\mathcal{A}$.

We then explain in the following two corruption cases how adversarial actions translate to efficient simulation in the ideal world.

---

[1] This notion is already present in other context. For example, it refers to functions with low (multiplicative) circuit size and depth, which can be efficiently computed using MPC protocols.

Case 1a. In this case, the adversary may actively control any strict subset $\mathcal{I}$ of the provers and passively control the verifier. The simulator S^{zk} in this case runs as follows:

1. It first simulates the preparation phase of $\Pi^{\pi}_{R^m}$. In particular, let $w^1_{\mathcal{I}}, \ldots, w^{t+1}_{\mathcal{I}}$ be the extracted witness of virtual parties simulated by $\mathcal{A}$ returned by S^{π}, the outer simulator S^{zk} computes and sends $w_{\mathcal{I}} = \sum_j w^j_{\mathcal{I}}$ to ideal functionality $\mathcal{F}^{zk}_{R^m}$ and sends the result $y \in \{0, 1\}$ to $\mathcal{A}$ via S^{π}. In addition, the simulator S^{zk} relays any aborting command of $\mathcal{A}$ to $\mathcal{F}^{zk}_{R^m}$.
2. Then through the simulation of the ideal commitment oracle $\mathcal{F}^{com}$, simulator S^{zk} can observe the committed views $V_{\mathcal{I}}$ from $\mathcal{A}$. By these views and the previous simulation of π, S^{zk} can define a consistency graph G: one node for each virtual party and two nodes are connected iff. they are inconsistent.
3. Then S^{zk} simulates an honest verifier and sends (sid, abort) to $\mathcal{F}^{zk}_{R^m}$ if inconsistency is detected.
4. Otherwise, S^{zk} sends (sid, contine) and concludes the simulation process.

Next, we argue the effectiveness of the above simulation. Consider the following three cases.

First of all, if $|G.E| = 0$ (i.e. no inconsistency) then correctness of π ensures the above simulation is correct.

The second case is $0 < |G.E| \le t$. First, we claim verifier will abort with the same probability in both worlds. This holds because the simulation of the verifier is perfect (since it does not require any trapdoor or correlation). Conditioned on verifier does not abort, we then claim the verifier in both worlds always output the same y except with negligible probability.

The effectiveness of S^{π} implies that in the real world honest provers (who at least controls $t + 1$ virtual parties) output y as in the ideal world except with negligible probability. Thus the probability of a real verifier being convinced on false output $\bar{y}$ is smaller than that of a random challenge is "concentrated on" $\mathcal{A}$ controlled views (denoted as Miss), which is negligible. In particular we have

$$\Pr[\bar{y} \leftarrow V] \le \Pr[\mathsf{Miss}] \le \frac{\binom{(m-1)(t+1)}{t}}{\binom{m(t+1)}{t}} \le \left(1 - \frac{1}{m-1}\right)^t = \mathsf{negl}(\lambda) \ .$$

Finally, if $|G.E| > t$, then G must have a minimal matching bigger than $t/2$. And thus the verifier (whether real or simulated) will abort except with $(t/n)^t = 2^{-\Omega(\lambda)}$ probability, which means the two worlds have the same behavior except with negligible probability.

Case 1b. In this case, the adversary $\mathcal{A}$ only passively controls the verifier. Notice that

- the verifier only observes t views in its transcript;
- the active-$(t + 1) \cdot (m - 1)$ security of π implies a passive simulator that generates any t views given output y.

Together this implies the passive simulation of $\mathcal{A}$'s view, in this case, is efficient.

Case 2. In this case the adversary actively controls all provers. The simulator S^{zk} runs the following steps (since all provers are corrupted, the preparation phase does not need to be simulated):

1. From the input to $\mathcal{F}^{com}$, S^{zk} can efficiently compute its consistency graph G.
2. Let VC be a minimal vertex cover of G. If $|\mathsf{VC}| \geq t$ it sends (sid, abort) to $\mathcal{F}^{zk}_{R^m}$.
3. Otherwise, it uses S^π to extract inputs w_{VC} from virtual parties in VC. It then sends w_{VC} and $w_{\overline{\mathsf{VC}}}$ (inputs of parties outside VC) to $\mathcal{F}^{zk}_{R^m}$, and gets output $y \in \{0,1\}$.
4. It then simulates an honest verifier and sends (sid, abort) if inconsistency is detected and (sid, continue) otherwise.

Next, we argue the effectiveness of simulation. From the arguments in Case 1a, it holds when the consistency graph has a minimal vertex cover of size $> t$ then the verifier will abort in the real world. Together with the fact that the simulation of the verifier is perfect, we conclude that the verifier will abort with the same probability (except with negligible difference) in both worlds.

Conditioned on abort does not occur, we claim that honest parties will output the same in both worlds, which suffices for proving the effectiveness of the above simulation. This holds because the effectiveness of S^π implies that $y = C(w_{\mathsf{VC}}, w_{\overline{\mathsf{VC}}})$ as returned by $\mathcal{F}^{zk}_{R^m}$ is indistinguishable from outputs in the real execution of π (as reported in $\mathcal{F}^{com}$). And thus views corresponding to $\overline{\mathsf{VC}}$ output y and the probability that honest parties output $\bar{y}$ is at most $1/\binom{n}{t}$ which is negligible.

Proof (of Theorem 2). The optimal threshold security of π implies simulation against passive corruption is efficient. And thus we only have to focus on the case of active corruption on *all* provers. In this case the simulator S^{zk} perform the following steps:

1. From inputs to $\mathcal{F}^{com}$ in every ℓ rounds, S^{zk} simulates the honest verifier's check and sends (sid, abort) if inconsistency is detected.
2. If the previous step does not abort, then the verifier checks every ℓ inputs to $\mathcal{F}^{com}$ and (sid, abort) if no such $w : y = C(w, x)$ is found where y is the verifier's output.
3. S^{zk} sends w to $\mathcal{F}^{zk}_{R^m}$ and concludes the simulation.

As argued in the previous proof, simulation of the honest verifier is perfect, and thus the verifier will abort with the same probability in both worlds. Conditioned on abort does not occur, we claim that honest verifier always returns the output y returned by $\mathcal{F}^{zk}_{R^m}$ except with negligible probability.

The only difference is the case that during simulation, the simulated verifier does not abort and outputs y for which S^{zk} cannot extract a corresponding w. This implies that inputs w for every ℓ rounds would results $\bar{y}$, in other words, inconsistency exists in every round. But by the parameter setting, this occurs except with probability $(t/t+1)^\ell < 2^{-\lambda}$.

References

[AHIV17] Ames, S., Hazay, C., Ishai, Y., Venkitasubramaniam, M.: Ligero: lightweight sublinear arguments without a trusted setup. In: Thuraisingham et al. [TEMX17], pp. 2087–2104

[AO12] Asharov, G., Orlandi, C.: Calling out cheaters: covert security with public verifiability. In: Wang, X., Sako, K. (eds.) ASIACRYPT 2012. LNCS, vol. 7658, pp. 681–698. Springer, Heidelberg (2012). https://doi.org/10.1007/978-3-642-34961-4_41

[BBC19] Boneh, D., Boyle, E., Corrigan-Gibbs, H., Gilboa, N., Ishai, Y.: Zero-knowledge proofs on secret-shared data via fully linear PCPs. In: Boldyreva and Micciancio [BM19], pp. 67–97

[BCC16] Bootle, J., Cerulli, A., Chaidos, P., Groth, J., Petit, C.: Efficient zero-knowledge arguments for arithmetic circuits in the discrete log setting. In: Fischlin, M., Coron, J.-S. (eds.) EUROCRYPT 2016. LNCS, vol. 9666, pp. 327–357. Springer, Heidelberg (2016). https://doi.org/10.1007/978-3-662-49896-5_12

[BCS16] Ben-Sasson, E., Chiesa, A., Spooner, N.: Interactive Oracle proofs. In: Hirt, M., Smith, A. (eds.) TCC 2016. LNCS, vol. 9986, pp. 31–60. Springer, Heidelberg (2016). https://doi.org/10.1007/978-3-662-53644-5_2

[BCS19] Baum, C., Cozzo, D., Smart, N.P.: Using TopGear in overdrive: a more efficient ZKPoK for SPDZ. In: Paterson, K.G., Stebila, D. (eds.) SAC 2019. LNCS, vol. 11959, pp. 274–302. Springer, Cham (2020). https://doi.org/10.1007/978-3-030-38471-5_12

[BDO14] Baum, C., Damgård, I., Orlandi, C.: Publicly auditable secure multi-party computation. In: Abdalla, M., De Prisco, R. (eds.) SCN 2014. LNCS, vol. 8642, pp. 175–196. Springer, Cham (2014). https://doi.org/10.1007/978-3-319-10879-7_11

[BF90] Babai, L., Fortnow, L.: A characterization of $\sharp P$ arithmetic straight line programs. In: FOCS 1990 [FOC90], pp. 26–34

[BFH20] Bhadauria, R., Fang, Z., Hazay, C., Venkitasubramaniam, M., Xie, T., Zhang, Y.: Ligero++: a new optimized sublinear IOP. In: Ligatti, J., Ou, X., Katz, J., Vigna, G. (eds.) ACM CCS 20, pp. 2025–2038. ACM Press, November 2020

[BFM88] Blum, M., Feldman, P., Micali, S.: Non-interactive zero-knowledge and its applications (extended abstract). In: STOC 1988 [STO88], pp. 103–112

[BGIN19] Boyle, E., Gilboa, N., Ishai, Y., Nof, A.: Practical fully secure three-party computation via sublinear distributed zero-knowledge proofs. In: Cavallaro, L., Kinder, J., Wang, X., Katz, J. (eds.) ACM CCS 2019, pp. 869–886. ACM Press, November 2019

[BGIN20] Boyle, E., Gilboa, N., Ishai, Y., Nof, A.: Efficient fully secure computation via distributed zero-knowledge proofs. In: Moriai, S., Wang, H. (eds.) ASIACRYPT 2020. LNCS, vol. 12493, pp. 244–276. Springer, Cham (2020). https://doi.org/10.1007/978-3-030-64840-4_9

[BGKW88] Ben-Or, M., Goldwasser, S., Kilian, J., Wigderson, A.: Multi-prover interactive proofs: how to remove intractability assumptions. In: STOC 1988 [STO88], pp. 113–131

[BGW88] Ben-Or, M., Goldwasser, S., Wigderson, A.: Completeness theorems for non-cryptographic fault-tolerant distributed computation (extended abstract). In: STOC 1988 [STO88], pp. 1–10

[BM19]   Boldyreva, A., Micciancio, D. (eds.): CRYPTO 2019. LNCS, vol. 11694. Springer, Cham (2019). https://doi.org/10.1007/978-3-030-26954-8References [BM19, FOC90, STO88, TEMX17] are given in the list but not cited in the text. Please cite these in text or delete these from the list.

[BOSS20] Baum, C., Orsini, E., Scholl, P., Soria-Vazquez, E.: Efficient constant-round MPC with identifiable abort and public verifiability. In: Micciancio, D., Ristenpart, T. (eds.) CRYPTO 2020. LNCS, vol. 12171, pp. 562–592. Springer, Cham (2020). https://doi.org/10.1007/978-3-030-56880-1_20

[CCD88]   Chaum, D., Crépeau, C., Damgård, I.: Multiparty unconditionally secure protocols (extended abstract). In: STOC 1988 [STO88], pp. 11–19

[CDG17]   Chase, M., et al.: Post-quantum zero-knowledge and signatures from symmetric-key primitives. In: Thuraisingham et al. [TEMX17], pp. 1825–1842

[CGGN17] Campanelli, M., Gennaro, R., Goldfeder, S., Nizzardo, L.: Zero-knowledge contingent payments revisited: attacks and payments for services. In: Thuraisingham et al. [TEMX17], pp. 229–243

[FGMv02] Fitzi, M., Gisin, N., Maurer, U., von Rotz, O.: Unconditional byzantine agreement and multi-party computation secure against dishonest minorities from scratch. In: Knudsen, L.R. (ed.) EUROCRYPT 2002. LNCS, vol. 2332, pp. 482–501. Springer, Heidelberg (2002). https://doi.org/10.1007/3-540-46035-7_32

[FLS90]   Feige, U., Lapidot, D., Shamir, A.: Multiple non-interactive zero knowledge proofs based on a single random string (extended abstract). In: FOCS 1990 [FOC90], pp. 308–317

[FOC90]   31st FOCS. IEEE Computer Society Press, October 1990

[FS84]   Fiat, A., Shamir, A.: Polymorphic arrays: a novel VLSI layout for systolic computers. In: 25th FOCS, pp. 37–45. IEEE Computer Society Press, October 1984

[FS87]   Fiat, A., Shamir, A.: How to prove yourself: practical solutions to identification and signature problems. In: Odlyzko, A.M. (ed.) CRYPTO 1986. LNCS, vol. 263, pp. 186–194. Springer, Heidelberg (1987). https://doi.org/10.1007/3-540-47721-7_12

[GGPR13] Gennaro, R., Gentry, C., Parno, B., Raykova, M.: Quadratic span programs and succinct NIZKs without PCPs. In: Johansson, T., Nguyen, P.Q. (eds.) EUROCRYPT 2013. LNCS, vol. 7881, pp. 626–645. Springer, Heidelberg (2013). https://doi.org/10.1007/978-3-642-38348-9_37

[GKR08]   Goldwasser, S., Kalai, Y.T., Rothblum, G.N.: Delegating computation: interactive proofs for muggles. In: Ladner, R.E., Dwork, C. (eds.) 40th ACM STOC, pp. 113–122. ACM Press, May 2008

[GMO16]   Giacomelli, I., Madsen, J., Orlandi, C.: ZKBoo: faster zero-knowledge for Boolean circuits. In: Holz, T., Savage, S. (eds.) USENIX Security 2016, pp. 1069–1083. USENIX Association, August 2016

[GMR85]   Goldwasser, S., Micali, S., Rackoff, C.: The knowledge complexity of interactive proof-systems (extended abstract). In: 17th ACM STOC, pp. 291–304. ACM Press, May 1985

[GMW86]   Goldreich, O., Micali, S., Wigderson, A.: Proofs that yield nothing but their validity and a methodology of cryptographic protocol design (extended abstract). In: 27th FOCS, pp. 174–187. IEEE Computer Society Press, October 1986

[GMW91] Goldreich, O., Micali, S., Wigderson, A.: Proofs that yield nothing but their validity or all languages in NP have zero-knowledge proof systems. J. ACM **38**(3), 691–729 (1991)

[Gro10] Groth, J.: Short pairing-based non-interactive zero-knowledge arguments. In: Abe, M. (ed.) ASIACRYPT 2010. LNCS, vol. 6477, pp. 321–340. Springer, Heidelberg (2010). https://doi.org/10.1007/978-3-642-17373-8_19

[HKK19] Hong, C., Katz, J., Kolesnikov, V., Lu, W., Wang, X.: Covert security with public verifiability: faster, leaner, and simpler. In: Ishai, Y., Rijmen, V. (eds.) EUROCRYPT 2019. LNCS, vol. 11478, pp. 97–121. Springer, Cham (2019). https://doi.org/10.1007/978-3-030-17659-4_4

[IKOS07] Ishai, Y., Kushilevitz, E., Ostrovsky, R., Sahai, A.: Zero-knowledge from secure multiparty computation. In: Johnson, D.S., Feige, U. (eds.) 39th ACM STOC, pp. 21–30. ACM Press, June 2007

[IPS08] Ishai, Y., Prabhakaran, M., Sahai, A.: Founding cryptography on oblivious transfer – efficiently. In: Wagner, D. (ed.) CRYPTO 2008. LNCS, vol. 5157, pp. 572–591. Springer, Heidelberg (2008). https://doi.org/10.1007/978-3-540-85174-5_32

[Kil92] Kilian, J.: A note on efficient zero-knowledge proofs and arguments (extended abstract). In: 24th ACM STOC, pp. 723–732. ACM Press, May 1992

[KKW18] Katz, J., Kolesnikov, V., Wang, X.: Improved non-interactive zero knowledge with applications to post-quantum signatures. In: Lie, D., Mannan, M., Backes, M., Wang, X. (eds.) ACM CCS 2018, pp. 525–537. ACM Press, October 2018

[KM15] Kolesnikov, V., Malozemoff, A.J.: Public verifiability in the covert model (almost) for free. In: Iwata, T., Cheon, J.H. (eds.) ASIACRYPT 2015. LNCS, vol. 9453, pp. 210–235. Springer, Heidelberg (2015). https://doi.org/10.1007/978-3-662-48800-3_9

[Lin16] Lindell, Y.: How to simulate it - a tutorial on the simulation proof technique. Cryptology ePrint Archive, Report 2016/046 (2016). http://eprint.iacr.org/2016/046

[Mic94] Micali, S.: CS proofs (extended abstracts). In: 35th FOCS, pp. 436–453. IEEE Computer Society Press, November 1994

[STO88] 20th ACM STOC. ACM Press, May 1988

[SV15] Schoenmakers, B., Veeningen, M.: Universally verifiable multiparty computation from threshold homomorphic cryptosystems. In: Malkin, T., Kolesnikov, V., Lewko, A.B., Polychronakis, M. (eds.) ACNS 2015. LNCS, vol. 9092, pp. 3–22. Springer, Cham (2015). https://doi.org/10.1007/978-3-319-28166-7_1

[TEMX17] Thuraisingham, B.M., David, E., Tal, M., Xu, D. (eds.): ACM CCS 2017. ACM Press, October/November (2017)

[XZZ19] Xie, T., Zhang, J., Zhang, Y., Papamanthou, C., Song, D.: Libra: succinct zero-knowledge proofs with optimal prover computation. In: Boldyreva and Micciancio [BM19], pp. 733–764

[ZXZS20] Zhang, J., Xie, T., Zhang, Y., Song, D.: Transparent polynomial delegation and its applications to zero knowledge proof. In: 2020 IEEE Symposium on Security and Privacy, pp. 859–876. IEEE Computer Society Press, May 2020

Complexity and Performance of Secure Floating-Point Polynomial Evaluation Protocols

Octavian Catrina[✉][iD]

Politehnica University of Bucharest, Bucharest, Romania
ocatrina@elcom.pub.ro

Abstract. Secure computation provides cryptographic protocols for collaborative applications with private inputs and outputs. In this paper, we examine a collection of protocols for secure evaluation of polynomials using secure floating-point arithmetic. The main goal is to provide a comparative analysis of their construction, complexity, performance, and tradeoffs in different application settings. The analysis demonstrates the performance gains that can be obtained by evaluating the polynomials using optimized secure multi-operand arithmetic instead of relying on generic constructions based on two-operand arithmetic. It also examines the relations between performance and complexity metrics for different execution environments (LAN, Internet), floating-point precision, and problem sizes. These protocols are part of a framework for secure multiparty computation with fixed-point and floating-point numbers based on Shamir secret sharing and related techniques.

Keywords: Secure multiparty computation · Secret sharing · Secure floating-point arithmetic · Polynomial evaluation

1 Introduction

Secure computation is a branch of cryptography that helps collaborative applications to protect the privacy of their inputs and outputs (e.g., to satisfy legal or business privacy requirements). Applications like statistical analysis, data mining, and various optimizations compute with real numbers and need the accuracy and dynamic range offered by floating-point numbers [2,4–6,15]. Improving the performance of secure floating-point computation is a difficult challenge.

In this paper, we examine a collection of protocols that evaluate polynomials with private inputs and output, based on the secure floating-point arithmetic protocols presented in [8,9,11]. An immediate application is the secure evaluation of various mathematical functions by polynomial approximation.

Optimizing secure computation involves a combination of factors: amount of exchanged data, interaction rounds, parallel execution, local processing, and pre-processing. Improving some factors can degrade the others, so there are various optimization tradeoffs (e.g., rounds versus amount of data and local processing).

© Springer Nature Switzerland AG 2021
E. Bertino et al. (Eds.): ESORICS 2021, LNCS 12973, pp. 352–369, 2021.
https://doi.org/10.1007/978-3-030-88428-4_18

The effects of these factors on the protocols' performance depend to a large extent on the execution environment, the application, and the implementation.

The protocols discussed in this paper are part of a framework for secure multiparty computation using Shamir secret sharing and related techniques, in the semi-honest model. The framework supports secure fixed-point and floating-point arithmetic with arbitrary precision and offers alternative solutions for the building blocks, with different complexity tradeoffs. The floating-point arithmetic protocols share the basic framework with the protocols in [1], but use simpler algorithms enabled by building blocks with lower (and constant) number of rounds, introduced in [7,9]. These building blocks offer a combination of complexity metrics aimed at improving the performance for a broader range of execution environments (network delay and bandwidth) and application requirements (precision and problem size). The floating-point protocols used in [5,15] rely on a different framework, based on additive sharing. Their building blocks have low communication, but higher (logarithmic) number of rounds.

The benefits offered by optimized secure multi-operand arithmetic for polynomial evaluation were initially explored in [8,10]. The protocols presented in this paper achieve better performance by using improved secure arithmetic [9,11] and adapting to different contexts by controlling certain tradeoffs. However, the main goal is to provide a comparative analysis of their construction, complexity, tradeoffs, and performance in different application settings.

The analysis demonstrates the improvements that can be obtained by evaluating the polynomials using optimized multi-operand floating-point arithmetic protocols [8,11] instead of relying on two-operand protocols [9] and generic constructions. It also clarifies the performance effects of certain design tradeoffs and shows that different protocol variants should be considered for different execution environments, floating-point precision, and problem sizes.

The paper is structured as follows. Section 2 provides an overview of the secure computation model, data encoding, and building blocks. Section 3 presents the protocols for polynomial evaluation with private floating-point inputs and outputs and their complexity. The results of the performance analysis are presented in Sect. 4, followed by conclusions in Sect. 5.

2   Secure Floating-Point Arithmetic

Secure Computation Model. The protocols rely on standard primitives for secure computation using Shamir secret sharing [13] and related techniques [12] and offer perfect or statistical privacy, assuming perfectly secure communication.

Secure arithmetic in a finite field $\mathbb{F}$ is provided by primitives based on Shamir secret sharing over $\mathbb{F}$, with perfect privacy against a passive threshold adversary that corrupts t out of n parties (the parties follow strictly the protocol and any $t + 1$ parties can reconstruct a secret, while t or less parties cannot distinguish it from random values in $\mathbb{F}$). Addition/subtraction of shared elements of $\mathbb{F}$ is locally computed by adding/subtracting the shares. Input sharing, output reconstruction, and multiplication require interaction between parties.

To overcome the limitations of secure arithmetic with shared data, the protocols combine secret sharing with additive or multiplicative hiding, with perfect privacy or statistical privacy with security parameter κ: for a shared variable $[\![x]\!]$, the parties jointly generate a shared random value $[\![r]\!]$, compute $[\![y]\!] = [\![x]\!] + [\![r]\!]$ or $[\![y]\!] = [\![x]\!] \cdot [\![r]\!], x \neq 0$, and reveal y (like one-time pad encryption with key r).

Complexity Metrics. The complexity analysis is based on two metrics that focus on interaction. Communication complexity counts the invocations of three primitives during which every party sends a share to the others: input sharing, multiplication, and secret reconstruction. Round complexity is the number of sequential invocations. The first metric accounts for the amount of data and local processing involved in the execution of the interactive primitives. The second metric takes into account the effects of other communication delays. The pseudocode of the protocols is annotated with the number of rounds followed by the number of interactive primitives.

The running time is reduced by executing in parallel, in one round, interactive primitives that are causally independent. All shared random values used in a task are precomputed in parallel. Part of them are generated without interaction, using Pseudo-random Replicated Secret Sharing (PRSS) [12] and its integer variant (RISS) [14] (random field elements, integers, and sharings of 0). With PRSS, the precomputation needs only one round. A variant that needs two rounds but is usually faster generates the shared random bits in a small field and then converts them to the larger field required by the protocol.

Data Encoding. The secure computation framework supports arbitrary-precision secure arithmetic with integer, fixed-point, and floating-point data types. A variable can be seen as a tuple that consists of its value, secret or public, encoded in a field $\mathbb{F}$, and public parameters that determine the type's range and accuracy. The protocols discussed in this paper use the field $\mathbb{Z}_q$, with prime q large enough for all data types. To distinguish different representations of a value, we denote $\tilde{x}$ a fixed-point number, $\bar{x}$ the integer value that encodes $\tilde{x}$, x the field element that encodes $\bar{x}$, and $[\![x]\!]$ a sharing of secret x; a floating-point number is denoted $\hat{x}$. The notation $x = (condition)? \, a : b$ means that x is assigned the value a when $condition = true$ and b otherwise. The data types are defined as follows.

Binary values $x \in \{0, 1\}$ are encoded as the field's values 0 and 1. This allows efficient secure evaluation of Boolean functions using secure arithmetic in $\mathbb{F}$. We denote $[\![a]\!] \wedge [\![b]\!] = [\![a]\!][\![b]\!] = [\![a \wedge b]\!]$ (AND), $[\![a]\!] \vee [\![b]\!] = [\![a]\!] + [\![b]\!] - [\![a]\!][\![b]\!] = [\![a \vee b]\!]$ (OR) and $[\![a]\!] \oplus [\![b]\!] = [\![a]\!] + [\![b]\!] - 2[\![a]\!][\![b]\!] = [\![a \oplus b]\!]$ (XOR).

The sets of integers are $\mathbb{Z}_{\langle k \rangle} = \{\bar{x} \in \mathbb{Z} \mid \bar{x} \in [-2^{k-1}, 2^{k-1} - 1]\}$. Integer values are encoded in $\mathbb{Z}_q$ by the function $\mathsf{fld} : \mathbb{Z}_{\langle k \rangle} \mapsto \mathbb{Z}_q$, $\mathsf{fld}(\bar{x}) = \bar{x} \bmod q$, for $q > 2^{k+\kappa}$, where κ is the security parameter (fld maps $\bar{x} \in [-2^{k-1}, -1]$ to $x \in [q - 2^{k-1}, q - 1]$). This encoding enables efficient secure integer arithmetic based on secure arithmetic in $\mathbb{Z}_q$: for any $\bar{x}_1, \bar{x}_2 \in \mathbb{Z}_{\langle k \rangle}$ and $\odot \in \{+, -, \cdot\}$, the protocols compute $\bar{x}_1 \odot \bar{x}_2 = \mathsf{fld}^{-1}(\mathsf{fld}(\bar{x}_1) \odot \mathsf{fld}(\bar{x}_2))$; also, if $\bar{x}_2 \mid \bar{x}_1$ then $\bar{x}_1 / \bar{x}_2 = \mathsf{fld}^{-1}(\mathsf{fld}(\bar{x}_1) \cdot \mathsf{fld}(\bar{x}_2)^{-1})$.

Table 1. Complexity of the main building blocks used in this paper [7,9].

Protocol	Rounds online	Primitives online	Primitives in precomputation round
$\mathsf{Div2m}(\llbracket a \rrbracket, k, m)$	3	$m + 2$	$3m$
$\mathsf{Div2mP}(\llbracket a \rrbracket, k, m)$	1	1	m
$\mathsf{PreDiv2m}(\llbracket a \rrbracket, k, m)$	3	$2m + 1$	$4m$
$\mathsf{PreDiv2mP}(\llbracket a \rrbracket, k, m)$	1	1	m
$\mathsf{Int2Mask}(\llbracket x \rrbracket, k)$	1	$k - 1$	$2k - 3$
$\mathsf{Pow2Inv}(\llbracket x \rrbracket, m)$	4	$3m$	$6m - 2$
$\mathsf{LTZ}(\llbracket a \rrbracket, k)$	3	$k + 1$	$3k$

The sets of fixed-point numbers are $\mathbb{Q}^{FX}_{\langle k, f \rangle} = \{ \tilde{x} \in \mathbb{Q} \mid \tilde{x} = \bar{x} \cdot 2^{-f}, \bar{x} \in \mathbb{Z}_{\langle k \rangle}, f < k \}$. Fixed-point values are mapped to $\mathbb{Z}_{\langle k \rangle}$ by the function int : $\mathbb{Q}^{FX}_{\langle k, f \rangle} \mapsto \mathbb{Z}_{\langle k \rangle}$, $\bar{x} = \mathsf{int}_f(\tilde{x}) = \tilde{x} \cdot 2^f$ and then encoded in $\mathbb{Z}_q$ as described above.

The sets of floating-point numbers are $\mathbb{Q}^{FL}_{\langle l, g \rangle} = \{ \hat{x} \in \mathbb{Q} \mid \hat{x} = (1-2s) \cdot \bar{v} \cdot 2^{\bar{p}}, \bar{v} \in [2^{\ell-1}, 2^\ell - 1] \cup \{0\}, \bar{p} \in \mathbb{Z}_{\langle g \rangle}, s, z \in \{0, 1\} \}$, where $\bar{v}$ is the normalized significand, $\bar{p}$ is the signed exponent, $s = (\hat{x} < 0)? \ 1 : 0$, and $z = (\hat{x} = 0)? \ 1 : 0$, all encoded in $\mathbb{Z}_q$ as described above. If $\hat{x} = 0$ then $\bar{v} = 0$, $z = 1$, and $\bar{p} = -2^{g-1}$.

Secure multiplication and division require a modulus $q > 2^{2k+\kappa}$ for $\tilde{x} \in \mathbb{Q}^{FX}_{\langle k, f \rangle}$ and $q > 2^{2\ell+\kappa}$ for $\hat{x} \in \mathbb{Q}^{FL}_{\langle \ell, g \rangle}$. The protocols support arbitrary precision arithmetic. The applications usually need $k \in [32, 128]$, $f \in [0, k]$, $\ell \in [16, 64]$ and $g \in [8, 15]$, depending on range and accuracy requirements.

Building Blocks. Fixed-point and floating-point arithmetic protocols are constructed using a small set of building blocks that compute $\bar{b} = 2^m \bar{a}$ and $\bar{c} \approx \bar{a}/2^m$, for secret $\bar{a}, \bar{b}, \bar{c} \in \mathbb{Z}_{\langle k \rangle}$ and public or secret integer $m \in [0, k-1]$. Table 1 lists the main building blocks and their complexity (see [7,9] and their references).

If m is public then $2^m \bar{a}$ is a local operation and $\bar{a}/2^m$ is computed by $\mathsf{Div2m}$ or $\mathsf{Div2mP}$. $\mathsf{Div2m}$ rounds to $-\infty$, while $\mathsf{Div2mP}$ rounds probabilistically to the nearest integer[1]. We denote their outputs $\lfloor \bar{a}/2^m \rfloor$ and $\lfloor \bar{a}/2^m \rceil$, respectively. $\mathsf{Div2mP}$ is much more efficient. The rounding error is $|\delta| < 1$ and $\delta = 0$ if 2^m divides $\bar{a}$. LTZ computes $s = (\bar{a} < 0)? \ 1 : 0 = -\lfloor \bar{a}/2^{k-1} \rfloor$ using $\mathsf{Div2m}$.

If m is secret then $2^m \bar{a}$ and $\bar{a}/2^m$ can be computed using two methods:

- The first method computes $\{x_i\}_{i=0}^{k-1}$, $x_i = (m = i)? \ 1 : 0$, using $\mathsf{Int2Mask}$ [10] and $\bar{d}_i = \{ \lfloor \bar{a}/2^i \rceil \}_{i=0}^{k-1}$ using $\mathsf{PreDiv2mP}$ (or $\{ \lfloor \bar{a}/2^i \rfloor \}_{i=0}^{k-1}$ with $\mathsf{PreDiv2m}$). Then, it computes $2^m \bar{a} = \bar{a} \sum_{i=0}^{k-1} x_i 2^i$ and $\bar{a}/2^m = \sum_{i=0}^{k-1} x_i \bar{d}_i$. $\mathsf{PreDiv2mP}$ and $\mathsf{PreDiv2m}$ are efficient generalizations of $\mathsf{Div2mP}$ and $\mathsf{Div2m}$ [7].

---

[1] $\mathsf{Div2mP}$ returns $\bar{c} = \lfloor \bar{a}/2^m \rfloor + u$, where $u \in \{0, 1\}$ and $u = 1$ with probability $p = \frac{\bar{a} \bmod 2^m}{2^m}$. For example, if $\bar{a} = 46$ and $m = 3$ then $\bar{a}/2^m = 5.75$; the output is $\bar{c} = 6$ with probability $p = 0.75$ or $\bar{c} = 5$ with probability $1 - p = 0.25$.

Table 2. Protocol complexity for inputs and outputs in $\mathbb{Q}^{FL}_{\langle \ell,g \rangle}$, $\lambda = \lceil \log \ell \rceil$, $\mu = \lceil \log m \rceil$, where m is the number of terms/factors in sums/products or the polynomial degree.

Protocol	Rounds online	Primitives: online computation and precomputation round	Modulus
AddFL [9]	18	$5\ell + 3\lambda + 3g + 25$	$> 2^{2\ell+1+\kappa}$
		$10\ell + 6\lambda + 3g$	
MulFL [9]	5	$\ell + 7$	$> 2^{2\ell+\kappa}$
		$4\ell + 3$	
SumGFL [11]	18μ	$(m-1)(5\ell + 3\lambda + 3g + 25)$	$> 2^{2\ell+1+\kappa}$
		$(m-1)(10\ell + 6\lambda + 3g)$	
SumFL [11]	$4\mu + 17$	$m(3\lambda + 2g + 7) + 5(\ell + \mu)$	$> 2^{2\ell+\mu+\kappa+1}$
		$m(\ell + 6\lambda + 6g + 5) + 10(\ell + \mu)$	
ProdGFL [8]	5μ	$(m-1)(\ell + 6)$	$> 2^{2\ell+\kappa}$
		$(m-1)(4\ell + 3)$	
ProdFL1 [8]	$\mu + 6$	$2\ell + 7(m-1)$	$> 2^{2\ell+m+\kappa-2}$
		$(m-1)(\ell + 6) + 4\ell$	
PolySGFL	$23\mu + 5$	$m(7\ell + 3\lambda + 3g + 39) - \ell - 7$	$> 2^{2\ell+\kappa}$
		$m(18\ell + 6\lambda + 3g + 6) - 4\ell - 3$	
PolySBFL	$9\mu + 18$	$m(\ell + 3\lambda + 2g + 11) + 4\ell + 5\mu$	$> 2^{2\ell+\kappa+2}$
		$m(5\ell + 6\lambda + 6g + 6) + 6\ell + 10\mu + 3$	
PolySOFL	$4\mu + 19$	$m(3\log(\ell + m) + 2g + 17) + 5\ell$	$> 2^{2\ell+2m+\kappa}$
		$m(3\ell + m + 6\log(\ell + m) + 6g + 13) + 9\ell + 10\mu$	
PolyPGFL	$5\mu + 18$	$m(6\ell + 3\lambda + 3g + 31) - \ell - 6$	$> 2^{2\ell+\kappa}$
		$m(14\ell + 6\lambda + 3g + 3) - 4\ell - 3$	
PolyPOFL	$\mu + 24$	$m(5\ell + 3\lambda + 3g + 32) + 2\ell - 7$	$> 2^{2\ell+m+\kappa-2}$
		$m(11\ell + 6\lambda + 3g + 6\lambda + 6) + 3\ell - 6$	

- The second method computes $\bar{y} = 2^m$ and $\mathsf{fld}(\bar{y})^{-1}$ (multiplicative inverse of $\bar{y}$'s encoding in $\mathbb{Z}_q$) with Pow2Inv [9] and then $2^m \bar{a} = \bar{a}\bar{y}$ and $\lfloor \bar{a}/2^m \rfloor = \lfloor \mathsf{fld}^{-1}(\mathsf{fld}(2^k \bar{a})\mathsf{fld}(\bar{y})^{-1})/2^k \rfloor$.

With standard primitives, a multiplication followed by additive hiding, $d \leftarrow \mathsf{Reveal}(\llbracket a \rrbracket \llbracket b \rrbracket + \llbracket r \rrbracket)$, needs 2 interactions and 2 rounds. We avoid the first interaction by randomizing the share products: for all $i \in [1, n]$, party i computes $\llbracket c \rrbracket_{2t,i} \leftarrow \llbracket a \rrbracket_i \llbracket b \rrbracket_i + \llbracket 0 \rrbracket_{2t,i}$, where $\llbracket 0 \rrbracket_{2t,i}$ are pseudo-random shares of 0 generated with PRZS(2t) [12]. We denote $\llbracket a \rrbracket * \llbracket b \rrbracket$ this local operation. Now the computation needs a single interaction: $d \leftarrow \mathsf{RevealD}(\llbracket a \rrbracket * \llbracket b \rrbracket + \llbracket r \rrbracket)$, where RevealD is the secret reconstruction protocol for polynomials of degree $2t$. Most of the protocols listed in Table 1 start with additive hiding of the input. We add variants of these protocols for input shared with a random polynomial of degree $2t$, and distinguish them by the suffix 'D' (they use RevealD instead of Reveal).

Floating-Point Arithmetic. The protocols for two-operand and multi-operand addition and multiplication are listed in Table 2. Their specifications and performance are presented in [8,9,11]. We summarize relevant aspects of the two-operand protocols. The other protocols will be discussed in the next section.

The protocol AddFL computes $\hat{a} = \hat{a}_1 + \hat{a}_2$ with secret inputs and output [9]. Let $\bar{v}_1' = (1 - 2s_1)\bar{v}_1$ and $\bar{v}_2' = (1 - 2s_2)\bar{v}_2$. Assume $\bar{p}_1 \geq \bar{p}_2$ and let $\Delta = \bar{p}_1 - \bar{p}_2$ (if $\bar{p}_1 < \bar{p}_2$ the inputs are swapped). The protocol computes $\bar{v}'$ and $\bar{p}'$ so that $\bar{v}'2^{\bar{p}'} \approx \bar{v}_1'2^{\bar{p}_1} + \bar{v}_2'2^{\bar{p}_2}$. It consists of two main tasks. The first task aligns the significands' radix points and adds them: $\bar{v}_i' = 2\bar{v}_i'$, $\bar{v}' = \bar{v}_1' + \lfloor\bar{v}_2'/2^\Delta\rceil \in [-4(2^\ell - 1), 4(2^\ell - 1)]$, $\bar{p}' = \bar{p}_1 - 1$. Setting $\bar{v}_i' = 2\bar{v}_i'$ reduces the effects of rounding errors for $\Delta = 1$. The second task normalizes $\bar{v}'$ so that $\hat{a} \in \mathbb{Q}_{\langle\ell,g\rangle}^{FL}$. Both tasks are expensive, so addition is (by far) the slowest secure floating-point operation.

AddFL can align the radix point using Int2Mask or Pow2Inv. We use the second method, which is faster, although it needs 2 more rounds [9].

The protocol MulFL computes $\hat{a} = \hat{a}_1\hat{a}_2$ with secret inputs and output [9]. It firsts computes $\bar{v}_3 = \bar{v}_1\bar{v}_2$, $\bar{p}_3 = \bar{p}_1 + \bar{p}_2$, $s = s_1 \oplus s_2$, and $z = z_1 \vee z_2$, then normalizes $\bar{v}_3$ so that $\hat{a} \in \mathbb{Q}_{\langle\ell,g\rangle}^{FL}$. Since $\bar{v}_3 \in [2^{2\ell-2}, 2^{2\ell} - 2^{\ell+1} + 1] \cup \{0\}$, the normalization consists of 3 cases: if $\bar{v}_3 < 2^{2\ell-1}$ then $\bar{v} = \lfloor\bar{v}_3/2^{\ell-1}\rceil$ and $\bar{p} = \bar{p}_3 + \ell - 1$, otherwise $\bar{v} = \lfloor\bar{v}_3/2^\ell\rceil$ and $\bar{p} = \bar{p}_3 + \ell$; if $\bar{v} = 0$ then $\bar{p} = \bar{p}(1 - z) - z2^{g-1}$.

A partial normalization computes only $\bar{v} = \lfloor\bar{v}_3/2^{\ell-1}\rceil \in [2^{\ell-1}, 2^{\ell+1} - 3] \cup \{0\}$ and $\bar{p} = \bar{p}_3 + \ell - 1$ (first case). This avoids an expensive secure comparison, but if $\bar{v}_3 \geq 2^{2\ell-1}$ the bitlength grows by 1 bit (it cuts off $\ell - 1$ bits instead of ℓ).

The optimized protocols for products and powers discussed in the next section use Protocol 1, MulPFL. This variant of MulFL computes the significand $\bar{v}$ and the exponent $\bar{p}$ of $\hat{a}_1\hat{a}_2$ with full or partial normalization for input significands with up to $\ell + \ell'$ bits. For full normalization ($\rho = 1$), SelDiv2mPD computes both $\bar{v}' = \lfloor\bar{v}_1\bar{v}_2/2^{\ell-1}\rceil$ and $\bar{v}'' = \lfloor\bar{v}_1\bar{v}_2/2^\ell\rceil$ with a single interactive operation [8]. Step 3 computes $b = (\bar{v}' < 2^\ell)?\ 1 : 0$ and step 4 selects $\bar{v} = (b = 1)?\ \bar{v}' : \bar{v}''$. Partial normalization ($\rho \neq 1$) computes only $\bar{v} = \lfloor\bar{v}_1\bar{v}_2/2^{\ell-1}\rceil$ using Div2mPD. This reduces the online complexity to just 1 round and 1 interactive operation, at the cost of increasing the significand's bitlength by at most 1 bit.

Protocol 1: MulPFL($\{[\![v_i]\!], [\![p_i]\!]\}_{i=1}^2, \ell, g, \ell', \rho$)

---

1   **if** $\rho = 1$ **then**

2    $([\![v']\!], [\![v'']\!]) \leftarrow$ SelDiv2mPD($[\![v_1]\!] * [\![v_2]\!], 2(\ell + \ell'), \{\ell - 1, \ell\}$);   // 1; 1

3    $[\![b]\!] \leftarrow$ LTZ($[\![v']\!] - 2^\ell, \ell + 1$);   // 3; $\ell + 2$

4    $[\![v]\!] \leftarrow [\![b]\!]([\![v']\!] - [\![v'']\!]) + [\![v'']\!]$;   // 1; 1

5    $[\![p]\!] \leftarrow [\![p_1]\!] + [\![p_2]\!] + \ell - [\![b]\!]$;

6   **else**

7    $[\![v]\!] \leftarrow$ Div2mPD($[\![v_1]\!] * [\![v_2]\!], 2(\ell + \ell'), \ell - 1$);   // 1; 1

8    $[\![p]\!] \leftarrow [\![p_1]\!] + [\![p_2]\!] + \ell - 1$;

9   **return** $([\![v]\!], [\![p]\!])$;

---

3   Secure Polynomial Evaluation

We consider two cases of secure polynomial evaluation. In the first case, the polynomial is defined by its coefficients and we evaluate $\hat{y} = P(\hat{x}) = \sum_{i=0}^m \hat{a}_i\hat{x}^i$. In the second case, it is defined by its real-valued roots and we evaluate $\hat{y} = P(\hat{x}) = \prod_{i=1}^m(\hat{x} - \hat{a}_i)$. The coefficients, roots, variable, and output are secret

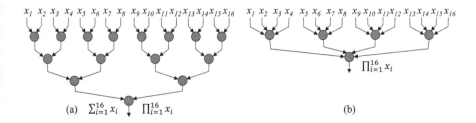

Fig. 1. Generic algorithms for secure evaluation of $\sum_{i=1}^{m} \hat{x}_i$ and $\prod_{i=1}^{m} \hat{x}_i$.

floating-point numbers encoded in $\mathbb{Z}_q$ as described in Sect. 2: $\{\hat{a}_i\}_{i=0}^{m} \in \mathbb{Q}_{\langle \ell, g \rangle}^{FL}$, $\hat{a}_i = (1 - 2s_i)\bar{v}_i 2^{\bar{p}_i}$, $\hat{x} \in \mathbb{Q}_{\langle \ell, g \rangle}^{FL}$, $\hat{x} = (1 - 2s)\bar{v} 2^{\bar{p}}$, and $\hat{y} \in \mathbb{Q}_{\langle \ell, g \rangle}^{FL}$, $\hat{y} = (1 - 2s')\bar{v}' 2^{\bar{p}'}$.

The design of polynomial evaluation protocols must take into account the specific features of secure floating-point arithmetic [9]: addition is much slower than multiplication; floating-point normalization is expensive; performance is substantially improved by parallel execution of interactive primitives.

Traditional polynomial evaluation algorithms are optimized based on other assumptions [17]. For a polynomial of degree m, the widely used Horner algorithm computes m multiply-add operations (optimal) in m iterations. Estrin's parallel algorithm needs only $\lfloor \log m \rfloor + 1$ iterations and the number of operations is almost optimal: m multiply-add operations and $\lfloor \log m \rfloor$ squares. Estrin's algorithm is more suitable for secure computation, but still computes m expensive secure floating-point additions, so the only improvement is the reduced number of rounds. Both algorithms can take advantage of fused multiply-add operations offered by modern processors, but the improvement obtained by optimizing secure multiply-add floating-point operations is rather small.

A more promising approach uses protocols optimized for multi-operand floating-point arithmetic, discussed in the next sections. Table 2 lists the main protocols and their complexity.

3.1 Generic Protocols for Secure Polynomial Evaluation

The protocols PolySGFL and PolyPGFL evaluate $\sum_{i=0}^{m} \hat{a}_i \hat{x}^i$ and $\prod_{i=1}^{m} (\hat{x} - \hat{a}_i)$, respectively, using AddFL, MulFL, and generic algorithms for sums, products, and powers, called SumGFL, ProdGFL, and PowAllGFL, respectively. These algorithms minimize the number of operations and execute many of them in parallel to reduce the running time.

SumGFL evaluates $\sum_{i=1}^{m} \hat{a}_i$ using AddFL and the algorithm with binary tree structure in Fig. 1a. The algorithm computes $m - 1$ operations (optimal) in $\lceil \log m \rceil$ iterations. Each iteration takes as input a vector, splits it into pairs of elements, adds them in parallel and returns the results in a vector of half length. ProdGFL evaluates $\prod_{i=1}^{m} \hat{a}_i$ using MulFL and the same algorithm as SumGFL.

PowAllGFL evaluates $\{\hat{x}^i\}_{i=1}^{m}$ using MulFL and the algorithm in Fig. 2. This algorithm computes $m - 1$ multiplications (optimal) in $\mu = \lceil \log m \rceil$ iterations.

Therefore, the protocol PolySGFL computes $\{\hat{x}^i\}_{i=1}^{m}$ using PowAllGFL, the terms $\{\hat{a}_i \hat{x}^i\}_{i=1}^{m}$ using MulFL, in parallel, and then $\hat{a}_0 + \sum_{i=1}^{m} \hat{a}_i \hat{x}^i$ using SumGFL.

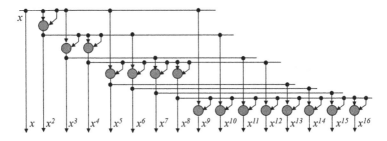

Fig. 2. Generic algorithm for secure evaluation of $\{\hat{x}^i\}_{i=1}^m$.

The protocol PolyPGFL computes the factors $\{\hat{x} - \hat{a}_i\}_{i=1}^m$ using AddFL, in parallel, and then $\prod_{i=1}^m (\hat{x} - \hat{a}_i)$ using ProdGFL.

Both protocols compute m secure floating-point additions, but PolyPGFL runs them in parallel, instead of $\lceil \log m \rceil$ iterations, so it needs fewer rounds. Also, PolyPGFL computes $m - 1$ secure floating-point multiplications, instead of $2m - 1$, so the number of interactive primitives is also reduced. However, the communication complexity is strongly dominated by the m additions.

A generic protocol based on Estrin's algorithm, PolyEGFL, is obtained using the tree structure in Fig. 1a, a multiply-add operation with MulFL and AddFL, and a square in parallel with each iteration [8]. PolyEGFL is slightly more efficient than PolySGFL: it removes 5 rounds and $m - \lceil \log m \rceil$ multiplications. We can simplify the multiply-add operation, but the performance gain is modest.

3.2 Optimized Protocols for Polynomials Defined by Coefficients

The protocol PolySFL, discussed in the following, improves PolySGFL by computing $\{\hat{x}^i\}_{i=1}^m$ and $\{\hat{a}_i \hat{x}^i\}_{i=1}^m$ using multiplications with partial normalization instead of full normalization (as explained in Sect. 2) and then $\sum_{i=0}^m \hat{a}_i \hat{x}^i$ using the protocol SumFL, specially optimized for multi-operand addition, instead of SumGFL (Table 2).

Computing $\{\hat{x}^i\}_{i=1}^m$ with partial normalization increases the bitlength of the significands to $\ell_i \in [\ell, \ell + i - 1]$ bits and requires a larger modulus q, able to encode integers of $2\ell + m - 2$ bits (for the last multiplication, before division by $2^{\ell-1}$). The larger modulus complicates the integration in applications: either run the entire application with the large modulus, or add share conversions to the product protocol. Both approaches have important disadvantages. We are interested in more flexible solutions, that limit the growth of the modulus.

Protocol 2, PowAllFL, computes the significands and exponents $\{\bar{v}_i, \bar{p}_i\}_{i=1}^m$ of $\{\hat{x}^i\}_{i=1}^m$ using MulPFL and the algorithm in Fig. 2. Let $\mu = \lceil \log m \rceil$. Iteration $i \in [1, \mu - 1]$ computes in parallel $\gamma = 2^{i-1}$ multiplications: $\hat{x}_{\gamma+j} = \hat{x}_\gamma \hat{x}_j = \hat{x}^{\gamma+j}$, for $j \in [1, \gamma]$. Iteration μ computes the remaining $\beta = m - 2^{\mu-1}$ multiplications.

The parameter $\theta \in [0, \mu]$ controls the tradeoff between the protocol's complexity and the significands' bitlength: full normalization for $i \leq \theta$ ($\rho = 1$, bitlength grows $\ell' = 0$ bits) and partial normalization for $i > \theta$ ($\rho = 0$, bitlength grows by 0 or 1 bits per multiplication, up to $\ell' = 2^{i-\theta} - 1$ bits).

Protocol 2: PowAllFL($[\![v]\!], [\![p]\!], \ell, g, m, \theta$)

1 $([\![v_1]\!], [\![p_1]\!]) \leftarrow ([\![v]\!], [\![p]\!]); \mu \leftarrow \lceil \log m \rceil;$
2 **foreach** $i \in [1, \mu]$ **do**
3      $\gamma \leftarrow 2^{i-1}; \beta \leftarrow (i < \mu)? \gamma : m - \gamma;$
4      $\rho \leftarrow (i \leq \theta)? 1 : 0; \ell' \leftarrow (i \leq \theta)? 0 : 2^{i-\theta} - 1;$
5   **foreach** $j \in [1, \beta]$ **do**
6          $([\![v_{\gamma+j}]\!], [\![p_{\gamma+j}]\!]) \leftarrow$ MulPFL($[\![v_\gamma]\!], [\![p_\gamma]\!], [\![v_j]\!], [\![p_j]\!], \ell, \ell', \rho$);
7 **return** $\{[\![v_i]\!], [\![p_i]\!]\}_{i=1}^m;$

The protocol SumFL, described in [10,11], is an efficient generalization of AddFL for $m > 2$ inputs. The goal is to compute $\bar{v}'$ and $\bar{p}'$ so that $\bar{v}'2^{\bar{p}'} \approx \sum_{i=1}^m (1 - 2s_i)\bar{v}_i 2^{\bar{p}_i}$. SumFL aligns the radix points of the m significands to the largest exponent and then adds them, by computing: $\bar{p}' = \max(\{p_i\}_{i=1}^m)$, $\Delta_i = \bar{p}' - \bar{p}_i$, $c_i = (\Delta_i < \ell + 1)? 1 : 0$, $\bar{v}'_i = (1 - 2s_i)\bar{v}_i$, and $\bar{v}' = \sum_{i=1}^m \lfloor 2\bar{v}'_i c_i / 2^{\Delta_i} \rfloor$. Then, it normalizes $\bar{v}'$ using the same protocol as AddFL. Before normalization, the maximum bitlength of the sum of m significands is only $\ell + \lceil \log m \rceil + 1$, so the growth of the significands is not a concern. The complexity is substantially reduced by simplifying the radix-point alignment and normalizing only the final result. SumFL can align the radix point using either Int2Mask, or Pow2Inv. We use the second method, which is faster, although it needs 3 more rounds [11].

Protocol 3, PolySFL, evaluates $\sum_{i=0}^m \hat{a}_i \hat{x}^i$ for $\{\hat{a}_i\}_{i=0}^m = \{\bar{v}_i, \bar{p}_i, \bar{s}_i, \bar{z}_i\}_{i=0}^m$ and $\hat{x} = \langle \bar{v}, \bar{p}, \bar{s}, \bar{z} \rangle$. Step 1 computes the significands and the exponents $\{\bar{v}'_i, \bar{p}'_i\}_{i=1}^m$ of $\{\hat{x}^i\}_{i=1}^m$ using PowAllFL and the tradeoff parameter $\theta \in [0, \mu]$. Steps 2–7 compute $\{\hat{a}_i \hat{x}^i\}_{i=1}^m = \{\bar{v}''_i, \bar{p}''_i, \bar{s}''_i, \bar{z}''_i\}_{i=1}^m$, multiplying the powers and the coefficients with partial normalization: steps 2 and 6 compute the flags $z''_i = (\hat{a}_i \hat{x}^i = 0)? 1 : 0 = z \vee z_i$ and the sign bits $s''_i = (\hat{a}_i \hat{x}^i < 0)? 1 : 0 - (i \bmod 2 = 1)? s_i : s \oplus s_i$; step 4 computes $\bar{v}''_i = \lfloor \bar{v}_i \bar{v}'_i / 2^{\ell-1} \rfloor$; and step 5 computes $\bar{p}''_i = (\hat{a}_i \hat{x}^i \neq 0)? \bar{p}'_i + \bar{p}_i : -2^{g-1}$. Due to partial normalizations, the significands of $\{\hat{a}_i \hat{x}^i\}_{i=1}^m$ have the bitlength $\ell_i \in [\ell, \ell + \lceil i/2^\theta \rceil]$. Step 8 computes $\sum_{i=0}^m \hat{a}_i \hat{x}^i$ using a slightly modified version of SumFL that takes on input significands with maximum bitlength $\ell' \geq \ell$ and normalizes the output to ℓ bits (here, $\ell' = \ell + \lceil m/2^\theta \rceil$).

Protocol 3: PolySFL($[\![v]\!], [\![p]\!], [\![s]\!], [\![z]\!], \{[\![v_i]\!], [\![p_i]\!], [\![s_i]\!], [\![z_i]\!]\}_{i=0}^m, \ell, g, \theta$)

1 $\{[\![v'_i]\!], [\![p'_i]\!]\}_{i=1}^m \leftarrow$ PowAllFL($[\![v]\!], [\![p]\!], \ell, g, m, \theta$) ;   *// $\mu + 4\theta; (\ell+3)(2^\theta - 1) + m$*
2 **foreach** $i \in [1, m]$ **do** $[\![z''_i]\!] \leftarrow [\![z]\!] \vee [\![z_i]\!];$ *// $0; m$*
3 **foreach** $i \in [1, m]$ **do**
4      $[\![v''_i]\!] \leftarrow$ Div2mPD($[\![v_i]\!] * [\![v'_i]\!], 2\ell + \lceil m/2^\theta \rceil - 1, \ell - 1$) ;   *// $1; 1(m)$*
5      $[\![p''_i]\!] \leftarrow ([\![p'_i]\!] + [\![p_i]\!])(1 - [\![z''_i]\!]) - [\![z''_i]\!]2^{g-1}$;   *// $0; 1(m)$*
6      $[\![s''_i]\!] \leftarrow (i \bmod 2 = 1)? [\![s_i]\!] : [\![s]\!] \oplus [\![s_i]\!]$;   *// $0; 0.5(m)$*
7 $([\![v''_0]\!], [\![p''_0]\!], [\![s''_0]\!]) \leftarrow ([\![v_0]\!], [\![p_0]\!], [\![s_0]\!]);$
8 $([\![v']\!], [\![p']\!], [\![s']\!], [\![z']\!]) \leftarrow$ SumFL($\{[\![v''_i]\!], [\![p''_i]\!], [\![s''_i]\!]\}_{i=0}^m, \ell + \lceil m/2^\theta \rceil, \ell, g$);
9 **return** $([\![v']\!], [\![p']\!], [\![s']\!], [\![z']\!]);$

The larger significands of the partially normalized terms $\{\hat{a}_i \hat{x}^i\}_{i=1}^m$ increase the complexity of SumFL. The radix-point alignment takes on input significands with up to $\ell + \lceil m/2^\theta \rceil$ bits (instead of ℓ bits) and needs a field able to encode integers of $2(\ell + \lceil m/2^\theta \rceil)$ bits. Also, the input of the final normalization is a significand with up to $\ell + \lceil m/2^\theta \rceil + \theta + 1$ bits[2] (instead of $\ell + \lceil \log m \rceil + 1$ bits).

Table 2 lists the complexity of two PolySFL configurations: PolySBFL, where $\theta = \lceil \log m \rceil$, so all powers are fully normalized, and PolySOFL, where $\theta = 0$, so all powers are partially normalized. PolySOFL eliminates $4 \log m$ rounds by partial normalization of the powers and $\log m$ rounds by computing in parallel the powers and the largest exponent in SumFL. For $\theta = 0$, the larger significands increase the complexity of SumFL and require a larger modulus. However, for small $\theta > 0$, PolySFL can efficiently compute most of the multiplications and also limit the growth of the significands and the modulus[3].

3.3   Optimized Protocols for Polynomials Defined by Roots

For the second case of polynomial evaluation, $\prod_{i=1}^{m}(\hat{x} + \hat{a}_i)$, we can improve PolyPGFL by replacing ProdGFL with Protocol 4, ProdFL1. This variant uses the same generic algorithm as ProdGFL, depicted in Fig. 1a, but multiplies with partial normalization and fully normalizes only the final result.

The algorithm executes $\theta = \lceil \log m \rceil$ iterations, with inputs and outputs stored in the vector $\{\hat{a}_j\}_{j=0}^{m-1} = \{v_j, p_j, s_j, z_j\}_{j=0}^{m-1}$. Iteration i starts with α inputs and computes in parallel $\beta = \lfloor \alpha/2 \rfloor$ multiplications with partial normalization (steps 4–7): $\bar{v}_j = \lfloor \bar{v}_{2j} \bar{v}_{2j+1}/2^{\ell-1} \rfloor$; $z_j = (\hat{a}_j = 0)?\ 1 : 0 = z_{2j} \vee z_{2j+1}$; $s_j = (\hat{a}_j < 0)?\ 1 : 0 = s_{2j} \oplus s_{2j+1}$; $\bar{p}_j = \bar{p}_{2j} + \bar{p}_{2j+1} + (\ell - 1)$. If the input vector of an iteration has an odd number of elements, the last element is moved to the output vector and processed in the next iteration (steps 8–9). Step 10 normalizes the final result using the protocol NormProdFL, described in [8].

Protocol 4: ProdFL1($\{[\![v_i]\!], [\![p_i]\!], [\![s_i]\!], [\![z_i]\!]\}_{i=0}^{m-1}, \ell, g$)

---

1 $\theta \leftarrow \lceil \log m \rceil$; $\alpha \leftarrow m$; $u \leftarrow 0$;
2 **foreach** $i \in [1, \theta]$ **do**
3 $\quad \beta \leftarrow \lfloor \alpha/2 \rfloor$; $u \leftarrow \alpha \bmod 2$;
4 $\quad$ **foreach** $j \in [0, \beta - 1]$ **do**
5 $\quad\quad [\![v_j]\!] \leftarrow \mathsf{Div2mPD}([\![v_{2j}]\!] * [\![v_{2j+1}]\!], 2(\ell + i), \ell - 1)$; $\qquad$ // 1;1
6 $\quad\quad [\![s_j]\!] \leftarrow [\![s_{2j}]\!] \oplus [\![s_{2j+1}]\!]$; $[\![z_j]\!] \leftarrow [\![z_{2j}]\!] \vee [\![z_{2j+1}]\!]$; $\qquad$ // 0;2
7 $\quad\quad [\![p_j]\!] \leftarrow [\![p_{2j}]\!] + [\![p_{2j+1}]\!] + (\ell - 1)$;
8 $\quad$ **if** $u = 1$ **then** $([\![v_\beta]\!], [\![p_\beta]\!], [\![s_\beta]\!], [\![z_\beta]\!]) \leftarrow ([\![v_{\alpha-1}]\!], [\![p_{\alpha-1}]\!], [\![s_{\alpha-1}]\!], [\![z_{\alpha-1}]\!])$;
9 $\quad \alpha \leftarrow \beta + u$;
10 $([\![v]\!], [\![p]\!]) \leftarrow \mathsf{NormProdFL}([\![v_0]\!], [\![p_0]\!], [\![z_0]\!], \ell, m - 1)$; $\qquad$ // 6;2ℓ + 4(m − 1)
11 **return** $([\![v]\!], [\![p]\!], [\![s_0]\!], [\![z_0]\!])$;

---

[2] This bound is determined as follows: Let $\{\bar{v}_i\}_{i=0}^{m}$ the significands of $\{\hat{a}_i \hat{x}^i\}_{i=0}^{m}$ after radix-point alignment, with up to $\ell + \lceil i/2^\theta \rceil$ bits, and $\sigma = \lceil m/2^\theta \rceil$. SumFL computes $\sum_{i=0}^{m} \bar{v}_i = \bar{v}_0 + \sum_{k=0}^{\sigma-2} \sum_{t=1}^{2^\theta} \bar{v}_{k2^\theta + t} + \sum_{t=1}^{m \bmod 2^\theta} \bar{v}_{(\sigma-1)2^\theta + t} < 2^\ell + 2^{\theta+\ell+1} \sum_{k=0}^{\sigma-2} 2^k + 2^{\ell+\sigma}(m \bmod 2^\theta) < 2^{\ell+\sigma+\theta+1}$. So the maximum bitlength is $\ell + \lceil m/2^\theta \rceil + \theta + 1$ bits.

[3] For example, if $m = 64$ and $\theta = 0$ the modulus grows by 128 bits. If $\theta = 3$, it grows by 16 bits, at the cost of fully normalizing 7 out of 127 multiplications.

NormProdFL normalizes a significand of $\ell_m \in [\ell, \ell + m - 1]$ bits and is relatively complex. Also, ProdFL1 needs a larger modulus q, able to encode integers of $2(\ell + m/2 - 1)$ bits (for the last multiplication, before division by $2^{\ell-1}$). We can limit the growth of the significands by computing the product as shown in Fig. 1b, where a node of the tree multiplies $t > 2$ inputs using ProdFL1.

Protocol 5, ProdFL2, is based on this idea. Let $\theta = \lceil \log_t m \rceil$. For $i \in [1, \theta - 1]$, the iterations compute in parallel products of t factors (steps 2–8) and iteration θ computes the product of all the remaining factors (step 9). Two iterations are usually sufficient: compute $\beta = \lfloor m/t \rfloor$ products of t factors and then a product of $t' = \beta + (m - \beta t)$ factors. Thus, NormProdFL normalizes signficands of up to $\ell' \in [\ell, \ell + \max(t, t') - 1]$ bits and the maximum bitlength is $2\ell + \max(t, t') - 2$.

Protocol 5: ProdFL2($\{[\![v_i]\!], [\![p_i]\!], [\![s_i]\!]\}_{i=0}^{m-1}, t, \ell, g$)

---

1   $\theta \leftarrow \lceil \log_t m \rceil$; $\alpha \leftarrow m$;

2   **foreach** $i \in [1, \theta - 1]$ **do**

3     $\beta \leftarrow \lfloor \alpha/t \rfloor$; $u \leftarrow 1 + \alpha \bmod t$;

4   **foreach** $j \in [0, \beta - 1]$ **do**

5       $([\![v_j]\!], [\![p_j]\!], [\![s_j]\!], [\![z_j]\!]) \leftarrow$ ProdFL1($\{[\![v_k]\!], [\![p_k]\!], [\![s_k]\!], [\![z_k]\!]\}_{k=tj}^{tj+t-1}, \ell, g$);

6   **foreach** $j \in [0, u - 1]$ **do**

7       $([\![v_{\beta+j}]\!], [\![p_{\beta+j}]\!], [\![s_{\beta+j}]\!], [\![z_{\beta+j}]\!]) \leftarrow ([\![v_{t\beta+j}]\!], [\![p_{t\beta+j}]\!], [\![s_{t\beta+j}]\!], [\![z_{t\beta+j}]\!])$;

8     $\alpha \leftarrow \beta + u$;

9   $([\![v]\!], [\![p]\!], [\![s]\!], [\![z]\!]) \leftarrow$ ProdFL1($\{[\![v_k]\!], [\![p_k]\!], [\![s_k]\!], [\![z_k]\!]\}_{k=0}^{\alpha-1}, \ell, g$);

10   **return** $([\![v]\!], [\![p]\!], [\![s]\!], [\![z]\!])$;

Given a target value for the maximum integer bitlength ℓ', the tradeoff parameter t should be chosen to minimize β, hence the number of expensive normalizations with NormProdFL. Table 2 lists the complexity of PolyPFL for $t = m$, called PolyPOFL. In this case, ProdFL2 is identical to ProdFL1. PolyPOFL needs fewer rounds than PolyPGFL, but the modulus is $m - 2$ bits longer. If $t < m$ then the modulus is only $\max(t, t') - 2$ bits longer, at the cost of more rounds and interactive primitives, due to $\beta = \lfloor m/t \rfloor$ additional executions of NormProdFL[4].

4 Performance Measurements

The protocols' running time was measured for secure computation with 3 parties and different floating-point precision, polynomial degrees, and communication settings. The protocols support arbitrary precision arithmetic, so the applications can select a tradeoff between precision and performance according to their requirements. We examined these tradeoffs by running tests for standard single precision, $\ell = 24$ and $g = 8$ bits, and double precision, $\ell = 53$ and $g = 11$ bits.

---

[4] For example, if $m = 64$ and $t = 64$ the modulus grows by 62 bits. If $t = 16$ it grows by 14 bits and $\beta = t' = 4$. However, if $t = 16$ then ProdFL2 needs 6 more rounds and $\beta(2\ell + 4(t - 1))$ more interactive primitives.

Table 3. Modulus bitlength for tests with PolyFL variants.

Significand length (ℓ)	24				53			
Polynomial degree (m)	8	16	32	64	8	16	32	64
PolySGFL (SG)	96	96	96	96	152	152	152	152
PolySBFL (SB)	96	96	96	96	152	152	152	152
PolySOFL1 (S1)	136	136	168	240	192	192	224	288
PolySOFL2 (S2)	120	120	120	120	176	176	176	176
PolyPOFL1 (P1)	112	112	128	160	168	168	192	224
PolyPOFL2 (P2)	112	112	112	112	168	168	168	168

The secure computation was carried out by 3 computers with 3.6 GHz CPU, running Linux 18.04, connected to an Ethernet switch (each party on its own computer). We analyzed the relations between running time, complexity metrics, and network bandwidth and delay, by testing the protocols in two network settings: LAN, with high bandwidth and low delay, and Internet, with moderate end-to-end bandwidth and delay. For LAN tests, the computers were connected to an Ethernet switch with 1 Gbps data rate (950 Mbps TCP data rate, 0.35 ms round-trip time). For Internet tests, they were connected to an Ethernet switch with 100 Mbps data rate and the Linux tool NetEm emulated a network path with 10 ms one-way delay (95 Mbps TCP data rate, 20.7 ms round-trip time).

The running time was measured for polynomials of degree $m \in \{8, 16, 32, 64\}$. Figure 3 and Fig. 4 show the online running time and the total time (including the precomputation) for PolySGFL (SG) and the following optimized protocols:

- PolySFL variants: PolySBFL (SB), $\theta = 0$, fully normalized powers; PolySOFL1 (S1), $\theta = \lceil \log m \rceil$, partially normalized powers; PolySOFL2 (S2), combination of fully and partially normalized powers, $\theta = (m \leq 16)? \lfloor \frac{\log m}{2} \rfloor - 1 : \lfloor \frac{\log m}{2} \rfloor$.
- PolyPFL variants: PolyPOFL1 (P1), $t = m$, product of m factors; PolyPOFL2 (P2), two iterations, products of up to t factors, $t = (m \geq 16)? 16 : 8$.

Table 3 lists the bitlength of the modulus for each setting, adjusted according to the maximum integer bitlength. Table 4 lists the complexity of the protocols' implementations for single and double precision and $m \in \{16, 32, 64\}$: the number of online rounds, with theoretical minimum between brackets; the number of bytes sent by party i to party $j \neq i$, online and during the precomputation[5].

The total running time includes online computation and precomputation time. The online complexity and running time offer more useful information about the performance of an application that uses these protocols. The precomputation needed by the entire application can be implemented as a single

---

[5] Differences between the measured values in Table 4 and those computed based on Table 2 are due to simplified complexity formulas, implementation tradeoffs between round optimization and modularity, and precomputation optimizations. Table 4 lists between brackets the minimum number of rounds computed using the exact formulas.

Table 4. Complexity of the PolyFL implementations used in the experiments.

Protocol	$\ell = 24$ $g = 8$			$\ell = 53$ $g = 11$		
	Online rounds	Online bytes	Precomp. bytes	Online rounds	Online bytes	Precomp. bytes
$m = 16$	$\theta = 1$	$t = 16$				
PolySGFL (SG)	125 (115)	47602	107792	125 (115)	140161	287336
PolySBFL (SB)	61 (58)	15446	46628	61 (58)	38321	108803
PolySOFL1 (S1)	45 (39)	16550	44368	45 (38)	30438	82674
PolySOFL2 (S2)	49 (43)	14420	40404	49 (47)	27164	77564
PolyPOFL1 (P1)	30 (28)	44268	85662	30 (10)	120370	213248
PolyPOFL2 (P2)	30 (28)	44268	85662	30 (10)	120370	213248
$m = 32$	$\theta = 2$	$t = 16$				
PolySGFL (SG)	150 (138)	95580	216762	150 (138)	281454	577960
PolySBFL (SB)	70 (67)	29040	89920	70 (67)	71398	209600
PolySOFL1 (S1)	50 (43)	37406	98476	50 (43)	62176	170640
PolySOFL2 (S2)	58 (51)	26250	76736	58 (51)	47898	145990
PolyPOFL1 (P1)	31 (29)	100476	185144	31 (29)	272672	464736
PolyPOFL2 (P2)	36 (34)	88982	172630	36 (34)	242004	430030
$m = 64$	$\theta = 3$	$t = 16$				
PolySGFL (SG)	175 (161)	191516	434734	175 (161)	564122	1159292
PolySBFL (SB)	79 (76)	56121	176367	79 (76)	137372	411024
PolySOFL1 (S1)	55 (47)	107754	261560	55 (47)	148480	394200
PolySOFL2 (S2)	67 (59)	49842	149687	67 (59)	93560	290332
PolyPOFL1 (P1)	32 (30)	250230	427893	32 (30)	633408	1035421
PolyPOFL2 (P2)	38 (36)	178062	345034	38 (36)	484204	858728

parallel computation that generates shared random values. Moreover, it can be independently optimized by improving its algorithms and implementation.

The secure computation framework offers alternative solutions for the building blocks, with different tradeoffs between complexity metrics. The protocols discussed here use solutions with smaller, constant, number of rounds and more precomputation, to offer better balanced performance over a broader range of communication environments and applications. The relative contribution of the precomputation to the total running time is smaller in the Internet than in LANs, since the number of rounds has stronger effects than local processing. However, parallel computation of (very) large batches may be faster with building blocks optimized for less local processing and exchanged data, at the cost of larger, logarithmic, number of rounds [16]. Assessing the combined effects of tradeoffs between complexity metrics (focused on interaction), field size, and local processing requires experiments matching potential deployment scenarios.

The results show that PolySFL is much faster than PolySGFL for all tested configurations (PolySBFL, PolySOFL1, and PolySOFL2) and all test settings. The performance gain grows with m and ℓ, so it also scales up better. PolySBFL achieves a large improvement relative to PolySGFL, by computing more efficiently the dot product between powers and coefficients, using SumFL instead of SumGFL and partially normalized multiplications. This agrees with the predictions of the

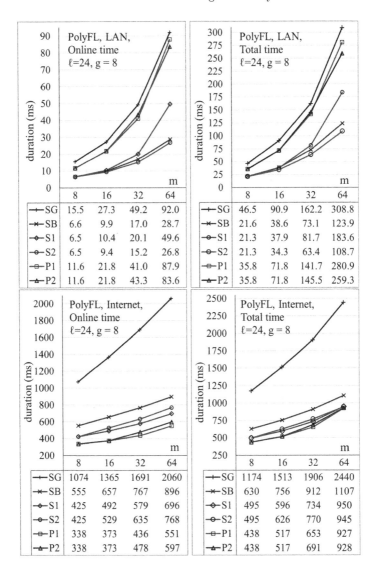

Fig. 3. Single precision, online and total running-time in LAN and Internet.

complexity analysis. The complexity of PolySGFL is strongly dominated by two-operand additions, so replacing them with optimized multi-operand addition substantially reduces the number of rounds and interactive primitives and the amount of exchanged data and local processing (Tables 2, 4).

PolySOFL1 tries to improve PolySBFL by computing the powers with partial normalization. However, this increases the complexity of SumFL and requires a larger modulus. In LANs, local processing has an important contribution to the running time, so PolySOFL1 becomes slower than PolySBFL when the difference

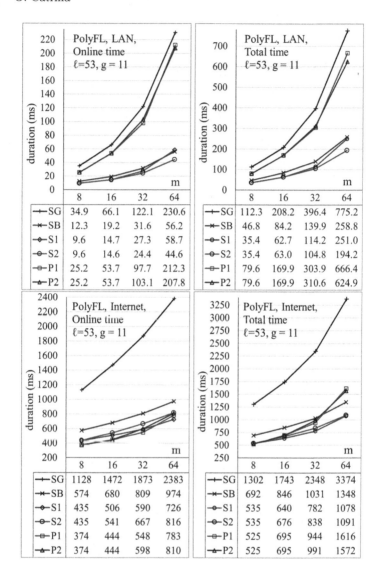

Fig. 4. Double precision, online and total running-time in LAN and Internet.

between modulus sizes grows (large m and small ℓ). For Internet communications, the running time is dominated by the network delay, so PolySOFL1 is faster than PolySBFL in all settings, due to the smaller number of rounds.

PolySOFL2 limits the growth of the integers and the modulus (Table 3) at the cost of additional rounds (Table 4). PolySOFL2 is faster than PolySBFL for all settings. In LANs, it is also faster than PolySOFL1, because the low delay attenuates the effects of the additional rounds. It is somewhat slower in the

Internet, due to the longer transfer delay, but this performance difference could be compensated by the cost of integrating PolySOFL1 in applications.

The running time of PolySFL protocols is dominated by the evaluation of the sum. The techniques that optimize the evaluation of powers and products, although effective for their own tasks, provide a relatively modest improvement. On the other hand, PowAllFL and ProdFL are useful for other applications.

The protocol families PolySFL and PolyPFL can be considered solutions to different problems: evaluating $\sum_{i=0}^{m} \hat{a}_i \hat{x}^i$ and $\prod_{i=1}^{m} (\hat{x} - \hat{a}_i)$, respectively. However, when the application can choose between the two polynomial representations, they become alternative (and hence competing) solutions to the same problem.

PolyPFL protocols have lower round complexity due to parallel computation of the m secure floating-point additions. However, they cannot take advantage of optimized multi-operand addition, like the PolySFL protocols, so they need a larger amount of exchanged data and local processing (Table 4). In LANs, their running time is strongly dominated by additions and the low delay attenuates the benefits of the smaller number of rounds. Thus, they are slightly faster than PolySGFL and much slower than the PolySFL protocols. The opposite occurs for Internet communications, where the transfer delay is much longer: the PolyPFL protocols offer the best performance, due to the smaller number of rounds. However, their advantage diminishes for larger ℓ and m.

The tradeoff parameter of PolyPOFL2 was set to $t = 16$. For $m \in \{8, 16\}$ the two variants of PolyPFL are actually identical. For $m \in \{32, 64\}$, PolyPOFL2 avoids further growth of the modulus (Table 3) and reduces the amount of exchanged data (Table 4). Its running time is similar to PolyPOFL1, despite the larger number of rounds. Therefore, PolyPOFL2 achieves its main goal, limiting the size of the module for large m, without performance degradation.

The precision of the floating-point numbers affects the performance in two ways: higher precision requires a larger modulus as well as more interactive primitives (Table 2). This increases both local processing and the amount of exchanged data (Table 4). The performance difference between single and double precision is more important for LAN communications, mainly due to the effects of local processing. The difference is reduced for Internet communications, because the number of rounds has stronger effects on the running time and, for these protocols, the number of rounds does not depend on precision.

5   Conclusions

The paper presents two families of secure computation protocols that evaluate polynomials with secret floating-point inputs and output: the PolySFL protocols evaluate $\sum_{i=0}^{m} \hat{a}_i \hat{x}^i$, while the PolyPFL protocols evaluate $\prod_{i=1}^{m} (\hat{x} - \hat{a}_i)$. A first goal was to show how these protocols are constructed, by integrating and adapting protocols for two-operand and multi-operand floating-point addition and multiplication introduced in previous work [8,9,11]. However, the main goal was to provide a comprehensive joint analysis of their complexity and performance, that includes the relations between running time, complexity metrics, network bandwidth and delay, floating-point precision, and polynomial degree.

Traditional polynomial evaluation algorithms are not suitable for secure computation because they are optimized according to different, incompatible assumptions. A more promising approach takes advantage of efficient multi-operand floating-point addition and multiplication protocols [8,11]. The polynomial evaluation protocols discussed in this paper improve the initial proposals [8,10] by using faster secure arithmetic and enabling tradeoffs that can improve the performance for different execution environments and application requirements.

The comparative complexity and performance analysis shows that these protocols are substantially faster than variants that rely on two-operand arithmetic and generic constructions for sums, powers, and products. The running time is strongly dominated by secure floating-point addition, so the main performance gain is obtained by optimizing the evaluation of sums and dot products. The techniques for optimizing powers and products, although effective for their own tasks, offer relatively modest improvements for polynomial evaluation. Overall, PolySFL protocols offer better performance for the majority of the test settings, while PolyPFL protocols are faster for Internet communications.

The performance measurements agree, essentially, with the predictions of the complexity analysis based on abstract metrics focused on interaction. However, the running time is strongly affected by the execution environment (network performance and parallel processing), so we need experiments to better understand the effects of local computation and tradeoffs between complexity metrics. Complexity and performance agree better for Internet communications, but the effects of interactions are attenuated in LANs, so local processing and implementation optimizations have a more important contribution to the running time.

Arbitrary precision secure arithmetic allows the applications to select the tradeoff between accuracy and performance that best matches their requirements. Moreover, it enables optimizations that require flexibility for the significands' length. The optimized polynomial evaluation protocols rely on the ability to compute sums, powers, and products with significands of different bitlengths.

Future work will consider applications of these protocols (e.g., secure evaluation of mathematical functions by polynomial approximation) and alternative building blocks, with lower communication, local processing, and precomputation. Another interesting issue is to examine to what extent the building blocks used by these protocols can be efficiently adapted to other secure computation frameworks, e.g., to take advantage of stronger security models supported by [3].

Acknowledgements. Part of this work was supported by POC72/1/2, nr.127454, "SECREDAS Support Project", contract 7/1.1.3H/6.01.2020, associated to the EUs Horizon 2020 ECSEL Joint Undertaking research project SECREDAS.

References

1. Aliasgari, M., Blanton, M., Zhang, Y., Steele, A.: Secure computation on floating point numbers. In: 20th Annual Network and Distributed System Security Symposium (NDSS 2013) (2013)

2. Aliasgari, M., Blanton, M., Bayatbabolghani, F.: Secure computation of hidden Markov models and secure floating-point arithmetic in the malicious model. Int. J. Inf. Secur. **16**(6), 577–601 (2017). https://doi.org/10.1007/s10207-016-0350-0

3. Aly, A., et al.: SCALE and MAMBA documentation. https://homes.esat.kuleuven. be/~nsmart/SCALE/. Accessed Apr 2020

4. Aly, A., Smart, N.P.: Benchmarking privacy preserving scientific operations. In: Deng, R.H., Gauthier-Umaña, V., Ochoa, M., Yung, M. (eds.) ACNS 2019. LNCS, vol. 11464, pp. 509–529. Springer, Cham (2019). https://doi.org/10.1007/978-3-030-21568-2_25

5. Bogdanov, D., Kamm, L., Laur, S., Sokk, V.: Rmind: a tool for cryptographically secure statistical analysis. IEEE Trans. Dependable Secure Comput. **15**(03), 481–495 (2018)

6. Bogdanov, D., Niitsoo, M., Toft, T., Willemson, J.: High-performance secure multiparty computation for data mining applications. Int. J. Inf. Secur. **11**(6), 403–418 (2012). https://doi.org/10.1007/s10207-012-0177-2

7. Catrina, O.: Round-efficient protocols for secure multiparty fixed-point arithmetic. In: 12th International Conference on Communications (COMM 2018), pp. 431–436. IEEE (2018)

8. Catrina, O.: Optimization and tradeoffs in secure floating-point computation: products, powers, and polynomials. In: 6th Conference on the Engineering of Computer Based Systems (ECBS 2019), pp. 7:1–7:10. ACM (2019)

9. Catrina, O.: Evaluation of floating-point arithmetic protocols based on Shamir secret sharing. In: Obaidat, M.S. (ed.) ICETE 2019. CCIS, vol. 1247, pp. 108–131. Springer, Cham (2020). https://doi.org/10.1007/978-3-030-52686-3_5

10. Catrina, O.: Optimizing secure floating-point arithmetic: sums, dot products, and polynomials. Proc. Rom. Acad. (Ser. A) **21**(1), 21–28 (2020)

11. Catrina, O.: Performance analysis of secure floating-point sums and dot products. In: 13th International Conference on Communications (COMM 2020), pp. 465–470. IEEE (2020)

12. Cramer, R., Damgård, I., Ishai, Y.: Share conversion, pseudorandom secret-sharing and applications to secure computation. In: Kilian, J. (ed.) TCC 2005. LNCS, vol. 3378, pp. 342–362. Springer, Heidelberg (2005). https://doi.org/10.1007/978-3-540-30576-7_19

13. Cramer, R., Damgård, I., Nielsen, J.B.: Secure Multiparty Computation and Secret Sharing. Cambridge University Press, Cambridge (2015)

14. Damgård, I., Thorbek, R.: Non-interactive proofs for integer multiplication. In: Naor, M. (ed.) EUROCRYPT 2007. LNCS, vol. 4515, pp. 412–429. Springer, Heidelberg (2007). https://doi.org/10.1007/978-3-540-72540-4_24

15. Kamm, L., Willemson, J.: Secure floating point arithmetic and private satellite collision analysis. Int. J. Inf. Secur. **14**(6), 531–548 (2015). https://doi.org/10.1007/s10207-014-0271-8

16. Kerik, L., Laud, P., Randmets, J.: Optimizing MPC for robust and scalable integer and floating-point arithmetic. In: Clark, J., Meiklejohn, S., Ryan, P.Y.A., Wallach, D., Brenner, M., Rohloff, K. (eds.) FC 2016. LNCS, vol. 9604, pp. 271–287. Springer, Heidelberg (2016). https://doi.org/10.1007/978-3-662-53357-4_18

17. Knuth, D.E.: The Art of Computer Programming, volume 2: Seminumerical Algorithms, 3rd edn. Addison-Wesley, Boston (1997)

SERVAS! Secure Enclaves via RISC-V Authenticryption Shield

Stefan Steinegger[1]([envelope]), David Schrammel[1], Samuel Weiser[1], Pascal Nasahl[1], and Stefan Mangard[1,2]

[1] Graz University of Technology, Graz, Austria
{stefan.steinegger,david.schrammel,samuel.weiser,
pascal.nasahl,stefan.mangard}@iaik.tugraz.at
[2] Lamarr Security Research, Graz, Austria

Abstract. Isolation is a long-standing security challenge. Privilege rings and virtual memory are increasingly augmented with capabilities, protection keys, and powerful enclaves. Moreover, we are facing an increased need for physical protection, e.g., via transparent memory encryption, resulting in a complex interplay of various security mechanisms. In this work, we tackle the isolation challenge with a new extensible isolation primitive called authenticryption shield that unifies various isolation policies. By using authenticated memory encryption, we streamline the security reasoning towards cryptographic guarantees. We showcase the versatility of our approach by designing and prototyping SERVAS – a novel enclave architecture for RISC-V. SERVAS facilitates a new efficient and secure enclave memory sharing mechanism. While the memory encryption constitutes the main overhead, invoking SERVAS enclave requires only 3.5x of a simple syscall instead of 71x for Intel SGX.

1 Introduction

Today, software vulnerabilities are omnipresent and penetrate the whole software stack, e.g., application software [52] and operating systems [12,27]. To reduce their impact, different isolation mechanisms can separate privileges [19], isolate individual processes [35], protect virtual machines [5,6], and segregate applications into smaller parts, also denoted as in-process isolation. Typical in-process isolation mechanisms are segmentation [31] and capabilities [61], memory coloring (e.g., protection keys) [30,49,55], or enclaves. Enclaves give strong security guarantees even in the event of a system compromise and found ample resonance both in academia [11,15,18,39,53,57] and industry [9,24,43]. In addition, cloud computing increasingly demands physical protection, for which modern CPUs provide transparent memory encryption [6,43]. Having proper integrity protection can cause worst-case throughput penalties of over 400% for Intel SGX [28].

Unfortunately, due to the zoo of isolation mechanisms, reasoning about their security becomes increasingly complex. For example, an application might depend on protection keys in combination with the Memory Management Unit

© Springer Nature Switzerland AG 2021
E. Bertino et al. (Eds.): ESORICS 2021, LNCS 12973, pp. 370–391, 2021.
https://doi.org/10.1007/978-3-030-88428-4_19

(MMU) and the memory mappings configured by the operating system [35]. Unifying these isolation mechanisms is desirable from a security standpoint, but most cover only a subset of scenarios. For example, Intel SGX isolates unprivileged user code, but its memory encryption is not utilizable for other purposes.

In this work, we first simplify the overall security reasoning by introducing a strong and generic isolation primitive. Second, we explore our primitive's synergies and features. Third, we use it to design a novel enclave architecture.

New Isolation Primitive. We unify various isolation policies with our novel RISC-V Authenticryption Shield (RVAS). By using memory encryption, we map isolation properties to the well-studied field of cryptography. More specifically, encryption ensures that the CPU and the memory are in a particular state. *Thus, RVAS achieves memory isolation with cryptographic guarantees.*

We design RVAS atop the RISC-V architecture. RVAS builds upon authenticated memory encryption whose associated data input, which we call encryption tweak, is exposed to software. This encryption tweak represents a security context composed of software-defined and CPU-internal components. It serves to achieve domain separation and can enforce a variety of different isolation mechanisms simultaneously, e.g., privilege separation, virtual memory protection, segmentation, and page coloring, etc. Traditionally, each of these mechanisms needs to securely store trusted metadata (e.g., the address mapping or the page colors). *RVAS implicitly secures this metadata by feeding it into the encryption tweak.* A proper generalization of encryption tweaks is non-trivial.

SERVAS Enclaves are our novel enclave system atop RVAS. SERVAS protects enclaves against software and physical attacks by means of RVAS encryption. In contrast, Intel SGX uses memory encryption only against *physical* attacks, while *software* attacks are prevented through a trusted metadata storage – the so-called EPCM [31]. Our design makes the EPCM obsolete, which yields two advantages: First, we remove trust from the address translation, *i.e.*, the MMU and the Translation Lookaside Buffer (TLB) configuration, and our security argument boils down to encryption tweaks. Second, SGX enclaves can typically only use 128 MB of encrypted physical memory [26]. RVAS encryption can be applied to the whole DRAM and also to non-enclave code.

SERVAS introduces the novel concept of secure sharing of enclave memory, a key requirement for many application scenarios but impractical with current enclave systems (e.g., requiring costly software-based encryption). SERVAS enables secure zero-cost memory sharing by sharing encryption tweaks.

We prototype RVAS on an FPGA using an open-source encryption core. A small stateless Security Monitor (SM) running in RISC-V machine mode ensures a proper tweak configuration. Invoking SERVAS enclaves only takes 3.5x the time of a syscall. Our evaluation indicates an overhead of 16.7% to 24.5% over the used encryption core. An extended version of this paper is available [51], and we plan to open-source our prototype[1]. In summary, our contributions are:

---
[1] https://github.com/IAIK/servas.

- A generic isolation primitive using authenticated memory encryption.
- A novel enclave architecture called SERVAS.
- A novel and fast and secure memory sharing mechanism between enclaves.
- An evaluation of the prototype implementation of SERVAS.

2 Challenges of Memory Isolation

Here, we give an overview of the most widely used isolation schemes and present their challenges concerning security and functional limitations we want to overcome. This paves the way for understanding the RVAS and SERVAS design.

Process Isolation requires privilege separation between the operating system (OS) and processes and isolating processes from each other. Privilege separation is achieved via privilege rings protecting CPU resources from unprivileged access. The OS also needs to configure the virtual memory subsystem:
Challenge C_1: "The privileged software must ensure that the virtual memory mappings of all unprivileged processes (i) cannot access privileged memory, and (ii) are not unintentionally aliasing with each other."

Segmentation is a fine-grained in-process isolation mechanism using address ranges. Segmentation forms the basis of hardware capabilities [61]. However, these systems are not suitable for enforcing cross-application policies, e.g., protecting cryptographic keys from other applications or the OS.
Challenge C_2: "Segmentation should allow flexible cross-application policies."

Memory Coloring is another in-process isolation mechanism labeling each memory block with a "color". If the color is loaded, the memory becomes accessible. Unfortunately, the number of colors is often quite limited [47] and not suitable to enforce cross application policies, e.g., for shared memory.
Challenge C_3: "Memory coloring should provide significantly more colors and also allow cross-application policies."

Memory Mapping Protection is needed to protect enclaves from the OS:
Challenge C_4: "The memory mapping of enclaves must be protected against privileged software." This is challenging because privileged software is in charge of managing enclaves. E.g., manipulating the page tables could cause data pages to become executable. Three security invariants need to hold here:

- **Attribute Invariant $\mathcal{IA}$**: *"Enclave pages must only be mapped with their intended page table attributes."*
- **Spatial Invariant $\mathcal{IS}$**: *"A physical enclave page must only be mapped to its corresponding virtual page."*
- **Temporal Invariant $\mathcal{IT}$**: *"At any time for every virtual enclave page, there must be at most one valid physical page mapping."*

$\mathcal{IT}$ specifically addresses double mapping attacks, where the attacker could silently replace the page to replay old data.

Protected Sharing is typically achieved via shared memory. However, the hard isolation boundary of enclaves prohibits secure, shared memory by design: *Challenge $\mathcal{C}_5$: "Shared memory must allow for efficient and confidential interaction between different enclaves."*

Memory Encryption. The DRAM can be attacked via passive [8,29] and active [36] physical attacks. Encrypted and authenticated DRAM is necessary to protect data from physical attacks. Memory encryption should not be restricted to specific code (e.g., enclaves) or specific parts of the DRAM. *Challenge $\mathcal{C}_6$: "The DRAM shall be hardened against active and passive physical attacks."*

3   RISC-V Authenticryption Shield (RVAS)

RVAS presents a generic mechanism to cryptographically enforce the challenges expressed in Sect. 2. At its core, it uses an authenticated Memory Encryption Engine (MEE) for encrypting the DRAM and incorporates a security context into its associated data. If encrypted data is accessed with the wrong security context, the MEE triggers an authentication error. Since the MEE gives cryptographic security guarantees for detecting authentication issues, the security argumentation boils down to one question: *Who controls the security context?*

The composition of the security context arguably lies at the heart of RVAS. For readability, we also call it "tweak" in the rest of the paper. The tweak consists of both software- and CPU-defined components, allowing for fine-grained, unforgeable isolation. In this section, we discuss the tweak composition, how RVAS solves the challenges from Sect. 2, and the requirements for the MEE.

3.1   RVAS Tweak Design

Our tweak design comprises five components explained in the following, each of which can be selectively enabled, depending on the specific use case.

Integrity Counter. The MEE maintains integrity counters for each memory block, which it increments at each write operation. Integrating the counter into the tweak ensures that the correct memory block is used at any time and thus, prevents reverting the memory to a previous state (*i.e.*, replay attacks).

Segmentation and Address Information holds metadata about the accessed address and whether it matches software-defined segments that can be configured at each privilege level. This allows to protect the page mapping, in particular the address translation, and page ordering and prevents double mappings. The address information can hold an absolute address or an offset relative to one of the segments. Each segment has a base address and a size and belongs to a privilege level. Depending on which segment(s) the address belongs to, the segment bitmap, which is also included in the tweak, is set. This further acts as a domain separation and influences which memory color is used.

Privilege Level. Including the CPU privilege level (e.g., M-mode, S-mode, U-mode) in the tweak ensures that memory is only accessible at a specific level.

Page Table Attributes such as read, write and execute permissions are included in the tweak to prevent undetected altering of the page mapping.

Memory Color. This field is extremely versatile and can be configured by software on each privilege level. By choosing appropriate colors, one can segregate memory pages at runtime and facilitate sharing across security domains.

3.2   Solving the Challenges

Process Isolation with RVAS could significantly enhance the security of processes, e.g., inside encrypted virtual machines [6]. Two components solve Challenge $\mathcal{C}_1$: First, we use the CPU privilege level in the tweak to achieve privilege separation, *i.e.*, *without the need for inspecting page tables*. Second, we use an OS-chosen process identifier in the tweak's memory color field to separate processes. By using RISC-V's Supervisor User Memory (SUM) bit to temporarily force the privilege level to U-mode in the tweak, the OS can be granted temporary access to user memory (e.g., for syscall handling). Of course for an enclave system one would disable this feature.

In-process Isolation. To solve the segmentation challenge $\mathcal{C}_2$ for cross-privilege policies, we can supply information from all privilege levels to the tweak's *Segment and Address Information* field. A segment-relative address offset in the tweak makes these policies compatible between different applications (*i.e.*, different address spaces), as we will show for cross-enclave shared memory.

To solve the memory coloring challenge $\mathcal{C}_3$, we support a vast number of 2^{80} colors (cf. 16 for Intel MPK [55]). Thus, RVAS makes trusted metadata storages for memory colors (*i.e.*, tagged memory) obsolete [64]. We will show how RVAS achieves brute-force resistance when using colors as a shared secret.

Enclaves are the most complex isolation technique discussed in this paper and involve the challenges $\mathcal{C}_2$ – $\mathcal{C}_6$. Current enclave systems like Intel SGX [43] use trusted metadata stores, *i.e.*, the Enclave Page Cache Map (EPCM), to ensure the attribute- $\mathcal{IA}$, the spatial- $\mathcal{IS}$, and the temporal invariant $\mathcal{IT}$. However, the EPCM has a few drawbacks: (1) It increases the Trusted Computing Base (TCB). (2) It takes up memory. (3) The enclave's TLB entries must be flushed during context switches [17,31]. (4) It permits only a single owner enclave for each page, precluding flexible enclave memory sharing.

We leverage RVAS to solve challenge $\mathcal{C}_4$ and make the EPCM obsolete: First, we guarantee $\mathcal{IA}$ by feeding the *page table attributes* into the tweak. Second, we enforce $\mathcal{IS}$ and $\mathcal{IT}$ by using the *segmentation and address information* and the *memory color* field in the tweak. Thus, that pages can only be mapped correctly to their legitimate enclave. More details are given in Sect. 4.3.

To solve the protected sharing challenge $\mathcal{C}_5$, we combine the memory color field ($\mathcal{C}_3$) with an enclave-defined segment ($\mathcal{C}_2$) for specifying the shared memory.

The memory color essentially comprises a shared secret established between two or more enclaves that want to communicate. The relative addressing of segments allows the enclave to choose the exact location of the shared memory. Only if the memory color and the segment is set up correctly, the enclaves will have the same encryption tweak and, thus, can access the shared memory.

Memory Encryption protects against active and passive physical attacks, thus solving challenge $\mathcal{C}_6$. For RVAS, an MEE needs to fulfill three properties: (1) confidentiality, authenticity, and integrity of the data, (2) replay protection, (3) the used cryptographic primitive must be tweakable. Integrity is typically ensured by storing authentication codes in a tree structure. The replay protection from (2) is usually done via authenticated counters that are typically fed into the encryption scheme as a tweak or nonce [17,23,54,59,60]. To fulfill (3), we require a tweakable block cipher or authenticated encryption scheme with a sufficiently large tweak size (*i.e.*, associated data), such as [21,62]. E.g., SGX's underlying MEE would require changes to fulfill the third property.

4   SERVAS

SERVAS is an innovative enclave architecture and, thus, the most complex RVAS use case we present. As shown in Fig. 1, SERVAS consists of the RISC-V Authenticryption Shield (RVAS) and a software Security Monitor (SM). The SM is the trusted intermediary that handles the enclave's lifecycle, acting as a universal entry and exit point and manages the RVAS encryption tweak via an Instruction Set Architecture (ISA) extension.

SERVAS follows SGX's design choices to keep a minimal TCB while simultaneously avoiding the drawbacks of large trusted metadata storages (*i.e.*, the EPCM). Instead, we feed the relevant security metadata into the RVAS tweak. By carefully controlling the tweak, SERVAS maintains cryptographic segregation of various security domains. SERVAS also enables dynamic enclave memory and secure sharing of enclave memory, avoiding costly software-based encryption [7].

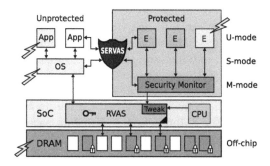

Fig. 1. SERVAS protects enclaves (*E*) from applications (*App*), the OS, and physical attacks. Thunderbolts mark the attack surface. RVAS encrypts and authenticates pages in the untrusted DRAM.

4.1 Threat Model

SERVAS protects code and data inside enclaves against a powerful, privileged software and physical attacker (cf. Intel SGX [17,43]). Non-enclave software (*i.e.*, the OS or user applications) is viewed as untrusted and can be attacker controlled. The OS can launch rogue enclaves. Our Trusted Computing Base (TCB) comprises software and hardware components: On the software side, we trust the enclaves and a small Security Monitor (SM). The enclave developer is responsible for avoiding vulnerabilities in the enclave code [13,40]. The SM is an integral part of our CPU hardware, similar to Intel SGX's microcode implementation [17]. It can be protected via a trusted on-chip ROM or a secure boot mechanism [38].

On the hardware side, anything outside the System on Chip (SoC) (e.g., the CPU and RVAS) is untrusted. In particular, the attacker can tamper with the DRAM, mount bus probing, cold-boot [29], or fault attacks on the encrypted DRAM [33], which are detected by RVAS' authenticated encryption.

Denial-of-service attacks are outside of our threat model. It is up to the OS and the applications to invoke an enclave. Whether performed in software or hardware, side-channel attacks are an orthogonal challenge, for which plenty of literature is available that could also be applied to SERVAS [15,16,20,54,58].

4.2 Enclave Life Cycle

SERVAS enclaves are built on top of RVAS and our Security Monitor (SM). The SMprovides an API for managing all phases of an enclave's life cycle, namely, initialization, entering, interruption, exiting, attestation and sealing.

Enclaves are identified via their so-called Enclave Identifier (EncID), which is computed via a cryptographic authentication code over the enclave binary (cf. SGX's MRENCLAVE [17]). Enclave binaries are encrypted with ASCON and a per CPU key. Similarly to SecureBlue++ [14] this implicitly attestates the enclave and allows for embedding secrets without the need for remote attestation and provisioning. During loading, the SMcompares the cryptographic authentication code. If the enclave binary was corrupted, the SMwill yield a different EncID and the SMwill refuse to execute the enclave.

User-mode applications can load and run enclaves within their own virtual address space, for which the SMassigns a unique Runtime Identifier (RTID) to each running enclave. For entering an enclave, the SMconfigures its tweak and transfers control to its single developer-specified entry point. An interrupt causes the SMto save the enclave's register state on private enclave memory and wipe the registers. Resuming from interruption and exiting an enclave is analogous. To store enclave secrets, the SMprovides a sealing functionality based on a key-derivation function involving the EncID and a per-CPU key. For more details about the enclave life cycle, we refer to our extended paper version [51].

4.3   Enclave Memory Management

Security of the enclave memory hinges on the *spatial* ($\mathcal{IS}$), *temporal* ($\mathcal{IT}$), and *attribute invariant* ($\mathcal{IA}$), as specified in Sect. 2, which need to hold over the whole enclave's lifecycle. To achieve these invariants, our trusted SMexclusively controls parts of the RVAS tweak. In particular, the initialization of enclave memory can only be done by the SM, for which it can override most parts of the RVAS tweak as if the enclave itself initialized the memory. Similarly, the SMcan invalidate an enclave page by writing it under a different tweak.

In the following, we show how to secure static and dynamic enclave page mappings and achieve shared memory and swapping.

Static Page Mapping and Code Sharing. Our three invariants protect static enclave pages, *i.e.*, code and data sections, from OS compromise. $\mathcal{IA}$ is ensured by adding page attributes to the tweak. To keep $\mathcal{IS}$, we link between virtual and physical enclave pages, as follows: An SM-controlled address segment distinguishes enclave memory from the rest. Any enclave memory access includes the segment-relative virtual address offset in the tweak. This field guarantees a correct address translation and also accounts for position-independent enclaves.

To ensure $\mathcal{IT}$ for private enclave memory, we put the enclave's unique Runtime Identifier (RTID) into the tweak's memory color field. This field binds each enclave page to exactly one enclave instance. Developers can optionally deduplicate enclave code to help reduce memory load and TLB pressure. In this case, we use the Enclave Identifier (EncID) instead of the Runtime Identifier (RTID) inside the tweak. To enforce $\mathcal{IT}$, these code pages need to be read-only and shared between enclave instances of the same binary only (*i.e.*, the same EncID).

Dynamic Page Mapping. SERVAS enclaves may use dynamic memory, which has been allocated by the host user-mode application. In principle, our security invariants are upheld in the same way as for static page mappings. However, the invariant $\mathcal{IT}$ requires special care to prevent double mapping attacks since dynamic mappings change during runtime: The enclave (runtime) keeps track of all of its valid page mappings *inside* the enclave's address range, e.g., in a private bitmap similar to SGX [42]. Thus, when the enclave receives new memory from the host, it can verify the mapping. Therefore, the enclave effectively acknowledges each dynamic memory page before it is initialized by the SMto be used. If an enclave releases dynamic memory, it explicitly invokes the SM, which invalidates the page content, e.g., by destroying its integrity. This prevents use-after-free scenarios and upholds $\mathcal{IT}$.

Data Sharing. SERVAS introduces a novel concept of data sharing between enclaves. Shared data memory is writable and can be used for data exchange at native speed (*i.e.*, without copying or re-encryption [7]). This memory is realized via a shared secret, supplied as memory color, that enclaves can directly manage. However, the SMcan assist in establishing the secret between enclaves, e.g., as a trusted entity attesting the enclaves. Upholding our security invariants for data sharing is critical and highlights the versatility of our RVAS design. Enclaves can enforce the invariants by simply configuring the shared memory and keeping the shared secret confidential. Data sharing also seamlessly scales to multiple enclaves. A user-mode segment register points to the desired shared virtual memory range to prevent double mapping attacks (e.g., aliasing shared-with private pages) and upholding $\mathcal{IT}$.

Swapping. In contrast to Intel SGX, SERVAS allows using the full DRAM for enclaves, nevertheless, out-of-memory situations can occur. To ensure the SM's correct operation and maintain our security invariants, we exclude enclave shared memory and SM-related pages from being swapped. In order to swap an enclave page, the OS provides a temporary page to the SM. The SMre-encrypts the page-to-swap to the temporary page. Next, the SMinvalidates the original physical enclave page in order to uphold $\mathcal{IT}$. The involved metadata (authentication tag, nonce, virtual address, range information, page permissions) are saved on a page only accessible to the SM. This metadata pins the page's version and prevents any roll-back attacks. Swap-in of enclave pages is analogous.

5   SERVAS Implementation Details

In this section, we detail our SERVAS implementation, shown in Fig. 2a. We discuss our instruction set changes with the tweak construction and page types and caching considerations and an encryption bypass option.

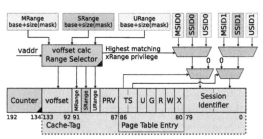

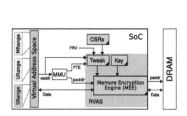

(a)   **Blocks   with   black corners show components that are part of RVAS.**

(b) **SERVAS tweak composition, including replay-protection counters, tweak select (TS), privilege mode (PRV), etc.**

Fig. 2. Overview of RVAS and the tweak construction for the MEE.

5.1 Instruction Set Extension

RVAS adds minimal changes to the RISC-V Instruction Set Architecture (ISA): We add Control and Status Registers (CSRs) to set RVAS' tweak in software. Moreover, we add an authentication exception that is raised whenever decryption fails with an integrity check error during a read, write, or fetch operation.

We add the segmentation registers MRange, SRange, and URange for the machine-, supervisor-, and user-mode, respectively, as seen in Fig. 2b. Each segment is defined by a base and a size in the virtual address space. The SM uses MRange to declare an enclave's memory. SRange and URange can be used for different purposes (e.g., shared memory). To include software-controllable Session Identifiers (SIDs) for page coloring, we add xSID0 and xSID1 CSRs.

Tweak Override. We provide additional tweak override registers that allow the SM to cryptographically initialize a page without trusting the OS-supplied page mapping. These registers can override any tweak parameters used by RVAS, except for the RVAS-managed integrity counters. Thus, any memory accesses by lesser-privileged modes must adhere to the same tweak used for initialization.

5.2 Tweak

RVAS incorporates CPU state information into the MEE via the tweak, including integrity counters, page mapping, and privilege information, range checks, and SIDs (cf. Fig. 2b). SERVAS uses a tweak size of 192 bits, as follows:

Counter. Similar to SGX's 56-bit counters, we reserve 58 tweak bits for *integrity counters* to protect against replay attacks, which are not exposed to software.

xRange. We use a bitmap with three bits to encode whether the accessed address is within URange, SRange, or MRange, respectively. If an address matches xRange segments, their tweak bits are set. The bits act as a domain separation and influence the SID and voffset selection. The most unprivileged matching xRange (e.g., URange) then determines the voffset calculation and the choice of the xSID registers.

voffset is the virtual address offset computed from the trusted base address of the effective matching xRange register at cache line granularity. Intel SGX protects the page mapping by linking the virtual- and physical address in the EPCM. For SERVAS enclaves, the page mapping is protected with the voffset, which is relative to the base of a segment. Additionally, the segment is uniquely identified with a SID. Combined, this ensures that the virtual mapping is correct, *i.e.*, as initialized by the SM. For 48-bit virtual addresses [56] and 64 B cache lines [17], this results in 42 bit.

PRV encodes the current privilege level of the CPU in two bits and ensures the memory can only be accessed at a specific level.

Page Table Entry (PTE). We include seven page table attribute bits from the page table entry (PTE) in the tweak to ensure they represent their initialized configuration. These attributes cover the user mode (U), global mapping (G), read, write and execute privileges (RWX), and software-defined reserved tweak select (TS) for selecting the effective SID register.

Session Identifier (SID). We allocate 80 bit for SIDs useable for defining memory colors and ensure a certain execution context. The active xRange determines whether MSID, SSID, or USID is used. TS determines whether one or both xSID0 and xSID1 registers are used. When using, both the effective SID is truncated to 80 bit.

5.3   Page Types

SERVAS defines five page types via a specific tweak combination (cf. Table 1):

PT_NORMAL marks untrusted memory outside of all xRange segments. It adheres to the PTE and can optionally be encrypted (cf. our encryption bypass).

PT_ENCLAVE denotes private enclave pages within the MRange, having any suitable combination of PTE page permissions. The TS bits specify the use of the MSID0 register, holding the unique SM-defined RTID Identifier.

PT_SHCODE shares non-writable pages between different instances of the same enclave to reduce memory and TLB pressure. This type adheres to the MRange and uses the MSID1 CSR, which holds the unique EncID of the enclave.

PT_SHDATA shares non-executable data between enclaves and resides in the enclave-configured URange. The *virtual address offset* is calculated relative to URange and ensures cross-enclave accessibility. The TS bits select the USID0 and USID1 CSRs, into which enclaves load an 80-bit shared secret before accessing the shared memory. The SMhelps in establishing the shared secret.

PT_MONITOR stores dynamic metadata for each enclave and thread (cf. SECS and TCS [17]) and is only accessible by the SMin M-mode. Note, that enclave code is not protected via PT_MONITOR but instead via Physical Memory Protection (PMP).

5.4   Security Monitor (SM)

The SMruns in machine mode (which is loosely comparable to CPU microcode used for Intel SGX logic) and protects itself using the RISC-V PMP. Our prototype has a tiny code size of 1253 Lines of Code (LoC), of which 381 LoC are used by the ASCON implementation (which is used for computing, e.g., the EncID and the sealing key). Therefore, it is small enough to be stored in on-chip SRAM, without the need for encryption.

In principle, the SMcan run completely stateless and only requires a small (approx. 1KiB) stack. Enclave management data is stored in dynamically allocated PT_MONITOR pages. The SMmaintains a 64 bit monotonic counter to allocate a unique RTID per enclave. One could also sample the RTID from the RISC-V hardware performance counters, e.g., the elapsed CPU cycles `mcycle`.

5.5   Caching

In our so-called *inline variant*, we cache the RVAS tweaks in the data and instruction caches. This caching allows the match of the currently active tweak with the cache line and ensures that the entire tweak can be reconstructed for any writeback operations. We store $b_{SERVAS} = 134$ tweak bits in each of the N_{cache} cache lines, covering the xRange-, PTE-, PRV-, SID-, and voffset bits. Since the MEE manages the integrity counters, they need no caching. This totals $S_{Data}, S_{Instr} = b_{SERVAS} \cdot N_{cache}$ additional cache bits.

Cache Optimization. For real-world scenarios, tweaks can be deduplicated into a separate Tweak Cache (TC) [34] to shrink the caching overhead in the *main caches*. The TC is linked with the main caches via a tweak index of $b_{tweakidx}$ bits. We propose a set-associative TC whose set index is derived from the tweak via a pseudorandom non-linear function, e.g., a lightweight cryptographic primitive [50,58]. This allows for efficient identification of already inserted tweaks, and only one additional cycle for the tweak comparison may be required. If a TC entry is removed, all associated cache lines need to be flushed.

Table 1. Tweak decision table: • denotes arbitrary values.

MRange	SRange	URange	PRV	PTE	TS	SID	Label
0	0	0	•	•	•	•	PT_NORMAL
1	0	0	U	•	01	MSID0	PT_ENCLAVE
1	0	0	U	!W	10	MSID1	PT_SHCODE
0	0	1	U	!X	11	USID0+1	PT_SHDATA
•	•	•	M	rw	•	0	PT_MONITOR

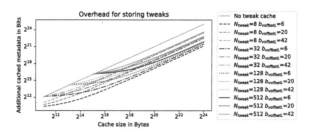

Fig. 3. Tweak cache compared to the inline variant (512*bit* cache lines) for different TC configurations (N_{tweak}, $b_{voffsetL}$). Lower is better.

The exact TC parameterization depends on the expected workload (*i.e.*, the number of tweaks required in parallel). As another optimization, the $b_{voffset}$ can be split between main caches ($b_{voffsetL}$) and the TC ($b_{voffsetH}$), resulting in a number of *tweak zones* per enclave. Moreover, we must consider two constraints: (1) more ways in the TC require additional parallel comparator logic, and (2) the overall cached tweak bits must be less than for the inline variant. To handle (1) there should be no more ways in the TC as in the main cache. Addressing (2) depends on the size of tweak zones, the size of the main caches, and the TC's size. The number of entries N_{tweak} in the TC determines the width of the index $b_{tweakidx}$. We also include a valid bit b_{valid}:

$$S_{DataOpt}, S_{InstrOpt} = (b_{voffsetL} + b_{tweakidx}) \cdot N_{cache} \tag{1}$$

$$S_{tweakcache} = (b_{valid} + b_{SERVAS} - b_{voffsetL}) \cdot N_{tweak} \tag{2}$$

We evaluate the storage overhead as a function of N_{cache} with 512 bit cache lines for different N_{tweak} and $b_{voffsetL}$ in Fig. 3. We observe that each N_{tweak} has the same break-even point for all $b_{voffsetL}$. After that, smaller $b_{voffsetL}$ reduce the overhead more. With larger caches $b_{voffsetL}$, becomes the dominating factor and clusters them into groups. This effect is less pronounced for $b_{tweakidx}$ due to its smaller size. However, as an example, a TC with $N_{tweak} = 128$ entries could reduce the storage overhead from 137 216 bit to 42 368 bit by about 69% for the CVA6 CPU with its 64 kB main cache and 1 GB tweak zones ($b_{voffsetL} = 20$).

5.6   Encryption Bypass Optimization

Our prototype encrypts the whole system's physical memory. To improve performance, one could also apply RVAS encryption only to pages (e.g., enclaves) that require this protection. This can be achieved by using the xRange registers to decide if a request has to go through the MEE or access the memory directly.

A limitation of the encryption bypass is that the inherent overhead of the integrity protection trees introduced by the MEE persists. Making the trees sparse could address this problem, but no such open-source memory encryption schemes have been proposed to the best of our knowledge.

6   Security Analysis

This section analyzes how RVAS's tweak (cf. Sect. 2) cryptographically enforces the challenges of memory isolation C_1-C_6. Attacks aim at breaking the *attribute-* (IA), *spatial-* (IS), or *temporal invariant* (IT).

6.1   Attacks on Physical Memory

An OS or physical attacker can access the physical memory via software or by mounting bus probing or cold-boot attacks [29]. However, RVAS's encryption prevents data access. Performing roll-back attacks or move encrypted data around to violate the invariant IT is mitigated by RVAS' integrity counters.

6.2   Attacks on Virtual Memory

Memory Isolation. Enclaves run in the virtual memory of a host application. Hence a rogue enclave, host, or OS could try to access enclave data. SERVAS supplies unforgeable (e.g., MRange, MSID) or enclave-private data to the memory color field of RVAS. Without a correct tweak, RVAS fails and traps to the SM.

Page Mapping Attacks. The OS has full control over the page table entries (PTEs) (challenge C_4, cf. Sect. 2), allowing for a range of attacks:

Downgrade or Remapping Attacks. The OS can map an unprotected page or another enclave's page to an address in the enclave's MRange to leak data or divert the control flow and violate IA, IT or IS. However, the combination of SM-controlled MRange registers, PTE bits, and the session identifier (e.g., the Runtime Identifier (RTID) or the Enclave Identifier (EncID)) ensure that any rogue pages in the MRange fail RVAS' integrity check.

Swapping Attacks. The OS can create a copy of an enclave page via the swapping mechanism to attempt to violate the temporal invariant IT. SERVAS mitigates this attack by invalidating the original page before the swapped-out copy is given to the OS. A similar attack attempts a roll-back by swapping-out a page twice and providing the older copy during swap-in. This is prevented by the latest authentication tag of the swapped out copy on a PT_MONITOR page.

Shared Data Page Attacks. Enclave shared memory faces two attacks from the OS: (1) Replace an enclave page with a shared memory page to trick the enclave into leaking its secrets. (2) The OS and malicious enclave cooperate to brute-force the 80 bit key. To prevent (1), the enclave must explicitly set the URange CSR and the key before shared memory is active. Scenario (2) is an online attack on shared memory only. It can be made practically infeasible by (A) terminating the attacker enclave, as loading the enclave acts as dynamic rate-limiting, or (B) performing explicit rate-limiting in the SMexception handler.

384   S. Steinegger et al.

Shared Code Page Attack. To deduplicate non-writable pages between different instances of the same enclave, the Enclave Identifier (EncID) is used as the memory color. An attacker can run an offline attack to create an enclave with a colliding EncID, which refers to finding a second pre-image to a cryptographic authentication code. Using a 128 bit EncID could completely eliminate this attack. However, SERVAS only supports an 80 bit SID. To achieve practical security, the EncID could be truncated using a key derivation function that involves a secret CPU key.

7   Evaluation

Our prototype is based on the CVA6 [63] platform, a 64-bit RISC-V CPU. For SERVAS, we extended this platform with the RVAS ISA extensions, the storage of tweaks in its write-through cache tag, and an MEE for RVAS. We increased the default cache line size from 16 B to 64 B, a common choice for many CPUs. We use MEMSEC [59], an open-source framework supporting various encryption schemes for the MEE. To fulfill our requirements (cf. Sect. 3), we configured MEMSEC to use ASCON-128 and extend it to process the tweak as ASCON's associated data. We use ASCON-128 for RVAS as it is the only cipher that is supported by the MEMSEC framework in TEC-Tree mode. MEMSEC is placed between the cache and the memory controller to encrypt all data transparently.

7.1   Performance Overhead

We ran a set of macrobenchmarks on a Linux 5.10 kernel on the CVA6 CPU to evaluate the performance. We use BEEBS [46] and CoreMark [22] as benchmarks. We excluded the `crc32`, `ludcmp`, `st`, `matmult-float`, and `rijndael` benchmarks from BEEBS, since they caused lockups on the unmodified CPU. We use the geometric mean to aggregate all BEEBS benchmarks into a single metric in Fig. 4. Detailed results are given in Appendix A. For the fast-running CoreMark, we plot the mean over 1 000 runs (with 10 internal iterations), while for the slower BEEBS, we average over 25 runs (with 4 internal iterations). We cannot run more heavyweight benchmarks due to the prototype's resource constraints (256 MB accessible DRAM and 50 MHz CPU frequency).

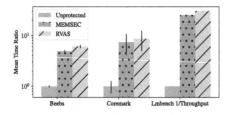 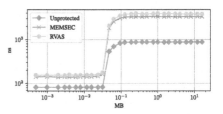

Fig. 4. Left: Benchmarking the CVA6 core using no memory encryption, MEMSEC, or RVAS. Right: Memory read-write latency.

Table 2. Micro-benchmarking results for SERVAS.

	Cycles median	Relative to getpid
Syscall getpid	10 403	1.0x
SERVAS SM Call "null"	9 030	0.9x
SERVAS Enter	18 865	1.8x
SERVAS Exit	17 391	1.7x
SERVAS Create	280 052	26.9x
Context Switch Sem.	238 781	23.0x

Figure 4 depicts our performance results normalized to an unprotected baseline, *i.e.*, CVA6 without any memory encryption. The overhead stems primarily from MEMSEC in TEC-tree mode. RVAS adds two calls to Ascon's permutation function to process the tweak in the MEE. RVAS' overhead is 16.7% for CoreMark, 20.0% for LMbench [44] and 24.5% for BEEBS compared to MEMSEC. Figure 4 shows the results of the read-write latency test of LMbench. This benchmark measures the latency for differently sized data chunks and visualizes the impact of CVA6's 32 kB L1 data cache and the latency of the external DDR3 memory. MEMSEC increases the average latency for a memory access from 850 ns to 3300 ns. The two additional rounds in RVAS only increase the latency by another 290 ns on average. These results are encouraging, given that we instantiated our RVAS prototype with the general-purpose MEMSEC encryption framework. We discuss possible optimizations in Sect. 7.3.

We evaluate SERVAS using the microbenchmarks shown in Table 2. We repeat each test 10 000 times to reduce scheduling- and cache-related differences. We compare the number of cycles for `eenter`/`eexit` with a simple "getpid" system call to get the switching overhead. The "null SM call" is the equivalent of a getpid system call that forms the baseline overhead for SM calls, but instead of calling into the OS, we invoke the SM. Calling an enclave function only takes 3.5x the time of a simple system call. This call includes the time for entering (18 865 cycles), executing a function with a fixed return value, and exiting (17 391 cycles) the enclave. Process-based context switching, using a semaphore and shared memory for synchronization, takes 23.0x of a simple system call. For comparison, entering and exiting an Intel SGX enclave takes 71x the time of a system call [37], thus being significantly slower than invoking a SERVAS enclave.

7.2   Hardware Overhead

We synthesize our modified CVA6 for a Xilinx Kintex-7 series FPGA. The hardware overhead of RVAS consists of the MEE, the ISA extension, and the augmented cache. The design's lookup tables (LUTs) increase by 20.27% and the flip-flops by 19.13%. 61.84 s% of the additional LUTs result from the MEE, 37.26% from the extended cache, and the rest from the ISA extension. Each cache line is tagged with 125 bit for the memory encryption tweak. The overhead in the cache is 25% for 512-bit cache lines. However, this overhead could be reduced by using the optimizations in Sect. 5.5.

7.3 Prototype Limitations

Our RVAS prototype is not optimized for performance. Due to a lack of openly available high-performance MEEs with authentication, we used the MEM-SEC [59] framework. Its storage overhead is analyzed in [59]. The MEE significantly impacts the overall performance (cf. Fig. 4). According to ARM, full memory encryption has a runtime overhead of 7.5% to 25% and a storage overhead of 7.8% to 26.7% [48]. Intel SGX memory encryption is good for medium workloads but might cause worst-case throughput penalties of 400% [28]. Given recent advances in RISC-V, we expect open-source, high-performance MEEs in the future. The bypass optimization Sect. 5.6 could also improve the system performance.

8   Related Work

Intel SGX [17,43] is a set of x86 instructions to interact with enclaves. Unlike SGX, SERVAS dynamically reuses the whole physical memory instead of being limited to the statically allocated 128 MB *Processor Reserved Memory*. Furthermore, SERVAS does not require a trusted metadata storage (*i.e.*, SGX's *Enclave Page Cache Map*) but instead feeds this metadata directly into the encryption.

CrypTag [45] feeds the upper pointer bits into an authenticated encryption engine to achieve memory safety. In contrast, RVAS supports various policies and incorporates information on the CPU state as specified by an SM(cf. Sect. 3) and adds the necessary logic to enforce these policies. The cache area overhead of CrypTag is up to 20%, which is comparable with RVAS.

VAULT [53] makes Intel SGX's EPC available to the full system memory to reduce paging overhead. Unlike SERVAS, VAULT does not overcome SGX's limitation regarding efficient shared memory.

SMARTS [60] implements a Memory Protection Unit as a framework that partially encrypts the memory and partitions the physical DRAM into three regions. In contrast, SERVAS is not bound to a static boot-time memory configuration.

AMD Secure Encrypted Virtualization (SEV) [5,6] describe CPU extensions to run virtual machines in untrusted environments. Unlike RVAS, SEV's memory encryption does neither provide integrity protection nor authentication.

Intel MKTME [32] transparently encrypts memory pages based on one of 64 different encryption keys indicated by the PTE. It does not provide cryptographic authentication and relies on a trusted hypervisor.

Other Systems. Sanctum [18], Keystone [39], and CURE [11] are other recent enclave and TEE designs tackling unique challenges. However, in contrast to SERVAS, these designs do not explicitly protect the external memory from physical attacks using memory encryption.

9   Future Work

We see usage scenarios of RVAS beyond traditional enclaves to provide, for example, fine-grained intra-enclave isolation and system-level enclaves. SERVAS could be used to supersede other protection mechanisms such as memory protection keys [31], pointer authentication [41], pointer tagging [10], and memory coloring [45]. SERVAS specifies configuration registers on each privilege level. These registers can allow for additional protection in the kernel by creating kernel-level enclaves. Our current prototype implementation uses ASCON as it is a lightweight cryptographic primitive already available in MEMSEC. However, realizing RVAS with other encryption primitives, such as AES, would be possible but requires additional analysis, which we leave open for future work.

Remote Attestation is a method to ensure the authenticity of the enclave [25] before provisioning secrets to it. Similar to SecureBlue++ [14], SERVAS loads already encrypted enclaves. Thus, they can embed their secrets directly in the code without the need for a remote attestation service. Based on these secrets, one can easily establish a remote attestation protocol.

10   Conclusion

This paper presented an innovative isolation primitive called authenticryption shield that unifies traditional and advanced isolation policies and offers potential for future security applications. This primitive is built on top of an authenticated memory encryption scheme, thus giving cryptographic isolation guarantees. We demonstrated our design and prototype for RISC-V called SERVAS, which allows for native and secure sharing between enclaves. We show how a small Security Monitor with only 1253 LoC can manage all enclaves throughout their life-cycle with our ISA extension. We prototyped and thoroughly assessed SERVAS's performance on the CVA6 RISC-V hardware and showed that entering or exiting takes only about 3.5x of a getpid syscall.

Acknowledgments. This project has received funding from the European Research Council (ERC) under the European Union's Horizon 2020 research and innovation programme (grant agreement No 681402) and by the Austrian Research Promotion Agency (FFG) via the competence center Know-Center (grant number 844595), which is funded in the context of COMET - Competence Centers for Excellent Technologies by BMVIT, BMWFW, and Styria. Furthermore, this work has been supported by the Austrian Research Promotion Agency (FFG) via the project ESPRESSO, which is funded by the province of Styria and the Business Promotion Agencies of Styria and Carinthia.

A   Detailed Evaluation Results

See Fig. 5.

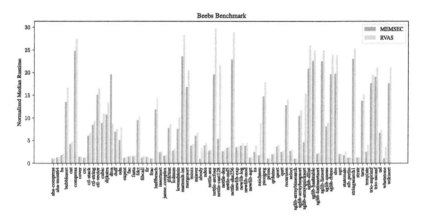

Fig. 5. RVAS performance on the BEEBS benchmark suite compared to MEMSEC, both normalized to an unprotected implementation.

References

1. USENIX Annual Technical Conference, USENIX ATC 2019, Renton, WA, USA, 10–12 July 2019 (2019)
2. 28th USENIX Security Symposium, USENIX Security 2019, Santa Clara, CA, USA, 14–16 August 2019 (2019)
3. 29th USENIX Security Symposium, USENIX Security 2020, 12–14 August 2020 (2020)
4. ACM/IEEE 41st International Symposium on Computer Architecture, ISCA 2014, Minneapolis, MN, USA, 14–18 June 2014 (2014)
5. Advanced Micro Devices Inc.: AMD secure encrypted virtualization (SEV) (2020). https://developer.amd.com/sev/
6. Advanced Micro Devices Inc.: AMD SEV-SNP: strengthening VM isolation with integrity protection and more (2020). https://www.amd.com/system/files/TechDocs/SEV-SNP-strengthening-vm-isolation-with-integrity-protection-and-more.pdf
7. Anati, I., Gueron, S., Johnson, S., Scarlata, V.: Innovative technology for CPU based attestation and sealing. In: HASP 2013, vol. 13, p. 7 (2013)
8. Andzakovic, D.: Extracting BitLocker keys from a TPM (2019). https://pulsesecurity.co.nz/articles/TPM-sniffing
9. Arm Limited: ARM security technology, building a secure system using TrustZone technology (2009). http://infocenter.arm.com/help/topic/com.arm.doc.prd29-genc-009492c/PRD29-GENC-009492C_trustzone_security_whitepaper.pdf. Ref. no. PRD29-GENC-009492C

10. Arm Limited: Armv8.5-a memory tagging extension (2020). https://developer.arm. com/-/media/Arm%20Developer%20Community/PDF/Arm_Memory_Tagging_ Extension_Whitepaper.pdf
11. Bahmani, R.: CURE: a security architecture with customizable and resilient enclaves. CoRR abs/2010.15866 (2020)
12. Beer, I.: An iOS zero-click radio proximity exploit odyssey (2020). https:// googleprojectzero.blogspot.com/2020/12/an-ios-zero-click-radio-proximity.html
13. Biondo, A., Conti, M., Davi, L., Frassetto, T., Sadeghi, A.: The guard's dilemma: efficient code-reuse attacks against Intel SGX. In: USENIX Security 2018, pp. 1213–1227 (2018)
14. Boivie, R.: SecureBlue++: CPU support for secure execution (2020). https:// dominoweb.draco.res.ibm.com/reports/rc25287.pdf
15. Bourgeat, T., Lebedev, I.A., Wright, A., Zhang, S., Arvind, Devadas, S.: MI6: secure enclaves in a speculative out-of-order processor. In: MICRO 2019, pp. 42–56 (2019). https://doi.org/10.1145/3352460.3358310
16. Busi, M., et al.: Provably secure isolation for interruptible enclaved execution on small microprocessors. In: CSF 2020, pp. 262–276 (2020). https://doi.org/10.1109/ CSF49147.2020.00026
17. Costan, V., Devadas, S.: Intel SGX explained. IACR Cryptol. ePrint Arch. **2016**, 86 (2016)
18. Costan, V., Lebedev, I.A., Devadas, S.: Sanctum: minimal hardware extensions for strong software isolation. In: USENIX Security 2016, pp. 857–874 (2016)
19. Dautenhahn, N., Kasampalis, T., Dietz, W., Criswell, J., Adve, V.S.: Nested kernel: an operating system architecture for intra-kernel privilege separation. In: ASPLOS 2015, pp. 191–206 (2015). https://doi.org/10.1145/2694344.2694386
20. Dessouky, G., Frassetto, T., Sadeghi, A.: HybCache: hybrid side-channel-resilient caches for trusted execution environments. In: USENIX Security 2020 [3], pp. 451–468 (2020)
21. Dobraunig, C., Eichlseder, M., Mendel, F., Schläffer, M.: Ascon v1.2. Submission to the CAESAR Competition (2016). https://ascon.iaik.tugraz.at/files/asconv12. pdf
22. EEMBC: Coremark (2020). https://www.eembc.org/coremark/
23. Elbaz, R., Champagne, D., Lee, R.B., Torres, L., Sassatelli, G., Guillemin, P.: TEC-Tree: a low-cost, parallelizable tree for efficient defense against memory replay attacks. In: Paillier, P., Verbauwhede, I. (eds.) CHES 2007. LNCS, vol. 4727, pp. 289–302. Springer, Heidelberg (2007). https://doi.org/10.1007/978-3-540-74735-2_20
24. Five, H.: MultiZone security for RISC-V (2020). https://hex-five.com/multizone-security-sdk/
25. Francillon, A., Nguyen, Q., Rasmussen, K.B., Tsudik, G.: A minimalist approach to remote attestation. In: DATE 2014, pp. 1–6 (2014). https://doi.org/10.7873/ DATE.2014.257
26. Gjerdrum, A.T., Pettersen, R., Johansen, H.D., Johansen, D.: Performance of trusted computing in cloud infrastructures with Intel SGX. In: CLOSER 2017, pp. 668–675 (2017). https://doi.org/10.5220/0006373706680675
27. Goodin, D.: Attackers exploit 0-day vulnerability that gives full control of Android phones (2019). https://arstechnica.com/information-technology/ 2019/10/attackers-exploit-0day-vulnerability-that-gives-full-control-of-android-phones/

28. Göttel, C.: Security, performance and energy trade-offs of hardware-assisted memory protection mechanisms. In: SRDS 2018, pp. 133–142 (2018). https://doi.org/10.1109/SRDS.2018.00024

29. Halderman, J.A., et al.: Lest we remember: cold boot attacks on encryption keys. In: USENIX Security 2008, pp. 45–60 (2008)

30. Hedayati, M., et al.: Hodor: intra-process isolation for high-throughput data plane libraries. In: USENIX ATC 2019 [1], pp. 489–504 (2019)

31. Intel Corporation: Intel 64 and IA-32 Architectures Software Developer's Manual, vol. 3 (3A, 3B & 3C): System Programming Guide (325384) (2016)

32. Intel Corporation: Intel Architecture Memory Encryption Technologies Specification. Ref: # 336907-002US. Rev: 1.2 (2019)

33. Jang, Y., Lee, J., Lee, S., Kim, T.: SGX-bomb: locking down the processor via rowhammer attack. In: SysTEX 2017, pp. 5:1–5:6 (2017). https://doi.org/10.1145/3152701.3152709

34. Joannou, A., et al.: Efficient tagged memory. In: ICCD 2017, pp. 641–648 (2017). https://doi.org/10.1109/ICCD.2017.112

35. Jomaa, N., Nowak, D., Grimaud, G., Hym, S.: Formal proof of dynamic memory isolation based on MMU. In: TASE 2016, pp. 73–80 (2016). https://doi.org/10.1109/TASE.2016.28

36. Kim, Y., et al.: Flipping bits in memory without accessing them: an experimental study of DRAM disturbance errors. In: ISCA 2014 [2], pp. 361–372. https://doi.org/10.1109/ISCA.2014.6853210

37. Koning, K., Chen, X., Bos, H., Giuffrida, C., Athanasopoulos, E.: No need to hide: protecting safe regions on commodity hardware. In: EUROSYS 2017, pp. 437–452 (2017). https://doi.org/10.1145/3064176.3064217

38. Kossifidis, N.: Secure boot notes (2020). https://lists.riscv.org/g/tech-tee/message/288. E-mail #288 from the tech-teelists.riscv.org group from 2 June 2020

39. Lee, D., Kohlbrenner, D., Shinde, S., Asanovic, K., Song, D.: Keystone: an open framework for architecting trusted execution environments. In: EUROSYS 2020, pp. 38:1–38:16 (2020). https://doi.org/10.1145/3342195.3387532

40. Lee, J., et al.: Hacking in darkness: return-oriented programming against secure enclaves. In: USENIX Security 2017, pp. 523–539 (2017)

41. Liljestrand, H., Nyman, T., Wang, K., Perez, C.C., Ekberg, J., Asokan, N.: PAC it up: towards pointer integrity using ARM pointer authentication. In: USENIX Security 2019 [2], pp. 177–194 (2019)

42. McKeen, F., et al.: Intel Software Guard Extensions (Intel SGX) support for dynamic memory management inside an enclave. In: HASP 2016, pp. 1–9 (2016)

43. McKeen, F., et al.: Innovative instructions and software model for isolated execution. In: HASP 2013, p. 10 (2013). https://doi.org/10.1145/2487726.2488368

44. McVoy, L.W., Staelin, C.: lmbench: portable tools for performance analysis. In: USENIX ATC 1996, pp. 279–294 (1996)

45. Nasahl, P., Schilling, R., Werner, M., Hoogerbrugge, J., Medwed, M., Mangard, S.: CrypTag: thwarting physical and logical memory vulnerabilities using cryptographically colored memory. In: ASIA CCS 2021: ACM Asia Conference on Computer and Communications Security, Virtual Event, Hong Kong, 7–11 June 2021, pp. 200–212 (2021). https://doi.org/10.1145/3433210.3453684

46. Pallister, J., Hollis, S.J., Bennett, J.: BEEBS: open benchmarks for energy measurements on embedded platforms. CoRR abs/1308.5174 (2013)

47. Park, S., Lee, S., Xu, W., Moon, H., Kim, T.: libmpk: Software abstraction for intel memory protection keys (Intel MPK). In: USENIX ATC 2019 [1], pp. 241–254 (2019)

48. Roberto-Maria, A.: Memory protection for the ARM architecture (2020). https://rwc.iacr.org/2020/slides/Avanzi.pdf. Presented at Real World Crypto 2020
49. Schrammel, D., et al.: Donky: domain keys - efficient in-process isolation for RISC-V and x86. In: USENIX Security 2020 [3], pp. 1677–1694 (2020)
50. Seznec, A., Bodin, F.: Skewed-associative caches. In: Bode, A., Reeve, M., Wolf, G. (eds.) PARLE 1993. LNCS, vol. 694, pp. 305–316. Springer, Heidelberg (1993). https://doi.org/10.1007/3-540-56891-3_24
51. Steinegger, S., Schrammel, D., Weiser, S., Nasahl, P., Mangard, S.: SERVAS! secure enclaves via RISC-V authenticryption shield. CoRR abs/1802.09085 (2021)
52. Szekeres, L., Payer, M., Wei, T., Song, D.: SoK: eternal war in memory. In: S&P 2013, pp. 48–62 (2013). https://doi.org/10.1109/SP.2013.13
53. Taassori, M., Shafiee, A., Balasubramonian, R.: VAULT: reducing paging overheads in SGX with efficient integrity verification structures. In: ASPLOS 2018, pp. 665–678 (2018). https://doi.org/10.1145/3173162.3177155
54. Unterluggauer, T., Werner, M., Mangard, S.: MEAS: memory encryption and authentication secure against side-channel attacks. J. Cryptogr. Eng. **9**(2), 137–158 (2018). https://doi.org/10.1007/s13389-018-0180-2
55. Vahldiek-Oberwagner, A., Elnikety, E., Duarte, N.O., Sammler, M., Druschel, P., Garg, D.: ERIM: secure, efficient in-process isolation with protection keys (MPK). In: USENIX Security 2019 [2], pp. 1221–1238 (2019)
56. Waterman, A., Asanović, K.: The RISC-V instruction set manual, volume II: privileged architecture, document version 20190608-priv-msu-ratified (2019). https://riscv.org/specifications/privileged-isa/
57. Weiser, S., Werner, M., Brasser, F., Malenko, M., Mangard, S., Sadeghi, A.: TIMBER-V: tag-isolated memory bringing fine-grained enclaves to RISC-V. In: NDSS 2019 (2019)
58. Werner, M., Unterluggauer, T., Giner, L., Schwarz, M., Gruss, D., Mangard, S.: ScatterCache: thwarting cache attacks via cache set randomization. In: USENIX Security 2019 [2], pp. 675–692 (2019)
59. Werner, M., Unterluggauer, T., Schilling, R., Schaffenrath, D., Mangard, S.: Transparent memory encryption and authentication. In: FPL 2017, pp. 1–6 (2017). https://doi.org/10.23919/FPL.2017.8056797
60. Wong, M.M., Haj-Yahya, J., Chattopadhyay, A.: SMARTS: secure memory assurance of RISC-V trusted SoC. In: HASP 2018, pp. 6:1–6:8 (2018). https://doi.org/10.1145/3214292.3214298
61. Woodruff, J., et al.: The CHERI capability model: revisiting RISC in an age of risk. In: ISCA 2014 [4], pp. 457–468 (2014). https://doi.org/10.1109/ISCA.2014.6853201
62. Wu, H., Preneel, B.: AEGIS: a fast authenticated encryption algorithm v1.1. Submission to the CAESAR Competition (2016). https://competitions.cr.yp.to/round3/aegisv11.pdf
63. Zaruba, F., Benini, L.: The cost of application-class processing: energy and performance analysis of a Linux-ready 1.7-GHz 64-Bit RISC-V core in 22-nm FDSOI technology. IEEE Trans. Very Large Scale Integr. Syst. **27**, 2629–2640 (2019). https://doi.org/10.1109/TVLSI.2019.2926114
64. Zeldovich, N., Kannan, H., Dalton, M., Kozyrakis, C.: Hardware enforcement of application security policies using tagged memory. In: OSDI 2008, pp. 225–240 (2008)

Privacy

Privacy-Preserving Gradient Descent for Distributed Genome-Wide Analysis

Yanjun Zhang, Guangdong Bai[✉], Xue Li, Caitlin Curtis, Chen Chen, and Ryan K. L. Ko

The University of Queensland, St Lucia, QLD, Australia
g.bai@uq.edu.au

Abstract. Genome-wide analysis, which provides perceptive insights into complex diseases, plays an important role in biomedical data analytics. It usually involves large-scale human genomic data, and thus may disclose sensitive information about individuals. While existing studies have been conducted against data exfiltration by external malicious actors, this work focuses on the emerging identity tracing attack that occurs when a dishonest insider attempts to re-identify obtained DNA samples. We propose a framework named vFRAG to facilitate privacy-preserving data sharing and computation in genome-wide analysis. vFRAG mitigates privacy risks by using vertical fragmentations to disrupt the genetic architecture on which the adversary relies for re-identification. The fragmentation significantly reduces the overall amount of information the adversary can obtain. Notably, it introduces no sacrifice to the capability of genome-wide analysis—we prove that it preserves the correctness of gradient descent, the most popular optimization approach for training machine learning models. We also explore the efficiency performance of vFRAG through experiments on a large-scale, real-world dataset. Our experiments demonstrate that vFRAG outperforms not only secure multiparty computation (MPC) and homomorphic encryption (HE) protocols with a speedup of more than 221x for training neural networks, but also noise-based differential privacy (DP) solutions and traditional non-private algorithms in most settings.

1 Introduction

Advances in biomedical data analytics over the last few decades have enabled inexpensive large-scale and whole genome studies. *Genome-wide analysis*, such as genome-wide association studies (GWAS) and genome-wide complex trait analysis (GCTA), plays an important role in assisting with predicting health risks, enabling preventative and personalized medicine, and investigating natural selection and population differences [27]. As a data-driven study, genome-wide analysis typically requires a large sample size to confirm differences with statistical confidence. Sharing genomic data on a large scale thus becomes essential. This however raises privacy concerns, as much sensitive information, including health status and family relationships, can be derived from the human genome.

© Springer Nature Switzerland AG 2021
E. Bertino et al. (Eds.): ESORICS 2021, LNCS 12973, pp. 395–416, 2021.
https://doi.org/10.1007/978-3-030-88428-4_20

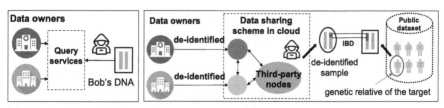

(a) Membership inference.   (b) Identity tracing.

Fig. 1. Genetic privacy breaches overview.

Indeed, various genetic privacy breaches and attacks [8,9] have highlighted the urgent need to enhance privacy in the analysis.

In the research area of genetic privacy, our community has been focusing on detecting and defending against the membership inference [12,18,25]. It aims to reveal the presence of an individual's genome in a dataset (e.g., a dataset of HIV patients' DNA sequences) that the adversary has partial or blackbox access through Beacon systems [12] or trained machine learning models [25] (Fig. 1a). In this work, we target an emerging but overlooked privacy threat known as the *identity tracing* [9]. It occurs in a data sharing scheme when the adversary is an insider such as dishonest participants or cloud service providers, shown in Fig. 1b. Through the data sharing scheme, the adversary could gain access to the datasets which in most instances have been conducted de-identification, and attempts to re-identify individuals in them.

The adversary's re-identification tactic is to exploit the *correlations* among genomic data. Due to the existence of the correlations, even though the personal identifiers (such as name and address) have been removed from the datasets, the inherent correlations among genomic data could still put an individual's privacy at risk. Figure 1b illustrates a representative attack scenario which exploits the genetic inheritance laws, the most fundamental correlation. The adversary applies a sophisticated tactic called *long-range familial search* (LFS) which detects the target's genetic relatives from identity-retaining datasets by matching the *identical-by-descent* (IBD) segments of DNA [9]. Having known the genetic relatives, the adversary is able to narrow down the target's identity.

LFS is a de facto investigative tool by law enforcement to trace suspects due to its re-identification capacity. In a notable case, LFS was used to successfully trace the Golden State Killer in 2018 [9]. With the explosion[1] of public consumer genomics services (such as GEDmatch and MyHeritage[2]) which allow users to upload raw genotype files for genetic analysis including searching for their genetic relatives, privacy threats of utilizing LFS against normal individuals are greatly exacerbated - as the growth of available datasets (refer to the public dataset in Fig. 1b) significantly increases the probability that an LFS identifies individuals.

---

[1] There have been around 26 million tests sold in 2019 [24].
[2] https://www.gedmatch.com/; https://www.myheritage.com/.

This presents an urgent demand for privacy-preserving solutions that take the correlations into account.

The existing techniques of preserving privacy for *general-purpose* data analytics, including differentially private (DP) deep learning frameworks [3,16,39], and cryptographic technologies such as homomorphic encryption (HE) [5,30] or secure multiparty computation (MPC) [17,36], may not be applicable to genome-wide analysis due to their inherent limitations. The former ones are usually based on additive noise mechanisms which perturb the original data/models and consequently affect model accuracy to a certain extent. This is often prohibitive given the high accuracy required by genome-wide analysis. The HE and MPC prevent plaintext data disclosure, and are able to compute identical results from the cyphertext as from the plaintext, but they are known to be limited by nontrivial computational or communicational overhead.

Our Solution. We propose vFRAG, which is a distributed framework for preserving privacy in collaborative genome-wide analysis. vFRAG achieves high efficiency via distributing computation throughout multiple *unnecessarily trustworthy* nodes, and privacy preservation via an innovative *DNA sequence fragmentation*. The proposed fragmentation is a *vertical* partitioning and reassembling of DNA segments, designated against the privacy risk of identity tracing.

The insight of the proposed fragmentation is to disrupt the *genetic architecture*[3] where the correlations stem from. This seemingly straightforward strategy inherently suits DNA sequence data, given that a DNA sequence is essentially a $(A|T|G|C)^*$ string and its "semantics" are reflected by the occurrence of variants at particular locations (i.e., loci). In the human genome, the effect size of single variation associated with the heritability is small. In other words, a person's phenotypic heritability, e.g., his/her susceptibility to disease, depends more on the combined effect of all the associated genes than on one particular genetic variation [27]. Therefore, the proposed fragmentation can significantly reduce the chance of an adversary fully obtaining the information about the heritability in genome.

vFRAG also addresses the fundamental challenge of privacy-utility tradeoff. Given the vertically partitioned datasets, most primitive functionalities and algorithms used in genome-wide analysis, such as genetic relationship matrix estimation [34] and genotype clustering [4], can be *parallelized*. This can be formalized as the *parallel correctness* that an analysis in our framework reaches the same results as in a centralized way. We demonstrate that our parallelization of gradient descent (Sect. 3) and other primitive functionalities (Appendix B) preserves this property. In such a way, our fragmentation results in *no* sacrifice to those analyses relying on them, e.g., any machine learning algorithm based on gradient descent for optimization.

Contributions. We summarize the main contributions of this work as follows.

---

[3] *Genetic architecture* refers to the underlying genetic basis and its variational properties that are responsible for broad-sense heritability [26].

1. A Privacy-Preserving Framework. We propose a novel framework υFRAG for privacy-preserving sharing of DNA data in large-scale genome-wide analysis. υFRAG is characterized by its capabilities of privacy preservation and verifiably correct computation for genome-wide analysis.

2. A Novel Privacy-preserving Technique and its Quantitative Analysis. To the best of our knowledge, our work is the first to use DNA sequence fragmentation for mitigating the genetic privacy threat. The evaluation of the privacy preservation in υFRAG is twofold. In a high level, we construct a formal model to quantitatively evaluate the overall amount of information leaked to the adversary. In the individual level, we propose ϵ-indistinguishability - a variant model of ϵ-local differential privacy, and prove that the vertical fragmentation provide a bound for the adversary's capacity in distinguishing individuals.

3. Experimental Evaluation. We conduct experiments on a real-world dataset, showing the significant improvement of efficiency by our framework compared with the MPC/HE algorithms and a state-of-the-art noise-based DP solution.

2   System Design

2.1 υFRAG Overview

Figure 2a demonstrates the architecture and workflow of υFRAG. It provides a distributed sharing network for the participants (local owners) to assemble their local DNA sequence datasets for large-scale analysis. The network is comprised of an aggregation node A (the blue node in Fig. 2a) and a worker node layer that includes s worker nodes $S^1, ..., S^s$ (the green and grey nodes). The original datasets are split into fragments locally before they leave their owners. These fragments are then transferred to the worker nodes. Each of them separately processes a few fragments and reports its single-point result to the aggregation node, which synthesizes the analysis results and sends them to the recipients.

The rationale to fragment the dataset in a vertical manner is to hinder malicious or compromised worker nodes from gaining the complete DNA sequence (x_t) and IBD segments. Below we define the mask operation for the fragmentation. Let X be a dataset of $\mathbb{S}^{m \times n}$, and $x_{ij} \in X$ represents the genotype on the jth SNP of ith individual. Let $Mask = \{M^1, ..., M^s\}$ be a set of s vectors of $[0|1]^n$ (denoting a n-dimensional vector comprising of 0 and 1) s.t., $M^1 \vee ... \vee M^s = [1]^n$.

Definition 1 *(Mask Operation $\odot$ for Vertical Fragmentation). Given a mask $M^l = [mask_1^l, ..., mask_n^l]$ ($l \in \{1, ..., s\}$), $X \odot M^l$ produces a dataset X^l, whose element x_{ij}^l in X^l is generated by*

$$x_{ij}^l = \begin{cases} x_{ij}, & if\ mask_j^l = 1 \\ drop, & if\ mask_j^l = 0 \end{cases} \tag{1}$$

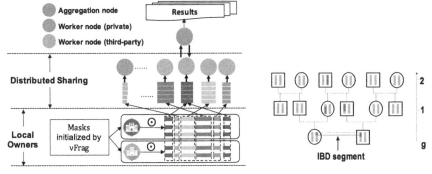

(a) The architecture and workflow of vFRAG.   (b) Example of an IBD segment.

Fig. 2. System design.

The *Mask* is initialized by vFRAG and distributed to each participant for them to generate fragments. By applying the mask operation with each vectors in *Mask*, participants produce s new datasets, $X^1, ..., X^s$, and each is then dispatched to a worker node. Note that participants do not have to assemble their original datasets for fragmentation; instead, each X^l is constructed in node S^i from individual fragments, as shown by the colored rectangles in Fig. 2a. The genome-wide analysis functionalities are then achieved by the collaboration between the worker nodes and the aggregation node. Initialization of the mask is the key to disrupt the genetic architecture. In vFRAG, this is determined by the fragmentation strategy (detailed in Sect. 5).

2.2 Attacker Model and Assumptions

We assume an honest-but-curious adversary $\mathcal{A}$ who may control t out of s worker nodes, where $t \leq s$. For the sake of simplicity, our privacy analysis in Sect. 5 considers an aggregation node out of the adversary's control. Such an aggregator can be accommodated with a private server or a private cloud instance in reality, as it is designed to be free from any computation-intensive task. In Sect. 7, we show that even though it is compromised, the identity tracing attack is unlikely (with a negligible probability) to derive the original DNA sequence for re-identification.

Let δ denote the proportion of trusted worker nodes, i.e., $\delta = (s-t)/s$. Each worker nodes holds a fragment $X^l = X \odot M^l$, and X has been anonymized such that the identifiers of its samples are removed. We assume the adversary also has access to a publicly available datasets $\mathcal{D}$ which comprise genotyped individuals. Given an arbitrary DNA sequence from $\{X^l\}|_{S^l \text{ is under } \mathcal{A}\text{'s control}}$ denoted by x_t, the adversary attempts to re-identify x_t's subject (referred to as the *target*) by searching for the target and/or its genetic relatives from $\mathcal{D}$. We parameterize this re-identification with the gth degree of genetic relatives, where $g \geq 1$ ($g = 1$ for target him/herself or siblings, $g = 2$ for first cousins, and so on) [4].

---

[4] For readability, a table of notations is included as Appendix A.

Below we brief the attack techniques the adversary can use, and leave their models in Sect. 4.

- **LFS Attack.** LFS makes use of the *IBD segments*, which are DNA segments inherited by persons having a common ancestor, for re-identification. Figure 2b shows an IBD segment co-inherited from a common ancestor two generations back. IBD segments indicate the genetic distance of two individuals, and are measured in *centiMorgans* (*cM*). The higher the number of centiMorgans of IBD segments, the more significant the match is, i.e., the higher probability that target and the matched individual have inherited from a recent ancestor [9]. As a result, the capacity of LFS can be regarded as the probability of the two individuals sharing *sufficient* detectable IBD segments.
- **Genotype Imputation.** We also take into account the *genotype imputation* technique that could infer the missing genotypes of a DNA sequence based on the remaining genotypes [7]. It could be abused by the sophisticated adversary to learn more fragments based on those it obtained.

3   Privacy-Preserving Gradient Descent

To retain the capability of genome-wide analysis, vFRAG must reach exactly the same result as a traditional non-distributed framework does when operating any computation. We formalize this as the *parallel correctness* of parallelized computation with respect to the vertical fragmentation.

Definition 2 *(Parallel Correctness).* *Given a function $\mathcal{F}$ which takes as input a genomic dataset $X \in \mathbb{S}^{m \times n}$, assume a fragmentation strategy partitions X into a set of fragments X^l ($l = \{1, ..., s\}$), and each of them is associated with a worker node $S^l \in S$, where S is the set of worker nodes interacting with an aggregation node A. The parallelized $\mathcal{F}$ in vFRAG, denoted by $\mathcal{F}'$, is parallely correct if $\mathcal{F}'(\{(S^l, X^l), A\}_{S^l \in S}) = \mathcal{F}(X)$.*

In the following, we present vFRAG's computation of gradient descent, the optimization that most analyses rely on, and prove its parallel correctness. We note that our computation also works on SGD, in which X^l denotes a randomly selected training sample or a subset of training samples.

We let $\mathcal{F}_{GD}(J, X)$ denote the gradient descent optimization applied on the dataset X with cost function J. J is defined as $J(\sigma(XW), y, W)$, where W denotes coefficient matrix and σ is the hypothesis function which is determined by the learning model. In logistic regression, σ is usually a sigmoid function, while in neural networks, it is a composite function known as the forward propagation. The optimal solution of W, denoted as W_*, is derived by the optimization $\arg\min_W J(\sigma(XW), y, W)$, and W is updated as $W := W - \alpha \frac{\partial J}{\partial W}$.

In vFRAG, the parallelized gradient descent optimization, denoted by $\mathcal{F}'_{GD}$, is designed as the following steps.

- ***Initialization.*** At the beginning of the task, the fragments $X^l \in \mathbb{R}^{m \times d_l}$ ($l \in \{1, ..., s\}$) are assigned to the corresponding S^l, and S^l randomly initializes its $W^l \in \mathbb{R}^{d_l \times H}$ which is associated with X^l.

- **Step 1.** Each S^l computes $X^l W^l$, and sends $X^l W^l$ to the aggregation node.
- **Step 2.** The aggregation node computes $XW = \sum_{l=1}^{s} X^l W^l$, and the gradient Δ, which is the gradient of the cost function J with respect to XW, i.e., $\Delta = \frac{\partial J}{\partial XW}$. Then it sends Δ back to each worker node.
- **Step 3.** Each S^l updates the respective coefficient $W^l := W^l - \alpha X^{l^T} \Delta$.

Step 1–3 repeat for the next iterations until convergence.

The following theorem demonstrates that if $\mathcal{F}_{GD}(J, X) = (W_*, \eta)$, i.e., if the non-distributed optimization outputs W_* that makes J converge to a local/global minimum η, then executing $\mathcal{F}'_{GD}(\{(J, S^l, X^l), Agg\}_{S^l \in S})$ on $X^1, ..., X^s$ in vFRAG with the same hyper settings (such as step size, model structure, initialization) will also output W_* that makes J converge to η.

Theorem 1. $\mathcal{F}'_{GD}$ *is parallelly correct.*

Proof. Let W_i denote the model parameters of $\mathcal{F}_{GD}$ at the ith training iteration. Let $W'_i = |\{W^l_i\}|_{l \in \{1,..,s\}}$ denote the vertical concatenation on $\{W^l_i\}_{l \in \{1,..,s\}}$, i.e., the model parameters of $\mathcal{F}'_{GD}$ at the ith training iteration. The theorem can be proved by induction as follows.

- **Base case:** $W_0 = W'_0$ by assumption of hyper setting.
- **Inductive step:** In $\mathcal{F}_{GD}$, the ith ($i \geq 1$) training iteration update W_i as

$$W_i = W_{i-1} - \alpha \frac{\partial J}{\partial W_{i-1}} = W_{i-1} - \alpha \frac{\partial J}{\partial (XW_{i-1})} \frac{\partial XW_{i-1}}{\partial W_{i-1}}$$
$$= W_{i-1} - \alpha X^T \frac{\partial J}{\partial (XW_{i-1})}. \tag{2}$$

In $\mathcal{F}'_{GD}$, each node S_l updates its local W^l_i as

$$W^l_i = W^l_{i-1} - \alpha X^{l^T} \Delta = W^l_{i-1} - \alpha X^{l^T} \frac{\partial J}{\partial (XW'_{i-1})}.$$

Since $W'_i = |\{W^l_i\}|_{l \in \{1,..,s\}}$ and $X = |\{X^l\}|_{l \in \{1,..,s\}}$, we have in $\mathcal{F}'_{GD}$ that

$$W'_i = |\{(W^l_{i-1} - \alpha X^{l^T} \frac{\partial J}{\partial (XW'_{i-1})})\}|_{l \in \{1,..,s\}} = W'_{i-1} - \alpha X^T \frac{\partial J}{\partial (XW'_{i-1})}. \tag{3}$$

Comparing Eq. 2 and 3, W_i and W'_i are updated with the same equation. Hence, $W_i = W'_i$. Thus, $\mathcal{F}_{GD} = \mathcal{F}'_{GD} = (W_*, \eta)$. □

4 Modeling Attacks for Privacy Analysis

In this section and Sect. 5, we assess the privacy-preservation of vFRAG's distributed gradient descent. We starts with modeling the proposed attacks (cf. Sect. 2.2), and leave the privacy analysis in Sect. 5.

4.1 Modeling the LFS Attack

We adopt a Shannon entropy based measurement to investigate the amount of information the adversary can obtain. Shannon entropy has been extensively employed as a metric to evaluate privacy-preserving mechanisms [8,28,31,32], due to its capability of quantifying the expected contribution of a piece of data in reducing the uncertainty of the target's identity among the base population.

We assume the target's record in a genome-wide analysis study is randomly sampled from a defined population with the size denoted by N. This therefore translates to $log_2 N$ bits of entropy. Take the US population as an example. With the population of 329 million in 2019, the uncertainty of a random sample's identity can be measured as 28.2 bits of entropy. Denote γ as the mean number of children per mating pair. Conditioned that a successful match between the target and a genetic relative at g^{th} degree, the amount of bits of information obtained by the adversary can be derived as $h(g) = log_2 N - log_2 \sum_{k=1}^{g} \gamma^k = log_2 \frac{N}{\sum_{k=1}^{g} \gamma^k}$. For example, if the LFS successfully matches the target or his/her siblings ($g = 1$) from the US population (where $\gamma = 2.5$), the adversary gains 26.88 bits of information. In other words, the uncertainty of target's identity is reduced to 1.32 bit. Then, we can formulate the expected entropy bits gained by the LFS attack as the function of generation degree g as $H(g) = h(g)Pr(identify)$, where the $Pr(identify)$ is the probability of a successful match between the target and a random individual at g^{th} degree. The $H(g)$ is taken as the indicator of the capacity of the LFS attack, and thus the core of our privacy analysis becomes to determine the $Pr(identify)$.

A successful match between the target and a random individual depends on the conditions that these two individuals are genetic relatives, and they share detectable IBD segments [9]. Therefore, $Pr(identify)$ can be derived from calculating the following two probabilities: 1) $Pr(shared)$, the probability of the target and a random individual sharing a pair of ancestors at g^{th} degree given $N(g)$ which is the population size of the generation at g^{th} degree, and 2) $Pr(match|g)$, the probability that these two individuals share *sufficient* IBD segments to be detected given the public dataset $\mathcal{D}$ of size R. Here the sufficiency is defined as the IBD matching parameters - to declare a match between the target and an individual in $\mathcal{D}$, there should be at least c IBD segments, each of which is of length $\geq v(cM)$.

To identify the target, the adversary needs to find at least t matches from $\mathcal{D}$. Thus, $Pr(identify)$ can be formulated as $Pr(identify) = 1 - \sum_{k=0}^{t-1} B(k; R, Pr(shared) \cdot Pr(match|g))$, where B is the probability mass function of the binomial distribution. Below, we give $Pr(shared)$ and $Pr(match|g)$:

$$Pr(shared) = \frac{2^{2g-2}}{N(g)} \prod_{g'=1}^{g-1} (1 - \frac{2^{2g'-2}}{N(g')}),$$

$$Pr(match|g) = 1 - \sum_{k=0}^{c-1} B(k; 2Lg + 22, \frac{Pr(IBD)}{2^{2g-2}}),$$

$$(4)$$

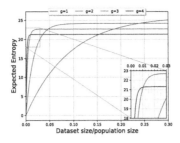

Fig. 3. Attack performance for varying dataset sizes. (Color figure online)

where $Pr(IBD)$ denotes the probability of the shared IBD segment length to exceed v, and L is the total genome length, which is roughly $3,500\ cM$ [23]. The derivation of $Pr(shared)$ and $Pr(match|g)$ is detailed in our technical report [1].

Quantifying Privacy Threat of LFS. We now are able to quantify privacy threat of the LFS attack when vFRAG is not applied. We first derive $Pr(IBD)$ in the scenario where the adversary has the access to the full genome of the target. As the length of the IBD segment is exponentially distributed with a mean of $1/(2g)\ cM$ [23], the probability density function (PDF) of the length of IBD segments is: $Pr(x) = 2ge^{-2gx}$. Therefore, the probability of the shared IBD segment length exceeding v is $Pr(IBD) = \int_{v}^{\infty} 2ge^{-2gx}dx = e^{-2vg}$.

With this, we explore the performance of LFS for various public dataset sizes, taking the aforementioned US population (329 million and $\gamma = 2.5$) as a case study. In general, as the dataset size increases, the LFS attack acquires higher entropy, as is shown in Fig. 3. When the dataset includes around 30% of the population, the attacker is able to achieve 25.9 bits (the magenta line). We also notice that in the cases where the dataset size is small, a greater g is more favorable to the attacker. When the public dataset covers less than 1% of the population, the best performance (21.3 bits) is achieved by the re-identification of the third cousins (the blue line). This may be because the number of distant relatives in the population is greater than close ones. For example, in Fig. 2b, the circle in level 0 has seven relatives with g = 2 whereas two with g = 1. As a result, when the size is small, the probability of successfully searching a distant relative is higher. Nevertheless, as the coverage of the dataset goes higher, identifying closer relatives gives the attacker more significant bits.

It is worth noting that the privacy threat is becoming worse in the real world, with the increasing number of consumer genomics services for searching identified genetic relatives. For example, with GEDmatch, which is a public available database that contains around one million DNA profiles (0.3% of the target population), LFS is able to achieve up to 19 bits of entropy (the blue line in the zoomed view of Fig. 3). The expected entropy further rises to 22.5 bits if the genetic dataset reaches the scale that covers 2% of the US population (the green line in the zoomed view of Fig. 3).

4.2   Modeling the Genotype Imputation

Next, we modeling the genotype imputation that infers (part of) missing geno-types of the target by matching the observed ones with a reference panel of haplotypes. A haplotype refers to a set of SNPs found on the same chromo-some. Haplotype reference panels are widely used for genotype imputation [7]. The model typically used for the inference is a Hidden Markov Model (HMM) in which the hidden states are a sequence of pairs of haplotypes in a reference panel [7]. That is,

$$Pr(G|H) = \sum_{Z^{(1)}, Z^{(2)}} Pr(G|Z^{(1)}, Z^{(2)}, H) \cdot Pr(Z^{(1)}, Z^{(2)}|H), \qquad (5)$$

where $H = \{H_1, ..., H_K\}$ is a set of K known haplotypes (the reference panel), $H_i = \{H_{i1}, ..., H_{in}\}$ is a single haplotype and $H_{ij} \in \{0, 1\}$ (0/1 stand for ref-erence and alternative genotype respectively). $G = \{G_1, ..., G_n\}$ denotes the genotype data on the target individual, and $G_i \in \{0, 1, missing\}$. $Z^{(1)} = \{Z_1^{(1)}, ..., Z_n^{(1)}\}$ and $Z^{(2)} = \{Z_1^{(2)}, ..., Z_n^{(2)}\}$ are the two sequences of hidden states at the n sites (i.e., loci) and $Z_l^{(j)} \in \{1, ..., K\}$. Intuitively, these hidden states can be regarded as pairs of haplotypes in the set H that are copied to form the genotype G.

The first term $Pr(G|Z^{(1)}, Z^{(2)}, H)$ in Eq. 5 defines the emission probabil-ities λ in HMM, which allows for mutation at each SNP. The second term $Pr(Z^{(1)}, Z^{(2)}|H)$ models the transition probability ρ. It reflects the linkage dis-equilibrium between two alleles and determines how $Z^{(1)}$ and $Z^{(2)}$ transits from H_i to H_j along the sequence. When calculating the state probability for loci with missing genotypes, λ is cancelled out and only the transition probability ρ plays a role. The transition probability ρ is dominated by the genetic distance, i.e., the longer the genetic distance between the observed genotypes, the larger the probability $(1 - \rho)$ for $Z^{(1)}$ and $Z^{(2)}$ transiting from one reference haplotype to others [7]. Therefore, with a growing number of missing genotypes in the IBD segments which is proportional to the genetic distance, the probability $(1 - \rho)$ increases. This results in more possible candidates for the imputation, and thus reduces the expected number of accurately imputed genotypes.

Here, we provide the upper bound of the expected number of accurately imputed genotypes (denoted as $\overline{T}$) with respect to the number of missing geno-types (denoted as τ) as

$$\overline{T} < \frac{K}{1 - \rho} K^{-\frac{1-\rho}{K}\tau} \prod_{i=1}^{\tau} MAF_i \sum_{k=0}^{\tau} \binom{\tau}{k} (\tau - k), \qquad (6)$$

where MAF_i is the minor allele frequency of the ith missing genotype (theoreti-cally $MAF_i \leq 0.5$). The derivation of Inequality 6 can be found in our technical report [1]. The evaluation the privacy preservation assumes that the adversary applies the genotype imputation by default, implying that the adversary knows

$\overline{T}$ extra genotypes. We further set $MAF_i = 0.5$ (such setting gives the adversary advantage as it leads to a large $\overline{T}$), such that Inequality 6 is simplified as

$$\overline{T} < \frac{\tau K}{2(1-\rho)} K^{-\frac{1-\rho}{K}\tau}. \tag{7}$$

5   Analysis of Privacy Preservation

With the models of attacks, we then analyze the privacy preservation of υFRAG against the adversary who has compromised a proportion of nodes. We outline our evaluation from the following two levels.

- **Collection Level: Reduction of Overall Information Leakage** (Sect. 5.1). We quantify information leakage reduction of two typical fragmentation strategies. Through the comparison with the baseline, we show that the information leakage to the adversary exponentially decreases with the growth in the proportion of trusted nodes.
- **Individual Level: Indistinguishability among Individuals** (Sect. 5.2). Information entropy is suitable for measuring the information leakage of a system as a whole, but less capable on individuals. As a complementary, we define ϵ-*indistinguishability* - a variant model of local differential privacy. We prove such indistinguishability provides the bound of an adversary's capacity of distinguishing an individual target based on the information obtained from the fragments (including those inferred by the genotype imputation).

5.1   The Collection-Level Analysis

Analysis on Random Fragmentation Strategy. First, we consider a scenario of *random sampling* that the individuals in the public dataset are randomly selected from a defined population. In this scenario, υFRAG applies a random fragmentation on the dataset. Assuming the adversary has applied the genotype imputation, the expected length of IBD segments held by the adversary is increased from $1/2g$ to $(1 + \frac{\overline{T}}{n})/2g$, in which $\frac{\overline{T}}{n}$ is the imputation rate. Then, the PDF of the length of IBD segments after the imputation is $Pr(x)_{adversary} = \frac{2g}{1+\overline{T}/n}e^{-\frac{2g}{1+\overline{T}/n}x}$. The probability of this IBD segment's length to exceed v is $Pr(IBD)_{impute} = \int_v^\infty \frac{2g}{1+\overline{T}/n}e^{-\frac{2g}{1+\overline{T}/n}x}dx = e^{-\frac{2vg}{1+\overline{T}/n}}$. In the random fragmentation setting, the probability for the adversary to hold this segment is $1 - \delta$. Therefore, the probability of the adversary holding a detectable IBD segment in this scenario, denoted by $Pr(IBD)_1$, can be calculated as:

$$Pr(IBD)_1 = (1 - \delta)e^{-\frac{2vg}{1+\overline{T}/n}}. \tag{8}$$

Combining $Pr(IBD)_1$ with Eq. 4, we can derive the probability for the adversary to match the target and his/her relative sharing at least c detectable (at least length v) IBD segments, denoted as $Pr(match|g)_1$, as

$$Pr(match|g)_1 = 1 - \sum_{k=0}^{c-1} B(k; 2Lg + 22, \frac{Pr(IBD)_1}{2^{2g-2}})$$

$$= 1 - \sum_{k=0}^{c-1} B(k; 2Lg + 22, (1-\delta)\frac{e^{-\frac{2vg}{1+\overline{T}/n}}}{2^{2g-2}}). \tag{9}$$

Thus, the expected value of entropy bits gained by the adversary who controls $(1 - \delta)$ proportion of nodes, denoted as $H'(g)_1$, can be formulated as

$$H'(g)_1 = h(g)\big(1 - \sum_{k=0}^{t-1} B\left(k; R, Pr(shared) \cdot Pr(match|g)_1\right)\big). \tag{10}$$

Analysis on IBD-targeting Fragmentation Strategy. We then consider a more realistic scenario wherein the individuals in the dataset are selected from particular families or particular areas/suburbs (such as the patient data of a hospital whose patients are usually from nearby suburbs). In this scenario, data owners can provide prior knowledge of their data (such as pedigree information and family distributions), such that vFRAG is able to identify the locations of the IBD segments and deliberately split them during the fragmentation.

With this strategy, the chance that adversary holds the full IBD segments is significantly reduced compared to the random fragmentation. Since each IBD segment is fragmented, the expected length of IBD segments held by the adversary is reduced from $(1 + \frac{\overline{T}}{n})/(2g)$ to $(1-\delta)(1 + \frac{\overline{T}}{n})/(2g)$. The PDF of the length of IBD segments then becomes $Pr(x)_{adversary} = \frac{2g}{(1-\delta)(1+\overline{T}/n)}e^{-\frac{2g}{(1-\delta)(1+\overline{T}/n)}x}$. Therefore, in this scenario, the probability of the adversary holding a detectable IBD segment $Pr(IBD)_2$ is

$$Pr(IBD)_2 = e^{-\frac{2vg}{(1-\delta)(1+\overline{T}/n)}}. \tag{11}$$

With this, the probability that two individuals share enough IBD segments to be detected, denoted as $Pr(match|g)_2$, can be calculated as

$$Pr(match|g)_2 = 1 - \sum_{k=0}^{c-1} B(k; 2Lg + 22, \frac{Pr(IBD)_2}{2^{2g-2}})$$

$$= 1 - \sum_{k=0}^{c-1} B(k; 2Lg + 22, \frac{e^{-\frac{2vg}{(1-\delta)(1+\overline{T}/n)}}}{2^{2g-2}}). \tag{12}$$

All in all, the expected entropy bits gained by the adversary in IBD-targeting fragmentation, denoted as $H'(g)_2$, can be calculated as

$$H'(g)_2 = h(g)\big(1 - \sum_{k=0}^{t-1} B\left(k; R, Pr(shared) \cdot Pr(match|g)_2\right)\big). \tag{13}$$

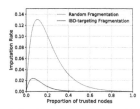
(a) Genotype imputation in both strategies

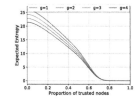
(b) Entropy reduction in random strategy

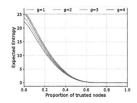
(c) Entropy reduction in IBD-targeting strategy

Fig. 4. Information leakage reduction.

Quantifying Information Leakage Reduction. We first explore the capacity of genotype imputation in both random and IBD-targeting fragmentation strategies according to Inequality 7. Our quantification is based on the 1000 Genomes Project dataset (Phase 3) [2] - a widely used reference dataset for genotype imputation; we set $K = 2,504$ which is the sample size of the dataset, and set ρ to 0.85 in the random strategy and 0.5 in the IBD-targeting strategy according to Das et al. [7]. As shown in Fig. 4a, the capacity of genotype imputation in the random strategy is lower than that in the IBD-targeting strategy. This is because the latter, which deliberately splits the IBD segments, further increases the genetic distance such that the upper bound of $\overline{T}$ (Inequality 7) is decreased. It also can be found that the imputation rate rises faster in the random strategy when the adversary controls $\geq 90\%$ nodes ($0 \leq \delta \leq 10\%$), with less missing genotypes in the IBD regions. However, with the further growth of trusted nodes, the imputation rate exponentially decreases in both strategies.

Next, we evaluate the privacy preservation in υFRAG. We keep the same setting of population size (329 million) and $\gamma = 2.5$. In addition, we fix the dataset size as 30% of the target population, as this gives the adversary an advantage according to Fig. 3. The genotype imputation is considered in our evaluation by incorporating the imputation rate into Eq. 10 and Eq. 13 respectively. As shown in Fig. 4b and 4c, with the growth of trusted nodes, the expected entropy bits achieved by the attack rapidly decreases. When the network reaches 20% honest nodes, the expected entropy bits gained by the attack reduce to 17.96 and 11.26 in random fragmentation strategy and IBD-targeting fragmentation strategy respectively. When the network reaches an honest majority ($\delta \geq 0.5$), the attack can achieve only 8.95 bits of entropy in random fragmentation, and 1.14 bits of entropy in IBD-targeting fragmentation. In other words, the uncertainty for the attack to identify an individual remains 19.25 bits (28.2–8.95) and 27.06 bits (28.2–1.14), which equals to a random guess among 623,487 people and 139.9 million people respectively.

5.2 The Individual-Level Analysis

We define ϵ-*indistinguishability* to evaluate the privacy preservation from the level of indistinguishability of individual data items.

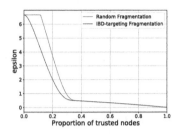

Fig. 5. ϵ-indistinguishability in both strategies

Definition 3 *(ϵ-Indistinguishability). Let ϵ be a positive real number and $\mathcal{G}$ be a randomized algorithm that processes dataset X and $\mathcal{D}$. The algorithm $\mathcal{G}$ is said to provide ϵ-indistinguishability if for data items $d_1, d_2 \in \mathcal{D}$ and $x \subseteq Range(\mathcal{G}(X))$*

$$Pr(\mathcal{G}(d_1) = x) \leq e^\epsilon Pr(\mathcal{G}(d_2) = x). \tag{14}$$

As is shown, the definition of ϵ-indistinguishability is essentially a variant of ϵ-local differential privacy (LDP), which is yet a variant model of differential privacy with added restriction to the indistinguishability of individual data items [6,10]. The difference is that, the indistinguishability in our model is measured from the *adversarial view*, i.e., the outputs space of $\mathcal{G}$ on individual data items from the two datasets accessible by the adversary (referring to fragments produced by $\mathcal{G}(X)$ and the public dataset $\mathcal{D}$), whereas the indistinguishability in the original LDP is measured directly on the output space of $\mathcal{G}$ on individual data items.

Let AF_i be the allele frequency of the ith SNP, d denote the number of SNPs from the target that the adversary is able to access, and $\mathcal{D}$ denote the dataset comprised of R genotyped individuals. The following theorem states that our *mask operation* $\odot$ makes vFRAG satisfy ϵ-indistinguishability.

Theorem 2. *The vertical fragmentation makes vFRAG satisfy ϵ-indistinguishability where $\epsilon = \ln((1 - \sum\limits_{k=0}^{1} B(k, R, \prod\limits_{i=1}^{d} AF_i))^{-1})$.*

Proof. Assume the adversary is able to access $\boldsymbol{x} \in \{A, T, C, G\}^d$, which is a randomized output generated by the mask operation $\odot$ for vertical fragmentation in vFRAG. The probability of observing at least t times of $\boldsymbol{x}$ in the dataset $\mathcal{D}$ of size R is $(1 - \sum\limits_{k=0}^{t} B(k, R, Pr(\boldsymbol{x}|\mathcal{D})))$, where $Pr(\boldsymbol{x}|\mathcal{D}) = \prod\limits_{i=1}^{d} Pr(\boldsymbol{x}_i|\mathcal{D}) = \prod\limits_{i=1}^{d} AF_i$.

Then, $\frac{Pr[(d_1 \odot Mask) = \boldsymbol{x}]}{Pr[(d_2 \odot Mask) = \boldsymbol{x}]} = \frac{1 - \sum\limits_{k=0}^{1} B(k, R, Pr(\boldsymbol{x}|d_1))}{1 - \sum\limits_{k=0}^{1} B(k, R, Pr(\boldsymbol{x}|d_2))} \leq \frac{1}{1 - \sum\limits_{k=0}^{1} B(k, R, \prod\limits_{i=1}^{d} AF_i)}$. Thus, we

have $\epsilon = \ln((1 - \sum\limits_{k=0}^{1} B(k, R, \prod\limits_{i=1}^{d} AF_i))^{-1})$.

We explore the privacy level ϵ each strategy can achieve. We keep the same setting of the dataset size, i.e., 30% of the target population, and set the number of SNPs in the genome-wide analysis as 5,000. As reported in 1000 Genomes Project, the majority of variants in the human genome have a minor allele frequency $< 0.5\%$ [2], we take the upper bound of the minor allele frequency 0.5% and set the $\bar{AF} = 99.5\%$ in the evaluation. This gives the adversary more advantage as $\bar{AF}$ in the real world can be even larger than in this setting. The parameter d, which is the number of SNPs obtained by the adversary, is set after the adversary has applied genotype imputation.

Figure 5 shows the privacy parameter ϵ against the proportion of the trusted nodes in both strategies. vFRAG can achieves $\epsilon = 3.72$ and $\epsilon = 2.02$ in the random and IBD-targeting strategies respectively, when the adversary controls 80% of the nodes ($\delta = 0.2$). When the network reaches an honest majority, ϵ is reduced to 0.406 and 0.405 respectively. As the definition of ϵ-indistinguishability is adopted from LDP, we demonstrate a comparable privacy gain with that of the state-of-the-art systems achieving LDP, such as Apple's DP framework with $\epsilon = \{2, 4, 8\}$ [6] and Google's RAPPOR with $\epsilon = ln(3)$ [10].

6   Performance Evaluation

We implement vFRAG in C++. It uses the Eigen library [11] to handle matrix operations, and ZeroMQ library [15] for distributed messaging. Our experiments use the 1000 Genomes Project dataset [2], which is a public dataset providing a comprehensive description of human genetic variation. The experiments are conducted on 62,042 SNPs on Y-chromosome from 1,233 male samples.

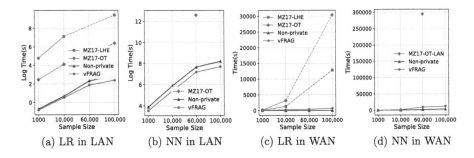

(a) LR in LAN   (b) NN in LAN   (c) LR in WAN   (d) NN in WAN

Fig. 6. Efficiency comparison with the baseline and MPC/HE solutions.

To be representative, vFRAG is executed on both LAN and WAN network settings. The LAN setting captures the scenario where two or more institutions collaboratively execute computations on their own private inputs. In such scenario, the involved parties usually communicate over fast dedicated links. In our experiments, the average network bandwidth is set as 1 GB/s. The WAN setting, on the other hand, simulates a scenario where individual participants share their

Table 1. Comparison with DP solution ($m = 32661, n = 124$).

	FDML	vFRAG-LAN
Linear regression	99 s	0.76 s
Neural network	110 s	139.53 s

Table 2. Overhead breakdown of linear regression and neural network ($n = 784$).

	Linear regression			Neural network		
	Computation	Communication		Computation	Communication	
		LAN	WAN		LAN	WAN
m = 1,000	0.4 s	0.0085 s	44.9 s	37.6 s	3.8 s	395.2 s
m = 10,000	1.2 s	0.5 s	264.4 s	225.9 s	1.6 s	1395.2 s
m = 60,000	5.7 s	0.8 s	402.9 s	1312.7 s	15.1 s	8143.9 s
m = 100,000	9.5 s	1.5 s	681.3 s	2167.9 s	23.2 s	10140.6 s

genomic data over public network infrastructure. The average network latency (one-way) is set as 183.19 ms, and the average throughput is 8.75 MB/s.

We take the performance of traditional non-privacy-preserving frameworks as the baseline, given that it is the most common practice in existing genome-wide analysis. We also show the performance of other existing privacy-preserving mechanisms, including cryptographic based methods (MZ17 [22]) and differential privacy mechanisms (FDML [16]). MZ17 considers MPC/HE solutions for privacy preserving machine learning algorithms based on oblivious transfer (OT) and linearly homomorphic encryption (LHE), and FDML is a state-of-the-art additive noise based DP framework which also employs in the scenario of distributed features, the same as vFRAG.

Figure 6 and Table 1 summarize our efficiency comparison with the baseline, MZ17, and FDML respectively. Table 2 lists the overhead breakdown to computation and communication. Generally, vFRAG significantly outperforms the MPC/HE solutions, and also outperforms the baseline and the state-of-the-art DP solution in most settings.

LR. We follow the same experimental settings as [22] (including machine specifications, network settings, and batch/epoch sizes). As shown in Fig. 6, vFRAG significantly outperforms MZ17, and even faster than the baseline in the LAN setting. For example, vFRAG takes 10.93 s with sample size $m = 100,000$ (Fig. 6a), while it takes 594.95 s in MZ17-OT and 17.21s in the baseline. In the WAN setting (Fig. 6c), vFRAG achieves 690.74 s with $m = 100,000$. It is 19x faster than the MPC solutions in MZ17-LHE, which takes 12,841.2 s with the same sample size. vFRAG also outperforms FDML (Table 1), due to the significant savings on the computational cost compared with the additive noise mechanism.

NN. We implement a fully connected NN with a sigmoid function as the activation function. It has the same structure as that in MZ17. In the LAN setting (Fig. 6b), vFRAG achieves 1,327.72 s (22.1 min) with sample size $m = 60,000$, while MZ17-OT takes 294,239.7 s (more than 81 h)[5]. In the WAN setting (Fig. 6d), our framework still remains practical. It achieves 9,456.53 s with sample size $m = 60,000$. In contrast, it is not yet practical for MZ17 to train NN in the WAN setting due to the massiveness of interaction and communication. We also plot the MZ17-OT-LAN result (294,239.7 s) in Fig. 6d. It can be found that even when running our framework in the WAN setting, vFRAG is still much more efficient than the MPC solutions in MZ17 running on the LAN setting.

In comparison with the DP solution, vFRAG NN achieves similar performance with FDML (Table 1). We note that FDML NN only considers a fully connected NN *within* each worker node while merging the local predictions in a composite model, whereas vFRAG uses a fully connected NN over *all* the features, thus leading to a more complex model.

Overhead Analysis. Computation overhead of vFRAG is in line with its complexity of $\mathcal{O}(d_l m)$ (where d_l and m are the number of SNPs and samples in X^l respectively), and communication cost is in linear with $\mathcal{O}(d_l m s)$ (where s is the number of local nodes). More nodes lead to a smaller d_l but a larger s. The memory consumption of vFRAG, same as its centralized counterpart, is only related to the size of X and weight W.

7   Discussion

Our privacy analysis (Sect. 5) is conducted under a trustworthy aggregator. In this section, we explore the impact of a compromised aggregator.

The aggregator in vFRAG has access to only the intermediate results but none of any local data. According to the derivation in our previous work [37] (refer to its Theorem 1), the overall knowledge of the aggregator can obtain is $\{X^l W^l, X^l (X^l)^T\}$, where $X^l W^l$ is the aggregator's own input, and $X^l (X^l)^T$ is the additional information that can be inferred from the training iterations. We then quantify the impact of colluding parties including the compromised aggregator. Given the knowledge of $\{X^l W^l, X^l (X^l)^T\}$, the probability of computing the original input X^l or W^l, is not greater than $1/(r!)$, where r is the rank of X^l (refer to Theorem 2 of [37]). Since X^l is a matrix of m samples with d_l SNPs, the rank r of X^l is the number of unique DNA sequence in X^l. We can formulate the probability of the number of duplicated sequence being no more than K, i.e., the rank $r > (d_l - K)$, as $Pr(r > (d_l - K)) = \sum_{k=0}^{K} B(k; d_l, (1 - \bar{AF})^{d_l})$, where $\bar{AF}$ denotes the expected allele frequency, and $(1 - \bar{AF})^{d_l}$ is the probability of a DNA sequence being identical to the reference genome.

With it, we can estimate the probability of the attacker deriving X^l or W^l, given d_l. We let $\bar{AF} = 0.00397$ as reported in the 1000 Genomes Project dataset

---

[5] Only the performance with $m = 60,000$ in the LAN setting is reported in [22].

[2]. When d_l exceeds 120, which is common in real-world genome-wide analysis datasets, the probability of $r > 32$ (i.e., the probability of deriving X^l or W^l being less than $1/(32!)$) is 0.9965. This implies that it is unlikely for the compromised aggregator to derive the original data of honest parties.

8 Related Work

In this section, we summarize existing privacy-preserving techniques which can be divided into the following categories.

Cryptographic Solutions. Cryptographic solutions, such as HE and MPC [5, 17,22,38], enable computation without disclosing data in plaintext. Several studies have been conducted to enable multiple entities to train machine learning models with privacy preservation over the input data. For example, Wan et al. [13] proposes a MPC-based solution for privacy-preserving gradient descent. In [36], a secure protocol is presented to calculate the delta function in the back-propagation training.

Differential Privacy. DP is another methodology that constitutes a strong standard for privacy guarantees for algorithms on aggregate databases [3,16,39]. Several studies have explored the differentially private release of common summary statistics of GWAS data (such as the allele frequencies of cases and controls, χ^2-statistic and P values [35,40]) or shifting the original locations of variants [19]. Recently, a study proposes a novel differential privacy mechanism named SVT^2 for mitigating membership inference attacks against DNA methylation data [12]. Recently, Hartmann et al. [14] proposes a noise-based DP framework which provides differential privacy with very small noise addition by adding and canceling noise among clients.

Distributed Deep Learning Framework. Our work is related to but different from distributed deep learning frameworks [33]. Existing work focuses either on the reduction of the training time of deep neural network models [29], or on the theoretical convergence speed in the distributed computing environment [20].

9 Conclusion

In this paper, we presented υFRAG, a privacy preserving framework for distributed genome-wide analysis. υFRAG mitigates privacy risks by using a vertical DNA sequence fragmentation to disrupt the genetic architecture on which the adversary relies for re-identification. We demonstrated the privacy preservation of υFRAG from both collection level (overall information leakage reduction) and individual level (indistinguishability among individuals). Our experiments on large-scale datasets showed that υFRAG outperforms state-of-the-art cryptography-based with a speedup of more than 221x for training neural networks. Our work sheds a light on the privacy preservation in genome-wide analysis. For sequential data (like DNA sequences), disrupting the order and location dependency could be a promising solution.

Acknowledgment. We thank our shepherd Erman Ayday and the anonymous reviewers for their insightful comments to improve this manuscript. This work is partly supported by the University of Queensland under the UQ Cyber Initiative Strategic Research Seed Funding 4018264-01-299-21-618071.

Appendix A   Notation Table

Table 3 summarizes the notations defined in this paper.

Table 3. Notation table

Notation	Domain	Explanation	Notation	Domain	Explanation
SNP	/	Single-nucleotide polymorphism	γ	$\mathbb{R}$	Mean value of children per couple
X	$\mathbb{S}^{m \times n}$	Centralized training dataset	ρ	$\mathbb{R}$	Transition probability in HMM
W	$\mathbb{R}^{n \times H}$	Centralized coefficient matrix	N	$\mathbb{Z}$	Size of a general population
x_{ij}	$\mathbb{S}$	Genotype of jth SNP of ith sample	$\overline{T}$	$\mathbb{R}$	Expected value of imputation accuracy
X^l	$\mathbb{S}^{m \times d_l}$	Vertical partition of X	τ	$\mathbb{Z}$	The number of missing genotypes
W^l	$\mathbb{R}^{d_l \times H}$	Coefficient matrix associated with X^l	R	$\mathbb{Z}$	Size of the public dataset
S^l, A	$\mathbb{Z}$	Worker node and aggregation node	K	$\mathbb{Z}$	Size of the reference haplotypes panel
δ	$\mathbb{R}$	Proportion of trusted worker nodes	$(M)AF$	$\mathbb{R}$	(Minor) allele frequency
g	$\mathbb{Z}$	Degree of genetic relatives	ϵ	$\mathbb{R}$	Privacy parameter
J, σ	/	Cost function and hypothesis function	$\odot$	/	*Mask* operation
Δ	$\mathbb{R}^{m \times H}$	Gradient of J w.r.t XW	$B()$	/	PMF of binomial distribution

Appendix B   Functionalities in Genome-Wide Analysis

In this section, we briefly introduce the functionalities commonly used in the analysis.

Summary Statistics. Summary statistics are used to summarize the observations on the genome-wide data. Commonly used summary statistics include the missingness statistics ($U_{i,miss}/n$, where $U_{i,miss}$ is the number of missing SNPs of ith sample), allele frequency ($c/2m$, where c is the total number of allele for each SNP), and Hardy-Weinberg equilibrium ($\{(p^2 + 2pq + q^2 == 1)\}$, where p^2 is the frequency of homozygous dominant genotype, pq is the frequency of heterozygous genotype, and q^2 is the frequency of homozygous recessive genotype) [21].

Basic Association Analysis. The basic association analysis for GWAS checks on any particular SNP. If one type of the variant (i.e., one allele) is more frequent in individuals with a disease, the variant is said to be associated with the disease. Commonly used statistics include standard χ^2 test and the Cochran-Armitage test, which performs the tests with respect to each SNP.

Genetic Relationship Matrix (GRM). GRM is developed for addressing the *missing heritability* problem by estimating the variance explained by all the SNPs on a chromosome or on the whole genome for a complex trait [34]. The genetic relationship between individuals β and ζ can be estimated by $\frac{1}{n}\sum_{i=1}^{n}\frac{(x_{\beta i}-2p_i)(x_{\zeta i}-2p_i)}{2p_i(1-p_i)}$, where $x_{\beta i}$ is the genotype of ith SNP of βth individual, and p_i is the frequency of the reference allele.

Classification Models Such as Neural Networks. Machine/deep learning algorithms, such as various NNs, are commonly used in genome-wide analysis. For example, they can be used to fit the effects of all the SNPs as random effects to estimate the total amount of phenotypic variance [34], or applied in genotype clustering and ethnicity prediction [4].

The former three functionalities are relatively simple to parallelize than machine learning algorithms, as the statistics with respect to each SNP can directly apply on the vertically partitioned dataset. Therefore, in this work, we focused on the latter.

References

1. vFrag. https://sites.google.com/view/vfrag
2. 1000 Genomes Project Consortium: A global reference for human genetic variation. Nature **526**(7571), 68 (2015)
3. Abadi, M., et al.: Deep learning with differential privacy. In: Proceedings of the 2016 ACM SIGSAC Conference on Computer and Communications Security, pp. 308–318. ACM (2016)
4. Angermueller, C., Pärnamaa, T., Parts, L., Stegle, O.: Deep learning for computational biology. Mol. Syst. Biol. **12**(7), 878 (2016)
5. Bogdanov, D., Kamm, L., Laur, S., Sokk, V.: RMIND: a tool for cryptographically secure statistical analysis. IEEE Trans. Dependable Secure Comput. **15**, 481–495 (2016)
6. Cormode, G., Jha, S., Kulkarni, T., Li, N., Srivastava, D., Wang, T.: Privacy at scale: local differential privacy in practice. In: Proceedings of the 2018 International Conference on Management of Data, pp. 1655–1658 (2018)
7. Das, S., et al.: Next-generation genotype imputation service and methods. Nat. Genet. **48**(10), 1284–1287 (2016)

8. Erlich, Y., Narayanan, A.: Routes for breaching and protecting genetic privacy. Nat. Rev. Genet. **15**(6), 409 (2014)
9. Erlich, Y., Shor, T., Pe'er, I., Carmi, S.: Identity inference of genomic data using long-range familial searches. Science **362**(6415), 690–694 (2018)
10. Erlingsson, Ú., Pihur, V., Korolova, A.: Rappor: randomized aggregatable privacy-preserving ordinal response. In: Proceedings of the 2014 ACM SIGSAC Conference on Computer and Communications Security, pp. 1054–1067. ACM (2014)
11. Guennebaud, G., Jacob, B., et al.: Eigen v3 (2010). http://eigen.tuxfamily.org
12. Hagestedt, I., et al.: MBeacon: privacy-preserving beacons for DNA methylation data. In: NDSS (2019)
13. Han, S., Ng, W.K., Wan, L., Lee, V.C.: Privacy-preserving gradient-descent methods. IEEE Trans. Knowl. Data Eng. **22**(6), 884–899 (2009)
14. Hartmann, V., West, R.: Privacy-preserving distributed learning with secret gradient descent. arXiv preprint arXiv:1906.11993 (2019)
15. Hintjens, P.: ZeroMQ: Messaging for Many Applications. O'Reilly Media Inc., Sebastopol (2013)
16. Hu, Y., Niu, D., Yang, J., Zhou, S.: FDML: a collaborative machine learning framework for distributed features. In: Proceedings of the 25th ACM SIGKDD International Conference on Knowledge Discovery & Data Mining, pp. 2232–2240 (2019)
17. Jagadeesh, K.A., Wu, D.J., Birgmeier, J.A., Boneh, D., Bejerano, G.: Deriving genomic diagnoses without revealing patient genomes. Science **357**(6352), 692–695 (2017)
18. Jia, J., Salem, A., Backes, M., Zhang, Y., Gong, N.Z.: MemGuard: defending against black-box membership inference attacks via adversarial examples. In: Proceedings of the 2019 ACM SIGSAC Conference on Computer and Communications Security, pp. 259–274 (2019)
19. Johnson, A., Shmatikov, V.: Privacy-preserving data exploration in genome-wide association studies. In: Proceedings of the 19th ACM SIGKDD International Conference on Knowledge Discovery and Data Mining, pp. 1079–1087. ACM (2013)
20. Lian, X., Huang, Y., Li, Y., Liu, J.: Asynchronous parallel stochastic gradient for nonconvex optimization. In: Advances in Neural Information Processing Systems, pp. 2737–2745 (2015)
21. Marees, A.T., et al.: A tutorial on conducting genome-wide association studies: quality control and statistical analysis. Int. J. Methods Psychiatric Res. **27**(2), e1608 (2018)
22. Mohassel, P., Zhang, Y.: SecureML: a system for scalable privacy-preserving machine learning. In: 2017 IEEE Symposium on Security and Privacy (SP), pp. 19–38. IEEE (2017)
23. Ralph, P., Coop, G.: The geography of recent genetic ancestry across Europe. PLoS Biol. **11**(5), e1001555 (2013)
24. Regalado, A.: MIT technology review. https://www.technologyreview.com/2019/02/11/103446/more-than-26-million-people-have-taken-an-at-home-ancestry-test/
25. Salem, A., Zhang, Y., Humbert, M., Berrang, P., Fritz, M., Backes, M.: ML-Leaks: model and data independent membership inference attacks and defenses on machine learning models. arXiv preprint arXiv:1806.01246 (2018)
26. Timpson, N.J., Greenwood, C.M., Soranzo, N., Lawson, D.J., Richards, J.B.: Genetic architecture: the shape of the genetic contribution to human traits and disease. Nat. Rev. Genet. **19**(2), 110 (2018)
27. Visscher, P.M., et al.: 10 years of GWAS discovery: biology, function, and translation. Am. J. Human Genet. **101**(1), 5–22 (2017)

28. Wang, K., Zhang, J., Bai, G., Ko, R., Dong, J.S.: It's not just the site, it's the contents: intra-domain fingerprinting social media websites through CDN bursts. In: Proceedings of the Web Conference 2021, pp. 2142–2153 (2021)
29. Wang, S., Pi, A., Zhou, X.: Scalable distributed DL training: batching communication and computation. In: Proceedings of AAAI (2019)
30. Wang, S., et al.: HEALER: homomorphic computation of exact logistic regression for secure rare disease variants analysis in GWAS. Bioinformatics **32**(2), 211–218 (2015)
31. Wang, Y., Huang, Z., Mitra, S., Dullerud, G.E.: Differential privacy in linear distributed control systems: entropy minimizing mechanisms and performance trade-offs. IEEE Trans. Control Netw. Syst. **4**(1), 118–130 (2017)
32. Wang, Y.-X., Lei, J., Fienberg, S.E.: On-average KL-privacy and its equivalence to generalization for max-entropy mechanisms. In: Domingo-Ferrer, J., Pejić-Bach, M. (eds.) PSD 2016. LNCS, vol. 9867, pp. 121–134. Springer, Cham (2016). https://doi.org/10.1007/978-3-319-45381-1_10
33. Xing, E.P., Ho, Q., Xie, P., Wei, D.: Strategies and principles of distributed machine learning on big data. Engineering **2**(2), 179–195 (2016)
34. Yang, J., Lee, S.H., Goddard, M.E., Visscher, P.M.: GCTA: a tool for genome-wide complex trait analysis. Am. J. Human Genet. **88**(1), 76–82 (2011)
35. Yu, F., Fienberg, S.E., Slavković, A.B., Uhler, C.: Scalable privacy preserving data sharing methodology for genome-wide association studies. J. Biomed. Inform. **50**, 133–141 (2014)
36. Yuan, J., Yu, S.: Privacy preserving back-propagation neural network learning made practical with cloud computing. IEEE Trans. Parallel Distrib. Syst. **25**(1), 212–221 (2014)
37. Zhang, Y., Bai, G., Li, X., Curtis, C., Chen, C., Ko, R.K.L.: PrivColl: practical privacy-preserving collaborative machine learning. In: Chen, L., Li, N., Liang, K., Schneider, S. (eds.) ESORICS 2020. LNCS, vol. 12308, pp. 399–418. Springer, Cham (2020). https://doi.org/10.1007/978-3-030-58951-6_20
38. Zhang, Y., Bai, G., Li, X., Nepal, S., Ko, R.K.: Confined gradient descent: Privacy-preserving optimization for federated learning. arXiv preprint arXiv:2104.13050 (2021)
39. Zhang, Y., Bai, G., Zhong, M., Li, X., Ko, R.: Differentially private collaborative coupling learning for recommender systems. IEEE Intell. Syst. **36**, 16–24 (2020)
40. Zhang, Y., Zhao, X., Li, X., Zhong, M., Curtis, C., Chen, C.: Enabling privacy-preserving sharing of genomic data for GWASs in decentralized networks. In: Proceedings of the Twelfth ACM International Conference on Web Search and Data Mining, pp. 204–212. ACM (2019)

Privug: Using Probabilistic Programming for Quantifying Leakage in Privacy Risk Analysis

Raúl Pardo[1(✉)], Willard Rafnsson[1], Christian W. Probst[2], and Andrzej Wąsowski[1]

[1] IT University of Copenhagen, Copenhagen, Denmark
{raup,wilr,wasowski}@itu.dk
[2] Unitec Institute of Technology, Auckland, New Zealand
cprobst@unitec.ac.nz

Abstract. Disclosure of data analytics results has important scientific and commercial justifications. However, no data shall be disclosed without a diligent investigation of risks for privacy of subjects. PRIVUG is a tool-supported method to explore information leakage properties of data analytics and anonymization programs. In PRIVUG, we reinterpret a program probabilistically, using off-the-shelf tools for Bayesian inference to perform information-theoretic analysis of the information flow. For privacy researchers, PRIVUG provides a fast, lightweight way to experiment with privacy protection measures and mechanisms. We show that PRIVUG is accurate, scalable, and applicable to a range of leakage analysis scenarios.

1 Introduction

However high the value of data becomes, we cannot ignore the risks that data disclosure presents to personal privacy. Consequently, general privacy protection methods like differential privacy [18], comprehensibility and communication of privacy issues [32], industrial processes for data management [22], and debugging and analyzing privacy risk problems in program code [9,11,12] have become intensive areas of research. This paper falls into this last group; we present tools for data scientists who create data analysis programs and would like to disclose the results of the computation. Our primary goal is to create a method that supports a *privacy debugging process*, *i.e.* assessing effectiveness of such algorithms, and indeed of any calculations on the data, for concrete programs and datasets, in the style of debuggers. We want to help *identifying* and *explaining* the leakage risks, as the first step towards eliminating them.

As an example, consider the following Scala program that, given a list of names and ages, computes the mean age of the persons in a map-reduce style:

Work partially supported by the Danish Villum Foundation through Villum Experiment project No. 00023028 and New Zealand Ministry of Business, Innovation and Employment – Hīkina Whakatutuki through Smart Ideas project No. UNIT1902.

© Springer Nature Switzerland AG 2021
E. Bertino et al. (Eds.): ESORICS 2021, LNCS 12973, pp. 417–438, 2021.
https://doi.org/10.1007/978-3-030-88428-4_21

```
1 def agg (records: List[(String,Double)]): Double =
2   records.map    { (n, a) => (a, 1) }
3         .reduce { (x, y) => (x._1 + y._1, x._2 + y._2) }
4         .map    { (sum, count) => sum / count }
```

Let the age of each individual be the sensitive secret in this example. One attack could be that underage individuals can be identified. An analyst would like to ask: How much of sensitive information leaks when the mean is disclosed? In what situations is this leak not ignorable? What kind of attackers may discover the secret by observing the mean?

PRIVUG is an analysis method for privacy risks in data processing. A data analyst using PRIVUG models an attacker's knowledge about the secret as a probability distribution. PRIVUG re-interprets the program as an information transformer that operates on distributions instead of concrete inputs. The analyst analyzes the attacker's confidence about the secret, using a combination of probability queries, standard information-theoretic measures, and visualizations. She explores and assesses the information leakage to the result of the program by varying attacker knowledge, the queries and the leakage measures. For our example, the analyst may learn that the leakage is ignorable if the subjects are drawn from general population, but if the attacker knows that they come from a homogeneous group, she could, for example, conclude that a specific individual is under age.

Since PRIVUG is based on probabilistic reasoning, it can be facilitated by *probabilistic programming*, a lively field in data science, with many tools available. PRIVUG is not tied to any particular probabilistic programming framework. In this paper, we implement queries, measures, and visualization in Figaro [35] and PyMC3 [40]. For programs seen as functions, a probabilistic programming framework can automatically build a Bayesian model which represents the information transform. This transform supplemented by a model of attacker can be used to explore re-identification risks [14].

PRIVUG offers three distinct advantages over state of the art tools for privacy risk analysis: (i) It focuses on the analysis of programs not data, which means that a what-if analysis can be performed before data is available, or without authorizing access to a sensitive database. (ii) It is largely automatable using off-the-shelf systematic Monte-Carlo inference tools already used by data analysts, but which have not been used for this purpose before. (iii) PRIVUG is easy to extend with new estimators of leakage thus serves as a good test-bed for privacy mechanism research. To the best of our knowledge, PRIVUG as a method and probabilistic programming as a platform are the only basis that can offer such versatility at this point. Our contributions include:

1. A widely applicable and extensible method, PRIVUG, to analyze privacy risks. The first such method based on probabilistic programming frameworks.
2. An implementation of PRIVUG in Figaro and PyMC3, the first versatile tool supporting such a wide range of measures over continuous and discrete inputs and outputs.

name	zip	birthday	sex	diag.
Alice	2300	15.06.1954	F	ill
Bob	2305	15.06.1954	M	healthy
Carol	2300	09.10.1925	F	healthy
Dave	2310	01.01.2000	M	ill

$\xrightarrow{\text{ano}}$

zip	birthday	sex	diag.
2300	**15.06.1954**	**F**	ill
2305	15.06.1954	M	healthy
2300	09.10.1925	F	healthy
2310	01.01.2000	M	ill

zip	birthday	sex	diag.
2300	**15.06.1954**	**F**	ill
2305	15.06.1954	M	healthy
2300	09.10.1925	F	healthy
2310	01.01.2000	M	ill

$\oplus$

name	zip	birthday	sex
Mark	2450	30.09.1977	M
Rose	2870	24.12.1985	F
Alice	**2300**	**15.06.1954**	**F**
Dave	2310	01.01.2000	M

$\rightsquigarrow$ Alice is ill

Fig. 1. Privacy violation: the data is anonymized (ano), then the diagnosis of Alice is recovered by an attacker who links the result with another data set ($\oplus$).

name	age
Alice	42
Bob	25
Carol	25
Dave	25

$\xrightarrow{\text{agg}}$ 29.25 $\oplus$

name	age
Alice	$\mathcal{N}(40,3)$
Bob	$\mathcal{N}(23,10)$
Carol	$\mathcal{N}(23,10)$
Dave	$\mathcal{N}(23,10)$

$\rightsquigarrow$ Alice's age is $\mathcal{N}(41,2.5)$

Fig. 2. Privacy violation: the program computes a mean of ages, the mean is released, but an attacker with prior knowledge can reduce the uncertainty regarding Alice's age.

3. An empirical evaluation of the accuracy, scalability, and applicability of PRIVUG for analyzing systems of different size and complexity, showing that probabilistic programming is an excellent base for implementing leakage analysis tools.

We evaluate applicability, accuracy, and scalability of PRIVUG, using well known privacy mechanisms (differential privacy, k-anonymity, naive anonymization) and synthetic cases that can be scaled up for higher dimensionality and using. Our experiments demonstrate PRIVUG's versatility to realize many analysis scenarios, and its interoperability with existing tools (by integrating external estimators). The source code and experiment data is available at https://bitbucket.org/itu-square/privug-experiments. The repository contains additional experiments showing the use of PRIVUG in a realistic case study: an experiment using the differential privacy library OpenDP (https://opendp.org/).

2 Overview

We consider data disclosure programs seen as functions that transform an input dataset to an output. The output is then disclosed to a third party, called an attacker. The aggregation example `agg` from the introduction translates a database with two columns: name (`String`) and age (`Double`) to a number representing mean age which is then published. The second running example, `ano`, *anonymizes* medical records in a dataset. The input data has five columns: name, zip code, birthday, sex, and diagnosis. The program simply drops the name column, before the data is released to an attacker:

```
1 def ano (records: List[(Name,Zip,Day,Sex,Diag)]): List[(Zip,Day,Sex,Diag)] =
2   records.map { (n, z, b, s, d) => (z, b, s, d) }
```

Suppose that in the anonymization example, subjects have not consented to disclosure of their diagnosis. Despite anonymization, the diagnosis of individuals may be revealed by a *linking attack* (see Fig. 1). If an attacker has access to a dataset with zip codes, birthdays, sex, and, crucially, names, a simple join could reveal the names of the individuals from the disclosed medical records. Zip code, birthday, and sex form a quasi-identifier in both datasets. (Sweeney famously joined medical records disclosed by the Group Insurance Commission with a voter registration list to reveal the health record data of the then-governor of Massachusetts [42].) Similarly, suppose that in the aggregation example (`agg`) users have not consented that their age is disclosed. Despite the disclosed data being an aggregate, it carries some information about individual ages. If you knew that Alice is around 40, as modeled by a Normal distribution in Fig. 2, then after learning the average, your uncertainty decreases: the final mean age raises, and the standard deviation decreases, making extreme values of Alice's age less likely.

PRIVUG aims to help data scientists investigate the information revealed to an attacker from the output of a program. We frame this scenario as an adversarial problem. We assume a *threat model* in which an information theoretical attacker has some prior knowledge about the input, has access to the program code, and observes the output. There are no bounds on the computational resources available to the attacker when analyzing the posterior knowledge to learn information about the secret input, e.g., probability of an outcome or event.

We model this scenario using probabilistic programming. First, we build a probabilistic model of the *prior knowledge* of the attacker. Intuitively, the prior of the attacker captures what she knows, with (un)certainty, about the input of the program before observing the output. We then express the attacker's view of the program, by transforming the program to operate on probabilistic models of datasets instead of actual data. We do this by lifting the algorithm into the probability monad [36]. Next, we introduce *observations* modeling the concrete output of the program that the attacker sees. Observations constrain the prior of the attacker and produce the *posterior knowledge* of the attacker, *i.e.*, what the attacker knows about the input. We use Bayesian inference to estimate the posterior, Figaro for Scala [35] and PyMC3 [40] for Python, but many other probabilistic frameworks can be used (Pyro [3], Tensorflow Probability [17], Anglican [43], etc.). Finally, we *analyze* the posterior to quantify how much the attacker learns by observing the output. This lets us determine whether specific attackers are capable of learning specific things, to assess the risk of disclosing the output of the program.

3 PRIVUG

We present each step of the PRIVUG method in detail. We model disclosure problems probabilistically and express models directly in a probabilistic programming language to enable automatic analysis. Let $D(X)$ denote a distribution over a set X. We write $x \sim D(X)$ to denote that random variable x is distributed according to $D(X)$; thus $x \sim \mathcal{U}(0, 10)$ means that x is uniformly distributed from 0 to 10. In a programming language, this corresponds to x = Uniform(0,10). We also use composition operators of the language to define y in terms of x, define a distribution over datasets, and so on.

Step 1: Attacker Knowledge (Prior). We model the prior knowledge of an attacker as a probability distribution over the possible input values of the program. In the agg program the input ranges over an array of pairs (name,age). Therefore, attacker prior knowledge is defined as a distribution over lists of pairs, $D(\text{List}[(\text{String},\text{Double})])$. Consider the following two examples of attackers:

k_{al} The *knows-a-lot* attacker knows that the input dataset contains exactly four rows and that the age of all individuals, except Alice, is 55.2. This is modeled by distributions $\mathcal{C}(4)$ for the size and $\mathcal{C}(55.2)$ for the age column.

k_{ab} The *knows-just-a-bit* attacker knows that the input has approximately hundred entries ($|records| \sim \mathcal{B}(300, 1/3)$, a binomial distribution), and that the average age of an individual in the list is 55 (distributed with $\mathcal{N}(55.2, 3.5)$).

Both attackers know that Alice's record is in the dataset, and that no other record in the dataset has that name. They do not know anything about Alice's age upfront: all ages from 0 to 100 are equally likely, a uniform distribution $\mathcal{U}(0, 100)$. Implementations of k_{al} and k_{ab} are shown below, the differences highlighted in bold. Here, Element[T] denotes a distribution over T, and FixedSizeArrayElement[T] denotes a distribution over fixed-but-unknown-size arrays of Ts. When sampled, k_{ab} yields an array of random size, containing (String,Double) pairs. The first pair represents Alice.

```
1  def prior_kal: FixedSizeArrayElement[(String,Double)] =
2    VariableSizeArray (Constant (4), i => for
3      n <- if i==0 then Constant ("Alice") else Uniform (names: _*)
4      a <- if i==0 then Uniform (0,100) else Constant (55.2)
5    yield (n, a))

7  def prior_kab: FixedSizeArrayElement[(String,Double)] =
8    VariableSizeArray (Binomial (300, 0.3), i => for
9      n <- if i==0 then Constant ("Alice") else Uniform (names: _*)
10     a <- if i==0 then Uniform (0,100) else Normal (55.2,3.5)
11   yield (n, a))
```

Step 2: Attacker Prediction (Program). We obtain the attacker's prediction of the output of running a program by transforming—*i.e.* lifting—the program to operate on distributions instead of concrete datasets, and applying it to the attacker model. Let $\mathcal{D}(X)$ denote the set of distributions on set X. Since distributions form a monad [36], several useful functions are well defined on distributions, including **lift** that, here, has type

$$\textbf{lift} : (A \to B) \to (\mathcal{D}(A) \to \mathcal{D}(B)).$$

A function from A to B becomes a function from distributions over A to distributions over B. Recall that the type of agg is List[(String, Double)] → Double. The lifting of agg has type: $\mathcal{D}(\text{List}[(\text{String, Double})]) \to \mathcal{D}(\text{Double})$. In Figaro:

```
1 def agg_p (records: FixedSizeArrayElement[(String,Double)]): Element[Double] =
2   records.map    { (n, a) => (a, 1) }
3         .reduce { (x, y) => (x._1 + y._1, x._2 + y._2) }
4         .map    { (sum, count) => sum / count }
```

Note that only types change; $\mathcal{D}$ is Element in Figaro, and FixedSizeArrayElement[T] is an efficient implementation of $\mathcal{D}(\text{List}[\text{T}])$. For a distribution over input datasets, agg_p yields a distribution over average ages (Double). Running agg_p on a prior modeling the attacker's knowledge yields the attacker's prediction of the average age. Formally, the distribution of the output (the attacker prediction) is defined as $P(o) = \int_x P(o|x)P(x)dx$. See the extended version of this paper [33] for the semantic details of computing $P(o)$.

Step 3: Attacker Observation. We use *observations* to condition the attacker's prediction of the output. Since the prediction depends on the prior, conditioning it conditions the prior, and updates the attacker's knowledge about the input. We write $P(x \,|\, E)$ to denote the conditional distribution of x given evidence E. Let $x \sim D(X)$, the evidence E is a predicate over X. For instance, we write $P(x \,|\, 4 < x < 8)$ to denote the conditional distribution where only the outcomes x in the interval $(4; 8)$ are possible. We use conditions to model attacker observations of the output. For our aggregation example, to assert that the attacker observes 55.3, we define the predicate E as (x : Double) => (55.295<=x && x<55.305) as evidence on the prediction. The observation is typically known as *likelihood function* [26], and it is modeled as a distribution (denoted as $P(E|x)$) assigning high probability to the values satisfying E. For instance, for the observation above we define $P(E|x)$ equals $1/0.005$ for $55.295 \leq x \leq 55.305$ and 0 otherwise. In Scala, the predicate E is written as an anonymous function stating that the output is within 0.005 from 55.3. We cannot assert that the output is exactly 55.3, since the output space is continuous; each individual outcome occurs with probability zero. In Figaro, we set E on prediction o with o.setCondition(E).

Step 4: Attacker Posterior. We use Bayesian inference to compute the updated attacker's knowledge upon the observation. We put together the elements of our model using the Bayes rule as follows:

Table 1. Posterior analysis summary. Results of each measure for the two attackers.

		k_{al}	k_{ab}			k_{al}	k_{ab}
Expectation	$E[a\|o \approx 55.3]$	55.60	64.000	Standard deviation	$\sigma[a\|o \approx 55.3]$	0.01	14.00
Probability query	$P(a\|o \approx 55.3)$	0.00	0.004	Shannon entropy	$H(a\|o \approx 55.3)$	-3.08	5.83
KL-divergence	$D_{KL}(a\|o \approx 55.3 \parallel a)$	5.64	0.770	Mutual information	$I(a;o)$	9.37	0.60

$$\underbrace{P(x,o\mid E)}_{posterior} = \underbrace{P(E\mid x,o)}_{observation} \cdot \overbrace{P(o|x) \cdot \underbrace{P(x)}_{prior}}^{prediction} \cdot P(E)^{-1} \tag{1}$$

Our goal is to use the attacker prior $P(x)$ (step 1), attacker prediction $P(x,o) = P(o|x)P(x)$ (step 2), and observation $P(E|x,o)$ (step 3) to compute the posterior knowledge $P(x,o|E)$. Note that the equation above is expressed in terms of the joint distribution of the random variables for input x and output o. The marginal distributions can be obtained by integrating out the corresponding variables.

We use Markov Chain Monte Carlo (MCMC) methods [38] to estimate the posterior distribution by generating samples from a probabilistic program. MCMC algorithms are simulation methods that efficiently generate samples from the high density intervals of the target distribution, in our case $P(x,o|E)$. We refer the interested readers to Robert and Casella [38] for details. We consider only terminating programs; as no samples can be generated from nonterminating programs using these methods. We remark that MCMC methods do not require computing or specifying the normalization factor $P(E)^{-1}$. Their convergence conditions are well-known [21], but the number of samples determines their accuracy. In Sect. 4, we evaluate the accuracy and efficiency of several MCMC methods for this application. In Figaro, we use the MCMC algorithm *importance sampling* [35]. Let a and o denote Alice's age and the outcome in the aggregation example. If we define the evidence $E = $ "$o \approx 55.3$" on the prediction as above, `Importance(10000, a)` produces 10000 samples that estimate the distribution $P(a \mid o \approx 55.3)$.

Step 5: Leakage (Posterior Analysis). We analyze the posterior distribution to investigate what the attacker learns. Table 1 shows an overview of analyses for the `agg` example. Using multiple measures gives a multi-perspective analysis for complex problems.

To query the probability $P(x \mid \varphi)$ of a random variable x satisfying a predicate φ, in Figaro we write `alg.probability`(x,φ) where `alg` is the inference algorithm. Other available queries estimate the histogram of the attacker's posterior, its expectation, and variance. The probability query allows to estimate whether an attacker learns a fact, effectively encoding a knowledge-based security policy check (Sect. 5). The strengths of an attack checking if Alice is underage in the `agg` example is captured by the query: $P(a < 18 \mid o \approx 55.3)$. The prior probability of $a < 18$ is 0.17. It reduces to 0.004 for k_{ab} and to 0 for k_{al} in the posterior. Both attackers can conclude that Alice is an adult. To visualize information gain, we plot the *kernel density estimates* [41]. Figure 4m plots the age of Alice in the prior $P(a)$ and the posterior $P(a \mid o \approx 55.3)$ for k_{al}. Figure 4n shows the same for o = agg_p(prior_kab). The plots confirm that k_{al} can make stronger conclusions than k_{ab}; the posterior of the former is taller and narrower than the one of the latter; note the y-axis scale. The uniform prior has expected value $E[a] \approx 50$ and standard deviation $\sigma_a \approx 29$. As listed in Table 1, the posterior expectation increases to 55.60 for k_{al} with standard deviation 0.01: k_{al} effectively learns a from the output. For k_{ab} the posterior has larger standard deviation (14), so k_{ab}'s uncertainty about the age of Alice is greatly reduced, yet remains high.

Moving beyond measuring and visualizing probability, we quantify attacker's learning using quantitative information flow measures: entropy, KL-divergence, mutual information, and Bayes risk. These and other measures are added to PRIVUG as libraries, which estimate the corresponding measure using the samples of the MCMC algorithm of Step 4.

Shannon's *entropy* quantifies the uncertainty about the value of a random variable (*e.g.*, [24, 30]). A decrease in entropy from prior to posterior signifies an increase in knowledge. Entropy (in bits) is defined as $H(x) = \sum_{x \in X} P(x) \log_2 P(x)$ for discrete random variables. Since PRIVUG works with an inferred distribution, we estimate the entropy using the classic algorithm [1], which is known to be accurate and easy to implement. In the agg example, the entropy of a in the prior is $H(a) = 6.67$ bits. At the same time, the conditional entropy of a in the posterior for k_{ab} is $H(a \mid o \approx 55.3) = 5.84$ bits. The attacker gained 0.83 bits of information about the age of Alice. For k_{al}, the posterior entropy is $H(a \mid o \approx 55.3) = -3.08$. Here the difference is 9.75 bits, twelve times more than what k_{al} learned. (The entropy of a continuous variable (replace $\sum$ with $\int$ above), *differential entropy*, can be negative [1].) Clearly, k_{al} is an example of an attacker able to amplify the disclosed information thanks to its additional pre-existing knowledge—a situation often referred to as a *linking attack*. The ability of k_{ab} in this respect is much weaker. PRIVUG allows experimenting with the attacker space in this way, to let the data controller understand what attacks are successful, and then assess whether they are of concern.

Relative entropy [28] or *KL-divergence* measures how much two distributions differ. In Bayesian inference, the KL-divergence of a posterior $P(x)$ and a prior $Q(x)$, defined as $D_{KL}(P \| Q) = \sum P(x) \log_2(P(x)/Q(x))$, expresses the amount of "*information lost when Q is used to approximate P*" [6, page 51]. Thus, KL-divergence is a measure of information gained by revising one's knowledge of the prior to the posterior. As with entropy, since we are working with an inferred distribution, we can estimate KL-divergence from samples. We use the algorithm by Wang *et al.* [44]. For the aggregation example, the KL-divergence between the posterior and prior of a is a measure of the amount of information that the attacker gained about Alice's age by observing the output of the program. For k_{ab}, $D_{KL}(a \mid o \approx 55.3 \| a) = 0.77$. For k_{al}, on the other hand, $D_{KL}(a \mid o \approx 55.3 \| a) = 5.64$. These results indicate that the observation yields an information gain of 0.77 bits for k_{ab} and 5.64 bits for k_{al}. More important is the difference; k_{al} gains over 7 times more information than k_{ab}. In Sect. 4 we show how KL-divergence can be used to measure utility when programs add noise to their output.

Mutual information between two random variables x, y, defined as $I(x; y) = \sum_{y \in Y} \sum_{x \in X} P(x, y) \log_2(P(x, y)/P(x)P(y))$, measures the reduction of the uncertainty of x by the knowledge of y [15]. We estimate $I(i; o)$ where i is a secret input and o a public output (the attacker's prediction) to quantify how much information o shares with i. Mutual information is well studied as a quantitative information flow measure (cf. Sect. 5). A privacy protection mechanism typically aims at minimizing $I(i; o)$. In PRIVUG, we use the mutual information estimator [25] provided by SKlearn [34] for continuous variables and Leaki-Est [11] for discrete variables. In our example, we have $I(a; o) = 9.37$ bits for k_{al} and $I(a; o) = 0.60$ bits for k_{ab}. This is consistent with our intuition: when the attacker knows everything about the input except for Alice's age, observing the output greatly reduces their uncertainty.

PRIVUG can incorporate estimators of other measures. In Sect. 4 we show that other tools can be incorporated on the example of F-BLEAU [9], to estimate *Bayes risk*—the expected probability of an attacker guessing a secret (s) by observing the output of the program (o); formally: $1 - \sum_{o \in O} \max_{s \in S} P(o|s)P(s)$ for random variables s and o [2].

This way we determine if specific attackers are capable of learning secrets, and assess whether disclosing the output of the program poses a privacy risk. Figure 3 gives an overview of the steps in the PRIVUG method. PRIVUG's intended users are data analysts with knowledge in statistics and probabilistic modeling. These users are typically trained in probabilistic programming, an essential part of their toolbox (*e.g.*, [21]). This makes it easy to perform steps 1, 3, and 4. Step 2 typically requires simply updating the datatypes of the input (as in agg and ano). The analyst may, however, need to change the program to ensure differentiability, or replace some operators with their probability counterparts. These are the same techniques that data analysts use to create advanced probabilistic models and analyses. Step 5's probability queries, visualizations, and distribution statistics such as expected value or variance, are likewise familiar to data analysts. The interpretation of leakage does, however, require privacy-specific expertise (information theory, quantitative information flow).

The results and conclusions drawn do depend on the to choice of prior. The prior models what an attacker knows about the input of the program, the secondary knowledge that *linked* with the observed output can lead to privacy violations. The analysis may report no leakage if priors do not reflect the real information that an attacker has access to. Ideally, priors should be informed from real world data. For instance, if the program takes as input a set of records of US citizens, then it is advisable to inform priors from publicly available sources, *e.g.*, the US census. Alternatively, probabilistic programming frameworks can be used to automatically learn underlying distributions from data with better accuracy than simply using the empirical distributions [21]. For mutual information and multiplicative Bayes capacity (a derived measure from Bayes risk, it has been shown that running the analysis with uniform priors uncovers leakage if it exists, see [13, Theorem 4] and [2, Theorem 7.2]. This result can be used with

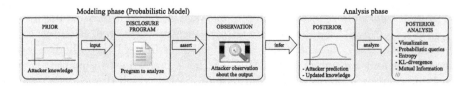

Fig. 3. Overview of the steps in PRIVUG method.

good effect to detect leakage, but not to estimate its magnitude, which can be estimated using PRIVUG.

4   Evaluation

RQ1: Can PRIVUG Analyze Common Privacy Mechanisms? We analyze three (modern and traditional) privacy mechanisms in PRIVUG. The purpose is twofold: i) Demonstrate the applicability of PRIVUG, and ii) Serve as templates for data analysts.

Differential Privacy. Consider a company computing the mean income of employees with `agg` and releasing the output publicly. To protect the anonymity of employees, they add Laplacian noise to the output; a popular mechanism to enforce differential privacy [18,19]. We use PRIVUG to explore trade-offs between privacy protection and data utility by varying the values of parameters. We assume a dataset of 200 incomes. The company have previously released some data on 195 of the 200 incomes, so it is publicly known that they are between $80k and $90k ($\mathcal{U}(80, 90)$). There are 5 new employees of which no income information is known ($\mathcal{U}(10, 200)$). The program to analyze is an extension of `agg` that adds Laplacian noise to the output: $o \sim \text{agg} + \mathcal{L}(0, \Delta\text{agg}/\epsilon)$ where Δagg denotes the *sensitivity*. This is known to preserve ϵ-differential privacy [19, Thm. 3.6]. Sensitivity captures the magnitude by which a single entry can change the output. The program with the mechanism incorporated takes as input the `epsilon` (ϵ) and a set of `records`, returning the average income. The implementation in Figaro after lifting is:

```
1 def dp_agg (epsilon: Double, records: FixedSizeArrayElement[(String,Double)]) =
2    val delta  = Constant(200.0)/records.length
3    val lambda = Constant(epsilon)/delta
4    val X = continuous.Exponential(lambda)
5    val Y = Flip(0.5) // <- Bernoulli
6    val laplaceNoise = If(Y, X*Constant(-1.0), X)
7    agg(records) ++ laplaceNoise
```

Since the maximum income is 200k, the sensitivity (`delta`) is $200/|records|$. We construct the Laplace distribution from an exponential and a Bernoulli distributions in lines 2–6 using a standard construction. Line 7 adds the noise to the result of `agg`.

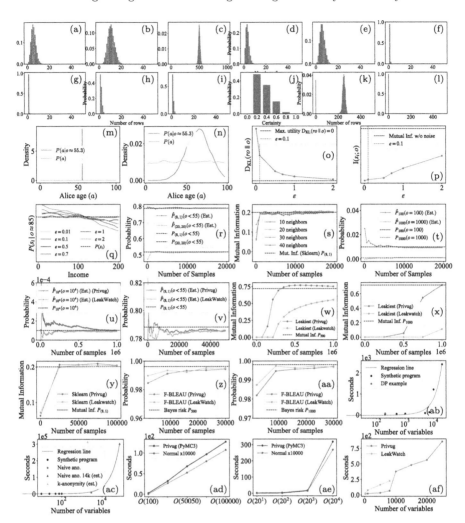

Fig. 4.   Analysis results. *Naive Anonymization:* Quasi-identifier analysis (a) zip, (b) day, (c) sex, (d) zip+sex, (e) day+sex, (f) zip+day, (g) zip+day+sex. Large datasets: (h) zip+day, (i) zip+day+sex. Sensitive attribute analysis: (j) Chance of learning that governor is ill if 5 share his zip. *k-anonymity:* Number of rows matching governor's attributes ($k = 2$): (k) sex, (l) any other attribute combination. *Aggregate example:* Prior and posterior knowledge of age of Alice (distributions): (m) k_{al}, (n) k_{ab}. *Differential privacy:* (o) Utility, (p) Mutual Information, (q) Probability Queries. **Convergence of PRIVUG.** (r) Probability query (Continuous), (s) Mutual Information (Continuous), (t) Probability query (Discrete). *Comparison w/ LeakWatch:* Probability queries (u) Discrete $P_{10000}(o = 10000)$, (v) Continuous $P_{(8,1)}(o < 55)$. Mutual Information (w) Discrete P_{500} in LeakiEst, (x) Discrete P_{1000} in LeakiEst, (y) Continuous $P_{(8,1)}$ in SKlearn. Bayes Risk: (z) Discrete P_{500} in F-BLEAU, (aa) Discrete P_{1000} in F-BLEAU. **Scalability of PRIVUG.** Inference time: (ab) Continuous random variables, (ac) Discrete random variables. Time complexity on `f(arr,c)`: (ad) Increasing $n \in (10^2, 10^5)$ for $O(n)$, (ae) Increasing $c \in (1,4)$ for $O(20^c)$. *Comparison w/Leak-Watch:* (af) $P_{(8,1)}$. (Color figure online)

The Laplacian mechanism includes a notion of accuracy to quantify utility (e.g., [19, Thm 3.8]). Unconventionally, we opt for measuring utility as KL-divergence between the output with noise (o) and without (ro). The reason is that KL-divergence can be applied to any method based on perturbing the output of the program (demonstrating broad applicability of our currently-supported measures). High KL-divergence indicates low utility as it represents loss of information wrt. the noiseless output. Maximum utility is achieved when KL-divergence equals 0. We observe in Fig. 4o an exponential decay of KL-divergence as ϵ increases, consistent with the intuition that small values of ϵ result in high noise and reduced utility. The graph suggests that decrements in ϵ for $\epsilon < 0.5$ may impact utility strongly.

Now we evaluate how ϵ influences the flow of information from the income of new employees (s_i) to the output (o). Mutual information is 0 if one is independent of the other (*i.e.* no information flow). Figure 4p plots mutual information for different values of ϵ. The dashed line shows the baseline, *i.e.* mutual information when the output has no added noise. This shows mutual information increases linearly with ϵ.

Finally, we use a *probability query* to evaluate the effect of ϵ on statistical information that an attacker can learn about the new members in the dataset. Differential privacy does not focus on protecting this type of information—it focuses on protecting the presence of a record in the dataset. Yet it is useful to quantify the effect of the noise on attacker knowledge. Suppose running dp_agg with $\epsilon = 0.5$ yields 85k as a result. Suppose privacy regulations disallow revealing income data without employee consent. The company would like to determine, whether revealing this result could breach the regulation. In PRIVUG, we analyze the distribution $P(s_i \mid o \approx 85)$ to determine this. Figure 4q shows the distributions for different values of ϵ. The dashed line marks the baseline, *i.e.*, the probability distribution before the observation. The blue line corresponds to the run with $\epsilon = 0.5$. Since this line is not parallel with the baseline, there is evidence of an increase in knowledge. The other lines show that any $\epsilon > 0.1$ increases the knowledge about the salary of the new employees. Consequently, releasing the average 85k computed using $\epsilon = 0.5$ will result in a violation of the regulation.

In summary, we have discovered that releasing the average income 85k with $\epsilon > 0.1$ reveals information about the salary of new employees. Thus, for $\epsilon = 0.5$, the company must seek consent from employees. Mutual information increases linearly with ϵ, and for $\epsilon < 0.5$ is notably low. Utility exhibits an exponential decay as ϵ decreases. This decay is especially pronounced with $\epsilon < 1$, showing the impact of the added noise on utility.

Naive Anonymization We quantify how strongly an attacker can determine the diagnosis of an individual (the governor) by observing the output of ano from Sect. 2. Though this mechanism has well-known privacy flaws, it is still commonly used. Thus, we illustrate how PRIVUG is used to effectively find these flaws. First, we define the prior. In Figaro:

```
1 def p : FixedSizeArrayElement[(Name,Zip,Day,Sex,Diag)] =
2   VariableSizeArray (Constant (1000), i => for
3     n <- if i==0 then Constant (GNAME) else Uniform (names:_*)
4     z <- if i==0 then Constant (GZIP)  else Uniform (zips:_*)
5     b <- if i==0 then Constant (GDAY)  else Uniform (days:_*)
6     s <- if i==0 then Constant (GSEX)  else Uniform (Male,Female)
7     d <- if i==0 then Constant (GILL)  else If (Flip (.2), Ill, Healthy)
8   yield (n,z,b,s,d))
```

Name is an identifier for an individual. For the sake of clarity, we assume that Zip, Day and Sex are non-sensitive attributes, and Diag is sensitive. Name, Zip, Day and Sex are uniformly distributed, and Diag is Ill with probability 0.2. The first row in the dataset is fixed, containing the governor's record. The prior fixes a dataset size of 1000 records.

The lifted version of ano follows. Note that, compared to ano, only the type changed.

```
1 def ano_p (records : FixedSizeArrayElement[(Name,Zip,Day,Sex,Diag)]) =
2   records.map { (n, z, b, s, d) => (z, b, s, d) }
```

First, we assess re-identification risk. We check whether an attacker can uniquely identify an individual's row using *quasi-identifiers*, which enables linking attacks. We inspect subsets of attributes to determine how uniquely they identify subjects. We query for the probability of a certain number x of rows in the output satisfying a predicate φ, where φ models which attributes we want to match with the governor. For example: probability(x,(v:Int) => v == 5), where x = output.count(φ), yields the probability that there are 5 such rows ($x = 5$). Figures 4a to 4g show the results. The governor is most likely to share zip code with ~5 rows, and sex with ~500 rows. With more attributes (*e.g.* zip+day, zip+day+sex) it becomes likely that only the governor's record has those values. Disclosing those together thus poses significant re-identification risk.

Next, we assess positive disclosure risk [29]: Can the attacker determine the diagnosis of an individual (w/o necessarily identifying its row)? Consider the following property of datasets, $\forall r \in D \cdot \psi(r) \implies r.d = $ Ill, which stipulates that all records satisfying ψ are ill. We instantiate ψ in various ways; with $\psi(r) = (r.z = $ GZIP$)$, the property stipulates that all records with the governor's zip code are ill. We compute the probability that this property holds for the anonymized dataset by issuing a forall query on the posterior. Column 2 in Table 2 displays the result. Like in the original case study [42], we conclude that with access to the governor's zip code, birthday, and sex (last row), an attacker can determine the diagnosis of the governor with high probability (98%). Unlike in the original study, we concluded this for all datasets satisfying our prior model.

We assess whether the dataset size affects our risk analyses. We re-run quasi-identifier and positive disclosure analyses for a dataset size of 14000—closer to Sweeney's [42]. This probabilistic model contains 70000 random variables (5 variables per row, 14000 rows). Our results (cf. Fig. 4i) are close to those originally reported [42]: There is a 71% probability that no other record shares the gov-

Table 2. Probability of learning governor's diagnosis.

Query	Prob. naive	Prob. 14k	Prob. k-ano
$P(\forall r \in D \cdot r.z = \text{GZIP} \implies r.d = \text{I11})$	.02000	.00	.0
$P(\forall r \in D \cdot r.b = \text{GDAY} \implies r.d = \text{I11})$	.00006	.00	.0
$P(\forall r \in D \cdot r.s = \text{GSEX} \implies r.d = \text{I11})$	.00000	.00	.0
$P(\forall r \in D \cdot r.z = \text{GZIP} \wedge r.b = \text{GDAY} \implies r.d = \text{I11})$	.96000	.51	.0
$P(\forall r \in D \cdot r.z = \text{GZIP} \wedge r.s = \text{GSEX} \implies r.d = \text{I11})$	.16000	.00	.0
$P(\forall r \in D \cdot r.b = \text{GDAY} \wedge r.s = \text{GSEX} \implies r.d = \text{I11})$	.01800	.00	.0
$P(\forall r \in D \cdot r.z = \text{GZIP} \wedge r.b = \text{GDAY} \wedge r.s = \text{GSEX} \implies r.d = \text{I11})$	.98000	.71	.0

ernor's zip code, birthday, and sex. For zip code and birthday (cf. Fig. 4h) the probability is 51%. Positive disclosure analysis shows a decrease in the probability of learning the diagnosis (column 3 in Table 2). These results indicate that, for this program and prior, increasing the size of the dataset does not uncover new privacy risks (in fact, smaller datasets are more vulnerable).

Finally, we assess how certain the attacker is about the governor's diagnosis. Say the dataset contains 5 records with the governor's zip code (cf. Fig. 4a). Suppose that out of those 5 people, k are ill. Then the probability of the governor being ill is $k/5$. Notably, if all 5 are ill, then the attacker is certain that the the governor is ill. This corresponds to the query $P(\text{output.count}(\varphi \wedge \psi) = k \mid \text{output.count}(\varphi) = 5)$, where φ and ψ are predicates; ψ is true iff the record is ill, and φ iff it has the governor's zip code. We use setCondition to observe that output.count$(\varphi) = 5$. Figure 4j shows the result. The first bar (0.2) reflects the prior probability, so there is 50% chance that the attacker learns nothing from an actual data set. However, there is a 50% chance that the belief of an attacker in a positive diagnosis grows: 0.4 with 35% probability, etc. This demonstrates that PRIVUG can not only reason about the risk of an attacker learning something with certainty, but about decrease of uncertainty as well.

k-Anonymity. We analyze an algorithm that produces a k-anonymous dataset of health records. That is, for any combination of attributes, at least k rows in the dataset share those attribute values [42]. This case study illustrates the use of PRIVUG for a non-trivial program with quadratic complexity. In terms of privacy analysis, we compare the results of running the program with $k = 2$ to those of naive anonymization above.

We start by presenting the prior and program. We use the same prior as ano_p above, but with a dataset size of 500 records (due to sampling performance, see RQ3). As for the program, we implemented k_ano, which takes as parameter k and a dataset, and outputs a k-anonymous dataset. The lifted version of k_ano has type (**lift** k_ano) : $\mathcal{D}(\text{Int, List[(Name,Zip,Day,...)]}) \rightarrow \mathcal{D}(\text{List[(Zip,Day,...)]})$. Due to space contraints, we refer interested readers to our code repository for implementation details.

We analyze re-identification and positive disclosure risks. Figure 4k shows that the number of records in the output dataset matching the governor's sex in the input, is like we saw before (cf. Fig. 4c), save for the rare (~3.5%) occasion where sex was part of some quasi-identifier. In those instances, k_ano *masked* Sex, replacing everyone's Sex with * to enforce 2-anonymity. Figure 4l shows that for any other attribute combination, none of the records in the output share those attribute values with the governor's values from the input. Thus, k_ano always mask Zip and Day. Regarding positive disclosure, the risk of learning the governor's diagnosis is 0 for any attribute combination (column 4 in Table 2), since k_ano always mask Zip and Day.

In summary, k_ano eliminates disclosure risk compared to ano. However, k_ano destroys most (or all) utility; when Sex also gets anonymized, then only the distribution on Diag remains (which is public). With PRIVUG, an analyst can thus investigate the privacy-utility tradeoff of changes made to a program, and compare programs for disclosure risk.

RQ2: Does PRIVUG Produce Accurate Results? How Fast Does It Converge? We study the convergence and accuracy of PRIVUG for continuous and discrete variables, as the type of variables affects convergence—different methods are used for the continuous and discrete case [21]. The goal is to confirm that PRIVUG's results are accurate, and check how effective the sampling methods are for the leakage estimation problem. In total, we have successfully driven five different estimators with PRIVUG samples derived from program code and priors: probability queries (continuous and discrete), mutual information (SKlearn, LeakiEst), Bayes Risk (F-BLEAU). All the estimators behaved as expected, PRIVUG converges to correct results (dashed black lines in the plots of Fig. 4 represent ground truth obtained in a pen-and-paper analysis). Furthermore, PRIVUG meets and exceeds performance of the main competing sampler for programs, LeakWatch [12], without inheriting some of its disadvantages: It is not bound to a single execution environment (JVM), it is naturally extensible with probabilistic programming ecosystem, and it is much more lightweight (very little code is required).

In all these experiments, 5000 samples give accurate results (except for Leaki-Est that requires >500k samples for large domain spaces). This is reassuring regarding the validity of experiments executed for RQ1. We generated 10k samples for dp_agg and ano; sufficient to obtain accurate results. For 14k dataset size with ano and k_ano, we only generated 1000 samples, due to the long running time. Still, since we only used discrete probability queries there, 1000 samples shall approximate the correct result well (Fig. 4t). Below we provide key details on the experiments leading to the above conclusions.

We start with continuous problems and the most popular sampler for such (NUTS [23], Hamiltonian). We use a program that computes the average o of random variables $s, p_1, ..., p_{200}$ distributed as $s \sim \mathcal{N}(42, \sigma_s)$ and $p_i \sim \mathcal{N}(55, \sigma_p)$. We vary σ_s and σ_p to control sample dispersion. We check how many samples are needed to accurately answer probability and mutual information queries. Figure 4r shows the accuracy for the probability query $P(o < 55)$ for $\sigma_s = 8, \sigma_p = 1$ and $\sigma_s = \sigma_p = 20$, labeled as $P_{(8,1)}$ and $P_{(20,20)}$ in the graph. The error is below

0.01 after 5000 samples in both cases. Increasing the dispersion does not impact convergence. We also estimate mutual information for $P_{(8,1)}$. After 5000 samples the estimation error drops below 0.02 (Fig. 4s). The mutual information estimator of SKlearn uses k-nearest neighbour distance, but we observe no significant impact when varying k. For discrete variables, we use a program that adds two input variables $x, y \sim \mathcal{U}(0, n)$ giving the output $o \sim x+y$, and sample with Metropolis algorithm, the method of choice for discrete problems (Importance sampling performs comparably). Figure 4t shows accuracy of the probability query $P(o=n)$ with $n = 100, 1000$. After 5000 samples the estimation error drops below 0.01 for both values of n, indicating that the support of x and y does not significantly impact convergence. We evaluate convergence of *mutual information* for this case using LeakiEst. Less than 5000 samples suffice for LeakiEst to converge. Finally, we also check the convergence of *Bayes risk* estimation using the state-of-the-art F-BLEAU estimator [9] driven by Metropolis sampling in PRIVUG. As few as 1000 samples suffice for F-BLEAU to converge.

We make LeakWatch, the most similar work to PRIVUG, drive the same estimators as above and compare with PRIVUG. LeakWatch does not directly support continuous inputs or Bayes risk. We have extracted the sample sets generated by LeakWatch and manually implemented the queries. We test the same estimators with LeakWatch as above. Figures 4u and 4v show convergence of *probability queries* for the discrete system with an input domain of size 10000, P_{10000}, and for the continuous system, $P_{(8,1)}$. Figures 4z and 4aa show convergence using F-BLEAU to estimate *Bayes risk*. Figures 4w and 4x show the convergence of using LeakiEst to estimate *mutual information*. For continuous random variables, we use the SKlearn estimator (Fig. 4y). In all these cases except for mutual information queries (Figs. 4w and 4x), the two samplers perform comparably. Strikingly, in Fig. 4x, PRIVUG needs 300k fewer samples to start converging; much less than LeakWatch which has been specifically designed to work with LeakiEst!

RQ3: Does PRIVUG Scale? Does Program Complexity Impact Running Time? We evaluate how long it takes for NUTS (continuous) and Metropolis (discrete) samplers to produce two chains of 10000 samples for synthetic programs of increasing size. As the efficiency of MCMC sampling depends on the dimensionality of the domain, we use the example from RQ2, but scaled up to 20000 variables (continuous: $(s + p_1 + p_2 + \ldots + p_{20000})/20001$, and discrete: $x + y_1 + y_2 + \ldots + y_{20000}$). This number permits modeling large and complex systems. We include several realistic programs in the scalability experiment: naive anonymization, k-anonymity and differential privacy, see RQ1 details. Figures 4ab and 4ac show the data points measured. The blue line overlays the main tendency of the measurements, black points correspond to the above synthetic programs, and the remaining symbols refer to the realistic programs. We run the experiments on a machine with 8x1.70 GHz cores, 16 GB RAM, except for the two experiments with naive anonymization, which have been run on 8x3.60 GHz machine with 32 GB RAM.

Execution time of synthetic programs in Fig. 4ac follows a linear trend. The red point corresponds to the naive anonymization case with 5000 variables. This data point follows the linear trend of synthetic programs, with run-time exceeding 2 h. Interestingly, inference for continuous variables is more efficient, as Hamiltonian samplers can leverage continuity to generalize faster [23]. We can generate samplers for a model with 20000 random variables in around 40 min (Fig. 4ab). Notably, the differential privacy case exhibits particularly low execution time (red in Fig. 4ab), consistent with the trend of the synthetic examples. The purple and orange triangles correspond to the naive anonymization with a dataset of size 14k, and to the k-anonymity case, respectively. To account for low sampling performance, we generated only 1000 samples for each and scaled the time linearly to place it in the graph. Both cases took over 5 h (80 h after scaling).

The k-anonymity program is an interesting outlier: even with a small database of 500 entries. The exponential k-anonymity algorithm used to produce each sample dominates the cost of inference. This leads us to ask how the subject program impacts the execution time of PRIVUG. We use the Metropolis sampler in this experiment, since it performed slower above. To this end, we use a program $f(arr, c) \triangleq \sum_{0..c} \sum_{i \in arr} i$ with running time $O(n^c)$ for $n = |arr|$ (see our code repository for the implementation). Increasing n and c induces linear and exponential growth respectively. We compare the running time of generating 10000 samples with f in PRIVUG against 10000 executions of f without PRIVUG. Figure 4ad and 4ae show similar execution times for both. Thus the execution time of PRIVUG is dominated by the number of samples requested and the cost of running the subject program, but the Metropolis sampler itself incurs no significant overhead.

Finally, we compare the scalability of PRIVUG and LeakWatch, by measuring the execution time to generate 20000 samples for $P_{(8,1)}$ with increasing number of variables. Figure 4af shows that up to 9000 variables, both perform comparably well—with PRIVUG slightly faster. However, LeakWatch crashes from out-of-memory errors on cases with more than 10000 variables. In contrast, PRIVUG exhibits much better scalability; it runs out of memory after 30000 variables.

In summary, PRIVUG can handle complex programs without introducing major overhead over the subject program's running time. PRIVUG scales better than LeakWatch, making it better fit for larger systems and more complex priors. This is largely due to probabilistic programming frameworks being heavily optimized by the data science community. We thus advocate use of these framework in information leakage research.

Table 3. Overview of leakage quantification tools. Legend: **KSP** = knowledge-based security policy; **custom** = custom input language; [a]Cherubin [8] lays the foundation to handle continuous input but this has not been implemented; [b]we show how to handle continuous and discrete KSP and mutual information with LeakWatch in Sect. 4—this was not demonstrated originally [12]; [c]via integrated 3rd party tools (F-BLEAU/LeakiEst/SKlearn) and pmf estimation for discrete input/output. ? = not studied.

	Random variable type				Input type	Tool capabilities			Supported quantitative information flow measures					
	Input		Output			exact	sampling	estimation	KSP	entropy	min-entropy	mutual-inf	Bayes-risk	KL-diverg
	disc.	cont.	disc.	cont.										
LeakiEst [11]	✓		✓	✓	set of samples			✓			✓	✓		
F-BLEAU [9]	✓	(✓)[a]	✓	✓	set of samples			✓			✓		✓	
SPIRE [27]	✓		✓		custom: PSI	✓				✓				
DKBP [31]	✓		✓		custom: Polyhedra	✓				✓				
QUAIL [5]	✓		✓		custom: QUAIL	✓						✓		
HyLeak [4]	✓		✓		custom: QUAIL 2.0		✓	✓				✓		
LeakWatch [12]	✓	(✓)[b]	✓	✓	Java		✓	✓	(✓)[b]		(✓)[c]	(✓)[b,c]		
Privug (this work)	✓	✓	✓	✓	Java/Scala/Python	?	✓	✓	✓	✓	(✓)[c]	(✓)[c]	(✓)[c]	✓

5   Related Work and Concluding Remarks

We have shown that probabilistic programming with Monte-Carlo Bayesian inference is a promising basis for implementing privacy risk and data leakage analyses. Privug analyses follow a well-defined architecture: modeling attackers, extracting models by lifting programs, and using a state-of-the-art sampler to drive an estimator. We know of no similarly broad competing framework to compare against. Several tools exist to quantify leakage using probabilistic reasoning. Table 3 provides a detailed comparison. The first 4 columns specify the type of input/output variables; Privug fully supports discrete and continuous distributions (unlike existing tools that mostly focus on discrete variables). The fifth column indicates whether the tool works on a (externally generated) set of samples, a custom specification language or a general purpose programming language; Privug works directly on general purpose programming languages. Columns 6–8 indicate whether the tool can perform exact analytical inference, sample from distributions (e.g., via naive sampling or MCMC), or can estimate leakage measures; in Privug we can perform all of these, but we have not studied exact inference in this paper. The last 6 columns show whether the tools support the corresponding measures; all of them are supported by Privug (unlike any other existing tool). In the following, we discuss the existing tools in two groups, white- and black-box. These tools are highly-specific; they feature a design and architecture of samplers and estimators highly optimized for a single purpose. In contrast, the idea of Privug is to build on a broad platform of probabilistic programming, which has not been used for this purpose before, and to reuse as many components as possible to provide a comprehensive assessment of a program.

Black-box methods estimate leakage by analyzing a set of input/output pairs of the system. LeakiEst [11] estimates min-entropy [37] and mutual information [15] using frequentist statistics, *i.e.*, counting the relative frequency of the outputs given inputs. F-BLEAU [9] and its generalization [39] use nearest neighbor classifiers to estimate Bayes risk [7] and g-leakage [2]. Classifiers can exploit patterns in the data and scale better than LeakiEst for large output spaces. Black-box tools require a set of independent and identically distributed samples over inputs. Obtaining such a sample is not easy as discussed by Chothia et al. [12]. PRIVUG automates this process, obtaining synergy with black-box methods in two ways: (i) black-box methods can be used easily within PRIVUG (Sect. 4); (ii) black-box methods can leverage the well-studied sampling mechanisms [38] used in PRIVUG to produce the set of samples they work on. Section 4 shows that LeakiEst converges faster using PRIVUG than with LeakWatch for mutual information queries.

White-box methods exploit the source code of the program to compute leakage analytically or via sampling. We distinguish white-box methods working on *custom specification languages* from those working on *general purpose programming languages*. Custom specification languages are languages designed for program analysis and are typically not directly executable. Mardziel et al. introduce abstract probabilistic polyhedra to capture attacker beliefs, and define transformations over the polyhedra to analytically obtain the revised belief of the attacker after observing an output of the program [31]. They are able to check whether queries to a database violate a knowledge-based security policy. SPIRE [27] uses the symbolic inference engine PSI [20] to analytically compute the updated beliefs of an attacker given an observation. Then, it uses Z3 [16] to verify whether a knowledge-based security policy holds. QUAIL performs forward state exploration of a program to construct a Markov chain capturing its semantics, which is then used to compute mutual information [5]. HyLeak is an evolution of QUAIL to use hybrid statistical estimation [4]. The method works on the control flow graph of the program. It first uses several symbolic reductions to simplify the program, then applies standard statistical reasoning via sampling. These works support programs with discrete inputs and outputs. In contrast, PRIVUG handles *discrete and continuous inputs and outputs*. In principle, it also allows obtaining analytical solutions, *e.g.*, using variable elimination (in Figaro) [35] but we have not explored this. Unlike HyLeak, we do not reduce the program graph, but Hamiltonian samplers compute gradients of the model (probabilistic program) to improve sampling effectiveness. QUAIL computes mutual information; HyLeak computes mutual information and Shannon entropy. Others support only analysis of knowledge-based security policies [27,31].

PRIVUG is, perhaps, the first work whose goal is supporting estimation of many measures for programs written not in custom specification languages, but in *general purpose programming languages* (Python, Scala, and Java via the Scala interface). LeakWatch samples a Java program and uses LeakiEst to estimate mutual information and min-entropy leakage [12]. There are several differences between PRIVUG and LeakWatch. First, PRIVUG uses efficient and scalable Bayesian inference methods as opposed to LeakWatch that relies on direct sampling from target distributions. We found that the Bayesian methods used in PRIVUG scale better (Sect. 4). We also found that LeakiEst, the estimator Leak-Watch was designed for, converges faster when using PRIVUG's samples (Sect. 4).

Bayesian inference is proven to be very effective in the presence of conditions [38], which are not directly available in LeakWatch. Second, LeakWatch relies on its users to select appropriate Pseudo-Random Number Generators (PRNGs). The authors recommend java.security.SecureRandom [10], which only support sampling from uniform and normal distributions. In contrast, probabilistic programming frameworks (used in PRIVUG) support a wide range of probability distributions with high quality PRNGs. This emphasizes another key contribution of this work for leakage research: It is beneficial to build on top of strong statistical and probabilistic platforms over custom solutions, with Bayesian probabilistic programming being one such platform.

References

1. Ahmad, I.A., Lin, P.-E.: A nonparametric estimation of the entropy for absolutely continuous distributions (corresp.). IEEE Trans. Inf. Theory **22**(3), 372–375 (1976)
2. Alvim, M., Chatzikokolakis, K., McIver, A., Morgan, C., Palamidessi, C., Smith, G.: The Science of Quantitative Information Flow. Springer, Cham (2020). https://doi.org/10.1007/978-3-319-96131-6
3. Bingham, E.: Pyro: deep universal probabilistic programming. J. Mach. Learn. Res. **20**, 28:1-28:6 (2019)
4. Biondi, F., Kawamoto, Y., Legay, A., Traonouez, L.-M.: Hybrid statistical estimation of mutual information and its application to information flow. Formal Aspects Comput. **31**(2), 165–206 (2018). https://doi.org/10.1007/s00165-018-0469-z
5. Biondi, F., Legay, A., Traonouez, L.-M., Wasowski, A.: QUAIL: a quantitative security analyzer for imperative code. In: Sharygina, N., Veith, H. (eds.) CAV 2013. LNCS, vol. 8044, pp. 702–707. Springer, Heidelberg (2013). https://doi.org/10.1007/978-3-642-39799-8_49
6. Burnham, K.P., Anderson, D.R.: Model Selection and Multimodel Inference: A Practical Information-Theoretic Approach. Springer, New York (2002). https://doi.org/10.1007/b97636
7. Chatzikokolakis, K., Palamidessi, C., Panangaden, P.: On the Bayes risk in information-hiding protocols. J. Comput. Secur. **16**(5), 531–571 (2008)
8. Cherubin, G.: Black-box security: measuring black-box information leakage via machine learning. Ph.D. thesis, Royal Holloway, University of London (2018)
9. Cherubin, G., Chatzikokolakis, K., Palamidessi, C.: F-BLEAU: fast black-box leakage estimation. In: SP 2019, pp. 835–852. IEEE (2019)
10. Chothia, T., Kawamoto, Y., Novakovic, C.: LeakWatch: pseudorandom number generators example. https://www.cs.bham.ac.uk/research/projects/infotools/leakwatch/examples/prng.php
11. Chothia, T., Kawamoto, Y., Novakovic, C.: A tool for estimating information leakage. In: Sharygina, N., Veith, H. (eds.) CAV 2013. LNCS, vol. 8044, pp. 690–695. Springer, Heidelberg (2013). https://doi.org/10.1007/978-3-642-39799-8_47
12. Chothia, T., Kawamoto, Y., Novakovic, C.: LeakWatch: estimating information leakage from Java programs. In: Kutyłowski, M., Vaidya, J. (eds.) ESORICS 2014. LNCS, vol. 8713, pp. 219–236. Springer, Cham (2014). https://doi.org/10.1007/978-3-319-11212-1_13
13. Chothia, T., Kawamoto, Y., Novakovic, C., Parker, D.: Probabilistic point-to-point information leakage. In: CSF 2013, pp. 193–205. IEEE (2013)

14. Clarkson, M.R., Myers, A.C., Schneider, F.B.: Belief in information flow. In: CSFW 2005, pp. 31–45. IEEE (2005)
15. Cover, T.M., Thomas, J.A.: Elements of Information Theory, 2nd edn. Wiley, New York (2006)
16. de Moura, L., Bjørner, N.: Z3: an efficient SMT solver. In: Ramakrishnan, C.R., Rehof, J. (eds.) TACAS 2008. LNCS, vol. 4963, pp. 337–340. Springer, Heidelberg (2008). https://doi.org/10.1007/978-3-540-78800-3_24
17. Dillon, J.V.: Tensorflow distributions. CoRR, abs/1711.10604 (2017)
18. Dwork, C., McSherry, F., Nissim, K., Smith, A.: Calibrating noise to sensitivity in private data analysis. In: Halevi, S., Rabin, T. (eds.) TCC 2006. LNCS, vol. 3876, pp. 265–284. Springer, Heidelberg (2006). https://doi.org/10.1007/11681878_14
19. Dwork, C., Roth, A.: The algorithmic foundations of differential privacy. Found. Trends Theor. Comput. Sci. 9(3–4), 211–407 (2014)
20. Gehr, T., Misailovic, S., Vechev, M.: PSI: exact symbolic inference for probabilistic programs. In: Chaudhuri, S., Farzan, A. (eds.) CAV 2016. LNCS, vol. 9779, pp. 62–83. Springer, Cham (2016). https://doi.org/10.1007/978-3-319-41528-4_4
21. Gelman, A., Carlin, J.B., Stern, H.S., Dunson, D.B., Vehtari, A., Rubin, D.B.: Bayesian Data Analysis. CRC Press, Boca Raton (2013)
22. Hargitai, V., Shklovski, I., Wasowski, A.: Going beyond obscurity: organizational approaches to data anonymization. PACMHCI 2(CSCW), 66:1–66:22 (2018)
23. Hoffman, M.D., Gelman, A.: The No-U-Turn sampler: adaptively setting path lengths in Hamiltonian Monte Carlo. J. Mach. Learn. Res. 15(1), 1593–1623 (2014)
24. Köpf, B., Basin, D.A.: An information-theoretic model for adaptive side-channel attacks. In: CCS 2007, pp. 286–296 (2007)
25. Kraskov, A., Stögbauer, H., Grassberger, P.: Estimating mutual information. Phys. Rev. E 69, 066138 (2004)
26. Kruschke, J.: Doing Bayesian Data Analysis: A Tutorial with R, JAGS, and Stan. Academic Press, Cambridge (2014)
27. Kucera, M., Tsankov, P., Gehr, T., Guarnieri, M., Vechev, M.T.: Synthesis of probabilistic privacy enforcement. In: CCS 2017, pp. 391–408. ACM (2017)
28. Kullback, S., Leibler, R.A.: On information and sufficiency. Ann. Math. Stat. 22(1), 79–86 (1951)
29. Machanavajjhala, A., Kifer, D., Gehrke, J., Venkitasubramaniam, M.: L-diversity: privacy beyond k-anonymity. ACM Trans. Knowl. Discov. Data 1(1), 1–52 (2007)
30. Malacaria, P.: Assessing security threats of looping constructs. In: POPL 2007, pp. 225–235. ACM (2007)
31. Mardziel, P., Magill, S., Hicks, M., Srivatsa, M.: Dynamic enforcement of knowledge-based security policies using probabilistic abstract interpretation. J. Comput. Secur. 21(4), 463–532 (2013)
32. Nadon, G., Feilberg, M., Johansen, M., Shklovski, I.: In the user we trust: unrealistic expectations of Facebook's privacy mechanisms. In: SMSociety 2018 (2018)
33. Pardo, R., Rafnsson, W., Probst, C., Wasowski, A.: Privug: using probabilistic programming for quantifying leakage in privacy risk analysis. arXiv preprint arXiv:2011.08742 (2021)
34. Pedregosa, F., et al.: Scikit-learn: machine learning in Python. J. Mach. Learn. Res. 12, 2825–2830 (2011)
35. Pfeffer, A.: Practical Probabilistic Programming. Manning Publications Co., New York (2016)
36. Ramsey, N., Pfeffer, A.: Stochastic lambda calculus and monads of probability distributions. In: POPL 2002 (2002)

37. Rényi, A., et al.: On measures of entropy and information. In: 4th Berkeley Symposium on Mathematical Statistics and Probability (1961)
38. Robert, C.P., Casella, G.: Monte Carlo Statistical Methods. Springer, New York (2004). https://doi.org/10.1007/978-1-4757-4145-2
39. Romanelli, M., Chatzikokolakis, K., Palamidessi, C., Piantanida, P.: Estimating g-leakage via machine learning. In: CCS 2020. ACM (2020)
40. Salvatier, J., Wiecki, T.V., Fonnesbeck, C.: Probabilistic programming in Python using PyMC3. PeerJ Comput. Sci. **2**, e55 (2016)
41. Silverman, B.W.: Density Estimation for Statistics and Data Analysis, vol. 26. CRC Press, Boca Raton (1986)
42. Sweeney, L.: k-anonymity: a model for protecting privacy. Int. J. Uncertainty Fuzziness Knowl. Based Syst. **10**(5), 557–570 (2002)
43. Tolpin, D., van de Meent, J.-W., Yang, H., Wood, F.D.: Design and implementation of probabilistic programming language Anglican. In: IFL 2016 (2016)
44. Wang, Q., Kulkarni, S.R., Verdú, S.: Divergence estimation of continuous distributions based on data-dependent partitions. IEEE Trans. Inf. Theory **51**(9), 3064–3074 (2005)

Transparent Electricity Pricing
with Privacy

Daniël Reijsbergen[(✉)], Zheng Yang[(✉)] [iD], Aung Maw, Tien Tuan Anh Dinh,
and Jianying Zhou

Singapore University of Technology and Design, Singapore, Singapore
daniel_reijsbergen@sutd.edu.sg, zheng.yang@rub.de

Abstract. Smart grids leverage data from smart meters to improve
operations management and to achieve cost reductions. The fine-grained
meter data also enable pricing schemes that simultaneously benefit electricity retailers and users. Our goal is to design a practical dynamic
pricing protocol for smart grids in which the rate charged by a retailer
depends on the total demand among its users. Realizing this goal is
challenging because neither the retailer nor the users are trusted. The
first challenge is to design a pricing scheme that incentivizes consumption
behavior that leads to lower costs for both the users and the retailer. The
second challenge is to prevent the retailer from tampering with the data,
for example, by claiming that the total consumption is much higher than
its real value. The third challenge is data privacy, that is, how to hide the
meter data from adversarial users. To address these challenges, we propose a scheme in which peak rates are charged if either the total or the
individual consumptions exceed some thresholds. We formally define a
privacy-preserving transparent pricing scheme (PPTP) that allows honest users to detect tampering at the retailer while ensuring data privacy.
We present two instantiations of PPTP, and prove their security. Both
protocols use secure commitments and zero-knowledge proofs. We implement and evaluate the protocols on server and edge hardware, demonstrating that PPTP has practical performance at scale.

1 Introduction

Smart meters, the building blocks of smart grids, allow electricity retailers to
measure their customers' power use at a frequency that is far beyond the capabilities of traditional meters, which rely on sporadic manual readouts. One important use case for a higher data frequency is that it enables more accurate and
informative bills. The high measurement frequency also enables advanced electricity *pricing*. Since the retailer's costs are highest during periods of high network demand, it is often profitable to incentivize users to spread their demand
across the day by charging them different rates during *peak* and *off-peak* periods.
This is ultimately also beneficial for the customers themselves because a retailer
with lower costs can offer more competitive prices.

© Springer Nature Switzerland AG 2021
E. Bertino et al. (Eds.): ESORICS 2021, LNCS 12973, pp. 439–460, 2021.
https://doi.org/10.1007/978-3-030-88428-4_22

Pricing schemes that are based on fixed peak and off-peak rates do not make full use of the smart meter's potential, which includes the ability to receive up-to-date pricing information that reflects network conditions observed by the retailer. To improve on this, *dynamic* pricing schemes [14] allow the retailer to anticipate periods of high electricity demand, e.g., heatwaves or major sporting events, and incentivize users to shift their loads away from these periods. In this set-up, the retailer shares pricing information with the meters at the start of each operational cycle (e.g., at midnight), which can then be forwarded to a smart home hub that coordinates high-demand activities (e.g., charging an electric vehicle) across the household. In return, the meter periodically sends measurements back to the retailer, and after a number of *operational cycles* – an operational cycle typically lasts a single day – the user is presented with an electricity bill that reflects the power usage and prices throughout the cycles. However, prior research [2,14] has found that users are uncomfortable with pricing schemes that they perceive to be overly complex or risky.

Our goal is to design a practical dynamic pricing protocol. This is challenging because neither the retailers nor the users are trusted. In particular, the first challenge is to design a pricing scheme that can simultaneously reduce the costs of the retailer and the users – i.e., that the retailer is able to charge higher prices during periods when the actual demand is high across the network. The second challenge is to prevent the retailer from giving wrong information about network-level demand – i.e., that it cannot tamper with the aggregate measurements from the meters. The third challenge is to share network-level information without revealing the users' privacy-sensitive measurements to other users – i.e., that an honest-but-curious user cannot learn other users' measurements.

The latter two challenges have been studied in the related literature, e.g., by Shi et al. [13] and others [1,6]. However, these works use a different threat model than the one that is most relevant in our setting. For example, in the work by Shi et al. [13] the retailer is not trusted with knowledge of individual users' measurements. Since the retailer in our model needs the measurements anyway to compute the bills, we can afford a more relaxed trust assumption, namely that the privacy requirement only applies to honest-but-curious users. Another difference is that Shi et al. [13] do not consider strict integrity of the aggregate data – therefore, in their setting random noise can be added to measurements, but allowing this in our setting would mean that the retailer can increase its profits by inflating the aggregate value. In summary, our threat model gives us opportunities to design a more efficient privacy-preserving protocol, while at the same time necessitating the protection of measurement integrity.

To address the above challenges, we present a privacy-preserving and transparent pricing (PPTP) scheme. The scheme addresses the first challenge by charging a peak or off-peak rate depending on the *actual* network demand. This protects the retailer from the risk of financial losses during a demand surge while being fully transparent to the user. It is predictable for the user as network demand under normal circumstances can be predicted with reasonable accuracy given historical data [9]. To address the second challenge, we require the retailer to share verifiable proofs about users' measurements. To address the third challenge, we use zero-knowledge range proofs that do not reveal the underlying measurements, e.g., Bulletproofs [4]. We formalize the security definition of PPTP and present two instantiations: a baseline protocol that shares the full set of range proofs with each user, and a more efficient one that uses Merkle trees and which uses concepts from related work on Certificate Transparency [5,7]. We prove the security of both instantiations, and evaluate their performance on a server and on edge devices. The results show that PPTP achieves practical performance at scale.

In summary, we make the following contributions.

1. We present a dynamic pricing protocol for smart grids that reduces the cost for both the retailer and users.
2. We define a privacy-preserving and transparent pricing (PPTP) scheme that ensures integrity of the retailer when computing dynamic prices. PPTP protects confidentiality of the meter data against malicious users.
3. We instantiate two PPTP protocols and prove their security properties.
4. We implement the two protocols and demonstrate their performance at scale using a server and Raspberry Pi hardware.

Throughout this paper, we use the notation $[k]$ to denote $\{1, \ldots, k\}$ for $k \in \mathbb{N}$. A summary of the other notation used in the paper can be found in Table 1. The structure of the paper is as follows. In Sect. 2, we present our model of the system's cost and price structure. The network model, threat model, and

Table 1. Summary of the notation used in this paper.

Symbol	Values	Meaning
n	$\mathbb{N}$	Number of users
k	$\mathbb{N}$	Number of time periods per operational cycle
$p_{i\,t}$	$\mathbb{N}$	Rate charged to user $i \in [n]$ in period $t \in [k]$
B_i	$\mathbb{N}$	Bill of user $i \in [n]$
α_t	$\mathbb{N}$	Peak rate in period $t \in [k]$
β_t	$\{0, \ldots, \alpha_t\}$	Off-peak rate in period $t \in [k]$
γ_t	$\{0, n\delta_t - 1\}$	System peak rate threshold in period $t \in [k]$
δ_t	$\mathbb{N}$	Individual peak rate threshold in period $t \in [k]$
$y_{i\,t}$	$\mathbb{N}$	Raw measurement of user $i \in [n]$ in period $t \in [k]$
$x_{i\,t}$	$\{0, \delta_t\}$	Truncated measurement of user $i \in [n]$ in period $t \in [k]$
$r_{i\,t}$	$\mathcal{R}_c$	Random secret of user $i \in [n]$ in period $t \in [k]$
$c_{i\,t}$	$\mathcal{C}_c$	Commitment of $x_{i\,t}$
$\pi_{i\,t}$		Zero-knowledge proof that $x_{i\,t} \in [0, \delta_t]$
x_t^*	$\{0, n\delta_t\}$	Sum of $\min(x_{i\,t}, \delta_t)$ for all $i \in [n]$ in period $t \in [k]$
c_t^*	$\mathcal{C}_c$	Sum of $c_{i\,t}$ for all $i \in [n]$ in period $t \in [k]$
π_t^*		Zero-knowledge proof that $x_t^* \in [0, \gamma_t]$

requirements are presented in Sect. 3. The two PPTP instantiations are presented in Sects. 4 and 5. We present the experimental results in Sect. 6 and discuss related work in Sect. 7. Section 8 concludes the paper.

2 Electricity Pricing

Power Usage and Cost Model. For the meter readings, we consider a single operational cycle (typically a day) that is divided into k time periods – e.g., if each operational cycle lasts for one day and $k = 24$, then each time period corresponds to an hour. Let $y_{it} \in \mathbb{N}$ be the reading by the smart meter of customer $i \in [n]$ in period $t \in [k]$ – note that measurements can be represented as integers through rounding, e.g., a power use of 2.72 kWh in a period can be represented as '272' if measurements are rounded to two decimals. Let $\vec{y}_t = (y_{1t}, \ldots, y_{nt})$ denote the readings in t. The readings reflect the customer's energy consumption, which for every period equals the sum of all the *loads* run in that period. A load is an electricity-consuming job, typically related to a specific appliance, that can be represented by its required duration (in terms of periods) per operational cycle, and its energy use per period. We consider two types of loads: *controllable* and *must-run* loads [11,12]. The customer is free to choose when to run the controllable loads, but the must-run loads must be executed in their assigned time periods. If the electricity prices p_t depend on the time period $t \in [k]$, then the goal of each customer $i \in [n]$ is to divide her controllable runs over the operational cycle such that her total electricity bill $B_i = \sum_{t=1}^{k} p_t y_{it}$ is minimal.

The retailer's goal is to maximize its profit, which is the difference between its revenues U and its costs C. The retailer's total revenues in a cycle equal the sum of the bills of its customers, i.e., $U(\vec{y}_t, \ldots, \vec{y}_k) = \sum_{t=1}^{k} \sum_{i=1}^{n} p_t y_{it}$. Its costs depend on the network demand, because a higher network demand means that more energy needs to be purchased on the electricity market. In this work, we do not consider other fixed costs such as fees paid to the grid operators. As a result, the total costs in a cycle are given by $C(\vec{y}_t, \ldots, \vec{y}_k) = \sum_{t=1}^{k} C_t(\vec{y}_t)$, where $C_t(\vec{y}_t)$ denotes the total costs in period t as a function of the demand in t.

We make the following two assumptions about the retailer's cost function. First, the costs may depend on the time period, which captures fluctuations in energy supply throughout the day, e.g., due to solar panels which require daylight to operate. Second, the marginal costs are an increasing function of the total demand $s_t = \sum_{i=1}^{n} y_{it}$ – i.e., if the amount of energy purchased during a period goes up, then so does the cost per unit of energy. This captures the fact that when demand exceeds the maximum capacity of the power generators, they must resort to limited reserves [15] or operate beyond capacity which increases the generators' long-term maintenance costs [12].

Pricing Model. It follows from the two assumptions above that the retailer has minimal costs if demand is high during periods with low prices, and the demand within a single period does not become too high. The retailer cannot directly control the demand of its customers in each period, but it can *incentivize* them to perform load balancing through a pricing mechanism that rewards customers for keeping the retailer's costs low.

The problem of pricing mechanism design has been studied extensively in the literature [8,14]. The most common design is *peak load pricing*: for each period $t \in [k]$ there is a different rate that depends on energy market prices and historical demand in t. Although such a scheme incentivizes customers to shift controllable loads away from the peak periods, they still have no incentive to spread demand across the different non-peak periods. A more refined pricing mechanism is *real-time pricing with inclining block rates* (RTPIBR) [9], in which the price paid by customer $i \in [n]$ during period $t \in [k]$ is given by

$$p_{it}(\vec{y}_t) = \begin{cases} \alpha_t & \text{if } y_i > \gamma_t, \\ \beta_t & \text{otherwise.} \end{cases} \tag{1}$$

Here, α_t is period t's penalty rate, β_t is period t's normal rate, and γ_t is the customer's usage threshold in period t. In words, in addition to the different prices per period, the customer is also charged a penalty if her demand in a single period is too high. Although this is an improvement over peak load pricing, it does not take into account the total network demand. Although the customers are motivated to shift loads over several non-peak periods to avoid the penalty rate in a single period, they could all shift it to the same non-peak periods, which would lead to unnecessarily high demand in those periods.

We propose a pricing scheme that takes the total demand into account. Our scheme allows users to learn the expected demand from previous operational cycles and allocate their controllable loads accordingly. At the start of each cycle, the cycle's penalty prices α_t, normal prices β_t, network demand thresholds γ_t, and individual demand thresholds δ_t are fixed for all $t \in [k]$ and made available to all the entities, e.g., by posting them on a public bulletin board. δ_t represents the maximum contribution of a single user to the network demand. Without this bound, a handful of heavy-use customers could report an energy use that exceeds γ_t, and the peak rate would apply regardless of the consumption of the other customers. The price p_{it} paid by user i during period t is then given by

$$p_{it}(\vec{y}_t) = \begin{cases} \alpha_t & \text{if } \sum_{j=1}^{n} \min(y_{jt}, \delta_t) > \gamma_t \text{ or } y_{it} > \delta_t, \\ \beta_t & \text{otherwise.} \end{cases} \tag{2}$$

This is similar to (1), except that the penalty rate is charged depending on the total demand among the retailer's users *and* whether the individual demand exceeds a threshold. In the following, we write $x_{it} = \min(y_{it}, \delta_t)$ and $x_t^* = \sum_{i=1}^{n} x_{it}$, and we write $p(y_{it}, x^*)$ instead of $p_{it}(\vec{y}_t)$ because each user's rate only depends on her own measurement and the sum.

Example. We consider n users who have the same must-run demand profile every day (taken from [11]). Each user has a single controllable load—namely the charging of an electric vehicle—which consumes 1 kW for six consecutive hours. We consider three different usage patterns: (a) all consumers schedule the load at 6PM, (b) all consumers schedule the load at midnight, and (c) half of the consumers schedule the load at midnight and the other half at noon. These patterns are shown in Figs. 1a, 1b, and 1c, respectively. The retailer's increasing marginal costs imply that its costs are highest in pattern (a), lower in (b), and lowest in (c). Using a na"1ve pricing scheme – i.e., a constant price – all three patterns have the same costs for users since they are charged the same rate in all cases. Using peak load pricing [11], in which a peak rate is charged between 2PM and 8PM and an off-peak rate between 10PM and 7PM, it is no longer optimal for all consumers to run the load at 6PM. Instead, they may all shift their loads to midnight in order to get the lowest bills, as shown in Fig. 1b. Using RTPIBR, we can impose that consumers also pay the peak rate whenever their demand in a period exceeds $\gamma = 1\,kW$. However, although this increases the bill of every user, they are not motivated to spread loads over the day as the user still pays a similar rate regardless of whether she schedules her load at midnight or at noon. Using our pricing scheme in Eq. 2, which charges the peak rate in periods where the network-level demand exceeds nkW, the users are motivated to spread their load to different periods. It can be seen in Fig. 1c that both the users and retailer incur low cost, because the users pay the normal rate, and the retailer has low marginal cost due to a balanced network demand.

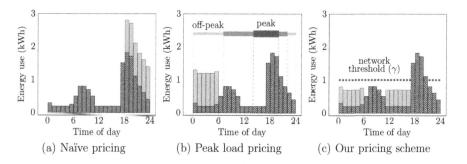

Fig. 1. Demand over time of an *average* user. Blue and red bars represent demand due to must-run and controllable loads, respectively. (Color figure online)

3   System and Security Model

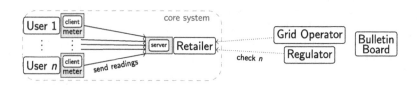

Fig. 2. Entities in our system.

System Model. Figure 2 depicts the different entities in our system. There is one power *retailer* and n *customers* (or users). The retailer purchases electricity from power generators on the wholesale electricity market, and pays a fee to one or more *grid operators* for the use of their transmission and distribution networks. We assume that the regulator and grid operators know n, but that they are unable to observe the individual or total consumption of the retailer's users.[1] The retailer runs a *server*, and each user owns a smart *meter*, which runs a software application called a *client* that communicates with the server.

At the end of each period $t \in [k]$, each smart meter $i \in [n]$ sends the raw reading y_{it} to the retailer via a secure and highly available channel. At the end of the operational cycle, the retailer uses the same channel to send to each user a statement containing the total bill $B_i \in \mathbb{N}$, and for each period $t \in [k]$ both y_{it} and the sum x_t^*. The customer can then verify that $B_i = \sum_{t=1}^{k} p_{it}(y_{it}, x_t^*)x_{it}$. However, the customer cannot verify x_t^*, which may allow the retailer to charge the peak rate incorrectly.

Threat Model. The retailer is adversarial and interested in convincing users of accepting an incorrect bill $\tilde{B}_i$ such that $\tilde{B}_i > B_i$. We assume that the meters are secure, i.e., they produce readings that match the user's true power consumption – otherwise, honest users would be able to report this to the regulator. The retailer can collude with a number of *adversarial users* who may generate arbitrary readings. Users can be adversarial because they have been bribed by the retailer, or they can be Sybil users created by the retailer. We assume that the regulator would notice if the retailer would create too many Sybils, so this number is limited in our model. Non-adversarial users are honest-but-curious, i.e., they will faithfully follow the protocol as described, but will attempt to use the information shared with them to learn the readings of other users. Finally, there is a public bulletin board which provides immutable and tamper-evident storage, e.g., a public blockchain.

Given this threat model, our first goal is allow users to *detect incorrect bills*. In particular, let B_i^* be the bill for user i if each adversarial user j reports $x_{jt} = \delta_t$ in each period $t \in [k]$. An incorrect bill $\tilde{B}_i$ then satisfies $\tilde{B}_i > B_i^*$. In other words, the adversarial users should not be able to influence individual bills beyond reporting the maximum. Another goal is to *hide private readings* x_{it} from other honest-but-curious users. The final goal is *efficiency*, that is, the protocol can support a large number of users with practical performance.

3.1   Security Model

We let κ be the security parameter by κ, and $\emptyset$ be the empty string. When X is a set, $x \overset{\$}{\leftarrow} X$ denotes the action of sampling an element uniformly at random from X. Let $\|$ denote an operation that concatenates two strings.

We define a privacy-preserving, transparent pricing (PPTP) scheme as one that consists of the four algorithms below.

---

[1] Although the grid operators will typically perform their own high-level measurements for system monitoring, e.g., using phasor measurement units, they will not be able to distinguish between the customers of different retailers in a small area.

$(P_{tp}, k_r) \leftarrow$ Initialize(1^κ): run by the retailer. It takes as input the security parameter κ, and outputs the system parameters P_{tp} and a secret key $k_r \in \mathcal{SK}_{tp}$ where $\mathcal{SK}_{tp}$ is the secret key space.

$(r_{it})_{i \in [n]} \leftarrow$ SlotSecretGen(P_{tp}, k_r, t): run by the retailer. It takes as input the system parameters P_{tp}, the secret key k_r, and the time slot t, and outputs slot secrets $(r_{it})_{i \in [n]} \in \mathcal{SS}_{tp}$ for n users, where $\mathcal{SS}_{tp}$ is the slot secret space.

$E_t \leftarrow$ EvidenceGen($P_{tp}, k_r, (x_{it})_{i \in [n]}, t$): run by the retailer. It takes as input the system parameters P_{tp}, secret key k_r, and the measurements $(x_{it})_{i \in [n]} \in \mathcal{V}_{tp}$ of each user i for time t, and outputs an evidence $E_t \in \mathcal{E}_{tp}$. Here, $\mathcal{E}_{tp}$ is the evidence space and $\mathcal{V}_{tp}$ is the measurement space.

$\{0, 1\} \leftarrow$ EvidenceVrf($P_{tp}, r_{it}, x_{it}, E_t, t$): run by each user. It takes as input the system parameters P_{tp}, slot secret r_{it}, measurement x_{it} of user i for time t, and the evidence E_t, and outputs TRUE or FALSE.

Given $(P_{tp}, k_r) :=$ Initialize(1^κ), $(r_{it})_{i \in [n]} :=$ SlotSecretGen(P_{tp}, k_r), a set of valid measurements $(x_{it})_{i \in [n]} \in \mathcal{V}_{tp}$ for time slot t, the scheme is correct if EvidenceVrf($(P_{tp}, r_{jt}, x_{jt},$ EvidenceGen($P_{tp}, k_r, (x_{it})_{i \in [n]}, t), t) = 1$, for any slot secret $r_{jt} \in (r_{it})_{i \in [n]}$ and the corresponding measurement $x_{jt} \in (x_{it})_{i \in [n]}$.

3.2 Security Properties

We define two properties of PPTP: *transparency* and *privacy*. For simplicity, we focus on a single operational cycle.

Transparency. This property means that each honest user $i \in [n]$ is able to verify that a bill $\tilde{B}_i$ is incorrect if $\tilde{B}_i > B_i^*$, where B_i^* is the worst-case bill defined earlier in the section. Furthermore, the user can check if $\tilde{B}_i$ contains an incorrect measurement $\bar{x}_{it}$, i.e., $\bar{x}_{it} > x_{it}$ or $\bar{x}_{it} > \delta_t$. Finally, a dishonest user cannot blame the retailer for misbehavior if it has behaved honestly.

We formulate transparency through a two-stage game $\text{Game}_{\text{PPTP}, \mathcal{A}}^{\text{Trans}}$ running between a challenger and an adversary $\mathcal{A}$. In the first stage, the adversary can run the PPTP scheme herself with the secret key k_r and measurements of her own choice, and outputs a time slot t^* as challenge request. The challenger then randomly samples a set of honest measurements $\vec{x}_{t^*} = (x_{it^*})_{i \in [n]} \xleftarrow{\$} \mathcal{V}_{tp}$ which are sent to $\mathcal{A}$. The goal of $\mathcal{A}$ is to generate a valid evidence $\bar{E}_{t^*}$ for a set of measurements $\vec{\bar{x}}_{t^*} = (\bar{x}_{it^*})_{i \in [n]}$, such that $\vec{\bar{x}}_{t^*} \neq \vec{x}_{t^*}$, which can pass the verification for an honest user j^*'s measurement $x_{j^*, t^*} \in \vec{x}_{t^*}$, meaning that EvidenceVrf($P_{tp}, r_{j t^*}, x_{j t^*}, \bar{E}_{t^*}, t^*) = 1$.

Privacy. This property means that a user i cannot learn privacy-sensitive meter readings x_{jt} of another user $j \in [n] \backslash \{i\}$ for any $t \in [k]$.

We define a game $\text{Game}_{\text{PPTP}, \mathcal{A}}^{\text{Priv}}$ to formulate the privacy via indistinguishability. The adversary $\mathcal{A}$ chooses measurements $(x_{it})_{i \in [n], t \in [k]}$ for all users, and an honest user j^* and time slot t^* as the challenge in the game. The challenger selects two values $x_{j^* t^*}^0, x_{j^* t^*}^0$ that lead to the same bills for all users $i \neq j^*$. Specifically, it sets $x_{j^* t^*}^0 := x_{j^* t^*}$, and $x_{j^* t^*}^1 \xleftarrow{\$} \mathcal{V}_{tp}$, such that $x_{j^*, t^*}^0 \neq x_{j^*, t^*}^1$ and $(\bigwedge_{i=1, i \neq j^*}^n B_i^0 = B_i^1) = 1$, where $B_i^b =$

$p_{it^*}(x_{it^*}, x_{t^*}^{b,*})x_{it^*} + \sum_{t=1,t\neq t^*}^{k} p_{it}(x_{it}, x_t^*)x_{it}$ and $x_{t^*}^{b,*} = \min(x_{j^*,t^*}^b, d_{t^*}) + \sum_{i=1,i\neq j^*}^{n} \min(x_{it^*}, d_{t^*})$. Next, the challenger generates the evidence for time t^* based on $(x_{it^*})_{i\in[n],i\neq j^*}||x_{j^*t^*}^b$ and $b \xleftarrow{\$} \{0,1\}$. The goal of $\mathcal{A}$ in this game is to distinguish whether her measurement $x_{j^*t^*}$ is used to generate the challenge evidence E_{t^*}. Note that the constraint that the values chosen by the challenger leads to the same bill for users $i \neq j^*$ is important. Otherwise, the distinct bills would allow the adversary to trivially distinguish the bit b. During the game, the adversary can ask oracle $\mathcal{O}_{EG}$ to get the evidences for any measurements, and oracle $\mathcal{O}_C$ to reveal the slot secrets. But it cannot ask either $\mathcal{O}_{EG}(\cdot, t^*)$ or $\mathcal{O}_C(j^*, t^*)$.

$\text{Game}_{\text{PPTP},\mathcal{A}}^{\text{Trans}}(\kappa)$	$\text{Game}_{\text{PPTP},\mathcal{A}}^{\text{Priv}}(\kappa)$
$\text{QL} := \emptyset$	$\text{QL} := \emptyset;\ \text{CL} := \emptyset;\ b \xleftarrow{\$} \{0,1\}$
$(P_{\text{tp}}, k_r) \leftarrow \text{Initialize}(1^\kappa)$	$(P_{\text{tp}}, k_r) \leftarrow \text{Initialize}(1^\kappa)$
$(state, t^*) \leftarrow \mathcal{A}(P_{\text{tp}}, k_r)$	$(state, j^*, t^*, (x_{it})_{i\in[n],t\in[k]}) \leftarrow \mathcal{A}^{\mathcal{O}_{EG}(\cdot,\cdot),\mathcal{O}_C(\cdot,\cdot)}(P_{\text{tp}})$
$\vec{x}_{t^*} = (x_{it^*})_{i\in[n]} \xleftarrow{\$} \mathcal{V}_{\text{tp}}$, s.t., $x_{it^*} \leq \delta_t$ for $i \in [n]$	$x_{j^*t^*}^0 := x_{j^*t^*}$
$(\bar{E}_{t^*}, (\bar{x}_{it^*})_{i\in[n]}, j^*) \leftarrow \mathcal{A}(P_{\text{tp}}, k_r, state, (x_{it^*})_{i\in[n]})$	$x_{j^*t^*}^1 \xleftarrow{\$} \mathcal{V}_{\text{tp}}$, s.t., $(x_{j^*t^*}^0 \neq x_{j^*t^*}^1)$ and $(\bigwedge_{i=1,i\neq j}^{n} B_i^0 = B_i^1) = 1$
$\vec{\bar{x}}_{t^*} = (\bar{x}_{it^*})_{i\in[n]}$	where $B_i^b = p_{it^*}(x_{it^*}, x_{t^*}^{b,*})x_{it^*} + \sum_{t=1,t\neq t^*}^{k} p_{it}(x_{it}, x_t^*)x_{it}$
$\text{Return } (\vec{x}_{t^*} \neq \vec{\bar{x}}_{t^*}) \wedge (\bigvee_{i=1}^n \bar{x}_{it^*} > \delta_t)$	and $x_{t^*}^{b,*} = \min(x_{j^*,t^*}^b, \delta_{t^*}) + \sum_{i=1,i\neq j^*}^{n} \min(x_{it^*}, \delta_{t^*})$
$\wedge (\bar{E}_{t^*} = \text{EvidenceGen}(P_{\text{tp}}, k_r, (\bar{x}_{it^*})_{i\in[n]}, t^*))$	$E_{t^*} := \text{EvidenceGen}(P_{\text{tp}}, k_r, ((x_{it^*})_{i\in[n]\backslash j^*}||x_{j^*,t^*}^b, t^*))$
$\wedge (\text{EvidenceVrf}(P_{\text{tp}}, r_{j^*t^*}, x_{j^*t^*}, \bar{E}_{t^*}, t^*) = 1)$	$b' \leftarrow \mathcal{A}^{\mathcal{O}_{EG}(\cdot,\cdot),\mathcal{O}_C(\cdot,\cdot)}(P_{\text{tp}}, E_{t^*}, state)$
	$\text{Return } (b = b') \wedge (t^* \notin \text{QL}) \wedge (r_{j^*,t^*} \notin \text{CL})$
$\mathcal{O}_{EG}((x_{it})_{i\in[n]}, t)$	$\mathcal{O}_C(i, t)$
$E_t := \text{EvidenceGen}(P_{\text{tp}}, k_r, (x_{it})_{i\in[n]}, t)$	$(r_{it})_{i\in[n]} := \text{SlotSecretGen}(P_{\text{tp}}, k_r, t)$
$(E_t, t, (x_{it})_{i\in[n]}) \rightarrow \text{QL}$	$r_{it} \rightarrow \text{CL}$
$\text{Return } E_t$	$\text{Return } r_{it}$

Definition 1. *A privacy-preserving transparent pricing scheme* PPTP *is secure if the advantages* $\text{Adv}_{\text{PPTP},\mathcal{A}}^{\text{Trans}}(\kappa) = \Pr[\text{Game}_{\text{PPTP},\mathcal{A}}^{\text{Trans}} = 1]$ *and* $\text{Adv}_{\text{PPTP},\mathcal{A}}^{\text{Priv}}(\kappa) = \left|\Pr[\text{Game}_{\text{PPTP},\mathcal{A}}^{\text{Priv}}(\kappa) = 1] - 1/2\right|$ *of any PPT adversaries* $\mathcal{A}$ *in the corresponding games are negligible.*

4 Baseline Protocol

In this section, we present a simple instantiation of PPTP. This baseline protocol meets the security definition above. In particular, the retailer creates a commitment and zero-knowledge range proof for each user's measurement, and shares the full set of commitments and proofs with all users. Each honest user verifies all the steps of the protocol to detect misbehavior. This protocol incurs a large performance overhead, which we address in next section with a more efficient protocol. In the following, we focus on the algorithms for a single time period $t \in [k]$, and discuss how to generalize it to a full operation cycle.

4.1 Preliminaries

We briefly review the syntax and security properties of the cryptographic primitives used in our protocol.

Commitment Scheme. A commitment scheme COM consists of two algorithms. COM.Setup(1^κ) takes as input the security parameter 1^κ, and outputs commitment parameters P_c. The algorithm COM.Commit(P_c, v, r) takes as input parameters P_c, a value v, and randomness r, and outputs a commitment c. The scheme is *hiding* when c reveals nothing of the committed value, and *binding* when the commitment cannot be opened with two different random values. The scheme is *collision-resistant* if for any $(v_0, v_1) \in \mathcal{V}_c$ and $(r_0, r_1) \in \mathcal{R}_c$ such that $v_0 \neq v_1$, the probability that COM.Commit(P_c, v_0, r_0) = COM.Commit(P_c, v_1, r_1) is negligible. Finally, the scheme is (additively) homomorphic if, for any $(v_0, v_1) \in \mathcal{V}_c$ and $(r_0, r_1) \in \mathcal{R}_c$, we have

$$\text{COM.Commit}(P_c, v_0, r_0) + \text{COM.Commit}(P_c, v_1, r_1) = \text{COM.Commit}(P_c, v_0 + v_1, r_0 + r_1).$$

Non-interactive Zero-Knowledge. Let R_{zk} be an efficiently computable relation of the form $(st, w) \in R_{zk}$, where st is the statement and w is the witness of st. A non-interactive proof system NIZK for R_{zk} consists of three algorithms. NIZK.Setup(1^κ) which takes as input the security parameter 1^κ and outputs the system parameters P_{zk}. NIZK.Prv(P_{zk}, st, w) takes as input system parameters P_{zk} and a pair (st, w) and outputs a proof π. NIZK.Vrf(P_{zk}, st, π) takes as input P_{zk}, a statement st, and a proof π, and outputs TRUE (1) or FALSE (0).

The proof system NIZK satisfies *zero-knowledge* if the generated proofs reveal nothing regarding the corresponding witnesses, and *simulation-extractability* if for any proof generated by the adversary, there exists an efficient algorithm to extract the corresponding witnesses with a trap door. In this work, we use NIZK over the family of relations $R_{zk} = (\mathcal{RL}_{v_{max}})_{v_{max} \in \mathbb{N}}$, where v_{max} can be either γ_t or δ_t, and

$$\mathcal{RL}_{v_{max}} = \{((c, v_{max}), (v, r)) | c = \text{COM.Commit}(P_c, v, r) \land v \in [0, v_{max}]\}.$$

Pseudo-random Functions. A pseudo-random function (PRF) family consists of two algorithms. PRF.KGen(1^κ) is takes as input the security parameter 1^κ and outputs a random key k. PRF.Eval(k, x) is takes as input the random key k and a message x, and outputs a pseudo-random value r.

4.2   Instantiation

The four main algorithms of Sect. 3 are instantiated as follows.

$(P_{tp}, k_r) \leftarrow$ Initialize(1^κ): this algorithm generates the secret key $k_r :=$ PRF.KGen(1^κ), and initializes the commitment and non-interactive zero-knowledge schemes as $P_c :=$ COM.Setup(1^κ) and $P_{zk} :=$ NIZK.Setup(1^κ), respectively. The retailer publishes the system parameters $P_{tp} = (P_c, P_{zk}, \alpha_t, \beta_t, \gamma_t, \delta_t)$ and keeps the secret key k_r private.

$(r_{it})_{i \in [n]} \leftarrow$ SlotSecretGen(P_{tp}, k_r, t): this algorithm uses the retailer's secret key to generate the slot secrets as $r_{it} :=$ PRF.Eval($k_r, i||t$) for $i \in [n]$. Each slot secret r_{it} is sent to the corresponding user i via a secure channel and is stored privately by the retailer and user i.

$E_t \leftarrow$ EvidenceGen$(P_{tp}, (x_{it}, r_{it})_{i \in [n]}, t)$: this algorithm computes for each user $c_{it} :=$ COM.Commit(P_c, x_{it}, r_{it}) and generates the proof $\pi_{it} :=$ NIZK.Prv(P_{zk}, st, w) for the statement $st = (c_{it}, \delta_t)$ and witness $w = (x_{it}, r_{it})$. The retailer computes the sum of the values $x_t^* = \sum_{i=1}^{n} x_{it}$, the sum of the random seeds $r_t^* = \sum_{i=1}^{n} r_{it}$, $c_t^* :=$ COM.Commit(P_c, x_t^*, r_t^*), and a proof $\pi_t^* :=$ NIZK.Prv(P_{zk}, st, w) for $st = (c_t^*, \gamma_t)$ and witness $w = (x_t^*, r_t^*)$. Finally, the retailer shares $E_t = (c_t^*, \pi_t^*, (c_{it}, \pi_{it})_{i \in [n]})$ with each user, and puts a hash $h_t = H(E_t)$ on the bulletin board.

$\{0, 1\} \leftarrow$ EvidenceVrf$(P_{tp}, r_{it}, x_{it}, E_t, t)$: this algorithm executes four subroutines, each taking parts of $E_t = (c_t^*, \pi_t^*, (c_{it}, \pi_{it})_{i \in [n]})$ as input, and returns TRUE if all four subroutines return 1.

> $\{0, 1\} \leftarrow$ VerifyConsistency(E_t, h): computes $\bar{h} = H(E_t)$, and outputs TRUE if $\bar{h} = h$, and FALSE otherwise.
>
> $\{0, 1\} \leftarrow$ VerifyCommitment(P_c, x_{it}, c_{it}, t): computes $\bar{c}_{it} :=$ COM.Commit (P_c, x_{it}, r_{it}) and outputs TRUE if $\bar{c}_{it} = c_{it}$, and FALSE otherwise.
>
> $\{0, 1\} \leftarrow$ VerifySum$(P_{zk}, c_t^*, \pi_t^*, (c_{it})_{i \in [n]})$: computes $\bar{c}_t^* = \sum_{i=1}^{n} c_{it}$. It checks if $\bar{c}^* = c^*$. It then checks that c^* and π_t^* match, and executes NIZK.Vrf(P_{zk}, st, π_t^*) for the statement $st = (c^*, \gamma_t)$. The functions outputs TRUE if all three checks are successful, and FALSE otherwise.
>
> $\{0, 1\} \leftarrow$ VerifyRangeProofs$(P_{zk}, (c_{it}, \pi_{it})_{i \in [n]})$: checks that for each i, the commitment c_{it} and the proof π_t match, then executes NIZK.Vrf(P_{zk}, st, π_{it}) for the statement $st = (c_{it}, \delta_t)$. It outputs TRUE if all proofs are valid and match the commitment, and FALSE otherwise.

Operational Cycles. For a full operational cycle, the protocol above is executed for every time period $t \in [k]$. The retailer computes B_i and sends it to each user $i \in [n]$, who then verifies the bill since she knows x_{it} and x_t^* for each time period.

4.3 Security Analysis

The baseline protocol described in this section is secure according to Definition 1. The proofs for the following two theorems are included in the Appendix B.

Theorem 1. *If the commitment scheme* COM *is additively homomorphic and satisfies binding property, and non-interactive zero-knowledge proof system* NIZK *is simulation-extractable, then the baseline protocol provides transparency.*

Theorem 2. *If the commitment scheme* COM *is additively homomorphic and satisfies hiding property, the non-interactive zero-knowledge proof system* NIZK *provides zero-knowledge, and pseudo-random function family* PRF *is secure, then the baseline protocol satisfies privacy.*

4.4   Performance Analysis

We analyze the computation cost of the protocol in terms of the number of invocations to the cryptographic functions, and the bandwidth cost in terms of the sizes of the messages sent over the network. We ignore the initiation cost and the cost of users sending measurements to the retailer, as these are independent of the implementation. In the following, M_c, M_π, M_h respectively denote the message size of the commitments, proofs, and hashes.[2]

The total costs per time slot for each entity are summarized in Table 2. The server has to execute the COM.Commit and NIZK.Prv $n + 1$ times in the EvidenceGen algorithm: n times for each client's measurement x_{it} and once for the sum x_t^*. The $n + 1$ commitments and proofs are sent to each of the n clients, meaning that a message of size $(n + 1)(M_c + M_\pi)$ is sent n times. The server also computes $H(E_t)$, and sends this hash to the bulletin board. Each client receives a single message of size $n(M_c + M_\pi)$, and downloads the hash from the bulletin board for verification. The client then 1) verifies the commitment of its own measurement by executing COM.Commit and checking whether its output matches the value sent by the retailer, 2) executes NIZK.Vrf on each of the proofs, and 3) check whether the hash of the result matches the one on the bulletin board. The load on the bulletin board consists of receiving a single hash from the retailer, and sending it to the n users.

Table 2. Performance cost of the baseline solution.

Entity	Computation			Bandwidth
	COM.Commit	NIZK.Prv	NIZK.Vrf	
Server	$n + 1$	$n + 1$	0	$n(n + 1)(M_c + M_\pi) + M_h$
Client	1	0	$n + 1$	$(n + 1)(M_c + M_\pi) + M_h$
Bulletin board	0	0	0	$(n + 1)M_h$

4.5   Discussion

We consider the computation cost at the server, which increases linearly in n, to be acceptable because the server is often equipped with powerful CPUs, and the operations are parallelizable. The bandwidth cost increases quadratically, but the server can offload the messages to a cloud storage or content delivery network that can distribute the messages in a scalable and cost-effective fashion. We discuss a blockchain-based extension to the baseline protocol that reduces the costs at the client, which is important since the clients are likely running on edge devices close to the meters, or even running directly on the meter firmware.

---

[2] Some range proof techniques, e.g., Bulletproofs [4], allow for the aggregation of multiple proofs over the same range, leading to reduced bandwidth costs.

Table 3. Performance cost of the blockchain solution. BC represents the processing of read requests at the blockchain smart contract. M_{bc} is the message containing the blockchain proof that a commitment is stored in the chain.

Entity	Computation				Bandwidth
	COM.Commit	NIZK.Prv	NIZK.Vrf	BC	
Server	$n+1$	$n+1$	0	0	$(n+1)(M_c + M_\pi)$
Client	1	0	0	1	$M_c + M_{bc}$
Bulletin board	0	0	$n+1$	$n+1$	$(2n+1)M_c + nM_{bc} + (n+1)M_\pi$

We note that for verification, only the VerifyCommitment algorithm requires the private input. In other words, most of the verification can be done publicly by another party without compromising client privacy. The VerifyRangeProof algorithm, which is the most expensive, can therefore be performed by a trusted third party with more resources than the client. As a first improvement over the baseline solution, we propose to leverage a blockchain as the trusted party, and implement the range proof verification in a *smart contract*.

The server sends the proofs and commitments to a blockchain smart contract, which executes VerifyConsistency, VerifySum, and VerifyRangeProofs. If the verifications pass, the blockchain stores the messages. The client i only computes the commitment c_{it} using its own measurement x_{it}, and verifies that it was included in the blockchain by reading blockchain storage directly without incurring consensus overhead. The client does not need to run NIZK.Vrf on any of the other users' range proofs, but the trade-off here is that the blockchain incurs significant overhead: generating n proofs for read requests from the user, and executing the smart contract for verification. We summarize the cost for each entity in Table 3 in the Appendix.

5 Merkle Tree Protocol

As discussed in Sect. 4.5, the baseline solution of Sect. 4 can be improved by offloading all range proof verification to a trusted third party such as the bulletin board. However, this puts a large computational burden on the bulletin board – far beyond the capacity of, for example, the Ethereum blockchain. In this section, we take inspiration from Certificate Transparency [5] and describe another PPTP instantiation based on a modified Merkle tree. The protocol reduces the communication and computation costs at the user, and therefore is more practical. In each period the retailer sends to each user a proof of the inclusion and a range proof for the sum x_t^*, which due to the homomorphism of our commitment scheme corresponds to the value in the root of the tree.

5.1 Overview

Merkle trees are an extension of *binary trees*. For any node v, let LEFT(v) be its first child and RIGHT(v) its second child. If node v has no second child, then

$\text{RIGHT}(v) = 0$, and if it also has no first child then $\text{LEFT}(v) = 0$. In the original Merkle tree, each node v contains a hash value h_v of its children. We modify it by storing at each node v a commitment c_v. For each user $i \in [n]$ we set the commitment in the ith leaf equal to $c_i = \text{COM.Commit}(P_c, x_{it}, r_{it})$. The commitments in the other nodes are computed as:

$$c_v = c_{\text{LEFT}(v)} + c_{\text{RIGHT}(v)}, \tag{3}$$

such that and $c_0 = \text{COM.Commit}(P_c, 0, 0)$. The inclusion proof for node i includes the root, i's leaf, the intermediate nodes that lie on the path between them, and the children of these nodes. Figure 3 shows an example, where the green nodes represent the path between the leaf and the root and the yellow nodes the children of those nodes.

Assumptions. In this section, we describe a protocol that is secure under the following assumptions. There are a number of powerful entities, called *auditors*, that perform verification on behalf of the users. In the following, we assume that auditors do not share measurements themselves (although in practice a single entity may act as a user and an auditor). At least one auditor is honest, and at most f are dishonest. Furthermore, the maximum time for an auditor to finish its verification and have its messages stored on the bulletin board, T, is known. We discuss other protocols that do not rely on auditors in the Appendix A.

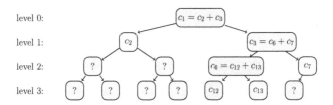

Fig. 3. Example of a modified Merkle tree with 7 leaves.

5.2 Instantiation

The four algorithms of Sect. 3 are instantiated as follows.

Initialize, SlotSecretGen: they are the same as in Sect. 4.

$E_t \leftarrow \text{EvidenceGen}(P_{\text{tp}}, (x_{it}, r_{it})_{i \in [n]}, t)$: this algorithm constructs a Merkle tree described above, using these measurements and slot randomness as input. For each user, the evidence E_t contains the inclusion proof G and a zero-knowledge proof π_t^* that the sum x_t^* (whose commitment c_t^* is the root of G) is within the range $[0, \gamma_t]$. For auditors, the evidence also includes the commitments and range proofs (c_{it}, π_{it}) for all leaf nodes $i \in [n]$. The retailer also uploads the commitment in the root node to the public bulletin board as c_h.

$\{0, 1\} \leftarrow \mathsf{EvidenceVrf}(P_{\mathsf{tp}}, r_{it}, x_{it}, E_t, t)$: this algorithm consists of two phases. In the first phase, it execute the following subroutines.

$\{0, 1\} \leftarrow \mathsf{VerifyConsistency}(G, c_h)$: verifies that the value of c_h on the bulletin board matches with the root of the inclusion proof G.

$\{0, 1\} \leftarrow \mathsf{VerifyCommitment}(P_c, r_{it}, x_{it}, G)$: if the user is an auditor, returns TRUE. Else, it computes $\bar{c}_{it} := \mathsf{COM.Commit}(P_c, x_{it}, r_{it})$, and verifies that $\bar{c}_{it} = c_v$, where v is the leaf node in the user's inclusion proof G.

$\{0, 1\} \leftarrow \mathsf{VerifyInclusionProof}(G)$: if the user is an auditor, returns TRUE. Else, it verifies that the inclusion proof is valid, i.e., that the commitment c in each intermediate core node $v \in G$ indeed follows from applying (3) to the commitments in v's children.

$\{0, 1\} \leftarrow \mathsf{VerifySum}(P_{\mathsf{zk}}, G, \pi_t^*)$: if the user is an auditor, returns TRUE. Else, it verifies that the proof π_t^* matches the commitment c_t^* in the root of G, and executes $\mathsf{NIZK.Vrf}(P_{\mathsf{zk}}, st, \pi_t^*)$ for the statement $st = (c_t^*, \gamma_t)$.

$\{0, 1\} \leftarrow \mathsf{VerifyTree}(P_{\mathsf{zk}}, (c_{it}, \pi_{it})_{i \in [n]})$: if the user is not an auditor, returns TRUE. Else, it executes $\mathsf{VerifyRangeProofs}(P_{\mathsf{zk}}, (c_{it}, \pi_{it})_{i \in [n]})$ from Sect. 4 for each user $i \in [n]$. Then, it checks whether the non-leaf nodes of the tree are correct, i.e., whether they follow from applying (3). It returns TRUE if all checks are successful, and FALSE otherwise.

In the second phase, if the user is an auditor, it signs and publishes a message to the bulletin board: a failed range proof for a leaf node if it exists, the value 1 if all four subroutines in the fist phase succeed, or an empty message otherwise. The algorithm then returns true or false depending on the result of the first phase. The non-auditor user checks if there is a proof of incorrect range in the bulletin board, if yes, it verifies the proof and returns false. Otherwise, it waits until there are $f + 1$ signed empty messages on the bulletin and returns TRUE, or returns FALSE after time T.

5.3 Security Analysis

We show that this protocol is a secure PPTP, by proving the following theorems. The proofs are included in the Appendix.

Theorem 3. *If the commitment scheme* COM *is additively homomorphic and satisfies binding property, and non-interactive zero-knowledge proof system* NIZK *is simulation-extractable, and the assumptions about f and T hold, then the Merkle tree protocol provides transparency.*

Theorem 4. *With the same assumptions in Theorem 2, the Merkle tree protocol satisfies privacy.*

5.4 Performance Analysis

We analyze the performance of the Merkle tree protocol using the same metrics as in the analysis of the baseline protocol. For simplicity, we assume $n = 2^m$ for

Table 4. Performance cost of the Merkle tree solution, assuming $m = \log_2(n)$ and $f + 1$ auditors who each report to the bulletin board. Note that a user can simultaneously act as a normal client and as an auditor.

Entity	Computation			Bandwidth
	COM.Commit	NIZK.Prv	NIZK.Vrf	
Server	$2n - 1$	$n + 1$	0	$(n + 1)(f + 1)(M_c + M_\pi) + n(2m + 1)M_c$
Normal Client	1	0	1	$(2m + 1)M_c + (f + 1)M_{bc}$
Auditor	0	0	n	$(n + 1)(M_c + M_\pi) + M_{bc}$
Bulletin board	0	0	0	$(n + 1)(f + 1)M_{bc}$

some $m \in \mathbb{N}$, so that the total number of nodes in the tree equals $2^{m+1} - 1 = 2n - 1$. The retailer generates commitments for all $2n - 1$ nodes and generates range proofs for the root and the n leaf nodes. It only sends the commitments for the nodes in the inclusion proof – this consists of $m = \log_2 n$ nodes on the path and $m + 1$ children, so $2m + 1$ in total. Table 4 summarizes the cost.

We can also extend the protocol to use a blockchain as described in Sect. 4.5. In particular, we can offload the range proofs to the smart contracts, hence making the blockchain an auditor.

6 Implementation

We implement both the baseline and Merkle tree protocol in Go. To do so, we extend the zero-knowledge range proof library by Morais et al. [10].[3] In particular, we use their implementation of Bulletproofs [4] which uses Pedersen commitment with the secp256k1 elliptic curve [3] as a commitment scheme. We parallelize proof generations and verification by exploiting Go's multi-threading. We release the source code for our experiments at https://github.com/aungmawjj/zkrp.

We evaluate the performance of our protocols in terms of the computation and bandwidth cost. We also examine how the performance scales with more hardware resources. There are no baselines from the related literature in our evaluation, because we are unaware of other protocols that address the same problem and have the same security guarantee as ours. We run the retailer's server on AWS EC2 with varying numbers of cores. We run the client on a Raspberry Pi (RPI) 3 with 4 CPUs and 1 GB RAM.

Results. Figures 4a, 4b, and 4c compare the costs of the two protocols, with varying numbers of users, using a VM with 8 cores for the server. Proof generation takes just as long for both protocols, so the lines overlap – in particular, for $n = 16\,384$, it takes 289 s for the two protocols to generate the proofs. In Fig. 4b, the auditor runs on the same VM as the server. The verification time and communication cost at the client increase linearly for the baseline, but only

---

[3] https://github.com/ing-bank/zkrp

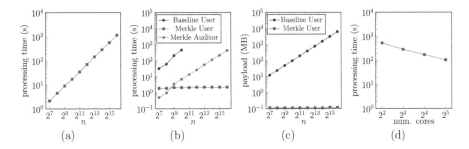

Fig. 4. (a) Proof generation times, (b) proof verification times, (c) network cost. Experiments taking longer than 20 min are not included. (d) Proof generation times for $n = 2^{14}$.

logarithmically for the Merkle tree protocol. Even with $n = 1\,024$, verification takes 460 s for the baseline, which is significant considering that it must be done k times per operational cycle. In contrast, the Merkle tree protocol takes 2.1 s.

Figure 4d shows that both protocols scale well, in terms of the proof generation cost, with more CPU cores. With $n = 16\,384$, the time for Merkle tree solution reduces from 492 s with 8 cores, to only 167 s with 32 cores.

We remark that the client cost is practical, for example with $n = 65\,536$ it takes 2.2 s to verify a single proof of roughly 110 kB and check 33 commitments. However, this cost increases linearly with k. As a large value of k implies fine-grained pricing, there is a trade-off between performance and how fine-grained the pricing scheme can be.

7   Related Work

Shi et al. [13] propose a privacy-preserving protocol that can be applied to smart meters. As mentioned in the introduction, their threat model is different from ours, as we allow the retailer to know individual users' measurements, but not to distort them. Another difference is that their method is unable to decrypt if a single meter is offline. In our setting, the retailer can set the measurements of offline users to any value that does not exceed δ_t, but offline users otherwise have no impact. Ács and Castelluccia [1] propose a related scheme for smart meters that is able to decrypt when some meters fail, although the protocol requires additional steps to do so. Erkin and Tsudik [6] consider a setting for sharing meter data that is entirely peer-to-peer, i.e., without a retailer/aggregator.

Zhang et al. [16] propose INTEGRIDB, which allows data owners to outsource SQL queries on their databases in a secure way. Their approach – which uses sorted Merkle trees – can be used to store sums and perform range proofs on measurement data, but they use a different system and threat model than the one in Sect. 3. In particular, range proofs in their setting require that the values in the leaves of the tree are sorted, but whereas their setting has an entity that checks the structure of the tree (the 'data owner'), there is no such entity in our model as the auditors do not know the leaves' underlying measurements.

Chase and Meiklejohn [5] define the first formal security model for provable transparency. Our formalization of transparency is adapted from their model but with additional constraints on electricity measurements and bills. Unlike Chase and Meiklejohn's model, we particularly formulate the privacy definition in conjunction with transparency. Nevertheless, we leverage auditors as in [5] to facilitate the proof verification in the Merkle tree scheme.

8   Conclusions

We have introduced Privacy-Preserving Transparency Pricing (PPTP) schemes, which incentivize consumers to schedule their electricity in a way that reduces the costs for both the retailer and the users. We showed that our scheme is secure against retailer misbehavior while preserving user privacy. Our scheme can support tens of thousands of users while remaining computationally feasible on low-capacity devices. In our scheme, the retailer is only able to increase its profits to the extent allowed by the number of adversarial users, which is limited. That is, the retailer can inflate demand to a degree determined by the fraction of adversarial users and δ_t, the maximum value for readings. This allows the retailer to occasionally charge higher prices, but only if the system-level threshold γ_t would not be exceeded if the adversarial users were to report their true usage, but exceeded if the adversarial users report the maximum usage δ_t.

Our future work includes improving the protocol further to support even larger numbers of users. We note that our approach can be extended to other situations in which it is beneficial for users to pay fees based on network-level demand – e.g., water or gas distribution networks. We also believe that our method generalizes to systems with multiple retailers, but we leave this as future work. Another interesting direction for future work is to investigate how quickly user behavior settles into a stable and efficient pattern given the dynamic pricing scheme presented in Sect. 2. We believe that this will mainly depend on 1) the degree to which user behavior fluctuates between cycles, and 2) the exact strategy that users use to move controllable loads from high-demand to low-demand periods. Regarding the former, we know from [9] that the demand in a day can be predicted with high accuracy using the demand in the previous week. The latter is a game theory question, but we expect (partially) random strategies to perform well: e.g., if the demand in some period exceeds the threshold due to a change in usage patterns, then each user shifts each of her controllable loads in the high-demand periods to a low-demand period with some probability $\tilde{p}$.

Acknowledgment. This research/project is supported by the National Research Foundation (NRF), Prime Minister's Office, Singapore, under its National Cybersecurity R&D Programme and administered by the National Satellite of Excellence in Design Science and Technology for Secure Critical Infrastructure, Award No. NSoE DeST-SCI2019-0009. This research is also supported by A*STAR under its RIE2020 Advanced Manufacturing and Engineering (AME) Industry Alignment Fund - Pre Positioning (IAF-PP) Award A19D6a0053. Any opinions, findings and conclusions or recommendations expressed in this material are those of the author(s) and do not reflect the views of A*STAR. Finally, we thank the anonymous reviewers whose comments helped improve the paper.

Appendix A: A Protocol Without Auditors

We describe a protocol that relies on users randomly checking each other's proofs. The only difference to the protocol presented in Sect. 5 is the EvidenceVrf algorithm. In particular, the EvidenceVrf($P_{tp}, r_{it}, x_{it}, E_t, t$) algorithm consists of two phases. In the first phase, it executes the subroutines of EvidenceVrf from Sect. 5 where the user is not an auditor. In the second phase, the user randomly picks z other users, and then requests the inclusion proof G_j and runs VerifyRangeProofs(P_{zk}, c_{jt}, π_{jt}) and VerifyInclusionProof(G_j) for every user j that it picks. If the range proof verification fails for j, the user publishes the invalid inclusion proof of j to the bulletin board. If the verification succeeds for all z users, then the user waits for a certain time T and checks if the bulletin board contains any incorrect range proof. The algorithm returns true if there is no such proof, and false otherwise.

Theorem 5. *Let h be the number of honest users who each check z proofs of other users, and let f be the number of malicious users whose committed value exceeds δ_t, such that $h + f \leq n$. Let T be a bound on the amount of time before any evidence of misbehavior appears on the bulletin board. If the commitment scheme* COM *is additively homomorphic and satisfies the binding property, and if the non-interactive zero-knowledge proof system* NIZK *is simulation-extractable, then the above protocol achieves transparency for sufficiently large h or z.*

Proof of Theorem 5. In the following, we assume that in each period t, each user i draws the same number of other users z from $[n]\setminus\{i\}$ without replacement (as there is no need to check the same proof twice). The number U_i of incorrect leaves that are drawn by i is then a random variable with the *hypergeometric distribution*, i.e.,

$$\mathbb{P}(U_i = u) = \binom{f}{u}\binom{n-f-1}{z-u} / \binom{n-1}{z}.$$

By substituting $u = 0$, the probability that user i draws 0 incorrect leaves can therefore be shown to be equal to $\frac{(n-f-1)!}{(n-f-z-1)!} / \frac{(n-1)!}{(n-z-1)!} = \prod_{i=0}^{z-1}\frac{n-f-i-1}{n-i-1}$ which is bounded by $\left(\frac{n-f-1}{n-1}\right)^z$ because the highest element in the product occurs at $i = 0$. If h honest nodes perform this experiment, then the probability that none of them detect an error is therefore at most $\left(\frac{n-f-1}{n-1}\right)^{hz}$ because the honest nodes perform their experiment independently. This is therefore an upper bound on the probability of failure, i.e., not detecting misbehavior, and the bound vanishes if $h \to \infty$ or $z \to \infty$.

Appendix B: Security Proofs

In the following, we present the proofs of the corresponding theorems.

Proof of Theorem 1. We give a sketch of proof here due to shortness of space. Recall that in the transparency game the adversary has to generate at least a dishonest measurement such that $\bar{x}_{i\,t^*} > d_t$. First, we claim that the commitment $C^*_{i\,t^*} = \mathsf{COM.Commit}(\mathrm{P_c}, \bar{x}_{i\,t^*}, r_{i\,t^*})$ of $\bar{x}$ has a negligible probability to collide with the commitment $C_{i\,t^*} = \mathsf{COM.Commit}(\mathrm{P_c}, x_{i\,t^*}, r_{i\,t^*})$ of the honest (challenge) measurement $x_{i\,t^*}$, i.e., $C^*_{i\,t^*} = C_{i\,t^*}$. Since if such a collision occurs with non-negligible probability, we could build an efficient algorithm $\mathcal{B}$ which runs the transparency-adversary $\mathcal{A}$ as a subroutine to break the binding security property of COM. Therefore, there is no ambiguity about the committed measurements after each user's confirmation of the corresponding commitment. Next, we show that no adversary $\mathcal{A}$ can produce a proof $\pi^*_{i\,t^*}$ for a false statement $\bar{x}_{i\,t^*} > d_t$ which may lead to a false bill $B^*_{j^*} > B_j$ where B_j is the bill determined by the challenge measurements. Note that the condition $\bar{x}_{i\,t^*} > d_t$ implies that it belongs to a relation which does not belong to the honest relation $\mathcal{RL}$ for $x_{i\,t^*}$. Obviously, if $\mathcal{A}$ can generate a false zero knowledge proof $\pi^*_{i\,t^*}$ for $\bar{x}_{i\,t^*}$, so we can make use of $\mathcal{A}$ to break the simulation-extractability of NIZK.

Proof of Theorem 2. We first reduce the security to that of the pseudo-random function PRF by replacing the slot secret $r_{j^*\,t^*}$ (which is supposed to compute the challenge evidence E_{t^*}) with a uniform random value. If there is an adversary $\mathcal{A}$ which can distinguish this modification, then we could make use of $\mathcal{A}$ to build an efficient algorithm $\mathcal{B}$ to break the security of PRF. Since the slot secret $r_{j^*\,t^*}$ is uniform random now, this can enable us to reduce the security to the hiding property of commitment scheme. Namely, if there exists an adversary $\mathcal{A}$ which can distinguish the bit b in the privacy game, we can build an efficient algorithm $\mathcal{B}$ running $\mathcal{A}$ to break the hiding property of the commitment scheme. $\mathcal{B}$ can return the bit b' obtained from $\mathcal{A}$ to the commitment-challenger to win the game. Now, we use a simulator of NIZK to generate the zero-knowledge proof for challenge measurements $(x^0_{j^*\,t^*}, x^1_{j^*\,t^*})$ without using the corresponding witness. Similarly, any adversary which distinguishes this change, can be used to break the zero-knowledge property of NIZK. Since the NIZK does not leak any information of the committed measurement, so we can always use $x^1_{j^*\,t^*}$ (which is random) to generate the challenge evidence. Note that from the compromised slot secrets at the time t^*, the adversary can learn at most $n-1$ measurements. But our scheme does not reveal the sum the measurements, so the adversary cannot directly get the measurement used for computing $c_{j^*\,t^*}$ and $\pi_{j^*\,t^*}$. Namely, we change the challenge evidence to be one which is independent of the bit b, so the advantage of the adversary is zero after all the above changes. In a nutshell, due to the security of the building blocks, the adversary can only have negligible advantage in breaking our baseline scheme.

Proof of Theorem 3. The commitments of leaf nodes are generated identically to those of baseline scheme. By our assumption there are at most f dishonest auditors, so there must have at least one auditor's verification result (on the entire Merkle tree) among those $f + 1$ signed results published on bulletin board within required time T is faithful. If the Merkle tree if correctly built, then those leaf nodes' commitments are bind to the measurements from users except for a negligible property due to the binding property of the commitment scheme. Besides, the additively homomorphic property does not affect the binding property of the aggregated non-leaf nodes in the Merkle tree, which implies each commitment of the corresponding correctly commit the sum of the committed values of its children. With a similar argument in the proof of Theorem 1, the zero-knowledge proofs for the non-leaf nodes would not deviate from the range of the corresponding committed value except for a negligible property because of the simulation-extractable property. Hence, we can conclude that the Merkle tree scheme achieves transparency.

Proof of Theorem 4. Since the adversary can reveal at most $n - 1$ slot secrets of users at the challenge time t^*, she can learn $n - 1$ measurements of the compromised users. In this case, only the challenge measurement $x^b_{j^*, t^*}$ and the sum of its parent node in the Merkle tree is unknown to the adversary. Note that the sub-tree involving the challenge user j^* and its sibling forms is identical to the baseline scheme with just two users. So if there exists an adversary $\mathcal{A}$ who can breaks the privacy of the baseline scheme with users $n' = 2$, then we can make use of it to build an efficient algorithm $\mathcal{B}$ to break the privacy of the Merkle tree scheme. It is not hard to see that $\mathcal{B}$ can forward the challenge measurements from $\mathcal{A}$ to its privacy-challenger to receive back the challenge evidence for simulating the challenge response to $\mathcal{A}$. All other queries from $\mathcal{A}$ can be simulated based on the secrets chosen by $\mathcal{B}$. In a nutshell, the privacy of the Merkle tree scheme is implied by that of the baseline scheme.

References

1. Ács, G., Castelluccia, C.: I have a DREAM! (DiffeRentially privatE smArt Metering). In: Filler, T., Pevný, T., Craver, S., Ker, A. (eds.) IH 2011. LNCS, vol. 6958, pp. 118–132. Springer, Heidelberg (2011). https://doi.org/10.1007/978-3-642-24178-9_9

2. Allcott, H.: Real time pricing and electricity markets. Working paper, Harvard University (2009)

3. Brown, D.: Standards for efficient cryptography 2 (SEC 2). Technical report, Certicom (2010)

4. Bünz, B., Bootle, J., Boneh, D., Poelstra, A., Wuille, P., Maxwell, G.: Bulletproofs: short proofs for confidential transactions and more. In: 2018 IEEE Symposium on Security and Privacy (SP), pp. 315–334. IEEE (2018)

5. Chase, M., Meiklejohn, S.: Transparency overlays and applications. In: CCS, pp. 168–179. ACM (2016)

6. Erkin, Z., Tsudik, G.: Private computation of spatial and temporal power consumption with smart meters. In: Bao, F., Samarati, P., Zhou, J. (eds.) ACNS 2012. LNCS, vol. 7341, pp. 561–577. Springer, Heidelberg (2012). https://doi.org/10.1007/978-3-642-31284-7_33

7. Laurie, B.: Certificate transparency. Commun. ACM **57**(10), 40–46 (2014)
8. Luh, P., Ho, Y., Muralidharan, R.: Load adaptive pricing: an emerging tool for electric utilities. IEEE Trans. Autom. Control **27**(2), 320–329 (1982)
9. Mohsenian-Rad, H., Leon-Garcia, A.: Optimal residential load control with price prediction in real-time electricity pricing environments. IEEE Trans. Smart Grid **1**(2), 120–133 (2010)
10. Morais, E., Koens, T., Van Wijk, C., Koren, A.: A survey on zero knowledge range proofs and applications. SN Appl. Sci. **1**(8), 946 (2019)
11. Pedrasa, M.A.A., Spooner, T.D., MacGill, I.F.: Coordinated scheduling of residential distributed energy resources to optimize smart home energy services. IEEE Trans. Smart Grid **1**(2), 134–143 (2010)
12. Samadi, P., Mohsenian-Rad, H., Schober, R., Wong, V.W.: Advanced demand side management for the future smart grid using mechanism design. IEEE Trans. Smart Grid **3**(3), 1170–1180 (2012)
13. Shi, E., Chan, T.H., Rieffel, E., Chow, R., Song, D.: Privacy-preserving aggregation of time-series data. In: NDSS (2011)
14. Vardakas, J.S., Zorba, N., Verikoukis, C.V.: A survey on demand response programs in smart grids: pricing methods and optimization algorithms. IEEE Commun. Surv. Tutor. **17**(1), 152–178 (2014)
15. Wood, A.J., Wollenberg, B.F., Sheblé, G.B.: Power Generation, Operation, and Control. Wiley, New York (2013)
16. Zhang, Y., Katz, J., Papamanthou, C.: IntegriDB: verifiable SQL for outsourced databases. In: ACM CCS (2015)

CoinJoin in the Wild
An Empirical Analysis in Dash

Dominic Deuber$^{(\boxtimes)}$ and Dominique Schröder

Friedrich-Alexander University Erlangen-Nürnberg, Erlangen, Germany
{dominic.deuber,dominique.schroeder}@fau.de

Abstract. CoinJoin is the predominant means to enhance privacy in non-private cryptocurrencies, such as Bitcoin. The basic idea of Coin-Join is to create transactions that combine equal-valued coins of multiple users. This mixing of coins aims to prevent linkage of the users' transactional in- and outputs. The cryptocurrency Dash employs a built-in CoinJoin service and, therefore, is ideal for empirically studying Coin-Join. This paper presents the first empirical analysis of Dash, which reveals that over 40% of all private transactions can be de-anonymized depending on underlying assumptions. The main issue of these attacks is the coin-aggregation problem, i.e. the need to combine outputs of several CoinJoin transactions. The coin aggregation problem is not specific to Dash and affects other cryptocurrencies as empirical evidence in Bitcoin suggests. We show that the logical solution to the problem, namely CoinJoin transactions with non-fixed arbitrary values, suffers from other privacy weaknesses. We propose a novel mixing algorithm to mitigate the need for coin aggregation without introducing additional privacy vulnerabilities. In contrast to prior mixing algorithms, our approach removes the need for fixed values by dynamically creating equal-valued CoinJoin transactions. The mixing algorithm is not specific to Dash, and integration into other cryptocurrencies, especially into Bitcoin, is possible.

Keywords: Anonymous transactions · Linking heuristics · De-anonymization · Mixing

1 Introduction

More and more it seems as if cryptocurrencies have come to stay and are not mere hype. The most widely used cryptocurrency Bitcoin [1] is often perceived to provide anonymity. However, Bitcoin is not anonymous as it is possible to link addresses that belong to the same user [18,34,38]. The goal of mixing protocols is the prevention of these linkage attacks. *CoinJoin* [32] is the most widely used protocol. It combines inputs and outputs from multiple users and creates a random permutation that hides the correlation between input and output addresses and, thus, between users. Even though Monero [13] and Zcash [16] are two cryptocurrencies that achieve privacy by design, it is crucial to study and improve *CoinJoin* for two reasons. First, Bitcoin is still the most commonly used cryptocurrency, especially in the dark web [24], and supports *CoinJoin* to improve

© Springer Nature Switzerland AG 2021
E. Bertino et al. (Eds.): ESORICS 2021, LNCS 12973, pp. 461–480, 2021.
https://doi.org/10.1007/978-3-030-88428-4_23

privacy without requiring to swap coins to a more privacy-preserving currency. Second, Monero and Zcash are already banned in South Korea [26], and there is a risk that other jurisdictions will follow. If privacy-preserving currencies are banned, *CoinJoin* on top of Bitcoin is among the only possibilities for people in the corresponding jurisdictions to add privacy to their cryptocurrency activities.

The cryptocurrency Dash [4] employs a built-in *CoinJoin* mechanism. Dash has not been researched before, although Dash has a market capitalization of over four billion USD, is the second-largest cryptocurrency with built-in privacy features, and the third most established privacy coin for transactions in the dark web [24]. By the beginning of 2021 Dash's blockchain accounted for approximately 1.4 million blocks including over 31 million transactions.

1.1 Empirical Analysis of Anonymity

We present the first empirical analysis of anonymity in Dash that combines new and existing attacks to evaluate Dash's anonymity level and gain insights on *CoinJoin* and its privacy. We introduce a novel attack that we call Backlink attack. In essence, Backlink attack carefully combines *multi-input heuristic* [18, 34,38] and a newly developed heuristic to find address clusters.

We put forward the DC attack, which is a modification of the *cluster-intersection attack* according to Goldfeder *et al.* [25]. The DC attack revealed a fundamental problem with *CoinJoin*, namely the coin aggregation problem. As Dash uses fixed values in their *CoinJoin* transactions, users generally need to aggregate coins of several *CoinJoin* transactions that fuel the attack. To ascertain whether the coin aggregation problem is also present in other cryptocurrencies, we analyze the impact of our attacks for Bitcoin.

Results: It was found that 15.1% of non-mixing transactions that spend private coins are linkable by the Backlink attack. In terms of address clusters, applying the newly developed heuristic reduces the number of clusters by almost two-third compared to only applying the *multi-input heuristic*. By applying the DC attack, we were able to link over 40% of Dash's private transactions depending on the underlying assumptions of the attack.

In Bitcoin, around 23% of all transactions which spend outputs from a *CoinJoin* transactions contain backlinks. In addition, more than one-tenth of all transactions do so from *CoinJoin* transactions spend from at least two different *CoinJoin* transactions, which indicates that coin aggregation is also a problem in Bitcoin.

1.2 Cookie Monster Mixing

Our analysis suggests that the privacy issues in Dash result from the fact that Dash only supports equal-valued mixing with fixed values and allows users to combine their coins in a way that might de-anonymize them. We analyze arbitrary-value *CoinJoin* as proposed by Maurer *et al.* [31] and show that it has other privacy weaknesses, which is why it is not a suitable way to solve the coin aggregation problem. To remove the issue of only fixed values being mixed without introducing additional privacy vulnerabilities, we propose a novel mixing algorithm that we call Cookie Monster Mixing. The algorithm is inspired by the cookie monster problem [22] and removes the need to split and combine coins before and after mixing. Thus, the information that multiple coins of different mixing transactions belong together is no longer present *on-chain*. As a consequence, *cluster-intersection attacks* without additional *off-chain* information are no longer possible. We have formalized the problem as an integer quadratic problem and propose an efficient greedy algorithm to solve it. A prototype implementation reinforces the practical efficiency. Through experimentation, we have validated that the greedy algorithm is nearly optimal.

1.3 Responsible Disclosure

We reported our findings to the Dash Core Group, one of the organizations working for the Dash network, and declared our willingness to support the implementation of the suggested countermeasures. With Dash Core Release 0.16.0.1 [6], Dash has implemented some of our suggested countermeasures to improve privacy.

1.4 Related Work

A major concern of *CoinJoin* is that the users need to trust an external mixing service that creates the transaction. Alternative approaches to mitigating this weakness have been proposed, such as *CoinShuffle* [39] or its more efficient successor *CoinShuffle++* [40]. For Ethereum, a trustless tumbler Möbius has been presented that achieves mixing through a smart contract based on ring signatures and stealth addresses [33].

While *CoinJoin* is a mixing service that can be used as an extension of traditional cryptocurrencies, new privacy-preserving cryptocurrencies have also evolved, spearheaded by Monero [13] and Zcash [16]. Monero is based on the CryptoNote protocol [42] and mainly uses ring-confidential transactions [36] to achieve privacy. Conversely, Zcash is based on the Zerocash protocol [20] and mainly uses zero-knowledge, succinct, non-interactive arguments of knowledge to achieve privacy. The anonymity of both cryptocurrencies has since then been subject to analyses [29,30,35,37].

Goldfeder *et al.* [25] showed that *CoinJoin* transactions in Bitcoin are vulnerable to the so-called *cluster-intersection attack*. Kalodner *et al.* [27] experimentally validated the applicability of the *cluster-intersection attack* to Dash on simulated transactions. In contrast, we apply the attack to the entire Dash blockchain data. To do so, however, we needed to refine it, as there are several underlying assumptions to take into account.

The major services for *CoinJoin* in Bitcoin are Wasabi Wallet [15], Samourai Wallet [14] and JoinMarket [12]. All distinguish between *pre-* and *post-*mixing. However, Wasabi and Samourai require fixed output values and thus might benefit from the flexibility Cookie Monster Mixing provides in building their *CoinJoin* transactions. JoinMarket allows for flexible output values, albeit in a different setting. Its protocol distinguishes between takers and makers where the taker pays the makers to participate in the mixing.

2   Preliminaries

In this section, we briefly explain concepts necessary to understand our attacks and countermeasures. We introduce transactions, the *multi-input heuristic* and *CoinJoin* followed by a high-level description of the *cluster-intersection attack*.

2.1   Transaction

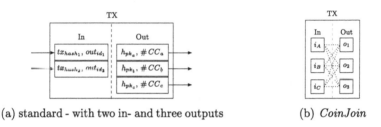

(a) standard - with two in- and three outputs   (b) *CoinJoin*

Fig. 1. Transaction

A transaction consists of a list of inputs and outputs. In simple terms, an output comprises an amount of a given cryptocurrency CC and the hash h_{pk} of a public key pk, which is also called an address. Inputs are references to outputs of previous transactions. A transaction with two inputs and three outputs is depicted in Fig. 1a. The two inputs refer to the outputs at indices out_{id_1} and out_{id_2} of transactions with hashes tx_{hash_1} and tx_{hash_2} respectively. Each output o_i for $i \in [a, b, c]$ of the transaction specifies an address h_{pk_i} and an amount $\#CC_i$ of the cryptocurrency. To spend an output o_i of this transaction in a succeeding transaction, a public key pk must be provided whose hash equals h_{pk_i} and a signature that verifies for pk. It is common for a transaction to have multiple in- and outputs, as the input value needs to be spent completely. For example, if the inputs amount to 5 CC but the user only wants to spend 4 CC to h_{pk_a} and h_{pk_b}, they will create an output o_c to send back the remaining 1 CC to an address they control (h_{pk_c}), which is also called *change* (address). Outputs that can be referenced by a transaction, but have not yet been, are called *unspent-transaction outputs*.

2.2   Multi-Input Heuristic

If a transaction has multiple inputs, the following address-linking heuristic can be applied.

Heuristic 21 *(multi-input heuristic* [18, 34, 38]*).* *All addresses referred to in the inputs of a transaction are controlled by the same entity.*

The reason is that the computation of the signature of each input requires the knowledge of the secret key. Other heuristics take advantage of the fact that coins can only be spent in their entirety with the spending user usually sending back the remaining amount of the cryptocurrency to a *change* address they control [18, 34, 38]. Linking addresses results in sets of addresses, so-called address clusters, which are likely controlled by the same entity.

2.3 *CoinJoin*

The basic idea of *CoinJoin* [32] is special *CoinJoin* transactions, which combine the in- and outputs of multiple users. An example of such a transaction is shown in Fig. 1b. The transaction has three inputs and three outputs from three different users A, B and C. Here, we assume that all in- and outputs have the same value. By merely examining the transaction it is not possible to determine which input i_x for $x \in [A, B, C]$ belongs to which output o_y for $y \in [1, 2, 3]$. As the inputs are controlled by three different users, the *multi-input heuristic* (Heuristic 21) cannot be applied.

2.4 Cluster-Intersection Attack

Goldfeder *et al.* [25] showed that *CoinJoin* transactions in Bitcoin are vulnerable to the so-called *cluster-intersection attack*, which works as follows. For each output of a *CoinJoin* transaction, its anonymity set is determined by inspecting the inputs of the transaction as, ideally, each input could be the origin of each output. The anonymity set contains all possible address clusters that might be the output's origin. Additional information may likely reveal that the same entity controls certain outputs of different *CoinJoin* transactions. In that case, the corresponding anonymity sets can be intersected, *i.e.* address clusters that are present in all sets can be identified. If there is only one address cluster in the intersection, this cluster might be the origin of those outputs. Additional information revealing that the same entity controls certain outputs of different *CoinJoin* transactions can, for instance, be a single transaction spending such outputs. Then, the information follows from the *multi-input heuristic* (Heuristic 21) and thus is *on-chain* information. Furthermore, it is also possible that the payment recipient can derive the information *off-chain*, as seen in the following example. Imagine a merchant receives two payments from the same customer, and each of the payments is the output of a different *CoinJoin* transaction. If the anonymity sets of both outputs only have a single address cluster in common, the merchant can assume that this cluster belongs to the customer.

3 Dash

In this section, we introduce Dash and explain how it addresses privacy in its PrivateSend feature as a necessary prerequisite for our attacks in Sect. 4.

3.1   Overview

The cryptocurrency Dash, having forked from Bitcoin in 2014 [5], follows the same basic structure: the decentralized transaction ledger is maintained in a peer-to-peer network that uses a consensus mechanism to agree on new transactions. The transactions are organized in blocks and the ledger is often called blockchain; the nodes in the consensus mechanism are called *miners*. They are rewarded for their participation through block rewards, *i.e.*, newly generated units of the cryptocurrency and transaction fees. Dash differs from Bitcoin mainly by implementing a native *CoinJoin* feature, PrivateSend, and a feature that reduces the time it takes until a transaction can be considered final, InstantSend. Both features are achieved by so-called *masternodes*, which are special nodes participating in the Dash network. In contrast to *miners*, *masternodes* do not directly participate in the consensus mechanism but mainly provide PrivateSend and InstantSend as a service. They are rewarded for their services with fees. Additionally, they also receive parts of the block rewards in so-called *Coinbase TXs*. InstantSend solves the problem of confirmation time that is present in Bitcoin. To do so, a quorum of *masternodes* locks the inputs of a proposed transaction, which leads to competing transactions being rejected [8]. We do not consider InstantSend in the rest of the paper, as we are concentrating on privacy.

3.2   PrivateSend

PrivateSend is a service provided by *masternodes* to prevent the linkage of addresses from different transaction outputs potentially belonging to the same entity. Put in simple terms, PrivateSend implements *CoinJoin* (see Sect. 2.3). There are several services that support the process of finding other users to group with in order to build a *CoinJoin* transaction. In an ideal scenario, only these services learn the input-output mapping, *i.e.*, the mapping of inputs to corresponding outputs.

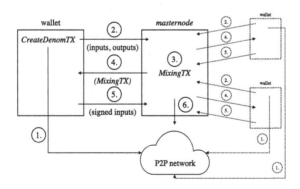

Fig. 2. PrivateSend mixing procedure

The mixing process of Dash is depicted in Fig. 2 and works as follows: a user's wallet splits the value of some *unspent-transaction outputs* in a *CreateDenom-TX*, and sends it to the network ①. This step is a necessary prerequisite, as mixing in Dash requires equal and fixed values. Next, the wallet reports a mixing request to a randomly selected *masternode* ②. This request includes certain *unspent-transaction outputs* of the *CreateDenomTX* as inputs and equally as many outputs with addresses that the wallet controls. If enough other users (dashed lines) also reported their request to the *masternode*, it builds a *Mixing-TX* ③, consisting of all of the users' input-output pairs. At this point, the *masternode* reports the *MixingTX* back to each user's wallet ④, such that it can sign the inputs. Before doing so, the wallet ensures that the outputs initially reported in its request are contained in the list of outputs of the *MixingTX*. This check is crucial in guaranteeing that the *masternode* cannot steal any coins by replacing outputs with its own. If each wallet only signs so long as the check is successful, the *masternode* cannot redirect money to their addresses since the sum of the input values must exactly match the sum of the output values in *MixingTXs*. The reason is that the fees required for mixing are decoupled from the *Mixing-TXs* and therefore omitted for the sake of simplicity. After each wallet has signed their inputs and sent the signatures to the *masternode* ⑤, the *masternode* can send the *MixingTX* to the network ⑥. Each wallet then has *private unspent-transaction outputs*, which can be used as inputs for further mixing rounds or spent in *PrivateSendTXs*, the final transaction type used in PrivateSend. A *PrivateSendTX* is a transaction, whereby the wallet implementation ensures that it only spends *private unspent-transaction outputs* from *MixingTXs*.

4   Empirical Anonymity Analysis

In this section, we analyze the anonymity provided by *CoinJoin* in the context of Dash and Bitcoin. For the analysis of Dash, we ran a Dash full node, version 0.16.1.1 [6] and build an analysis pipeline using BlockSci [28] with version 0.5.0. First, we retrieved the raw blockchain data up to December 31, 2020, which corresponds to a chain of 1 397 530 blocks. Then we detected the type of transactions that are relevant for our attacks. In the backlink attack, we linked address clusters based on the *multi-input heuristic* (see Heuristic 21) and a new clustering heuristic. Finally, we refined the *cluster-intersection attack* by adding false-positive rejection mechanisms and addressing uncertainty about its underlying assumptions to make the attack applicable to Dash (DC attack). The differences of our analysis of Bitcoin are stated in Appendix A.

4.1   Transaction Type Detection

We ran a transaction type detection algorithm for the identification of relevant transactions for PrivateSend. This algorithm processes the data retrieved from our full node, and it takes advantage of the fact that the *mixing denominations* in Dash are of the form 1.00001×10^k for $k \in [-3, \ldots, 1]$. Due to this structure, it seems unlikely that it would not be a *mixing denomination* if we were to encounter such a value. As a consequence, our detection mechanism should produce few to no false positives. By design of our detection mechanism, a transaction can only have one type, *i.e.*, there is no ambiguity. We consider each transaction that does not match any of the following types to be an *OtherTX*. *MixingTX* is a transaction with equally many inputs and outputs, all with the same denomination. This is due to the fact that the fee is decoupled from mixing. Thus, there is exactly one output for each input. We additionally require that there are at least three inputs as at least three participants are required for mixing (see Dash's whitepaper [23]). *CreateDenomTX* is a transaction that is not a *MixingTX* if there are at least two outputs, while one output needs to have one of the *mixing denominations*. Furthermore, we allow at most two *non-mixing-denominated* outputs since one of them might be the *change* output and thus of arbitrary value. The other might be a special output required to pay mixing fees. *PrivateSendTX* is a transaction that is not a *MixingTX* if it has more than one input and all the inputs are *mixing denominations*. However, we only consider it a *PrivateSendTX* if it has exactly one output since a *PrivateSendTX* does not allow *change* [10].

In Fig. 3 the transactions are listed by their type, where the total number of transactions was 31 563 841. Only 0.4% (110 846) of all transactions are *PrivateSendTXs*.
Bitcoin. In Bitcoin, we found that out of 493 118 000 transactions, 1 767 452 (0.4%) were *CoinJoinTXs* (the counterpart of Dash's *MixingTXs*). For the transactions entering into and spending from *CoinJoinTXs*, we detected 5 865 534 (1.2%) *PreCoinJoinTXs* and 7 228 843 (1.5%) *PostCoinJoinTXs*.

CoinbaseTXs	4.4%
PrivateSendTXs	0.4%
MixingTXs	10.1%
CreateDenomTXs	1.5%
OtherTXs	83.6%

Fig. 3. Dash transaction types

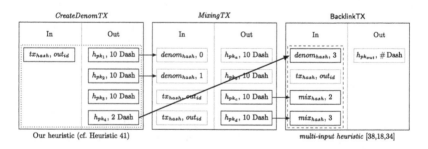

Fig. 4. Backlink analysis

4.2 Backlink Attack

We introduce the Backlink attack, which directly links addresses occurring in the output of a *MixingTX*, *i.e.*, linking them to output addresses of a *CreateDenomTX*. There are transactions in Dash that spend outputs of *MixingTXs* and at the same time outputs of *CreateDenomTXs*. We call such a transaction a BacklinkTX and the output of the *CreateDenomTX* a backlink. Such a transaction is shown in Fig. 4. The transaction's first input is a reference to the fourth output of the *CreateDenomTX*, which is the backlink.[1] Thus, as a direct result of the *multi-input heuristic* (see Heuristic 21), the addresses of the *MixingTX*, h_{pk_c} and h_{pk_d}, are linkable, as under the assumptions of the *multi-input heuristic* there is a link to h_{pk_4}, which is an output address of the *CreateDenomTX*.

However, the linkable addresses can be further linked as all input and all output addresses of a *CreateDenomTX* are most likely controlled by the same entity. The reason for this is that *CreateDenomTXs* are generated by a user's wallet. This leads to the following address clustering heuristic:

Heuristic 41. *All in- and output addresses of a* CreateDenomTX *are controlled by the same entity.*

As a result, h_{pk_c} and h_{pk_d} of the BacklinkTX in Fig. 4 can not only be linked to h_{pk_4} (*multi-input heuristic*, dashed line) but also to h_{pk_1} to h_{pk_3} and to the address corresponding to the output of tx_{hash} at index out_{id} (Heuristic 41, dotted line). Note that reasonable clustering results are only achieved by combining both heuristics. Applying the *multi-input heuristic* would allow linking to the backlink. However, without Heuristic 41, the backlink address would, in general, be in a single cluster and not reveal any additional information about the user's transaction history before mixing.

To detect backlinks, we do the following. We first iterate over all transactions. Then, we check each transaction as to whether it has inputs referencing *MixingTXs* as well as inputs referencing *CreateDenomTXs*. To identify the corresponding clusters, we add our heuristic to the clustering module of BlockSci, which already implements the *multi-input heuristic*.

We found that out of the 174 834 transactions that are not *MixingTXs* but spend mixing outputs, 26 402 (15.1%) have backlinks. In terms of addresses from the outputs of *MixingTXs*, we found that out of 6 833 911 addresses, 836 230 (12.2%) are linkable. Applying only the *multi-input heuristic* resulted in 23 580 clusters. We reduced that number by almost two thirds by additionally applying our Heuristic 41, which resulted in only 7 920 clusters.

Bitcoin. The attack slightly differs in Bitcoin as there are no explicit *CreateDenomTXs*. Instead of *CreateDenomTXs*, we consider the *PreCoinJoinTXs*. Thus, a BacklinkTX in Bitcoin is a *PostCoinJoinTX* with at least one input from a *PreCoinJoinTX*. We found that out of 7 228 843 *PostCoinJoinTXs*, 1 674 070 (23.2%) have backlinks. This shows that backlinks are also present and even more problematic in Bitcoin.

4.3   DC Attack

We introduce the DC attack as a modification of the *cluster-intersection attack* (Sect. 2.4). First, we give a high-level description of the *cluster-intersection attack*

---

[1] Note that the reference says $[denom_{hash}, 3]$ to refer to the fourth output as indexing starts with 0.

in the context of Dash, followed by a discussion of which modifications are necessary to apply the attack. Finally, we present the Dash *cluster-intersection attack* (DC attack).

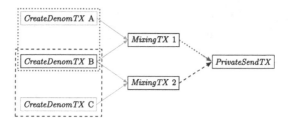

Fig. 5. Cluster intersection in Dash

An overview of the *cluster-intersection attack* in Dash is depicted in Fig. 5. The *PrivateSendTX* has inputs from both *MixingTX* 1 and *MixingTX* 2. If we trace back the inputs, the set of *CreateDenomTXs* that can be reached from the *MixingTX* 1 input contains *CreateDenomTX* A and *CreateDenomTX* B. Likewise, the set reachable from the *MixingTX* 2 input contains *CreateDenom-TX* B and *CreateDenomTX* C. If we intersect the sets, *CreateDenomTX* B is the only *CreateDenomTX* remaining.

Modifications. For actual transaction data, we do not know how many rounds users have been mixing for and whether the mixing originated from a single linkable address cluster [19,25]. Thus, we need to modify the attack. To compensate for not knowing how many rounds of mixing the inputs of a *PrivateSendTX* took, we consider a range of mixing rounds. To address the assumption that all inputs originated from a single cluster, we developed a two-fold approach.

First, we add a mechanism to reject a cluster if there is a subset of inputs that would result in another cluster. This cluster can be seen as an *alternative* explanation for the subset of inputs. The minimum size of the subset is adjustable via a parameter (*alt*). If, for example, ground-truth data indicated that clusters containing 90% of the inputs are common, then an *alt* value of 80% could be suitable for blockchain analysts to safeguard the evidential value of their findings. In that case, the analysts would reject a cluster, if 80% or more of the inputs could be explained by another cluster.

Second, we add a mechanism to detect some obvious false positives that are based on the following observation. A cluster cannot have more Dash spent in its *PrivateSendTXs* than have been created in its *CreateDenomTXs*. This is why we compute a *mix balance* for each cluster as follows. Firstly, we sum the value of all outputs of *CreateDenomTXs* that are spent in *MixingTXs*. Then, we subtract the value of all inputs of a transaction that is not a *MixingTX* but is spending from *MixingTXs*. In simple terms, we determine the value that has been input into mixing and subtract the value that has been spent after mixing. Suppose the attack now suggests linking two clusters, such that the sum of their *mix balances* is negative. In that case, we know that we either encountered a false positive or that our clustering of pre-mix addresses was incomplete. In either case, we must reject the result because the two cases cannot be distinguished without ground-truth data.

This results in the Dash *cluster-intersection attack* (DC attack), which is a modified version of the algorithm proposed by Goldfeder *et al.* [25]. The algorithm is stated in Algorithm 1. The LEN method always returns the number of elements of the passed argument. The algorithm's input is a *PrivateSendTX ptx* and the parameter *alt* as described above. We set the starting value for the number of rounds r to 2, since 2 is the minimum number of mixing rounds required in Dash. The maximal possible number of rounds changed at the begin-

---

Algorithm 1. DC attack

procedure DC_ATTACK(*ptx*, *alt*)
  candidate = *None*
  $r = 2$
  max_r = DETERMINE_MAX_ROUNDS(*ptx*)
  while $r \leq max_r$ **do**
    clusts = $\emptyset$
    for *inp* $\in$ *ptx.inps* **do**
      clusts[*inp*] = EXTRACT_CLUSTS(r, *inp*)
    intersec = $\bigcap\limits_{inp \in ptx.inps}$ *clusts*[*inp*]
    if LEN(*intersec*) == 1 **then**
      if CORR_REJ(*intersec*, *alt*, *clusts*) **then**
        candidate = GET(*intersec*)
      break
  if BALANCE_CONF(*candidate*) **then**
    return *candidate*
  return *None*

---

ning of 2019 from 8 to 16 with protocol version 0.13.0.0 [7]. Thus, to prevent the algorithm from detecting obvious false positives, we determine for every *PrivateSendTX*, the maximal possible number of rounds max_r in DETERMINE_MAX_ROUNDS as follows. We retrieve the block in which the transaction occurred. If the year extracted from the block's timestamp is greater than 2018, we set max_r to 16 and 8 otherwise. Next, the algorithm iterates over all rounds. In every round, for each input, all clusters that are attainable within r rounds of mixing are determined (EXTRACT_CLUSTS). Then, the intersection *intersec* of all found cluster sets is computed. If there is exactly one cluster in the intersection, we perform an additional check, CORR_REJ. This checks whether there is a subset of the inputs whose size is greater than or equal to *alt* of LEN(*ptx.inps*), which would lead to a different cluster than *intersec*. If this is not the case, *candidate* is set to the cluster in *intersec* (GET). The loop is left regardless of CORR_REJ. Finally, we check that *candidate* is not a false positive according to the *mix balance*, which is performed by BALANCE_CONF and works as explained above.

The results of the DC attack are shown in Fig. 6. Setting parameter *alt* to 100% corresponds to complete certainty in the assumption that all inputs resulted from one linkable cluster. In that case, no alternative explanation is taken into account and over 40% of the *PrivateSendTXs* are linkable. In the case of *alt* being equal to 0%, all results would be rejected by definition.

Bitcoin. Goldfeder *et al.* already demonstrated the applicability of the *cluster-intersection attack* in Bitcoin [25]. Thus, the crucial question in this work

alt (%)	10	20	30	40	50	60	70	80	90	100
linkable (%)	0.2	0.7	2.2	4.1	5.6	11.9	17.5	22.4	32.1	43.8

Fig. 6. DC attack linkable *PrivateSendTXs* for parameter *alt* ranging from 10% to 100%

is whether there is *on-chain* information fueling the attack. The special vulnerability to cluster intersection in Dash results from the fact that users need to aggregate value in *PrivateSendTXs*. Thus, a *PrivateSendTXs* has several inputs from different *MixingTXs* in general that can be seen as such *on-chain* information.

To determine whether such *on-chain* information is also present in Bitcoin, we did the following. We checked for every *PostCoinJoinTXs* whether there are inputs from at least two different *CoinJoinTXs*. If this was the case, there was *on-chain* information as it is possible to intersect the anonymity sets of the different *CoinJoinTXs*. We found that out of the 7 228 843 *PostCoinJoin-TXs*, 919 532 (12.7%) have inputs from at least two different *CoinJoinTXs*. This indicates that the coin aggregation problem is also present in Bitcoin.

5 Enhancing Privacy of Mixing

We show how to enhance the privacy of mixing and discuss direct countermeasures to mitigate the vulnerability to the Backlink attack. After discussing why fundamental changes to Dash seem unavoidable to prevent the DC attack, we propose a new mixing algorithm that removes the vulnerability to the *cluster-intersection attack*. This algorithm is of independent interest as it is not specific to Dash.

5.1 Preventing backlinks

The anonymity problems that come with backlinks are approachable within the design of Dash and Bitcoin. First, not all outputs of a *CreateDenomTX* must be input to *MixingTXs*. There may be *change*, such as discussed above in the example of Fig. 4. Additionally, Dash allows for *CoinControl*, *i.e.* letting users in their wallet manually select inputs of a transaction [9]. While this is a useful feature, in the case of a user creating a BacklinkTX, we recommend explicitly warning them as backlinks remove the anonymity gained by mixing. A user's wallet should strictly separate any coins from *CreateDenomTXs* and those originating from a *MixingTX*. This idea is incorporated in the Bitcoin fungibility framework ZeroLink [17] that distinguishes a *pre-mix* and a *post-mix* wallet. With version 0.16.0.1 [6] Dash improved its user interface following our recommendations after we disclosed our findings to them.

5.2 Cookie Monster Mixing

The vulnerability to the *cluster-intersection attack* results from the coin aggregation problem, that is the need to combine coins of different mixes. In Dash, this is a consequence of restricting the mixing to specific values. The logical solution would be to allow arbitrary values. However, arbitrary-value mixing suffers from privacy weaknesses caused by value analysis as discussed in Appendix B. Thus, we propose a new mixing algorithm, Cookie Monster Mixing. The basic principle behind Cookie Monster Mixing is to create a *MixingTX* where there are at least k outputs with the same value and k is the anonymity level the transaction should provide. This is related to the cookie monster problem [22]. Given a set of jars filled with various numbers of cookies, the cookie monster wants to eat all the cookies. However, the cookie monster has to proceed in rounds, select a subset of jars, and eat the same number of cookies from each jar in this subset. The goal is to eat the cookies in as few rounds as possible. In contrast, the objective in Cookie Monster Mixing is to maximize the number of cookies for a fixed number of rounds under constraints instead of minimizing rounds.

In Cookie Monster Mixing, a mixing service provider takes the role of the cookie monster, while the jars are inputs with a specific value of the cryptocurrency to be mixed. In Dash, the *masternodes* act as mixing service providers. Deviating from the cookie monster problem, let the number of rounds r be fixed. In each round $j \in \{1, \ldots, r\}$, the mixing service provider may choose a target value t_j and a subset of the input values from which t_j is subtracted. The subtracted value is added to the output set, while the objective is to maximize the total output value. Intuitively that relates to maximizing the total value of anonymous coins. Additionally, there are two constraints. First, the size of the subset of inputs selected per round needs to be at least k. Second, each selected input needs to have a value at least as large as t_j. Together the constraints ensure that the outputs determined via t_j have at least an anonymity set size of k as they have the same value and thus might have originated from any of the inputs selected in that round.

Integer Quadratic Problem. The problem can be formulated as the following integer quadratic problem (IQP).

Constants

- $v_1, \ldots, v_n$: non-negative integers (values of n inputs)
- k: positive integer (minimum number of values to select per round)

Variables

- $x_1, \ldots, x_n$: $0 - 1$ vectors of length r (where x_i denotes the rounds in which value v_i has been selected)
- t: non-negative integer vector of length r (target values to be subtracted)

$$maximise \sum_{i=1}^{n} \langle x_i, t \rangle \tag{1}$$

$$s.t. \ \langle x_i, t \rangle \le v_i, \text{for each } i \in \{1, \ldots, n\} \tag{2}$$

$$\sum_{i=1}^{n} x_{i,j} \ge k, \text{for each } j \in \{1, \ldots, r\} \tag{3}$$

The Objective (1) is to maximize the total anonymized value, while Constraints (2) and (3) ensure that it is actually possible to subtract t_j from the selected inputs and that at least k inputs are selected per round j respectively.

Greedy Algorithm. We propose a greedy algorithm that approximates the integer quadratic problem. It is stated in Algorithm 2. The input to the algorithm is a list of input values in_vals, as well as k and r as defined above. in_vals can be obtained from the multiset of inputs I by replacing each input with its value. LEN returns the number of elements in a list and EXTRACT_K_LARGEST extracts the kth largest element of a list. The

---

Algorithm 2. Greedy solver

---

procedure SOLVER(in_vals, k, r)
  if LEN(in_vals) $< k$ $||$ $r == 0$ **then**
    return $\emptyset$
  $target\_vals = \emptyset$
  $tmp\_vals = \emptyset$
  $r_{val} =$ EXTRACT_K_LARGEST(k, in_vals)
  $target\_vals.add(r_{val})$
  for $val \in in\_vals$ **do**
    if $val > r\_val$ **then**
      $tmp\_vals.add(val - r_{val})$
    else if $val < r\_val$ **then**
      $tmp\_vals.add(val)$
  return $target\_vals.concat($SOLVER($tmp\_vals, k, r - 1$))

---

algorithm returns $target\_vals$, which is a list of values referring to the target values t_j of the integer quadratic problem.

As long as the abort criterion (*i.e.*, LEN(in_vals) $< k$ $||$ $r == 0$) is not fulfilled, the algorithm extracts the kth largest element of in_vals, which is assigned to r_{val}. Since this element can be seen as the target value of the greedy algorithm in that round, it is added to $target\_vals$. Then, the input values are updated as follows. In case a value is greater than r_{val}, their difference is added to tmp_vals. Otherwise, if the value is smaller than r_{val}, the value itself is added to tmp_val. If they are equal, the value is omitted. This behavior corresponds to inherently selecting all possible inputs per round in terms of the integer quadratic problem. The algorithm runs in polynomial time. There are at most r recursive calls and the runtime of each call is mainly determined by the time it takes to extract the kth largest element of a list. If this is implemented by sorting, the algorithm runs in $\mathcal{O}(r \cdot n \log n)$.

Our greedy algorithm is not optimal, which can be seen by the following example. Let $in\_vals = [2, 2, 1], k = 2$ and $r = 2$. In the first round, the algorithm extracts 2 as the second largest element and adds it to $target\_vals$, while 1 is added to tmp_vals. In the recursive call, $\emptyset$ is returned, as the length in_vals is 1 and thus smaller than k which satisfies the abort criteria. Consequently, the output value achieved in terms of Objective (1) is only 4, as $target\_vals = [2]$ and the greedy algorithm inherently selects all possible inputs per round, which are the first two of in_vals in the first round. The optimum 5, however, is achieved by setting $a_1 = a_2 = x_{1,1} = x_{2,1} = x_{3,1} = x_{1,2} = x_{2,2}$ to 1 and $x_{3,2}$ to 0.

Evaluation of Algorithm 2. To measure the quality of our greedy algorithm in terms of maximizing Objective (1), we evaluated it against the optimal solution. Therefore we modelled the integer quadratic problem as given by Objective (1) and Constraints (2) and (3) in IBM's Optimization Programming Language (OPL) and used the mixed integer optimizer from IBM LOG CPLEX Optimization Studio V12.10.0 [11].

For the values of the inputs (in_vals), we first considered all clusters of $CreateDenomTXs$ retrieved by applying the *multi-input heuristic* and Heuristic 41 as discussed in Sect. 4.2. For each cluster, we summed up the values of all outputs that were referenced by $MixingTXs$. This results in a distribution of Dash that users were mixing in the past. It is therefore better suited for evaluation than purely random values. We varied both, r and the number of inputs that we chose randomly from the distribution. We set k to 3 following the Dash whitepaper, which suggests at least three participants per mixing round [23]. The results are shown in Fig. 7a averaged over 100 runs indicating that Fig. 2 is nearly as good as the optimal solution. The average wall-clock time of the solver is reported in Fig. 7b. In contrast, Algorithm 2 took less than a second for each choice of parameters. Therefore, particularly for multiple inputs and rounds, using a solver is infeasible, which is why Algorithm 2 should be used instead.

		r	
$|in\_vals|$	3	4	5
5	98.8%	98.5%	98.1%
10	98.2%	98.4%	98.3%
15	97.0%	97.2%	98.3%
20	96.1%	95.8%	97.7%

(a) Avg. performance of Algorithm 2 w.r.t Objective (1)

		r	
$|in\_vals|$	3	4	5
5	0.02	0.02	0.28
10	0.03	0.27	7.80
15	0.07	7.51	68.71
20	0.15	5.98	180.14

(b) Avg. wall-clock time of optimizer in minutes

Fig. 7. Evaluation of Algorithm 2 against optimizer

Using Cookie Monster Mixing removes the need for splitting and aggregating coins *before* and *after* mixing. Thus, the *on-chain* information that multiple coins of different mixes belong together is no longer present, preventing the DC attack. To prevent *cluster-intersection attacks* from *off-chain* information as well, Cookie Monster Mixing needs to be combined with privacy-aware wallets and browsers.

Acknowledgments. We would like to thank Christoph Egger, Paul Gahman, Viktoria Ronge and Kyle Soska for their helpful comments as well as all the reviewers of this work for their constructive feedback. Work was supported by Deutsche Forschungsgemeinschaft (DFG, German Research Foundation) under reference number 442893093 and as part of the Research and Training Group 2475 "Cybercrime and Forensic Computing" (grant number 393541319/ GRK2475/1-2019).

A   Differences in the Analysis in Bitcoin

This section highlights the general differences in the analysis of Bitcoin and Dash. For Bitcoin, we ran a full node, version 0.20.0 [2] and used BlockSci [28] with version 0.7.0. We retrieved the raw blockchain data corresponding to a chain of 612 793 blocks with 493 118 000 transactions.

The main difference occurs in the transaction type detection as Bitcoin neither knows *CreateDenomTXs* nor *PrivateSendTXs*. Thus, besides the *CoinJoinTXs*, we also consider *PreCoinJoinTXs* and *PostCoinJoinTXs*. A *PreCoinJoinTX* is any transaction that has at least one output being referenced by a *CoinJoinTX*. Likewise, a *PostCoinJoinTX* is any transaction referencing at least one output of a *CoinJoinTX*. We further exclude all *CoinJoinTXs* from *PreCoinJoinTXs* and *PostCoinJoinTXs*. In comparison with Dash, the *CoinJoinTXs* would correspond to *MixingTXs*, the *PreCoinJoinTXs* to the *CreateDenomTXs*, and the *PostCoinJoinTXs* to the *PrivateSendTXs*. Detecting *PostCoinJoinTXs* and *PreCoinJoinTXs* is straightforward once *CoinJoinTXs* are detected. However, the detection of *CoinJoinTXs* is difficult as there are multiple different *CoinJoin* services in Bitcoin (*e.g.* [12,14,15]) that neither require the number of inputs and outputs to be the same nor restrict their inputs to specific denominations as is the case in Dash. BlockSci already implements a *CoinJoin* detection mechanism which, however, is tailored to JoinMarket [12] transactions and therefore does not recognize the transactions of other *CoinJoin* services such as Wasabi Wallet [15] or Samurai Wallet [14]. For this reason, we adapted the *CoinJoin* detection mechanism of the open-source Blockstream Bitcoin explorer [21] as it is capable of detecting *CoinJoinTXs* of several services. However, we also adopted the elements of BlockSci's algorithm [3] that were not specific to JoinMarket.

Our algorithm is stated in Algorithm 3. The algorithm returns *True* if the provided transaction tx is (most likely) a *CoinJoin* transaction. The LEN method returns the number of elements of the passed argument, MIN and MAX work as expected. OCC computes the number of occurrences of the value val in the provided *outputs*. OCC_MOST returns the number of

---
Algorithm 3. *CoinJoin* detection

---
procedure COJO_DETECTION(tx)
  if LEN($tx.inps$) < 2 $||$ LEN($tx.outs$) < 3 **then**
    return *False*
  $target =$ MIN(MAX(LEN($tx.outs$)$/2, 2), 5)$
  $found = False$
  for $out \in tx.outs$ **do**
    if $out.val == 546$ $||$ $out.val == 2730$ **then**
      return *False*
    if OCC($val, tx.outs$) $>= target$) **then**
      $found = True$
  if OCC_MOST($tx.outs$) $<$ OCC_UNIQ($tx.outs$) **then**
    return *False*
  return *found*

---

occurrences of the value that occurs the most while OCC_UNIQ returns the number of unique output values. The first thing the algorithm does is check whether the transaction has at least two inputs and three outputs. The reason for this is that mixing requires at least two participants. At least one participant generally receives some change, which is why there is always at least one additional output aside from the two mixed ones. Next, a *target* between two and five is computed. This is used to check whether there are at least *target* many outputs with the same value, where *target* corresponds to half the number of outputs but is kept between two and five as done by Blockstream [21]. As suggested by BlockSci, a transaction with so-called *dust* outputs is unlikely a *CoinJoin* transaction, which is why output values should not be equal to 546 or 2 730 [3]. These values are the smallest possible output values allowed by Bitcoin Core depending on the version. The last check is to prevent false positives as there needs to be at least as many equal-valued outputs as there are unique ones. The reason is that in a *CoinJoinTX* unique outputs should only be change outputs.

B   Limitations to Arbitrary-Value Mixing

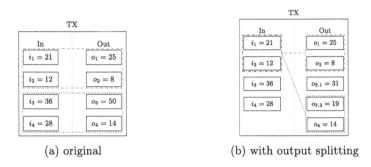

(a) original   (b) with output splitting

Fig. 8. *CoinJoin* transaction

We proposed Cookie Monster Mixing (see Sect. 5.2) as arbitrary-value mixing is not a suitable solution for the coin aggregation problem due to privacy weaknesses based on value analysis. When mixing coins with an arbitrary value, outputs can usually be linked to the corresponding inputs by inspecting the values, as discussed by Maurer *et al.* [31]. Considering the *CoinJoin* transaction in Fig. 8a taken from Maurer *et al.* [31], the transaction can only consist of the two sub-transactions (dotted line and dashed line), such that it is possible to link inputs i_1 and i_2 to outputs o_1 and o_2, as well as i_3 and i_4 to o_3 and o_4, respectively. To prevent this linkage, Maurer *et al.* [31] propose output-splitting algorithms. Given two transactions, their basic splitting algorithm works by calculating the difference between the sums of the corresponding output lists. Next, one of the outputs of the list with the larger sum is split to produce this difference [31]. Thus, multiple input-output relations are possible. Applied to the two sub-transactions in Fig. 8a, the algorithm results in the transaction depicted in Fig. 8b. Output o_3 in Fig. 8a has been split in $o_{3.1}$ and $o_{3.2}$ such that i_1 and i_2 belong to either o_1 and o_2 or $o_{3.2}$ and o_4. The reason is that the sum of the values of i_1 and i_2 equals 33, as do the sums of o_1 and o_2 as well as $o_{3.2}$ and o_4.

However, even if output-splitting results in multiple potential input-output relations, it is still possible to determine the actual input-output relation by inspecting the values. In Fig. 8b, i_1 and i_2 are far more likely to result in o_1 and o_2 than in $o_{3.1}$ and o_4. The reason is that under the assumption that one of the outputs is *change*, input i_2 would not have been required as i_1 is larger than 19 ($o_{3.1}$) and 14 (o_4).

As their basic output-splitting algorithm does not affect the input linkability, that is i_1 and i_2 as well as i_3 and i_4 are linkable, Maurer *et al.* [31] propose a version of the algorithm that implements input shuffling. Instead of using the difference between the sums of the corresponding output lists, the sum of a random subset of inputs is used to split the outputs. Thereby, the number of inputs is a parameter of the algorithm. In terms of Fig. 8a, the input shuffling algorithm might employ the sum of i_1, i_2 and i_4. While this seems to be an improvement over the basic algorithm, it is especially dangerous if the inputs are linkable by heuristics. Intuitively, the gained privacy relies on an ambiguity on the input side, which is introduced by using the sum of a random subset in output splitting. However, if it is known which inputs belong together, there is no gain in privacy at all.

References

1. Bitcoin. https://bitcoin.org/
2. Bitcoin release v0.20.0. https://bitcoin.org/en/release/v0.20.0
3. Blocksci source code. https://github.com/citp/BlockSci
4. Dash. https://www.dash.org/
5. Dash core repository. https://github.com/dashpay/dash
6. Dash core repository release history. https://github.com/dashpay/dash/releases
7. Dash core version 0.13.0.0. https://github.com/dashpay/dash/blob/master/doc/release-notes/dash/release-notes-0.13.0.md
8. Dash developer documentation. https://dashcore.readme.io/docs
9. Dash wallet documentation - coin control. https://docs.dash.org/en/stable/wallets/dashcore/advanced.html
10. Dash wallet documentation - privatesend and instantsend. https://docs.dash.org/en/stable/wallets/dashcore/privatesend-instantsend.html
11. Ibm log cplex optimization studio vol 12.10.0. https://www.ibm.com/products/ilog-cplex-optimization-studio
12. Joinmarket. https://github.com/JoinMarket-Org/joinmarket-clientserver
13. Monero. https://www.getmonero.org/
14. Samourai wallet. https://samouraiwallet.com
15. Wasabi wallet. https://wasabiwallet.io
16. Zcash. https://z.cash/
17. Zerolink - the bitcoin fungibility framework. https://github.com/nopara73/ZeroLink
18. Androulaki, E., Karame, G., Roeschlin, M., Scherer, T., Capkun, S.: Evaluating user privacy in Bitcoin. In: Sadeghi [41], pp. 34–51
19. Kaikkonen, A.: Evaluating the privacy of privatesend (2018). https://www.dash.org/forum/threads/evaluating-the-privacy-of-privatesend.32472/

20. Ben-Sasson, E., et al.: Zerocash: decentralized anonymous payments from bitcoin. In: 2014 IEEE Symposium on Security and Privacy, pp. 459–474. IEEE Computer Society Press (2014)

21. Blockstream: Bitcoin explorer source code. https://github.com/Blockstream/esplora

22. Braswell, L.M., Khovanova, T.: The cookie monster problem. In: The Mathematics of Various Entertaining Subjects: Research in Recreational Math, p. 231 (2015)

23. Duffield, E., Diaz, D.: Dash: a payments-focused cryptocurrency. https://github.com/dashpay/dash/wiki/Whitepaper

24. European Cybercrime Center (EC3): Internet organised crime threat assessment (2020). https://www.europol.europa.eu/activities-services/main-reports/internet-organised-crime-threat-assessment-iocta-2020

25. Goldfeder, S., Kalodner, H., Reisman, D., Narayanan, A.: When the cookie meets the blockchain: privacy risks of web payments via cryptocurrencies. In: Proceedings on Privacy Enhancing Technologies 2018, no. 4, pp. 179–199 (2018). https://content.sciendo.com/view/journals/popets/2018/4/article-p179.xml

26. Ikeda, S.: South Korea's new crypto AML law bans trading of "privacy coins" (monero, zcash). https://www.cpomagazine.com/data-privacy/south-koreas-new-crypto-aml-law-bans-trading-of-privacy-coins-monero-zcash/

27. Kalodner, H., Goldfeder, S., Chator, A., Möser, M., Narayanan, A.: BlockSci: design and applications of a blockchain analysis platform. arXiv preprint arXiv:1709.02489 (2017)

28. Kalodner, H.A., et al.: BlockSci: design and applications of a blockchain analysis platform. In: Capkun, S., Roesner, F. (eds.) USENIX Security 2020, pp. 2721–2738. USENIX Association (2020)

29. Kappos, G., Yousaf, H., Maller, M., Meiklejohn, S.: An empirical analysis of anonymity in zcash. In: Enck, W., Felt, A.P. (eds.) USENIX Security 2018, pp. 463–477. USENIX Association (2018)

30. Kumar, A., Fischer, C., Tople, S., Saxena, P.: A traceability analysis of Monero's blockchain. In: Foley, S.N., Gollmann, D., Snekkenes, E. (eds.) ESORICS 2017. LNCS, vol. 10493, pp. 153–173. Springer, Cham (2017). https://doi.org/10.1007/978-3-319-66399-9_9

31. Maurer, F.K., Neudecker, T., Florian, M.: Anonymous CoinJoin transactions with arbitrary values. In: 2017 IEEE Trustcom/BigDataSE/ICESS, pp. 522–529 (2017)

32. Maxwell, G.: CoinJoin: bitcoin privacy for the real world (2013). https://bitcointalk.org/index.php?topic=279249

33. Meiklejohn, S., Mercer, R.: Möbius: trustless tumbling for transaction privacy. PoPETs 2018(2), 105–121 (2018)

34. Meiklejohn, S., et al.: A fistful of bitcoins: characterizing payments among men with no names. In: Proceedings of the 2013 Conference on Internet Measurement Conference, pp. 127–140. ACM (2013)

35. Möser, M., et al.: An empirical analysis of traceability in the Monero blockchain. PoPETs 2018(3), 143–163 (2018)

36. Noether, S., Mackenzie, A., Lab, T.: Ring confidential transactions. Ledger 1, 1–18 (2016)

37. Quesnelle, J.: On the linkability of Zcash transactions. arXiv e-prints arXiv:1712.01210 (2017)

38. Ron, D., Shamir, A.: Quantitative analysis of the full Bitcoin transaction graph. In: Sadeghi [41], pp. 6–24

39. Ruffing, T., Moreno-Sanchez, P., Kate, A.: CoinShuffle: practical decentralized coin mixing for bitcoin. In: Kutyłowski, M., Vaidya, J. (eds.) ESORICS 2014. LNCS, vol. 8713, pp. 345–364. Springer, Cham (2014). https://doi.org/10.1007/978-3-319-11212-1_20

40. Ruffing, T., Moreno-Sanchez, P., Kate, A.: P2P mixing and unlinkable bitcoin transactions. In: NDSS 2017. The Internet Society (2017)

41. Sadeghi, A.R. (ed.): FC 2013, LNCS, vol. 7859. Springer, Heidelberg (2013)

42. Van Saberhagen, N.: Cryptonote v 2.0 (2013)

One-Time Traceable Ring Signatures

Alessandra Scafuro$^{(\boxtimes)}$ and Bihan Zhang

North Carolina State University, Raleigh, USA
ascafur@ncsu.edu

Abstract. A ring signature allows a party to sign messages anonymously on behalf of a group, which is called ring. *Traceable* ring signatures are a variant of ring signatures that limits the anonymity guarantees, enforcing that a member can sign anonymously at most one message *per tag*. Namely, if a party signs two different messages for the *same tag*, it will be de-anomymized. This property is very useful in decentralized platforms to allow members to anonymously endorse statements in a controlled manner.

In this work we introduce *one-time traceable* ring signatures, where a member can sign anonymously only one message. This natural variant suffices in many applications for which traceable ring signatures are useful, and enables us to design a scheme that only requires a few hash evaluations and outperforms existing (non one-time) schemes.

Our one-time traceable ring signature scheme presents many advantages: it is *fast*, with a signing time of less than 1 s for a ring of 2^{10} signers (and much less for smaller rings); it is *post-quantum resistant*, as it only requires hash evaluations; it is *extremely simple*, as it requires only a black-box access to a generic hash function (modeled as a random oracle) and no other cryptographic operation is involved. From a theoretical standpoint our scheme is also the first anonymous signature scheme based on a black-box access to a symmetric-key primitive. All existing anonymous signatures are either based on specific hardness assumptions (e.g., LWE, SIS, etc.) or use the underlying symmetric-key primitive in a non-black-box way, i.e., they leverage the circuit representation of the primitive.

1 Introduction

Ring signatures, introduced by Kalai, Rivest and Shamir in [33], allow a party to anonymously sign a message on behalf of a group chosen in a spontaneous manner among a set of public keys. The crucial property of ring signatures that set them apart from group signatures [13] is that there is no manager who creates the keys, managing the group and de-anonymizing if necessary. In ring signatures, a party can generate its own pair of keys and the ring is simply the set of published public keys. Furthermore, at signing time, a signer can choose any subset of the published keys as a ring for its own signature, and no other party

---

A. Scafuro—Research supported by NSF grants #1718074 and NSF #1764025.

E. Bertino et al. (Eds.): ESORICS 2021, LNCS 12973, pp. 481–500, 2021.
https://doi.org/10.1007/978-3-030-88428-4_24

is able to de-anonymize it. Ring signatures are therefore particularly suitable for decentralized systems and have received renewed attention lately with the development of blockchains [29,30]. For instance, ring signatures could be used as a building block for a decentralized governance of a blockchain. In [36] for example, the goal is to provide a mechanism to vote on projects that should be funded with the blockchain treasury. In such an application, ring signatures could be used as a preliminary step to anonymously endorse projects that should be later considered for voting.

However, the lack of a manager in ring signatures enable members to abuse of their anonymity. In the example above, a member who wants to push a certain project, could anonymously compute multiple signatures endorsing the same project. Due to the anonymity guarantees, the other members cannot distinguish whether this project is endorsed by a single member or by multiple members[1].

Traceable Ring Signatures. To overcome the unrestricted anonymity provided by ring signatures, Fujisaki and Suzuki in [19] introduced *traceable* ring signatures, where each message is associated to a 'tag' (a tag can be thought as a topic of discussion) and a party can anonymously sign only one message per tag. Specifically, traceable ring signatures provide an algorithm, called Trace, such that if Alice prepares two signatures σ, σ' for messages m and m' w.r.t the same tag, Trace will output the public key of Alice. Note, however, that if Alice computes two signatures σ, σ' for the *same* message m (signatures can be randomized) w.r.t. the same tag, the two signatures will be linked but Alice's identity will *not* be revealed. This property is called tag-linkability.

A downside of tag-linkability so defined is that a malicious party who just wants *to disrupt* the system, can mount a simple denial-of-service attack by continuously sending multiple signatures of the same message. While these signatures will be linked and then discarded, the identity of the attacker will not be revealed. Hence, the bad actor can keep the parties busy verifying and discarding signatures.

Traceable ring signatures have been constructed from the DDH assumption by Fujisaki and Suzuki [18,19] and from bilinear maps by Ho Au et al. in [2]. Such hardness assumptions however are not post-quantum resistant [34]. Only very recently, Branco and Mateus [10] provided the first[2] post-quantum resistant traceable ring signatures. Their construction is based on the syndrome decoding problem, a classical problem in coding theory that is conjectured to be post-quantum resistant. This scheme relies on the Fiat-Shamir heuristic and is proved secure in the classic random oracle model [5]. However, their construction is quite inefficient, with signature size of $240\,\text{KB}\cdot N$, where N is the size of the ring, which

---

[1] A similar problem motivated the concept of *threshold* ring signatures [11], where a signature can be computed only if a least t members agree. This is very specific to applications where a *quorum* is required, and is not suitable in more general applications where we just want to enable members to express their opinion anonymously.

[2] Post-quantum *linkable* ring signatures existed in the literature before – and we discuss them in Sect. 2. However, they do *not* provide traceability.

would translate in 24 MB with a ring of just 100 people. Signing time estimations are not provided in [10], but they are expected to be high.

Hence, the state-of-the-art of traceable ring signature offers only one scheme that is post-quantum resistant, but such scheme is currently impractical.

In this work we mitigate this situation by constructing a practical post-quantum resistant traceable ring signature scheme that only requires hash-function evaluations. Our key insight is to *enforce a one-time flavor* that gives us traceability almost for free, at the expenses of reusability. As we discuss below, this might not be a limitation and is an acceptable compromise in some applications where traceable ring signatures can be used. We elaborate on our contribution next.

1.1 Our Contribution

We introduce *one-time* traceable ring signatures and we construct them from a random oracle only. One-time means that the security properties – unforgeability, anonymity, non-frameability – are guaranteed only as long as a signer uses the secret key at most once. This allows us to provide a stronger public traceability guarantee that prevents denial-of-service attacks. Concretely, differently from the previous tag-linkability property achieved in [10,19], our public traceability property guarantees that if Alice signs twice, her identity will be revealed *even if she signed the same message*.

The one-time flavor can be a feature rather than a limitation in settings where signatures are used to endorse statements. Furthermore, our one-time traceable signature can be extended to many-time assuming a common public immutable state (e.g., the blockchain), using standard techniques that we discuss later in this section.

Our one-time traceable ring signature scheme advances the state of the art both from a practical and a theoretical perspective. From a practical standpoint the signing algorithm is extremely fast, requiring *less than a second* even for a ring of 1024 signers (see Table 1), and could be practical for applications such as the blockchain treasury decision discussed above (we stress however that we don't expect it to be suitable for applications such as anonymous payments).

Table 1. Signature size and running times of our one-time traceable ring signature scheme Σ_{OTS} (described in Fig. 1) when $\mathcal{H}$ and G are instantiated with SHA3, and security parameter $\lambda = 128$.

Ring Size	Signature Size	Signing Time (sec)
2^6	131 KB	0.034
2^7	262 KB	0.068
2^8	524 KB	0.135
2^9	1 MB	0.273
2^{10}	2 MB	0.760

The signature size of our scheme is $N \cdot \lambda^2$ *bits* (where N is the ring size and λ is the security parameter) and outperforms the size of the post-quantum secure traceable signature of [10] (which size is $N \cdot 240$ KB). For instance, for a ring of size 100, our scheme produces a signature of 204 KB versus the 24,000 KB required by the scheme of [10]. In Table 3 we compare the running time and size with various existing anonymous signatures that are linkable but not traceable (see Sect. 1.3 for details).

Finally, our signature scheme is *extremely simple*, and can be easily understood by anyone who understands the security properties of an hash-function modeled as a random oracle. We see this as an important advantage of our scheme since it makes it less prone to implementation errors and more agile (since we use the hash function as an oracle, it is easy to swap between implementations).

From a theoretical standpoint, our signature scheme is the first (one-time) ring signature that uses a hash function in a *black-box* way. Existing ring signatures rely on hardness assumptions that have a trapdoor flavor and hence require structure, e.g., trapdoor one-way permutation [33] or Cameleon Hash Plus [3] [27] functions. Others rely on specific hardness assumptions such as RSA [15], DDH [19,25] or Ring-LWE, NTRU, SIS/ISIS [4,27,35], syndrome, LWE [8,10]. The only ring signatures based on generic symmetric-key type of assumption, such as pseudo-random functions (PRF), rely on zero-knowledge proofs (e.g., [21]) and use the underlying primitive in a non-black-box manner. See Remark 1 for further discussions on non-black-box usage of cryptographic primitives.

Finally, our signature scheme reduces the gap between what we can achieve from black-box access to symmetric-key primitives in the *non*-anonymous setting and the anonymous setting. Indeed, it is well known that in the regular, *non*-anonymous, setting we can construct one-time signature schemes given only black-box access to a hash function [22,28] [4]. In contrast, in the anonymous setting, *even for one-time security*, no construction was known. (But we stress again that it is known from *non*-black-box use of symmetric-key primitives).

Remark 1. Black-box vs Non-black-box Usage of a Cryptographic Primitive. Ring signatures can be constructed generically using zero-knowledge proofs as follow. To sign a message on for a ring of N public keys, simply compute a non-interactive zero-knowledge proof of knowledge of the secret key associated to one of the N public keys. While this approach allows one to use *any* one-way function, note that the size of the resulting zero-knowledge proof *depends* on the specific one-way function that one chooses. Hence, different one-way functions lead to different performances in both size and running time. As a consequence, to improve performances, existing works (e.g., [21]) use less standard one-way

---

[3] Chameleon Hash Plus were introduced in [27], it is a special hash function equipped with a trapdoor such that given *any* value y, a party P can produce x' s.t. $H(pk_P, x') = y$.

[4] Precisely, one-way functions are sufficient for one-time signatures, hash functions are used for succinctness and reusability.

functions, such as lowMC [1], that yield shorter zero-knowledge proofs. In contrast, when a primitive is used only as an oracle, that is, in a black-box manner, the signature size is *independent* of the complexity of the particular choice of the primitive, but it depends only on the security parameter and how it relates with the output size of the function. The concrete running times will vary of course with the actual implementation of the oracle, but not the size. Even more, if the oracle is implemented via hardware (e.g., GPU), the running time is dramatically reduced. Finally, note that hardware implementation of the primitive cannot be leveraged when the primitive is used in a non-black-box manner.

On the One-time Flavor. We observe that, when an immutable shared state is available – as it is the case in a blockchain system – the one-time flavor is not a strong limitation since the common state can be leveraged to bootstrap the one-time use to many-time use, following standard techniques. For instance, consider the scenario where members associated with the governance of a blockchain are identified with a permanent public key. Whenever there is a topic of discussion on which the members are asked to give opinions, members can create a one-time, *per-topic* key and sign this key using their permanent key. Once all interested members have published their per-topic key (or a certain time has elapsed), the ring has formed. Each party can now sign their message anonymously on behalf of the ring for the specific topic, and no party can express more than one opinion/vote on the topic without being caught. This process can be bootstrapped so that when anonymously signing a message for topic 1, the party also signs the next one-time public key for topic 2, that will be added to the next ring.

1.2   Our Technique

The idea behind our traceable one-time ring signature scheme is simple. It leverages the equivocability of Naor's bit commitment scheme [31].

To start, let us recall Naor's commitment scheme. This scheme consists of two rounds. The first round is a random string R of 3λ bits, chosen by the receiver of the commitment, where λ is the security parameter. The second round is the commitment c computed as follows: $c := G(s) \oplus (b \cdot R)$, where G is a Pseudorandom Generator (PRG) with expansion from λ to 3λ bits, and $(b \cdot R)$ means the multiplication of each bit of R with the bit b, where b is the bit the sender wants to commit to. To *open* a commitment c (computed over the string R), the sender simply sends the PRG seed s (that was used to computed c). From the seed s, the receiver can then infer if the bit committed in c was 0 or 1 by simply trying to recompute c as either $G(s)$ ($b = 0$) or $G(s) \oplus R$ ($b = 1$). Naor's bit commitment scheme is statistically binding. However, if the string R instead of being chosen at random, were computed in an *"equivocal mode"*, that is, as $R = G(s_0) \oplus G(s_1)$, for two random seeds s_0, s_1, the commitment can be computed in such a way that can be equivocated, that is, opened as 0 or 1. This is done as follows: to commit, one always sends $c = G(s_0)$. Then in the decommitment phase, one sends s_0 if it wishes to open to bit 0 and s_1 otherwise. The seeds s_0, s_1 are therefore *trapdoors* that can allow the sender to open the same commitment c adaptively to either 0 or 1. Naor's bit commitment can be straightforwardly extended to string commitment. To commit a λ-bit string equivocally, one simply needs λ strings $(R_1, \ldots, R_\lambda)$ computed in *"equivocal mode"*. As we will see shortly, these strings will be the public key in our traceable ring signature.

Given this equivocation property of Naor's commitment, we can immediately create a one-time *traceable ring* signature as follows.

Public Key of a Member. When a member $\mathcal{U}_i$ wants to join the system, it will compute strings $(R_1, \ldots, R_\lambda)$ in *equivocal mode* and set them to be their public key. More precisely, to generate its own pair of public and private signing key, a ring member $\mathcal{U}_i$ proceeds as follows. It chooses λ pairs of random seeds $s_{i,j}^0$ and $s_{i,j}^1$, for $j \in [\lambda]$ (each seed is λ bits) and computes the j-th component of its public key as $pk_{i,j} := G(s_{i,j}^0) \oplus G(s_{i,j}^1)$. The final public key that $\mathcal{U}_i$ publishes is $\mathbf{pk}_i = (pk_{i,1}, \ldots, pk_{i,\lambda})$, and it has size $\lambda(3\lambda)$. The values $s_{i,j}^0$ and $s_{i,j}^1$ are the secret trapdoors that $\mathcal{U}_i$ will use as a secret key to sign a message.

Ring. A ring R of N public keys therefore corresponds to the vector of keys $(\mathbf{pk}_1, \ldots, \mathbf{pk}_N)$, where each $\mathbf{pk}_i - (pk_{i,1}, \ldots, pk_{i,\lambda})$, is the vector of λ first rounds of Naor's commitment chosen by member $\mathcal{U}_i$ and computed in equivocal mode.

Signature. To sign a message m, on behalf of the ring R of size $|\mathsf{R}| = N$, a user $\mathcal{U}_i$ will proceed as follows. It will choose N random strings $x_1, \ldots, x_N$, one on behalf of each member of the chosen ring R, while it sets $x_i = 0$. Then, it will commit to each string x_q using the public key of member $\mathcal{U}_q$. Indeed, recall that the public key of $\mathbf{pk}_q$ is nothing but the first round of Naor's scheme that can be used by anyone to compute a commitment to a string. Hence, the signer $\mathcal{U}_i$ will compute N commitments $\mathbf{c}_1, \ldots, \mathbf{c}_N$, using the N public keys in R, and the i-th commitment is computed in equivocal mode. Once the commitments are fixed, the signer evaluates the random oracle $\mathcal{H}$ on input the message m to be signed, the ring R, and the commitments $\mathbf{c}_1, \ldots, \mathbf{c}_N$ just computed. It then obtains the value $z = \mathcal{H}(m, \mathsf{R}, \mathbf{c}_1, \ldots, \mathbf{c}_N)$ which is called the *target*. Note, the target z is a completely random string (due to the properties of the random oracle $\mathcal{H}$), that is sampled independently of the strings $x_1, \ldots, x_N$ committed in $\mathbf{c}_1, \ldots, \mathbf{c}_N$. After the target z is learnt, in order for the signature to be accepted, the signer must somehow show that the xor of the openings of all commitments $x_1 \oplus \cdots \oplus x_N$ is equal to z. Since $x_1 \oplus \cdots \oplus x_N$ were committed before the random oracle evaluation, this relation does not hold (with all but negligible probability). Hence, in order for the signer to satisfy the xor relation, it needs to equivocate at least one commitment. Since the signer $\mathcal{U}_i$ knows the trapdoors associated to the public key $\mathbf{pk}_i$, it can indeed equivocate the i-th commitment $\mathbf{c}_i$ so that it opens to a new string x_i^* that satisfies the xoring relation above.

The actual signature will consist only of openings, i.e., the PRG seeds, of the N string commitments. Note that among these PRG seeds, which are computed on-the-fly at random, there are the secret PRG seeds (i.e., $s_{i,j}^0$ or $s_{i,j}^1$) that $\mathcal{U}_i$ had chosen when computing its public key, and that are used specifically to equivocate the commitment. Looking ahead this means that upon a signature $\mathcal{U}_i$ is exposing a share of the secret key. If the same $\mathcal{U}_i$ tries to sign twice, it will end up using the other share and hence it will be traced. Our scheme is formally described in Fig. 1.

Note that the idea of using some form of "trapdoor primitive", in combination with a target value z computed via the random oracle, is not new at all. In fact it is the pillar of most ring signatures. Trapdoors, however, are typically connected to cryptographic objects that have some structure and all previous works that follow this design did require specific structured assumptions (e.g., Discrete Log, Syndrome Decoding, Lattices, etc.). The new insight of our paper is simply that, in the settings where traceability is required, one-time trapdoors can suffice, and we show that they can be derived *very cheaply* from an *unstructured object* such as the random oracle.

Security of Our Scheme. Next, we provide the intuition behind the security guarantees that our scheme provides. First, we discuss the security definition we adopt. We use the standard definition of traceable ring signature of [19], and *adapt it* to the *one-time* setting. Informally, a traceable one-time ring signature must satisfy the following properties: (1) anonymity, as long a party signs *up to one message* no-one can distinguish her identity, (2) traceability: there exists an algorithm Trace that given two signatures σ_1, σ_2 over a ring R, it outputs an identity $pk \in$ R if both σ_1, σ_2 were computed with the secret associated to pk; (3) exculpability (also knows as non-frameability): no malicious party should be able to "frame" an honest party pk who signed only once; (4) one-time unforgeability: no malicious party can sign on behalf of a party who signed only once (this property is implied by exculpability and traceability).

We briefly argue why our scheme satisfy the above security properties.

Anonymity is guaranteed by the random oracle properties. Indeed, the only difference between a signature computed by member $\mathcal{U}_i$ and one computed by member $\mathcal{U}_j$ is in the position where the equivocation seeds are placed. If a signature is coming from $\mathcal{U}_i$, in position i we observe the equivocation seeds (either $s_{i,j}^0$ or $s_{i,j}^1$) used to computed the public key $\mathbf{pk}_i$, while for any other position $q \neq i$ we observe random PRG seeds that have no connection with how the public keys $\mathbf{pk}_q$ was computed. If the signature was computed by $\mathcal{U}_j$ we will observe the same but in position j. Now, first observe that the equivocation seeds ($s_{i,j}^0$ and $s_{i,j}^1$) were chosen uniformly at random when the public key was computed. Then observe that in the one-time setting, the adversary see at most one signature from each party. Hence it will only observe at most one equivocation seed (and never both). Computationally, an equivocation seed picked when computing the public key $\mathbf{pk}_i$ is distributed as a random PRG seed computed on the fly for the commitment on behalf $\mathbf{pk}_q$. Hence, given any signature, it is computationally infeasible to tell where the secret keys are placed (the formal argument is provided in Lemma 1).

Traceability follows directly from the fact that to successfully sign, a member $\mathcal{U}_i$ must use, and hence reveal, one of its equivocation seeds. If $\mathcal{U}_i$ computes two *distinct* signatures (even on the same message) σ, σ', it must hold that they had two different targets z, z'. Due to the random oracle properties, these target must be different in many positions. Now, recall that, in order to sign, a member $\mathcal{U}_i$ must equivocate the bit commitments $\mathbf{c}_i$ to hit a bit string x_i^* that satisfy the xor relation with the target. Now, if there are two targets z, z' that differ in many positions, this means that there is at least on bit, say j, of x_i^* such that the j-th bit of x_i^* should be equal to 0 to accommodate for target z for σ while it should be 1 to accommodate for target z' for σ'. This will require to use seed $s_{i,j}^0$ in signature σ and seed $s_{i,j}^1$ signature σ'. Using σ, σ' it is therefore possible to recompute the j-th component of $\mathcal{U}_i$'s public key and hence de-anonymize these signatures.

Exculpability holds because in order to successfully frame a signer with public key $\mathbf{pk}_l$, the adversary needs to find two seeds s, s' such that $pk_{l,j} = G(s') \oplus G(s)$ for some index j. This is computationally infeasible (due to the one-way property of the random oracle), even if the adversary has observed one signature from $\mathbf{pk}_l$ – and therefore she has seen one of the seeds – and even if the adversary can create public keys maliciously and adaptively on honest public keys and signatures.

On Post-quantum Security. Our proof of security is carried in the classic random oracle model (ROM). Namely it assumes that a post-quantum adversary only has classical access to the Random Oracle (i.e., cannot make queries in superposition). This is consistent with all previous (traceable) ring signatures (e.g., [8,10,27]) that aimed at post-quantum security. The *Quantum* ROM [9], introduced by Boneh et al., considers an adversary that has quantum access to the Random Oracle and can make queries in superposition. In this setting, the practice of *programming* the Random Oracle, which is standard in the classic ROM, cannot be always applied and must be performed and analyzed very carefully. Exciting recent work [16,26] show techniques that facilitate the use programming in the QROM, paving the way to closing the gap between proofs in the classic ROM and QROM. We leave it as a future work to provide a security analysis of our scheme in the QROM model.

1.3   Performance Comparison

We compare our scheme with most recent traceable and linkable ring signatures that are post-quantum resistant (in the classic random oracle model). Specifically, we compare with the traceable ring signatures of Branco and Mateus [10] based on syndrome decoding, the linkable ring signatures Calamari and Falafl of Beullens et al. [8] that are based on isogeny and LWE, and the linkable ring signature Raptor [27] by Lum Ho Au and Zhang, based on NTRU and SIS. We compare w.r.t. hardness assumptions (Table 2) and performances. The latter are measured in terms of signature size and signing time (Table 3). We stress that this *is not an apple to apple comparison*, firstly, because our scheme provides only one-time security while the others provide many-time unforgeability and non-frameability, and secondly, because [8] and [27] are not traceable. In terms of assumptions, thanks to the one-time setting, our scheme uses the minimum assumption – only a random oracle —, while all other schemes require specific hardness assumption *in addition to* a random oracle. We also stress that, like ours, all such works only consider the classic random oracle, and leave it as a future work to analyze the scheme in the quantum random oracle model. For the running times, since our scheme only requires hash function evaluations, it is the fastest [5]. For the signature size, our scheme outperforms the traceable signature of [10] and it is asymptotically better than the linkable ring signatures of [27]. Calamari and Felafl [8] however have *much better* signature size than ours (but they are not traceable). For our implementation we used an Intel(R) Core(TM) i7-5600U CPU @ 2.60 GHz, using only a single core and 1 GB of RAM. We instantiated the random oracle with SHA3 implemented in GO[6].

Public Key and Signature Size. We recall that the public key is $3\lambda^2$ bits (as explained in Sect. 1.1). Hence, for $\lambda = 128$, the public key of each party is fixed to be 6 KB. Computing a public key only consists in choosing 2λ seeds, computing 2λ PRG evaluations and xoring. The signature size depends on the size N of the ring, and is computed as $N \cdot \lambda^2$.

Table 2. Hardness Assumptions used in most recent post-quantum secure linkable/traceable ring signatures. Our work provides one-time security.

	Hardness assumptions	Random Oracle
Branco et al. [10]	Syndrome Decoding	YES
Calamari [8]	Isogeny CSIDH-512	YES
Falafl [8]	Lattices MSIS MLWE	YES
Raptor [27]	Lattices NTRU	YES
This work	none	YES

Table 3. This table shows how the signature size and running time varies with the size of the ring N, when the security parameter is 128 bits. (Note that for Raptor [27], the reported values are for only 100 bits of security), with 64 bits of quantum security.

	(Ring Size) N					
	2^3		2^6		2^{10}	
Branco et al. [3]	1920 KB	–	1536 KB	–	245 MB	–
Calamari [8]	5.4 KB	79 s	8.3 KB	16 min	10 KB	2.7 hrs
Falafl [8]	30 KB	<1 s	32 KB	1 s	33 KB	9 s
Raptor [27]	11 KB	0.017 s	82 KB	>0.06 s	1.3 MB	–
This work	**16 KB**	**0.004 s**	**131 KB**	**0.03 s**	**1 MB**	**0.7 s**

---

[5] Note that this is true even if we add to the signature time, the time to computed the public key.

[6] https://godoc.org/golang.org/x/crypto/sha3#ShakeSum128.

2   Related Work

In this section we review the literature on ring signatures. Most of the existing work are not traceable, hence they are not directly relevant to our result.

Ring Signatures. Ring signatures were introduced by Rivest, Shamir and Tauman in [33]. Their construction is based on any trapdoor permutation (or trapdoor function) and is proved in the ROM [5]. Bender, Katz and Morselli in [6] formalized ring signatures more carefully and showed a scheme based on general assumptions and ZAPs (i.e., two-round witness indistinguishable proofs) treating the underlying cryptographic primitives in a non-black-box manner. Libert et al. in [23] construct the first ring signature with size logarithmic in the ring from a lattice-based accumulator. Groth and Kohlweiss [20] show how to construct logarithmic ring signatures from 1-out-N commit-and-prove scheme from DDH assumption, this scheme was improved by Libert, Peters and Qian in [24]. Chandran, Groth, and Sahai [12] show a ring signature scheme with signature size $O(\sqrt{N})$ based on the on composite order groups with a bilinear maps. Dodis et al. [15] provides a constant-size ring signature scheme based on RSA accumulators and the strong RSA assumption, and Nguyen [32] extends it with a pairing-based accumulator. Derler, Ramacher and Slamanig [14] show the first ring sub-linear ring signature scheme based only on symmetric primitives. Their construction is in the random oracle model, it is non-black-box and non-linkable. Katz, Kolesnikov and Wang [21] later provided optimized zero-knowlege proofs that can be used to build shorter and faster ring signature for a pseudo-random function only, used in a non-black-box manner. Lattice-based ring signatures have been shown in [27] by Lu, Ho Au and Zhang from the SIS and NTRU assumption. Beullens in [7] shows more efficient Sigma protocols for the MQ, PKP and SIS problems, that yield to the construction of more efficient ring signatures based on the same problem. Beullens, Katsumata and Pintore in [8] and Esgin et al. [17] construct efficient ring signatures from the isogenies and lattices problem. The scheme shown in [8] scale very well with the number of signers, by using the Merkle Tree in a very elegant way and avoiding using the circuit of the hash function. Unfortunately, signing (and verification) time is very high, with 79s for a ring as small as 8 people for the isogeny-based signature. This is due to the fact that the construction requires the parties to perform expensive group "actions". For the lattice-based implementation the bottleneck is not the lattice arithmetic, but rather the use of symmetric primitives (i.e. hashing, commitments and expanding seeds).

Linkable Ring Signatures. Linkable Ring Signatures were introduced by Liu, Wei and Wong in [25]. They differ from traceable ring signatures in that they only allow to detect that two signatures are linked – i.e., computed by the same signer – but the identity of the signer is never revealed. Post-quantum resistant linkable ring signatures have been provided in [4,27,35], which have large signatures and withstand a somewhat weaker adversary who cannot maliciously craft its keys.

Very recently, the Calamari and Falafl shown by Beullens et al. [8] yield much shorter linkable ring signatures, though the running times are not practical in some cases (see Sect. 1.3). These schemes are not traceable.

Traceable Ring Signatures. Traceable ring signatures were introduced by Fujisaki and Suzuki in [19], who constructed them based on the DDH assumption and the Fiat-Shamir heuristic, in the ROM. Fujisaki [18] presents a sub-linear scheme (where the size of the signature is $O(\sqrt{N})$ if N is the size of the ring), which trades the RO assumption with the assumption that there exists a trusted common reference string (CRS). Ho Au et al. in [2] propose a construction based on bilinear maps. All such constructions are based on variants of the hardness of the discrete logarithm problem, and are not post-quantum resistant.

3 Definitions

Notation. We use notation $[n]$ to denote the set $\{1, \ldots, n\}$. We use $y \leftarrow \mathsf{F}(x)$ to indicate y is the output of a randomized algorithm F on input x and $y := \mathsf{F}(x)$ if F is a deterministic algorithm. PPT stands for "probabilistic polynomial time". A function negl is *negligible* if for every positive polynomial p there is an integer n_0 such that for all integers $n > n_0$ it holds that $\mathsf{negl}(n) \leq \frac{1}{p(n)}$.

3.1 One-Time Traceable Ring Signatures

One-time Traceable Ring Signatures. A ring signature is a signature computed on behalf of a group of N public keys $pk_1, \ldots, pk_N$, called the ring. To compute a ring signature, a signer must know one of the corresponding secret keys, e.g., sk_i. Ring signatures provide two properties: unforgeability and anonymity. Unforgeability means that only members of the ring can produce valid signatures. Anonymity means that given a ring signature σ on behalf of the ring $\mathsf{R} \subset \{pk_1, pk_2, \ldots\}$ it is infeasible to distinguish which secret key was actually used to compute the signature. For simplicity of exposition we will always assume that the ring is the set of all N public keys. A *traceable* ring signature [19] poses *restrictions* on the number of times a signer can anonymously sign a certain message. Namely, if a signer signs a message two times, then the two messages will be linked. We introduce *one-time* traceable ring signatures where all security properties hold assuming that a secret key is used at most once. We adapt the definition of traceable ring signatures of [19] to the one-time setting, and we provide a stronger traceability guarantee.

Definition 1. *A one-time traceable ring signature scheme is a tuple of PPT algorithms* (GenKey, RSign, RVer, Trace) *where:*

- **Key Generation:** $(pk_i, sk_i) \leftarrow \mathsf{GenKey}(1^\lambda)$ *A randomized algorithm run by a user $\mathcal{U}_i$. It takes in input the security parameter λ and outputs a verification key pk_i and a secret key sk_i.*

- **Signing Algorithm:** $(R, \sigma, m) \leftarrow RSign(R, m, sk_l)$ *On input a ring* $R \subseteq \{ pk_1, \ldots, pk_N \}$, *a message* m *and a secret key* sk_l, *it outputs a signature* σ. *We assume that* $|R| \geq 2$ *and each public key in the ring is distinct.*
- **Verification Algorithm:** $b \leftarrow RVer(R, m, \sigma)$ *it verifies a signature* σ *for message* m *and w.r.t ring* R. *It outputs 1 if the signature verifies, 0 otherwise.*
- **Trace:** $Trace(R, m_1, \sigma_1, m_2, \sigma_2)$ *on input two distinct signatures* σ_1 *and* σ_2 *on messages* m_1, m_2 *it outputs either "indep" or* $pk \in R$.

Completeness. A one-time traceable ring signature scheme is complete if: for all $(pk_i, sk_i) \leftarrow GenKey(1^\lambda)$, for all $R \subseteq \{pk_1, \ldots, pk_N\}$, for all $\sigma \leftarrow RSign(R, m, sk_l)$ s.t. $l \in [N]$: $Pr[RVer(R, m, \sigma) \rightarrow 1] = 1$

One-time Anonymity. This property guarantees that if an honest signer computes a single signature w.r.t an arbitrary ring R, the secret key used by the signer is anonymous w.r.t the honest public keys present in the ring R. To capture this, and following the definition of anonymity provided in [19], in the one-time anonymity game $Exp_{\mathcal{A},\Pi}^{OneTimeAnon}$ all keys are maliciously computed by the adversary $\mathcal{A}$, except for two keys (pk_0, pk_1) which are honestly generated by the challenger. In the challenge phase, the adversary chooses a ring R, containing the keys pk_0 and pk_1, and a message m to sign. The challenger returns a signature σ^* which is computed with one of the secret keys sk_b where b is chosen at random. The adversary wins if it guesses the bit correctly. To capture the one-time setting, our adversary cannot observe any previous signature from pk_0 or pk_1. Concerning the other public keys besides pk_0, pk_1, note that the adversary "chooses" the ring R, hence it is assumed that the adversary controls those public keys and can obtain any signature computed by these *other* public keys (again, this follows the definition of [19])[7]. Also notes that the adversary gets at most one signature. This capture the fact that anonymity is guaranteed if the honest party only signs at most once in an absolute sense. If the party uses the same secret keys with different rings, no anonymity is guaranteed.

Experiment $Exp_{\mathcal{A},\Pi}^{OneTimeAnon}(1^\lambda)$

- Generate keys. Run $(pk_0, sk_0) \leftarrow GenKey(1^\lambda)$ and $(pk_1, sk_1) \leftarrow GenKey(1^\lambda)$ and send (pk_0, pk_1) to $\mathcal{A}$.
- Challenge phase. Upon receiving a message m and a ring R of public keys from the adversary proceed as follows. If pk_0, pk_1 are in R, pick bit $b \leftarrow \{0, 1\}$ and output $\sigma^* \leftarrow Sign(R, m, sk_b)$.
- (Decision). When $\mathcal{A}$ outputs b', output 1 iff $b = b'$.

Definition 2 (One-time Anonymity). *A one-time traceable ring signature scheme* Π *is anonymous if for all PPT adversaries* $\mathcal{A}$, *there exists a negligible function* negl *such that:* $Pr\left[Exp_{\mathcal{A},\Pi}^{OneTimeAnon}(1^\lambda) = 1\right] \leq \frac{1}{2} + negl(\lambda)$.

---

[7] A stronger anonymity definition introduced in [6] demands that an adversary cannot break anonymity of a honest ring signature even if it knows the secret keys all honest parties. As remarked in [19] (Remark 2.3), this property cannot be achieved in combination with public traceability.

Public Traceability. Traceability is a security property that protects the system against malicious users. To capture this, in the security game we assume that all keys are computed by the adversary, and we want that, given N adversarially-crafted keys, it should be infeasible for the adversary to produce $N+1$ signatures on $N + 1$ distinct messages *without being traced*. We note that our definition is stronger than the traceability definition of [19]. Indeed, in the latter, traceability is considered a correctness property and not a security concern. Thus, [19] only guarantees that two messages signed with the same secret key are linkable, but the identity of the malicious signer is not necessarily revealed. Instead, in our definition, we guarantee that if the same secret key is used twice, to compute two distinct signatures, the corresponding public key is detected and revealed by the Trace algorithm. The security game $\mathsf{Exp}^{\mathsf{Trace}}$ is formally defined below.

Experiment $\mathsf{Exp}_{\mathcal{A},\Pi}^{\mathsf{Trace}}(1^\lambda)$

1. $\mathcal{A}$ on input the security parameter 1^λ outputs a ring R of N public keys, and a list of $N + 1$ *distinct* signatures for the same ring R:
   $\{(m_1, \sigma_1), \ldots, (m_{N+1}, \sigma_{N+1})\}$.
2. Return 1 if:
   (a) $\mathsf{RVer}(\mathsf{R}, m_i, \sigma_i) = 1$ for all $i \in [N + 1]$ and
   (b) $\mathsf{Trace}(\mathsf{R}, m_i, \sigma_i, m_j, \sigma_j) \notin \mathsf{R}$ for all $i, j \in [N + 1]$, where $i \neq j$

Definition 3 (Traceability). *A one-time ring signature scheme Π is traceable if for all PPT adversaries $\mathcal{A}$, there exists a negligible function* negl *such that:*

$$Pr\left[\mathsf{Exp}_{\mathcal{A},\Pi}^{\mathsf{Trace}}(1^\lambda) = 1\right] \leq \mathsf{negl}(\lambda)$$

One-time Exculpability (Non-frameability). This property guarantees that if an honest ring member signed at most once, it cannot be framed. To capture this, we consider a target public key pk that is honestly generated, while all other keys are maliciously generated by the adversary. The goal of the adversary is to generate rings R, R′ and two signatures σ, σ' such that algorithm Trace will output the target key pk. The adversary can ask for one signature computed by pk on an arbitrary ring and message. More formally, the experiment is described below:

Experiment $\mathsf{Exp}_{\mathcal{A},\Pi}^{\mathsf{Frame}}(1^\lambda)$

1. Generate target key. Run $(pk, sk) \leftarrow \mathsf{GenKey}(1^\lambda)$ and send pk to $\mathcal{A}$.
2. Signature request. Upon receiving m, S, pk from the adversary, where S is a set of arbitrary public keys and m is the message the adversary wants to see signed. If $pk \in S$ then output $\sigma \leftarrow \mathsf{Sign}(S, m, sk)$.
3. Output. Upon receiving (R, m, σ) and $(\mathsf{R}, m', \sigma')$ from the adversary. Output 1 if $\mathsf{Trace}(\mathsf{R}, m, \sigma, m', \sigma') = pk$.

Definition 4 (One-time Exculpability (Non-frameability)). *A one-time traceable ring signature scheme Π is exculpable (non-frameable) if for all PPT adversaries $\mathcal{A}$, there exists a negligible function* negl *such that:*

$$Pr[\mathsf{Exp}_{\mathcal{A},\Pi}^{\mathsf{Frame}}(1^\lambda) = 1] \leq \mathsf{negl}(\lambda)$$

Remark. One can also consider a more general experiment where there are several target honest keys. In this case the adversary could ask for signatures for each target party and then attempt to frame one of them. As remarked in [19] a construction satisfying the simpler experiment with one target key would satisfy also the more general one.

One-time Unforgeability. As noted in [19] (see Theorem 2.6, Pag. 8) if a signature scheme is traceable and exculpable, then it is also unforgeable. The intuition on why this is true is that, if it was not the case, namely, if the scheme is exculpable but not forgeable, then the adversary producing the forgery can be used to break exculpability and frame an honest user. On the other hand, if the forgery could not be used to frame the honest user, then this means that the scheme is not traceable. Thus, in this paper we will not explicitly prove unforgeability.

4   One-Time Traceable Ring Signature Scheme

The high-level idea of our one-time traceable ring signature scheme has been provided in Sect. 1.1. In this section we describe the scheme formally and provide the formal security proof.

Notation. For a bit string x we use notation $x[j]$ to denote the j-th bit of x. We use the subscript notation $pk_{i,j}$ to denote the j-th element of vector $\mathbf{pk}_i$. Namely, $\mathbf{pk}_i = (pk_{i,1}, \ldots, pk_{i,\lambda})$. Let $H : \{0,1\}^* \rightarrow \{0,1\}^\lambda$ and $G : \{0,1\}^\lambda \rightarrow \{0,1\}^{3\lambda}$ be two random oracles. The one-time traceable signature scheme $\Sigma_{\mathsf{OTS}} = (\mathsf{GenKey}, \mathsf{RSign}, \mathsf{RVer}, \mathsf{Trace})$ is described in Fig. 1.

Theorem 1. *If $\mathcal{H} : \{0,1\}^* \rightarrow \{0,1\}^\lambda$ and $G : \{0,1\}^\lambda \rightarrow \{0,1\}^{3\lambda}$ are random oracles, then scheme $\Sigma_{\mathsf{OTS}} = (\mathsf{GenKey}, \mathsf{RSign}, \mathsf{RVer}, \mathsf{Trace})$ in Fig. 1 is a one-time traceable ring signature.*

One-time Anonymity. If a signature is computed by signer $\mathbf{pk}_l$, this means that the l-th set of commitments is equivocal, while the others are not. Recall that being equivocal means that each seed $r_{l,j}$ provided as part of the signatures has the property that $pk_{l,j} = G(r_{l,j}) \oplus G(\tilde{r}_{l,j})$ for some $\tilde{r}_{l,j}$. For any other $l' \neq l$ instead no such $\tilde{r}_{l',j}$ is known. Hence, in order to break anonymity, an adversary should be able to distinguish whether the seeds present/do not present such property. We prove that it is infeasible for any PPT adversary to distinguish if this is the case through a sequence of hybrid games. We do so by considering a mental experiment where the signature is computed by programming the random oracle rather than using the equivocation property of Naor's commitment. In such experiment, no secret key is used, all commitments are opened

---

One-Time Traceable Ring Signature Scheme: Σ_{OTS}

Key Generation $\mathsf{GenKey}(1^\lambda)$: A member $\mathcal{U}_i$ joins the system as follows:
  1. Pick 2λ seeds: $s_{i,j}^0 \leftarrow \{0,1\}^\lambda$, $s_{i,j}^1 \leftarrow \{0,1\}^\lambda$ for $j \in [\lambda]$.
  2. Set $pk_{i,j} := G(s_{i,j}^0) \oplus G(s_{i,j}^1)$, and $sk_{i,j} = (s_{i,j}^0, s_{i,j}^1)$.
  3. Output public key $\mathbf{pk}_i = (pk_{i,1}||\ldots||pk_{i,\lambda})$ and secret key $\mathbf{sk}_i = (sk_{i,1}, \ldots, sk_{i,\lambda})$.

Signature $\mathsf{RSign}(\mathsf{R}, \mathbf{sk}_l, m)$. A member $\mathcal{U}_l$ signs a message as follows.
  1. Parse $\mathsf{R} = (\mathbf{pk}_1, \ldots, \mathbf{pk}_N)$. Parse the secret key $\mathbf{sk}_l = (s_{l,1}^0, s_{l,1}^1, \ldots, s_{l,\lambda}^0, s_{l,\lambda}^1)$.
  2. For all $i \neq l$
     (a) Commit to a random string $x_i \in \{0,1\}^\lambda$ using the i-th public key $\mathbf{pk}_i$.
        i. For $j \in [\lambda]$, commit to the j-th bit of x_i: (1) pick a seed $r_{i,j} \leftarrow \{0,1\}^\lambda$; (2) compute $c_{i,j} := G(r_{i,j}) \oplus (x_i[j] \cdot pk_{i,j})$.
        ii. Set $\mathbf{c}_i := [c_{i,1}, \ldots, c_{i,\lambda}]$.
  3. For $i = l$, set $\mathbf{c}_l := [G(s_{l,1}^0), \ldots, G(s_{l,\lambda}^0)]$.
  4. Compute target $z := \mathcal{H}(\mathsf{R}, m, \mathbf{c}_1, \ldots, \mathbf{c}_N)$.
  5. Compute adjustment string $x_l^* := \bigoplus_i x_i \oplus z$. (Recall, x_i were defined in Step 2a)
  6. Equivocate the l-th commitments $\mathbf{c}_l$ so that they open to x_l^*. Namely: set seed $r_{l,j}$ as $r_{l,j} := s_{l,j}^{x_l[j]}$ for each $j \in [\lambda]$.
  7. Signatures $\sigma := (x_i[j], r_{i,j})_{i \in [N], j \in [\lambda]}$. Output (R, σ, m).

Verification $\mathsf{RVer}(\mathsf{R}, \sigma, m)$.
  1. Parse $\mathsf{R} = (\mathbf{pk}_1, \ldots, \mathbf{pk}_N)$, where the i-th key is: $\mathbf{pk}_i = (pk_{i,1}, \ldots, pk_{i,\lambda})$. If keys are not all distinct (or are not of the correct size) abort.
  2. Parse $\sigma = (r_{i,j}, x_i[j])_{i \in [N], j \in [\lambda]}$.
  3. Compute commitments: if $x_i[j] = 0$ set $c_{i,j} := G(r_{i,j})$, else set $c_{i,j} := G(r_{i,j}) \oplus pk_{i,j}$. Set $\mathbf{c}_i = (c_{i,1}, \ldots, c_{i,\lambda})$.
  4. Compute $z' := \mathcal{H}(\mathsf{R}, m, \mathbf{c}_1, \ldots, \mathbf{c}_N)$. If $z' = \bigoplus_{i \in N} x_i$ accept the signature, else reject.

Trace $\mathsf{Trace}(\mathsf{R}, m_1, \sigma_1, m_2, \sigma_2)$.
  1. Parse $\sigma_1 = (a_{i,j}, \alpha_{i,j})_{i \in [N], j \in [\lambda]}$.
  2. Parse $\sigma_2 = (b_{i,j}, \beta_{i,j})_{i \in [N], j \in [\lambda]}$.
  3. If there exist a public key $\mathbf{pk}_i \in \mathsf{R}$ and a j such that $G(\alpha_{i,j}) \oplus G(\beta_{i,j}) = pk_{i,j}$ then output $(1, \mathbf{pk}_i)$. Else output 0.

Fig. 1. One-time traceable ring signature scheme Σ_{OTS}.

without a trapdoor, hence, a signature carries no information about the signer. The formal proof consists of a sequence of hybrid games, from the real experiments $\mathsf{Exp}_{\mathcal{A}, \Sigma_{\mathsf{OTS}}}^{\mathsf{OneTimeAnon}}(1^\lambda)$ where signatures are computed using the secret keys and equivocating the commitment, to the final experiment, where all signatures are computed by programming the random oracle and no commitment is equivocated.

Lemma 1 (One-time Anonymity). *If $\mathcal{H} : \{0,1\}^* \rightarrow \{0,1\}^\lambda$ is a random oracle and $G : \{0,1\}^\lambda \rightarrow \{0,1\}^{3\lambda}$ is a PRG, then scheme Σ_{OTS} achieves one-time anonymity according to Definition 2.*

Proof. Towards a contradiction, assume that there exists a PPT adversary $\mathcal{A}$ that wins game $\mathsf{Exp}_{\mathcal{A},\Sigma_{\mathsf{OTS}}}^{\mathsf{OneTimeAnon}}(1^\lambda)$ with non-negligible probability $p(\lambda)$. We show an adversary that distinguishes the output of G with the same probability. The proof goes by hybrid arguments, and leverage the programmability of the random oracle $\mathcal{H}$.

Hybrid 0. Real World Experiment. Hybrid H_0 corresponds to experiment $\mathsf{Exp}_{\mathcal{A},\Sigma_{\mathsf{OTS}}}^{\mathsf{OneTimeAnon}}(1^\lambda)$ instantiated with Σ_{OTS}. By contradicting hypothesis we assume that there is a PPT adversary $\mathcal{A}$ that wins game $\mathsf{Exp}_{\mathcal{A},\Sigma_{\mathsf{OTS}}}^{\mathsf{OneTimeAnon}}(1^\lambda)$ with probability $1/2 + p(\lambda)$.

Hybrid 1. Programming $\mathcal{H}$ and Avoiding Equivocation. In this experiment we slightly modify the computation of the signature in the following way. The value z is not computed as $z := \mathcal{H}(S, m, \mathbf{c}_1, \ldots, \mathbf{c}_N)$. Instead, in this experiment the challenger fixes values $(x_1, \ldots, x_N)$ and computes $z = \bigoplus x_l$. Later, the challenger programs the output of the RO so that when queried with input $q = (\mathsf{R}, m, \mathbf{c}_1, \ldots, \mathbf{c}_N)$ it outputs z. The commitments $\mathbf{c}_l$ associated to public key $\mathbf{pk}_l$ however are still computed as equivocal and the secret key is used to open them, however, the value x_l that must be opened to is defined in advance. Note that in this experiment the challenger can abort if two events happen: Event 1: the adversary queried a value $q = (\mathsf{R}, m, \mathbf{c}_1, \ldots, \mathbf{c}_N)$ before seeing the signature. Event 2: the value z chosen by the challenger was already used to answer previous random oracle queries.

Analysis. The difference between experiment H_0 and H_1 is only in the way the output of $\mathcal{H}$ is computed. H_0 and H_1 are distinguishable only if Event 1 or Event 2 happens, which happen with negligible probability as we show in Lemma 2 and Lemma 3.

Lemma 2. *If $\mathcal{H}$ is modeled as a programmable random oracle, $Pr[Event\ 1] \leq \frac{t}{2^{N\lambda^2}}$, where t is the number of queries to $\mathcal{H}$.*

Proof. Event 1 happens when adversary $\mathcal{A}$ queries the RO with input $q = (\mathsf{R}, m, \mathbf{c}_1, \ldots, \mathbf{c}_N)$ and later exactly the same commitments $(\mathbf{c}_1, \ldots, \mathbf{c}_N)$ are generated by the challenger. Since each $\mathbf{c}_i$ is a Naor's commitment and is the output of the RO on a randomly chosen seed, the probability that $\mathcal{A}$ queried values $\mathbf{c}_1, \ldots, \mathbf{c}_N$ prior to see the signature corresponds to guessing such values, which happens with probability less than $\frac{1}{2^{N\lambda^2}}$.

Lemma 3. *If $\mathcal{H}$ is modeled as a programmable random oracle, $Pr[Event\ 2] \leq \frac{t}{2^\lambda}$, where t is the number of queries to $\mathcal{H}$.*

Proof. Event 2 happens when the output z chosen by the oracle challenger was already provided as the output of $\mathcal{H}$ from previous queries. Since each output of $\mathcal{H}$ is simulated by sampling a string uniformly at random in $\{0,1\}^\lambda$, this events happen with probability $\frac{t}{2^\lambda}$ where t is the (polynomial) number of queries.

Hybrid 2. Replacing Honest Public Keys with Truly Random Strings. In Hybrid H_2 the honest keys are truly random strings instead of the xor of two pseudorandom values. Note that since the random oracle is programmed, there is no need for trapdoors in this experiment. An adversary distinguishing H_2 from H_1 can be reduced to a PRG distinguisher. Since no secret key exist in the system, no identity can be leaked in this experiment. This concludes the proof of one-time anonymity. □

Traceability. This property guarantees that if two signatures were computed by the same signer, they will be linked and the identity of the signer detected. To win the traceability game $\mathsf{Exp}^{\mathsf{Trace}}$, an adversary must provide a ring R of N keys and $N + 1$ distinct signatures $\sigma_1, \ldots, \sigma_{N+1}$ on $N + 1$ messages $m_1, \ldots, m_{N+1}$, such that for any pair (m_a, σ_a), (m_b, σ_b), $\mathsf{Trace}(\mathsf{R}, m_a, \sigma_a, m_b, \sigma_b)$ outputs 0, i.e., no pairs of signatures is linkable. Intuitively, this is not possible since, in order to compute $N + 1$ distinct signatures the adversary needs to compute at least $N + 1$ equivocal commitments and thus use the trapdoor twice, hence revealing which key was used.

We now argue this claim more formally. First, recall that according to the Trace procedure two distinct signatures σ_a, σ_b for messages m_a, m_b are linked when the following condition is satisfied: There exists a tuple a, b, i, j, such that: $G(r_{i,j}^a) \oplus G(r_{i,j}^b) = K_{i,j}$.

Now, assume that an adversary is able to provide $N + 1$ distinct signatures w.r.t the same ring $R = (K_1, \ldots, K_N)$ of *adversarially chosen* keys. Namely, the adversary provides:

$$\sigma_1 = \quad m^1, z^1 \qquad (x_{i,j}^1, r_{i,j}^1)_{i \in [N], j \in [\lambda]}$$
$$\ldots \ldots \qquad \ldots \qquad \ldots \ldots$$
$$\sigma_N = \quad m^{N+1}, z^{N+1} \qquad (x_{i,j}^{N+1}, r_{i,j}^{N+1})_{i \in [N], j \in [\lambda]}$$

Recall that to verify a signature σ_δ the verifier computes for each i, j, $c_{i,j}^\delta = G(r_{i,j}^\delta) \oplus x_i^\delta[j] \cdot K_{i,j}$ and then checks that: $z^\delta = \mathcal{H}(m^\delta, c_{i,j}^\delta)_{i \in [N], j \in [\lambda]}$. Now, since the signatures are distinct, each must have a different target z. Since $\mathcal{H}$ is modelled as a RO, the following observations hold:

1. For each pair a, b, values z^a, z^b differ in at least $v \geq \lambda/2$ positions w.h.p. because they are the output of $\mathcal{H}$.
2. For any δ, adversary learns z^δ only after being committed to the values $x_i^\delta[j]$.
3. Due to (1) and (2) the adversary needs to equivocate at least one bit commitment to guarantee that $\bigoplus_{i,j} x_i^\delta[j] = z^\delta$.
4. To equivocate one commitment $c_{i,j}^\delta$ which is either $G(r_{i,j}^\delta)$ or $G(r_{i,j}^\delta) \oplus K_{i,j}$, one needs to provide *another* seed $r_{i,j}^*$ such that $K_{i,j} = G(r_{i,j}^k) \oplus G(r_{i,j}^*)$.

The above observations simply tell us that in each signature there is at least one equivocal opening, that is, a real seed $r_{i,j}^\delta$ such that $K_{i,j} = G(r_{i,j}^\delta) \oplus G(r')$. If the adversary provided only N signatures, this means that for each signature one seed (trapdoor) has been provided. Now if the adversary provided $N + 1$ signatures then, for at least one of the keys the other seed must have been provided. In which case, that public key is linked. To complete the proof, we need to discard the possibility that an adversary is able to find multiple pairs of seeds that yield to the same public key $K_{i,j}$. Namely, the adversary could find two pairs $r_{i,j}^1, r_{i,j}^2, r_{i,j}^3, r_{i,j}^4$ such that $K_{i,j} = G(r_{i,j}^1) \oplus G(r_{i,j}^2)$ and $K_{i,j} = G(r_{i,j}^3) \oplus G_{r_{i,j}^4}$.

Since G is modeled as a Random Oracle, then the probability of finding such tuple is negligible.

Exculpability (Non-frameability). In the exculpability game the adversary participates at the same experiment as the anonymity experiment $\mathsf{Exp}^{\mathsf{OneTimeAnon}}$ but without the challenge phase. The goal of the adversary here is to output two signatures (R, m, σ) and (R, m', σ') with $m \neq m'$ such that there exists a *honest public key* $\mathbf{pk}_i \in \mathbb{H}$ such that: (1) $\mathbf{pk}_i \in R \cap R'$; (2) $\mathsf{SigVfy}(R, m, \sigma) = \mathsf{SigVfy}(R', m', \sigma') = 1$; (3) $\mathsf{Trace}(R, m, \sigma, m', \sigma') = \mathbf{pk}_i, 1$.

Recall the algorithm Trace shown in Fig. 1. The condition for linking a key $pk_{i,j}$ is that for two seeds $\alpha_{i,j}$ and $\beta_{i,j}$ it holds that: $G(\alpha_{i,j}) \oplus G(\beta_{i,j}) = pk_{i,j}$. Note that in $\mathsf{Exp}^{\mathsf{OneTimeAnon}}$ the adversary is able to observe at most one signature computed under secret key $\mathbf{pk}_i$, and thus he is able to learn at most one seed $s_{i,j}^b$ for each $j \in [\lambda]$. From this view the adversary can win the exculpability in two ways: (1) Finding the preimage of $pk_{i,j} \oplus G(s_{i,j}^b)$, (2) Finding two seeds α and β such that $G(\alpha) \oplus G(\beta) = pk_{i,j}$. In both cases the adversary is breaking the security of the PRG. The formal proof follows the same hybrid arguments shown for one-time anonymity (Lemma 1). The idea is to replace each honest public key $pk_{i,j}$ with a truly random string, and equivocating by programming the output $\mathcal{H}$. In this hybrid world, the adversary wins exculpability only by finding two seeds that satisfying the linkability equation, which corresponds to break the statically binding property of Naor's commitment.

One-Time Unforgeability. This property is implied by one-time exculpability and one-time traceability (see [19], Theorem 2.6 of).

References

1. Albrecht, M.R., Rechberger, C., Schneider, T., Tiessen, T., Zohner, M.: Ciphers for MPC and FHE. In: Oswald, E., Fischlin, M. (eds.) EUROCRYPT 2015. LNCS, vol. 9056, pp. 430–454. Springer, Heidelberg (2015). https://doi.org/10.1007/978-3-662-46800-5_17

2. Au, M.H., Liu, J.K., Susilo, W., Yuen, T.H.: Secure id-based linkable and revocable-iff-linked ring signature with constant-size construction. Theor. Comput. Sci. **469**, 1–14 (2013)

3. El Bansarkhani, R., Misoczki, R.: G-Merkle: a hash-based group signature scheme from standard assumptions. In: Lange, T., Steinwandt, R. (eds.) PQCrypto 2018. LNCS, vol. 10786, pp. 441–463. Springer, Cham (2018). https://doi.org/10.1007/978-3-319-79063-3_21

4. Baum, C., Lin, H., Oechsner, S.: Towards practical lattice-based one-time linkable ring signatures. IACR Cryptology ePrint Archive 2018:107 (2018)

5. Bellare, M., Rogaway, P.: Random oracles are practical: a paradigm for designing efficient protocols. In: Ashby, V. (ed.) ACM CCS 93, pp. 62–73. ACM Press (November 1993)

6. Bender, A., Katz, J., Morselli, R.: Ring signatures: stronger definitions, and constructions without random oracles. In: Halevi, S., Rabin, T. (eds.) TCC 2006. LNCS, vol. 3876, pp. 60–79. Springer, Heidelberg (2006). https://doi.org/10.1007/11681878_4

7. Beullens, W.: Sigma protocols for MQ, PKP and SIS, and fishy signature schemes. In: Canteaut, A., Ishai, Y. (eds.) EUROCRYPT 2020. LNCS, vol. 12107, pp. 183–211. Springer, Cham (2020). https://doi.org/10.1007/978-3-030-45727-3_7

8. Beullens, W., Katsumata, S., Pintore, F.: Calamari and falafl: logarithmic (linkable) ring signatures from isogenies and lattices. In: Moriai, S., Wang, H. (eds.) ASIACRYPT 2020. LNCS, vol. 12492, pp. 464–492. Springer, Cham (2020). https://doi.org/10.1007/978-3-030-64834-3_16

9. Boneh, D., Dagdelen, Ö., Fischlin, M., Lehmann, A., Schaffner, C., Zhandry, M.: Random oracles in a quantum world. In: Lee, D.H., Wang, X. (eds.) ASIACRYPT 2011. LNCS, vol. 7073, pp. 41–69. Springer, Heidelberg (2011). https://doi.org/10.1007/978-3-642-25385-0_3

10. Branco, P., Mateus, P.: A traceable ring signature scheme based on coding theory. In: Ding, J., Steinwandt, R. (eds.) PQCrypto 2019. LNCS, vol. 11505, pp. 387–403. Springer, Cham (2019). https://doi.org/10.1007/978-3-030-25510-7_21

11. Bresson, E., Stern, J., Szydlo, M.: Threshold ring signatures and applications to Ad-hoc groups. In: Yung, M. (ed.) CRYPTO 2002. LNCS, vol. 2442, pp. 465–480. Springer, Heidelberg (2002). https://doi.org/10.1007/3-540-45708-9_30

12. Chandran, N., Groth, J., Sahai, A.: Ring signatures of sub-linear size without random oracles. In: Arge, L., Cachin, C., Jurdziński, T., Tarlecki, A. (eds.) ICALP 2007. LNCS, vol. 4596, pp. 423–434. Springer, Heidelberg (2007). https://doi.org/10.1007/978-3-540-73420-8_38

13. Chaum, D., van Heyst, E.: Group signatures. In: Davies, D.W. (ed.) EUROCRYPT 1991. LNCS, vol. 547, pp. 257–265. Springer, Heidelberg (1991). https://doi.org/10.1007/3-540-46416-6_22

14. Derler, D., Ramacher, S., Slamanig, D.: Post-quantum zero-knowledge proofs for accumulators with applications to ring signatures from symmetric-key primitives. In: Lange, T., Steinwandt, R. (eds.) PQCrypto 2018. LNCS, vol. 10786, pp. 419–440. Springer, Cham (2018). https://doi.org/10.1007/978-3-319-79063-3_20

15. Dodis, Y., Kiayias, A., Nicolosi, A., Shoup, V.: Anonymous identification in *Ad Hoc* groups. In: Cachin, C., Camenisch, J.L. (eds.) EUROCRYPT 2004. LNCS, vol. 3027, pp. 609–626. Springer, Heidelberg (2004). https://doi.org/10.1007/978-3-540-24676-3_36

16. Don, J., Fehr, S., Majenz, C., Schaffner, C.: Security of the fiat-shamir transformation in the quantum random-oracle model. In: Boldyreva, A., Micciancio, D. (eds.) CRYPTO 2019. LNCS, vol. 11693, pp. 356–383. Springer, Cham (2019). https://doi.org/10.1007/978-3-030-26951-7_13

17. Esgin, M.F., Steinfeld, R., Liu, J.K., Liu, D.: Lattice-based zero-knowledge proofs: new techniques for shorter and faster constructions and applications. In: Boldyreva, A., Micciancio, D. (eds.) CRYPTO 2019. LNCS, vol. 11692, pp. 115–146. Springer, Cham (2019). https://doi.org/10.1007/978-3-030-26948-7_5

18. Fujisaki, E.: Sub-linear size traceable ring signatures without random oracles. In: Kiayias, A. (ed.) CT-RSA 2011. LNCS, vol. 6558, pp. 393–415. Springer, Heidelberg (2011). https://doi.org/10.1007/978-3-642-19074-2_25

19. Fujisaki, E., Suzuki, K.: Traceable ring signature. In: Okamoto, T., Wang, X. (eds.) PKC 2007. LNCS, vol. 4450, pp. 181–200. Springer, Heidelberg (2007). https://doi.org/10.1007/978-3-540-71677-8_13

20. Groth, J., Kohlweiss, M.: One-Out-of-Many Proofs: or how to leak a secret and spend a coin. In: Oswald, E., Fischlin, M. (eds.) EUROCRYPT 2015. LNCS, vol. 9057, pp. 253–280. Springer, Heidelberg (2015). https://doi.org/10.1007/978-3-662-46803-6_9

21. Katz, J., Kolesnikov, V., Wang, X.: Improved non-interactive zero knowledge with applications to post-quantum signatures. In: ACM SIGSAC CCS 2018, pp. 525–537 (2018)
22. Lamport, L.: Constructing digital signatures from a one-way function. Technical report. CSL-98, SRI International Palo Alto (1979)
23. Libert, B., Ling, S., Nguyen, K., Wang, H.: Zero-knowledge arguments for lattice-based accumulators: logarithmic-size ring signatures and group signatures without trapdoors. In: Fischlin, M., Coron, J.-S. (eds.) EUROCRYPT 2016. LNCS, vol. 9666, pp. 1–31. Springer, Heidelberg (2016). https://doi.org/10.1007/978-3-662-49896-5_1
24. Libert, B., Peters, T., Qian, C.: Logarithmic-size ring signatures with tight security from the DDH assumption. In: Lopez, J., Zhou, J., Soriano, M. (eds.) ESORICS 2018. LNCS, vol. 11099, pp. 288–308. Springer, Cham (2018). https://doi.org/10.1007/978-3-319-98989-1_15
25. Liu, J.K., Wei, V.K., Wong, D.S.: Linkable spontaneous anonymous group signature for Ad Hoc groups. In: Wang, H., Pieprzyk, J., Varadharajan, V. (eds.) ACISP 2004. LNCS, vol. 3108, pp. 325–335. Springer, Heidelberg (2004). https://doi.org/10.1007/978-3-540-27800-9_28
26. Liu, Q., Zhandry, M.: Revisiting post-quantum fiat-shamir. In: Boldyreva, A., Micciancio, D. (eds.) CRYPTO 2019. LNCS, vol. 11693, pp. 326–355. Springer, Cham (2019). https://doi.org/10.1007/978-3-030-26951-7_12
27. Lu, X., Au, M.H., Zhang, Z.: Raptor: a practical lattice-based (linkable) ring signature. In: Deng, R.H., Gauthier-Umaña, V., Ochoa, M., Yung, M. (eds.) ACNS 2019. LNCS, vol. 11464, pp. 110–130. Springer, Cham (2019). https://doi.org/10.1007/978-3-030-21568-2_6
28. Merkle, R.C.: A certified digital signature. In: Brassard, G. (ed.) CRYPTO 1989. LNCS, vol. 435, pp. 218–238. Springer, New York (1990). https://doi.org/10.1007/0-387-34805-0_21
29. Monero: Monero, a secure, private and untraceable digital currency (2016)
30. Nakamoto, S.: Bitcoin: a peer-to-peer electronic cash system. (2012):28, 2008
31. Naor, M.: Bit commitment using pseudo-randomness. In: Brassard, G. (ed.) CRYPTO 1989. LNCS, vol. 435, pp. 128–136. Springer, New York (1990). https://doi.org/10.1007/0-387-34805-0_13
32. Nguyen, L.: Accumulators from bilinear pairings and applications. In: Menezes, A. (ed.) CT-RSA 2005. LNCS, vol. 3376, pp. 275–292. Springer, Heidelberg (2005). https://doi.org/10.1007/978-3-540-30574-3_19
33. Rivest, R.L., Shamir, A., Tauman, Y.: How to leak a secret. In: Boyd, C. (ed.) ASIACRYPT 2001. LNCS, vol. 2248, pp. 552–565. Springer, Heidelberg (2001). https://doi.org/10.1007/3-540-45682-1_32
34. Shor, P.W.: Algorithms for quantum computation: discrete logarithms and factoring. In: Foundations of Computer Science, 1994 Proceedings., 35th Annual Symposium on, pp. 124–134. IEEE (1994)
35. Alberto Torres, W.A., et al.: Post-quantum one-time linkable ring signature and application to ring confidential transactions in blockchain (Lattice RingCT v1.0). In: Susilo, W., Yang, G. (eds.) ACISP 2018. LNCS, vol. 10946, pp. 558–576. Springer, Cham (2018). https://doi.org/10.1007/978-3-319-93638-3_32
36. Zhang, B., Oliynykov, R., Balogun, H.: A treasury system for cryptocurrencies: enabling better collaborative intelligence. In: Network and Distributed System Security Symposium, NDSS (2019)

PACE with Mutual Authentication – Towards an Upgraded eID in Europe

Patryk Kozieł, Przemysław Kubiak, and Mirosław Kutyłowski[✉]

Wrocław University of Science and Technology, Wrocław, Poland
{patryk.koziel,przemyslaw.kubiak,miroslaw.kutylowski}@pwr.edu.pl

Abstract. In this paper we present modifications to the protocols PACE (Password Authenticated Connection Establishment) and PACE CAM (PACE with Chip Authentication Mapping) from International Civil Aviation Organization (ICAO) specification. We show that with slight changes it is possible to convert PACE (which is limited to password authentication) and PACE CAM (where only the chip is strongly authenticated) to a full-fledged authentication where apart from password authentication both the terminal and the chip are authenticated in a strong cryptographic way.

The new protocols provide better privacy protection and resilience against key leakage than the previous protocols and are implementation friendly. The idea is not to reveal an exponent (as in case of PACE CAM) – instead, we reuse the Diffie-Hellman key exchange for static Diffie-Hellman authentication in the PACE protected channel.

The proposed fine tuning of the schemes adopted by ICAO for biometric passports may contribute to the future European eID practice, since the ICAO standards have been chosen by the EU as an obligatory basic platform for official personal identity documents issued since August 2021 in all EU countries.

Keywords: eID · Electronic identity document · ICAO · PAKE · PACE · Mutual Authentication · Privacy

1 Introduction

1.1 Role of eIDs

Nowadays using electronic identity documents for accessing various electronic services becomes more and more popular. A primary example are different types of e-Government services like accessing medical information of a patient, interacting with tax authorities or with financial institutions. As electronic identity documents with a strong cryptographic layer became widely deployed, they can be used in a large number of new scenarios. Every connection to remote service that requires sending sensitive data like name, date of birth or ID number can be realized by the means of standardized and secure usage of electronic credentials issued by government agencies and available via personal identity documents.

© Springer Nature Switzerland AG 2021
E. Bertino et al. (Eds.): ESORICS 2021, LNCS 12973, pp. 501–519, 2021.
https://doi.org/10.1007/978-3-030-88428-4_25

Enabling to present such tokens by a physical person may also help with and facilitate many day-to-day activities. A good example would be using vending machines where age verification is needed in case of buying age-restricted goods.

1.2   New Regulations for eIDs

There are many European countries that have started providing electronic personal identity documents (eIDs) for their citizens already many years ago, with prominent examples of Germany and Estonia. However, in many cases eIDs issued in one country are not suitable for using as an electronic token in another country due to lack of international technical coordination in designing the eIDs. To solve this problem, European Union decided to enforce a common basic platform to be implemented on European eIDs and issued Regulation 2019/1157 [13], which applies directly in all member states regardless of the national law. This regulation requires all eIDS issued after August 2, 2021 to implement PACE protocol from International Civil Aviation Organization (ICAO) specification [8] intended for Machine Readable Travel Documents (MRTDs). PACE was intended for travel documents such as e-passports, aiming to facilitate automatic border control (e-Booths) while securing against potential privacy attacks. PACE is Password Authenticated Connection Establishment protocol based on a password authenticated key exchange protocol (PAKE), and designed by the German Federal Office for Information Security (BSI) [4]. The goal of PACE is to establish a shared secret key between two parties sharing a password, and use it subsequently for communication between these parties. PACE can be divided into four phases:

1. A random nonce encrypted with a key derived from a password known to the document holder is sent to the reader. The document holder inputs the password to the reader (terminal) so the reader can also derive the key and retrieve the nonce. (In practice, the password is optically scanned from the machine-readable zone of the document).
2. There is a procedure of establishing a generator to be used in the next phase for deriving the secret key. There a few options how to do it. We focus on one of two options from the ICAO specification – so called GM (General Mapping), which is basically a Diffie-Hellman key establishment with additional usage of the nonce from Phase 1.
3. Based on the generator from Phase 2, the actual main session key is derived again using the Diffie-Helmann protocol. From this shared main key, the keys for encryption and message authentication codes are derived.
4. Protocol parties exchange tags ensuring that the parties derived the same keys and that the execution has not been manipulated by a man-in-the-middle.

Details of PACE will be recalled on Fig. 1 where we introduce an extension of PACE.

Besides enforcing the usage of PACE on eIDs, Regulation [13] also allows for extensions of PACE to be deployed on eIDs alongside the obligatory basic version. This possibility provides means for greatly expanding functionalities of eIDs and is one of the rationales for the solution we propose in this paper.

Regulation [13] creates a situation where extending PACE while preserving backwards compatibility is one of the most pragmatic ways to realize additional functionalities on a personal identity card. It is also likely that this strategy will not result in deep incompatibilities between the eIDs issued by different parties. Also this strategy is less endangered by patent threats and future regulations.

Later on we will use terms *chip* and *terminal* for the parties participating in the protocol as they are more general than *eID* and *reader*. The classic setup - border control - is eID with a chip and a reader that simultaneously plays the role of a terminal. However, it is possible to execute PACE remotely, so that a reader is merely a man-in-the middle enabling forwarding messages sent by the terminal and the chip.

1.3   Rationale for Including Mutual Authentication

Currently ICAO includes in its specification PACE-CAM - a version of PACE that provides chip authentication. We extend this protocol in two versions to provide a way to use PACE with additional mutual authentication. It means that not only the chip is authenticated in front of the terminal, but also the terminal is authenticated in front of the chip. We propose two versions of the protocol that are suitable for different scenarios (with more in-depth explanation in Sect. 2).

There are many scenarios where the need for mutual authentication is a basic application requirement. This concerns any remote service that requires sending potentially sensitive data, when both the server and the user need a way to authenticate the other. This could be in particular health care systems or next generation systems for financial services. Among others, in this case it is crucial to strongly authenticate the terminals in order to prevent phishing attacks.

Mutual authentication in PACE adds another layer of security to the protocol. We propose how to achieve this goal without major modifications of the protocol and without big computational overhead in comparison with regular PACE, reusing currently used operations. The important feature is that one can update PACE to PACE-MA(-light) even without the consent of ICAO as it is backwards compatible and the regulation [13] allows that.

1.4   Other extensions and Modifications of PACE

An interesting modification of the PACE protocol has been presented in [11] – it uses one-time pad as encryption method during the first phase of PACE. It seems to be be quite controversial, but it turns out for instance that it doubles the expected number of trials in the brute force attack on the password.

Quite early, the authors of PACE have started the work on extending the protocol towards strong authentication. Bender et al. [1] introduced a protocol called PACE|AA. It is the first extension of PACE protocol enabling active authentication of the chip. For this purpose PACE was interleaved with Schnorr or DSA signatures. Hanzlik et al. [6] proposed a simplified version of PACE|AA protocol – which achieves an implicit authentication binding the random numbers from PACE to the public key instead of using signatures. Moreover, a leakage-resilient version derived by slightly modifying the PACE protocol was introduced, in which the secret key is secure even when all ephemeral values are leaked. Slightly later Bender et al. published paper [3] describing two slightly different protocols (addition version and multiplication version), where one version is in fact identical with [6]. The protocols from [3,6] achieve active authentication of the eID with just one additional message. The multiplication version was included in the standard Supplemental Access Control (SAC) and then renamed as PACE-CAM protocol, where CAM is short for Chip Authentication Mapping [8]. The algorithm was patented by the German government [5].

PACE-CAM protocol can only work with the Generic Mapping and cannot use the more efficient Integrated Mapping. To this end, Hanzlik and Kutyłowski [7] proposed PACE-CAM v2 protocol based on bilinear maps, which can work with both Generic Mapping and Integrated Mapping while having the same efficiency as PACE-CAM on the side of the chip. Those works however do not support mutual authentication, they focus rather on one-sided chip authentication.

PACE can be converted to a proof of presence or a signing protocol. For eID it has been implicitly done already in [1]. For the terminal, it has been recently proposed in [10], where it has been proposed to build a pool of cryptographic schemes for eIDs based on a common core of the ICAO standard and reusing intensively the same code.

On the other hand, there are discussions and activities (LDS2) aiming to provide the next generation of ePassports, enabling for instance issuing electronic visas and storing them on the passport. For those future functionalities new cryptographic engines will be necessary, in particular authentication of involved parties should be achieved on much higher level of security than today.

2   PACE with Mutual Authentication

The following strategy may ease upgrading cryptographic protocols that are already widely deployed. Assume that we have a protocol $\mathcal{A}$ that should be upgraded to a protocol $\mathcal{A}^+$. The implementation and deployment of $\mathcal{A}^+$ would be much easier when the following conditions are fulfilled:

- the steps of $\mathcal{A}$ are executed by $\mathcal{A}^+$ in exactly the same way, or they are modified so that if a party A executes $\mathcal{A}$ while the other party B executes $\mathcal{A}^+$, then from the point of view of A there is a correct execution of $\mathcal{A}$, while B recognizes that the partner A runs the old version $\mathcal{A}$ and may smoothly adjust to the situation.
- if an additional mechanism introduced by $\mathcal{A}^+$ requires executing computationally hard operations, one should reuse – whenever possible – the steps of $\mathcal{A}$ without violating the original protocol.

This approach has the following consequences:

– adopting the software to the new protocol version might be much easier,
– security analysis of $\mathcal{A}^+$ may reuse security analysis of $\mathcal{A}$; hopefully, restarting security analysis from scratch can be avoided.

The presented strategy is a standard industrial practice. Proposing new mechanisms made from scratch, when there are many tools already deployed and accepted in regulations, is bound to be a practical failure due to high costs, necessary effort and long time-to-market.

PACE CAM is an example of this pragmatic approach. Additional operations come at the end and they do not require exponentiation (which is the most time consuming operation). Moreover, if for PACE we can determine when the protocol parties reach an accepting state at the protocol termination, then the same applies to PACE CAM at the moment when the PACE phase terminates.

In this paper we follow the same strategy. However, now the reuse-mechanism is different. The proposed mutual authentication protocols reuse the strings X_A and X_B from the first Diffie-Hellman key exchange. Now, apart from that, we use X_A and X_B for static Diffie-Hellman authentication that is executed at the very end of the protocol. Note that for PACE CAM the chip presents an exponent and not a group member to the terminal. Moreover, the exponent must be presented in full to the terminal, as the terminal cannot compute it itself.

We are going to present two protocols. The first one, presented in Sect. 2.1 follows the same approach as PACE CAM: until the last phase of the protocol, the execution is indistinguishable or identical to the plain PACE. The second protocol, presented in Sect. 2.2, reduces the number of messages – their number is the same as in case of the original PACE. However, now the tags T_A, T_B are created in a modified way. Nevertheless, we are still talking about a MAC based construction, so the previous security arguments still apply.

A good point is that if the terminal is executing the plain PACE, but the chip is executing the modified protocol, then at this moment the chip can immediately fall back to the plain PACE. If the terminal is executing the modified protocol but the chip is executing the plain PACE, then the current connection fails and another try is necessary to enable the terminal to fall back to the plain PACE.

Finally, let us observe that one can provide hybrid versions of the protocol from Sect. 2.2. By skipping some parameters one can get only authentication of the terminal or only authentication of the chip. This might be useful for instance in the situations where the chip should check authenticity of a terminal, however revealing identity of the chip is unnecessary. In this case, a fallback to a weaker authentication is a security requirement according to the data minimality principle of GDPR [12].

2.1 PACE with Mutual Authentication

In Fig. 1 we describe the first extension of PACE with mutual authentication, called PACE-MA.

In this protocol the chip and the terminal will authenticate each other after the completion of the PACE protocol. The authentication strategy is as follows:

- the chip uses the strings X_B sent by the terminal during Phase 2 for execution of the static Diffie-Hellman authentication protocol,
- first the token $K_A = X_B^x$ is computed, subsequently it is hashed (mainly for saving the space, but also for repelling potential algebraic attacks),
- the hash $H_3(K_A)$ together with the certificate cert(X) of the chip are sent encrypted to the terminal.
- only the terminal can decrypt this message (as a secure session key was used for encryption), so nobody but the terminal will learn the identity of the chip by inspecting the certificate cert(X). The terminal can recompute K_A on its side just like in case of the standard static Diffie-Hellman protocol.

The PKI framework may be chosen by the document issuer and standard solutions are applicable in this case. In particular, we can follow the approach of PACE-CAM.

The procedure to authenticate the terminal is exactly the same, only the arguments are mirrored: $X_A, y,$ cert(Y) are used instead of $X_B, x,$ cert(X).

The order of the messages C_A and C_B has been chosen according to the order once preferred by the German information security authorities: first the terminal should present its identity. This gives the chip an opportunity to decide, whether to disclose own identity. Such an approach is conformant with the principles of the GDPR regulation [12]: chip identity usually fall to the category of *personal data* of the chip owner, while the identity of the terminal is usually the identity of an element of an infrastructure. So we get a good example of a framework where a data subject is controlling to whom the personal data are presented. Of course, the protocol enables changing the order of these messages which corresponds to the order: chip authentication first, then terminal authentication (this approach has also been used in the past in the context of electronic identity documents).

2.2   A Lightweight Version

In this section we consider a lightweight version of PACE MA, named PACE-MA-light, and the details are given in Fig. 2. The main difference between this scheme and PACE-MA is that:

- the last phase (exchanging the ciphertexts C_A and C_B) and the phase of exchanging the tags T_A, T_B are merged together,
- the MACs corresponding to the tags T_A and T_B are computed now with one additional parameter: namely K_A and K_B, correspondingly,
- additionally, the public key certificate is sent together with the MAC; in order to protect the information about identity of the chip and the terminal, these data are encrypted with a session key that is known exclusively to the chip and the terminal.

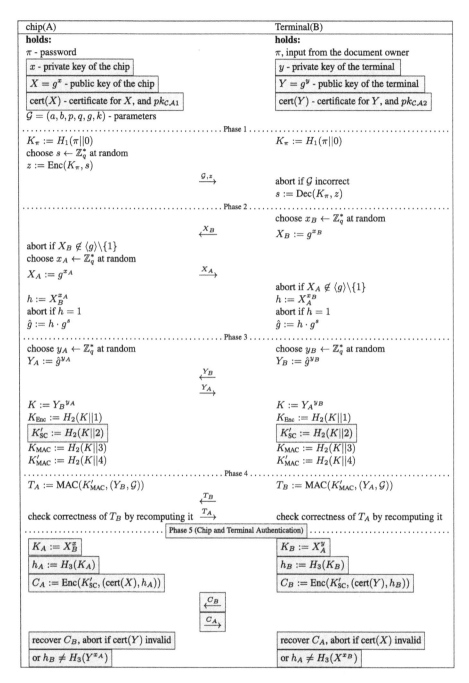

Fig. 1. PACE-MA – an extension of PACE with mutual authentication, H_1, H_2, H_3 denote here hash functions, their range is given by the context. Gray boxes indicate the changes specific to PACE-MA, the rest of the protocol is the original PACE.

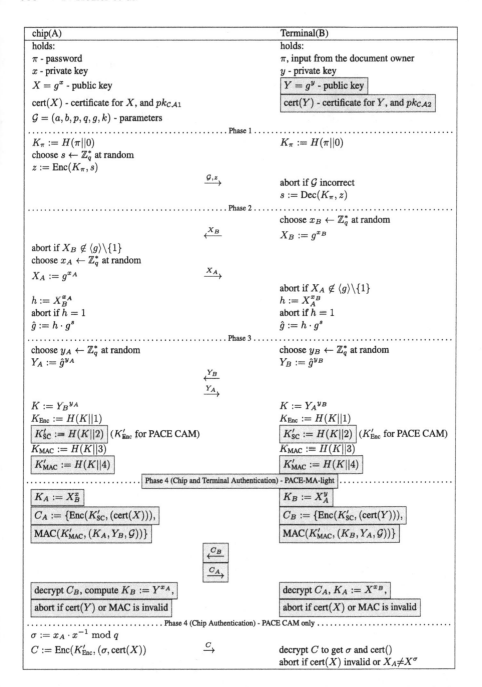

Fig. 2. PACE MA-light– an extension of PACE with mutual authentication with the same number of messages as for the plain PACE. PACE-MA-light changes to PACE-CAM are in gray boxes and additionally last phases for PACE-MA-light and PACE CAM are separated.

As before, the identity information is not sent until the main key K is established. Unlike PACE-MA, the identity information is sent by the terminal, before it learns that the chip shares the same key K. It could be a potential issue, because potentially it may ease tracing the terminal (note that the role of the terminal can be played by a mobile unit assigned to a physical person, so the personal data protection rules do apply!). However, the certificate is encrypted with the key that can be derived by the chip, only if the chip and the terminal have used the same password. More sensitive information about the chip identity is sent after the chip authenticates and accepts the terminal according to its current policy. This is much better than in case of PACE CAM, where the chip reveals and proves its identity based only on the fact that the terminal shares the same password.

2.3   Backwards Compatibility

Let us consider the situation where either the terminal or the chip runs the plain PACE scheme while the other party runs PACE-MA or PACE-MA-light.

Terminal Executing PACE. Assume first that the terminal is executing the plain PACE while the chip expects it to execute either PACE-MA or PACE-MA-light. Note that in both cases the chip may recognize that the terminal is running the plain PACE before the chip sends the first message specific to PACE-MA(-light) – namely C_B. Moreover, until this moment the chip has been executing exactly the same steps as in case of the plain PACE, so it can immediately switch to the plain PACE, if the current policy of chip allows for that. (Note that the chip may disable any connection with an unverified terminal).

Chip Executing PACE, Terminal Executing PACE-MA. Note that until the end of Phase 3 both the terminal and the chip execute the plain PACE, so in particular a secure connection based on a shared password will be successfully established. Then, the terminal will send the message C_B, which is not expected by the chip. It will be treated as a payload message and decrypted with K_{Enc}. The result will be garbage, as the encryption and decryption keys used do not match. According to the current policy on the application level, the chip may either interrupt the connection, or respond that the message has not been understood. In either case, the terminal will learn that the chip is not running PACE-MA – if a message is returned, then the terminal first decrypts it with K'_{SC} hoping that this is a correct C_A. Since the result will not have the correct form (starting with a garbage and not a certificate), the terminal may continue with decryption with the key K_{Enc} and then see the response of the chip. At this moment the terminal may interrupt the connection or proceed, depending on its policy – e.g. transferring sensitive data to the chip may require more than a password based authentication.

Chip Executing PACE, Terminal Executing PACE-MA-light. In this case the situation is slightly more complicated. The chip receives C_B consisting of a ciphertext and a MAC. Even if the ciphertext is ignored, the examination of the MAC yields a negative result. Indeed, the chip recomputes the MAC on input $(Y_A, \mathcal{G})$, while the terminal has used $(K_B, Y_A, \mathcal{G})$. Thereby chip will fail to establish a connection. Consequently, the terminal will eventually learn that the connection failed. In this case the terminal still has the option to downgrade to the plain PACE and attempt to connect once more, if its current policy allows for that.

The situation discussed above is on one hand inevitable, if extra data are to be sent. On the other hand, we need to be careful not to install extra exceptions and interpretations while running the plain PACE, as in this case we could not leverage on security properties of PACE.

3   Security and Privacy Issues

In this section we provide a sketch of crucial security properties of the proposed schemes. Here, we take the properties of PACE (declared in [2,9]) and derive the properties of the extensions without starting the analysis from scratch. As PACE-MA-light modifies the last phase of PACE, some modifications in the original proofs are necessary. As for this preliminary version, we can only sketch why the same arguments should apply, and postpone the details until a detailed (and long) version of [9] becomes available.

3.1   Fragility

Protocol *fragility* is a very useful feature that in many scenarios may simplify greatly the security analysis. It implies that any active man-in-the-middle attack results in a protocol failure except for a negligible probability. Thereby we may disregard immediately all man-in-the-middle active attacks and concentrate on passive ones. Fragility is inherently connected with the construction of the protocol itself, specifically with the expected format of the received messages and the event of breaking the session in case of abnormality detection by one of the parties.

Definition 1. *We say that protocol P is* fragile *when any modification of the communication done by an active man-in-the-middle adversary leads to a session failure, except for a negligible probability.*

As stated in [9], the plain PACE has a property very close to fragility. The only modification that does not lead to a protocol failure is raising X_A and X_B to the same power by the adversary. In this case the chip and the terminal share the same session key K and accept the session, even if their points of view are slightly different. Any other modification, in particular during the first two phases, leads to a failure. In contrast to PACE:

Proposition 1. *PACE-MA and PACE-MA-light are fragile.*

Before we start a detailed argument let us observe that after phase 3 all messages depend deterministically on what has been sent and received so far. Hence the manipulations need to be done in phases 1–3, and later the messages need only to be adjusted to the values from phases 1–3.

First let us show Proposition 1 for PACE-MA. Now, messages exchanged by the parties in PACE-MA are essentially the same as in PACE up to the beginning of the last phase which does not occur for PACE. Up to this moment the same conditions for aborting the connection apply as in case of PACE, so the only case that may escape protocol failure is raising X_A and X_B to the same power $\alpha \neq 1$. Now consider the last phase and the message C_B. Let us give the adversary $\mathcal{A}$ an extra power at this point - assume that $\mathcal{A}$ can decrypt C_B and retrieve h_B. At this point to produce C_B that would be valid for the chip, $\mathcal{A}$ has to replace $h_B = H_3(K_B) = H_3(g^{x_A \cdot \alpha \cdot y})$ by $H_3(g^{x_A \cdot y})$. According to Diffie-Hellman assumption, $\mathcal{A}$ cannot derive K_B and even distinguish it from a random value. So if H_3 is correlated input secure hash function, it is infeasible for $\mathcal{A}$ to derive $H_3(g^{x_A \cdot y})$ from h_B. So the connection fails if $\alpha \neq 1$ and Proposition 1 holds for PACE-MA.

Now let us turn out attention to PACE-MA-light. Here we also can say that the adversary cannot do more than to raise X_A and X_B to the same power α without breaking the session. Indeed, C_B and C_A contain MAC values for all values occurring in the definition of the tags T_B and T_A. So the same argument as in [9] show that any other manipulation up to this point leads to a protocol failure. However note that now MAC contains K_B. If the adversary raised X_A and X_B to the same power α, he would need to transform MAC of $(g^{x_A \cdot \alpha \cdot y}, Y_A, \mathcal{G})$ to MAC of $(g^{x_A \cdot y}, Y_A, \mathcal{G})$. Just as in case of PACE-MA, this is infeasible.

Corollary 1. *Any man-in-the-middle attack against PACE-MA(-light) can be reduced to a passive attack.*

3.2 Protection of Secrets

An authentication process must not leak the secrets that are used to authenticate a protocol party. First note that no such threats exist for the keys x and y. These values are used to compute K_A and K_B which in turn are arguments for a hash function or a MAC. The values K_A and K_B are computed themselves by the verifying parties, so there is no added information, if the verifying party follows the protocol (and knows the discrete logarithm of, respectively, X_B and X_A). If the verifying party $\mathcal{P}$ does not follow the protocol and does not know the discrete logarithm mentioned, then in particular $\mathcal{P}$ cannot derive the session key K of PACE. Consequently, in case of PACE-MA $\mathcal{P}$ cannot decrypt, respectively, C_B or C_A and learn h_B or h_A. For PACE-MA-light, $\mathcal{P}$ can learn the MAC on respectively K_B or K_A, but obtained with a key K'_{MAC} which is not distinguishable from a random one.

The really hard case is protection of the password π. It has a small entropy and therefore a brute force attack applies: a terminal may initiate connections with the chip trying one by one all possible passwords. Similarly, the chip may interact with a terminal after the password of another chip I has been input to the terminal. In this case we need to check whether a protocol run may indicate what is the password for I.

PACE-MA(-light) inherits the following property from PACE:

Property 1. If the chip and the terminal hold different passwords π, π' and it is not true that

$$\mathrm{Enc}(K_\pi, \mathrm{Dec}(K_{\pi'}, z)) = z, \tag{1}$$

then they derive different values of the session key K and consequently the connection fails.

The above property is non-trivial and holds also if a party (a chip or a terminal) does not follow the protocol. Consequently, the information from a protocol trial run is that either the passwords used satisfy (1) (if the connection is established), or they fail to satisfy (1) (if the connection fails). (An interesting observation is that typically the chip may try more than 1 password in this way [9]).

An attack may also have an offline form: first, an adversary $\mathcal{A}$ can analyze the messages exchanged in a protocol run by the chip and an honest terminal. Second, if $\mathcal{A}$ was active himself, he can analyze the message exchanged and parameters he used in order to find a matching password.

These attacks fail for PACE. The key reason for this property is the method of deriving the generator $\hat{g}$: it is a product of h (a Diffie-Hellman key exchange result from Phase 2, where neither part knows the discrete logarithm) and the element g^s, where s depends on the password. An active adversary will know the exponent y_A or y_B it has used in the failed protocol execution. In order to match a different password and check the resulting key K, adversary $\mathcal{A}$ would need to derive the discrete logarithm of either Y_A or Y_B with respect to the new candidate for $\hat{g}$ based on the corresponding discrete logarithm for $\hat{g}$ used during protocol execution. It has been shown that this is infeasible. Moreover, $\mathcal{A}$ can be given the session key K and nevertheless it will be still infeasible to derive the right password.

In case of PACE-MA(-light) the situation is slightly more complicated since the protocol delivers some extra data during the authentication phase. However, we could emulate all these messages if we provide $\mathcal{A}$ the secret keys x', y', the public keys $g^{x'}$, $g^{y'}$ and the session key K and thereby get a reduction argument: if there is an algorithm $\mathcal{A}$ finding the password based on K and ephemeral data of one side of the failed protocol execution of PACE-MA(-light), then we could create an algorithm $\mathcal{A}'$ finding the password for the plain PACE.

3.3   Impersonation

It may seem that resistance to impersonation is obvious due to execution of double static Diffie-Hellman protocol (derivation of K_A and K_B and a proof of their knowledge). However, this is not that simple. Potentially it could happen that an adversary man-in-the-middle $\mathcal{A}$ could compute the same session key K

as the terminal and the chip. Then $\mathcal{A}$ could simply forward the authentication information created by the honest parties in the last phase and finally hijack the connection to either the terminal or the chip (this may require jamming the signal of the other party). In this way $\mathcal{A}$ may either pretend to be the verified chip against the terminal, or $\mathcal{A}$ may pretend to be the verified terminal against the chip.

The key property inherited by PACE-MA(-light) from the plain PACE is that except for a negligible probability it may not occur that the chip, the terminal and $\mathcal{A}$ derive the same key K. As the first phases are the same for the extended protocols, this property holds PACE-MA(-light) just like for PACE.

So the only option left for $\mathcal{A}$ is to run separately the protocol with the chip and with the terminal. Note that in these executions X_A used by the chip cannot be reused by $\mathcal{A}$ as its X_A while talking to the terminal (knowledge of the discrete logarithm of X_A is necessary to derive the session key). The same applies to X_B. However finally $\mathcal{A}$ has to present a MAC (or hash) derived from K_B. The terminal sends to $\mathcal{A}$ the value that $\mathcal{A}$ can compute itself (as he knows the discrete logarithm of X_A that it has sent to the terminal). However, the value expected by the chip is X_A^y for X_A chosen by the chip. As $\mathcal{A}$ neither knows the discrete logarithm of this X_A nor the private key y, $\mathcal{A}$ must fail to provide the right value with a very high probability.

3.4   Security of the Session Key

We have to guarantee that it is safe to encrypt data with the key K_{Enc} derived by the chip and by the terminal during a successful protocol execution. For this purpose it is enough to show that an adversary observing the protocol execution up to the end of the last phase and given either the real K_{Enc} or a random key K_{Enc}, cannot distinguish which option has been chosen.

At this point let us recall that both PACE-MA and PACE-MA-light are *fragile* in the sense of Definition 1, so we only consider a passive adversary $\mathcal{A}$. Moreover, we have already pointed that it is impossible that the adversary $\mathcal{A}$ learns this key by an active interaction.

Note that for PACE-MA(-light) there are additional messages or data exchanged with respect to PACE. So potentially, they might be used for testing K_{Enc}. We can only increase the chances of the adversary if we provide him the secret keys x, y as well as the genuine keys K'_{SC} and K'_{MAC}. In this case all authentication messages are redundant, as $\mathcal{A}$ can compute them himself.

Note that the key K_{Enc} and the keys K'_{SC} and K'_{MAC} are correlated according to the protocol specification: they are obtained as hash values $H_2(K\|1)$, $H_2(K\|2)$, $H_2(K\|4)$. However, if H_2 is a correlated input secure hash function, it is infeasible to determine whether K'_{SC} is the next correlated value $H_2(K\|1)$ given $H_2(K\|2)$ and $H_2(K\|4)$, unless one can extract K. In our case, one cannot extract K from K'_{SC} and K'_{MAC} due to preimage resistance of H_2, while on the other hand $\mathcal{A}$ cannot derive K from the transcript of the first 3 phases of PACE due to hardness of the CDH problem.

3.5   Resistance to Tracing

One of the major goals of the designers of PACE was privacy protection. As a wireless communication can be easily tapped by an arbitrary observer, there is a serious threat that an observer would analyze the messages exchanged and find out who is communicating with whom. Note that in some situations the identity of the terminal might be easy to guess. Potentially, it could ease finding out the identity of the chip, who typically is the main target of the attack.

In case of the plain PACE the only identity based information is the password used. In case of mutual authentication we have additionally the secret keys of the terminal and the chip and the keys K_A, K_B derived with them. The property we are aiming for is tracing resistance – unless it is explicitly designed for a correct protocol run, it should impossible to derive which identity specific data has been used.

Note 1. Let us note that there are limitations for active tracing resistance in case of plain PACE. An adversarial terminal $\mathcal{A}$ can initiate connections with the chip (in case that chip does not need to be activated somehow by its user, e.g. by pulling out of the cover acting as a Faraday cage). $\mathcal{A}$ does not know the right password (as the goal of the attack is to find the password), but $\mathcal{A}$ can run a brute force attack or probe with passwords already seen in various locations. In particular, if the adversary is controlling a terminal where Alice opens a legitimate session using her chip, then the adversary learns her password π and can use it in different locations in order to trace Alice. Note that this attack does not work so easily in case of PACE-MA(-light). Indeed, if the chip implements a policy restricting communication to a fixed set of terminals, then after receiving C_B and authenticating the terminal, the chip has an opportunity to break the connection. Until this moment the message sent by the chip are random elements distributed independently of the identity of the chip, so the adversarial terminal learns nothing but that it has been rejected according to the chip's policy or due to a wrong password.

In general, defining tracing resistance is hard, due to multiple attack scenarios, including in particular the cases when one of the protocol participants (e.g. a terminal) does not follow literally the protocol or there are executions where the passwords used by the chip and the terminal do not match and consequently the session fails. Nevertheless, a failed session could potentially provide valuable information about the identity of the protocol participants.

Apparently, PACE has been designed having in mind all these problems and the identity information was carefully postponed to the later phases of the execution:

Property 2. Until the tags T_A, T_B are sent during an execution of PACE, the probability distribution for the messages sent are independent of the password or passwords used by the terminal and the tag.

This property holds for PACE-MA(-light) as well, since the first two phases are identical with PACE.

Passive Observer. For PACE-MA(-light) a potential source of identity information might be the elements K_A, K_B. They are not sent in clear, but for a moment assume that they are. An adversary observing a protocol execution and the public key X of a potential chip, would have to decide whether (X_B, X, K_A) is a Diffie-Hellman triple. This is infeasible as long as the observer does not know x_B or x. A similar argument applies for K_B. Unfortunately, a terminal may deliberately weaken the execution and enable an observer to detect that the owner of X is participating in the protocol run. It would suffice to choose x_B so that the observer can guess it. As only the x_B component would be weak, the final session key would remain safe against the observer.

Fortunately, the identity specific information is protected by the session key. In case of PACE-MA we may observe that the tags T_A, T_B cannot serve a source of information for tracing, as this part is identical with PACE and PACE is claimed to be secure against passive tracing. The only source of trouble might be the ciphertexts C_A and C_B. However, these are ciphertexts obtained with the key K'_{SC}. Now untraceability depends on semantic security of the encryption scheme. The key itself should be secure if the terminal and the chip honestly execute Phase 3. In this case the observer cannot distinguish between an honest execution of the protocol and a virtual executions where the terminal and the chip jointly choose K at random. If H_2 is a cryptographic hash function, then we may assume that it is impossible to check whether $K'_{SC} = H_2(K\|2)$ or it has been chosen at random. So the observer cannot see the difference between the virtual executions just described and the executions where also K'_{SC} is chosen at random. It follows that C_A and C_B are useless for tracing, provided that semantically secure encryption scheme is used.

In case of PACE-MA-light the situation is slightly different as we do not execute the whole PACE – its last phase has been modified. Now instead of the tags T_A and T_B some ciphertexts obtained with the key K'_{SC} are sent. Following the same argument as before we may conclude that the observer cannot extract more information than as in the case when K'_{SC} is chosen at random.

Active Tracing. Another scenario for tracing is that an attacker interacts with a chip or a terminal, say D, aiming to find its identity. The target is to find a password and/or the public key of this device.

If the password is known, then of course nothing can prevent the attacker to establish a connection and thereby confirm the identity of D. If the attacked side is the terminal, then C_B is sent before C_A and regardless of the policy applied by the terminal the identity of the terminal is revealed. If the attacked side is the chip (which is the typical case), then the terminal must disclose and prove its identity first. Now the chip has an opportunity to refuse to send C_A, if the connection does not comply with the policy of the chip.

We see that we are left with attempts to trace without knowing the password. However, then we fall into already discussed category of attacks that aim to retrieve some information about the password.

3.6 Simultability

One of important questions concerning privacy protection is whether the authentication is limited to the parties that are intended to be recipients of the authentication proof. We have to guarantee that

(a) an observer cannot convince a third party – possibly holding some private information not available to the observer – that a given party participated in an interaction,

(b) no participant (i.e. a terminal or a chip) can convince a third party that an interaction with the other protocol party has occurred. In this case the party presenting a proof may reveal not only the messages exchanged, but also some own data – e.g. the secret ephemerals used, such as s, x_A, x_B, y_A, y_B, as well as the data derived from the private keys x, y. The protocol participant may also be obliged by the third party to use some particular values determined by the third party.

Note 2. What we cannot exclude is that given an interaction T observed by a possibly malicious observer Eve (so that Eve can be sure that the messages have been really exchanged between some chip and terminal). Later, one of the participants of execution T may prove that it took part in execution T and played a given role. This occurs by simply revealing either x_A or x_B. If it must be shown to Eve that the connection has not failed, then it suffices to reveal own ephemerals as well as a proof that K_B (in case of the terminal) or K_A (in case of chip) is correct. Any ZKP protocol for equality of discrete logarithms for (g, Y, X_A, K_B) or, respectively, (g, X, X_B, K_A) can be used for this purpose. In particular, one can convince Eve that a particular password π has been used.

The properties from point (a) and (b) can be derived from the following observation. Anybody can create a valid full transcript of a protocol run, including all private values created by the protocol participants. Namely, given a password π one has to choose the ephemerals s, x_A, x_B, y_A, y_B and compute the values occurring in the protocol. In case of K_B and K_A we do not need to proceed as the terminal and, respectively, the chip, but we compute them as it is done during verification of the tags. All we need is to know the certificates for X and Y.

Obviously this solves the case (a). For case (b), let us observe that Eve may oblige the terminal or the chip to behave in a certain way. However, the protocol participant has to know the ephemerals on own side, as otherwise the protocol would fail. In this case the prover may simulate the second protocol participant and cheat Eve.

4 PACE-MA Versus PACE-CAM

In this section we discuss shortly some practical problems regarding implementation issues, deployment strategies and relation to the existing standards such as PACE CAM.

Time Complexity. First let us note that the protocol PACE-MA provides authentication for the cost of additional operations. On each side these are the following main activities that may be attributed to authentication:

- CDH (or ECDH) executed for computing K_A and K_B, (2 executions)
- hashing of K_A and of K_B (2 hashings),
- encryption and decryption for C_A and C_B, (1 encryption, 1 decryption)
- certificate verification (ECDSA signature verification).

A trial implementation on an old MULTOS smartcard resulted in the runtime of about 900 ms for these operations, so perfectly acceptable for practical applications.

Note that in case of PACE CAM for authentication in one direction we need one modular division, one ECDH for verification, one encryption, one decryption and one certificate verification. If we implement PACE CAM in a way resistant to leakage, then we get one more ECDH instead of the modular division. So the extra operations are almost the same as for PACE-MA.

The computation time is acceptable – and there is no need for further optimization, as the connection should not be established faster than in, say $2\,s^1$.

Operations. Very important issue, also from the point of view of real time complexity, is what operations are executed. The standard computational complexity characteristics may not apply for the sheer reason that certain cryptographic operations might be hardware supported and executed very fast. Therefore modular exponentiation might be much faster than modular multiplication, if the later is not supported by cryptographic co-processor. Definitely, exponentiation/scalar multiplication of a EC point belong to the set of operations that are to be implemented on the co-processor on any reasonable cryptographic smart card. Modular multiplication and division do not belong to a standard suite of algorithms supported by smart cards.

Another issue related to the choice of operations used by a scheme is the space complexity. To this end we understand the space not only as space in the volatile memory nedded to execute the algorithm, but mainly as the place necessary to store the code for executing these operations in the non-volatile memory. This memory is scarce and frequently a substantial implementation bottleneck. PACE-MA(-light) does not use any operation that should not already been implemented on a smart card running PACE.

Leakage. Implementing modular division is not only problematic from the point of view of a memory usage. Note that it must be implemented so that any side channel leakage (e.g. power consumption) is not betraying the arguments used. In case of PACE CAM this is particularly critical, as one of the arguments is directly the secret key. Therefore, any ad hoc implementation of this operation

---

[1] Such a delay is necessary to make brute force attacks harder and to convince the user that some computation is really taking place.

might be risky. In case of PACE-MA(-light) we are not using any operation involving the secret keys apart from what should be available on a cryptographic co-processor. PACE CAM can be implemented in this way too (see [6]), but then the code for PACE should be modified as well (implying necessity for renewing software certification).

Another point of concern is leakage of ephemeral values. For PACE CAM leakage of ephemeral values stored during the protocol execution reveals the secret key of the chip. In case of PACE-MA(-light) this is not the case. Note that the leakage to be concerned is not only side channel information, but also a backdoor in the pseudorandom number generator used by the terminal or by the chip. Therefore one can somewhat reduce the requirements of tamper resistance and quality of PRNG.

PACE-MA(-light) and PACE-CAM with Terminal Authentication. Important property making PACE-MA(-light) more desirable solution than PACE-CAM with Terminal Authentication is the fact that the latter case provides means for tracing attacks when the terminal simply disconnects after authenticating the chip. Additionally, comparing PACE-MA(-light) to PACE-CAM rather than to PACE CAM followed by Terminal Authentication makes sense for the scenario of replacing already widely deployed PACE CAM with PACE-MA(-light).

Extended Privacy Guarantees. One particular property of PACE-MA is that after executing the first 4 phases a protocol participant can create itself the message that has to authenticate the other protocol participant (this message is either C_A or C_B, depending on the protocol side). In case of PACE CAM this is infeasible.

This property may be useful due to some subtle privacy protection concerns. Assume for instance that an adversary has installed a unit that has both access to the wireless channel and the ephemeral values created by the terminal (the later can be easily achieved, e.g. via a backdoor in the PRNG of the terminal). Such a scenario is not unrealistic, especially in case of authoritarian regimes aiming to spy on and control the citizens.

In case of PACE-MA(-light) one can easily trick the adversary. Namely, it can create the message C_A itself and transmit it over the wireless channel.

For the reason described, the adversary discussed above may receive a communication transcript indicating that Bob has been talking to Alice, while in reality Bob has been executing PACE-MA with Eve. The only drawback of this approach is that Eve is not authenticated, apart from password authentication – but always this authentication may be provided by an application level. The most important point is that PACE-MA enables to escape the powerful surveillance attacks of the art described by cheating the spying party at any moment.

References

1. Bender, J., Dagdelen, Ö., Fischlin, M., Kügler, D.: The PACE|AA protocol for machine readable travel documents, and its security. In: Keromytis, A.D. (ed.) FC 2012. LNCS, vol. 7397, pp. 344–358. Springer, Heidelberg (2012). https://doi.org/10.1007/978-3-642-32946-3_25
2. Bender, J., Fischlin, M., Kügler, D.: Security analysis of the PACE key-agreement protocol. In: Samarati, P., Yung, M., Martinelli, F., Ardagna, C.A. (eds.) ISC 2009. LNCS, vol. 5735, pp. 33–48. Springer, Heidelberg (2009). https://doi.org/10.1007/978-3-642-04474-8_3
3. Bender, J., Fischlin, M., Kügler, D.: The PACE|CA protocol for machine readable travel documents. In: Bloem, R., Lipp, P. (eds.) INTRUST 2013. LNCS, vol. 8292, pp. 17–35. Springer, Cham (2013). https://doi.org/10.1007/978-3-319-03491-1_2
4. BSI: Technical guideline TR-03110 v2.21 - advanced security mechanisms for machine readable travel documents and eidas token (2016). https://www.bsi.bund.de/EN/Publications/TechnicalGuidelines/TR03110/BSITR03110.html
5. Dennis Kügler, J.B.: Method for authentication, RF chip document, RF chip reader and computer program products. Patent US20140157385A1 (2014)
6. Hanzlik, L., Krzywiecki, Ł, Kutyłowski, M.: Simplified PACE|AA protocol. In: Deng, R.H., Feng, T. (eds.) ISPEC 2013. LNCS, vol. 7863, pp. 218–232. Springer, Heidelberg (2013). https://doi.org/10.1007/978-3-642-38033-4_16
7. Hanzlik, L., Kutyłowski, M.: Chip authentication for E-passports: PACE with chip authentication mapping v2. In: Bishop, M., Nascimento, A.C.A. (eds.) ISC 2016. LNCS, vol. 9866, pp. 115–129. Springer, Cham (2016). https://doi.org/10.1007/978-3-319-45871-7_8
8. ICAO: Machine Readable Travel Documents - Part 11: Security Mechanism for MRTDs. Doc 9303 (2015)
9. Kutyłowski, M., Kubiak, P.: Privacy and security analysis of PACE GM protocol. In: 18th IEEE International Conference On Trust, Security And Privacy In Computing And Communications/13th IEEE International Conference On Big Data Science And Engineering, TrustCom/BigDataSE 2019, Rotorua, New Zealand, 5–8 August 2019, pp. 763–768. IEEE (2019). https://doi.org/10.1109/TrustCom/BigDataSE.2019.00110
10. Kutyłowski, M., Kubiak, P., Kozieł, P., Cao, Y.: Poster: eID in Europe - password authentication revisited. In: Yan, Z., Tyson, G., Koutsonikolas, D. (eds.) IFIP Networking Conference, IFIP Networking 2021, Espoo and Helsinki, Finland, 21–24 June 2021, pp. 1–3. IEEE (2021). https://doi.org/10.23919/IFIPNetworking52078.2021.9472856
11. Shenets, N.N., Trukhina, E.E.: X-PACE: modified password authenticated connection establishment protocol. Autom. Control Comput. Sci. **51**(8), 972–977 (2017)
12. The European Parliament and the Council of the European Union: Regulation (EU) 2016/679 of the European Parliament and of the Council of 27 April 2016 on the protection of natural persons with regard to the processing of personal data and on the free movement of such data, and repealing Directive 95/46/EC (General Data Protection Regulation). Off. J. Eur. Union **119**(1) (2016)
13. The European Parliament and the Council of the European Union: Regulation (EU) 2019/1157—strengthening the security of identity cards and of residence documents issued to eu citizens and their family members exercising their right of free movement. Off. J. Eur. Union **188**(67) (2019)

Differential Privacy

Secure Random Sampling in Differential Privacy

Naoise Holohan and Stefano Braghin[(⊠)]

IBM Research Europe, Dublin, Ireland
naoise@ibm.com, stefanob@ie.ibm.com

Abstract. Differential privacy is among the most prominent techniques for preserving privacy of sensitive data, oweing to its robust mathematical guarantees and general applicability to a vast array of computations on data, including statistical analysis and machine learning. Previous work demonstrated that concrete implementations of differential privacy mechanisms are vulnerable to statistical attacks. This vulnerability is caused by the approximation of real values to floating point numbers. This paper presents a practical solution to the finite-precision floating point vulnerability, where the inverse transform sampling of the Laplace distribution can itself be inverted, thus enabling an attack where the original value can be retrieved with non-negligible advantage.

The proposed solution has the advantages of being (i) mathematically sound, (ii) generalisable to any infinitely divisible probability distribution, and (iii) of simple implementation in modern architectures. Finally, the solution has been designed to make side channel attack infeasible, because of inherently exponential, in the size of the domain, brute force attacks.

Keywords: Differential privacy · Random numbers · Computational complexity

1 Introduction

The generation of random samples from probability distributions is a well-studied field, and is an ever-present feature in programming languages and random number generators alike. Random sampling is especially important in the field of differential privacy, where specially-calibrated random noise is used to protect published data from unwanted inference. However, while the definition and analysis of differential privacy is typically viewed in the theoretical, real-valued world of mathematics, translating its rigorous guarantees to the floating-point world of computers requires special attention.

Work by Mironov in 2012 [22] was the first to point to significant vulnerabilities in floating point implementations of differential privacy, which allow

© Springer Nature Switzerland AG 2021
E. Bertino et al. (Eds.): ESORICS 2021, LNCS 12973, pp. 523–542, 2021.
https://doi.org/10.1007/978-3-030-88428-4_26

for catastrophic destruction of the much-vaunted privacy guarantees. Using naïve sampling of the Laplace distribution, Mironov was able to exploit holes in the output space to reconstruct the original input from a finite list of candidate inputs. Being able to reconstruct a single value with certainty is a blatant breach of differential privacy, which should guarantee uncertainty on any query. In this paper, we further extend Mironov's approach to present a novel attack on the Gaussian mechanism (Sect. 2.4).

It is well-known that the cardinality of the real line $\mathbb{R}$ is the same as that of the unit interval on the real line, $[0, 1]$, which allows for precise sampling using the inverse transform method. For floating-point numbers however, there are many more numbers on the real line than there are in the unit interval, which results in the holes that Mironov used in the attack. Typical defences against this vulnerability eliminate these holes by limiting the output space, using such techniques as the "snapping mechanism" [22], and sampling from the discrete analogue of the distribution [6, 14], but these require much more complex code to implement.

In this paper, we seek an alternative defence – that of computational complexity. The attack presented by Mironov relies on an attacker inverting the sampling procedure to test the feasibility of candidate inputs. Although random samples generated from a single random number (*e.g.*, the Laplace distribution) are vulnerable to this attack, samples generated by two or more random numbers (*e.g.*, the Gaussian distribution) are less vulnerable. By generating samples from multiple random numbers, we can render the attack sufficiently costly so as to be impractical on today's computers.

We demonstrate how this approach can be implemented with ease for the Laplace and Gaussian distributions (both popular in differential privacy), and a large family of probability distributions. The approach can be extended to systems of reduced precision (*e.g.*, single- and half- precision floating point), and allows for any desired level of complexity to be achieved.

Given that data is commonly stored as floating point numbers, we believe there is value in developing tools that reflect this reality. Equally, we are cognisant of the need to develop simple solutions to these complex tasks, to allow for easy implementation, adoption, generalisation and understanding of the techniques. As described in [8]:

> Fast programs are seldom short, and short programs are likely to be slow. But it is also true that long programs are often not elegant and more error-prone. Short smooth programs survive longer and are understood by a larger audience.

The rest of the paper is organised as follows. Section 2 describe the required background information. The guiding principles to this paper are then given in Sect. 3, with the specifics presented in Sect. 4. Example implementations are given in Sect. 5 and the protection provided is explored in

Sect. 6 After reviewing the state of the art in Sect. 7, the contribution is summarised in Sect. 8.

2 Background

This section will give a brief outline of the vulnerability presented in [22], alongside an example attack implementation and its extension to attacking Gaussian sampling, and the current state-of-the-art in mitigating against the attack.

2.1 Floating Point Numbers

To begin, we give a very brief outline of floating point numbers. Floating point numbers take their inspiration from scientific notation to store a wide range of numbers in binary format. Double-precision floating points (also known as *doubles*) occupy 64 bits of storage, comprising 1 bit for the sign, 11 bits for the exponent and the remaining 52 bits for the fraction or mantissa. The corresponding real number for a given double is given by

$$(-1)^{\text{sign}}(1.b_{51}b_{50}\ldots b_0)_2 \times 2^{e-1023},$$

where $b_0, \ldots, b_{51} \in \{0, 1\}$ are the bits of the mantissa, and $e \in \mathbb{N}$ is the non-negative integer exponent. This format allows for the representation of numbers between 10^{-308} and 10^{308}, with varying degrees of granularity.

The IEEE standard[1] gives an algorithm for addition, subtraction, multiplication, division, and square root and requires that implementations produce the same result as that algorithm.

The standard specifies that floating-point numbers are represented as base 2 fractions. For example, the value 0.001_2 represents the decimal value $\frac{0}{2} + \frac{0}{4} + \frac{1}{8}$. Nonetheless, not all decimal fractions can be represented exactly as binary fractions. Thus, the decimal floating-point numbers are approximated to the binary floating point. For example, in base-2, $\frac{1}{10}$ is represented as the infinitely-repeating value $0.0001100110011\ldots$

The standard provides information about the error introduced by both the representation and operations that can be performed. For example, the addition (and subtraction) operation can be performed by converting the operands to the same exponent, and then summing (or subtracting) the mantissa. On the other hand, multiplications can be computed by multiplying the mantissa of both operands and adding the exponents.

These operation introduce a rounding error, as the values need to be converted and as multiplications are performed. Moreover, the standard specifies various rounding modes, including round to nearest (where ties round

---

[1] ANSI/IEEE Std 754–2019 http://754r.ucbtest.org.

to the nearest even digit in the required position, the most commonly used), round away from zero, round up (toward $+\infty$), round down (toward $-\infty$), and round toward zero (*i.e.*, truncation).

The amount of error can be quantified [13] to a *machine epsilon* (generally denoted as E_{mach}), that depends on the actual precision used in the representation. For example, single precision floating point (32 bits) have a machine epsilon equal to $2^{-23} \approx 1.19 \times 10^{-7}$, while double precision floating point numbers (64 bits) have a machine epsilon equal to $2^{-52} \approx 2.22 \times 10^{-16}$.

2.2 Random Number Sampling

When sampling random numbers from a probability distribution, the common starting point is to take a (many) random number(s) from the unit interval and transform them to sample from the given distribution. Although the unit interval can be sampled with increasing granularity closer to zero, the typical practice is to sample from a multiple of a small number. For example, the Python programming language returns a multiple of 2^{-53} when sampling from the unit interval.

Inverse transform sampling is a popular method to sample from certain probability distributions, by taking the inverse of the Cumulative Distribution Function (CDF) or Cumulative Mass Function (CMF). For example, given a CDF $F(x) : \mathbb{R} \to [0, 1]$ from which we want to sample, and whose inverse $F^{-1}(x) : [0, 1] \to \mathbb{R}$ is known, then given $U \sim \mathcal{U}(0, 1)$, we have

$$\mathbb{P}(F^{-1}(U) \leq x) = \mathbb{P}(U \leq F(x)) = F(x),$$

for $x \in \mathbb{R}$, noting that $\mathbb{P}(U \leq u) = u$ for a uniform variate $U \sim \mathcal{U}(0, 1)$ and $u \in [0, 1]$.

2.3 Mironov Attack

Noting that there are only 2^{53} possible uniform variates to be generated and 2^{64} floating point numbers, there is an immediate difficulty in covering the output space with the image of a transformation. Without additional randomness, it is impossible for the inverse transform sampling method to fully cover the real line. This was demonstrated in [22], where the author confirmed that gaps appear in the output space between the outputs of consecutive uniform variates. Mironov formulated an attack that could successfully reconstruct an entire database, with certainty, under specific conditions.

The CDF of the standard Laplace distribution is given by

$$F_{\text{Lap}}(x) = \begin{cases} \frac{1}{2}e^x & \text{if } x \leq 0, \\ 1 - \frac{1}{2}e^{-x} & \text{if } x > 0, \end{cases} \tag{1}$$

with which we can calculate its inverse:

$$F_{\mathrm{Lap}}^{-1}(u) = (-1)^{\lfloor u \rfloor_1} \log(1 - 2|u - 0.5|), \tag{2}$$

where $\lfloor \cdot \rfloor_k$ denotes rounding to the nearest multiple of $k \in \mathbb{R}$. A Laplace variate can then be generated using $F_{\mathrm{Lap}}^{-1}(U) \sim \mathrm{Lap}(0,1)$, by first sampling a uniform variate $U \sim U(0,1)$. We present an example algorithm for attacking a single value in a dataset in Algorithm 1.

Input: Attack target v, DP query Q using the Laplace mechanism with implementation (2), finite candidate set $\mathcal{C}$

Output: Attack result $c \in \mathcal{C}$

1 **while** $|\mathcal{C}| > 1$ **do**
2      $q = Q(v)$
3   **for** $c \in \mathcal{C}$ **do**
4         $u = \lfloor F_{\mathrm{Lap}}(q - c) \rceil_{2^{-p}}$
5   **if** $F_{\mathrm{Lap}}^{-1}(u) + c \neq q$ **then**
6   remove c from $\mathcal{C}$
7   **end**
8   **end**
9 **end**
10 **return** *remaining element* $c \in \mathcal{C}$

Algorithm 1: Example algorithm implementing the Mironov attack

---

Critical to this attack is the ability to compute the inverse of the sampling procedure (*i.e.*, the CDF, given in (2), in the case of inverse transform sampling). The success of this attack is therefore independent of the precision of the uniform variate, and can be executed whenever the sampling function can be inverted.

2.4 Gaussian Attack

We now show an extension of the Mironov attack to the Gaussian distribution, one which we believe to be novel. This attack can be performed on Gaussian variates sampled using the popular Box-Muller transform [4]. Given two uniform variates $U_1, U_2 \sim \mathcal{U}(0,1)$, the Box-Muller transform returns two independent Gaussian samples $N_1, N_2 \sim N(0,1)$ as follows:

$$N_1 = \sqrt{-2\log(1 - U_1)}\cos(2\pi U_2), \tag{3a}$$

$$N_2 = \sqrt{-2\log(1 - U_1)}\sin(2\pi U_2). \tag{3b}$$

Knowing both N_1 and N_2, we can recover U_1 and U_2 as follows:

$$U_1 = 1 - e^{-\frac{N_1^2 + N_2^2}{2}}, \tag{4a}$$

$$U_2 = \frac{1}{2\pi} \left(\arctan\left(\frac{N_2}{N_1}\right) + \pi \mathbb{1}_{\{N_1 < 0\}} \right). \tag{4b}$$

The same inversion technique as described in Algorithm 1 can be used to eliminate candidates and determine the true input, noting that q and u in Lines 2, 4 and 5 will be vectors of two values each.

Getting two values from a mechanism utilising the Box-Muller transform can be done by executing the same query twice in succession. Ensuring both values are from the same Box-Muller operation, and determining which is associated with the cos and which is associated with the sin can be done by examining the source code and executing a simple timing attack. It is a common implementation to return the first variate to the user, while caching the second variate to be returned the next time the function is called [24]. The calculation overhead in the first step can be measured to determine the phasing to implement the attack.

This attack can be mitigated against by discarding one of the variates, or by using both variates in an output of $\frac{1}{\sqrt{2}}(N_1 + N_2)$.

2.5 Existing Defences

To mitigate against the attack, Mironov proposed the *snapping mechanism* to sample a noisy output with Laplace-like additive noise. The snapping mechanism involves snapping the noisy output to the nearest factor of the scale of the noise, resulting in a significant reduction in granularity of the output. For example, given a privacy budget $\epsilon = 2^{-5}$, the only outputs will be multiples of $2^5 = 32$. Alongside the reduction in granularity, the snapping mechanism is also cumbersome to implement, requiring a custom approach to sampling from the unit interval, as well as clipping and rounding operations.

Another approach is to sample from the discrete analogue of the desired distribution, thereby giving more control to the user on the discretisation of the output [6,14]. [14] in particular offers solutions for the Laplace and Gaussian distributions, but requires complex sampling procedures. It is not clear if it is simple, or possible, to adapt their solution to other probability distributions.

While there are many algorithms to sample from the discrete Gaussian distribution [6,18], all common random number generator packages produce floating-point Gaussian variates, making the implementation of such solutions more complex.

3 General Principles

In this section we present the general principles of the proposed solution. We first make the following assumptions in analysing the protections provided by our approach:

Assumption 1. *Mechanism source code is public.*

Assumption 2. *Uniform variates are generated using a cryptographically-secure pseudorandom number generator (CSPRNG).*

Assumption 3. *Uniform variates are generated as multiples of 2^{-p} for some fixed $p \in \mathbb{N}_{>0}$.*
Hence, for $U \sim \mathcal{U}(0,1)$, we have

$$U \in [0,1) \cap \left(2^{-p}\mathbb{N}\right). \tag{5}$$

Assumption 1 ensures that we cannot achieve security of random number generation through obscurity, and that the protections are an inherent characteristic of the system. Assumption 2 ensures that an attacker cannot predict forthcoming uniform variates, as can be done with some standard Pseudo-Random Number Generators (PRNGs) (*e.g.*, the Mersenne-Twister PRNG). Assumption 3 simplifies some of the analysis of this paper, and aligns with random number generation in many programming languages.

For clarity, we define the set of uniform variates as follows for a given precision p.

Definition 1 (Uniform variates) . *Given $p \in \mathbb{N}$, we define*

$$\mathbb{U} = [0,1) \cap (2^{-p}\mathbb{N}),$$

the set of all multiples of 2^{-p} in the half-open unit interval $[0,1)$.
This denotes the set of uniform variates in many programming languages. For example, in the Python programming language, $p = 53$.

Although the holes in the output space of the random number generation provide the key to the attack as shown in Sect. 2.3, it relies on the invertibility of the sampling procedure to execute efficiently. If the sampling procedure can be made non-injective (and consequently, non-invertible), then any sampled variate could be the result of more than one combination of uniform variate(s). Therefore, satisfying the non-equality condition of Line 5 in Algorithm 1 would require searching through all possible uniform variate combinations that approximately give equality in Line 5 (up to floating point rounding errors).

We can flesh out the details of this using the Gaussian distribution as an example.

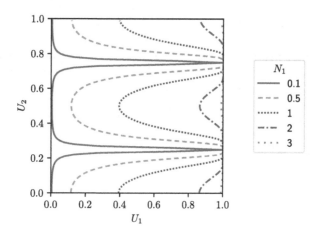

Fig. 1. Level curves of (6) for given values of N_1.

Example 1 (Gaussian distribution) . Consider samples from the Gaussian distribution, as given in Sect. 2.4. Although it is possible to reconstruct U_1 and U_2 knowing both outputs from the Box-Muller transform, we can show that knowing a single Box-Muller output is not sufficient to execute the Mironov attack in a single step. Suppose N_1 is known to have originated from (3a), and we wish to determine U_1 and U_2 from which it came. We can write

$$U_1(U_2) = 1 - e^{-\frac{N_1^2}{2\cos^2(2\pi U_2)}}, \tag{6}$$

allowing us to solve for U_1 given U_2. We can similarly write U_2 as a function of U_1.

As shown in Algorithm 1, we need only find a single pair $U_1, U_2 \in \mathbb{U}^2$ that gives equality in Line 5 in order to retain that candidate as feasible. On the real line, any pair $U_1, U_2 \in [0, 1)$ satisfying (6) will give equality for Line 5. However, due to floating point rounding errors and the limited precision of values $U \in \mathbb{U}$, we need to search through $\mathbb{U}^2$ to find values that satisfy the equality down to the bit of least precision. Figure 1 shows the level curves of (6), illustrating the paths through the grid of $(U_1, U_2) \in \mathbb{U}^2$ that would be traversed in a typical execution of the attack.

This example prompts two questions:

1. Can we extend the protection offered to Gaussian variates, beyond that of searching through 2^p uniform variates?
2. Can this approach be adopted for other probability distributions? Particularly, ones with injective sampling procedures (*e.g.*, the Laplace distribution)?

If we can use our choice of $n \in \mathbb{N}$ uniform variates to generate a single sample from a given distribution, then a brute-force attack (similar to

Example 1) would require on the order of $2^{p(n-1)}$ 'checks'. In essence, it would require fixing $(n-1)$ of the variates, and running an inversion attack (*e.g.*, using (6) in the case of the Gaussian distribution) on the nth variate. Importantly, for a linear increase in the time to sample a variate, the cost of executing the attack will increase exponentially.

Additionally, this approach can be extended to systems of reduced precision. Single- and half- precision systems use only 32 and 16 bits respectively to represent a floating point number, compared to the 64 bits allocated for double-precision floating point numbers. For example, Graphical Processing Units (GPUs) typically use lower-precision floating point numbers in their calculations, making attacks such as Example 1 more feasible.

In implementing such an approach, we can take some inspiration from the subset sum problem in computer science. The subset sum problem asks, given a multiset A of positive integers ($a \in \mathbb{N}$ for each $a \in A$), and a target $T \in \mathbb{Z}$, is there a subset $A' \subseteq A$ such that $\sum_{a \in A'} a = T$? It is known that the subset sum problem is NP-complete [10], making it intractable to solve when the set A is large.

Luckily, there is a branch of probability theory that we can exploit in this context – infinite divisibility.

4   Divisibility of Probability Distributions

Our approach relies on simple and effective ways to generate random numbers from a given distribution using many uniform variates. As explained in Sect. 3, simply increasing the number of random bits used to generate a random sample from a distribution is not sufficient to protect against inversion attacks. Instead, we seek to increase the number of uniform variates used to generate a single random sample.

A probability distribution P is *divisible*, if there exists a distribution Q such that, given independent $X_1, X_2 \sim Q$, we have $X_1 + X_2 \sim P$. P is *infinitely divisible* if, for any $n \in \mathbb{N}$, there exists a distribution R_n such that independent $X_i \sim R_n$ for each $i \in [n]$ satisfy $\sum_{i=1}^{n} X_i \sim P$.

Probability distributions that are infinitely divisible therefore allow the greatest flexibility in increasing the complexity of this defence. Fortunately, the two most popular distributions used in differential privacy are infinitely divisible.

4.1   Preliminaries

For every $i \in \mathbb{N}$, we adopt the following notation for these common distributions:

- $N_i \sim \mathcal{N}(0,1)$ is a collection of independent (standard) Gaussian random variables, and,

– $U_i \sim \mathcal{U}(0,1)$ is a collection of independent uniform random variables on the unit interval.

Formulations of the probability distributions used in this section are given in Appendix A,

For any $n \in \mathbb{N}$, we let $[n] = [1,n] \cap \mathbb{N}$ denote the positive integers up to and including n.

We note that when sampling uniformly from the unit interval, random number generators typically sample from $[0,1)$ (*i.e.*, excluding 1). This range is undesirable when computing $\log(U_1)$, and instead we use $\log(1-U_1)$, since $1 - U_1 \in (0,1]$ lies within the domain of logarithms.

Finally, we limit our analysis to standard distributions, those with zero location and unit scale parameters. These standard distributions can be scaled and translated as appropriate to get a distribution of a specific mean and variance (see Appendix A).

4.2   Gaussian Distribution

It is well-known that the Gaussian distribution is infinitely divisible. Given that the sum of two Gaussians is Gaussian ($N_1 \pm N_2 \sim \mathcal{N}(0,2)$), we can generate a standard Gaussian from $n > 0$ standard Gaussians:

$$\frac{1}{\sqrt{n}} \sum_{i=1}^{n} N_i \sim \mathcal{N}(0,1). \tag{7}$$

This property of divisibility allows for the sampling of Gaussians with ease for any $n \in \mathbb{N}$. Additionally, decomposing any other probability distribution as a function of Gaussians will allow for the subsequent decomposition into any finite number of Gaussians.

4.3   Laplace Distribution

The Laplace distribution is infinite divisible using the gamma distribution.

Proposition 1 (Laplace divisibility [20]). *Given an integer $n \geq 1$, and $X_i, Y_i \sim \Gamma\left(\frac{1}{n}, 1\right)$ for each $i \in [n]$, then*

$$\sum_{i=1}^{n} (X_i - Y_i) \sim \mathrm{Lap}(0,1).$$

The case of $n = 1$ gives the decomposition of the Laplace distribution as the difference of two exponential distributions.

Corollary 1. *Given $E_1, E_2 \sim \mathrm{Exp}(1)$,*

$$E_1 - E_2 \sim \mathrm{Lap}(0,1). \tag{8}$$

Proof. Noting that $\Gamma(1,1) \sim \mathrm{Exp}(1)$ completes the proof.

The special case of $n = 2$ also deserves special attention.

Corollary 2. *Given independent samples of the standard Gaussian distribution, $N_1, N_2, N_3, N_4 \sim \mathcal{N}(0,1)$,*

$$\frac{1}{2}\left(N_1^2 - N_2^2 + N_3^2 - N_4^2\right) \sim \mathrm{Lap}(0,1). \tag{9}$$

Proof. The chi-squared distribution with 1 degree of freedom is related to the gamma distribution (given $X \sim \chi^2(1)$, then $\frac{1}{2}X \sim \Gamma\left(\frac{1}{2},1\right)$). Furthermore, it is known that a squared sample from the Gaussian distribution is chi-squared ($N_1^2 \sim \chi^2(1)$). Combining these two observations completes the proof.

The Laplace distribution can be decomposed in many other ways, as given in [20, Table 2.3], one of which is of particular interest in our context:

Proposition 2. *Given independent samples of the standard Gaussian distribution, $N_1, N_2, N_3, N_4 \sim \mathcal{N}(0,1)$,*

$$N_1 N_2 - N_3 N_4 \sim \mathrm{Lap}(0,1). \tag{10}$$

Proof. We note that $Z = N_1 N_2$ has a characteristic function $\phi_Z(t) = (1 + t^2)^{-\frac{1}{2}}$. This gives the characteristic function for (10) of

$$\phi_{N_1 N_2 - N_3 N_4}(t) = \phi_Z(t)\phi_Z(-t) = (1 + t^2)^{-1},$$

which corresponds to the standard Laplace distribution.

We therefore have two methods to sample from the Laplace distribution as a composition of four standard Gaussians. Each Gaussian can be further decomposed using (7).

5 Sampling Implementations

There are many ways to sample from the Gaussian distribution [24]. We restrict our analysis to the Box-Muller transform [4], owing to its simplicity, compactness, exactness and ubiquity among programming languages.

The polar method [3] of the Box-Muller transform was developed to avoid the costly sin and cos calculations. Other methods have been proposed to eliminate the similarly costly log and $\sqrt{\cdot}$ calculations [2,5]. These modifications are typically reserved for low-level languages or machine code, because the added complexity can slow computation time in higher-level languages [1]. Given our focus on high-level languages, such as Python, analysis of these variants is beyond the scope of this paper.

In this section, we offer simple implementation examples in Python, using standard libraries. We hope these examples will be sufficient to enable the reader to port the code to their desired language.

5.1 Gaussian Sampling

As noted in Sect. 2.4, a naïve implementation of the Box-Muller transform in sampling from the Gaussian distribution presents vulnerabilities. The question therefore arises of how best to protect Gaussian samples from the Mironov attack, and there are two immediate considerations:

1. Discard one of the pair of Box-Muller samples, or
2. Make use of both samples, noting that $\frac{1}{\sqrt{2}}(N_1 + N_2) \sim \mathcal{N}(0,1)$.

Both of these choices are mathematically identical (albeit with the outputs $\frac{\pi}{4}$ out of phase[2]), but it may be a more elegant implementation using standard libraries to opt for the second option. Extending this choice to generating Gaussian samples from multiple Box-Muller draws, using the infinite divisibility described in Sect. 4.2, we use $2n$ samples[3] from the Box-Muller transform, and divide the result by $\sqrt{2n}$. This can be implemented in Python as follows, after importing the math and random libraries:

```
1   sum(gauss(0, 1) for i in range(2 * n)) / sqrt(2 * n)
```

Readers are encouraged to discard the first result from Box-Muller before sampling in this way, to ensure no carry-over of uniform variates from a previous draw, which may have already been successfully attacked.

Importantly, the time taken in the generation of a standard Gaussian variate from n uniform variates increases linearly with n, whereas the attack complexity as described in Sect. 3 increases exponentially in n, given as $2^{p(n-1)}$. A small increase in computation overhead to sample the variates gives an exponential increase in attack complexity.

5.2 Laplace Sampling

We ignore the decomposition of the Laplace distribution into the difference of two exponential variates, and skip straight to the decomposition into Gaussians.

As such, we are interested in the forms given in Corollary 2 and Proposition 2. In both these cases, we can safely use two samples from Box-Muller to generate the Laplace sample, since squaring-and-summing or multiplying Box-Muller samples breaks the invertibility given in Sect. 2.4. Empirical analysis has shown (10) to be the faster option, as (9) requires two additional multiplication operations. In Python, this can be implemented as follows after importing the random library:

---

[2] Since $\cos(\theta) + \sin(\theta) = \sqrt{2}\cos\left(\theta - \frac{\pi}{4}\right)$.

[3] We need only use n samples for sampling procedures that do not share uniform variates between executions, for example the normalvariate method in Python's random library, which uses the Kinderman-Monahan sampling procedure [19].

```
1  gauss(0, 1) * gauss(0, 1) - gauss(0, 1) * gauss(0, 1)
```

However, doing so will introduce some redundancy in the uniform variates, which presents an opportunity for those willing to write their own subroutines.

Theorem 1. *Given independent uniform variates $U_1, U_2, U_3, U_4 \sim \mathcal{U}(0,1)$,*

$$\log(1 - U_1)\cos(\pi U_2) + \log(1 - U_3)\cos(\pi U_4) \sim \text{Lap}(0,1). \tag{11}$$

Proof. Firstly with (9), we can write the difference of squared outputs from the Box-Muller transform as follows,

$$N_1^2 - N_2^2 = -2\log(1 - U_1)\left(\cos^2(2\pi U_2) - \sin^2(2\pi U_2)\right) \tag{12}$$
$$= -2\log(1 - U_1)\cos(4\pi U_2), \tag{13}$$

using the double-angle formula $\cos(2\theta) = cos^2(\theta) - \sin^2(\theta)$.

Also, since $-\cos(4\pi U_2) \sim \cos(\pi U_2)$ when $U_2 \sim \mathcal{U}(0,1)$, owing to the periodicity of $\cos$, we get the desired result. Analysis of (10) gives a similar representation.

In Python, this can be implemented as follows after importing the math and random libraries:

```
1  log(1 - random()) * cos(pi * random()) + log(1 - random()) * cos(pi
       * random())
```

Remark 1: We observe that $U_2 \in [0,1)$ in a floating-point environment, which results in an asymmetric output for $\cos(\pi U_2) \in (-1,1]$. We can eliminate this asymmetry by using the first bit of randomness of U_2 to sample the sign, and then using the remaining bits to sample the magnitude, giving

$$\cos(\pi U_2) \sim (-1)^{\lceil U_2 \rceil_1} \cos\left(\pi\left(U_2 \bmod \frac{1}{2}\right)\right)$$

in real number arithmetic, with an output space of $[-1,1] \setminus \{0\}$ when $U_2 \in [0,1)$. This can be implemented in Python as follows:

```
1  u2 = random()
2  copysign(cos(pi * (u2 % 0.5)), u2 - 0.5)
```

Remark 2: The representation in Theorem 1 brings two benefits over sampling naïvely with Box-Muller: (i) reduced redundancy in the $\cos$ argument (using Box-Muller, the first two random bits of U_2 and U_4 are redundant), and, (ii) greater computational efficiency (empirical evidence suggests a halving in the time taken to sample).

5.3 Choosing n

In choosing the number, n, of uniform variates to use in sampling a single Laplace or Gaussian variate, we take inspiration from current standards in cryptography. The Advanced Encryption Standard (AES) supports key sizes of 128, 192 and 256 bits, corresponding with search spaces of sizes 2^{128}, 2^{192} and 2^{256} respectively. Thus, it will take $O(key\ size)$ steps for a polynomial adversary to enumerate, and test, all possible keys.

In order to achieve a similar search space size for our application, assuming a precision of $p = 53$ (as in Python), we require $n = 4, 5$ and 6 respectively. We consider it sufficient to use $n = 4$ in most applications, corresponding to the implementation of Theorem 1. This standard has been adopted in the implementation of the Laplace, Gaussian and other mechanisms[4] in the diffprivlib open source library [16].

The effect of n on the time it takes to sample from the Laplace distribution is shown in Fig. 2. Despite using four times as many uniform variates, the implementation of Theorem 1 only takes twice as long as the naïve sampling with a single uniform variate. Using the native math and random libraries is costly for larger n, owing to Python's slow for loops. Numpy's C codebase [25] allows for fast computation even for large n, and can be further leveraged to produce multiple samples in parallel, with superior per-sample computation time than naïve sampling. The code for these simulations is given in Appendix B.

6 Gaussian Attack Complexity

We briefly revisit the brute force attack on the Gaussian distribution in Example 1 to highlight the robustness of the proposed approach. Given a single Gaussian variate, we know from Example 1 that we can write U_1 as a function of U_2. This allows us to estimate a lower bound on the number of checks required on a given variate N_1, since we know that $U_1, U_2 \in \mathbb{U} \subset [0, 1)$. We stress that this is only a lower bound, as rounding errors in floating point arithmetic would typically require the checking of adjacent uniform variates.

For example, using (6), given $U_2 \in [0, 1)$, we have

$$U_1 \in \left[1 - e^{-\frac{N_1^2}{2}}, 1\right),$$

allowing us to reduce the search space to $U_1 \in \mathbb{U} \cap [1 - e^{-\frac{N_1^2}{2}}, 1)$ We can therefore approximate the number of checks as $e^{-\frac{N_1^2}{2}} 2^p$.

---

[4] https://github.com/IBM/differential-privacy-library/tree/main/diffprivlib/mechanisms.

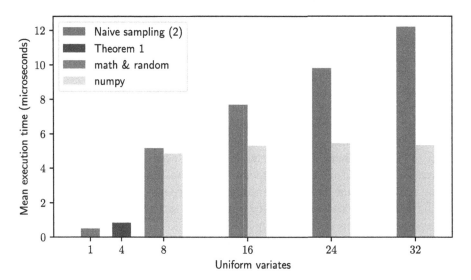

Fig. 2. Mean execution time for sampling a single standard Laplace variate, in microseconds (μs), over 5 000 000 runs in Python.

Knowing that $N_1 \sim \mathcal{N}(0,1)$, we can get the expected number of checks as follows:

$$\mathbb{E}[\text{checks}] = 2^p \int e^{-\frac{x^2}{2}} f(x)dx = 2^p C \int e^{-\frac{(\sqrt{2}x)^2}{2}}dx = 2^p \frac{C}{\sqrt{2}} \int e^{-\frac{x^2}{2}} dx \quad (14)$$

$$= \frac{2^p}{\sqrt{2}} = 2^{p-\frac{1}{2}}, \quad (15)$$

where $f(x)$ denotes the probability density function of the standard Gaussian distribution $\mathcal{N}(0,1)$ and C is the normalisation constant (see Appendix A.2).

This demonstrates the robustness of the approach, with (15) confirming that the complexity of the attack only decreases by a small constant from the theoretical limit. While outlying values lead to smaller search spaces, their vanishingly small probabilities of being sampled result in a small aggregate impact.

7   Related Work

The original attack on the Laplace mechanism, which also inspired this work, was first presented in [22]. Subsequent work on the subject in [12], where the authors analyse the situation of infinite-precision semantic at the implementation level. The authors present results arguing that in general there are violations of the differential privacy property, proposing a variation of the differential privacy definition leading to a degradation of the privacy level.

Thorough examination of randomness required for differential privacy is presented in [11], where the authors analyse various techniques for random number generation, presenting a picture of strengths and limitations of the commonly used sources of randomness.

Other work in [9] and [23] analyse theoretical and practical limitations of the source of randomness used in differential privacy. In particular [9] presents an cryptographic requirements for real randomness, and describe the analogies existing in differential privacy.

In [12] the authors show the violation of differential privacy property caused by the approximation introduced by the finite-precision representation of continuous data. The authors also present the conditions under which limited by acceptable privacy guarantees can be provided, under only a minor degradation of the privacy level.

[15] describes several different kinds of covert-channel attacks for differential privacy frameworks. The authors present possible countermeasures with particular focus on one specific solution based on a new primitive called *predictable transactions*.

[7] presents a systematic study of a fundamental limitation of locally differentially private protocols with respect to their vulnerability to adversarial manipulation. The authors also present a solution to provide increased security via a protocol that deploys local differential privacy and reinforces it with cryptographic techniques.

Finally, [17] presents a study similar to the one first introduced in [22], but concentrate on the exponential mechanism of McSherry and Talwar [21].

8 Conclusion

In this paper we have presented an alternative defence to a particular floating point vulnerability in differential privacy. The solution we presented, using the infinite divisibility of probability distributions, is simple to understand, quick and easy to implement, difficult to attack, and generalisable to different probability distributions and system precisions. Of particular interest is the ability to generate samples from the Laplace distribution in a single statement of code (Sect. 5.2), with strong attack guarantees. We believe this is an important contribution to the literature on differential privacy in mitigating some of the risks associated with operating in a floating point environment.

Acknowledgments. The authors wish to thank David Malone (Hamilton Institute, Maynooth University) for useful discussions at the beginning of this project.

Appendix

A   Probability Density Functions

The following probability distributions are referenced in Sect. 4.

A.1   Uniform Distribution

The uniform distribution on the interval $[a, b] \subset \mathbb{R}$, $-\infty < a < b < \infty$, is given by the Probability Density Function (PDF)

$$f_{\mathcal{U}(a,b)}(x) = \begin{cases} \frac{1}{b-a} & \text{if } x \in [a, b], \\ 0 & \text{otherwise.} \end{cases}$$

We make use of the uniform distribution $\mathcal{U}(0, 1)$ on the unit interval $[0, 1]$.

A.2   Gaussian Distribution

The Gaussian distribution with mean μ and variance σ^2 is given by the PDF

$$f_{\mathcal{N}(\mu,\sigma)}(x) = \frac{1}{\sigma\sqrt{2\pi}} e^{-\frac{1}{2}\left(\frac{x-\mu}{\sigma}\right)^2}.$$

We refer to the case when $\mu = 0$ and $\sigma = 1$ as the *standard Gaussian distribution*. If $N \sim \mathcal{N}(0, 1)$, then $\sigma N + \mu \sim \mathcal{N}(\mu, \sigma)$.

A.3   Laplace Distribution

The Laplace distribution with mean μ and variance $2b^2$ is given by the PDF

$$f_{\text{Lap}(\mu,b)}(x) = \frac{1}{2b} e^{-\frac{|x-\mu|}{b}}.$$

We refer to the case when $\mu = 0$ and $b = 1$ as the *standard Laplace distribution*. If $L \sim \text{Lap}(0, 1)$, then $bL + \mu \sim \text{Lap}(\mu, b)$.

A.4   Exponential Distribution

The exponential distribution with mean $\frac{1}{\lambda}$ and variance $\frac{1}{\lambda^2}$ is given by the PDF

$$f_{\text{Exp}(\lambda)}(x) = \lambda e^{-\lambda x}.$$

We refer to the case when $\lambda = 1$ as the *standard exponential distribution*. If $E \sim \text{Exp}(1)$, then $\frac{E}{\lambda} \sim \text{Exp}(\lambda)$.

A.5   Gamma Distribution

The gamma distribution with mean $k\theta$ and variance $k\theta^2$ is given by the PDF

$$f_{\Gamma(k,\theta)}(x) = \frac{1}{\Gamma(k)\theta^k} x^{k-1} e^{-\frac{x}{\theta}}.$$

If $G \sim \Gamma(k, \theta)$, then $cG \sim \Gamma(k, c\theta)$ for any $c > 0$.

A.6   Chi-Squared Distribution

The chi-squared distribution with $k \in \mathbb{N}$ degrees of freedom is given by the PDF

$$f_{\chi^2(k)}(x) = \frac{1}{2^{\frac{k}{2}} \Gamma\left(\frac{k}{2}\right)} x^{\frac{k}{2}-1} e^{-\frac{x}{2}}.$$

B   Code Samples

The following code samples were used in estimating execution time for different implementations. This code was run using Python 3.8.6.

B.1   Naïve Sampling

The naïve standard Laplace sampling given by (2) was implemented using:

```
1  def laplace_naive():
2      u = random()
3      return copysign(log(1 - 2 * abs(u - 0.5)), u - 0.5)
```

B.2   Theorem 1 Sampling

The implementation of Theorem 1 was given by:

```
1  def laplace_theorem1():
2      return log(1 - random()) * cos(pi * random()) + log(1 - random()
       ) * cos(pi * random())
```

B.3   Sampling with math and random

We combine the Gaussian and Laplace sampling procedures from (7) and (2) to generate standard Laplace samples from $8n$ uniform variates using the math and random libraries as follows:

```
1  def gaussian_sum(n=1):
2      return sum(normalvariate(0, 1) for i in range(n))
3
4  def laplace_math_and_random(n=1):
5      return (gaussian_sum(n) * gaussian_sum(n) - gaussian_sum(n) *
       gaussian_sum(n)) / n
```

B.4   Sampling with Numpy

Finally, we present an implementation of the same procedure using the popular Numpy package, leveraging its C-based code for faster computations with larger n:

```
1  import numpy as np
2
3  def laplace_numpy(n=1):
4      g1, g2, g3, g4 = np.random.standard_normal(size=(4, 2 * n)).sum(
         axis=1)
5      return (g1 * g2 - g3 * g4) / 2 / n
```

References

1. Ahrens, J.H., Dieter, U.: Computer methods for sampling from the exponential and normal distributions. Commun. ACM **15**(10), 873–882 (1972)
2. Ahrens, J.H., Dieter, U.: Efficient table-free sampling methods for the exponential, Cauchy, and normal distributions. Commun. ACM **31**(11), 1330–1337 (1988)
3. Bell, J.R.: Algorithm 334: normal random deviates. Commun. ACM **11**(7), 498 (1968)
4. Box, G.E.P., Muller, M.E.: A note on the generation of random normal deviates. Ann. Math. Stat. **29**(2), 610–611 (1958)
5. Brent, R.P.: Fast normal random number generators on vector processors. Technical report TR-CS-93-04, Department of Computer Science, The Australian National University, Canberra, 0200 ACT, Australia (1993)
6. Canonne, C.L., Kamath, G., Steinke, T.: The discrete Gaussian for differential privacy. In: Larochelle, H., Ranzato, M., Hadsell, R., Balcan, M.F., Lin, H. (eds.) Advances in Neural Information Processing Systems, vol. 33, pp. 15676–15688. Curran Associates, Inc. (2020). https://proceedings.neurips.cc/paper/2020/file/b53b3a3d6ab90ce0268229151c9bde11-Paper.pdf
7. Cheu, A., Smith, A., Ullman, J.: Manipulation attacks in local differential privacy. arXiv preprint arXiv:1909.09630 (2019)
8. Devroye, L.: Non-uniform Random Variate Generation. Springer, New York (1986). https://doi.org/10.1007/978-1-4613-8643-8
9. Dodis, Y., López-Alt, A., Mironov, I., Vadhan, S.: Differential privacy with imperfect randomness. In: Safavi-Naini, R., Canetti, R. (eds.) CRYPTO 2012. LNCS, vol. 7417, pp. 497–516. Springer, Heidelberg (2012). https://doi.org/10.1007/978-3-642-32009-5_29
10. Garey, M.R., Johnson, D.S.: Computers and Intractability: A Guide to the Theory of NP-Completeness. W. H. Freeman and Company, New York (1979)
11. Garfinkel, S.L., Leclerc, P.: Randomness concerns when deploying differential privacy. In: Proceedings of the 19th Workshop on Privacy in the Electronic Society. WPES 2020, pp. 73–86. Association for Computing Machinery, New York (2020)

12. Gazeau, I., Miller, D., Palamidessi, C.: Preserving differential privacy under finite-precision semantics. Theoret. Comput. Sci. **655**, 92–108 (2016). Quantitative Aspects of Programming Languages and Systems (2013–14)
13. Goldberg, D.: What every computer scientist should know about floating-point arithmetic. ACM Comput. Surv. (CSUR) **23**(1), 5–48 (1991)
14. Google Differential Privacy Team: Secure noise generation. github.com/google **1**(1), 1–14 (2020)
15. Haeberlen, A., Pierce, B.C., Narayan, A.: Differential privacy under fire. In: USENIX Security Symposium, vol. 33 (2011)
16. Holohan, N., Braghin, S., Mac Aonghusa, P., Levacher, K.: Diffprivlib: the IBM differential privacy library. arXiv e-prints 1907.02444 [cs.CR], July 2019
17. Ilvento, C.: Implementing the exponential mechanism with base-2 differential privacy. In: Proceedings of the 2020 ACM SIGSAC Conference on Computer and Communications Security, pp. 717–742 (2020)
18. Karney, C.F.F.: Sampling exactly from the normal distribution. ACM Trans. Math. Softw. **42**(1), 1–14 (2016)
19. Kinderman, A.J., Monahan, J.F.: Computer generation of random variables using the ratio of uniform deviates. ACM Trans. Math. Softw. **3**(3), 257–260 (1977)
20. Kotz, S., Kozubowski, T., Podgorski, K.: The Laplace Distribution and Generalizations: A Revisit with Applications to Communications, Economics, Engineering, and Finance. Springer, Heidelberg (2012)
21. McSherry, F., Talwar, K.: Mechanism design via differential privacy. In: 2007 48th Annual IEEE Symposium on Foundations of Computer Science. FOCS 2007, pp. 94–103. IEEE (2007)
22. Mironov, I.: On significance of the least significant bits for differential privacy. In: Proceedings of the 2012 ACM Conference on Computer and Communications Security. CCS 2012, pp. 650–661. Association for Computing Machinery, New York (2012)
23. Mironov, I., Pandey, O., Reingold, O., Vadhan, S.: Computational differential privacy. In: Halevi, S. (ed.) CRYPTO 2009. LNCS, vol. 5677, pp. 126–142. Springer, Heidelberg (2009). https://doi.org/10.1007/978-3-642-03356-8_8
24. Thomas, D.B., Luk, W., Leong, P.H., Villasenor, J.D.: Gaussian random number generators. ACM Comput. Surv. **39**(4), 11-es (2007)
25. van der Walt, S., Colbert, S.C., Varoquaux, G.: The NumPy array: a structure for efficient numerical computation. Comput. Sci. Eng. **13**(2), 22–30 (2011)

Training Differentially Private Neural Networks with Lottery Tickets

Lovedeep Gondara$^{(\boxtimes)}$, Ricardo Silva Carvalho, and Ke Wang

Department of Computing Science, Simon Fraser University,
British Columbia, Canada
lgondara@sfu.ca

Abstract. We propose the differentially private lottery ticket hypothesis (DPLTH). An end-to-end differentially private training paradigm based on the lottery ticket hypothesis, designed specifically to improve the privacy-utility trade-off in differentially private neural networks. DPLTH, using high-quality winners privately selected via our custom score function outperforms current methods by a margin greater than 20%. We further show that DPLTH converges faster, allowing for early stopping with reduced privacy budget consumption and that a single publicly available dataset for ticket generation is enough for enhancing the utility on multiple datasets of varying properties and from varying domains. Our extensive evaluation on six public datasets provides evidence to our claims.

Keywords: Differential privacy · Lottery ticket hypothesis · Differential privacy in neural networks

1 Introduction

Learning while preserving the privacy of the contributing users is a priority for neural networks trained on sensitive data. Especially, when it is known that neural networks tend to "remember" training data instances [3,9,23,25]. Differential privacy [6] has become the *de facto* standard for protecting an individual's privacy in machine learning. Differentially private training of neural networks ensures that the model does not unduly disclose any sensitive information. The most often used approach to achieve this goal is the method of gradient perturbation, where we add controlled noise to the gradients during the training phase. Differentially Private Stochastic Gradient Descent (DPSGD) [1] is the current state-of-the-art, used extensively for training privacy-preserving neural networks. DPSGD, however, falls short on the utility front [10], the main reason for which we discuss below.

DPSGD, for a given minibatch, first computes the per-observation gradient, $g(x_i)$, and then clips $g(x_i)$ in l_2 norm, $g(x_i)/\max(1, \|g(x_i)\|_2/C)$ (Line 6 in [1], Algorithm 1). We can see that the norm will be large (proportional to the number of model parameters), especially for a multi-layer neural network, leading to a

© Springer Nature Switzerland AG 2021
E. Bertino et al. (Eds.): ESORICS 2021, LNCS 12973, pp. 543–562, 2021.
https://doi.org/10.1007/978-3-030-88428-4_27

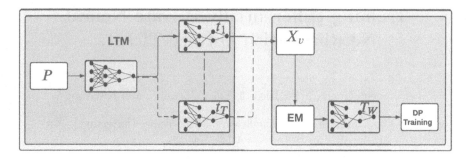

Fig. 1. The differentially private lottery ticket hypothesis (DPLTH). We divide the mechanism into two distinct *blocks*, green block is where we generate lottery tickets $([t_1, \cdots, t_T])$ using the lottery ticket mechanism with a public dataset P. This block does not utilize any sensitive information, hence we do not concern ourselves with privacy in this block. The orange block is where the sensitive dataset X is used. We use its validation split X_v to measure performance of each lottery ticket $t_i, [i \in 1, \cdots, T]$, and use our custom score function with Exponential Mechanism (EM) to select a winning ticket (T_w). The winning ticket is then trained with differential privacy and released as the final model. (Color figure online)

large clipping impact on the gradient, resulting in smaller clipped-gradient magnitude, easily overwhelmed by noise, which is required for preserving differential privacy. This leads to diminished utility, especially, for the scenarios where we require tight privacy [10].

An obvious solution is to minimize the number of model parameters while maximizing the model's utility. This, however, is non-trivial for differentially private neural networks, especially when we need to balance privacy and utility. Recently, it has been shown that there exist smaller sub-networks within large neural networks, which when trained in isolation provide similar utility as the large networks [7,8]. The phenomenon, known as the lottery ticket hypothesis represents a neural network pruning paradigm, where pruned network architectures via iterative magnitude pruning with their weights set back to their original values are known as the lottery tickets. This offers an encouraging step towards finding small, high-utility architectures. But, directly using the lottery ticket hypothesis with differential privacy is non-trivial as we need to ensure the complete process (from ticket generation, ticket selection, to training the winning ticket) is end-to-end differentially private.

As a potential solution to improve the privacy-utility bottleneck in differentially private neural networks, we propose the Differentially Private Lottery Ticket Hypothesis (DPLTH) (Fig. 1). To ensure differential privacy in DPLTH, we use a *three-tiered* approach. In phase 1 (green block in Fig. 1), we create the lottery tickets using a publicly available dataset (P), this ensures that the tickets (ticket architecture) do not contain any sensitive information. In phase 2 (orange block in Fig. 1), we calculate the performance of each ticket (accuracy) using the validation partition of the sensitive dataset (X_v). Then we proceed to select the winning ticket with differential privacy, defined as a function of the ticket's performance and the number of model parameters. This step is carefully designed to ensure that we pick the winner with a small number of model parameters and high utility (via our custom score function, details in Sect. 3.3). After differentially private selection of the winning ticket, our phase 3 (orange block in Fig. 1) trains the winning architecture with differential privacy using the training partition of X. Our main contributions are as follows:

1. We propose DPLTH, the differentially private lottery ticket hypothesis, an end-to-end differentially private method based on the lottery ticket hypothesis (Sect. 3).
2. With the aid of the winning ticket, selected via our custom score function (Sect. 3.3), we show that DPLTH significantly improves the privacy-utility trade-off over the state-off-the-art.
3. Due to the reduced noise in DPLTH, we show that DPLTH converges at a significantly faster rate compared to *full* DPSGD, leading to a smaller privacy budget consumption and better utility if early stopping is desired (Sect. 4.5).
4. Success of DPLTH hinges on an assumption that a ticket generated using P will "work" with X. Using six real-life datasets, we show that the constraint of the public dataset (P) availability for ticket generation is easy to work with. We show that the ticket generated from a single dataset (P) is *enough* for significantly improved utility for multiple datasets with varying properties (such as from out of domain/different data type datasets) (Sect. 4.4, Sect. 4.7)[1].

2 Preliminaries

We use this section to provide preliminary introduction to differential privacy and the lottery ticket hypothesis.

2.1 Differential Privacy

Differential privacy [6] provides us with formal and provable privacy guarantees, with the intuition that a randomized algorithm behaves similarly on "similar" input datasets, formally

Definition 1 (Differential privacy [6]). *A randomized mechanism* $\mathcal{M} : D^n \to \mathbb{R}^d$ *preserves* (ϵ, δ)-*differentially privacy if for any pair of* neighbouring databases $(X, X' \in D^n)$ *such that* $d(X, X') = 1$, *and for all sets* $\mathcal{S}$ *of possible outputs:*

$$Pr[\mathcal{M}(X) \in \mathcal{S}] \leq e^\epsilon Pr[\mathcal{M}(X') \in \mathcal{S}] + \delta$$

---

[1] Code for DPLTH will be made publicly available at https://github.com/lgondara/DPLTH.

Intuitively, Definition 1 states that for any pair of two neighboring datasets, X, X', differing on any one row, a randomized mechanism $\mathcal{M}$'s outcome does not change by more than a multiplicative factor of e^ϵ. Moreover, the guarantee fails with probability no larger than δ. If $\delta = 0$, we have pure-ϵ differential privacy.

The Exponential Mechanism (EM) [15] is a well-known tool for providing differential privacy. Defined by a range $\mathcal{R}$, privacy parameter ϵ, and a score function $u : \mathcal{X}^N \times \mathcal{R} \to \mathbb{R}$ that maps a dataset to the utility scores, given a dataset $D \in \mathcal{X}^N$, the EM defines a probability distribution over $\mathcal{R}$ according to the utility score. In other words, the EM is more likely to output some $r \in \mathcal{R}$ with higher utility scores, formally

Definition 2 (Exponential Mechanism [15]). *The exponential mechanism $\mathcal{M}(D, u, \mathcal{R})$ selects and outputs an element $r \in \mathcal{R}$ with probability proportional to*

$$\exp\left(\frac{\epsilon u(D, r)}{2\Delta u}\right)$$

where ϵ is the privacy budget and Δu is the sensitivity of the score function.

$$\Delta u = \max_{r \in \mathcal{R}} \max_{X, X': \|X - X'\|_1 \leq 1} |u(X, r) - u(X', r)|$$

In terms of privacy guarantees, the exponential Mechanism provides pure-ϵ differential privacy [15].

2.2 Lottery Ticket Hypothesis

The Lottery Ticket Hypothesis was proposed by Frankle & Carbin [7], where interestingly, it was shown that randomly initialized neural networks contain small subnetworks (models), which when trained in isolation, can provide similar utility as the full network. Formally,

Definition 3 (The Lottery Ticket Hypothesis [7]). *A randomly-initialized, dense neural network contains a subnetwork that is initialized such that when trained in isolation it can match the test accuracy of the original network after training for at most the same number of iterations.*

To get the subnetworks, we train a network for $\mathcal{I}$ iterations, prune $\rho\%$ of its weights (of smallest magnitude), and reset the weights of the pruned network to the original initialization, to be trained again. This process ensures that for n rounds, each round prunes $\rho^{1/n}\%$ of the weights. Such pruned, small subnetworks (denoted by t_is), are known as the lottery tickets, and the lottery tickets with high utility are the winners from the lottery ticket mechanism.

3   Differentially Private Lottery Ticket Hypothesis

3.1   Overview

We start by providing an overview of DPLTH. Using a publicly available dataset P and the non-private lottery ticket hypothesis, we generate and store multiple lottery tickets ($[t_1, t_2, \cdots, t_T]$), each with a varying number of model parameters. Before we move further, we would like to emphasize the importance of using a publicly available dataset P. We use P instead of X (the sensitive dataset) for ticket generation as if we were to use X (as in the general, non-private setting of lottery ticket mechanism [7,8]), even if the tickets only contain the architecture (pruning information) with weights reverted to their initial random values [7], the architecture of the winning ticket can potentially leak sensitive information. We clarify this point with an example: Suppose that the sensitive dataset X is such that during the ticket generating phase, all of the first ζ parameters of the model are zero and hence are pruned under the current setup, but a neighboring dataset X' is such that one of those first ζ parameters isn't zero so it is not pruned. Releasing the chosen ticket created using X can thus break our privacy guarantees.

After ticket generation using P, we use the validation part of X (X_v) to estimate each ticket's performance (example: accuracy score). Using the performance as one of the parameters, we use our custom score function (details follow) to *privately* select a winning ticket (T_w), where our score function ensures the desired balance between the number of model parameters and the model utility. After selecting the winner, we train the winning architecture using the training partition of X with differential privacy. Our total privacy cost, hence, is composed of two separate parts, selecting the winning ticket and training the winning ticket. We present the complete process succinctly as Algorithm 1 followed by a walk-through.

3.2   DPLTH Walkthrough

Phase 1 (Generating Lottery Tickets): We start with generating lottery tickets required for DLPTH using a publicly available dataset P. At this stage, as we are not yet concerned about privacy, we use the standard, non-private lottery ticket mechanism with P and generate T lottery tickets ($t_i; i \in [1, \cdots, T]$). Specifically, we use the iterative pruning version of the lottery ticket mechanism, where using the pruning parameter, ρ, at each ticket iteration, we remove $\rho\%$ of model parameters with the smallest magnitude. This results in T tickets with a successively smaller number of model parameters.

Phase 2 (Selecting a Winning Ticket with Differential Privacy): After ticket generation, we record the performance of each ticket on the validation split of the sensitive dataset (X_v) and store the resulting accuracy ($a_i, i \in [1, T]$) along with the fraction of model parameters ($c_i, i \in [1, T]$) in the ticket. For further

Algorithm 1 Differentially Private Lottery Ticket Hypothesis (DPLTH)

Require: Public dataset: P, Sensitive dataset: X, Total privacy budget: (ϵ, δ), Pruning percent: ρ, Number of tickets: T, Ticket training iterations: $\mathcal{T}$, final DP model training iterations: I, Neural Network: f, Initial model parameters: θ_0, Initial mask: m, Privacy budget for ticket selection: ϵ_1, Privacy budget for ticket training: (ϵ_2, δ), Constant for score function: ν, Minibatch size: L, Clipping factor: C, Learning rate: η

Phase 1 – Generating Lottery Tickets

1: **procedure** LTG(f, m, θ_0)
2:     Randomly initialize $f(P, m \odot \theta_0)$; $m = 1^{|\theta_0|}$
3:     **for** $i \in T$ **do**
4:         Train $f(P, m \odot \theta_0)$ for $\mathcal{T}$ iterations, to get $f(P, m \odot \theta_{\mathcal{T}})$
5:         Prune $\rho\%$ of parameters from $\theta_{\mathcal{T}}$, creating a new mask m'
6:         Reset the remaining parameters to their values in θ_0
7:         $f(P, m' \odot \theta_0)$ is the lottery ticket
8:         Store the mask m_i', initial parameters θ_0, and proportion of remaining model parameters c_i
9:         Let $m = m'$
10:     **end for**
11:     **return** $\mathcal{C}, M, \theta_0$ ▷ The collection of parameter proportions, masks, and initial parameters; $c_i \in \mathcal{C}, m_i' \in M; i \in [1, T]$
12: **end procedure**

Phase 2 – Selecting a Winning Ticket

13: **procedure** DPWT($\mathcal{C}, \epsilon_1$)
14:     Calculate the performance of lottery tickets on the validation partition of X (X_v) and store the accuracies $[a_i \in \mathcal{A}, i \in 1, \cdots, T]$
15:     Calculate score $\mathcal{S}(\mathcal{C}, \mathcal{A}) = \mathcal{A}(1 - \nu\mathcal{C})$
16:     Select a winning ticket, T_w, with probability, $P = \dfrac{\exp(\frac{\epsilon_1 \mathcal{S}}{2\Delta})}{\sum_T \exp(\frac{\epsilon_1 \mathcal{S}}{2\Delta})}$
17:     **return** T_w
18: **end procedure**

Phase 3 – Training the Winning Ticket

19: **procedure** DPTWT(T_w)
20:     Initialize the network, f, with mask and initial values from the winning ticket T_w
21:     **for** $k \in I$ **do**
22:         Take a minibatch with sampling probability L/N
23:         For each $x_i \in L$, compute gradient $g_k(x_i) = \nabla_{\theta_k} \mathcal{L}(\theta_k, x_i)$
24:         $\hat{g}_k = \frac{1}{L}(\sum_i g_k(x_i)/\max(1, \frac{\|g_k(x_i)\|_2}{C}) + \mathcal{N}(0, \sigma^2 C^2 I))$
25:         $\theta_{k+1} \to \theta_k - \eta_k \hat{g}_k$
26:     **end for**
27: **end procedure**

use, we also store the mask m'_i from each ticket and the randomly initialized model parameters θ_0.

Now we need to select the winning ticket, which we will train from scratch with differential privacy on the training partition of X. However, picking a winner is non-trivial for two reasons, *first* as the tickets are evaluated using sensitive data, we cannot directly pick a winner, that is, we need differential privacy for selecting the winning ticket, and *second*, we need to pick a winner such that the winner has an adequate balance between the number of model parameters (smaller the better) and the model performance (higher the better). As a solution, we use the Exponential Mechanism (EM) [15] to pick our winner with differential privacy. And to balance the number of model parameters and the utility, we define our custom score function using the combination of the accuracy achieved by the ticket on X_v and the proportion of parameters left in the network.

$$S(\mathcal{C}, \mathcal{A}) = \mathcal{A} \times (1 - (\nu \mathcal{C})) \tag{1}$$

Where $\mathcal{A}$ is the classification accuracy on X_v for the given network configuration (ticket), $\mathcal{C}$ is the proportion of remaining weights in the network, and ν is a constant (further details in Sects. 3.3 and 3.4).

Phase 3 (Training the Winning Ticket with Differential Privacy): After we select our winning ticket with differential privacy in phase 2, now we need to train our *winner* architecture so the final model is differentially private. We do so by using the differentially private stochastic gradient descent (DPSGD) [1] for the training of our winning ticket. This, in contrast to the *full* DPSGD (with the full network), now only trains a *sub-network* with a significantly small number of model parameters. And hence provides significantly better utility, reasons for which we discussed at length in the Introduction. Our extensive empirical evaluation in Sect. 4 provides evidence for this claim.

Next, we provide formal privacy guarantees for DPLTH. We start with introducing the EM for DPLTH with our custom score function.

3.3   Differential Privacy Guarantees of DPLTH

As seen in Algorithm 1, our first phase of generating candidate tickets is non-private. Differential privacy comes into play in phase 2, where we evaluate the tickets on X_v and pick a winning ticket. Hence, we start with privacy guarantees of phase 2.

Selecting a Winning Ticket: For the Exponential Mechanism (EM), as discussed in preliminaries, we need to define a score/utility function that assigns a higher score to *good* outputs. For DPLTM, using the score function as described in Sect. 3.2, we sample our winning ticket with probability

$$P = \frac{\exp(\frac{\epsilon_1 S}{2\Delta})}{\sum_T \exp(\frac{\epsilon_1 S}{2\Delta})} \tag{2}$$

where P is the probability of picking a ticket, ϵ_1 is the privacy budget for EM, and Δ is the sensitivity of the score/utility function. Tickets with *higher* score function have a higher probability of getting selected compared to the tickets with a lower score.

Lemma 1. *Sensitivity (Δ) of the score function, $\mathcal{S}$, is $|1 - \nu|$, for $\nu \neq 1$.*

Proof. We can write the score function as

$$\begin{aligned}
\mathcal{S}(\mathcal{C}, \mathcal{A}) &= \mathcal{A} \times (1 - (\nu \mathcal{C})) \\
&= \mathcal{A} - \mathcal{A}\nu\mathcal{C}
\end{aligned} \tag{3}$$

Using the definition of neighbouring datasets, we have the sensitivity as

$$|\max((\mathcal{A} - \mathcal{A}\nu\mathcal{C})) - (\mathcal{A}' - \mathcal{A}'\nu\mathcal{C}'))| \tag{4}$$

where $\mathcal{A}', \mathcal{C}'$ are "neighbouring" to $\mathcal{A}, \mathcal{C}$.

$$\begin{aligned}
&\leq |\max(\mathcal{A} - \mathcal{A}\nu\mathcal{C} - \mathcal{A}' + \mathcal{A}'\nu\mathcal{C}')| \\
&\leq |\max(\mathcal{A} - \mathcal{A}' - \nu(\mathcal{A}\mathcal{C} - \mathcal{A}'\mathcal{C}'))|
\end{aligned} \tag{5}$$

using $\nu \neq 1$, for the worse case scenarios ($\mathcal{A}, \mathcal{C} = 1, \mathcal{A}', \mathcal{C}' = 0$, and $\mathcal{A}, \mathcal{C} = 0, \mathcal{A}', \mathcal{C}' = 1$), we get $\mathcal{S}(\mathcal{C}, \mathcal{A}) = |1 - \nu|$ □

Theorem 1. *Phase 2 (Selecting a winning ticket) is (ϵ_1) - differentially private.*

Proof. Proof is an instantiation of EM with our custom score function and is provided in the Appendix for completeness. □

Training the Winning Ticket. After we select our winning ticket with differential privacy in phase 2. Our next step is to train the winning architecture in a differentially private fashion. For this step, we use the training process same as DPSGD [1]. Specifically, after calculating the per-observation gradients for a minibatch, we clip the gradients (line 25 in Algorithm 1) by their l_2 norm, scaled by a constant C to enforce sensitivity, and then add appropriate Gaussian noise to ensure differential privacy, formally

Theorem 2. *Phase 3 (Training the winning ticket) is (ϵ_2, δ) - differentially private, if we chose $\sigma \geq C \dfrac{L/N \sqrt{I \log(1/\delta)}}{\epsilon_2}$*

Proof. Proof is an instatiation of Theorem 1 from Abadi et al. [1] using ϵ_2 and I and is omitted here for space constraints. □

Putting It All Together. After generating the lottery tickets, selecting the winner with differential privacy, and the differentially private training of the winning ticket, we are now ready to put it all together and state the overall privacy guarantees of our proposed DPLTH.

Theorem 3. *Algorithm 1 is (ϵ, δ) - differentially private, with $\epsilon > 0, \delta > 0$ where* $\epsilon = (\epsilon_1 + \epsilon_2)$

Proof. We have already shown that phase 2 is (ϵ_1)-differentially private and phase 3 is (ϵ_2, δ)-differentially private. Using the *naive* composition [6][2], it is easy to see that the Algorithm 1 is (ϵ, δ)-differentially private, with $\epsilon = \epsilon_1 + \epsilon_2$ and $\delta = \delta$. $\qquad\square$

3.4   Discussion

We use this section to discuss some interesting properties of DPLTH. The first observation is the seamless integration of differential privacy with the lottery ticket hypothesis, making it accessible for implementation. In the non-private setting, we know that the lottery tickets either perform at-par or slightly worse than the *full model* [7,8], however, in the differentially private regime, DPLTH provides significantly better utility compared to DPSGD on the full model (Experiments in Sect. 4 support this claim).

The success of our method hinges on the two crucial aspects. *First*, that the lottery tickets generated using a public dataset P will *work* with the sensitive dataset X, and more so that the lottery tickets with a significantly small number of model parameters will have high utility on X. [16] has shown that in the non-private setting, tickets often generalize across *similar* datasets. However, no such result is known in the differential privacy setting. In addition to providing similar empirical evidence in the case of differential privacy, we further show that we can extend this property of lottery tickets to out of domain and to *completely* different dataset types (such as from image to tabular data) via the use of carefully designed initial lottery ticket setup (details in Sect. 4.3).

Second, it is vital for our method that out of all available tickets, the probability of selecting the winner with a small number of model parameters and high accuracy is high. Our custom utility function ($\mathcal{S}$) strives to achieve this goal by ensuring that the selection process does not degenerate to uniform random sampling. In particular, the utility function assigns more weight to the models with high accuracy and a small number of model parameters, where the importance of either is modulated using the constant ν, large ν assigns more weight to $\mathcal{C}$ (proportion of model parameters in the ticket). For good utility with tight privacy, we advocate using large values for ν as most tickets have comparative performance, hence it is in our best interest to select the ticket with a small number of model parameters. We further show in Sect. 4.6 that our score function works as intended and the sampled tickets using the score function have better performance than random sampling from the available tickets.

Also, as we observe from Theorem 3, the total privacy budget for our method is composed of two parts. The privacy budget from the EM phase used to select the winning ticket and the privacy budget to train the winning ticket. Hence, we need to decide on the overall privacy budget split. That is, the portion of the

---

[2] As we are only composing two mechanisms, advanced composition is not necessary.

budget to allocate to the drawing of the winning ticket and the portion of the privacy budget for the training of the winning ticket. We advocate dedicating a *large* proportion of the privacy budget to the training of the winning ticket and a small portion for selecting the winning ticket. With our custom utility function, a small privacy budget suffices for selecting a *good* ticket (empirical evidence provided in Sect. 4). A question the readers might ask: Why can't we train the full network with differential privacy when generating lottery tickets using dataset X? That is, why do we need non-private tickets using P? The answer is simple, as differential privacy composes by iteration for minibatch stochastic gradient descent, training multiple networks using the methodology described in Algorithm 1 would result in a large privacy budget leading to noisier models, providing worse utility compared to our proposed method.

4   Experiments

Now we provide empirical evidence on five real-world datasets that are *in domain*, *out of domain*, and *out of type* compared to the public dataset P to support our claim that our proposed method (DPLTH) significantly outperforms full DPSGD. We begin by describing the datasets.

4.1   Datasets

For our empirical evaluation, we use six real-world datasets (one as a publicly available dataset P and five as the sensitive datasets X).

Public Dataset (P). We use **MNIST** [11] as our initial publicly available dataset P, used to generate the lottery tickets. For ticket generation, we use the training partition of MNIST. We further show in Sect. 4.7 that *other* datasets work just as well when used as P.

Sensitive Datasets (X). We use five datasets as our sensitive datasets (X), for which we are concerned about privacy preservation. Datasets are carefully chosen to evaluate our proposed method with varying relations between P and X. Dataset **Kannada-MNIST** [20] contains data on handwritten digit recognition, where digits are written in Kannada (an Indian language). The digits have a varying degree of similarity and overlap with MNIST, hence this dataset is classified as *in domain*. We use three *out of domain* datasets compared to P (MNIST) where dataset **Fashion-MNIST** [26] is a dataset of Zalando's article images, associated with a label from ten classes (clothing items, fashion accessories, etc.); dataset **Kuzushiji-MNIST** [5] has images spanning ten classes with one from each column of hiragana characters; dataset **COOS** [12] consists of the 64×64 microscopic images of mouse cells, with the target being to classify between two biological entities (Endoplasmic Reticulum, Golgi, Peroxisomes, Early Endosome vs Inner Mitochondrial Membrane, Cytosol, Nuclear Envelope).

Dataset **ISOLET** has data on spoken letters with the outcome being correctly classifying each observation into one of twenty-six letters. This dataset contains spectral coefficients, contour features, sonorant features, pre-sonorant features, and post-sonorant features related to audio, hence is *completely* different from previous datasets (all were image) and P (MNIST), we call this dataset *out of domain/out of type*. Further dataset details are provided in Table 1.

Table 1. Dataset details, Attributes is the dataset dimensionality, Observations are the number of rows, Class is the number of classes in the classification target, and the Property is the relation of the dataset with P.

Dataset	Attributes	Observations	Class	Property
Fashion-MNIST	784	60000	10	Out of domain
Kuzushiji-MNIST	784	60000	10	Out of domain
ISOLET	617	7797	26	Out of domain/type
Kannada-MNIST	784	60000	10	In domain
COOS	4096	50000	2	Out of domain

4.2 Competitor

Our competitor is the *full DPSGD*, that is the implementation of DPSGD on the complete, unpruned network. This also represents the current best practice and state-of-the-art in differentially private neural networks. We use the terms DPSGD and full DPSGD interchangeably in the following sections to refer to our competitor. We also use a non-private baseline with the same architecture to provide us with an upper bound on the best achievable performance with the architecture used.

4.3 Setup

For generating lottery tickets (phase 1) using MNIST (our P), our implementation is based on the publicly available source code[3]. Our underlying base model is a fully connected neural network with three layers with the same architecture as in the publicly available code from [7]. Hidden layers use ReLU [17] as the activation function. The learning rate is kept fixed at 0.1 and the minibatch size is kept fixed at 400. We set the pruning percent, ρ, at 30% for the first two layers and 20% for the last layer. This means that for each subsequent ticket, the model will prune 30% of the weights compared to the previous ticket for the first two layers and 20% of the weights for the final layer. To generate lottery tickets, the mechanism is run for 5000 iterations ($\mathcal{I}$) for each ticket.

---

[3] https://github.com/google-research/lottery-ticket-hypothesis.

For datasets COOS and ISOLET, as they both have different input dimensionality and the number of output classes, we add two additional layers (one after the input and one before the output) when generating lottery tickets using P, these layers act as projection layers for our desired dimensionality. This allows us to generalize the lottery ticket generation for *any* given dataset with arbitrary input/output dimensionality using a fixed public dataset P.

If the input dataset does not have a predefined train/test/validation partition, we use a 70/10/20 split, with 10% of the dataset used as the validation split, 20% of the dataset used as the test split, and 70% of the dataset used as the training set. For robust comparison, all models are run for 10 iterations and we report the average results on the test partition along with their standard errors.

For differentially private training of the lottery tickets and to train our competitor, the DPSGD's implementation is based on the publicly available source code[4]. The clipping norm for DPSGD and DPLTH is set at a constant value of 1 for all experiments. Minibatch size for DP training is kept fixed at 100. All the rest of the hyperparameters, including the underlying model architecture are the same for DPSGD and DPLTH to ensure a fair comparison. Differentially private training is run for 50 epochs. For privacy, δ is kept fixed at 10^{-5} with ϵ varied as required and reported. For our proposed method, the privacy budget split is set at 90/10. That is, we reserve 90% of the privacy budget for the differentially private training of the winning ticket and 10% for the differentially private selection of the winning ticket. ν is kept fixed at 50 for all experiments.

4.4   Main Comparison

Figure 2 shows the results of our main comparison with DPSGD. First and the obvious observation is that our proposed model (DPLTH, blue line) significantly outperforms our competitor (DPSGD, red line) with an average 23% margin of improvement over all settings and datasets, and performs *close* to the non-private version (horizontal dashed line). The improvement over DPSGD is noteworthy as DPSGD has a 10% extra privacy budget compared to DPLTH as DPSGD does not involve DP ticket selection. This provides evidence for our earlier claim that our proposed method provides significantly better utility compared to DPSGD. The second observation is as the privacy budget gets tighter (ϵ decreases), our proposed method (DPLTH) retains good utility, with the performance of DPLTH still significantly higher than DPSGD, even when comparing DPLTH at $\epsilon = 0.4$ while keeping DPSGD fixed at $\epsilon = 1$. The performance gap is specifically larger for ISOLET, as full DPSGD suffers from worse utility degradation when dataset size is small, due to the interplay between the clipping and sampling probability (See Algorithm 1 and Theorem 1 of [1]).

The utility boost with DPLTH is observed due to the reasons discussed in the introduction. That is, in DPLTH, we consistently select the *winning architecture* with a small number of model parameters and high performance on X_v

---

[4] https://github.com/tensorflow/privacy.

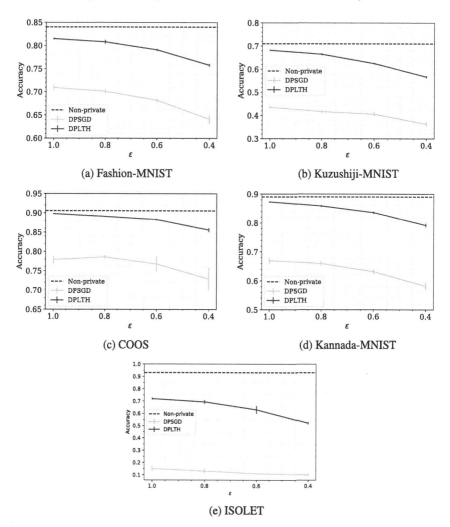

Fig. 2. Comparing our proposed method (DPLTH, blue line) with DPSGD (red line). Horizontal dashed line is the performance of the non-private model. We observe that our proposed model significantly outperforms DPSGD by a wide margin for all privacy budgets. Y-axis limits are adjusted per-figure to aid visualization. (Color figure online)

compared to the full model used in DPSGD[5]. Hence the norm clipping has a relatively diminished impact on DPLTH's performance compared to DPSGD, leading to overall better utility and robust models. This also aids in faster convergence for our method, which has its own added advantages. We study the convergence/privacy trade-off in detail in the next section.

---

[5] DPLTH consistently selects winning tickets with total parameters $\leq 10\%$ of the full model.

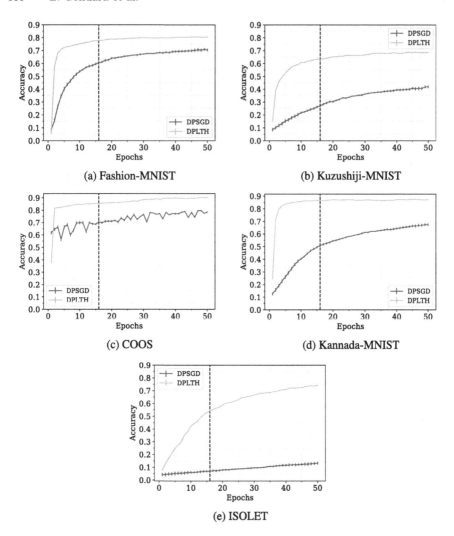

Fig. 3. Comparing convergence of our proposed DPLTH and DPSGD. We observe that our proposed method converges significantly faster compared to DPSGD. Vertical dashed line signifies the point where half of the privacy budget is spent. We observe that our proposed method can be used with early stopping while providing good utility with reduced privacy consumption.

4.5 Convergence and Early Stopping

As we briefly mentioned above, DPLTH provides *faster* convergence compared to full DPSGD, and hence allows for early stopping with reduced consumption of the total privacy budget. This is a very desirable property for *practical* applications, where one might want to begin with an estimate of the number of iterations required for convergence/utility from a non-private analysis, but if the desired utility is reached early on during training, one can stop the training and output the resulting model which now has stronger privacy guarantees compared to the model that is allowed to run for full training duration. Early stopping with reduced privacy budget consumption is made possible by keeping track of the privacy loss at each iteration and stopping when the desired accuracy/privacy budget is reached. Here we investigate our claim of faster convergence in DPLTH in detail. We keep the experimental setup the same as in the previous section, with the privacy budget to start training being fixed at $\epsilon = 1, \delta = 10^{-5}$. This provides us with the maximum number of iterations for the training process.

Figure 3 shows the results. The plots show the accuracy as the function of the number of epochs. We observe that irrespective of the dataset, DPLTH (blue line) converges significantly faster than DPSGD (red line). The vertical dashed line in the figures shows the scenario if we were to use early stopping when the total privacy consumption for DPLTH is half of the total privacy budget. For such a scenario where early stopping is desired, it is noteworthy that DPLTH provides a performance improvement of >30% compared to DPSGD with the utility loss less than 7% compared to running the training for the full privacy budget. A brief insight into this performance gain is as follows: As the updates in DPLTH are inherently less noisy due to the reduced number of model parameters, DPLTH converges much faster using less number of iterations compared to the full DPSGD, which utilizes *noisier* updates.

4.6   Investigating the Score Function

We have discussed at length the properties of our proposed score function and have argued that it selects *good* tickets. We use this section to provide empirical evidence for the claim, to answer the question, "What is the impact of using our score function for selecting a winning ticket?". That is, is our score function performing better than a randomly selected ticket? If not, then we do not need to *waste* privacy budget on the ticket selection. For evaluation, we use the tightest privacy budget with $\epsilon = 0.4$ as we would expect our score function to perform worse at this setting compared to a larger privacy budget, and we compare the average accuracy achieved by our proposed method using the "winning tickets" compared to a randomly selected ticket.

Table 2 shows the results. We observe that the winning ticket selected via our custom score function has a significant advantage over the use of a randomly sampled ticket, with our winning ticket significantly and consistently outperforming the randomly selected ticket on all datasets. Our selection method outperforms random sampling even though with a randomly sampled ticket, we save 10% of the privacy budget, meaning the differentially private training of the ticket in case of a randomly sampled ticket has 10% extra privacy budget compared to the winning ticket selected by our method. This finding enforces our claim that using a "winning" ticket with fewer model parameters and high performance, we can achieve a good privacy-utility trade-off for differentially private neural networks, and that our custom score function does a good job in selecting such a ticket.

Table 2. Comparing accuracy of our winning ticket and a randomly sampled ticket. We observe that using the winning ticket selected via our custom score function has significant advantage over the use of a randomly sampled ticket.

Dataset	Winning	Random
Fashion-MNIST	**0.76**	0.70
Kuzushiji-MNIST	**0.58**	0.51
COOS	**0.86**	0.81
Kannada-MNIST	**0.79**	0.73
ISOLET	**0.43**	0.32

4.7   Robustness to P

So far, we have seen that our proposed method significantly outperforms DPSGD on all datasets and for all privacy budgets while providing faster convergence. However, all of the evidence we have presented so far has relied on MNIST for being the publicly available dataset P, used to generate the lottery tickets. A natural question arises around the robustness of our proposed method when the underlying P changes.

We use this section to explore this phenomenon in detail, where we change P from MNIST to Fashion-MNIST, a significantly harder dataset [26] that has image samples for clothing and fashion accessories. We keep all other settings the same as our main comparison and we move MNIST to be one of our sensitive datasets. Hence, similar to our other comparisons, we have five sensitive datasets and one publicly available dataset.

Figure 4 shows the results. We observe that by changing P from MNIST to fashion-MNIST, the overall results look similar to Sect. 4.4, further providing evidence to our earlier claim that our proposed method is *robust* with respect to the P used, that is, the requirement of having a publicly available dataset P for our method is easily met.

5   Related Work

Our related work mainly falls into two categories. First is the prior work related to the lottery ticket mechanism, and the second is related to the differential privacy in neural networks.

The lottery ticket hypothesis as introduced in [7] provides evidence that there exist subnetworks within a large network, which when trained in isolation, can perform at-par with the large network. The hypothesis has been formally proven in [13] and has been further extended in [8], where the initial idea is improved to work on larger, deeper networks. Lottery ticket mechanism since has been further explored, it has been shown that the winning tickets can be used across datasets [16], and that the tickets occur in other domains as well, such as in NLP [4,29].

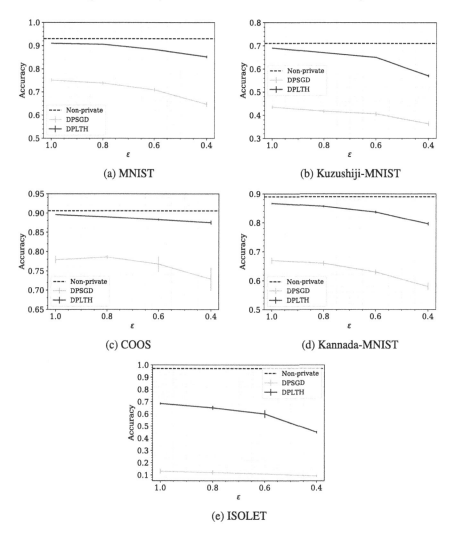

Fig. 4. Impact of changing P from MNIST to fashion-MNIST. We observe similar performance as shown in our main comparison providing evidence to our claim that the requirement of P in our proposed method can be easily met.

Perturbing the learning process to provide differential privacy has been studied in various contexts [1,21,22,24], where gradients are perturbed during the gradient descent, so the resulting weight updates, and hence the model itself is differentially private. Differentially private stochastic gradient descent (DPSGD), proposed by Abadi et al. [1], is the most popular and most often used method for differentially private training for a wide variety of neural networks [2,14,27]. DPSGD, however, falls short on the utility front, as the noise required for preserving privacy in DPSGD scales up proportional to the model size, discussed at length in the Introduction. There have been various improvements proposed to enhance the utility of DPSGD [18,19], we would like to note that these are tangential to our proposed method and our method can be built on the top of such enhancements, further boosting model utility.

6   Conclusion

We have proposed DPLTH, an end-to-end differentially private version of the lottery ticket hypothesis. Using our custom score function to select differentially private winning tickets, we have shown that DPLTH significantly outperforms DPSGD on a variety of datasets, tasks, and privacy budgets. We have shown that DPLTH converges faster compared to DPSGD, leading to reduced privacy budget consumption with improved utility if early stopping is desired. We have further shown that DPLTH is robust to the choice of P. For our future work, we would like to incorporate recent advances in lottery ticket literature, such as using *early bird* tickets [28] to reduce computation time, using the tickets reverted to trained weights after k iterations instead of reverting to the original, random values, to generalize to larger networks and datasets [8], etc. We would further like to focus on the detailed study of the mechanism when used for differentially private transfer and generative learning and to further improve the utility guarantees.

Acknowledgements. This research is in part supported by a CGS-D award and a discovery grant from Natural Sciences and Engineering Research Council of Canada.

Appendix

Theorem 1. *Phase 2 (Selecting a winning ticket) is (ϵ_1) - differentially private.*

Proof. We consider the scenario where the EM outputs some element $r \in \mathcal{R}$ on two neighbouring datasets, X, X'.

$$\frac{Pr[\mathcal{M}(X, u, \mathcal{R}) = r]}{Pr[\mathcal{M}(X', u, \mathcal{R}) = r]} = \frac{\left(\dfrac{\exp(\dfrac{\epsilon_1 u(X, r)}{2\Delta u})}{\sum_{r' \in \mathcal{R}} \exp(\dfrac{\epsilon_1 u(X, r')}{2\Delta u})}\right)}{\left(\dfrac{\exp(\dfrac{\epsilon_1 u(X', r)}{2\Delta u})}{\sum_{r' \in \mathcal{R}} \exp(\dfrac{\epsilon_1 u(X', r')}{2\Delta u})}\right)} \tag{6}$$

$$= \left(\frac{\exp(\dfrac{\epsilon_1 u(X, r)}{2\Delta u})}{\exp(\dfrac{\epsilon_1 u(X', r)}{2\Delta u})}\right) \cdot \left(\frac{\sum_{r' \in \mathcal{R}} \exp(\dfrac{\epsilon_1 u(X, r')}{2\Delta u})}{\sum_{r' \in \mathcal{R}} \exp(\dfrac{\epsilon_1 u(X', r')}{2\Delta u})}\right) \tag{7}$$

$$= \exp\left(\frac{\epsilon_1(u(X,r') - u(X',r'))}{2\Delta u}\right) \cdot \left(\frac{\sum_{r'\in\mathcal{R}}\exp(\frac{\epsilon_1 u(X,r')}{2\Delta u})}{\sum_{r'\in\mathcal{R}}\exp(\frac{\epsilon_1 u(X',r')}{2\Delta u})}\right) \tag{8}$$

$$\leq \exp(\frac{\epsilon_1}{2}) \cdot \exp(\frac{\epsilon_1}{2}) \cdot \left(\frac{\sum_{r'\in\mathcal{R}}\exp(\frac{\epsilon_1 u(X,r')}{2\Delta u})}{\sum_{r'\in\mathcal{R}}\exp(\frac{\epsilon_1 u(X',r')}{2\Delta u})}\right) \tag{9}$$

$$\leq \exp(\epsilon_1) \tag{10}$$

$\square$

References

1. Abadi, M., et al.: Deep learning with differential privacy. In: Proceedings of the 2016 ACM SIGSAC Conference on Computer and Communications Security, pp. 308–318. ACM (2016)
2. Beaulieu-Jones, B.K., Wu, Z.S., Williams, C., Greene, C.S.: Privacy-preserving generative deep neural networks support clinical data sharing. BioRxiv, p. 159756 (2017)
3. Carlini, N., Liu, C., Kos, J., Erlingsson, Ú., Song, D.: The secret sharer: measuring unintended neural network memorization & extracting secrets. arXiv preprint arXiv:1802.08232 (2018)
4. Chen, T., et al.: The lottery ticket hypothesis for pre-trained BERT networks. arXiv preprint arXiv:2007.12223 (2020)
5. Clanuwat, T., Bober-Irizar, M., Kitamoto, A., Lamb, A., Yamamoto, K., Ha, D.: Deep learning for classical Japanese literature (2018)
6. Dwork, C., McSherry, F., Nissim, K., Smith, A.: Calibrating noise to sensitivity in private data analysis. In: Halevi, S., Rabin, T. (eds.) TCC 2006. LNCS, vol. 3876, pp. 265–284. Springer, Heidelberg (2006). https://doi.org/10.1007/11681878_14
7. Frankle, J., Carbin, M.: The lottery ticket hypothesis: finding sparse, trainable neural networks. arXiv preprint arXiv:1803.03635 (2018)
8. Frankle, J., Dziugaite, G.K., Roy, D.M., Carbin, M.: The lottery ticket hypothesis at scale. arXiv preprint arXiv:1903.01611 (2019)
9. Fredrikson, M., Jha, S., Ristenpart, T.: Model inversion attacks that exploit confidence information and basic countermeasures. In: Proceedings of the 22nd ACM SIGSAC Conference on Computer and Communications Security, pp. 1322–1333. ACM (2015)
10. Jayaraman, B., Evans, D.: Evaluating differentially private machine learning in practice. In: 28th USENIX Security Symposium (USENIX Security 2019), pp. 1895–1912 (2019)
11. LeCun, Y., Cortes, C.: MNIST handwritten digit database (2010). http://yann.lecun.com/exdb/mnist/
12. Lu, A.X., Lu, A.X., Schormann, W., Ghassemi, M., Andrews, D.W., Moses, A.M.: The cells out of sample (COOS) dataset and benchmarks for measuring out-of-sample generalization of image classifiers. arXiv preprint arXiv:1906.07282 (2019)
13. Malach, E., Yehudai, G., Shalev-Schwartz, S., Shamir, O.: Proving the lottery ticket hypothesis: pruning is all you need. In: International Conference on Machine Learning, pp. 6682–6691. PMLR (2020)

14. McMahan, H.B., Ramage, D., Talwar, K., Zhang, L.: Learning differentially private recurrent language models. arXiv preprint arXiv:1710.06963 (2017)
15. McSherry, F., Talwar, K.: Mechanism design via differential privacy. In: 48th Annual IEEE Symposium on Foundations of Computer Science (FOCS 2007), pp. 94–103. IEEE (2007)
16. Morcos, A.S., Yu, H., Paganini, M., Tian, Y.: One ticket to win them all: generalizing lottery ticket initializations across datasets and optimizers. arXiv preprint arXiv:1906.02773 (2019)
17. Nair, V., Hinton, G.E.: Rectified linear units improve restricted Boltzmann machines. In: Proceedings of the 27th International Conference on Machine Learning (ICML 2010), pp. 807–814 (2010)
18. Nasr, M., Shokri, R., et al.: Improving deep learning with differential privacy using gradient encoding and denoising. arXiv preprint arXiv:2007.11524 (2020)
19. Papernot, N., Thakurta, A., Song, S., Chien, S., Erlingsson, Ú.: Tempered sigmoid activations for deep learning with differential privacy. arXiv preprint arXiv:2007.14191 (2020)
20. Prabhu, V.U.: Kannada-MNIST: a new handwritten digits dataset for the Kannada language. arXiv preprint arXiv:1908.01242 (2019)
21. Rajkumar, A., Agarwal, S.: A differentially private stochastic gradient descent algorithm for multiparty classification. In: Artificial Intelligence and Statistics, pp. 933–941 (2012)
22. Shokri, R., Shmatikov, V.: Privacy-preserving deep learning. In: Proceedings of the 22nd ACM SIGSAC Conference on Computer and Communications Security, pp. 1310–1321. ACM (2015)
23. Song, C., Ristenpart, T., Shmatikov, V.: Machine learning models that remember too much. In: Proceedings of the 2017 ACM SIGSAC Conference on Computer and Communications Security, pp. 587–601. ACM (2017)
24. Song, S., Chaudhuri, K., Sarwate, A.D.: Stochastic gradient descent with differentially private updates. In: 2013 IEEE Global Conference on Signal and Information Processing, pp. 245–248. IEEE (2013)
25. Wu, X., Fredrikson, M., Jha, S., Naughton, J.F.: A methodology for formalizing model-inversion attacks. In: 2016 IEEE 29th Computer Security Foundations Symposium (CSF), pp. 355–370. IEEE (2016)
26. Xiao, H., Rasul, K., Vollgraf, R.: Fashion-MNIST: a novel image dataset for benchmarking machine learning algorithms (2017)
27. Xie, L., Lin, K., Wang, S., Wang, F., Zhou, J.: Differentially private generative adversarial network. arXiv preprint arXiv:1802.06739 (2018)
28. You, H., et al.: Drawing early-bird tickets: towards more efficient training of deep networks. arXiv preprint arXiv:1909.11957 (2019)
29. Yu, H., Edunov, S., Tian, Y., Morcos, A.S.: Playing the lottery with rewards and multiple languages: lottery tickets in RL and NLP. arXiv preprint arXiv:1906.02768 (2019)

Locality Sensitive Hashing with Extended Differential Privacy

Natasha Fernandes[1,2] , Yusuke Kawamoto[3(✉)] , and Takao Murakami[3]

[1] Macquarie University, Sydney, Australia
[2] Inria, École Polytechnique, IPP, Palaiseau, France
[3] National Institute of Advanced Industrial Science and Technology (AIST),
Tokyo, Japan

Abstract. Extended differential privacy, a generalization of standard differential privacy (DP) using a general metric, has been widely studied to provide rigorous privacy guarantees while keeping high utility. However, existing works on extended DP are limited to few metrics, such as the Euclidean metric. Consequently, they have only a small number of applications, such as location-based services and document processing.

In this paper, we propose a couple of mechanisms providing extended DP with a different metric: *angular distance* (or *cosine distance*). Our mechanisms are based on locality sensitive hashing (LSH), which can be applied to the angular distance and work well for personal data in a high-dimensional space. We theoretically analyze the privacy properties of our mechanisms, and prove extended DP for input data by taking into account that LSH preserves the original metric only approximately. We apply our mechanisms to friend matching based on high-dimensional personal data with angular distance in the local model, and evaluate our mechanisms using two real datasets. We show that LDP requires a very large privacy budget and that RAPPOR does not work in this application. Then we show that our mechanisms enable friend matching with high utility and rigorous privacy guarantees based on extended DP.

Keywords: Local differential privacy · Locality sensitive hashing · Angular distance · Extended differential privacy

1 Introduction

Extended differential privacy (extended DP), a.k.a. $d_\mathcal{X}$-*privacy* [13], is a privacy notion that provides rigorous privacy guarantees while enabling high utility. Extended DP is a generalization of standard DP [20,21] in that the adjacency

The authors are ordered alphabetically. This work was supported by the French-Japanese project LOGIS within the Inria Equipes Associées program, by an Australian Government RTP Scholarship (2017278), by ERATO HASUO Metamathematics for Systems Design Project (No. JPMJER1603), JST, and by JSPS KAKENHI Grant Number JP19H04113.

© Springer Nature Switzerland AG 2021
E. Bertino et al. (Eds.): ESORICS 2021, LNCS 12973, pp. 563–583, 2021.
https://doi.org/10.1007/978-3-030-88428-4_28

relation (regarded as the Hamming distance) is generalized to a metric. A well-known application is geo-indistinguishability [4,7,9], an instance of extended DP for two-dimensional Euclidean space. Geo-indistinguishability guarantees that a user's location is indistinguishable from any location within a certain radius (e.g., within 5km) in the local model, in which each user obfuscates her own data and sends it to a data collector. It can also be regarded as a *relaxation* of DP in the local model (local DP or LDP [19]) to make two locations within a certain radius indistinguishable (whereas LDP makes arbitrary locations indistinguishable). Consequently, extended DP results in much higher utility than LDP, e.g., for a task of estimating geographic population distributions [4].

Since extended DP is defined using a general metric, it can potentially have a wide range of applications. However, the range of actual applications is limited by the particular metrics for which extended DP mechanisms have been designed. For example, the existing works on locations [4,7,9], documents [25], range queries [53], and linear queries [32] are designed for the Euclidean metric, the Earth Mover's metric, the l_1 metric, and the summation of privacy budgets for attributes, respectively. However, there have been no known extended DP mechanisms designed for the angular distance (or cosine distance).

For example, consider friend matching (or friend recommendation) based on personal data (e.g., locations, rating history) [10,14,16,35,36,38,44,47]. In the case of locations, we can create a vector of visit-counts where each value is the visit-count on the corresponding Point of Interest (POI). Users with similar vectors have a high probability of establishing new friendships [54]. Therefore, we can use the POI vector to recommend a new friend. Similarly, we can recommend a new friend based on the similarity of their item rating vectors, since this identifies users with similar interests [2]. Because the distance between vectors in such applications is usually given by the angular distance (or equivalently, the cosine distance) [2], the angular distance is a natural choice for the utility measure and the metric for extended DP.

In this paper, we focus on friend matching in the local model, and propose two mechanisms providing extended DP with the angular distance. Our mechanisms are based on *locality sensitive hashing* (LSH) [28,49], which can be applied to a wide range of metrics including the angular distance. Our first mechanism, LapLSH, uses the multivariate Laplace mechanism [25] to generate noisy vectors, and then hashes them into buckets using LSH as post-processing. Our second mechanism, LSHRR, embeds personal data into a binary vector using LSH, and then applies Warner's randomized response [52] for each bit of the binary vector.

The privacy analysis of extended DP is challenging especially for LSHRR. This is because LSH does not precisely preserve the original metric; it *approximates* the original metric via hashing. We theoretically analyze the privacy properties of our mechanisms, showing that they provide extended DP for the input. We also note that much existing work on privacy-preserving LSH [3,15,46] fails to provide rigorous guarantees about user privacy. We point out, using a toy example, how the lack of rigorous guarantees can lead to privacy breaches.

We evaluate our mechanisms using two real datasets. We show that LDP requires a very large privacy budget ϵ. This comes from the fact that LDP expresses an upper bound on the privacy guarantee for all inputs. In contrast, extended DP is a finer-grained notion than LDP in that it describes the privacy guarantee for inputs at various distances. In fact, we show that extended DP enables friend matching with a much smaller privacy budget than LDP for close inputs.

We also explain why RAPPOR [23] and the generalized RAPPOR [51], which are state-of-the-art LDP mechanisms, cannot be applied (either completely lose utility or are computationally infeasible) to friend matching. In short, the Bloom filter used in RAPPOR is not a metric-preserving hashing, and therefore cannot guarantee utility w.r.t. the metric distance between user vectors. This is further elaborated in Sect. 7.4.

Contributions. Our main contributions are as follows:

- We propose two mechanisms providing extended DP with the angular distance: LapLSH and LSHRR. We show that LSH itself does not provide privacy guarantees and could result in complete privacy collapse in some situations. We then prove that our mechanisms provide rigorous guarantees of extended DP. In particular, we show that the distribution of the LSHRR's privacy loss can be characterized as extended notions of concentrated DP [22] and probabilistic DP [39] with input distance. To our knowledge, this work is the first to provide extended DP with the angular distance.
- We apply our mechanisms to friend matching based on rating history and locations. Then we compare LSHRR with LapLSH using two real datasets. We show that LSHRR provides higher (resp. lower) utility than LapLSH for a high-dimensional (resp. low-dimensional) vector. We also show that LDP requires a very large privacy budget ϵ, and RAPPOR does not work for friend matching. Finally, we show that LSHRR provides high utility for a high-dimensional vector (e.g., 1000-dimensional rating/location vector) in the medium privacy regime [1,55] of extended DP, and therefore enables friend matching with rigorous privacy guarantees and high utility.

All proofs on the technical results can be found in the preprint [26].

2   Related Work

2.1   Extended DP

As explained in Sect. 1, there are a number of existing extended DP mechanisms [4,7,9,25,32,53] designed for other metrics (e.g., the Euclidean metric, the l_1 metric), which cannot be applied to the angular distance. To our knowledge, our mechanisms are the first to provide extended DP with the angular distance.

In addition, most of the studies on extended DP have studied low-dimensional data such as two-dimensional [4,7,9,32] and six-dimensional [53] data. One exception is the work in [25], which proposed the multivariate Laplace mechanism for 300-dimensional vectors. In this paper, we apply our mechanisms to vectors in 1000-dimensions (much larger than any existing work), and show that our LSHRR provides high utility for such high-dimensional data.

2.2 Privacy-Preserving Friend Matching

A number of studies [10,14,16,35,36,38,44,47] have been made on algorithms for privacy-preserving friend matching (or friend recommendation). Many of them (e.g., [16,38,44,47]) use cryptographic techniques such as homomorphic encryption and secure multiparty computation. However, such techniques require high computational costs or focus on specific algorithms, and are not suitable for a more complicated calculation of distance such as the angular distance between two rating/location vectors.

The techniques in [10,14,35,36] are based on perturbation. The mechanisms in [10,35,36] do not provide DP or its variant, whereas that in [14] provides DP. The technique in [14], however, is based on social graphs and cannot be applied to our setting, where a user's personal data is represented as a rating vector or visit-count vector. Moreover, DP-based friend matching in social graphs can require prohibitive trade-offs between utility and privacy [10,40].

Similarly, DP mechanisms based on each user's high-dimensional rating/location vector require a very large privacy budget (e.g., $\varepsilon \geq 250$ [37], $\varepsilon \geq 2 \times 10^4$ [42]) to provide high utility. In contrast, our extended DP mechanisms provide meaningful privacy guarantees in high-dimensional spaces with high utility, since extended DP is a finer-grained notion than DP, as explained in Sect. 1.

We also note that a privacy-preserving clustering algorithm in [45] and an item recommendation algorithm in [48] cannot be applied to friend matching.

2.3 Privacy-Preserving LSH

Finally, we note that some studies have proposed privacy-preserving LSH [3,8,15, 29,45,46,56]. However, some of them [3,15,46] only apply LSH and claim that it protects user privacy because LSH is a kind of non-invertible transformation. In Sect. 4, we show that the lack of rigorous guarantees can lead to privacy breaches. Nissim and Stemmer [45] proposed clustering algorithms based on LSH and the heavy-hitters algorithm. However, their algorithms focus on clustering such as k-means clustering and cannot be applied to friend matching.

Aumüller et al. [8] proposed a privacy-preserving LSH algorithm that can be applied to friend matching. Specifically, they focused on a similarity search problem under the Jaccard similarity using up to 2000-dimensional vectors, and proposed an LDP algorithm based on MinHash. After the submission of our paper to a preprint [26], two related papers [29,56] have been published. Zhang et al. [56] proposed an LDP algorithm for rating prediction based on MinHash and knowledge distillation. Hu et al. [29] proposed an LDP algorithm based on LSH for federated recommender system.

Our work differs from [8,29,56] in the following points. First, [8,29,56] only analyzed LDP for hashes, and did not conduct a more challenging analysis of extended DP for inputs. In contrast, our work provides a careful analysis of extended DP, given that LSH preserves the original metric only approximately. We also show that extended DP requires a much smaller privacy budget than LDP. Second, we compared LSHRR with LapLSH in detail, and show that LSHRR (resp. LapLSH) is more suitable for high (resp. low) dimensional data.

3 Preliminaries

In this section, we introduce notations and recall background on locality sensitive hashing (LSH), privacy measures, and privacy protection mechanisms.

Let d_{euc} be the Euclidean distance between real vectors, i.e., $d_{\mathrm{euc}}(\boldsymbol{x},\boldsymbol{x}') = \|\boldsymbol{x}-\boldsymbol{x}'\|_2$. We write $\mathcal{V}$ for the set of all binary data of length κ, i.e., $\mathcal{V}=\{0,1\}^\kappa$. The *Hamming distance* between $\boldsymbol{v},\boldsymbol{v}'\in\mathcal{V}$ is: $d_{\mathcal{V}}(\boldsymbol{v},\boldsymbol{v}')=\sum_{i=1}^\kappa |v_i - v_i'|$.

We denote the *set of all probability distributions* over a set $\mathcal{S}$ by $\mathbb{D}\mathcal{S}$. Let $N(\mu,\sigma^2)$ be the normal distribution with mean μ and variance σ^2. Let $A:\mathcal{X}\to \mathbb{D}\mathcal{Y}$ be a randomized algorithm from a finite set $\mathcal{X}$ to another $\mathcal{Y}$, and $A(x)[y]$ (resp. by $A(x)[S]$) be the probability that A maps x to y (resp. an element of S).

3.1 Locality Sensitive Hashing (LSH)

We denote by $\mathcal{X}$ the set of all possible input data. We introduce the notion of a *(normalized) dissimilarity function* $d_{\mathcal{X}}:\mathcal{X}\times\mathcal{X}\to[0,1]$ over $\mathcal{X}$ such that two inputs $\boldsymbol{x}$ and $\boldsymbol{x}'$ have less dissimilarity $d_{\mathcal{X}}(\boldsymbol{x},\boldsymbol{x}')$ when they are closer, and that $d_{\mathcal{X}}(\boldsymbol{x},\boldsymbol{x}')=0$ when $\boldsymbol{x}=\boldsymbol{x}'$. If $d_{\mathcal{X}}$ is symmetric and subadditive, it is a metric.

A *locality sensitive hashing (LSH)* [28] is a family of functions in which the probability of two inputs $\boldsymbol{x},\boldsymbol{x}'$ having different 1-bit outputs is proportional to $d_{\mathcal{X}}(\boldsymbol{x},\boldsymbol{x}')$.

Definition 1 (Locality sensitive hashing). A *locality sensitive hashing (LSH) scheme* w.r.t. a dissimilarity function $d_{\mathcal{X}}$ is a family $\mathcal{H}$ of functions from $\mathcal{X}$ to $\{0,1\}$ coupled with a probability distribution $D_{\mathcal{H}}$ such that for any $\boldsymbol{x},\boldsymbol{x}'\in\mathcal{X}$,

$$\Pr_{h\sim D_{\mathcal{H}}}[h(\boldsymbol{x})\neq h(\boldsymbol{x}')] = d_{\mathcal{X}}(\boldsymbol{x},\boldsymbol{x}'), \tag{1}$$

where h is chosen from $\mathcal{H}$ according to the distribution $D_{\mathcal{H}}$. By using independently chosen functions $h_1,h_2,\ldots,h_\kappa$, the *κ-bit LSH function* $H:\mathcal{X}\to\mathcal{V}$ is:

$$H(\boldsymbol{x}) = (h_1(\boldsymbol{x}), h_2(\boldsymbol{x}), \ldots, h_\kappa(\boldsymbol{x})). \tag{2}$$

We denote by $H^*:\mathcal{X}\to\mathbb{D}\mathcal{V}$ the randomized algorithm that draws a κ-bit LSH H from the distribution $D_{\mathcal{H}}^\kappa$ and outputs the hash value $H(\boldsymbol{x})$ of a given input $\boldsymbol{x}$.

3.2   Examples of LSHs

There are a variety of LSH families corresponding to useful metrics, such as the angular distance [5,12], Jaccard metric [11], and l_p metric with $p \in (0,2]$ [18]. In this work, we focus on LSH families for the angular distance.

A *random-projection-based hashing* is a one-bit hashing with the domain $\mathcal{X} \overset{\text{def}}{=} \mathbb{R}^n$ and a random vector $\boldsymbol{r} \in \mathbb{R}^n$ that defines a hyperplane through the origin. Formally, we define a *random-projection-based hashing* $h_{\text{proj}} : \mathbb{R}^n \to \{0,1\}$ by:

$$h_{\text{proj}}(\boldsymbol{x}) = \begin{cases} 0 & (\text{if } \boldsymbol{r}^\top \boldsymbol{x} < 0) \\ 1 & (\text{otherwise}) \end{cases}$$

where each element of $\boldsymbol{r}$ is independently chosen from the standard normal distribution $N(0,1)$. By (2), a κ-bit LSH function H_{proj} is built from one-bit hashes $h_{\text{proj}_1}, \ldots, h_{\text{proj}_\kappa}$ that are generated from independent hyperplanes $\boldsymbol{r}_1, \ldots, \boldsymbol{r}_\kappa$.

The random-projection-based hashing h_{proj} is an LSH w.r.t. the *angular distance* $d_\theta : \mathbb{R}^n \times \mathbb{R}^n \to [0,1]$ defined by:

$$d_\theta(\boldsymbol{x}, \boldsymbol{x}') = \tfrac{1}{\pi} \cos^{-1} \left(\tfrac{\boldsymbol{x}^\top \boldsymbol{x}'}{\|\boldsymbol{x}\| \|\boldsymbol{x}'\|} \right) \tag{3}$$

For example, $d_\theta(\boldsymbol{x}, \boldsymbol{x}') = 0$ iff $\boldsymbol{x} = \boldsymbol{x}'$, while $d_\theta(\boldsymbol{x}, \boldsymbol{x}') = 1$ iff $\boldsymbol{x} = -\boldsymbol{x}'$. $d_\theta(\boldsymbol{x}, \boldsymbol{x}') = 0.5$ exactly when the two vectors $\boldsymbol{x}$ and $\boldsymbol{x}'$ are orthogonal, namely, $\boldsymbol{x}^\top \boldsymbol{x}' = 0$.

3.3   Approximate Nearest Neighbor Search

We recall the nearest neighbor search (NNS) problem and its utility measures.

Given a dataset $S \subseteq \mathcal{X}$, the *nearest neighbor search (NNS)* for an $x_0 \in S$ is the problem of finding the closest $x \in S$ to x_0 w.r.t. a metric $d_\mathcal{X}$ over $\mathcal{X}$. A *k-nearest neighbor search (k-NNS)* is the problem of finding the k closest points.

A naive and exact approach to k-NNS is to perform pairwise comparisons of data points, requiring $O(|S|)$ operations. Approaches to improve this computational inefficiency shift the problem to space inefficiency [6]. An alternative approach [30] is to employ LSH to perform *approximate* NNS efficiently. To evaluate the utility, we use the average distance of returned nearest neighbors from the data point x_0 compared with the average distance of true nearest neighbors.

Definition 2 (Utility loss). Let A be an approximate algorithm that produces approximate k nearest neighbors $N \subseteq S$ for a data point $x_0 \in S$ in terms of a metric $d_\mathcal{X}$. The *average utility loss* for N w.r.t. the true nearest neighbors T is given by: $\mathcal{U}_A(S) = \frac{1}{k} \sum_{x \in N} d_\mathcal{X}(x_0, x) - \frac{1}{k} \sum_{x \in T} d_\mathcal{X}(x_0, x)$.

3.4   Privacy Measures and Privacy Mechanisms

Extended Differential Privacy. [13,34] guarantees that when two inputs x and x' are closer, their corresponding output distributions are less distinguishable.

In this paper, we propose a more generalized definition using a function δ over $\mathcal{X}$ and an arbitrary function ξ over $\mathcal{X}$ instead of a metric. The main reason for this generalization is that LSH preserves the metric over the input only probabilistically and approximately, hence cannot fit to [13]'s standard definition.

Definition 3 (Extended differential privacy). Given two functions $\xi : \mathcal{X} \times \mathcal{X} \to \mathbb{R}_{\geq 0}$ and $\delta : \mathcal{X} \times \mathcal{X} \to [0, 1]$, a randomized algorithm $A : \mathcal{X} \to \mathbb{D}\mathcal{Y}$ provides (ξ, δ)-*extended differential privacy (XDP)* if for all $x, x' \in \mathcal{X}$ and for any $S \subseteq \mathcal{Y}$,

$$A(x)[S] \leq e^{\xi(x,x')} A(x')[S] + \delta(x, x'),$$

where the probability is taken over the random choices in A.

We abuse notation and write δ when $\delta(x, x')$ is a constant. When $\xi(x, x')$ is also a constant ε, the definition gives the (standard) *differential privacy* (DP). When $\xi(x, x') = d_{\mathcal{X}}(x, x')$ and $\delta(x, x') = 0$, the definition gives $d_{\mathcal{X}}$-privacy in [13]. In later sections, we instantiate the metric $d_{\mathcal{X}}$ with the angular distance d_θ.

Finally, we recall some popular privacy protection mechanisms.

Definition 4 (Laplace mechanism [21]). For an $\varepsilon \in \mathbb{R}_{>0}$ and a metric $d_{\mathcal{X}}$ over $\mathcal{X} \cup \mathcal{Y}$, the $(\varepsilon, d_{\mathcal{X}})$-*Laplace mechanism* is the randomized algorithm $Q_{\mathsf{Lap}} : \mathcal{X} \to \mathbb{D}\mathcal{Y}$ that maps an input x to an output y with probability $\frac{1}{c} \exp(-\varepsilon d_{\mathcal{X}}(x, y))$ where $c = \int_{\mathcal{Y}} \exp(-\varepsilon d_{\mathcal{X}}(x, y))\, dy$.

Examples of the $(\varepsilon, d_{\mathcal{X}})$-Laplace mechanism include the one-dimensional [21] and the multivariate Laplace mechanism [25], both equipped with the Euclidean metric. The $(\varepsilon, d_{\mathcal{X}})$-Laplace mechanism provides $(\varepsilon d_{\mathcal{X}}, 0)$-XDP.

Definition 5 (Randomized response [52]). The ε-*randomized response* (ε-RR) is the randomized algorithm $Q_{\mathsf{rr}} : \{0, 1\} \to \mathbb{D}\{0, 1\}$ that maps a bit b to another b' with probability $\frac{e^\varepsilon}{e^\varepsilon + 1}$ if $b' = b$, and with probability $\frac{1}{e^\varepsilon + 1}$ otherwise.

The ε-RR provides ε-DP. Erlingsson et al. [23] introduce the *RAPPOR*, which first uses a Bloom filter to produce a hash value and then applies the RR to each bit of the hash value. The RAPPOR provides ε-DP in the local model.

4 Privacy Properties of LSH

Several works in the literature make reference to the privacy-preserving properties of LSH [3,17,46]. The privacy guarantee attributed to LSH mechanisms hinges on its hash function, which 'protects' an individual's private attributes by revealing only their hash bucket. We now apply a formal analysis to LSH and explain why LSH implementations do not provide strong privacy guarantees, and could, in some situations, result in complete privacy collapse for the individual.

Modeling LSH. We present a simple example to show how privacy breaks down. Consider the set of secret inputs $\mathcal{X} = \{(0, 1), (1, 0), (1, 1)\}$ whose element represents whether an individual rated two movies A and B. Then an LSH is modeled as a probabilistic channel $h^* : \mathcal{X} \to \mathbb{D}\{0,1\}$ that maps a secret input to a binary observation.

For brevity, we deal with a single random-projection-based hashing h in Sect. 3.2. That is, we randomly choose a vector r representing the normal to a hyperplane, and given an input $x \in \mathcal{X}$, the hash function h outputs 0 if $r^\top x < 0$ and 1 otherwise. For example, if $r = (1, -\frac{1}{2})$ is chosen, h is defined as:

$$h : \mathcal{X} \to \{0,1\}$$
$$(0,1) \mapsto 0$$
$$(1,0) \mapsto 1$$
$$(1,1) \mapsto 1$$

In fact, there are 6 possible (deterministic) hash functions for any choice of the vector r, corresponding to hyperplanes that separate different pairs of points:

h_1	h_2	h_3
$(0,1) \mapsto 1$	$(0,1) \mapsto 0$	$(0,1) \mapsto 1$
$(1,0) \mapsto 0$	$(1,0) \mapsto 1$	$(1,0) \mapsto 0$
$(1,1) \mapsto 0$	$(1,1) \mapsto 1$	$(1,1) \mapsto 1$

h_4	h_5	h_6
$(0,1) \mapsto 0$	$(0,1) \mapsto 1$	$(0,1) \mapsto 0$
$(1,0) \mapsto 1$	$(1,0) \mapsto 1$	$(1,0) \mapsto 0$
$(1,1) \mapsto 0$	$(1,1) \mapsto 1$	$(1,1) \mapsto 0$

Each of h_1, h_2, h_3, and h_4 occurs with probability $1/8$, while h_5 and h_6 each occur with probability $1/4$. The resulting channel h^*, computed as the probabilistic sum of these deterministic hash functions, turns out to leak no information on the secret input (i.e., all outputs have equal probability conditioned on each input). This indicates that the channel h^* is perfectly private. However, in practice, LSH may require the release of the choice of the vector r (e.g. [17])[1], that is, the choice of hash function is leaked. Notice that in our example, h_1 to h_4 correspond to deterministic mechanisms which leak exactly 1 bit of the secret, while h_5 and h_6 leak nothing. In other words, with 50% probability, 1 bit of the 2-bit secret is leaked. Furthermore, h_1 and h_2 leak the secret $(0,1)$ exactly, and h_3 and h_4 leak $(1,0)$ exactly. Thus, the release of r destroys the privacy guarantee.

The Guarantee of LSH. In general, for any number of hash functions and any length of input, an LSH which releases its choice of hyperplanes also leaks its choice of deterministic mechanism. This means that it leaks the equivalence classes of the secrets. Such mechanisms belong to the 'k-anonymity'-style of privacy mechanisms which promise privacy by hiding secrets in equivalence classes of size at least k. These have been shown to be unsafe due to their failure to compose well [24,27,33]. This failure leads to the potential for linkage or intersection attacks by an adversary armed with auxiliary information. For this reason, we consider compositionality an essential property for a privacy-preserving system. LSH with hyperplane release does not provide such privacy guarantees.

---

[1] In fact, since the channel on its own leaks nothing, there *must* be further information released in order to learn anything useful from this channel.

5   LSH-Based Privacy Mechanisms

In this section, we propose two privacy protection mechanisms called *LSHRR* and *LapLSH*. The former is an extension of RAPPOR [23] w.r.t. LSH, and the latter is constructed using the Laplace mechanism and LSH.

Construction of LSHRR. We introduce the *LSH-then-RR privacy mechanism* (*LSHRR*) as the randomized algorithm that (i) randomly chooses a κ-bit LSH function H, (ii) computes the κ-bit hash value $H(\boldsymbol{x})$ of a given input $\boldsymbol{x}$, and (iii) applies the randomized response to each bit of $H(\boldsymbol{x})$.

To formalize this, we define the (ε, κ)-*bitwise RR* Q_{brr}, which applies the randomized response Q_{rr} to each bit of the input independently. Formally, $Q_{\mathsf{brr}} : \mathcal{V} \to \mathbb{D}\mathcal{V}$ maps a bitstring $\boldsymbol{v} = (v_1, v_2, \dots, v_\kappa)$ to another $\boldsymbol{y} = (y_1, y_2, \dots, y_\kappa)$ with probability $Q_{\mathsf{brr}}(\boldsymbol{v})[\boldsymbol{y}] = \prod_{i=1}^{\kappa} Q_{\mathsf{rr}}(v_i)[y_i]$. Then LSHRR is defined as follows.

Definition 6 (LSHRR). The ε-*LSH-then-RR privacy mechanism* (*LSHRR*) instantiated with a κ-bit LSH function $H : \mathcal{X} \to \mathcal{V}$ is the randomized algorithm $Q_H : \mathcal{X} \to \mathbb{D}\mathcal{V}$ defined by $Q_H = Q_{\mathsf{brr}} \circ H$. Given a distribution $D_{\mathcal{H}}^\kappa$ of the κ-bit LSH functions, the ε-LSHRR w.r.t. $D_{\mathcal{H}}^\kappa$ is defined by $Q_{\mathsf{LSHRR}} = Q_{\mathsf{brr}} \circ H^*$.

LSHRR deals with two kinds of randomness: (a) the randomness in choosing a (deterministic) LSH function H from $D_{\mathcal{H}}^\kappa$ (e.g., the random seed $\boldsymbol{r}$ in the random-projection-based hashing h_{proj}), and (b) the random noise added by the bitwise RR Q_{brr}. We can assume that each user of this privacy mechanism selects an input $\boldsymbol{x}$ independently of both kinds of randomness, since they wish to protect their own privacy when publishing $\boldsymbol{x}$.

In practical settings, the same LSH function H is often used to produce hash values of different inputs; namely, multiple hash values are dependent on an identical hash seed (e.g., a service provider would generate a hash seed so that multiple users can share the same H to compare their hash values). Furthermore, the adversary might obtain the LSH function H (or the seed $\boldsymbol{r}$ used to produce H), and might learn a set of possible inputs that produce the same hash value $H(x)$ without knowing the actual input x. Therefore, the hash value $H(x)$ might reveal partial information on the input x (see Sect. 4), and the bitwise RR Q_{brr} is crucial in guaranteeing privacy (see Sect. 6 for our privacy analyses).

On the other hand, Q_{brr} causes errors in the Hamming distance as follows:

Proposition 1 (Error bound). *For any $x, x' \in \mathcal{X}$, the expected error in the Hamming distance satisfies* $\mathbb{E}[|d_\mathcal{V}(Q_H(x), Q_H(x')) - d_\mathcal{V}(H(x), H(x'))|] \leq \frac{2\kappa}{1+e^\varepsilon}$ *where the expectation is taken over the randomness in the bitwise RR.*

Construction of LapLSH. We also propose the *Laplace-then-LSH privacy mechanism* (LapLSH) as the randomized algorithm that (i) randomly chooses a κ-bit LSH function H, (ii) applies the multivariate Laplace mechanism Q_{Lap} to $\boldsymbol{x}$, and (iii) computes the κ-bit hash value $H(Q_{\mathsf{Lap}}(\boldsymbol{x}))$.

Definition 7 (LapLSH). The $(\varepsilon, d_{\mathcal{X}})$-*Laplace-then-LSH privacy mechanism* (*LapLSH*) with a κ-bit LSH function $H : \mathcal{X} \to \mathcal{V}$ is the randomized algorithm $Q_{\mathsf{Lap}H} : \mathcal{X} \to \mathbb{D}\mathcal{V}$ defined by $Q_{\mathsf{Lap}H} = H \circ Q_{\mathsf{Lap}}$. The $(\varepsilon, d_{\mathcal{X}})$-LapLSH w.r.t. a distribution $D_{\mathcal{H}}^{\kappa}$ of the κ-bit LSH functions is defined by $Q_{\mathsf{LapLSH}} = H^* \circ Q_{\mathsf{Lap}}$.

LapLSH also deals with the two kinds of randomness discussed above, and the Laplace mechanism Q_{Lap} is crucial in guaranteeing privacy. One of the main differences from LSHRR is that LapLSH adds noise directly to the input before applying LSH whereas LSHRR adds noise after applying LSH to the input.

In Sect. 7 we implement the multivariate Laplace mechanism with the input domain $\mathcal{X} = \mathbb{R}^n$ and Euclidean distance d_{euc} described in [25]; namely, we generate additive noise by constructing a unit vector uniformly at random over the n-dimensional unit sphere $\mathbb{S}^n$, scaled by a random value generated from the gamma distribution with shape n and scale $^1/_\varepsilon$.

6   Privacy Analyses of the Mechanisms

We provide an analysis of the privacy guarantees provided by our mechanisms in two operational scenarios: (i) w.r.t. an already-chosen LSH function (e.g., where it has been generated by a service provider), and (ii) w.r.t. all possible choices of the LSH function (e.g., prior to its instantiation by a particular service provider). Note that our analysis is general in that it does not rely on specific metrics or hashing algorithms for LSH.

6.1   LSHRR's Privacy W.r.t. the Particular LSH Function

We first show the privacy guarantee for LSHRR w.r.t. the particular LSH function used by the service provider. This type of privacy is defined using the Hamming distance $d_{\mathcal{V}}$ between the hash values of given inputs, and the degree of privacy depends on the actual selection of the LSH function H (or the hash seeds $\boldsymbol{r}$), which we assume is available to the adversary. Since LSH preserves the original metric $d_{\mathcal{X}}$ only approximately, we obtain XDP guarantee w.r.t. a pseudo-metric $d_{\varepsilon H}$ that approximates $d_{\mathcal{X}}$ as follows.

Proposition 2 (XDP of Q_H). Let $H : \mathcal{X} \to \mathcal{V}$ be a κ-bit LSH function, and $d_{\varepsilon H}$ be the pseudometric over $\mathcal{X}$ defined by $d_{\varepsilon H}(\boldsymbol{x}, \boldsymbol{x}') = \varepsilon d_{\mathcal{V}}(H(\boldsymbol{x}), H(\boldsymbol{x}'))$ for $\boldsymbol{x}, \boldsymbol{x}' \in \mathcal{X}$. Then the ε-LSHRR Q_H instantiated with H provides $(d_{\varepsilon H}, 0)$-XDP.

However, we cannot compute $d_{\varepsilon H}$ or the degree of XDP in Proposition 2 until H has been computed. To overcome this unclear guarantee of privacy, in Sect. 6.2 we show a useful privacy guarantee that can be evaluated without requiring H (or hash seeds) generated by the service provider.

Note that the $\kappa\varepsilon$-DP of LSHRR is obtained as the worst case of Proposition 2, i.e., when the hamming distance between vectors is maximum due to an "unlucky" choice of hash seeds or very large distance $d_{\mathcal{X}}(\boldsymbol{x}, \boldsymbol{x}')$ between the inputs $\boldsymbol{x}, \boldsymbol{x}'$. The following proposition guarantees the privacy independently of the actual choice of H.

Proposition 3 (Worst-case privacy of Q_H). *For a κ-bit LSH function H, the ε-LSHRR Q_H instantiated with H provides $\kappa\varepsilon$-DP.*

6.2 LSHRR's Privacy W.r.t. the Distribution of LSH Functions

Next, we show LSHRR's privacy guarantee w.r.t. any possible LSH function that may be generated. This type of privacy guarantee is useful in a variety of scenarios. For example, a privacy analyst could evaluate the expected degree of privacy before the service provider fixes the LSH function or hash seeds. For another example, the seeds may be stored in tamper-resistant hardware privately.

The privacy guarantee without relying on specific LSH functions or hash seeds is modeled as a probability distribution of degrees of XDP over the random choice of seeds. Then this can be characterized as an extension of concentrated DP [22] and probabilistic DP [39] with input distance, yielding the XDP guarantee.

In the privacy analysis, we deal with the situation where multiple users produce hash values by employing the same hash seeds, as seen in typical applications such as approximate NNS. Then we define privacy notions for the mechanisms that share randomness among them.

Formally, we denote by $A_r : \mathcal{X} \to \mathbb{D}\mathcal{Y}$ a randomized algorithm A with a shared input $r \in \mathcal{R}$. Given a distribution λ over a finite set $\mathcal{R}$ of shared input, we denote by $A_\lambda : \mathcal{X} \to \mathbb{D}\mathcal{Y}$ the randomized algorithm that draws a shared input r from λ and behaves as A_r; i.e., $A_\lambda(x)[y] = \sum_{r \in \mathcal{R}} \lambda[r] A_r(x)[y]$. Then we extend the notion of privacy loss [22] with shared randomness as follows.

Definition 8 (Privacy loss). For a randomized algorithm $A_r : \mathcal{X} \to \mathbb{D}\mathcal{Y}$ with a shared input r, the *privacy loss* on $y \in \mathcal{Y}$ w.r.t. $x, x' \in \mathcal{X}$, $r \in \mathcal{R}$ is defined by:

$$\mathcal{L}_{x,x',y,r} = \ln\left(\frac{A_r(x)[y]}{A_r(x')[y]}\right),$$

where the probability is taken over the random choices in A_r. Given a distribution λ over $\mathcal{R}$, the *privacy loss random variable* $\mathcal{L}_{x,x'}$ of x over x' w.r.t. λ is the real-valued random variable representing the privacy loss $\mathcal{L}_{x,x',y,r}$ where a *shared randomness r* is sampled from λ and y is sampled from $A_r(x)$.

To characterize the privacy loss random variable $\mathcal{L}_{x,x'}$ for LSHRR, we introduce an extension of CDP [22] wth input distance $d(x, x')$ as follows.

Definition 9 (CXDP). Let $\mu \in \mathbb{R}_{\geq 0}$, $\tau \in \mathbb{R}_{>0}$, $\lambda \in \mathbb{D}\mathcal{R}$, and $d : \mathcal{X} \times \mathcal{X} \to \mathbb{R}_{\geq 0}$ be a metric. A random variable Z over $\mathbb{R}$ is τ-*subgaussian* if for all $s \in \mathbb{R}$, $\mathbb{E}[\exp(sZ)] \leq \exp(\frac{s^2\tau^2}{2})$. A randomized algorithm $A_\lambda : \mathcal{X} \to \mathbb{D}\mathcal{Y}$ provides (μ, τ, d)-*mean-concentrated extended differential privacy (CXDP)* if for all $x, x' \in \mathcal{X}$, the privacy loss random variable $\mathcal{L}_{x,x'}$ of x over x' w.r.t. λ satisfies that $\mathbb{E}[\mathcal{L}_{x,x'}] \leq \mu d(x, x')$, and that $\mathcal{L}_{x,x'} - \mathbb{E}[\mathcal{L}_{x,x'}]$ is τ-subgaussian.

Then we obtain the following CXDP guarantee for LSHRR.

Proposition 4 (CXDP of Q_{LSHRR}). *The ε-LSHRR provides $(\varepsilon\kappa, \frac{\varepsilon\kappa}{2}, d_\mathcal{X})$-CXDP.*

To clarify the implication of CXDP, we introduce an extension of probabilistic DP [39] with input distance, which we call PXDP. Intuitively, (ξ, δ)-PXDP guarantees $(\xi, 0)$-XDP with probability $1 - \delta$.

Definition 10 (PXDP). Let $\lambda \in \mathbb{DR}$, $\xi : \mathcal{X} \times \mathcal{X} \to \mathbb{R}_{\geq 0}$, and $\delta : \mathcal{X} \times \mathcal{X} \to [0, 1]$. A randomized algorithm $A_\lambda : \mathcal{X} \to \mathbb{DY}$ provides (ξ, δ)-*probabilistic extended differential privacy (PXDP)* if for all $x, x' \in \mathcal{X}$, $\Pr[\mathcal{L}_{x,x'} > \xi(x, x')] \leq \delta(x, x')$. We abuse notation to write δ when $\delta(x, x')$ is constant.

In Appendix B, we show that CXDP implies PXDP and that PXDP implies XDP. Based on these, we show that LSHRR provides PXDP and XDP as follows.

Theorem 1 (PXDP/XDP of Q_{LSHRR}). *Let $\delta \in \mathbb{R}_{>0}$, $\varepsilon' = \varepsilon\sqrt{\frac{-\ln\delta}{2}}$, and $\xi(x, x') = \varepsilon\kappa d_\mathcal{X}(x, x') + \varepsilon'\sqrt{\kappa}$. The ε-LSHRR provides (ξ, δ)-PXDP, hence (ξ, δ)-XDP.*

For our experimental evaluation, we show a privacy guarantee that gives tighter bounds but requires the parameters dependent on the inputs x and x'.

Proposition 5 (Tighter bound for PXDP/XDP). *For $a, b \in \mathbb{R}_{>0}$, let $D_{\text{KL}}(a\|b) = a \ln \frac{a}{b} + (1 - a) \ln \frac{1-a}{1-b}$. For an $\alpha \in \mathbb{R}_{>0}$, we define:*

$$\xi_\alpha(x, x') = \varepsilon\kappa(d_\mathcal{X}(x, x') + \alpha)$$
$$\delta_\alpha(x, x') = \exp\big(-\kappa D_{\text{KL}}(d_\mathcal{X}(x, x') + \alpha \| d_\mathcal{X}(x, x'))\big).$$

Then the ε-LSHRR provides $(\xi_\alpha, \delta_\alpha)$-PXDP, hence $(\xi_\alpha, \delta_\alpha)$-XDP.

6.3   Privacy Guarantee for LapLSH

Finally, we also show that LapLSH provides XDP. This is immediate from the fact that XDP is preserved under the post-processing by an LSH function.

Proposition 6 (XDP of Q_{LapH} and Q_{LapLSH}). *The $(\varepsilon, d_\mathcal{X})$-LapLSH Q_{LapH} with a κ-bit LSH function H provides $(\varepsilon d_\mathcal{X}, 0)$-XDP. The $(\varepsilon, d_\mathcal{X})$-LapLSH Q_{LapLSH} w.r.t. a distribution $D_\mathcal{H}^\kappa$ of the κ-bit LSH functions also provides $(\varepsilon d_\mathcal{X}, 0)$-XDP.*

7   Experimental Evaluation

We show an experimental evaluation of LSHRR and LapLSH on two real datasets: MovieLens [41] and FourSquare [54]. Our goal is to determine the utility of these mechanisms when compared with a (slow but accurate) true nearest neighbor search. As a baseline, we also show the performance of vanilla (non-private) LSH.

(a) MovieLens Dataset

(b) Foursquare Dataset

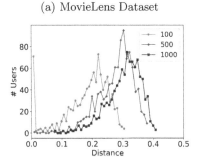
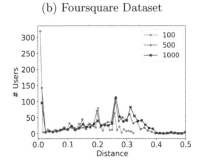

Fig. 1. Distributions of angular distances d_θ to nearest neighbor for $k = 1$ for each user, plotted for vectors with dimensions 100, 500 and 1000. The distance 0.5 represents orthogonal vectors; i.e., having no items in common. The privacy guarantee for users is a function of the distance d_θ to their nearest neighbors.

7.1 Datasets and Experimental Setup

Our problem of interest is *privacy-preserving friend matching (or friend recommendation)*. In this scenario, we are given a dataset of users in which each user is represented as a (real-valued) vector of attributes. The data curator's goal is to recommend k friends for each user based on their k-nearest neighbors.

For our experiments, we used the following two datasets:

MovieLens. The MovieLens 25m dataset [41] contains 162000 users with ratings across 62000 movies, with ratings ranging from 1 to 5. We normalized the scores, i.e., to mean 0, and gave unseen movies a score of 0. For each user, we constructed a rating vector that consists of the user's rating for each movie.

Foursquare. The Foursquare dataset (Global-scale Check-in Dataset with User Social Networks) [54] contains 90048627 check-ins by 2733324 users on POIs all over the world. We extracted 107091 POIs in New York and 10000 users who have visited at least one POI in New York. For each user, we constructed a visit-count vector, which consists of a visit-count value for each POI.

For both datasets, we generated input (rating/visit-count) vectors of length $n = 100, 500, 1000$ to evaluate the effectiveness of LSH. Reduced vector lengths were used because LSH has poor utility for larger vector lengths and the utility of our mechanisms requires a good baseline utility for LSH.

We computed the k nearest neighbors w.r.t. the angular distance d_θ for 1000 users for $k = 1, 5, 10$ using standard NNS (i.e., pairwise comparisons over all inputs). The distributions of True Nearest Neighbor distances are shown in Fig. 1.

κ-bit LSH (for $\kappa = 10, 20, 50$) was implemented using the *random-projection-based hashing*. For each user, we then computed their k nearest neighbors for $k = 1, 5, 10$ using the Hamming distance on bitstrings. To compute the overall (ξ, δ)-XDP guarantee as per Proposition 5, we fixed $\delta = 0.01$ and $d_\theta = 0.1$ and varied ε to generate ξ values in the range 0.1 to 20.

Figure 1 shows that about 43% (resp. 16%) of input vectors with 100 (resp. 1000) dimensions are within the distance of 0.1 in the Foursquare dataset. Thus, extended DP with $d_\theta = 0.1$ is useful to hide such input vectors.

7.2   Comparing Privacy and Utility

We use the angular distance d_θ as our utility measure, i.e., to determine similar users for the purposes of recommendations. For utility loss, we use Definition 2 instantiated with the angular distance d_θ. We compare the utility loss of each mechanism w.r.t. a comparable privacy guarantee, namely the overall privacy budget $\varepsilon d_{\mathrm{euc}}(\boldsymbol{x}, \boldsymbol{x}')$ for LapLSH and $\xi_\alpha(\boldsymbol{x}, \boldsymbol{x}')$ for LSHRR (Proposition 5). However, as LSHRR's privacy guarantee depends on the angular distance d_θ and LapLSH's depends on d_{euc}, they cannot be compared directly. For comparison using the same metric, we use the relationship between the Euclidean and angular distances for normalized vectors $\boldsymbol{x}, \boldsymbol{x}'$:

$$d_{\mathrm{euc}}(\boldsymbol{x}, \boldsymbol{x}') = \sqrt{2 - 2\cos(\pi \cdot d_\theta(\boldsymbol{x}, \boldsymbol{x}'))} . \qquad (4)$$

We normalized input vectors to length 1 (noting that the normalization does not affect the angular distance, hence utility), and transformed $\varepsilon d_{\mathrm{euc}}(\boldsymbol{x}, \boldsymbol{x}')$ into $\xi_\alpha(\boldsymbol{x}, \boldsymbol{x}')$ using (4) (Since $\xi_\alpha(\boldsymbol{x}, \boldsymbol{x}')$ depends on α and $d_\theta(\boldsymbol{x}, \boldsymbol{x}')$, we perform comparisons against various reasonable ranges of these variables).

We note that the trade-off between privacy and utility means that users with similar profiles will be indistinguishable from each other, whereas users with very different profiles can be distinguished. This is an inherent trade-off determined by the correlation between the sensitive and useful information to be released.

7.3   Experimental Results

We compared the performance of LapLSH and LSHRR with that of vanilla LSH in Fig. 2. We observe that LSHRR outperforms LapLSH when the dimension of the input vector is $n = 100$, 500, or 1000. This is because LapLSH needs to add noise for each element of the input vector (even if the vector is sparse and includes many zero elements) and the total amount of noise is very large in high-dimensional data. In contrast, when the vector length is $n = 50$, LapLSH ($\kappa = 50$ bits) outperforms LSHRR ($\kappa = 50$ bits). We conjecture that this is because the total amount of noise used in LapLSH is small for low-dimensional data whereas LSHRR needs to add a large amount of noise for each element of the hash when the hash length κ is large. We expect LapLSH performance to improve further over LSHRR for smaller values of n.

Interestingly, we observe that although the performance of LSH degrades as the hash length κ decreases, the performance of LSHRR and LapLSH both remain relatively stable. This is mainly because when κ is 5 times larger, the amount of information expressed by the hash can be roughly 5 times larger whereas the amount of noise added to each bit is also 5 times larger. When the privacy budget is $\xi = 20$, the performance of LSHRR on larger bit-lengths

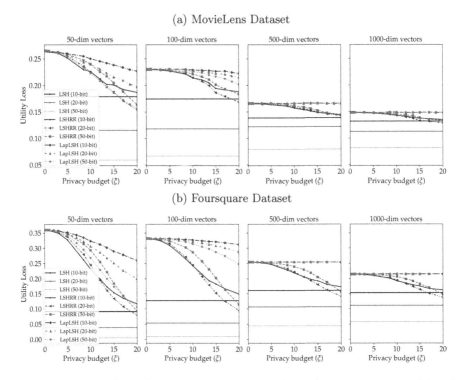

Fig. 2. Utility loss (y-axis) versus privacy budget ξ (x-axis) for LSHRR, LapLSH and LSH on n-dimensional vectors. ξ is computed for various κ, and $d_\theta = 0.1$.

($\kappa = 20$ or 50) overtakes the performance of 10-bit LSHRR. This is because the utility loss of LSHRR is bounded below by the utility loss of the corresponding LSH; i.e., LSHRR converges to LSH with the same hash length κ as ξ increases.

Figure 2 also shows that when the total privacy budget ξ is around 2, LSHRR achieves lower utility loss than a uniformly random hash, i.e., LSHRR when the total privacy budget is 0. LSHRR achieves much lower utility loss when the total privacy budget is around 5. We can interpret the value of the total privacy budget in terms of the flip probability in the RR. For example, when we use the 20-bit hash, the total privacy budget of 5 for $d_\theta = 0.05$ corresponds to the case in which the RR flips each bit of the hash with the probability approx. 0.27. Therefore, we flip around 5-bits on average out of 20-bits in this case.

We also note that the total privacy budget used in our experiments is much smaller than the privacy budget ϵ previously used in the low privacy regime [31]. Specifically, Kairouz *et al.* [31], and subsequent works (e.g., [1,43,50,55]) refer to $\epsilon = \ln |\mathcal{X}|$ as a privacy budget in the low privacy regime. Since our experiments deal with high-dimensional data, a privacy budget of $\ln |\mathcal{X}|$ would be extremely large. For example, when we use the 1000-dimensional rating vector in the MovieLens dataset, the privacy budget in the low privacy regime is: $\epsilon =$

$\ln |\mathcal{X}| = \ln 5^{1000} = 1609$. The total privacy budget in our experiments ($\xi \leq 20$) is much smaller than this value, and falls into the *medium privacy regime* [1,55].

Note that LDP requires a much larger privacy budget than extended DP. For example, by Proposition 5, when $\kappa = 50$ and $d_\theta = 0.05$ (resp. 0.1), the total privacy budget $\xi = 20$ in extended DP corresponds to the total privacy budget 120 (resp. 80) in LDP. More details are shown in Appendix A.

Finally, we compare LSHRR with LapLSH in terms of time complexity and general applicability. For time complexity, LapLSH requires $O(n\kappa)$ operations (construction of n-dimensional noise, then κ-bit hashing). In contrast, LSHRR requires $O(m\kappa)$ operations, where m is the number of non-zero elements in the input vector (κ-bit hashing on m non-zero elements followed by κ-randomized response). Since $m \ll n$ in practice, LSHRR is significantly more efficient.

For general applicability, LSHRR can be used with other metrics such as the Jaccard metric [11], Earth Mover's metric [12], and l_p metric [18] by choosing a suitable LSH function, whereas LapLSH is designed for the Euclidean metric only. Thus, LSHRR has more potential applications than LapLSH.

In summary, we find that LSHRR is better than LapLSH in terms of both time complexity and general applicability, and provides high utility with a reasonable privacy level for a high-dimensional data (100 dimensions or more).

7.4   Inapplicability of the RAPPOR

We finally explain that neither the RAPPOR [23] nor the generalized RAPPOR [51] can be used for friend matching based on high-dimensional personal data. These mechanisms apply a Bloom filter to an input vector before applying the randomized response. Typically, this Bloom filter is a hash function that neither allows for efficiently finding an input from its hash value, nor preserves the metric $d_{\mathcal{X}}$ over the inputs. For instance, [23] uses MD5 to implement the Bloom filter.

Let us consider two approaches to perform the nearest neighbor search using RAPPOR: *comparing two hash values* and *comparing two input vectors*.

In the first approach, the data collector calculates the Hamming distance between obfuscated hash values. Then the utility is completely lost, because the Bloom filter does not preserve the metric $d_{\mathcal{X}}$ over the inputs. Hence we cannot recommend friends based on the proximity of input vector in this approach.

In the second approach, the data collector tries to invert obfuscated hash values to the original input vector, and calculates the angular distance between the input vectors to find nearest neighbors. Since the Bloom filter may not allow for efficiently finding an input from its hash value, the data collectors need to perform exhaustive searches, i.e., to compute the hash values of all possible input data $\mathcal{X}$. However, this is computationally intractable when the input domain $\mathcal{X}$ is very large. In particular, our setting deals with high-dimensional input data (e.g., $|\mathcal{X}| = 5^{1000}$ in the 1000-dimensional MovieLens rating vector), and thus it is computationally infeasible to invert hash values into input vectors.

In summary, the first approach (comparing two hashes) results in a complete loss of utility, and the second approach (comparing two input vectors) is computationally infeasible when the input data are in a high-dimensional space.

Therefore, the RAPPOR cannot be applied to our problem of friend matching. The same issue applies to a generalized version of the RAPPOR [51].

In contrast, our mechanisms can be applied to friend matching even when $|\mathcal{X}|$ is very large, because LSH allows us to approximately compare the distance between the input vectors without computing them from their hash values.

8   Conclusion

In this paper, we proposed two extended DP mechanisms LSHRR and LapLSH. We showed that LSH itself does not provide privacy guarantees and could result in complete privacy collapse in some situations. We then proved that LSHRR and LapLSH provide rigorous guarantees of extended DP. To our knowledge, this work is the first to provide extended DP with the angular distance.

By experiments with real datasets, we show that LSHRR outperforms LapLSH on high-dimensional data. We also show that LSHRR provides high utility for a high-dimensional vector, thus enabling friend matching with rigorous privacy guarantees and high utility.

A   Total Privacy Budgets in Extended DP and LDP

Table 1 shows total privacy budgets in extended DP and LDP calculated from Proposition 5 and the fact that the angular distance is 0.5 or smaller.

For example, when $d_\theta = 0.05$ and $\kappa = 10$, 20, and 50, the total privacy budget $\xi = 20$ in extended DP corresponds to the total privacy budget of 55, 79, and 120, respectively, in LDP.

Table 1. Total privacy budgets in extended DP (XDP) and LDP when $d_\theta = 0.05$ or 0.1, $\kappa = 10$, 20, or 50, and $\delta = 0.01$.

(a) $d_\theta = 0.05$				
Total privacy budget ξ in XDP	1	5	10	20
Total privacy budget in LDP ($\kappa = 10/20/50$)	3/4/6	14/20/30	28/40/60	55/79/120
(b) $d_\theta = 0.1$				
Total privacy budget ξ in XDP	1	5	10	20
Total privacy budget in LDP ($\kappa = 10/20/50$)	2/3/4	10/14/20	21/28/40	42/57/80

B   More Details on the Privacy Analyses

We show the relationships among CXDP, PXDP, and XDP as follows. See the preprint version [26] of this paper for the proofs.

Lemma 1 (CXDP $\Rightarrow$ PXDP). Let $\mu \in \mathbb{R}_{\geq 0}$, $\tau \in \mathbb{R}_{>0}$, $\lambda \in \mathbb{DR}$, $A_\lambda : \mathcal{X} \to \mathbb{DY}$, and d be a metric over $\mathcal{X}$. Let $\delta \in (0, 1]$, $\varepsilon = \tau\sqrt{-2\ln\delta}$, and $\xi(x, x') = \mu d(x, x') + \varepsilon$. If A_λ provides (μ, τ, d)-CXDP, then it provides (ξ, δ)-PXDP.

Lemma 2 (PXDP $\Rightarrow$ XDP). Let $\lambda \in \mathbb{DR}$, $A_\lambda : \mathcal{X} \to \mathbb{DY}$, $\xi : \mathcal{X} \times \mathcal{X} \to \mathbb{R}_{\geq 0}$, and $\delta : \mathcal{X} \times \mathcal{X} \to [0, 1]$. If A_λ provides (ξ, δ)-PXDP, it provides (ξ, δ)-XDP.

Next, we present the proofs for some of the main results as follows. See the preprint [26] of this paper for the proofs of the other technical results.

Proof (of Proposition 4*).* For a κ-bit LSH function $H \in \mathcal{H}^\kappa$,

$$
\begin{aligned}
Q_H(\boldsymbol{x})[y] &= Q_{\mathsf{brr}}(H(\boldsymbol{x}))[y] \\
&\leq e^{\varepsilon d_\mathcal{V}(H(\boldsymbol{x}), H(\boldsymbol{x}'))} Q_{\mathsf{brr}}(H(\boldsymbol{x}'))[y] \quad \text{(by XDP of BRR)} \\
&= e^{\varepsilon d_\mathcal{V}(H(\boldsymbol{x}), H(\boldsymbol{x}'))} Q_H(\boldsymbol{x}')[y].
\end{aligned}
$$

Let Z be the random variable defined by $Z \stackrel{\text{def}}{=} d_\mathcal{V}(H(\boldsymbol{x}), H(\boldsymbol{x}'))$ where $H = (h_1, h_2, \ldots, h_\kappa)$ is distributed over $\mathcal{H}^\kappa$, namely, the seeds of these LSH functions are chosen randomly. Then $0 \leq Z \leq \kappa$, and Z follows the binomial distribution with mean $\mathbb{E}[Z] = \kappa d_\mathcal{X}(\boldsymbol{x}, \boldsymbol{x}')$. Then the random variable $\varepsilon Z - \mathbb{E}[\varepsilon Z]$ is centered, i.e., $\mathbb{E}[\varepsilon Z - \mathbb{E}[\varepsilon Z]] = 0$, and ranges over $[-\varepsilon\kappa d_\mathcal{X}(\boldsymbol{x}, \boldsymbol{x}'), \varepsilon\kappa(1 - d_\mathcal{X}(\boldsymbol{x}, \boldsymbol{x}'))]$. Hence it follows from Hoeffding's lemma that:

$$
\mathbb{E}[\exp(t(\varepsilon Z - \mathbb{E}[\varepsilon Z]))] \leq \exp\left(\tfrac{t^2}{8}(\varepsilon\kappa)^2\right) = \exp\left(\tfrac{t^2}{2}\left(\tfrac{\varepsilon\kappa}{2}\right)^2\right).
$$

Hence by definition, $\varepsilon Z - \mathbb{E}[\varepsilon Z]$ is $\frac{\varepsilon\kappa}{2}$-subgaussian. Therefore, the LSH-based mechanism Q_{LSHRR} provides $(\varepsilon\kappa, \frac{\varepsilon\kappa}{2}, d_\mathcal{X})$-CXDP. $\qquad\square$

Proof (of Theorem 1*).* Let $\alpha = \sqrt{\frac{-\ln\delta}{2\kappa}}$. Let Z be the random variable defined by $Z \stackrel{\text{def}}{=} d_\mathcal{V}(H(\boldsymbol{x}), H(\boldsymbol{x}'))$ where $H = (h_1, h_2, \ldots, h_\kappa)$ is distributed over $\mathcal{H}^\kappa$. Then Z follows the binomial distribution with mean $\mathbb{E}[Z] = \kappa d_\mathcal{X}(\boldsymbol{x}, \boldsymbol{x}')$. Hence it follows from Chernoff-Hoeffding theorem that $\Pr[Z \geq \kappa(d_\mathcal{X}(\boldsymbol{x}, \boldsymbol{x}') + \alpha)] \leq \exp(-2\kappa\alpha^2) = \delta$. Hence $\Pr[\varepsilon Z \geq \varepsilon\kappa d_\mathcal{X}(\boldsymbol{x}, \boldsymbol{x}') + \varepsilon'\sqrt{\kappa}] \leq \delta$. Therefore Q_{LSHRR} provides (ξ, δ)-PXDP. By Lemma 2, Q_{LSHRR} provides (ξ, δ)-XDP. $\qquad\square$

Proof (of Proposition 5*).* Let Z be the random variable defined by $Z \stackrel{\text{def}}{=} d_\mathcal{V}(H(\boldsymbol{x}), H(\boldsymbol{x}'))$ where $H = (h_1, h_2, \ldots, h_\kappa)$ is distributed over $\mathcal{H}^\kappa$. By Chernoff-Hoeffding theorem, $\Pr[Z \geq \kappa(d_\mathcal{X}(\boldsymbol{x}, \boldsymbol{x}') + \alpha)] \leq \delta_\alpha(\boldsymbol{x}, \boldsymbol{x}')$. Then $\Pr[\varepsilon Z \geq \xi_\alpha(\boldsymbol{x}, \boldsymbol{x}')] \leq \delta_\alpha(\boldsymbol{x}, \boldsymbol{x}')$. Therefore Q_{LSHRR} provides $(\xi_\alpha, \delta_\alpha)$-PXDP. By Lemma 2, Q_{LSHRR} provides $(\xi_\alpha, \delta_\alpha)$-XDP. $\qquad\square$

References

1. Acharya, J., Sun, Z., Zhang, H.: Hadamard response: Estimating distributions privately, efficiently, and with little communication. In: AISTATS, pp. 1120–1129 (2019)

2. Aggarwal, C.C.: Recommender Systems. Springer, Heidelberg (2016). https://doi.org/10.1007/978-3-319-29659-3
3. Aghasaryan, A., Bouzid, M., Kostadinov, D., Kothari, M., Nandi, A.: On the use of LSH for privacy preserving personalization. In: TrustCom, pp. 362–371 (2013)
4. Alvim, M.S., Chatzikokolakis, K., Palamidessi, C., Pazii, A.: Invited paper: local differential privacy on metric spaces: optimizing the trade-off with utility. In: CSF, pp. 262–267 (2018). https://doi.org/10.1109/CSF.2018.00026
5. Andoni, A., Indyk, P., Laarhoven, T., Razenshteyn, I., Schmidt, L.: Practical and optimal LSH for angular distance. In: NIPS, pp. 1–9 (2015)
6. Andoni, A., Indyk, P., Razenshteyn, I.: Approximate nearest neighbor search in high dimensions. In: ICM, pp. 3287–3318. World Scientific (2018)
7. Andrés, M.E., Bordenabe, N.E., Chatzikokolakis, K., Palamidessi, C.: Geo-indistinguishability: differential privacy for location-based systems. In: CCS, pp. 901–914. ACM (2013). https://doi.org/10.1145/2508859.2516735
8. Aumüller, M., Bourgeat, A., Schmurr, J.: Differentially private sketches for Jaccard similarity estimation. CoRR abs/2008.08134 (2020)
9. Bordenabe, N.E., Chatzikokolakis, K., Palamidessi, C.: Optimal geo-indistinguishable mechanisms for location privacy. In: CCS, pp. 251–262 (2014)
10. Brendel, W., Han, F., Marujo, L., Jie, L., Korolova, A.: Practical privacy-preserving friend recommendations on social networks. In: WWW, pp. 111–112 (2018)
11. Broder, A.Z., Charikar, M., Frieze, A.M., Mitzenmacher, M.: Min-wise independent permutations. J. Comput. Syst. Sci. **60**, 630–659 (2000)
12. Charikar, M.S.: Similarity estimation techniques from rounding algorithms. In: STOC, pp. 380–388 (2002)
13. Chatzikokolakis, K., Andrés, M.E., Bordenabe, N.E., Palamidessi, C.: Broadening the scope of differential privacy using metrics. In: De Cristofaro, E., Wright, M. (eds.) PETS 2013. LNCS, vol. 7981, pp. 82–102. Springer, Heidelberg (2013). https://doi.org/10.1007/978-3-642-39077-7_5
14. Chen, L., Zhu, P.: Preserving the privacy of social recommendation with a differentially private approach. In: SmartCity, pp. 780–785. IEEE (2015)
15. Chen, X., Liu, H., Yang, D.: Improved LSH for privacy-aware and robust recommender system with sparse data in edge environment. EURASIP J. Wirel. Commun. Netw. **2019**(1), 1–11 (2019). https://doi.org/10.1186/s13638-019-1478-1
16. Cheng, H., Qian, M., Li, Q., Zhou, Y., Chen, T.: An efficient privacy-preserving friend recommendation scheme for social network. IEEE Access **6**, 56018–56028 (2018)
17. Chow, R., Pathak, M.A., Wang, C.: A practical system for privacy-preserving collaborative filtering. In: ICDM Workshops, pp. 547–554 (2012)
18. Datar, M., Immorlica, N., Indyk, P., Mirrokni, V.S.: Locality-sensitive hashing scheme based on p-stable distributions. In: SCG, pp. 253–262 (2004)
19. Duchi, J.C., Jordan, M.I., Wainwright, M.J.: Local privacy and statistical minimax rates. In: FOCS, pp. 429–438 (2013)
20. Dwork, C.: Differential privacy. In: ICALP, pp. 1–12 (2006)
21. Dwork, C., McSherry, F., Nissim, K., Smith, A.: Calibrating noise to sensitivity in private data analysis. In: Halevi, S., Rabin, T. (eds.) TCC 2006. LNCS, vol. 3876, pp. 265–284. Springer, Heidelberg (2006). https://doi.org/10.1007/11681878_14
22. Dwork, C., Rothblum, G.N.: Concentrated differential privacy. CoRR abs/1603.01887 (2016)
23. Úlfar Erlingsson, Pihur, V., Korolova, A.: RAPPOR: randomized aggregatable privacy-preserving ordinal response. In: CCS, pp. 1054–1067 (2014)

24. Fernandes, N., Dras, M., McIver, A.: Processing text for privacy: an information flow perspective. In: Havelund, K., Peleska, J., Roscoe, B., de Vink, E. (eds.) FM 2018. LNCS, vol. 10951, pp. 3–21. Springer, Cham (2018). https://doi.org/10.1007/978-3-319-95582-7_1
25. Fernandes, N., Dras, M., McIver, A.: Generalised differential privacy for text document processing. In: POST, pp. 123–148 (2019)
26. Fernandes, N., Kawamoto, Y., Murakami, T.: Locality sensitive hashing with extended differential privacy. CoRR abs/2010.09393 (2020). https://arxiv.org/abs/2010.09393
27. Ganta, S.R., Kasiviswanathan, S.P., Smith, A.: Composition attacks and auxiliary information in data privacy. In: KDD, pp. 265–273. ACM (2008)
28. Gionis, A., Indyk, P., Motwani, R.: Similarity search in high dimensions via hashing. In: VLDB, pp. 518–529 (1999)
29. Hu, H., Dobbie, G., Salcic, Z., Liu, M., Zhang, J., Lyu, L., Zhang, X.: Differentially private locality sensitive hashing based federated recommender system. Concurr. Comput. Pract. Exp. 1–16 (2020)
30. Indyk, P., Motwani, R.: Approximate nearest neighbors: towards removing the curse of dimensionality. In: STOC, pp. 604–613 (1998)
31. Kairouz, P., Bonawitz, K., Ramage, D.: Discrete distribution estimation under local privacy. In: ICML, pp. 2436–2444 (2016)
32. Kamalaruban, P., Perrier, V., Asghar, H.J., Kaafar, M.A.: Not all attributes are created equal: d_x-private mechanisms for linear queries. In: Proceedings on Privacy Enhancing Technologies (PoPETs), vol. 2020, no. 1, pp. 103–125 (2020)
33. Kawamoto, Y., Murakami, T.: On the anonymization of differentially private location obfuscation. In: ISITA, pp. 159–163. IEEE (2018)
34. Kawamoto, Y., Murakami, T.: Local obfuscation mechanisms for hiding probability distributions. In: Sako, K., Schneider, S., Ryan, P.Y.A. (eds.) ESORICS 2019. LNCS, vol. 11735, pp. 128–148. Springer, Cham (2019). https://doi.org/10.1007/978-3-030-29959-0_7
35. Li, M., Ruan, N., Qian, Q., Zhu, H., Liang, X., Yu, L.: SPFM: scalable and privacy-preserving friend matching in mobile clouds. IEEE Internet Things J. **4**(2), 583–591 (2017)
36. Liu, C., Mittal, P.: LinkMirage: enabling privacy-preserving analytics on social relationships. In: NDSS (2016)
37. Liu, Z., Wang, Y.X., Smola, A.J.: Fast differentially private matrix factorization. In: RecSys, pp. 171–178 (2015)
38. Ma, X., Ma, J., Li, H., Jiang, Q., Gao, S.: ARMOR: a trust-based privacy-preserving framework for decentralized friend recommendation in online social networks. Futur. Gener. Comput. Syst. **79**, 82–94 (2018)
39. Machanavajjhala, A., Kifer, D., Abowd, J.M., Gehrke, J., Vilhuber, L.: Privacy: theory meets practice on the map. In: ICDE, pp. 277–286. IEEE (2008)
40. Machanavajjhala, A., Korolova, A., Sarma, A.D.: Personalized social recommendations - accurate or private? VLDB **4**(7), 440–450 (2020)
41. MovieLens 25m Dataset. https://grouplens.org/datasets/movielens/25m/. Accessed 2020
42. Murakami, T., Hamada, K., Kawamoto, Y., Hatano, T.: Privacy-preserving multiple tensor factorization for synthesizing large-scale location traces with cluster-specific features. Proc. Priv. Enhancing Technol. **2021**(2), 5–26 (2021)
43. Murakami, T., Kawamoto, Y.: Utility-optimized local differential privacy mechanisms for distribution estimation. In: USENIX Security, pp. 1877–1894 (2019)

44. Narayanan, A., Thiagarajan, N., Lakhani, M., Hamburg, M., Boneh, D., et al.: Location privacy via private proximity testing. In: NDSS, vol. 11 (2011)
45. Nissim, K., Stemmer, U.: Clustering algorithms for the centralized and local models. In: Algorithmic Learning Theory, pp. 619–653 (2019)
46. Qi, L., Zhang, X., Dou, W., Ni, Q.: A distributed locality-sensitive hashing-based approach for cloud service recommendation from multi-source data. IEEE J. Sel. Areas Commun. **35**(11), 2616–2624 (2017)
47. Samanthula, B.K., Cen, L., Jiang, W., Si, L.: Privacy-preserving and efficient friend recommendation in online social networks. Trans. Data Priv. **8**(2), 141–171 (2015)
48. Shin, H., Kim, S., Shin, J., Xiao, X.: Privacy enhanced matrix factorization for recommendation with local differential privacy. IEEE Trans. Knowl. Data Eng. **30**(9), 1770–1782 (2018)
49. Wang, J., Liu, W., Kumar, S., Chang, S.F.: Learning to hash for indexing big data - a survey. Proc. IEEE **104**(1), 34–57 (2016)
50. Wang, S., et al.: Mutual information optimally local private discrete distribution estimation. CoRR abs/1607.08025 (2016). https://arxiv.org/abs/1607.08025
51. Wang, T., Blocki, J., Li, N., Jha, S.: Locally differentially private protocols for frequency estimation. In: USENIX Security, pp. 729–745 (2017)
52. Warner, S.L.: Randomized response: a survey technique for eliminating evasive answer bias. J. Am. Stat. Assoc. **60**(309), 63–69 (1965)
53. Xiang, Z., Ding, B., He, X., Zhou, J.: Linear and range counting under metric-based local differential privacy. In: ISIT, pp. 908–913 (2020)
54. Yang, D., Qu, B., Yang, J., Cudre-Mauroux, P.: Revisiting user mobility and social relationships in LBSNs: a hypergraph embedding approach. In: WWW, pp. 2147–2157 (2019)
55. Ye, M., Barga, A.: Optimal schemes for discrete distribution estimation under local differential privacy. In: ISIT, pp. 759–763 (2017)
56. Zhang, Y., Gao, N., Chen, J., Tu, C., Wang, J.: PrivRec: user-centric differentially private collaborative filtering using LSH and KD. In: Yang, H., Pasupa, K., Leung, A.C.-S., Kwok, J.T., Chan, J.H., King, I. (eds.) ICONIP 2020. CCIS, vol. 1332, pp. 113–121. Springer, Cham (2020). https://doi.org/10.1007/978-3-030-63820-7_13

Zero Knowledge

MLS Group Messaging: How Zero-Knowledge Can Secure Updates

Julien Devigne[1,2], Céline Duguey[1,2(✉)], and Pierre-Alain Fouque[2,3]

[1] DGA Maîtrise de l'information, Bruz, France
julien.devigne@intradef.gouv.fr
[2] Irisa, Rennes, France
{celine.duguey,pierre-alain.fouque}@irisa.fr
[3] Univ Rennes1, CNRS, Rennes, France

Abstract. The Messaging Layer Security (MLS) protocol currently developed by the Internet Engineering Task Force (IETF) aims at providing a secure group messaging solution. MLS aims for end-to-end security, including Forward Secrecy and Post Compromise Secrecy, properties well studied for one-to-one protocols. It proposes a tree-based regular asynchronous update of the group secrets, where a single user can alone perform a complete update. A main drawback is that a malicious user can create a denial of service attack by sending invalid update information.

In this work, we propose a solution to prevent this kind of attacks, giving a checkpoint role to the server that transmits the messages. In our solution, the user sends to the server a proof that the update has been computed correctly, without revealing any information about this update. We use a Zero-Knowledge (ZK) protocol together with verifiable encryption as building blocks. As a main contribution, we provide two different ZK protocols to prove knowledge of the input of a pseudo random function implemented as a circuit, given an algebraic commitment of the output and the input.

Keywords: Cryptographic protocols · Messaging Layer Security - MLS · Secure messaging · Zero-knowledge

1 Introduction

Secure messaging protocols have been widely adopted over the last few years. The privacy offered by encrypted communication seduces billions of users worldwide. A significant number of application providers have settled their security on the Double Ratchet Algorithm [37], often identified as Signal. This protocol provides End-to-End confidentiality, as well as Forward Secrecy (FS) and Post Compromise Secrecy (PCS). The Double Ratchet however is dedicated to one-to-one communications. MLS targets secure *group* messaging and is developed by the IETF. The goal is to obtain similar security properties as those in one-to-one protocols. The group keys are computed and regularly updated in a

© Springer Nature Switzerland AG 2021
E. Bertino et al. (Eds.): ESORICS 2021, LNCS 12973, pp. 587–607, 2021.
https://doi.org/10.1007/978-3-030-88428-4_29

protocol called TreeKEM, based on a tree structure: each member of the group is represented by a tree leaf and the group secret is given by the tree root. To perform an update, a user sends to the other leaves secret information which depend on their position in the tree. In this paper, we are concerned with an open problem identified in the MLS draft: how to be sure that each user receives a valid update information? In other words: how to be sure that the updating user is not cheating? The current protocol provides verification elements for each user to check whether the update he received is valid, but it does not prevent a malicious updater to send misformed update information to all or part of the group. Such attacks would prevent the updating process, seriously damaging FS and PCS properties, that seduce the users. Consequently, we propose a solution in which the users only receive valid updates: the server which transmits the update messages can check their validity before forwarding them. The server is given a check-point role and has no more power to create an update, malicious or not, than in the original protocol. Hence we only add a layer of security, through the server, without modifying the core of MLS. A main building block of our solution is a ZK protocol, inspired from the recent multi party computation (MPC) in the head solutions [27,30,34].

Our Contribution. As a first contribution, we show how to combine a ZK protocol with a verifiable encryption solution to solve the open problem identified in the IETF draft for MLS, in a light version of the protocol. The idea is to enable an intermediate server to perform a blind verification (on encrypted and committed data) that each update information sent by the updater is correctly computed. The ZK proof is provided on a statement that mixes a circuit evaluation (an HKDF derivation, defined in [36]) and an algebraic commitment (typically a Pedersen commitment, described in [38]). The verifiable encryption scheme proves to the server (*i.e.* the verifier) that the encrypted data is the one that is committed to and verified in the proof.

As a second contribution, we propose two ZK protocols for statements that compose an algebraic commitment and the circuit computation of a pseudorandom function family (PRF) f. More precisely, we prove the knowledge of a secret witness x such that public commitments C_x, C_y are algebraic commitments of x and $f(x)$, with $f(x)$ remaining secret. Our approach is based on the MPC in the head paradigm, introduced in [30]. We consider the recent ZK proof system ZKBoo [27] and its improvements ZKBoo++ [18] as well as KKW [34]. Our first approach is directly inspired by a recent work of Backes *et al.* [6]. The first step is to provide commitments to the bits of the secret input and output. Then, we call the algebraic properties of the commitment scheme to link those bits with values used in the circuit proof. Our second approach consists in considering a Boolean circuit that computes a tag $t = f(x) + ax$. The proof on this circuit binds the secret input and output to the tag value. In a second step, we use the homomorphic properties of the commitment to show that the committed values are also bound by t. Finally, we invoke properties of the function f to show that their exists only one solution to the tag equation.

Previous works, in particular [19] and [1], have proposed solutions for such algebraic and circuit composition statements. However, the former is inherently interactive and the latter uses SNARKs, where the burden of the proof is mainly on the prover side, which does not fit our use case as smartphones have resources to be saved.

Related Work. *Secure Messaging,* and more particularly Ratcheted Key Exchange (RKE), have been widely studied (*e.g.* [3,9,31,33,39]) since the first analysis of the Signal protocol [22]. Literature for the group version is more limited. In [21] Cohn Gordon *et al.* introduced the notion of Asynchronous Ratcheted Trees (ART). These ART are Diffie Hellman based binary trees in which the update process of a node involves entropy coming from both its children. In MLS, the underlying TreeKEM protocol is inspired by ART. A main difference is that a single leaf can generate the update data for each of its ancestor nodes. TreeKEM has been initially formalized in the technical paper [11] and has then evolved to reach the actual description available on the prevailing draft 11 [7]. Alwen *et al.* formalize in [4] a Continuous Group Key Agreement (CGKA) derived from the two-party Continuous Key Agreement defined in [3]. They provide a security model for CGKA and show that TreeKem does not achieve optimal FS and PCS security, but prove that using updatable public key encryption can lead to a better security. Our solution is compatible with this improvement. In [2], Alwen *et al.* focus on the addition and revocation process. Finally, Brzuska *et al.* provide in [12] an analyse of the current draft 11, considering both TreeKem and the Key Schedule on top of it.

Zero-Knowledge (ZK) proofs, have proved to be a powerful tool in cryptography, since their conception in the mid 1980s. It has been shown that ZK proofs exist for any NP language. However, efficient ZK protocols are designed for a small class of language and do not extend to any NP languages. Sigma protocols (Σ-protocols), clearly described in [23], are very efficient for proving algebraic relations, whereas other protocols have been designed for proving statements that can be expressed as a circuit. Among them, Garbled Circuits based schemes, as introduced in [32], which are inherently interactive, and SNARKs, as designed in [26,28,35]. SNARKs are non-interactive arguments (with computational soundness) of knowledge with small proofs and light verification: the burden of the proof is on the prover side. They are proven secure in the common reference string (CRS) model: a common trusted public input has to be shared by the prover and the verifier. Practical implementations based on pairings are in use in real life protocols such as cryptocurrencies. STARK proofs [10] remove the CRS requirement but the prover's algebraic computations are still linear in the circuit size. The MPC in the head paradigm, introduced in [30], leads to very efficient proof system without CRS. The seminal paper [27] introducing ZKBoo proposes the first efficient ZK proof of a hash function computation. Further works significantly optimize the efficiency, such as Ligero [5], ZKBoo++ [18] and KKW [34] (developed for the post quantum signature scheme Picnic) or [29].

In real life however, many applications need to provide proofs on statements that mix algebraic and non algebraic parts. Expressing the algebraic part as a circuit would considerably increase the circuit size and reduce the efficiency. One could express each gate of a circuit as an algebraic relation that can be proven with a Σ-protocol, but this solution is clearly non desirable as circuits for hashing may have thousands of gates. Considering this, combining efficiently algebraic and non algebraic proofs has revealed to be an important challenge.

In [19], Chase *et al.* propose two constructions, based on Garbled Circuits, to provide a circuit proof on a committed input. Our solutions are close to theirs in the sense that their first proposal uses bit wise commitment on an secret input, and their second proposal includes a one-time mac computation in the circuit to be garbled. However, their proposal heavily relies on the garbling protocol and can not be transposed to the non interactive setting.

More recently, Agrawal *et al.* in [1] propose a solution for modular composition of algebraic and non algebraic proofs. Their solution is non interactive, based on Sigma protocols and QAP-based SNARKs. As explained in their work, the "key ingredient [they] need from a SNARK construction is that the proof contains a multi-exponentiation of the input/output". They compose it with a proof that the exponents in a multi-exponentiation correspond to values committed to in a collection of commitments. From this result, they show how to obtain proofs for AND, OR and composition of two statements, either algebraic or circuit. The small proofs and the light verification step of SNARKS are desirable for privacy-preserving credentials or crypto-currencies proofs of solvency. But the prover's high computational effort is not adapted to our application where the verifier turns out to have a larger computation power than the prover.

Finally, Backes *et al.* propose in [6] an extended version of ZKBoo++ that allows algebraic commitments on the secret input of the circuit. Their protocol is non interactive and the computational cost is balanced between the prover and the verifier. Their solution requires to commit to each bit of the secret input and to commit to internal values of the ZKBoo++ circuit proof. We extend their result to the case of a committed output in our first zero-knowledge solution. We focus on the MPC in the head paradigm in order to provide proofs in which the amount of work is balanced between both parties.

Organization of the Paper. In Sect. 2, we recall the definitions concerning ZK proofs, commitment schemes, and verifiable encryption. In Sect. 3, we present the protocol MLS, focusing on the process to update the group secret, and we describe our solution to improve the security of the update mechanism. The Sect. 4 is dedicated to our two protocols, CopraZK and (bitwise) ComInOutZK, for proving knowledge of the preimage of a PRF function when only commitments of the input and the output are publicly available.

2   Backgrounds

Zero-Knowledge. Consider an NP relation $\mathcal{R}$, *i.e.* given a witness w and an input x, $\mathcal{R}(x, w) = 1$ can be decided in polynomial time. Let $\mathcal{L}$ be the language associated to $\mathcal{R}$, $\mathcal{L} = \{x | \exists w \text{ such that } \mathcal{R}(x, w) = 1\}$. A ZK proof of knowledge for $\mathcal{L}$ allows a prover to convince a verifier, that he knows a witness w for x, without revealing w. It shall be correct (if the prover and the verifier are honest, the verifier always accepts), sound (an efficient extractor that interacts with a corrupted prover can exhibit a valid witness except with negligible probability), and zero-knowledge (no information on w leaks from the proof). Following the notation of [14], we write $\mathsf{PK}\{w_1, \ldots w_s : \mathcal{R}(w_1, \ldots, w_s, x_1 \ldots x_t) = 1\}$ to denote the proof of knowledge of the secret witnesses $w_1, \ldots w_s$ that satisfy the relation $\mathcal{R}$ with the public values $x_1, \ldots, x_t$.

Σ-**Protocols.** These are specific three moves proofs of knowledge. The prover first sends a commitment value q, receives a challenge e and answers with a value t. Given (x, a, e, t), the verifier accepts or not. Those protocol provide correctness, s-special soundness (given s transcripts with common commitments and distinct challenges, one can extract a witness) and honest-verifier ZK (the verifier is suppose to generate the challenge honestly). They can be turned into a non-interactive proof using Fiat-Shamir transformation [25]. In this case the special-honest verifier clause disappears and the verification step consists in reconstructing the challenge from the received data.

Commitment Schemes. A commitment scheme involves a *Committer* and a *Receiver* who share public parameters. On entrance a message x and an additional opening information r, the commitment protocol produces a value $c = \mathsf{Com}(x, r)$ such that c shall not reveal any information about x; this is the hiding property. The *Committer* can open its commitment c by revealing r and x with the property that only the secret x shall produce a valid opening for c; this is the binding property. For our first ZK protocol, we will require an extra property, called equivocality. A commitment is equivocable if there exists a trapdoor T such that, given a commitment C, its opening information, and T, it is possible to open C to any value. Equivocality comes with a specific extractor that, given two different openings (x_1, r_1), (x_2, r_2) to a single commitment C, can extract the trapdoor T. The Pedersen commitment scheme [38] is an equivocable scheme with unconditional hiding and computational binding. It is routinely used because it interacts nicely with linear relations. This scheme is defined as follows: let $\mathbb{G}$ be a cyclic group of prime order q, P a generator and $Q \in \mathbb{G}$ such that the discrete log of Q in base P is unknown. Then, $\mathsf{Com}(x) = xP + rQ$ where r is sampled at random in $\mathbb{Z}_q$. Let C_1, C_2 be commitments to values x_1, x_2. If $a, b \in \mathbb{Z}_q$ are public values, then one can efficiently prove the following: $PK\{x_1, x_2, r_1, r_2 : C_1 = x_1 P + r_1 Q \wedge C_2 = x_2 P + r_2 Q \wedge a x_1 + x_2 = b \mod q\}$. The trapdoor for equivocality is given by the discrete log of Q in base P.

MPC in the Head. Ishai *et al.* introduced in [30] a new paradigm for ZK proofs, called MPC in the head. This solution reveals to be very competitive in terms of efficiency for ZK proofs performed on circuits. The idea is that the prover performs a virtual MPC and obtains several views. He commits to these views and opens only a sub-part of them required by the verifier. ZKBoo [27] generalizes IKOS to any relation $\mathcal{R}_\phi$ defined by a function $\phi : X \to Y$ ($\mathcal{R}_\phi(y, x) \leftrightarrow y = \phi(x)$), as long as the function ϕ can be computed in a specific manner identified as a (2,3)-decomposition. The prover first shares its secret input x into $(x_1, x_2, x_3) = \mathsf{Share}(x)$ such that $x = x_1 \oplus x_2 \oplus x_3$. Then he runs the MPC and obtains three distinct views w_1, w_2, w_3 and from each of this view he gets an output share $y_i = \mathsf{Output}(w_i), i \in \{1, 2, 3\}$ such that $y_1 \oplus y_2 \oplus y_3 = \phi(x)$.

Verifiable Encryption. Verifiable encryption aims at convincing a verifier that an encrypted data satisfies some properties without leaking any information about the data itself. In such 2-party protocol, a prover and a verifier share in a common input string a public key encryption scheme Enc, a public key pk for Enc, and a public value y. At the end, the verifier either accepts and obtains the encryption of a secret value x under pk such that x and y verify some relation $\mathcal{R}$ or rejects. It is worth noticing that the prover does not need the secret key sk, that usually belongs to a third party. Verifiable encryption often appears in the domain of anonymous credentials, fair exchange signatures, or verifiable secret sharing [40]. In [13], Camenish and Damgård describe how to provide a proof that an encrypted value is a valid signature, using any semantically secure encryption scheme. The idea is to take advantage of the $\varSigma$-protocol for a relation $\mathcal{R}(r, y)$, to prove that an encrypted value is the witness x for this relation. In our application, we need to prove that the data that is encrypted, x, is the one that is linked by a Pedersen commitment $C_x = y$. As a Pedersen commitment comes with an associated $\varSigma$-protocol, the Camenish-Damgård scheme applies naturally. There are interesting ways towards more efficient schemes, *e.g.* [20] or [16]. However, the main benefit of the Camenish-Damgård solution is that we can still use the encryption scheme required in MLS specification. We denote by $\mathsf{VerifEnc_{Enc,}}_{pk}(m : r)$ the encryption of a message m (using randomness r) under the public key pk with the encryption scheme Enc and the associated proof. We omit the randomness r when it is not necessary to explicitly mention it.

3   MLS Updates

We explain how the MLS update mechanism works and our more secure solution.

3.1   Message Layer Security

MLS is a protocol currently under development by the IETF to provide an End-to-End secure group messaging application. The idea is to enable a group of users to share a common secret that can be updated regularly by any member. One of the open issues in the IETF draft is that the validity of an update message can only be checked *after* it has been received. This open issue is clearly identified in the current draft 11 ([7], Sect. 15.5). However, to our knowledge, there is still no solution to this problem. Currently in MLS, the authors require an hybrid public key encryption (HPKE) scheme, as designed in [8], composed of a key encapsulation mechanism (KEM) to transmit a symmetric key k and an AEAD encryption scheme that encrypts the data under k, as well as a key derivation function. In the rest of this work, we denote by $\mathsf{Enc}_{pk}(m : r)$ the HPKE encryption of a message m under the public key pk using randomness r.

The asymmetric part of Enc is based on an elliptic curve E defined on a finite field $\mathbb{Z}/p\mathbb{Z}$ with base point P of order a prime q. MLS also supposes the existence of a broadcast channel for each group, which distributes the messages to each group member, conserving the order.

TreeKem. MLS key exchange TreeKem is based on a binary tree structure (Fig. 1) where users correspond to leaves and each node is associated to a secret value. Each user U has a long term identity signing key and an initial key package for the encryption scheme Enc (both certified by a PKI). We will simply represent the key package as a public/private key pair (pk_U, sk_U).

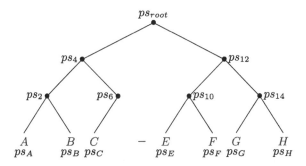

Fig. 1. A view of the MLS tree. Nodes are implicitly numbered from left to right, independently from their height. Leaves are associated to a user represented as a letter. Each node i has a secret ps_i. A leaf secret is indexed with its user name.

The group key is derived from the root secret. Each child node knows the secret of each of its ancestors and only of its ancestors. To each node i corresponds a path secret ps_i and a secret and public key $sk_i, pk_i = \mathsf{deriveKeyPair}(ps_i)$ (in the original protocol the keys are derived from an intermediate node secret ns_i itself derived from ps_i. We present a lighter version for the simplicity of the exposure but the complete version is compatible with our solution.)

The derivation depends on the elliptic curve (see Appendix A). We define, w.l.o.g, $(sk_i, pk_i) = \mathsf{deriveKeyPair}(ps_i) = (\mathsf{deriveSK}(ps_i), \mathsf{deriveSK}(ps_i)P)$ where deriveSK is a PRF. A user knows the secrets ps_i and sk_i in his direct path, composed of himself and his direct ancestors. Moreover, each user keeps an up-to-date global view of the tree, as a hash value of each node's public information.

Updates. To update the tree, a user B generates a new secret ps'_B. The path secrets in the direct path will be successively derived from ps'_B. We note $\mathsf{H}_p(ps_i)$ for the function $\mathsf{HKDF} - \mathsf{expand}(ps_i, \text{``path''}, \text{``''}, Hash.length)$. The update mechanism is given in Fig. 2. When B updates its secret $ps_B \to ps'_B$, he first computes the new node data for each node on his path:

- $ps'_2 = \mathsf{H}_p(ps'_B)$, $pk_2 = \mathsf{deriveSK}(ps'_2) \cdot P$
- $ps'_4 = \mathsf{H}_p(ps'_2)$, $pk_4 = \mathsf{deriveSK}(ps'4) \cdot P$
- $ps'_{root} = \mathsf{H}_p(ps'_4)$, $pk_{root} = \mathsf{deriveSK}(ps'_{root}) \cdot P$

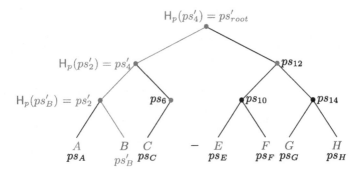

Fig. 2. Update process. User B updates its secrets. Path secrets are updated along its direct path (in red). The update secrets are sent to its copath nodes (in green). (Color figure online)

Then he sends for each node on its copath the necessary secret material for the users under this node to perform the same update. Following our example in Fig. 2, B has to send ps_2' to A, ps_4' to nodes C and 6 and ps_{root}' to nodes $E, 10, F, 12, G, 14, H$. As a child knows the secret key sk_i for each of its ancestors, B will only have to encrypt ps_2' under pk_A, ps_4' under pk_6 and ps_{root}' under pk_{12}.

From ps_2' (respectively ps_4'), A (resp. C) shall be able to compute the root secret. From this root secret is derived an epoch secret S_{E+1}. Before sending his Commit, B computes S_{E+1} and uses it to produce a confirmation key. This value shall enable A and C to check that they have derived the correct root secret and so, that they received a correct update. Other mechanisms such as the transmission of the updated view of the tree, or of intermediate hash values are provided for a user to check that he received a correct update. All those mechanisms enable a verification after receiving the update information.

Hence, either the update is adopted only once some members have confirmed that they received a valid update - at least one member in the subtree of each node in the update copath, as recommended in draft 11. This can imply a huge latency, if some users are seldom online, and non valid updates can lead to a denial of service. Or the update is validated without feedback and the users that received non valid secret values are ejected from the group *de facto*. In both case, this seriously hampers with the security of the service provided by the protocol.

3.2   Securing MLS Updates

We now explain how to combine a ZK protocol and a verifiable encryption to secure the update process in MLS. We first focus on a single step of the update process (a user updates his direct parent) and then explain how this solution can be extended to the global tree.

Server-Checking in MLS. As described in Fig. 2, let assume that B generates a new secret ps_B' and computes:

- deriveKeyPair(ps'_B) to obtain a new key package and $C_B = \mathsf{Com}(ps_{B'}, r_{B'})$;
- $ps'_2 = \mathsf{H}_p(ps'_B)$ the new secret for node 2 and $C_2 = \mathsf{Com}(\mathsf{H}_p(ps'_B), r_2)$;
- $(sk'_2, pk'_2) = \mathsf{deriveKeyPair}(ps'_2)$ the new keys for node 2 and the corresponding $C_{sk'_2} = \mathsf{Com}(\mathsf{deriveSK}(\mathsf{H}_p(ps'_B)), r_{sk'_2})$.

Suppose there exists a ZK protocol which, given public values C_x and C_y, provides the following proof: $\mathsf{PK}\{x, r_x, r_y : C_x = \mathsf{Com}(x, r_x) \wedge C_y = \mathsf{Com}(f(x), r_y)\}$ for any PRF f. Then B can send to the server the public values C_B, C_2, $C_{sk'_2}$, pk'_2 together with a proof $\Pi_2 = \mathsf{PK}\{ps'_B, r_{B'}, r_2, r_{sk'_2} : C_B = \mathsf{Com}(ps'_B, r_{B'}) \wedge C_2 = \mathsf{Com}(\mathsf{H}_p(ps'_B), r_2) \wedge C_{sk'_2} = \mathsf{Com}(\mathsf{deriveSK}(\mathsf{H}_p(ps'_B)), r_{sk'_2}) \wedge pk'_2 = \mathsf{deriveSK}(ps'_2)P\}$ (the last part of the proof being a classic discrete log proof).

On another side, verifiable encryption (detailed in Sect. 2) allows to link the message encrypted with $\mathsf{VerifEnc}$ with the data committed in C_2. To sum up, B will send for a node update, the public values C_B, C_2, $C_{sk'_2}$, and pk'_2, the proof Π_2 together with $\mathsf{VerifEnc}_{\mathsf{Enc}, pk_A}(ps'_2)$. If the server accepts the proof, then he transmits the public key pk'_2 as well as $\mathsf{VerifEnc}_{\mathsf{Enc}, pk_A}(ps'_2)$ to A.

To extend the proof to the complete tree, one has to repeat the above steps for each level. To certify the update value ps'_4 corresponding to the parent node 4, B will send the server values C_4, $C_{sk'_4}$, pk'_4, the proof $\Pi_4 = PK\{ps'_2, r_2, r_4, r_{sk'_4} : C_2 = \mathsf{Com}((ps'_2), r_2) \wedge C_4 = \mathsf{Com}(\mathsf{H}_p(ps'_2), r_4) \wedge C_{sk_4} = \mathsf{Com}(\mathsf{deriveSK}(\mathsf{H}_p(ps'_2)), r_{sk'_4}) \wedge pk'_4 = \mathsf{deriveSK}(\mathsf{H}_p(ps'_2))P\}$ together with $\mathsf{VerifEnc}_{\mathsf{Enc}, pk_6}(ps'_4)$. The crucial point is that, as the commitment C_2 is linked with ps'_B in Π_2, it can be used as a base value for Π_4 and so on. Some special care must be taken as we commit, in a group of order q prime, to an element $sk \in \{0,1\}^{256}$ that does not lie naturally in $\mathbb{Z}/q\mathbb{Z}$. We explain how to handle with this in Appendix A.

About the Server. Several reasons appear for calling on a third party. Firstly, this central node with the largest computational power is the one that can discard invalid updates with the most efficiency. If one relies on users to check for the validity of the data they received, this means that one must wait for each user to process the update and to send back an acknowledgement. As a user can be off-line for a long time, this can be very inefficient. Another solution would be to allow users to adopt the update as soon as they are individually convinced it is correct, while providing a "backup solution". This would probably imply keeping old keys and drastically impoverish FS.

Secondly, in MLS architecture, all the update encrypted messages are gathered and sent as one big message to all the users. It may be of interest to think of a solution where only the needed encryption is sent to a specific user. In this case, only the server will see all the messages together. He is then the only one able to perform a verification on a global proof to see whether all the updates are correctly generated from a single secret seed.

4   ZK for a PRF on Committed Input and Output

In this section, we provide two protocols to prove the knowledge of an input x and randoms r_x, r_y, such that, for a public values C_x, C_y, and a function f

evaluated as a circuit, $C_x = \mathsf{Com}(x, r_x)$ and $C_y = \mathsf{Com}(f(x), r_y)$. Recall that efficient ZK proofs for a function evaluation are operated on a circuit, whereas efficient commitments are algebraic. Consequently, we want to achieve the best of both worlds by combining a proof on a circuit and algebraic commitments.

Our first solution, ComInOutZK (Committed Input and Output ZK) is directly inspired from [6], which provides a proof of a circuit evaluation on a committed input and public output. We extend their work to a committed output.

Our second solution, CopraZK (Commitment and PRF alternative ZK), requires some specific properties on the function f. We consider the circuit that computes $f(x, m) + \alpha x$ where x is the key of the PRF and α is determined by the commitment values. Calling some PRF-related properties, and the homomorphic properties of the commitment, we show that the values committed in C_x and C_y must be those that appear in the circuit evaluation.

We compare in Table 1 our two solutions with the SNARK based solution of [1]. CopraZK adds a negligible number of algebraic operations. The prover performs 4 multiplications on the curve (public key operations) and 8 computations in $\mathbb{Z}/q\mathbb{Z}$ (symmetric operations). For the verifier, 6 computations on the curve and 2 ln $\mathbb{Z}/q\mathbb{Z}$ are needed. Considering ZKBoo, the prover effort is $\mathcal{O}(\sigma|F|)$ symmetric operations, where $|F|$ is the number of AND gates of the circuit and σ the number of rounds. Our solution requires $\mathcal{O}(\sigma(|F| + |mod|)) + 8$ symmetric operations and 4 public key operations, where $|mod|$ is the size of the circuit for a modular addition which is negligible compared to $|F|$. The computational cost is dominated by the symmetric part and finally, our solution requires on the prover side ($\mathcal{O}(\sigma|F|)$ symmetric operations. The size of the proof and the work on the verifier's side are also dominated by the circuit part. One inconvenient is that the security proof requires non usual hypothesis on the function f.

On the opposite side, ComInOutZK is valid for any circuit, only requires equivocality of the commitment scheme, which is a common hypothesis, and leaves the circuit evaluation untouched. But it requires a non negligible number of algebraic commitments. Considering $|x|$ (respectively $|y|$) the bit size of the input (of the output), we obtain on the prover side $\mathcal{O}(|x| + |y| + 2\sigma)$ public key operations and $\mathcal{O}(\sigma|F|)$ symmetric operations. The verifier's work is equivalent. The proof size of ZKBoo is augmented with $\mathcal{O}(|x| + |y| + 6\sigma)$ curve points which is asymptotically $\mathcal{O}((|x| + |y| + \lambda)\lambda)$ as σ augments with λ.

On the Challenge Size. When we expose our solutions, in both case we mention a unique challenge, that is used for the algebraic Σ-protocol and for the ZKBoo proof. This means that the challenge space size for the Σ-protocol is 3 and that we shall perform $\lambda/3$ rounds to obtain a soundness error in $2^{-\lambda}$. The Σ-protocol can benefit from a larger challenge space, that allows for a single round. As explained in [6], it is possible to define distinct challenges $e_\rho \in \{1, 2, 3\}$ for each ZKBoo round and a global challenge $e = \sum_{i=1}^{\sigma} 3^i e_i$ for the algebraic Σ-protocols, hence the algebraic part of the proof can be performed a single time.

Table 1. Efficiency of the different solutions for circuit proof on committed input and output. *pub* stands for the cost of a public key operation (multiplication on the curve), while *sym* stands for the cost of a symmetric operation. $|F|$ is the circuit size, $|x|$ the input size and $|y|$ the output size. In most applications, $|F| \gg (|x|, |y|, \lambda)$.

	Non inter- active	No CRS	Prover's work	Verifier's work	Proof size
SNARK based [1]	Yes	No	$\mathcal{O}((|F| + \lambda) \cdot pub)$	$\mathcal{O}((|x| + |y| + \lambda) \cdot pub)$	λ
CopraZK	Yes	Yes	$\mathcal{O}(|F|\lambda \cdot sym)$	$\mathcal{O}(|F|\lambda \cdot sym)$	$\mathcal{O}(|F|\lambda)$
ComInOutZK	Yes	Yes	$\mathcal{O}(|F|\lambda \cdot sym + (|x| + |y| + \lambda) \cdot pub)$	$\mathcal{O}(|F|\lambda \cdot sym + (|x| + |y| + \lambda) \cdot pub)$	$\mathcal{O}((|F| + |x| + |y| + \lambda)\lambda)$

4.1 ComInOutZK: A Bit-Wise Solution

In [6], the authors propose a non interactive proof $PK\{x : C_x = Com(x, r_x) \wedge y = f(x)\}$ based on bit commitments and ZKBoo++. Their optimized solution increases the ZKBoo++ prover's and verifier's work with $\mathcal{O}(|x| + \sigma)$ exponentiations and multiplications on the group $\mathbb{G}$ of order q chosen for the commitment, where $|x|$ is the number of bits of the input x and σ is the number of rounds in ZKBoo++. The proof size grows by $\mathcal{O}(|x| + \sigma)$ group elements and $\mathcal{O}(|x| + \sigma)$ elements in $\mathbb{Z}/q\mathbb{Z}$. We adapt this strategy in the case of a committed output. As the output of the circuit, y, shall remain secret, we will not be able to call ZKBoo++ as a full black box. This is of prime importance when we prove the zero-knowledge property.

The work of Backes *et al.* and our extension rely on a result given by the homomorphic property of a commitment scheme such as Pedersen scheme. For any scalar k, and any two commitments $Com(x, r_x)$, $Com(y, r_y)$, $k \cdot Com(x, r_x) + Com(y, r_y) = Com(kx + y, kr_x + r_y)$. For any commitment $C_b = Com(b, r_b)$ to a secret bit b and any public bit β, one can easily compute the commitment of $b \oplus \beta$ as follows: if $\beta = 0$, $C_{b \oplus \beta} = C_b$ and if $\beta = 1$ then $C_{b \oplus \beta} = Com(1, 0) - C_b = Com(1 - b, -r_b)$. For any $x = \sum_{i=0}^{|x|-1} 2^i x[i]$, denote $C_{x[i]} = Com(x[i], r_{x[i]})$ a commitment to the i-th bit of x. Then $\sum_{i=0}^{|x|-1} 2^i C_{x[i]}$ is a valid commitment to x with opening randomness $\sum_{i=0}^{|x|-1} 2^i r_{x[i]}$. And one can easily compute a commitment to $x \oplus \beta$ for an element β as $C_{x \oplus \beta} = \sum_{i=0}^{|x|-1} 2^i C_{x[i] \oplus \beta[i]}$, with opening randomness $\sum_{i=0}^{|x|-1} 2^i (-1)^{\beta[i]} r_{x[i]}$.

We describe in Fig. 3 the protocol on committed output only (ComOutZK), for readability reasons. Combining Backes *et al.* protocol for committed input and ours for committed output leads to ComInOutZK.

Let f be a function: $\mathbb{Z}_2^\ell \rightarrow \mathbb{Z}_2^\ell$, $\mathbb{G}$ be a group of prime order q, such that $2^\ell \leq p$. There is a natural embedding $\mathbb{Z}_2^\ell \hookrightarrow \mathbb{G}$. Let P be a generator for this

The *Prover* knows x, $y = f(x)$, and r_y such that $C_y = \mathsf{Com}(f(x), r_y)$. The *Verifier* knows the statement C_y.

Prover

Commit phase

1. samples random $r_{y[j]}$ and commits to the bits of y : $C_{y[j]} = \mathsf{Com}(y[j], r_{y[j]})$ for $j \in [0, |y|]$.
2. computes the commit phase a_{Π_j} for the proofs $\Pi_j = PK\{y[j], r_{y[j]} : C_{y[j]} = \mathsf{Com}(y[j], r_{y[j]}) \wedge y[j] \in \{0, 1\}\}$ for $j \in [0, |y|]$.

for $\rho \in [1, \sigma]$:

3. samples random seeds k_1^ρ, k_2^ρ, k_3^ρ.
4. generates the shares $x_1^\rho, x_2^\rho, x_3^\rho = \mathsf{Share}(x, k_1^\rho, k_2^\rho)$ such that $x = x_1^\rho \oplus x_2^\rho \oplus x_3^\rho$.
5. simulates the MPC to obtain three views $w_1^\rho, w_2^\rho, w_3^\rho$.
6. evaluates $y_i^\rho = \mathsf{Output}(w_i^\rho)$, $i \in \{1, 2, 3\}$.
7. commits to the views : $c_i^\rho = h(w_i^\rho, k_i^\rho)$, $i \in \{1, 2, 3\}$.
8. samples random $r_{y_i^\rho}$ and commits to the outputs : $C_{y_i^\rho} = \mathsf{Com}(y_i^\rho, r_{y_i^\rho})$, $i \in \{1, 2, 3\}$.

$a = ((C_{y_1^\rho}, C_{y_2^\rho}, C_{y_3^\rho}, c_1^\rho, c_2^\rho, c_3^\rho)_\sigma, (C_{y[j]})_{|y|}, (a_{\Pi_j})_{|y|})$

Challenge : $c = h(a)$

Response phase

1. computes the responses z_{Π_j} for the proofs Π_j

for $\rho \in [1, \sigma]$:

2. $b^\rho = (C_{y_{e+2}^\rho}, c_{e+2}^\rho)$
3. $z^\rho = (w_{e+1}^\rho, k_e^\rho, k_{e+1}^\rho, r_{y_e^\rho}, r_{y_{e+1}^\rho})$
4. $\beta^\rho = y_e^\rho \oplus y_{e+1}^\rho$
5. $C_z^\rho = \sum_{i=0}^{|y|-1} 2^i C_{y[i] \oplus \beta^\rho[i]}$
6. $r_z^\rho = r_{y_{e+2}^\rho} - \sum_{i=0}^{|y|-1} 2^i (-1)^{\beta[i]} r_{y[i]}$

return $p = (e, (b^\rho, z^\rho, r_z^\rho)_\rho), (z_{\Pi_j})_j$

....

Verifier(a, p)

1. Parses p as e, $(b^\rho, z^\rho, r_z^\rho)_\sigma$
2. Parses a as $(C_{y_1^\rho}, C_{y_2^\rho}, C_{y_3^\rho}, c_1^\rho, c_2^\rho, c_3^\rho)_\sigma, (C_{y[j]})_{|y|}, a_{\Pi_j})$
3. Reconstructs the proof Π_j (computes a_Π from $(z_{\Pi_j})_j$)
4. Rejects if $C_y \neq \sum_{i=0}^{|y|-1} 2^i C_{y[i]}$

for $\rho \in [1, \sigma]$:

5. runs the MPC protocol to reconstruct w_e^ρ from $w_{e+1}^\rho, k_e^\rho, k_{e+1}^\rho$
6. obtains $y_e^\rho = \mathsf{Output}(w_e)$, $y_{e+1}^\rho = \mathsf{Output}(w_{e+1})$
7. Computes $\beta^\rho = y_e \oplus y_{e+1}$
8. Computes $C_z^\rho = \sum_{i=0}^{|y|} 2^i C_{y[i] \oplus \beta^\rho[i]}$
9. Rejects if $C_{y_{e+2}^\rho} \neq \mathsf{Com}(0, r_z) + C_z^\rho$

Reconstructs a and reject if $e \neq h(a)$

Fig. 3. The ComOutZK protocol. Combining this protocol with the same mechanism on the input given in [6] leads to ComInOutZK. The reconstruct step of the verification consists in computing the commitment a from the response data and check its validity with the challenge. Only the values in a that can not be reconstructed need being sent.

group and Q an element of $\mathbb{G}$ such that $\log_P(Q)$ is unknown. We consider a hash function $\mathsf{h} : \mathbb{Z}_2^* \to \mathbb{Z}_2^{\ell*}$ and Com be the Pedersen commitment scheme.

The Theorem 1 states the security of our bitwise solution.

Theorem 1. *Given that ZKBoo and the Π_j are Σ protocols with 3-special soundness and honest verifier Zero Knowledge property, and Com is a homomorphic and equivocal commitment scheme, then the protocol described in Fig. 3 is a Σ-protocol with 3-special soundness and honest verifier property.*

Proof of the Security of $\mathsf{ComInOutZK}$. We study separately the three properties a Σ-protocol should verify.

Correctness. Assuming the *Prover* and the *Verifier* execute the protocol as described, the *Verifier* never meets a rejection cause and then always accepts.

Soundness. Consider an algorithm $\mathcal{E}xt$ that has access to three distinct accepting executions of the protocol on the same commit phase: (a, e_1, p_1), (a, e_2, p_2), and (a, e_3, p_3), $e_1 \neq e_2 \neq e_3$, for a public statement C_y. We show that $\mathcal{E}xt$ can exhibit a witness (x^*, r^*) such that $C_y = \mathsf{Com}(f(x^*), r^*)$. We can not directly call the Extractor from ZKBoo++ as we do not exactly execute ZKBoo. In our protocol, the *Verifier* does not have access to the output of the circuit. However, we show that this difference does not prevent $\mathcal{E}xt$ from succeeding. We describe in the following how $\mathcal{E}xt$ works.

Firstly, from the distinct transcripts $\mathcal{E}xt$ can obtain three pairs of shares $x_{e_1}, x_{e_1+1}, x_{e_2}, x_{e_2+1}, x_{e_3}, x_{e_3+1}$. He also gets three pairs of output values $y_{e_1}, y_{e_1+1}, y_{e_2}, y_{e_2+1}, y_{e_3}, y_{e_3+1}$ and the corresponding randomness $r_{y_{e_1}}, r_{y_{e_1+1}}, r_{y_{e_2}}, r_{y_{e_2+1}}, r_{y_{e_3}}, r_{y_{e_3+1}}$. From the common commitment a, $\mathcal{E}xt$ gets $C_{y_1}, C_{y_2}, C_{y_3}$. As the three transcripts are accepting, $\mathcal{E}xt$ knows that (considering, w.l.o.g., $e_1 = 1, e_2 = 2, e_3 = 3$):

$$C_{y_1} = \mathsf{Com}(y_{e_1}, r_{y_{e_1}}) = \mathsf{Com}(y_{e_3+1}, r_{y_{e_3}+1}).$$
$$C_{y_2} = \mathsf{Com}(y_{e_2}, r_{y_{e_2}}) = \mathsf{Com}(y_{e_1+1}, r_{y_{e_1}+1}).$$
$$C_{y_3} = \mathsf{Com}(y_{e_3}, r_{y_{e_3}}) = \mathsf{Com}(y_{e_2+1}, r_{y_{e_2}+1}).$$

Then, if one of this equality verifies with different openings, then, due to the equivocability of the commitment scheme, $\mathcal{E}xt$ can extract the trapdoor. Then he can consider any value $\tilde{x}$, compute $\tilde{y} = f(\tilde{x})$ and compute the appropriate randomness to open C_y to $\tilde{y}$.

Now we consider the case when the equalities on the commitments traduce equalities of the openings. $\mathcal{E}xt$ thus obtains three values $y_1 = y_{e_1} = y_{e_3+1}$, $y_2 = y_{e_2} = y_{e_1+1}$, $y_3 = y_{e_3} = y_{e_2+1}$ and a single $y^* = y_1 \oplus y_2 \oplus y_3$. From then, as in the original ZKBoo proof he can execute back the MPC protocol and obtain three shares $x_1 = x_{e_1} = x_{e_3+1}$, $x_2 = x_{e_2} = x_{e_1+1}$, $x_3 = x_{e_3} = x_{e_2+1}$ and a single $x^* = x_1 \oplus x_2 \oplus x_3$ such that $y^* = f(x^*)$.

Now $\mathcal{E}xt$ needs to extract a randomness r^* that opens C_y to y^*. Using as a subroutine the extractors for the proofs Π_j, $\mathcal{E}xt$ obtains couples $(y'[j], r_{y'[j]})$ for $j \in [0, |y| - 1]$. From the protocol, as the transcripts are accepting ones,

$\mathcal{E}xt$ knows that $C_y = \sum_{i=0}^{|y'|-1} 2^i \mathsf{Com}(y'[i], r_{y'[i]})$. $\mathcal{E}xt$ selects one transcript, for instance e_1. He computes $\beta = y_{e_1} \oplus y_{e_1+1}$ and $C_z = \sum_{i=0}^{|y'|-1} 2^i C_{y'[i] \oplus \beta[i]} = \sum_{i=0}^{|y'|-1} 2^i \mathsf{Com}(y'[i] \oplus \beta[i], (-1)^{\beta[i]} r_{y'[i]})$. By the protocol, $C_z = C_{y_{e_1+2}} - \mathsf{Com}(0, r_z)$. If $\sum_{i=0}^{|y'|-1} 2^i (y'[i] \oplus \beta[i]) \neq y_{e_1+2}$ and/or $\sum_{i=0}^{|y'|-1} 2^i (-1)^{\beta[i]} r_{y'[i]} \neq r_{y_{e_1+2}} - r_z$, then again, $\mathcal{E}xt$ obtains the trapdoor of the commitment scheme and can open C_y to the value he wishes. Otherwise $\sum_{i=0}^{|y'|-1} 2^i (y'[i] \oplus \beta[i]) = y_{e_1+2}$ and $\sum_{i=0}^{|y'|-1} 2^i (y'[i]) = y_{e_1+2} \oplus \beta = y_{e_1+2} \oplus y_{e_1} \oplus y_{e_1+1} = f(x^*)$. Finally, $\sum_{i=0}^{|y'|-1} 2^i r_{y'[i]}$ opens C_y to $f(x^*)$ and the extractor is done. The running time of the extractor is bounded by the time of running back the MPC protocol (as for the ZKBoo extractor) + the running time of the extractors $\mathcal{E}xt_{\Pi_j}$ + computing one XOR and one commitment. Considering that an extractor for ZKBoo and the extractor for the proofs Π_j run in polynomial time, $\mathcal{E}xt$ also runs in polynomial time.

Zero-Knowledge. We consider a simulator $\mathcal{S}im$ that, on input a public statement C_y, shall produce a transcript (a, e, p). As for the soundness, we cannot call directly the ZKBoo simulator, $\mathcal{S}im_{ZKB}$, as the output of the circuit is not part of the statement. $\mathcal{S}im$ runs as follows: he sets e and he samples random tapes k_e, k_{e+1} and random input shares x_e, x_{e+1}. Then he runs the protocol as normal except that, when he meets a binary multiplication gate in the circuit, he cannot compute the real value of the view w_{e+1} (because it would depend on the third view that he cannot compute because he does not know x) so he samples it at random. This is indistinguishable form the real execution as binary multiplication gates are, in a correct execution, randomized with an element from k_{e+2} that the *Verifier* cannot compute. $\mathcal{S}im$ obtains output values y_e, y_{e+1}. He samples random r_e, r_{e+1}, computes $C_{y_e} = \mathsf{Com}(y_e, r_e)$ and $C_{y_{e+1}} = \mathsf{Com}(y_{e+1}, r_{e+1})$.

In a second step, he samples random $|y| - 1$ bit values $y[j], j \in [1, |y| - 1]$ and associated randomness $r_y[j]$ and computes $C_{y[j]} = \mathsf{Com}(y[j], r[j])$. He executes the proofs Π_j with challenge e. Then he evaluates $C_y[0] = C_y - \sum_{j=1}^{|y|-1} C_{y[j]}$. Using the simulator for the proof Π_0, $\mathcal{S}im$ obtains a transcript for Π_0 for a challenge e'. If $e' \neq e$ he runs $\mathcal{S}im_{\Pi_0}$ again. Given that Π_0 is honest verifier, there is a non negligible probability that $e' = e$ within a polynomial time. Defining $\beta = y_e \oplus y_{e+1}$, $\mathcal{S}im$ can compute $C_{y[i] \oplus \beta[i]}$ only from the knowledge of $C_{y[i]}$ and $\beta[i]$. Now $\mathcal{S}im$ samples $r_z \in \mathbb{Z}_p$ and computes $C_{y_{e+2}} = \sum_{j=0}^{|y|-1} C_{y[i] \oplus \beta[i]} + \mathsf{Com}(0, r_z)$. He now has all the elements to produce an accepting transcript.

The transcript of the ZKBoo part of the proof is indistinguishable form a real execution. The elements that $\mathcal{S}im$ produces itself are commitments that will not be opened, hence, by the hiding property of the commitment, the complete simulated transcript is indistinguishable form a real execution of the protocol.

4.2   A Second Solution: CopraZK

Let us denote by $\mathsf{Func}(\mathcal{D}, \mathcal{R})$ the set of all functions from $\mathcal{D}$ to $\mathcal{R}$ and by $\mathsf{FF}(\mathcal{K}, \mathcal{D}, \mathcal{R})$ the set of all function families with parameter (key) in $\mathcal{K}$, domain $\mathcal{D}$ and range $\mathcal{R}$. We write $f : \mathcal{K} \times \mathcal{D} \to \mathcal{R}$ for a function family in $\mathsf{FF}(\mathcal{K}, \mathcal{D}, \mathcal{R})$ (and

Let C_y, C_x be public commitments and m a public message. The *Prover* wants to convince the *Verifier* that he knows x, r_x, r_y such that $C_x = \mathsf{Com}(x, r_x)$ and $C_y = \mathsf{Com}(f(x, m), r_y)$.

Prover

Commit phase:
1. computes $\alpha = \mathsf{h}(C_x \| C_y)$.
2. computes $t = f(x, m) + \alpha x \mod q$.
3. Evaluates the commit phase output a_Π for the Σ protocol $\Pi = PK\{x, r_x, y, r_y : C_x = xP + r_x Q \wedge C_y = yP + r_y Q \wedge t = y + \alpha x\}$

for $\rho \in [1, \sigma]$ (ZKBoo part):
4. samples random tapes $k_1^\rho, k_2^\rho, k_3^\rho$.
5. generates the shares $x_1^\rho, x_2^\rho, x_3^\rho = \mathsf{Share}(x, k_1^\rho, k_2^\rho)$ such that $x = x_1^\rho \oplus x_2^\rho \oplus x_3^\rho$.
6. evaluates the MPC protocol on the circuit Circ that, on entrance values entry (x, a), evaluates $t = f(x, m) + \alpha x \mod q$ and obtains three views $w_1^\rho, w_2^\rho, w_3^\rho$.
7. obtains the output shares : $o_1^\rho = t_1, o_2^\rho = t_2, o_3^\rho = t_3$ such that $t = t_1^\rho \oplus t_2^\rho \oplus t_3^\rho$.
8. commits to the views : $c_1^\rho = \mathsf{h}(w_1^\rho, k_1^\rho), c_2^\rho = \mathsf{h}(w_2^\rho, k_2^\rho), c_3^\rho = \mathsf{h}(w_3^\rho, k_3^\rho)$.

$a = t, (c_1^\rho, c_2^\rho, c_3^\rho, o^\rho = (o_1^\rho, o_2^\rho, o_3^\rho))_\rho, a_\Pi$.

Challenge: $e = \mathsf{h}(a)$

Response phase:
1. computes the response z_Π for the proof Π

for $\rho \in [1, \sigma]$:
2. $b^\rho = (o_{e+2}^\rho = t_{e+2}, c_{e+2}^\rho)$
3. $z^\rho = (w_{e+1}^\rho, k_e^\rho, k_{e+1}^\rho)$

returns $p = (e, (b^\rho, z^\rho)_\rho, z_\Pi)$

. . . .

Verifier(a, p)
1. parses p as $e, (b^\rho, z^\rho)_\rho, z_\Pi$
2. parses a as $t, (c_1^\rho, c_2^\rho, c_3^\rho, o^\rho = (o_1^\rho, o_2^\rho, o_3^\rho))_\rho, a_\Pi$
3. computes α
4. reconstruct the proof Π

for $\rho \in [1, \sigma]$ (Verifying the ZKBoo proof):
5. runs the MPC protocol to reconstruct w_e^ρ from $w_{e+1}^\rho, k_e^\rho, k_{e+1}^\rho$
6. obtains $t_e^\rho = \mathsf{Output}(w_e), t_{e+1}^\rho = \mathsf{Output}(w_{e+1})$
7. computes $t_{e+2}^\rho = t \oplus t_e^\rho \oplus t_{e+1}^\rho$.

reconstructs a and rejects if $e \neq \mathsf{h}(a)$

Fig. 4. Our protocol `CopraZK`.

call it a function, by ease of language). Let f be a function: $\mathbb{Z}_2^\ell \times \mathbb{Z}_2^* \to \mathbb{Z}_2^\ell$ and m a public input, $m \in \mathbb{Z}_2^*$. Let $\mathbb{G}$ be a group of prime order q, such that $2^\ell \leq q$. Let P be a generator for this group and Q an element of $\mathbb{G}$ such that $\log_P(Q)$ is unknown. Let h be a hash function $\mathbb{Z}_2^* \to \mathbb{Z}_2^{\ell*}$ and Com be the Pedersen commitment scheme. They are the public parameters of the protocol.

Let C_x, C_y be public commitments, known to the verifier. The main idea is to consider the circuit that computes the tag $t = f(x, m) + \alpha x$ where α is a public coefficient derived from the commitment values C_x and C_y. A MPC in the head proof on this circuit ensures that t is correctly computed from a secret value x known to the prover. Considering Pedersen commitments, we complete the circuit proof with an algebraic proof that the committed values in C_x and C_y verify the relation t. This linear relation plus the properties of f defined below, bind the values of C_x and C_y such that the verifier can be convinced that the value committed in C_y is equal to the evaluation of f on the value committed in C_x. A complete description is given in Fig. 4. We depict our protocol using ZKBoo for the circuit part, but the proof adapts to any circuit based ZK proof.

Theorem 2 states the security of CopraZK, that is settled on two properties of the family f. The correlation intractability [15] of its dual function $\tilde{f}$ (when the role of the input and the key are switched) and a glider-PRF (general linear input deviation resistant PRF) security that states that an adversary gains no knowledge on x when given $f(x, m) + \alpha x$. We provide more information on those properties and a sketch of proof in Appendix B.

Theorem 2. *Given that ZKBoo and the Π_j are Σ protocols with 3 (respectively 2) special soundness and honest verifier Zero Knowledge property (in their interactive form), that Com is a homomorphic commitment scheme, and that f is a glider-PRF function family such that $\tilde{f}$ is correlation intractable relatively to relations $\{R_{a,b} : \{x, y : y = ax + b\}\}$, then the protocol described in Fig. 4 is a Σ-protocol with 3-special soundness and full Zero-Knowledge.*

5   Conclusion

In this work we provide a concrete solution to a practical problem that appears in the MLS specification. We describe how existing cryptographic tools such as ZK proofs and verifiable encryption can be combined to secure the update process. As the regular update of the group secret is the key to obtain the FS and PCS properties, we think our solution may be of interest.

Additionally, we propose two protocols to obtain ZK proofs on circuit with committed input and output, such that our improvement proposal for MLS is settled on protocols as efficient as possible. Hence, an interesting way for future work is in the optimization of the verifiable encryption. The CL framework, introduced by Castagnos and Laguillaumie in [17] and enriched with Zero-Knowledge properties in [16], that considers a cyclic group $\mathbb{G}$ where the DDH assumption holds together with a subgroup F of $\mathbb{G}$ where the discrete logarithm problem is easy, may provide novel and efficient solutions.

A   Key Size and Group Orders in MLS Updates

In [7], several suitable cipher suites are described. We focus on one of them for a practical example, for a 128-bit security level. This suite uses X25519 for ECDH computation and SHA256 as a hash function (and base function for HKDF implementation). Following [24], the private key sk is obtained from a 256-bit string of secure random data $(sk[0], sk[1], \ldots, sk[255])$ by applying the following transform: $sk[0]\& = 248$, $sk[31]\& = 127$ and $sk[31]| = 64$. One obtains, when interpreted as an integer value in little endian, a scalar of the form $2^{254} + 8 \cdot \ell, \ell \in [\![0; 2^{251} - 1]\!]$. We design by deriveSK the application of SHA256 followed by the above transformation such that for any 32-byte sequence of random data X, deriveSK(X) is a valid secret key for X25519. This encoding can be integrated in the circuit computing the last derivation. The public key is obtained by multiplying the secret key by the base point of the curve: given a 32-byte secret X, DeriveKeyPair$(X) = ($deriveSK$(X),$ deriveSK$(X)P)$. We adopt this notation independently from the curve targeted.

Group Order and Commitments. In our proofs, we consider commitments and discrete logarithm proofs in cyclic groups of order q, and circuits input and output that naturally lie in F_q. This may not be the case. Considering X25519 key derivation derived above, a new user's secret ps'_B is a random element in $\{0, 1\}^{256}$, which, when interpreted as an integer, can be larger than q. As explained in [6], it is possible to consider $ps'_B \mod q$ for the commitment and to include to a modular computation in the circuit. If q is close enough to 2^{256} then it is a simple comparison and subtraction. This requires around 2 000 gates, which is negligible compared to our circuit size. Another solution is to directly sample ps'_B in F_q. This can be done by rejection sampling or as follow: sample X sufficiently big compared to $\log_2(q)$ $(\log_2(X) > \log_2(q) + 64$ as advised by the NIST for instance), then simply considering $X \mod q$ can be done with a negligible bias. For all the intermediate values in the tree, the first method can be applied. The last step is the commitment of the secret key $sk = $ Encode(X). For this element, we directly consider the encoding provided with the curve. The commitment C_{sk} of sk in a group of order q will result in the same implicit reduction modulo q than the computation of the public key. Then we can produce an AND ZK proof that the value committed to in C_{sk} is the discrete log of the pk: $PK\{sk : C_{sk} = skP + rQ \wedge pk = skP\}$.

B   Security of Our Zero-Knowledge Protocols

We present a sketch of proof for the security of CopraZK given in Theorem 2. It is settled on two properties for the function family f. Firstly, we need its dual function $\tilde{f}$ to be correlation intractable with respect to the family of relations $\mathcal{R}_{a,b} : \{x, y : y = ax + b\}$ for a, b random values. Correlation intractability was introduced in [15] and says that, for any relation in the family $\mathcal{R}_{a,b}$, for any random key x, an adversary has a negligible probability to find an input m such that $(m, f(x, m))$ satisfies the relation. Secondly, we need to be sure that the tag does not leak information on the key. We define a general linear input deviation resistant PRF (glider-PRF) as follows:

Definition 1 (glider-PRF security). *A function family $f \in \mathsf{FF}(\mathcal{K}, \mathcal{D}, \mathcal{R})$ (with appropriate domain and range) is said to be a* glider-PRF *if for all PPT adversary $\mathcal{A}$, and a random $\alpha \leftarrow_{\$} \mathcal{R}$, there exists a negligible function* negl *such that:*

$$\Pr\left[x \leftarrow \mathcal{A}(\alpha)^{\mathcal{O}_g} : g \leftarrow_{\$} \mathsf{F}(\mathcal{D}, \mathcal{R})\right] - \Pr\left[x \leftarrow \mathcal{A}(\alpha)^{\mathcal{O}_{f(k,\cdot)+\alpha\cdot}} : k \leftarrow_{\$} \mathcal{K}\right] \leq \mathsf{negl}(\lambda)$$

As we use Fiat-Shamir to get an non interactive protocol, our proof is settled in the Random Oracle Model (ROM), which would satisfy our hypothesis. However, it seems contradictory to idealize as a random oracle the PRF f that is concretely described as a circuit in the ZKBoo part of the protocol. Hence, the ROM hypothesis only applies to the hash function h that generates the challenge and the correlation intractability and glider-PRF properties provide a way to formalize a security proof when only some properties of the random oracle are needed. The correctness of the protocol follows by inspection.

3-Special Soundness. From the 2-special soundness of the Sigma protocol Π, one extract $\tilde{x}, \tilde{y}, \tilde{r}_x, \tilde{r}_y$ such that $C_x = \tilde{x}P + \tilde{r}_x Q, C_y = \tilde{y}P + \tilde{r}_y Q$ and $t = \alpha\tilde{x} + \tilde{y}$. From the 3-special soundness of ZKBoo, one extracts x' such that $t = f(x', m) + \alpha x'$, where t is a fixed value, the same as the one for the proof Π. Correlation intractability of $\tilde{f}$ ensures that $x' \neq \tilde{x}$ happens with negligible probability. We note that the correlation intractability of $\tilde{f}$ requires the input of f to be randomized. In MLS, this supposes considering a random value (for instance the hash of the tree view) instead of the constant 0.

Zero Knowledge. We build a simulator $\mathcal{S}im$ as follows: $\mathcal{S}im$ sample a random value $t \leftarrow_{\$} \mathbb{Z}/q\mathbb{Z}$. Then he calls the Simulator of ZKBoo, $\mathcal{S}im_{ZKBoo}$, as a subroutine and obtains a transcript $(a_{ZKBoo,e,z_{ZKBoo}})$. Then he calls the simulator for the Sigma protocol Π, $\mathcal{S}im_{\Pi}$, as a second subroutine, on the challenge e and obtains a second transcript (a_{Π}, e, z_{Π}) (as $\mathcal{S}im_{\Pi}$ shall work for any challenge). If f is glider-PRF-secure, then sampling a random t is indistinguishable from the real distribution of t and finally, the output distribution of $\mathcal{S}im$ is indistinguishable from the real execution output. In the context of MLS, the tag t must be accessible to the server only. A user who would receive its valid update and access the tag could compute the secret of its child, which he should not.

References

1. Agrawal, S., Ganesh, C., Mohassel, P.: Non-interactive zero-knowledge proofs for composite statements. In: Shacham, H., Boldyreva, A. (eds.) CRYPTO 2018. LNCS, vol. 10993, pp. 643–673. Springer, Cham (2018). https://doi.org/10.1007/978-3-319-96878-0_22
2. Alwen, J., et al.: Keep the dirt: tainted TreeKEM, adaptively and actively secure continuous group key agreement. Cryptology ePrint Archive, Report 2019/1489 (2019). https://eprint.iacr.org/2019/1489
3. Alwen, J., Coretti, S., Dodis, Y.: The double ratchet: security notions, proofs, and modularization for the signal protocol. In: Ishai, Y., Rijmen, V. (eds.) EUROCRYPT 2019. LNCS, vol. 11476, pp. 129–158. Springer, Cham (2019). https://doi.org/10.1007/978-3-030-17653-2_5

4. Alwen, J., Coretti, S., Dodis, Y., Tselekounis, Y.: Security analysis and improvements for the IETF MLS standard for group messaging. In: Micciancio, D., Ristenpart, T. (eds.) CRYPTO 2020. LNCS, vol. 12170, pp. 248–277. Springer, Cham (2020). https://doi.org/10.1007/978-3-030-56784-2_9

5. Ames, S., Hazay, C., Ishai, Y., Venkitasubramaniam, M.: Ligero: lightweight sublinear arguments without a trusted setup. In: Thuraisingham, B.M., Evans, D., Malkin, T., Xu, D. (eds.) ACM CCS 2017, pp. 2087–2104. ACM Press, Oct/Nov 2017. https://doi.org/10.1145/3133956.3134104

6. Backes, M., Hanzlik, L., Herzberg, A., Kate, A., Pryvalov, I.: Efficient noninteractive zero-knowledge proofs in cross-domains without trusted setup. In: Lin, D., Sako, K. (eds.) PKC 2019. LNCS, vol. 11442, pp. 286–313. Springer, Cham (2019). https://doi.org/10.1007/978-3-030-17253-4_10

7. Barnes, R., Beurdouche, B., Millican, J., Omara, E., Cohn-Gordon, K., Robert, R.: The messaging layer security (MLS) protocol. https://datatracker.ietf.org/doc/draft-ietf-mls-protocol/

8. Barnes, R., Bhargavan, K., Lipp, B., Wood, C.: Hybrid public key encryption (2021). https://datatracker.ietf.org/doc/html/draft-irtf-cfrg-hpke-12

9. Bellare, M., Singh, A.C., Jaeger, J., Nyayapati, M., Stepanovs, I.: Ratcheted encryption and key exchange: the security of messaging. In: Katz, J., Shacham, H. (eds.) CRYPTO 2017. LNCS, vol. 10403, pp. 619–650. Springer, Cham (2017). https://doi.org/10.1007/978-3-319-63697-9_21

10. Ben-Sasson, E., Bentov, I., Horesh, Y., Riabzev, M.: Scalable, transparent, and post-quantum secure computational integrity. Cryptology ePrint Archive, Report 2018/046 (2018). https://eprint.iacr.org/2018/046

11. Bhargavan, K., Barnes, R., Rescorla, E.: TreeKEM: asynchronous decentralized key management for large dynamic groups (2018)

12. Brzuska, C., Cornelissen, E., Kohbrok, K.: Cryptographic security of the MLS RFC, Draft 11. Cryptology ePrint Archive, Report 2021/137 (2021). https://ia.cr/2021/137

13. Camenisch, J., Damgård, I.: Verifiable encryption, group encryption, and their applications to separable group signatures and signature sharing schemes. In: Okamoto, T. (ed.) ASIACRYPT 2000. LNCS, vol. 1976, pp. 331–345. Springer, Heidelberg (2000). https://doi.org/10.1007/3-540-44448-3_25

14. Camenish, J., Stadler, M.: Proof systems for general statements about discrete logarithms (1997)

15. Canetti, R., Goldreich, O., Halevi, S.: The random oracle methodology, revisited. Cryptology ePrint Archive, Report 1998/011 (1998). http://eprint.iacr.org/1998/011

16. Castagnos, G., Catalano, D., Laguillaumie, F., Savasta, F., Tucker, I.: Two-party ECDSA from hash proof systems and efficient instantiations. In: Boldyreva, A., Micciancio, D. (eds.) CRYPTO 2019. LNCS, vol. 11694, pp. 191–221. Springer, Cham (2019). https://doi.org/10.1007/978-3-030-26954-8_7

17. Castagnos, G., Laguillaumie, F.: Linearly homomorphic encryption from DDH. In: Nyberg, K. (ed.) CT-RSA 2015. LNCS, vol. 9048, pp. 487–505. Springer, Cham (2015). https://doi.org/10.1007/978-3-319-16715-2_26

18. Chase, M., et al.: Post-quantum zero-knowledge and signatures from symmetric-key primitives. In: Thuraisingham, B.M., Evans, D., Malkin, T., Xu, D. (eds.) ACM CCS 2017, pp. 1825–1842. ACM Press, Oct/Nov 2017. https://doi.org/10.1145/3133956.3133997

19. Chase, M., Ganesh, C., Mohassel, P.: Efficient zero-knowledge proof of algebraic and non-algebraic statements with applications to privacy preserving credentials. In: Robshaw, M., Katz, J. (eds.) CRYPTO 2016. LNCS, vol. 9816, pp. 499–530. Springer, Heidelberg (2016). https://doi.org/10.1007/978-3-662-53015-3_18

20. Chase, M., Perrin, T., Zaverucha, G.: The signal private group system and anonymous credentials supporting efficient verifiable encryption. Cryptology ePrint Archive, Report 2019/1416 (2019). https://eprint.iacr.org/2019/1416

21. Cohn-Gordon, K., Cremers, C., Garratt, L., Millican, J., Milner, K.: On ends-to-ends encryption: asynchronous group messaging with strong security guarantees. Cryptology ePrint Archive, Report 2017/666 (2017). http://eprint.iacr.org/2017/666

22. Cohn-Gordon, K., Cremers, C.J.F., Dowling, B., Garratt, L., Stebila, D.: A formal security analysis of the signal messaging protocol. In: 2017 IEEE European Symposium on Security and Privacy, EuroS&P 2017, Paris, France, 26–28 April 2017, pp. 451–466 (2017). https://doi.org/10.1007/s00145-020-09360-1

23. Damgård, I.: On sigma protocols (2010)

24. Bernstein, D.J.: A state-of-the-art Diffie Hellman function. https://cr.yp.to/ecdh.html

25. Fiat, A., Shamir, A.: How to prove yourself: practical solutions to identification and signature problems. In: Odlyzko, A.M. (ed.) CRYPTO 1986. LNCS, vol. 263, pp. 186–194. Springer, Heidelberg (1987). https://doi.org/10.1007/3-540-47721-7_12

26. Gennaro, R., Gentry, C., Parno, B., Raykova, M.: Quadratic span programs and succinct NIZKs without PCPs. In: Johansson, T., Nguyen, P.Q. (eds.) EUROCRYPT 2013. LNCS, vol. 7881, pp. 626–645. Springer, Heidelberg (2013). https://doi.org/10.1007/978-3-642-38348-9_37

27. Giacomelli, I., Madsen, J., Orlandi, C.: ZKBoo: faster zero-knowledge for Boolean circuits. In: Holz, T., Savage, S. (eds.) USENIX Security 2016, pp. 1069–1083. USENIX Association, August 2016

28. Groth, J.: Short pairing-based non-interactive zero-knowledge arguments. In: Abe, M. (ed.) ASIACRYPT 2010. LNCS, vol. 6477, pp. 321–340. Springer, Heidelberg (2010). https://doi.org/10.1007/978-3-642-17373-8_19

29. Gvili, Y., Ha, J., Scheffler, S., Varia, M., Yang, Z., Zhang, X.: TurboIKOS: improved non-interactive zero knowledge and post-quantum signatures. Cryptology ePrint Archive, Report 2021/478 (2021). https://eprint.iacr.org/2021/478

30. Ishai, Y., Kushilevitz, E., Ostrovsky, R., Sahai, A.: Zero-knowledge from secure multiparty computation. In: Johnson, D.S., Feige, U. (eds.) 39th ACM STOC, pp. 21–30. ACM Press, June 2007. https://doi.org/10.1145/1250790.1250794

31. Jaeger, J., Stepanovs, I.: Optimal channel security against fine-grained state compromise: the safety of messaging. In: Shacham, H., Boldyreva, A. (eds.) CRYPTO 2018. LNCS, vol. 10991, pp. 33–62. Springer, Cham (2018). https://doi.org/10.1007/978-3-319-96884-1_2

32. Jawurek, M., Kerschbaum, F., Orlandi, C.: Zero-knowledge using garbled circuits: how to prove non-algebraic statements efficiently. In: Sadeghi, A.R., Gligor, V.D., Yung, M. (eds.) ACM CCS 2013, pp. 955–966. ACM Press, November 2013. https://doi.org/10.1145/2508859.2516662

33. Jost, D., Maurer, U., Mularczyk, M.: Efficient ratcheting: almost-optimal guarantees for secure messaging. Cryptology ePrint Archive, Report 2018/954 (2018). https://eprint.iacr.org/2018/954

34. Katz, J., Kolesnikov, V., Wang, X.: Improved non-interactive zero knowledge with applications to post-quantum signatures. In: Lie, D., Mannan, M., Backes, M., Wang, X. (eds.) ACM CCS 2018, pp. 525–537. ACM Press, October 2018. https://doi.org/10.1145/3243734.3243805

35. Kilian, J.: A note on efficient zero-knowledge proofs and arguments (extended abstract). In: 24th ACM STOC, pp. 723–732. ACM Press, May 1992. https://doi.org/10.1145/129712.129782

36. Krawczyk, H.: Cryptographic extraction and key derivation: the HKDF scheme. In: Rabin, T. (ed.) CRYPTO 2010. LNCS, vol. 6223, pp. 631–648. Springer, Heidelberg (2010). https://doi.org/10.1007/978-3-642-14623-7_34

37. Marlinspike, M., Perrin, T.: The double ratchet algorithm. Signal's web site (2016)

38. Pedersen, T.P.: Non-interactive and information-theoretic secure verifiable secret sharing. In: Feigenbaum, J. (ed.) CRYPTO 1991. LNCS, vol. 576, pp. 129–140. Springer, Heidelberg (1992). https://doi.org/10.1007/3-540-46766-1_9

39. Poettering, B., Rösler, P.: Towards bidirectional ratcheted key exchange. In: Shacham, H., Boldyreva, A. (eds.) CRYPTO 2018. LNCS, vol. 10991, pp. 3–32. Springer, Cham (2018). https://doi.org/10.1007/978-3-319-96884-1_1

40. Stadler, M.: Publicly verifiable secret sharing. In: Maurer, U. (ed.) EUROCRYPT 1996. LNCS, vol. 1070, pp. 190–199. Springer, Heidelberg (1996). https://doi.org/10.1007/3-540-68339-9_17

More Efficient Amortization of Exact Zero-Knowledge Proofs for LWE

Jonathan Bootle[1], Vadim Lyubashevsky[1], Ngoc Khanh Nguyen[1,2(✉)], and Gregor Seiler[1,2]

[1] IBM Research, Zurich, Switzerland
nkn@zurich.ibm.com
[2] ETH Zurich, Zurich, Switzerland

Abstract. We propose a practical zero-knowledge proof system for proving knowledge of short solutions $\mathbf{s}, \mathbf{e}$ to linear relations $\mathbf{As} + \mathbf{e} = \mathbf{u} \pmod{q}$ which gives the most efficient solution for two naturally-occurring classes of problems. The first is when $\mathbf{A}$ is very "tall", which corresponds to a large number of LWE instances that use the same secret $\mathbf{s}$. In this case, we show that the proof size is independent of the height of the matrix (and thus the length of the error vector $\mathbf{e}$) and rather only linearly depends on the length of $\mathbf{s}$. The second case is when $\mathbf{A}$ is of the form $\mathbf{I} \otimes \mathbf{A}'$, which corresponds to proving many LWE instances (with different secrets) that use the same samples $\mathbf{A}'$. The length of this second proof is square root in the length of $\mathbf{s}$, which corresponds to a square root of the length of all the secrets. Our constructions combine recent advances in "purely" lattice-based zero-knowledge proofs with the Reed-Solomon proximity testing ideas present in some generic zero-knowledge proof systems – with the main difference that the latter are applied directly to lattice instances without going through intermediate problems.

Keywords: Lattices · Zero-knowledge proofs · LWE · Amortization

1 Introduction

Zero-knowledge proofs, in which a prover convinces a verifier of knowledge of a witness to the fact that an instance belongs to a language, are an integral cryptographic building block. For relations among values (e.g. public keys, ciphertexts, commitments, etc.) stemming from classical cryptography based on the hardness of discrete logarithm and factoring, there exist many very efficient (even succinct) zero-knowledge proofs. When it comes to proving relations between public and secret information for *lattice* primitives, however, the landscape of efficient zero-knowledge proofs is significantly less advanced. The fundamental lattice problem upon which most of lattice cryptography rests is the LWE problem, which states that it is hard to distinguish a uniformly random tuple $(\mathbf{A}, \mathbf{u})$

The full version of this paper is available at https://eprint.iacr.org/2020/1449.

E. Bertino et al. (Eds.): ESORICS 2021, LNCS 12973, pp. 608–627, 2021.
https://doi.org/10.1007/978-3-030-88428-4_30

and $(\mathbf{A}, \mathbf{u} = \mathbf{As} + \mathbf{e})$, where the coefficients of $\mathbf{s}$ and $\mathbf{e}$ are small. The main techniques of this paper will prove knowledge of $\mathbf{s}$ and $\mathbf{e}$ with small coefficients[1] that satisfy

$$\mathbf{As} + \mathbf{e} = \mathbf{u}. \tag{1}$$

As is typical with zero-knowledge proofs, there is no one technique that is best for all scenarios. Similarly, our proofs in this paper will not be the shortest for all the parametrizations of the above equation, but they will be the most compact for some important parameter settings which intuitively correspond to simultaneously proving many LWE instances at the same time.

1.1   Prior Work

Relaxed Proofs. The most efficient proofs of equations of the form as in (1) work over some polynomial ring $\mathcal{R}_q = \mathbb{Z}_q[X]/(X^d + 1)$ rather than over $\mathbb{Z}_q$, and are able to prove knowledge of vectors of polynomials $\bar{\mathbf{s}}, \bar{\mathbf{e}}$ with small coefficients (but larger than the ones in $\mathbf{s}$ and $\mathbf{e}$) and a polynomial $\bar{c}$ with $-1/0/1$ coefficients satisfying $\mathbf{A}\bar{\mathbf{s}} + \bar{\mathbf{e}} = \bar{c}\mathbf{t}$. While not exactly proving (1), this zero-knowledge proof is enough to obtain very efficient lattice-based digital signatures (e.g. [DKL+18]) and rather efficient commitment schemes with zero-knowledge openings [BDL+18]. Another variation of the proof is just like above except there is no multiplicative factor $\bar{c}$. Such proofs are particularly efficient in the amortized setting [BBC+18] and are useful as a preprocessing step in certain multi-party protocols [BCS19] or in voting protocols where the authorities perform many simultaneous proofs [dPLNS17].

While the above relaxations of the relation in (1) have found some useful applications, especially when they are used in standalone protocols (e.g. [EZS+19,EKS+20]), they are not very useful for proving relations in schemes for which the parameters have been optimally set according to some external constraints. Because such relaxed proofs only prove knowledge of larger $\bar{\mathbf{s}}$ and $\bar{\mathbf{e}}$ than the ones used by an honest prover, we must increase the sizes of other parameters (like q and n, m) in order to obtain the same security level, solely for the purpose of being compatible with the (possibly seldom-used) zero-knowledge proofs. In order to avoid this inefficiency, it is necessary to have a proof which proves that the secrets are in exactly the same range as is used by the honest prover.

Exact Proofs. One technique for getting short and exact proofs of (1) was given in [dPLS19] where the idea is to first convert (1) to an equivalent (statistically-hiding) discrete-logarithm relation, and then prove knowledge of exponents corresponding to the coefficients of $\mathbf{s}, \mathbf{e}$ using Bulletproofs [BCC+16,BBB+18]. The

---

[1] If the coefficients of $\mathbf{s}$ are unrestricted, as in some applications of LWE, then the proof will be slightly more efficient because we do not have to prove the shortness of $\mathbf{s}$. If $\mathbf{s}$ has a size-restricted distribution, but different from $\mathbf{e}$, then we can apply the transformation of [ACPS09] to convert the instance to one where the distribution of the secret is the same as of the error.

resulting proof is just a few kilobytes, but has the shortcomings of being (very) slow and not fully quantum-safe. In particular, both the prover and the verifier are required to perform on the order of hundreds of thousands of exponentiations, even for fairly modest sizes of the parameters in (1), which requires a few dozen seconds and does not scale well for larger instances. In terms of quantum-security, while the proof is statistical zero-knowledge, soundness is only based on the hardness of the discrete logarithm problem.

Another strategy uses information-theoretic proof systems such as PCPs, interactive PCPs [KR08,BCS16], or interactive oracle proofs (IOPs) [BCS16, RRR16]. In these proof systems, the verifier does not read the prover's messages in their entirety, but rather makes a sublinear number of queries to individual message positions for verification. Given a suitable PCP or IOP, one can convert it into a sublinear-sized cryptographic argument by following the approach of Kilian [Kil92] and Micali [Mic00]. In the resulting argument, the prover commits to each of their proof messages using a Merkle tree, and opens individual message positions using Merkle paths. Thus, security is based solely on collision resistant hash functions, which are quantum-safe.

Various prior works (e.g. [BCR+19, AHIV17, BCG+17]) produce such arguments by designing IOPs for the R1CS or circuit satisfiability problems, which are NP complete. To prove other relations, one must first convert them into suitable problem instances. Unfortunately, directly applying these arguments to lattice relations (e.g. via conversion to R1CS) can be extremely resource-intensive. For example, [BCOS20] reported that constructing a group signature using the arguments from [BCR+19] resulted in rather short outputs (of about 100 KB), but they were not able to sign due to the (cloud) PC running out of memory. Thus, to better use this strategy, one should design PCPs and IOPs which target (1) directly. The work of [BCG+17] gives one way of doing this, by giving IOPs which simulate the behaviour of zero-knowledge arguments that use homomorphic commitments. More precisely, [BCG+17] shows how to compile 'ideal linear commitment' (ILC) protocols, a type of information-theoretic protocol, into IOP protocols, by encoding each of the prover's messages using an error-correcting code. Taking the ILC-to-IOP and IOP-to-argument transformations together, gives an 'encode-then-hash' method for committing to messages which acts essentially like a homomorphic commitment scheme.

Our approach uses some of the algebraic techniques from previous lattice-based works, which design zero-knowledge arguments for (1) directly based on homomorphic, lattice-based commitments. The main difference is that we replace the the lattice-based commitments with the 'encode-then-hash' commitment scheme implicit in [BCG+17]. This scheme is asymptotically more efficient than when using lattice-based commitments (which are linear in the size of the message), but has a large additive overhead. This overhead grows logarithmically in the number of instances, and linearly in the size of the domain of the errors in (1). We show that when the errors come from a small domain, then the overhead is amortized away as the number of instances grows.

The main difference between our work and IOP constructions such as [BCR+19, AHIV17, BCG+17] is that we do not require a (possibly costly) reduction to the intermediate R1CS problem, instead taking inspiration from lattice-based protocols (e.g. [BLS19]) which handle (1) with only a small number of commitments.

Until recently, the shortest fully quantum-safe proofs for proving the exact version of (1) have been direct adaptations [KTX08, LNSW13] of Stern's original protocol [Ste93] for proving knowledge of low-weight code-words over $\mathbb{Z}_2$. The work of [Beu20] used a cut-and-choose approach to leverage the larger field size in (1) to obtain a more efficient generalization of Stern's protocol. Using very different techniques, the works of [BLS19, YAZ+19] achieved a slightly shorter proof for (1) when the secret coefficients are chosen from the set $\{-1, 0, 1\}$. For $n = m = 1024$, and $q \approx 2^{32}$, the proofs (with 2^{-128} soundness error) are around 400 KB long. Further building on these results, the proof of [ENS20] is a little under 50 KB, and a recent improvement in [LNS21] reduces it by another 30%.

For direct comparisons with the results in this paper, we also computed the parameter sizes using the techniques in [ENS20, LNS21] for $n = m = 2048, q \approx 2^{60}$, and 2^{-57} soundness. The proof size for these parameters is around 45 KB.[2]

1.2   Our Results

In this work we give *exact proofs* for several scenarios in which one needs to prove many LWE instances. The first case is proving (1) for the case where $\mathbf{A}$ is a tall matrix. In our running example, $\mathbf{A} \in \mathbb{Z}_q^{n \times m}$ where $m = 2048$ and $n = 64 \cdot 2048$. This can be seen as 64 LWE instances where the dimensions of $\mathbf{A}$ are a square 2048×2048. A simple example where this comes up in practice is when one encrypts a long message using a symmetric LWE encryption scheme (e.g. for FHE applications) or if encrypting a message to different public keys using the same randomness (as in e.g. [PVW08, KKPP20])[3].

In Fig. 1, we give the proof size and running time for our problem instance, where the dependence is on the size of the set from which the coefficients of $\mathbf{s}$ and $\mathbf{e}$ are chosen. In the example from [ENS20] mentioned at the end of the last section, these were chosen from the set $\{-1, 0, 1\}$ of size 3. Thus from the first

---

[2] We point out that the parameters n and m from this paper do not correspond to those with the same name from [ENS20, Appendix B.1]. The length of the secret $\mathbf{s}$ in [ENS20] already includes the error vector. So even though the length of the secret is 2048 there, it is actually broken down into a vector of dimension 1024 which gets multiplied by $\mathbf{A}$, and another 1024 dimensional vector, which is the error. Thus the secret length we are comparing to in this paper is twice as large as in the original [ENS20]. The comparisons to [ENS20] for other dimensions/modulus would be fairly similar.

[3] Incorporating a message vector $\mathbf{m}$ in (1) simply involves rewriting $\mathbf{e} = \mathbf{e}' + [q/2] \cdot \mathbf{m}$ where $\mathbf{e}'$ is the LWE error.

Size of Secret Set	Proof Size (KB)	Prover Time (sec)	Verifier Time (sec)
4	217	0.78	0.06
8	232	1.12	0.06
16	262	1.77	0.06
32	322	3.13	0.07
64	442	6.03	0.08
128	682	12.97	0.10
256	1162	31.27	0.15

Fig. 1. Proof sizes and single-core running times (implemented in C++ using NTL [Sho], running on a Skylake processor) for the proof system in Fig. 2 when $\mathbf{A} \in \mathcal{R}_q^{64 \times 1}$ (i.e. 64 Ring-LWE instances) where $\mathcal{R}_q = \mathbb{Z}_q[X]/(X^d + 1)$ for $q \approx 2^{60}$ and $d = 2048$. The values of τ and l (see Sect. 3 for their definitions) are 512 and 2^{19}, respectively. The secret vectors (over $\mathcal{R}_q$) $\mathbf{s}, \mathbf{e}$ each have coefficients coming from a set of a size specified in the first column rather than coming from the set $\{-1, 0, 1\}$ as specified in Fig. 2, so the protocol has to be adjusted as described in the caption of that Figure. The soundness error is around 2^{-57}, so one may need to repeat the proof twice to achieve cryptographic soundness. This will roughly double the proof size and running time. The size of the commitment/ciphertext $\mathbf{u}$ is 960 KB. The proof sizes would be the same if $\mathbf{A}$ were an unstructured matrix in $\mathbb{Z}_q^{n \times m}$ where $n = 64 \cdot 2048$ and $m = 2048$. The running times, however, would be higher because one can no longer use NTT for performing fast multiplications $\mathbf{As}$. For the same parameters, the proof size per 2048×2048 dimensional instance (of which there are 64 in our example proof) from [ENS20] is 45 KB, and about 30% smaller using improvements from [LNS21], when the size of the secret set is 3.

line of Fig. 1,[4] we see that the amortized proof is about 3 KB per instance, which is about an order of magnitude improvement in size.

The second scenario for which we provide improved proofs is for the case when we have many equations as in (1) with the same public randomness $\mathbf{A}$ but different $\mathbf{s}$ and $\mathbf{e}$. In a way, it complements our first result in which the LWE instances had the same secret, but different public randomness. In this scenario, we give a proof that is square root in the size of the secret, and it produces proofs that are several times smaller than the non-amortized version. We did not implement this scheme, but as it uses essentially the same operations as the one in our first scenario, the running times should be comparable in practice.

1.3   Technical Overview

As mentioned previously, the strategy employed in our basic protocol uses ideas from the lattice-based schemes of [BLS19, YAZ+19] in combination with the 'encode-then-hash' commitment scheme implicit in [BCG+17]. This latter building block of the proof is an additively-homomorphic commitment scheme Com

---

[4] The secret size in the first line is chosen from 4 elements, rather than 3 as in [ENS20]. Reducing the set to 3 will not give us any noticeable reduction.

committing to vectors in $\mathbb{Z}_q^m$ and possessing an efficient ZKPoK of the committed value. That is, if $S = \mathtt{Com}(\mathbf{s})$ and $T = \mathtt{Com}(\mathbf{t})$, then for any $c \in \mathbb{Z}_q$, $\mathbf{s} + \mathbf{t}c = \mathtt{Open}(S + Tc)$. For now, let us treat $\mathtt{Com}$ as a black box. Let $\mathbf{1}$ be a vector all of whose coefficients are 1, and for two vectors $\mathbf{v}, \mathbf{w} \in \mathbb{Z}_q^m$, let $\mathbf{v} \circ \mathbf{w}$ denote the component-wise product of $\mathbf{v}$ and $\mathbf{w}$. We will now give a simplified version of the protocol in Fig. 2 where the prover is trying to convince the verifier that $\mathbf{s}, \mathbf{e} \in \{0, 1\}^m$.

The prover starts out by choosing a uniformly-random masking vector $\mathbf{t} \in \mathbb{Z}_q^m$ and creating a commitment $T = \mathtt{Com}(\mathbf{t})$ and $S = \mathtt{Com}(\mathbf{s})$. At the end of the protocol, the prover will eventually send the polynomial $\mathbf{t}X + \mathbf{s}$ evaluated at the challenge $X = x \in \mathbb{Z}_q$. If we write $\mathbf{f} = \mathbf{t}X + \mathbf{s}$, then

$$\mathbf{f} \circ (\mathbf{f} - \mathbf{1}) = (\mathbf{t} \circ \mathbf{t})X^2 + \mathbf{t} \circ (2\mathbf{s} - \mathbf{1})X + \mathbf{s} \circ (\mathbf{s} - \mathbf{1}) \qquad (2)$$

If all the coefficients in $\mathbf{s}$ are $0/1$, then the constant term will be 0; and so the equation $\frac{1}{X} \cdot \mathbf{f} \circ (\mathbf{f} - \mathbf{1})$ will be the linear equation $\mathbf{v}_1 X + \mathbf{v}_0$ where $\mathbf{v}_1 = \mathbf{t} \circ \mathbf{t}$ and $\mathbf{v}_0 = \mathbf{t} \circ (2\mathbf{s} - \mathbf{1})$. The prover creates commitments $V_1 = \mathtt{Com}(\mathbf{v}_1)$ and $V_0 = \mathtt{Com}(\mathbf{v}_0)$.

The prover also defines

$$\mathbf{d} = \mathbf{u} - \mathbf{A}\mathbf{f} = \mathbf{u} - \mathbf{A}\mathbf{s} - \mathbf{A}\mathbf{t}X = \mathbf{e} - \mathbf{A}\mathbf{t}X, \qquad (3)$$

which satisfies

$$\mathbf{d} \circ (\mathbf{d} - \mathbf{1}) = (\mathbf{A}\mathbf{t}) \circ (\mathbf{A}\mathbf{t})X^2 + (\mathbf{A}\mathbf{t}) \circ (\mathbf{1} - 2\mathbf{e})X + \mathbf{e} \circ (\mathbf{e} - \mathbf{1}). \qquad (4)$$

Therefore $\frac{1}{X} \cdot \mathbf{d} \circ (\mathbf{d} - \mathbf{1})$ will also be a linear equation if and only if all the coefficients of $\mathbf{e}$ are $0/1$. The prover similarly creates commitments $W_1 = \mathtt{Com}((\mathbf{A}\mathbf{t}) \circ (\mathbf{A}\mathbf{t}))$ and $W_0 = \mathtt{Com}((\mathbf{A}\mathbf{t}) \circ (\mathbf{1} - 2))$.

We now begin the description of the interactive protocol. The prover sends the commitments S, T, V_0, V_1, W_0, W_1, and the verifier picks a uniformly-random challenge $x \in \mathbb{Z}_q \setminus \{0\}$. The prover responds with $\mathbf{f} = \mathbf{t}x + \mathbf{s}$ and zero-knowledge proofs of knowledge of the committed values in S, T, V_0, V_1, W_0, W_1, and zero-knowledge proofs that

$$\mathbf{f} = \mathtt{Open}(Tx + S) \qquad (5)$$

$$\frac{1}{x} \cdot (\mathbf{f}) \circ (\mathbf{f} - \mathbf{1}) = \mathtt{Open}(V_1 x + V_0) \qquad (6)$$

$$\frac{1}{x} \cdot (\mathbf{u} - \mathbf{A}\mathbf{f}) \circ (\mathbf{u} - \mathbf{A}\mathbf{f} - \mathbf{1}) = \mathtt{Open}(W_1 x + W_0) \qquad (7)$$

The first proof implies knowledge of some $\mathbf{s}, \mathbf{t}$ satisfying $\mathbf{f} = \mathbf{t}x + \mathbf{s}$. Via a Schwartz-Zippel argument, the second proof, together with (2), implies that $\mathbf{s}$ has $0/1$ coefficients. Similarly, the third proof and (3) imply that $\mathbf{u} - \mathbf{A}\mathbf{s}$ has $0/1$ coefficients. Since the verifier has $\mathbf{f}$ and $\mathbf{u}$, he can verify all three proofs (as well as the proofs of knowledge of the committed values) and conclude that the prover knows $\mathbf{s}, \mathbf{e}$ with $0/1$ coefficients such that $\mathbf{A}\mathbf{s} + \mathbf{e} = \mathbf{u}$. The soundness error of this proof is approximately $1/q$, and so if q is not very large, the proof needs to be repeated several times for soundness amplification.

The Commitment Scheme. We will use the 'encode-then-hash' commitment scheme resulting from combining the two transformations from ILC-to-IOP and from IOP-to-arguments given in [BCG+17]. This can be viewed as an interactive commitment scheme (which can be made non-interactive using the Fiat-Shamir transform) in which the vectors to which we would like to commit, appended with some randomness, are first encoded using a linear error-correcting code (a Reed-Solomon code). If the length of the codeword is l, then the prover creates l hash-based commitments where the input to the ith commitment are all the elements in the ith position of all codewords. These commitments are then hashed into a Merkle tree and the root is transmitted as the final commitment. Proving knowledge of committed values is done via a "cut-and-choose" approach where the verifier sends a random set of size τ and asks the prover to open the codeword in those τ positions. If τ is smaller than the number of randomness positions, then revealing τ positions of the codeword information-theoretically hides the message and so the commitment scheme is hiding.

The verifier can then check whether (5) is satisfied restricted to the τ positions opened by the prover, and due to the fact that $\mathbf{f}$ is given in the clear, one can conclude using a cut-and-choose argument and some properties of Reed-Solomon codes that the values committed in T and S are indeed close to valid codewords (and thus can be decoded to some $\mathbf{s}$ and $\mathbf{t}$), and $\mathbf{f}$ is really the linear combination $\mathbf{t}x + \mathbf{s}$. The same arguments are used to show that (6) and (7) are satisfied.

Amortizing When the Public Randomness is Fixed. An expensive part of our protocol is proving that the correct positions in the Merkle tree have been opened. Each of the τ positions that are opened require the prover to give a path to the root of the tree, which consists of $\log l$ hash function outputs – if one uses SHA-256, then one needs to $32\tau \log l$ bytes for this part of the proof. In general, τ is a small multiple of the security parameter (in practice, ≈ 512) while l is a small multiple of the length of the vectors that are being committed to. In the scheme implemented in Fig. 1, $l \approx 2^{19}$, and therefore just the tree opening would require close to 300 kB. One can optimize this by having multiple roots, (which lowers the number of levels), but this is still the most expensive part of the proof when the size of the secret set is not too large.

A significant saving can be achieved when the matrix $\mathbf{A}$ is the same for all the equations $\mathbf{A}\mathbf{s}_j + \mathbf{e}_j = \mathbf{u}_j$ for $j = 1, \ldots, r$. Then all the secret vectors $\mathbf{s}_j$ can be packed into only one masked opening $\mathbf{f} = x_0\mathbf{t} + \sum_j x_j\mathbf{s}_j$ where the secret vectors are separated by different challenges x_j. The verifier can then still compute $\mathbf{d} = \sum_j x_j\mathbf{u}_j - \mathbf{A}\mathbf{f} = -x_0\mathbf{A}\mathbf{t} + \sum_j x_j\mathbf{e}_j$, which is a masked opening of all the error vectors $\mathbf{e}_j$ in the same form as $\mathbf{f}$. The masked opening $\mathbf{f}$ is the second biggest part of our basic protocol after the Merkle tree paths and so amortizing its size over many equations gives a further saving of about a factor of 2 in the per-equation cost. Now, if one computes a quadratic expression of the form $\mathbf{f} \circ (\mathbf{f} - \sum_j x_j\mathbf{1})$ then the terms x_j^2 vanish if and only if the $\mathbf{s}_j$ have binary coefficients. We take the challenges x_j to be evaluations $x_j = \ell_j(x)$ of Lagrange interpolation polynomials at the same evaluation point x. This has the advantage that the number of non-vanishing garbage terms that appear in the quadratic expression (i.e. the terms to which we need to commit and transmit the commitments) for proving $0/1$ scales only linearly in r, as will be explained in Sect. 4. If one has m^2 secret coefficients distributed over m vectors, each of length m, then our final amortized protocol has communication cost of order m, i.e. of order square root in the number of secret coefficients. This is because there is only one masked opening $\mathbf{f}$ of length m for all m^2 secret coefficients.

2   Preliminaries

Notation. Let q be a prime. We write $\mathbb{Z}_q$ for the ring of integers modulo q. Bold letters as in $\mathbf{v} \in \mathbb{Z}_q^l$ will denote vectors over $\mathbb{Z}_q$ and matrices will be written as regular capital letters M.

Reed-Solomon Codes. Let l, k' be positive integers. Let $\zeta_1, \dots, \zeta_l$ be distinct elements of $\mathbb{Z}_q^{\times}$. The subspace $\mathcal{C} \subset \mathbb{Z}_q^l$ of $\mathbb{Z}_q^l$ of degree k' consisting of all l-tuples $\mathsf{Enc}\,(f) = (f(\zeta_1), \dots, f(\zeta_l))$ where f is a polynomial of degree less than k' with coefficients in $\mathbb{Z}_q$ is a so-called *Reed-Solomon* code. We write $d(\mathbf{V}, \mathbf{W})$ for the Hamming distance between two elements of $\mathbb{Z}_q^l$. Since a polynomial of degree less than k' can have at most $k' - 1$ roots, it is clear that the minimum distance between codewords in $\mathcal{C}$ is $d = l - k' + 1$. This means that if $\mathbf{V}$ is a vector in $\mathbb{Z}_q^l$ that we know has distance at most $(d-1)/2$ from $\mathcal{C}$, then the vector can be uniquely decoded to the closest codeword in $\mathcal{C}$.

The usefulness of Reed-Solomon codes in zero-knowledge proofs stems from the following facts.

Firstly, the encoding function is homomorphic. More precisely, polynomial addition and multiplication translate to coefficient-wise addition and multiplication on the codewords.

Secondly, assume that the prover has committed to several codewords. Then, suppose that the verifier is allowed to see a small number, say τ, of openings of random positions of his choice from all of the committed codewords. If he now checks that a random linear combination of these positions coincide with the positions of a fixed known codeword, then he will be convinced that the prover has honestly committed to codewords with sufficiently few errors that they decode to polynomials whose linear combination is the same as the decoding of the known codeword.

Moreover, if the k' coefficients of the input polynomials consist of m message coefficients and τ randomness coefficients, then the τ openings do not reveal any information about the message coefficients. We explain this in more detail in Appendix A.

We will write $\mathsf{Enc}\,(\mathbf{m}, \mathbf{r})$ to denote the Reed-Solomon codeword corresponding to the input polynomial $f = \sum_{i=0}^{m-1} \mathbf{m}_i X^i + X^m \sum_{i=0}^{\tau-1} \mathbf{r}_i X^i$ with message coefficients $\mathbf{m}$ and randomness coefficients $\mathbf{r}$. We will also extend this notation in the straight-forward way to split the input polynomial into even more coefficient vectors.

So, in summary, Reed-Solomon codes offer a way to commit to message vectors with the ability to prove linear relations between these vectors in zero-knowledge. We perform hash-based commitments to codewords with the technique from [BCG+17] that we recall in the next paragraphs.

Commitments. Let Commit be a commitment scheme with message space $\mathbb{Z}_q^r$ and randomness space R. Let $M = (\mathbf{m}_1 \, \mathbf{m}_2 \, \ldots \, \mathbf{m}_l)$ be a matrix made up of column vectors $\mathbf{m}_i \in \mathbb{Z}_q^r$. Let $\rho = (\rho_1 \, \rho_2 \, \ldots \, \rho_l)$ be a list of random strings $\rho_i \in R$.

Define CommitCols to be the function which takes M and ρ as input and returns the list of commitments Commit$(\mathbf{m}_i; \rho_i)$.

In our protocols, we will instantiate Commit with the folklore hash-based commitment scheme where Commit$(\mathbf{m}_i; \rho_i) = h(\rho_i || \mathbf{m}_i)$, for a hash-function $h \colon \{0,1\}^* \to \{0,1\}^{256}$, and randomness ρ_i uniformly sampled from $\{0,1\}^{128}$. When h is modelled as a random-oracle, Commit is a computationally-hiding and computationally-binding commitment scheme (see e.g. [MF21, Proposition 8.12]).

Merkle Trees. We will commit to many Reed-Solomon codewords $\mathbf{H}_i \in \mathcal{C}$, $i = 1, \ldots, r$, in the following way. Firstly, take the codewords to be the rows of the matrix $M = (\mathbf{H}_i) \in \mathbb{Z}_q^{r \times l}$. Secondly, apply CommitCols to commit to the columns of M. Finally, produce a Merkle tree with all these column commitments as leaves. This means that the commitments CommitCols$(M; \rho)$ are taken to be the leaves of a binary tree of height $\log l$ where each inner node is the hash of its two children. This results in a single hash $\mathcal{M} = \text{Merkle}(\text{CommitCols}(M; \rho))$ at the root of the tree. This gives a commitment to all codewords $\mathbf{H}_i$ and allows simultaneous opening of all codewords at arbitrary positions $j \in [l]$ by revealing the position j of every codeword and the nodes in the Merkle tree that are needed to compute the path to the root node $\mathcal{M}$. For $I \subset [l]^\tau$ we will later write MerklePaths$|_I$ for the set of all nodes in the Merkle tree needed to compute the paths for all codeword position in I. This construction is binding because if it were possible to produce two different openings at the same position then there would be a hash collision somewhere on the path to the root of the Merkle tree. The construction is hiding because the unopened leaves are all hiding commitments, and so the nodes in the Merkle paths which are derived from them do not leak any information about the unopened codeword entries.

3   Basic Protocol

In this section, we present our basic protocol tailored towards single LWE instances, where the solution has entries lying in $\{-1, 0, 1\}$. The protocol can incorporate larger sets in the obvious way, as explained in the caption of Fig. 2. At a high level, it implements the strategy used in [BLS19] and explained in the introduction. But it uses Reed-Solomon codes to instantiate the commitment scheme and their associated zero-knowledge proofs, rather than lattice-based commitments.

Proof systems using code-based commitment schemes often require a proximity test, to prove that the (possibly malicious) values hashed by the prover are close to codewords, and therefore represent valid encodings of messages. Following [RVW13], this is often done by checking that an auxiliary random linear combination of the committed and possibly noisy codewords is itself close to the code. Previously, [BKS18] investigated the use of the structured linear combination $(1, x)$ for some random x, in proximity testing. We will use the same strategy for proximity testing with powers of x as part of our scheme.[5]

We cannot use a structured linear combination in the amortised case since with this strategy, the probability that the verifier can catch a cheating prover decreases as the number of committed secrets increases. Our amortised result thus uses a random linear combination of all of the hashed vectors to prove that each hashed vector is close to a codeword.

The complete protocol is given in Fig. 2.

Theorem 3.1 (Completeness). *The protocol in Fig. 2 is perfectly complete.*

Proof. This follows from a careful inspection of the protocol. □

Theorem 3.2 (Special Honest Verifier Zero Knowledge). *There exists an efficient simulator S which, given values for the random challenges x and I from the protocol in Fig. 2, outputs a protocol transcript whose distribution is indistinguishable from that of a real transcript from the interaction between an honest prover and an honest verifier.*

The proof of Theorem 3.2 is included in the full version of this paper [BLNS20].

Theorem 3.3 (Knowledge Soundness). *Let $C \subset \mathbb{Z}_q^l$ be a Reed-Solomon code of dimension $k' = 2m + n + \tau$ and length l with encoding function $\mathsf{Enc}()$. Let $k' \leq k \leq l$. Suppose that there is an efficient deterministic prover $\mathcal{P}^*$ that convinces the honest verifier $\mathcal{V}$ on input $\mathbf{A}, \mathbf{u}$ to accept with probability*

$$\varepsilon > 2\max\left\{2\left(\frac{k}{l-\tau}\right)^\tau, \frac{2}{q-1} + \left(1 - \frac{k-k'}{9l}\right)^\tau, 2\left(1 - \frac{2(k-k')}{3l}\right)^\tau, \frac{12}{q-1}\right\}.$$

Then, there exists a probabilistic extraction algorithm $\mathcal{E}$ which, given rewindable black-box access to $\mathcal{P}^*$, produces a witness $\mathbf{s} \in \{-1, 0, 1\}^m$ such that $\mathbf{u} - \mathbf{As} \in \{-1, 0, 1\}^n$ or finds a hash collision in expected time at most $64T$ where $T := \frac{3}{\varepsilon} + \frac{k-\tau}{\varepsilon/2-(k/(l-\tau))^\tau}$ and running $\mathcal{P}^*$ once is assumed to take unit time.

The proof of Theorem 3.3 is included in the full version of this paper [BLNS20].

---

[5] From a technical perspective, [BKS18, Theorem 4.1] proves that except with small probability, these structured linear combinations have the same distance from the code as the maximum distance of all the codewords in the linear combination. Here, we can tolerate some decrease in the distance in our soundness proof, and prove a weaker result via a simpler method. See the full version of this paper for details.

Prover $\mathcal{P}$'s input: $\mathbf{A} \in \mathbb{Z}_q^{n \times m}, \mathbf{u} \in \mathbb{Z}_q^n, \mathbf{s} \in \{-1, 0, 1\}^m$ and $\mathbf{e} \in \{-1, 0, 1\}^n$ such that $\mathbf{u} = \mathbf{As} + \mathbf{e}$.

Verifier $\mathcal{V}$'s input: $\mathbf{A} \in \mathbb{Z}_q^{n \times m}, \mathbf{u} \in \mathbb{Z}_q^n$.

The protocol proceeds as follows.

$\mathcal{P}$:

- The prover samples $\mathbf{t} \leftarrow \mathbb{Z}_q^m$ and computes the polynomials $\mathbf{f}(X) = \mathbf{t}X + \mathbf{s}$ and $\mathbf{d}(X) = \mathbf{u} - \mathbf{Af}(X)$.
- The prover computes the polynomials

$$\frac{1}{X}\mathbf{f}(X) \circ [\mathbf{f}(X) - \mathbf{1}^m] \circ [\mathbf{f}(X) + \mathbf{1}^m] = \mathbf{v}_2 X^2 + \mathbf{v}_1 X + \mathbf{v}_0 \ , \text{ and}$$

$$\frac{1}{X}\mathbf{d}(X) \circ [\mathbf{d}(X) - \mathbf{1}^n] \circ [\mathbf{d}(X) + \mathbf{1}^n] = \mathbf{w}_2 X^2 + \mathbf{w}_1 X + \mathbf{w}_0 \ .$$

- The prover samples $\mathbf{r}_0, \mathbf{r}_1, \mathbf{r}_2 \leftarrow \mathbb{Z}_q^\tau$ and computes the encodings

$$\mathbf{H}_2 = \mathsf{Enc}\left(\mathbf{0}^m, \mathbf{v}_2, \mathbf{w}_2, \mathbf{r}_2\right), \ \mathbf{H}_1 = \mathsf{Enc}\left(\mathbf{t}, \mathbf{v}_1, \mathbf{w}_1, \mathbf{r}_1\right) \text{ and } \mathbf{H}_0 = \mathsf{Enc}\left(\mathbf{s}, \mathbf{v}_0, \mathbf{w}_0, \mathbf{r}_0\right) \ .$$

- The prover sets $E = \begin{pmatrix} \mathbf{H}_2 \\ \mathbf{H}_1 \\ \mathbf{H}_0 \end{pmatrix}$, samples randomness ρ for CommitCols, and computes $\mathcal{M} = \mathsf{Merkle}(\mathsf{CommitCols}(E; \rho))$.

$\mathcal{P} \to \mathcal{V}$: The prover sends $\mathcal{M}$ to the verifier.

$\mathcal{P} \leftarrow \mathcal{V}$: The verifier samples $x \leftarrow \mathbb{Z}_q^\times$ and sends x to the prover.

$\mathcal{P} \to \mathcal{V}$: The prover computes $\bar{\mathbf{f}} = \mathbf{f}(x)$ and $\bar{\mathbf{r}} = \mathbf{r}_2 x^2 + \mathbf{r}_1 x + \mathbf{r}_0$ and sends them to the verifier.

$\mathcal{P} \leftarrow \mathcal{V}$: The verifier samples $I \leftarrow [l]^\tau$ such that $|I| = \tau$ and sends I to the prover.

$\mathcal{P} \to \mathcal{V}$: The prover computes $E|_I$, $\rho|_I$ and $\mathsf{MerklePaths}_I$ and sends them to the verifier.

$\mathcal{V}$:

- The verifier checks $E|_I$ and $\rho|_I$ against $\mathcal{M}$ and $\mathsf{MerklePaths}_I$.
- The verifier computes $\bar{\mathbf{d}} = \mathbf{u} - \mathbf{A}\bar{\mathbf{f}}$ and checks whether

$$\mathsf{Enc}\left(\bar{\mathbf{f}}, \frac{1}{x}\bar{\mathbf{f}} \circ [\bar{\mathbf{f}} - \mathbf{1}^m] \circ [\bar{\mathbf{f}} + \mathbf{1}^m], \frac{1}{x}\bar{\mathbf{d}} \circ [\bar{\mathbf{d}} - \mathbf{1}^n] \circ [\bar{\mathbf{d}} + \mathbf{1}^n], \bar{\mathbf{r}}\right)\Bigg|_I \overset{?}{=} \mathbf{H}_2|_I x^2 + \mathbf{H}_1|_I x + \mathbf{H}_0|_I \ .$$

Fig. 2. Simple hash-based proof of knowledge of a ternary solution to a linear equation over $\mathbb{Z}_q$. To use a secret set S of size b different from $\{-1, 0, 1\}$, one would change $\frac{1}{X}\mathbf{f}(X) \circ [\mathbf{f}(X) - \mathbf{1}^m] \circ [\mathbf{f}(X) + \mathbf{1}^m]$ to $\frac{1}{X}\bigcirc_{i \in S}[\mathbf{f}(X) - i^m] = \sum \mathbf{v}_j X^j$. The analogous of this is done for the line $\frac{1}{X}\mathbf{d}(X) \circ [\mathbf{d}(X) - \mathbf{1}^n] \circ [\mathbf{d}(X) + \mathbf{1}^n]$. One would also accordingly increase the number of terms $\mathbf{r}_j$ and the number of rows $\mathbf{H}_j = \mathsf{Enc}\left(\mathbf{0}^m, \mathbf{v}_j, \mathbf{w}_j, \mathbf{r}_j\right)$.

Remark 3.4 (on the parameter k). The parameter k in Theorem 3.3 is not used by the prover and verifier algorithms, but only by the extraction algorithm $\mathcal{E}$. In more detail, the extraction algorithm $\mathcal{E}$ attempts to collect openings for k out of the l entries of each committed codeword. The extraction algorithm attempts to decode the partial codewords obtained in order to find a witness.

Analysing the probability that $\mathcal{E}$ can decode these codewords leads to the dependence of ε on k. This indirectly affects the proof size, as choosing k to reduce the knowledge soundness error ε means that the proof requires fewer parallel repetitions to achieve negligible soundness. This also applies to our amortised protocol.

Asymptotically, when $l = ck'$ for some constant $c > 1$, one could set $k = c'k'$ for constant $c' \in (1, c)$. For concrete parameters, we choose the value of k in our basic and amortised protocols using computer experiments.

3.1 Proof Size and Concrete Parameter Choices

For one iteration of the proof in Fig. 2 the prover has to send the linear masked secrets $\bar{\mathbf{f}} \in \mathbb{Z}_q^m$ and $\bar{\mathbf{r}} \in \mathbb{Z}_q^\tau$, and open the 3 codewords $\mathbf{H}_j$ at τ positions, with the randomness that was used to commit to them. Together these are $m + 4\tau$ elements of $\mathbb{Z}_q$, and τ bitstrings of commitment randomness, each of size 128 bits. Moreover, the prover has to send the initial commitment $\mathcal{M}$ and τ Merkle paths. As specified in the protocol this needs $1 + \tau\lceil \log l \rceil$ 32-byte hashes per iteration. It is obvious that the latter can be optimized by splitting the tree with l leaves into h trees with l/h leaves each. This results in shorter Merkle paths at the costs of h root hashes in the commitment $\mathcal{M}$. Concretely, with this optimization in one iteration of the protocol $h + \tau\lceil \log(l/h) \rceil$ hashes need to be sent. In total we see that one iteration of the protocol has a bandwidth requirement of

$$\left((m + 4\tau)\lceil \log(q) \rceil + 128\tau + 256 \left(h + \tau \left\lceil \log\left(\frac{l}{h}\right) \right\rceil \right) \right) \Big/ 8192$$

kilobytes.

4   Amortized Protocol for a Fixed Public Randomness

A closer look at the communication cost of the protocol from the previous section shows that the initial commitment and the Merkle paths are actually responsible for the majority of the proof size.

Now, the size of the Merkle trees does not depend on the number of Reed-Solomon codewords that the prover commits to, since each leaf can be the hash of codeword positions from arbitrarily many codewords. It is therefore clear that when one has to prove many (different) equations $\mathbf{u}_j = \mathbf{A}_j\mathbf{s}_j + \mathbf{e}_j$ for $j = 1, \ldots, r$ at once, then one can commit to all of the codewords in the corresponding proofs using only one set of Merkle trees. Moreover, when the individual proofs are executed in a parallel fashion where the same challenges are used in all parallel proofs, then one also only needs one set of τ Merkle paths for all the proofs. So we see that the protocol in Fig. 2 can be operated in a simple amortized mode which has a total size of

$$\left(r(m + 4\tau)\lceil \log(q) \rceil + 128\tau + 256 \left(h + \tau \left\lceil \log\left(\frac{l}{h}\right) \right\rceil \right) \right) \Big/ 8192$$

kilobytes for r equations.

In this section we improve on this result by giving a sublinear amortized proof protocol that allows to prove $r = O(m)$ equations $\mathbf{u}_j = \mathbf{A}\mathbf{s}_j + \mathbf{e}_j$ with the same matrix $\mathbf{A}$ and a total number of $O(m^2)$ secret coefficients in size that scales only with the square root m of the number of secret coefficients. As an independent generalization, the protocol of this section allows to directly prove that the coefficients of the secret lie in an arbitrary interval $\{0, \ldots, b-1\}$. We chose not do this in the basic protocol from Sect. 3 to keep that protocol as simple as possible.

The key technique for the sublinearity is to replace the r masked secrets $\bar{\mathbf{f}}_j = x\mathbf{t}_j + \mathbf{s}_j$ of total length rm by a single length-m packed vector that masks all secrets $\mathbf{s}_j$ at once. After the Merkle tree roots for the commitment and the Merkle tree paths, the masked secret $\bar{\mathbf{f}}$ is the next largest element of the basic proof protocol. So by being able to amortize its size over many equations we can also significantly improve the concrete per-equation cost. One way of doing this is to separate the secret vectors with independent challenges $x_j \in \mathbb{Z}_q$ and use $\bar{\mathbf{f}} = \sum_{j=0}^{r} x_j \mathbf{s}_j$, where $\mathbf{s}_0$ now is the single masking vector. So then $\bar{\mathbf{f}}$ is the evaluation of a multivariate polynomial in r indeterminates. This is compatible with the lattice equations because we assume that they use the same matrix $\mathbf{A}$. The verifier can compute

$$\sum_{j=1}^{r} x_j \mathbf{u}_j - \mathbf{A}\bar{\mathbf{f}} = -x_0 \mathbf{A}\mathbf{s}_0 - \sum_{j=1}^{r} x_j \mathbf{e}_j$$

which is a masking of the error vectors with masking vector $\mathbf{e}_0 = -\mathbf{A}\mathbf{s}_0$. The problem with this approach is that when we work with equations of degree b in these polynomials to prove that all $\mathbf{s}_j$ and $\mathbf{e}_j$ have coefficients in $\{0, \ldots, b-1\}$, we arrive at multivariate polynomials of total degree b that contain on the order of r^b monomials. So this means we need to commit to that many garbage terms and prove openings of these commitments which has communication cost on the order of r^b. On the other hand, the multivariate Schwartz-Zippel lemma still only gives that a multivariate polynomial of total degree b vanishes at a random point with probability b/q so we do not profit from the large challenge space of size q^r in the soundness error.

Therefore a better approach is to not use independent challenges x_j but instead choose them to be evaluations of Lagrange interpolation polynomials at the same evaluation point as in [GGPR13].

So let $a_1, \ldots, a_r$ be distinct interpolation points in $\mathbb{Z}_q$. Then, for $j \in \{1, \ldots, r\}$, let

$$\ell_j(X) = \prod_{i \neq j} \frac{X - a_i}{a_j - a_i}$$

be the jth Lagrange interpolation polynomial and let $\ell_0(X) = \prod_{j=1}^{r}(X - a_j)$.

By polynomial interpolation every polynomial $f \in \mathbb{Z}_q[X]/(\ell_0(X))$ can be written uniquely as a linear combination of $\ell_j(X)$'s, i.e.

$$f(X) = \sum_{j=1}^{r} \lambda_j \ell_j(X)$$

with $\lambda_j \in \mathbb{Z}_q$. Since $\ell_j(X)^2 \equiv \ell_j(X) \pmod{\ell_0(X)}$ and $\ell_i(X)\ell_j(X) \equiv 0 \pmod{\ell_0(X)}$ for all $i,j \in \{1,\ldots,r\}$, $i \neq j$, multiplication is coefficient-wise in this representation. That is,

$$f(X)^2 = \sum_{j=1}^{r} \lambda_j^2 \ell_j(X).$$

Now, higher-degree polynomials $f \in \mathbb{Z}_q[X]/(\ell_0(X)^b)$ can be written uniquely as a linear combination of the polynomials $\{\ell_j(X)\ell_0(X)^i\}_{i=0,j=1}^{b-1,r}$. For our application, this means that when we separate the secret vectors using Lagrange polynomials, i.e.

$$\bar{\mathbf{f}} = \sum_{j=0}^{r} \ell_j(x)\mathbf{s}_j,$$

then equations of degree b in $\bar{\mathbf{f}}$ will only contain br terms $\mathbf{v}_{i,j}\ell_j(x)\ell_0(x)^i$ for $j \in \{1,\ldots,r\}$, $i \in \{0,\ldots,b-1\}$. So this is again linear in r and suffices for our sublinearity result.

After we have replaced the individual masked secrets $\bar{\mathbf{f}}_j$ by just one, note that we need $r+1$ commitments to the secret vectors in order to prove that $\bar{\mathbf{f}}$ is correctly formed whereas the range proofs for the secret coefficients need br commitments to the garbage terms in the equations of degree b in $\bar{\mathbf{f}}$ or $\bar{\mathbf{d}}$. So we don't want to put the secret vectors and the garbage terms in the same Reed-Solomon codewords as we have done in the basic protocol in Sect. 3. This would only prove that $\bar{\mathbf{f}}$ is the evaluation of a polynomial of degree $br-1$ instead of a polynomial of degree r, which is bad for large b as it results in a higher soundness error. Splitting the codewords into several smaller ones has the downside that more openings need to be sent. Therefore for small b it would actually be better not to do this.

The last difference to the basic protocol is that for technical reasons already explained in Sect. 3, the prover sends an auxiliary masking of a random linear combination with independent coefficients of all of the messages in the codewords. This is necessary since the prover commits to many more codewords and he must prove that they are really close to codewords. Using a variant of the technique of the basic protocol and leverage the linear combination of the codewords with $\ell_j(x)$ as coefficients would result in a much larger soundness error.

The complete sublinear protocol is given in Fig. 3. We only use one Reed-Solomon code of dimension $k' = m + \tau$ and length l and also use it for the shorter message vectors of length $n \leq m$ by padding these vectors with zeroes. We analyze the protocol in the following theorems.

Theorem 4.1 (Completeness). *The protocol in Fig. 3 is perfectly complete.*

Proof. This follows by inspection of the protocol. $\qquad\square$

Theorem 4.2 (Special Honest Verifier Zero Knowledge). *There exists an efficient simulator $\mathcal{S}$ which given values for the random challenges x, β, γ, δ,*

Prover $\mathcal{P}$'s input: $\mathbf{A} \in \mathbb{Z}_q^{n \times m}$, $\mathbf{u}_1, \ldots, \mathbf{u}_r \in \mathbb{Z}_q^n$, $\mathbf{s}_1, \ldots, \mathbf{s}_r \in \{0, \ldots, b-1\}^m$ and $\mathbf{e}_1, \ldots, \mathbf{e}_r \in \{0, \ldots, b-1\}^n$ such that $\mathbf{u}_j = \mathbf{A}\mathbf{s}_j + \mathbf{e}_j$ for all $j \in [r]$.

Verifier $\mathcal{V}$'s input: $\mathbf{A} \in \mathbb{Z}_q^{n \times m}$, $\mathbf{u}_1, \ldots, \mathbf{u}_r \in \mathbb{Z}_q^n$.

The protocol proceeds as follows.

$\mathcal{P}$:

- The prover samples $\mathbf{s}_0 \leftarrow \mathbb{Z}_q^m$ and computes the polynomials

$$\mathbf{f}(X) = \sum_{j=0}^r \mathbf{s}_j \ell_j(X) \qquad \text{and} \qquad \mathbf{d}(X) = \sum_{j=1}^r \mathbf{u}_j \ell_j(X) - \mathbf{A}\mathbf{f}(X) \ .$$

- The prover computes the polynomials

$$\frac{1}{\ell_0(X)} \bigcirc_{i=0}^{b-1} \left[\mathbf{f}(X) - i\mathbf{1}\right] = \sum_{i=0}^{b-1}\sum_{j=1}^r \mathbf{v}_{i,j} \ell_j(X)\ell_0(X)^i \ , \text{ and}$$

$$\frac{1}{\ell_0(X)} \bigcirc_{i=0}^{b-1} \left[\mathbf{d}(X) - i\mathbf{1}\right] = \sum_{i=0}^{b-1}\sum_{j=1}^r \mathbf{w}_{i,j} \ell_j(X)\ell_0(X)^i \ .$$

- The prover samples $\mathbf{y} \leftarrow \mathbb{Z}_q^m$ and $\mathbf{r}^y \leftarrow \mathbb{Z}_q^\tau$, and computes the encoding $\mathbf{Y} = \mathsf{Enc}\,(\mathbf{y}, \mathbf{r}^y)$.
- For $j = 0, 1, \ldots, r$, the prover samples $\mathbf{r}_j^s \leftarrow \mathbb{Z}_q^\tau$ and computes the encoding $\mathbf{S}_j = \mathsf{Enc}\,(\mathbf{s}_j, \mathbf{r}_j^s)$.
- For $i = 0, \ldots, b-1$ and $j = 1, \ldots, r$, the prover samples $\mathbf{r}_{i,j}^v$, $\mathbf{r}_{i,j}^w \in \mathbb{Z}_q^\tau$ and computes the encodings

$$\mathbf{V}_{i,j} = \mathsf{Enc}\,(\mathbf{v}_{i,j}, \mathbf{r}_{i,j}^v) \qquad \text{and} \qquad \mathbf{W}_{i,j} = \mathsf{Enc}\,(\mathbf{w}_{i,j}, \mathbf{r}_{i,j}^w) \ .$$

- The prover sets $S = \begin{pmatrix} \mathbf{S}_0 \\ \vdots \\ \mathbf{S}_r \end{pmatrix}$, $V = \begin{pmatrix} \mathbf{V}_{0,1} \\ \vdots \\ \mathbf{V}_{b-1,r} \end{pmatrix}$ and $W = \begin{pmatrix} \mathbf{W}_{0,1} \\ \vdots \\ \mathbf{W}_{b-1,r} \end{pmatrix}$, samples randomness ρ for CommitCols, and computes

$$\mathcal{M} = \mathsf{Merkle}\left(\mathsf{CommitCols}\left(\begin{pmatrix} \mathbf{Y} \\ S \\ V \\ W \end{pmatrix}\right); \rho\right) \ .$$

$\mathcal{P} \to \mathcal{V}$: The prover sends $\mathcal{M}$ to the verifier.

$\mathcal{P} \to \mathcal{V}$: The verifier samples $x \leftarrow \mathbb{Z}_q \setminus \{a_1, \ldots, a_r\}$, $\beta \leftarrow \mathbb{Z}_q^{r+1}$, $\gamma \leftarrow \mathbb{Z}_q^{rb}$ and $\delta \leftarrow \mathbb{Z}_q^{rb}$ and sends them to the prover.

$\mathcal{P} \to \mathcal{V}$: The prover computes vectors

$$\bar{\mathbf{f}} = \mathbf{f}(x) \ , \qquad \bar{\mathbf{f}}^f = \sum_{j=0}^r \mathbf{r}_j^s \ell_j(x) \ , \qquad \bar{\mathbf{r}}^v = \sum_{i=0}^{b-1}\sum_{j=1}^r \mathbf{r}_{i,j}^v \ell_j(x)\ell_0(x)^{i+1} \ ,$$

$$\bar{\mathbf{r}}^w = \sum_{i=0}^{b-1}\sum_{j=1}^r \mathbf{r}_{i,j}^w \ell_j(x)\ell_0(x)^{i+1} \ , \qquad \bar{\mathbf{z}} = \mathbf{y} + \sum_{j=0}^r \beta_j \mathbf{s}_j + \sum_{i=0}^{b-1}\sum_{j=1}^r (\gamma_{i,j}\mathbf{v}_{i,j} + \delta_{i,j}\mathbf{w}_{i,j}) \ , \text{ and}$$

$$\bar{\mathbf{r}}^z = \mathbf{r}^y + \sum_{j=0}^r \beta_j \mathbf{r}_j^s + \sum_{i=0}^{b-1}\sum_{j=1}^r (\gamma_{i,j}\mathbf{r}_{i,j}^v + \delta_{i,j}\mathbf{r}_{i,j}^w) \ ,$$

and sends them to the verifier.

$\mathcal{P} \leftarrow \mathcal{V}$: The verifier samples $I \leftarrow [l]^\tau$ such that $|I| = \tau$ and sends I to the prover.

$\mathcal{P} \to \mathcal{V}$: The prover computes $\mathbf{Y}|_I$, $S|_I$, $V|_I$, $W|_I$, $\rho|_I$ and $\mathsf{MerklePaths}_I$, and sends them to the verifier.

$\mathcal{V}$:

- The verifier checks $\mathbf{Y}|_I$, $S|_I$, $V|_I$, $W|_I$ and $\rho|_I$ against $\mathcal{M}$ and $\mathsf{MerklePaths}_I$.
- The verifier computes $\bar{\mathbf{d}} = \sum_{j=1}^r \mathbf{u}_j \ell_j(x) - \mathbf{A}\bar{\mathbf{f}}$ and checks whether

$$\mathsf{Enc}\left(\bar{\mathbf{f}}, \bar{\mathbf{r}}^f\right)\big|_I \stackrel{?}{=} \sum_{j=0}^r \ell_j(x)\mathbf{S}_j|_I \ , \qquad \mathsf{Enc}\left(\bigcirc_{i=0}^{b-1}\left[\bar{\mathbf{f}} - i\mathbf{1}^m\right], \bar{\mathbf{r}}^v\right)\big|_I \stackrel{?}{=} \sum_{i=0}^{b-1}\sum_{j=1}^r \ell_j(x)\ell_0(x)^{i+1}\mathbf{V}_{i,j}|_I \ ,$$

$$\mathsf{Enc}\left(\bigcirc_{i=0}^{b-1}\left[\bar{\mathbf{d}} - i\mathbf{1}^n\right], \bar{\mathbf{r}}^w\right)\big|_I \stackrel{?}{=} \sum_{i=0}^{b-1}\sum_{j=1}^r \ell_j(x)\ell_0(x)^{i+1}\mathbf{W}_{i,j}|_I \ , \text{ and} \quad \mathsf{Enc}\,(\bar{\mathbf{z}}, \bar{\mathbf{r}}^z)|_I \stackrel{?}{=} \mathbf{Y}|_I + \sum_{j=0}^r \beta_j \mathbf{S}_j|_I + \sum_{i=0}^{b-1}\sum_{j=1}^r (\gamma_{i,j}\mathbf{V}_{i,j} + \delta_{i,j}\mathbf{W}_{i,j}|_I) \ .$$

Fig. 3. Sublinear hash-based proof of knowledge of short solutions to many linear equations over $\mathbb{Z}_q$.

and I from the protocol in Fig. 3, outputs a protocol transcript whose distribution is indistinguishable from that of a real transcript from the interaction between an honest prover and an honest verifier.

The proof of Theorem 4.2 is included in the full version of this paper [BLNS20].

Theorem 4.3 (Knowledge Soundness). *Let* $\mathcal{C} \subset \mathbb{Z}_q^l$ *be a Reed-Solomon code of dimension* $k' = \max(n, m) + \tau$ *and length* l *with encoding function* $\mathsf{Enc}\,()$. *Let* $k' \leq k \leq l$. *Suppose that there is an efficient deterministic prover* $\mathcal{P}^*$ *that convinces the honest verifier* $\mathcal{V}$ *on input* $\mathbf{A}, \mathbf{u}_j$ *to accept with probability*

$$\varepsilon > 2\max\left\{ 2\left(\frac{k}{l-\tau}\right)^\tau, \frac{1}{q-r} + \left(1 - \frac{k-k'}{6l}\right)^\tau, 2\left(1 - \frac{2(k-k')}{3l}\right)^\tau, \frac{2(b+1)r}{q-r} \right\}.$$

Then, there exists an efficient probabilistic extraction algorithm $\mathcal{E}$ *which, given rewindable black-box access to* $\mathcal{P}^*$, *either produces vectors* $\mathbf{s}_j \in \{0, \ldots, b-1\}^m$ *such that* $\mathbf{u}_j - \mathbf{A}\mathbf{s}_j \in \{0, \ldots, b-1\}^n$ *for all* $j = 1, \ldots, r$ *or finds a hash collision in expected time at most* $64T$ *where* $T := \frac{3}{\varepsilon} + \frac{k-\tau}{\varepsilon/2 - (k/(l-\tau))^\tau}$ *and running* $\mathcal{P}^*$ *once is assumed to take unit time.*

The proof of Theorem 4.3 is included in the full version of this paper [BLNS20].

The parameter k is used as part of the strategy for the knowledge extractor $\mathcal{E}$, but not in the protocol itself, as discussed in Remark 3.4.

4.1 Proof Size

In one execution of the protocol in Fig. 3 the prover sends 6 masked secret vectors $\bar{\mathbf{f}} \in \mathbb{Z}_q^m$, $\bar{\mathbf{z}}$, and $\bar{\mathbf{r}}^\iota \in \mathbb{Z}_q^\tau$ for $\iota = f, v, w, z$ for all r equations with a total of $2m + 4\tau$ $\mathbb{Z}_q$-coefficients. Then he also sends τ codeword positions from all of the $(2b + 1)r + 1$ codewords in the protocol, and τ bitstrings of commitment randomness, each of size 128 bits. Note that from the soundness error in Theorem 4.3 it is clear that τ does not need to increase with the number of equations. So this part only scales linearly in r. Finally, the number of hashes sent is exactly the same as in the single-equation protocol from Sect. 3. That is, the prover sends $h + \tau\lceil log(l/h)\rceil$ 32-byte hashes. In summary, we see that the protocol has a bandwidth requirement of

$$\left((2m + ((2b+1)r + 5)\tau)\lceil \log q \rceil + 128\tau + 256\left(h + \tau\left\lceil \log\left(\frac{l}{h}\right)\right\rceil\right) \right) \Big/ 8192$$

kilobytes. Asymptotically, when we have $r = O(m)$ equations with m secret coefficients each, so $O(m^2)$ secret coefficients in total, we see that the communication cost is of order $O(m)$, which is the square root of the number of secret coefficients. To be a little more precise, the parameter m is multiplied by $2\log q$, while the parameter r is multiplied by $(2b+1)\tau\log q$. Thus the optimal setting of parameters occurs roughly when $m \approx b\tau r$. If the scenario in which we need to apply our proof system does not have this optimal relation between m and r because r is too large, we can transform our instance into one that does. For example, we can transform several relations of the form $\mathbf{u}_1 = \mathbf{A}\mathbf{s}_1 + \mathbf{e}_1, \ldots, \mathbf{u}_j = \mathbf{A}\mathbf{s}_j + \mathbf{e}_j$ into one relation

$$\begin{bmatrix} \mathbf{A} & 0 & \cdots & 0 & 0 \\ & & \cdots & & \\ & & \cdots & & \\ & & \cdots & & \\ & & \cdots & & \\ 0 & 0 & \cdots & 0 & \mathbf{A} \end{bmatrix} \cdot \begin{bmatrix} \mathbf{s}_1 \\ \cdots \\ \cdots \\ \cdots \\ \mathbf{s}_j \end{bmatrix} + \begin{bmatrix} \mathbf{e}_1 \\ \cdots \\ \cdots \\ \cdots \\ \mathbf{e}_j \end{bmatrix} = \begin{bmatrix} \mathbf{u}_1 \\ \cdots \\ \cdots \\ \cdots \\ \mathbf{u}_j \end{bmatrix} \tag{8}$$

If we combine j relations into one in such manner, then the magnitude of m and n increase by a factor of j, while the number of equations r gets reduced by this same factor. By picking the j strategically, one can therefore end up with $m \approx b\tau r$ for the new values of m and r.

Example. Since the proof system in this section is multiple instances of the example from [BLS19, ENS20] (using the same public randomness matrix $\mathbf{A}$), we compare the amortized output size to those papers. As an example, we consider the case where $(q, R, N, M) = (\approx 2^{32}, 1026, 1024, 1024)$ and one wants to prove

$$\mathbf{u}_j = \mathbf{A}\mathbf{s}_j + \mathbf{e}_j \text{ and } \mathbf{s}_j, \mathbf{e}_j \in \{-1, 0, 1\}^M \text{ for } j \in [r] \text{ and } \mathbf{A} \in \mathbb{Z}_q^{N \times M}.$$

We take the value R larger than optimal to illustrate how one can use the idea from above (i.e. (8)) to optimally rearrange the equations. Firstly, note that for every divisor d of R,[6] we can define vectors

$$\mathbf{s}_i^* = \begin{pmatrix} \mathbf{s}_{(i-1)d+1} \\ \vdots \\ \mathbf{s}_{id} \end{pmatrix}, \mathbf{e}_i^* = \begin{pmatrix} \mathbf{e}_{(i-1)d+1} \\ \vdots \\ \mathbf{e}_{id} \end{pmatrix}, \mathbf{u}_i^* = \begin{pmatrix} \mathbf{u}_{(i-1)d+1} \\ \vdots \\ \mathbf{u}_{id} \end{pmatrix}$$

for $i \in [r/d]$ and a matrix $\mathbf{A}^* = \mathbf{I}_d \otimes \mathbf{A}$, where $\mathbf{I}_d$ is the $d \times d$ identity matrix. Clearly, our problem is reduced to proving that each $\mathbf{s}_i, \mathbf{e}_i \in \{-1, 0, 1\}^{Md}$ and

$$\mathbf{u}_i^* = \mathbf{A}^* \mathbf{s}_i^* + \mathbf{e}_i^* \text{ for } i \in [R/d].$$

Now, we can apply our protocol from Fig. 3 for $(b, n, m, r) = (3, N, Md, R/d)$ and find an appropriate divisor d to minimize the proof size per equation.

In this example, we pick $d = 18$, hence $r = 57$. The last term in the expression for the soundness error in Theorem 4.3 limits it to at least 2^{-24}. So we search for parameters k, l and τ under the constraint that the soundness error stays below 2^{-24}. Then 5 iterations of the protocol give a negligible soundness error of less than 2^{-120}. Our search for such parameters minimizing the proof size resulted in

$$k = 50304, \quad l = 55809, \quad \text{and} \quad \tau = 176.$$

With these parameters and $h = 2\tau$, the total proof size for all 5 iterations is 2384 kilobytes. So this translates to an amortized cost of 2.32 kilobytes per equation, which is a noticeable improvement over the 47 KB proof size in [ENS20].

Acknowledgements. We would like to thank anonymous reviewers for their useful feedback. This work was supported by the SNSF ERC Transfer Grant CRETP2-166734 FELICITY.

A   The Hiding Property of Reed-Solomon Codes

We show that when $\mathbf{r}$ is sampled uniformly at random from $\mathbb{Z}_q^\tau$, then any τ entries of the Reed-Solomon encoding $\mathsf{Enc}(\mathbf{m}, \mathbf{r})$ corresponding to the input polynomial $f = \sum_{i=0}^{m-1} \mathbf{m}_i X^i + X^m \sum_{i=0}^{\tau-1} \mathbf{r}_i X^i$ follow the uniform distribution over $\mathbb{Z}_q^\tau$.

---

[6] If d is not a divisor of R, we can pad the last equation with zeroes.

Let $\zeta_1, \ldots, \zeta_l$ be distinct elements of $\mathbb{Z}_q^\times$ used as the evaluation points for the Reed-Solomon code. We can write the encoding $\mathsf{Enc}\,(\mathbf{m}, \mathbf{r})$ as a matrix multiplication:

$$
\mathsf{Enc}\,(\mathbf{m}, \mathbf{r}) = \begin{bmatrix} 1 & \zeta_1 & \zeta_1^2 & \cdots & \zeta_1^{m-1} \\ 1 & \zeta_2 & \zeta_2^2 & \cdots & \zeta_2^{m-1} \\ \vdots & \vdots & \vdots & \ddots & \vdots \\ 1 & \zeta_l & \zeta_l^2 & \cdots & \zeta_l^{m-1} \end{bmatrix} \mathbf{m} + \begin{bmatrix} \zeta_1^m & \cdots & \zeta_1^{m+\tau-1} \\ \zeta_2^m & \cdots & \zeta_2^{m+\tau-1} \\ \vdots & \ddots & \vdots \\ \zeta_l^m & \cdots & \zeta_l^{m+\tau-1} \end{bmatrix} \mathbf{r} = A\mathbf{m} + B\mathbf{r}
$$

Let I be a subset of $[l]$ with $|I| = \tau$, and let $B(I)$ be the submatrix of B formed by restricting to the rows in I. Observe $B(I)$ forms a Vandermonde matrix where the i-th row has been multiplied by ζ_i^m. Since the ζ_i are distinct and non-zero, $B(I)$ is invertible. Hence, if $\mathbf{r}$ is sampled uniformly at random from $\mathbb{Z}_q^\tau$, then $B(I)\mathbf{r}$ is uniformly distributed over $\mathbb{Z}_q^\tau$. This argument shows that any τ entries of $\mathsf{Enc}\,(\mathbf{m}, \mathbf{r})$ are uniformly distributed.

References

[ACPS09] Applebaum, B., Cash, D., Peikert, C., Sahai, A.: Fast cryptographic primitives and circular-secure encryption based on hard learning problems. In: Halevi, S. (ed.) CRYPTO 2009. LNCS, vol. 5677, pp. 595–618. Springer, Heidelberg (2009). https://doi.org/10.1007/978-3-642-03356-8_35

[AHIV17] Ames, S., Hazay, C., Ishai, Y., Venkitasubramaniam, M.: Ligero: lightweight sublinear arguments without a trusted setup. In: ACM Conference on Computer and Communications Security - CCS 2017, pp. 2087–2104 (2017)

[BBB+18] Bünz, B., Bootle, J., Boneh, D., Poelstra, A., Wuille, P., Maxwell, G.: Bulletproofs: short proofs for confidential transactions and more. In: IEEE Symposium on Security and Privacy - IEEE S&P 2018, pp. 315–334 (2018)

[BBC+18] Baum, C., Bootle, J., Cerulli, A., del Pino, R., Groth, J., Lyubashevsky, V.: Sub-linear lattice-based zero-knowledge arguments for arithmetic circuits. In: Shacham, H., Boldyreva, A. (eds.) CRYPTO 2018. LNCS, vol. 10992, pp. 669–699. Springer, Cham (2018). https://doi.org/10.1007/978-3-319-96881-0_23

[BCC+16] Bootle, J., Cerulli, A., Chaidos, P., Groth, J., Petit, C.: Efficient zero-knowledge arguments for arithmetic circuits in the discrete log setting. In: Fischlin, M., Coron, J.-S. (eds.) EUROCRYPT 2016. LNCS, vol. 9666, pp. 327–357. Springer, Heidelberg (2016). https://doi.org/10.1007/978-3-662-49896-5_12

[BCG+17] Bootle, J., Cerulli, A., Ghadafi, E., Groth, J., Hajiabadi, M., Jakobsen, S.K.: Linear-time zero-knowledge proofs for arithmetic circuit satisfiability. In: Takagi, T., Peyrin, T. (eds.) ASIACRYPT 2017. LNCS, vol. 10626, pp. 336–365. Springer, Cham (2017). https://doi.org/10.1007/978-3-319-70700-6_12

[BCOS20] Boschini, C., Camenisch, J., Ovsiankin, M., Spooner, N.: Efficient post-quantum snarks for RSIS and RLWE and their applications to privacy. In: International Conference on Post-Quantum Cryptography - PQCrypto 2020, pp. 247–267 (2020)

626   J. Bootle et al.

[BCR+19] Ben-Sasson, E., Chiesa, A., Riabzev, M., Spooner, N., Virza, M., Ward, N.P.: Aurora: transparent succinct arguments for R1CS. In: Ishai, Y., Rijmen, V. (eds.) EUROCRYPT 2019. LNCS, vol. 11476, pp. 103–128. Springer, Cham (2019). https://doi.org/10.1007/978-3-030-17653-2_4

[BCS16] Ben-Sasson, E., Chiesa, A., Spooner, N.: Interactive Oracle proofs. In: Hirt, M., Smith, A. (eds.) TCC 2016. LNCS, vol. 9986, pp. 31–60. Springer, Heidelberg (2016). https://doi.org/10.1007/978-3-662-53644-5_2

[BCS19] Baum, C., Cozzo, D., Smart, N.P.: Using TopGear in overdrive: a more efficient ZKPoK for SPDZ. In: Paterson, K.G., Stebila, D. (eds.) SAC 2019. LNCS, vol. 11959, pp. 274–302. Springer, Cham (2020). https://doi.org/10.1007/978-3-030-38471-5_12

[BDL+18] Baum, C., Damgård, I., Lyubashevsky, V., Oechsner, S., Peikert, C.: More efficient commitments from structured lattice assumptions. In: Catalano, D., De Prisco, R. (eds.) SCN 2018. LNCS, vol. 11035, pp. 368–385. Springer, Cham (2018). https://doi.org/10.1007/978-3-319-98113-0_20

[Beu20] Beullens, W.: Sigma protocols for MQ, PKP and SIS, and fishy signature schemes. In: Canteaut, A., Ishai, Y. (eds.) EUROCRYPT 2020. LNCS, vol. 12107, pp. 183–211. Springer, Cham (2020). https://doi.org/10.1007/978-3-030-45727-3_7

[BKS18] Ben-Sasson, E., Kopparty, S., Saraf, S.: Worst-case to average case reductions for the distance to a code. In: Computational Complexity Conference - CCC 2018, pp. 1–23 (2018)

[BLNS20] Bootle, J., Lyubashevsky, V., Nguyen, N.K., Seiler, G.: More efficient amortization of exact zero-knowledge proofs for LWE. IACR Cryptology ePrint Archive, Report 2020/1449 (2020)

[BLS19] Bootle, J., Lyubashevsky, V., Seiler, G.: Algebraic techniques for short(er) exact lattice-based zero-knowledge proofs. In: Boldyreva, A., Micciancio, D. (eds.) CRYPTO 2019. LNCS, vol. 11692, pp. 176–202. Springer, Cham (2019). https://doi.org/10.1007/978-3-030-26948-7_7

[DKL+18] Ducas, L., et al.: Crystals-Dilithium: a lattice-based digital signature scheme, pp. 238–268 (2018)

[dPLNS17] del Pino, R., Lyubashevsky, V., Neven, G., Seiler, G.: Practical quantum-safe voting from lattices. In: ACM Conference on Computer and Communications Security - CCS 2017, pp. 1565–1581 (2017)

[dPLS19] del Pino, R., Lyubashevsky, V., Seiler, G.: Short discrete log proofs for FHE and Ring-LWE ciphertexts. In: Lin, D., Sako, K. (eds.) PKC 2019. LNCS, vol. 11442, pp. 344–373. Springer, Cham (2019). https://doi.org/10.1007/978-3-030-17253-4_12

[EKS+20] Esgin, M.F., et al.: Practical post-quantum few-time verifiable random function with applications to algorand. IACR Cryptology ePrint Archive, Report 2020/1222 (2020)

[ENS20] Esgin, M.F., Nguyen, N.K., Seiler, G.: Practical exact proofs from lattices: new techniques to exploit fully-splitting rings. In: Moriai, S., Wang, H. (eds.) ASIACRYPT 2020. LNCS, vol. 12492, pp. 259–288. Springer, Cham (2020). https://doi.org/10.1007/978-3-030-64834-3_9

[EZS+19] Esgin, M.F., Zhao, R.K., Steinfeld, R., Liu, J.K., Liu, D.: Matrict: efficient, scalable and post-quantum blockchain confidential transactions protocol. In: ACM Conference on Computer and Communications Security - CCS 2019, pp. 567–584 (2019)

[GGPR13] Gennaro, R., Gentry, C., Parno, B., Raykova, M.: Quadratic span programs and succinct NIZKs without PCPs. In: Johansson, T., Nguyen, P.Q. (eds.) EUROCRYPT 2013. LNCS, vol. 7881, pp. 626–645. Springer, Heidelberg (2013). https://doi.org/10.1007/978-3-642-38348-9_37

[Kil92] Kilian, J.: A note on efficient zero-knowledge proofs and arguments. In: ACM Symposium on the Theory of Computing - STOC 1992, pp. 723–732 (1992)

[KKPP20] Katsumata, S., Kwiatkowski, K., Pintore, F., Prest, T.: Scalable ciphertext compression techniques for post-quantum KEMs and their applications. In: Moriai, S., Wang, H. (eds.) ASIACRYPT 2020. LNCS, vol. 12491, pp. 289–320. Springer, Cham (2020). https://doi.org/10.1007/978-3-030-64837-4_10

[KR08] Kalai, Y.T., Raz, R.: Interactive PCP. In: Aceto, L., Damgård, I., Goldberg, L.A., Halldórsson, M.M., Ingólfsdóttir, A., Walukiewicz, I. (eds.) ICALP 2008. LNCS, vol. 5126, pp. 536–547. Springer, Heidelberg (2008). https://doi.org/10.1007/978-3-540-70583-3_44

[KTX08] Kawachi, A., Tanaka, K., Xagawa, K.: Concurrently secure identification schemes based on the worst-case hardness of lattice problems. In: Pieprzyk, J. (ed.) ASIACRYPT 2008. LNCS, vol. 5350, pp. 372–389. Springer, Heidelberg (2008). https://doi.org/10.1007/978-3-540-89255-7_23

[LNS21] Lyubashevsky, V., Nguyen, N.K., Seiler, G.: Shorter lattice-based zero-knowledge proofs via one-time commitments. In: Garay, J.A. (ed.) PKC 2021. LNCS, vol. 12710, pp. 215–241. Springer, Cham (2021). https://doi.org/10.1007/978-3-030-75245-3_9

[LNSW13] Ling, S., Nguyen, K., Stehlé, D., Wang, H.: Improved zero-knowledge proofs of knowledge for the ISIS problem, and applications. In: Kurosawa, K., Hanaoka, G. (eds.) PKC 2013. LNCS, vol. 7778, pp. 107–124. Springer, Heidelberg (2013). https://doi.org/10.1007/978-3-642-36362-7_8

[MF21] Mittelbach, A., Fischlin, M.: The Theory of Hash Functions and Random Oracles - An Approach to Modern Cryptography. Springer, Cham (2021)

[Mic00] Micali, S.: Computationally sound proofs. SIAM J. Comput. 30(4), 1253–1298 (2000)

[PVW08] Peikert, C., Vaikuntanathan, V., Waters, B.: A framework for efficient and composable oblivious transfer. In: Wagner, D. (ed.) CRYPTO 2008. LNCS, vol. 5157, pp. 554–571. Springer, Heidelberg (2008). https://doi.org/10.1007/978-3-540-85174-5_31

[RRR16] Reingold, O., Rothblum, G.N., Rothblum, R.D.: Constant-round interactive proofs for delegating computation. In: ACM Symposium on the Theory of Computing - STOC 2016, pp. 49–62 (2016)

[RVW13] Rothblum, G.N., Vadhan, S.P., Wigderson, A.: Interactive proofs of proximity: delegating computation in sublinear time. In: ACM Symposium on the Theory of Computing - STOC 2013, pp. 793–802 (2013)

[Sho] Victor Shoup. https://www.shoup.net/ntl/

[Ste93] Stern, J.: A new identification scheme based on syndrome decoding. In: Stinson, D.R. (ed.) CRYPTO 1993. LNCS, vol. 773, pp. 13–21. Springer, Heidelberg (1994). https://doi.org/10.1007/3-540-48329-2_2

[YAZ+19] Yang, R., Au, M.H., Zhang, Z., Xu, Q., Yu, Z., Whyte, W.: Efficient lattice-based zero-knowledge arguments with standard soundness: construction and applications. In: Boldyreva, A., Micciancio, D. (eds.) CRYPTO 2019. LNCS, vol. 11692, pp. 147–175. Springer, Cham (2019). https://doi.org/10.1007/978-3-030-26948-7_6

Zero Knowledge Contingent Payments for Trained Neural Networks

Zhelei Zhou[1], Xinle Cao[1], Jian Liu[1,2(✉)], Bingsheng Zhang[1,2(✉)], and Kui Ren[1,3]

[1] Zhejiang University, Hangzhou, China
{zl_zhou,xinle,liujian2411,bingsheng,kuiren}@zju.edu.cn
[2] ZJU-GTTX Joint Research Laboratory for Cyber Security, Hangzhou, China
[3] Key Laboratory of Blockchain and Cyberspace Governance of Zhejiang Province, Hangzhou, China

Abstract. Nowadays, neural networks have been widely used in many machine learning tasks. In practice, one might not have enough expertise to fine-tune a neural network model; therefore, it becomes increasingly popular to outsource the model training process to a machine learning expert. This activity brings out the needs of fair model exchange: if the seller sends the model first, the buyer might refuse to pay; if the buyer pays first, the seller might refuse to send the model or send an inferior model. In this work, we aim to address this problem so that neither the buyer nor the seller can deceive the other. We start from Zero Knowledge Contingent Payment (ZKCP), which is used for fair exchange of digital goods and payment over blockchain, and extend it to *Zero Knowledge Contingent Model Payment* (ZKCMP). We then instantiate our ZKCMP with two state-of-the-art NIZK proofs: zk-SNARKs and Libra. We also propose a random sampling technique to improve the efficiency of zk-SNARKs. We extensively conduct experiments to demonstrate the practicality of our proposal.

1 Introduction

Deep neural networks have recently gained much popularity due to their record-breaking performance on a wide range of machine learning tasks such as pattern recognition [5], medical diagnosis [9] and credit-risk assessment [3]. It is well-known that the final performance of a neural network model highly depends on its training data. However, the data owners usually do not have enough expertise to fine-tune the model, thereby they would like to outsource the training process to some machine learning (ML) experts. This gives ML experts an opportunity to monetize their skills, but brings the challenge of *fairly exchanging the model*: if the seller (i.e., ML expert) returns the model first, the buyer might refuse to pay the honorarium; if the buyer pays first, the seller might refuse to provide the model or provide an inferior model. In this paper, we aim to address this problem so that neither the buyer nor the seller can cheat the other.

© Springer Nature Switzerland AG 2021
E. Bertino et al. (Eds.): ESORICS 2021, LNCS 12973, pp. 628–648, 2021.
https://doi.org/10.1007/978-3-030-88428-4_31

Our starting point is *zero knowledge contingent payment* (ZKCP), which allows fair exchange of digital goods and payments over Bitcoin. Most cryptocurrencies like Bitcoin and Ethereum allow a payer to make a payment by specifying a condition that needs to be met in order for the money to be redeemed by the payee. One example of such conditions is a *hash-locked transaction* [2], where a payment can be redeemed by presenting a SHA256 preimage of a hash value. In ZKCP, the seller first encrypts the digital goods s as a ciphertext c and sends it to the buyer together with the hash of the encryption key $y := \mathsf{SHA256}(k)$. Then, the buyer makes a hash-locked transaction requiring the seller to post k to the blockchain to redeem the payment. Meanwhile, the buyer can decrypt c and obtain the purchased information. Moreover, the seller is required to prove that c really encrypts the "desired information" and the preimage of y is the encryption key, via a zero-knowledge (ZK) proof [13], which guarantees that the proof does not leak anything about s and k.

In our case, the digital goods s is a trained neural network, and the "desired information" means that s reaches a certain level of accuracy. We introduce a new notion named *zero knowledge contingent model payment* (ZKCMP), the whole procedure of which is as follows: (i) the buyer sends the training dataset to the seller; (ii) the seller trains a model s and commits it to the buyer, denoted as $c = \mathsf{Enc}(k, s)$ and $y = \mathsf{hash}(k)$; (iii) the buyer sends the testing dataset together with desired accuracy acc to the seller; (iv) the seller evaluates the model on the testing dataset; (v) the seller sends a ZK proof, proving that "the preimage of y can decrypt c and gets the previously committed model s, which achieves an accuracy of acc when being evaluated on the testing dataset"; (vi) the buyer verifies the proof and posts a hash-locked transaction for y; (vii) the seller redeems the payment by posting k to the blockchain.

For the ZK proof, we investigate both zk-SNARKs [6] and Libra [17]. The challenge for zk-SNARKs is that the proof generation phase is time-consuming and memory-consuming since it involves billions of gates for running a neural network over the testing dataset. To this end, we propose a *random sampling* technique to reduce the computational overhead for generating a proof, while still keeping the exchange secure and fair. The challenge for Libra is that the layered arithmetic circuit being used can only have a single output, thereby cannot support the proof for both accuracy and encryption. To conquer this, we construct separate arithmetic circuits for different output, and use zero-knowledge polynomial commitment to connect them (i.e., commit the I/O of each circuit so that circuits can be connected in a zero-knowledge way). A common challenge for both zk-SNARKs and Libra is that proving the final accuracy of the neural network is non-trivial. We design a customized circuit by composing a series of matrix operations so that the final accuracy can be proved efficiently. We summarize our contribution as follows:

- We propose a new notion named *zero knowledge contingent model payment* (ZKCMP), which allows fair exchange of a trained machine learning model and a cryptocurrency payment (e.g., Bitcoin) (cf. Sect. 3).
- We instantiate ZKCMP with zk-SNARKs and Libra respectively, which involves a series of sophistic circuit designs (cf. Sect. 4).

- We propose a random sampling technique to improve the efficiency of zk-SNARKs (cf. Sect. 4.1).
- We provide a full-fledged implementation and conduct experiments extensively (cf. Sect. 6).

2   Preliminaries

Notations. Let λ be the security parameter. Let $\mathsf{negl}(\cdot)$ denote a negligible function. Let PRF be a pseudorandom function. Let $\mathbb{F}$ be a finite field of prime order. We denote $[x]$ as the set $\{1, 2, \ldots, x\}$. We denote $\vec{1}_n$ as the vector $(1, \ldots, 1) \in \mathbb{F}^n$. Let $\mathcal{M}$ be a trained model, we denote w as the model parameter. We denote $\mathcal{D} := \{\langle x_i, L_i \rangle\}_{i \in n}$ (where x_i is the data sample entry, and L_i is its corresponding label) of size n.

Commitment Scheme. A commitment scheme consists of:

- $\mathsf{Setup}(1^\lambda)$. It is the public parameter generation algorithm that takes input as the security parameter λ, and it outputs public parameter pp (to be used by the other algorithms implicitly).
- $\mathsf{Commit}(m; r)$. It is the commitment generation algorithm that takes input as: the message m, the random coin r. It outputs commitment-opening pair (E, d). When r is not important, we use $\mathsf{Commit}(m)$ for simplicity.
- $\mathsf{Verify}(c, d, m)$. It is the verification algorithm that takes input as: the commitment c, the opening d, the message m. It outputs a bit $b \in \{0, 1\}$, indicating acceptance or rejection.

A commitment scheme should be simultaneously binding and hiding, and let $\mathsf{Adv}_{\mathsf{COM}}^{\mathcal{A}, Hide}(\lambda)$ and $\mathsf{Adv}_{\mathsf{COM}}^{\mathcal{A}, Bind}(\lambda)$ denote the corresponding adversarial advantage. In this work, we instantiate COM with salted SHA256. In particular, we pick a random $r \leftarrow \{0, 1\}^\lambda$, and commit to m by $E \leftarrow \mathsf{SHA256}(m||r)$, the opening is set as $d := (m, r)$.

Non-interactive Zero-Knowledge (NIZK) Proofs. Let $\mathcal{R}$ be an efficiently decidable binary relation, which defines the NP language $\mathcal{L} := \{\mathsf{st}|\ \exists\mathsf{wit} : (\mathsf{st}, \mathsf{wit}) \in \mathcal{R}\}$. A NIZK proof system $\mathsf{NIZK}_\mathcal{R}$ for $\mathcal{R}$ consists of:

- $\mathsf{Setup}(1^\lambda)$. It is the common reference string (CRS) generation algorithm that takes input as the security parameter λ, and it outputs a CRS crs.
- $\mathsf{Prove}(crs, \mathsf{st}, \mathsf{wit})$. It is the proof generation algorithm that takes input as: the CRS crs, statement st, witness wit. It outputs a proof π.
- $\mathsf{Verify}(crs, \mathsf{st}, \pi)$. It is the verification algorithm that takes input as: the CRS crs, statement s, proof π. It outputs a bit $b \in \{0, 1\}$.

Definition 1 (NIZK). *A triple of algorithms* $\mathsf{NIZK}_\mathcal{R} := (\mathsf{Setup}, \mathsf{Prove}, \mathsf{Verify})$ *is a NIZK proof for the relation* $\mathcal{R}$ *if the following properties holds:*

- **Perfect Completeness.** *We say that a NIZK system for $\mathcal{R}$ is perfectly complete if for any adversary $\mathcal{A}$, we have:*

$$Pr\left[\begin{array}{l} crs \leftarrow \mathsf{Setup}(1^{\lambda}); (\mathsf{st}, \mathsf{wit}) \leftarrow \mathcal{A}(crs); \\ \pi \leftarrow \mathsf{Prove}(crs, \mathsf{st}, \mathsf{wit}) \end{array} : (\mathsf{st}, \mathsf{wit}) \notin \mathcal{R} \vee \mathsf{Verify}(crs, \mathsf{st}, \pi) = 1 \right] = 1$$

- **Computational Soundness.** *We say that a NIZK system for $\mathcal{R}$ is computationally sound if for any PPT adversary $\mathcal{A}$, the adversarial advantage $\mathsf{Adv}_{\mathsf{NIZK}}^{\mathcal{A},Sound}(\lambda)$ is:*

$$Pr\left[\begin{array}{l} crs \leftarrow \mathsf{Setup}(1^{\lambda}); \\ (\mathsf{st}, \pi) \leftarrow \mathcal{A}(crs) \end{array} : \mathsf{Verify}(crs, \mathsf{st}, \pi) = 1 \wedge \mathsf{st} \notin \mathcal{L} \right] = \mathsf{negl}(\lambda)$$

- **Computational Zero-Knowledge.** *We say that a NIZK system for $\mathcal{R}$ is computationally zero-knowledge if there exists a pair of PPT simulators $(\mathsf{Sim}_1, \mathsf{Sim}_2)$ such that for any PPT adversary $\mathcal{A}$, the adversarial advantage $\mathsf{Adv}_{\mathsf{NIZK}}^{\mathcal{A},ZK}(\lambda)$ is:*

$$\left| Pr\left[\begin{array}{l} crs \leftarrow \mathsf{Setup}(1^{\lambda}): \\ \mathcal{A}^{\mathsf{Prove}(crs,\cdot,\cdot)}(crs) = 1 \end{array}\right] - Pr\left[\begin{array}{l} (crs^*, \mathsf{td}) \leftarrow \mathsf{Sim}_1(1^{\lambda}): \\ \mathcal{A}^{\mathsf{Sim}^*(crs^*,\mathsf{td},\cdot,\cdot)}(crs^*) = 1 \end{array}\right] \right| = \mathsf{negl}(\lambda)$$

Where the oracle $\mathsf{Sim}^*(crs^*, \mathsf{td}, \mathsf{st}, \mathsf{wit}) := \mathsf{Sim}_2(crs^*, \mathsf{st}, \mathsf{td})$ for $(\mathsf{st}, \mathsf{wit}) \in \mathcal{R}$ and the oracle outputs $\perp$ if $(\mathsf{st}, \mathsf{wit}) \notin \mathcal{R}$.

In practice, the relation decision algorithm is instantiated by a circuit $\mathcal{C}_{\mathcal{R}}(\mathsf{st}, \mathsf{wit})$, which outputs 1 if $(\mathsf{st}, \mathsf{wit}) \in \mathcal{R}$; otherwise, it outputs 0.

zk-SNARKs. Zero-knowledge succinct non-interactive arguments of knowledge (zk-SNARKs) [6] is a type of widely used NIZK proof systems. It achieves succinct proof size and verification time, whereas the proving cost is heavy. zk-SNARKs can be used to prove the satisfaction problem of a system of rank-1 quadratic equations over a finite field $\mathbb{F}$. See more details in [4].

Definition 2. *Denote N_g the number of rank-1 quadratic equations, N_v the number of variables, and ℓ the statement size. A system of rank-1 quadratic equations over $\mathbb{F}$ is a tuple $\mathcal{S} = ((a_j, b_j, c_j)_{j=1}^{N_g}, \ell, N_v)$ where $a_j, b_j, c_j \in \mathbb{F}^{1+N_v}$ and $\ell \leq N_v$. Such a system S is satisfiable with an input $x \in \mathbb{F}^{\ell}$ if there is a witness $w \in \mathbb{F}^{N_v - \ell}$ such that: $\forall j \in [N_g], \langle a_j, (1, x, w) \rangle \cdot \langle b_j, (1, x, w) \rangle = \langle c_j, (1, x, w) \rangle$. In such a case, we write $\mathcal{S}(x, w) = 1$.*

In brief, zk-SNARKs aims to prove the relation $\mathcal{R}_S = \{(x, w) \in \mathbb{F}^{\ell} \times \mathbb{F}^{N_v - \ell} : \mathcal{S}(x, w) = 1\}$ holds. In this article, we call the system of rank-1 quadrtic equations as *constraint system*, the rank-1 quadratic equation as *constraint equation* to make our expression clear.

Libra. Libra [17] is a zero-knowledge proof system that is designed for layered arithmetic circuits. The performance of Libra is competitive, it has very fast prover time and succinct proof size/verification time. Libra uses zero-knowledge

GKR protocol [12] and zero-knowledge verifiable polynomial delegation scheme (zkVPD) [18] as two main building blocks. The construction for non-interactive version of Libra is presented in Fig. 1. In Appendix A, we provide brief description of its main building blocks.

Non-interactive Libra for $\mathcal{C}(\mathsf{st}, \mathsf{wit}) = 1$

Libra.Setup(1^λ):

- Generate $(pp, vp) \leftarrow$ zkVPD.KeyGen(1^λ);
- Output $crs := (pp, vp)$;

Libra.Prove($\mathsf{st}, \mathsf{wit}, \mathcal{C}$):

- Select a random bivariate polynomial R;
- Compute $\overline{\mathsf{wit}}$ which is defined as Eq. 2;(cf. Eq. 2 in Appendix A)
- Pick random $r \leftarrow \mathbb{F}$;
- Commit $Com \leftarrow$ zkVPD.Commit($\overline{\mathsf{wit}}, r, pp$);
- Generate GKR proof [12] π_0 showing $\mathcal{C}(\mathsf{st}, \mathsf{wit}) = 1$;
- Compute $(e_1, e_2) \leftarrow$ hash(st, π_0, Com);
- For $i \in \{1, 2\}$: generate proof $(y_i, \pi_i) \leftarrow$ zkVPD.Open($\overline{\mathsf{wit}}, e_i, r, pp$);
- Output $\pi := (Com, \pi_0, y_1, \pi_1, y_2, \pi_2)$;

Libra.Verify(π):

- Compute $(e_1, e_2) \leftarrow$ hash(st, π_0, Com);
- Return 1 if and only if:
    - The GKR proof π_0 is verified;
    - For $i \in \{1, 2\}$:
        * zkVPD.Verify(Com, e_i, y_i, π_i, vp) = 1;
        * $y_i \leftarrow \overline{\mathsf{wit}}(e_i)$;

Fig. 1. Non-interactive Libra for $\mathcal{C}(\mathsf{st}, \mathsf{wit}) = 1$

3   Design Overview

A Brief Introduction to ZKCP. ZKCP [1,7] is a blockchain based fair exchange protocol. For the most common scenarios, the seller $\mathcal{S}$ has some digital goods s which the buyer $\mathcal{B}$ wants to purchase on condition that $f(s) = 1$ for a verification function $f : \{0,1\}^\lambda \mapsto \{0,1\}$. In the off-chain phase, $\mathcal{S}$ uses a symmetric encryption Enc to encrypt s with a random key k and publishes the ciphertext $c \leftarrow \mathsf{Enc}(s, k)$ and the committed key $E \leftarrow \mathsf{SHA256}(k)$ together with a ZK proof showing $\mathsf{SHA256}(k) = E \ \wedge \ f(\mathsf{Enc}^{-1}(c, k)) = 1$. If the proof is correct, $\mathcal{B}$ and $\mathcal{S}$ then enter the on-chain phase using a hash-locked transaction [2]. Even through ZKCP has been extensively explored by both researchers and practitioners, to the best of our knowledge, there is still no formalization so far. For the first time, we formalize the syntax of ZKCP as follows:

- $pp \leftarrow$ Setup(1^λ): It is the public parameter generation algorithm that takes input as: the security parameter 1^λ, and it outputs the public parameter pp.

- Invoke $crs \leftarrow$ NIZK.Setup(1^λ);
- Output $pp := crs$.
- $(c, E, d, \pi) \leftarrow$ Prove(pp, s): It is the prove algorithm that takes input as: the public parameter pp, the digital file s. It then outputs the ciphertext c, a commitment-opening pair (E, d) and a proof π.
  - Sample a random key $k \leftarrow \{0,1\}^\lambda$;
  - Generate $c \leftarrow$ Enc(s, k), where Enc is a symmetry encryption;
  - Commit to the key $(E, d) \leftarrow$ COM.Commit(k);
  - Generate $\pi \leftarrow$ NIZK.Prove($pp, (c, E), (k, s)$);
  - Output (c, E, d, π).
- $b \leftarrow$ Verify(pp, c, E, π). It is the verification algorithm that takes input as: the public parameter pp, the ciphertext c, the commitment E, and the proof π. It then outputs a bit $b \in \{0,1\}$, indicating acceptance or rejection.
  - Output $b \leftarrow$ NIZK.Verify($pp, (c, E), \pi$).
- $\mathcal{F}_{ex}$[COM]. It is the the trusted exchange functionality to guarantee the fairness and security of the payment. As depicted in Fig. 2, when $\mathcal{B}$ sends instruction (Commit, v, E) to $\mathcal{F}_{ex}$[COM], where v is the payment amount, and E is the committed key, $\mathcal{F}_{ex}$[COM] checks $\mathcal{B}$'s account balance $Acc_\mathcal{B} \geq v$ and then stores E. When $\mathcal{S}$ sends instruction (Redeem, k, d) to $\mathcal{F}_{ex}$[COM], where k is the key and d is the opening, $\mathcal{F}_{ex}$ calls COM to check the validity. If COM.Verify(E, d, k) = 1, $\mathcal{F}_{ex}$[COM] transfers v from $\mathcal{B}$'s account balance $Acc_\mathcal{B}$ to $\mathcal{S}$'s account balance $Acc_\mathcal{S}$. $\mathcal{F}_{ex}$[COM] can be instantiated by hash-locked transaction.

The exchange functionality $\mathcal{F}_{ex}$[COM]

It is parameterized with a commitment scheme COM.
The buyer $\mathcal{B}$'s account balance: $Acc_\mathcal{B}$;
The seller $\mathcal{S}$'s account balance: $Acc_\mathcal{S}$;

Description:

- Upon receiving (Commit, v, E) from $\mathcal{B}$:
  - Assert $Acc_\mathcal{B} \geq v$;
  - Store E;
- Upon receiving (Redeem, k, d) from $\mathcal{S}$:
  - Assert COM.Verify(E, d, k) = 1;
  - Set $Acc_\mathcal{S} := Acc_\mathcal{S} + v$;
  - Set $Acc_\mathcal{B} := Acc_\mathcal{B} - v$;
  - Send k to $\mathcal{B}$.

Fig. 2. The exchange functionality $\mathcal{F}_{ex}$[COM]

From ZKCP to ZKCMP. We extend the idea of ZKCP to a specific class of problems: paying for qualified trained models. Consider such a scenario, $\mathcal{S}$ has a trained model $\mathcal{M}$ which $\mathcal{B}$ wants to purchase. Since the model structure is a common knowledge, they only need to exchange the model parameters, denoted as w. However, the original ZKCP protocol is not sufficient for our purpose. This is because in practice $\mathcal{B}$ may want to test the accuracy of $\mathcal{M}$ w.r.t his own testing dataset $\mathcal{D}$ before paying for it; however, according to the ZKCP protocol, $\mathcal{S}$ can provide the encrypted model after seeing the testing dataset, which nullifies the testing soundness.

To address this issue, we propose a new notion named *zero knowledge contingent model payments* (ZKCMP). Intuitively, let us focus on the Prove. Prove serves two purposes: (i) send the encryption of the digital goods, so $\mathcal{S}$ cannot change it latter; (ii) prove the digital goods satisfies the requirement. We introduce a new algorithm Seal to seal the the model parameter w to separate these two purposes. The separation is important, since $\mathcal{S}$ must perform Seal(w) before $\mathcal{B}$ sending his testing dataset $\mathcal{D}$. After receiving $\mathcal{D}$, $\mathcal{S}$ generates a proof to prove the accuracy of $\mathcal{M}$.

The workflow of ZKCMP is presented in Fig. 3. Before the protocol starts, Setup(1^λ) is invoked by a trusted entity to generate pp. It is then sent to both $\mathcal{B}$ and $\mathcal{S}$. To prevent $\mathcal{S}$ from cheating, $\mathcal{S}$ is required to seal the model parameters w by invoking $(c, E, d) \leftarrow$ Seal(w) and send the sealed model c and the committed key E to $\mathcal{B}$. In this way, $\mathcal{S}$ cannot modify the model later. $\mathcal{B}$ randomly picks a testing dataset $\mathcal{D} := \{\langle x_i, L_i \rangle\}_{i \in n}$ by invoking $\mathcal{D} \leftarrow$ Sample(n) and sends $\mathcal{D}$ to $\mathcal{S}$ together with a threshold τ. After receiving $\mathcal{D}$, $\mathcal{S}$ evaluates the model on $\mathcal{D}$ by $F(w, x_i) = y_i \wedge \mathsf{argmax}(y_i) = L_i$, where F is the model prediction function corresponding to $\mathcal{M}$, and y_i is the final model output. argmax is used for the transformation from final model output to its corresponding label. Then $\mathcal{S}$ is required to prove that the accuracy of the trained model $\mathcal{M}$ on $\mathcal{D}$ exceeds the threshold τ as well as E is the commitment of k and c is the encryption of w with k. $\mathcal{S}$ obtains the proof π by invoking $\pi \leftarrow$ Prove($pp, c, E, w, k, \mathcal{D}, \tau$) and sends π back to $\mathcal{B}$. After that, $\mathcal{B}$ checks the validity of π by invoking $b \leftarrow$ Verify($pp, c, E, \mathcal{D}, \tau, \pi$). If $b = 1$, $\mathcal{B}$ sends (Commit, v, E) to the trusted exchange functionality $\mathcal{F}_{ex}$[COM]. $\mathcal{S}$ can receive the payment by submitting (k, d) to $\mathcal{F}_{ex}$[COM]; $\mathcal{F}_{ex}$[COM] will then send (k, d) to $\mathcal{B}$. Then $\mathcal{B}$ can obtain the model parameters $w \leftarrow$ Ext(c, k). To prevent redundancy, we present the syntax of ZKCMP that differs from ZKCP.

- $(c, E, d) \leftarrow$ Seal(w). It is the model sealing algorithm that takes input as: the model parameters w, and it outputs the sealed model c, the commitment-opening pair (E, d).
  - Sample a random key $k \leftarrow \{0, 1\}^\lambda$;
  - Compute $(w_1, \ldots, w_\ell) \leftarrow$ Convert(w), where Convert is a function mapping model parameter w into strings (c.f. Sect. 4.2);
  - For $i \in [\ell]$:
    * Generate $ks_i \leftarrow$ PRF(k, i);
    * Set $c_i := w_i \oplus ks_i$;
  - Commit to the key by $(E, d) \leftarrow$ COM.Commit(k);
  - Output $(c := (c_1, \ldots, c_\ell), E, d)$;
- $\pi \leftarrow$ Prove($pp, c, E, w, k, \mathcal{D}, \tau$). It is the prove algorithm that takes input as: the public parameter pp, the sealed model c, the committed key E, the model

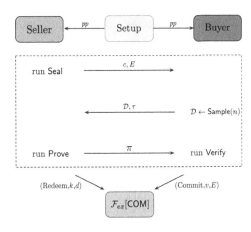

Fig. 3. Our designed protocol

parameter w, the key k, the testing dataset $\mathcal{D}$, and the threshold τ. It then outputs a proof π.

- Compute $I = \{i \mid F(w, x_i) = y_i \wedge \mathsf{argmax}(y_i) = L_i\}$;
- Output $\pi \leftarrow \mathsf{NIZK.Prove}(pp, (c, E, \mathcal{D}, \tau), (w, k))$;

- $b \leftarrow \mathsf{Verify}(pp, c, E, \mathcal{D}, \tau, \pi)$. It is the verification algorithm that takes input as: the public parameter pp, the sealed model c, the committed key E, the testing dataset $\mathcal{D}$, the threshold τ and the proof π. It then outputs a bit $b \in \{0, 1\}$, indicating acceptance or rejection.
  - Output $b \leftarrow \mathsf{NIZK.Verify}(pp, (c, E, \mathcal{D}, \tau), \pi)$;

A ZKCMP protocol Π is a three-party protocol: the buyer $\mathcal{B}$, the seller $\mathcal{S}$, and a trusted functionality $\mathcal{F}_{ex}$. We denote with $[a, b] \leftarrow \langle \mathcal{B}(F, \tau), \mathcal{S}(w, F, \tau), \mathcal{F}_{ex} \rangle$ the event that at the end of Π, $\mathcal{B}$ gets a and $\mathcal{S}$ gets b, where a, b can be $\perp$ meaning that the parties reject the execution, and neither party will learn any information. We denote with $\mathcal{E}_v$ the event that $Acc_{\mathcal{S}}$ increases v. We define the view of $\mathcal{B}$ as his money v and all the messages exchanged during the protocol: $View_{\mathcal{B}} := [v \| Message \langle \mathcal{B}(F, \tau), \mathcal{S}(w, F, \tau), \mathcal{F}_{ex} \rangle \| Out \langle \mathcal{B}(F, \tau), \mathcal{S}(w, F, \tau), \mathcal{F}_{ex} \rangle]$.

Definition 3. *A ZKCMP protocol Π satisfies the following properties.*

- ***Completeness.*** *We say a ZKCMP protocol Π is complete if for any $(w, \mathcal{D})$ such that $|I| \geq n \cdot \tau$, where $I := \{i \mid i \in [n] \wedge F(w, x_i) = y_i \wedge argmax(y_i) = L_i\}$, the following holds:*

$$\Pr \left[\begin{array}{c} pp \leftarrow \mathsf{Setup}(1^\lambda); \\ (c, E) \leftarrow \mathsf{Seal}(w); \\ \pi \leftarrow \mathsf{Prove}(pp, c, E, w, k, \mathcal{D}, \tau) \end{array} : \begin{array}{c} \mathsf{Verify}(pp, c, E, \mathcal{D}, \tau, \pi) = 1 \wedge \\ [k, \mathcal{E}_v] \leftarrow \langle \mathcal{B}(F, \tau), \mathcal{S}(w, F, \tau), \mathcal{F}_{ex} \rangle \end{array} \right] = 1$$

- ***ε-soundness.*** *We say a ZKCMP protocol Π is ε-sound, $\varepsilon \geq 0$, if for any possibly malicious PPT $\hat{\mathcal{S}}$, if at the end of the protocol $\hat{\mathcal{S}}$'s account balance $Acc_{\hat{\mathcal{S}}}$*

increases with non-negligible probability, then there exists an PPT extractor $\mathsf{Ext}_{\hat{S}}$ *which outputs* $\hat{w}$ *s.t.*

$$\tau - \frac{1}{n}|\{i|F(\hat{w}, x_i) = y_i' \wedge \mathsf{argmax}(y_i') = L_i\}| \leq \varepsilon$$

– **Zero-knowledge.** *We say a ZKCMP protocol* Π *is zero-knowledge, if for any possibly malicious PPT* $\hat{\mathcal{B}}$, *there exists a PPT simulator* $\mathsf{Sim}_{\hat{\mathcal{B}}}$ *s.t.*

$$\mathsf{Sim}_{\hat{\mathcal{B}}}(1^\lambda) \overset{c}{\approx} View_{\hat{\mathcal{B}}}(1^\lambda)$$

4   Instantiation

In this section, we give two efficient solutions to instantiate ZKCMP for trained neural networks respectively: (i) zk-SNARKs and (ii) Libra. We use the neural network in CryptoNets [8] as an example and it can be expressed as:

$$w^{(3)}(w^{(2)}(w^{(1)}x + b^{(1)})^2 + b^{(2)})^2 + b^{(3)} = y \wedge \mathsf{argmax}(y) = L \qquad (1)$$

where $w^{(i)}, b^{(i)}$ $\forall i \in [3]$ are the model parameters. Note that both zk-SNARKs and Libra works in $\mathbb{F}$, while neural networks require floating-point arithmetic. A simple solution is to scale the floating-point numbers up to integers by multiplying the same constant to all values and drop the fractional parts [14].

In Prove, $\mathcal{S}$ aims to give a NIZK proof for the statement:

$$\exists w, k, \text{s.t.} \ \forall i \in [\ell], \ c_i = w_i \oplus \mathsf{PRF}(k, i) \ \wedge \ \mathsf{COM.Verify}(E, d, k) = 1 \ \wedge$$

$$\frac{1}{n}|\{i \mid w^{(3)}(w^{(2)}(w^{(1)}x_i + b^{(1)})^2 + b^{(2)})^2 + b^{(3)} = y_i \ \wedge \ \mathsf{argmax}(y_i) = L_i\}| \geq \tau$$

To generate a NIZK proof, $\mathcal{S}$ constructs a circuit for the statement. The circuit consists of two components, which we describe in their specific context:

1. **Proof of accuracy**: Prove $I = \{i \mid F(w, x_i) = y_i \ \wedge \ \mathsf{argmax}(y_i) = L_i\}$ and $|I| > n \cdot \tau$;
2. **Proof of encryption**: Prove $\forall i \in [\ell]$: $ks_i \leftarrow \mathsf{PRF}(k, i) \ \wedge \ c_i := w_i \oplus ks_i$ and $(E, d) \leftarrow \mathsf{COM.Commit}(k)$;

Remark. COM is used only once while PRF is frequently invoked, so we instantiate PRF with a lightweight hash function MiMC7 and instantiate COM with SHA256 (with the random nonce) due to Bitcoin restrictions.

4.1 zk-SNARKs-Based Solution

Our first approach is based on zk-SNARKs and we give a high level description of our approach here. $\mathcal{S}$ transforms the statement into the format of constraint system described in Sect. 2. $\mathcal{S}$ then constructs a circuit to show the correctness of every constraint equation in the constraint system. The proof size of zk-SNARKs is a small constant, which means low communication between $\mathcal{S}$ and $\mathcal{B}$. However, naively using zk-SNARKs to generate NIZK proofs for neural networks can be quite time-consuming and memory-consuming. The performance bottleneck lies in the huge computation of $w^{(3)}(w^{(2)}(w^{(1)}x_i + b^{(1)})^2 + b^{(2)})^2 + b^{(3)} = y_i$ which means enormous constraint equations need to be added into the constraint system. In addition, the computation of I is not trivial.

We conclude the main challenge for this approach in the following:

- How to reduce the computation of $w^{(3)}(w^{(2)}(w^{(1)}x_i + b^{(1)})^2 + b^{(2)})^2 + b^{(3)} = y_i$ while maintain the soundness;
- How to show the correct computation of $I = |\{i \mid w^{(3)}(w^{(2)}(w^{(1)}x_i + b^{(1)})^2 + b^{(2)})^2 + b^{(3)} = y_i \wedge \mathsf{argmax}(y_i) = L_i\}|$ and prove $|I| \geq n \cdot \tau$.

Reducing Computational Complexity. Generally speaking, in zk-SNARKs, all the constraint equations need to be added to a constraint system to maintain the soundness. Intuitively, we would like to check a subset of the constraint equations whereas the soundness error are still tolerated. We introduce a Sampling algorithm to reduce the computation.

As described in Sect. 2, the constraint system over $\mathbb{F}$ is denoted as $Q = ((a_j, b_j, c_j)_{j=1}^{N_g}, N)$. Sampling takes input as the original constraint system Q, a selecting parameter u, and it outputs a reduced constraint system Q' (cf. Fig. 4).

Sampling algorithm: $Q' \leftarrow \mathsf{Sampling}(Q, u)$

Input: Original constraint system $Q = ((a_j, b_j, c_j)_{j=1}^{N_g}, l, N_v)$, selecting parameter u

Outputs: Reduced constraint system $Q' = ((a_j, b_j, c_j)_{j=1}^{u \cdot N_g}, l, N_v)$

Description:

- $\mathsf{Sampling}(Q, u)$:
  - Sample a random set $T \subset [N_g]$, where $|T| = u \cdot N_g$;
  - For $k \in [u \cdot N_g]$:
    * Select a random constrain equation $(a_{T_k}, b_{T_k}, c_{T_k})$ from Q;
    * Add $(a_{T_k}, b_{T_k}, c_{T_k})$ into Q'
  - Output $Q' := ((a_{T_k}, b_{T_k}, c_{T_k})_{k=1}^{u \cdot N_g}, l, N_v)$.

Fig. 4. Sampling algorithm: $Q' \leftarrow \mathsf{Sampling}(Q, u)$

Now, we construct a constraint system for our example neural network and apply Sampling to reduce the computation. According to Eq. 1, we divide the model into four layers: (i) $x^{(1)} = (w^{(1)}x + b^{(1)})^2$; (ii) $x^{(2)} = (w^{(2)}x^{(1)} + b^{(2)})^2$; (iii) $y = w^{(3)}x^{(2)} + b^{(3)}$; (iv) $L = \mathsf{argmax}(y)$. We take the third layer $y = w^{(3)}x^{(2)} + b^{(3)}$, where $w^{(3)} \in \mathbb{F}^{10 \times 100}, x^{(2)} \in \mathbb{F}^{100}, b^{(3)} \in \mathbb{F}^{10}$ and $y \in \mathbb{F}^{10}$ (we use specific numbers here for better explaination), as the example to show how these constraints are produced.

We first define the following variables: $(1, S, w^{(3)}, x^{(2)}, b^{(3)}, y)$, where $S = (S_{(1)}, ..., S_{(1000)}), w^{(3)} = (w^{(3)}_{(1,1)}, w^{(3)}_{(1,2)}, ..., w^{(3)}_{(10,99)}, w^{(3)}_{(10,100)}), x^{(2)} = (x^{(2)}_{(1)}, ..., x^{(2)}_{(100)}), b^{(3)} = (b^{(3)}_{(1)}, ..., b^{(3)}_{(10)}), y = (y_{(1)}, ..., y_{(100)})$. Then we rewrite $y = w^{(3)}x^{(2)} + b^{(3)}$ in the terms of two operations as follows:

– **Inner Product** (i.e. $w^{(3)}x^{(2)} = S$): It produces the constraint equations:
  - For $i \in [10]$:
    * $S_{((i-1) \times 100 + 1)} = w^{(3)}_{(i,1)} \cdot x^{(2)}_{(1)};$
    * $S_{((i-1) \times 100 + j)} = w^{(3)}_{(i,j)} \cdot x^{(2)}_{(i)} + S_{((i-1) \times 100 + j - 1)}, 1 < j \leq 100$
– **Addition** (i.e. $S + b^{(3)} = y$): It produces the constraint equations:
  - For $i \in [10]$: $y_{(i)} = S_{(100 \times i)} + b^{(3)}_{(i)};$

Note that, the constraints equations we described above are produced by a single test case. Our goal is to evaluate the model on a large testing dataset, so we need Sampling to reduce the computation. We denote the set of constraints equations produced by test case x_i as s_i, and apply Sampling to each s_i to get the reduced constraint system Q'.

Remark. In our construction, u is generally set to a small value, such as 3%. With Sampling, the computation can be largely reduced, and we show the soundness error is acceptable in Sect. 5.

Computing $|I|$. After computing the model output $\forall i \in [n] : y_i \in \mathbb{F}^m$, we use it to compute $|I|$. Here we present algorithms VCompute to compute $|I|$ and show whether $|I| \geq n \cdot \tau$ without revealing I:

– VComputing(y, L, τ):
  - For $i \in [n]$:
    * Find the maximum value of y_i: $y_{i,max} \leftarrow \mathsf{max}(y_i);$
    * Construct $d_i \in \mathbb{Z}^m_2$ as follows:
      · For $k \in [m]$: set $d_{i,k} = 1$ iff $y_{i,k} \geq y_{i,max}$; otherwise, set $d_{i,k} = 0;$
    * Add the constraint equation $\sum_{k=1}^m d_{i,k} = 1$ to $Q';$
  - Compute $|I| = \sum_{i=1}^n d_{i,L_i}$, and add it to $Q';$
  - Output 1 iff $|I| \geq n \cdot \tau$; otherwise, output 0.

Remark. With overwhelming probability, there is a unique index j such that $y_{i,j} = y_{i,max}$. If there are more than one entry reaching the maximum value, it means the model cannot determine which entry is the correct output. In case of such a rare occurrence, we may choose a rule in advance (e.g. random selection) to ensure that there is only one index j such that $d_{i,j} = 1$. A similar situation may occur in the Libra-based solution, and we take the same approach.

4.2 Libra-Based Solution

We first give a high level description. $\mathcal{S}$ commits to the witness w, k at the beginning. Then $\mathcal{S}$ constructs multiple circuits which consist of two main components: (i) evaluate accuracy of the model; (ii) encrypt the model parameter $w := (w^{(1)}, w^{(2)}, w^{(3)}, b^{(1)}, b^{(2)}, b^{(3)})$. Note that, in the latter part, the model parameter $w^{(i)} \in \mathbb{F}^{n_i \times m_i}, b^{(i)} \in \mathbb{F}^{n_{i+3} \times m_{i+3}}, \forall i \in [3]$, needs to be converted into $(w_1, \ldots, w_\ell) \in \mathbb{F}^\ell$ for efficient encryption. This leads to a subtle issue: how to show the consistency between model parameter $w^{(i)}, b^{(i)}, \forall i \in [3]$, and the converted model parameter $(w_1, \ldots, w_\ell) \in \mathbb{F}^\ell$.

For this approach, our main effort is to show:

- How to show the correct computation of $|I|$ and prove $|I| \geq n \cdot \tau$;
- How to combine multiple circuits with the purpose of maintaining zero-knowledge property.

Computing $|I|$. $\mathcal{S}$ constructs three circuits as follows.

- $\mathcal{C}_1 : F(w, x) = y$, where $y \in \mathbb{F}^{n \times m}$.
- $\mathcal{C}_2 : \mathsf{argmax}(y) = L'$, where $L' \in \mathbb{F}^{n \times m}$.
- $\mathcal{C}_3 : \mathsf{Judge}(L', L, \tau) = r$, where $r \in \mathbb{F}$.

Unlike Sect. 4.1, we present the ground-truth label L in the form of one-hot vectors. After computing $y \leftarrow w_3(w_2(w_1 x + b_1)^2 + b_2)^2 + b_3$ using $\mathcal{C}_1$, $\mathcal{S}$ computes the predicted label L' in the following way:

- $\mathsf{argmax}(y)$:
  - For $i \in [n]$:
    * Find the maximum value of y_i: $y_{i,max} \leftarrow \mathsf{max}(y_i)$;
    * Compute $y_{i,mid} \leftarrow y_{i,max} - 1$;
    * Compute $L'_i \leftarrow relu(y_i - y_{i,mid} \cdot \vec{1}_m)$, where $relu(x) = \mathsf{max}(0, x)$;
  - Output the predicted label $L' := (L'_1, \ldots, L'_n)$, where $L' \in \mathbb{F}^{n \times m}$.

With overwhelming probability, there is only one entry is non-zero (i.e. 1) in L'_i. If not, approach described in Sect. 4.1 will be taken. $\mathcal{S}$ can prove $L' \leftarrow \mathsf{argmax}(y)$ by $\pi_2 \leftarrow \mathsf{Libra.Prove}(L', y, \mathcal{C}_2)$, and $\mathcal{B}$ can validate it by $b \leftarrow \mathsf{Libra.Verify}(\pi_2)$. The algorithm mentioned later can be proved and verified using Libra (cf. Fig. 1) in the similar way. Then $\mathcal{S}$ can judge whether the model accuracy exceeds the threshold τ:

- $\mathsf{Judge}(L', L, \tau)$:
  - Compute $\delta \leftarrow relu(L' - L)$;
  - Compute $|\delta| \leftarrow \vec{1}_n^T \cdot \delta \cdot \vec{1}_m$;
  - Compute $|I| \leftarrow n - |\delta|$;
  - Output $r \leftarrow relu(n \cdot \tau - |I|)$.

If $r = 0$, it means that $|I| \geq n \cdot \tau$, that is, this model meets $\mathcal{B}$'s requirement.

Converting w. For efficient encryption, the model parameter $w^{(i)} \in \mathbb{F}^{n_i \times m_i}, b^{(i)} \in \mathbb{F}^{n_{i+3} \times m_{i+3}}, \forall i \in [3]$, needs to be converted into $(w_1, \ldots, w_\ell) \in \mathbb{F}^\ell$. Without loss of generality, we resize $w^{(i)}$ and $b^{(i)}$ into matrix with the same number of columns denoted as m'. Then $\mathcal{S}$ can convert w as follows:

- Convert(w) :
    - Resize the model parameter into the same column m': $\forall i \in [3], w^{(i)} \in \mathbb{F}^{\ell_i \times m'}, b^{(i)} \in \mathbb{F}^{\ell_{i+3} \times m'}$, and set $\ell := \sum_{i=1}^{6} \ell_i, \ell_0 := 0$;
    - Set $B := (\beta, \beta^2, \ldots, \beta^{m'})^T$, where β is a public variable to control the precision of w;
    - Compute $\forall i \in [3], w^{(i)} \cdot B = (w_{l_{i-1}+1}, \cdots, w_{l_i})^T, b^{(i)} \cdot B = (w_{l_{i+2}+1}, \cdots, w_{l_{i+3}})^T$;
    - Output $ws := (w_1, \ldots, w_\ell) \in \mathbb{F}^\ell$.

Remark. In the above algorithm, we assume there exists m' such that $m' | n_i m_i, \forall i \in [6]$. If the original model parameter does not have enough entries to fill $\ell_i m'$ entries of the resized version, we just pad 0.

Putting the Pieces Together. In order to prove the whole process, $\mathcal{S}$ constructs multiple circuits as follows:

- Component 1: proof of accuracy
    - $\mathcal{C}_1 : F(w, x) = y$.
    - $\mathcal{C}_2 : \mathsf{argmax}(y) = L'$.
    - $\mathcal{C}_3 : \mathsf{Judge}(L', L, \tau) = r$.

- Component 2: proof of encryption
    - $\mathcal{C}_4 : \mathsf{Convert}(w) = ws$.
    - $\mathcal{C}_5 : \forall i \in [\ell], \mathsf{PRF}(k, i) = ks_i$.
    - $\mathcal{C}_6 : \mathsf{COM.Commit}(k) = (E, d)$.
    - $\mathcal{C}_7 : \forall i \in [\ell], w_i \oplus ks_i = c_i$.

These circuits are connected in the way shown in Fig. 5. However, the output of a circuit may be the input of another which should be kept private. Our solution is to use zkVPD scheme (cf. Appendix A) to connect the circuits.

Take the component 2 as an example. The prover $\mathcal{P}$ first computes $\overline{w}, \overline{k}, \overline{ws}$ and $\overline{ks}$ defined as Eq. 2 and commits to them using zkVPD.Commit. After the verifier $\mathcal{V}$ receiving a claim about the output of $\mathcal{C}_7$, that is c, she computes $\overline{c}$ and evaluates it on u where u is randomly selected. Then $\mathcal{P}$ and $\mathcal{V}$ will reduce $\overline{c}(u)$ layer by layer recursively until it reaches the input layer. At the end, $\mathcal{V}$ queries the evaluations of $\overline{ws}(p), \overline{ks}(q)$ using zkVPD.Open where p and q are randomly selected by $\mathcal{V}$, and validates them by zkVPD.Verify. If zkVPD.Verify outputs 1, $\mathcal{P}$ and $\mathcal{V}$ continue to deal with $\mathcal{C}_4$ and $\mathcal{C}_5$. For $\mathcal{C}_4$, $\mathcal{V}$ uses $\overline{ws}(p)$ as the start point instead of evaluating on a random point. Then they will reduce $\overline{ws}(p)$ layer by layer to complete the protocol. For $\mathcal{C}_5$, the similar approaches will be applied for $\overline{ks}(q)$. The construction above can be made non-interactive by applying Fiat-Shamir heuristic[10]. The non-interactive version of Libra based on a 254-bit prime field can provide a security level of 100+ bits [17].

5   Security Analysis

Security analysis of Sampling. We now examine the soundness of our reduced constraint system Q'. As defined in Sect. 3, if the system is ε-sound with accuracy τ, then the real model accuracy is bounded by $(\tau - \epsilon, 1]$. Recall the proof has two components: (i) show the prover knows a set of model parameters w such that

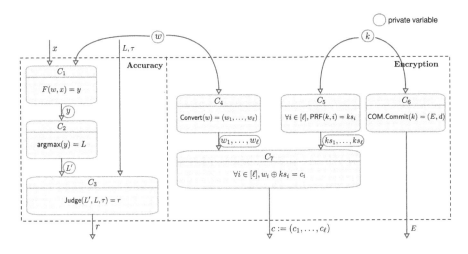

Fig. 5. The circuits designed for Libra

$(c, E, d) \leftarrow \mathsf{Seal}(w)$ and (ii) show the prover knows a set of model parameters w' such that

$$|\{i \,|\, F(w', x_i) = y_i \,\wedge\, argmax(y_i) = L_i\}| \geq n \cdot \tau \ .$$

In general, an adversary may perform the following two types of attacks:

- **Inconsistent model parameters attack.** In this attack, the adversary try to use inconsistent $w \neq w'$ between the encrypted model and the testing model to produce a valid proof, whereas $F(w', x_i)$ is correctly computed.
- **Model execution tampering attack.** In this attack, the adversary try to tamper the model execution $F(w', x_i) = y_i$ by modifying the intermediate variable values during the computation.

Lemma 1. *Let u be the selecting parameter, n be the testing dataset size. Denote $\mathsf{Adv}_{\mathsf{NIZK}}^{\mathcal{A},Sound}(\lambda)$ as the soundness advantage of the underlying NIZK proof system. The probability that any PPT adversary can success with the inconsistent model parameters attack is*

$$\mathsf{Adv}_{\mathsf{NIZK}}^{\mathcal{A},Sound}(\lambda) + (1 - \mathsf{Adv}_{\mathsf{NIZK}}^{\mathcal{A},Sound}(\lambda)) \cdot (1 - u)^n.$$

Proof. We assume that the adversary cannot break the soundness of the underlying NIZK system. Every parameter in w will be checked at least once in constraint equations set s_i. Since we select $N'_g \cdot u$ constraint equations from s_i to check, the probability for adversary to escape from capturing in a single test case is $(1 - u)$. With n test cases, the probability is $(1 - u)^n$.   □

Lemma 2. *Let u be the selecting parameter, n be the testing dataset size. Denote $\mathsf{Adv}_{\mathsf{NIZK}}^{\mathcal{A},Sound}(\lambda)$ as the soundness advantage of the underlying NIZK proof system. The probability that any PPT adversary can success with the model execution tampering attack is*

$$\mathsf{Adv}_{\mathsf{NIZK}}^{\mathcal{A},Sound}(\lambda) + (1 - \mathsf{Adv}_{\mathsf{NIZK}}^{\mathcal{A},Sound}(\lambda)) \cdot (1 - u)^{n \cdot \varepsilon}.$$

Proof. Here we adapt the weakest assumption: adversary only needs to change one intermediate variable value to influence accuracy. Denote there are n test cases in $\mathcal{D}$ and adversary changes M test cases to influence accuracy, and we have $\varepsilon = \frac{M}{n}$. Denote the probability that the adversary escapes from capturing is p. In our assumption, there is one constraint can not be satisfied in each constraints set produced by M test cases. Similar to the proof of Lemma 1, the probability p is $(1 - u)^M$. Replace M with $n \cdot \varepsilon$, the equation $p = (1 - u)^{n \cdot \varepsilon}$ holds.   □

Remark. As shown in Fig. 6, when $n = 10000$, if the prover deviates the model accuracy from τ for 1%, she will be caught with at least 95% probability.

Security Analysis of Main Construction. We examine the security of our construction. Intuitively, the security of our ZKCMP protocol largely depends on the soundness and zero-knowledge properties of underlying NIZK proofs. We also assume COM and PRF are a secure commitment scheme and secure pseudorandom function, respectively. More formally, we prove the security of our construction by the following theorem, and its proof is provided in Appendix B.

Theorem 1. *Let* $\mathsf{PRF} : \{0,1\}^\lambda \times \{0,1\}^\lambda \mapsto \{0,1\}^{\mu(\lambda)}$ *be a secure pseudorandom function, and* $\mathsf{COM} : \{0,1\}^* \mapsto \{0,1\}^\lambda$ *be a commitment scheme. The protocol described in Sect. 3 with* $\mathcal{F}_{ex}[\mathsf{COM}]$ *as depicted in Fig. 2 is perfect complete, 0-sound, and computational zero-knowledge if the underlying* NIZK *protocol is perfect complete, computational sound, and computational zero-knowledge.*

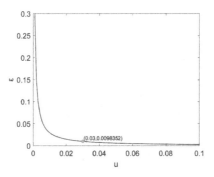

Fig. 6. Fix $p = 0.95$ and $n = 10000$, the relation between ε and u.

6   Implementation and Experiments

We fully implement the proposed instantiations and evaluate the neural network described in CryptoNets [8] on MNIST dataset. All experiments are conducted on the same machine that has 80 Intel Xeon E5-2680 v4 vCPUs@2.5 GHz with 700GB RAM and is running on Ubuntu.

Efficiency of Sampling. We conduct experiments to demonstrate the efficiency of our proposed Sampling technique. Fixing selecting parameter $u = 3\%$, the results are shown in Table 1 and Fig. 7. The results show that it is able to reduce the cost of proof generation significantly.

Performance of Our Solutions. Since Prove and Verify account for main cost, we focus on describing them. We compare our instantiations in terms of prover time, verifier time and proof size. Fixing selecting parameter $n = 10000, u = 3\%$, the experiment results are shown in Table 2 and Fig. 8. For zk-SNARKs based solution, its proof size is a small constant (1019 bits) while its prover time (5781.95 s) and verifier time (18.5781 s) is acceptable. For Libra based solution, although proof size is larger (104.4257 KB), it costs much less in both prover time (1034.1239 s) and verifier time (0.4413 s).

Table 1. Performance of Sampling

Image number		5	10	15	20	25	30
Prover time(s)	Original	42.4675	80.6847	135.829	161.769	220.973	272.984
	Sampling	2.72504	4.43177	5.82092	7.50026	8.54351	10.4192
Verifier time(s)	Original	0.01525	0.021936	0.028138	0.035503	0.041257	0.054159
	Sampling	0.0152	0.021861	0.027569	0.034297	0.040474	0.049441

Table 2. Performance of solutions

Image number		0	2000	4000	6000	8000	10000
Prover time(s)	zk-SNARKs	464.36	1466.78	2593.56	3773.49	4503.66	5781.95
	Libra	11.8639	202.9769	392.7659	609.2089	799.3409	1034.1239
Verifier time(s)	zk-SNARKs	0.0126	3.8566	8.0160	11.9275	16.0533	18.5781
	Libra	0.1546	0.4067	0.4268	0.4440	0.4449	0.4413
Proof size(KB)	zk-SNARKs	0.9951	0.9951	0.9951	0.9951	0.9951	0.9951
	Libra	50.1967	97.4724	99.7902	102.1080	102.2080	104.4257

7 Related Work

SafetyNets [11] is a framework that enables a computationally weak client to outsource neural network inferences to an untrusted server (cloud), and allows the server to prove the correctness of the inference results using interactive proof. In this scenario, clients knows both the model and the input data, whereas in our case both the model and the input data has to be committed to the verifiers. Slalom [16] is a framework that allows neural network evaluations inside

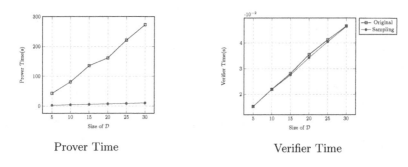

Prover Time   Verifier Time

Fig. 7. Performance of Sampling

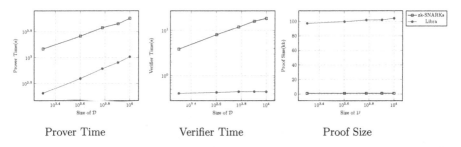

Prover Time   Verifier Time   Proof Size

Fig. 8. Performance of our instantiations

trusted execution environments (TEEs), and the matrix multiplication layers are outsourced to an untrusted GPU without compromising integrity or privacy. They use a lightweight way for verification but it is limited to linear layers and requires TEEs. In [19], Zhao et al. proposed to use zk-SNARKs naively to valid neural network prediction. The prover commits to the value of all intermediate layers, and the verifier validates one random layer with a zk-SNARKs proof. This scheme neither provide negligible soundness nor support validation for large testing dataset.

8   Conclusion

In this paper, we address the problem of fair model exchange by proposing a new concept called Zero Knowledge Contingent Model Payment (ZKCMP). We investigate two state-of-the-art NIZK proofs: zk-SNARKs and Libra, and use them as the main building block to instantiate our ZKCMP protocol respectively. In particular, we propose a random sampling technique to improve the efficiency of zk-SNARKs. Therefore, our proposal is able to support validation for large testing dataset. To demonstrate the practicality of our proposal, we have conducted extensive experiments.

Acknowledgment. This work is supported by the Key (Keygrant) Project of Chinese Ministry of Education. (No. 2020KJ010201) and the National Natural Science Foundation of China (Grant No. 62072401, 62002319, U20A20222). It is also supported by the "Open Project Program of Key Laboratory of Blockchain and Cyberspace Governance of Zhejiang Province" and GTTX Network Technology Co., Limited. The work is also supported in part by Zhejiang Key R&D Plans (Grant No. 2021C01116).

A The Main Building Blocks of Libra

zkVPD Scheme. A zkVPD scheme [18] allows a verifier to delegate the computation of polynomial evaluations to a powerful prover without leaking any sensitive information, and validates the result in time that is constant or logarithmic to the size of the polynomial. Let $\mathcal{F}$ be a family of l-variate polynomial over $\mathbb{F}$. A zkVPD for $f \in \mathcal{F}$ and $\mathbf{t} \in \mathbb{F}^l$ consists of the following algorithms:

- $(pp, vp) \leftarrow \mathsf{KeyGen}(1^\lambda)$
- $com \leftarrow \mathsf{Commit}(f, r_f, pp)$
- $\{0, 1\} \leftarrow \mathsf{Check}(com, vp)$
- $(y, \pi) \leftarrow \mathsf{Open}(f, t, r_f, pp)$
- $\{0, 1\} \leftarrow \mathsf{Verify}(com, t, y, \pi, vp)$

GKR Protocol. Using sumcheck protocol [15] as a main building block, Goldwasser *et al.* [12] constructed an interactive protocol for layered arithmetic circuits with size C and depth d. We denote the number of gates in the i-th layer as C_i and let $c_i = \lceil \log_2 S_i \rceil$. We then define a function $V_i : \{0, 1\}^{c_i} \to \mathbb{F}$ that takes a binary string $b \in \{0, 1\}^{c_i}$ as input and returns the output of gate b in layer i. Therefore, V_0 corresponds to the output of the circuit and V_D corresponds to the input. Then we extend V_i to its *multilinear extension*.

Definition 4 (Multi-linear Extension). *Let $V : \{0, 1\}^l \to \mathbb{F}$ be a function. The multilinear extension of V is the unique polynomial $\widetilde{V} : \mathbb{F}^l \to \mathbb{F}$ such that $\widetilde{V}(x_1, x_2, \ldots, x_l) = V(x_1, x_2, \ldots, x_l)$ for all $(x_1, x_2, \ldots, x_l) \in \{0, 1\}^l$. $\widetilde{V}$ can be expressed as:*

$$\widetilde{V}(x_1, x_2, \ldots, x_l) = \sum_{b \in \{0,1\}^l} \prod_{i=1}^{l} ((1 - x_i)(1 - b_i) + x_i b_i) \cdot V(b),$$

where b_i is i-th bit of b.

To ensure zero knowledge, $\mathcal{P}$ masks the polynomial $\widetilde{V}_i$ and the sumcheck protocol by adding random polynomials. In particular, for layer i, $\mathcal{P}$ selects a random bivariate polynomial $R_i(x_1, z)$ and defines

$$\overline{V}_i(x_1, \ldots, x_{c_i}) = \widetilde{V}_i(x_1, \ldots, x_{c_i}) + Z_i(x_1, \ldots, x_{c_i}) \cdot \sum_{z \in \{0,1\}} R_i(x_1, z), \quad (2)$$

where $Z_i(x) = \prod_{i=1}^{c_i} x_i(1 - x_i)$, so $Z_i(x) = 0, \forall x \in \{0, 1\}^{c_i}$. Since R_i is randomly selected, revealing evaluations of $\overline{V}_i$ does not leak information about $\widetilde{V}_i$. A random polynomial $\delta_i(x, y, z)$ is also selected to mask the sumcheck protocol. In this way, the sumcheck protocol will not leak information and thus be zero knowledge. See more details in [17].

B   Proof of Theorem 1

Proof. For perfect completeness, since the underlying NIZK is perfect complete, it is straightforward that the verification Verify would return 1, and $\mathcal{F}_{ex}$ guarantees that the buyer $\mathcal{B}$ will receive k when the event $\mathcal{E}_m$ occurs.

For 0-soundness, the event $\mathcal{E}_v$ occurs when the potentially malicious seller $\hat{\mathcal{S}}$ produces an accepting proof π and submits (Redeem, k, d) to $\mathcal{F}_{ex}$[COM]; By the soundness of the underlying NIZK protocol, with overwhelming probability, the model parameter $w := (w_1, \ldots, w_\ell)$ can satisfy $|\{i \mid F(w, x_i) = y_i \land \mathsf{argmax}(y_i) = L_i\}| \geq n \cdot \tau$, where $\forall i \in [\ell] : w_i = c_i \oplus \mathsf{PRF}(k, i) \land$ COM.Verify$(E, d, k) = 1$. Moreover, due to the binding property of the commitment scheme COM, k cannot be changed afterwards. Therefore, we can construct an extractor $\mathsf{Ext}_{\hat{\mathcal{S}}}$ that takes input as $\{c_i\}_{i \in [\ell]}$ and k from the out-going messages of $\hat{\mathcal{S}}$, and outputs the model as $w_i = c_i \oplus \mathsf{PRF}(k, i)$.

For computational zero-knowledge, we first construct a simulator Sim works as follows.

- During Setup:
  - Invoke $(\mathsf{crs}^*, \mathsf{td}) \leftarrow \mathsf{NIZK.Sim}_1(1^\lambda)$;
  - Output $pp := \mathsf{crs}^*$;
- During Seal:
  - Pick a random key $k^* \leftarrow \{0, 1\}^\lambda$;
  - Compute $(E^*, d^*) \leftarrow \mathsf{COM.Commit}(k^*)$;
  - For $i \in [\ell]$, compute $c_i^* \leftarrow \{0, 1\}^{\mu(\lambda)}$, where $\mu(\lambda) := |c_i|$;
  - Output $(c^* := (c_1^*, \ldots, c_\ell^*), E^*)$;
- During Prove:
  - Invoke $\pi^* \leftarrow \mathsf{NIZK.Sim}_2(pp, (c^*, E^*, \mathcal{D}, \tau), \mathsf{td})$;
  - Output π^*;

Lemma 3. *The adversary's view output by the simulator Sim as described above is indistinguishable from the real view with advantage*

$$\mathsf{Adv}_{\mathsf{NIZK}}^{\mathcal{A}, ZK}(1^\lambda) + \mathsf{Adv}_{\mathsf{COM}}^{\mathcal{A}, Hide}(1^\lambda) + \ell \cdot \mathsf{Adv}_{\mathsf{PRF}}^{\mathcal{A}}(1^\lambda).$$

Proof. We prove Lemma 3 by the sequence of hybrids $\mathcal{H}_0, \ldots, \mathcal{H}_3$ as follows.

Hybrid $\mathcal{H}_0$: it is the real view.

Hybrid $\mathcal{H}_1$: it is the same as Hybrid $\mathcal{H}_0$, except during Setup, $\mathsf{NIZK.Sim}_1(1^\lambda)$ is used to generate the simulated CRS crs^*; during Prove, π^* is generated by $\mathsf{NIZK.Sim}_2(pp, (c, E, \mathcal{D}, \tau), \mathsf{td})$ instead of the real proof.

Claim 1. *If the underlying NIZK proof system is computationally zero-knowledge with advantage* $\mathsf{Adv}_{\mathsf{NIZK}}^{\mathcal{A}, ZK}(1^\lambda)$, *then the view of Hybrid* $\mathcal{H}_1$ *is indistinguishable from the view of Hybrid* $\mathcal{H}_0$ *with distinguishing advantage* $\mathsf{Adv}_{\mathsf{NIZK}}^{\mathcal{A}, ZK}(1^\lambda)$.

Proof. By Definition 1, it is straightforward that if an adversary $\mathcal{A}$ can distinguish $\mathcal{H}_1$ from $\mathcal{H}_0$ with advantage $\mathsf{Adv}_{\mathsf{NIZK}}^{\mathcal{A}, ZK}(1^\lambda)$, then $\mathcal{A}$ can break the zero-knowledge property of the underlying NIZK proof system with the same advantage. $\qquad\square$

Hybrid $\mathcal{H}_2$: it is the same as Hybrid $\mathcal{H}_1$, except during Seal, replace (E^*, d^*) as COM.Commit(k^*) instead of COM.Commit(k).

Claim 2. *If the distinguishing advantage of the* COM *hiding property is* $\mathsf{Adv}_{\mathsf{COM}}^{\mathcal{A},Hide}(1^\lambda)$, *then the view of Hybrid* $\mathcal{H}_2$ *is indistinguishable from the view of Hybrid* $\mathcal{H}_1$ *with distinguishing advantage* $\mathsf{Adv}_{\mathsf{COM}}^{\mathcal{A},Hide}(1^\lambda)$.

Proof. It is straightforward by direct reduction. □

Hybrid $\mathcal{H}_3$: it is the same as Hybrid $\mathcal{H}_2$, except during Seal, for $i \in [\ell]$, replace c_i^* as $\{0,1\}^{\mu(\lambda)}$ instead of $w_i \oplus \mathsf{PRF}(k,i)$.

Claim 3. *If the distinguishing advantage of* PRF *is* $\mathsf{Adv}_{\mathsf{PRF}}^{\mathcal{A}}(1^\lambda)$, *then the view of Hybrid* $\mathcal{H}_3$ *is indistinguishable from the view of Hybrid* $\mathcal{H}_2$ *with distinguishing advantage* $\ell \cdot \mathsf{Adv}_{\mathsf{PRF}}^{\mathcal{A}}(1^\lambda)$.

Proof. First of all, the distribution of $D_i := c_i^* \oplus w_i$ is the uniformly random. Since the distinguishing advantage of D_i and $\mathsf{PRF}(k,i)$ is bounded by the advantage of PRF $\mathsf{Adv}_{\mathsf{PRF}}^{\mathcal{A}}(1^\lambda)$, by hybrid argument, the overall distinguishing advantage of $\mathcal{H}_3$ and $\mathcal{H}_2$ is bounded by $\ell \cdot \mathsf{Adv}_{\mathsf{PRF}}^{\mathcal{A}}(1^\lambda)$. □

Hybrid $\mathcal{H}_3$ is the simulated view; therefore, the overall distinguishing advantage is $\mathsf{Adv}_{\mathsf{NIZK}}^{\mathcal{A},ZK}(1^\lambda) + \mathsf{Adv}_{\mathsf{COM}}^{\mathcal{A},Hide}(1^\lambda) + \ell \cdot \mathsf{Adv}_{\mathsf{PRF}}^{\mathcal{A}}(1^\lambda)$. □

This concludes the proof. □

References

1. The first successful zero-knowledge contingent payment (2016). https://bitcoincore.org/en/2016/02/26/zero-knowledge-contingent-payments-announcement/
2. Hashlock (2016). https://en.bitcoin.it/wiki/Hashlock
3. Angelini, E., di Tollo, G., Roli, A.: A neural network approach for credit risk evaluation. Q. Rev. Econ. Finan. **48**(4), 733–755 (2008). https://doi.org/10.1016/j.qref.2007.04.001
4. Ben-Sasson, E., Chiesa, A., Genkin, D., Tromer, E., Virza, M.: SNARKs for C: verifying program executions succinctly and in zero knowledge. In: Canetti, R., Garay, J.A. (eds.) CRYPTO 2013. LNCS, vol. 8043, pp. 90–108. Springer, Heidelberg (2013). https://doi.org/10.1007/978-3-642-40084-1_6
5. Bishop, C.M.: Pattern Recognition and Machine Learning (Information Science and Statistics). Springer, Heidelberg (2006)
6. Bitansky, N., Canetti, R., Chiesa, A., Tromer, E.: From extractable collision resistance to succinct non-interactive arguments of knowledge, and back again. In: ITCS 2012, pp. 326–349. Association for Computing Machinery, New York (2012)
7. Campanelli, M., Gennaro, R., Goldfeder, S., Nizzardo, L.: Zero-knowledge contingent payments revisited: attacks and payments for services. In: CCS 2017, pp. 229–243 (2017)
8. Dowlin, N., Gilad-Bachrach, R., Laine, K., Lauter, K., Naehrig, M., Wernsing, J.: Cryptonets: applying neural networks to encrypted data with high throughput and accuracy. Technical report, February 2016

9. Fakoor, R., Ladhak, F., Nazi, A., Huber, M.: Using deep learning to enhance cancer diagnosis and classification. In: Proceedings of the International Conference on Machine Learning, vol. 28. ACM, New York (2013)

10. Fiat, A., Shamir, A.: How to prove yourself: practical solutions to identification and signature problems. In: Odlyzko, A.M. (ed.) CRYPTO 1986. LNCS, vol. 263, pp. 186–194. Springer, Heidelberg (1987). https://doi.org/10.1007/3-540-47721-7_12

11. Ghodsi, Z., Gu, T., Garg, S.: SafetyNets: verifiable execution of deep neural networks on an untrusted cloud. In: Advances in Neural Information Processing Systems, vol. 30, pp. 4672–4681. Curran Associates, Inc. (2017)

12. Goldwasser, S., Kalai, Y.T., Rothblum, G.N.: Delegating computation: interactive proofs for muggles. J. ACM **62**(4), 1–64 (2015)

13. Goldwasser, S., Micali, S., Rackoff, C.: The knowledge complexity of interactive proof systems. SIAM J. Comput. **18**(1), 186–208 (1989)

14. Liu, J., Juuti, M., Lu, Y., Asokan, N.: Oblivious neural network predictions via MiniONN transformations. In: CCS 2017, pp. 619–631. Association for Computing Machinery, New York (2017)

15. Lund, C., Fortnow, L., Karloff, H.: Algebraic methods for interactive proof systems. J. ACM **39**(4) (1999)

16. Tramer, F., Boneh, D.: Slalom: fast, verifiable and private execution of neural networks in trusted hardware. arXiv preprint arXiv:1806.03287 (2018)

17. Xie, T., Zhang, J., Zhang, Y., Papamanthou, C., Song, D.: Libra: succinct zero-knowledge proofs with optimal prover computation. In: Boldyreva, A., Micciancio, D. (eds.) CRYPTO 2019. LNCS, vol. 11694, pp. 733–764. Springer, Cham (2019). https://doi.org/10.1007/978-3-030-26954-8_24

18. Zhang, Y., Genkin, D., Katz, J., Papadopoulos, D., Papamanthou, C.: VSQL: verifying arbitrary SQL queries over dynamic outsourced databases. In: 2017 IEEE Symposium on Security and Privacy (SP), pp. 863–880. IEEE (2017)

19. Zhao, L., et al.: VeriML: enabling integrity assurances and fair payments for machine learning as a service. arXiv preprint arXiv:1909.06961 (2019)

Key Exchange

Identity-Based Identity-Concealed Authenticated Key Exchange

Huanhuan Lian[1], Tianyu Pan[1], Huige Wang[1,2(✉)], and Yunlei Zhao[1,3(✉)]

[1] School of Computer Science, Fudan University, Shanghai, China
{wanghuige,ylzhao}@fudan.edu.cn
[2] Anhui Science and Technology University, Bengbu, China
[3] State Key Laboratory of Integrated Services Networks, Xidian University, Xi'an, China

Abstract. Identity-based authenticated key exchange (ID-AKE) allows two parties (whose identities are just their public keys) to agree on a shared session key over open channels. At ESORICS 2019, Tomida et al. proposed a highly efficient ID-AKE protocol, referred to as the TFNS19-protocol, under the motivation of providing authentication and secure communication for huge number of low-power IoT devices. The TFNS19-protocol currently stands for the most efficient ID-AKE based on bilinear pairings, where each user remarkably performs only a single pairing operation. But it does not consider users' identity privacy, and the security is based on relatively non-standard assumptions.

In this work, we formulate and design identity-based identity-concealed AKE (IB-CAKE) protocols. Here, identity concealment means that the session transcript does not leak users' identity information. We present a simple and highly practical IB-CAKE protocol, which is computationally more efficient than the remarkable TFNS19-protocol in total. We present a new security model for IB-CAKE, and show it is stronger than the ID-eCK model used for the TFNS19-protocol. The security of our IB-CAKE protocol is proved under relatively standard assumptions in the random oracle model, assuming the security of the underlying authenticated encryption and the gap bilinear Diffie-Hellman (Gap-BDH) problem. Finally, we provide the implementation results for the proposed IB-CAKE scheme, and present performance benchmark.

Keywords: Identity-based cryptography · Identity privacy · IoT authentication

1 Introduction

Authentication key exchange (AKE) provides confidentiality, authentication and integrity protection for communication. It plays a fundamental role in modern cryptography and serves as a bridge between public key cryptography and symmetric cryptography, as well as becomes the core mechanism for the network security protocol. Traditional authenticated key agreement based on public key

© Springer Nature Switzerland AG 2021
E. Bertino et al. (Eds.): ESORICS 2021, LNCS 12973, pp. 651–675, 2021.
https://doi.org/10.1007/978-3-030-88428-4_32

infrastructure (PKI) needs relatively complex key management. Identity-based authenticated key exchange (ID-AKE) protocols allow two parties to establish a session key based on their identities over an open network. Compared to PKI-based AKE, the ID-AKE scheme directly uses the users' identities as the public keys so that the key management and distribution can be significantly simplified.

Since Shamir's seminal work [22] of the concept of identity-based cryptography, identity-based AKE has been extensively studied. The first identity-based key agreement protocol was suggested in [15,16], and it was constructed by using the same key pair format as Shamir's original identity-based signature. In 2001, Boneh and Franklin [4] proposed a secure and practical identity-based encryption scheme based on weil pairing. In 2002, from the IBE scheme proposed in [4], Smart [24] proposed the first ID-based authenticated key agreement under the assumption of bilinear pairings. Following these works, a variety of provably secure ID-AKE protocols were proposed [3,5,8–10,14,23,25–28]. Though there exist efficient ID-AKE protocols like the one proposed in [10] that does not use pairings, but requires pre-key-issue, i.e., secret key needs to be issued by KGC before parties start a session [25]. In this work, we focus on constructing highly efficient ID-AKE protocols based on bilinear pairings. In this line, the ID-AKE protocol proposed by Tomida et al. at ESORICS 2019 [25], referred to as the TFNS19-protocol, may stand for the current state of the art *in efficiency*. The structure of TFNS19-protocol is briefly described in Appendix B. For the TFNS19-protocol, each user remarkably performs only a single pairing operation. Indeed, the TNFS19-protocol was introduced under the motivation of providing authentication and secure communication for huge number of low-power IoT devices. However, the security of TFNS-19 is proved in the ID-eCK model under the relatively less standard assumptions of XDHT and q-Gap-BCA in the quantum random oracle model.

In many applications of mobile Internet, the user's identity is considered to be sensitive information that should be protected during communications. Indeed, many cryptographic standards like TLS 1.3 [18], QUIC [20] and EMV [7] mandate identity concealment now. However, most of the existing ID-AKE protocols do not concern this privacy problem. This raises the following open question: can we come up with an efficient ID-AKE protocol that simultaneously enjoys: (1) single pairing operation by each user, (2) identity concealment, and (3) provable security based on relatively standard assumptions? What's more, to the best of our knowledge, there exists no appropriate security definition framework for ID-AKE with identity concealment.

Our Contributions. In this work, we solve the above question. Specifically, we present the first identity-based identity-concealed AKE protocol (IB-CAKE, for short), which enjoys the following advantageous features:

- It is highly efficient: each user needs to perform a single pairing operation. Moreover, the scheme does not need master public key. Compared with the TFNS19-protocol, our scheme can be computationally more efficient in total. For example, the TFNS19-protocol generates traditional master public key that performs one exponentiation operation, the secret key generation for each user requires an extra modular inverse operation that is also relatively expensive, and also the computation of session key in TFNS19-protocol is also relatively more complex than ours.

- It provides forward identity privacy for all the users. Specifically, users' identity privacy is kept even if all of their static secret keys are exposed.
- Our scheme works in the post-specified ID setting, where peer's identity information is unknown to the initiator user when the protocol run starts. In comparison, the TFNS19 protocol works in the pre-specified ID setting, where peer's identity information must be known before the protocol run.
- In addition, the proposed scheme also has the following advantages: perfect forward security, strong resilience to ephemeral state exposure, i.e., x-security; and reasonable deniability.

We present a new security model for IB-CAKE, and show it is stronger than the ID-eCK model used in [25] for the TFNS19-protocol. The security of our IB-CAKE protocol is proved under relatively standard assumptions in the random oracle model, assuming the security of the underlying authenticated encryption and the gap bilinear Diffie-Hellman (Gap-BDH) problem. Finally, we also provide the implementation results for the IB-CAKE scheme and demonstrate its practical feasibility.

2 Preliminaries

2.1 Notation

We denote the integer number by $\mathbb{Z}$. For prime p, $\mathbb{Z}_p$ denotes field $\mathbb{Z}/p\mathbb{Z}$. A string or value α means a binary number, and $|\alpha|$ is its binary length. Let $a := b$ denote a simple assignment statement, which means assigning b to a, and $x \parallel y$ be the concatenation of two elements $x, y \in \{0,1\}^*$. For a finite set S, $s \leftarrow S$ is the operation of picking an element uniformly at random from S. For a probability distribution D, $s \leftarrow D$ is the operation of picking an element according to D. We overload the notion for probabilistic or stateful algorithms, writing $V \leftarrow \mathsf{Alg}$ to mean that algorithm Alg runs and outputs value V.

2.2 Bilinear Pairings and Assumptions

Definition 1 (Bilinear Pairing [21]). *Let $\mathbb{G}_1$, $\mathbb{G}_2$ and $\mathbb{G}_T$ be three multiplicative groups of the same prime order q, and g_1, g_2 be generators of $\mathbb{G}_1$ and $\mathbb{G}_2$, respectively, and an admissible bilinear pairing $e : \mathbb{G}_1 \times \mathbb{G}_2 \to \mathbb{G}_T$, which has the following properties:*

- *Bilinear: $\forall a, b \leftarrow \mathbb{Z}_q^*$, and $\forall \hat{g}_1 \leftarrow \mathbb{G}_1, \hat{g}_2 \leftarrow \mathbb{G}_2$, $e(\hat{g}_1{}^a, \hat{g}_2{}^b) = e(\hat{g}_1, \hat{g}_2)^{ab}$ holds.*
- *Non-degenerate: $\exists \hat{g}_1 \in \mathbb{G}_1, \hat{g}_2 \in \mathbb{G}_2$, such that $e(\hat{g}_1, \hat{g}_2) \neq 1_{\mathbb{G}_T}$.*
- *Computable: $\forall \hat{g}_1 \in \mathbb{G}_1, \hat{g}_2 \in \mathbb{G}_2$, $e(\hat{g}_1, \hat{g}_2)$ is efficiently computable.*

Generally, there are three types of bilinear pairing:

Type I: $\mathbb{G}_1 = \mathbb{G}_2$, it is also called symmetric bilinear pairing.

Type II: There is an efficiently computable isomorphism either from $\mathbb{G}_1$ to $\mathbb{G}_2$ or from $\mathbb{G}_2$ to $\mathbb{G}_1$.

Type III: There exists no efficiently computable isomorphism between $\mathbb{G}_1$ and $\mathbb{G}_2$.

Definition 2 (Bilinear Diffie-Hellman (BDH) [13]**).** *The bilinear Diffie-Hellman (BDH) problem in* $\langle \mathbb{G}_1, \mathbb{G}_T, e \rangle$ *is to compute* $e(g,g)^{abc} \in \mathbb{G}_T$, *given* $(g, g^a, g^b, g^c) \in \mathbb{G}_1^4$, *where* $a, b, c \leftarrow \mathbb{Z}_q^*$. *The BDH assumption says that no PPT algorithm can solve the BDH problem with non-negligible probability.*

Definition 3 (Gap Bilinear Diffie-Hellman (Gap-BDH) [1,13]**).** *The gap bilinear Diffie-Hellman (Gap-BDH) problem is to compute* $e(g,g)^{abc} \in \mathbb{G}_T$, *given* $(g, g^a, g^b, g^c) \in \mathbb{G}_1^4$, *where* $a, b, c \leftarrow \mathbb{Z}_q^*$, *but with the help of a decisional bilinear Diffie-Hellman (DBDH) oracle for* $\mathbb{G}_1 = \langle g \rangle$ *and* $\mathbb{G}_T$. *Here on arbitrary input* $(A = g^a, B = g^b, C = g^c, T) \in \mathbb{G}_1^3 \times \mathbb{G}_T$, *the DBDH oracle outputs 1 if and only if* $T = e(g,g)^{abc}$. *The Gap-BDH assumption says that no PPT algorithm can solve the Gap-BDH problem with non-negligible probability.*

2.3   Authenticated Encryption

We follow [2,11,17] to review the authenticated encryption (AE) security notion. Briefly speaking, an authenticated encryption scheme transforms a message m and a public header information h (e.g., a packet header, an IP address, some predetermined nonce or initial vector) into a ciphertext c in such a way that c provides both privacy (of m) and authenticity (of c and h) [19].

Let $\mathsf{SE} = (\mathsf{K}_{se}, \mathsf{Enc}, \mathsf{Dec})$ be a symmetric encryption scheme and let $\mathcal{A}$ be an adversary. The probabilistic polynomial-time (PPT) algorithm K_{se} takes as input a security parameter κ and samples a key K from a finite and no-empty set $\mathcal{K}$. The polynomial-time (randomized or stateful) encryption algorithm $\mathsf{Enc} : \mathcal{K} \times \{0,1\}^* \times \{0,1\}^* \to \{0,1\}^* \cup \{\bot\}$, and the (deterministic) polynomial-time decryption algorithm $\mathsf{Dec} : \mathcal{K} \times \{0,1\}^* \to \{0,1\}^* \cup \{\bot\}$ satisfy: for any $K \leftarrow \mathcal{K}$, any associated data $\mathsf{H} \in \{0,1\}^*$ and any message $m \in \{0,1\}^*$, if $\mathsf{Enc}_K(h,m)$ outputs $c \neq \bot$, $\mathsf{Dec}_K(c)$ always outputs m.

Table 1 details a security length-hiding authenticated-encryption game. We define the AEAD-advantage (of $\mathcal{A}$) to be $\mathbf{Adv}_{\mathsf{SE}}^{\mathrm{lh\text{-}ae}}(\mathcal{A}) = |2 \cdot \Pr[\mathrm{LHAE}_{\mathsf{SE}}^{\mathcal{A}} \Rightarrow \mathrm{true}] - 1|$. Let LHAE1 (resp. LHAE0) be the LHAE game except with b set to one (resp. zero). Then a standard argument gives that $\mathbf{Adv}_{\mathsf{SE}}^{\mathrm{lh\text{-}ae}}(\mathcal{A}) = \Pr[\mathrm{LHAE1}_{\mathsf{SE}}^{\mathcal{A}} \Rightarrow \mathrm{true}] - \Pr[\mathrm{LHAE0}_{\mathsf{SE}}^{\mathcal{A}} \Rightarrow \mathrm{flase}]$. We say that AEAD is LHAE-secure when the advantage of all adversaries consuming "reasonable" resources is "small" (where "reasonable" and "small" can be quantified in a concrete security setting).

Table 1. Length-hiding AEAD security game

main LHAE$_{SE}$:	Enc(ℓ, h, m_0, m_1):	Dec(h, c):
$K \leftarrow \mathcal{K}_{se}$	$c_0 \leftarrow \text{Enc}_K(\ell, h, m_0)$	If $b = 1 \wedge c \notin \mathcal{C}$ then
$b \leftarrow 0, 1$	$c_1 \leftarrow \text{Enc}_K(\ell, h, m_1)$	return $\text{Dec}_K(h, c)$
$b' \leftarrow \mathcal{A}^{\text{Enc,Dec}}$	If $c_0 = \bot$ or $c_1 = \bot$	return $\bot$
return $(b' = b)$	return $\bot$	
	set $\mathcal{C} = c_b$; return $\mathcal{C}$	

3 Security Model

In traditional security models for identity-based cryptosystem, to a large extent
the security definitions rely on users' identity to define session matching, which
are not suitable for our identity-concealed protocol. In this section, we present
a strong security model for our identity-based identity-concealed authenticated
key exchange (IB-CAKE), which integrates the identity privacy and identity-
based AKE together and is applicable to identity-based CAKE scenarios. The
model allows a more powerful concurrent man-in-the-middle (CMIM) adversary
with adaptive party registration and strong capability of secrecy exposure.

3.1 System and Adversary Setting

Let n denotes the largest numbers of users. Suppose $\{ID_1, ..., ID_n\}$ =
HONEST $\cup$ DISHONEST are all users in the system. There is also a set
CORRUPTED $\subseteq$ HONEST for indicating honest yet corrupted users. All the sets
HONEST, DISHONEST and CORRUPTED may be initialized to be non-empty,
and adaptively evolve during the attack. Each user has a long-term ID-based
public/private key pair, in which the public key just is her identity information
and the private key is computed (associated with her identity information) and
preserved secretly by a key generator center(KGC). For presentation simplicity,
we assume that all users in the system have public identity information of equal
length. But our security model and protocol constructions can be extended to
the general case of different lengths of identities, by incorporating length-hiding
authenticated encryption in the underlying security model and protocol constructions.

Session. Each session has a session-identifier SID that is simply assigned by
an incremental counter. Setting session identifier via a counter is only for distinguishing messages being delivered to different sessions, which is just an artifact
in the security model. Each session, with session-identifier SID, keeps in private a local state $peer_{SID}$ (for indicating the interacting peer player), a local
state ST_{SID} (for storing the intermediate randomness) and a local state SK_{SID}
(for storing session-key), all of which are originally initialized to be the empty
string (meaning "undefined") and are assigned during the session run according
to protocol specifications.

We say that a session is completed if its owner computes a session key, where the last session message has been sent or received. We say that a session is incomplete (or on-going), if the session owner is still waiting for the next protocol message. We say that a session is aborted if it stops in the middle of session run because of some abnormal event (e.g., failure in authentication, etc.) according to the protocol specifications. Whenever a session is aborted, all its local states are removed from memory. Whenever a session SID is completed, ST_{SID} is removed from memory but SK_{SID} is still kept in private. A session can also be expired, and for expired sessions the session-keys are also canceled.

Adversary. The adversary denoted by $\mathcal{A}$ in the security model is modeled as a PPT algorithm which has access to all the participants' oracles. Participant oracles only respond to queries by the adversary and do not communicate directly among themselves, i.e., there exist at least a benign adversary who simply passes messages between participants faithfully. A party's private information is not accessible to the adversary; however, the leakage of private information is captured via the following adversary queries.

Here we keep a counter CTR_I that is initiated to be 0 in the following queries, and embed the same challenge bit b used by the initiator (also embed the same challenge b used by the responder). We give the operations of initiator about the queries, the processing for the role of responder is similar to that of initiator case.

- **Start**(ID_i) Upon receiving an instruction "(**Start**, ID_i)", $1 \leq i \leq n$, for an honest yet uncorrupted user with identity ID_i (i.e., $ID_i \in$ HONEST \ CORRUPTED), the challenger sets the counter CTR_I as $CTR_I := CTR_I + 1$, creates a session for the user with identity $ID_i \in \{0,1\}^*$ with session identifier $SID_I := CTR_I$, and returns back $(SID_I, M_{SID_I}^{(1)})$, where $M_{SID_I}^{(1)}$ denotes the first protocol message for the session SID_I kept at initiator for the user with identity ID_i indicated by adversary. It also creates and keeps some local states in private, which are the peer $peer_{SID_I}$ (for indicating the peer it is interacting), an intermediate randomness state ST_{SID_I} and session-key SK_{SID_I} for session SID_I.
- **Send**(SID_I, M_I) Upon receiving a tuple "(SID_I, M_I)", the challenger first checks whether the session SID_I exists or not, if not, it ignores; else it treats M_I as the incoming message for session SID_I, and responds with the next protocol message if M_I is not the last protocol message for that session; otherwise, it works according to the protocol specification.
- **STReveal**(SID_I) Upon receiving a pair "$(SID_I, \textbf{STReveal})$", the challenger checks whether the session SID_I exists or not, if not, it ignores; else it responds with the session state ST_{SID_I} for the session SID_I if the session is not completed, otherwise it returns back "$\perp$".
- **Test**(ID_{t_0}, ID_{t_1}) Upon receiving "(**Test**, ID_{t_0}, ID_{t_1})" for $ID_{t_0}, ID_{t_1} \in$ HONEST, where $1 < t_0 \neq t_1 < n$, the challenger randomly chooses $b \leftarrow \{0,1\}$ and sets $ID_t = ID_{t_b}$, and runs just as receiving the "(**Start**, ID_t) instruction, where the session-identifier is denoted as SID_T for convenience. We stress that the Test-type query can be made by the adversary for only once

during its attack, exclusively against initiator or responder (but not both of them).

- **SKReveal**(SID_I) Upon receiving a pair "(SID_I, **SKReveal**)", the challenger checks whether the session SID_I exists or not, if not, it ignores; else if $SID_I \neq SID_T$, and SID_I has been completed yet not expired, it returns the session key SK_{SID_I}; if $SID_I = SID_T$, it returns SK_{SID_I} if $b = 1$, otherwise it returns a value taken uniformly at random from $\{0,1\}^{SKlen}$ where $SKlen$ is the length of session key.

- **Peer**(SID_I) Upon receiving "SID_I", it returns back the value stored in $peer_{SID_I}$ if SID_I is an existing session, otherwise the query is ignored.

- **StaKeyReveal**(ID_i) Upon receiving "ID_i", $1 \leq i \leq n$, it returns back the static-key of ID_i if $ID_i \in$ HONEST; otherwise, the query is ignored.

- **Corrupt**(ID_i) Upon receiving an identity "ID_i" for $1 \leq i \leq n$, if $ID_i \in$ HONEST (otherwise, the query is ignored), it returns back static secret-key, intermediate randomness, and session-key in the storage part for ID_i, and sets CORRUPTED = CORRUPTED $\cup \{ID_i\}$. That is, we allow the adversary to adaptively corrupt honest users.

- **Create**(ID_i) Upon receiving a pair "(ID_i, **Create**)" for $1 \leq i \leq n$, where ID_i is a new user not in HONEST $\cup$ DISHONEST. When this oracle gets the identity ID_i, it returns back the private key for ID_i, and sets HONEST = HONEST$\cup ID_i$. That is, we allow the adversary to adaptively create the users in the system.

- **MSKReveal**() The challenger responds with the master key msk of KGC, from which the adversary learns the static key of any given identity ID.

During the attack, the adversary $\mathcal{A}$ schedules all the oracle queries adaptively as it wishes. We note that in our security model the adversary has the ability to make other queries such as **Corrupt** and **Peer** but the security model of protocol [25] does not. At the end of the attack, $\mathcal{A}$ outputs a bit b'.

Note that we require that **Test** query can be performed only once, against an oracle that is in the accepted state (see below), and the test-session has not been previously asked a **SKReveal** query or a **Corrupt** query.

An oracle may be in one of the following states (it cannot be in more than one state).

- Accepted. If the oracle decides to accept a session key, after receipt of properly formatted messages.
- Rejected. If the oracle decides not to accept and aborts the run of the protocol.
- Opened. If the **SKReveal** query has been performed against this oracle for its last run of the protocol (its current session key is revealed).
- Corrupted. If a **Corrupt** query has ever been performed against the Corrupt oracle.

3.2   Definition of Security

In our model, the label of a session is defined to be a substring of the session transcript.

Definition 4 (Matching Session). *Two sessions are matching, if they have the same session label.*

Let SID_T be the completed test-session held at the user with identity $ID_t = ID_{t_b}$ and $peer_{SID_T} = ID_k \in \text{HONEST}$ for $1 \leq k \leq n$. Denote by SID'_T its matching session if the matching session exists, which may be still on-going. We say that the test-session is exposed during the attack, if any of the following events occurs.

- ID_{t_0} or ID_{t_1} is corrupted via the **Corrupt** query.
- The query **SKReveal**(SID_T) is made, or if the matching session SID'_T exists the query **SKReveal**(SID'_T) is made.
- The query **StaKeyReveal**(ID_{t_0}) or **StaKeyReveal**(ID_{t_1}) is made, and ST_{SID_T} is exposed via the query **STReveal**(SID_T).
- If the matching session SID'_T exists, the query **StaKeyReveal**(ID_k) and **STReveal**(SID'_T) are both made;[1] else, the query **StaKeyReveal**(ID_k) is made.
- The query **Peer**(SID'_T) is made if the matching session SID'_T exists.

Note that, for unexposed test-session, it may be the case: the static-secret key of ID_{t_0} and ID_{t_1} are exposed, and $ST_{SID'_T}$ is exposed (in the case the matching session exists). If $\mathcal{A}$ made the query **MSKReveal**(), we consider $\mathcal{A}$ as having queried both **StaKeyReveal**(ID_t) (where $ID_t = ID_{t_0}$ or $ID_t = ID_{t_1}$) and **StaKeyReveal**(ID_k), but it does not imply that the users are corrupted.

Remark 1. Similar to the eCK model, in our security model the session state and the static-secret key are viewed as ephemeral secret and long-term secret, respectively. Indeed, for the same session, if both the static-secret key and the ephemeral session state are exposed, then the session-key of this session will be exposed. But as our security model is eCK-like, we allow the adversary to expose the static-secret key of one session and the ephemeral session state of another different session. Consider the following scenario. For the unexposed test-session SID_T, if the matching session SID'_T exists, our security model allows that both the static-secret key of the test-session (via the **StaKeyReveal**(ID_t) query) and the ephemeral session state of the matching session (via the **STReveal**(SID'_T) query) may be exposed. In addition, when a session is completed, the ephemeral session state will be erased from memory, but the session key usually further exists much longer in the memory (e.g., for the subsequent authentication and channel communications) until the session expires. Therefore, we need to separate the oracles for session-state reveal and session-key reveal queries.

Definition 5 (Strong IB-CAKE-security). *A two-party key exchange protocol is strongly IB-CAKE secure, if for any PPT adversary $\mathcal{A}$ defined as above, and for any sufficiently large security parameter, the following holds:*

- **Label-security.** *Any of the following events occurs with negligibility probability:*

---

[1] If SID'_T exists, whether exposing either the static keys of ID_{t_0}, ID_{t_1} and ID_k via the **StaKeyReveal**(ID_i) oracle, or exposing the states of session SID_T and SID'_T via the **STReveal**(SID) oracle, does not necessarily expose the test-session.

- *There exist more than two sessions of the same session label.*
- *There exist two matching sessions: session SID held at a user with identity ID_i and session SID' held at a user with identity ID_j such that any of the following events occurs:*
  - *(1) ID_i and ID_j plays the same session role (i.e., both of them are initiator or responders).*
  - *(2) $SK_{SID} \neq SK_{SID'}$.*
  - *(3) $peer_{SID} \neq \perp \wedge peer_{SID} \neq ID_j$, or $peer_{SID'} \neq \perp \wedge peer_{SID'} \neq ID_i$.*

We remark that label-security is w.r.t any PPT adversary who can, in particular, expose the long-term private key of all honest users and expose the local states of all existing sessions.

- **ID-concealed session-key (IC-SK) security.** The adversary makes an arbitrary sequence of the queries described above. On condition that the test-session SID_T (held at the uncorrupted user ID_t) is completed and unexposed, the following quantities are all hold:
  - **Impersonation security.** The probability that the test-session has no matching session is negligible. Specifically, if the unexposed test-session has no matching session, the static secret key of the honest peer player ID_k must be unexposed via **StaKeyReveal**(ID_k) according to the definition of unexposed session. In this case, if the test-session is successfully completed without a matching session, the honest peer player ID_k must be impersonated by the adversary in the test-session.
  - **ID-SK indistinguishability.** $|Pr[b' = b] - \frac{1}{2}|$ is negligible. ($|Pr[b' = b] - \frac{1}{2}| \leq negl(1^\kappa)$)

We note that label-security implies the security against unknown key share (UKS) attack. Conditioned on the test-session is completed and unexposed[2], the impersonation security (which means the test-session has matching session) and the ID-SK indistinguishability security (which means the real session-key and random session-key are indistinguishable) together imply perfect forward security (PFS). The ID-SK indistinguishability also implies forward ID-privacy.

Comparison with ID-eCK security model used in [25]. Compared with the ID-eCK security model used in [25] for the TFNS19-protocol, our security model has the following merits besides capturing forward ID-privacy, which makes our security definition stronger than that of ID-eCK.

- In our model, the adversary is allowed to have access to the **Corrupt** oracle and the **Peer** oracle, which are not allowed in the ID-eCK model.
- Our security model integrates label security, impersonation security and ID-SK indistinguishability, where the later two altogether imply perfect forward security. On the one hand, we note that the TFNS19-protocol does not satisfy our label security. Specifically, label security requires that the matching session must exist, but in the security model of TFNS19-protocol, the

---

[2] The unexposed case implies that the static secret-keys of both ID_t and ID_k could be exposed.

matching session does not necessarily exist. On the other hand, as TFNS19 is HMQV[12]-like AKE protocol, it does not provide perfect forward security.

– At the onset of its attack, in the ID-eCK model the adversary can select the identities only for honest parties, while in our model the adversary is allowed to select additional identities such as dishonest ones and corrupted ones.

4   Construction of IB-CAKE Protocol

In this section, we present the protocol construction for identity-based identity-concealed authenticated key exchange (IB-CAKE) with mutual authentication, which is described as follows.

Let κ be a secure parameter, $\mathbb{G}_1$ and $\mathbb{G}_T$ be two multiplicative bilinear map groups of the same prime order q such that the discrete algorithm problems in $\mathbb{G}_1$ and $\mathbb{G}_T$ are intractable, g be a generator of $\mathbb{G}_1$, $\hat{e} : \mathbb{G}_1 \times \mathbb{G}_1 \to \mathbb{G}_T$ be a bilinear pairing over $\mathbb{G}_1$ and $\mathbb{G}_T$. Denote $1_{\mathbb{G}_1}$ and $1_{\mathbb{G}_T}$ the identity element of $\mathbb{G}_1$ and $\mathbb{G}_T$, by $\mathbb{G}_1/1_{\mathbb{G}_T}$ the set of elements of $\mathbb{G}_1$ except $1_{\mathbb{G}_T}$. Let $SE = (K_{se}, Enc, Dec)$ be an authenticated encryption with associated data (AEAD) scheme, where $\mathcal{K} = \{0,1\}^\kappa$ is the key space of K_{se}. Let $H : \{0,1\}^* \to \mathbb{Z}_q^*$ and $H_1 : \{0,1\}^* \to \mathbb{G}_1$ be one-way collision-resistant hash functions modeled as random oracles, and $KDF : \{0,1\}^* \to \{0,1\}^{p(\kappa)}$ be a key derivation function, where $p(\kappa)$ is a polynomial in κ. The key generator center produces the system's public parameters and the master secret key msk. And it generates the private key $SK_i = H_1(ID_i)^{msk}$ for the user with identity ID_i. For presentation simplicity, we denote by Alice the anonymous session initiator, whose public identity and private key are ID_A and $SK_A = (H_1(ID_A))^{msk}$, and by Bob the session responder, whose public identity and private key are ID_B and $SK_B = (H_1(ID_B))^{msk}$, where msk is the master secret key of KGC. The protocol structure of IB-CAKE using type-I pairing is depicted in Fig. 1.

In the following, let A be a session initiator and B be a session responder.

– The initiator A selects $r_A \leftarrow \mathbb{Z}_q^*$, computes $x = H(SK_A, r_A)$ and $X = (H_1(ID_A))^x$. It sends X to B.
– Upon receiving X, B checks whether $X \in \mathbb{G}_1/1_{\mathbb{G}_1}$ and aborts if not. B selects $r_B \leftarrow \mathbb{Z}_q^*$, computes $y = H(SK_B, r_B)$ and $Y = (H_1(ID_B))^y$. Then B sets the primary secret $PS_B = e(X, SK_B)^y$, derives keys $(K_1, K_2) \leftarrow KDF(PS_B, X \parallel Y)$ and computes $C_B = Enc_{K_1}(ID_B, y)$. Finally, B sends (Y, C_B) to A.
– Upon receiving (Y, C_B), A sets primary secret $PS_A = e(SK_A, Y)^x$, derives keys $(K_1, K_2) \leftarrow KDF(PS_A, X \parallel Y)$ and decrypts the ciphertext C_B by using K_1 to get the identity ID_B and y. Then A verifies if $y \in Z_q^*$ and $Y = (H_1(ID_B))^y$, if successful, it computes $C_A = Enc_{K_1}(ID_A, x)$ and the session key is set to be K_2. Finally, A sends C_A to B.
– Upon receiving C_A, B runs $Dec_{K_1}(C_A) \to (ID_A, x)$. Then it verifies if $x \in Z_q^*$ and $X = (H_1(ID_A))^x$, if successful, session key is set to be K_2.

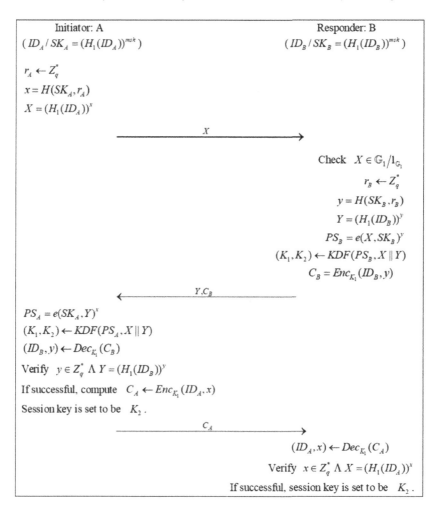

Fig. 1. Construction of IB-CAKE with Type-I bilinear mapping

In the execution of IB-CAKE protocol, the second-round message sent by sever contains the ciphertext which can be decrypted by client, then the client can check whether y and Y are valid or not, from which it achieves the authentication of sever. Similarly, the server authenticates the identity of user after receiving the third-round message. Therefore, this proposed scheme realizes the property of mutual authentication.

Correctness. It suffices to indicate that honest parties can obtain the same session key. We have $PS_A = e(SK_A, Y)^x = e(H_1(ID_A)^{msk}, H_1(ID_B)^y)^x = e(H_1(ID_A), H_1(ID_B))^{x \cdot y \cdot msk}$ and $PS_B = e(SK_B, X)^y = e(H_1(ID_B)^{msk}, H_1(ID_A)^x)^y = e(H_1(ID_B), H_1(ID_A))^{x \cdot y \cdot msk}$. Thus they derive the same session keys using the function KDF. This completes the correctness argument.

We note that the above IB-CAKE scheme is constructed in the symmetric pairing (Type-I) setting, where the bilinear map e is defined over $\mathbb{G}_1$ and $\mathbb{G}_T$, i.e., $e : \mathbb{G}_1 \times \mathbb{G}_1 \to \mathbb{G}_T$. In practice, using asymmetric bilinear groups (Type-II and Type-III) is most practical for pairing implementations, where e is defined as $e : \mathbb{G}_1 \times \mathbb{G}_2 \to \mathbb{G}_T$. The straightforward extensions to Type-II and Type-III pairings are presented in Appendix A.

5   Security Analysis of IB-CAKE

In this section, we present the security analysis for identity-based identity-concealed authenticated key exchange (IB-CAKE) with mutual authentications. Due to the space limitation, we focus on the security proof of our IB-CAKE construction with symmetric bilinear groups. The extension to the asymmetric bilinear groups is straightforward. In the following security analysis, both the KDF and the hash functions H, H_1 are performed as random oracle (RO).

Theorem 1. *Assume the $AEAD = (Enc, Dec)$ scheme is AE-secure and the $Gap - BDH$ assumption holds, then the proposed scheme IB-CAKE in Sect. 4 is strong IB-CAKE secure in the random oracle model.*

Proof. For each session run of the IB-CAKE protocol (at either Initiator or Responder), define the session label to be "$X \parallel Y$". Two sessions (whether they are complete or not) are matching if they have the same session label. Note that, for honestly generated X and Y, with overwhelming probability $X \neq Y$. Observe that the two messages "$X \parallel Y$" uniquely determine the parties nonce and identities as well as the key PS which in turn determines the authentication key K_1 and application key K_2. In addition, the two messages determine the two parties authentication messages C_A and C_B if the peer reached the acceptance state.

5.1   Proof of Label Security

The label-security is proved as follows. Firstly, it is trivial to check that the probability that more than two sessions share the same session label is negligible. We consider any pair of matching sessions: session SID held at user ID_i and session SID' held at user ID_j. Label matching (with $X \neq Y$) implies that, with overwhelming probability, ID_i and ID_j cannot play the same session role (since two different identities playing the same role will initially violate the definition of matching session). Since the intermediate values $PS_i = \hat{e}(SK_i, Y)^x$ and $PS_j = \hat{e}(SK_j, X)^y$, the AEAD-key/session-key pairs $(K_1, K_2) = KDF(PS_i, X \parallel Y)$ and $(K_1, K_2) = KDF(PS_j, X \parallel Y)$ can be derived from the same label $X \parallel Y$, and it is easy to see that $PS_i = PS_j$. Thus we conclude that the two matching sessions must have the same session-key.

Without loss of generality, assume that ID_i (holding session SID) is initiator and ID_j (holding the matching session SID') is responder. Next, we prove that the probability of $peer_{SID} \neq \perp \wedge peer_{SID} \neq ID_j$, or $peer_{SID'} \neq \perp \wedge peer_{SID'} \neq ID_i$, is negligible. Note that, for IB-CAKE protocol, it may be the case that $peer_{SID} = ID_j$ but $peer_{SID'} = \perp$. Specifically, consider that the third-round message sent by the initiator ID_i in session SID is dropped by adversary, which causes $peer_{SID} = ID_j$ but $peer_{SID'} = \perp$. We note that such a cutting-last-message attack is unavoidable. Let $X = (H_1(ID_i))^x$ (sent by the user ID_i in session SID) and $Y = (H_1(ID_j))^y$ (sent by the user ID_j in session SID'), and suppose that $peer_{SID} \neq \perp \wedge peer_{SID} \neq ID_j$, or $peer_{SID'} \neq \perp \wedge peer_{SID'} \neq ID_i$. This implies that there exists a PPT adversary who can successfully open $Y = (H_1(ID_j))^y$ into (ID_k, y') for $ID_k \neq ID_j$ in session SID such that $Y = (H_1(ID_j))^y = (H_1(ID_k))^{y'}$, or can open $X = (H_1(ID_i))^x$ into (ID_b, x') for $ID_b \neq ID_i$ in session SID' such that $X = (H_1(ID_i))^x = (H_1(ID_b))^{x'}$. However, according to Lemma 1, either case can occur with at most negligible probability. This completes the proof of the label security. Note that, our label security still holds, even if the adversary is allowed to obtain the master secret key by querying the **MSKReveal** oracle.

Lemma 1. *Assuming that the functions $H_1 : \{0,1\}^* \to \mathbb{G}_1$ and $H : \{0,1\}^* \to \mathbb{Z}_q^*$ are both random oracles, there does not exist a PPT algorithm which can output $\{ID_j, y \in \mathbb{Z}_q^*\}$ and $\{ID_k, y' \in \mathbb{Z}_q^*\}$, where $\{ID_j, y\} \neq \{ID_k, y'\}$, with non-negligible probability such that $(H_1(ID_j))^y = (H_1(ID_k))^{y'}$.*

Proof. Assuming that the functions $H_1 : \{0,1\}^* \to \mathbb{G}_1$ and $H : \{0,1\}^* \to \mathbb{Z}_q^*$ are random oracles, for any pair of different $\{ID_j, y\}$ and $\{ID_k, y'\}$, the probability that $(H_1(ID_j))^y = (H_1(ID_k))^{y'}$ is described as follows.

$$\Pr[H_1(ID_j) = H_1(ID_k), y = y'] = \frac{1}{q-1}$$
$$\Pr[H_1(ID_j) \neq H_1(ID_k), y \neq y'] = \frac{1}{(q-1)(q-2)} \cdot \frac{1}{(q-2)}$$
$$\Pr[(H_1(ID_j))^y = (H_1(ID_k))^{y'}] = \frac{1}{q-1} + \frac{1}{(q-1)(q-2)^2}$$

Then, for any PPT algorithm who makes at most t times oracle queries to H_1 and H, where t is polynomial in $|q|$, the probability it outputs a pair of different (ID_j, y) and (ID_k, y') such that $(H_1(ID_j))^y = (H_1(ID_k))^{y'}$ is at most $\frac{t^2}{2(q-1)} + \frac{t^2}{2(q-1)(q-2)^2}$, which is obviously negligible.

5.2 Proof of ID-Concealed Session-Key Security

In the following, we continue to present the proof of the ID-concealed session-key security.

Let SID_T be the completed unexposed test-session held at the user $ID_t = ID_{t_b}$ with session-label $X \parallel Y$ and $peer_{SID_T} = ID_k \in \mathsf{HONEST}$, $1 \leq k \leq n$. Denote by SID_T' its matching session (in case it exists), which may be still on-going. As the test-session SID_T is completed and unexposed, it means that: (1) ID_{t_0} and ID_{t_1} are not corrupted; (2) The static secret key of ID_{t_0} and ID_{t_1} are unexposed, or ST_{SID_T} is unexposed; (3) If the matching session SID'_T exists, the static secret key of ID_k is unexposed or $ST_{SID'_T}$ is unexposed; (4) Neither the session-key of SID_T nor that of SID'_T (in case the matching session exists) is exposed; (5) $peer_{SID'_T}$ is unexposed (in case the matching session exists).

The ID-concealed session-key security is reduced to the AEAD security and the Gap-BDH assumption. Before proceeding the security analysis, we first clarify the use of the DBDH-oracle in ensuring the consistency of the KDF random oracle. Specifically, we consider a simulator $\mathcal{S}$ who wants to simulate, with the aid of a DBDH-oracle, the peer user $peer_{SID_T}$ (suppose it is ID_k) of the test-session, as well as the user ID_t in the test-session SID_T. The input of $\mathcal{S}$ includes a given value g^c, where $c \leftarrow Z_q^*$ is defined to be the master secret key but is unknown to $\mathcal{S}$.

- Simulation of the test-session SID_T. If the test-session SID_T is run at Initiator, denote by $ID_t = ID_A$ the test-session holder for presentation simplicity. When the adversary queries the static secret key SK_{ID_A} of ID_A, the simulator $\mathcal{S}$ generates SK_{ID_A} and answers as follows. $\mathcal{S}$ first checks whether the adversary has queried the hash oracle H_1 for ID_A, if so, the simulator retrieves the value a_1 used for responding to the query $H_1(ID_A)$, i.e., $g^{a_1} = H_1(ID_A)$; otherwise, $\mathcal{S}$ selects a fresh a_1 randomly and sets $g^{a_1} = H_1(ID_A)$. Next, the simulator uses a_1 and g^c to compute $SK_{ID_A} = (g^c)^{a_1}$. Then the simulator $\mathcal{S}$ chooses $X \leftarrow \mathbb{G}_1/1_{\mathbb{G}_1}$, and gets access to the DBDH-oracle $\mathcal{O}_{DBDH}(\cdot, \cdot, \cdot, \cdot)$. In the first round of SID_T, $\mathcal{S}$ sends X to the responder. After receiving (Y, C_B) in the second round of the test-session, $\mathcal{S}$ checks whether $(X \parallel Y, (K_1, K_2))$ has been recorded in the list $\mathcal{L}_{DBDH}$: if "yes", $\mathcal{S}$ just uses K_1 to decrypt C_B; if "not", $\mathcal{S}$ randomly generates $(K_1, K_2) \leftarrow (0,1)^\kappa \times (0,1)^\kappa$ by itself and records $(X \parallel Y, (K_1, K_2))$ into the list $\mathcal{L}_{DBDH}$. From this point on, for each RO-query of the form $KDF(PS, X \parallel Y)$ made by the adversary $\mathcal{A}$, where PS is supposed to be $BDH(X, Y, g^c)$ (where the master secret-key is set as $msk = c$). $\mathcal{S}$ queries DBDH-oracle with (SK_{ID_A}, Y, g^x, PS), where $SK_{ID_A} = (H_1(ID_A))^c$. If $\mathcal{O}_{DBDH}$ outputs "yes", $\mathcal{S}$ returns the already stored (K_1, K_2) to the adversary $\mathcal{A}$; otherwise, random answer is returned.

- If the test-session SID_T is run at Responder, denote by $ID_t = ID_B$ the holder of the test-session for simplicity. When the adversary queries the static secret key SK_{ID_B} of ID_B, the simulator $\mathcal{S}$ generates SK_{ID_B} and answers as follows. $\mathcal{S}$ first checks whether the adversary has queried the hash oracle H_1 for ID_B, if so, the simulator retrieves the value a_2 used for responding to the query $H_1(ID_B)$, i.e., $g^{a_2} = H_1(ID_B)$; otherwise, $\mathcal{S}$ selects a fresh a_2 randomly and sets $g^{a_2} = H_1(ID_B)$. Next, the simulator uses a_2 and g^c to compute $SK_{ID_B} = (g^c)^{a_2}$. Then the simulator takes $Y \leftarrow \mathbb{G}_1/1_{\mathbb{G}_1}$ as input, and has access to the DBDH-oracle $\mathcal{O}_{DBDH}(\cdot, \cdot, \cdot, \cdot)$. After receiving X in the first round of SID_T, $\mathcal{S}$ checks $X \in \mathbb{G}_1/1_{\mathbb{G}_1}$, and checks whether $(X \parallel Y, (K_1, K_2))$ has been recorded in the list $\mathcal{L}_{DBDH}$: if "yes", $\mathcal{S}$ will abort, which occurs with at most negligible probability in the RO model; if "not", $\mathcal{S}$ randomly generates (K_1, K_2) by itself and records $(X \parallel Y, (K_1, K_2))$ into the list $\mathcal{L}_{DBDH}$. From this point on, for each RO-query of the form $KDF(PS, X \parallel Y)$ made by the adversary $\mathcal{A}$, where PS is supposed to be $PS = BDH(X, Y, g^c)$, and queries its DBDH-oracle with (X, SK_{ID_B}, g^y, PS), where $SK_{ID_B} = (H_1(ID_B))^c$. If $\mathcal{O}_{DBDH}$ outputs "yes", $\mathcal{S}$ returns the already stored (K_1, K_2) to the adversary; otherwise, random answer is returned.

It is easy to check that, in the random oracle model where KDF is assumed to be an RO. With overwhelming probability the simulation of $peer_{SID_T}$ and the test-session by $\mathcal{S}$ is perfect.

Impersonation Security. Next, we prove the impersonation security which means the probability that the test session SID_T has no matching session is negligible. Suppose an efficient adversary $\mathcal{A}$ could successful impersonate the honest user ID_k in the completed and unexposed test-session SID_T, while no matching session exists. We distinguish two cases according to whether SID_T is run at Initiator or Responder, and present the outline of proof.

The first case, denote Case-1, is that SID_T is run at Initiator. In this case, for presentation simplicity, we denote $ID_t = ID_A$ as the test-session holder and $ID_k = ID_B$ as the peer user $peer_{SID_T}$. Firstly, by Lemma 1, we have that with overwhelming probability Y was never generated and sent by ID_B in any existing session. Otherwise, by the fact that the test-session is successfully completed, it implies the adversary can solve the discrete logarithm problem. Then, the impersonation security is reduced to the AEAD security and the Gap-BDH assumption in the RO model. Specifically, the Gap-BDH solver $\mathcal{S}$ takes (ID_B, X, g^c) as input, where $X \leftarrow \mathbb{G}_1/1_{\mathbb{G}_1}$, $\mathcal{S}$ defines the master secret key $msk = c$ (note that c is unknown to $\mathcal{S}$), and its goal is to $BDH(X, H_1(ID_B), g^c)$ with a DBDH-oracle. Towards this goal, it randomly guesses the peer user $peer_{SID_T} = ID_k = ID_B$ with probability $\frac{1}{n}$ by taking $k \leftarrow \{1, ..., n\}$, generates the secret-keys for all the honest users in the system except ID_B.

Upon receiving "($\textbf{Test}, ID_{t_0}, ID_{t_1}$)" for uncorrupted $ID_{t_0}, ID_{t_1} \in \mathsf{HONEST}$, where $1 \leq t_0 \neq t_1 \leq n$, it sets $ID_t = ID_{t_b}$, $\mathcal{S}$ just sends X, the element given in its input, to $\mathcal{A}$ as the first-round message of the test-session. As $\mathcal{S}$ knows the secret-keys of all the other users except ID_k, and Case-1 assumes that secret-key of ID_k is unexposed and no matching session exists for SID_T, $\mathcal{S}$ can perfectly answer all the other queries made by $\mathcal{A}$ regarding **StaKeyReveal, Corrupt, Create** and **Peer**. When the **MSKReveal** is queried, $\mathcal{S}$ aborts the experiment. It is easy to check that the view of $\mathcal{A}$ under the run of $\mathcal{S}$ is identical to that in its real attack, where KDF is assumed to be an RO. Moreover, as clarified above regarding the simulation of $peer_{SID_T}$ and test-session SID_T, $\mathcal{S}$ can well simulate the actions of ID_B. In the test-session SID_T, $\mathcal{S}$ sends X in the first round. Denote by (X, Y) the session label of the completed test-session SID_T, and by (Y, C_B) the AEAD ciphertext sent by $\mathcal{A}$ in the second round of SID_T. Case-1 means that Y was not generated by user ID_B, but the decryption of C_B gives (ID_B, y) such that $y \in \mathbb{Z}_q^*$ and $Y = (H_1(ID_B))^y$, where y may be generated by $\mathcal{A}$ itself and $\mathcal{A}$ made the RO-query $H_1(ID_B)$. Denote by $(K_1, K_2) = KDF(PS, X \parallel Y)$. As we assume SID_T has no matching session and Y was not sent by ID_B, with overwhelming probability the AEAD ciphertext $Enc_{K_1}(ID_B, y)$ was not sent in any existing session other than the test-session. By the AEAD security, the adversary $\mathcal{A}$ must have made the oracle query $KDF(PS, X \parallel Y)$, where $PS = e(X, SK_{ID_B})^y = BDH(X, Y, g^c)$ that can be checked with the DBDH oracle. Consequently, $\mathcal{S}$ gets $PS = BDH(X, Y, g^c) = e(H_1(ID_A)^x, H_1(ID_B)^y)^c$ and $\mathcal{S}$ decrypts C_B with the key K_1 to get y, from which it computes $BDH(X, H_1(ID_B), g^c) = e(H_1(ID_A)^x, H_1(ID_B))^c = e(H_1(ID_A)^x, H_1(ID_B)^y)^{c \cdot \frac{1}{y}} = PS^{\frac{1}{y}}$, which violates the Gap-BDH assumption.

The second case, denoted Case-2, is that SID_T is run at Responder. In this case, for presentation simplicity, we denote $ID_t = ID_B$ the test-session holder, and by $ID_k = ID_A$ the peer user $peer_{SID_T}$. Let $X \parallel Y$ be the session label of SID_T, where X is sent by the adversary $\mathcal{A}$ who is impersonating the honest user ID_A and Y is sent by the uncorrupted user ID_B. The impersonation security in this case is still reduced to the AEAD security and the Gap-BDH assumption in the RO model.

Assuming there exists a PPT adversary $\mathcal{A}$ such that Case-2 occurs with non-negligible probability. In this case, the Gap-BDH solver $\mathcal{S}$ takes (Y, ID_A, g^c) as input, where $Y \leftarrow \mathbb{G}_1/1_{\mathbb{G}_1}$, and its goal is to compute $BDH(Y, H_1(ID_A), g^c)$ with the aid of DBDH oracle. Towards this goal, it randomly guesses the peer user ID_A with successful probability $\frac{1}{n}$, generates the secret-key for all the honest users in the system except ID_A. As clarified above regarding the simulation for $peer_{SID_T}$ and the test-session, $\mathcal{S}$ can well simulate ID_A. In the test-session SID_T, after receiving X in the first round, and getting Y which is the value given in $\mathcal{S}$'s input, $\mathcal{S}$ then generates the accompanying AEAD ciphertext C_B, where the underlying keys (K_1, K_2) are set by $\mathcal{S}$ itself with the aid of the DBDH oracle to ensure the consistency of KDF as clarified above regarding the $peer_{SID_T}$ simulation. Finally, $\mathcal{S}$ sends $\{Y, C_B\}$ in the second round of the test-session SID_T. Denote by C_A the AEAD ciphertext sent by the adversary $\mathcal{A}$ in the third-round of SID_T, which is decrypted to be (ID_A, x) using the key K_1 such that $x \in \mathbb{Z}_q^*$ and $X = (H_1(ID_A))^x$ as we assume SID_T is complete. Note that, in the RO model, with overwhelming probability the RO-query $H_1(ID_A)$ has been made before $\mathcal{A}$ sends X in the first round of SID_T; otherwise, SID_T will fail in the third round with overwhelming probability (while SID_T is assumed to be complete). Also note that the RO-query $H_1(ID_A)$ may not be made by $\mathcal{A}$ itself. For example, consider that: the RO-query $H_1(ID_A)$ is generated by ID_A in a non-matching session, where x is, however, exposed to $\mathcal{A}$. Note that, as we assume the test-session has no matching session, the underlying AEAD-key K_1 used in SID_T is independent of the AEAD-keys in all the other sessions. By the AEAD security in the RO model, conditioned on $\mathcal{S}$ successfully breaks the impersonation security with non-negligible probability in Case-2, $\mathcal{S}$ will get $PS = BDH(X, Y, g^c) = e(H_1(ID_A)^x, H_1(ID_B)^y)^c$, from which it computes $BDH(Y, H_1(ID_A), g^c) = e(H_1(ID_B)^y, H_1(ID_A))^c = e(H_1(ID_A)^x, H_1(ID_B)^y)^{c \cdot \frac{1}{x}} = PS^{\frac{1}{x}}$, which violates the Gap-BDH assumption. This finishes the proof of impersonation security.

ID-SK Indistinguishability. Finally, we prove the ID-SK indistinguishability. The proof of impersonation security has already established that the test-session SID_T has matching session SID'_T, where they share the same session label $X \parallel Y$. By the AEAD security, in order to break the ID-SK indistinguishability the CMIM adversary $\mathcal{A}$ has to make the RO-query $KDF(PS = BDH(X, Y, g^c), X \parallel Y)$ with non-negligible probability. It is then reduced to the Gap-BDH assumption in the RO model, where the proof is similar to, but actually simpler than, the proof for impersonation security.

Here, for presentation simplicity, one of $\{peer_{SID_T}, ID_t\}$ denotes ID_A and the other denotes ID_B for presentation simplicity. The Gap-BDH solver $\mathcal{S}$ takes as input (U, V), where $U, V \leftarrow \mathbb{G}_1/1_{\mathbb{G}}$, and its goal is to compute $BDH(U, V, g^c)$ with DBDH oracle. The public key and secret key of ID_t are generated by $\mathcal{S}$ itself, while the hash of public-key of $peer_{SID_T}$ and the DH-component to be sent by ID_t in SID_T are set to be (U, V), i.e., the input given to $\mathcal{S}$. From $PS = BDH(X, Y, g^c) = e(SK_B, X)^y$ because $\mathcal{S}$ knows (SK_A, y) or (SK_B, x), $\mathcal{S}$ can compute $BDH(U, V, g^c)$ that is either $BDH(X, H_1(ID_B), g^c)$ or $BDH(Y, H_1(ID_A), g^c)$, which violates the Gap-BDH assumption.

Finally, we would like highlight the role of generating x and y from the random oracle H on inputs of both the static-secret key and the ephemeral nonce, i.e., $x = H(SK_A, r_A)$ and $y = H(SK_B, r_B)$. This is a common trick for provable security in the eCK-like model. But we stress that the role of this trick is different for the TFNS19-protocol [25] and for our protocol. Specifically, in the eCK-like model, exposing the ephemeral session states of both the test-session and the matching-session is allowed. Note that, according to the protocol structure of the TFNS19-protocol [25] (reviewed in Appendix B), its primary secrecy (PS) can be computed merely from (x, y) and some public values, specifically $PS = g_T^{(x+d_A)(y+d_B)}$, from which the session-key can be derived. So, in the security model of [25], the values x and y are not allowed to be both exposed, and only the values r_A and r_B are specified to be the session states to be exposed. But for our IB-CAKE protocol, the primary secrecy PS cannot be computed from (x, y) and public values. Indeed, we note that our IB-CAKE protocol remains provable security in the model proposed in [25] without the above trick, i.e., by directly setting $x = r_A$ and $y = r_B$. This means that our protocol can be more efficient with respect to the TFNS19 security model [25]. However, this trick is indeed necessary for the stronger security model proposed in this work. Specifically, it is critical for the security of ID-SK indistinguishability and particularly for ID-privacy. In more details, as $X = H_1(ID_A)^x$ and $Y = H_1(ID_B)^y$, if the value x or y *in the test-session* is exposed via the **STReveal** query, the adversary can easily compute $H_1(ID_A) = X^{x^{-1}}$ or $H_1(ID_B) = Y^{y^{-1}}$, which will leak the identity information of the holder of the test-session. Specifically, the adversary can distinguish ID_{t_0} and ID_{t_1} of the test-session with the value x or y obtained by querying the **STReveal** oracle. However, if $x = H(SK_A, r_A)$ and $y = H(SK_B, r_B)$ and the session states to be exposed are specified to be r_A and r_B, the above attack fails as the adversary is not allowed to expose both the ephemeral session state and the static secret key of the test-session, and hence cannot derive x or y of the test-session.

6 Comparison and Implementation

Now we give a comparison between an identity-based authenticated key exchange scheme [25] (TFNS19-protocol, for short) and our proposed scheme based on asymmetric bilinear pairings of Type-III (for more references see [6]), in terms of efficiency and functionalities. The comparison is briefly summarized in Table 2.

Table 2. Comparisons between IB-CAKE and TFNS19-protocol

	IB-CAKE	TFNS19-protocol [25]
no master public-key	✓	×
x-security	✓	✓
forward ID-privacy	✓	×
perfect forward security	✓	×
post-specified ID	✓	×
mutual authentication	✓	×
assumption	Gap-BDH, AEAD	XDHT, q-Gap-BCA

In comparison with the TFNS19-protocol [25], IB-CAKE scheme has stronger security. IB-CAKE protocol provides x-security, that is, the primary secret PS is still hidden without the knowledge of the static secret key although the secret x is exposed. Furthermore, in IB-CAKE protocol, the initiator doesn't need to know the peer's identity before starting a protocol. While in the TFNS19-protocol, the peer's identity information must be known before the protocol run. Compared with TFNS19-protocol, our proposed scheme also enjoys many nice properties such as forward ID-privacy, perfect forward security and mutual authentication. In addition, we argue that our IB-CAKE protocol is more efficient than the TFNS19-protocol. For example, the TFNS19-protocol generates traditional master public key that performs one exponentiation operation, the secret key generation for each user requires an extra modular inverse operation that is also relatively expensive.

We now provide proof-of-concept implementations for our IB-CAKE scheme and TFNS19-protocol [25], and show efficiency through implementation. The implementation is done on the platform of AMD Ryzen 7 4800H with Radeon Graphics 2.90 GHz CPU at 8 GB RAM running on the Ubuntu 20.04.2 LTS operation system. To better compare the two schemes, we implemented the two schemes based on the same pairing specified in the PBC library. Our program uses C++ language, and uses the PBC library and OPENSSL library. H is implemented by using "HMAC" method from OPENSSL library, H_1 is implemented

Table 3. Space size

	msk	sk	pk	m	c	K_2
Size(byte)	40	128	128	32	216	128

Table 4. Implementation benchmarks

	IB-CAKE	TFNS19-protocol [25]
KGC (ms)	3.787154	7.005497
CPU_1 (million)	1.106735	1.9894491
Both Parties (ms)	12.838818	14.019664
CPU_2 (million)	3.596742	3.977965

by using "SHA256" method from OPENSSL library, and H_2 is implemented by using "blake2s256" method from OPENSSL library. The message and key size are listed in Table 3. It shows the sizes of master secret-key msk, static secret-key sk, public-key pk, plaintext m, ciphertext c and session-key K_2. The computational performance of our scheme and TFNS19-protocol [25] is presented in Table 4. It shows the average performance by executing the protocol 10000 iterations, where the running time of the key generation phase includes the generations of master public key mpk, and the secret keys of both users SK_A and SK_B. Table 4 also includes the number of CPU clock cycle by KGC (CPU_1) and by the two parties (CPU_2), respectively. The implementation results show that our IB-CAKE scheme takes less than TFNS19-protocol whether in KGC or in the key exchange phase between the two parties. Moreover, our proposed scheme is implemented for mutual explicit authentications (while the TFNS19-protocol only achieves implicit authentications). The experiment results show that our scheme has practical applicability.

Acknowledgement. We are grateful to Prof. Satoshi Obana for shepherding on our submission, and for all the anonymous referees of ESORICS 2021 for their constructive and insightful review comments. We thank Shiyu Shen, Pengfei Shi and Hongbing Wang for many helpful discussions. This work was supported by National Key Research and Development Program of China (Grant No. 2017YFB0802000), National Natural Science Foundation of China (Grant Nos. U1536205, 61472084 and NSFC61702007), Shanghai Innovation Action Project under Grant No. 16DZ1100200, Shanghai Science and Technology Development Funds under Grant No. 16JC1400801, Shandong Provincial Key Research and Development Program of China (Grant Nos. 2017CXG0701 and 2018CXGC0701), and Foundations (Grant Nos. 2019M661360 (KLH2301024), gxbjZD27, KJ2018A0533, XWWD201801, ahnis20178002).

A Structures of IB-CAKE Protocol with Asymmetric Bilinear Pairing

A.1 Protocol Structure with Bilinear Pairing of Type-II

For the construction of our IB-CAKE protocol with Type-II bilinear pairing, an additional efficient publicly computable isomorphism ψ is required. Let κ be a secure parameter, $\mathbb{G}_1$, $\mathbb{G}_2$ and $\mathbb{G}_T$ be three multiplicative bilinear map groups of the same prime order q such that the discrete algorithm problems in $\mathbb{G}_1$, $\mathbb{G}_2$ and $\mathbb{G}_T$ are intractable, g_1 be a generator of $\mathbb{G}_1$, $g_2 = \psi(g_1)$ be a generator of $\mathbb{G}_2$, the isomorphism ψ is for the purpose of mapping an element from $\mathbb{G}_1$ to $\mathbb{G}_2$, $\hat{e} : \mathbb{G}_1 \times \mathbb{G}_2 \rightarrow \mathbb{G}_T$ be a bilinear pairing. Let $SE = (K_{se}, Enc, Dec)$ be an authenticated encryption with associated data (AEAD) scheme, where $\mathcal{K} = \{0,1\}^\kappa$ is the key space of K_{se}. Let $H : \{0,1\}^* \rightarrow \mathbb{Z}_q^*$ and $H_1 : \{0,1\}^* \rightarrow \mathbb{G}_1$ be one-way collision-resistant cryptographic hash functions modeled as random oracles and $KDF : \{0,1\}^* \rightarrow \{0,1\}^{p(\kappa)}$ be a key derivation function which is also modeled as a random oracle, where $p(\kappa)$ is a polynomial of κ. The KGC first produces the system's public parameters and the master secret key msk. Then it generates the private key $SK_i = H_1(ID_i)^{msk}$ for the user with identity ID_i. For presentation simplicity, we denote by Alice the anonymous session initiator, whose public identity and private key are ID_A and $SK_A = (H_1(ID_A))^{msk}$, and by Bob the session responder, whose public identity and private key are ID_B and $SK_B = (H_1(ID_B))^{msk}$. The structure is described in Fig. 2.

- The initiator A selects $r_A \leftarrow \mathbb{Z}_q^*$, computes $x = H(SK_A, r_A)$ and $X = (H_1(ID_A))^x$. It sends X to B.
- Upon receiving X, B checks whether $X \in \mathbb{G}_1/1_{\mathbb{G}_1}$ and aborts if not. B selects $r_B \leftarrow \mathbb{Z}_q^*$, computes $y = H(SK_B, r_B)$ and $Y = (H_1(ID_B))^y$. Then B sets the primary secret $PS_B = e(X, \psi(SK_B))^y$, derives keys $(K_1, K_2) \leftarrow KDF(PS_B, X \parallel Y)$ and computes $C_B = Enc_{K_1}(ID_B, y)$. Finally, B sends (Y, C_B) to A.
- Upon receiving (Y, C_B), A sets primary secret $PS_A = e(SK_A, \psi(Y))^x$, derives keys $(K_1, K_2) \leftarrow KDF(PS_A, X \parallel Y)$ and decrypts the ciphertext C_B by using K_1 to get the identity ID_B and y. Then A verifies if $y \in Z_q^*$ and $Y = (H_1(ID_B))^y$, if so, it computes $C_A = Enc_{K_1}(ID_A, x)$ and the session key is set to be K_2. Finally, A sends C_A to B.
- Upon receiving C_A, B runs $Dec_{K_1}(C_A) \rightarrow (ID_A, x)$. Then it verifies if $x \in Z_q^*$ and $X = (H_1(ID_A))^x$, if so, the session key is set to be K_2.

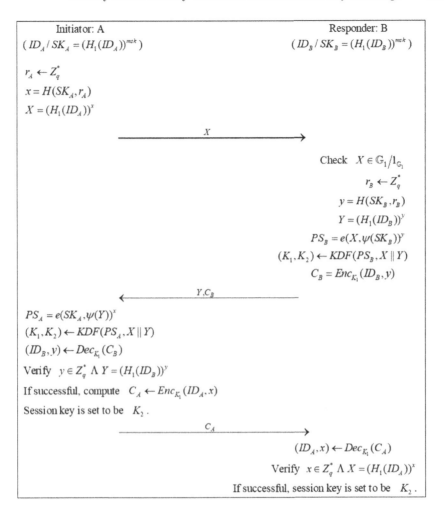

Fig. 2. Construction of IB-CAKE with Type-II bilinear mapping

A.2   Protocol Structure with Bilinear Pairing of Type-III

For the construction of our IB-CAKE protocol with Type-III bilinear pairing, the private key SK of any user ID is replaced by a pair of key (SK^I, SK^R), where SK^I is used when the user is an initiator in a session and SK^R is used when the user is a responder in a session. Let κ be a secure parameter, $\mathbb{G}_1$, $\mathbb{G}_2$ and $\mathbb{G}_T$ be three multiplicative bilinear map groups of the same prime order q such that the discrete algorithm problems in $\mathbb{G}_1$, $\mathbb{G}_2$ and $\mathbb{G}_T$ are intractable, g_1 be a generator of $\mathbb{G}_1$, g_2 be a generator of $\mathbb{G}_2$, $\hat{e} : \mathbb{G}_1 \times \mathbb{G}_2 \to \mathbb{G}_T$ be a bilinear pairing. Let $H : \{0,1\}^* \to \mathbb{Z}_q^*$, $H_1 : \{0,1\}^* \to \mathbb{G}_1$ and $H_2 : \{0,1\}^* \to \mathbb{G}_2$ be one-way collision-resistant cryptographic hash functions modeled as random oracles. Our IB-CAKE protocol structure using Type-III bilinear pairing is described in Fig. 3.

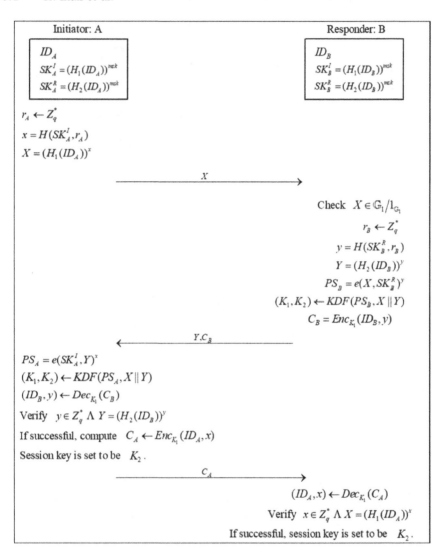

Fig. 3. Construction of IB-CAKE with Type-III bilinear mapping

In the following, let A be a session initiator and B be a session responder.

- The initiator A selects $r_A \leftarrow \mathbb{Z}_q^*$, computes $x = H(SK_A^I, r_A)$ and $X = (H_1(ID_A))^x$. It sends X to B.
- Upon receiving X, B checks whether $X \in \mathbb{G}_1/1_{\mathbb{G}_1}$ and aborts if not. B selects $r_B \leftarrow \mathbb{Z}_q^*$, computes $y = H(SK_B^R, r_B)$ and $Y = (H_2(ID_B))^y$. Then B sets the primary secret $PS_B = e(X, SK_B^R))^y$, derives keys $(K_1, K_2) \leftarrow KDF(PS_B, X \parallel Y)$ and computes $C_B = Enc_{K_1}(ID_B, y)$. Finally, B sends (Y, C_B) to A.

- Upon receiving (Y, C_B), A computes primary secret $PS_A = e(SK_A^I, Y)^x$, derives keys $(K_1, K_2) \leftarrow KDF(PS_A, X \parallel Y)$ and decrypts the ciphertext C_B under the secret value K_1 to get the identity ID_B and y. Then A verifies if $y \in Z_q^*$ and $Y = (H_2(ID_B))^y$, if so, it computes $C_A = Enc_{K_1}(ID_A, x)$ and the session key is set to be K_2. Finally, A sends C_A to B.
- Upon receiving C_A, B runs $Dec_{K_1}(C_A) \rightarrow (ID_A, x)$. Then it verifies if $x \in Z_q^*$ and $X = (H_1(ID_A))^x$, if so, the session key is set to be K_2.

B   Review of the TFNS19-Protocol

The structure of the TFNS19-protocol [25] is described in Fig. 4. In this protocol, the three hash functions are defined as: $H, H_1, H_2 : \{0,1\}^* \rightarrow \mathbb{Z}_p, H_3 : \{0,1\}^* \rightarrow \{0,1\}^\kappa$.

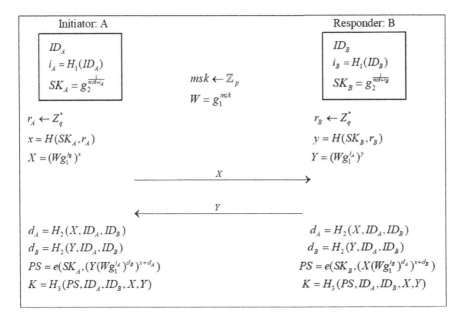

Fig. 4. Construction of TFNS19-protocol [25]

References

1. Baek, J., Safavi-Naini, R., Susilo, W.: Efficient multi-receiver identity-based encryption and its application to broadcast encryption. In: Vaudenay, S. (ed.) PKC 2005. LNCS, vol. 3386, pp. 380–397. Springer, Heidelberg (2005). https://doi.org/10.1007/978-3-540-30580-4_26

2. Bellare, M., Namprempre, C.: Authenticated encryption: relations among notions and analysis of the generic composition paradigm. J. Cryptol. **21**, 469–491 (2008). https://doi.org/10.1007/s00145-008-9026-x
3. Blazy, O., Chevalier, C.: Non-interactive key exchange from identity-based encryption. In: ARES 2018, pp. 13:1–13:10. ACM, Hamburg (2018)
4. Boneh, D., Franklin, M.: Identity-based encryption from the weil pairing. In: Kilian, J. (ed.) CRYPTO 2001. LNCS, vol. 2139, pp. 213–229. Springer, Heidelberg (2001). https://doi.org/10.1007/3-540-44647-8_13
5. Boyd, C., Cliff, Y., Gonzalez Nieto, J., Paterson, K.G.: Efficient one-round key exchange in the standard model. In: Mu, Y., Susilo, W., Seberry, J. (eds.) ACISP 2008. LNCS, vol. 5107, pp. 69–83. Springer, Heidelberg (2008). https://doi.org/10.1007/978-3-540-70500-0_6
6. Boyd, C., Mathuria, A., Stebila, D.: Protocols for Authentication and Key Establishment, 2nd edn. Springer, Heidelberg (2020). https://doi.org/10.1007/978-3-662-09527-0
7. Brzuska, C., Smart, N.P., Warinschi, B., Watson, G.J.: An analysis of the EMV channel establishment protocol. In: ACM CCS 2013, pp. 373–386. ACM Press, Berlin (2013)
8. Chen, L., Cheng, Z., Smart, N.P.: Identity-based key agreement protocols from pairings. Int. J. Inf. Secur. **6**(4), 213–241 (2007). https://doi.org/10.1007/s10207-006-0011-9
9. Daniel, R.M., Rajsingh, E.B., Silas, S.: An efficient eCK secure identity based two party authenticated key agreement scheme with security against active adversaries. Inf. Comput. **275**, 104630 (2020)
10. Fiore, D., Gennaro, R.: Making the Diffie-Hellman protocol identity-based. In: Pieprzyk, J. (ed.) CT-RSA 2010. LNCS, vol. 5985, pp. 165–178. Springer, Heidelberg (2010). https://doi.org/10.1007/978-3-642-11925-5_12
11. Krawczyk, H., Paterson, K.G., Wee, H.: On the security of the TLS protocol: a systematic analysis. In: Canetti, R., Garay, J.A. (eds.) CRYPTO 2013. LNCS, vol. 8042, pp. 429–448. Springer, Heidelberg (2013). https://doi.org/10.1007/978-3-642-40041-4_24
12. Krawczyk, H.: HMQV: a high-performance secure Diffie-Hellman protocol. In: Shoup, V. (ed.) CRYPTO 2005. LNCS, vol. 3621, pp. 546–566. Springer, Heidelberg (2005). https://doi.org/10.1007/11535218_33
13. Libert, B., Quisquater, J.-J.: Identity based undeniable signatures. In: Okamoto, T. (ed.) CT-RSA 2004. LNCS, vol. 2964, pp. 112–125. Springer, Heidelberg (2004). https://doi.org/10.1007/978-3-540-24660-2_9
14. Ni, L., Chen, G., Li, J., Hao, Y.: Strongly secure identity-based authenticated key agreement protocols without bilinear pairings. Inf. Sci. **367–368**, 176–193 (2016)
15. Okamoto, E., Tanaka, K.: Key distribution system based on identification information. IEEE J. Sel. Areas Commun. **7**(4), 481–485 (1989)
16. Okamoto, E.: Key distribution systems based on identification information. In: Pomerance, C. (ed.) CRYPTO 1987. LNCS, vol. 293, pp. 194–202. Springer, Heidelberg (1988). https://doi.org/10.1007/3-540-48184-2_15
17. Paterson, K.G., Ristenpart, T., Shrimpton, T.: Tag size *does* matter: attacks and proofs for the TLS record protocol. In: Lee, D.H., Wang, X. (eds.) ASIACRYPT 2011. LNCS, vol. 7073, pp. 372–389. Springer, Heidelberg (2011). https://doi.org/10.1007/978-3-642-25385-0_20
18. Rescorla, E.: The transport layer security (TLS) protocol version 1.3, RFC 8446 (2018)

19. Rogaway, P.: Authenticated-encryption with associated-data. In: CCS 2002, pp. 98–107. ACM, Washington (2002)
20. Roskind, J.: Quick UDP internet connections: Multiplexed stream transport over UDP, **1**(2), 77–94 (2012). https://www.chromium.org/quic
21. Sakai, R., Ohgishi, K., Kasahara, M.: Cryptosystem based on pairings. In: Symposium on Cryptography and Information Security (SCIS), pp. 26–28 (2000)
22. Shamir, A.: Identity-based cryptosystems and signature schemes. In: Blakley, G.R., Chaum, D. (eds.) CRYPTO 1984. LNCS, vol. 196, pp. 47–53. Springer, Heidelberg (1985). https://doi.org/10.1007/3-540-39568-7_5
23. Shim, K.: Efficient ID-based authenticated key agreement protocol based on the Weil pairing. Electron. Lett. **39**(8), 653–654 (2003)
24. Smart, N.P.: Identity-based authenticated key agreement protocol based on Weil pairing. Electron. Lett. **38**(13), 630–632 (2002)
25. Tomida, J., Fujioka, A., Nagai, A., Suzuki, K.: Strongly secure identity-based key exchange with single pairing operation. In: Sako, K., Schneider, S., Ryan, P.Y.A. (eds.) ESORICS 2019. LNCS, vol. 11736, pp. 484–503. Springer, Cham (2019). https://doi.org/10.1007/978-3-030-29962-0_23
26. Wu, J.-D., Tseng, Y.-M., Huang, S.-S.: An identity-based authenticated key exchange protocol resilient to continuous key leakage. IEEE Syst. J. **13**(4), 3968–3979 (2019)
27. Xie, M., Wang, L.: One-round identity-based key exchange with perfect forward security. Inf. Process. Lett. **112**(14–15), 587–591 (2012)
28. Zhang, J., Huang, X., Wang, W., Yue, Y.: Unbalancing pairing-free identity-based authenticated key exchange protocols for disaster scenarios. IEEE Internet Things J. **6**(1), 878–890 (2019)

Privacy-Preserving Authenticated Key Exchange: Stronger Privacy and Generic Constructions

Sebastian Ramacher⬤, Daniel Slamanig$^{(\boxtimes)}$⬤, and Andreas Weninger

AIT Austrian Institute of Technology, Vienna, Austria
{sebastian.ramacher,daniel.slamanig,andreas.weninger}@ait.ac.at

Abstract. Authenticated key-exchange (AKE) protocols are an important class of protocols that allow two parties to establish a common session key over an insecure channel such as the Internet to then protect their communication. They are widely deployed in security protocols such as TLS, IPsec and SSH. Besides the confidentiality of the communicated data, an orthogonal but increasingly important goal is the protection of the confidentiality of the identities of the involved parties (aka privacy). For instance, the Encrypted Client Hello (ECH) mechanism for TLS 1.3 has been designed for exactly this reason. Recently, a series of works (Zhao CCS'16, Arfaoui et al. PoPETS'19, Schäge et al. PKC'20) studied privacy guarantees of (existing) AKE protocols by integrating privacy into AKE models. We observe that these so called privacy-preserving AKE (PPAKE) models are typically strongly tailored to the specific setting, i.e., concrete protocols they investigate. Moreover, the privacy guarantees in these models might be too weak (or even are non-existent) when facing active adversaries.

In this work we set the goal to provide a single PPAKE model that captures privacy guarantees against different types of attacks, thereby covering previously proposed notions as well as so far not achieved privacy guarantees. In doing so, we obtain different "degrees" of privacy within a single model, which, in its strongest forms also capture privacy guarantees against powerful active adversaries. We then proceed to investigate (generic) constructions of AKE protocols that provide strong privacy guarantees in our PPAKE model. This includes classical Diffie-Hellman type protocols as well as protocols based on generic building blocks, thus covering post-quantum instantiations.

1 Introduction

Authenticated key exchange (AKE) protocols are among the most important cryptographic building blocks to enable secure communication over insecure networks. Essentially, an AKE allows two parties A and B, in possession of long term key pairs $(\mathsf{pk}_A, \mathsf{sk}_A)$ and $(\mathsf{pk}_B, \mathsf{sk}_B)$ respectively, to authenticate each other and securely establish a common session key. Security should thereby even hold in the presence of active attackers, which may intercept, read, alter, replay, or

© Springer Nature Switzerland AG 2021
E. Bertino et al. (Eds.): ESORICS 2021, LNCS 12973, pp. 676–696, 2021.
https://doi.org/10.1007/978-3-030-88428-4_33

drop any message transmitted between these parties. Moreover, in state-of-the-art protocols one requires security of the session key (i.e., confidentiality) of past interactions of A and B, even if attackers are able to compromise the long term secrets sk_A and sk_B. This is typically denoted as perfect forward secrecy (PFS). In current real world applications, such AKE protocols typically rely on the Diffie-Hellman (DH) protocol and digital signatures and are widely deployed in security protocols such as TLS, IPsec and SSH. The emerging threat of the feasibility of powerful quantum computers additionally revived the interest in AKE protocols that do not rely on DH key exchange, but instead are based generically on public key encryption (PKE) or key encapsulation mechanisms (KEMs) [16,18,31].

Privacy in AKE. While confidentiality of communicated data is the prime target for a security protocol, another important property is the confidentiality of the identities of the parties involved in the AKE. We will call this goal of hiding the identities from external parties privacy.[1] Schäge et al. [30] recently coined the term privacy-preserving authenticated key exchange (PPAKE) for AKE protocols with such privacy guarantees. While the study of PPAKE is an interesting subject on its own right, we currently can observe an increasing interest in such features in real world protocols. For instance, TLS 1.3 [27] aims to protect the identities of the server and client by encrypting messages as soon as possible during the authentication and in particular hiding the certificate sent by the server. Besides, many other protocols such as QUIC, IPsec IKE, SSH and certain patterns of the Noise protocol framework [26] aim to protect identity-related information such as identities, public keys or digital signatures. This is usually done by running an anonymous DH handshake where the derived keying material is then used to encrypt all subsequent messages (essentially the SIGMA-R template [21]). Moreover, the recent proposal of Encrypted Client Hello (ECH) mechanism for TLS encrypts the initial client message (the ClientHello) [28] with the aim of hiding the target domain for a given connection from attackers listening on the network. We also want to note that over the years various protocols have been designed to provide some intuitive identity protection measures, such as SKEME [20] or the SIGMA-I and SIGMA-R variants of the SIGMA protocol family [21]. The work of Schäge et al. [30], for instance, formally analyzes the privacy guarantees of SIGMA-R as used in IKEv2 within IPSec.

Relevance of PPAKE in Practice. From the above mentioned protocols that try to conceal identifying information, in particular encrypted Server Name Indication (ESNI) and its successor ECH have demonstrated its usefulness in practice. Especially when considering network censorship, ESNI/ECH can help to thwart censorship [7]. Consequently, all ESNI protected TLS connections have been blocked in China.[2] In general, one can observe a push towards an Internet

---

[1] We note that key-exchange protocols that hide the identity of one party even from the peer in the key exchange (e.g., as in [13,24]) are outside the scope of this work.

[2] https://www.zdnet.com/article/china-is-now-blocking-all-encrypted-https-traffic-using-tls-1-3-and-esni/.

infrastructure that reduces the amount of identifiable information. DNS over HTTPS/TLS [15,17] for instance helps in hiding identifying information associated to a connection from an adversary listening to public network traffic.

While in the above cases typically only one party, i.e., the server, is authenticated, with the Internet-of-Things (IoT) [14,29] or FIDO2 [3,12] we see an adoption of mutually authenticated AKE protocols and interest towards identity privacy. For instance, Wu et al. [33] study protocols for private service discovery and private mutual authentication in both the IoT and the mobile landscape (with a case study on Apple AirDrop). Similarly, many VPN implementations also offer the ability to configure certificate-based client authentications during the initial handshake which is also the only option in WireGuard [10,11] to establish connections.

Previous Work on PPAKE. To the best of our knowledge, the first work that specifically addresses privacy in key agreement is by Aiello et al. [1]. Informally, their privacy property wants to achieve that protocols must not reveal the identity of a participant to any unauthorized party, including an active attacker that attempts to act as the peer. They concretely propose two protocols, where one protects the identity of the initiator from an active attacker and the second one that of the responder. However, we note that this privacy property is neither modeled nor rigorously analyzed. Another informal discussion of how to achieve "identity concealment" by encrypting the identities was even earlier mentioned by Canetti and Krawczyk in [6]. Later Zhao in [34] introduced the notion of identity-concealed authenticated key exchange (CAKE), which enforces the notion of forward identity-privacy (which we simply call forward privacy) and some form of man-in-the-middle (MITM) privacy for completed sessions.

Recently, Schäge et al. [30] provided a PPAKE model, which similarly to Zhao [34] incorporates forward privacy and some form of MITM privacy for completed sessions, but considers a different setting. In their model, the identity of any two communicating parties are known (so it is visible who communicates with whom), but each party has two additional identities associated to it and it should be hard to figure out which identities the parties are using. Consequently, this model is tailored to a specific setting, e.g., where one server hosts multiple virtual machines or services and these identities need to be protected. Schäge et al. then use their model to analyze the privacy of the IKEv2 protocol [19]. Also recently Arfaoui et al. [2] investigate privacy in TLS 1.3 including session resumption. They capture a weaker notion of privacy than what is required by forward privacy, as they do not allow any corruptions. Their model also only considers uni-lateral authentication and models privacy as a separate property using the concept of a virtual identifier known from privacy analysis of RFID protocols (cf. [30] for a discussion why this is not desirable). Interestingly, none of the previously proposed formal models (including [34]) considers strong active adversaries against the privacy of the AKE protocols. To be more precise, while they actually allow active attacks, they only allow the adversaries to attack accepted sessions. And for any reasonable AKE, this essentially boils down to passive attacks (we will discuss this in more detail in Sect. 2).

Our Contribution. Subsequently, we briefly summarize our contributions:

- We revisit privacy in context of AKE and introduce a comprehensive PPAKE model building upon and extending the recent AKE model in [8]. It is more general than the recent PPAKE by Schäge et al. [30] and among variants of privacy notions known from previous works [30,34] supports stronger notions against active adversaries.
- The main contribution of this work is that we deal with *incomplete session attacks*, i.e., active MITM adversaries that learn the identity of one party but are unable to then complete the protocol run. This is typically due to the inability to authenticate themselves, which is caused by a lack of secret key material. The models and protocols of Schäge et al. [30] and Zhao [34], as noted by the authors, do not prevent such attacks. In each case the adversary can create the first message(s) of either the initiator or the responder without having access to the user's long-term secret key. This is due to the fact that the first messages only serve the purpose of exchanging ephemeral randomness, e.g., via an anonymous DH key exchange. Then the other side will authenticate itself, allowing the adversary to trivially learn the identity. We stress that this attack can be done by any MITM adversary without corrupting any user.
- We present generic constructions of PPAKE protocols with strong privacy guarantees. Our constructions rely on standard primitives such as public-key encryption or key-encapsulation mechanisms, signature schemes and unauthenticated two-move key exchange protocols. Thus, our constructions can be instantiated with post-quantum secure building blocks. In contrast, previous works exclusively focused on DH based protocols.

2   On Modeling Privacy in AKE

There are different privacy properties that are considered to be relevant, some of which that can and others that cannot be covered within PPAKE. In this section we discuss these issues, highlight aspects that have not been considered so far in PPAKE models and present a comprehensive overview of the different privacy properties and their relations.

2.1   What Can(not) Be Handled by PPAKE

Identity-related information such as client specific identifiers, public keys (certificates in particular) and digital signatures can be used by an adversary to break privacy. All these information are available on the layer of the AKE protocol, but there are clearly other network dependent information outside the AKE layer and our model, e.g., network addresses such as IP or MAC addresses, that allow adversaries to break privacy. Consequently, as discussed in [30] for PPAKE, the assumptions on the network are stronger than those required by network anonymization protocols like Tor [9]. Latter implement an overlay network and provide privacy against an adversary who controls large parts of the underlying network (i.e., the Internet) but not the complete network, as well as parts of the overlay network (e.g., Tor) itself.

PPAKE considers an adversary that is weaker and in particular assumes an active MITM attacker that controls a large, but well-defined part of the network. Consequently, one omits the consideration of network identifiers like IP or MAC addresses in PPAKE. This firstly allows to make the model simpler and independent of any network technology and topology. Secondly, as argued in [30], by using trustworthy proxies at the entry points of the adversary controlled network the usefulness of these information to an adversary can be significantly reduced. Nevertheless, we argue that even in case of absence of such proxies PPAKE still provides a meaningful countermeasure to large scale privacy attacks. In particular, it is easily possible to record identity-related information such as certificates (which can simply be parsed locally) on the AKE layer. Consequently, compared to basing the analysis on network address information, which might be additionally complicated by Network Address Translation (NAT), this is much more efficient and easily leads to a unique identification of the entities.

While it is clear that fully hiding all identity information is not possible in practice, privacy can only be lost. Consequently, guaranteeing an adequate level of privacy via PPAKE is a first step to reduce privacy risks.

2.2   Privacy Goals in PPAKE

Now we are going to discuss privacy goals relevant to PPAKE and distill a set of privacy properties from that. Unlike previous works [2,30,34], which basically design PPAKE models in a way that they allow to analyze a specific AKE protocol (family) such as used in TLS 1.3 or IKEv2, in this work we ask what are desirable properties and how to design PPAKE protocols providing strong privacy guarantees. In doing so we do not consider a single privacy notion (as done in previous work), but propose a set of privacy notions that allow to cover properties relevant to diverse use-cases.

Roughly, we can classify privacy attacks in either *passive* or *active* attacks and whether we either consider only *completed sessions* or we allow even *incomplete sessions* to be the target of an attack. Thereby, a passive adversary only behaves passive during the session establishment but can corrupt parties after the session-establishment. Note that for incomplete sessions, a purely passive adversary is not reasonable and is thus not considered. Active adversaries and incomplete sessions are however reasonable, i.e., actively trying to identify peers that are establishing a session which might already provide a sufficient amount of compromising information. Nevertheless, such notions have not been considered in previous models. See Table 1 for an overview.

Passive Adversaries. We start with a property that is implicitly covered by the privacy notion in previous PPAKE [30,34]. We call it forward privacy and it can be seen as the privacy analogue of forward secrecy. Namely, it requires that for any completed session even if an adversary can later on corrupt the long term secrets of all parties, the identities of the actual parties that were involved in the session are not revealed.

Table 1. Type of adversary $\mathcal{A}$ and state of the attacked session. ($\times$) denotes no corruption; ($\checkmark$) denotes corruption of all but the users in the target session (i.e., the session to be attacked); ($\checkmark\checkmark$) denotes corruption of *all* users. Corruption always refers to the long-term secrets.

	Completed session	Incomplete session
Passive $\mathcal{A}$	Forward privacy ($\checkmark\checkmark$)	—
Active $\mathcal{A}$	Completed-session privacy ($\checkmark$)	(Weak) 2-way MITM privacy ($\times$)
		Strong 2-way MITM privacy ($\checkmark$)

For instance, the signed DH protocol does not provide any privacy, but one could imagine to add public-key encryption (PKE), i.e., party A sends g^x in plain but the value $\mathsf{Sig}_{\mathsf{sk}_A}(g^x \| id_B)$ is encrypted under the public key of B and vice versa (this pattern is similar to what is done to achieve identity protection in SKEME [20]). This will conceal the identities from any eavesdropper as long as no corruptions happen. If, however, the long-term secret keys of A and B corresponding to their PKE public keys are leaked, their identities are clearly revealed from a recorded transcript. The same holds for other protocols such as KEA or KEA+ [22] when in addition all messages are encrypted with a PKE.

Note that with such a fix (that unfortunately does not give forward privacy), the initiator, besides needing to know the responders identity, would also needs to know its public key. However, we want to stress that this is a quite reasonable assumption as in many scenarios the public keys can already be deployed on the devices or can be fetched from key repositories. Clearly, in the latter case it is not advisable to do this immediately before running the AKE as this yields another channel that leaks privacy relevant information. But in many real world settings, e.g., Encrypted Client Hello (ECH) in TLS 1.3, responder's public keys are assumed to be fetched out-of-band.

Active Adversaries. First, we note that several works [1,2,21] state that active adversaries against privacy are hard to handle:

"...it is not possible for a protocol to protect both the initiator and the responder against an active attacker; one of the participants must always go first." [1]

However, this statement seems to implicitly assume that the parties do not know public keys of the other parties beforehand or have no means to detect whether the public keys are revoked. Recent PPAKE models [30,34] indeed achieve privacy against active adversaries, though in only a limited setting. In particular, they consider active man-in-the-middle (MITM) adversaries but restrict them to completed sessions and thus requiring the involved entities have not been corrupted, i.e., the respective long term secret keys are not compromised/revoked.

To illustrate this, we consider a template analyzed in [30] representing a variant of the SIGMA protocol family [21] covering protocols such as TLS 1.3, QUIC, IPsec IKE or SSH. In particular, the SIGMA-R protocol that is designed to provide receiver identity protection is investigated. This template uses an

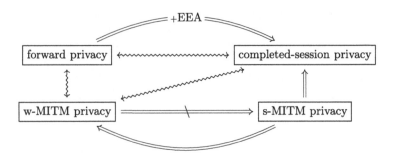

Fig. 1. Overview of implications and separations between privacy notions. ↭ denotes two incomparable properties and EEA denotes explicit entity authentication.

anonymous DH key exchange, i.e., party A sends g^x for ephemeral x and party B responds with g^y for ephemeral y. Subsequently, parties authenticate using digital signatures, where these authentication messages are encrypted using a symmetric key derived from the shared secret g^{xy}. This protocol can provide privacy against active MITM attackers, but only if the session completes (requiring that the involved entities are not corrupted). So this only can happen "after the fact". Nevertheless, it is easy to see that for incomplete sessions there is no privacy guarantee as the initiator "goes first" and thus anyone can identify the initiator. Schäge et al. in [30] explicitly discuss this limitation of their model which allows to always reveal the server identity in TLS or QUIC or the client identity in IPsec IKE and mention that *"It is therefore conceivable to formalize a stronger property for the secrecy of identities selected by the responder which does not rely on session acceptance."* Indeed, this is a setting we want to cover with our privacy notion. Consequently, we will formalize adequate properties for privacy against active adversaries even if sessions are not completed.

Summarizing, such a stronger notion cannot work in the PPAKE model by Schäge et al. in [30]. Also the model and the protocols by Zhao [34] do not consider adversaries that do not need to know the long-term secret key to perform the attack (and thus only consider completed sessions). Note there are simple attack strategies against these protocols that do not require the attacker to obtain any long-term keys or otherwise compromise any party and can be performed by anyone. But we stress that such attacks are outside the model of [34].

Previous PPAKE models only achieve the notion of active MITM attacks against completed sessions (which implicitly covers forward privacy), but not against incomplete sessions. In order to also capture such attacks, we introduce the notion of MITM privacy in two flavors. The first and easier to achieve variant allows adversaries to also attack incomplete sessions but require that no user corruption happens. The second and stronger notion removes this requirement and also allows corruption of users (clearly with exception of the attacked ones). Looking ahead, to achieve MITM privacy requires that even in case of failure protocol messages that look like real protocol messages needs to be send.

Whether this notion is meaningful consequently depends on the context of the use of the protocol and might not be meaningful if used within some higher level protocols where the required behavior cannot be realized.

In Fig. 1 we provide an overview of the privacy notions captured in this paper and how they relate to each other (cf. Sect. 3.2 for a formal treatment). We note that completed-session privacy essentially reflects the privacy notions proposed by Zhao [34] as well as Schäge et al. [30].

Initiator and Responder Privacy. Another aspect, which typically depends on the structure of the protocol as well as the application, is whether privacy only holds for either the initiator or the responder or both of them. For instance, in the most common TLS application scenario clients do not authenticate and thus, unless client authentication is used, only responder privacy is important. Schäge et al. in [30] model privacy in a way that the adversary can explicitly trigger (via a bit) whether to attack the initiator or the responder. In our model, we also consider both aspects simultaneously (which we denote as 2-way privacy), but the adversary controls whom to attack by means of how it engages with the respective oracles. We discuss how to restrict the adversary in our model to model either initiator or responder privacy in the next section.

3   Our PPAKE Model

3.1   Security Model

Our formal security model builds upon the model in [8] which we extend to cover privacy features. Like [8], our model accounts for key impersonation (KCI) security and weak forward secrecy and we use their notion of origin-oracle partnering. We note that [8] avoid no-match attacks [23] as their concrete protocol's messages only contain group elements and deterministic functions of them. We consider the generic countermeasure from [23] by including all exchanged messages (the context) in the final key derivation.

Execution Environment. We consider μ parties $1, \ldots, \mu$. Each party P_i is represented by a set of oracles, $\{\pi_i^1, \ldots, \pi_i^\ell\}$, where each oracle corresponds to a session, i.e., a single execution of a protocol role, and where $\ell \in \mathbb{N}$ is the maximum number of protocol sessions per party. Each oracle π_i^s is equipped with a randomness tape r_i^s containing random bits, but is otherwise deterministic. Each oracle π_i^s has access to the long-term key pair $(\mathsf{sk}_i, \mathsf{pk}_i)$ of party P_i[3] and to the public keys of all other parties, and maintains a list of internal state variables that are described in the following:

- Pid_i^s ("peer id") stores the identity of the intended communication partner. We assume the initiator of a protocol to know who she contacts, hence for the initiator this value is set immediately. Due to the nature of PPAKE the responder might not immediately know the identity of the initiator, hence for the responder this value is initialized to $\bot$ and only set once he receives a message containing the initiator's identity.

---

[3] This might contain various private and public keys for signatures and encryption.

- $\Psi_i^s \in \{\emptyset, \mathsf{Accept}, \mathsf{Reject}\}$ indicates whether π_i^s has successfully completed the protocol execution and "accepted" the resulting key.
- k_i^s stores the session key computed by π_i^s
- $\mathsf{role}_i^s \in \{\emptyset, \mathsf{Initiator}, \mathsf{Responder}\}$ indicates π_i^s's role during the protocol execution.

For each oracle π_i^s these variables are initialized to the empty string $\emptyset$. The computed session key is assigned to the variable k_i^s if and only if π_i^s reaches the Accept state, that is we have $k_i^s \neq \emptyset \Leftrightarrow \Psi_i^s = \mathsf{Accept}$. Furthermore the environment maintains three initially empty lists $\mathsf{L_{corr}}$, $\mathsf{L_{Send}}$ and $\mathsf{L_{SessKey}}$ of all corrupted parties, sent messages and session keys respectively.

Partnering. We use the following partnering definitions (cf. [8]).

Definition 1 (Origin-oracle). *An oracle π_j^t is an origin-oracle for an oracle π_i^s if $\Psi_j^t \neq \emptyset$, $\Psi_j^s = \mathsf{Accept}$ and the messages sent by π_j^t equal the messages received by π_i^s, i.e., if $\mathsf{sent}_j^t = \mathsf{recv}_i^s$.*

Definition 2 (Partner oracles). *We say that two oracles π_i^s and π_j^t are partners if (1) each is an origin-oracle for the other; (2) each one's identity is the other one's peer identity, i.e., $\mathsf{Pid}_i^s = j$ and $\mathsf{Pid}_j^t = i$; and (3) they do not have the same role, i.e., $\mathsf{role}_i^s \neq \mathsf{role}_j^t$.*

Oracles and Attacker Model. The adversary $\mathcal{A}$ interacts with the oracles through queries. It is assumed to have full control over the communication network, modeled by a $\mathsf{Send}(i, s, m)$ query which allows it to send arbitrary messages to any oracle. The adversary is also granted a number of additional queries that model the fact that various secrets might get lost or leaked. The queries are described in detail below.

- $\mathsf{Send}(i, s, m)$: This query allows $\mathcal{A}$ to send an arbitrary message m to oracle π_i^s. The oracle will respond according to the protocol specification and its current internal state. To start a new oracle, the message m takes the form: $(\mathsf{START} : \mathsf{role}, j)$: If π_i^s was already initialized before, return $\perp$. Otherwise this initializes π_i^s in the role role, having party P_j as its intended peer. Thus, it sets $\mathsf{Pid}_i^s := j$ and $\mathsf{role}_i^s := \mathsf{role}$. If π_i^s is started in the initiator role (role = Initiator), then it outputs the first message of the protocol. All $\mathsf{Send}(i, s, m)$ calls are recorded in the list $\mathsf{L_{Send}}$.
- $\mathsf{RevLTK}(i)$: For $i \leq \mu$, this query returns the long-term private key sk_i of party P_i. After this query, P_i and all its protocol instances π_i^s (for any s) are said to be *corrupted* and P_i is added to $\mathsf{L_{corr}}$.
- $\mathsf{RegisterLTK}(i, \mathsf{pk}_i)$: For $i > \mu$, this query allows the adversary to register a new party P_i with the public key pk_i. The adversary is not required to know the corresponding private key. After the query, the pair (i, pk_i) is distributed to all other parties. Parties registered by $\mathsf{RegisterLTK}(i, \mathsf{pk}_i)$ (and their protocol instances) are corrupted by definition and are added to $\mathsf{L_{corr}}$.

– RevSessKey(i, s): This query allows the adversary to learn the session key derived by an oracle. If $\Psi_i^s =$ Accept, return k_i^s. Otherwise return a random key k^* and add (π_i^s, k^*) to $\mathsf{L_{SessKey}}$. After this query, π_i^s is said to be revealed. If this query is called for an oracle π_i^s, while there is an entry (π_j^t, k^*) in $\mathsf{L_{SessKey}}$, so that π_i^s and π_j^t have matching conversations, then k^* is returned.[4]

Security. Formally, we have a security game, played between an adversary $\mathcal{A}$ and a challenger $\mathcal{C}$, where $\mathcal{A}$ can issue the queries defined above. Additionally, it is given access to a special query $\mathsf{Test}(m)$, which, depending on a secret bit b chosen by the challenger, either returns real or random keys (for key indistinguishability) or an oracle to communicate with one of two specified parties in the sense of a left-or-right oracle for the privacy notions. The goal of the adversary is to guess the bit b. The adversary is only allowed to call $\mathsf{Test}(m)$ once and we distinguish the following two cases:

– Case $m = (\mathsf{TestKeyIndist}, i, s)$: If $\Psi_i^s \neq$ Accept, return $\perp$. Else, return k_b where $k_0 = k_i^s$ and $k_1 \xleftarrow{\$} \mathcal{K}$ is a random key. After this query, oracle π_i^s is said to be tested.
– Case $m = (Y, i, j), Y \in \{\mathsf{Test\text{-}w\text{-}MITMPriv}, \mathsf{Test\text{-}s\text{-}MITMPriv}, \mathsf{TestForwardPriv},$ $\mathsf{TestCompletedSessionPriv}\}, i, j \leq \mu$: Create a new Party $P_{i|j}$ with identifier $i|j$. This party has all properties of P_i (if $b = 0$) or P_j (if $b = 1$), but no active sessions. The public key of $P_{i|j}$ is not announced to the adversary and the query $\mathsf{RevLTK}(i|j)$ always returns $\perp$. Furthermore create exactly one session $\pi_{i|j}^1$. Return the new handle $i|j$.

One-Way Privacy. The second case in $\mathsf{Test}(m)$ above models two-way privacy, i.e., we are considering that privacy needs to hold for the initiator and the responder. In case of one-way privacy, i.e., the privacy only holds either for the initiator or the responder (depending on the protocol), we need to restrict the adversary in a way such that the first message sent to $\pi_{i|j}^1$ via $\mathsf{Send}(i|j, 1, m)$ must be a START command. Analogously, we can model scenarios where we only consider privacy of the responder involved in a session.

Security Experiment. The experiment $\mathsf{Exp}_{\mathsf{PPAKE},\mathcal{A}}^{\mathsf{X}}$ is defined as follows.

1. Let μ be the number of parties in the game and ℓ the number of sessions per user. $\mathcal{C}$ begins by drawing a random bit $b \xleftarrow{\$} \{0, 1\}$ and generating key pairs $\{(\mathsf{sk}_i, \mathsf{pk}_i) \mid 1 \leq i \leq \mu\}$ as well as oracles $\{\pi_i^s \mid 1 \leq i \leq \mu, 1 \leq s \leq \ell\}$.
2. $\mathcal{C}$ now runs $\mathcal{A}$, providing all the public keys as input. During its execution, $\mathcal{A}$ may adaptively issue $\mathsf{Send}(i, s, m)$, $\mathsf{RevLTK}(i)$, $\mathsf{RevSessKey}(i, s)$ and $\mathsf{RegisterLTK}(i, \mathsf{pk}_i)$ queries any number of times and the $\mathsf{Test}(m)$ query once.
3. Depending on what argument Y the $\mathsf{Test}(m)$ oracle was called with, we require the corresponding property below to hold through the entire game.
   (a) $\mathsf{TestKeyIndist}$: The tested oracle remains fresh (cf. Definition 3).
   (b) $\mathsf{Test\text{-}w\text{-}MITMPriv}$: No oracle is ever corrupted.

---

[4] Note that the bookkeeping and consistent answers for matched sessions are required to avoid trivial distinguishers in case of cross tunnel attacks (cf. Sect. 3.3).

(c) Test-s-MITMPriv: P_i and P_j are never corrupted. Furthermore we require that $\mathsf{Pid}_{i|j}^1 = \bot$ or $\mathsf{Pid}_{i|j}^1 = k$ for some k, while P_k is never corrupted.

(d) TestForwardPriv: The returned oracle $\pi_{i|j}^1$ has a partner oracle π_k^r at the end of the game. Furthermore no oracle besides π_k^r may be instructed to start a protocol run with intended partner $P_{i|j}$.

(e) TestCompletedSessionPriv: The returned oracle $\pi_{i|j}^1$'s state is Accept at the end of the game. Let $k = \mathsf{Pid}_{i|j}^1$. P_k are not corrupted, RevSessKey$(i|j, 1)$ was never queried and RevSessKey(k, r) (for any π_k^r that has matching conversations) was never queried.

Furthermore no oracle besides π_k^r may be instructed to start a protocol run with intended partner $P_{i|j}$.

4. The game ends when $\mathcal{A}$ terminates with output b', representing the guess of the secret bit b. If $b' = b$, output 1. Otherwise output 0.

Definition 3 (Freshness). *An oracle π_i^s is fresh if*

1. RevSessKey(i, s) *has not been issued*
2. *no query* RevSessKey(j, t) *has been issued, where π_j^t is a partner of π_i^s.*
3. Pid_i^s *was:*
   (a) not corrupted before π_i^s accepted if π_i^s has an origin-oracle, and
   (b) not corrupted at all if π_i^s has no origin-oracle.

PPAKE Security. The above model can be parameterized by allowing or prohibiting the different types of Test(m) queries. This leads to the following:

Definition 4. *A key-exchange protocol Γ is called X for if for any PPT adversary $\mathcal{A}$ with access to the oracle* Test(m) *with queries of the form defined below, the advantage function*

$$\mathsf{Adv}_\Gamma^X(\lambda) := \left| \Pr\left[\mathsf{Exp}_{PPAKE,\mathcal{A}}^X(\lambda) = 1 \right] - \frac{1}{2} \right|$$

is negligible in λ, where

- $\mathcal{A}$ *queries* TestKeyIndist: $X = secure$.
- $\mathcal{A}$ *queries* Test-w-MITMPriv: $X = 2\text{-way MITM private}$.
- $\mathcal{A}$ *queries* Test-s-MITMPriv: $X = strongly\ 2\text{-way MITM private}$.
- $\mathcal{A}$ *queries* TestForwardPriv: $X = forward\ private$.
- $\mathcal{A}$ *queries* TestCompletedSessionPriv: $X = completed\text{-session private}$.

In the above definition, secure corresponds to having indistinguishable session keys, weak forward secrecy and security against key compromise impersonation (KCI). We now show how to integrate explicit entity authentication in our model, which allows to simplify the proofs of the protocols in Sect. 4. Therefore, we require the following:

Definition 5 (Matching Conversation). *Let Π be an N-message two-party protocol in which all messages are sent sequentially.*

- If a session oracle π_i^s sent the last message of the protocol, then π_j^t is said to have matching conversations to π_i^s if the first $N - 1$ messages of π_i^s's transcript agrees with the first $N - 1$ messages of π_j^t's transcript.
- If a session oracle π_i^s received the last message of the protocol, then π_j^t is said to have matching conversations to π_i^s if all N messages of π_i^s's transcript agrees with π_j^t's transcript.

We define implicit authentication through the fact that even a MITM adversary would not be able to derive the session key. This can be done in two moves. Explicit authentication is characterized by the fact that, additionally to providing implicit authentication, the protocol fails if a party does not possess a valid secret key, i.e., an active MITM adversary.

Definition 6 (Explicit entity authentication). *On game* $\mathsf{PPAKE}_{\mathcal{A}}^{2\text{-way-priv}}$ *define* $\mathsf{break}_{\mathsf{EA}}$ *to be the event that there exists an oracle* π_i^s *for which all the following conditions are satisfied.*

1. π_i^s *has accepted, that is,* $\Psi_i^s = \mathsf{Accept}$.
2. $\mathsf{Pid}_i^s = j$ *and party* j *is not corrupted.*
3. *There is no oracle* π_j^t *having:*
   (a) matching conversations to π_i^s *and*
   (b) $\mathsf{Pid}_j^t = i$ *and*
   (c) $\mathsf{role}_j^t \neq \mathsf{role}_i^s$

Definition 7. *A key-exchange protocol* Γ *has explicit authentication, if, for any PPT adversary* $\mathcal{A}$, *the event* $\mathsf{break}_{\mathsf{EA}}$ *(see Definition 6) occurs with at most* $\mathsf{negl}(\lambda)$ *probability.*

3.2   Relation Between Privacy Notions

Subsequently, we investigate the relations between the different privacy notions (as informally shown in Fig. 1).

Lemma 1. *Strong 2-way MITM privacy is strictly stronger than (weak) 2-way MITM privacy.*

Proof. This immediately follows from the tighter restrictions put on the attacker in the (weak) 2-way MITM privacy test. Furthermore, there are protocols that are (weak) 2-way MITM anonymous but not strongly 2-way MITM anonymous (see, e.g., Π_{ss} in Protocol 1). ☐

Lemma 2. *The 2-way MITM privacy notions are independent of forward privacy.*

Proof. Note that the privacy notions do not allow corruptions of the test oracle and forward privacy does not allow the attacker modify any sent messages (i.e. does not allow the attack to act as an active MITM). Π_{PKE}^2 (see Protocol 3) for instance is strongly 2-way MITM private (see Theorem 4) and hence also (weakly) 2-way MITM private, but it is not forward private as the identities are only encrypted using long term keys. On the other hand a protocol that runs the classic Diffie-Helman key exchange followed by transmitting their identities symmetrically encrypted would reach forward privacy, but no 2-way MITM privacy, as any MITM adversary could simply run the protocol.   □

Completed-session privacy is implied by the other privacy notions: if a protocol is strong MITM private or has explicit authentication and is forward private, then it also provides completed session-privacy. The following lemma shows the implication starting from strong MITM privacy.

Lemma 3. *Let Γ be a PPAKE protocol. If Γ is strong MITM private, then it is completed-session private.*

Proof. Strong 2-way MITM privacy test puts less restrictions on the attacker.□

Finally, the following Theorem covers completed-session privacy from explicit authentication and forward privacy.

Theorem 1. *Let Γ be a PPAKE protocol. If Γ has explicit authentication and is forward private, then it is completed-session private.*

Proof. Assume for contradiction that some Γ has explicit authentication and is forward private, but is not completed-session private. This means a PPT-adversary $\mathcal{A}$ is able to call TestCompletedSessionPriv and not violate the imposed restrictions, while also correctly guessing the challenge bit b with non-negligible probability. Since Γ is forward private, the adversary violates a necessary restriction for calling TestForwardPriv while correctly guessing the challenge bit b. (Note that otherwise the exact same adversary $\mathcal{A}$ breaks forward privacy by simply using the argument TestForwardPriv instead).

It follows that after $\mathcal{A}$ is done, $\pi_{i|j}^1$ does not have a partner oracle with non-negligible probability. As per requirement of winning TestCompletedSessionPriv, there is the oracle $\pi_{i|j}^1$ which has accepted and party P_k, where $k = \mathsf{Pid}_{i|j}^1$, is not corrupted. Due to Γ providing explicit authentication, there is an oracle π_k^r s.t. π_k^r has matching conversations to $\pi_{i|j}^1$, $\mathsf{Pid}_k^r = i|j$ and $\mathsf{role}_k^r \neq \mathsf{role}_{i|j}^1$ (see Definition 6 detailing explicit entity authentication). Then $\mathcal{A}$ could simply not drop the last message (if it did before) thereby making $\pi_{i|j}^1$ and π_k^r have matching conversations to each other. This also makes $\pi_{i|j}^1$ and π_k^r be partnered to each other, without making it less likely for $\mathcal{A}$ to correctly guess the challenge bit b. Hence $\mathcal{A}$ is able to break forward privacy, which is a contradiction.   □

3.3   Discussion and Limitations of Our PPAKE Model

Completed Session Privacy. TestCompletedSessionPriv is intended to represent the privacy notions of the literature, specifically Schäge et al. [30] and Zhao [34]. The only addition we made is the requirement that "no oracle besides π_k^r may be instructed to start a protocol run with intended partner $P_{i|j}$". This is a necessary addition since due to the nature of our model there are other-wise trivial attacks against a large class of protocols: First of all the adversary makes the test oracle complete its session without interfering and hence fulfills the experiment's requirements. It then corrupts both of the test oracle's possible identities. Finally it instructs a new oracle to initiate the protocol with the test oracle being the intended recipient, but answers all messages itself using the information obtained with the corruptions. If the imitator at any point uses the intended recipient's public key, e.g. for PKE, then the adversary learns the test oracle's identity.

This problem does not exist in the model of [30], since they let each initiator determine the identity of the test oracle (if configured correspondingly), instead of having the identity of the test oracle fixed throughout the entire experiment. We note that while [30] always model two identities per party, in our model every party only has a single identity.[5]

Revocation. In our model, corruptions are immediately publicly known. While this is an idealization, defending against secret corruptions is infeasible, since an adversary could perfectly impersonate the corrupted user.

As typically done in AKE, we do not formally cover revocation of long term keys in our model. There is previous work that explicitly models revocation for AKE protocols [5], but we want to avoid this added complexity since at this point we are not interested in the specifics of the respective revocation mechanism. Nevertheless, we note that for any revocation mechanism, the revocation status of a communication partner can only be checked after they revealed their identity. For this reason, we model strong MITM privacy so that the adversary can corrupt users as long as it does not openly identify itself as that user.

MITM Cross Tunnel Attack. We now discuss a generic MITM attack on privacy that does not require the corruption of any party, dubbed *MITM cross tunnel attack*. The goal of the attack is to de-anonymize a party that acts as a responder in the protocol. Specifically, the attack targets MITM privacy (both weak and strong). Let the responder be called $P_{i|j}$ and $\pi^1_{i|j}$ its corresponding session. Assume π^r_k is trying to communicate with $\pi^1_{i|j}$, but the adversary is a MITM in that communication channel. Assume at the same time, the adversary is MITM on another channel, where it knows that some π^z_y is trying to communicate with π^s_i. The adversary now relays all messages of π^z_y (of the second channel) to $\pi^1_{i|j}$ (of the first channel) and vice versa. Clearly, if either party produces an error or otherwise noticeably changes its behavior (e.g. by initiating the protocol again), then the adversary knows that $\pi^1_{i|j}$ cannot be the intended partner of π^z_y. Therefore $P_{i|j}$ must be P_j.

Defining protocols such that the parties – from an eavesdropper's view – do not behave noticeably different on errors (e.g. a party cannot decrypt a received ciphertext) prevents this attack as well as trivial distinguishers in case a party is revoked. Specifically, protocols need to continue similar to a normal execution,

---

[5] Clearly, one could however group parties to generate virtual parties with more identities in our model though.

but with randomly sampled messages and the sessions are internally marked as invalid. Our protocols in Sect. 4 are designed to counter these attacks. As noted before, fully preventing this attack in practice is only possible if higher level protocols do not reveal the session status, e.g. by restarting the AKE protocol.

4   Constructing PPAKE with Strong Privacy

In this section we discuss generic construction methodologies to achieve weak and strong MITM privacy, respectively. While not made explicit, all protocols are assumed to behave indistinguishable to real executions (from an eavesdropper's view) even if some verification (indicated using ▮▮▮ boxes) fails, i.e., either a random bitstring or encryption of a random message is returned. Also, we assume that communication partners check the revocation status of the respective peers prior to engaging in a session initiation. All used encryption schemes are required to be length-hiding (cf. [32]), which we make explicit in the theorems.

User Certification and PKIs. In our protocols Cert_A indicates a certificate that binds the identity of A to the long term public key(s). We assume all users have their keys certified by some certification authority (CA) and that there is a mechanism in place for checking the revocation status of certificates. All these features are typically realized via a public-key infrastructure (PKI), i.e., PKIX. As already mentioned, we do not make such a mechanism explicit in our model.

4.1   Achieving Weak MITM Private PPAKE Using Shared Secrets

For the first protocol, we assume all honest parties belong to the same group and have a shared secret s only known to the members of the group. In terms of our model, the shared secret s is part of the secret keys and can hence be compromised by corrupting any party. With this shared secret, we can preserve anonymity against an active MITM adversary, that does not have access to s. But compromise of s does not endanger the usual key indistinguishability. The idea is to derive all session keys by additionally including this shared secret. So, even an active MITM attacker will be unable to use its knowledge of its share of the ephemeral keys due to the lack of knowledge of s. The scheme extending anonymous Diffie-Hellman with a shared secret and encrypted transfer of the peer's certificates is presented in Protocol 1. Similar to the protocols we discuss later, this protocol can also be rewritten in terms of any unauthenticated KE replacing the ephemeral DH shares and a signature scheme replacing the long term keys. We can show the following:

Theorem 2. *If the Oracle Diffie-Hellman (ODH) assumption holds and symmetric encryption scheme Ω is SE-LH-IND-CCA-secure, then Π_{ss} in Protocol 1 provides explicit entity authentication, is secure, weakly 2-way MITM private and forward private.*

Alice: $\mathrm{Cert}_A = (A = g^a, \dots)$	**Bob:** $\mathrm{Cert}_B = (B = g^b, \dots)$
$\mathsf{sk}_A = (a, s)$	$\mathsf{sk}_B = (b, s)$

$x \overset{\$}{\leftarrow} \mathbb{Z}_p$ $\xrightarrow{\quad m_1 = g^x \quad}$ $y \overset{\$}{\leftarrow} \mathbb{Z}_p$

$k' \leftarrow H(g^{xy}, g^x, g^y, s)$

$c_2 \leftarrow E_{k'}(\mathrm{Cert}_B)$

$k' \leftarrow H(g^{xy}, g^x, g^y, s)$ $\xleftarrow{\quad m_2 = (g^y, c_2, U) \quad}$ $U \leftarrow H(g^{xb}, g^{xy}, g^x, g^y, c_2, s)$

verify B, Cert_B, U

$c_3 \leftarrow E_{k'}(\mathrm{Cert}_A)$

$V \leftarrow H(g^{ya}, g^{xy}, g^x, g^y, m_2, s)$ $\xrightarrow{\quad m_3 = (c_3, V) \quad}$ verify Cert_A, V

$k \leftarrow H(g^{xy}, g^{xb}, g^{ya}, s, (m_i)_{i=1}^3)$ $k \leftarrow H(g^{xy}, g^{xb}, g^{ya}, s, (m_i)_{i=1}^3)$

Protocol 1: Protocol Π_{ss} with shared secret s, using symmetric encryption $\Omega = (E, D)$.

For the proof we refer to the full version. Similar to the protocols from Wu et al. [33], the protocol in Protocol 1 is useful for managed groups. While their approach based on prefix encryption (PE) built from identity-based encryption (IBE) is more expressive, only their second protocol is able to provide weak MITM privacy. Our protocol highlights that weak MITM privacy can be obtained using less heavy tools than IBE. Note that Wu et al. [33] also require a trusted party (e.g., the CA) to generate and hand out secret keys to users. So this can be regarded as being similar to having a shared secret as in our approach.

4.2   Generic Construction of Strongly MITM Private PPAKE

Next, we introduce a protocol that achieves MITM privacy, in this case even strong MITM privacy, without relying on a shared secret. For this protocol and the protocol in Sect. 4.3, we consider a setting where the public keys (certificates) of responders are known a priori. Therefore, the initiator has all the information including all public keys of the responder available. Note however, that the first message cannot contain the initiator's certificate. Otherwise, if the long-term key of the responder is compromised, privacy of the initiator cannot be guaranteed (a trade-off that we make in Sect. 4.3). So, authentication of the initiator can only be performed after establishing an initial session key.

Similar to Π_{ss} we run a two-move KE and let the initiator sample a nonce which takes over the role of the shared secret of Π_{ss}, i.e., the (temporary) session keys are derived from the nonces and the result of the two-move KE. However, we now encrypt the nonce under the receivers public key. Moreover, after the initial shared key has been computed, the initiator is able to send its certificate to the responder and authenticate itself using a signature (which is encrypted together with the senders certificate). The protocol is depicted in Protocol 2.

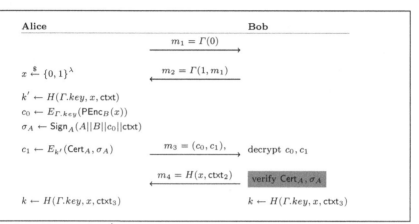

Protocol 2: Protocol Π_{PKE}^4, using an unauthenticated KE Γ, PKE PKE = (PEnc, PDec), symmetric encryption $\Omega = (E, D)$, signature scheme $\Sigma =$ (Sign, Verify), ctxt = $m_1 \| m_2$, ctxt$_2$ = $A\|B\|$ctxt$\|m_3$, and ctxt$_3$ = ctxt$_2\|m_4$.

We note that due to active attacks the PKE is required to provide key-privacy, i.e., be PKE-IK-CCA-secure. Otherwise, an active attacker may determine the senders identity purely by means of the PKE ciphertext. This additional requirement on the PKE is fulfilled by many natural schemes (cf. [4,25]). Moreover, to obtain forward privacy the PKE ciphertext needs to be encrypted using the key from the anonymous two-move KE.[6]

Theorem 3. *If KE Γ is unauthenticated and secure, the PKE PKE is PKE-IND-CCA- and PKE-IK-CCA-secure, symmetric encryption scheme Ω is SE-LH-IND-CCA-secure, and the signature scheme Σ is EUF-CMA-secure, then Π_{PKE}^4 provides explicit entity authentication, is secure, strongly MITM private and forward private.*

For the proof we refer to the full version.

4.3   Two-Move PPAKE Protocol Without Forward Privacy

Finally, let us now present a two move variant of Π_{PKE}^4. Here, the initiator already includes the certificate in the first message and thus allows the responder to respond with a message encrypted with respect to the initiators public key and thus the protocol is authenticated after two moves. The resulting protocol, Π_{PKE}^2, is depicted in Protocol 3 and achieves strong MITM privacy, but obviously forward privacy can not be satisfied by this construction. In comparison to Π_{PKE}^4, the construction also requires the PKE to be length-hiding. Note though, when using anonymous DH as in Π_{ss} one can avoid the signatures.

---

[6] Otherwise an adversary obtaining all long-term PKE keys could simply try to test-decrypt. Omitting this countermeasure would require non-standard properties from the PKE, i.e.,. decryptions of ciphertexts under a key can also be decrypted with other keys and yield meaningful messages.

Alice		Bob
$x \leftarrow \Gamma(0)$		
$\sigma_A \leftarrow \mathsf{Sign}_A(x, \mathsf{Cert}_B)$	$m_1 = \mathsf{PEnc}_B(x, \mathsf{Cert}_A, \sigma_A)$ $\xrightarrow{}$	decrypt m_1 and verify σ_A
		$y \leftarrow \Gamma(1, x)$
decrypt m_2 and verify σ_B	$m_2 = \mathsf{PEnc}_A(y, \sigma_B)$ $\xleftarrow{}$	$\sigma_B \leftarrow \mathsf{Sign}_B(x, y)$
$k \leftarrow H(\Gamma.key, m_1, m_2)$		$k \leftarrow H(\Gamma.key, m_1, m_2)$

Protocol 3: Protocol Π^2_{PKE} using a PKE PKE, an unauthenticated KE Γ, and a signature scheme Σ. where Certs contain Σ and PKE public keys.

Theorem 4. *If KE Γ is secure, the PKE PKE is length-hiding, PKE-IND-CCA- and PKE-IK-CCA-secure, and the signature scheme Σ is EUF-CMA-secure, then Π^2_{PKE} provides explicit entity authentication, is secure, strongly MITM private and completed-session private.*

For the proof we refer to the full version.

5 Discussion and Future Work

In Table 2, we present an overview of the protocols presented in Sect. 4. All protocols provide completed-session privacy as well as weak MITM privacy, but for forward privacy and strong MITM privacy the picture looks different. Due the use of shared secret in Π_{ss}, strong MITM privacy does not hold. Yet this approach can be viewed as mitigation strategy for existing protocols to at least guarantee weak MITM privacy guarantees (e.g., for the IoT setting as targeted in [33]). For the PKE-based approach Π^4_{PKE} we require more than two moves to achieve forward privacy, but all other notions can already be achieved with the two move protocol Π^2_{PKE}.

Our motivation in this work was primarily to investigate the space of meaningful privacy notions and whether there are protocols that satisfy strong notions of privacy. An interesting question is the efficiency and privacy trade-off of concretely instantiated protocols as well as a strengthening of the model to support session state reveal queries. Currently only trivial ones would be supported and thus we decided to omit this feature. Another interesting direction, as done for

Table 2. Comparison of our protocols. "ss" denotes the requirement of a shared secret and "pk" the requirement to know the public key of the intended responder upfront.

	ss	pk	forward priv.	comp.-ses. priv.	w.-MITM	s.-MITM	# moves
Π_{ss}	✓	✗	✓	✓	✓	✗	3
Π^2_{PKE}	✗	✓	✗	✓	✓	✓	2
Π^4_{PKE}	✗	✓	✓	✓	✓	✓	4

IKE v2 in [30], is to study which privacy properties deployed AKE protocols satisfy or how they can be modified in a way that they provide strong privacy guarantees.

Acknowledgements. This work was supported by the European Union's Horizon 2020 research and innovation programme under grant agreement n°826610 (COMP4DRONES) and n°861696 (LABYRINTH) and by the Austrian Science Fund (FWF) and netidee SCIENCE under grant agreement P31621-N38 (PROFET).

References

1. Aiello, W., et al.: Just fast keying: key agreement in a hostile internet. ACM Trans. Inf. Syst. Secur. **7**(2), 242–273 (2004)
2. Arfaoui, G., Bultel, X., Fouque, P.A., Nedelcu, A., Onete, C.: The privacy of the TLS 1.3 protocol. PoPETs **2019**(4), 190–210 (2019). https://doi.org/10.2478/popets-2019-0065
3. Barbosa, M., Boldyreva, A., Chen, S., Warinschi, B.: Provable security analysis of FIDO2. Cryptology ePrint Archive, Report 2020/756 (2020). https://eprint.iacr.org/2020/756
4. Bellare, M., Boldyreva, A., Desai, A., Pointcheval, D.: Key-privacy in public-key encryption. In: Boyd, C. (ed.) ASIACRYPT 2001. LNCS, vol. 2248, pp. 566–582. Springer, Heidelberg (2001). https://doi.org/10.1007/3-540-45682-1_33
5. Boyd, C., Cremers, C., Feltz, M., Paterson, K.G., Poettering, B., Stebila, D.: ASICS: authenticated key exchange security incorporating certification systems. In: Crampton, J., Jajodia, S., Mayes, K. (eds.) ESORICS 2013. LNCS, vol. 8134, pp. 381–399. Springer, Heidelberg (2013). https://doi.org/10.1007/978-3-642-40203-6_22
6. Canetti, R., Krawczyk, H.: Security analysis of IKE's signature-based key-exchange protocol. In: Yung, M. (ed.) CRYPTO 2002. LNCS, vol. 2442, pp. 143–161. Springer, Heidelberg (2002). https://doi.org/10.1007/3-540-45708-9_10 https://eprint.iacr.org/2002/120/
7. Chai, Z., Ghafari, A., Houmansadr, A.: On the importance of encrypted-SNI (ESNI) to censorship circumvention. In: FOCI @ USENIX. USENIX Association (2019)
8. Cohn-Gordon, K., Cremers, C., Gjøsteen, K., Jacobsen, H., Jager, T.: Highly efficient key exchange protocols with optimal tightness. In: Boldyreva, A., Micciancio, D. (eds.) CRYPTO 2019. LNCS, vol. 11694, pp. 767–797. Springer, Cham (2019). https://doi.org/10.1007/978-3-030-26954-8_25
9. Dingledine, R., Mathewson, N., Syverson, P.F.: Tor: the second-generation onion router. In: Blaze, M. (ed.) USENIX Security 2004, pp. 303–320. USENIX Association, August 2004
10. Donenfeld, J.A.: WireGuard: next generation kernel network tunnel. In: NDSS 2017. The Internet Society, Feb/Mar 2017
11. Dowling, B., Paterson, K.G.: A cryptographic analysis of the WireGuard protocol. In: Preneel, B., Vercauteren, F. (eds.) ACNS 2018. LNCS, vol. 10892, pp. 3–21. Springer, Cham (2018). https://doi.org/10.1007/978-3-319-93387-0_1
12. Fan, K., Li, H., Jiang, W., Xiao, C., Yang, Y.: U2F based secure mutual authentication protocol for mobile payment. In: ACM TUR-C, pp. 27:1–27:6. ACM (2017)

13. Goldberg, I., Stebila, D., Ustaoglu, B.: Anonymity and one-way authentication in key exchange protocols. Des. Codes Cryptogr. **67**(2), 245–269 (2013)
14. Gross, H., Hölbl, M., Slamanig, D., Spreitzer, R.: Privacy-aware authentication in the Internet of Things. In: Reiter, M., Naccache, D. (eds.) CANS 2015. LNCS, vol. 9476, pp. 32–39. Springer, Cham (2015). https://doi.org/10.1007/978-3-319-26823-1_3
15. Hoffman, P.E., McManus, P.: DNS queries over HTTPS (DoH). RFC **8484**, 1–21 (2018)
16. Hövelmanns, K., Kiltz, E., Schäge, S., Unruh, D.: Generic authenticated key exchange in the quantum random oracle model. In: Kiayias, A., Kohlweiss, M., Wallden, P., Zikas, V. (eds.) PKC 2020. LNCS, vol. 12111, pp. 389–422. Springer, Cham (2020). https://doi.org/10.1007/978-3-030-45388-6_14
17. Hu, Z., Zhu, L., Heidemann, J.S., Mankin, A., Wessels, D., Hoffman, P.E.: Specification for DNS over transport layer security (TLS). RFC **7858**, 1–19 (2016)
18. Hülsing, A., Ning, K.C., Schwabe, P., Weber, F., Zimmermann, P.R.: Post-quantum WireGuard. Cryptology ePrint Archive, Report 2020/379 (2020). https://eprint.iacr.org/2020/379
19. Kaufman, C., Hoffman, P.E., Nir, Y., Eronen, P., Kivinen, T.: Internet key exchange protocol version 2 (IKEv2). RFC **7296**, 1–142 (2014)
20. Krawczyk, H.: SKEME: a versatile secure key exchange mechanism for internet. In: NDSS, pp. 114–127. IEEE (1996)
21. Krawczyk, H.: SIGMA: the 'SIGn-and-MAc' approach to authenticated Diffie-Hellman and its use in the IKE protocols. In: Boneh, D. (ed.) CRYPTO 2003. LNCS, vol. 2729, pp. 400–425. Springer, Heidelberg (2003). https://doi.org/10.1007/978-3-540-45146-4_24
22. Lauter, K., Mityagin, A.: Security analysis of KEA authenticated key exchange protocol. In: Yung, M., Dodis, Y., Kiayias, A., Malkin, T. (eds.) PKC 2006. LNCS, vol. 3958, pp. 378–394. Springer, Heidelberg (2006). https://doi.org/10.1007/11745853_25
23. Li, Y., Schäge, S.: No-match attacks and robust partnering definitions: defining trivial attacks for security protocols is not trivial. In: Thuraisingham, B.M., Evans, D., Malkin, T., Xu, D. (eds.) ACM CCS 2017, pp. 1343–1360. ACM Press, Oct/Nov 2017. https://doi.org/10.1145/3133956.3134006
24. Øverlier, L., Syverson, P.: Improving efficiency and simplicity of Tor circuit establishment and hidden services. In: Borisov, N., Golle, P. (eds.) PET 2007. LNCS, vol. 4776, pp. 134–152. Springer, Heidelberg (2007). https://doi.org/10.1007/978-3-540-75551-7_9
25. Paterson, K.G., Srinivasan, S.: Building key-private public-key encryption schemes. In: Boyd, C., González Nieto, J. (eds.) ACISP 2009. LNCS, vol. 5594, pp. 276–292. Springer, Heidelberg (2009). https://doi.org/10.1007/978-3-642-02620-1_20
26. Perrin, T.: The noise protocol framework (2017). https://noiseprotocol.org
27. Rescorla, E.: The transport layer security (TLS) protocol version 1.3. RFC **8446**, 1–160 (2018)
28. Rescorla, E., Oku, K., Sullivan, N., Wood, C.A.: TLS encrypted client hello. Internet-Draft draft-ietf-tls-esni-07, Internet Engineering Task Force, June 2020. https://datatracker.ietf.org/doc/html/draft-ietf-tls-esni-07. Work in Progress
29. dos Santos, G.L., Guimaraes, V.T., da Cunha Rodrigues, G., Granville, L.Z., Tarouco, L.M.R.: A DTLS-based security architecture for the internet of things. In: ISCC, pp. 809–815. IEEE (2015)

30. Schäge, S., Schwenk, J., Lauer, S.: Privacy-preserving authenticated key exchange and the case of IKEv2. In: Kiayias, A., Kohlweiss, M., Wallden, P., Zikas, V. (eds.) PKC 2020. LNCS, vol. 12111, pp. 567–596. Springer, Cham (2020). https://doi.org/10.1007/978-3-030-45388-6_20

31. Schwabe, P., Stebila, D., Wiggers, T.: Post-quantum TLS without handshake signatures. In: Ligatti, J., Ou, X., Katz, J., Vigna, G. (eds.) ACM CCS 2020, pp. 1461–1480. ACM Press, November 2020. https://doi.org/10.1145/3372297.3423350

32. Tezcan, C., Vaudenay, S.: On hiding a plaintext length by preencryption. In: Lopez, J., Tsudik, G. (eds.) ACNS 2011. LNCS, vol. 6715, pp. 345–358. Springer, Heidelberg (2011). https://doi.org/10.1007/978-3-642-21554-4_20

33. Wu, D.J., Taly, A., Shankar, A., Boneh, D.: Privacy, discovery, and authentication for the Internet of Things. In: Askoxylakis, I., Ioannidis, S., Katsikas, S., Meadows, C. (eds.) ESORICS 2016. LNCS, vol. 9879, pp. 301–319. Springer, Cham (2016). https://doi.org/10.1007/978-3-319-45741-3_16

34. Zhao, Y.: Identity-concealed authenticated encryption and key exchange. In: Weippl, E.R., Katzenbeisser, S., Kruegel, C., Myers, A.C., Halevi, S. (eds.) ACM CCS 2016, pp. 1464–1479. ACM Press, October 2016. https://doi.org/10.1145/2976749.2978350

Multi-party Computation

Correlated Randomness Teleportation via Semi-trusted Hardware—Enabling Silent Multi-party Computation

Yibiao Lu[1], Bingsheng Zhang[1(✉)], Hong-Sheng Zhou[2], Weiran Liu[3],
Lei Zhang[3], and Kui Ren[1,4]

[1] Zhejiang University, Hangzhou, China
{luyibiao,bingsheng,kuiren}@zju.edu.cn
[2] Virginia Commonwealth University, Richmond, USA
hszhou@vcu.edu
[3] Alibaba Group, Hangzhou, China
weiran.lwr@alibaba-inc.com, zongchao.zl@taobao.com
[4] Key Laboratory of Blockchain and Cyberspace Governance of Zhejiang Province,
Hangzhou, China

Abstract. With the advancement of the *trusted execution environment* (TEE) technologies, hardware-supported secure computing becomes increasingly popular due to its efficiency. During the protocol execution, typically, the players need to contact a third-party server for remote attestation, ensuring the validity of the involved trusted hardware component, such as Intel SGX, as well as the integrity of the computation result. When the hardware manufacturer is not fully trusted, sensitive information may be leaked to the third-party server through backdoors, steganography, and kleptography, etc. In this work, we introduce a new security notion called *semi-trusted hardware model*, where the adversary is allowed to passively or maliciously corrupt the hardware. Therefore, she can learn the input of the hardware component and might also tamper its output. We then show how to utilize such semi-trusted hardwares for *correlated randomness teleportation*. When the semi-trusted hardware is instantiated by Intel SGX, to generate 10k random OT's, our protocol is 24X and 450X faster than the EMP-IKNP-ROT in the LAN and WAN setting, respectively. When SGX is used to teleport Garbled circuits, the resulting two-party computation protocol is 5.3-5.7X and 43-47X faster than the EMP-SH2PC in the LAN and WAN setting, respectively, for the AES-128, SHA-256, and SHA-512 evaluation. We also show how to achieve malicious security with little overhead.

Keywords: MPC · Semi-trusted hardware model · Garbled circuit

1 Introduction

In secure multi-party computation (MPC), two or more players want to collectively compute a function and receive its output without revealing their inputs

© Springer Nature Switzerland AG 2021
E. Bertino et al. (Eds.): ESORICS 2021, LNCS 12973, pp. 699–720, 2021.
https://doi.org/10.1007/978-3-030-88428-4_34

to the other players. In the past decades, MPC has gradually transitioned from theory to practice, and it has been widely used in many security critical real-world applications, such as private set intersection and secure auction. In spite of its success, MPC is still not efficient for complicated real-time tasks due to its computational overhead and high communication cost. Meanwhile, recent development of trusted execution environment (TEE) technologies, such as Intel SGX and ARM TrustZone, enables a new approach for privacy-preserving computation. Hardware-supported secure computing can greatly accelerate an MPC process by avoiding expensive cryptographic operations. However, this kind of construction introduces additional hardware setup assumptions that require new trust roots, e.g., Intel. Recent exposure of Intel source code [5] raises a security concern on possible backdoors contained in its design. When the hardware manufacturer is not fully trusted, sensitive information may be leaked through backdoors, steganography and kleptography, etc. For instance, Intel SGX uses the remote attestation mechanism to ensure the validity of the enclave execution environment and the integrity of the computation result. More specifically, Intel's (anonymous) attestation is based on an anonymous group signature scheme called Intel Enhanced Privacy ID (EPID) [11]. To verify that an outcome is computed by a pre-agreed program in a genuine SGX, Quoting Enclave (QE) will produce a quote by signing the report with the group signature. The users then need to contact the remote Intel Attestation Service (IAS) (or some other alternative servers) for verification. If Intel is malicious, sensitive information may be leaked from the SGX component to the IAS through the signatures, using for example kleptography techniques. (Currently, Intel SGX uses 4096-bit RSA signatures.) That means the input of SGX might be revealed to the adversary.

When the hardware provider is not allied with the MPC participants, is it possible to still use potentially malicious leaky hardware components to accelerate MPC executions with privacy assurance? In this work, we answer this question affirmatively.

New Model. We introduce a new semi-trusted hardware model, where the adversary $\mathcal{A}$ is allowed to passively or maliciously corrupt the hardware ideal functionality $\mathcal{F}_{\mathsf{HW}}$. $\mathcal{F}_{\mathsf{HW}}$ is parameterized with a probabilistic polynomial time (PPT) interactive Turing machine (ITM) M, which specifies its functionality. When the hardware functionality $\mathcal{F}_{\mathsf{HW}}$ is passively corrupted, the adversary $\mathcal{A}$ can learn all the incoming messages received by $\mathcal{F}_{\mathsf{HW}}$; when $\mathcal{F}_{\mathsf{HW}}$ is maliciously corrupted, in addition to leaning the incoming messages, the adversary $\mathcal{A}$ can replace the original M with an arbitrary ITM M*; namely, $\mathcal{A}$ can fully control the execution of $\mathcal{F}_{\mathsf{HW}}$.

We note that the existing remote attestation model [18], tamper-proof hardware token models [9,12], and *server-aided* model [15] are different from our model. When hardware is fully trusted, unlike the remote attestation model, our $\mathcal{F}_{\mathsf{HW}}$ does not sign its output. Moreover, the existing model does not address hardware leakage as well as malicious corruptions.

Our Constructions. We show semi-trusted hardware can still be used to significantly improve the efficiency of an MPC protocol by reducing the communication. The main idea is to use semi-trusted hardware for those MPC computation that does not depend on the actual protocol inputs; thus no sensitive information is leaked to the hardware components. We propose a new notion called *correlated randomness teleportation*, where the sender can teleport a large amount of correlated randomness to the receiver with little communication. Take random OT (ROT) generation as an example, assume the Receiver uses an SGX-enabled machine, while there is no special hardware requirement to the Sender. During the ROT protocol, the Sender only needs to send a random seed k_1 to the Receiver's SGX enclave via a secure channel, and the Receiver also sends a random seed k_2 to the enclave locally. Both parties can then generate polynomially many ROT copies without any further communication. Namely, for a ROT copy, the Sender locally computes $R_{\mathsf{ctr}}^0 \leftarrow \mathsf{PRF}_{k_1}(\mathsf{ctr}, 0)$ and $R_{\mathsf{ctr}}^1 \leftarrow \mathsf{PRF}_{k_1}(\mathsf{ctr}, 1)$ from the seed k_1 using some pseudo-random function PRF, where ctr is the counter; meanwhile, the SGX generates the ROT choice bit b_{ctr} from the seed k_2 using some pseudo-random number generator PRG, and then it computes $R_{\mathsf{ctr}}^{b_{\mathsf{ctr}}} \leftarrow \mathsf{PRF}_{k_1}(\mathsf{ctr}, b_{\mathsf{ctr}})$. The SGX locally outputs $\{R_{\mathsf{ctr}}^{b_{\mathsf{ctr}}}\}_{\mathsf{ctr}}$ to the Receiver.

Garbled circuit (GC) can also be viewed as a type of correlated randomness. With our technique, the communication between the 2PC players can also be dramatically reduced. We assume the GC Evaluator uses an SGX-enabled machine, while there is no special hardware requirement to the GC Garbler. Note that, the main cost of a GC-based 2PC protocol is the transmission of the garbled tables of the entire circuit. Analogously, during the GC protocol, the Garbler sends a random seed k_1 to the Evaluator's SGX enclave via a secure channel. The SGX can then internally generate the garbled tables and locally outputs them to the Evaluator without network communication. The only communication needed is for transmitting the input labels from the Garbler to the Evaluator. The overall communication is linear to the input size and independent of the circuit size.

Remark. We would like to emphasize that naively using the secure hardware components, such as SGX, and a simulatable private garbling scheme in a black-box fashion to prepare GC in an offline phase won't result in a simulatable 2PC protocol. This is because the simulator cannot extract the malicious Evaluator's input in the offline phase, yet it needs to learn the MPC output (from the ideal functionality) to invoke the GC simulator (cf. Definition 2) to produce the (fake) GC tables in the real/hybrid world. The protocol should invoke the secure hardware component at the right moment along with the 2PC protocol execution.

Efficiency. We mainly compare the performance of our protocols with the well-known EMP-toolkit maintained by Wang *et al.* [20]. Table 1 shows the performance comparison between the passively secure IKNP OT extension protocol [8] implemented in EMP-toolkit [20] and our silent ROT protocol (semi-honest security). We perform the experiments on an SGX-enabled Dell OptiPlex 7080 equipped with an Intel Core 8700 CPU @ 3.20 GHz with 32 GB RAM. In the LAN setting (Bandwidth: 1Gbps, Delay: 1ms), our silent ROT protocol is 22-39X faster w.r.t. the sender's running time and 9-14X faster w.r.t. the receiver's

Table 1. Performance comparison of the ROT protocols. Result obtained from Dell OptiPlex 7080 (Intel Core 8700 CPU @ 3.20 GHz, 32 GB RAM, OS: Ubuntu 18.04 LTS). LAN: 1 Gbps bandwidth, 0.1 ms delay. WAN: 100 Mbps bandwidth, 25 ms delay.

# ROT	Network	Sender's running time (in ms)		Receiver's running time (in ms)	
		EMP-IKNP-ROT [20]	Our ROT	EMP-IKNP-ROT [20]	Our ROT
1×10^4	LAN	2.889	0.074	3.908	0.162
	WAN	26.331	0.079	76.358	0.169
1×10^5	LAN	17.790	0.780	19.355	1.575
	WAN	150.502	0.795	200.030	1.477
1×10^6	LAN	154.373	6.182	150.621	15.910
	WAN	1451.043	6.402	1495.294	16.032
1×10^7	LAN	1507.961	51.616	1451.562	103.937
	WAN	13859.934	51.280	13963.502	103.435
1×10^8	LAN	15030.832	505.289	14470.057	995.987
	WAN	138028.607	501.757	137034.187	980.795

Table 2. Performance comparison of the generation, transmission and evaluation process of the garbled circuit in the semi-honest setting 2PC protocol. Result obtained from the same experiment environment as in Table 1. It shows the running time (in ms) for evaluating AES-128, SHA-256, and SHA-512 circuits 1000 times, respectively.

Circuit	Network	EMP-SH2PC [20] time (in ms)			Our 2PC protocol time (in ms)		
		Garbler	Comm.	Evaluator	Garbler	Comm.	Evaluator (SGX+PC)
AES-128	LAN	246.557	1742.094	229.339	10.171	≈0	243.730 + 174.916
	WAN	265.919	18335.009	234.264	9.875	≈0	255.275 + 177.637
SHA-256	LAN	829.398	6135.087	776.880	26.310	≈0	805.893 + 583.828
	WAN	839.626	64433.208	777.284	28.981	≈0	804.904 + 581.166
SHA-512	LAN	2434.915	15745.170	2388.890	52.110	≈0	2061.712 + 1549.076
	WAN	2303.479	163362.579	2418.025	52.373	≈0	2072.215 + 1551.586

Table 3. Performance comparison of the computation process of the malicious setting 2PC protocol. Result obtained from the same experiment environment as in Table 1. It shows the running time (in ms) for evaluating AES-128, SHA-256, and SHA-512 circuits once, respectively.

Circuit	Network	EMP-AG2PC [20] running time (in ms)				Ours (in ms)	
		Garb. offline	Garb. online	Eval. offline	Eval. online	Garbler	Evaluator
AES-128	LAN	94.744	5.185	92.055	5.193	3.100	6.311
	WAN	1345.708	53.440	1240.956	53.385	30.124	61.457
SHA-256	LAN	210.676	6.303	201.701	6.272	10.373	15.633
	WAN	2299.404	52.474	2196.297	52.440	47.756	86.059
SHA-512	LAN	435.581	9.634	423.302	9.593	25.756	34.944
	WAN	4095.115	56.471	4044.428	56.426	70.139	112.336

running time than the EMP-IKNP-ROT [20]. In the WAN setting (Bandwidth: 100 Mbps, Delay: 25 ms), our silent ROT protocol is 189-333X faster w.r.t. the sender's running time and 93-451X faster w.r.t. the receiver's running time than the EMP-IKNP-ROT.

Table 2 shows the performance comparison between EMP-SH2PC [20] and our semi-honest setting silent 2PC protocol. (EMP-SH2PC provides an efficient semi-honest 2PC implementation based on Yao's GC protocol with half-gates [22] optimization.) We perform the experiments on this same machine as above. We test the garbling time, the garbled tables transmission time, and the evaluation time separately, as for the Garbler in our protocol, the garbling time is the time to generate input wire labels. We omit the time of transmitting seeds and wire labels in both protocols. Since in our protocol, the garbling process is performed in the SGX enclave at the evaluator side, we split the evaluator running time of our protocol into two parts: (i) the SGX running time and (ii) normal mode CPU running time. The garbler running time is the time to generate the input wire labels. We take the AES-128, SHA-256, and SHA-512 circuit evaluation as benchmarks. In the LAN setting, our silent 2PC protocol is 5.3-5.7X faster than the EMP-SH2PC [20]. In the WAN setting, our silent 2PC protocol is 43-47X faster than the EMP-SH2PC.

Table 3 shows the performance comparison between EMP-AG2PC [20] and our malicious setting silent 2PC protocol. (EMP-AG2PC implements an efficient maliciously secure two-party computation protocol, authenticated garbling [21].) We perform the experiments on this same machine as above. We take the AES-128, SHA-256, and SHA-512 circuit evaluations as benchmarks, and the results are the average of 100 tests. All the one-time expenses are omitted, e.g., creating enclave in our protocol and initialize $\mathcal{F}_{pre}$ in EMP-AG2PC. EMP-AG2PC consists of three computing phases: (i) function independent offline phase, (ii) function dependent offline phase and (iii) online phase. (i) and (ii) are collectively called offline phase. In the LAN setting, our silent 2PC protocol is 17-32X faster w.r.t. the garbler's running time and 12-15X faster w.r.t. the evaluator's running time than the EMP-AG2PC [20]. In the WAN setting, our silent PC protocol is 46-59X faster w.r.t. the garbler's running time and 21-36X faster w.r.t. the evaluator's running time than the EMP-AG2PC.

2 Preliminaries

Notation. Throughout this paper, we use the following notations and terminologies. Let $\lambda \in \mathbb{N}$ be the security parameter. We abbreviate *probabilistic polynomial time* as PPT, and *interactive Turing machine* as ITM. Let $\text{poly}(\cdot)$ and $\text{negl}(\cdot)$ be a polynomially-bounded function and negligible function, respectively. We assume each party has a unique PID. For readability, we refer P_i as the PID for the party P_i. Suppose $f(x_1, x_2) = y$ is a function (circuit). Denote $f.n_1$ and $f.n_2$ as the input size of x_1 and x_2, respectively. Let $f.n = f.n_1 + f.n_2$. Denote $f.m$ as the size of the output y and $f.N$ as the overall wire number in f. For notation simplicity, we also use n_1, n_2, n, m, N to represent $f.n_1, f.n_2, f.n, f.m, f.N$ when there will be no ambiguity.

Garbling Scheme. As defined in [3], a garbling scheme GC consists of the following PPT algorithms (Gb, En, Ev, De).

- $\mathsf{Gb}(1^\lambda, f)$ is the garbling algorithm that takes input as the security parameter $\lambda \in \mathbb{N}$ and a circuit f, and it returns a garbled circuit F, encoding information e, and decoding information d.
- $\mathsf{En}(e, x)$ is the encoding algorithm that takes input as the encoding information e and an input x, and it returns a garbled input X.
- $\mathsf{Ev}(F, X)$ is the evaluation algorithm that takes input as the garbled circuit F and the garbled input X, and it returns a garbled output Y.
- $\mathsf{De}(d, Y)$ is the decoding algorithm that takes input as the decoding information d and the garbled output Y, and it returns the output y.

A garbling scheme $\mathsf{GC} := (\mathsf{Gb}, \mathsf{En}, \mathsf{Ev}, \mathsf{De})$ is called projective if e consists of $2f.n$ wire labels. For the i-th input bit, we denote the corresponding wire labels as (X_i^0, X_i^1). Let $e := \{(X_i^0, X_i^1)\}_{i \in [n]}$; the encoding algorithm $\mathsf{En}(e, x)$ simply outputs $X_i^{x[i]}, i \in [n]$, where $x[i]$ is the i-th bit of x.

Analogously, a garbling scheme is called output-projective if d consists of 2 labels for each output bits, which can be denoted as (Z_i^0, Z_i^1). Let $d := \{(Z_i^0, Z_i^1)\}_{i \in [m]}$; the decoding algorithm $\mathsf{De}(d, Y)$ outputs $y[i], i \in [m]$, where $y[i]$ is the i-th bit of y s.t. $Z_i^{y[i]} = Y_i$.

In this work, we assume the garbling scheme GC is both projective and output-projective.

Definition 1 (Correctness [3]). *We say a garbling scheme* $(\mathsf{Gb}, \mathsf{En}, \mathsf{Ev}, \mathsf{De})$ *is correct if for all functions f and input x:*

$$\Pr[(F, e, d) \leftarrow \mathsf{Gb}(1^\lambda, f) : \mathsf{De}(d, \mathsf{Ev}(F, \mathsf{En}(e, x))) = f(x)] = 1 .$$

Definition 2 (Simulatable Privacy [3]). *We say a garbling scheme* $(\mathsf{Gb}, \mathsf{En}, \mathsf{Ev}, \mathsf{De})$ *is simulatable private if for all functions f and input x, there exists a PPT simulator* Sim *such that for all PPT adversary $\mathcal{A}$ the following holds:*

$$\Pr \begin{bmatrix} (F_0, e_0, d_0) \leftarrow \mathsf{Gb}(1^\lambda, f); X_0 \leftarrow \mathsf{En}(e, x); \\ (F_1, X_1, d_1) \leftarrow \mathsf{Sim}(1^\lambda, f(x), \Phi(f)); \\ b \leftarrow \{0, 1\}; b^* \leftarrow \mathcal{A}(F_b, X_b, d_b) : b = b^* \end{bmatrix} = \mathsf{negl}(\lambda) .$$

where Φ is the side-information function.

Yao's GC Optimizations and Our Choice. Throughout the past decades, several optimization techniques have been proposed to improve the efficiency of Yao's garbled circuit (GC). In this section, we examine a few Yao's GC optimizations and analyze their suitability for our work to achieve the best performance, the concrete performance analysis is taken from the work of Zahur *et al.* [22].

In the classical garbling scheme, the GC generator needs to invoke the hash function H 4 times for each gate to create a garbled table consists of 4 ciphertexts. The GC evaluator also needs to invoke H up to 4 times for each gate to decrypt all these ciphertexts and obtains an output wire label.

Beaver *et al.* [2] introduced a technique called *point-and-permute*. By appending a select bit to each wire label, one can easily determine the places of the

---

Functionality $\mathcal{F}_{2pc}^{f}$

It interacts with players $\mathcal{P} := \{P_1, P_2\}$ and the adversary $\mathcal{S}$. Let $\mathcal{P}_c$ be the set of corrupted parties. Initially, set $\mathcal{P}_c = \emptyset$.

Compute:

- Upon receiving (COMPUTE, sid, x_i) from party $P_i \in \mathcal{P}$:
  - If $P_i \in \mathcal{P}_c$, send a notification (COMPUTENOTIFY, sid, x_i, P_i) to $\mathcal{S}$;
    Otherwise, send a notification (COMPUTENOTIFY, sid, $|x_i|$, P_i) to $\mathcal{S}$;
  - If it has received x_1 from P_1 and x_2 from P_2:
    * Compute $y \leftarrow f(x_1, x_2)$;
  - Send (OUTPUT, sid, P_2) to adversary $\mathcal{S}$:
    * Upon receiving (DELIVER, sid, P_2) from $\mathcal{S}$, it sends (COMPUTE, sid, y) to P_2;

Corruption handling:

- Upon receiving (CORRUPT, sid, P_i) from the adversary $\mathcal{S}$, if $P_i \in \mathcal{P}$:
  - Set $\mathcal{P}_c := \mathcal{P}_c \cup \{P_i\}$;
  - Send (INPUT, sid, x_i, P_i) to $\mathcal{S}$ if x_i is already defined;

Fig. 1. Functionality $\mathcal{F}_{2pc}^{f}$

corresponding ciphertexts. Therefore, for a garbled table, the GC evaluator can decide which ciphertext to decrypt according to the select bit and only invoke H once. Nevertheless, each garbled table still contains 4 ciphertexts, and it takes 4 H invocations to generate. We adopt this technique in our design, as it greatly reduces the GC evaluator's computational cost, and it is compatible with other optimizations.

Naor *et al.* [17] introduced a *garbled row-reduction* technique known as GRR3 to reduce the garbled table size. The main idea is to fix 1 of the 4 ciphertexts, e.g., the top one, in each garbled table to be 0, and thus can be eliminated. In our construction, the memory of the enclave is limited, and this technique can reduce memory usage of GC generation.

Kolesnikov *et al.* [14] introduced the *free-XOR* technique. This technique allows us to garble and evaluate XOR gates for free. To do this, the offset between each wire's 0-label and 1-label in the entire circuit is fixed to Δ. Therefore, one can generate or evaluate an XOR gate via a simple XOR operation. This technique can greatly improve the performance of our scheme.

We note that, in a conventional 2PC setting, the other optimization techniques, such as *GRR2* [19] and *half-gates* [22], may be helpful to further improve scheme performance. However, GRR2 is not compatible with free-XOR. Although half-gates is compatible with the aforementioned three optimizations, it is not ideal for our construction. The reason is that the main benefit of half-gates is to reduce the non-XOR gate garbled table size to 2, but it needs 2 H invocations to evaluate. Whereas, in our design, the GC size is not the bottleneck of our overall performance, because the GC table is transmitted between the SGX enclave and the host locally. While, without half-gates, each non-XOR gate garbled table only needs 1 H invocation to evaluate.

Semi-trusted Hardware Functionality $\mathcal{F}_{\mathrm{HW}}[\mathsf{M}]$

It interacts with players $\mathcal{P} := \{P_1, P_2\}$ and the adversary $\mathcal{A}$. It is parameterized with a PPT ITM M and a Boolean flag corrupted.
Initially, set corrupted := false.

- Upon receiving (CORRUPT, sid, M*) from $\mathcal{A}$:
  - Set corrupted := true;
  - If M* $\neq \emptyset$, replace M := M*;
- Upon receiving (RUN, sid, x_i) from party $P_i \in \mathcal{P}$:
  - If corrupted = true:
    * Send leakage message (RUNNOTIFY, sid, x_i, P_i) to $\mathcal{A}$;
  - If corrupted = false:
    * Send notification message (RUNNOTIFY, sid, P_i) to $\mathcal{A}$;
  - When (RUN, sid, x_1) and (RUN, sid, x_2) are both received:
    * Run $(y_1, y_2) \leftarrow \mathsf{M}(x_1, x_2)$;
    * For $i \in \{1, 2\}$, send (Run, sid, y_i) to P_i;

Fig. 2. The semi-trusted hardware functionality $\mathcal{F}_{\mathrm{HW}}[\mathsf{M}]$

3   Security Model

Simulation-Based Security. Our security model follows the simulation paradigm, which lays down a solid foundation for designing and analyzing protocols secure against attacks in an arbitrary *network* execution environment (therefore it is also known as *network aware security model*). Roughly speaking, in a simulation-based security model, protocols are carried out over multiple interconnected machines; to capture attacks, a network adversary $\mathcal{A}$ is introduced, which is allowed to corrupt some machines (i.e., have the full control of all physical parts of some machines); in addition, $\mathcal{A}$ is allowed to partially control the communication tapes of all uncorrupted machines, that is, it sees all the messages sent from and to the uncorrupted machines and controls the sequence in which they are delivered. Then, a protocol ρ is a secure implementation of a functionality $\mathcal{F}$, if it satisfies that for every network adversary $\mathcal{A}$ attacking an execution of ρ, there is another adversary $\mathcal{S}$—known as the simulator—attacking the ideal process that uses $\mathcal{F}$ (by corrupting the same set of machines), such that, the executions of ρ with $\mathcal{A}$ and that of $\mathcal{F}$ with $\mathcal{S}$ makes no difference to any network execution environment.

<u>The Ideal World Execution.</u> In the ideal world, P_1 and P_2 only communicate with an ideal functionality $\mathcal{F}_{2\mathrm{pc}}^f$ during the execution. As depicted in Fig. 1, party $P_i \in \mathcal{P}$ sends (COMPUTE, sid, x_i) to the functionality $\mathcal{F}_{2\mathrm{pc}}^f$, and $\mathcal{F}_{2\mathrm{pc}}^f$ sends a notification (COMPUTENOTIFY, sid, x_i, P_i) to the adversary $\mathcal{S}$ if P_i is corrupted; Otherwise, $\mathcal{F}_{2\mathrm{pc}}^f$ leaks the input size (COMPUTENOTIFY, sid, $|x_i|$, P_i) to $\mathcal{S}$. When both parties' inputs are received, $\mathcal{F}_{2\mathrm{pc}}^f$ computes $y \leftarrow f(x_1, x_2)$. It then sends (COMPUTE, sid, y) to P_2 if the adversary $\mathcal{S}$ allows. For corruption handling, if the adversary $\mathcal{S}$ corrupts party $P_i \in \mathcal{P}$, $\mathcal{F}_{2\mathrm{pc}}^f$ adds P_i to the set of corrupted parties, $\mathcal{P}_c$, and leaks P_i's input x_i to $\mathcal{S}$ if it is already defined.

Description of M^{ROT}

M$^{\mathsf{ROT}}(x_1, x_2)$:

- Parse $x_1 = \langle \ell_1, k_1 \rangle$ and $x_2 = \langle \ell_2, k_2 \rangle$;
- Assert $\ell_1 = \ell_2$;
- Generate $(b_1, \ldots, b_{\ell_1}) \leftarrow \mathsf{PRG}(k_2)$;
- For $i \in [\ell_1]$:
  - Generate $R_i^{b_i} \leftarrow \mathsf{PRF}_{k_1}(i, b_i)$;
  - [M] Generate $R_i^{b_i \oplus 1} \leftarrow \mathsf{PRF}_{k_1}(i, b_i \oplus 1)$;
  - [M] Set $\sigma_i^{b_i \oplus 1} := H(R_i^{b_i \oplus 1})$;
- [S] Return $y_1 := \emptyset$ and $y_2 := \{R_i^{b_i}\}_{i \in [\ell_1]}$;
- [M] Return $y_1 := \emptyset$ and $y_2 := (\{R_i^{b_i}\}_{i \in [\ell_1]}, \{\sigma_i^{b_i \oplus 1}\}_{i \in [\ell_1]})$;

Fig. 3. Description of M^{ROT}

The Real World Execution. The real/hybrid world protocol Π uses a semi-trusted hardware components, which are modeled as the ideal functionality $\mathcal{F}_{\mathsf{HW}}$. Later, we will discuss how $\mathcal{F}_{\mathsf{HW}}$ is instantiated by Intel SGX in practice. For notation simplicity, we define $\mathcal{F}_{\mathsf{HW}}$ as a template, and specify the required functionalities in the description of a PPT Turing machine M. We use $\mathcal{F}_{\mathsf{HW}}[\mathsf{M^{GC}}]$ in our semi-honest/malicious setting protocol $\Pi_{\mathsf{2pc}}^{\mathsf{GC}}$.

3.1 Semi-trusted Hardware Model

We introduce a new notion, called *semi-trusted hardware model*. Unlike the conventional trusted hardware model, the semi-trusted hardware functionality $\mathcal{F}_{\mathsf{HW}}[\mathsf{M}]$ shown in Fig. 2 can be corrupted by the adversary $\mathcal{A}$. The functionality $\mathcal{F}_{\mathsf{HW}}[\mathsf{M}]$ is parameterized with a PPT ITM M and a Boolean flag corrupted to indicate whether the hardware is corrupted. The parties P_1 and P_2 can invoke $\mathcal{F}_{\mathsf{HW}}[\mathsf{M}]$ to compute $(y_1, y_2) \leftarrow \mathsf{M}(x_1, x_2)$ by sending the input x_1 and x_2 respectively to $\mathcal{F}_{\mathsf{HW}}$.

However, the adversary $\mathcal{A}$ is allowed to corrupt $\mathcal{F}_{\mathsf{HW}}$ via the (CORRUPT, sid, M*) command. When $\mathcal{A}$ is a semi-honest adversary, it sets M$^* = \emptyset$. In execution, if $\mathcal{F}_{\mathsf{HW}}$ is corrupted, it will leak each party's input to $\mathcal{A}$. When $\mathcal{A}$ is a malicious adversary, M* can be arbitrarily defined by $\mathcal{A}$ (not necessarily PPT), and $\mathcal{F}_{\mathsf{HW}}$ computes $(y_1, y_2) \leftarrow \mathsf{M}^*(x_1, x_2)$ instead. After the computation, $\mathcal{F}_{\mathsf{HW}}$ sends the output y_1 to the party P_1 and y_2 to the party P_2.

4   Correlated Randomness Teleportation

Correlated randomness is widely used in the MPC offline protocols to achieve better online efficiency. In practice, correlated randomness can be generated and distributed by a trusted server. However, this approach still needs huge communication between the trusted server and the players to deliver those correlated random copies. In this section, we show it is possible to utilize a semi-trusted

---

Protocol Π_{ROT}

Protocol description:

- Upon receiving (COMPUTE, sid, $x_2 := \ell$) from the environment $\mathcal{Z}$, the party P_2:
  - Pick random $k_2 \leftarrow \{0,1\}^\lambda$;
  - Generate $(b_1, \ldots, b_\ell) \leftarrow \text{PRG}(k_2)$;
  - Send (Run, sid, $\langle \ell, k_2 \rangle$) to $\mathcal{F}_{\text{HW}}[\text{M}^{\text{ROT}}]$;
- Upon receiving (COMPUTE, sid, $x_1 := \ell$) from the environment $\mathcal{Z}$, the party P_1:
  - Pick random $k_1 \leftarrow \{0,1\}^\lambda$;
  - For $i \in [\ell]$:
    - Generate $R_i^0 \leftarrow \text{PRF}_{k_1}(i, 0)$ and $R_i^1 \leftarrow \text{PRF}_{k_1}(i, 1)$;
    - [M] Set $\sigma_i^0 := H(R_i^0)$ and $\sigma_i^1 := H(R_i^1)$;
  - [M] Set $\tau := H(\{\sigma_i^0, \sigma_i^1\}_{i \in [\ell]})$;
  - [S] Send (Run, sid, $\langle \ell, k_1 \rangle$) to $\mathcal{F}_{\text{HW}}[\text{M}^{\text{ROT}}]$;
  - [M] Send (Run, sid, $\langle \ell, k_1 \rangle$) to $\mathcal{F}_{\text{HW}}[\text{M}^{\text{ROT}}]$ and send τ to P_2;
  - Return (COMPUTE, sid, $\{R_i^0, R_i^1\}_{i \in [\ell]}$) to the environment $\mathcal{Z}$;
- [S] Upon receiving (Run, sid, $\{R_i^{b_i}\}_{i \in [\ell]}$), the party P_2:
  - Return (COMPUTE, sid, $\{R_i^{b_i}\}_{i \in [\ell]}$) to the environment $\mathcal{Z}$;
- [M] Upon receiving (Run, sid, $(\{R_i^{b_i}\}_{i \in [\ell]}, \{\hat{\sigma}_i^{b_i \oplus 1}\}_{i \in [\ell]})$) from $\mathcal{F}_{\text{HW}}[\text{M}^{\text{ROT}}]$ and receiving τ from P_1, the party P_2:
  - For $i \in [\ell]$, set $\hat{\sigma}_i^{b_i} := H(R_i^{b_i})$;
  - Set $\hat{\tau} := H(\{\hat{\sigma}_i^0, \hat{\sigma}_i^1\}_{i \in [\ell]})$;
  - Assert $\hat{\tau} = \tau$;
  - Return (COMPUTE, sid, $\{R_i^{b_i}\}_{i \in [\ell]}$) to the environment $\mathcal{Z}$;

Fig. 4. The semi-honest/malicious setting Π_{ROT} in the $\mathcal{F}_{\text{HW}}[\text{M}^{\text{ROT}}]$-hybrid model

hardware to teleport correlated randomness with little ($O(\lambda)$) communication. Take two-party computation as an example. Without loss of generality, suppose $\mathcal{F}_{\text{HW}}$ is located at P_2's side with fast local connections, e.g., $\mathcal{F}_{\text{HW}}$ is instantiated with P_2's SGX. In the following, we provide Random OT teleportation and GC teleportation protocols to illustrate our idea.

4.1   Random OT Teleportation

Description of M^{ROT}. We now define the Turing machine M^{ROT} for $\mathcal{F}_{\text{HW}}$ in Fig. 3. We use [S] (or [M]) labels to indicate instructions only included in the machine used in the semi-honest (or malicious) setting protocol. Unlabeled instructions are performed in both settings.

When P_1 sends $\langle \ell_1, k_1 \rangle$ and P_2 sends $\langle \ell_2, k_2 \rangle$, M^{ROT} parses their inputs to obtain the ROT seeds k_1, k_2 and the number of ROT to be generated ℓ_1, ℓ_2, and it asserts P_1 and P_2 send the same number $\ell_1 = \ell_2$. Subsequently, M^{ROT} use k_2 to generate the ROT select bits by $(b_1, \ldots, b_{\ell_1}) \leftarrow \text{PRG}(k_2)$. Then, M^{ROT} computes $R_i^{b_i} \leftarrow \text{PRF}_{k_1}(i, b_i)$, for $i \in [\ell_1]$. In the semi-honest setting, M^{ROT} can simply returns the ROT copies $\{R_i^{b_i}\}_{i \in [\ell_1]}$ to P_2.

In the malicious setting, in addition to generate the ROT copies, M^{ROT} needs to produce some verification messages. More specifically, after generating a ROT copy $R_i^{b_i}$, M^{ROT} also generates $R_i^{b_i \oplus 1} \leftarrow \text{PRF}_{k_1}(i, b_i \oplus 1)$, and it sets

$\sigma_i^{b_i \oplus 1} := H(R_i^{b_i \oplus 1})$ as the verification message. In the end, $\mathsf{M}^{\mathsf{ROT}}$ returns the ROT messages $\{R_i^{b_i}\}_{i \in [\ell_1]}$ and the verification messages $\{\sigma_i^{b_i \oplus 1}\}_{i \in [\ell_1]}$ to P_2.

Description of Π_{ROT}. We depict our semi-honest/malicious setting protocol in Fig. 4, where ℓ is the number of ROT copies P_1 and P_2 want to generate. We use [S] (or [M]) labels to indicate instructions only included in the semi-honest (or malicious) setting protocol. Other instructions not labeled should be included in both settings.

The Semi-honest Setting. In the semi-honest setting protocol, the party P_2 first picks a random $k_2 \leftarrow \{0,1\}^\lambda$ as its ROT seed, and it uses this seed to generate $(b_1, \ldots, b_\ell) \leftarrow \mathsf{PRG}(k_2)$ as the ROT select bits. Then, P_2 sends $(\mathsf{Run}, \mathsf{sid}, \langle \ell, k_2 \rangle)$ to $\mathcal{F}_{\mathrm{HW}}[\mathsf{M}^{\mathsf{ROT}}]$. The party P_1 also picks a random $k_1 \leftarrow \{0,1\}^\lambda$ as its ROT seed, and it uses this seed to generate $R_i^0 \leftarrow \mathsf{PRF}_{k_1}(i, 0)$ and $R_i^1 \leftarrow \mathsf{PRF}_{k_1}(i, 1)$, for $i \in [\ell]$. Subsequently, P_1 sends $(\mathsf{Run}, \mathsf{sid}, \langle \ell, k_1 \rangle)$ to $\mathcal{F}_{\mathrm{HW}}[\mathsf{M}^{\mathsf{ROT}}]$, and it returns $(\mathrm{COMPUTE}, \mathsf{sid}, \{R_i^0, R_i^1\}_{i \in [\ell]})$ to the environment $\mathcal{Z}$. After that, P_2 receives the ROT copies $\{R_i^{b_i}\}_{i \in [\ell]}$ from $\mathcal{F}_{\mathrm{HW}}[\mathsf{M}^{\mathsf{ROT}}]$.

The Malicious Setting. In the malicious setting protocol, the party P_2 first picks a random $k_2 \leftarrow \{0,1\}^\lambda$ as its ROT seed, and it uses this seed to generate $(b_1, \ldots, b_\ell) \leftarrow \mathsf{PRG}(k_2)$ as the ROT select bits. Then, P_2 sends $(\mathsf{Run}, \mathsf{sid}, \langle \ell, k_2 \rangle)$ to $\mathcal{F}_{\mathrm{HW}}[\mathsf{M}^{\mathsf{ROT}}]$. The party P_1 also picks a random $k_1 \leftarrow \{0,1\}^\lambda$ as its ROT seed. For $i \in [\ell]$, P_1 generates $R_i^0 \leftarrow \mathsf{PRF}_{k_1}(i, 0)$ and $R_i^1 \leftarrow \mathsf{PRF}_{k_1}(i, 1)$, and it sets $\sigma_i^0 := H(R_i^0)$ and $\sigma_i^1 := H(R_i^1)$. Subsequently, it sets a hash value of all these hash values $\tau := H(\{\sigma_i^0, \sigma_i^1\}_{i \in [\ell]})$. P_1 then sends $(\mathsf{Run}, \mathsf{sid}, \langle \ell, k_1 \rangle)$ to $\mathcal{F}_{\mathrm{HW}}[\mathsf{M}^{\mathsf{ROT}}]$ and sends τ to P_2, and it returns $(\mathrm{COMPUTE}, \mathsf{sid}, \{R_i^0, R_i^1\}_{i \in [\ell]})$ to the environment $\mathcal{Z}$. After that, P_2 receives the ROT copies $\{R_i^{b_i}\}_{i \in [\ell]}$ and hash values $\{\hat{\sigma}_i^{b_i \oplus 1}\}_{i \in [\ell]}$ from $\mathcal{F}_{\mathrm{HW}}[\mathsf{M}^{\mathsf{ROT}}]$ and τ from P_1. For $i \in [\ell]$, P_2 sets $\hat{\sigma}_i^{b_i} := H(R_i^{b_i})$. At last, P_2 sets $\hat{\tau} := H(\{\hat{\sigma}_i^0, \hat{\sigma}_i^1\}_{i \in [\ell]})$ and asserts $\hat{\tau} = \tau$ to check these hash values.

Security. When SGX is malicious, it may produce incorrect $R_i^{b_i}$: To check the correctness of $R_i^{b_i}$ at a low communication cost while preventing P_1 from learning b_i, we let P_1 and SGX collaboratively generate verification messages. More specifically, SGX will send hash values of R_i^0 and R_i^1 to P_2 (since P_2 can generate $H(R_i^{b_i})$ by itself, only $H(R_i^{b_i \oplus 1})$ is needed). Meanwhile, P_1 computes and sends $\tau = H(\{H(R_i^{b_i}), H(R_i^{b_i \oplus 1})\}_{i \in [\ell]})$ to P_2. This hash value τ can be used to verify the validity of SGX's outputs later. Due to space limitation, the full proof can be found in the full version.

4.2 GC Teleportation with Applications to Silent 2PC

Description of M^{GC}. We now define the Turing machine M^{GC} for $\mathcal{F}_{\mathrm{HW}}$ that will be used for our 2PC protocol in the semi-honest/malicious adversarial setting (cf. Fig. 5). We use [S] (or [M]) labels to indicate instructions only included in the machine used in the semi-honest (or malicious) setting protocol. Unlabeled instructions are performed in both settings.

Description of M^{GC}

$\mathsf{M}^{\mathsf{GC}}(x_1, x_2)$:

- Parse $x_1 = \langle k, f_1 \rangle$ and $x_2 = \langle f_2, \{x^0_{2,i}\}_{i \in [f_2.n_2]}\rangle$;
- Assert $f_1 = f_2$;
- Set $f^*(x_1, (x^0_2, x^1_2)) = f_1(x_1, x^0_2 \oplus x^1_2)$;
- Generate $(F, e, d) \leftarrow \mathsf{Gb}(1^\lambda, f^*; k)$;
- Parse $e = \{(X^0_i, X^1_i)\}_{i \in [f^*.n]}$;
- [M] For $i \in [f^*.n_2]$, set $\sigma^0_i := H(X^0_{i+f^*.n_1})$ and $\sigma^1_i := H(X^1_{i+f^*.n_1})$;
- [S] Return $y_1 := \emptyset$ and $y_2 := (F, d, \{X^{x^0_{2,i}}_{i+f^*.n_1}\}_{i \in [f_2.n_2]})$;
- [M] Return $y_1 := \emptyset$ and $y_2 := (F, d, \{X^{x^0_{2,i}}_{i+f^*.n_1}\}_{i \in [f_2.n_2]}, \{\sigma^0_i, \sigma^1_i\}_{i \in [f^*.n_2]})$;

Fig. 5. Description of M^{GC}

When P_1 sends $\langle k, f_1 \rangle$ and P_2 sends $\langle f_2, \{x^0_{2,i}\}_{i \in [f_2.n_2]}\rangle$, M^{GC} parses their inputs to obtain the GC seed k, the circuit to be computed and P_2's secret-shared input x^0_2. M^{GC} asserts P_1 and P_2 send the same circuit $f_1 = f_2$, and use f_1 to generate a function $f^*(x_1, (x^0_2, x^1_2)) = f_1(x_1, x^0_2 \oplus x^1_2)$. M^{GC} then generates the garbled circuit by $(F, e, d) \leftarrow \mathsf{Gb}(1^\lambda, f^*; k)$, and it parses the encoding information $e = \{(X^0_i, X^1_i)\}_{i \in [f^*.n]}$ to get the input wire labels. In the semi-honest setting, M^{GC} can simply returns (F, d) and the wire label of x^0_2 to P_2.

In the malicious setting, in addition to generate the GC copy, M^{GC} needs to produce some verification messages. More specifically, after parsing the encoding information, M^{GC} sets $\sigma^0_i := H(X^0_{i+f^*.n_1})$ and $\sigma^1_i := H(X^1_{i+f^*.n_1})$, for $i \in [f^*.n_2]$. These hash values $\{\sigma^0_i, \sigma^1_i\}_{i \in [f^*.n_2]}$ can help P_2 to verify that it receives the correct input wire labels from P_1 in the subsequent execution. In the end, M^{GC} returns $(F, d, \{X^{x^0_{2,i}}_{i+f^*.n_1}\}_{i \in [f_2.n_2]}, \{\sigma^0_i, \sigma^1_i\}_{i \in [f^*.n_2]})$ to P_2.

Instantiation of M^{GC}. In practice, M^{GC} can be instantiated by just running an SGX enclave on the P_2 side. P_1 will remotely interact with P_2's SGX enclave via a secure channel established by remote attestation. As introduced in Sect. 2, we adopt three GC optimizations, respectively are point-and-permute, GRR3 and free-XOR. For the point-and-permute, we set the least significant bits of the wire labels as the select bits, and arrange the garbled table according to these bits. For the GRR3 optimization, we set the 0-label of the output wire as the first row of the garbled table, and XOR each row with this 0-label, then the first row becomes an all 0 string and thus can be eliminated. And the free-XOR optimization is implemented as described.

Description of $\Pi^{\mathsf{GC}}_{\mathsf{2pc}}$. We depict our semi-honest/malicious setting protocol in Fig. 6, where f is the function that P_1 and P_2 want to jointly compute, as described in Sect. 2, n_1, n_2 and n are the input size of P_1, the input size of P_2 and the overall input size, respectively. In addition, we define a modified function $f^*(x_1, (x^0_2, x^1_2)) = f(x_1, x^0_2 \oplus x^1_2)$, in which x^0_2 and x^1_2 are the additive secret shares of P_2's original input x_2. This idea of splitting P_2's inputs is from the work of Mohassel et al. [16], in their setting, there are two garblers and

---

Protocol $\Pi_{2\text{pc}}^{\text{GC}}$

We define $f^*(x_1, (x_2^0, x_2^1)) = f(x_1, x_2^0 \oplus x_2^1)$, both x_2^0 and x_2^1 are P_2's inputs, so $n_1^* = n_1, n_2^* = 2n_2, n^* = n_1^* + n_2^*$.

- Upon receiving (COMPUTE, sid, $x_2 := (x_{2,1}, \ldots, x_{2,n_2})$) from $\mathcal{Z}$, the party P_2:
  - For $i \in [n_2]$, pick random $x_{2,i}^0 \leftarrow \{0,1\}$, and set $x_{2,i}^1 := x_{2,i} \oplus x_{2,i}^0$;
  - Send (Run, sid, $\langle f, \{x_{2,i}^0\}_{i \in [n_2]} \rangle$) to $\mathcal{F}_{\text{HW}}[\text{M}^{\text{GC}}]$ and $\{x_{2,i}^1\}_{i \in [n_2]}$ to P_1;
- Upon receiving (COMPUTE, sid, $x_1 := (x_{1,1}, \ldots, x_{1,n_1})$) from the environment $\mathcal{Z}$ and $\{x_{2,i}^1\}_{i \in [n_2]}$ from P_2, P_1:
  - Pick random $k \leftarrow \{0,1\}^\lambda$;
  - Generate $(F, e, d) \leftarrow \text{Gb}(1^\lambda, f^*; k)$;
  - Parse $e = \{(X_i^0, X_i^1)\}_{i \in [n^*]}$;
  - [M] For $i \in [n_2^*]$, set $\sigma_i^0 := H(X_{i+n_1}^0)$ and $\sigma_i^1 := H(X_{i+n_1}^1)$;
  - [M] Send $\tau := H(F, d, \{\sigma_i^0, \sigma_i^1\}_{i \in [n_2^*]})$ to P_2;
  - Send (Run, sid, $\langle k, f \rangle$) to $\mathcal{F}_{\text{HW}}[\text{M}^{\text{GC}}]$, and send
    $\{Z_i = X_i^{x_{1,i}}\}_{i \in [n_1]}, \{Z_{i+n_1+n_2} = X_{i+n_1+n_2}^{x_{2,i}^1}\}_{i \in [n_2]}$ to P_2;
- Upon receiving (Run, sid, $(\hat{F}, \hat{d}, \{Z_{i+n_1} = X_{i+n_1}^{x_{2,i}^0}\}_{i \in [n_2]})$) (and [M] $\{\hat{\sigma}_i^0, \hat{\sigma}_i^1\}_{i \in [n_2^*]}$) from $\mathcal{F}_{\text{HW}}[\text{M}^{\text{GC}}]$, and receiving $\{Z_i\}_{i \in [n_1]}, \{Z_{i+n_1+n_2}\}_{i \in [n_2]}$ (and [M] τ) from P_1, party P_2:
  - [M] Set $\hat{\tau} := H(\hat{F}, \hat{d}, \{\hat{\sigma}_{0,i}^0, \hat{\sigma}_{0,i}^1\}_{i \in [n_2^*]})$;
  - [M] Assert $\hat{\tau} = \tau$;
  - [M] For $i \in [n_2]$, assert $\hat{\sigma}_i^{x_{2,i}^0} = H(Z_{i+n_1})$ and $\hat{\sigma}_{i+n_2}^{x_{2,i}^1} = H(Z_{i+n_1+n_2})$;
  - Evaluate $Y \leftarrow \text{GC.Ev}(\hat{F}, (Z_1, \ldots, Z_{n^*}))$;
  - Decode $y \leftarrow \text{GC.De}(\hat{d}, Y)$;
  - Return (COMPUTE, sid, y) to the environment $\mathcal{Z}$;

Fig. 6. The semi-honest/malicious setting protocol $\Pi_{2\text{pc}}^{\text{GC}}$ in the $\mathcal{F}_{\text{HW}}[\text{M}^{\text{GC}}]$-hybrid model

one evaluator, and the evaluator secret-shares its inputs and sends shares to the garblers. We use [S] (or [M]) labels to indicate instructions only included in the semi-honest (or malicious) setting protocol. Other instruction not labeled should be included in both the semi-honest setting protocol and the malicious setting protocol.

The Semi-honest Setting. In the semi-honest setting protocol, the party P_2 first secret shares its input $x_{2,i}$ as $x_{2,i} = x_{2,i}^0 \oplus x_{2,i}^1$, and it sends (Run, sid, $\langle f, \{x_{2,i}^0\}_{i \in [n_2]} \rangle$) to $\mathcal{F}_{\text{HW}}[\text{M}^{\text{GC}}]$ and $\{x_{2,i}^1\}_{i \in [n_2]}$ to P_1. After receiving the secret shares of P_2's inputs $\{x_{2,i}^1\}_{i \in [n_2]}$, P_1 picks a random $k \leftarrow \{0,1\}^\lambda$ as the seed of GC, it generates a GC with this seed by $(F, e, d) \leftarrow \text{Gb}(1^\lambda, f^*; k)$ and it parses the input wire labels by $e = \{(X_i^0, X_i^1)\}_{i \in [n^*]}$. Then, P_1 sends (Run, sid, $\langle k, f \rangle$) to $\mathcal{F}_{\text{HW}}[\text{M}^{\text{GC}}]$, and it sends the input wire labels of its own inputs $\{Z_i = X_i^{x_{1,i}}\}_{i \in [n_1]}$ and P_2's input shares $\{Z_{i+n_1+n_2} = X_{i+n_1+n_2}^{x_{2,i}^1}\}_{i \in [n_2]}$ to P_2. Subsequently, P_2 receives the garbled tables F, the decoding information d and the input wire labels of $\{x_{2,i}^0\}_{i \in [n_2]}$ from $\mathcal{F}_{\text{HW}}[\text{M}^{\text{GC}}]$, and it receives P_1's input wire labels and the input wire labels of $\{x_{2,i}^1\}_{i \in [n_2]}$, it evaluates the garbled circuit by $Y \leftarrow \text{GC.Ev}(F, (Z_1, \ldots, Z_{n_1+2n_2}))$, and decodes the output value by $y \leftarrow \text{GC.De}(d, Y)$.

The Malicious Setting. In the malicious setting protocol, the party P_2 first secret shares its input $x_{2,i}$ as $x_{2,i} = x_{2,i}^0 \oplus x_{2,i}^1$, and it sends $(\mathsf{Run}, \mathsf{sid}, \langle f, \{x_{2,i}^0\}_{i \in [n_2]} \rangle)$ to $\mathcal{F}_{\mathrm{HW}}[\mathsf{M^{GC}}]$ and $\{x_{2,i}^1\}_{i \in [n_2]}$ to P_1. After receiving the secret shares of P_2's inputs $\{x_{2,i}^1\}_{i \in [n_2]}$, P_1 picks a random $k \leftarrow \{0,1\}^\lambda$ as the seed of GC, it generates a GC with this seed by $(F, e, d) \leftarrow \mathsf{Gb}(1^\lambda, f^*; k)$ and it parses the input wire labels by $e = \{(X_i^0, X_i^1)\}_{i \in [n^*]}$. Then, P_1 computes the hash values of all P_2's input wire labels, $\sigma_i^0 := H(X_{i+n_1}^0)$ and $\sigma_i^1 := H(X_{i+n_1}^1)$, for $i \in [n_2^*]$, in addition, it computes another hash value of these all hash values and the garbled circuit by $\tau = H(F, d, \{\sigma_i^0, \sigma_i^1\}_{i \in [n_2^*]})$. After that, P_1 sends $(\mathsf{Run}, \mathsf{sid}, \langle k, f \rangle)$ to $\mathcal{F}_{\mathrm{HW}}[\mathsf{M^{GC}}]$, and it sends the hash value τ, the input wire labels of its own inputs $\{Z_i = X_i^{x_{1,i}}\}_{i \in [n_1]}$ and P_2's input shares $\{Z_{i+n_1+n_2} = X_{i+n_1+n_2}^{x_{2,i}^1}\}_{i \in [n_2]}$ to P_2. Subsequently, P_2 receives the garbled tables F, the decoding information d, the input wire labels of $\{x_{2,i}^0\}_{i \in [n_2]}$ and the hash values of all its input wire labels $\{\hat{\sigma}_i^0, \hat{\sigma}_i^1\}_{i \in [n_2^*]}$ from $\mathcal{F}_{\mathrm{HW}}[\mathsf{M^{GC}}]$, and it receives τ, P_1's input wire labels and the input wire labels of $\{x_{2,i}^1\}_{i \in [n_2]}$. Then, P_2 checks the message sent by $\mathcal{F}_{\mathrm{HW}}[\mathsf{M^{GC}}]$ with the hash value τ, and it verifies that $\mathcal{F}_{\mathrm{HW}}[\mathsf{M^{GC}}]$ and P_1 sends the correct input wire labels using the hash values from $\mathcal{F}_{\mathrm{HW}}[\mathsf{M^{GC}}]$. At last, P_2 evaluates the garbled circuit by $Y \leftarrow \mathsf{GC.Ev}(F, (Z_1, \ldots, Z_{n_1+2n_2}))$, and decodes the output value by $y \leftarrow \mathsf{GC.De}(d, Y)$.

5   Security

In this section, we first examine why our schemes are secure at the high level, and then formally state the security of our semi-honest/malicious setting protocol $\Pi_{\mathsf{2pc}}^{\mathsf{GC}}$ in Theorem 1/Theorem 2, respectively, where we restrict the adversary $\mathcal{A}$ to only corrupt one of the following entities (i) the semi-trusted hardware functionality, (ii) player P_1 and (iii) player P_2.

In our protocols, P_2's input x_2 is secretly shared as $x_2 = x_2^0 \oplus x_2^1$, and P_2 sends x_2^0 to $\mathcal{F}_{\mathrm{HW}}[\mathsf{M^{GC}}]$ and x_2^1 to P_1. $\mathcal{F}_{\mathrm{HW}}[\mathsf{M^{GC}}]$ and P_1 will not be corrupted simultaneously, so the adversary can not learn P_2's input value.

In the semi-honest setting, the view of $\mathcal{F}_{\mathrm{HW}}[\mathsf{M^{GC}}]$ is the MPC function f, a random input share of x_2 and the seed of the garbled circuit, f is already known to the environment $\mathcal{Z}$ and the adversary $\mathcal{A}$; therefore, no additional information would be leaked to the adversary $\mathcal{A}$. Since $\mathcal{F}_{\mathrm{HW}}[\mathsf{M^{GC}}]$ could only be passively corrupted, the correctness of the garbled circuit and the wire labels of P_2's secret shared input are preserved. The input privacy of protocol $\Pi_{\mathsf{2pc}}^{\mathsf{GC}}$ is guaranteed by the simulatable privacy property of the underlying garbling scheme GC. In the malicious setting, $\mathcal{F}_{\mathrm{HW}}[\mathsf{M^{GC}}]$, P_1, and P_2 may be maliciously corrupted. The main design principle is as follows. In P_2's point of view, either $\mathcal{F}_{\mathrm{HW}}[\mathsf{M^{GC}}]$ or P_1 could be corrupted. Note that our protocol does not provide accountability, i.e., when the protocol abort, we are not required to identify which party is guilty. Thus, P_2 can use messages generated by $\mathcal{F}_{\mathrm{HW}}[\mathsf{M^{GC}}]$ and messages sent by P_1 to carry out a mutual verification, and it aborts if any inconsistency is detected. More specifically, the wire labels of P_2's secret shared input x_2^0 and x_2^1

are checked using hash values $\sigma_i^0 := H(X_{i+n_1}^0)$ and $\sigma_i^1 := H(X_{i+n_1}^1)$ generated by $\mathcal{F}_{\mathrm{HW}}[\mathsf{M}^{\mathsf{GC}}]$. The correctness of the garbled circuit and the hash values are ensured by another hash value $\tau = H(F, d, \{\sigma_i^0, \sigma_i^1\}_{i \in [n_2^*]})$.

Theorem 1. *If* $\mathsf{GC} := (\mathsf{Gb}, \mathsf{En}, \mathsf{Ev}, \mathsf{De})$ *is a secure simulatable private garbling scheme, protocol* $\Pi_{2\mathsf{pc}}^{\mathsf{GC}}$ *(semi-honest setting) described in Fig. 6 securely realizes* $\mathcal{F}_{2\mathsf{pc}}^f$ *as described in Fig. 1 in the* $\mathcal{F}_{\mathrm{HW}}[\mathsf{M}^{\mathsf{GC}}]$*-hybrid model against any PPT semi-honest adversaries who can corrupt one of the following entities: (i)* $\mathcal{F}_{\mathrm{HW}}[\mathsf{M}^{\mathsf{GC}}]$*, (ii)* P_1*, or (iii)* P_2 *with static corruption.*

Theorem 2. *If* $H : \{0,1\}^* \mapsto \{0,1\}^\lambda$ *is a collision resistant hash function, and* $\mathsf{GC} := (\mathsf{Gb}, \mathsf{En}, \mathsf{Ev}, \mathsf{De})$ *is a secure simulatable private garbling scheme, protocol* $\Pi_{2\mathsf{pc}}^{\mathsf{GC}}$ *(malicious setting) described in Fig. 6 securely realizes* $\mathcal{F}_{2\mathsf{pc}}^f$ *as described in Fig. 1 in the* $\mathcal{F}_{\mathrm{HW}}[\mathsf{M}^{\mathsf{GC}}]$*-hybrid model against any PPT malicious adversaries who can corrupt one of the following entities: (i)* $\mathcal{F}_{\mathrm{HW}}[\mathsf{M}^{\mathsf{GC}}]$*, (ii)* P_1*, or (iii)* P_2 *with static corruption.*

The proofs are provided in Appendix A.1.

6   Implementation and Benchmarks

Our protocol is implemented in C++ using Intel SGX SDK on Linux. We use AES-NI for the PRF algorithm. We perform the experiments on an SGX-enabled Dell OptiPlex 7080 equipped with an Intel Core 8700 CPU @ 3.20 GHz with 32.0 GB RAM, running Ubuntu 18.04 LTS. We evaluate all protocols in two simulated network settings: (i) a LAN setting with 1 Gbps bandwidth and 0.1 ms delay and (ii) a WAN setting with 100 Mbps bandwidth and 25 ms delay.

To test the performance of our semi-honest ROT generation protocol, we compared our protocol with the implementation of the IKNP OT extension protocol [8] in EMP-OT [20]. Table 1 shows the performance comparison for generating 10^4 to 10^8 copies of ROT, where the result is the average of 10 tests.

Table 4. Details of the benchmark Bristol Fashion circuit

Circuit	# wire	# gate	# AND gate	# P_1's input	# P_2's input	# output
AES-128	36919	36663	6400	128	128	128
SHA-256	135841	135073	22573	256	256	256
SHA-512	351153	349617	57947	512	512	512

To test the performance of the 2PC protocols, our benchmarks use three Bristol Fashion format circuits [1], and the details are provided in Table 4.

For the semi-honest setting protocol, we compared our protocol with EMP-SH2PC [20] (EMP-SH2PC provides an efficient semi-honest 2PC implementation based on Yao's GC protocol with half-gates [22] optimization); for the malicious setting protocol, we compared our protocol with EMP-AG2PC [20] (EMP-AG2PC implements an efficient maliciously secure two-party computation protocol, authenticated garbling [21]). Table 2 shows the performance comparison for evaluating the aforementioned benchmark circuits for 1000 times using the semi-honest setting protocols, and the results are the average of 10 tests. Table 3 shows the performance comparison for evaluating the benchmark circuits once using the malicious version, and the results are the average of 100 tests.

7   Related Work

As mentioned above, there are several hardware models proposed in the literature, such as the remote attestation model [18] and the tamper-proof hardware token models [9,12]. However, the existing model does not address hardware leakage as well as malicious corruptions. Mohassel et al. [15] proposed a scheme that enables efficient secure computation on mobile phones. Their protocol is constructed in a *Server-Aided* setting, where a semi-honest (covert) server who does not collude with protocol players is used to accelerate computation. However, their objective is to save computation, while our goal is to reduce communication. Moreover, in our model, the hardware can be maliciously corrupted. Järvinen et al. [10] used hardware token to reduce the cost of the OT process in standard GC protocols. In their protocol, a sender generates a garbled circuit and it uses hardware tokens, e.g. One-Time Memory (OTM) tokens, to store the GC encoding information, the garbled circuit and the hardware tokens are collectively called One-Time Program (OTP), which is a non-interactive version of GC protocol. In our work, we also remove the OT process, but to keep sensitive information away from the enclave, we secret-share P_2's input and sends the shares to P_1 and SGX. A similar idea can be found in Mohassel et al. [16]. Kolesnikov [13] used hardware tokens to construct an efficient OT protocol. This work considers the client-server setting where the server is the sender and the client is the receiver. The server can deploy a hardware token in the client side, and the client can obtain messages by querying the token. Our work provides a more efficient malicious setting protocol, instead of the cut-and-choose technique.

There have been some Intel SGX-based MPC solutions. Gupta et al. [7] proposed protocols using Intel SGX for SFE problem which is secure in the semi-honest model, and show how to improve their protocol's security.. The naive solution is to let the players enter their inputs to the enclave, and they reduce the data leakage problem by using SGX to convert plaintexts to ciphertexts (e.g. wire labels) and vice versa, but the enclave still knows the input values. They notice the problem that the players need to trust hardware supplier when using Intel SGX, but don't give a feasible solution. Felsen et al. [6] proposed an Intel SGX-based secure function evaluation (SFE) approach in which private inputs are sent to enclave. In their protocol, only the inputs and the outputs need to be transferred, the communication complexity of their protocol is optimal up to an additive constant. They evaluate the Boolean circuit representation of the function in enclave to provide security with regards to software side-channel attacks. Choi et al. [4] consider the possibility of SGX being compromised and want to protect the most sensitive data in any case. They propose a hybrid SFE-SGX protocol which consists of calculation in SGX enclave and standard cryptographic techniques. The function to be evaluated is partitioned into several round functions, in the odd rounds, the computation is executed in the enclave and the player Bob (the remote party) only provide less sensitive inputs, in the even rounds, a scheme based on garbled circuit is used and Bob provides more sensitive data. These works focus on the efficiency of the Intel SGX-based solutions, and the main security concern is the side-channel attack problem. Providing private information to enclave is an inevitable step of their protocols; therefore, private information may be leaked in our setting.

8   Conclusion

In this work, we investigate the problem where the trusted hardware manufacturer is not fully trusted, and the hardware components may leak sensitive information to the remote servers. In our model, the adversary is allowed to passively or maliciously corrupt the hardware component. We present several correlated randomness teleportation protocols, such as ROT and GC generation with applications to silent MPC, where the communication only depends on the input size regardless the circuit size. The resulting protocols are significantly faster than the EMP-IKNP-ROT, EMP-SH2PC and EMP-AG2PC.

Acknowledgments. Bingsheng Zhang is supported by the "Open Project Program of Key Laboratory of Blockchain and Cyberspace Governance of Zhejiang Province" and the National Natural Science Foundation of China (Grant No. 62072401). Hong-Sheng Zhou acknowledges support by NSF grant CNS-1801470, a Google Faculty Research Award and a research gift from Ergo Platform. This work is also supported by Alibaba Group through Alibaba Innovative Research Program.

A   Appendix

A.1   Security Proof of Our Main Theorems

Due to space limitation, we only provide the security proof for malicious setting.

Proof. To prove Theorem 2, we construct a simulator $\mathcal{S}$ such that no non-uniform PPT environment $\mathcal{Z}$ can distinguish between (i) the real execution $\text{EXEC}_{\Pi_{2pc}^{GC}, \mathcal{A}, \mathcal{Z}}^{\mathcal{F}_{HW}[M^{GC}]}$ where the parties $\mathcal{P} := \{P_1, P_2\}$ run protocol Π_{2pc}^{GC} in the $\mathcal{F}_{HW}[M^{GC}]$-hybrid model and the corrupted parties are controlled by a dummy adversary $\mathcal{A}$ who simply forwards messages from/to $\mathcal{Z}$, and (ii) the ideal execution $\text{EXEC}_{\mathcal{F}_{2pc}^{f}, \mathcal{S}, \mathcal{Z}}$

where the parties P_1 and P_2 interact with functionality $\mathcal{F}_{2pc}^f$ in the ideal world, and corrupted parties are controlled by the simulator $\mathcal{S}$. We consider following cases.

Case 1: $\mathcal{F}_{HW}[\mathsf{M}^{GC}]$ is corrupted; P_1 and P_2 are honest.

Simulator. The simulator $\mathcal{S}$ internally runs $\mathcal{A}$, forwarding messages to/from the environment $\mathcal{Z}$. $\mathcal{S}$ simulates the interface of $\mathcal{F}_{HW}[\mathsf{M}^{GC}]$ as well as honest parties P_1 and P_2. In addition, the simulator $\mathcal{S}$ simulates the following interactions with $\mathcal{A}$.

- Upon receiving $(\textsc{ComputeNotify}, \mathsf{sid}, |x_2|, P_2)$ for an honest party P_2 from the external $\mathcal{F}_{2pc}^f$, the simulator $\mathcal{S}$ picks random $x_{2,i}^0 \leftarrow \{0,1\}$, for $i \in [n_2]$, and it sends $(\mathsf{Run}, \mathsf{sid}, \langle f, \{x_{2,i}^0\}_{i \in [n_2]}\rangle)$ to $\mathcal{F}_{HW}[\mathsf{M}^{GC}]$ on behave of P_2.
- Upon receiving $(\textsc{ComputeNotify}, \mathsf{sid}, |x_1|, P_1)$ for an honest party P_1 from the external $\mathcal{F}_{2pc}^f$, the simulator $\mathcal{S}$ picks random $k \leftarrow \{0,1\}^\lambda$, and it sends $(\mathsf{Run}, \mathsf{sid}, \langle k, f\rangle)$ to $\mathcal{F}_{HW}[\mathsf{M}^{GC}]$ on behave of P_1. $\mathcal{S}$ then generate $(F, e, d) \leftarrow \mathsf{Gb}(1^\lambda, f^*; k)$ and parse $e = \{(X_i^0, X_i^1)\}_{i \in [n^*]}$. Subsequently, for $i \in [n_2^*]$, $\mathcal{S}$ sets $\sigma_i^0 := H(X_{i+n_1}^0)$ and $\sigma_i^1 := H(X_{i+n_1}^1)$, and it sets $\tau = H(F, d, \{\sigma_i^0, \sigma_i^1\}_{i \in [n_2^*]})$. $\mathcal{S}$ then sends τ to the simulated party P_2 on behave of P_1.
- Upon receiving $(\mathsf{Run}, \mathsf{sid}, Q_i)$ from the party $P_i \in \mathcal{P}$ via the interface of $\mathcal{F}_{HW}[\mathsf{M}^{GC}]$, $\mathcal{S}$ acts as $\mathcal{F}_{HW}[\mathsf{M}^{GC}]$ to send $(\textsc{RunNotify}, \mathsf{sid}, Q_i, P_i)$ to $\mathcal{A}$. $\mathcal{S}$ then simulates the $\mathcal{F}_{HW}[\mathsf{M}^{GC}]$ functionality as defined.
- When the simulated party P_2 receives $(\hat{F}, \hat{d}, \{X_{i+n_1}^{x_{2,i}^0}\}_{i \in [n_2]}, \{\hat{\sigma}_i^0, \hat{\sigma}_i^1\}_{i \in [n_2^*]})$ from $\mathcal{F}_{HW}[\mathsf{M}^{GC}]$ and receives τ from the simulated P_1, P_2 computes $\hat{\tau} = H(\hat{F}, \hat{d}, \{\hat{\sigma}_{0,i}^0, \hat{\sigma}_{0,i}^1\}_{i \in [n_2^*]})$ and asserts $\hat{\tau} = \tau$. Thereafter, $\mathcal{S}$ fetches the internal GC label information (F, e, d) from the simulated P_1. For $i \in [n_2]$, $\mathcal{S}$ acts as P_2 to assert $Z_{i+n_1} = X_{i+n_1}^{x_{2,i}^0}$.
- Upon receiving $(\textsc{Output}, \mathsf{sid}, P_2)$ from the external $\mathcal{F}_{2pc}^f$, the simulator $\mathcal{S}$ returns $(\textsc{Deliver}, \mathsf{sid}, P_2)$ if and only if all the checks are valid.

Indistinguishability. Assume the communication between P_1 and P_2 is via the secure channel functionality $\mathcal{F}_{SC}$, the views of $\mathcal{A}$ and $\mathcal{Z}$ in $\mathrm{EXEC}_{\Pi_{2pc}^{GC}, \mathcal{A}, \mathcal{Z}}^{\mathcal{F}_{HW}[\mathsf{M}^{GC}]}$ and $\mathrm{EXEC}_{\mathcal{F}_{2pc}^f, \mathcal{S}, \mathcal{Z}}$ are identical except the scenario where the real-world output y is different from the ideal-world output y'. This happens when the malicious $\mathcal{F}_{HW}[\mathsf{M}^{GC}]$ provides inconsistent information, yet she manages to pass all the hash validations. It means that the adversary provides at least one different hash preimage that would hashes to the same value as the original preimage. Therefore, the simulator and the adversary can jointly outputs two messages $m_1 \neq m_2$ such that $H(m_1) = H(m_2)$. Assume H is a collision resistant cryptographic hash function, the views of $\mathcal{A}$ and $\mathcal{Z}$ in $\mathrm{EXEC}_{\Pi_{2pc}^{GC}, \mathcal{A}, \mathcal{Z}}^{\mathcal{F}_{HW}[\mathsf{M}^{GC}]}$ and $\mathrm{EXEC}_{\mathcal{F}_{2pc}^f, \mathcal{S}, \mathcal{Z}}$ are indistinguishable.

Case 2: P_1 is corrupted; P_2 and $\mathcal{F}_{HW}[\mathsf{M}^{GC}]$ are honest.

Simulator. The simulator $\mathcal{S}$ internally runs $\mathcal{A}$, forwarding messages to/from the environment $\mathcal{Z}$. $\mathcal{S}$ simulates the interface of $\mathcal{F}_{\mathrm{HW}}[\mathsf{M}^{\mathsf{GC}}]$ as well as honest P_2. In addition, the simulator $\mathcal{S}$ simulates the following interactions with $\mathcal{A}$.

- Upon receiving $(\textsc{ComputeNotify}, \mathsf{sid}, |x_2|, P_2)$ from the external $\mathcal{F}^f_{\mathsf{2pc}}$, the simulator $\mathcal{S}$ picks random $x^0_{2,i} \leftarrow \{0,1\}$, for $i \in [n_2]$, and it sends $(\mathsf{Run}, \mathsf{sid}, \langle f, \{x^0_{2,i}\}_{i\in[n_2]}\rangle)$ to $\mathcal{F}_{\mathrm{HW}}[\mathsf{M}^{\mathsf{GC}}]$ on behave of P_2. For $i \in [n_2]$ $\mathcal{S}$ sends random $\hat{x}^1_{2,i} \leftarrow \{0,1\}$ to P_1 on behave of P_2.
- Upon receiving $(\mathsf{Run}, \mathsf{sid}, \langle k, f\rangle)$ from P_1 and $(\mathsf{Run}, \mathsf{sid}, \langle f, \{x^0_{2,i}\}_{i\in[n_2]}\rangle)$ from P_2, $\mathcal{S}$ acts as $\mathcal{F}_{\mathrm{HW}}[\mathsf{M}^{\mathsf{GC}}]$ to set $f^*(x_1, (x^0_2, x^1_2)) = f_1(x_1, x^0_2 \oplus x^1_2)$ and generate the garbled circuit by $(F, e, d) \leftarrow \mathsf{Gb}(1^\lambda, f^*; k)$. $\mathcal{S}$ then parse $e = \{(X^0_i, X^1_i)\}_{i\in[n_1+2n_2]}$ and sends $(F, d, \{X^{x^0_{2,i}}_{i+n_1}\}_{i\in[n_2]}, \{\sigma^0_i, \sigma^1_i\}_{i\in[n^*_2]})$ to the simulated party P_2 on behave of $\mathcal{F}_{\mathrm{HW}}[\mathsf{M}^{\mathsf{GC}}]$.
- When the simulated party P_2 receives $\{Z_i\}_{i\in[n_1]}, \{Z_{i+n_1+n_2}\}_{i\in[n_2]}$ and τ from P_1, $\mathcal{S}$ acts as P_2 to compute $\hat{\tau} = H(F, d, \{\sigma^0_i, \sigma^1_i\}_{i\in[n^*_2]})$ and assert $\hat{\tau} = \tau$. Thereafter, $\mathcal{S}$ fetches the internal GC label information (F, e, d) from the simulated $\mathcal{F}_{\mathrm{HW}}[\mathsf{M}^{\mathsf{GC}}]$. For $i \in [n_2]$, $\mathcal{S}$ acts as P_2 to assert $Z_{i+n_1+n_2} = X^{x^1_{2,i}}_{i+n_1+n_2}$. In addition, $\mathcal{S}$ uses the internal GC label information (F, e, d) and $\{Z_i\}_{i\in[n_1]}$ to extract P_1's input x^*_1, and it sends $(\textsc{Compute}, \mathsf{sid}, x^*_1)$ to the external $\mathcal{F}^f_{\mathsf{2pc}}$ on behave of P_1.
- Upon receiving $(\textsc{Output}, \mathsf{sid}, P_2)$ from the external $\mathcal{F}^f_{\mathsf{2pc}}$, the simulator $\mathcal{S}$ returns $(\textsc{Deliver}, \mathsf{sid}, P_2)$ if and only if all the checks are valid and $\mathcal{A}$ allows P_2 to finish the protocol execution and obtains y.

Indistinguishability. The indistinguishability is proven through a series of hybrid worlds $\mathcal{H}_0, \ldots, \mathcal{H}_2$.

Hybrid $\mathcal{H}_0$: It is the real protocol execution $\textsc{EXEC}^{\mathcal{F}_{\mathrm{HW}}[\mathsf{M}^{\mathsf{GC}}]}_{\Pi^{\mathsf{GC}}_{\mathsf{2pc}}, \mathcal{A}, \mathcal{Z}}$.

Hybrid $\mathcal{H}_1$: $\mathcal{H}_1$ is the same as $\mathcal{H}_0$ except that in $\mathcal{H}_1$, P_2 sends random $\{\hat{x}^1_{2,i}\}_{i\in[n_2]}$ to P_1, instead of $\{x^1_{2,i} := x^0_{2,i} \oplus x_{2,i}\}_{i\in[n_2]}$.

Claim. $\mathcal{H}_1$ and $\mathcal{H}_0$ are perfectly indistinguishable.

Proof. Since $\{x^0_{2,i}\}_{i\in[n_2]}$ are random bits picked by P_2, the distribution of $\{\hat{x}^1_{2,i}\}_{i\in[n_2]}$ and $\{x^1_{2,i}\}_{i\in[n_2]}$ are identical. Therefore, $\mathcal{H}_1$ and $\mathcal{H}_0$ are perfectly indistinguishable.

Hybrid $\mathcal{H}_2$: $\mathcal{H}_2$ is the same as $\mathcal{H}_1$ except that in $\mathcal{H}_2$, P_2 fetches the internal GC label information (F, e, d) from the simulated $\mathcal{F}_{\mathrm{HW}}[\mathsf{M}^{\mathsf{GC}}]$, and it checks if $Z_{i+n_1+n_2} = X^{x^1_{2,i}}_{i+n_1+n_2}$; otherwise, $\mathcal{S}$ aborts.

Claim. If H is a collision resistant cryptographic hash function, $\mathcal{H}_2$ and $\mathcal{H}_1$ are indistinguishable.

Proof. The difference between $\mathcal{H}_1$ and $\mathcal{H}_2$ is that in $\mathcal{H}_1$, P_2 only checks $H(Z_{i+n_1+n_2})$; whereas, in $\mathcal{H}_2$, P_2 directly checks if $Z_{i+n_1+n_2} = X_{i+n_1+n_2}^{x_{2,i}^1}$. It is easy to see when H is a collision resistant cryptographic hash function, $\mathcal{H}_2$ and $\mathcal{H}_1$ are indistinguishable.

The adversary's view of $\mathcal{H}_2$ is identical to the simulated view $\mathrm{EXEC}_{\mathcal{F}_{2\mathrm{pc}}^f, \mathcal{S}, \mathcal{Z}}$. Therefore, it is perfectly indistinguishable.

Case 3: P_2 is corrupted; P_1 and $\mathcal{F}_{\mathrm{HW}}[\mathsf{M}^{\mathsf{GC}}]$ are honest.

Simulator. The simulator $\mathcal{S}$ internally runs $\mathcal{A}$, forwarding messages to/from the environment $\mathcal{Z}$. $\mathcal{S}$ simulates the interface of $\mathcal{F}_{\mathrm{HW}}[\mathsf{M}^{\mathsf{GC}}]$ as well as honest P_1. In addition, the simulator $\mathcal{S}$ simulates the following interactions with $\mathcal{A}$.

- Upon receiving $(\textsc{ComputeNotify}, \mathsf{sid}, |x_1|, P_1)$ from the external $\mathcal{F}_{2\mathrm{pc}}^f$ and receiving $\{x_{2,i}^1\}_{i \in [n_2]}$ from P_2, the simulator $\mathcal{S}$ picks random $k \leftarrow \{0,1\}^\lambda$, and it sends $(\mathsf{Run}, \mathsf{sid}, \langle k, f \rangle)$ to $\mathcal{F}_{\mathrm{HW}}[\mathsf{M}^{\mathsf{GC}}]$ on behave of P_1.
- Upon receiving $(\mathsf{Run}, \mathsf{sid}, \langle k, f \rangle)$ from P_1 and $(\mathsf{Run}, \mathsf{sid}, \langle f, \{x_{2,i}^0\}_{i \in [n_2]} \rangle)$ from P_2, $\mathcal{S}$ computes P_2's input $x_{2,i}^* := x_{2,i}^0 \oplus x_{2,i}^1$, for $i \in [n_2]$. After that, it sends $(\textsc{Compute}, \mathsf{sid}, x_2^*)$ to the external $\mathcal{F}_{2\mathrm{pc}}^f$ on behave of P_2.
- Upon receiving $(\textsc{Compute}, \mathsf{sid}, y)$ from the external $\mathcal{F}_{2\mathrm{pc}}^f$ for P_2, the simulator $\mathcal{S}$ sets $f^*(x_1, (x_2^0, x_2^1)) = f_1(x_1, x_2^0 \oplus x_2^1)$ and uses the GC simulator to generate $(F', X', d') \leftarrow \mathsf{Sim}(1^\lambda, y, \Phi(f^*))$. $\mathcal{S}$ then uses X' as the wire labels to generate $\{Z_i\}_{i \in [n_1 + 2n_2]}$ as $Z_i := X_i'$. $\mathcal{S}$ picks $2n_2$ random numbers $\hat{Z}_i \leftarrow \{0,1\}^\lambda$. For $i \in [n_2]$, $\mathcal{S}$ sets $\sigma_i^{x_{2,i}^0} := H(Z_{i+n_1})$, $\sigma_i^{x_{2,i}^0 \oplus 1} := H(\hat{Z}_i)$, $\sigma_{i+n_2}^{x_{2,i}^1} := H(Z_{i+n_1+n_2})$ and $\sigma_{i+n_2}^{x_{2,i}^1 \oplus 1} := H(\hat{Z}_{i+n_2})$. Subsequently, $\mathcal{S}$ sets $\tau = H(F', d', \{\sigma_i^0, \sigma_i^1\}_{i \in [n_2^*]})$. At last, $\mathcal{S}$ sends $\{Z_{i+n_1}\}_{i \in [n_2]}$ as the wire label of x_2^0, (F', d') as the GC tables and decode information and $\{\sigma_i^0, \sigma_i^1\}_{i \in [n_2^*]}$ as the hash values of P_2's wire labels to P_2 on behave of $\mathcal{F}_{\mathrm{HW}}[\mathsf{M}^{\mathsf{GC}}]$, and it sends $\{Z_i\}_{i \in [n_1]}$, $\{Z_{i+n_1+n_2}\}_{i \in [n_2]}$ and τ to P_2 on behave of P_1.

Indistinguishability. The indistinguishability is proven through a series of hybrid worlds $\mathcal{H}_0, \ldots, \mathcal{H}_2$.

Hybrid $\mathcal{H}_0$: It is the real protocol execution $\mathrm{EXEC}_{\Pi_{2\mathrm{pc}}^{\mathsf{GC}}, \mathcal{A}, \mathcal{Z}}^{\mathcal{F}_{\mathrm{HW}}[\mathsf{M}^{\mathsf{GC}}]}$.

Hybrid $\mathcal{H}_1$: $\mathcal{H}_1$ is the same as $\mathcal{H}_0$ except that $\mathcal{H}_1$ generates different hash values by $\sigma_i^{x_{2,i}^0 \oplus 1} := H(\hat{Z}_i)$ and $\sigma_{i+n_2}^{x_{2,i}^1 \oplus 1} := H(\hat{Z}_{i+n_2})$, for $i \in [n_2]$, where $\{\hat{Z}_i\}_{i \in [2n_2]}$ are random values.

Claim. If H is a collision resistant cryptographic hash function, $\mathcal{H}_1$ and $\mathcal{H}_0$ are indistinguishable.

Proof. The difference between $\mathcal{H}_0$ and $\mathcal{H}_1$ is that in $\mathcal{H}_0$, $\sigma_i^{x_{2,i}^0 \oplus 1} := H(X_{i+n_1}^{x_{2,i}^0 \oplus 1})$ and $\sigma_{i+n_2}^{x_{2,i}^1 \oplus 1} := H(X_{i+n_1+n_2}^{x_{2,i}^1 \oplus 1})$; whereas, in $\mathcal{H}_1$, $\sigma_i^{x_{2,i}^0 \oplus 1} := H(\hat{Z}_i)$ and $\sigma_{i+n_2}^{x_{2,i}^1 \oplus 1} := H(\hat{Z}_{i+n_2})$. It is easy to see when H is a collision resistant cryptographic hash function, $\mathcal{H}_1$ and $\mathcal{H}_0$ are indistinguishable.

Hybrid $\mathcal{H}_2$: $\mathcal{H}_2$ is the same as $\mathcal{H}_1$ except that $\mathcal{H}_2$ generates $(F', X', d') \leftarrow$ $\mathsf{Sim}(1^\lambda, y, \Phi(f^*))$, and then it uses X' as the wire labels to generate $\{Z_i\}_{i \in [n_1 + 2n_2]}$. $\mathcal{F}_{\mathrm{HW}}[\mathsf{M}^{\mathsf{GC}}]$ also sends (F', d') as the GC tables and decoding information to P_2.

Claim. If GC is simulatable private with adversarial distinguishing advantage $\mathsf{Adv}_{\mathsf{GC}}^{\mathsf{prv.sim},\Phi,\mathsf{Sim}}(\mathcal{A}, \lambda)$, then $\mathcal{H}_1$ and $\mathcal{H}_0$ are indistinguishable with distinguishing advantage $\mathsf{Adv}_{\mathsf{GC}}^{\mathsf{prv.sim},\Phi,\mathsf{Sim}}(\mathcal{A}, \lambda)$.

Proof. By the requirement of simulatable privacy in Definition 2, $(F', X', d') \leftarrow$ $\mathsf{Sim}(1^\lambda, y, \Phi(f^*))$ should be indistinguishable from the real one except for the adversarial distinguishing advantage $\mathsf{Adv}_{\mathsf{GC}}^{\mathsf{prv.sim},\Phi,\mathsf{Sim}}(\mathcal{A}, \lambda)$.

The adversary's view of $\mathcal{H}_2$ is identical to the simulated view $\mathrm{EXEC}_{\mathcal{F}_{2pc}^f, \mathcal{S}, \mathcal{Z}}$.

Therefore, if GC is simulatable private, the views of $\mathcal{A}$ and $\mathcal{Z}$ in $\mathrm{EXEC}_{\Pi_{2pc}^{\mathsf{GC}}, \mathcal{A}, \mathcal{Z}}^{\mathcal{F}_{\mathrm{HW}}[\mathsf{M}^{\mathsf{GC}}]}$ and $\mathrm{EXEC}_{\mathcal{F}_{2pc}^f, \mathcal{S}, \mathcal{Z}}$ are indistinguishable with distinguishing advantage

$$\mathsf{Adv}_{\mathsf{GC}}^{\mathsf{prv.sim},\Phi,\mathsf{Sim}}(\mathcal{A}, \lambda) = \mathsf{negl}(\lambda) \ .$$

References

1. Archer, D., et al.: 'Bristol Fashion' MPC Circuits (2020). https://homes.esat. kuleuven.be/~nsmart/MPC/. Accessed 5 Jan 2021
2. Beaver, D., Micali, S., Rogaway, P.: The round complexity of secure protocols. In: Proceedings of the Twenty-Second Annual ACM Symposium on Theory of Computing, pp. 503–513 (1990)
3. Bellare, M., Hoang, V.T., Rogaway, P.: Foundations of garbled circuits. In: Proceedings of the 2012 ACM Conference on Computer and Communications Security, pp. 784–796 (2012)
4. Choi, J.I., et al.: A hybrid approach to secure function evaluation using SGX. In: Proceedings of the 2019 ACM Asia Conference on Computer and Communications Security, pp. 100–113 (2019)
5. Dan, G., Jim, S.: More than 20 GB of Intel source code and proprietary data dumped online. [EB/OL]. https://arstechnica.com/information-technology/2020/08/intel-is-investigating-the-leak-of-20gb-of-its-source-code-and-private-data/. Accessed 30 Aug 2020
6. Felsen, S., Kiss, Á., Schneider, T., Weinert, C.: Secure and private function evaluation with Intel SGX. In: Proceedings of the 2019 ACM SIGSAC Conference on Cloud Computing Security Workshop, pp. 165–181 (2019)
7. Gupta, D., Mood, B., Feigenbaum, J., Butler, K., Traynor, P.: Using Intel software guard extensions for efficient two-party secure function evaluation. In: Clark, J., Meiklejohn, S., Ryan, P.Y.A., Wallach, D., Brenner, M., Rohloff, K. (eds.) FC 2016. LNCS, vol. 9604, pp. 302–318. Springer, Heidelberg (2016). https://doi.org/10.1007/978-3-662-53357-4_20
8. Ishai, Y., Kilian, J., Nissim, K., Petrank, E.: Extending oblivious transfers efficiently. In: Boneh, D. (ed.) CRYPTO 2003. LNCS, vol. 2729, pp. 145–161. Springer, Heidelberg (2003). https://doi.org/10.1007/978-3-540-45146-4_9

9. Järvinen, K., Kolesnikov, V., Sadeghi, A.-R., Schneider, T.: Embedded SFE: offloading server and network using hardware tokens. In: Sion, R. (ed.) FC 2010. LNCS, vol. 6052, pp. 207–221. Springer, Heidelberg (2010). https://doi.org/10.1007/978-3-642-14577-3_17

10. Järvinen, K., Kolesnikov, V., Sadeghi, A.-R., Schneider, T.: Garbled circuits for leakage-resilience: hardware implementation and evaluation of one-time programs. In: Mangard, S., Standaert, F.-X. (eds.) CHES 2010. LNCS, vol. 6225, pp. 383–397. Springer, Heidelberg (2010). https://doi.org/10.1007/978-3-642-15031-9_26

11. Johnson, S., Scarlata, V., Rozas, C., Brickell, E., Mckeen, F.: Intel® software guard extensions: EPID provisioning and attestation services. White Paper 1(1–10), 119 (2016)

12. Katz, J.: Universally composable multi-party computation using tamper-proof hardware. In: Naor, M. (ed.) EUROCRYPT 2007. LNCS, vol. 4515, pp. 115–128. Springer, Heidelberg (2007). https://doi.org/10.1007/978-3-540-72540-4_7

13. Kolesnikov, V.: Truly efficient string oblivious transfer using resettable tamper-proof tokens. In: Micciancio, D. (ed.) TCC 2010. LNCS, vol. 5978, pp. 327–342. Springer, Heidelberg (2010). https://doi.org/10.1007/978-3-642-11799-2_20

14. Kolesnikov, V., Schneider, T.: Improved garbled circuit: free XOR gates and applications. In: Aceto, L., Damgård, I., Goldberg, L.A., Halldórsson, M.M., Ingólfsdóttir, A., Walukiewicz, I. (eds.) ICALP 2008. LNCS, vol. 5126, pp. 486–498. Springer, Heidelberg (2008). https://doi.org/10.1007/978-3-540-70583-3_40

15. Mohassel, P., Orobets, O., Riva, B.: Efficient server-aided 2PC for mobile phones. Proc. Privacy Enhanc. Technol. 2016(2), 82–99 (2016)

16. Mohassel, P., Rosulek, M., Zhang, Y.: Fast and secure three-party computation: the garbled circuit approach. In: Proceedings of the 22nd ACM SIGSAC Conference on Computer and Communications Security, pp. 591–602 (2015)

17. Naor, M., Pinkas, B., Sumner, R.: Privacy preserving auctions and mechanism design. In: Proceedings of the 1st ACM Conference on Electronic Commerce, pp. 129–139 (1999)

18. Pass, R., Shi, E., Tramèr, F.: Formal abstractions for attested execution secure processors. In: Coron, J.-S., Nielsen, J.B. (eds.) EUROCRYPT 2017. LNCS, vol. 10210, pp. 260–289. Springer, Cham (2017). https://doi.org/10.1007/978-3-319-56620-7_10

19. Pinkas, B., Schneider, T., Smart, N.P., Williams, S.C.: Secure two-party computation is practical. In: Matsui, M. (ed.) ASIACRYPT 2009. LNCS, vol. 5912, pp. 250–267. Springer, Heidelberg (2009). https://doi.org/10.1007/978-3-642-10366-7_15

20. Wang, X., Malozemoff, A.J., Katz, J.: EMP-toolkit: efficient MultiParty computation toolkit (2016). https://github.com/emp-toolkit/. Accessed 5 Jan 2021

21. Wang, X., Ranellucci, S., Katz, J.: Authenticated garbling and efficient maliciously secure two-party computation. In: Proceedings of the 2017 ACM SIGSAC Conference on Computer and Communications Security, pp. 21–37 (2017)

22. Zahur, S., Rosulek, M., Evans, D.: Two halves make a whole. In: Oswald, E., Fischlin, M. (eds.) EUROCRYPT 2015. LNCS, vol. 9057, pp. 220–250. Springer, Heidelberg (2015). https://doi.org/10.1007/978-3-662-46803-6_8

Polynomial Representation Is Tricky: Maliciously Secure Private Set Intersection Revisited

Aydin Abadi[1]([✉]), Steven J. Murdoch[1], and Thomas Zacharias[2]

[1] University College London, London, England
aydin.abadi@ucl.ac.uk, s.murdoch@ucl.ac.uk
[2] University of Edinburgh, Edinburgh, Scotland
thomas.zacharias@ed.ac.uk

Abstract. Private Set Intersection protocols (PSIs) allow parties to compute the intersection of their private sets, such that nothing about the sets' elements beyond the intersection is revealed. PSIs have a variety of applications, primarily in efficiently supporting data sharing in a privacy-preserving manner. At Eurocrypt 2019, Ghosh and Nilges proposed three efficient PSIs based on the polynomial representation of sets and proved their security against active adversaries. In this work, we show that these three PSIs are susceptible to several serious attacks. The attacks let an adversary (1) learn the correct intersection while making its victim believe that the intersection is empty, (2) learn a certain element of its victim's set beyond the intersection, and (3) delete multiple elements of its victim's input set. We explain why the proofs did not identify these attacks and propose a set of mitigations.

1 Introduction

A Private Set Intersection protocol (PSI) lets mutually distrustful parties compute the intersection of their private sets such that nothing, about the sets' elements, beyond the result is revealed. PSIs have been studied extensively due to their numerous real-world applications to reduce online harm by preserving the Internet users' privacy, to some extent. For instance, they have been used in (a) contact tracing schemes that prevent the further spread of COVID-19 [16], (b) certain Google technologies that find target audiences for marketing campaigns [24] or check compromised credentials [35], (c) online gaming [10], and (d) remote diagnostics [9].

At Eurocrypt 2019, Ghosh and Nilges [20] proposed three PSIs (i.e., two-party, multi-party, and threshold multi-party) that are designed to remain secure against active adversaries. These protocols are efficient as they are primarily based on symmetric-key primitives and polynomial representation of sets, and avoid using zero-knowledge proofs usually utilised in the protocols that consider active adversaries. The three PSIs have been defined and proven secure in the

© Springer Nature Switzerland AG 2021
E. Bertino et al. (Eds.): ESORICS 2021, LNCS 12973, pp. 721–742, 2021.
https://doi.org/10.1007/978-3-030-88428-4_35

well-known Universal Composability (UC) paradigm [12]. To date, their multi-party protocol is the most efficient multi-party PSI designed to remain secure in the presence of active adversaries.

Our Contributions. We identify *three attacks* that can be mounted on all the three "maliciously secure" PSIs in [20]. In particular, we show an adversary can successfully carry out the following attacks:

1. Attack 1: learning the result, i.e., sets' intersection, while making its honest counter-party believe that there is no element in the intersection.
2. Attack 2: learning a certain element (not necessarily in its set) of the honest party's set beyond the sets' intersection.
3. Attack 3: deleting multiple elements of its counter-party's input set.

Our attacks' analysis indicates that Attack 1 always succeeds (except with a negligible probability), also Attacks 2 and 3 succeed with a non-negligible probability (when the sets' universe size is polynomial or constant in the security parameter). We show that these attacks are feasible in terms of cost to the attacker. We identify several flaws in the protocols' *design* and *proofs* that led to the attacks remaining undetected. Accordingly, we propose a set of candidate *mitigations*. At a high level, most of the issues we identify are the result of a single case: *inappropriate use of polynomial representation*. This representation has been widely used in various cryptographic schemes beyond PSIs, such as in secret sharing [34], error-correcting codes [33], e-voting [27], or secure multi-party computation [25]. Nevertheless, our findings provide evidence that special care should be taken when polynomial representation is utilised in protocols that should remain secure against active adversaries. We hope our work will be used as a reference point by future researchers who need to integrate this representation into their protocols, to avoid (at least) the issues we highlight.

2   Related Work

PSIs were first introduced by Freedman *et al.* [17] that were mainly based on Paillier homomorphic encryption and polynomial representation of sets. Since then, numerous PSIs have been proposed. They can be broadly divided into *traditional* and *delegated* categories.

In *traditional* PSIs, e.g., protocols in [7,13,14,17,20–23,29,30,37], data owners interactively compute the result using their local data. Currently, the protocol of Kolesnikov *et al.* in [29] is the fastest two-party PSI, which is secure against a semi-honest (or passive) adversary. It relies on an oblivious pseudorandom function and Cuckoo hashing. Recently, Pinkas *et al.* in [31] proposed an efficient PSI that is secure against a stronger (i.e., malicious/active) adversary. It is based on Cuckoo hashing, oblivious transfer, and a new data structure called probe-and-XOR of strings. Moreover, there have been efforts to improve the communication cost in PSIs, through fully homomorphic encryption and batching techniques [14] and additive homomorphic encryption, oblivious linear function evaluation, and polynomial representation [21]. Very recently, a new PSI has been proposed that achieves a better balance between communication and computation costs [13]. It relies on oblivious transfer, hashing, and symmetric-key primitives. Since the above schemes support only two parties, researchers proposed multi-party PSIs to let more than two parties efficiently compute the intersection. The multi-party PSIs in [22,23,30] have been designed to be secure against passive adversaries. To date, the protocol in [30] is the most efficient multi-party PSI secure against passive adversaries. Also, the multi-party PSIs in [7,20,37] have been designed to remain secure against active adversaries. There are two PSIs proposed in [37]. As their authors admit, one of them leaks (non-trivial) information and another one requires the involvement of two non-colluding servers, which is a strong assumption. Also, the PSI of Efraim *et al.* in [7] offers a weaker security guarantee and has a higher communication cost than the multi-party PSI in [20] does (as the authors admit). To date, the multi-party protocol in [20] is the most efficient multi-party PSI designed to be secure against active adversaries.

In *delegated* PSIs, e.g., in [1,3–5,26,36,38], an additional third party is involved to perform a part of the intersection computation and/or to store parties' encrypted sets. They can be divided into schemes that support (a) one-off delegation, e.g., in [26,38], that requires parties to re-encode their data locally for each computation and (b) repeated delegation, e.g., in [1,3–5,36], that lets parties reuse their outsourced data without locally re-encoding it for each computation.

3   Background

In this section, we present the definitions and techniques used in the PSIs proposed by Ghosh and Nilges [20]. This work proposes three PSIs: (a) two-party, (b) multi-party, and (c) threshold multi-party. These PSIs use (a) polynomials to represent set elements, which lets parties compute the intersection in a privacy-preserving way, and (b) Oblivious Polynomial Addition (OPA) to let parties randomise each other's input polynomials. The OPA itself uses two primitives; namely, Oblivious Linear Function Evaluation (OLE) and enhanced OLE.

For the sake of simplicity, we will focus on and analyse the two-party PSI. In the following sections, we describe three attacks that can be mounted on it. The other two PSIs are susceptible to similar attacks. We use κ as the security parameter. As in the original work, we consider finite fields $\mathbb{F}$ that are exponential in the size of the security parameter, κ. A function is negligible (in κ) if it is asymptotically smaller than any inverse polynomial function. By $[n]$ we denote the set $\{1, \ldots, n\}$. The size of a set S is denoted by $|S|$ and set elements' universe is denoted by $\mathcal{U}$. We say the universe size, $|\mathcal{U}|$, is: (a) large, if $|\mathcal{U}|$ is exponential in κ, (b) medium, if $|\mathcal{U}|$ is polynomial in κ, and (c) small, if $|\mathcal{U}|$ is constant in κ.

3.1   Representing Sets by Polynomials

The idea of using a polynomial to represent a set's elements was proposed by Freedman *et al.* in [17]. Since then, the idea has been widely used, e.g., in [1,3–

5,21,28]. In this representation, set elements $S = \{s_1, ..., s_d\}$ are defined over $\mathbb{F}$ and set S is represented as a polynomial of form: $\mathbf{p}(x) = \prod_{i=1}^{d}(x - s_i)$, where $\mathbf{p}(x) \in \mathbb{F}[X]$ and $\mathbb{F}[X]$ is a polynomial ring. Often a polynomial, $\mathbf{p}(x)$, of degree d is represented in the "coefficient form" as follows: $\mathbf{p}(x) = a_0 + a_1 \cdot x + ... + a_d \cdot x^d$. The form $\prod_{i=1}^{d}(x - s_i)$ is a special case of the coefficient form. As shown in [8,28], for two sets $S^{(A)}$ and $S^{(B)}$ represented by polynomials $\mathbf{p}_A$ and $\mathbf{p}_B$ respectively, their product, which is polynomial $\mathbf{p}_A \cdot \mathbf{p}_B$, represents the set union, while their greatest common divisor, $gcd(\mathbf{p}_A, \mathbf{p}_B)$, represents the set intersection. For two degree-d polynomials $\mathbf{p}_A$ and $\mathbf{p}_B$, and two degree-d random polynomials $\boldsymbol{\gamma}_A$ and $\boldsymbol{\gamma}_B$ whose coefficients are picked uniformly at random from the field, it is proven in [8,28] that: $\boldsymbol{\theta} = \boldsymbol{\gamma}_A \cdot \mathbf{p}_A + \boldsymbol{\gamma}_B \cdot \mathbf{p}_B = \boldsymbol{\mu} \cdot gcd(\mathbf{p}_A, \mathbf{p}_B)$, where $\boldsymbol{\mu}$ is a uniformly random polynomial, and polynomial $\boldsymbol{\theta}$ contains only information about the elements in $S^{(A)} \cap S^{(B)}$, and contains no information about other elements in $S^{(A)}$ or $S^{(B)}$.

Polynomials can also be represented in the "point-value form". In particular, a polynomial $\mathbf{p}(x)$ of degree d can be represented as a set of m ($m > d$) point-value pairs $\{(x_1, y_1), ..., (x_m, y_m)\}$ such that all x_i are distinct non-zero points and $y_i = \mathbf{p}(x_i)$ for all i, $1 \leq i \leq m$. If x_i are fixed, then we can represent polynomials as a vector $\vec{\boldsymbol{y}} = [y_1, ..., y_m]$. Polynomials in point-value form have been used previously in PSIs [1,3–5,21,30]. A polynomial in this form can be converted into coefficient form via polynomial interpolation, e.g., using Lagrange interpolation [6]. Moreover, one can add or multiply two polynomials, in point-value form, by adding or multiplying their corresponding y-coordinates. In this case, the polynomial interpolated from the result would be the two polynomials' addition or product. Often PSIs that use this representation assume that all x_i are picked from $\mathbb{F} \setminus \mathcal{U}$.

3.2   Oblivious Linear Function Evaluation

Oblivious Linear function Evaluation (OLE) is a two-party protocol that involves a sender and receiver. In OLE, the sender has two inputs $a, b \in \mathbb{F}$ and the receiver has input $c \in \mathbb{F}$, and the protocol allows the receiver to learn only $s = a \cdot c + b \in \mathbb{F}$, while the sender learns nothing. The PSIs in [20] that we analyse in this paper, sometimes invoke the OPA primitive, explained in the following section, which itself makes a black-box call to the OLE in [18]. Since the OLE has been proven secure in the UC framework, other caller protocols can make calls to OLE's ideal functionality, denoted by $\mathcal{F}_{\text{OLE}}$. The OPA also uses an enhanced version of the above OLE. The enhanced OLE and its ideal functionality are denoted by OLE$^+$ and $\mathcal{F}_{\text{OLE}^+}$, respectively. OLE$^+$ ensures that the receiver cannot learn anything about the sender's inputs, even if it sets its input to 0. We refers readers to the paper's full version [2], for $\mathcal{F}_{\text{OLE}}$, $\mathcal{F}_{\text{OLE}^+}$, and OLE$^+$.

3.3   Oblivious Polynomial Addition

Ghosh and Nilges [20] propose Oblivious Polynomial Addition (OPA) which can be seen as a variant of OLE, where parties' inputs are polynomials (instead of the field's elements). In particular, in this scheme two parties are involved, sender and receiver. The sender has two polynomials $\mathbf{r}$ and $\mathbf{u}$ and the receiver has a single polynomial, $\mathbf{p}$. The scheme allows the two parties to compute a linear combination of their inputs, i.e., $\mathbf{s} = \mathbf{p} \cdot \mathbf{r} + \mathbf{u}$, and lets the receiver learn the result, $\mathbf{s}$. The security of OPA requires that (a) nothing about the sender's input polynomials is leaked to the receiver (even if the receiver inserts a 0 polynomial), (b) nothing about the receiver's input polynomial and result is leaked to the sender, and (c) a malicious party who acts arbitrarily is detected by its counter-party, with a high probability. The OPA is presented in Fig. 1.

- **Public parameters**: a vector of distinct non-zero elements: $\vec{x} = [x_1, \ldots, x_{2d+1}]$
1. **Computing** $\mathbf{s}(x) = \mathbf{p}(x) \cdot \mathbf{r}(x) + \mathbf{u}(x)$, where the sender has $\mathbf{r}(x), \mathbf{u}(x)$ and the receiver has $\mathbf{p}(x)$ as inputs, $deg(\mathbf{u}) \leq 2d, deg(\mathbf{r}) = d, deg(\mathbf{p}) \leq d$.
   (a) Sender: $\forall j, 1 \leq j \leq 2d + 1$, computes $r_j = \mathbf{r}(x_j)$ and $u_j = \mathbf{u}(x_j)$. Then, it inserts (r_j, u_j) into $\mathcal{F}^{(j)}_{\text{OLE}^+}$.
   (b) Receiver: $\forall j, 1 \leq j \leq 2d + 1$, computes $p_j = \mathbf{p}(x_j)$. Then, it inserts every p_j into $\mathcal{F}^{(j)}_{\text{OLE}^+}$ and receives $s_j = p_j \cdot r_j + u_j$. It interpolates a polynomial $\mathbf{s}(x)$ using pairs (x_j, s_j). Next, it checks if $deg(\mathbf{s}) \leq 2d$. Otherwise, it aborts.
2. **Consistency check**:
   (a) Sender: picks a random $x^* \xleftarrow{\$} \mathbb{F}$, and sends it to the receiver.
   (b) Receiver: picks random values $f, v \xleftarrow{\$} \mathbb{F}$ and inserts them into an instance of $\mathcal{F}_{\text{OLE}}$, denoted by $\mathcal{F}^1_{\text{OLE}}$. It inserts $(\mathbf{p}(x^*), -\mathbf{s}(x^*) + f)$ into another instance of $\mathcal{F}_{\text{OLE}}$, say $\mathcal{F}^2_{\text{OLE}}$.
   (c) Sender: picks a random value $t \xleftarrow{\$} \mathbb{F}$, and inserts it to $\mathcal{F}^1_{\text{OLE}}$ that sends $c = f \cdot t + v$ to the sender. It also inputs $\mathbf{r}(x^*)$ into $\mathcal{F}^2_{\text{OLE}}$ that sends $\bar{f} = \mathbf{r}(x^*) \cdot \mathbf{p}(x^*) - \mathbf{s}(x^*) + f$ to the sender which sums it with $\mathbf{u}(x^*)$. This yields $f' = \mathbf{r}(x^*) \cdot \mathbf{p}(x^*) - \mathbf{s}(x^*) + f + \mathbf{u}(x^*)$. The sender sends f' to the receiver.
   (d) Receiver: It aborts if $f' \neq f$; otherwise, it sends v to the sender.
   (e) Sender: It aborts if $f' \cdot t + v \neq c$.
3. Receiver: picks x_r and runs similar consistency check with the sender.

Fig. 1. Oblivious Polynomial Addition (OPA) protocol [20]

3.4   Two-Party PSI

In this section, we describe the two-party PSI of Ghosh and Nilges [20] that has been designed to be secure against an active adversary. The protocol mainly utilises polynomial representation of sets and OPA. At a high level, in this protocol, each party generates a polynomial that represents its set. After that, each party randomises its counter-party's polynomial. To do so, a party (as a sender) picks two random polynomials and inserts them into the OPA. The other party (as a receiver) inserts into the OPA its polynomial that represents its set; in return, it receives its polynomial in a randomised form. The parties switch their role and run the OPA again. Next, they exchange messages that allow them to find the result (intersection) polynomial whose roots contain the sets' intersection. Each party evaluates the result polynomial at every element of its set and considers the element in the intersection, if the evaluation's result is zero.

To check the result's correctness, the parties participate in an efficient "output verification" phase. In this phase, parties A and B pick random values z and q respectively. Then, a party evaluates its polynomials at its random element (say z) which yields a small set of values. It sends the result to its counter-party, which (a) combines the messages that the other party sent, (b) evaluates the result polynomial at z, (c) checks if the values generated in the previous two steps are equal, and (d) accepts the result if they are equal. The two-party PSI is presented in Fig. 2. There is a minor difference between the two-party PSI presented in [20] and Fig. 2. Namely, in Fig. 2 we replaced the OPA's ideal functionality $\mathcal{F}_{OPA}$ with the actual protocol, OPA. This change (that does not affect the protocol at all) helps clarify the explanation of our attacks.

Each party $I \in \{A, B\}$ has a set $S^{(I)}$, where $m = max(|S^{(A)}|, |S^{(B)}|) + 1$.

1. **PSI Computation**
   (a) Party $I \in \{A, B\}$: represents its set elements (i.e., all $s_j^{(I)} \in S^{(I)}$) as a degree-m polynomial: $\mathbf{p}_I = \boldsymbol{\omega}_I(x) \cdot \prod_{j=1}^{\ddot{o}} (x - s_j^{(I)})$, where $\boldsymbol{\omega}_I(x)$ is a random polynomial and $\ddot{o} = |S^{(I)}|$. Each party $I \in \{A, B\}$ picks three random polynomials: $\mathbf{r}_I, \mathbf{u}_I$ and $\mathbf{r}'_I$, where the degree of $\mathbf{u}_I$ is $2m$ and the degree of $\mathbf{r}_I$ and $\mathbf{r}'_I$ is m.
   (b) The parties invoke OPA where party A inserts $\mathbf{r}_A, \mathbf{u}_A$ and party B inserts $\mathbf{p}_B$ to OPA, which outputs $\mathbf{s}_B = \mathbf{p}_B \cdot \mathbf{r}_A + \mathbf{u}_A$ to party B.
   (c) The parties again invoke OPA, this time party A inserts $\mathbf{p}_A$ while party B inserts $\mathbf{r}_B, \mathbf{u}_B$ to OPA that outputs $\mathbf{s}_A = \mathbf{p}_A \cdot \mathbf{r}_B + \mathbf{u}_B$ to party A.
   (d) Party A sends $\mathbf{s}'_A = \mathbf{s}_A - \mathbf{u}_A + \mathbf{p}_A \cdot \mathbf{r}'_A$ to party B.
   (e) Party B computes: $\mathbf{p}_\cap = \mathbf{s}'_A + \mathbf{s}_B + \mathbf{p}_B \cdot \mathbf{r}'_B - \mathbf{u}_B = \mathbf{p}_A \cdot \mathbf{r}'_A + \mathbf{p}_A \cdot \mathbf{r}_B + \mathbf{p}_B \cdot \mathbf{r}_A + \mathbf{p}_B \cdot \mathbf{r}'_B$. It sends the result polynomial, $\mathbf{p}_\cap$, to party A.
   (f) To find the intersection, party I evaluates polynomial $\mathbf{p}_\cap$ at every element of its set, $s_j^{(I)}$, and considers the element in the intersection if $\mathbf{p}_\cap(s_j^{(I)}) = 0$.

2. **Output Verification**
   (a) Parties A and B pick random values $z, q \xleftarrow{\$} \mathbb{F}$ respectively and send them to their counter-party.
   (b) Party B sends $\alpha_B = \mathbf{p}_B(z)$, $\beta_B = \mathbf{r}_B(z)$, and $\delta_B = \mathbf{r}'_B(z)$ to party A.
   (c) Party A checks if: $\mathbf{p}_\cap(z) \stackrel{?}{=} \mathbf{p}_A(z) \cdot (\beta_B + \mathbf{r}'_A(z)) + \alpha_B \cdot (\mathbf{r}_A(z) + \delta_B)$.
   (d) Party A sends $\alpha_A = \mathbf{p}_A(q)$, $\beta_A = \mathbf{r}_A(q)$, and $\delta_A = \mathbf{r}'_A(q)$ to party B.
   (e) Party B checks if: $\mathbf{p}_\cap(q) \stackrel{?}{=} \mathbf{p}_B(q) \cdot (\beta_A + \mathbf{r}'_B(q)) + \alpha_A \cdot (\mathbf{r}_B(q) + \delta_A)$.

Fig. 2. Two-party PSI in [20]

4   Attack 1: Making Honest Party Learn Incorrect Result

In this section, we describe an attack scenario in which an adversary crafts certain messages in the PSI, that ultimately would allow that party to learn the actual result, i.e., the intersection, while (a) making its honest counter-party believe that there is no element in the intersection, and (b) not having misbehaviour detected. Thus, this attack allows the adversary to affect the PSI's correctness. The issue stems from a flaw in the protocol that lets a party include in the result a polynomial which is *not re-randomized* by its counter-party.

4.1   Attack Description

Without loss of generality, we let party B be malicious. Our focus will be on the two-party PSI, presented in Fig. 2. Both parties honestly perform steps 1a–1d. However, B in step 1e, as part of computing polynomial $\mathbf{p}_\cap$, instead of summing $\mathbf{s}'_A$ with the product $\mathbf{p}_B \cdot \mathbf{r}'_B$, it sums $\mathbf{s}'_A$ with another random polynomial $\mathbf{r}''_B$ of degree $2m$ and then honestly adds the rest of the polynomials. So, now $\mathbf{p}_\cap$ is:

$$\begin{aligned} \tilde{\mathbf{p}}_\cap &= \mathbf{s}'_A + \mathbf{s}_B + \mathbf{r}''_B - \mathbf{u}_B \\ &= \mathbf{p}_A \cdot \mathbf{r}'_A + \mathbf{p}_A \cdot \mathbf{r}_B + \mathbf{p}_B \cdot \mathbf{r}_A + \mathbf{r}''_B \end{aligned} \qquad (1)$$

Party B sends $\tilde{\mathbf{p}}_\cap$ to A, in step 1e. In the "output verification" phase, both parties honestly take step 2a, to generate z and q. In step 2b, B honestly computes $\alpha_B = \mathbf{p}_B(z)$, $\beta_B = \mathbf{r}_B(z)$, but it sets $\delta_B = \mathbf{r}''_B(z) \cdot (\alpha_B)^{-1}$, instead of setting $\delta_B = \mathbf{r}'_B(z)$. It sends α_B, β_B, and δ_B to A which in step 2c:

1. evaluates the result polynomial, $\tilde{\mathbf{p}}_\cap$, at z that yields:

$$\tilde{\mathbf{p}}_\cap(z) = \mathbf{p}_A(z) \cdot \mathbf{r}'_A(z) + \mathbf{p}_A(z) \cdot \mathbf{r}_B(z) + \mathbf{p}_B(z) \cdot \mathbf{r}_A(z) + \mathbf{r}''_B(z)$$

2. generates value ζ as below (given messages α_B, β_B, and δ_B, sent by party B):

$$\begin{aligned} \zeta &= \mathbf{p}_A(z) \cdot (\beta_B + \mathbf{r}'_A(z)) + \alpha_B \cdot (\mathbf{r}_A(z) + \delta_B) \\ &= \mathbf{p}_A(z) \cdot (\mathbf{r}_B(z) + \mathbf{r}'_A(z)) + \mathbf{p}_B(z) \cdot (\mathbf{r}_A(z) + \mathbf{r}''_B(z) \cdot (\alpha_B)^{-1}) \\ &= \mathbf{p}_A(z) \cdot \mathbf{r}_B(z) + \mathbf{p}_A(z) \cdot \mathbf{r}'_A(z) + \mathbf{p}_B(z) \cdot \mathbf{r}_A(z) + \mathbf{r}''_B(z) \end{aligned}$$

3. checks if $\tilde{\mathbf{p}}_\cap(z)$ equals ζ, i.e., $\tilde{\mathbf{p}}_\cap(z) \stackrel{?}{=} \zeta$. If passed, then it accepts the result.

4.2   Attack Analysis

By using the above approach, malicious party B can pass the verification in the PSI and convince A to accept the manipulated result. Malicious party B can generate the correct result (i.e., sets' intersection) *for itself*, by honestly computing $\mathbf{p}_\cap$ in step 1e and following the protocol in step 1f. However, given manipulated result $\tilde{\mathbf{p}}_\cap$, presented in Eq. (1), honest party A cannot learn the actual sets' intersection, for the following reason. Let us rewrite the manipulated result as $\tilde{\mathbf{p}}_\cap = \gamma + \mathbf{r}''_B$, where $\gamma = \mathbf{p}_A \cdot \mathbf{r}'_A + \mathbf{p}_A \cdot \mathbf{r}_B + \mathbf{p}_B \cdot \mathbf{r}_A$. Note that polynomial γ encodes the actual result, as its roots contain the intersection of the sets. But, $\mathbf{r}''_B$ is a random polynomial of degree $2m$, so the probability that its roots contain all elements in the intersection is negligible in κ. In particular, the said probability is

$\frac{1}{|\mathbb{F}|^h}$, where h is the intersection cardinality (for a formal analysis, we refer readers to our paper's full version [2]). This means that the set of roots of polynomial $\tilde{\mathbf{p}}_\cap = \boldsymbol{\gamma} + \mathbf{r}''_B$ does not contain all common roots of both polynomials $\boldsymbol{\gamma}$ and $\mathbf{r}'_B$, except with a negligible probability. Thus, the manipulated polynomial, $\tilde{\mathbf{p}}_\cap$, does not represent the intersection of the sets. Accordingly, party A, which does not know $\mathbf{r}'_B$, cannot learn the correct result and the malicious party can succeed with a high probability, $Pr_1 = 1 - \frac{1}{|\mathbb{F}|^h}$. Attack 1 is efficient, as it requires the adversary to perform only $2m + 1$ extra modular additions and multiplications in total. We also examined the protocol's security proof. The inspection shows that the lack of analysis of the case where $\delta_B \neq \mathbf{r}'_B(z)$ in the proof, led to Attack 1. We refer readers to Appendix A.1 for a detailed analysis of the proof's flaw.

Extension to Multi-party Protocol. The security issue, identified in this section, is inherited by the multi-party PSI, presented in Fig. 10 in [20], because it uses the same verification mechanism. Specifically, in the multi-party PSI, a malicious party (except the central party, P_0) in step 3 of phase 3, replaces $\mathbf{p}_i \cdot \mathbf{r}'_i$ with $\mathbf{r}'_i$. To pass the verification, in step 2 of phase 5, it sets $\delta_i = \mathbf{r}'_i(x^*) \cdot (\alpha_i)^{-1}$, instead of setting $\delta_i = \mathbf{r}'_i(x^*)$, where x^* is a random value generated in step 1 of phase 5. For central party P_0 to mount a similar attack, it follows the instructions provided above for malicious party B. Since the threshold multi-party PSI makes a black-box call to the multi-party PSI, a similar attack we described in this section (and later sections) can be mounted to the threshold scheme too.

4.3 Candidate Mitigation

A closer look at the above attack reveals that the main source of the issue is the use of the polynomials' product $\mathbf{p}_I \cdot \mathbf{r}'_I$, in steps 1d and 1e, where the product is not re-randomized by the other party, and is a part of the result polynomial. Fortunately, the above issue can be efficiently addressed, for the two-party PSI, if the protocol is slightly adjusted. Nonetheless, addressing the issue for the multi-party PSI would require each party to interact with all other parties and so would add significant costs. The remedy for the two-party PSI relies on the idea that (1) each party randomizes its input polynomial, (2) each party re-randomizes its counter-party's input polynomial, and (3) the result polynomial consists of the sum of only the re-randomized input polynomials.

Next, we present the modified two-party PSI. We first describe the "PSI computation" phase. In step (a) party $I \in \{A, B\}$: represents its set elements $s_j^{(I)} \in S^{(I)}$ as a degree-m polynomial: $\mathbf{p}_I = \boldsymbol{\omega}_I(x) \cdot \prod_{j=1}^{\ddot{o}} (x - s_j^{(I)})$, where $\boldsymbol{\omega}_I(x)$ is a random polynomial and $\ddot{o} = |S^{(I)}|$. Each party I picks three random polynomials: $\mathbf{r}_I, \mathbf{u}_I$ and $\mathbf{r}'_I$, where the degree of $\mathbf{u}_I$ is $3m$ and the degree of $\mathbf{r}_I$ and $\mathbf{r}'_I$ is m. It also computes $\bar{\mathbf{p}}_I = \mathbf{p}_I \cdot \mathbf{r}'_I$. In step (b) the parties invoke OPA where party A inserts $\mathbf{r}_A, \mathbf{u}_A$ and party B inserts $\bar{\mathbf{p}}_B$ to OPA, which outputs $\mathbf{s}_B = \bar{\mathbf{p}}_B \cdot \mathbf{r}_A + \mathbf{u}_A$ to B. In step (c) the parties invoke OPA again, this time A inserts $\bar{\mathbf{p}}_A$ while B inserts

$\mathbf{r}_B, \mathbf{u}_B$ to OPA that outputs $\mathbf{s}_A = \bar{\mathbf{p}}_A \cdot \mathbf{r}_B + \mathbf{u}_B$ to A. In step (d) party A sends $\mathbf{s}'_A = \mathbf{s}_A - \mathbf{u}_A$ to B. In step (e) party B computes: $\mathbf{p}_\cap = \mathbf{s}'_A + \mathbf{s}_B - \mathbf{u}_B = \bar{\mathbf{p}}_A \cdot \mathbf{r}_B + \bar{\mathbf{p}}_B \cdot \mathbf{r}_A$. It sends $\mathbf{p}_\cap$ to A. In step (f) to find the intersection, party I evaluates polynomial $\mathbf{p}_\cap$ at every element of its set, $s_j^{(I)}$, and considers the element in the intersection if $\mathbf{p}_\cap(s_j^{(I)}) = 0$. Now we move to the "output verification" phase. In step (a) parties A and B pick random values $z, q \xleftarrow{\$} \mathbb{F}$ respectively and send them to their counter-party. In step (b) party B sends $\alpha_B = \bar{\mathbf{p}}_B(z)$ and $\beta_B = \mathbf{r}_B(z)$, to A. In step (c) party A checks if: $\mathbf{p}_\cap(z) \stackrel{?}{=} \bar{\mathbf{p}}_A(z) \cdot \beta_B + \alpha_B \cdot \mathbf{r}_A(z)$. In step (d) party A sends $\alpha_A = \bar{\mathbf{p}}_A(q)$ and $\beta_A = \mathbf{r}_A(q)$ to B. In step (e) party B checks if: $\mathbf{p}_\cap(q) \stackrel{?}{=} \bar{\mathbf{p}}_B(q) \cdot \beta_A + \alpha_A \cdot \mathbf{r}_B(q)$. In short, the scheme is now secure because (1) $\mathbf{p}_\cap$ leaks nothing beyond the intersection, (2) neither party knows its counter-party's random polynomials $\mathbf{r}_I, \mathbf{r}'_I$ and $\boldsymbol{\omega}_I$, (3) the evaluation of random polynomial $\boldsymbol{\omega}_I$ at a random point yields a random value, and (4) the result polynomial is the sum of only re-randomized input polynomials. In our paper's full version [2], we outline how the solution can be used for the multi-party PSI.

5   Attack 2: Learning Honest Party's Element Beyond the Intersection

In this section, we describe an attack scenario in which a malicious party in the PSI exploits the OPA as a subroutine to check if a certain element (not necessarily an element of its set) exists or not in its honest counter-party's set.

The attack violates the protocol's privacy by allowing the adversary to (a) learn an element of the honest party's set beyond the sets' intersection or (b) efficiently establish the presence or absence of an element in the honest party's set without completing the PSI and without allowing the honest party to learn anything about the other party's set. The source of the issue is that, in the OPA, a sender is given the ability to *independently* pick a random value. This lets a malicious sender pick a value of its choice, x'^*, and check if that element is in its honest counter-party's set, i.e., if it is a root of the honest party's input polynomial. In the attack, if x'^* is in the other party's set, then the adversary would *always* pass verifications; but, if x'^* is not in that set, then it would be detected. In the latter case, the adversary still learns the additional information that x'^* is not in its counter-party's set. For the sake of simplicity, in the attack's description below, we focus on a worst-case scenario where the adversary has no background knowledge of its counter-party's set, so it picks x'^* uniformly at random from $\mathcal{U}$. As we will show later, the adversary can conclude that x'^* is in the other party's set and escape from being detected with non-negligible probability, even if the element x'^* is picked randomly from $\mathcal{U}$, when the universe size is medium or small.

5.1   Attack Description

Consider the case where malicious party A guesses an element, $x'^* \xleftarrow{\$} \mathcal{U}$, of honest party B's set, $S^{(B)}$. To evaluate its guess, A participates in the PSI with B. A follows steps 1a and 1b of Fig. 2, and accordingly invokes the OPA. However, it deviates from some of the instructions in the OPA. In particular, both parties honestly take steps 1a and 1b of Fig. 1, where B's input, $\mathbf{p}$, is a polynomial that represents its set elements. But, in step 2a of Fig. 1, A instead of picking a uniformly random value, $x^* \xleftarrow{\$} \mathbb{F}$, uses x'^*, and sends that value to B which (given x'^*) follows the protocol in step 2b of Fig. 1. In step 2c of Fig. 1, A instead of inserting $\mathbf{r}(x'^*)$ to $\mathcal{F}^2_{\text{OLE}}$, it inserts an arbitrary value, w', to $\mathcal{F}^2_{\text{OLE}}$, where $w' \neq \mathbf{r}(x'^*)$. In this case, $\mathcal{F}^2_{\text{OLE}}$ outputs $\bar{f} = w' \cdot \mathbf{p}(x'^*) - \mathbf{s}(x'^*) + f$ to A which adds the output with $\mathbf{u}(x'^*)$, resulting in:

$$\begin{aligned} f' &= w' \cdot \mathbf{p}(x'^*) - \mathbf{s}(x'^*) + f + \mathbf{u}(x'^*) \\ &= w' \cdot \mathbf{p}(x'^*) - \mathbf{p}(x'^*) \cdot \mathbf{r}(x'^*) + f \end{aligned} \tag{2}$$

Both parties A and B honestly follow the rest of the OPA. If A correctly guesses the set element, then it holds that $\mathbf{p}(x'^*) = 0$, because the element would be a root of polynomial $\mathbf{p}$ which represents the set. If $\mathbf{p}(x'^*) = 0$, then by Eq. (2) it holds that $f' = f$. Therefore, the adversary can pass the check in step 2d of Fig. 1 and at this point can conclude that x'^* is in B's set.

5.2   Attack Analysis

In the PSI, when the adversary concludes that x'^* is in B's set, it can (a) honestly take the rest of the steps or (b) avoid doing so. In the former case, the adversary learns the intersection and finds out the guessed element is in the receiver's set, while the honest party learns only the intersection. In the latter case, it learns a single element of the honest party's set without completing the PSI that saves it costs too, while the honest party learns nothing, not even the intersection. So, in either case, the successful adversary learns more than its counter-party does. Note that a malicious B can also carry out the same attack as it is allowed to pick a (random) value of its choice in phase 3 of Fig. 1.

Recall, x'^* is picked uniformly at random from $\mathcal{U}$ and if x'^* is in the receiver's set, then the adversary can always pass the OPA's verification. So, the probability that it can confirm x'^* is in the other party's set and escape from being detected depends on the size of $\mathcal{U}$ and the set's cardinality. Specifically, the probability is $Pr_2 = \frac{|S^{(B)}|}{|\mathcal{U}|}$. The adversary can also find out x'^* is *not* in the other party's set with probability $Pr'_2 = 1 - \frac{|S^{(B)}|}{|\mathcal{U}|}$. In the majority of PSIs, there is no assumption made on the size of $\mathcal{U}$, e.g., in [1,3–5,13,14,20,26,29]. The universe size can be large, medium, or even small; for instance, the universe size of temperature, salary, age, and medical treatment is small [11,15]. Hence, the above adversary can confirm x'^* is in the other party's set without being caught with non-negligible probability, when the universe size is medium or small, whereas that probability would be only negligible if the universe size is large. Also, when the adversary possesses background knowledge of its counter-party's set, it can increase the above probability. The background knowledge could be a small set of elements likely to be in the other party's set. In this case, the adversary picks

x'^* from this set to mount the attack; this is in principle akin to the well-known online dictionary attack. Interestingly, Attack 2 does not impose any additional cost to the adversary. This attack was not identified in the protocol's security proof because the proof does not analyse the case where an adversary in the "consistency check" deviates from the protocol and still passes the verification. We refer readers to Appendix A.2 for further discussion on the proof's flaw.

Extension to Multi-party Protocol. In the multi-party PSI, each party $P \in \{P_1, ..., P_{n-1}\}$ separately participates in the OPA along with the central party, P_0. This means a malicious party P can use the above attack to check whether P_0 has a certain element. Similarly, P_0 can carry out the attack. The central party's attack will have more severe repercussions than P's attack, because in each run of the PSI, the central party can interact with and attack more parties (i.e., $n - 1$ parties) and accordingly can learn more information.

5.3   Candidate Mitigations

One may adjust the protocol such that once an honest receiver finds out $\mathbf{p}(x'^*) = 0$ it aborts, in step 2b of Fig. 1. However, this behavior itself would reveal to the malicious sender that it has correctly guessed the element. The above issue can be tackled by letting the parties run a coin-tossing protocol (secure against active adversaries) to compute x^*, which would add a small cost.

6   Attack 3: Deleting Honest Party's Set Elements

In this section, we show how an adversary can delete certain elements of its counter-party's input set during the PSI computation, which affects the protocol's correctness and privacy. Briefly, the attack lets a successful adversary conclude that a certain *set of elements* exist in its victim's set without letting the victim find those elements in the intersection. The probability that the adversary succeeds without being detected is non-negligible when set elements' universe size is medium or small. The main source of the issue is the use of *point-value* (polynomial) representation of sets. Before we elaborate on the attack, we present the following theorem that is in the core of the adversary's strategy in order to successfully mount its attack. We refer readers to Appendix B for the theorem's formal statement and proof.

Theorem 1 (informal). *A set of y-coordinates of a polynomial can be multiplied by a set of non-zero values, such that the polynomial interpolated from the product misses a specific root of the original polynomial.*

6.1   Attack Description

We first focus on deleting *a single element*. Later, we will show that the malicious party can delete *multiple elements*. We split the attack into three phases (a) set manipulation, (b) passing OPA's verification, and (c) passing PSI's verification.

Phase (a): Set Manipulation. This phase involves both the PSI and OPA. Assume that malicious party A guesses at least one of party B's set elements, say $s_1^{(B)}$, and wants to delete it from B's input. Similar to Attack 2, we assume $s_1^{(B)}$ is picked uniformly at random from $\mathcal{U}$. Loosely speaking, the idea behind the attack is that while the adversary takes steps of the OPA, as the PSI's subroutine, it also generates a *multiplicative inverse* of (y-coordinates of a polynomial representing) $s_1^{(B)}$ and delicately uses the inverse as part of its input. This ultimately cancels out the same element encoded in its counter-party's polynomial that is inserted into the same OPA. In particular, malicious party A honestly follows the PSI in step 1a to generate polynomials $\mathbf{p}_A, \mathbf{u}_A$, and $\mathbf{r}'_A$, with an exception; namely, now it picks a random polynomial, $\bar{\mathbf{r}}_A$, of degree $m - 1$ (instead of picking $\mathbf{r}_A$ of degree m). Then, in step 1b, party A sends $\bar{\mathbf{r}}_A$ and $\mathbf{u}_A$ to the OPA. Next, A performs as follows in step 1a of Fig. 1.

(i) evaluates $\bar{\mathbf{r}}_A$ at every element $x_j \in \vec{\boldsymbol{x}} = [x_1, ..., x_{2d+1}]$. This results in a vector of y-coordinates: $\vec{\boldsymbol{q}}_1 = [\bar{\mathbf{r}}_A(x_1), ..., \bar{\mathbf{r}}_A(x_{2d+1})]$.

(ii) constructs another polynomial of the following form: $x - s_1^{(B)}$. Recall, $s_1^{(B)}$ is the element it guessed. It evaluates the polynomial at every element x_j. This results in a vector of y-coordinates: $[(x_1 - s_1^{(B)}), ..., (x_{2d+1} - s_1^{(B)})]$.

(iii) generates the multiplicative inverse of each y-coordinate, that was computed in step (ii). This yields $\vec{\boldsymbol{q}}_2 = [(x_1 - s_1^{(B)})^{-1}, ..., (x_{2d+1} - s_1^{(B)})^{-1}]$.

(iv) multiplies the elements of vectors $\vec{\boldsymbol{q}}_1$ and $\vec{\boldsymbol{q}}_2$, component-wise. This yields $\vec{\boldsymbol{q}}_3 = [\bar{\mathbf{r}}_A(x_1) \cdot (x_1 - s_1^{(B)})^{-1}, ..., \bar{\mathbf{r}}_A(x_{2d+1}) \cdot (x_{2d+1} - s_1^{(B)})^{-1}]$.

(v) evaluates random polynomial $\mathbf{u}_A$, generated honestly in step 1a, at every element x_j. This results in $\vec{\boldsymbol{q}}_4 = [\mathbf{u}_A(x_1), ..., \mathbf{u}_A(x_{2d+1})]$.

(vi) sends every pair $(q_{3,j}, q_{4,j})$ to $\mathcal{F}_{\text{OLE+}}^{(j)}$, where $q_{3,j} \in \vec{\boldsymbol{q}}_3$ and $q_{4,j} \in \vec{\boldsymbol{q}}_4$.

This means that instead of sending $\mathbf{r}_A(x_j)$, malicious party A now sends $q_{3,j} = \bar{\mathbf{r}}_A(x_j) \cdot (x_j - s_1^{(B)})^{-1}$ to $\mathcal{F}_{\text{OLE+}}^{(j)}$. In this case, in step 1b of Fig. 1, honest party B (who inserted values $\mathbf{p}_B(x_j)$ into $\mathcal{F}_{\text{OLE+}}^{(j)}$) receives the following values from $\mathcal{F}_{\text{OLE+}}^{(j)}$. For every $j, 1 \leq j \leq 2d + 1$:

$$y_j = \mathbf{p}_B(x_j) \cdot q_{3,j} + q_{4,j}$$

$$= \underbrace{\left(\boldsymbol{\omega}_B(x_j) \cdot (x_j - s_1^{(B)}) \cdot \prod_{i=2}^{\ddot{o}}(x_j - s_i^{(B)})\right)}_{\mathbf{p}_B(x_j)} \cdot \underbrace{\left(\bar{\mathbf{r}}_A(x_j) \cdot (x_j - s_1^{(B)})^{-1}\right)}_{q_{3,j}} + \underbrace{\mathbf{u}_A(x_j)}_{q_{4,j}}$$

$$= \left(\boldsymbol{\omega}_B(x_j) \cdot \prod_{i=2}^{\ddot{o}}(x_j - s_i^{(B)})\right) \cdot \left(\bar{\mathbf{r}}_A(x_j)\right) + \mathbf{u}_A(x_j)$$

(3)

In the same step, party B uses pairs (x_j, y_j), $j \in [2d + 1]$, to interpolate a polynomial, $\mathbf{s}'_B$, that has the following form.

$$\mathbf{s}'_B = \left(\boldsymbol{\omega}_B(x) \cdot \prod_{i=2}^{\ddot{o}}(x - s_i^{(B)})\right) \cdot \left(\bar{\mathbf{r}}_A(x)\right) + \mathbf{u}_A(x)$$

(4)

Note that in the PSI, in step 1b of Fig. 2, honest party B will receive polynomial $\mathbf{s}'_B$ as the output of the OPA (if malicious party A manages to pass the OPA's verification; we will show it does). Furthermore, each value $(x_j - s_1^{(B)}) \cdot \prod_{i=2}^{\ddot{o}}(x_j - s_i^{(B)})$ in Eq. (3) has the same structure as each μ_j has in Theorem 1 (in Appendix B). Hence, according to Eqs. (3) and (4) and Theorem 1, malicious party A has managed to remove $s_1^{(B)}$ from roots of $\mathbf{p}_B$ used in the above step. This ultimately leads to the elimination of that element from the final result, i.e., the sets' intersection. To make that happen, A follows the PSI in steps 1c and 1d of Fig. 2 by honestly computing $\mathbf{s}'_A = \mathbf{s}_A - \mathbf{u}_A + \mathbf{p}_A \cdot \mathbf{r}'_A$, and sending $\mathbf{s}'_A$ to B. Given polynomials $\mathbf{s}'_B$ and $\mathbf{s}'_A$, party B, in step 1e of Fig. 2, follows the protocol and computes the result polynomial (presented below) that is supposed to encode the sets' intersection.

$$
\begin{aligned}
\mathbf{p}_\cap &= \mathbf{s}'_A + \mathbf{s}'_B + \mathbf{p}_B \cdot \mathbf{r}'_B - \mathbf{u}_B \\
&= \mathbf{p}_A \cdot \mathbf{r}'_A + \mathbf{p}_A \cdot \mathbf{r}_B + \left(\boldsymbol{\omega}_B \cdot \prod_{i=2}^{\ddot{o}}(x - s_i^{(B)}) \right) \cdot \bar{\mathbf{r}}_A + \mathbf{p}_B \cdot \mathbf{r}'_B
\end{aligned}
\tag{5}
$$

Nevertheless, as it is evident in Eq. (5), the result polynomial's roots do not include element $s_1^{(B)}$ with a high probability, even if both parties' sets contain it. Because the roots of polynomial $\left(\boldsymbol{\omega}_B \cdot \prod_{i=2}^{\ddot{o}}(x - s_i^{(B)}) \right)$ lack that element, due to malicious party A's manipulation described above.

For malicious party A to fully succeed, it also needs to pass two verifications, one in the OPA and the other in the PSI. Below, we explain how it can do so.

Phase (b): Passing OPA's Verification. This phase involves only the OPA. Since we have already covered steps 1a and 1b in the OPA (in the previous phase description) we will focus only on the "consistency check" in this protocol. Parties A and B honestly follow the OPA in steps 2a and 2b. So, malicious party A (as the sender) in step 2a honestly picks a random value x^* and sends it to honest party B (as the receiver). Then, B, in step 2b, picks random values f, v and inserts them into $\mathcal{F}^1_{\mathrm{OLE}}$. Party B inserts $(\mathbf{p}_B(x^*), -\mathbf{s}'_B(x^*) + f)$ into $\mathcal{F}^2_{\mathrm{OLE}}$. Recall, $\mathbf{s}'_B$ is the polynomial which was defined in Eq. (4). Party A in step 2c honestly picks a random value, t, and inserts it to $\mathcal{F}^1_{\mathrm{OLE}}$ that sends $c = f \cdot t + v$ back to the same party. But, A in the same step, sends $\bar{\mathbf{r}}_A(x^*) \cdot (x^* - s_1^{(B)})^{-1}$, instead of $\mathbf{r}_A(x^*)$, to $\mathcal{F}^2_{\mathrm{OLE}}$ that returns the following value to A.

$$\bar{f} = \bar{\mathbf{r}}_A(x^*) \cdot (x^* - s_1^{(B)})^{-1} \cdot \mathbf{p}_B(x^*) - \mathbf{s}'_B(x^*) + f$$

$$= \bar{\mathbf{r}}_A(x^*) \cdot (x^* - s_1^{(B)})^{-1} \cdot \underbrace{\left(\boldsymbol{\omega}_B(x^*) \cdot (x^* - s_1^{(B)}) \cdot \prod_{i=2}^{\ddot{o}} (x^* - s_i^{(B)}) \right)}_{\mathbf{p}_B(x^*)} - \mathbf{s}'_B(x^*) + f$$

$$= \bar{\mathbf{r}}_A(x^*) \cdot \left(\boldsymbol{\omega}_B(x^*) \cdot \prod_{i=2}^{\ddot{o}} (x^* - s_i^{(B)}) \right) - \mathbf{s}'_B(x^*) + f$$

$$= -\mathbf{u}_A(x^*) + f \tag{6}$$

Recall, polynomial $\mathbf{p}_B$, that was inserted by B, encodes all set elements of B, including $s_1^{(B)}$, whereas polynomial $\mathbf{s}'_B$ misses that specific element due to the party A's manipulation in Eq. (3). However, as it is indicated in Eq. (6), party A has managed to remove $x^* - s_1^{(B)}$ from $\mathbf{p}_B(x^*)$ too. This will let A escape from being detected, because the result (i.e., $\bar{f} = -\mathbf{u}_A(x^*) + f$) is what an honest party A would have computed. Malicious party A completes step 2c honestly, by adding $\mathbf{u}_A(x^*)$ to $\bar{f}$ (i.e., it computes $f' = \bar{f} + \mathbf{u}_A(x^*)$) and sending f' to B, which checks f' equals the random value, f, it initially picked in step 2b. By Eq. (6), $f' = \bar{f} + \mathbf{u}_A(x^*) = f$ holds; therefore, malicious party A has managed to pass this verification.

Phase (c): Passing PSI's Verification. Next, we show how malicious party A can also pass the verification in the PSI, i.e., in step 2d in Fig. 2. Our focus will be on the "output verification" in the PSI. At a high level, to pass this verification, A uses a similar trick that is used to pass the verification in the OPA. Specifically, in step 2a, both parties honestly agree on two values z and q. Then, in step 2b, party B honestly computes α_B, β_B, and δ_B and sends them to A which ignores the values and skips step 2c. Malicious party A, in step 2d, honestly generates $\alpha_A = \mathbf{p}_A(q)$ and $\delta_A = \mathbf{r}'_A(q)$; however, instead of setting $\beta_A = \mathbf{r}_A(q)$, it sets $\beta_A = \bar{\mathbf{r}}_A(q) \cdot (q - s_1^{(B)})^{-1}$. It sends α_A, δ_A, and β_A to B which acts honestly in step 2e. In particular, it:

1. evaluates the result polynomial, $\mathbf{p}_\cap$, at q which yields:

$$\mathbf{p}_\cap(q) = \mathbf{p}_A(q) \cdot \mathbf{r}'_A(q) + \mathbf{p}_A(q) \cdot \mathbf{r}_B(q) + \left(\boldsymbol{\omega}_B(q) \cdot \prod_{i=2}^{\ddot{o}} (q - s_i^{(B)}) \right) \cdot \bar{\mathbf{r}}_A(q) + \mathbf{p}_B(q) \cdot \mathbf{r}'_B(q)$$

2. generates value τ as below (given the three messages, sent by party A):

$$\tau = \mathbf{p}_B(q) \cdot (\beta_A + \mathbf{r}'_B(q)) + \alpha_A \cdot (\mathbf{r}_B(q) + \delta_A)$$

$$= \left(\boldsymbol{\omega}_B(q) \cdot \overset{\ddot{o}}{\underset{i=2}{\prod}}(q - s_i^{(B)}) \right) \cdot \bar{\mathbf{r}}_A(q) + \mathbf{p}_B(q) \cdot \mathbf{r}'_B(q) + \alpha_A \cdot \mathbf{r}_B(q) + \alpha_A \cdot \delta_A$$

$$= \left(\boldsymbol{\omega}_B(q) \cdot \overset{\ddot{o}}{\underset{i=2}{\prod}}(q - s_i^{(B)}) \right) \cdot \bar{\mathbf{r}}_A(q) + \mathbf{p}_B(q) \cdot \mathbf{r}'_B(q) + \mathbf{p}_A(q) \cdot \mathbf{r}_B(q) + \mathbf{p}_A(q) \cdot \mathbf{r}'_A(q)$$

3. checks if $\mathbf{p}_\cap(q)$ equals τ (i.e., $\mathbf{p}_\cap(q) \overset{?}{=} \tau$) and accepts the result, if the check passes.

As indicated above, it holds $\mathbf{p}_\cap(q) = \tau$. Hence, malicious party A can pass the verification in the PSI and convince B to accept the manipulated result.

Deleting Multiple Elements. Now we outline how malicious party A can delete *multiple elements* from its counter-party's set during the PSI. Let $S' = \{s_1^{(B)}, ..., s_k^{(B)}\}$ be a set of elements that malicious party A wants to delete from B's set, where $k \leq m$, every element $s_i^{(B)} \in S'$ is picked uniformly at random from $\mathcal{U}$. In the "set manipulation" phase, in the PSI step 1a, party A picks a random polynomial $\bar{\mathbf{r}}_A$ that now has a degree $m - k$. It performs as before in the rest of the same step. In step (ii), it constructs a polynomial that now has the form: $\prod_{i=1}^{k}(x - s_i^{(B)})$. In the same step, it evaluates the polynomial at every element x_j, which yields $[\prod_{i=1}^{k}(x_1 - s_i^{(B)}), ..., \prod_{i=1}^{k}(x_{2d+1} - s_i^{(B)})]$. It takes the rest of steps (iii)-(vi) as previously described in the set manipulation phase. The "passing OPA's verification" phase remains unchanged with the exception that, in (the OPA) step 2c, party A now sends $\bar{\mathbf{r}}_A(x^*) \cdot \prod_{i=1}^{k}(x^* - s_i^{(B)})^{-1}$ to $\mathcal{F}_{\text{OLE}}^2$. Similarly, the "passing PSI's verification" phase remains the same as before, with a difference that, in (the PSI) step 2d, party A now sets $\beta_A = \bar{\mathbf{r}}_A(q) \cdot \prod_{i=1}^{k}(q - s_i^{(B)})^{-1}$.

6.2   Attack Analysis

A trivial way for an adversary to delete certain elements from the intersection is to delete those elements from its own contributed set. However, there is a major difference between this trivial approach and Attack 3, in terms of the amount of information it learns. Specifically, if the adversary succeeds in Attack 3, it would conclude that its victim has all the deleted elements in its local set. On the contrary, it cannot learn such information by taking the above trivial approach. Moreover, there is a big difference between attacks 2 and 3, in terms of the amount of information the adversary learns. Namely, in the former it learns a *single* element while in the latter it learns *multiple* elements of its victim's set.

Recall, in Attack 3, the adversary always manages to pass the verifications in phases (b) and (c) if it correctly guesses $s_1^{(B)}$. So, its probability of success throughout Attack 3 boils down to correctly guessing that $s_1^{(B)}$ is in its counterparty's set. To compute that probability we can use the same analysis used for Attack 2 (in Sect. 5.2). As a result, the probability that the adversary successfully deletes a single element is $Pr_3 = \frac{|S^{(B)}|}{|\mathcal{U}|}$; in general, the probability that it can delete k elements is $Pr_3' = \frac{\prod\limits_{i=0}^{k-1} |S^{(B)}|-i}{|\mathcal{U}|^k}$. The adversary can succeed to delete a constant number of elements, k, with a non-negligible probability when the universe is of medium or small size, while that probability is negligible when the universe is of large size. Background knowledge, about the other party's set, would benefit the adversary in this attack too. Attack 3 is efficient, as it only imposes $4m + 6$ extra modular additions and multiplications to the adversary when it deletes a single element. The main two flaws in the protocols' proofs that led to Attack 3 is that, in the OPA's proof, the definition of a malformed input has been limited to only two cases (i.e., polynomial of incorrect degree or zero-polynomial); also, in the PSI's proof, it is assumed the only way the adversary can change an original value is via the addition operation, so the multiplication is never analysed. We refer readers to Appendix A.3 for a detailed discussion on the above flaws.

Extension to Multi-party Protocol. The above attack can also be applied to the multi-party PSI, because it uses the same OPA and verification mechanisms as the two-party PSI uses. Therefore, each malicious party $P \in \{P_1, ..., P_{n-1}\}$ can delete an honest central party's set element(s) or a malicious centralised party can delete set element(s) of every honest P, without being detected.

6.3   Candidate Mitigation

The primary cause of the vulnerability discussed is the use of point-value polynomial representation in the OPA. Specifically, during polynomial multiplication in the OPA where polynomials are presented in point-value form, an adversary can craft its input polynomial such that when it is multiplied by an honest party's polynomial, the product polynomial (after interpolation) misses a certain root. Therefore, it is natural to ask: *can the issue be avoided if polynomials in the coefficient form are used in the OPA?* This is indeed the case. Specifically, if the OPA requires the input polynomials to be in coefficient form, then regardless of how the adversary constructs its input polynomial, the product of the two parties' polynomials, generated in the OPA, preserves both polynomials' roots. We refer readers to the paper's full version [2] for a formal statement and proof. The above adjustment imposes to the OPA additional computation cost $O(m^2)$ that stems from multiplying two polynomials in coefficient form.[1] Thus, the

---

[1] To lower the polynomial multiplication cost to $O(m \log_2 m)$, one may use Fast Fourier Transform (FFT). However, as FFT uses point-value polynomial representation, further security analysis is required to ensure the attack would not be enabled again.

computation complexity of the two-party and multi-party PSIs would be higher. Specifically, it would be $O(m^2)$ for two-party and $O(n \cdot m^2)$ for multi-party PSIs, instead of $O(m \cdot \log m)$ and $O(n \cdot m \cdot \log m)$ as in the original protocol [20].

7   Conclusion and Future Work

Private set intersection (PSI) is a vital protocol with various real-world applications. At Eurocrypt 2019, Gosh and Nilges [20] proposed three PSIs: (a) two-party, (b) multi-party, and (c) threshold multi-party. To date, their multi-party protocol is the most efficient multi-party PSI designed to remain secure against active adversaries. In this work, we identified three attacks that can be mounted on all of these PSIs. The attacks let an adversary (1) learn the intersection while making its counter-party believe the intersection is empty, (2) learn a certain element of the honest party's set beyond the intersection, and (3) delete multiple elements of its counter-party's input set. We also identified various flaws in the protocols' design and security proofs and proposed a set of mitigations.

Our observation is that in all three attacks an adversary exploits two features of the protocols' design; namely, (a) the polynomial representation of sets and (b) polynomial-based consistency check. Our analysis indicated that the attacks could have been detected if, in the protocols' security proofs, there was a comprehensive study of (i) all checks, (ii) simulators' design, and (iii) malformed inputs' definition. We conclude that special care should be taken in the design and proof of PSIs that use the combination of the two aforementioned features.

Future research could investigate how the security of other protocols (e.g., noisy polynomial addition in [21]) that already used the schemes proposed in [20] could be affected by our findings. While our proposed mitigations add relatively low cost to the two-party PSI, they scale quadratically with the number of participants in the multi-party case. Designing efficient multi-party PSIs, secure against active adversaries, with linear costs is another interesting research line.

Acknowledgments. Aydin Abadi is supported by REPHRAIN: The National Research Centre on Privacy, Harm Reduction and Adversarial Influence Online, under UKRI grant: EP/V011189/1. Steven J. Murdoch is supported by The Royal Society under grant UF160505. Thomas Zacharias is supported by the Horizon 2020 project # 780477 (PRIViLEDGE).

A   Identified Flaws In The Security Proofs

Below, we briefly explain a set of flaws we identified in the security proofs of the paper's conference [20] and full [19] versions. These flaws made the three attacks undetected. We categorise the flaws in three classes based on their relevance to each attack. For the sake of simplicity, we exclude the hat symbol, " ˆ ", used in the original proofs. See our paper's full version [2] for a more detailed analysis.

A.1   Class 1: Not All Checks Have Been Included

In this section, we describe a flaw in the proof of two-party PSI (page 20 in [19]) that lets the environment use Attack 1 to distinguish the two worlds. Briefly, the flaw is that the proof does not consider the case where $\delta_B^* \neq \mathbf{r}'_B(z)$. Before we elaborate on it, we highlight two typos in "Hybrid" 1; namely, $\alpha_A^* \neq \mathbf{p}_A(z)$ and $\beta_A^* \neq \mathbf{r}_A(z)$ should have been $\alpha_B^* \neq \mathbf{p}_B(z)$ and $\beta_B^* \neq \mathbf{r}_B(z)$ respectively, as the proof is for corrupt party B. In Hybrid 2, it is stated that "an environment distinguishing Hybrid 1 and 2 must manage to send $\mathbf{p}_\cap^*$ such that $\mathbf{p}_\cap^* \neq \mathbf{p}_A \cdot (\mathbf{r}_B + \mathbf{r}'_A) + \mathbf{p}_B \cdot (\mathbf{r}'_B + \mathbf{r}_A)$ while passing the check in Step 5 [of Fig. 9] with non-negligible probability." The proof shows that the check fails *only* in the cases where $\alpha_B^* \neq \mathbf{p}_B(z)$ and $\beta_B^* \neq \mathbf{r}_B(z)$; therefore, $\delta_B^* \neq \mathbf{r}'_B(z)$ has been left out of the proof. The lack of such analysis leads to the following issue. As we have shown, the check does not fail for certain $\mathbf{p}_\cap$ and δ_B such that $\mathbf{p}_\cap \neq \mathbf{p}_A \cdot (\mathbf{r}_B + \mathbf{r}'_A) + \mathbf{p}_B \cdot (\mathbf{r}'_B + \mathbf{r}_A)$ and $\delta_B \neq \mathbf{r}'_B(z)$. So, the adversary can pass the check with a high probability in the real world (or Hybrid 0). The simulator, in Hybrid 2, detects this inconsistency (i.e., $\delta_B^* \neq \mathbf{r}'_B(z)$) according to Fig. 11 in [19]. But, the simulator in Hybrid 1 cannot detect it, as it only aborts if $\alpha_B^* \neq \mathbf{p}_B(z)$ or $\beta_B^* \neq \mathbf{r}_B(z)$. Thus, Hybrids 1 and 2 (likewise Hybrids 0 and 2) are distinguishable by the environment.

A.2   Class 2: Incomplete Simulator

In the proof of Lemma 4.1, i.e., OPA's security, in the paper's conference version [20], it is stated that "the only possibility for an environment to distinguish between the simulation and the real protocol is by succeeding in answering the check while using a malformed input, i.e. a polynomial of incorrect degree or 0-polynomials." We argue that this is not the only possible case. As we indicated in Attack 2, it is possible the adversary (in the real world) in the "consistency check" phase, deviates from the protocol and still passes the verification. This will ultimately let the environment distinguish the two worlds. Note, the proof should have included the simulation of the "consistency check" phase. Accordingly, the proof does not capture the case where w' of the form $w' \neq \mathbf{r}(x'^*)$ is used by the adversary. In the simulation of the consistency check, the simulator can detect when it is given $w' \neq \mathbf{r}(x'^*)$, as it has already extracted polynomial $\mathbf{r}$ from the adversary. But, in the real world, as we have shown, the adversary can pass the check when $w' \neq \mathbf{r}(x'^*)$ and a certain value, x'^*, is used in this phase. Hence, the environment can distinguish the two worlds. This issue arises because the proof does not analyse the case where the check, in the consistency check phase, is passed but $w' \neq \mathbf{r}(x'^*)$ is used in this phase.

A.3   Class 3: Incomplete Definition Of Malformed Input

Recall, the proof of Lemma 4.1 considers a malformed input if an input polynomial is (i) of incorrect degree or (ii) zero. The issue is that the proof shows only in these two cases the environment cannot distinguish the two worlds. We argue that an input can be malformed without satisfying conditions (i) or (ii). Similar to the description of Attack 3, let a corrupt sender (for all $j \in [2d + 1]$) send $q_{3,j} = \bar{\mathbf{r}}_A(x_j) \cdot (x_j - s_1^{(B)})^{-1}$ to $\mathcal{F}_{\text{OLE}^+}^{(j)}$ in the ideal world. This lets the simulator obtain all $q_{3,j}$ and interpolate a polynomial, $\mathbf{q}$. There would be two cases: (1) $deg(\mathbf{q}) > d$, or (2) $deg(\mathbf{q}) \leq d$. In case (1), the simulator aborts. But in the real protocol (in step 1b of Fig. 1) the honest party never aborts. Because, in general, polynomial $\mathbf{s}$ interpolated from $2d + 1$ pairs (x_j, s_j) always has degree at most $2d$ by Theorem 2. This issue lets the environment distinguish the two worlds. Now we move on to case (2). In the ideal world, in the consistency check phase, the simulator of the OPA is given random value x^* and $w'' = \bar{\mathbf{r}}_A(x^*) \cdot (x^* - s_1^{(B)})^{-1}$ and wants to check $w'' \stackrel{?}{=} \mathbf{q}(x^*)$. Note, the equation may not always hold; because factors $(x_j - s_1^{(B)})^{-1}$ of y-coordinates $q_{3,j}$ from which $\mathbf{q}$ was interpolated, are not directly generated by evaluating a polynomial at x_j's. The probability that $w'' = \mathbf{q}(x^*)$ depends on the choice of x^*. If the equation holds, then the simulator does not abort; also, the honest party does not abort as we showed in Attack 3. This is problematic, as the attack has been successfully mounted without being detected in both worlds. If $w'' \neq \mathbf{q}(x^*)$, the simulator aborts, but the honest party does not abort, as the adversary can pass the consistency check. So, the environment can distinguish the two worlds. This issue arises because, in the proof, the definition of a malformed input has been limited to only the above conditions (i) and (ii), and the proof never analyses the case where the check is passed while w'' (s.t., $w'' \neq \mathbf{r}(x'^*)$) is sent to $\mathcal{F}_{\text{OLE}}^2$.

The adversary in Attack 3, can pass the PSI's verification too. The issue is that in the PSI's proof (i.e., proof of Theorem 5.1 in [20]) when A is corrupt, the case where β_A is not the result of evaluating truly random polynomial $\mathbf{r}_A$ at z (i.e., $\beta_A \neq \mathbf{r}_A(z)$) is never analysed in detail and also it is assumed that the only way the adversary changes the original value is via a modular addition (i.e., $\alpha_A + e$); so, a modular multiplication is never considered as a part of the attack. But, as we showed, the adversary can multiply its input y-coordinates by certain values to affect the result's correctness and pass the verification.

B   Attack 3 Theorems

We first restate Theorem 2 that will be used by the main one, i.e., Theorem 1.

Theorem 2 *(Uniqueness of interpolating polynomial [32]). Let $\vec{\boldsymbol{x}} = [x_1, \ldots, x_v]$ be a vector of non-zero distinct elements. For v arbitrary values: $y_1, \ldots, y_v$ there is a unique polynomial: $\boldsymbol{\tau}$, of degree at most $v - 1$ such that: $\forall j, 1 \leq j \leq v : \boldsymbol{\tau}(x_j) = y_j$, where $x_j, y_j \in \mathbb{F}$.*

Informally, Theorem 1 states that a set of y-coordinates of a polynomial can be multiplied by a set of non-zero values, such that the polynomial interpolated from the product misses a specific root of the original polynomial.

Theorem 1. *Let $\vec{\boldsymbol{x}} = [x_1, \ldots, x_v]$ be a vector of non-zero distinct elements. Let $\boldsymbol{\mu} = \prod_{i=1}^{\ddot{o}} (x - e_i) \in \mathbb{F}[X]$ be a degree $\ddot{o} < v$ polynomial with $\ddot{o}$ distinct roots*

$e_1, \ldots, e_{\ddot{o}}$, and let $\mu_j = \boldsymbol{\mu}(x_j)$, where $1 \leq j \leq v$. For some $c \in [\ddot{o}]$ such that $e_c \notin \{x_1, \ldots, x_v\}$, let $\boldsymbol{\mu}'$ be a degree $\ddot{o} - 1$ polynomial interpolated from pairs $(x_1, \mu_1 \cdot (x_1 - e_c)^{-1}), \ldots, (x_v, \mu_v \cdot (x_v - e_c)^{-1})$. Then, $\boldsymbol{\mu}'$ will not have e_c as root, i.e. $\boldsymbol{\mu}'(e_c) \neq 0$.

Proof. For the sake of simplicity and without loss of generality, let $c = 1$. We can rewrite polynomial $\boldsymbol{\mu}$ as $\boldsymbol{\mu}(x) = (x - e_1) \cdot \prod_{i=2}^{\ddot{o}} (x - e_i)$. Then, every μ_j $(1 \leq j \leq v)$ can be written as: $\mu_j = (x_j - e_1) \cdot \prod_{i=2}^{\ddot{o}} (x_j - e_i)$. Accordingly, for every j, the product $\alpha_j := \mu_j \cdot (x_j - e_1)^{-1}$ has the form: $\alpha_j = \mu_j \cdot (x_j - e_1)^{-1} = \prod_{i=2}^{\ddot{o}} (x_j - e_i)$. Let $\boldsymbol{\mu}''$ be a degree $\ddot{o} - 1$ polynomial with $\ddot{o} - 1$ distinct roots identical to the roots of $\boldsymbol{\mu}$ excluding e_1, i.e., $\boldsymbol{\mu}''(e_1) \neq 0$. By the Polynomial Remainder Theorem, $\boldsymbol{\mu}''$ can be written as $\boldsymbol{\mu}''(x) = K \cdot \prod_{i=2}^{\ddot{o}} (x - e_i)$, where $K \in \mathbb{F} \setminus \{0\}$. So, it holds that $\forall j \in [v] : \boldsymbol{\mu}''(x_j) = K \cdot \prod_{i=2}^{\ddot{o}} (x_j - e_i) = K \cdot \alpha_j$. This implies that $\boldsymbol{\mu}''$ is a degree $\ddot{o} - 1$ polynomial interpolated from $(x_1, K \cdot \alpha_1), \ldots, (x_v, K \cdot \alpha_v)$. By its definition, the polynomial $\boldsymbol{\mu}'$ is interpolated from the pairs $(x_1, \alpha_1), \ldots, (x_v, \alpha_v)$. Thus, $K \cdot \boldsymbol{\mu}'$ is another degree $\ddot{o} - 1$ polynomial interpolated from $(x_1, K \cdot \alpha_1), \ldots, (x_v, K \cdot \alpha_v)$. Due to Theorem 2, we have that $\boldsymbol{\mu}'' = K \cdot \boldsymbol{\mu}'$, so $\boldsymbol{\mu}''(e_1) = K \cdot \boldsymbol{\mu}'(e_1) \Rightarrow \boldsymbol{\mu}'(e_1) = K^{-1} \cdot \boldsymbol{\mu}''(e_1)$. We also know that $K^{-1} \neq 0$ and $\boldsymbol{\mu}''(e_1) \neq 0$. Since $\mathbb{F}$ is an integral domain, it follows that $\boldsymbol{\mu}'(e_1) = K^{-1} \cdot \boldsymbol{\mu}''(e_1) \neq 0$.

$\square$

References

1. Abadi, A., Terzis, S., Metere, R., Dong, C.: Efficient delegated private set intersection on outsourced private datasets. IEEE TDSC (2018)
2. Abadi, A., Murdoch, S.J., Zacharias, T.: Polynomial representation is tricky: Maliciously secure private set intersection revisited (Full version) (2021). https://eprint.iacr.org/2021/1009.pdf
3. Abadi, A., Terzis, S., Dong, C.: O-PSI: delegated private set intersection on outsourced datasets. In: IFIP SEC (2015)
4. Abadi, A., Terzis, S., Dong, C.: VD-PSI: verifiable delegated private set intersection on outsourced private datasets. In: FC (2016)
5. Abadi, A., Terzis, S., Dong, C.: Feather: Lightweight multi-party updatable delegated private set intersection. IACR Cryptology ePrint Archive (2020)
6. Aho, A.V., Hopcroft, J.E.: The Design and Analysis of Computer Algorithms. Addison-Wesley Longman Publishing Co., Inc., Boston (1974)
7. Ben-Efraim, A., Nissenbaum, O., Omri, E., Paskin-Cherniavsky, A.: Psimple: Practical multiparty maliciously-secure private set intersection, ePrint Archive (2021)
8. Boneh, D., Gentry, C., Halevi, S., Wang, F., Wu, D.J.: Private database queries using somewhat homomorphic encryption. In: ACNS (2013)
9. Brickell, J., Porter, D.E., Shmatikov, V., Witchel, E.: Privacy-preserving remote diagnostics. In: CCS (2007)

10. Bursztein, E., Hamburg, M., Lagarenne, J., Boneh, D.: Openconflict: preventing real time map hacks in online games. In: IEEE S&P (2011)
11. Camenisch, J., Zaverucha, G.M.: Private intersection of certified sets. In: FC (2009)
12. Canetti, R.: Universally composable security: a new paradigm for cryptographic protocols. In: FOCS (2001)
13. Chase, M., Miao, P.: Private set intersection in the internet setting from lightweight oblivious PRF. In: CRYPTO (2020)
14. Chen, H., Laine, K., Rindal, P.: Fast private set intersection from homomorphic encryption. In: CCS (2017)
15. Cristofaro, E.D., Lu, Y., Tsudik, G.: Efficient techniques for privacy-preserving sharing of sensitive information. In: TRUST (2011)
16. Duong, T., Phan, D.H., Trieu, N.: Catalic: delegated PSI cardinality with applications to contact tracing. In: ASIACRYPT (2020)
17. Freedman, M.J., Nissim, K., Pinkas, B.: Efficient private matching and set intersection. In: EUROCRYPT (2004)
18. Ghosh, S., Nielsen, J.B., Nilges, T.: Maliciously secure oblivious linear function evaluation with constant overhead. In: ASIACRYPT (2007)
19. Ghosh, S., Nilges, T.: An algebraic approach to maliciously secure private set intersection (full version). ePrint Archive (2017). https://eprint.iacr.org/2017/1064
20. Ghosh, S., Nilges, T.: An algebraic approach to maliciously secure private set intersection. In: EUROCRYPT (2019)
21. Ghosh, S., Simkin, M.: The communication complexity of threshold private set intersection. In: CRYPTO (2019)
22. Hazay, C., Venkitasubramaniam, M.: Scalable multi-party private set-intersection. In: PKC (2017)
23. Inbar, R., Omri, E., Pinkas, B.: Efficient scalable multiparty private set-intersection via garbled bloom filters. In: SCN (2018)
24. Ion, M., et al.: On deploying secure computing: private intersection-sum-with-cardinality. In: IEEE EuroS&P (2020)
25. Ishai, Y., Kushilevitz, E.: Randomizing polynomials: a new representation with applications to round-efficient secure computation. In: FOCS (2000)
26. Kamara, S., Mohassel, P., Raykova, M., Sadeghian, S.: Scaling private set intersection to billion-element sets. In: FC (2014)
27. Katz, J., Myers, S.A., Ostrovsky, R.: Cryptographic counters and applications to electronic voting. In: EUROCRYPT (2001)
28. Kissner, L., Song, D.X.: Privacy-preserving set operations. In: CRYPTO (2005)
29. Kolesnikov, V., Kumaresan, R., Rosulek, M., Trieu, N.: Efficient batched oblivious PRF with applications to private set intersection. In: CCS (2016)
30. Kolesnikov, V., Matania, N., Pinkas, B., Rosulek, M., Trieu, N.: Practical multi-party private set intersection from symmetric-key techniques. In: CCS (2017)
31. Pinkas, B., Rosulek, M., Trieu, N., Yanai, A.: PSI from PaXoS: fast, malicious private set intersection. In: EUROCRYPT (2020)
32. Quarteroni, A., Sacco, R., Saleri, F.: Numerical Mathematics, vol. 37. Springer Science & Business Media, Heidelberg (2010)
33. Reed, I.S., Solomon, G.: Polynomial codes over certain finite fields. J. Soc. Ind. Appl. Math. **8**(2), 300–304 (1960)
34. Shamir, A.: How to share a secret. Commun. ACM **22**(11), 612–613 (1979)
35. Thomas, K., et al.: Protecting accounts from credential stuffing with password breach alerting. In: USENIX Security (2019)

36. Yang, X., Luo, X., Wang, X.A., Zhang, S.: Improved outsourced private set intersection protocol based on polynomial interpolation. Concurr. Comput. Pract. Exp. (2018)
37. Zhang, E., Liu, F., Lai, Q., Jin, G., Li, Y.: Efficient multi-party private set intersection against malicious adversaries. In: CCSW (2019)
38. Zhao, Y., Chow, S.S.M.: Can you find the one for me? Privacy-preserving match-making via threshold PSI. ePrint Archive (2018)

Posters

RIoTPot: A Modular Hybrid-Interaction IoT/OT Honeypot

Shreyas Srinivasa$^{(\boxtimes)}$, Jens Myrup Pedersen, and Emmanouil Vasilomanolakis

Aalborg University, Aalborg, Denmark
{shsr,jens,emv}@es.aau.dk

Abstract. Honeypots are often used as a proactive attack detection mechanism and as a source of threat intelligence data. However, many honeypots are poorly maintained and cumbersome to extend. Moreover, low-interaction honeypots are prone to fingerprinting attacks due to their limited emulation capabilities. Nonetheless, low-interaction honeypots are essential for environments with limited resources. In this paper, we introduce RIoTPot, a modular and hybrid-interaction honeypot for Internet-of-Things (IoT) and Operational Technology (OT) protocols mainly used in Industrial Control System environments. RIoTPot's modularity comes as a result of plug-n-play container services while its hybrid-interaction capability enables users to switch between low- and high-interaction modes. We deploy RIoTPot on the Internet, receive a large amount of attacks and discuss the results received on both low- and high-interaction modes.

1 Introduction

Honeypots are deceptive systems that simulate a seemingly vulnerable system to gather attacks. Over the years, many honeypot solutions have been proposed that are commonly classified to low-, medium- and high-interaction based on the level of interaction they offer to the adversary [2, 19]. Low- and medium-interaction honeypots, due to their limited emulation capabilities, are prone to honeypot fingerprinting that may limit their scope [18]. Honeypot fingerprinting refers to adversarial methods that allow for the identification of the honeypot nature of a system. Nevertheless, these two classes of honeypots are the most commonly deployed ones. Other common issues with honeypots include the lack of flexibility in extending/adapting them, the absence of support, and limited documentation.

Despite the aforementioned limitations, honeypots are an excellent defensive toolkit, especially with regard to the increasing number of IoT and OT attacks. With such protocols being consistently attacked, in both consumer [7] and commercial environments [5], deception mechanisms like honeypots offer an early warning system and a method to analyse adversaries' techniques [9, 12, 16].

Traditional honeypot simulations may run on virtualized environments like VMs, virtual containers (LXC), or even language-based virtual environments.

© Springer Nature Switzerland AG 2021
E. Bertino et al. (Eds.): ESORICS 2021, LNCS 12973, pp. 745–751, 2021.
https://doi.org/10.1007/978-3-030-88428-4

Kedrowitsch et al. made a first effort to propose the use of containers for honeypots [6]. The authors propose the usage of Linux containers as a platform to develop honeypots and compliment their proposal by comparing the detection methods of popular virtualization platforms against containers. Kedrowitsch et al. conclude that limitations exist in the use of either containers or virtual machines as a honeypot platform. A much recent proposal by Reti et al. introduces the use of container-based deception for honeypots [11]. The authors investigate the possibilities of container-based honeypots and introduce the concept of simulating container-escapes (fake network pivoting outside a container) as a deception technique. Both approaches suggest the use of container systems to achieve ease of deployment. Moreover, many open-source honeypots offer the possibility of a containerized deployment for ease of installation. Nevertheless, besides the aforesaid academic work there are not many actual honeypot implementations that make use of containers. Furthermore, all existing honeypots have a binary interaction level: they are either low-, medium-, or high-interaction [19].

In this paper, we present RIoTPot[1], a honeypot that: *i.)* breaks the traditional binary interaction paradigm, *ii.)* focuses on IoT and OT protocols, and *iii.)* is designed with a modular-by-design architecture. First, the hybrid-interaction level of RIoTPot aims at providing defenders flexibility by giving them the ability to utilize the appropriate interaction level based on their needs and capabilities. For instance, low constrained environments scale better with low interaction components while high interaction comes handy when deeper analysis of attack is required. Second, RIoTPot supports many IoT and OT protocols (i.e., Telnet, SSH, CoAP, Modbus, MQTT), with more to be implemented in the immediate future. At the moment, there are only a few real world honeypot implementations that focus on IoT [9, 15] and even fewer for OT [12, 17]. Lastly, the modularity of the honeypot comes from its architecture; each functionality of the honeypot is a plug-n-play component that can be edited, activated or deactivated based on the user's preferences.

2   RIoTPot Design

RIoTPot features a modular architecture that facilitates quick integration of new protocol simulation modules. A modular software architecture is a structural approach of building software components as modules by separating the the functionality of a program into independent, interchangeable modules, such that each contains everything necessary to execute only one aspect of the desired functionality [8]. Figure 1 shows the high level architecture of RIoTPot. The prominent modules in the architecture are the *RIoTPot core* module, the *packet capture and noise filter* module, the *low-interaction* modules, the *high-interaction* modules, and the *attack database*.

The *RIoTPot core* consists of the required components for the configuration, administration, and orchestration of the honeypot. In particular, the core module provides RIoTPot with all the required parameters at startup. This includes user

---

[1] https://github.com/aau-network-security/riotpot.

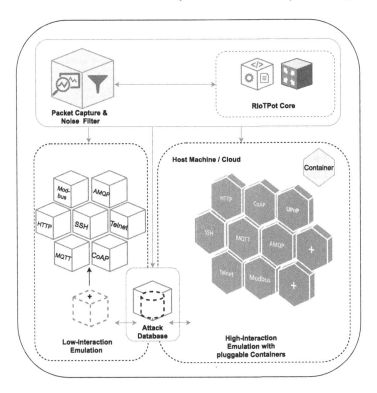

Fig. 1. High level architecture of RIoTPot

preferences for specific protocols, profile simulation, and the desired interaction level. In addition, the core is responsible for the network management for the high-interaction protocol services simulated on containers. The received attack traffic is forwarded to the respective container that hosts the protocol on which the attack was targeted. Furthermore, the core also facilitates the communication between itself and the containers, if hosted on a cloud environment.

For the *Packet capture and noise filter* module the attack capture component is responsible for storing the attack packets as *pcap* files, using *tcpdump*, which can be used for detailed analysis (e.g., deep packet inspection). The noise filter component filters out the traffic received from Internet-wide scanners like Shodan [14] and Censys [3]. This helps the honeypot administrator to concentrate on attacks that matter by removing the noise traffic generated by such services.

The *low-interaction mode* is achieved through independent packages, with each package simulating a specific protocol. RIoTPot is implemented in Go language [4] and facilitates the development of a modular architecture through packages. The packages act as plug-ins that can be added to the honeypot to extend the protocols simulated. For example, the *fakeshell* package emulates a system shell that can be leveraged by the SSH and the Telnet packages. The *fakeshell* package can be extended to include emulation of specific commands.

Furthermore, RIoTPot provides a template that can be used for integration of additional protocols. The *high-interaction mode* is achieved by emulating the protocols as services in container images. Hence, since a container implements the full protocol the honeypot provides the attacker with high interaction capabilities. The containers act as high-interaction modules that offer a full implementation of a protocol. Additional protocol services can be added by integrating containers with the desired protocol services. The hybrid-interaction mode further allows the user to emulate selective protocols on low or high-interaction levels. For example, the user can choose to have SSH in low-interaction mode and MQTT in high-interaction mode.

The *attack database* stores all the attack traffic received on the honeypot. The database is setup as an independent module to ensure data availability even if a honeypot module is down (e.g., due to a crash or DDoS attack). The database is accessible from the low-interaction and high-interaction modules for attack storage.

To sum up, the design of RIoTPot facilitates modularity through packages and containers as plugins. Furthermore, the modular architecture assists the hybrid-interaction model of RIoTPot.

3   Preliminary Results

The honeypot was deployed in both low and high interaction modes on two hosts in our lab. The hosts were assigned a public IP each, under an unfiltered network. We define an attack as any interaction with the honeypot as there is no production value whatsoever. However, we differentiate incoming traffic from well-known crawlers (e.g. Shodan). The attacks on the honeypots were recorded for a period of one week. In the low-interaction variant, the protocols SSH, Telnet, HTTP, MQTT, CoAP and Modbus were simulated through the plug-in packages, while the high-interaction variant simulated the MQTT protocol in a container. In addition to recording the attacks in the database, the hosts also had the *tcpdump* service running in the background to capture the attack packets for comprehensive analysis. A total of 7,587 attacks were observed across all the protocols simulated by RIoTPot.

Figure 2 shows the number of unique attacks received per protocol for a period of one week. MQTT-HI indicates the high-interaction mode of the MQTT protocol. We observe a trend in the number of attacks for all protocols. Furthermore, the number of attacks on the MQTT protocol in the high-interaction mode is higher in comparison to the low-interaction mode. Moreover, we observe recurring sessions from same suspicious actors on the high-interaction mode, that included topic creation, subscription and deletion, and modification of existing messages in topics which have not been observed on the low-interaction mode.

Figure 3 depicts the percentage of attacks from Internet-scanning engines (e.g., Shodan, Censys, Project Sonar [10], and ShadowServer [13]) in comparison to the attacks from suspicious sources. We observe an average of 25% of the total

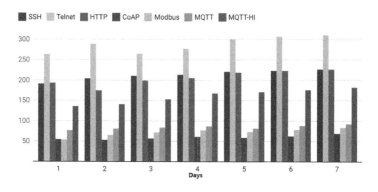

Fig. 2. Number of attacks on protocols per day

traffic originating from 19 common scanning engines[2]. Filtering out such traffic reduces noise and alert data fatigue for the administrators.

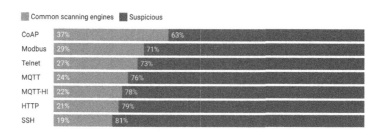

Fig. 3. Attack noise classification in percentage

4 Conclusion

In this paper, we introduce RIoTPot, a honeypot that features a hybrid-interaction model with a modular design for IoT and OT protocols. RIoTPot addresses the issue of limited interaction and flexibility, in addition to ease of deployment. Our preliminary results suggest that the honeypot is attractive to adversaries and is able to distinguish between suspicious traffic (traffic originating from attackers) and common scanning engines (traffic likely coming from Shodan-like systems). As future work, we aim to extend RIoTPot to support more IoT and OT protocols like UPnP, AMQP, XMPP, S7, DNP3, Fieldbus and Profibus. Furthermore, we intend to integrate threat intelligence reporting

---

[2] For a complete list of the supported scanning engines see: https://github.com/aau-network-security/riotpot#12-Noise-Filter.

through STIX to facilitate structured sharing of threat data [1]. Finally, we plan to perform a more extensive evaluation of RIoTPot with an emphasis on ICS environments.

References

1. Barnum, S.: Standardizing cyber threat intelligence information with the structured threat information expression (STIX). Mitre Corp. **11**, 1–22 (2012)
2. Bringer, M.L., Chelmecki, C.A., Fujinoki, H.: A survey: recent advances and future trends in honeypot research. Int. J. Comput. Netw. Inf. Secur. **4**(10), 63 (2012)
3. Censys: Censys search (2021). https://censys.io/
4. Golang: Go language (2021). https://golang.org/
5. Jiang, X., Lora, M., Chattopadhyay, S.: An experimental analysis of security vulnerabilities in industrial IoT devices. ACM Trans. Internet Technol. **20**(2) (2020). https://doi.org/10.1145/3379542
6. Kedrowitsch, A., Yao, D.D., Wang, G., Cameron, K.: A first look: using linux containers for deceptive honeypots. In: Proceedings of the 2017 Workshop on Automated Decision Making for Active Cyber Defense, SafeConfig 2017, pp. 15–22. Association for Computing Machinery, New York (2017). https://doi.org/10.1145/3140368.3140371
7. Mangino, A., Pour, M.S., Bou-Harb, E.: Internet-scale insecurity of consumer internet of things: an empirical measurements perspective. ACM Trans. Manage. Inf. Syst. **11**(4) (2020). https://doi.org/10.1145/3394504
8. Mohammed, M., Elish, M., Qusef, A.: Empirical insight into the context of design patterns: modularity analysis. In: 2016 7th International Conference on Computer Science and Information Technology (CSIT), pp. 1–6 (2016). https://doi.org/10.1109/CSIT.2016.7549474
9. Oosterhof, M.: Cowrie ssh/telnet honeypot (2016). https://github.com/micheloosterhof/cowrie
10. Research, R.: Project sonar (2021). https://www.rapid7.com/research/project-sonar/
11. Reti, D., Becker, N.: Escape the fake: Introducing simulated container-escapes for honeypots (2021)
12. Rist, L., Vestergaard, J., Haslinger, D., Pasquale, A., Smith, J.: Conpot ics/scada honeypot. Honeynet Project (conpot. org) (2013)
13. ShadowServer.org: Shadowserver.org (2021). https://www.shadowserver.org/
14. SHODAN: Shodan (2021). https://www.shodan.io/
15. Vasilomanolakis, E., et al.: This network is infected: hostage-a low-interaction honeypot for mobile devices. In: Proceedings of the Third ACM Workshop on Security and Privacy in Smartphones and Mobile Devices, pp. 43–48 (2013)
16. Vasilomanolakis, E., Karuppayah, S., Mühlhäuser, M., Fischer, M.: Hostage: a mobile honeypot for collaborative defense. In: Proceedings of the 7th International Conference on Security of Information and Networks, SIN 2014, pp. 330–333. Association for Computing Machinery, New York (2014). https://doi.org/10.1145/2659651.2659663
17. Vasilomanolakis, E., Srinivasa, S., Mühlhäuser, M.: Did you really hack a nuclear power plant? An industrial control mobile honeypot. In: 2015 IEEE Conference on Communications and Network Security (CNS), pp. 729–730. IEEE (2015)

18. Vetterl, A., Clayton, R.: Bitter harvest: systematically fingerprinting low- and medium-interaction honeypots at internet scale. In: 12th USENIX Workshop on Offensive Technologies (WOOT 2018). USENIX Association, Baltimore, August 2018. https://www.usenix.org/conference/woot18/presentation/vetterl
19. Zhang, L., Thing, V.: Three decades of deception techniques in active cyber defense - retrospect and outlook. Comput. Secur. **106**, 102288 (2021). https://doi.org/10.1016/j.cose.2021.102288. https://www.sciencedirect.com/science/article/pii/S0167404821001127

Towards Automatically Generating Security Analyses from Machine-Learned Library Models

Maria Kober$^{(\boxtimes)}$ and Steven Arzt

Fraunhofer Institute for Secure Information Technology, Darmstadt, Germany
{maria.kober,steven.arzt}@sit.fraunhofer.de

Abstract. Automatic code vulnerability scanners identify security antipatterns in application code, such as insecure uses of library methods. However, current scanners must regularly be updated manually with new library models, patterns, and corresponding security analyses. We propose a novel, two-phase approach called MOD4SEC for automatically generating static and dynamic code analyses targeting vulnerabilities based on library (mis)usage. In the first phase, we automatically infer semantic properties of libraries on a method and parameter level with supervised machine learning. In the second phase, we combine these models with high-level security policies. We present preliminary results from the first phase of MOD4SEC, where we identify security-relevant methods, with categorical f1-scores between 0.81 and 0.93.

Keywords: Vulnerability scanner · Vulnerability detection · Security analysis · Specialized domain language · Automated analysis · Mod4Sec

1 Introduction and Motivation

Implementation flaws are prevalent in software. While modern platforms and operating systems offer powerful APIs for sensitive security operations such as encryption or authentication, developers often misuse these APIs, leading to numerous vulnerabilities [1, 2]. Manual approaches like penetration tests or code reviews can detect such vulnerabilities but require substantial effort. They are therefore unsuitable for agile development processes with fast release cycles [9]. Automated code scanning [3, 4, 11, 13, 15, 16] can identify known antipatterns in code, but requires the respective patterns. If a scanner has no support for the respective API, i.e., no antipatterns to look for, the security vulnerability remains undetected. Such scanners need to be updated regularly with new antipatterns, which is largely a manual effort. For example, on popular platforms like Android more than 13,700 third-party libraries are used in apps additional to the Java Standard Library and Android SDK, according to our pre-study on 9,373 apps from the 2020 and 2021 Google Play Store. If only considering libraries that are used in at least 10% of Android apps, a code scanner must be kept up-to-date with 65 libraries, yet vulnerabilities regarding other libraries would remain

E. Bertino et al. (Eds.): ESORICS 2021, LNCS 12973, pp. 752–758, 2021.
https://doi.org/10.1007/978-3-030-88428-4

undetected. New library versions may become available in frequencies of several days to months [5, 17], leading to constant requirements for manual maintenance.

In this paper, we present our idea and vision for MOD4SEC, a novel approach for automatically inferring semantic models of individual libraries and platforms, i.e., API specifications, and linking them to security policies for program analyses. Library-agnostic security properties such as "cryptographic keys must not be hard-coded" change rarely. APIs, on the other hand, evolve. We therefore propose to automatically infer specific library models (e.g., "second parameter of method `encrypt()` in class A in library B is a cryptographic key") and match them to library-independent security properties (e.g., "RSA keys must be of 2048 bits or more"). This mapping is then used to automatically generate antipatterns for static and dynamic code analyses. These antipatterns are further processed to generate analysis code, so that scanners can detect violations of the security properties in apps that use libraries for which a model has been inferred.

This paper is organized as follows. Section 2 describes details of our vision. Section 3 presents details on and results of first experiments. Section 4 presents related work. Section 5 concludes this paper and points out future work.

2   Vision

Our vision is to automatically generate semantic models for libraries and platforms using machine learning, and to use these models to link generic security assets (keys, passwords, certificates, etc.) to concrete APIs. Thus, we are able to automatically generate static and dynamic code analyses, thereby reducing manual effort for tool developers and security analysts.

The core idea behind MOD4SEC is that security properties are derived from only a handful of core assets and concepts that usually remain unchanged for years. For example, the concept of a password is the same, regardless of how this password is used (e.g., for authentication or deriving an encryption key using a KDF). Likewise, authentication methods that consume passwords are equivalent from the point of a security scanner, regardless of the target of authentication, even though the APIs may look differently. We therefore propose to identify these generic concepts in implementations and documentations of APIs using machine learning and natural language processing.

In our proposed workflow, a security analyst only needs to reason about problems within the domain of security, fully abstracting from the concrete implementation of applications and programming libraries. The analyst specifies properties in terms of abstract domain knowledge such as "MD-4 must not be used as cryptographic hash function". The link back to code, i.e., identifying what should be checked within an application, is done using the auto-generated library models. As these models are auto-generated, they can easily be updated by the tool developer when new or updated libraries are available.

Figure 1 shows an overview of our approach, which consists of two phases. In the first phase, we generate the library models as explained in Sect. 2.1. In the second phase, we match them with security policies to generate static and dynamic analyses as explained in Sect. 2.2. Additionally, developers can give feedback on the analysis results, increasing the accuracy of the model over time.

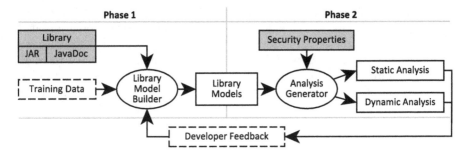

Fig. 1. The two phases of our vision. Input data to generate security analyses is denoted in gray. Data required solely for training is marked by dashed lines (Color figure online).

2.1   Phase 1: Generate Library Models

In the first phase, MOD4SEC uses supervised machine learning to automatically associate library methods and method parameters with pre-defined categories, e.g., "encryption" or "authentication" for methods, and "username", "crypto key" or "filename" for parameters. The learning algorithm learns on a set of implementation JAR files and the corresponding JavaDoc JARs. The resulting *Generic Domain Model*, an integral part of the *Library Model Builder* in Fig. 1, generalizes over all input libraries and is therefore library-agnostic. It can be re-used for classification whenever new or updated libraries become available. Thus, obtaining high-quality training data and training the model is a rare task, if not a one-time effort. Note that we train two different classifiers for method and parameter classification, thereby reducing complexity, as the set of parameter labels is category-specific, e.g., "crypto key" is not within "file access methods".

When classifying a concrete library, MOD4SEC uses the Generic Domain Model and takes the respective library as input. We call the resulting library-specific model, which describes the semantics of the individual methods and parameters inside the library, a *Library Model*. Thus, utilizing MOD4SEC's generic domain model results in one model per provided library and library version, which can seamlessly be integrated into code scanners and used with analyses.

2.2   Phase 2: Generate Security Analyses

In the second phase, MOD4SEC uses the library models to automatically generate static and dynamic code analyses for previously defined security policies. The key idea is to encode security properties in a language that can be mapped to specific functionalities in a particular analysis framework such as Soot [8], and to properties of the library models generated in phase 1 of MOD4SEC.

Table 1. Categorization results on three security categories.

Category	Precision	Recall	F1-score	# Samples
Cryptography	0.92	0.93	0.93	320
Authentication	0.83	0.78	0.81	161
Network/TLS	0.81	0.81	0.81	303
Other	0.99	0.99	0.99	10,412

Our proposed description language SECPLANG is declarative, i.e., it defines which properties should be checked. How properties are evaluated is up to the specific analysis framework. SECPLANG contains basic logic operations, and a small set of predefined functions and predicates, e.g., has(x) to check whether a collection x contains items, and $value_s$(y) resp. $value_d$(y) to statically resp. dynamically retrieve all values of parameter y of a program statement. We further define one auto-generated placeholder for each method parameter label of the library models, e.g., p-key references parameters labeled as cryptographic keys.

For example, the policy "crypto keys must not be hard-coded" can be encoded as encryption[not has ($value_s$(p-key))] for static analyses. During the analysis, all API calls that are of type encryption according to the library models of phase 1 are collected. The placeholders in the Boolean formula are replaced with the respective statement parameters. If the declaration of the API method is, e.g., encrypt(input, key, algorithm), and it is called as encrypt(a, b, c) in the code under analysis, the placeholder p-key in the Boolean formula of the security property is replaced with b because the second argument is the cryptographic key according to the library model. Evaluating the Boolean formula only requires invoking the correct building blocks of the analysis framework. In the example, a value analysis is invoked on variable b, modeled as predefined $value_s$-function in the formula. The predefined has-function checks whether $value_s$ returned at least one value, i.e., there is a hard-coded key.

3 Experiments and Preliminary Results

To evaluate the feasibility of our approach, we implemented a prototype for the first phase of MOD4SEC as described in Sect. 2.1. From the Maven central repository, we obtained cryptography, network, and authentication libraries. We hand-annotated 784 security-relevant methods in the Java Standard Library and in 11 relevant third-party libraries (altogether 3× cryptography, 5× network, 6× authentication), omitting method parameter annotation. We extracted JavaDoc and signatures for 11,196 methods with JavaParser. For supervised machine learning, we transformed input data to bags-of-words and used scikit-learn [12] with one fully connected neural network having one hidden layer with 16 nodes.

Table 1 presents the results of a stratified ten-fold cross-validation on our data set. The precision of MOD4SEC is between 0.81 and 0.99 for different categories. The recall is between 0.78 and 0.99, with an f1-score between 0.81 and 0.99. In

Table 2. Results for five subcategories of cryptography APIs.

Category	Precision	Recall	F1-score	# Samples
Cipher-configuration	0.74	0.90	0.81	61
Crypt. Randomness	1.00	0.88	0.93	8
En- & Decryption	0.75	0.71	0.73	21
Key creation	0.89	0.86	0.88	125
Signatures	0.84	0.72	0.78	29

total, more than three-quarters of all methods are categorized correctly and we are able to correctly identify a high number of security-relevant methods, even when those are a minority in the analyzed code.

To assess whether finer-grained categories are beneficial, we divided the cryptography category into several subcategories as shown in Table 2[1]. All subcategories have a precision between 0.74 and 1.0, and a recall between 0.71 and 0.9. These numbers indicate that it is possible to correctly distinguish individual cryptographic functionalities in libraries, making an essential part of the first phase of MOD4SEC applicable for software analysis.

Note that a simple keyword-search is not sufficient for our purpose. For example, the keyword "key" is present, amongst others, in the context of cryptographic keys, but also in key-value pairs in maps and object builders. When searching through our dataset for "key", we found 903 methods, which is almost thrice as much as there are cryptographic methods of interest and about six times the number of methods related to cryptographic keys, encryption, or decryption.

4   Related Work

Checking applications for specific misuses of security-sensitive APIs is common practice [3, 13, 15, 16]. CogniCrypt [6, 7] further assists developers with automatic code generation for using such APIs. FixDroid [11] evaluates code snippets against a database of known insecure code. PQL [10] allows for declarative queries on code the analyst is familiar with. All of these approaches rely on manually assembled patterns for APIs. In contrast, we propose a general approach for automatically generating analysis rules, based on a library-agnostic semantic domain model. SWAN_ASSIST [14] could be integrated in step 1 of MOD4SEC. It utilizes developer feedback to actively learn security-relevant methods.

5   Conclusion and Future Work

In this paper, we have presented our vision of MOD4SEC for automatically generating static and dynamic code analyses from generic security properties described

---

[1] Due to space limitations, we only include the most relevant subcategories. Hash and MAC APIs, for example, have fewer methods in our sample set.

in our newly introduced API-agnostic language SECPLANG. MOD4SEC uses machine learning for automatically generating library models, which then allow it to map generic security properties to concrete APIs. We presented first experimental results to demonstrate the feasibility of the first phase of our vision.

As future work, we will provide a full implementation and evaluation of our vision, including automatic classification for method parameters using machine learning. We plan to re-evaluate our preliminary results on a larger dataset and aim to increase MOD4SEC's precision and recall. Furthermore, we will extend MOD4SEC with additional categories of methods. We plan to formally describe SECPLANG and extend its scope to more complex security properties. We plan to build an implementation of the analysis generator for static and dynamic analyses on top of the Soot program analysis framework [8].

References

1. Chatzikonstantinou, A., Ntantogian, C., Karopoulos, G., Xenakis, C.: Evaluation of cryptography usage in android applications. In: Proceedings of the 9th EAI International Conference on Bio-inspired Information and Communications Technologies (formerly BIONETICS), pp. 83–90 (2016). https://doi.org/10.4108/eai.3-12-2015.2262471
2. Egele, M., Brumley, D., Fratantonio, Y., Kruegel, C.: An empirical study of cryptographic misuse in android applications. In: Proceedings of the 2013 ACM SIGSAC conference on Computer and communications security, pp. 73–84 (2013). https://doi.org/10.1145/2508859.2516693
3. Fahl, S., Harbach, M., Muders, T., Baumgärtner, L., Freisleben, B., Smith, M.: Why Eve and Mallory love android: an analysis of android SSL (in) security. In: Proceedings of the 2012 ACM Conference on Computer and Communications Security, pp. 50–61 (2012). https://doi.org/10.1145/2382196.2382205
4. Felderer, M., Büchler, M., Johns, M., Brucker, A.D., Breu, R., Pretschner, A.: Security testing: a survey. In: Advances in Computers, vol. 101, pp. 1–51. Elsevier (2016). https://doi.org/10.1016/bs.adcom.2015.11.003
5. Ihara, A., Fujibayashi, D., Suwa, H., Kula, R.G., Matsumoto, K.: Understanding when to adopt a library: a case study on ASF projects. In: Balaguer, F., Di Cosmo, R., Garrido, A., Kon, F., Robles, G., Zacchiroli, S. (eds.) OSS 2017. IAICT, vol. 496, pp. 128–138. Springer, Cham (2017). https://doi.org/10.1007/978-3-319-57735-7_13
6. Krüger, S., et al.: Cognicrypt: supporting developers in using cryptography. In: 2017 32nd IEEE/ACM International Conference on Automated Software Engineering (ASE), pp. 931–936. IEEE (2017)
7. Krüger, S., Späth, J., Ali, K., Bodden, E., Mezini, M.: CrySL: validating correct usage of cryptographic APIs. arXiv preprint arXiv:1710.00564 (2017)
8. Lam, P., Bodden, E., Lhoták, O., Hendren, L.: The soot framework for java program analysis: a retrospective. In: Cetus Users and Compiler Infastructure Workshop (CETUS 2011), October 2011
9. Maqsood, H.M., Bondavalli, A.: Agility of security practices and agile process models: an evaluation of cost for incorporating security in agile process models. In: ENASE 2020, pp. 331–338 (2020). https://doi.org/10.5220/0009356403310338

10. Martin, M., Livshits, B., Lam, M.S.: Finding application errors and security flaws using PQL: a program query language. ACM Sigplan Not. **40**(10), 365–383 (2005)

11. Nguyen, D.C., Wermke, D., Acar, Y., Backes, M., Weir, C., Fahl, S.: A stitch in time: supporting android developers in writing secure code. In: Proceedings of the 2017 ACM SIGSAC Conference on Computer and Communications Security, pp. 1065–1077 (2017). https://doi.org/10.1145/3133956.3133977

12. Pedregosa, F., et al.: Scikit-learn: machine learning in Python. J. Mach. Learn. Res. **12**, 2825–2830 (2011)

13. Piccolboni, L., Di Guglielmo, G., Carloni, L.P., Sethumadhavan, S.: Crylogger: Detecting crypto misuses dynamically. arXiv preprint arXiv:2007.01061 (2020)

14. Piskachev, G., Do, L.N.Q., Johnson, O., Bodden, E.: SwanSwan_assist: semi-automated detection of code-specific, security-relevant methods. In: 2019 34th IEEE/ACM International Conference on Automated Software Engineering (ASE), pp. 1094–1097. IEEE (2019). https://doi.org/10.1109/ASE.2019.00110

15. Saccente, N., Dehlinger, J., Deng, L., Chakraborty, S., Xiong, Y.: Project achilles: a prototype tool for static method-level vulnerability detection of java source code using a recurrent neural network. In: 2019 34th IEEE/ACM International Conference on Automated Software Engineering Workshop (ASEW).,pp. 114–121. IEEE (2019). https://doi.org/10.1109/ASEW.2019.00040

16. Shuai, S., Guowei, D., Tao, G., Tianchang, Y., Chenjie, S.: Modelling analysis and auto-detection of cryptographic misuse in android applications. In: 2014 IEEE 12th International Conference on Dependable, Autonomic and Secure Computing, pp. 75–80. IEEE (2014). https://doi.org/10.1109/DASC.2014.22

17. Suwa, H., Ihara, A., Kula, R.G., Fujibayashi, D., Matsumoto, K.: An analysis of library rollbacks: a case study of java libraries. In: 2017 24th Asia-Pacific Software Engineering Conference Workshops (APSECW), pp. 63–70. IEEE (2017). https://doi.org/10.1109/APSECW.2017.25

Jamming of NB-IoT Synchronisation Signals

Gabriela Morillo$^{(\boxtimes)}$ and Utz Roedig

School of Computer Science and Information Technology, University College Cork,
Cork, Ireland
{g.morillo,u.roedig}@cs.ucc.ie

Abstract. Narrowband-Internet of Things (NB-IoT) is a relatively novel Low Power Wide Area Network (LPWAN) radio technology used to deploy Internet of Things (IoT) infrastructures at scale. It is important that such deployments are resilient to attacks. In this work we describe how interference on the NB-IoT synchronisation signals - the initial communication steps - can be used to implement an effective Denial of Service (DoS) attack. Interference with the synchronisation prevents communication and may also allow an attacker to force a device to connect with a specific base station.

1 Introduction

Narrowband-Internet of Things (NB-IoT) is a Low Power Wide Area Network (LPWAN) radio technology defined by the 3rd Generation Partnership Project (3GPP) standard, Release-13 [1]. NB-IoT aims to support a large number of low-cost, low energy consumption, and low data rate devices operated in a large enhanced coverage area. NB-IoT is increasingly seen as the preferred future IoT technology as it is deployed as part of the existing Long-Term Evolution (LTE) infrastructure and uses a licensed band that enables reliable and future-proof deployments. NB-IoT provides several security mechanisms based on established mechanisms defined for LTE [2]. However, privacy and security in NB-IoT have yet received little research attention.

In this work we consider an adversary using a jamming device to disrupt NB-IoT communication. We consider an intelligent jammer that targets the initial communication steps of NB-IoT communication to have a maximum impact. Specifically we describe and investigate how a jammer can interfere with the Narrowband Primary Synchronisation Signal (NPSS) and Narrowband Secondary Synchronisation Signal (NSSS) which are used to initiate the NB-IoT contention-based random-access procedure. NPSS and NSSS perform time and frequency synchronisation, cell identity detection and acquisition of frame infrastructure information. NPSS is used to obtain symbol timing and Carrier Frequency Offset (CFO), while NSSS is used to obtain the Narrowband Physical Cell ID (NB-PCID). Interference with NPSS and NSSS can prevent an NB-IoT device to initiate communication with a base station (eNodeB). Furthermore, our experiments indicate that careful design of the interference signal could allow an attacker to force the User Equipment (UE) to recognise a specific NB-PCID.

© Springer Nature Switzerland AG 2021
E. Bertino et al. (Eds.): ESORICS 2021, LNCS 12973, pp. 759–763, 2021.
https://doi.org/10.1007/978-3-030-88428-4

Existing work has focused on LTE specific attacks. For example, Eygi et al. [3] describe a countermeasure against smart jamming attacks on LTE synchronisation signals. The authors point out the vulnerability of LTE to jamming attacks due to the broadcast nature of the channel. Their work is focused specifically on the LTE downlink synchronisation signals. As countermeasure a jamming detection is proposed based on the Neyman-Pearson theorem. Simulation results show lower jamming success and better cell id detection. Labib et al. [4] describe a mechanism to enhance the immunity of LTE Systems against spoofing. The work analyses spoofing of the LTE synchronisation signal where standard-compliant primary and secondary synchronisation sequences are transmitted by a fake cell. Several mitigation techniques are proposed. The simulation results show that LTE control channel spoofing is an effective DoS attack during the cell selection process.

To the best of our knowledge, there has not yet been an investigation of smart jamming attacks on the synchronisation signals in NB-IoT.

2   The UE and eNodeB Synchronisation Process

The full specification of the NB-IoT protocol was completed in June 2016 and is described in [5]. Here we describe only the synchronisation procedure.

When an NB-IoT device (the UE) becomes active, it synchronises with a base station (eNodeB) to establish a communication link. First, the UE needs to identify a suitable cell to attach to, and for this purpose, parameters such as symbol, subframe, and frame timing and carrier frequency synchronisation must be obtained.

The NB-IoT random access procedure is illustrated in Fig. 1. The process starts with the transmission of the NPSS and NSSS which are used by the UE to perform time and frequency synchronisation, cell identity detection and acquisition frame infrastructure information. The NPSS is used to obtain symbol timing and CFO, while the NSSS is used to obtain the NB-PCID.

After this step, the UE acquires the Master Information Block (MIB) carried by the Narrowband Broadcast Channel (NPBCH) which is transmitted in subframe 0 in every transmitted frame. The MIB provides scheduling information for the uplink and downlink data channels.

Then, the random-access procedure initiates when the UE sends a random access preamble through Narrowband Physical Random Access Channel (NPRACH). Several messages are exchanged between UE and eNodeB through the Narrowband Physical Downlink Shared Channel (NPDSCH) and Narrowband Physical Uplink Shared Channel (NPUSCH) to obtain scheduling information and identity parameters that allow the connection establishment [6].

3   Jamming the NB-IoT Synchronization Process

The NB-IoT standard defines that NPSS and NSSS are transmitted in specific subframes on an 80 ms repetition interval. Both signals are designed to allow

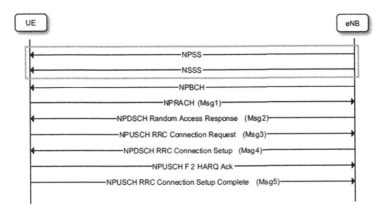

Fig. 1. NB-IoT random access procedure. Initial steps of a UE to establish communication with an eNodeB.

a device to use a unified synchronisation algorithm during initial acquisition without knowing the specific NB-IoT operation mode [6]. Therefore, to avoid collisions with LTE subframes, subframe 5 is used for the NPSS and subframe 9 is used for the NSSS. Also, in order to avoid a potential collision with the LTE Physical Downlink Control Channel (PDCCH), the subframes that carry NPSS or NSSS do not use the first three Orthogonal Frequency Division Multiplexing (OFDM) symbols. Thus, it leaves only 11 OFDM symbols per subframe available for NPSS and NSSS. The NPSS detection by the UE requires that the signal is detectable even with a very large frequency offset. Hence, all cells in an NB-IoT network use the same NPSS sequence. Consequently, a device only needs to search for one specific known NPSS sequence. Each of the 11 OFDM symbols in an NPSS subframe carries a copy of the base sequence. NB-IoT supports 504 unique NB-PCID indicated by the NSSS. Four different NSSS sequences are transmitted in an 80 ms repetition interval.

The NB-PCIDs is determined by a correlation algorithm using NPSS and NSSS which defines the peak correlation magnitude PEAK as the sum of the peak correlation magnitudes from time-domain NPSS detection and frequency-domain NSSS detection. PEAK is a scalar indicating the peak magnitude of the correlation used to detect a cell.

Adding a jamming signal to the NPSS and NSSS signal may have the effect that the correlation algorithm is still able to produce a result but the determined NB-PCID is incorrect. Jamming can be applied only to the NPSS and NSSS signal without the need to continuously jam the entire transmission channel.

4   Jamming Evaluation

To test the aforementioned jamming attack on the synchronisation signal, we use Matlab [7] with the LTE-Toolbox. The simulation fully synchronises, demodulates and decodes an NB-IoT downlink signal. A time-domain waveform of a

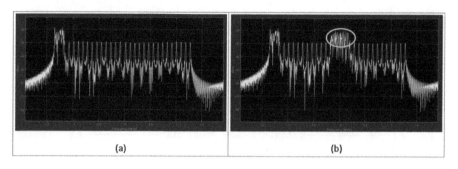

Fig. 2. Jamming attack on NB-IoT: (a) Standard transmission (b) Transmission with Jamming signal.

Reference Measurement Channel (RMC) is generated for an NPDSCH; the Matlab class used for this purpose is *NBIoTDownlinkWaveformGenerator*. Then, we introduce a jamming signal generated using a downlink 4G RMC waveform where we can adjust the signal power. The resulting signal received by the UE is the sum of the generated signal obtained from the base station plus the jamming signal.

Following the example, the frequency offset estimation and correction are performed through the *lteFrequencyOffset* and *lteFrequencyCorrect* methods. Afterwards, OFDM demodulation and channel estimation are executed. Finally, to decode the MIB, the RE corresponding to the NPBCH from the first subframe across all receive antennas and channel estimates are extracted.

In our simulation, if the power of the interference signal is above 13dB a successful modification of the NB-PCID is observed. From the experiment results, it is observed that if the power on the jammer is insufficient, the communication with the specific eNodeB is inhibited because the UE is not able to decode the MIB and get the scheduling information.

Figure 2(a) shows the transmission signal without a jamming signal. Here, the cell ID is accurately detected [NNCellID: 120], and the MIB is decoded correctly. At this point, the MIB parameters are extracted (NNCellID, NB Reference Signal, Number of Sufframe, HyperSuframe, Operation Mode, Additional Transmission SIB1).

In contrast, scenario Fig. 2(b) shows the signal with jammer, where it is observed that it is not possible to decode the MIB, and a wrong cell ID is displayed [NNCellID: 371].

5   Conclusions

We have shown that it is possible to interfere with the synchronisation signal used by NB-IoT devices (the UE) to establish communication with the base station. Thus, a simple selective jamming device can prevent communication of NB-IoT devices. Furthermore, our experiments indicate that careful design of the interference signal might enable an attacker to force the UE to recognise a specific NB-PCID. In our next steps, we will analyse how the jamming signal should be designed for this purpose. We also plan to investigate methods to detect the jamming of synchronisation signals and methods to make the detection of the NB-PCID more robust.

Acknowledgement. This publication has emanated from research conducted with the financial support of Science Foundation Ireland under Grant number 18/CRT/6222. For the purpose of Open Access, the author has applied a CC BY public copyright license to any Author Accepted Manuscript version arising from this submission.

References

1. Third Generation Partnership Project, 3GPP., : Cellular system support for ultra-low complexity and low throughput Internet of Things (CIoT) (Release 13). In: Technical Specification Group GSM/EDGE Radio Access Network, 3GPP TR 45.820 V13.1.0. (2015)
2. Cao, J., Yu, P., Ma, M., Gao, W.: Fast authentication and data transfer scheme for massive NB-IoT devices in 3GPP 5G network. IEEE IoT J. **6**, 1561–1575 (2019). https://doi.org/10.1109/JIOT.2018.2846803
3. Eygi, M., Karabulut-Kurt, G.: A countermeasure against smart jamming attacks on LTE synchronization signals. J. Commun. **15**, 626–632 (2020)
4. Labib, M., Marojevic, V., Reed, J., Zaghloul, A.: How to enhance the immunity of LTE systems against RF spoofing. In: 2016 International Conference on Computing, Networking and Communications (ICNC), pp. 1–65. (2016). https://doi.org/10.1109/ICCNC.2016.7440650
5. Third Generation Partnership Project Standardization of NB-IoT Completed. https://www.3gpp.org/news-events/3gpp-news/. Accessed 8 Jul 2021
6. Liberg, O., Sundberg, M., Wang, YO., Bergman, J., Sachs, J., Wikstrom, G.: Cellular Internet of Things from Massive Deployments to Critical 5G Applications, 2nd edn. (2020)
7. MATLAB: 9.7.0.1190202 (R2020b). The MathWorks Inc., Natick, Massachusetts (2020)

TPRou: A Privacy-Preserving Routing for Payment Channel Networks

Zijian Bao[1], Qinghao Wang[1,2], Yongxin Zhang[2,4], Hong Lei[1,3(✉)],
and Wenbo Shi[2]

[1] Hainan Nanhai Cloud Holding Co., Ltd., Chengmai 571924, China
{zijian,qinghao,leihong}@oxhainan.org
[2] School of Computer Science and Engineering, Northeastern University,
Shenyang 110001, China
shiwb@neuq.edu.cn
[3] School of Cyberspace Security, Hainan University, Hainan 570228, China
[4] Oxford-Hainan Blockchain Research Institute, Chengmai 571924, China

Abstract. Although cryptocurrencies have achieved great success in recent years, building large-scale fast payments is still a challenge. Payment channel networks (PCNs), as a practical solution to resolve this problem, can realize numerous off-chain settlements of transactions without heavy on-chain operations. The core of PCN is a routing scheme that discovers transaction paths with sufficient funds between the sender and receiver. However, the leakage of private information (*e.g.,* the identity of senders and receivers, transaction value) becomes one tricky issue. In this work, we proposed TPRou, a privacy-preserving PCN routing scheme leveraging trusted execution environments (TEEs), which can provide broader privacy guarantees than the state-of-the-art routing schemes. TPRou constructs redundant paths with different receivers to hide the identity of the receiver. Moreover, TPRou introduces a novel identity information transfer scheme, called an *encrypted identity chain*, to hide the identity of the sender and the receiver from the intermediate nodes in the payment path. Based on security analysis and performance evaluation, our result demonstrates that TPRou is able to achieve privacy-preserving payment with minimal overhead.

Keywords: Payment channel networks · Routing · Trusted execution environment (TEE) · Intel software guard extensions (SGX) · Blockchain

1 Introduction

Although cryptocurrencies have been widely concerned, their application is limited by pool scalability. For example, limited by the consensus mechanism

This study is supported by Finance Science and Technology Project in Hainan Province (No. ZDKJ2020009), the National Natural Science Foundation of China (Nos. 62072093 and U1708262), the Fundamental Research Funds for the Central Universities (No. N172304023).

ensuring the data consistency in an untrusted environment, Bitcoin can only process 7 transactions per second(tps), demonstrating a huge gap with the real scenarios of a payment system (*e.g.*, Visa handles 1500 tps).

The payment channel is a promising proposal to improve cryptocurrency scalability. It is a layer-two solution, combining on-chain and off-chain operation, to reduce blockchain burden while keeping the normal payment function. First, two users build a payment channel with a transaction to lock money on the chain. Then, they can reallocate this locked money off-chain fastly. Finally, one can send a transaction to close the channel with the latest money allocation plan.

Payment channels can be linked together to form a payment channel network (PCN), such as Lightning Network in Bitcoin. The core of PCN is a routing scheme that discovers payment paths between the sender and receiver. The existing PCN routing schemes can be classified into *non-landmark* and *landmark-based* schemes, according to the participation of noted nodes named *landmarks*. In the *non-landmark* schemes, the user itself is responsible for routing, introducing a heavy overhead of computation, storage and communication. The *landmark-based* schemes are more popular because it frees the users from these burdens. However, the landmark will acquire sensitive information such as the *transaction value and the identity of the senders and receivers*.

To tackle this problem, Moreno-Sanchez *et al.* [2] employ secret sharing and multi-party secure computation technologies to hinder transaction value. Moreover, SpeedyMurmurs [3] makes a further effort by providing higher overall performance while protecting the identity of the receiver. However, SpeedyMurmurs just split the value of the transaction without further protecting it, which raises the risk of privacy leakage. Resorting to *landmarks* to implement PCN routing while considering identity and transaction value privacy is a problem worth studying.

In this work, we present TPRou, a landmark-based routing scheme, finding the feasible paths and enable multi-hop payment with a manner of privacy-aware. It can provide broader privacy guarantees than the state-of-the-art routing schemes. Specifically, TPRou enforces the confidential data of routing in the trusted execution environment (TEE) controlled by the landmark node to prevent privacy leakage. To hide the receiver, TPRou constructs redundant paths with different receivers in the TEE. Moreover, TPRou introduces a novel identity information transfer scheme, called an *encrypted identity chain*, which is compatible with the multi-hop payment. It is capable of hiding the identity of the sender and the receiver from the intermediate nodes in the payment path. Finally, the security analysis and performance evaluation show that TPRou is able to achieve privacy-preserving payment with minimal overhead.

2   Our Design

We describe the key ideas of TPRou, including the *preparation, path building* and *executing payment* stages. The work flow is shown in Fig. 1. TPRou contains following entities: users (*e.g.*, senders, receivers and intermediate users) and

TEE-based landmarks (TLs). Since our scheme uses Intel SGX as the instance of TEE, we will default that TEE supports the features provided by SGX [1].

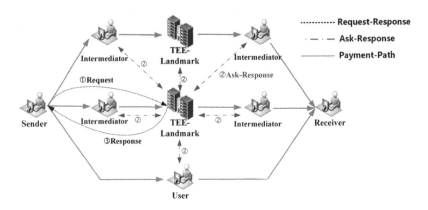

Fig. 1. An illustrative example of the path building stage of TPRou: Black lines show communications between the senders and TLs. Blue lines show communications between intermediate users and TLs. We consider a payment from a sender to a receiver. ① A sender sends a request to TL for a path to pay. ② The TL searches the intermediate users and asks them if they can meet the request of the sender. ③ The TL gives the sender a response including the feasible path.

Preparation Stage: In this stage, preparations are mainly carried out, such as TL nodes' joining the payment channel network, broadcasting their identities and related public keys to the entire network, and declaring that they will provide routing services for users. Any node can use remote attestation to authenticate the TL's identity and the code in the TEE to ensure trustworthiness. Moreover, a secure communication channel can be constructed between nodes and TLs. TL maintains a global topology of payment channel routing.

Path Building Stage: The sender sends a multi-hop routing request to the TL (① in Fig. 1). Then, TL constructs multiple payment paths (one is the real path and others are the redundant paths with pseudo receivers) according to the existing topology and verifies whether the path nodes meet the routing conditions, such as routable value and transaction fees (② in Fig. 1). Note that TL executes the breadth first search (BFS) algorithm in the TEE to construct the shortest path from the sender to the receiver. TL needs to record the round number of the enquiry to prove that the TEE owner does not deliberately abandon the path. If an available path is found, TL will enter the next stage. Otherwise, TL will inform the sender that there is no proper path (③ in Fig. 1).

Executing Payment Stage: In this stage, TL mainly informs the sender of path node information (③ in Fig. 1), including node identity and transaction fees. The sender builds a multi-hop payment request based on the above information.

In particular, to ensure the identity privacy of the sender and receiver among the intermediate users, the *encrypted identity chain* is designed. The sender built it with the nodes' public keys in an order from the receiver to the sender. The form of *encrypted identity chain* as follows:

$$CreID_i = \begin{cases} \{ID_{i+2}, CreID_{i+1}\}_{PKi+1}, & i \in [0, n-3] \\ \{ID_n\}_{PKi+1}, & i = n-2 \end{cases}$$

For example, in the path $\{node_{sed}, node_1, node_2, ..., node_{n-2}, node_{rec}\}$, the $node_4$ will receive the $\{ID_5, CreID_{4_{PK_4}}\}$ from $node_3$. The $node_4$ decrypts it with its secret key, obtains ID_5 (*i.e.*, its next hop) and $CreID_4$ (*i.e.*, the content for its next hop).

3   Security Analysis

In this section, we give a brief analysis to show how our scheme can achieve privacy protection. The Table 1 shows the comparison of PCN routing schemes.

Table 1. The comparison of PCN routing schemes

	SilentWhisper[2]	SpeedyMurmurs[3]	Spider[4]	**TPRou**
Types	Landmark	Landmark	Non-Landmark	Landmark
Sender's privacy	●	●	-	●
Receiver's privacy	○	●	-	●
Transaction value privacy	●	◑	○	●

● means that the schemes has the function, while ○ means not. ◑ means the schemes provides limited functionality.

Sender Privacy and Receiver Privacy. We improve the privacy-preserving of PCN routing in two ways. On the one hand, the confusion technique is used to hinder the identity of the receiver from the landmark. When sending a multi-hop payment request to the landmark, the sender sets multiple receivers in the **Path building stage**, so that landmark is impossible to directly determine which node is the real receiver. In previous work [2], the landmark only communicates with nodes in one path, it can easily determine the identity of the receiver. On the other hand, the *encrypted identity chain* is adopted to hinder the identity of the sender and the receiver from intermediate nodes. The next hop is encrypted by the node's public key, and only itself can decrypt it. Intermediate nodes only learn their neighbours (i.e., last hop and next hop) rather than the whole path.

Value Privacy. TPRou achieves value privacy whether the path exists or not. If the path exists, the transaction amount is added to the *encrypted identity chain*, and the remaining nodes cannot decrypt it. Otherwise, the transaction amount is encrypted by the key from TEE, and the TEE platform holder cannot decrypt it. In work [3], the transaction amount is divided into pieces rather than the protection of cryptography technology.

4 Performance Evaluation

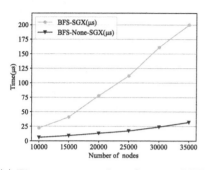
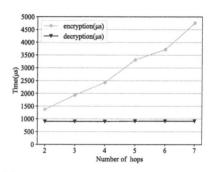

(a) Time cost comparisons between SGX and non-SGX environments

(b) Time cost of the *encrypted identity chain* algorithm with different hops

Fig. 2. The results of performance evaluation

To analyze the efficiency of TPROU, we implement our scheme using Intel SGX as the instance of TEE, and evaluate the performance of it. First, we implemented the BFS-based routing algorithm with different numbers of nodes (where 25,000 is similar to the number in Bitcoin's Lightning Network) in the SGX and non-SGX environment. Figure 2(a) shows that the execution time in SGX requires higher overhead, but such overhead is acceptable as several SGX-enabled landmarks that are profit-driven can cover the whole PCN.

Then, we implemented the *encrypted identity chain* algorithm based on the ECC algorithm (note that our scheme is compatible with any signature algorithm supported on any blockchain) and tested the overhead of multiple payments with different hop counts (2 to 7 hops which are the common range of the Lightning Network). Figure 2(b) shows the operation overhead of the sender (encryption) and the intermediate node (decryption). The encryption overhead increases linearly as the number of hops increases. And the decryption overhead is constant because each node only needs to decrypt once. In summary, our scheme is able to achieve privacy-preserving payment with minimal overhead.

5 Conclusion

In this work, we propose TPROU, a privacy-preserving payment channel network routing scheme. Thanks to TEE, the transaction value privacy is protected from the landmarks. To hide payment receivers, TPROU constructs redundant paths with different receivers in the TEE. We design an *encrypted identity chain* to hide transaction information in the payment process. The experiment shows that TPROU achieves privacy protection while maintaining low computation overhead.

References

1. Costan, V., Devadas, S.: Intel SGX explained. IACR Cryptol. ePrint Arch. **2016**(86), 1–118 (2016)
2. Malavolta, G., Moreno-Sanchez, P., Kate, A., Maffei, M.: SilentWhispers: enforcing security and privacy in decentralized credit networks. In: 24th Annual Network and Distributed System Security Symposium, NDSS (2017)
3. Roos, S., Moreno-Sanchez, P., Kate, A., Goldberg, I.: Settling payments fast and private: efficient decentralized routing for path-based transactions. In: 25th Annual Network and Distributed System Security Symposium, NDSS (2018)
4. Sivaraman, V., et al.: High throughput cryptocurrency routing in payment channel networks. In: 17th USENIX Symposium on Networked Systems Design and Implementation, NSDI (2020)

Determining Asset Criticality in Cyber-Physical Smart Grid

Yazeed Alrowaili$^{(\boxtimes)}$, Neetesh Saxena, and Pete Burnap

School of Computer Science and Informatics, Cardiff University, Cardiff, UK
{alrowailiyf, saxenan4, burnapp}@Cardiff.ac.uk

Abstract. Cybersecurity threats in smart grids have incredibly increased in the past years, and there is a strong need to protect these critical systems. Moreover, cyber-risk assessment and determining asset criticality are needed to apply the best remediation plan if the system is compromised. Still, due to the heterogeneity between operation technology (OT) and information technology, it is not easy to protect such a system altogether. Hence, the criticality of OT resources should be identified by their characteristics, helping operators understand that different assets can cause additional damage and require further protection or need more vital remediation plans. In this work, we proposed a methodology that can identify and indicates the frequency and impact of an asset in the system to determine its criticality. Moreover, the effectiveness and feasibility of the proposed method are evaluated by a 12-bus power system using the PowerWorld simulator by performing attacks on critical assets such as circuit breakers and evaluated their impact on the physical system. Finally, the test results demonstrate that targeting the most critical assets identified can severely impact the system while targeting the least critical assets is manageable.

Keywords: Smart grid · Cyber risks · Critical assets · Attack impact · OT

1 Introduction: Context and Motivation

Smart grids (SGs) can be classified as one of the many types of critical infrastructure. Moreover, it can monitor the flow of measurement units such as power from generation to consumption and match generation flow in real-time or near real-time by limiting and/or controlling any electrical load [1]. It provides control automation and transmit power from generation plants to transmission lines, distribution substations, and later to the consumers. Furthermore, cybersecurity threats targeting these systems have incredibly increased, and the failure to protect these OT assets will cause a significant impact [2]. According to the research analysis of the cyber-attack on the Ukrainian Power Grid done by E-ISAC and SANS ICS, on Dec. 23, 2015, there was a service outage on three energy companies that affected 225,000 customers for 3–7 h in 103 cities [3]. Moreover, the current focus on protecting such a system is either specified on listing the possible attacks or attack paths that can occur on the system or classifying the criticality of ICS assets from an IT or business perspective [4]. Yet, there is little focus on criticality evaluation based on the damage that can occur after a successful attack on OT assets under physical processes.

© Springer Nature Switzerland AG 2021
E. Bertino et al. (Eds.): ESORICS 2021, LNCS 12973, pp. 770–776, 2021.
https://doi.org/10.1007/978-3-030-88428-4

Contribution. Firstly, we proposed a new method that identifies and determines the criticality of OT assets within the physical system. Secondly, we evaluated the proposed method using the PowerWorld with a 12-bus case by performing attacks on critical assets, such as circuit breakers, and measured their impact on the physical system. Finally, we analysed the damage when the most critical and the least critical assets are zero-day at-tacked, gaining unauthorised access to the system by exploiting software vulnerability [5].

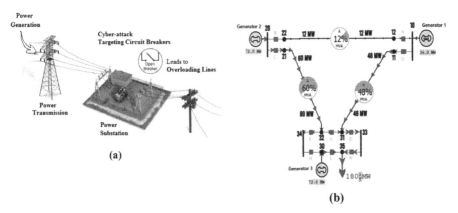

Fig. 1 (a) Smart grid substation system model. (b) 12-bus power system case normal scenario

2 Related Work

Attacks targeting assets at physical level are challenging to deal with, as evaluating assets criticality in a SG system should be specific to its characteristics. In this direction, Hasan et al. [6] proposed a method to detect and evaluate paths to critical energy delivery system nodes with network heterogeneity. However, the work uses logs and host logs, which mostly exist in IT systems. Corallo et al. [9] proposed a metric to evaluate assets criticality in the context of industry 4.0, aiming to recognise and assess the critical assets in ICS to protect them against cyber threats. However, this work was mainly focused on what impact can occur from a business perspective and quite limited in terms of offering a comprehensive evaluation for assets criticality in OT. Crespo et al. [10] proposed criticality evaluation in power line systems to offer a reliable, fast-maintained process in these systems by performing asset criticality evaluation and use the collected information to update the appropriate maintenance plan. Nevertheless, this work concentrates on assets maintenance strategy and determining its criticality they deal with, and the evaluation was also conducted on limited nodes. Recently, Vallant et al. [7] offer risk assessment methodology by identifying all possible vulnerabilities to cyber secure SG systems. However, the work focuses potential threats and the likelihood of successful attacks only. In order to fill the gaps in identifying asset criticality in OT systems and evaluating cyber risks impact on the physical systems, we not only proposed a method for discovering OT assets with most and least criticality, but also evaluating their impact on smart grid system using PowerWorld simulator.

3   Approach

Our aim is to propose a method that can identify the most critical assets in the physical system and evaluates adverse impact that may occur when the system is compromised.

3.1   System Model and Simulation Scenario

Figure 1(a) presents a power substation system model where an adversary can target critical assets such as circuit breakers or transformers to create physical and/or operational damage to the system. Further, Fig. 1(b) shows a test case of a 12-bus system regularly operated with normal scenario on the Powerworld simulator. Moreover, this case was used to show this study on critical components, and it contains 12 buses, 3 generators, 10 breakers and one load. Furthermore, the focus is identifying the most critical asset (circuit breakers), seen as red squares. When an adversary attacks critical circuit breakers, it will cause all generators to increase their reactive power *(Mvar)*, consequently reducing system reliability and efficiency, making the system to no longer supply load, which can cause a blackout [8].

3.2   Proposed Method

We present the proposed method to determine criticality of each asset in the smart grid system and evaluate their cyber impact using PowerWorld tool. This method can be generalized to other cyber-physical systems considering relevant devices and OT operational impact. Further, identify most and least critical assets (scanning devices and apply our method) and then apply risk assessment methodologies to analyse cyber risks, and evaluate their impact (e.g., simulation) on physical systems. In our scenario, we determine each circuit breaker based on its frequent occurrence in use while supplying power from a *generator* to the load using a specified path. Moreover, this can be applied by identifying all possible P paths that a generator *(i)* uses to transmit the power as per the load requirement, then assess how many times (how frequently) a circuit breaker *(i)* Cb_i is used in all paths. The criticality can be calculated as:

$$\text{Criticality} = Cb_i/P \tag{1}$$

Algorithm 1 Calculate Criticality of an Asset in Smart Grid

Input: All paths P for generator *(i)* & Number of frequent uses of Cb_i in all paths.
Output: Criticality score for Cb_i linked to a specified generator.

1: Let **P** denote total number of paths generator *(i)* uses to transmit the power to the load.
2: Let **Cb_i** indicate how many times circuit breaker *(i)* has been used in all paths **P**.
3: Applying *Equation (1)* listed above. *(where $0 \leq score \leq 1$)*
4: **if (**Cb_i score is > 0.5 *(meaning that Cb_i has appeared in more than half of paths)***) then**
5:     Declare most critical asset.
6: **else**
7:     Declare least critical asset.

Table 1. Shows all possible paths and circuit breakers that existed in each path generator *(1,2,3)* uses to transmit power to load.

ID		A	B	C	D	E	F	G	H	L	K
Gen1	Path 1	✓	✓	✓			✓	✓			✓
	Path 2				✓			✓			✓
	Path 3				✓	✓	✓		✓	✓	
Gen2	Path 1	✓	✓		✓			✓			✓
	Path 2		✓			✓			✓	✓	
	Path 3		✓				✓	✓			✓
Gen3	Path 1									✓	
	Path 2				✓	✓	✓	✓			✓

Table 1 shows the frequent use of circuit breakers in all paths for *generators 1, 2, and 3*. Moreover, applying *Algorithm 1* in all generators with the giving data will indicate that circuit breakers *(D, F, G, K)* are considered the critical asset for *generator 1*, and for *generator 2* are *(C, G, K)*. Moreover, circuit breaker *(L)* is considered critical as the other breakers since it is the only breaker used in a specific path with *generator 3*. Therefore, the most critical circuit breakers in this 12-bus system test case are *(D, F, G, C, K, L)*.

4   Experimental Results and Evaluation

This section shows an evaluation of our methodology when targeting the system's critical assets with zero-day attack and monitor generators reactive power *(Mvar)* for any changes.

4.1   System Operations Under No Attack Scenario

Table 2 shows generators information under a normal scenario, indicating that the measurements of *(Gen MW)* and *(Gen Mvar)* are normal and the system is under control, as shown in Fig. 1. We have kept *Gen MW* constant for our experiments and observing *Gen Mvar* values when targeting most vs. least critical assets in the system.

Table 2. Generators measurements on normal scenario

ID	Number of bus	Name of bus	Gen *MW*	Gen *Mvar*
1	10	10	36.00	1.23
2	20	20	72.00	1.88
3	30	30	72.00	2.97

4.2   System Operations Under Attack Scenario

Table 3 shows generators measurements when targeting the most critical circuit breakers [(F, L), C, D]. It can be seen that compromising the most critical breakers made the reactive power *(Gen Mvar)* for related generators increasing highly, which can cause overloaded transmission lines and/or overheating, as demonstrated in Fig. 2. For example, opening F and L circuit breakers (for generator 3) increases *Gen Mvar* (44.13 and 12.81) for generator 1 and 2, respectively, while it is further decreased for generator 3 (2.74) as compared to original *Gen Mvar* values from Table 2. As a result, line 10–20 and 10–33 are overloaded with 144% and 183%, respectively. This is true for other two cases as reflected in Fig. 2, when a circuit breaker C and D are opened in each case, which resulted into overloading lines 10–33 and 20–34 with 108%.

Table 3. Generator's measurements when targeting most critical circuit breaker (D), *(C)* or *(F, L)*

Gen ID	Gen *MW* for (F, L)	Gen *Mvar* for (F, L)	Gen *MW* for (C)	Gen *Mvar* for (C)	Gen *MW* for (D)	Gen *Mvar* for (D)
1	36.00	44.13	36.00	8.47	36.00	0.65
2	72.00	12.81	72.00	1.60	72.00	6.51
3	72.00	2.74	72.00	5.83	72.00	5.88

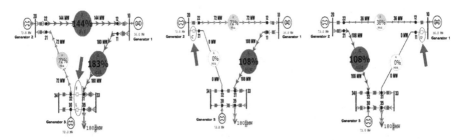

Fig. 2 Attacker compromises most circuit breakers in respective order *(F, L), (C), and (D)*

Further, Table 4 shows generators' measurements when targeting some of the least critical circuit breakers. Moreover, it can be seen that compromising the least critical breakers made the reactive power *(Gen Mvar)* for relevant generators increase slightly. Yet, it can be seen in Fig. 3 that the system is under control, and there are no threats or overload in transmission lines. As we can observe, line 10–20 is disconnected after opening A and B circuit breakers, whereas the lines 20–34 and 10–33 are with 72% and 36% capacity, respectively, once H circuit breaker is further opened.

Table 4. Generator's measurements when targeting the least critical circuit breakers *(A, B, H)*

Gen ID	Gen *MW for (A, B, H)*	Gen *Mvar for (A, B, H)*
1	36.00	0.66
2	72.00	2.61
3	72.00	3.25

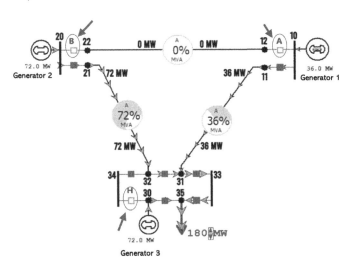

Fig. 3 Attacker compromises the least critical circuit breakers *(A, B, H)*

5   Conclusion and Future Work

In conclusion, this work has summarised the importance of protecting critical infrastructure with smart grid as a case study. Moreover, it emphasises an approach for determining and evaluating the criticality of assets located in OT at physical level. Furthermore, a simulation approach to evaluate the criticality of the physical smart grid system under attack scenarios is also presented, which reflects the potential impact on the physical system. After determining critical assets, our results show that targeting the most critical assets identified in this work can severely compromise the system, making transmission lines to be overloaded beyond their capacities. while targeting the least critical assets is manageable and transmission lines are within the specified range along with stability of the overall system. In the future, we aim to extend this work to determine critical assets at higher levels with a scalable system (e.g., 37-bus case). Moreover, we aim to build a comprehensive methodology to compute and quantify criticality for assets starting from enterprise until the process level assets associated with processes and operations.

References

1. European Commission: European Technology Platform, *Energy*, vol. 19, no. 3, p. 44 (2006). http://europa.eu.int/comm/research/energy. Accessed 22 Feb 2021
2. Ten, C., Manimaran, G., Liu, C.: Cybersecurity for critical infrastructures: attack and defense modeling. IEEE Trans. Syst. Man Cybern. Part A Syst. Hum. **40**(4), 853–865 (2010)
3. Lee, R.M., Assante, M.J., Conway, T.: Analysis of the cyber attack on the Ukrainian power grid defense use case. In: Electricity Information Sharing and Analysis Center, p. 36 (2016). https://ics.sans.org/media/E-ISAC_SANS_Ukraine_DUC_5.pdf.
4. Corallo, A., Lazoi, M., Lezzi, M., Pontrandolfo, P.: Cybersecurity challenges for manufacturing systems 4.0: assessment of the business impact level. IEEE Trans. Eng. Manage. (2021)
5. Frankenfield, J.: Zero-Day Attack Definition, 8 May 2020. https://www.investopedia.com/terms/z/zero-day-attack.asp . Accessed 10 Jul 2021
6. Hasan, K., Shetty, S., Ullah, S., Hassanzadeh, A., Hadar, E.: Towards optimal cyber defense remediation in energy delivery systems. In: IEEE GLOBECOM (2019)
7. Vallant, H., Stojanović, B., Božić, J., Hofer-Schmitz, K.: Threat modelling and beyond-novel approaches to cyber secure the smart energy system. Appl. Sci. **11**(11) (2021)
8. HYTEPS: Reduce your reactive power improves efficiency and saves costs, *HYTEPS* (2019). https://hyteps.com/power-quality/reactive-power/. Accessed 11 Jul 2021
9. Corallo, A., Lazoi, M., Lezzi, M.: Cybersecurity in the context of industry 4.0: a structured classification of critical assets and business impacts. Comput. Ind. **114**, 103165 (2020)
10. Crespo, A., et al.: Criticality analysis for improving maintenance, felling and pruning cycles in power lines. IFAC-PapersOnLine **51**(11), 211–216 (2018)

Signature-in-Signature: The Last Line of Defence in Case of Signing Key Compromise

Przemysław Błaskiewicz, Mirosław Kutyłowski, and Marcin Słowik$^{(\boxtimes)}$

Wrocław University of Science and Technology, Wrocław, Poland
Miroslaw.Kutylowski@pwr.edu.pl

Abstract. The standard approach for electronic signatures and seals is that Secure Signature Creation Devices are responsible for confidentiality of secret keys and remain under sole control of their owner. The eIDAS Regulation of EU follows this approach. However, once the private key gets compromised (e.g. by a faulty design of the signing device or powerful cryptanalysis of the public key), then the signature model becomes a deadly trap.

We address this problem by creating a second line of defence – when the signing key gets compromized we can still fish out the signatures created by a signature device. The proposed approach of *signature-in-signature* can be implemented in the standard Schnorr signature and can remain hidden until the examination of signatures after the signing key compromise.

Keywords: eIDAS · Advanced electronic signature · Electronic seal · SSCD · Schnorr signature · Key compromise · Forgery

To be used in business and administration, an electronic signature must have a legal status equivalent to that of handwritten signatures. For this purpose the lawmakers specify requirements for electronic signatures. The eIDAS regulation [6] provides such a framework for the whole EU. In particular, as all other legal frameworks, it focuses on secure signature creation devices (SSCD). An SSCD has to guarantee that the signatures corresponding to the public key of its owner can be created only by this SSCD and that the owner's consent is given prior to signature creation.

This approach leads to severe problems that are neglected in the legal framework and that are not sufficiently addressed by technical designs. One of the problems is that somebody may learn the private signing key allegedly stored only in the SSCD. There are multiple ways for this unfortunate event to happen. E.g., a powerful adversary may break the underlying scheme and reveal the key anonymously just to create a legal mess for his political or economical advantage. The keys might be compromised also by a faulty design of key generation procedure (e.g. Estonian eID case [5]), side-channel leakage (see e.g. [1]) etc. While there is an option for securing against leakage by appropriate design of cryptographic schemes (see e.g. [7]), nothing helps if the key is exposed by

© Springer Nature Switzerland AG 2021
E. Bertino et al. (Eds.): ESORICS 2021, LNCS 12973, pp. 777–782, 2021.
https://doi.org/10.1007/978-3-030-88428-4

successful cryptanalysis. If there is no secure record, e.g. in a distributed ledger, witnessing which signatures have been created by the attacked SSCD, or the list of signatures cannot be checked for completeness (cf. [3]), then we get into severe troubles regarding validity of signed documents.

Signature in Signature. Our approach of *signature-in-signature* aims to safeguard the legitimate signatures in case of revealing the signing key. The idea is that inside a regular signature (called *outer signature*) there is a hidden *inner signature*. For the inner signature neither the public key is presented nor its existence should be detectable. The public key for the inner signature is revealed at the moment when the standard signing key is compromised.

The key procedures of such a scheme are *signature creation* (subdivided into creation of the inner and outer signatures) and *signature re-validation* executed after revealing the signing key.

Once a signing key is revealed, we expect that we can challenge the validity of all signatures generated with that SSCD. However, the legal ruling is that a qualified signature remains valid if it has been created before the qualified certificates related to the signature was revoked. In practice however, a malicious forger rarely has interest in informing the victim about his success and the victim learns about the attack when it is already too late to revoke any certificates. On the other hand, invalidating en bloc all signatures created with a compromised key is also a very bad idea – it would enable the signer to cancel his past obligations.

What we propose is a scheme where a layman user holding a SSCD can come to a court of law, where via re-validation procedure the signatures created by the SSCD will be confirmed and the other signatures will be rejected.

While some approaches in the literature aim to reach this goal with dedicated schemes (e.g. fail-stop signatures), we aim to design a solution that can be incorporated into standard schemes, so that even up to the moment of re-validation it would be unknown whether this defense has been implemented by the SSCD.

In the following we show an example design based on inner and outer Schnorr signatures. Other designs (e.g. with inner BLS signature and outer DSA signature) are also possible.

1   Example Sig-in-Sig Scheme

Pseudorandomness of the First Component of the Schnorr Signature. Let $Z(M, x)$ denote the set of elements s such that there is a signature (s, e) of M and the private key x. Then $s \in Z(M, x)$ if there is k such that

$$s = k - x \cdot \text{Hash}(M, g^k) \mod q \tag{1}$$

where q is the order of the group used. We ask whether it is possible to recognize if $s \in Z(M, x)$, for a known x.

In the random oracle model we may treat Hash as a random function. Then the probability that (1) holds for given s and k is $\frac{1}{q}$, as the hash needs to have one particular value. So the probability that (1) does not hold for any k equals $(1 - \frac{1}{q})^q \approx \frac{1}{e}$. The probability that there are exactly i solutions k for (1) is $\binom{q}{i} \frac{1}{q^i} (1 - \frac{1}{q})^{q-i} < \frac{1}{i!}$. So we may assume that the number of solutions k for (1) is negligible with respect to q.

An algorithm $\mathcal{A}$ trying to answer whether $s \in Z(M, x)$ can make a limited number of queries T to the Hash oracle. The probability that every hash query for $\text{Hash}(M, g^k)$ yields a value different from $(k - s)/x \bmod q$ is at least $(1 - \frac{t}{q})^T$, where $t, T \ll q$. So the probability does not differ from 1 in a non-negligible way.

We may conclude that except for a negligible number of cases, $\mathcal{A}$ will ask the oracle for k's such that (1) does not hold. Nevertheless, $\mathcal{A}$ has to make the decision whether $s \in Z(M, x)$. In this situation $\mathcal{A}$ is forced to make a random guess.

This motivates the following assumption:

Proposition 1. *Let M be a message and let x be a private signing key for Schnorr signatures. Assume that given an element $s < q$ the problem is to decide whether there is k such that $s = k - x \cdot \text{Hash}(M, g^k) \bmod q$, or s has been chosen at random. Then any feasible algorithm $\mathcal{A}$ has at most negligible advantage to provide a correct answer to this problem.*

Schnorr Signature with Unknown Public Key. When a Schnorr signature (s, e) is created, then first the element $r = g^k$ is computed. One could design the scheme so that (s, r) is the signature instead of (s, e). With standard verification procedure in mind these seem to be equivalent. However, (s, r) enables immediately derivation of the public key X corresponding to the signature: $e := \text{Hash}(M, r)$, $X := (r/g^s)^{1/e}$. In case of the standard signature (s, e) in order to find X it is necessary to solve the equation

$$e = \text{Hash}(M, g^s \cdot X^e) \tag{2}$$

for unknown X. Note that for each Hash oracle call $\text{Hash}(M, r)$ one can derive a candidate for X which is $(r/g^s)^{1/\text{Hash}(M,r)}$. We see that finding a matching public key to the signature (s, e) of M is equivalent to finding an element r such that $\text{Hash}(M, r) = e$.

Proposition 2. *In the random oracle model for Hash, given (s, e), it is infeasible to derive the public key such that (s, e) is a Schnorr signature of a message M or to decide that there is no such public key. It is also infeasible to decide whether two alleged signatures (s_0, e_0) and (s_1, e_1) for messages M_0 and M_1 correspond to the same public key.*

Scheme Description. In this section we show how to insert a full signature into the random component of a Schnorr signature. Due to the signature size, this implies that either this inner signature must be constructed in a different way, or that it is generated over a smaller group. In this paper we follow the second approach as it is much simpler conceptually. A smaller group usually means a lower degree of security, however inner signatures are used only to separate the forged signatures from the signatures created by a legitimate SSCD. Moreover, the public key for inner signatures remains hidden until the re-validation phase so that attempts at breaking it are minimized.

Setup. Two groups for Schnorr signatures are used: the outer group $\mathcal{G}$ of prime order q and an inner group $\mathcal{P}$ of prime order ρ. The bit-length of q should be at least double of the bit-length of ρ in order to provide enough room for the inner signature. Generators g and γ are chosen for, respectively, $\mathcal{G}$ and $\mathcal{P}$. (Let us remark that the outer Schnorr signature can be replaced by any scheme, where the verifier can retrieve g^k for a number k chosen at random by the signatory).

Outer Key Generation: it is the same as in case of the regular Schnorr scheme. Let x be the private key and $X = g^x$ the public key for a device D.

Inner Key Generation: The owner of D creates a pair of keys (y, Y), where $Y = \gamma^y$ and $y < \rho$ is chosen at random.

Device Initialization: The owner uploads y to D.

Signature Creation: To sign a message M the following steps are executed:

1. Compute the inner Schnorr signature:
   (a) choose $\kappa < \rho$ at random,
   (b) compute $\epsilon := \mathrm{Hash}_\rho(M, \gamma^\kappa)$,
   (c) compute $\sigma := \kappa - y \cdot \epsilon \bmod \rho$, the first component of the inner Schnorr signature,
2. Compute the outer Schnorr signature:
   (a) $k := L(\sigma, \epsilon)$, where $L(\alpha, \beta)$ means encoding of numbers $\alpha, \beta < \rho$ by a single number smaller than q,
   (b) $e := \mathrm{Hash}_q(M, g^k)$,
   (c) $s := k - e \cdot x \bmod q$,
3. Output the signature (s, e) of M.

The hash functions Hash_ρ, Hash_q map into, respectively, $\mathbb{Z}_\rho$ and $\mathbb{Z}_q$.

Note 1. Any encoding function L can be used, however it should be invertible: given $L(\alpha, \beta)$ it should be possible to derive back α and β or a few candidates for them. For example, if $L(\alpha, \beta)$ can be defined as a number $z < q$ chosen at random from the numbers satisfying $z = \alpha \cdot \rho + \beta \bmod q$.

Note 2. The elements k used for the outer Schnorr signature are chosen in a particular way – they are not arbitrary random elements anymore. However, according to Proposition 2, it is infeasible to distinguish such k's from random strings if we apply the random oracle model for Hash_ρ.

Outer signature verification: the standard verification procedure is applied on input public key X and message M.

Re-validation of signatures: If the secret key x is leaked, then it is necessary to re-validate all signatures that pass the standard verification procedure. Once a list of such signatures is created, then the owner of D may reveal the public key Y and the following steps are executed for each signature (s, e) from the list:

- the original ephemeral k is recomputed as $k := s + e \cdot x \bmod q$,
- the alleged inner signature is retrieved as $(\sigma, \epsilon) := L^{-1}(k)$,
- (s, e) is validated iff (σ, ϵ) verifies positively with Y and M.

Note 3. Before the breach becomes public, an adversary $\mathcal{A}$ holding the key x may attempt to forge signatures of D. $\mathcal{A}$ may create easily outer signatures verifiable with X. However, in order to create a signature that will not be rejected during the re-validation phase, $\mathcal{A}$ has to create valid inner signatures as well.

If $\mathcal{A}$ can break X by cryptanalysis, then it is likely that he will be able to break Y as well, as the key length here is substantially shorter. However, Y is kept secret and the only input $\mathcal{A}$ may have are some inner signatures retrieved from the signatures created by D (note that $\mathcal{A}$ can compute them as he holds the secret key x). Fortunately, according to Proposition 2 it is infeasible to derive Y from inner signatures alone.

Note that a brute force attack to create a signature and test if it contains an inner signature verifiable with the same (unknown) key Y as signatures created by D is also infeasible. According to Proposition 2, there is no effective test of this kind.

Note 4. Of course, at the time of re-validation all signatures produced allegedly by D have to be presented. This follows from the fact that at this moment the adversary learns Y and thereby may attempt to forge inner signatures as well, after its successful cryptanalysis.

Of course, there is no need to *publish* the plaintexts of all signatures at this moment. It is enough to publish their hashes (or a root of the Merkle tree built on these hashes), before the re-validation procedure starts. Later, each signature can be inspected on demand. The hashes may be simply stored in a distributed ledger with no additional information attached.

Note 5. The Sig-in-Sign schemes based on Schnorr signatures can be extended so that we get an additional security feature which we call *chaining*: during re-validation procedure the SSCD owner must provide the full history of his signatures – otherwise it will become evident that he is hiding some of them. The idea is based on fluctuations of the inner signing key. A former scheme [3] of this kind has been based on a symmetric secret shared by the SSCD and the judge. Now we do not need such a shared key.

Note 6. For an interested reader, in the Appendix we provide an overview of some implementation options with the currently available (and recommended) algebraic structures such that the resulting scheme fulfils the requirements for both the outer and inner signature.

Final Remarks. Due to size constraints, this paper presents only a draft solution to the problem of securing signatures *after* their corresponding signing key has been compromised. An ongoing work is under way to present a full working solution with additional features.

At the same time, the authors wish to draw attention to the fact that it is not only the technical means that are required for such solutions to be implementable – both procedural as well as legal steps must be taken in unison, which will yield a functional solution to digital signature application in real life.

A   Appendix

In the table below we present some choice of standard groups that may be used to implement the example scheme described in Sect. 1 (Table 1).

Table 1. Example groups for signature-in-signature Schnorr based schemes.

Outer signature			Inner signature				
Sec level	Curve bits	Example curve	Sec level	Curve bits	Example curve	ρ^2/q	C.f
160	320	brainpoolP320t1	80	160	brainpoolP160t1	1.006	[4]
192	384	brainpoolP384t1	96	192	brainpoolP192t1	1.056	[4]
224	448	Curve448-Goldilocks	112	224	brainpoolP224t1	2.841	[2, 4]
256	512	brainpoolP512t1	128	256	brainpoolP256t1	0.660	[4]

References

1. Duc, A., Dziembowski, S., Faust, S.: Unifying leakage models: from probing attacks to noisy leakage. J. Cryptol. **32**(1), 151–177 (2019). https://doi.org/10.1007/s00145-018-9284-1
2. Hamburg, M.: Ed448-goldilocks, a new elliptic curve. IACR Cryptol. ePrint Arch. **2015**, 625 (2015). http://eprint.iacr.org/2015/625
3. Kubiak, P., Kutyłowski, M.: Supervised usage of signature creation devices. In: Lin, D., Xu, S., Yung, M. (eds.) Inscrypt 2013. LNCS, vol. 8567, pp. 132–149. Springer, Cham (2014). https://doi.org/10.1007/978-3-319-12087-4_9
4. Lochter, M., Merkle, J.: Elliptic curve cryptography (ECC) brainpool standard curves and curve generation. RFC **5639**, pp. 1–27 (2010)
5. Nemec, M., Sýs, M., Svenda, P., Klinec, D., Matyas, V.: The return of coppersmith's attack: practical factorization of widely used RSA moduli. In: Thuraisingham, B.M., Evans, D., Malkin, T., Xu, D. (eds.) Proceedings of the 2017 ACM SIGSAC CCS 2017, pp. 1631–1648. ACM (2017)
6. The European Parliament and the Council of the European Union: Regulation (EU) No 910/2014 of the European Parliament and of the Council of 23 July 2014 on electronic identification and trust services for electronic transactions in the internal market and repealing Directive 1999/93/EC (2014). http://eur-lex.europa.eu/legal-content/EN/TXT/?uri=uriserv:OJ.L_.2014.257.01.0073.01.ENG
7. Wu, J., Tseng, Y., Huang, S., Tsai, T.: Leakage-resilient certificate-based signature resistant to side-channel attacks. IEEE Access **7**, 19041–19053 (2019). https://doi.org/10.1109/ACCESS.2019.2896773

Author Index